W9-BNA-306

TD/STAT.29

UNITED NATIONS CONFERENCE ON TRADE AND DEVELOPMENT
Geneva

UNCTAD **HANDBOOK** OF STATISTICS

CONFERENCE DES NATIONS UNIES SUR LE COMMERCE ET LE DEVELOPPEMENT
Genève

MANUEL DE STATISTIQUES DE LA CNUCED

2004

UNITED NATIONS 2004 NATIONS UNIES
New York and Geneva New York et Genève

TD/STAT.29

UNITED NATIONS PUBLICATION
Sales No. E/F.05.II.D.4
ISBN 92-1-012058-2 ISSN 0251-9461

The *UNCTAD Handbook of Statistics* provides a comprehensive collection of statistical data relevant to the analysis of international trade, investment and development for the use of government officials, university and other research specialists, and others interested in these subjects. The publication is available in three complementary formats: printed copy, CD-ROM and on-line: (www.unctad.org/statistics/handbook).

While the complementary CD-ROM and Internet versions of the *Handbook* present the full time series of data, this printed publication focuses on recent statistics.

The tables, while largely based on existing international and national data sources, provide a compilation of data that is unique in the following ways:

♦ Wherever possible, data are presented in an analytical way, through the use of rank orderings, growth rates, shares and other special calculations, so as to facilitate their interpretation. Statistical classifications have been condensed into groupings of particular relevance to the analysis of trade and development.

♦ Time series of basic trade data cover periods that the UNCTAD secretariat considers to be particularly relevant to statistical and other applicable analysis.

♦ A number of the series shown represent UNCTAD secretariat estimates based on detailed research and analysis.

♦ Every effort has been made to take account of all available information in order to provide as complete coverage as possible for individual countries. In some cases this has involved secretariat judgements regarding data sources for a particular country.

Particular acknowledgement is made of the cooperation extended by the Statistics Division, Department of Economic and Social Affairs of the United Nations, as well as by other international organisations, in the preparation of this publication.

Le but du *Manuel de statistiques de la CNUCED* est de fournir, à l'intention des administrations nationales, des universitaires et autres spécialistes de la recherche, des organisations internationales, et de tous ceux que la question intéresse, l'ensemble de données statistiques essentielles à l'analyse du commerce mondial, de l'investissement et du développement. La publication est disponible dans trois formats complémentaires : l'édition imprimée, le CD-ROM et la version en ligne (www.unctad.org/statistics/handbook).

Comme les versions CD-ROM et Internet du *Manuel,* complémentaires à cette publication, présentent les séries chronologiques complètes, cette version imprimée fait davantage apparaître les données récentes.

Les tableaux, qui font appel principalement aux sources de données internationales et nationales existantes, forment un catalogue unique de statistiques établies de la manière suivante :

♦ Chaque fois que possible, les données ont été présentées d'une manière analytique, classées par ordre de grandeur, taux de croissance, parts et autres calculs spéciaux, afin d'en faciliter l'interprétation. Des groupements se prêtant particulièrement bien à l'analyse du commerce et du développement ont été réalisés au sein des nomenclatures statistiques.

♦ Les séries chronologiques de données de base sur le commerce couvrent des périodes que le secrétariat de la CNUCED considère être d'une importance particulière pour des analyses statistiques et autres analyses du sujet.

♦ Un certain nombre de séries correspondent à des estimations du secrétariat de la CNUCED fondées sur des recherches et des analyses détaillées.

♦ Le secrétariat s'est efforcé de tenir compte de tous les renseignements disponibles afin de brosser dans chaque cas un tableau aussi complet que possible de la situation. Ce faisant, il a parfois dû opérer un choix entre différentes sources de données pour tel ou tel pays.

Le secrétariat de la CNUCED tient à remercier la Division de statistique, Département des affaires économiques et sociales de l'ONU, et diverses organisations internationales du concours qu'elles ont apporté à la préparation de cette publication.

TABLE OF CONTENTS	TABLE DES MATIERES

www.unctad.org/statistics/handbook

www.unctad.org/statistics/handbook

PART ONE International merchandise trade	PREMIERE PARTIE Commerce international des marchandises

PART TWO Trade and commodity price indices	DEUXIEME PARTIE Indices du commerce et des prix des produits de base

These notes summarize the coverage of each part of the *Handbook* and highlight modifications as compared with previous issues.

The tables included in this book represent analytical summaries of the full time series contained in the *UNCTAD Handbook of Statistics 2004* presented on CD-ROM and on the Internet (www.unctad.org/statistics/handbook). This printed version includes more concise table formats, with the emphasis on recent information. In certain instances, the two electronic versions might have different figures from the printed volume, as they are published somewhat later and take into account more recent data.

PART ONE
International merchandise trade

Table 1.1A shows the value of total exports and imports for individual countries and for geographical groups, expressed in millions of dollars. The national system of reporting (general trade or special trade) and valuation is indicated.

The same data as in table 1.1A are shown in table 1.1B for different economic groupings.

Table 1.1C includes shares of exports and imports for different geographical and economic groups.

Growth rates of international trade, derived from tables 1.1A and 1.1B, are presented in tables 1.2A and 1.2B.

Table 1.3 contains trade balances (exports f.o.b. minus imports c.i.f.) and these balances as a percentage of imports by country, region and economic grouping.

Table 1.4 shows the relative importance of intra-trade in total trade of different trade or regional groupings, such as EU, ASEAN or MERCOSUR, by comparing their respective exports of goods within the group, the geographical region they belong to and the world. Thirty different trade groups are included in this analysis.

PART TWO
Trade and commodity price indices

The group of tables 2.1 (2.1A to 2.1F) shows volume and unit value indices for exports and imports, and the terms of trade and purchasing power of exports for developed and developing countries by region and economic grouping. The indices for individual developing economies are shown separately in table 8.1.

Table 2.2 includes aggregated price indices for primary commodity groups such as food, tropical beverages, vegetable oilseeds and oils, agricultural raw materials and minerals, ores and metals, as well as a combined price index in current US dollars. Also included are the annual and quarterly free-market price indices of selected commodities exported by developing economies. For reference, market prices in current dollars are shown for the base year. The table is based on data from the UNCTAD *Commodity Price Bulletin.*

PART THREE
Structure of international trade by region

Tables 3.1A and 3.1B show, respectively, the export and import structure of individual countries by main regions of origin and destination, in percentages. Data are presented for as many individual countries as possible, while trade partners are grouped in 13 major clusters according to the UNCTAD secretariat's judgement as to their relevance for the analysis of the direction of international trade.

The group of tables 3.2.1 presents the export structure by destination and by major commodity groups for the world and selected regions, while tables grouped under the 3.2.2 heading provide the same information for imports by origin. The total of all products is presented in dollar terms, while percentages are presented for different product groups. These sets of data provide detailed information on the trade network for the world, 22 regions of origin and 22 regions of destination for each of the 12 commodity groups shown. The commodity groups are based on the SITC (Rev. 2) classification. Figures in these tables are not strictly comparable with the trade data in table 1.1, mainly owing to more frequent revisions of the latter. The complete data on which the figures shown are based are contained in table 3.2 of the CD-ROM and the Internet version of the *UNCTAD Handbook of Statistics 2004.*

PART FOUR
Structure of international trade by product

Tables 4.1A and 4.1B show, respectively, the export and import structure of individual economies by commodity groups for selected years. The eight commodity groups shown, based on the SITC (Rev. 2) classification, are the following: all food items, agricultural raw materials, fuels, ores and metals, manufactured goods, chemical products, other manufactured goods, and machinery and transport equipment.

Tables 4.2A, B and C present the structure of exports for the world and for developed and developing economies at the SITC group (Rev. 2, 3-digit) level. The share of the commodity in the exports of the region and world is shown, as are its annual average growth rate and its difference from that of the world.

Table 4.2D shows the leading exports at the SITC group (Rev. 2, 3-digit) level for individual economies. Each commodity's share in the total exports of the countries, as well as in those of the region and the world, is also presented.

Table 4.2E summarizes information on the major exporters of 70 leading commodities among developing economies at the SITC group (Rev. 2, 3-digit) level.

PART FIVE
International trade in services

Table 5.1 presents the value of total trade in services by country, region and economic grouping. The figures refer to 11 principal service categories as defined in the IMF *Balance of Payments Manual* (1993, BPM 5). The aggregate figures presented also include the UNCTAD secretariat's estimates that are not shown separately. The commercial services, which exclude government services and follow the GATS definition, can be viewed as a memo item in table 5.2 on the CD-ROM or the Internet version of the *Handbook*. Given the general difficulties in statistically capturing certain aspects of the trade in services, the balance-of-payments figures presented here may be somewhat downward biased as compared with existing flows of the international trade in services.

Table 5.2A indicates 20 major exporters, among developing economies, for each of the 10 principal service categories as defined in the IMF *Balance of Payments Manual* (1993, BPM 5). Table 5.2B presents the same information for 20 major importers of services among developing economies. The sectors shown are transport, travel, communication, construction, computer and information services, insurance, financial services, royalties and licence fees, other business services, personal, cultural and recreational services. Government services n.i.e. are not included.

Table 5.3 focuses on tourism services. It presents, for individual economies and for recent years, the following statistics: value of tourism expenditure, number of overnight stays, number of arrivals and the average length of stay. All figures refer to non-resident tourists (inbound tourism).

PART SIX
International finance

Table 6.1A presents summaries of the current account of the balance of payments for individual countries and territories. Balance-of-payments current account data cover all transactions between residents and non-residents of a reporting economy, involving economic values and mainly concerning goods, services, income and current transfers. Following the table are notes that provide explanations of the categories and terminology employed.

Table 6.1B contains summaries of the capital and financial account of the balance of payments for individual economies. Capital and financial account figures, recorded as net values, cover transactions in foreign assets and liabilities. All valuation changes or other non-transaction modifications of net foreign assets are not reflected in these accounts. Capital account includes capital transfers and acquisition and disposal of non-produced, non-financial assets. Financial account covers investments (direct, portfolio and other) and reserve assets (monetary gold, SDRs, foreign exchange and others). The *Handbook* includes capital and financial account data for the first time in this edition. Detailed notes with explanations of categories and terminology used are provided after the table.

Table 6.2 contains information on foreign direct investment (FDI) inflows and outflows by country and regional grouping. These figures correspond to the Statistical Annexes of UNCTAD's *World Investment Report 2004: The Shift Towards Services*.

Tables 6.3A and B present information on major receivers and benefactors of workers' remittances among developing economies. They also show workers' remittances as percentages of international trade data. The IMF *Balance of Payments Manual (1993, BPM 5)* classifies workers' remittances separately from compensation of employees and from migrants' capital transfers. Table 6.3 includes all three categories in the values shown, in order to present a clearer picture of the flows that enter or exit economies via transfers by migrant workers.

Table 6.4 presents data on international reserves (total reserves minus gold) of developing economies by country, region and economic grouping. Other calculations included show months of imports that these reserves could finance at current import levels, as well as annual change in total reserves.

Table 6.5 gives a summary of the different types of official financial flows to developing economies by country, region and economic grouping. Flows from bilateral and multilateral sources are taken into account, as recorded by the Development Assistance Committee (DAC – OECD).

Table 6.6 shows data on the external indebtedness of developing economies by region and economic grouping. It also provides a detailed breakdown of public and publicly guaranteed debt by source of lending. External debt data in this table are based on the Debtor Reporting System (DRS), maintained by the World Bank.

PART SEVEN
Indicators of development

Table 7.1 provides information on population and density, area and total and per capita current GDP (in dollars) by country, region and economic grouping. The GDP per capita estimates in US dollars presented in this table are derived from data in national currency converted into dollars. Comparison of these series converted into current dollars through the use of official exchange rates is not always satisfactory owing to differences in price levels in individual economies.

Table 7.2 contains annual average growth rates of total and per capita real GDP at market prices by country, region and economic grouping.

Table 7.3 provides data on GDP by type of expenditure and kind of economic activity, by country, region and economic grouping.

Table 7.4 shows selected economic and social indicators for individual countries. It contains information on vital, health and environment statistics. This table presents the latest available figures for each indicator and makes it possible to compare countries on the basis of different aspects of socio-economic development at a given time. Among the indicators presented are urban population, infant mortality, life expectancy, access to adequate sanitation facilities, HIV/AIDS, emissions of carbon dioxide and total energy consumption.

Table 7.5 focuses on other socio-economic data related to education, labour force, gender and migration. The latest available figure is shown for each indicator, among which are: school enrolment, illiteracy rate, unemployment rate, employment by sector, number of migrants and gender perspective statistics.

Table 7.6 presents selected information and communication technology (ICT) indicators. It focuses on development and use of new technologies and on access to information and media by including indicators referring to the number of television sets, telephones, telecommunication costs, personal computers, the Internet, investment in telecommunications, etc.

PART EIGHT
Special studies

Table 8.1 contains tentative estimates of export and import unit value indices for individual developing economies, as well as the terms of trade and purchasing power of exports derived from them. The aggregates in table 2.1 have been calculated on the basis of the figures from this table.

Table 8.2A includes time series of export concentration and diversification indices for individual countries and territories and for regional groupings, while table 8.2B presents the same indices for imports.

Tables 8.3A and B provide the concentration and structural change indices for exports and imports by product at the SITC group (Rev. 2, 3-digit) level.

Table 8.4 presents average applied import tariff rates for major categories of non-agricultural and non-fuel products by individual markets and by groups of exporting countries.

Table 8.5 presents instability indices and trends in free-market prices for selected primary commodities that are of particular interest to developing economies.

Table 8.6 focuses on international maritime transport. It contains data on the world merchant fleet by flag of registration and by type of ship. This table, being published for the first time in the *Handbook*, contains consolidated time series that appeared in the various issues of UNCTAD *Review of Maritime Transport*.

OTHER NOTES AND EXPLANATION OF SYMBOLS

Because of rounding, details and percentages in tables do not necessarily add up to totals.

"Dollars" ($) refers to US dollars, unless otherwise stated.

Zero (0) means that the amount is nil or negligible.

The symbol underscore (_) indicates that the item is not applicable.

Two dots (..) indicate that the data are not available or are not separately reported.

Use of a hyphen (-) between years (e.g. 1985-1990) signifies the full period involved, including the initial and final years. Some exceptions are indicated in footnotes.

The country distributions presented on the following pages have been adopted for statistical convenience only and follow those used by the Statistics Division, Department of Economic and Social Affairs (DESA) of the United Nations.

The term *economies*, as used in this publication, covers regions, countries and territories.

A number of modifications have been introduced in country groupings as compared with the distributions of countries presented in the previous *Handbook*. The changes follow the enlargement of the European Union, as of 1 May 2004, and include consequent adjustments, particularly for the countries of Central and South-East Europe and those succeeding the former USSR. The cluster South-East Europe and Commonwealth of Independent States (CIS) has been newly introduced.

THREE MAIN GROUPS OF COUNTRIES / TERRITORIES

Developed economies:

In Europe:
  European Union:

Austria	Greece	Netherlands
Belgium	Hungary	Poland
Czech Republic	Ireland	Portugal
Cyprus	Italy	Slovakia
Denmark	Latvia	Slovenia
Estonia	Lithuania	Spain
Finland	Luxembourg	Sweden
France	Malta	United Kingdom of Great Britain and Northern Ireland
Germany		

  Other developed Europe:

Andorra	Holy See	Monaco
Channel Island	Iceland	Norway
Faeroe Islands	Isle of Man	San Marino
Gibraltar	Liechtenstein	Switzerland

In America: Canada and the United States of America

In Asia: Israel and Japan

In Oceania: Australia and New Zealand

South-East Europe and Commonwealth of Independent States (CIS):

South-East Europe:

Albania	Croatia	Serbia and Montenegro
Bosnia and Herzegovina	Romania	The former Yugoslav Republic of Macedonia
Bulgaria		

Commonwealth of Independent States (CIS):

Armenia	Kazakhstan	Tajikistan
Azerbaijan	Kyrgyzstan	Turkmenistan
Belarus	Republic of Moldova	Ukraine
Georgia	Russian Federation	Uzbekistan

Developing economies:

All other countries and territories in Africa, America, Asia and Oceania not specified above. For developing economies, the main regions have been further subdivided into subregions to provide additional information. The exact composition of each region is shown on the following pages. Possible exceptions to this classification in some of the *Handbook* tables are specified in footnotes.

A number of economic classifications have been used in the *UNCTAD Handbook of Statistics* in order to reflect more accurately differences among developing countries and territories, and thus to facilitate the analysis of socio-economic data. These classifications distinguish, in the first instance, between the major petroleum-exporting countries and other developing economies. The latter are in turn subdivided into two categories: (a) major exporters of manufactures, and (b) remaining economies distributed by major geographical regions.

The group "Major petroleum exporters" consists of all 11 OPEC member countries. In addition, 10 non-OPEC countries are included on the basis of the following criteria: the share of petroleum and petroleum products was not less than 50 per cent of their total exports, and exports of those products amounted to at least US$ 1.5 billion on average in the period 1999-2001. The Netherlands Antilles were added to the group in this year's *Handbook*, as this state satisfies the criteria cited for the given period.

The group "Major exporters of manufactures" consists of 12 economies included on the basis of the following criteria: the share

of manufactured products was not less than 50 per cent of total exports, and exports of those products amounted to at least US$ 20 billion on average in the period 1999-2001.

In addition, all developing economies have been classified, according to their per capita GDP in 2000, into three groupings: high-income, middle-income and low-income countries.

For further reference, the groups of "Least developed countries" (LDCs), "Heavily indebted poor countries" (HIPCs) and "Landlocked countries" are shown as memo items. Certain tables present the grouping "Developing countries excluding China", which refers to mainland China only. "Sub-Saharan Africa" (South Africa included) forms another memo item.

Trade groupings (e.g. ASEAN, EU, LAIA) are included in certain tables, which makes it possible to include groups that cut across regions, such as APEC.

All groups are presented on the basis of the latest information available in May 2004.

America   49

South America   14

Argentina	Ecuador	Peru
Bolivia	Falkland Islands (Malvinas)	Suriname
Brazil	French Guiana	Uruguay
Chile	Guyana	Venezuela
Colombia	Paraguay	

Other America   35

Anguilla	Dominican Republic	Netherlands Antilles
Antigua and Barbuda	El Salvador	Nicaragua
Aruba	Greenland	Panama
Bahamas	Grenada	Puerto Rico
Barbados	Guadeloupe	Saint Kitts and Nevis
Belize	Guatemala	Saint Lucia
Bermuda	Haiti	Saint Pierre and Miquelon
British Virgin Islands	Honduras	Saint Vincent and the Grenadines
Cayman Islands	Jamaica	Trinidad and Tobago
Costa Rica	Martinique	Turks and Caicos Islands
Cuba	Mexico	United States Virgin Islands
Dominica	Montserrat	

Africa   55

North Africa   6

Algeria	Libyan Arab Jamahiriya	Sudan
Egypt	Morocco	Tunisia

Other Africa   49

Angola	Gabon	Reunion
Benin	Gambia	Rwanda
Botswana	Ghana	Saint Helena
Burkina Faso	Guinea	Sao Tome and Principe
Burundi	Guinea-Bissau	Senegal
Cameroon	Kenya	Seychelles
Cape Verde	Lesotho	Sierra Leone
Central African Republic	Liberia	Somalia
Chad	Madagascar	South Africa
Comoros	Malawi	Swaziland
Congo	Mali	Togo
Côte d'Ivoire	Mauritania	Uganda
Democratic Republic of the Congo	Mauritius	United Republic of Tanzania
Djibouti	Mozambique	Zambia
Equatorial Guinea	Namibia	Zimbabwe
Eritrea	Niger	
Ethiopia	Nigeria	

Asia   40

West Asia   14

Bahrain	Lebanon	Syrian Arab Republic
Iran, Islamic Republic of	Palestinian territory	Turkey
Iraq	Oman	United Arab Emirates
Jordan	Qatar	Yemen
Kuwait	Saudi Arabia	

Other Asia   26

Afghanistan	India	Nepal
Bangladesh	Indonesia	Pakistan
Bhutan	Korea, Democratic People's Republic of	Philippines
Brunei Darussalam	Korea, Republic of	Singapore
Cambodia	Lao People's Democratic Republic	Sri Lanka
China	Malaysia	Thailand
China, Hong Kong SAR	Maldives	Timor-Leste
China, Macao SAR	Mongolia	Viet Nam
China, Taiwan Province of	Myanmar	

American Samoa	Micronesia, Federated States of	Samoa
Cook Islands	Nauru	Solomon Islands
Fiji	New Caledonia	Tokelau
French Polynesia	Niue	Tonga
Guam	Northern Mariana Islands	Tuvalu
Kiribati	Palau	Vanuatu
Marshall Islands	Papua New Guinea	Wallis and Futuna Islands

DISTRIBUTION OF DEVELOPING COUNTRIES / TERRITORIES BY ECONOMIC GROUPING

A. DISTRIBUTION OF DEVELOPING COUNTRIES / TERRITORIES BY MAJOR CATEGORY

Major petroleum exporters 21

Algeria*	Netherlands Antilles	**Major exporters of manufactures 12**
Angola	Nigeria*	Brazil
Bahrain	Oman	China
Brunei Darussalam	Qatar*	China, Hong Kong SAR
Congo	Saudi Arabia*	China, Taiwan Province of
Gabon	Syrian Arab Republic	India
Indonesia*	Trinidad and Tobago	Korea, Republic of
Iran, Islamic Republic of*	United Arab Emirates*	Malaysia
Iraq*	Venezuela*	Mexico
Kuwait*	Yemen	Philippines
Libyan Arab Jamahiriya*		Singapore

(* OPEC member country)

Thailand

Turkey

Remaining economies 132
All other developing countries / territories not listed among Major petroleum exporters or Major exporters of manufactures.

B. DISTRIBUTION OF DEVELOPING COUNTRIES / TERRITORIES BY INCOME GROUP

2000 per capita current GDP above US$ 4,500: High-income   50

American Samoa	French Guiana	Palau
Anguilla	French Polynesia	Puerto Rico
Antigua and Barbuda	Greenland	Qatar
Argentina	Grenada	Reunion
Aruba	Guadeloupe	Saint Kitts and Nevis
Bahamas	Guam	Saint Lucia
Bahrain	Korea, Republic of	Saint Pierre and Miquelon
Barbados	Kuwait	Saudi Arabia
Bermuda	Lebanon	Seychelles
British Virgin Islands	Libyan Arab Jamahiriya	Singapore
Brunei Darussalam	Martinique	Trinidad and Tobago
Cayman Islands	Mexico	Turks and Caicos Islands
Chile	Montserrat	United Arab Emirates
China, Hong Kong SAR	Netherlands Antilles	United States Virgin Islands
China, Macao SAR	New Caledonia	Uruguay
China, Taiwan Province of	Northern Mariana Islands	Venezuela
Falkland Islands (Malvinas)	Oman	

2000 per capita current GDP between US$ 1000 and US$ 4,500: Middle-income   50

Algeria	Gabon	Peru
Belize	Guatemala	Saint Helena
Bolivia	Iran, Islamic Republic of	Saint Vincent and the Grenadines
Botswana	Jamaica	Samoa
Brazil	Jordan	South Africa
Cape Verde	Malaysia	Suriname
Colombia	Maldives	Swaziland
Cook Islands	Marshall Islands	Syrian Arab Republic
Costa Rica	Mauritius	Thailand
Cuba	Micronesia, Federated States of	Tokelau
Dominica	Morocco	Tonga
Dominican Republic	Namibia	Tunisia
Ecuador	Nauru	Turkey
Egypt	Niue	Tuvalu
El Salvador	Palestinian territory	Vanuatu
Equatorial Guinea	Panama	Wallis and Futuna Islands
Fiji	Paraguay	

2000 per capita current GDP below US$ 1000: Low-income   65

Afghanistan	Guinea-Bissau	Nicaragua
Angola	Guyana	Niger
Bangladesh	Haiti	Nigeria
Benin	Honduras	Pakistan
Bhutan	India	Papua New Guinea
Burkina Faso	Indonesia	Philippines
Burundi	Iraq	Rwanda
Cambodia	Kenya	Sao Tome and Principe
Cameroon	Kiribati	Senegal
Central African Republic	Korea, Democratic People's	Sierra Leone
Chad	Republic of	Solomon Islands
China	Lao People's Democratic Republic	Somalia
Comoros	Lesotho	Sri Lanka
Congo	Liberia	Sudan
Côte d'Ivoire	Madagascar	Timor-Leste
Democratic Republic of the Congo	Malawi	Togo
Djibouti	Mali	Uganda
Eritrea	Mauritania	United Republic of Tanzania
Ethiopia	Mongolia	Viet Nam
Gambia	Mozambique	Yemen
Ghana	Myanmar	Zambia
Guinea	Nepal	Zimbabwe

C.   OTHER GROUPINGS (MEMO ITEMS)

Least developed countries (LDCs) 50, with respective year of inclusion in the grouping

Afghanistan	1971	Gambia	1975	Rwanda	1971
Angola	1994	Guinea	1971	Samoa	1971
Bangladesh	1975	Guinea-Bissau	1981	Sao Tome and Principe	1982
Benin	1971	Haiti	1971	Senegal	2001
Bhutan	1971	Kiribati	1986	Sierra Leone	1982
Burkina Faso	1971	Lao People's Democratic Republic	1971	Solomon Islands	1991
Burundi	1971	Lesotho	1971	Somalia	1971
Cambodia	1991	Liberia	1990	Sudan	1971
Cape Verde	1977	Madagascar	1991	Timor-Leste	2003
Central African Republic	1975	Malawi	1971	Togo	1982
Chad	1971	Maldives	1971	Tuvalu	1986
Comoros	1977	Mali	1971	Uganda	1971
Democratic Republic of the Congo	1991	Mauritania	1986	United Republic of Tanzania	1971
Djibouti	1982	Mozambique	1988	Vanuatu	1985
Equatorial Guinea	1982	Myanmar	1987	Yemen	1971
Eritrea	1994	Nepal	1971	Zambia	1991
Ethiopia	1971	Niger	1971		

Landlocked countries 31

Afghanistan	Kazakhstan	Rwanda
Armenia	Kyrgyzstan	Swaziland
Azerbaijan	Lao People's Democratic Republic	Tajikistan
Bhutan	Lesotho	Macedonia, the former Yugoslav
Bolivia	Malawi	Republic of
Botswana	Mali	Turkmenistan
Burkina Faso	Mongolia	Uganda
Burundi	Nepal	Uzbekistan
Central African Republic	Niger	Zambia
Chad	Paraguay	Zimbabwe
Ethiopia	Republic of Moldova	

Heavily indebted poor countries (HIPCs) 42

Angola	Gambia	Nicaragua
Benin	Guinea	Niger
Bolivia	Guinea-Bissau	Rwanda
Burkina Faso	Guyana	Sao Tome and Principe
Burundi	Honduras	Senegal
Cameroon	Kenya	Sierra Leone
Central African Republic	Lao People's Democratic Republic	Somalia
Chad	Liberia	Sudan
Comoros	Madagascar	Togo
Congo	Malawi	Uganda
Côte d'Ivoire	Mali	United Republic of Tanzania
Democratic Republic of the Congo	Mauritania	Viet Nam
Ethiopia	Mozambique	Yemen
Ghana	Myanmar	Zambia

DISTRIBUTION OF COUTRIES / TERRITORIES BY TRADE GROUPING

Europe

Group	Year of accession		Year of accession		Year of accession
EFTA (European Free Trade Association) 3		**EU (European Union) 25**			
Iceland	1960	Austria	1995	Latvia	2004
Norway	1960	Belgium	1957	Lithuania	2004
Switzerland	1960	Cyprus	2004	Luxembourg	1957
		Czech Republic	2004	Malta	2004
Euro Zone (of EU) 12		Denmark	1973	Netherlands	1957
Austria	2002	Estonia	2004	Poland	2004
Belgium	2002	Finland	1995	Portugal	1986
Finland	2002	France	1957	Slovakia	2004
France	2002	Germany	1957	Slovenia	2004
Germany	2002	Greece	1981	Spain	1986
Greece	2002	Hungary	2004	Sweden	1995
Ireland	2002	Ireland	1973	United Kingdom	1973
Italy	2002	Italy	1957		
Luxembourg	2002				
Netherlands	2002				
Portugal	2002				
Spain	2002				

America

Group	Year of accession	Group	Year of accession	Group	Year of accession
ANCOM (Andean Community) 5		**FTAA (Free Trade Area of the Americas) 34**		**LAIA (Latin American Integration Association) 12**	
Bolivia	1996	Antigua and Barbuda	1994	Argentina	1980
Colombia	1996	Argentina	1994	Bolivia	1980
Ecuador	1996	Bahamas	1994	Brazil	1980
Peru	1996	Barbados	1994	Chile	1980
Venezuela	1996	Belize	1994	Colombia	1980
		Bolivia	1994	Cuba	1999
CACM (Central American Common Market) 5		Brazil	1994	Ecuador	1980
Costa Rica	1962	Canada	1994	Mexico	1980
El Salvador	1961	Chile	1994	Paraguay	1980
Guatemala	1961	Colombia	1994	Peru	1980
Honduras	1961	Costa Rica	1994	Uruguay	1980
Nicaragua	1961	Dominica	1994	Venezuela	1980
		Dominican Republic	1994		
CARICOM (Caribbean Community) 15		Ecuador	1994	**MERCOSUR (Southern Common Market) 4**	
Antigua and Barbuda	1974	El Salvador	1994	Argentina	1994
Bahamas	1983	Grenada	1994	Brazil	1994
Barbados	1973	Guatemala	1994	Paraguay	1994
Belize	1974	Guyana	1994	Uruguay	1994
Dominica	1974	Haiti	1994		
Grenada	1974	Honduras	1994	**OECS (Organization of Eastern Caribbean States) 9**	
Guyana	1973	Jamaica	1994	Anguilla	1995
Haiti	1997	Mexico	1994	Antigua and Barbuda	1981
Jamaica	1973	Nicaragua	1994	British Virgin Islands	1984
Montserrat	1974	Panama	1994	Dominica	1981
Saint Kitts and Nevis	1974	Paraguay	1994	Grenada	1981
Saint Lucia	1974	Peru	1994	Montserrat	1981
Saint Vincent and the Grenadines	1974	Saint Kitts and Nevis	1994	Saint Kitts and Nevis	1981
Suriname	1995	Saint Lucia	1994	Saint Lucia	1981
Trinidad and Tobago	1973	Saint Vincent and the Grenadines	1994	Saint Vincent and the Grenadines	1981
		Suriname	1994		
NAFTA (North American Free Trade Agreement) 3		Trinidad and Tobago	1994		
Canada	1992	United States of America	1994		
Mexico	1992	Uruguay	1994		
United States of America	1992	Venezuela	1994		

Group	Year of accession
CEPGL (Economic Community of the Great Lakes Countries) 3	
Burundi	1976
Democratic Republic of the Congo	1976
Rwanda	1976
COMESA (Common Market for Eastern and Southern Africa) 20	
Angola	1994
Burundi	1994
Comoros	1994
Democratic Republic of the Congo	1994
Djibouti	1994
Egypt	1994
Eritrea	1994
Ethiopia	1994
Kenya	1994
Madagascar	1994
Malawi	1994
Mauritius	1994
Namibia	1994
Rwanda	1994
Seychelles	1994
Sudan	1994
Swaziland	1994
Uganda	1994
Zambia	1994
Zimbabwe	1994
UMA (Arab Maghreb Union) 5	
Algeria	1989
Libyan Arab Jamahiriya	1989
Mauritania	1989
Morocco	1989
Tunisia	1989

Group	Year of accession
ECOWAS (Economic Community of West African States) 15	
Benin	1975
Burkina Faso	1975
Cape Verde	1975
Côte d'Ivoire	1975
Gambia	1975
Ghana	1975
Guinea	1975
Guinea-Bissau	1975
Liberia	1975
Mali	1975
Niger	1975
Nigeria	1975
Senegal	1975
Sierra Leone	1975
Togo	1975
SADC (Southern African Development Community) 14	
Angola	1992
Botswana	1992
Democratic Republic of the Congo	1992
Lesotho	1992
Malawi	1992
Mauritius	1992
Mozambique	1992
Namibia	1992
Seychelles	1992
South Africa	1994
Swaziland	1992
United Republic of Tanzania	1992
Zambia	1992
Zimbabwe	1992

Group	Year of accession
ECCAS (Economic Community of Central African States) 11	
Angola	1999
Burundi	1983
Cameroon	1983
Central African Republic	1983
Chad	1983
Congo	1983
Democratic Republic of the Congo	1983
Equatorial Guinea	1983
Gabon	1983
Rwanda	1983
Sao Tome and Principe	1983
MRU (Mano River Union) 3	
Guinea	1973
Liberia	1973
Sierra Leone	1973
CEMAC (Economic and Monetary Community of Central Africa) 6	
Cameroon	1994
Central African Republic	1994
Chad	1994
Congo	1994
Equatorial Guinea	1994
Gabon	1994
UEMOA (West African Economic and Monetary Union) 8	
Benin	1994
Burkina Faso	1994
Côte d'Ivoire	1994
Guinea-Bissau	1994
Mali	1994
Niger	1994
Senegal	1994
Togo	1994

Group	Year of accession
ASEAN (Association of South-East Asian Nations) 10	
Brunei Darussalam	1967
Cambodia	1967
Indonesia	1967
Lao People's Democratic Republic	1967
Malaysia	1967
Myanmar	1967
Philippines	1967
Singapore	1967
Thailand	1967
Viet Nam	1967
GCC (Gulf Cooperation Council) 6	
Bahrain	1981
Kuwait	1981
Oman	1981
Qatar	1981
Saudi Arabia	1981
United Arab Emirates	1981

Group	Year of accession
Bangkok Agreement 6	
Bangladesh	1975
China	2001
India	1975
Lao People's Democratic Republic	1975
Republic of Korea	1975
Sri Lanka	1975
ECO (Economic Cooperation Organization) 10	
Afghanistan	1992
Azerbaijan	1992
Iran, Islamic Republic of	1985
Kazakhstan	1992
Kyrgyzstan	1992
Pakistan	1985
Tajikistan	1992
Turkey	1985
Turkmenistan	1992
Uzbekistan	1992

Group	Year of accession
MSG (Melanesia Spearhead Group) 4	
Fiji	1996
Papua New Guinea	1988
Solomon Islands	1988
Vanuatu	1988
SAARC (South Asian Association for Regional Cooperation) 7	
Bangladesh	1985
Bhutan	1985
India	1985
Maldives	1985
Nepal	1985
Pakistan	1985
Sri Lanka	1985

Group	Year of accession	Group	Year of accession	Group	Year of accession
APEC (Asia-Pacific Economic Cooperation) 21		**BSEC (Black Sea Economic Cooperation) 11**		**CIS (Commonwealth of Independent States) 12**	
Australia	1989	Albania	1992	Armenia	1991
Brunei Darussalam	1989	Armenia	1992	Azerbaijan	1991
Canada	1989	Azerbaijan	1992	Belarus	1991
Chile	1989	Bulgaria	1992	Georgia	1993
China	1989	Georgia	1992	Kazakhstan	1991
China, Hong Kong SAR	1989	Greece	1992	Kyrgyzstan	1991
China, Taiwan Province of	1989	Moldova, Republic of	1992	Republic of Moldova	1991
Indonesia	1989	Romania	1992	Russian Federation	1991
Japan	1989	Russian Federation	1992	Tajikistan	1991
Malaysia	1989	Turkey	1992	Turkmenistan	1991
Mexico	1989	Ukraine	1992	Ukraine	1991
New Zealand	1989			Uzbekistan	1991
Papua New Guinea	1989				
Peru	1989				
Philippines	1989				
Republic of Korea	1989				
Russian Federation	1989				
Singapore	1989				
Thailand	1989				
United States of America	1989				
Viet Nam	1989				

ABBREVIATIONS

APEC	Asia-Pacific Economic Cooperation
ASEAN	Association of South-East Asian Nations
BPM	*Balance of Payments Manual* (IMF)
BSEC	Black Sea Economic Cooperation
CACM	Central American Common Market
CARICOM	Caribbean Community
CEMAC	Economic and Monetary Community of Central Africa (formerly UDEAC)
CEPGL	Economic Community of the Great Lakes Countries
c.i.f.	cost, insurance and freight
CIS	Commonwealth of Independent States
COMESA	Common Market for Eastern and Southern Africa (formerly PTA)
DAC	Development Assistance Committee (of OECD)
DRS	Debtor Reporting System
ECCAS	Economic Community of Central African States
ECE	Economic Commission for Europe
ECO	Economic Cooperation Organisation
ECOWAS	Economic Community of West African States
EFTA	European Free Trade Association
ESCAP	Economic and Social Commission for Asia and the Pacific
ESCWA	Economic and Social Commission for Western Asia
EU	European Union
excl.	excluding
FAO	Food and Agriculture Organisation of the United Nations
FDI	foreign direct investment
f.o.b.	free on board
FTAA	Free Trade Area of the Americas
GATS	General Agreement on Trade in Services
GCC	Gulf Cooperation Council
GDP	gross domestic product
GFCF	gross fixed capital formation
GNP	gross national product
HIPC	heavily indebted poor countries
IEA	International Energy Agency
ILO	International Labour Organisation
IMF	International Monetary Fund
KTOE	kilotons of oil equivalent
LAIA	Latin American Integration Association
LDC	least developed countries
MERCOSUR	Southern Common Market
MRU	Mano River Union
MSG	Melanesia Spearhead Group
NAFTA	North American Free Trade Agreement
n.e.s.	not elsewhere specified
NIE	newly industrialized economies
n.i.e.	not included elsewhere
NPISHs	non-profit institutions serving households
OA	official aid
ODA	official development assistance
OE	oil equivalent
OECD	Organisation for Economic Co-operation and Development
OECS	Organisation of Eastern Caribbean States
OOF	other official flows
OPEC	Organisation of the Petroleum Exporting Countries
SAARC	South Asian Association for Regional Cooperation
SADC	Southern African Development Community
SAR	Special Administrative Region
SDR	special drawing rights
SITC	Standard International Trade Classification
TFYR	The former Yugoslav Republic (of Macedonia)
TNC	transnational corporation
TPES	total primary energy supply
UEMOA	West African Economic and Monetary Union
UMA	Arab Maghreb Union
UNAIDS	Joint United Nations Programme on HIV/AIDS
UNCTAD	United Nations Conference on Trade and Development
UN/DESA/SD	United Nations Department of Economic and Social Affairs, Statistics Division
UNESCO	United Nations Educational, Scientific and Cultural Organisation
UNICEF	United Nations Children's Fund
WHO	World Health Organisation
WTO	World Trade Organisation
WTO	World Tourism Organisation

Ces notes donnent des indications sur le contenu de chaque partie du *Manuel*, en particulier sur les modifications apportées par rapport aux précédentes éditions.

Les tableaux inclus dans cette publication constituent un résumé analytique des séries chronologiques complètes publiées dans le *Manuel de statistiques de la CNUCED 2004* sur CD-ROM et dans la version Internet (www.unctad.org/statistics/handbook). L'édition imprimée présente les mêmes tableaux dans un format concis, avec toutefois une place plus grande consacrée aux informations récentes. Les données dans les deux versions électroniques pourront, dans certains cas, être différentes de celles de la variante imprimée en raison de leur publication à une date ultérieure.

PREMIERE PARTIE
Commerce international des marchandises

Le tableau 1.1A donne la valeur des exportations et des importations totales de marchandises par pays et par groupements régionaux et économiques, exprimée en millions de dollars. Le système national d'enregistrement (commerce général ou commerce spécial) et d'évaluation est indiqué.

Les mêmes données sont présentées dans le tableau 1.1B pour des groupements économiques différents.

Le tableau 1.1C fait apparaître les parts dans les exportations et les importations de différents groupements géographiques et économiques.

Les taux de croissance calculés à partir des valeurs des tableaux 1.1A et 1.1B figurent aux tableaux 1.2A et 1.2B.

Le tableau 1.3 présente les balances commerciales (exportations f.a.b. moins importations c.a.f.), ainsi que ces mêmes balances en pourcentage des importations par pays, par régions et par groupements économiques.

Le tableau 1.4 indique l'importance relative des échanges intrarégionaux dans le commerce total des groupements commerciaux, comme l'UE, l'ANASE ou le MERCOSUR. Il présente la valeur de leurs exportations de marchandises au sein du groupement, ainsi que leur part dans le commerce régional et mondial. 30 groupes commerciaux sont inclus dans cette analyse.

DEUXIEME PARTIE
Indices du commerce et des prix des produits de base

Le groupe de tableaux 2.1 (2.1A à 2.1F) fournit les indices du volume et de la valeur unitaire des exportations et des importations, ainsi que des termes de l'échange et du pouvoir d'achat des exportations, pour les pays développés et les pays en développement par régions et par groupements économiques. Les indices concernant les économies en développement figurent au tableau 8.1.

Le tableau 2.2 donne les indices de prix agrégés pour des groupes de produits de base tels que les produits alimentaires, les boissons tropicales, les huiles et graines oléagineuses, les matières premières d'origine agricole, les minéraux, minerais et métaux ainsi qu'un indice de l'ensemble en dollars courants des Etats-Unis. Il contient également des indices annuels et trimestriels de prix sur le marché libre d'une sélection de produits de base exportés par les économies en développement. Pour mémoire, les prix du marché en dollars courants sont donnés pour l'année de base. Ce tableau a été établi à partir de données extraites du *Bulletin des prix des produits de base* de la CNUCED.

TROISIEME PARTIE
Structure du commerce international par régions

Les tableaux 3.1A et 3.1B présentent respectivement la structure des exportations et des importations des pays par régions d'origine et de destination. Le plus grand nombre possible de pays en développement sont inclus dans cette étude, tandis que les partenaires commerciaux sont regroupés en 13 groupes, considérés particulièrement importants pour analyser les flux du commerce international.

Le groupe de tableaux 3.2.1 indique la structure des exportations par destinations et par principaux groupes de produits pour le monde et pour certaines régions, tandis que les tableaux sous le titre 3.2.2 donnent les mêmes renseignements concernant les importations par origines. Ces ensembles de données fournissent les informations détaillées sur le réseau du commerce international pour le monde, 22 régions d'origine et 22 régions de destination, pour chacun de 12 groupes de produits présentés. Ces derniers se basent sur la classification CTCI (rév. 2). Les données dans ce tableau ne sont pas strictement comparables à celles du tableau 1.1, principalement en raison de la révision plus fréquente de ces dernières. Les données complètes à partir desquelles ces tableaux ont été composés sont disponibles dans le tableau 3.2 des versions CD-ROM et Internet du *Manuel de statistiques de la CNUCED 2004*.

QUATRIEME PARTIE
Structure du commerce international par produits

Les tableaux 4.1A et 4.1B font apparaître la structure des exportations et des importations des économies individuelles par catégories de produits pour une sélection d'années. Huit groupes de produits, qui se basent sur la classification CTCI (rév. 2), sont présentés : les produits alimentaires, les matières premières d'origine agricole, les combustibles, les minerais et métaux, les produits manufacturés, les produits chimiques, les articles manufacturés divers, ainsi que les machines et le matériel de transport.

Dans les tableaux 4.2A, B et C sont présentées respectivement les exportations du monde, des économies développées et de celles en développement, par groupes de la CTCI (rév. 2, position à trois chiffres). On y trouve également la part de chaque groupe de produits dans les exportations de la région et du monde, ainsi que le taux annuel moyen de croissance correspondant et l'écart de ce dernier par rapport au taux de croissance mondial.

Le tableau 4.2D fait apparaître, pour les différentes économies, les principaux produits qu'elles exportent (CTCI rév. 2, position à trois chiffres).La part de chaque produit dans le total des exportations du pays, de la région et du monde est également indiquée.

Le tableau 4.2E indique les plus gros exportateurs des 70 principaux produits exportés par les économies en développement (CTCI rév. 2, position à trois chiffres), ainsi que les parts correspondantes.

CINQUIEME PARTIE
Commerce international des services

Le tableau 5.1 présente la valeur des exportations et des importations des services par pays, par régions et par groupements économiques. Les services se divisent en 11 catégories principales, conformément à la définition du *Manuel de la balance des paiements* du FMI (1993, MBP 5). Les agrégats incluent les valeurs estimées par le secrétariat de la CNUCED qui ne sont pas présentées séparément. Les services commerciaux, qui excluent les services des administrations publiques et suivent la définition des AGCS, sont présentés pour mémoire dans le tableau 5.2 du *Manuel de statistiques de la CNUCED 2004* sur CD-ROM ou sur l'Internet. De manière générale, les difficultés à mesurer statistiquement la valeur du commerce des services persistent et les données de la balance des paiements peuvent être inférieures aux flux existants du commerce international des services.

Le tableau 5.2A fait apparaître les 20 plus gros exportateurs, parmi les économies en développement, pour chacune des 10 catégories principales de services, selon la définition du *Manuel de la balance des paiements* du FMI (1993, MBP 5). Le tableau 5.2B fournit les mêmes informations sur les 20 plus gros importateurs de services parmi les économies en développement. Les secteurs présentés sont : les transports, les voyages, les communications, le bâtiment et les travaux publics, l'informatique et l'information, les assurances, les services financiers, les redevances et droits de licence, les services personnels, culturels et relatifs aux loisirs et les services fournis ou reçus par les administrations publiques. Les services fournis ou reçus par les administrations publiques, n.c.a. ne sont pas inclus.

Le tableau 5.3 fait apparaître les données sur les services liés au tourisme en présentant, par pays et pour les années récentes, les statistiques suivantes : montant des dépenses des touristes, nombre des nuitées des touristes, nombre des arrivées et durée moyenne de séjour. Tous les indicateurs se réfèrent aux touristes non résidents.

SIXIEME PARTIE
Flux financiers internationaux

Le tableau 6.1A contient un état récapitulatif du «compte courant» des balances des paiements des pays et territoires individuels. Les données du compte des transactions courantes de la balance des paiements recouvrent toutes les transactions, entre entités résidentes et non résidentes, portant sur des valeurs économiques, concernant principalement les biens, les services, les revenus et les transferts courants. Des notes explicatives concernant les catégories et la terminologie employée se trouvent à la suite du tableau.

Le tableau 6.1B fait apparaître le sommaire du «compte de capital et d'opérations financières» des balances des paiements des pays et territoires individuels. Les chiffres des comptes de capital et des comptes financiers, rapportés en valeurs nettes, couvrent les transactions en avoirs et engagements étrangers. Toutes les réévaluations et autres variations d'avoirs et d'engagements qui ne reflètent pas des transactions sont exclues du compte de capital et d'opérations financières. Le compte de capital est subdivisé en transferts de capital et en acquisitions et cession d'avoirs non financiers non produits. Le compte financier recouvre les investissements (directs, de portefeuille et autres) et les avoirs de réserve (or monétaire, DTS, devises et autres créances). Ces statistiques sont présentées dans le Manuel pour la première fois. Les explications détaillées des catégories et de la terminologie utilisées sont présentées à la suite du tableau.

Le tableau 6.2 est consacré aux investissements directs en provenance de l'étranger (IDE) et présente les flux entrants et sortants par pays et par groupements régionaux. Ces chiffres correspondent aux données présentées dans l'Annexe statistique du *World Investment Report 2004: The Shift Towards Services,* de la CNUCED.

Les tableaux 6.3A et B fournissent des informations sur les principaux économies en développement destinataires et expéditeurs des envois de fonds des travailleurs. En plus, ils présentent les versements des travailleurs en pourcentage du commerce international. Le *Manuel de la balance des paiements* du FMI *(1993, MBP 5)* classifie séparément les versements des travailleurs, la rémunération des salariés et les transferts de capital des migrants. Les valeurs dans le tableau 6.3 incluent les trois catégories mentionnées, afin d'offrir une présentation plus exhaustive des flux entrants ou sortants d'une économie à travers les transferts réalisés par les travailleurs migrants.

Le tableau 6.4 fournit les données relatives aux réserves internationales (les réserves totales moins l'or) des économies en développement par pays, par régions et par groupements économiques. Les mois d'importation que ces réserves peuvent financer, dans la situation actuelle du commerce international du pays, sont également indiqués, ainsi que la variation annuelle des réserves totales.

Le tableau 6.5 fait apparaître la composition des flux financiers officiels vers les économies en développement par pays, par régions et par groupements économiques. Les flux bilatéraux et multilatéraux sont pris en compte, selon les publications du Comité d'aide au développement (CAD – OCDE).

Le tableau 6.6 contient des données sur la dette extérieure des économies en développement par régions et par groupements économiques, ainsi qu'une ventilation détaillée de la dette publique ou garantie par l'état par sources d'emprunt. Les données de la dette extérieure présentées dans ce tableau se basent sur le Système de notification des pays débiteurs (SNPD), géré par la Banque mondiale.

SEPTIEME PARTIE
Indicateurs du développement

Le tableau 7.1 fournit des renseignements sur le chiffre et la densité de la population, la superficie et le PIB courant total et par habitant (en dollars), par pays, par régions et par groupements économiques. Les estimations du PIB par habitant (en dollars) présentées dans ce tableau ont été obtenues à partir de données en monnaies nationales. Il n'est pas toujours satisfaisant de ramener la valeur de séries de ce type à une devise commune - le dollar des Etats-Unis - en appliquant les taux de change officiels, étant donné les différences de niveau de prix entre les économies individuelles.

Le tableau 7.2 indique les taux annuels moyens de croissance du PIB réel total et du PIB par tête d'habitant au prix de marché, par pays, par régions et par groupements économiques.

Le tableau 7.3 contient les données sur la structure du PIB par catégories de dépenses et par branches d'activité économique, par pays, par régions et par groupements économiques.

Le tableau 7.4 présente quelques indicateurs économiques et sociaux pour les différents pays. Il fournit des statistiques vitales, ainsi que celles relatives à la santé et l'environnement. Grâce aux dernières données disponibles, le tableau permet la comparaison des pays à travers différents aspects de leur développement socio-économique. Parmi les indicateurs présentés, on trouve : la population urbaine, la mortalité infantile, l'espérance de vie, la disponibilité des sanitaires, le VIH/SIDA, les émissions de dioxyde de carbone, la consommation totale d'énergie.

Le tableau 7.5 présente d'autres indicateurs socio-économiques par pays relatifs à l'éducation, à la main-d'œuvre, à l'égalité entre femmes et hommes et aux migrations. Les dernières données disponibles sont prises en compte pour tous les indicateurs parmi lesquels figurent : les inscriptions scolaires, l'éducation des femmes, l'analphabétisme, le taux de chômage, le taux de chômage féminin, la main-d'œuvre par secteur, le nombre de migrants.

Le tableau 7.6 contient une sélection de données relatives aux technologies de l'information et de la communication, qui se réfèrent au développement et à l'usage des nouvelles technologies, ainsi qu'à l'informatique et l'accès aux media. Le tableau inclut des indicateurs sur les postes téléviseurs, les téléphones, les ordinateurs personnels, l'Internet, l'investissement dans les télécommunications, etc.

HUITIEME PARTIE
Etudes spéciales

Le tableau 8.1 fait apparaître des estimations provisoires des indices de la valeur unitaire des exportations et des importations pour différents pays et territoires en développement, ainsi que les termes de l'échange et le pouvoir d'achat des exportations calculés à partir de ces indices. Les agrégats présentés dans le tableau 2.1 sont calculés à partir des estimations qui figurent ici.

Le tableau 8.2A contient les séries de données sur les indices de concentration et de diversification des exportations des pays et territoires individuels et des différents groupements régionaux. Le tableau 8.2B présente les mêmes indices pour les importations.

Les tableaux 8.3A et B fournissent les indices de concentration et de changements structurels des exportations et des importations par groupes de produits de la CTCI (rév. 2, position à trois chiffres).

Le tableau 8.4 contient les données sur les droits de douane moyens appliqués à l'importation des principales catégories de produits non-agricoles et non-pétroliers, par marchés individuels et par groupes de pays exportateurs.

Le tableau 8.5 présente les indices d'instabilité et les tendances des prix sur le marché libre d'une sélection de produits de base ayant une importance particulière pour les économies en développement.

Le tableau 8.6 concerne le transport maritime international. Il contient des données sur la flotte marchande mondiale par pavillons d'immatriculation et par types de navires. Ce tableau, qui paraît pour la première fois dans le *Manuel*, incorpore les informations consolidées provenant des différentes éditions de la publication *Review of Maritime Transport* de la CNUCED.

AUTRES NOTES ET EXPLICATIONS DES SYMBOLES

La somme des chiffres et des pourcentages indiqués dans les tableaux ne correspond pas nécessairement aux totaux en raison des arrondis.

Sauf indication contraire, le terme «dollar» s'entend du dollar des Etats-Unis d'Amérique.

Un zéro (0) signifie que le montant est nul ou négligeable.

Un tiret (_) signifie que la rubrique est sans objet.

Deux points (..) signifient que les données ne sont pas disponibles ou ne sont pas communiquées séparément.

Le trait d'union (-) entre deux millésimes (par exemple 1985-1990) indique qu'il s'agit de la période tout entière (y compris la première et la dernière année mentionnées). Les exceptions sont indiquées dans les notes de bas de page.

Les répartitions des pays, incluses dans les pages suivantes, sont adoptées uniquement pour des raisons de présentation statistique et sont celles qu'utilise la Division de statistique, Département des affaires économiques et sociales (DAES) de l'ONU.

Dans cette publication, le terme *économie* couvre les régions, les pays et les territoires.

En comparaison avec le *Manuel de statistiques de la CNUCED* de l'année précédente, la présente édition comporte quelques modifications, notamment dans la présentation des groupes de pays. Les changements suivent l'élargissement de l'Union européenne du 1 mai 2004 et incluent les ajustements conséquents, particulièrement concernant les pays d'Europe centrale et du Sud-Est et pays qui ont succédé de l'ex-URSS. Le nouveau groupement Europe du Sud-Est et Communauté des Etats indépendants (CEI) a été introduit.

TROIS GRANDS GROUPES DE PAYS / TERRITOIRES

Economies développées :

En Europe :
  Union européenne :

Allemagne	Grèce	Pays-Bas
Autriche	Hongrie	Pologne
Belgique	Irlande	Portugal
Chypre	Italie	République Tchèque
Danemark	Lettonie	Royaume-Uni de Grande-Bretagne et d'Irlande du Nord
Espagne	Lituanie	Slovénie
Estonie	Luxembourg	Slovaquie
Finlande	Malte	Suède
France		

  Autres pays développés d'Europe :

Andorre	Iles Féroé	Norvège
Gibraltar	Islande	Saint-Marin
Ile de Man	Liechtenstein	Saint-siège
Iles Anglo-Normandes	Monaco	Suisse

En Amérique : Canada et Etats-Unis d'Amérique

En Asie : Israël et Japon

En Océanie : Australie et Nouvelle-Zélande

Europe du Sud-Est et Communauté des Etats indépendants (CEI) :

Europe du Sud-Est :

Albanie	Croatie	Roumanie
Bosnie-Herzégovine	Macédoine, l'ex-République yougoslave de	Serbie-et-Monténégro
Bulgarie		

Communauté des Etats indépendants (CEI) :

Arménie	Géorgie	Ouzbékistan
Azerbaïdjan	Kazakhstan	Tadjikistan
Bélarus	Kirghizstan	Turkménistan
Fédération de Russie	Moldova, République de	Ukraine

Economies en développement :

Tous les autres pays et territoires d'Afrique, d'Amérique, d'Asie et d'Océanie non mentionnés ci-dessus. Les grandes régions couvrant l'ensemble des économies en développement ont été divisées en sous-régions pour permettre la présentation de statistiques plus détaillées. La composition de chaque région est présentée dans les pages suivantes. Les exceptions à ce classement que comportent quelques tableaux sont indiquées dans des notes.

Dans le *Manuel de statistiques de la CNUCED*, un certain nombre de classifications des pays et territoires sont utilisées afin de mieux faire ressortir les différences entre les économies en développement et ainsi faciliter l'analyse des données socio-économiques. Ces classifications distinguent, en premier lieu, les principaux pays exportateurs de pétrole des autres économies en développement. Ces derniers ont été à leur tour répartis en deux sous-catégories: (a) principaux exportateurs d'articles manufacturés et (b) autres économies. La rubrique «Autres économies» a été elle-même subdivisée d'après les principales régions géographiques.

Le groupement des «Principaux exportateurs de pétrole» comprend les 11 pays membres de l'OPEP et 10 pays non-membres de l'OPEP choisis en fonction des critères suivants : la part du pétrole et des produits pétroliers ne représentait pas moins de 50% de leurs exportations totales, et les exportations de ces produits s'élevaient à au moins 1,5 milliards de dollars en 1999 - 2001 en moyenne. Les Antilles néerlandaises ont été ajoutées à ce groupe dans la présente édition du *Manuel de statistiques de la CNUCED.*

Le groupement des «Principaux exportateurs d'articles manufacturés» comprend les économies sélectionnées en fonction

des critères suivants : la part d'articles manufacturés ne représentait pas moins de 50% de leurs exportations totales, et leurs exportations d'articles manufacturés avaient une valeur moyenne d'au moins 20 milliards de dollars en 1999 - 2001.

Les économies en développement sont aussi divisées en trois groupes de revenu (en fonction du PIB par habitant en 2000) : revenu élevé, revenu intermédiaire et revenu faible.

En plus, les groupements des «Pays les moins avancés» (PMA), «Pays pauvres très endettés» (PPTE) et «Pays enclavés» sont présentés pour mémoire. Certains tableaux incluent aussi le groupe des «Pays en développement, Chine non comprise», qui se réfère seulement à la Chine continentale. Les pays de «l'Afrique subsaharienne» (Afrique du Sud comprise) forment un autre groupe.

Les groupements commerciaux (par exemple Union européenne, ALADI, Accord de Bangkok) sont présentés dans un certain nombre de tableaux. Cela a permis de faire figurer des groupements à caractère interrégional tels la CEAP.

Les dernières informations disponibles au mois de mai 2004 ont été prises en compte pour présenter les groupements contenus dans ce *Manuel de statistiques.*

REPARTITION DES PAYS / TERRITOIRES EN DEVELOPPEMENT PAR REGIONS

Amérique 49

Amérique du Sud 14

Argentine
Bolivie
Brésil
Chili
Colombie
Equateur
Guyana
Guyane française
Iles Falkland (Malvinas)
Paraguay
Pérou
Suriname
Uruguay
Venezuela

Autres pays d'Amérique 35

Anguilla
Antigua-et-Barbuda
Antilles néerlandaises
Aruba
Bahamas
Barbade
Belize
Bermudes
Costa Rica
Cuba
Dominique
El Salvador
Grenade
Groenland
Guadeloupe
Guatemala
Haïti
Honduras
Iles Caïmanes
Iles Turques et Caïques
Iles Vierges américaines
Iles Vierges britanniques
Jamaïque
Martinique
Mexique
Montserrat
Nicaragua
Panama
Porto Rico
République dominicaine
Saint-Kitts-et-Nevis
Saint-Lucie
Saint-Pierre-et-Miquelon
Saint-Vincent-et-les Grenadines
Trinité-et-Tobago

Afrique 55

Afrique du Nord 6

Algérie
Egypte
Jamahiriya arabe libyenne
Maroc
Soudan
Tunisie

Autres pays d'Afrique 49

Afrique du Sud
Angola
Bénin
Botswana
Burkina Faso
Burundi
Cameroun
Cap-Vert
Comores
Congo
Côte d'Ivoire
Djibouti
Erythrée
Ethiopie
Gabon
Gambie
Ghana
Guinea
Guinée équatoriale
Guinée-Bissau
Kenya
Lesotho
Libéria
Madagascar
Malawi
Mali
Maurice
Mauritanie
Mozambique
Namibie
Niger
Nigéria
Ouganda
République centrafricaine
République démocratique du Congo
République-Unie de Tanzanie
Réunion
Rwanda
Sainte-Hélène
Sao Tomé-et-Principe
Sénégal
Seychelles
Sierra Leone
Somalie
Swaziland
Tchad
Togo
Zambie
Zimbabwe

Asie 40

Asie occidentale 14

Arabie saoudite
Bahreïn
Emirats arabes unis
Iran, République islamique d'
Iraq
Jordanie
Koweït
Liban
Oman
Qatar
République arabe syrienne
Territoire palestinien
Turquie
Yémen

Autres pays d'Asie 26

Afghanistan
Bangladesh
Bhoutan
Brunéi Darussalam
Cambodge
Chine
Chine, RAS de Hong Kong
Chine, RAS de Macao
Chine, Taiwan Province de
Corée, République populaire démocratique de
Corée, République de
Inde
Indonésie
Malaisie
Maldives
Mongolie
Myanmar
Népal
Pakistan
Philippines
République démocratique populaire lao
Singapour
Sri Lanka
Thaïlande
Timor-Leste
Viet Nam

Fidji	Kiribati	Polynésie française
Guam	Micronésie, Etats fédérés de	Samoa
Iles Cook	Nauru	Samoa américaines
Iles Mariannes du Nord	Nioué	Tokélaou
Iles Marshall	Nouvelle-Calédonie	Tonga
Iles Salomon	Palaos	Tuvalu
Iles Wallis et Futuna	Papouasie-Nouvelle-Guinée	Vanuatu

REPARTITION DES PAYS / TERRITOIRES EN DEVELOPPEMENT PAR GROUPEMENTS ECONOMIQUES

A. REPARTITION DES PAYS / TERRITOIRES EN DEVELOPPEMENT PAR GRANDES CATEGORIES

Principaux exportateurs de pétrole 21

Algérie*	Iraq*	**Principaux exportateurs d'articles manufacturés 12**
Antilles néerlandaises	Jamahiriya arabe libyenne*	Brésil
Angola	Koweït*	Chine
Arabie saoudite*	Nigéria*	Chine, Hong Kong RAS
Bahreïn	Oman	Chine, Taiwan Province de
Brunéi Darussalam	Qatar*	Corée, République de
Congo	République arabe syrienne	Inde
Emirats arabes unis*	Trinité-et-Tobago	Malaisie
Gabon	Venezuela*	Mexique
Indonésie*	Yémen	Philippines
Iran, République islamique d'*		Singapour
(* pays membre de l'OPEP)		Thaïlande
		Turquie

Autres économies 132

Tous les autres pays et territoires en développement non compris parmi les Principaux exportateurs du pétrole ou parmi Principaux exportateurs d'articles manufacturés.

B. REPARTITION DES PAYS / TERRITOIRES EN DEVELOPPEMENT PAR GROUPES DE REVENU

PIB courant par habitant supérieur à 4500 dollars en 2000 : Revenu élevé 50

Anguille	Grenade	Nouvelle-Calédonie
Antigua-et-Barbuda	Groenland	Oman
Antilles néerlandaises	Guadeloupe	Palaos
Arabie saoudite	Guam	Polynésie française
Argentine	Guyane française	Porto Rico
Aruba	Iles Caïmanes	Qatar
Bahamas	Iles Falkland (Malvinas)	Réunion
Bahreïn	Iles Mariannes du Nord	Saint-Kitts-et-Nevis
Barbade	Iles Turques et Caïques	Sainte-Lucie
Bermudes	Iles Vierges américaines	Saint-Pierre-et-Miquelon
Brunéi Darussalam	Iles Vierges britanniques	Samoa américaines
Chili	Jamahiriya arabe libyenne	Seychelles
Chine, Hong Kong RAS	Koweït	Singapour
Chine, Macao RAS	Liban	Trinité-et-Tobago
Chine, Taiwan Province de	Martinique	Uruguay
Corée, République de	Mexique	Venezuela
Emirats arabes unis	Montserrat	

PIB courant par habitant compris entre 1000 et 4 500 dollars en 2000 : Revenu intermédiaire 50

Afrique du Sud	Guinée équatoriale	Pérou
Algérie	Iles Cook	République arabe syrienne
Belize	Iles Marshall	République dominicaine
Bolivie	Iles Wallis et Futuna	Sainte-Hélène
Botswana	Iran, République islamique d'	Saint-Vincent-et-les Grenadines
Brésil	Jamaïque	Samoa
Cap-Vert	Jordanie	Suriname
Colombie	Malaisie	Swaziland
Costa Rica	Maldives	Territoire palestinien
Cuba	Maroc	Thaïlande
Dominique	Maurice	Tokélaou
Egypte	Micronésie, Etats fédérés de	Tonga
El Salvador	Namibie	Tunisie
Equateur	Nauru	Turquie
Fidji	Nioué	Tuvalu
Gabon	Panama	Vanuatu
Guatemala	Paraguay	

PIB courant par habitant inférieur à 1000 dollars en 2000 : Revenu faible 65

Afghanistan	Haïti	Pakistan
Angola	Honduras	Papouasie-Nouvelle-Guinée
Bangladesh	Iles Salomon	Philippines
Bénin	Inde	République démocratique populaire lao
Bhoutan	Indonésie	République centrafricaine
Burkina Faso	Iraq	République démocratique du Congo
Burundi	Kenya	République-Unie de Tanzanie
Cambodge	Kiribati	Rwanda
Cameroun	Lesotho	Sao Tomé-et-Principe
Chine	Libéria	Sénégal
Comores	Madagascar	Sierra Leone
Congo	Malawi	Somalie
Corée, République populaire démocratique de	Mali	Soudan
Côte d'Ivoire	Mauritanie	Sri Lanka
Djibouti	Mongolie	Tchad
Erythrée	Mozambique	Timor-Leste
Ethiopie	Myanmar	Togo
Gambie	Népal	Viet Nam
Ghana	Nicaragua	Yémen
Guinée	Niger	Zambie
Guinée-Bissau	Nigéria	Zimbabwe
Guyana	Ouganda	

C. AUTRES GROUPEMENTS (POUR MEMOIRE)

Pays les moins avancés (PMA) 50, avec l'année d'inclusion dans le groupe

Afghanistan	1971	Haïti	1971	République démocratique populaire lao	1971
Angola	1994	Iles Salomon	1991	République-Unie de Tanzanie	1971
Bangladesh	1975	Kiribati	1986	Rwanda	1971
Bénin	1971	Lesotho	1971	Samoa	1971
Bhoutan	1971	Libéria	1990	Sao Tomé-et-Principe	1982
Burkina Faso	1971	Madagascar	1991	Sénégal	2001
Burundi	1971	Malawi	1971	Sierra Leone	1982
Cambodge	1991	Maldives	1971	Somalie	1971
Cap-Vert	1977	Mali	1971	Soudan	1971
Comores	1977	Mauritanie	1986	Tchad	1971
Djibouti	1982	Mozambique	1988	Timor-Leste	2003
Erythrée	1994	Myanmar	1987	Togo	1982
Ethiopie	1971	Népal	1971	Tuvalu	1986
Gambie	1975	Niger	1971	Vanuatu	1985
Guinée	1971	Ouganda	1971	Yémen	1971
Guinée équatoriale	1982	République centrafricaine	1975	Zambie	1991
Guinée-Bissau	1981	République démocratique du Congo	1991		

Pays enclavés 31

Afghanistan	Lesotho	Paraguay
Arménie	Macédoine, ex-République yougoslave de	République centrafricaine
Azerbaïdjan		République démocratique populaire lao
Bhoutan	Malawi	Rwanda
Bolivie	Mali	Swaziland
Botswana	Moldova, République de	Tadjikistan
Burkina Faso	Mongolie	Tchad
Burundi	Népal	Turkménistan
Ethiopie	Niger	Zambie
Kazakhstan	Ouganda	Zimbabwe
Kirghizistan	Ouzbékistan	

Pays pauvres très endettés (PPTE) 42

Angola	Guyana	République démocratique du Congo
Bénin	Honduras	République démocratique populaire lao
Bolivie	Kenya	République-Unie de Tanzanie
Burkina Faso	Libéria	Rwanda
Burundi	Madagascar	Sao Tomé-et-Principe
Cameroun	Malawi	Sénégal
Comores	Mali	Sierra Leone
Congo	Mauritanie	Somalie
Côte d'Ivoire	Mozambique	Soudan
Ethiopie	Myanmar	Tchad
Gambie	Nicaragua	Togo
Ghana	Niger	Viet Nam
Guinée	Ouganda	Yémen
Guinée-Bissau	République centrafricaine	Zambie

REPARTITION DES PAYS / TERRITOIRES PAR GROUPEMENTS COMMERCIAUX

Europe

Groupe	Année d'adhésion
AELE (Association européenne de libre-échange) 3	
Islande	1960
Norvège	1960
Suisse	1960
Zone Euro (d'Union européenne) 12	
Allemagne	2002
Autriche	2002
Belgique	2002
Espagne	2002
Finlande	2002
France	2002
Grèce	2002
Irlande	2002
Italie	2002
Luxembourg	2002
Pays-Bas	2002
Portugal	2002

	Année d'adhésion		Année d'adhésion
UE (Union européenne) 25			
Allemagne	1957	Lettonie	2004
Autriche	1995	Lituanie	2004
Belgique	1957	Luxembourg	1957
Chypre	2004	Malte	2004
Danemark	1973	Pays-Bas	1957
Espagne	1986	Pologne	2004
Estonie	2004	Portugal	1986
Finlande	1995	République tchèque	2004
France	1957	Royaume-Uni	1973
Grèce	1981	Slovaquie	2004
Hongrie	2004	Slovénie	2004
Irlande	1973	Suède	1995
Italie	1957		

Amérique

Groupe	Année d'adhésion
ALADI (Association latino-américaine d'intégration) 12	
Argentine	1980
Bolivie	1980
Brésil	1980
Chili	1980
Colombie	1980
Cuba	1999
Equateur	1980
Mexique	1980
Paraguay	1980
Pérou	1980
Uruguay	1980
Venezuela	1980
ALENA (Accord de libre-échange nord-américain) 3	
Canada	1992
Etats-Unis d'Amérique	1992
Mexique	1992
CARICOM (Communauté des Caraïbes) 15	
Antigua-et-Barbuda	1974
Bahamas	1983
Barbade	1973
Belize	1974
Dominique	1974
Grenade	1974
Guyane	1973
Haïti	1997
Jamaïque	1973
Montserrat	1974
Sainte-Lucie	1974
Saint-Kitts-et-Nevis	1974
Saint-Vincent-et-les Grenadines	1974
Suriname	1995
Trinité-et-Tobago	1973

Groupe	Année d'adhésion
Communauté andine 5	
Bolivie	1996
Colombie	1996
Equateur	1996
Pérou	1996
Venezuela	1996
MCAC (Marché commun d'Amérique centrale) 5	
Costa Rica	1962
El Salvador	1961
Guatemala	1961
Honduras	1961
Nicaragua	1961
MERCOSUR (Marché commun austral) 4	
Argentine	1994
Brésil	1994
Paraguay	1994
Uruguay	1994
OECO (Organisation des Etats des Caraïbes orientales) 9	
Anguilla	1995
Antigua-et-Barbuda	1981
Dominique	1981
Grenade	1981
Iles vierges britanniques	1984
Montserrat	1981
Sainte-Lucie	1981
Saint-Kitts-et-Nevis	1981
Saint-Vincent-et-les Grenadines	1981

Groupe	Année d'adhésion
ZLEA (Zone de libre échange de l'Amérique) 34	
Antigua-et-Barbuda	1994
Argentine	1994
Bahamas	1994
Barbade	1994
Belize	1994
Bolivie	1994
Brésil	1994
Canada	1994
Chili	1994
Colombie	1994
Costa Rica	1994
Dominique	1994
El Salvador	1994
Equateur	1994
Etats-Unis	1994
Grenade	1994
Guatemala	1994
Guyana	1994
Haïti	1994
Honduras	1994
Jamaïque	1994
Mexique	1994
Nicaragua	1994
Panama	1994
Paraguay	1994
Pérou	1994
République dominicaine	1994
Sainte-Lucie	1994
Saint-Kitts-et-Nevis	1994
Saint-Vincent-et-les Grenadines	1994
Suriname	1994
Trinité-et-Tobago	1994
Uruguay	1994
Venezuela	1994

Afrique

Groupe	Année d'adhésion	Groupe	Année d'adhésion	Groupe	Année d'adhésion
CEDEAO (Communauté économique des Etats de l'Afrique de l'Ouest) 15		**CEPGL (Communauté économique des pays des Grands Lacs) 3**		**CDAA (Communauté de développement de l'Afrique australe) 14**	
Bénin	1975	Burundi	1976	Afrique du Sud	1994
Burkina Faso	1975	République démocratique		Angola	1992
Cap-Vert	1975	du Congo	1976	Botswana	1992
Côte d'Ivoire	1975	Rwanda	1976	Lesotho	1992
Gambie	1975			Malawi	1992
Ghana	1975	**COMESA (Marché commun des Etats de l'Afrique de l'Est et du Sud) 20**		Maurice	1992
Guinée	1975			Mozambique	1992
Guinée-Bissau	1975	Angola	1994	Namibie	1992
Libéria	1975	Burundi	1994	République démocratique	1992
Mali	1975	Comores	1994	du Congo	
Niger	1975	Djibouti	1994	République-Unie de Tanzanie	1992
Nigéria	1975	Egypte	1994	Seychelles	1992
Sénégal	1975	Erythrée	1994	Swaziland	1992
Sierra Leone	1975	Ethiopie	1994	Zambie	1992
Togo	1975	Kenya	1994	Zimbabwe	1992
		Madagascar	1994		
CEEAC (Communauté économique des Etats de l'Afrique centrale)11		Malawi	1994	**CEMAC (Communauté économique et monétaire de l'Afrique centrale) 6**	
Angola	1999	Maurice	1994		
Burundi	1983	Namibie	1994	Cameroun	1994
Cameroun	1983	Ouganda	1994	Congo	1994
Congo	1983	République démocratique		Gabon	1994
Gabon	1983	du Congo	1994	Guinée équatoriale	1994
Guinée équatoriale	1983	Rwanda	1994	République centrafricaine	1994
République centrafricaine	1983	Seychelles	1994	Tchad	1994
République démocratique		Soudan	1994		
du Congo	1983	Swaziland	1994	**UEMOA (Union économique et monétaire ouest-africaine) 8**	
Rwanda	1983	Zambie	1994		
Sao Tomé-et-Principe	1983	Zimbabwe	1994	Bénin	1994
Tchad	1983			Burkina Faso	1994
		UMA (Union du Maghreb arabe) 5		Côte d'Ivoire	1994
UFM (Union du fleuve Mano) 3		Algérie	1989	Guinée-Bissau	1994
Guinée	1973	Jamahiriya arabe libyenne	1989	Mali	1994
Libéria	1973	Maroc	1989	Niger	1994
Sierra Leone	1973	Mauritanie	1989	Sénégal	1994
		Tunisie	1989	Togo	1994

Asie

Groupe	Année d'adhésion	Groupe	Année d'adhésion	Groupe	Année d'adhésion
Accord de Bangkok 6		**ANASE (Association des nations de l'Asie du Sud-Est) 10**		**CCG (Conseil de coopération du Golfe) 6**	
Bangladesh	1975	Brunéi Darussalam	1967	Arabie saoudite	1981
Chine	2001	Cambodge	1967	Bahreïn	1981
Corée, République de	1975	Indonésie	1967	Emirats arabes unis	1981
Inde	1975	Malaisie	1967	Koweït	1981
République démocratique		Myanmar	1967	Oman	1981
populaire lao	1975	Philippines	1967	Qatar	1981
Sri Lanka	1975	République démocratique			
		populaire lao	1967	**SAARC (Association de l'Asie du Sud pour la coopération régionale) 7**	
ECO (Organisation de coopération économique) 10		Singapour	1967		
		Thaïlande	1967		
Afghanistan	1992	Viet Nam	1967	Bangladesh	1985
Azerbaïdjan	1992			Bhoutan	1985
Iran, République islamique d'	1985	**Groupe Fer de lance mélanésien 4**		Inde	1985
Kazakhstan	1992			Maldives	1985
Kirghizistan	1992	Fidji	1996	Népal	1985
Ouzbékistan	1992	Iles Salomon	1988	Pakistan	1985
Pakistan	1985	Papouasie-Nouvelle-Guinée	1988	Sri Lanka	1985
Tadjikistan	1992	Vanuatu	1988		
Turkménistan	1992				
Turquie	1985				

Groupe	Année d'adhésion
CEMN (Coopération économique de la Mer Noire) 11	
Albanie	1992
Arménie	1992
Azerbaïdjan	1992
Bulgarie	1992
Fédération de Russie	1992
Géorgie	1992
Grèce	1992
Moldova, République de	1992
Roumanie	1992
Turquie	1992
Ukraine	1992

Groupe	Année d'adhésion
CEAP (Coopération économique de l'Asie et du Pacifique) 21	
Australie	1989
Brunéi Darussalam	1989
Canada	1989
Chili	1989
Chine	1989
Chine, RAS de Hongkong	1989
Chine, Taiwan Province de	1989
Corée, République de	1989
Etats-Unis d'Amérique	1989
Fédération de Russie	1989
Indonésie	1989
Japon	1989
Malaisie	1989
Mexique	1989
Nouvelle-Zélande	1989
Papouasie-Nouvelle-Guinée	1989
Pérou	1989
Philippines	1989
Singapour	1989
Thaïlande	1989
Viet Nam	1989

Groupe	Année d'adhésion
CEI (Communauté des Etats indépendants) 12	
Arménie	1991
Azerbaïdjan	1991
Bélarus	1991
Fédération de Russie	1991
Géorgie	1993
Kazakhstan	1991
Kirghizistan	1991
Moldova, République de	1991
Ouzbékistan	1991
Tadjikistan	1991
Turkménistan	1991
Ukraine	1991

ABREVIATIONS

AASP	autres apports du secteur public
AELE	Association européenne de libre-échange
AGCS	Accord général sur le commerce des services
ALADI	Association latino-américaine d'intégration
ALENA	Accord de libre-échange nord-américain
ANASE	Association des nations de l'Asie du Sud-Est
anc.	ancien, ancienne, anciennement
AP	aide publique
APD	aide publique au développement
ATEP	Approvisionnements totaux en énergie primaire
CAD	Comité d'aide au développement (OCDE)
CARICOM	Communauté des Caraïbes
CCG	Conseil de coopération du Golfe
CDAA	Communauté de développement de l'Afrique australe
CEAP	Coopération économique de l'Asie et du Pacifique
CEDEAO	Communauté économique des Etats de l'Afrique de l'Ouest
CEE	Commission économique pour l'Europe
CEEAC	Communauté économique des Etats de l'Afrique centrale
CEI	Communauté des Etats indépendants
CEMAC	Communauté économique et monétaire de l'Afrique centrale (anc. UDEAC)
CEMN	Coopération économique de la Mer Noire
CEPGL	Communauté économique des pays des Grands Lacs
CESAP	Commission économique et sociale pour l'Asie et le Pacifique
CESAO	Commission économique et sociale pour l'Asie occidentale
c.a.f.	coût, assurance, fret
CNUCED	Conférence des Nations Unies sur le commerce et le développement
COMESA	Marché commun d'Afrique de l'Est et du Sud
CTCI	Classification type pour le commerce international
DTS	droits de tirage spéciaux
EP	équivalent de pétrole
f.a.b.	franco à bord
FAO	Organisation des Nations Unies pour l'alimentation et l'agriculture
FBCF	formation brute de capital fixe
FMI	Fonds monétaire international
IDE	Investissement direct étranger
IEA	Agence internationale de l'énergie
ISBLM	institutions sans but lucratif au service des ménages
LERY	L'ex-République yougoslave (de Macédoine)
KTEP	kilo tonnes d'équivalent de pétrole
MBP	*Manuel de la balance des paiements* (FMI)
MCAC	Marché commun d'Amérique centrale
MERCOSUR	Marché commun austral
MSG	Groupe Fer de lance mélanésien
n.c.a.	non classé ailleurs
n.d.a.	non dénommé ailleurs
NEI	nouvelles économies industrialisées
OCDE	Organisation de coopération et de développement économiques
OCE	Organisation de coopération économique
OECO	Organisation des Etats des Caraïbes orientales
OIT	Organisation internationale du travail
OMC	Organisation mondiale du commerce
OMS	Organisation mondiale de la santé
ONU/DAES/DS	Organisation des Nations Unies, Département des affaires économiques et sociales, Division de statistique
ONUSIDA	Programme commun des Nations Unies sur le VIH/SIDA
OPEP	Organisation des pays exportateurs de pétrole
PIB	produit intérieur brut
PMA	pays les moins avancés
PNB	produit national brut
PPTE	pays pauvres très endettés
RAS	région administrative spéciale
SAARC	Association de l'Asie du Sud pour la coopération régionale
SNPD	Système de notification des pays débiteurs
STN	société transnationale
UE	Union européenne
UEMOA	Union économique et monétaire des Etats de l'Afrique de l'Ouest
UFM	Union du fleuve Mano
UMA	Union du Maghreb arabe
UNESCO	Organisation des Nations Unies pour l'éducation, la science et la culture
UNICEF	Fonds des Nations Unies pour l'enfance
ZLEA	Zone de libre échange des Amériques

PART ONE

International merchandise trade

PREMIERE PARTIE

Commerce international des marchandises

1

2

3

4

5

6

7

8

Region, country or area	Exports - Exportations (f.o.b. / f.a.b.)								
	1980	1990	1995	1998	1999	2000	2001	2002	2003
WORLD	2031874	3491451	5137956	5458595	5667125	6364080	6121807	6396697	7443692
DEVELOPED ECONOMIES	1326934	2516733	3577831	3808849	3884412	4158604	4042000	4176111	4803196
DEVELOPING ECONOMIES	597931	845411	1425174	1519594	1653932	2034820	1908835	2038639	2410871
SOUTH-EAST EUROPE AND CIS	107008	129307	134952	130152	128780	170657	170972	181948	229625
DEVELOPED ECONOMIES: AMERICA	293300	521221	776940	896465	940544	1057760	990661	946254	996544
Canada	67734	127629	192197	214327	238446	276635	259858	252394	272739
United States	225566	393592	584743	682138	702098	781125	730803	693860	723805
DEVELOPED ECONOMIES: EUROPE	870291	1647209	2271972	2433544	2430151	2513023	2541678	2704370	3215218
EU 25	821020	1547400	2146174	2311802	2301923	2369069	2397741	2554030	3047551
EU 15	*782251*	*1510435*	*2062889*	*2203882*	*2193922*	*2247585*	*2263014*	*2400829*	*2849905*
Austria	17489	41135	57643	62742	64124	64155	66659	70860	87553
Belgium	..	..	175849	179078	178963	187850	190317	215782	255354
Belgium-Luxembourg	64656	118294	..	..	..	..	..	..	..
Denmark [1]	16749	37037	51478	48828	50399	50357	51046	56226	65934
Finland	14150	26571	39573	42963	41841	45473	42794	44650	52500
France [2]	116030	216591	284865	305788	302477	300041	297024	312287	365705
Germany [3]	192860	410104	523802	543397	542871	550150	571358	612598	748465
Germany (former Dem. Rep.)	17312	11842	–	–	–	–	–	–	–
Greece	5153	8105	10961	10732	10475	10747	9483	10315	13195
Ireland	8398	23747	44635	64477	71219	77081	83004	87419	92398
Italy	78104	170486	233998	245700	235175	239886	244210	253228	307959
Luxembourg	..	..	7750	7922	7895	7946	8238	8582	10192
Netherlands	84948	131775	196276	201374	200286	208782	216100	222269	258647
Portugal	4640	16422	23207	24814	25227	23274	24445	25523	30591
Spain	20720	55521	91046	109228	109964	113325	115155	123507	155994
Sweden	30906	57538	79801	84994	84812	86954	75833	81284	101233
United Kingdom	110137	185268	242006	271844	268193	281564	267349	276299	304185
New EU members 10	*38768*	*36965*	*83284*	*107920*	*108001*	*121484*	*134726*	*153202*	*197646*
Cyprus [4]	532	957	1229	1061	995	951	976	843	923
Czech Republic	–	–	21686	26418	26241	28996	33399	38486	48740
Czechoslovakia (former) [5]	14891	11654	–	–	–	–	–	–	–
Estonia [6]	–	–	1838	3131	2936	3133	3295	3444	4530
Hungary	8672	9596	12802	22992	24950	28016	30530	34512	42532
Latvia	–	–	1305	1811	1723	1865	2001	2284	2893
Lithuania [6]	–	–	2705	3711	3004	3810	4583	5564	7233
Malta	483	1130	1914	1834	1983	2442	1958	2225	2532
Poland	14191	13627	22895	27191	27397	31651	36092	41010	53537
Slovakia	–	–	8595	10721	10226	11889	12641	14478	21960
Slovenia	–	–	8316	9051	8546	8732	9252	10357	12767
Other developed Europe	49271	99809	125799	121742	128228	143953	143937	150340	167667
Faeroe Islands	178	385	362	437	468	470	580	540	656
Iceland	918	1592	1804	2050	2005	1891	2022	2228	2385
Norway	18542	34049	41992	40399	45455	60058	59192	59697	67480
Switzerland	29632	63784	81641	78856	80300	81534	82144	87876	97146
DEVELOPED ECONOMIES: ASIA	135979	299157	462162	410920	445161	510653	432544	446073	503394
Israel	5538	11576	19046	22993	25794	31404	29048	29347	31577
Japan	130441	287581	443116	387927	419367	479249	403496	416726	471817
DEVELOPED ECONOMIES: OCEANIA	27365	49146	66756	67920	68557	77168	77116	79413	88040
Australia	21944	39752	53111	55893	56080	63870	63387	65033	71544
New Zealand	5421	9394	13645	12027	12477	13297	13730	14380	16496

For sources and notes, see end of table.

1.1A Valeur des exportations et des importations par régions et par pays
Millions de dollars

Imports - Importations (c.i.f./ c.a.f.)									Régions, pays ou zones
1980	1990	1995	1998	1999	2000	2001	2002	2003	
2072819	3612808	5198096	5569982	5791619	6555066	6310769	6534518	7614588	MONDE
1470305	2638979	3573790	3922060	4112700	4536530	4370813	4493510	5191749	ECONOMIES DEVELOPPEES
495422	814142	1501427	1517206	1575352	1900383	1804472	1890493	2229506	ECONOMIES EN DEVELOPPEMENT
107091	159687	122879	130716	103567	118153	135484	150515	193332	EUROPE DU SUD-EST ET CEI
319528	640231	938893	1150419	1279623	1504086	1406471	1429929	1550431	ECONOMIES DEVELOPPEES : AMERIQUE
62544	123244	168041	206066	220183	244786	227291	227499	245021	Canada
256984	516987	770852	944353	1059440	1259300	1179180	1202430	1305410	Etats-Unis
971825	1695100	2194196	2384690	2405193	2536095	2502608	2603133	3114466	ECONOMIES DEVELOPPEES : EUROPE
917336	1596222	2079005	2264247	2288196	2415009	2382738	2481787	2979550	UE 25
876488	1561504	1974825	2117950	2144580	2256607	2213973	2294095	2740866	UE 15
24444	49088	66386	68183	69555	68972	70448	72849	88256	Autriche
..	..	159683	164669	164623	176970	178685	199304	235421	Belgique
71864	120314	..	..	..	..	..	..	..	Belgique-Luxembourg
19340	33248	45747	46347	44537	44369	44297	49284	56400	Danemark [1]
15635	27001	28114	32301	31617	33893	32108	33627	41605	Finlande
134889	234447	281440	290241	294928	310886	301646	311117	369768	France [2]
188002	346153	464271	471418	473539	495380	485967	491904	601713	Allemagne [3]
19082	10876	–	–	–	–	–	–	–	Allemagne (anc. Rép. Dém. d')
10548	19777	26795	29388	28720	29221	29928	31164	44375	Grèce
11153	20682	33064	44631	47194	51464	51295	51459	53291	Irlande
100741	181968	206040	218445	220323	238023	236086	244175	291227	Italie
..	..	9748	10237	11045	10716	11151	11549	13568	Luxembourg
88419	126475	176874	187747	187525	198291	194890	193698	232456	Pays-Bas
9309	25264	33306	38536	39825	38185	39415	38308	40835	Portugal
34078	87554	113319	133149	144436	152870	153607	163501	208512	Espagne
33438	54245	64741	68627	68755	72972	63477	66718	82728	Suède
115545	224412	265297	314031	317959	334396	320973	335438	380712	Royaume-Uni
40848	34719	104180	146297	143616	158402	168766	187692	238684	Nouveaux membres de l'UE 10
1202	2568	3694	3685	3618	3846	3923	4086	4466	Chypre [4]
–	–	26385	30338	29482	33852	38307	42773	56094	République tchèque
12774	13106	–	–	–	–	–	–	–	Tchécoslovaquie (anc.) [5]
–	–	2545	4613	4094	4241	4305	4810	6500	Estonie [6]
9245	8670	15380	25679	27923	31955	33725	37787	47602	Hongrie
–	–	1818	3191	2945	3184	3504	4053	5242	Lettonie
–	–	3649	5794	4835	5457	6353	7838	9841	Lituanie [6]
938	1961	2943	2668	2846	3399	2725	2839	3350	Malte
16690	8413	29050	46495	45903	48940	50275	55113	68004	Pologne
–	–	9225	13725	11888	13412	15501	17460	23735	Slovaquie
–	–	9492	10111	10083	10116	10148	10933	13851	Slovénie
54489	98878	115191	120443	116997	121085	119870	121346	134916	Autres économies développées d'Europe
223	296	315	387	˜470	518	560	510	645	Iles Féroé
999	1680	1756	2489	2503	2591	2253	2275	2789	Islande
16926	27221	32968	37473	34167	34392	32955	34890	39486	Norvège
36342	69681	80152	80094	79857	83584	84102	83672	91996	Suisse
151080	252162	365461	309826	344428	410915	384538	372711	419212	ECONOMIES DEVELOPPEES : ASIE
9784	16794	29579	29342	33166	31404	35449	35517	36282	Israël
141296	235368	335882	280484	311262	379511	349089	337194	382930	Japon
27871	51486	75240	77125	83456	85434	77196	87737	107641	ECONOMIES DEVELOPPEES : OCEANIE
22399	41985	61283	64630	69158	71529	63888	72690	89086	Australie
5472	9501	13957	12495	14299	13906	13308	15047	18555	Nouvelle-Zélande

Pour les sources et les notes, se reporter à la fin du tableau.

Region, country or area	Exports - Exportations (f.o.b. / f.a.b.)								
	1980	1990	1995	1998	1999	2000	2001	2002	2003
DEVELOPING ECONOMIES: AMERICA	111722	144750	225154	276644	294485	354111	342050	341578	375206
South America	*65623*	*86747*	*126999*	*137755*	*135506*	*162650*	*159755*	*158676*	*183163*
Argentina	8021	12353	20967	26441	23333	26341	26543	25709	29350
Bolivia	942	926	1101	1104	1051	1230	1285	1299	1573
Brazil	20132	31414	46506	51140	48011	55086	58223	60362	73084
Chile	4705	8373	16024	16323	17162	19210	18272	18177	21046
Colombia	3924	6766	10056	10890	11575	13043	12290	11911	12671
Ecuador	2481	2714	4307	4203	4451	4927	4678	5042	6039
French Guiana [2]	25	93	131	_	_	_	_	_	_
Guyana	389	257	455	484	523	498	478	493	634
Paraguay	310	959	919	1014	741	869	990	1164	1487
Peru	3898	3231	5492	5757	6087	6951	7007	7647	8954
Suriname	514	472	477	436	144	399	521	530	638
Uruguay	1059	1693	2106	2771	2237	2295	2060	1861	2197
Venezuela	19221	17497	18457	17193	20190	31802	27409	24482	25490
Other America	*46099*	*58003*	*98154*	*138888*	*158979*	*191462*	*182294*	*182902*	*192043*
Antigua and Barbuda	26	21	53	36	38	42	39	39	20
Aruba	..	28	15	29	29	173	149	128	166
Bahamas [7]	5009	238	176	300	462	576	423	446	425
Barbados	228	215	239	252	264	272	259	206	210
Belize	111	133	162	172	186	218	169	169	205
Bermuda	37	60	56	45	60	59	60	60	77
Costa Rica	1002	1448	3476	5526	6662	5850	5021	5253	6101
Cuba	5577	4910	1600	1512	1496	1760	1762	1500	1530
Dominica	10	55	45	62	56	54	43	42	39
Dominican Republic	962	735	872	880	805	966	805	834	1041
El Salvador	967	582	998	1256	1177	1332	1214	1238	1255
Greenland	211	452	364	255	289	263	277	310	354
Grenada	17	28	22	27	25	26	27	20	20
Guadeloupe [2]	107	118	157	_	_	_	_	_	_
Guatemala	1520	1163	2156	2582	2398	2696	2466	2232	2489
Haiti	226	160	110	320	334	318	274	280	347
Honduras	829	831	1220	1533	1164	1380	1324	1321	1332
Jamaica	963	1158	1427	1312	1240	1304	1220	1114	1398
Martinique [2]	117	272	223	_	_	_	_	_	_
Mexico	18031	40711	79542	117460	136391	166367	158547	160682	165396
Montserrat	1	2	3	4	5	1	1	2	2
Netherlands Antilles	5162	1790	1522	1562	1588	1895	2300	1571	2131
Nicaragua	451	331	457	573	545	645	592	596	676
Panama	361	340	625	784	822	860	911	846	864
Saint Kitts and Nevis	24	28	19	31	30	37	39	43	45
Saint Lucia	58	127	109	62	56	43	44	44	37
Saint Pierre and Miquelon	1	26	10	5	5	5	6	6	6
Saint Vincent and the Grenadines	15	83	43	50	49	47	41	38	38
Trinidad and Tobago	4077	1960	2455	2258	2804	4274	4280	3880	5840
DEVELOPING ECONOMIES: AFRICA	120051	108821	112114	105064	116762	146060	137962	142086	174236
North Africa	*44042*	*39278*	*35577*	*33114*	*38050*	*54025*	*50139*	*51383*	*63139*
Algeria	13871	12930	10240	9839	12525	22031	19350	19130	23000
Egypt	3046	4957	3450	3130	3559	4689	4128	4708	5357
Libyan Arab Jamahiriya	21910	13225	8975	6659	7947	12687	11187	10970	14900
Morocco	2441	4265	6881	7153	7367	6961	7144	7851	9080
Sudan	543	374	556	596	780	1807	1699	1850	2775
Tunisia	2231	3527	5475	5738	5872	5850	6631	6874	8027
Other Africa	*76009*	*69544*	*76537*	*71950*	*78712*	*92035*	*87824*	*90704*	*111097*
Angola	1883	3884	3723	3543	5157	7921	6534	7600	8661
Benin	63	288	420	407	422	392	374	448	554
Botswana	504	1785	2142	1948	2644	2712	2449	2510	3037
Burkina Faso	90	152	276	319	255	209	234	237	326
Burundi	65	75	106	65	54	50	39	30	38
Cameroon [8]	1384	2002	1630	1838	1526	1534	2101	2276	2904
Cape Verde	4	6	8	10	11	11	10	11	14
Central African Republic [8]	116	120	171	151	146	161	142	147	86

For sources and notes, see end of table.

Imports - Importations (c.i.f./ c.a.f.)									Régions, pays ou zones
1980	1990	1995	1998	1999	2000	2001	2002	2003	
125722	131553	252251	344902	333208	386209	377796	351521	367753	**ECONOMIES EN DEVELOPPEMENT : AMERIQUE**
66737	*57554*	*138602*	*167311*	*136901*	*150897*	*149678*	*122820*	*131731*	*Amérique du Sud*
10545	4078	20026	31381	25507	25154	20320	8990	13813	Argentine
665	687	1424	1983	1755	1830	1708	1770	1613	Bolivie
24961	22524	53783	60652	51759	58631	58351	49603	50665	Brésil
5797	7742	15900	19880	15988	18507	17832	17196	19413	Chili
4739	5590	13853	14635	10659	11539	12834	12738	13892	Colombie
2253	1865	4153	5576	3017	3721	5363	6431	6535	Equateur
255	786	752	–	–	–	–	–	–	Guyane française [2]
396	311	528	640	620	653	584	563	1021	Guyana
615	1352	2782	2471	1725	2050	1989	2085	2528	Paraguay
2499	3470	9300	9915	8152	8888	9080	9100	10504	Pérou
504	472	585	552	298	246	535	540	601	Suriname
1680	1343	2867	3811	3357	3466	3061	1964	2190	Uruguay
11827	7335	12650	15818	14064	16213	18022	11840	8955	Venezuela
58984	*73999*	*113649*	*177592*	*196307*	*235312*	*228118*	*228701*	*236022*	*Autres économies: Amérique*
88	255	346	385	414	400	375	375	365	Antigua-et-Barbuda
..	536	567	815	782	835	841	841	832	Aruba
7546	1112	1243	1873	1772	1764	1738	1527	1740	Bahamas [7]
525	704	771	1010	1108	1156	1087	1039	1133	Barbade
150	211	257	295	370	524	517	525	552	Belize
343	595	550	629	678	685	721	748	850	Bermudes
1540	1990	4090	6239	6355	6389	6569	7188	7643	Costa Rica
6505	6745	2825	4197	4365	4877	4838	4161	4776	Cuba
48	118	117	132	138	148	131	115	126	Dominique
1640	2062	3639	5631	5988	7379	5937	6050	6250	République dominicaine
966	1263	2853	3121	3140	3795	3866	3909	4382	El Salvador
328	445	421	397	418	347	303	310	361	Groenland
50	106	124	200	205	246	215	218	271	Grenade
679	1677	1887	–	–	–	–	–	–	Guadeloupe [2]
1598	1649	3293	4651	4382	4791	5607	6078	6488	Guatemala
375	332	653	797	1025	1036	1013	1130	1188	Haïti
1009	935	1643	2535	2676	2855	2942	2981	3276	Honduras
1171	1928	2818	3035	2899	3326	3360	3533	4128	Jamaïque
843	1710	1958	–	–	–	–	–	–	Martinique [2]
22144	43548	75858	130948	148648	182702	176185	176607	178503	Mexique
12	48	30	19	22	23	19	23	23	Montserrat
5676	2141	1841	2051	2019	2802	2783	2233	2607	Antilles néerlandaises
887	637	993	1492	1862	1805	1779	1795	2211	Nicaragua
1449	1539	2511	3398	3516	3379	2964	2982	3086	Panama
45	110	133	148	155	153	155	150	196	Saint-Kitts-et-Nevis
124	271	306	335	355	355	355	309	384	Sainte-Lucie
10	86	74	66	75	70	65	55	69	Saint-Pierre-et-Miquelon
57	136	136	193	201	163	186	174	200	Saint-Vincent-et-les Grenadines
3178	1109	1714	2999	2741	3308	3569	3643	4383	Trinité-et-Tobago
96437	103616	126681	133251	127325	129124	133159	135962	169248	**ECONOMIES EN DEVELOPPEMENT : AFRIQUE**
31552	*44952*	*46546*	*51590*	*48859*	*48566*	*49823*	*52941*	*60777*	*Afrique du Nord*
10559	9780	10250	9403	9162	9152	9700	10791	11926	Algérie
4860	16783	11760	16166	16022	14010	12756	12552	14764	Egypte
6777	5336	5392	5466	3861	3751	4458	5700	6466	Jamahiriya arabe libyenne
4255	6922	10023	10290	9925	11534	11038	11879	14618	Maroc
1576	619	1219	1915	1415	1553	2342	2493	2093	Soudan
3526	5513	7903	8350	8475	8567	9529	9526	10910	Tunisie
64885	*58665*	*80135*	*81661*	*78465*	*80558*	*83336*	*83020*	*108471*	*Autres économies: Afrique*
1328	1578	1468	2079	3109	3040	3179	3795	5313	Angola
331	265	746	736	749	613	602	679	743	Bénin
693	1947	1911	2387	2215	2469	1809	1950	2182	Botswana
359	536	455	732	678	611	656	739	855	Burkina Faso
168	231	234	158	118	148	139	129	157	Burundi
1602	1400	1199	1495	1318	1489	1852	1796	2148	Cameroun [8]
68	136	252	228	246	230	233	278	317	Cap-Vert
81	154	174	146	131	117	107	120	117	République centrafricaine [8]

Pour les sources et les notes, se reporter à la fin du tableau.

Region, country or area	Exports - Exportations (f.o.b. / f.a.b.)								
	1980	1990	1995	1998	1999	2000	2001	2002	2003
Chad	71	188	243	262	243	183	189	185	301
Comoros	11	18	11	4	5	7	14	19	11
Congo [8]	911	981	1173	1368	1560	2489	1990	2236	2599
Côte d'Ivoire	3135	3072	3806	4606	4662	3888	3946	5275	5844
Dem. Rep. of the Congo	2269	2326	1649	1180	933	760	940	1210	1242
Djibouti	13	25	14	12	12	12	54	85	63
Equatorial Guinea	14	62	86	439	709	1097	1634	1879	1823
Eritrea	..	..	81	28	17	19	19	52	52
Ethiopia [9]	425	298	423	561	467	486	455	480	617
Gabon [8]	2173	2204	2713	1916	2394	2462	2649	2100	2583
Gambia	31	32	18	21	12	16	9	10	7
Ghana	1257	891	1724	1795	1720	1660	1570	1840	2106
Guinea	401	671	702	693	636	666	731	886	517
Guinea-Bissau	11	19	44	27	51	62	63	54	69
Kenya	1245	1032	1879	2008	1747	1734	1944	2116	2411
Lesotho	58	62	160	194	173	220	282	365	477
Liberia	600	2207	820	425	469	329	245	227	230
Madagascar	401	318	507	538	584	824	928	486	655
Malawi	295	417	405	431	453	379	449	407	486
Mali	205	359	442	561	571	551	725	885	930
Mauritania	194	447	499	350	373	358	348	321	343
Mauritius	435	1194	1538	1645	1588	1557	1628	1801	1939
Mozambique	281	126	168	230	263	364	703	680	880
Namibia	..	1086	1409	1232	1234	1320	1179	1096	1214
Niger	566	283	288	334	287	283	272	279	339
Nigeria	25946	13596	12342	9855	13856	20975	17261	15107	22214
Reunion [2]	130	190	207	–	–	–	–	–	–
Rwanda	121	109	52	60	60	52	85	56	55
Sao Tome and Principe	17	4	5	5	2	3	3	5	7
Senegal	477	762	993	968	1027	920	1003	1067	1331
Seychelles	21	57	53	122	145	194	216	228	278
Sierra Leone	224	138	42	7	6	13	29	49	92
Somalia	141	150	170	197	191	193	285	297	351
South Africa [10]	25540	23568	27853	26362	26707	29983	29258	29723	36482
Swaziland	373	557	866	973	937	910	1054	937	1149
Togo	338	268	378	420	391	363	357	427	616
Uganda	345	152	461	501	519	460	456	443	562
United Republic of Tanzania	511	331	682	589	543	663	776	875	1222
Zambia	1305	1309	1040	1021	1063	666	985	930	1029
Zimbabwe	1409	1725	2114	1730	1887	1925	1207	2327	2354
DEVELOPING ECONOMIES: ASIA	363850	589025	1083353	1134268	1238778	1530565	1425281	1551653	1856878
West Asia	*202044*	*136605*	*152667*	*148313*	*186884*	*263661*	*242093*	*252264*	*319183*
Bahrain	3606	3761	4113	3270	4363	6195	5577	5786	6364
Iran, Islamic Republic of	7109	19305	18360	13118	21030	28461	23904	28186	38962
Iraq	26278	10314	496	5500	12800	20603	15905	13520	14548
Jordan	574	1064	1769	1802	1832	1899	2293	2770	3372
Kuwait	19842	7042	12785	9554	12164	19436	16203	15369	19371
Lebanon	955	494	656	662	677	715	870	1046	1524
Oman	2387	5508	6068	5508	7231	10852	11037	11172	11669
Qatar	5680	3293	3481	4880	7061	11594	10870	11032	13926
Saudi Arabia	109116	44417	50040	38822	50761	77583	68064	72550	93338
Syrian Arab Republic	2108	4212	3563	2890	3464	4634	5248	5540	5616
Turkey	2910	12959	21637	26974	26587	27775	31334	34561	46576
United Arab Emirates	20676	23544	27753	33835	36474	49835	47572	47275	60086
Yemen [11]	802	692	1945	1497	2440	4079	3215	3458	3832
Other Asia	*161806*	*452420*	*930686*	*985955*	*1051893*	*1266904*	*1183188*	*1299388*	*1537694*
Afghanistan	670	235	156	209	167	186	113	101	204
Bangladesh	759	1671	3733	5141	5458	6399	6085	6102	6991
Bhutan	17	70	103	108	116	103	106	108	108
Brunei Darussalam	4581	2213	2402	2058	2551	2855	2796	2901	3419
Cambodia	16	86	855	800	1129	1401	1571	1750	2106
China	18099	62091	148780	183712	194931	249203	266098	325591	437899
China, Hong Kong SAR	19752	82160	173750	174002	173885	201860	189894	200092	223762
China, Macao SAR	538	1701	1997	2141	2200	2539	2300	2356	2581
China, Taiwan Province of	19786	67079	111563	110518	121496	147777	122506	130457	144180

For sources and notes, see end of table.

Imports - Importations (c.i.f./ c.a.f.)									Régions, pays ou zones
1980	1990	1995	1998	1999	2000	2001	2002	2003	
74	286	365	356	316	315	679	997	826	Tchad
29	52	63	47	80	72	98	85	112	Comores
562	621	670	680	821	465	580	590	667	Congo [8]
2991	2098	2931	3346	2766	2402	2418	2456	3320	Côte d'Ivoire
1519	1739	1046	1230	1108	1035	702	980	1370	Rép. dém. du Congo
213	215	177	158	153	152	143	162	155	Djibouti
26	61	50	317	425	451	730	430	829	Guinée équatoriale
..	..	404	500	329	328	423	538	794	Erythrée
722	1081	1145	1517	1538	1262	1815	1666	2665	Ethiopie [9]
674	918	882	1103	841	994	859	1010	1155	Gabon [8]
165	188	182	228	192	187	134	148	183	Gambie
1129	1199	1907	2563	3480	2973	2480	2790	3450	Ghana
270	699	819	537	556	612	601	667	679	Guinée
55	86	133	63	51	49	62	58	69	Guinée-Bissau
2125	2223	2991	3197	2832	3105	3192	3245	3725	Kenya
427	673	985	863	781	728	681	785	1021	Lesotho
535	210	510	470	520	668	623	591	560	Libéria
764	566	628	693	742	997	955	603	964	Madagascar
439	575	475	515	673	532	563	695	647	Malawi
439	602	772	761	605	592	735	745	1130	Mali
286	220	494	359	305	324	374	356	354	Mauritanie
614	1618	1976	2073	2247	2093	1987	2168	2381	Maurice
800	878	704	790	1139	1158	1063	1350	1364	Mozambique
..	1163	1616	1648	1610	1550	1547	1450	1700	Namibie
594	389	374	471	394	393	370	400	551	Niger
16660	5627	8222	9211	8588	8721	11586	7547	10853	Nigéria
887	2133	2625	–	–	–	–	–	–	Réunion [2]
262	287	238	284	250	211	250	203	210	Rwanda
19	21	29	17	38	30	28	31	42	Sao Tomé-et-Principe
1052	1220	1412	1455	1564	1519	1730	1942	2454	Sénégal
99	187	233	384	434	342	476	420	430	Seychelles
427	149	133	95	81	149	182	264	303	Sierra Leone
435	81	268	280	340	343	449	454	526	Somalie
19700	18399	30546	29242	26696	29695	28248	29267	41084	Afrique du Sud [10]
625	664	1008	1083	1068	1046	1129	983	1060	Swaziland
551	581	594	588	489	485	516	579	844	Togo
293	288	1056	1416	1342	1536	1594	1111	1252	Ouganda
1258	1364	1675	1453	1556	1524	1712	1687	2193	République-Unie de Tanzanie
1088	1220	700	1087	822	993	1307	1253	1267	Zambie
1449	1839	2661	2621	2127	1810	1739	2829	3451	Zimbabwe
									ECONOMIES EN DEVELOPPEMENT : ASIE
269713	**573995**	**1116939**	**1033765**	**1109611**	**1379922**	**1288251**	**1397260**	**1685763**	
92403	*106712*	*134179*	*157622*	*155747*	*185428*	*172253*	*190670*	*226950*	*Asie occidentale*
3483	3712	3716	3566	3698	4634	4306	4985	5116	Bahreïn
12246	20322	12313	14323	12683	14347	17626	21180	27543	Iran, Rép. islamique d'
7477	7660	665	4400	6900	11153	11000	12000	10275	Iraq
2402	2600	3698	3828	3717	4597	4844	5020	6049	Jordanie
6533	3972	7790	8619	7617	7157	7869	9001	10794	Koweït
3650	2529	7278	7070	6207	6230	7293	6447	7171	Liban
1732	2681	4248	5682	4674	5040	5798	6005	6572	Oman
1423	1695	3398	3409	2500	3252	3758	4052	5163	Qatar
30171	24069	28091	30013	28011	30238	31223	32312	34822	Arabie saoudite
4124	2400	4709	3895	3832	3815	4752	5220	6360	République arabe syrienne
7910	22302	35709	45921	40671	54503	41399	49663	65637	Turquie
8746	11199	20984	24728	33231	38139	30075	32180	38403	Emirats arabes unis
2505	1571	1582	2167	2008	2324	2310	2604	3045	Yémen [11]
177310	*467283*	*982760*	*876144*	*953864*	*1194494*	*1115998*	*1206590*	*1458813*	*Autres économies: Asie*
841	936	368	373	411	550	551	950	1236	Afghanistan
2599	3618	6502	6974	7694	8360	8350	7914	9020	Bangladesh
50	81	112	134	182	203	191	165	171	Bhoutan
572	1001	2091	1552	1397	1505	1267	1640	1937	Brunéi Darussalam
180	164	1187	1166	1591	1939	2094	2314	2699	Cambodge
19941	53345	132084	140237	165699	225094	243553	295171	413062	Chine
22447	82490	192751	184518	179520	212805	201076	207644	231896	Chine, Hong Kong RAS
544	1539	2042	1955	2040	2255	2386	2530	2755	Chine, Macao RAS
19764	54831	103698	104946	110957	139927	107274	112758	127249	Chine, Taiwan Province de

Pour les sources et les notes, se reporter à la fin du tableau.

Region, country or area	Exports - Exportations (f.o.b. / f.a.b.)								
	1980	1990	1995	1998	1999	2000	2001	2002	2003
India	8586	17969	30630	33437	35667	42379	43347	49312	55982
Indonesia	21909	25675	45417	48848	48666	62124	56447	58120	62631
Korea, Dem. People's Republic of	..	1857	840	644	597	708	826	724	731
Korea, Republic of [12]	17512	65016	125058	132313	143685	172267	150439	162470	193817
Lao People's Dem. Rep.	28	79	311	370	311	330	331	298	378
Malaysia [13, 14]	12945	29452	73914	73255	84621	98229	88005	93265	99369
Maldives	8	53	50	74	64	76	76	90	113
Mongolia	403	661	473	345	358	466	448	448	529
Myanmar	477	328	860	1077	1136	1646	2381	3046	2613
Nepal	80	204	346	474	602	804	737	568	662
Pakistan	2618	5589	7992	8494	8424	9028	9238	9913	11930
Philippines	5741	8117	17502	29414	36576	39783	32664	36502	36502
Singapore [15]	19375	52730	118268	109895	114680	137804	121751	125177	145366
Sri Lanka	1062	1912	3798	4809	4594	5430	4816	4699	5125
Thailand	6505	23068	56439	54456	58440	69057	65113	68768	80522
Viet Nam	339	2404	5449	9361	11540	14449	15100	16530	20176
DEVELOPING ECONOMIES: OCEANIA	**2309**	**2815**	**4554**	**3618**	**3907**	**4083**	**3542**	**3322**	**4551**
American Samoa	127	311	272	415	345	346	383	397	456
Cook Islands	4	5	5	3	3	9	7	7	7
Fiji	470	497	619	510	610	584	538	499	593
French Polynesia	30	111	194	247	253	222	195	183	383
Guam	35	60	85	86	76	74	61	41	59
Kiribati	3	3	7	6	9	4	5	3	4
Nauru	65	60	28	20	36	28	13	9	9
New Caledonia	409	480	471	378	466	606	443	534	741
Papua New Guinea	1031	1177	2654	1772	1924	2096	1814	1549	2174
Samoa	17	9	9	15	20	14	16	14	15
Solomon Islands	74	70	168	126	126	69	47	58	74
Tonga	7	11	14	8	12	9	7	13	16
Tuvalu	..	1	0	0	0	0	0	0	0
Vanuatu	36	19	28	34	26	23	16	15	21
SOUTH-EAST EUROPE AND CIS	**107008**	**129307**	**134952**	**130152**	**128780**	**170657**	**170972**	**181948**	**229625**
South-East Europe	*30559*	*25130*	*20863*	*21747*	*21157*	*24704*	*25699*	*29351*	*37122*
Albania	..	224	202	205	264	261	305	330	453
Bosnia and Herzegovina [16]	–	–	24	593	748	1067	1082	1005	1150
Bulgaria	10372	4822	5359	4195	3964	4809	5115	5749	7534
Croatia	–	–	4633	4541	4303	4432	4666	4899	6162
Macedonia, TFYR	–	–	1204	1311	1192	1319	1154	1112	1351
Romania	11209	5775	7910	8300	8505	10367	11391	13876	17619
Serbia and Montenegro	–	–	1531	2604	2182	2450	1986	2380	2854
Yugoslavia, SFR (former)	8978	14308	–	–	–	–	–	–	–
CIS	–	–	*114089*	*108404*	*107624*	*145953*	*145273*	*152597*	*192503*
Armenia	–	–	271	221	232	294	343	507	678
Azerbaijan	–	–	637	606	930	1745	2314	2168	2592
Belarus	–	–	4803	7070	5909	7326	7451	8021	9964
Georgia [6]	–	–	151	191	238	331	320	349	447
Kazakhstan [6]	–	–	5250	5334	5872	8812	8639	9709	12900
Kyrgyzstan	–	–	409	514	454	505	476	486	582
Moldova, Republic of	–	–	739	632	463	471	570	660	875
Russian Federation [6]	–	–	82913	74884	75665	105565	103139	107110	134377
Tajikistan [6]	–	–	749	602	689	780	652	650	832
Turkmenistan [6]	–	–	1939	2186	2289	2333	1850	2016	2465
Ukraine [6]	–	–	13128	12637	11582	14573	16265	17957	23080
USSR (former)	76449	104177	–	–	–	–	–	–	–
Uzbekistan [6]	–	–	3100	3528	3302	3217	3255	2965	3710

For sources and notes, see next page.

Imports - Importations (c.i.f./ c.a.f.)									Régions, pays ou zones
1980	1990	1995	1998	1999	2000	2001	2002	2003	
14864	23580	34707	42980	46979	51523	50392	56517	70707	Inde
10834	21837	40630	27337	24003	33515	31010	25388	41682	Indonésie
..	2930	1270	1170	1212	1686	1847	1718	1750	Corée, Rép. populaire dém. de
22292	69844	135119	93282	119725	160481	141098	152126	178827	Corée, République de [12]
92	185	589	553	525	535	528	431	524	Rép. dém. populaire lao
10779	29258	77691	58272	65389	81963	73866	79869	81948	Malaisie [13, 14]
29	137	268	354	402	389	393	392	471	Maldives
548	924	415	503	513	615	630	680	777	Mongolie
357	273	1348	2695	2323	2401	2877	2348	2530	Myanmar
342	672	1333	1246	1422	1573	1473	1419	1754	Népal
5350	7376	11461	9308	10207	10864	10191	11233	13038	Pakistan
8291	13004	28341	31496	32568	37027	34921	37180	39502	Philippines
24007	60774	124507	104719	111060	134545	116000	116441	127934	Singapour [15]
2057	2688	5306	5905	5961	7177	5973	6105	6672	Sri Lanka
9214	33045	70786	42971	50342	61924	62058	64658	75809	Thaïlande
1314	2752	8155	11500	11742	15638	15999	19000	24863	Viet Nam
									ECONOMIES EN DEVELOPPEMENT :
3550	**4978**	**5556**	**5287**	**5208**	**5128**	**5266**	**5750**	**6743**	**OCEANIE**
95	360	200	247	188	222	239	298	292	Samoa américaines
23	52	49	38	37	50	47	40	40	Iles Cook
562	754	892	722	903	825	794	825	984	Fidji
547	929	1008	1018	926	976	1057	1293	1661	Polynésie française
400	410	516	659	459	554	673	527	662	Guam
17	27	34	33	41	40	41	43	40	Kiribati
12	38	28	11	13	27	21	25	20	Nauru
456	883	951	929	1006	925	931	1117	1361	Nouvelle-Calédonie
1176	1193	1452	1240	1233	1151	1073	1235	1297	Papouasie-Nouvelle-Guinée
63	81	95	97	115	106	130	135	137	Samoa
89	91	154	128	110	92	82	48	70	Iles Salomon
38	62	77	69	73	69	73	65	65	Tonga
..	4	6	10	8	5	4	11	16	Tuvalu
73	96	95	88	96	87	102	89	99	Vanuatu
107091	**159687**	**122879**	**130716**	**103567**	**118153**	**135484**	**150515**	**193332**	**EUROPE DU SUD-EST ET CEI**
38569	*39036*	*29497*	*35440*	*33556*	*36653*	*41711*	*47833*	*63013*	*Europe du Sud-Est*
..	423	714	829	1140	1091	1331	1504	1864	Albanie
–	–	950	2921	3274	3082	3217	3799	4900	Bosnie-Herzégovine [16]
9650	4710	5661	4949	5453	6505	7263	7987	10890	Bulgarie
–	–	7510	8383	7799	7887	9147	10714	14136	Croatie
–	–	1719	1915	1796	2085	1676	1928	2241	Macédoine, LERY
13843	9843	10278	11821	10392	13055	15561	17862	24003	Roumanie
–	–	2666	4622	3703	2950	3516	4040	4979	Serbie-et-Monténégro
15076	18871	–	–	–	–	–	–	–	Yougoslavie, RSF (anc.)
–	–	*93383*	*95276*	*70010*	*81500*	*93773*	*102682*	*130319*	*CEI*
–	–	674	902	800	882	874	991	1269	Arménie
–	–	668	1077	1036	1172	1431	1500	2626	Azerbaïdjan
–	–	5564	8549	6674	8646	8286	9092	11505	Bélarus
–	–	392	887	585	654	684	733	1061	Géorgie [6]
–	–	3807	4314	3655	5040	6446	6584	8327	Kazakhstan [6]
–	–	522	842	600	554	467	587	717	Kirghizistan
–	–	841	1024	586	776	897	1038	1351	Moldova, République de
–	–	60945	58015	39537	44862	53764	60520	74600	Fédération de Russie [6]
–	–	810	771	664	696	711	724	1014	Tadjikistan [6]
–	–	777	931	1001	1014	1150	1037	1242	Turkménistan [6]
–	–	15484	14676	11846	13956	15775	16977	23021	Ukraine [6]
68522	120651	–	–	–	–	–	–	–	URSS (anc.)
–	–	2900	3289	3028	3247	3287	2899	3585	Ouzbékistan [6]

Pour les sources et les notes, se reporter à la page suivante.

1.1A Value of exports and imports by region and country

1.1A Valeur des exportations et des importations par régions et par pays

Sources:

United Nations, *Yearbook of International Trade Statistics;* United Nations, *Monthly Bulletin of Statistics*; United Nations, Economic Commission for Europe; International Monetary Fund, *International Financial Statistics;* International Monetary Fund, *Direction of Trade Statistics*; World Trade Organization; Eastern Caribbean Central Bank; national sources and UNCTAD secretariat estimates.

Notes:

Figures in this table refer to total exports and total imports of goods. Data on trade in services are shown in table 5.1.
Unless otherwise specified, export values are free on board (f.o.b.) and import values cost, insurance and freight (c.i.f.).

Differences between data shown in this table and those shown in Part III are due to a variety of factors. For instance, imports arrive at destination and are registered with some time-lag from the date they were recorded as exports.
Consequently, total exports differ from total of imports. See notes in Part III.

Two trade systems are in common use: the *General Trade System* and the *Special Trade System*.

The General Trade System is used when the statistical territory of a compiling country coincides with its economic territory. Consequently, imports include all goods entering the economic territory of a compiling country and exports include all goods leaving the economic territory of a compiling country.

The *Special Trade System* is used when the statistical territory comprises only a particular part of the economic territory within which goods may be disposed without customs restriction (free circulation area).
Imports include all goods entering the free circulation area of a compiling country, which means cleared through customs for home use; exports include all goods leaving the free circulation area. However, goods entering and goods leaving an industrial free zone are not recorded since they have not been cleared through customs for home use. The products processed in free zones are also excluded from exports.

For further explanations, see United Nations, *International Merchandise Trade Statistics: Concepts and Definitions, Series M, No. 52, Revision 2.*

The trade flows shown in this table refer to the General Trade System, except for the countries and territories listed below which employ the Special Trade System:

Algeria; American Samoa; Argentina; Armenia; Austria; Belgium; Belgium-Luxembourg; Benin; Bosnia and Herzegovina; Botswana; Brunei Darussalam; Bulgaria; Burundi; Cameroon; Central African Republic; Chad; Chile; Comoros; Congo; Costa Rica; Côte d'Ivoire; Cuba; Czech Republic; Dem. Rep. of the Congo; Denmark; Dominica; Dominican Republic; Egypt; El Salvador; France; French Guiana; French Polynesia; Gabon; Greece; Grenada; Guadeloupe; Guatemala; Guyana; Honduras; Hungary; Iran, Islamic Rep. of; Iraq; Israel; Italy; Kazakhstan; Kuwait; Lao People's Dem. Rep.; Latvia; Liberia; Luxembourg; Madagascar; Mali; Martinique; Mauritania; Montserrat; Morocco; Netherlands Antilles; New Caledonia; Niger; Panama; Peru; Poland; Portugal; Qatar; Reunion; Romania; Saint Kitts and Nevis; Saint Lucia; Saint Vincent and the Grenadines; Samoa; Sao Tome and Principe; Saudi Arabia; Serbia and Montenegro; Sierra Leone; Slovakia; Slovenia; Solomon Islands; Spain; Switzerland; Syrian Arab Republic; Thailand; Macedonia, TFYR; Togo; Trinidad and Tobago; Turkey; Ukraine; Uzbekistan; Viet Nam;Yemen; Zambia.

Sources :

Organisation des Nations Unies, *Annuaire statistique du commerce international;* Organisation des Nations Unies, *Bulletin mensuel de statistique*; Organisation des Nations Unies, Commission économique pour l'Europe; Fonds monétaire international, *International Financial Statistics*; Fonds monétaire international, *Direction of Trade Statistics*; Organisation mondiale du commerce; Eastern Caribbean Central Bank; Sources nationales et estimations du secrétariat de la CNUCED.

Notes :

Les chiffres de ce tableau se réfèrent aux exportations et importations totales des biens. Les données sur le commerce des services sont présentées dans le tableau 5.1.
Sauf indications contraires, les valeurs des exportations sont franco à bord (f.a.b.) et celles des importations coût assurance et frêt (c.a.f.).

Les différences entre les données de ce tableau et les tableaux de la Partie III sont dues à divers facteurs. Par exemple, les importations des marchandises peuvent arriver à destination et être enregistrées bien après la date de leur enregistrement à l'exportation. Par conséquent, le total des exportations n'est pas égal au total des importations.

Deux systèmes d'enregistrement des marchandises sont couramment utilisés: le *Système du Commerce Général* et le *Système du Commerce Spécial.*

Le *Système du Commerce Général* est utilisé lorsque le territoire statistique d'un pays coïncide avec son territoire économique. Par conséquent, les importations comprennent tous les biens admis sur le territoire du pays déclarant et les exportations comprennent tous les biens qui le quittent.

Le *Système du Commerce Spécial* est utilisé lorsque le territoire statistique ne comprend qu'une partie du territoire économique à l'intérieur de laquelle les biens peuvent être écoulés librement sans restriction douanière (zone de libre circulation).
Les importations comprennent tous les biens qui entrent dans la zone de libre circulation du pays déclarant et donc qui ont été dédouanés pour mise à la consommation; les exportations comprennent tous les biens qui en sortent. Toutefois, les biens importés en vue d'un perfectionnement actif ainsi que les biens qui entrent ou qui sortent d'une zone franche industrielle ne sont pas enregistrés. Sont également exclus, les produits résultant du perfectionnement actif.

Pour de plus amples explications se référer à la publication des Nations Unies, *Statistiques du commerce international de marchandises: Concepts et définitions, Série M, n° 52, Révision 2.*

Les flux du commerce présentés dans ce tableau se réfèrent au Système du commerce général à l'exception des pays et territoires qui utilisent le Système du commerce spécial et dont la liste suit:

Algérie; Antilles néerlandaises; Arabie saoudite; Argentine; Arménie; Autriche; Belgique; Belgique-Luxembourg; Bénin; Bosnie-Herzégovine; Botswana; Brunéi Darussalam; Bulgarie; Burundi; Cameroun; Chili; Comores; Congo; Costa Rica; Côte d'Ivoire; Cuba; Danemark; Dominique; Egypte; El Salvador; Espagne; France; Gabon; Grenade; Grèce; Guadeloupe; Guatemala; Guyana; Guyane française; Honduras; Hongrie; Iles Salomon; Iran, Rép. islamique d'; Iraq; Israël; Italie; Kazakhstan; Koweït; Lettonie; Libéria; Luxembourg; Macédoine, LERY; Madagascar; Mali; Maroc; Martinique; Montserrat; Niger; Nouvelle-Calédonie; Ouzbékistan; Panama; Pérou; Pologne; Polynésie française; Portugal; Qatar; Rép. dém. du Congo; Rép. dém. populaire lao; République arabe syrienne; République centrafricaine; République dominicaine; République Tchèque; Réunion; Roumanie; Saint-Kitts-et-Nevis; Saint-Vincent-et-les-Grenadines; Sainte-Lucie; Samoa; Samoa américaines; Sao Tomé-et-Principe; Serbie-et-Monténégro; Sierra Leone; Slovaquie; Slovénie; Suisse; Tchad; Thaïlande; Togo; Trinité-et-Tobago; Turquie; Ukraine; Viet Nam; Yémen; Zambie.

1 Prior to 1985, General Trade.

2 From 1996, France data include trade of French Guiana, Guadeloupe, Martinique and Reunion.

3 Data prior to July 1990 pertain to the territorial boundaries of the Federal Republic of Germany prior to 3 October 1990.

4 Excluding military imports.

5 From 1985 onwards, data are not comparable to those shown for prior periods due to revisions of the koruna-to-US dollar exchange rate.

1 Avant 1985, Commerce général.

2 A partir de 1996, les données de la France incluent celles de la Guadeloupe, la Guyane française, la Martinique et la Réunion.

3 Les données relatives à la période antérieure à juillet 1990 correspondent aux limites territoriales de la République fédérale d'Allemagne d'avant le 3 octobre 1990.

4 Non compris les importations militaires.

5 A partir de 1985, les chiffres ne sont pas comparables à ceux des années antérieures à cause de révisions du taux de change de la couronne par rapport au dollar des Etats-Unis.

6   Prior to 1994, covers only trade with countries outside the CIS.

6   Avant 1994, concerne seulement le commerce avec les pays extérieurs à la CEI.

7   From 1990 onwards, trade statistics exclude certain oil and chemical products.

7   A partir de 1990, certains produits pétroliers et chimiques ne sont plus inclus dans les statistiques du commerce.

8   Inter-trade between the countries of the Customs Union (UDEAC) is excluded.

8   Non compris le commerce entre les pays de l'Union douanière (UDEAC).

9   Prior to 1993, data refer to Ethiopia (former), including Eritrea.

9   Avant 1993, les données se réfèrent à l'Ethiopie (anc.) y compris l'Erythrée.

10   Prior to 1998, data refer to the South African Common Customs Area, which includes Botswana, Lesotho, Namibia, South Africa and Swaziland. Beginning in 1998, trade data refer to South Africa only, excluding intra-trade of the South African Common Customs Area.

10   Avant 1998 les données du commerce se réfèrent à l'Union douanière de l'Afrique Australe qui comprend Botswana, Lesotho, Namibie, Afrique du Sud et Swaziland. A partir de 1998, les données se réfèrent uniquement à l'Afrique du Sud et excluent le commerce interne de l'Union.

11   Prior to 1990, data refer to Yemen, Arab Republic (former) and Yemen, Democratic Republic (former).

11   Avant 1990, les données se réfèrent à la République arabe du Yémen (anc.) et la République démocratique du Yémen (anc.).

12   Excluding imports of goods financed through foreign aid.

12   Non compris les biens d'importation financés par l'aide à l'étranger.

13   Inter-trade between the States of Malaysia included.

13   Y compris le commerce entre les Etats de la Malaisie.

14   Excluding military imports and offshore installations of petroleum industry.

14   Non compris les importations militaires et les installations près des côtes de l'industrie pétrolière.

15   Including trans-shipments to and from peninsular Malaysia.

15   Y compris les transbordements à destination et en provenance de la Malaisie péninsulaire.

16   Prior to 1998, data refer to the Federation of Bosnia and Herzegovina only. The other entity of Bosnia and Herzegovina, Republika Srpska, is not included.

16   Avant 1998, les données se réfèrent uniquement à la Fédération de Bosnie-Herzégovine. L'autre entité de la Bosnie-Herzégovine, Republika Srpska, n'est pas incluse.

1.1B Value of exports and imports by economic grouping
Millions of dollars

Economic grouping	Exports (f.o.b.) - Exportations (f.a.b.)								
	1980	1990	1995	1998	1999	2000	2001	2002	2003
WORLD	**2031874**	**3491451**	**5137956**	**5458595**	**5667125**	**6364080**	**6121807**	**6396697**	**7443692**
DEVELOPED ECONOMIES	1326934	2516733	3577831	3808849	3884412	4158604	4042000	4176111	4803196
DEVELOPING ECONOMIES	597931	845411	1425174	1519594	1653932	2034820	1908835	2038639	2410871
By major category									
Major petroleum exporters	319247	218043	238024	223972	277025	404787	359798	361985	441180
Other developing economies	278684	627368	1187150	1295622	1376907	1630033	1549037	1676655	1969691
Major exporters of manufactures	169375	492767	1003589	1096576	1174971	1407587	1327921	1447239	1702454
Remaining economies	109309	134602	183561	199046	201936	222447	221115	229416	267237
America	45099	51378	76672	87031	85501	94688	91291	90601	103265
Africa	53358	62002	72948	71885	73325	77495	78991	84943	100279
West Asia	1529	1558	2425	2464	2509	2614	3163	3816	4895
Other Asia	7014	16850	26963	34048	36695	43566	44128	46734	54246
By income group (per capita GDP in 2000)									
High-income	332608	459474	790842	820419	891427	1109121	1003099	1037703	1189029
Middle-income	127078	203944	319360	322223	349244	407971	392328	413578	488300
Low-income	138244	181992	314972	376953	413261	517727	513408	587358	733542
MEMO ITEM:									
Least developed countries	15301	19658	24323	25399	28825	35951	36043	38872	44226
Heavily indebted poor countries	24189	29649	37303	42079	45889	54702	55330	61373	71410
Landlocked countries	8398	10722	26896	27666	28527	32710	32287	34476	42714
TRADE GROUPINGS									
EUROPE									
EFTA	49093	99424	125437	121305	127760	143483	143357	149800	167011
European Union 25	821020	1547400	2146174	2311802	2301923	2369069	2397741	2554030	3047551
EU 15	782251	1510435	2062889	2203882	2193922	2247585	2263014	2400829	2849905
New EU members 10	38768	36965	83284	107920	108001	121484	134726	153202	197646
Euro Zone	607148	1218750	1689604	1798215	1790518	1828710	1868787	1987019	2378553
AMERICA									
ANCOM	30467	31134	39414	39147	43355	57952	52669	50380	54727
CACM	4768	4354	8306	11470	11946	11903	10618	10640	11854
CARICOM	11443	4776	5684	5486	5880	7791	7585	7066	9550
FTAA	393784	658220	998013	1169696	1231557	1407716	1328156	1284254	1367485
LAIA	88302	131546	207078	255807	272726	329880	319065	319836	348817
MERCOSUR	29522	46418	70499	81366	74322	84590	87816	89096	106118
NAFTA	311331	561932	856482	1013925	1076935	1224127	1149208	1106936	1161940
OECS	152	343	294	272	257	250	235	228	201
AFRICA									
CEPGL	2455	2510	1807	1304	1047	862	1063	1296	1335
COMESA	14204	19911	20335	19380	21201	25772	24012	26861	30950
ECCAS	9023	11956	11550	10825	12784	16712	16306	17724	20298
ECOWAS	33348	22743	22305	20449	24377	30338	26829	26802	35186
MRU	1225	3016	1564	1125	1111	1008	1005	1162	839
SADC	34884	38425	43803	41200	43725	49573	47660	50690	60450
CEMAC (UDEAC)	4668	5558	6016	5973	6579	7926	8705	8823	10296
UEMOA [1]	4884	5202	6648	7643	7666	6668	6974	8672	10007
UMA	40648	34394	32071	29738	34084	47887	44660	45146	55350
ASIA									
ASEAN	71916	144152	321417	329534	359650	427678	386160	406357	453081
Bangkok Agreement	46045	148738	312310	359782	384646	476009	471116	548472	700191
ECO	13308	38088	60229	61565	69742	82842	81775	90755	120754
GCC	161307	87565	104240	95869	118054	175496	159323	163183	204754
MSG	2020	2243	3940	2819	3152	3378	2857	2655	3603
SAARC	13129	27468	46651	52537	54924	64220	64404	70793	80910
INTERREGIONAL GROUPINGS									
APEC	625317	1331446	2351979	2496339	2656769	3109773	2870865	2957431	3335991
BSEC	29644	31886	143908	139576	138904	176938	180579	193582	247425
CIS	–	–	114089	108404	107624	145953	145273	152597	192503

Sources: Data are based on trade figures in table 1.1A.

Notes: For definition of country groupings, see "Distribution of countries and territories".

1 Formerly CEAO.

1.1B Valeur des exportations et des importations par groupements économiques
Millions de dollars

				Imports (c.i.f.) - Importations (c.a.f.)					Groupements économiques
1980	1990	1995	1998	1999	2000	2001	2002	2003	
2072819	3612808	5198096	5569982	5791619	6555066	6310769	6534518	7614588	**MONDE**
1470305	2638979	3573790	3922060	4112700	4536530	4370813	4493510	5191749	ECONOMIES DEVELOPPEES
495422	814142	1501427	1517206	1575352	1900383	1804472	1890493	2229506	ECONOMIES EN DEVELOPPEMENT
									Par principales catégories
147085	136564	173302	178500	175757	203563	205729	203718	244036	Principaux pays exportateurs de pétrole
348337	677578	1328125	1338706	1399595	1696820	1598744	1686775	1985470	Autres économies en developpement
206615	508544	1065033	1040941	1123318	1401124	1306173	1398237	1641739	Principaux pays exportateurs d'articles manufacturés
141722	169035	263091	297764	276277	295695	292571	288538	343731	Autres économies
57937	54896	106405	132436	113978	122554	118887	107594	122639	Amérique
59879	79756	99799	105308	100943	103001	102798	106529	132868	Afrique
6053	5129	10976	10898	9924	10827	12137	11467	13220	Asie occidentale
14303	24276	40356	43834	46225	54185	53483	57198	68260	Autres pays d'Asie
									Par catégories de revenus (PIB par habitant en 2000)
226319	406310	786653	795525	835815	1011162	914902	925546	1025598	Revenu élevé
144433	228653	393009	379564	365931	426169	409506	426459	492072	Revenu intermédiaire
124671	179179	321765	342118	373606	463051	480064	538488	711837	Revenu faible
									POUR MEMOIRE
24264	25516	34302	39355	40793	42596	45915	47005	55959	Pays les moins avancés
31552	31055	44067	55320	55632	59545	62816	67188	82235	Pays pauvres très endettés
10866	15609	32295	36724	32756	35585	37581	39393	48368	Pays enclavés
									GROUPEMENTS COMMERCIAUX
									EUROPE
54267	98582	114876	120056	116527	120567	119310	120836	134270	AELE
917336	1596222	2079005	2264247	2288196	2415009	2382738	2481787	2979550	Union européenne 25
876488	1561504	1974825	2117950	2144580	2256607	2213973	2294095	2740866	UE 15
40848	34719	104180	146297	143616	158402	168766	187692	238684	Nouveaux membres de l'UE 10
689082	1238723	1599041	1688945	1713330	1804871	1785226	1842655	2221027	Zone Euro
									AMERIQUE
21983	18947	41379	47925	37647	42190	47006	41879	41499	ANCOM
6001	6473	12871	18038	18414	19634	20762	21952	24000	MCAC
13893	6891	9107	11817	11298	12466	12826	12734	15122	CARICOM
430599	757014	1180239	1487148	1604473	1880656	1774697	1773079	1908665	ZLEA
94230	106279	215420	301264	288996	337577	329582	302485	313388	ALADI
37801	29296	79458	98313	82348	89300	83720	62642	69197	MERCOSUR
341672	683779	1014751	1281367	1428271	1686788	1582656	1606536	1728934	ALENA
423	1045	1192	1413	1490	1488	1436	1365	1564	OECO
									AFRIQUE
1949	2256	1518	1672	1476	1394	1091	1312	1737	CEPGL
18174	32927	31096	38771	38020	35814	36336	37360	44509	COMESA
6314	7296	6355	7866	8475	8294	9105	10081	12834	CEEAC
25624	13983	19441	21482	20960	20205	22927	19882	26312	CEDEAO
1231	1057	1462	1101	1157	1430	1406	1522	1543	UFM
30038	33844	47003	47456	45585	48014	46142	49612	65462	SADC
3018	3440	3340	4098	3852	3831	4806	4943	5742	CEMAC (UDEAC)
6371	5777	7416	8150	7297	6664	7088	7598	9966	UEMOA [1]
25402	27771	34062	33868	31728	33328	35098	38253	44274	UMA
									ASIE
65641	162292	355324	282260	300940	370993	340619	349269	399428	ANASE
61846	153260	314306	289930	346583	453170	449894	518263	678812	Accord de Bangkok
26347	50936	69334	81148	73955	91987	83259	96356	124965	ECO
52088	47328	68226	76016	79729	88459	83029	88536	100870	CCG
2356	3017	3543	3107	3348	3079	2982	3313	3810	MSG
25292	38153	59689	66900	72848	80089	76963	83744	101833	SAARC
									GROUPEMENTS INTERREGIONAUX
669769	1405218	2429323	2528854	2760301	3329565	3118812	3231392	3670027	CEAP
41951	57056	158160	169489	140765	166676	168907	189938	250698	CEMN
–	–	93383	95276	70010	81500	93773	102682	130319	CEI

Sources : Les totaux ont été calculés d'après les chiffres du tableau 1.1A.
Notes : Pour la définition des groupements, se reporter à la "Répartition des pays et territoires".

1 Anciennement CEAO.

1.1C Share of exports and imports by region and economic grouping
Percentage

Region and economic grouping	Exports - Exportations (f.o.b. / f.a.b.)										
	1980	1990	1995	1996	1997	1998	1999	2000	2001	2002	2003
WORLD	100.00	100.00	100.00	100.00	100.00	100.00	100.00	100.00	100.00	100.00	100.00
DEVELOPED ECONOMIES	65.31	72.08	69.64	68.69	67.89	69.78	68.54	65.34	66.03	65.29	64.53
DEVELOPING ECONOMIES	29.43	24.21	27.74	28.54	29.42	27.84	29.18	31.97	31.18	31.87	32.39
SOUTH-EAST EUROPE AND CIS	5.27	3.70	2.63	2.77	2.68	2.38	2.27	2.68	2.79	2.84	3.08
DEVELOPED ECONOMIES:											
America	14.43	14.93	15.12	15.43	16.28	16.42	16.60	16.62	16.18	14.79	13.39
Europe	42.83	47.18	44.22	43.81	42.23	44.58	42.88	39.49	41.52	42.28	43.19
Asia	6.69	8.57	9.00	8.05	7.99	7.53	7.86	8.02	7.07	6.97	6.76
Oceania	1.35	1.41	1.30	1.39	1.39	1.24	1.21	1.21	1.26	1.24	1.18
DEVELOPING ECONOMIES:											
By region											
America	**5.50**	**4.15**	**4.38**	**4.70**	**5.04**	**5.07**	**5.20**	**5.56**	**5.59**	**5.34**	**5.04**
South America	3.23	2.48	2.47	2.56	2.68	2.52	2.39	2.56	2.61	2.48	2.46
Other America	2.27	1.66	1.91	2.14	2.36	2.54	2.81	3.01	2.98	2.86	2.58
Africa	**5.91**	**3.12**	**2.18**	**2.33**	**2.28**	**1.92**	**2.06**	**2.30**	**2.25**	**2.22**	**2.34**
North Africa	2.17	1.12	0.69	0.73	0.73	0.61	0.67	0.85	0.82	0.80	0.85
Other Africa	3.74	1.99	1.49	1.60	1.55	1.32	1.39	1.45	1.43	1.42	1.49
Asia	**17.91**	**16.87**	**21.09**	**21.42**	**22.02**	**20.78**	**21.86**	**24.05**	**23.28**	**24.26**	**24.95**
West Asia	9.94	3.91	2.97	3.27	3.30	2.72	3.30	4.14	3.95	3.94	4.29
Other Asia	7.96	12.96	18.11	18.15	18.72	18.06	18.56	19.91	19.33	20.31	20.66
Oceania	**0.11**	**0.08**	**0.09**	**0.09**	**0.08**	**0.07**	**0.07**	**0.06**	**0.06**	**0.05**	**0.06**
By major category											
Major petroleum exporters	15.71	6.25	4.63	5.16	5.12	4.10	4.89	6.36	5.88	5.66	5.93
Other developing countries and territories	13.72	17.97	23.11	23.37	24.30	23.74	24.30	25.61	25.30	26.21	26.46
Major exporters of manufactures	8.34	14.11	19.53	19.72	20.53	20.09	20.73	22.12	21.69	22.62	22.87
Remaining economies	5.38	3.86	3.57	3.65	3.77	3.65	3.56	3.50	3.61	3.59	3.59
America	2.22	1.47	1.49	1.52	1.63	1.59	1.51	1.49	1.49	1.42	1.39
Africa	2.63	1.78	1.42	1.43	1.41	1.32	1.29	1.22	1.29	1.33	1.35
West Asia	0.08	0.04	0.05	0.05	0.04	0.05	0.04	0.04	0.05	0.06	0.07
Other Asia	0.35	0.48	0.52	0.57	0.61	0.62	0.65	0.68	0.72	0.73	0.73
By income group (per capita GDP in 2000)											
High-income	16.37	13.16	15.39	15.92	16.14	15.03	15.73	17.43	16.39	16.22	15.97
Middle-income	6.25	5.84	6.22	6.31	6.34	5.90	6.16	6.41	6.41	6.47	6.56
Low-income	6.80	5.21	6.13	6.31	6.94	6.91	7.29	8.14	8.39	9.18	9.85
MEMO ITEM:											
Least developed countries	0.75	0.56	0.47	0.50	0.49	0.47	0.51	0.56	0.59	0.61	0.59
Heavily indebted poor countries	1.19	0.85	0.73	0.79	0.80	0.77	0.81	0.86	0.90	0.96	0.96
Landlocked countries	0.41	0.31	0.52	0.56	0.57	0.51	0.50	0.51	0.53	0.54	0.57

Sources: Secretariat calculations based on sources listed in tables 1.1A and 1.1B.

Notes: For definitions of country groupings, see "Distribution of countries and territories".

1.1C Parts des régions et groupements économiques dans les exportations et les importations
En pourcentage

				Imports - Importations (c.i.f./ c.a.f.)							Régions et groupements économiques
1980	1990	1995	1996	1997	1998	1999	2000	2001	2002	2003	
100.00	100.00	100.00	100.00	100.00	100.00	100.00	100.00	100.00	100.00	100.00	**MONDE**
70.93	73.05	68.75	68.21	67.47	70.41	71.01	69.21	69.26	68.77	68.18	ECONOMIES DEVELOPPEES
23.90	22.53	28.88	29.17	29.88	27.24	27.20	28.99	28.59	28.93	29.28	ECONOMIES EN DEVELOPPEMENT
5.17	4.42	2.36	2.62	2.65	2.35	1.79	1.80	2.15	2.30	2.54	EUROPE DU SUD-EST ET CEI
											ECONOMIES DEVELOPPEES :
15.42	17.72	18.06	18.29	19.51	20.65	22.09	22.95	22.29	21.88	20.36	Amérique
46.88	46.92	42.21	41.46	39.98	42.81	41.53	38.69	39.66	39.84	40.90	Europe
7.29	6.98	7.03	6.98	6.55	5.56	5.95	6.27	6.09	5.70	5.51	Asie
1.34	1.43	1.45	1.47	1.43	1.38	1.44	1.30	1.22	1.34	1.41	Océanie
											ECONOMIES EN DEVELOPPEMENT :
											Par régions
6.07	**3.64**	**4.85**	**5.07**	**5.82**	**6.19**	**5.75**	**5.89**	**5.99**	**5.38**	**4.83**	**Amérique**
3.22	1.59	2.67	2.67	3.04	3.00	2.36	2.30	2.37	1.88	1.73	Amérique du Sud
2.85	2.05	2.19	2.40	2.78	3.19	3.39	3.59	3.61	3.50	3.10	Autres pays d'Amérique
4.65	**2.87**	**2.44**	**2.30**	**2.35**	**2.39**	**2.20**	**1.97**	**2.11**	**2.08**	**2.22**	**Afrique**
1.52	1.24	0.90	0.86	0.83	0.93	0.84	0.74	0.79	0.81	0.80	Afrique du Nord
3.13	1.62	1.54	1.45	1.52	1.47	1.35	1.23	1.32	1.27	1.42	Autres pays d'Afrique
13.01	**15.89**	**21.49**	**21.69**	**21.60**	**18.56**	**19.16**	**21.05**	**20.41**	**21.38**	**22.14**	**Asie**
4.46	2.95	2.58	2.74	2.90	2.83	2.69	2.83	2.73	2.92	2.98	Asie occidentale
8.55	12.93	18.91	18.95	18.70	15.73	16.47	18.22	17.68	18.46	19.16	Autres pays d'Asie
0.17	**0.14**	**0.11**	**0.11**	**0.10**	**0.09**	**0.09**	**0.08**	**0.08**	**0.09**	**0.09**	**Océanie**
											Par principales catégories
7.10	3.78	3.33	3.29	3.48	3.20	3.03	3.11	3.26	3.12	3.20	Principaux pays exportateurs de pétrole
16.80	18.75	25.55	25.88	26.40	24.03	24.17	25.89	25.33	25.81	26.07	Autres économies en développement
9.97	14.08	20.49	20.86	21.15	18.69	19.40	21.37	20.70	21.40	21.56	Principaux pays exportateurs d'articles manufacturés
6.84	4.68	5.06	5.02	5.26	5.35	4.77	4.51	4.64	4.42	4.51	Autres économies
2.80	1.52	2.05	2.04	2.28	2.38	1.97	1.87	1.88	1.65	1.61	Amérique
2.89	2.21	1.92	1.83	1.84	1.89	1.74	1.57	1.63	1.63	1.74	Afrique
0.29	0.14	0.21	0.22	0.21	0.20	0.17	0.17	0.19	0.18	0.17	Asie occidentale
0.69	0.67	0.78	0.82	0.82	0.79	0.80	0.83	0.85	0.88	0.90	Autres économies d'Asie
											Par catégories de revenus (PIB par habitant en 2000)
10.92	11.25	15.13	15.27	15.87	14.28	14.43	15.43	14.50	14.16	13.47	Pays à revenu élevé
6.97	6.33	7.56	7.54	7.52	6.81	6.32	6.50	6.49	6.53	6.46	Pays à revenu intermédiaire
6.01	4.96	6.19	6.36	6.49	6.14	6.45	7.06	7.61	8.24	9.35	Pays à revenu faible
											POUR MEMOIRE :
1.17	0.71	0.66	0.68	0.68	0.71	0.70	0.65	0.73	0.72	0.73	Pays les moins avancés
1.52	0.86	0.85	0.94	0.94	0.99	0.96	0.91	1.00	1.03	1.08	Pays pauvres très endettés
0.52	0.43	0.62	0.68	0.68	0.66	0.57	0.54	0.60	0.60	0.64	Pays enclavés

Sources : Calculs du secrétariat d'après les chiffres indiqués dans les tableaux 1.1A et 1.1B.

Notes : Pour la définition des groupements, se reporter à la "Répartition des pays et territoires".

Region, country or area	Exports - Exportations (f.o.b. / f.a.b.)										
	1980-90	1990-00	1980-85	1985-90	1990-95	1995-00	1998-99	1999-00	2000-01	2001-02	2002-03
WORLD	**6.0**	**6.6**	**-0.7**	**12.4**	**7.6**	**3.6**	**3.8**	**12.3**	**-3.8**	**4.5**	**16.4**
DEVELOPED ECONOMIES	7.3	5.7	0.2	13.1	6.6	2.7	2.0	7.1	-2.8	3.3	15.0
DEVELOPING ECONOMIES	3.2	9.0	-3.7	12.6	10.7	5.7	8.8	23.0	-6.2	6.8	18.3
SOUTH-EAST EUROPE AND CIS	2.9	6.7	3.2	1.9	4.8	1.8	-1.1	32.5	0.2	6.4	26.2
DEVELOPED ECONOMIES: AMERICA	**6.0**	**7.5**	**0.8**	**12.4**	**7.9**	**5.7**	**4.9**	**12.5**	**-6.3**	**-4.5**	**5.3**
Canada	6.8	8.3	6.5	8.2	8.7	6.9	11.3	16.0	-6.1	-2.9	8.1
United States	5.7	7.3	-1.1	14.0	7.7	5.2	2.9	11.3	-6.4	-5.1	4.3
DEVELOPED ECONOMIES: EUROPE	**7.6**	**5.3**	**-1.1**	**13.9**	**5.7**	**1.9**	**-0.1**	**3.4**	**1.1**	**6.4**	**18.9**
EU 25	**7.5**	**5.4**	**-1.1**	**13.9**	**5.8**	**1.9**	**-0.4**	**2.9**	**1.2**	**6.5**	**19.3**
EU 15	*7.8*	*5.1*	*-1.0*	*14.3*	*5.4*	*1.6*	*-0.5*	*2.5*	*0.7*	*6.1*	*18.7*
Austria	10.2	5.6	-0.3	17.3	5.5	2.7	2.2	0.1	3.9	6.3	23.6
Belgium	–	–	–	–	–	1.2	-0.1	5.0	1.3	13.4	18.3
Belgium-Luxembourg	7.8	–	-3.2	15.9	–	–	–	–	–	–	–
Denmark	9.0	3.6	0.4	15.2	5.7	-0.5	3.2	-0.1	1.4	10.2	17.3
Finland	7.4	7.7	-1.0	13.7	8.1	3.0	-2.6	8.7	-5.9	4.3	17.6
France	7.6	4.3	-2.7	15.3	4.3	1.3	-1.1	-0.8	-1.0	5.1	17.1
Germany	9.2	3.9	-1.0	15.7	3.8	1.2	-0.1	1.3	3.9	7.2	22.2
Germany (former Dem. Rep.)	0.1	–	7.9	-11.9	–	–	–	–	–	–	–
Greece	5.8	3.0	-0.7	10.8	4.4	-1.5	-2.4	2.6	-11.8	8.8	27.9
Ireland	12.8	13.8	5.3	18.0	12.8	12.3	10.5	8.2	7.7	5.3	5.7
Italy	8.7	4.6	-0.6	16.0	5.6	-0.2	-4.3	2.0	1.8	3.7	21.6
Luxembourg	–	–	–	–	–	1.5	-0.3	0.7	3.7	4.2	18.8
Netherlands	4.6	5.5	-1.7	10.9	7.2	1.1	-0.5	4.2	3.5	2.9	16.4
Portugal	15.1	5.2	5.3	22.8	5.4	0.4	1.7	-7.7	5.0	4.4	19.9
Spain	10.8	8.6	3.5	17.7	9.2	4.0	0.7	3.1	1.6	7.3	26.3
Sweden	8.1	6.0	0.1	13.0	5.4	1.3	-0.2	2.5	-12.8	7.2	24.5
United Kingdom	5.9	5.4	-2.1	12.7	4.6	2.3	-1.3	5.0	-5.1	3.4	10.1
New EU members 10	*1.0*	*13.6*	*-3.2*	*3.0*	*17.9*	*7.7*	*0.1*	*12.5*	*10.9*	*13.7*	*29.0*
Cyprus	4.7	1.1	-1.6	16.7	3.3	-6.5	-6.3	-4.4	2.6	-13.6	9.5
Czech Republic	–	–	–	–	–	6.3	-0.7	10.5	15.2	15.2	26.6
Czechoslovakia (former)	-0.3	–	-5.9	1.0	–	–	–	–	–	–	–
Estonia	–	–	–	–	–	11.4	-6.2	6.7	5.2	4.5	31.5
Hungary	1.4	12.7	-0.4	2.2	3.9	17.1	8.5	12.3	9.0	13.0	23.2
Latvia	–	–	–	–	–	7.1	-4.9	8.3	7.3	14.2	26.7
Lithuania	–	–	–	–	–	3.9	-19.1	26.8	20.3	21.4	30.0
Malta	9.2	6.3	-4.1	22.0	9.5	5.1	8.2	23.1	-19.8	13.7	13.8
Poland	1.4	9.9	-2.1	3.8	9.1	5.9	0.8	15.5	14.0	13.6	30.6
Slovakia	–	–	–	–	–	6.9	-4.6	16.3	6.3	14.5	51.7
Slovenia	–	–	–	–	–	1.2	-5.6	2.2	6.0	11.9	23.3
Other developed Europe	**7.9**	**3.9**	**-0.4**	**14.5**	**4.0**	**1.5**	**5.3**	**12.3**	**0.0**	**4.5**	**11.5**
Faeroe Islands	10.7	1.8	0.2	14.6	-2.9	5.2	7.1	0.4	23.4	-6.9	21.5
Iceland	7.9	3.1	-3.1	12.4	2.0	2.7	-2.2	-5.7	6.9	10.2	7.1
Norway	5.3	5.2	1.5	11.9	2.9	3.9	12.5	32.1	-1.4	0.9	13.0
Switzerland	9.5	3.1	-1.5	16.3	4.7	0.0	1.8	1.5	0.8	7.0	10.6
DEVELOPED ECONOMIES: ASIA	**8.9**	**4.4**	**5.5**	**10.2**	**8.8**	**1.5**	**8.3**	**14.7**	**-15.3**	**3.1**	**12.9**
Israel	8.8	10.3	1.9	13.5	11.0	9.6	12.2	21.8	-7.5	1.0	7.6
Japan	8.9	4.1	5.7	10.0	8.7	1.1	8.1	14.3	-15.8	3.3	13.2
DEVELOPED ECONOMIES: OCEANIA	**6.5**	**4.8**	**0.8**	**13.5**	**5.9**	**1.0**	**0.9**	**12.6**	**-0.1**	**3.0**	**10.9**
Australia	6.6	5.0	0.9	13.8	5.4	1.7	0.3	13.9	-0.8	2.6	10.0
New Zealand	6.2	3.9	0.5	11.9	7.9	-2.0	3.7	6.6	3.3	4.7	14.7

For sources and notes, see end of table.

16

Imports - Importations (c.i.f./ c.a.f.)											Régions, pays ou zones
1980-90	1990-00	1980-85	1985-90	1990-95	1995-00	1998-99	1999-00	2000-01	2001-02	2002-03	
6.1	**6.5**	**-0.5**	**12.4**	**7.0**	**3.9**	**4.0**	**13.2**	**-3.7**	**3.6**	**16.5**	**MONDE**
6.9	6.0	-0.3	12.8	5.4	4.5	4.9	10.3	-3.7	2.8	15.5	ECONOMIES DEVELOPPEES
4.2	8.3	-1.8	12.8	12.5	3.0	3.8	20.6	-5.1	4.8	17.9	ECONOMIES EN DEVELOPPEMENT
4.2	3.5	2.0	6.4	-0.8	-3.6	-20.8	14.1	14.7	11.1	28.5	EUROPE DU SUD-EST ET CEI
											ECONOMIES DEVELOPPEES : AMERIQUE
8.1	**9.1**	**6.6**	**8.5**	**8.5**	**9.4**	**11.2**	**17.5**	**-6.5**	**1.7**	**8.4**	
7.9	7.5	5.0	10.0	6.7	7.7	6.9	11.2	-7.2	0.1	7.7	Canada
8.2	9.5	6.9	8.2	8.9	9.8	12.2	18.9	-6.4	2.0	8.6	Etats-Unis
											ECONOMIES DEVELOPPEES : EUROPE
6.8	**4.8**	**-2.9**	**14.6**	**3.8**	**2.8**	**0.9**	**5.4**	**-1.3**	**4.0**	**19.6**	
6.7	**4.9**	**-2.9**	**14.6**	**3.9**	**2.9**	**1.1**	**5.5**	**-1.3**	**4.2**	**20.1**	**UE 25**
7.0	*4.4*	*-2.9*	*15.1*	*3.3*	*2.6*	*1.3*	*5.2*	*-1.9*	*3.6*	*19.5*	*UE 15*
8.7	4.1	-2.8	16.9	4.9	1.0	2.0	-0.8	2.1	3.4	21.2	Autriche
					1.7	0.0	7.5	1.0	11.5	18.1	Belgique
6.4	–	-4.6	15.3								Belgique-Luxembourg
6.8	3.9	-1.4	11.0	4.9	-0.4	-3.9	-0.4	-0.2	11.3	14.4	Danemark
6.9	4.8	-3.6	15.5	0.7	3.6	-2.1	7.2	-5.3	4.7	23.7	Finlande
6.5	3.4	-4.6	16.0	2.3	2.0	1.6	5.4	-3.0	3.1	18.9	France
7.1	3.4	-3.0	15.5	3.7	1.4	0.5	4.6	-1.9	1.2	22.3	Allemagne
-0.5		4.3	-11.9								Allemagne (anc. Rép. Dém. d')
6.6	4.5	-0.1	13.2	4.0	1.1	-2.3	1.8	2.4	4.1	42.4	Grèce
7.0	10.9	-2.5	15.3	8.9	9.5	5.7	9.1	-0.3	0.3	3.6	Irlande
6.9	3.2	-3.1	15.4	0.4	2.7	0.9	8.0	-0.8	3.4	19.3	Italie
					2.8	7.9	-3.0	4.1	3.6	17.5	Luxembourg
4.4	5.4	-3.6	11.4	5.6	2.1	-0.1	5.7	-1.7	-0.6	20.0	Pays-Bas
10.3	5.1	-4.9	26.6	3.7	3.3	3.4	-4.1	3.2	-2.8	6.6	Portugal
10.6	6.1	-2.9	24.6	3.0	6.2	8.5	5.8	0.5	6.4	27.5	Espagne
6.7	4.5	-3.1	13.8	2.4	2.1	0.2	6.1	-13.0	5.1	24.0	Suède
8.5	5.4	-0.5	15.9	2.9	4.3	1.3	5.2	-4.0	4.5	13.5	Royaume-Uni
0.2	*17.0*	*-3.6*	*0.9*	*24.4*	*8.0*	*-1.8*	*10.3*	*6.5*	*11.2*	*27.2*	*Nouveaux membres de l'UE 10*
7.6	4.3	1.9	17.3	5.9	-0.3	-1.8	6.3	2.0	4.2	9.3	Chypre
					3.8	-2.8	14.8	13.2	11.7	31.1	République tchèque
1.7	–	-2.0	2.9								Tchécoslovaquie (anc.)
					9.9	-11.3	3.6	1.5	11.7	35.1	Estonie
0.1	13.5	-2.8	-0.2	11.0	15.9	8.7	14.4	5.5	12.1	26.0	Hongrie
					11.1	-7.7	8.1	10.1	15.6	29.4	Lettonie
–	–	–	–	–	6.5	-16.6	12.9	16.4	23.4	25.6	Lituanie
8.1	4.4	-4.7	20.3	7.1	2.4	6.7	19.4	-19.8	4.2	18.0	Malte
-3.2	18.3	-5.9	-5.1	23.2	10.0	-1.3	6.6	2.7	9.6	23.4	Pologne
–	–	–	–	–	6.6	-13.4	12.8	15.6	12.6	35.9	Slovaquie
–	–	–	–	–	1.7	-0.3	0.3	0.3	7.7	26.7	Slovénie
											Autres économies développées d'Europe
8.0	**3.1**	**-2.6**	**14.1**	**2.2**	**0.9**	**-2.9**	**3.5**	**-1.0**	**1.2**	**11.2**	
7.1	6.2	4.3	1.9	-0.7	9.8	21.5	10.2	8.1	-8.9	26.5	Iles Féroé
6.6	5.5	-3.5	11.4	-1.5	8.3	0.6	3.5	-13.1	1.0	22.6	Islande
6.2	4.2	-2.6	9.8	3.1	0.4	-8.8	0.7	-4.2	5.9	13.2	Norvège
8.8	2.6	-2.7	16.2	2.0	0.8	-0.3	4.7	0.6	-0.5	10.0	Suisse
											ECONOMIES DEVELOPPEES : ASIE
5.1	**4.8**	**-1.6**	**14.0**	**7.0**	**0.3**	**11.2**	**19.3**	**-6.4**	**-3.1**	**12.5**	
5.9	6.9	-0.3	10.7	11.6	1.1	13.0	-5.3	12.9	0.2	2.2	Israël
5.1	4.6	-1.7	14.2	6.7	0.2	11.0	21.9	-8.0	-3.4	13.6	Japon
											ECONOMIES DEVELOPPEES : OCEANIE
6.2	**6.2**	**1.4**	**12.5**	**8.1**	**2.1**	**8.2**	**2.4**	**-9.6**	**13.7**	**22.7**	
6.4	6.4	1.4	12.9	8.0	2.7	7.0	3.4	-10.7	13.8	22.6	Australie
5.4	5.6	1.8	10.3	9.0	-0.7	14.4	-2.8	-4.3	13.1	23.3	Nouvelle-Zélande

Pour les sources et les notes, se reporter à la fin du tableau.

**1.2A   Annual average growth rates of exports and imports
         by region and country** (*continued*)
Percentage

Region, country or area	Exports - Exportations (f.o.b. / f.a.b.)										
	1980-90	1990-00	1980-85	1985-90	1990-95	1995-00	1998-99	1999-00	2000-01	2001-02	2002-03
DEVELOPING ECONOMIES:											
AMERICA	**1.7**	**10.3**	**-0.5**	**7.6**	**9.2**	**8.1**	**6.5**	**20.3**	**-3.4**	**-0.1**	**9.8**
South America	*2.3*	*7.0*	*-0.7*	*8.7*	*7.9*	*3.3*	*-1.6*	*20.0*	*-1.8*	*-0.7*	*15.4*
Argentina	2.1	10.1	-0.3	9.9	10.6	3.1	-11.8	12.9	0.8	-3.1	14.2
Bolivia	-2.0	4.3	-7.8	8.3	4.3	0.8	-4.8	17.0	4.5	1.1	21.2
Brazil	5.1	5.9	5.1	7.6	8.9	2.4	-6.1	14.7	5.7	3.7	21.1
Chile	8.1	9.4	-3.3	19.4	11.9	3.2	5.1	11.9	-4.9	-0.5	15.8
Colombia	7.8	7.3	0.0	11.0	7.3	4.4	6.3	12.7	-5.8	-3.1	6.4
Ecuador	-0.4	6.8	2.9	0.1	9.4	0.5	5.9	10.7	-5.0	7.8	19.8
French Guiana	10.1	_	6.7	18.3	11.2	_	_	_	_	_	_
Guyana	-2.8	8.4	-15.7	6.1	15.5	0.6	7.9	-4.8	-4.0	3.1	28.8
Paraguay	11.6	1.7	0.2	35.0	0.6	-3.9	-26.9	17.3	13.9	17.6	27.8
Peru	-1.5	9.0	-4.3	4.0	10.5	3.2	5.7	14.2	0.8	9.1	17.1
Suriname	-0.4	-2.4	-8.9	10.7	1.6	-12.5	-67.0	177.7	30.5	1.7	20.4
Uruguay	4.5	5.2	-4.3	13.5	4.6	0.7	-19.3	2.6	-10.2	-9.7	18.1
Venezuela	-4.4	5.5	-6.7	6.5	1.4	6.2	17.4	57.5	-13.8	-10.7	4.1
Other America	*0.8*	*14.1*	*-0.2*	*6.1*	*11.0*	*13.3*	*14.5*	*20.4*	*-4.8*	*0.3*	*5.0*
Antigua and Barbuda	-4.8	-0.4	-12.8	0.9	13.3	-3.4	4.5	11.1	-7.1	0.0	-48.7
Aruba	_	14.3	_	_	-13.8	53.8	0.4	491.9	-14.0	-13.7	29.3
Bahamas	-18.2	8.5	-13.3	-30.4	-7.1	30.3	54.0	24.6	-26.5	5.5	-4.8
Barbados	-3.0	3.9	13.9	-9.8	0.3	1.0	4.9	3.2	-4.8	-20.4	1.7
Belize	2.2	5.0	0.0	3.4	4.7	5.3	8.1	17.4	-22.8	-0.1	21.4
Bermuda	6.8	0.5	-3.2	12.4	-6.8	-1.1	33.3	-2.3	2.1	0.5	27.9
Costa Rica	4.6	17.0	-0.4	8.2	20.4	13.9	20.6	-12.2	-14.2	4.6	16.2
Cuba	-0.9	-1.5	2.5	-5.6	-13.3	-1.7	-1.1	17.7	0.1	-14.9	2.0
Dominica	15.8	0.6	19.9	10.6	-4.2	3.7	-10.2	-3.8	-19.0	-3.6	-6.8
Dominican Republic	-2.1	4.9	-6.3	2.8	2.0	-0.3	-8.5	20.0	-16.7	3.6	24.8
El Salvador	-4.6	10.1	-5.6	-5.5	12.1	5.2	-6.4	13.2	-8.9	2.0	1.4
Greenland	10.5	-3.7	-4.1	19.9	-4.1	-6.8	13.2	-9.0	5.3	11.9	14.2
Grenada	7.0	1.0	3.3	3.8	-2.8	5.0	-7.9	5.1	3.9	-25.9	-1.2
Guadeloupe	4.9	_	-5.6	9.7	4.4	_	_	_	_	_	_
Guatemala	-2.2	10.0	-5.6	2.0	11.6	5.0	-7.1	12.4	-8.5	-9.5	11.5
Haiti	-1.2	12.2	-2.9	-3.3	-10.5	31.7	4.5	-5.0	-13.7	2.2	23.6
Honduras	1.6	7.2	-1.2	1.1	6.2	0.9	-24.0	18.5	-4.0	-0.3	0.8
Jamaica	1.1	2.2	-10.0	16.6	3.9	-2.3	-5.5	5.1	-6.4	-8.7	25.6
Martinique	7.6	_	0.6	6.5	-4.0	_	_	_	_	_	_
Mexico	5.9	16.1	8.1	11.0	13.8	14.7	16.1	22.0	-4.7	1.4	2.9
Montserrat	-0.2	4.9	22.0	-12.3	17.7	-10.0	25.0	-80.0	0.0	100.0	0.0
Netherlands Antilles	-15.7	0.4	-23.3	12.0	-4.1	5.3	1.7	19.3	21.4	-31.7	35.6
Nicaragua	-5.8	10.3	-7.6	2.9	7.1	6.5	-4.9	18.3	-8.2	0.7	13.4
Panama	-0.5	9.6	-2.9	-1.1	14.1	6.1	4.9	4.6	5.9	-7.1	2.1
Saint Kitts and Nevis	3.4	2.6	-3.7	5.6	-6.9	12.5	-5.3	25.4	5.4	10.3	4.8
Saint Lucia	11.0	-10.1	-0.8	17.7	-3.6	-14.9	-10.5	-22.1	2.3	0.2	-17.3
Saint Pierre and Miquelon	_	-14.9	21.5	_	-26.9	-5.4	0.0	0.0	20.0	0.0	0.0
Saint Vincent and the Grenadines	16.2	-5.3	31.9	6.8	-12.0	2.1	-2.0	-2.9	-12.1	-8.0	0.0
Trinidad and Tobago	-9.4	6.9	-13.7	-0.2	2.7	8.9	24.2	52.4	0.1	-9.3	50.5
DEVELOPING ECONOMIES:											
AFRICA	**-1.3**	**3.0**	**-6.8**	**6.4**	**0.0**	**2.7**	**11.1**	**25.1**	**-5.5**	**3.0**	**22.6**
North Africa	*-2.6*	*2.6*	*-5.8*	*5.3*	*-2.7*	*5.3*	*14.9*	*42.0*	*-7.2*	*2.5*	*22.9*
Algeria	-4.4	3.0	-2.2	1.7	-6.3	10.4	27.3	75.9	-12.2	-1.1	20.2
Egypt	7.3	0.7	2.7	12.8	-6.4	3.9	13.7	31.7	-12.0	14.1	13.8
Libyan Arab Jamahiriya	-7.4	-2.2	-10.7	0.9	-7.6	2.0	19.3	59.7	-11.8	-1.9	35.8
Morocco	6.2	7.8	-2.6	14.0	8.7	0.8	3.0	-5.5	2.6	9.9	15.7
Sudan	-2.5	14.0	-4.9	6.2	11.3	20.7	30.9	131.6	-6.0	8.9	50.0
Tunisia	3.5	6.0	-6.4	16.0	8.4	1.6	2.3	-0.4	13.4	3.7	16.8
Other Africa	*-0.5*	*3.2*	*-7.4*	*7.1*	*1.4*	*1.4*	*9.4*	*16.9*	*-4.6*	*3.3*	*22.5*
Angola	6.5	6.1	4.1	15.7	-2.5	10.4	45.6	53.6	-17.5	16.3	14.0
Benin	18.8	3.3	33.7	15.4	7.7	-2.9	3.6	-7.1	-4.8	20.0	23.6
Botswana	18.8	4.8	14.6	16.9	2.7	2.7	35.7	2.6	-9.7	2.5	21.0
Burkina Faso	7.9	12.7	-2.9	12.6	9.3	-2.3	-20.1	-18.0	12.0	1.3	37.6
Burundi	2.5	-4.3	10.7	-10.0	7.2	-8.5	-15.9	-7.9	-23.0	-21.6	24.7
Cameroon	2.5	-2.0	-10.8	23.9	-4.6	-1.1	-17.0	0.5	37.0	8.3	27.6
Cape Verde	6.6	13.0	4.3	-1.4	5.8	1.8	9.8	-7.2	-7.3	11.6	23.6
Central African Republic	3.5	3.6	-3.6	10.4	6.9	-1.1	-3.3	9.8	-11.5	3.2	-41.3

For sources and notes, see end of table.

| Imports - Importations (c.i.f./ c.a.f.) | | | | | | | | | | | Régions, pays ou zones |
1980-90	1990-00	1980-85	1985-90	1990-95	1995-00	1998-99	1999-00	2000-01	2001-02	2002-03	
0.0	**11.5**	**-9.2**	**9.4**	**14.0**	**8.2**	**-3.4**	**15.9**	**-2.2**	**-7.0**	**4.6**	**ECONOMIES EN DEVELOPPEMENT : AMERIQUE**
-1.6	*10.8*	*-11.8*	*7.3*	*18.5*	*0.6*	*-18.2*	*10.2*	*-0.8*	*-17.9*	*7.3*	*Amérique du Sud*
-6.6	16.9	-19.1	-0.3	37.0	4.1	-18.7	-1.4	-19.2	-55.8	53.7	Argentine
-0.4	9.7	-4.6	-1.7	13.4	4.5	-11.5	4.3	-6.7	3.7	-8.9	Bolivie
-1.9	12.7	-11.8	8.8	18.3	0.2	-14.7	13.3	-0.5	-15.0	2.1	Brésil
2.8	10.3	-14.6	22.3	14.6	0.5	-19.6	15.8	-3.7	-3.6	12.9	Chili
0.0	9.7	-3.4	7.2	24.3	-4.8	-27.2	8.3	11.2	-0.8	9.1	Colombie
-1.3	7.8	-7.1	0.2	16.3	-3.4	-45.9	23.3	44.1	19.9	1.6	Equateur
11.5	_	0.4	24.9	-2.4	_	_	_	_	_	_	Guyane française
-3.3	7.9	-13.5	4.7	12.9	3.5	-3.2	5.4	-10.7	-3.6	81.5	Guyana
4.3	5.5	-3.6	17.8	15.1	-8.9	-30.2	18.8	-3.0	4.8	21.3	Paraguay
1.3	10.8	-8.9	8.8	19.9	-2.0	-17.8	9.0	2.2	0.2	15.4	Pérou
-5.5	-4.2	-13.6	10.1	1.4	-15.9	-46.0	-17.5	117.6	0.9	11.3	Suriname
-1.3	10.1	-17.9	12.7	17.1	2.9	-11.9	3.3	-11.7	-35.8	11.5	Uruguay
-3.2	5.3	-11.2	-1.4	6.0	7.0	-11.1	15.3	11.2	-34.3	-24.4	Venezuela
1.5	*11.9*	*-6.5*	*11.3*	*9.8*	*15.3*	*10.5*	*19.9*	*-3.1*	*0.3*	*3.2*	*Autres économies : Amérique*
10.9	4.3	10.5	5.6	5.9	3.3	7.5	-3.4	-6.3	0.0	-2.6	Antigua-et-Barbuda
_	5.6	_	_	2.1	9.4	-4.0	6.8	0.7	0.0	-1.1	Aruba
-14.3	7.0	-17.0	-14.6	1.1	7.9	-5.4	-0.5	-1.5	-12.1	14.0	Bahamas
1.6	7.2	3.8	3.6	0.5	8.6	9.7	4.3	-6.0	-4.4	9.0	Barbade
4.0	5.9	-4.4	13.6	3.1	14.4	25.3	41.7	-1.4	1.5	5.2	Belize
4.8	2.3	4.7	7.0	-0.6	4.8	7.7	1.1	5.3	3.7	13.7	Bermudes
4.5	13.9	-5.3	12.8	19.0	10.9	1.9	0.5	2.8	9.4	6.3	Costa Rica
1.5	2.5	5.2	-3.3	-15.3	11.2	4.0	11.7	-0.8	-14.0	14.8	Cuba
9.7	3.3	3.3	18.8	-1.5	4.1	4.6	7.2	-11.6	-12.0	8.9	Dominique
3.3	14.4	-2.5	9.0	13.6	14.7	6.3	23.2	-19.5	1.9	3.3	République dominicaine
2.4	11.1	0.0	6.0	17.4	5.8	0.6	20.9	1.9	1.1	12.1	El Salvador
5.9	-1.1	-2.0	7.0	-1.9	-3.5	5.2	-17.0	-12.7	2.3	16.4	Groenland
8.4	8.6	5.0	8.3	2.1	13.6	2.4	19.9	-12.5	1.4	24.2	Grenade
10.0	_	-0.4	19.3	0.5	_	_	_	_	_	_	Guadeloupe
0.6	11.0	-7.1	10.2	14.4	9.1	-5.8	9.3	17.0	8.4	6.8	Guatemala
-2.9	14.4	2.5	-6.1	6.6	11.5	28.6	1.1	-2.2	11.6	5.1	Haïti
0.6	13.8	-1.9	2.0	9.6	12.3	5.6	6.7	3.0	1.4	9.9	Honduras
2.8	7.0	-2.6	14.9	8.1	2.1	-4.5	14.7	1.0	5.1	16.8	Jamaïque
7.8	_	-4.5	18.0	1.8	_	_	_	_	_	_	Martinique
6.4	14.2	-7.4	21.1	12.8	18.4	13.5	22.9	-3.6	0.2	1.1	Mexique
14.6	-6.1	4.0	21.0	-8.4	-7.6	15.8	4.6	-17.4	21.1	0.0	Montserrat
-14.6	1.7	-21.1	9.6	-3.7	4.1	-1.6	38.8	-0.7	-19.8	16.8	Antilles néerlandaises
-3.1	11.7	0.0	-8.5	7.5	13.6	24.8	-3.0	-1.5	0.9	23.1	Nicaragua
-3.6	8.7	-1.6	-2.0	10.8	6.8	3.5	-3.9	-12.3	0.6	3.5	Panama
10.4	4.6	3.2	16.9	4.7	2.4	4.6	-1.3	1.3	-3.2	30.5	Saint-Kitts-et-Nevis
9.1	2.4	0.0	18.0	1.9	3.2	5.8	0.1	0.0	-13.0	24.2	Sainte-Lucie
36.8	-1.5	17.0	16.7	-3.5	-0.6	13.6	-6.7	-7.1	-15.4	26.4	Saint-Pierre-et-Miquelon
9.7	3.9	7.5	12.3	-0.6	6.5	4.2	-19.0	14.3	-6.2	14.9	Saint-Vincent-et-les Grenadines
-12.3	12.1	-14.5	-5.6	3.8	12.2	-8.6	20.7	7.9	2.1	20.3	Trinité-et-Tobago
-0.3	**3.6**	**-6.2**	**7.7**	**3.9**	**0.4**	**-4.5**	**1.4**	**3.1**	**2.1**	**24.5**	**ECONOMIES EN DEVELOPPEMENT : AFRIQUE**
2.7	*3.2*	*-0.3*	*8.1*	*2.1*	*1.3*	*-5.3*	*-0.6*	*2.6*	*6.3*	*14.8*	*Afrique du Nord*
-2.7	0.5	-1.9	0.4	2.4	-1.1	-2.6	-0.1	6.0	11.3	10.5	Algérie
12.6	4.7	14.9	11.8	-3.0	5.0	-0.9	-12.6	-9.0	-1.6	17.6	Egypte
-4.4	-2.4	-9.7	6.3	0.7	-8.7	-29.4	-2.9	18.9	27.9	13.4	Jamahiriya arabe libyenne
3.6	5.5	-2.9	12.6	6.9	2.5	-3.6	16.2	-4.3	7.6	23.1	Maroc
_	9.8	-11.9	_	13.7	3.3	-26.1	9.7	50.9	6.4	-16.0	Soudan
2.7	5.2	-5.1	15.1	7.3	2.1	1.5	1.1	11.2	0.0	14.5	Tunisie
-2.2	*4.0*	*-9.7*	*7.3*	*5.1*	*-0.1*	*-3.9*	*2.7*	*3.5*	*-0.4*	*30.7*	*Autres économies : Afrique*
0.8	7.8	-2.2	3.7	-1.3	14.3	49.5	-2.2	4.6	19.4	40.0	Angola
-4.9	9.7	-6.3	-8.3	21.8	-1.4	1.8	-18.2	-1.8	12.8	9.5	Bénin
9.0	2.7	-3.6	27.6	-1.9	6.2	-7.2	11.5	-26.7	7.8	11.9	Botswana
4.3	3.6	-4.0	6.9	-5.6	5.4	-7.3	-9.9	7.4	12.7	15.7	Burkina Faso
2.2	-6.9	2.3	2.3	-1.2	-6.2	-25.1	25.3	-5.8	-7.1	21.0	Burundi
0.1	1.9	-6.6	-0.7	-3.0	4.1	-11.8	13.0	24.4	-3.0	19.6	Cameroun
5.7	6.0	6.6	7.3	12.2	-1.0	7.9	-6.6	1.3	19.4	14.0	Cap-Vert
7.9	0.2	2.3	2.6	4.9	-6.0	-10.5	-10.7	-8.5	12.3	-3.0	République centrafricaine

Pour les sources et les notes, se reporter à la fin du tableau.

1.2A Annual average growth rates of exports and imports by region and country (continued)
Percentage

Region, country or area	Exports - Exportations (f.o.b. / f.a.b.)										
	1980-90	1990-00	1980-85	1985-90	1990-95	1995-00	1998-99	1999-00	2000-01	2001-02	2002-03
Chad	9.4	3.2	3.7	22.8	0.4	-3.5	-7.2	-24.8	3.2	-2.1	63.0
Comoros	2.8	-16.6	-1.8	2.1	-12.6	-10.0	18.2	47.5	98.6	39.2	-41.1
Congo	2.2	7.5	4.6	2.5	1.7	12.1	14.1	59.6	-20.1	12.4	16.2
Côte d'Ivoire	1.7	6.0	-0.5	-1.4	2.9	0.8	1.2	-16.6	1.5	33.7	10.8
Dem. Rep. of the Congo	2.7	-6.8	-1.5	6.7	-7.2	-14.8	-20.9	-18.5	23.7	28.7	2.6
Djibouti	11.3	-5.1	4.9	9.8	-11.7	-2.0	-1.2	0.7	336.3	57.9	-25.1
Equatorial Guinea	19.8	41.2	5.7	26.8	9.6	61.7	61.6	54.6	49.0	15.0	-3.0
Eritrea	–	–	–	–	–	-31.1	-38.3	9.1	0.7	173.4	0.4
Ethiopia	-1.1	11.5	-2.8	-1.3	12.0	2.9	-16.7	4.0	-6.3	5.5	28.6
Gabon	-3.9	1.3	-2.5	3.6	3.7	-5.0	25.0	2.9	7.6	-20.7	23.0
Gambia	6.8	-14.5	-6.6	0.3	-7.6	2.0	-41.2	32.1	-44.0	9.7	-30.0
Ghana	-2.7	9.0	-12.2	7.0	17.2	0.0	-4.2	-3.5	-5.4	17.2	14.4
Guinea	4.0	0.6	4.8	6.9	1.2	-1.6	-8.3	4.8	9.7	21.2	-41.7
Guinea-Bissau	4.2	13.6	1.6	10.6	33.3	8.6	91.0	21.6	1.1	-13.8	26.6
Kenya	-1.1	6.3	-4.6	-0.6	12.4	-2.6	-13.0	-0.8	12.1	8.9	13.9
Lesotho	3.7	12.4	-17.6	26.7	23.0	3.9	-11.0	27.5	28.2	29.4	30.7
Liberia	4.7	-12.6	-6.1	27.5	-15.5	-14.5	10.4	-29.9	-25.5	-7.4	1.3
Madagascar	-1.0	9.0	-5.4	1.8	9.7	8.6	8.5	41.1	12.7	-47.7	34.9
Malawi	2.0	0.9	-1.8	8.8	-3.7	-2.1	5.0	-16.2	18.5	-9.4	19.4
Mali	6.0	6.2	-7.9	18.6	4.6	5.7	1.7	-3.6	31.7	22.0	5.1
Mauritania	8.0	-2.2	11.6	4.0	2.5	-7.3	6.8	-4.0	-2.9	-7.6	6.7
Mauritius	14.4	3.6	1.2	19.5	4.8	-0.8	-3.5	-1.9	4.5	10.7	7.6
Mozambique	-9.6	9.6	-25.5	10.2	3.7	13.7	14.5	38.5	93.2	-3.3	29.4
Namibia	–	0.9	–	–	4.2	-2.3	0.1	7.0	-10.7	-7.0	10.8
Niger	-5.4	0.0	-15.0	-1.2	-2.8	-0.7	-14.1	-1.3	-3.7	2.6	21.2
Nigeria	-8.4	3.2	-13.6	3.5	-4.1	5.2	40.6	51.4	-17.7	-12.5	47.0
Reunion	4.7	–	-2.4	6.2	1.8	–	–	–	–	–	–
Rwanda	-0.9	-3.9	3.6	-8.3	-18.7	-1.0	0.2	-12.4	62.0	-34.4	-1.2
Sao Tome and Principe	-8.3	-6.1	-11.5	-8.5	1.8	-14.8	-53.7	25.1	-4.6	90.4	33.0
Senegal	3.5	4.0	4.8	5.3	5.1	-0.6	6.1	-10.5	9.1	6.3	24.8
Seychelles	9.3	15.5	8.6	18.1	-0.3	20.9	18.6	33.4	11.6	5.5	22.0
Sierra Leone	-2.4	-29.5	-8.2	-0.2	-17.7	-30.8	-5.6	107.7	122.6	67.8	89.6
Somalia	-1.1	6.5	-15.2	6.8	5.3	2.3	-3.1	1.0	47.7	4.3	18.1
South Africa	0.8	2.5	-7.5	7.2	3.3	-0.2	1.3	12.3	-2.4	1.6	22.7
Swaziland	4.7	5.9	-13.9	24.0	9.4	1.5	-3.7	-2.9	15.9	-11.1	22.6
Togo	1.1	6.7	-8.9	6.7	5.3	-1.6	-6.9	-7.3	-1.6	19.5	44.3
Uganda	-4.0	15.4	6.3	-16.2	25.3	-1.4	3.5	-11.3	-0.8	-3.0	27.0
United Republic of Tanzania	-5.1	7.4	-15.2	4.2	15.2	-4.2	-7.8	22.1	17.0	12.7	39.6
Zambia	0.9	-2.0	-11.7	17.8	-4.3	-5.7	4.1	-37.4	47.9	-5.6	10.7
Zimbabwe	2.5	2.6	-5.4	8.5	5.0	-4.0	9.1	2.0	-37.3	92.9	1.1
DEVELOPING ECONOMIES: ASIA	**4.7**	**9.5**	**-3.9**	**15.5**	**12.6**	**5.5**	**9.2**	**23.6**	**-6.9**	**8.9**	**19.7**
West Asia	*-6.1*	*5.8*	*-14.5*	*8.4*	*2.3*	*8.1*	*26.0*	*41.1*	*-8.2*	*4.2*	*26.5*
Bahrain	-3.3	3.5	-6.1	6.1	1.8	4.5	33.4	42.0	-10.0	3.7	10.0
Iran, Islamic Republic of	7.2	1.2	22.1	10.7	-0.6	4.9	60.3	35.3	-16.0	17.9	38.2
Iraq	-4.0	29.4	-10.2	0.2	-37.0	118.8	132.7	61.0	-22.8	-15.0	7.6
Jordan	6.2	6.6	4.1	8.4	9.8	1.0	1.6	3.7	20.7	20.8	21.7
Kuwait	-7.7	16.5	-10.6	-2.1	34.7	3.2	27.3	59.8	-16.6	-5.2	26.0
Lebanon	-5.6	4.1	-12.9	-0.2	2.3	0.6	2.3	5.6	21.8	20.2	45.7
Oman	3.3	5.5	7.1	12.3	2.4	7.5	31.3	50.1	1.7	1.2	4.5
Qatar	-8.7	10.3	-9.1	0.7	0.3	26.3	44.7	64.2	-6.2	1.5	26.2
Saudi Arabia	-13.4	3.1	-26.8	10.4	0.2	3.5	30.8	52.8	-12.3	6.6	28.7
Syrian Arab Republic	2.4	0.9	-4.7	22.8	-3.3	1.7	19.9	33.8	13.3	5.6	1.4
Turkey	14.0	9.2	19.6	11.8	10.4	4.9	-1.4	4.5	12.8	10.3	34.8
United Arab Emirates	-0.8	6.8	-9.0	10.9	2.8	11.2	7.8	36.6	-4.5	-0.6	27.1
Yemen	-3.2	20.6	-4.6	6.7	19.4	8.7	63.0	67.1	-21.2	7.5	10.8
Other Asia	*11.1*	*10.3*	*5.2*	*18.2*	*15.0*	*5.1*	*6.7*	*20.4*	*-6.6*	*9.8*	*18.3*
Afghanistan	-10.5	1.0	-3.1	-18.6	-7.2	2.4	-20.1	11.4	-39.3	-10.6	102.0
Bangladesh	7.8	15.7	5.3	11.9	16.9	11.1	6.2	17.2	-4.9	0.3	14.6
Bhutan	19.6	7.0	3.0	27.6	6.2	0.9	7.3	-11.4	3.1	2.3	-0.2
Brunei Darussalam	-9.3	0.9	-8.4	-3.8	-0.8	2.2	24.0	11.9	-2.1	3.8	17.8
Cambodia	18.0	26.8	9.3	32.6	49.4	12.9	41.1	24.1	12.1	11.4	20.3
China	12.8	14.5	7.6	18.3	18.7	10.0	6.1	27.8	6.8	22.4	34.5
China, Hong Kong SAR	16.8	8.3	8.8	23.7	15.9	1.6	-0.1	16.1	-5.9	5.4	11.8
China, Macao SAR	12.3	3.8	10.3	13.7	3.4	4.3	2.7	15.4	-9.4	2.5	9.6
China, Taiwan Province of	14.9	7.2	9.7	17.2	9.5	4.3	9.9	21.6	-17.1	6.5	10.5

For sources and notes, see end of table.

Imports - Importations (c.i.f./ c.a.f.)											Régions, pays ou zones
1980-90	1990-00	1980-85	1985-90	1990-95	1995-00	1998-99	1999-00	2000-01	2001-02	2002-03	
12.6	3.9	18.7	9.0	0.0	-2.3	-11.3	-0.3	115.3	46.9	-17.1	Tchad
5.7	1.6	6.0	6.4	1.5	4.6	70.1	-9.9	36.6	-13.7	32.0	Comores
2.7	2.7	3.1	-0.3	2.4	-10.9	20.6	-43.4	24.8	1.7	13.0	Congo
-1.5	3.5	-11.4	2.7	3.8	-2.7	-17.3	-13.2	0.7	1.6	35.2	Côte d'Ivoire
3.1	-0.4	-4.5	8.3	-13.3	-1.9	-9.9	-6.6	-32.2	39.6	39.8	Rép. dém. du Congo
-1.1	-4.3	-1.0	1.5	-3.6	-3.3	-3.5	-0.7	-5.5	13.2	-4.5	Djibouti
11.9	29.1	-8.8	18.3	-7.5	41.3	34.0	6.0	62.0	-41.1	92.8	Guinée équatoriale
–	–	–	–	–	-6.5	-34.1	-0.5	29.0	27.2	47.7	Erythrée
4.3	7.8	7.1	0.1	7.6	3.1	1.4	-18.0	43.8	-8.2	60.0	Ethiopie
1.1	2.4	1.4	0.2	-0.9	0.6	-23.7	18.2	-13.6	17.6	14.4	Gabon
2.5	0.2	-9.4	15.0	0.5	-2.7	-15.9	-2.4	-28.3	10.1	24.0	Gambie
0.6	8.3	-5.2	5.8	15.3	11.5	35.8	-14.6	-16.6	12.5	23.7	Ghana
9.7	-2.6	2.7	16.1	2.0	-5.7	3.6	10.2	-1.9	10.9	1.9	Guinée
5.2	-4.9	1.2	7.4	12.3	-17.9	-18.4	-3.9	25.7	-5.5	17.9	Guinée-Bissau
1.7	6.0	-8.2	9.6	4.9	0.1	-11.4	9.7	2.8	1.7	14.8	Kenya
3.5	0.6	-3.6	16.0	5.9	-6.7	-9.5	-6.9	-6.5	15.4	30.0	Lesotho
-7.2	11.1	-10.3	-2.8	16.1	2.6	10.6	28.5	-6.7	-5.1	-5.3	Libéria
-4.3	6.4	-14.2	7.5	3.5	8.4	7.2	34.3	-4.3	-36.9	59.9	Madagascar
3.3	-0.6	-7.8	17.8	-6.5	1.1	30.7	-21.0	5.8	23.5	-6.9	Malawi
2.7	2.1	-7.6	8.9	6.0	-5.6	-20.4	-2.2	24.1	1.4	51.7	Mali
-2.1	0.4	-5.4	-0.7	11.9	-9.6	-14.8	6.2	15.2	-4.6	-0.8	Mauritanie
12.9	3.8	-3.7	25.0	5.0	0.5	8.4	-6.9	-5.1	9.2	9.8	Maurice
0.1	1.2	-12.4	15.3	-1.8	11.4	44.2	1.7	-8.2	27.0	1.0	Mozambique
–	4.0	–	–	6.8	-1.1	-2.3	-3.7	-0.2	-6.3	17.2	Namibie
-3.5	0.7	-11.9	1.2	-1.9	0.3	-16.4	-0.3	-5.9	8.1	37.8	Niger
-15.6	3.1	-15.3	-5.5	1.7	3.3	-6.8	1.6	32.8	-34.9	43.8	Nigéria
11.0	–	-0.8	18.8	3.6	–	–	–	–	–	–	Réunion
2.7	-1.7	1.9	-0.9	-9.7	-2.1	-12.0	-15.5	18.4	-18.8	3.7	Rwanda
1.6	-0.8	-12.4	12.3	4.9	4.9	125.2	-22.3	-3.6	9.1	35.1	Sao Tomé-et-Principe
1.4	3.7	-4.1	8.1	1.1	2.0	7.5	-2.9	13.9	12.3	26.4	Sénégal
7.2	9.6	-0.8	14.8	5.5	7.3	13.1	-21.2	39.2	-11.7	2.2	Seychelles
-8.7	-4.2	-20.5	3.0	-2.2	-6.3	-14.6	84.9	21.8	45.2	14.8	Sierra Leone
-19.3	26.6	-11.5	-30.8	14.9	4.5	21.5	0.9	31.0	0.9	16.0	Somalie
-1.3	5.8	-10.6	11.0	9.6	-1.8	-8.7	11.2	-4.9	3.6	40.4	Afrique du Sud
-0.5	5.0	-11.3	16.6	7.3	0.6	-1.4	-2.1	7.9	-12.9	7.9	Swaziland
2.0	4.0	-13.3	15.0	-7.6	-5.6	-16.7	-0.9	6.4	12.1	45.8	Togo
4.5	21.0	1.6	1.0	37.6	6.8	-5.2	14.5	3.8	-30.3	12.6	Ouganda
-0.6	0.1	-10.9	7.2	2.7	-0.1	7.2	-2.1	12.4	-1.5	30.0	République-Unie de Tanzanie
0.0	0.3	-11.8	12.1	-10.1	5.8	-24.4	20.8	31.6	-4.1	1.1	Zambie
-0.5	1.9	-10.8	15.9	5.7	-8.2	-18.9	-14.9	-3.9	62.7	22.0	Zimbabwe
											ECONOMIES EN DEVELOPPEMENT : ASIE
6.7	8.1	2.4	14.9	13.5	2.0	7.3	24.4	-6.6	8.5	20.7	
-1.7	*4.8*	*-1.0*	*4.8*	*3.2*	*5.0*	*-1.2*	*19.1*	*-7.1*	*10.7*	*19.0*	*Asie occidentale*
-2.3	0.3	-3.3	4.8	-1.1	1.6	3.7	25.3	-7.1	15.8	2.6	Bahreïn
0.2	-6.5	0.9	11.5	-12.9	0.7	-11.5	13.1	22.9	20.2	30.0	Iran, Rép. islamique d'
-1.5	20.9	6.4	-2.5	-29.1	77.8	56.8	61.6	-1.4	9.1	-14.4	Iraq
-1.9	5.1	0.6	-1.8	8.2	1.7	-2.9	23.7	5.4	3.6	20.5	Jordanie
-4.1	5.5	-1.6	-4.6	13.3	-1.9	-11.6	-6.0	10.0	14.4	19.9	Koweït
-5.5	8.7	-8.1	2.9	21.5	-4.0	-12.2	0.4	17.1	-11.6	11.2	Liban
0.7	6.1	10.4	-2.3	8.9	3.0	-17.7	7.8	15.1	3.6	9.4	Oman
-1.4	7.4	-6.1	7.9	11.3	-1.7	-26.7	30.1	15.6	7.8	27.4	Qatar
-6.1	0.8	-3.9	1.4	-0.2	1.3	-6.7	8.0	3.3	3.5	7.8	Arabie saoudite
-8.5	3.6	-2.2	-9.3	17.3	-5.8	-1.6	-0.4	24.6	9.9	21.8	République arabe syrienne
9.3	10.3	7.1	13.6	8.7	5.4	-11.4	34.0	-24.0	20.0	32.2	Turquie
0.7	11.2	-7.1	12.7	13.8	11.9	34.4	14.8	-21.1	7.0	19.3	Emirats arabes unis
-5.0	0.6	-4.6	0.5	0.6	5.7	-7.3	15.7	-0.6	12.7	16.9	Yémen
10.0	*8.8*	*4.0*	*18.0*	*15.5*	*1.6*	*8.9*	*25.2*	*-6.6*	*8.1*	*20.9*	*Autres économies : Asie*
-0.1	-3.8	9.6	-8.0	-16.1	3.7	10.2	33.8	0.2	72.4	30.1	Afghanistan
3.6	10.3	-0.3	8.8	11.8	5.0	10.3	8.7	-0.1	-5.2	14.0	Bangladesh
5.7	8.6	8.5	0.4	4.6	12.1	36.1	11.4	-6.0	-13.4	3.8	Bhoutan
3.8	3.2	1.2	10.4	15.9	-10.1	-10.0	7.7	-15.8	29.4	18.1	Brunéi Darussalam
-3.1	25.2	-5.6	4.0	46.2	11.3	36.5	21.9	8.0	10.5	16.7	Cambodge
13.5	13.1	13.8	7.0	20.7	9.5	18.2	35.9	8.2	21.2	39.9	Chine
15.0	8.8	5.4	24.0	18.0	0.2	-2.7	18.5	-5.5	3.3	11.7	Chine, Hong Kong RAS
10.4	2.1	6.1	15.5	5.4	1.4	4.3	10.6	5.8	6.0	8.9	Chine, Macao RAS
12.4	8.5	0.8	24.6	12.6	5.0	5.7	26.1	-23.3	5.1	12.9	Chine, Taiwan Province de

Pour les sources et les notes, se reporter à la fin du tableau.

1.2A Annual average growth rates of exports and imports
by region and country (concluded)
Percentage

Region, country or area	Exports - Exportations (f.o.b. / f.a.b.)										
	1980-90	1990-00	1980-85	1985-90	1990-95	1995-00	1998-99	1999-00	2000-01	2001-02	2002-03
India	7.3	9.5	2.0	15.7	11.5	5.3	6.7	18.8	2.3	13.8	13.5
Indonesia	-0.9	8.1	-3.6	8.8	11.8	4.1	-0.4	27.7	-9.1	3.0	7.8
Korea, Dem. People's Republic of	–	-9.6	–	–	-15.6	-6.6	-7.3	18.6	16.7	-12.4	1.0
Korea, Republic of	15.1	10.1	11.5	18.1	12.8	5.5	8.6	19.9	-12.7	8.0	19.3
Lao People's Dem. Rep.	11.0	15.4	16.2	6.5	36.4	0.6	-15.9	6.3	0.3	-10.1	27.0
Malaysia	8.6	12.2	5.9	16.2	19.9	4.6	15.5	16.1	-10.4	6.0	6.5
Maldives	22.6	5.6	25.2	19.6	-2.4	7.1	-14.3	19.1	0.4	18.6	24.5
Mongolia	5.0	-1.3	11.7	-0.5	-4.5	-2.4	3.8	30.1	-3.8	-0.1	18.1
Myanmar	-7.6	14.4	-9.6	-2.5	21.6	14.3	5.4	44.9	44.7	27.9	-14.2
Nepal	8.1	10.7	9.6	5.3	11.2	17.8	27.0	33.7	-8.4	-23.0	16.7
Pakistan	8.1	4.3	0.3	14.2	6.1	0.8	-0.8	7.2	2.3	7.3	20.4
Philippines	3.9	18.9	-3.7	13.7	16.1	18.8	24.4	8.8	-17.9	11.8	0.0
Singapore	9.9	9.9	3.7	20.6	17.6	1.1	4.4	20.2	-11.7	2.8	16.1
Sri Lanka	5.4	11.3	6.1	7.7	15.4	6.4	-4.5	18.2	-11.3	-2.4	9.1
Thailand	14.0	10.5	1.5	28.0	18.7	3.2	7.3	18.2	-5.7	5.6	17.1
Viet Nam	18.9	22.7	16.1	29.6	19.5	19.7	23.3	25.2	4.5	9.5	22.1
DEVELOPING ECONOMIES: OCEANIA	**4.3**	**2.8**	**-2.6**	**9.2**	**11.6**	**-3.6**	**8.0**	**4.5**	**-13.3**	**-6.2**	**37.0**
American Samoa	8.9	1.4	7.2	9.0	-3.1	4.3	-16.9	0.3	10.7	3.7	14.8
Cook Islands	1.3	-0.1	-5.7	0.5	-2.8	10.6	-1.6	180.3	-23.3	2.6	0.0
Fiji	1.0	3.1	-7.9	9.6	5.3	-3.1	19.5	-4.2	-8.0	-7.2	18.8
French Polynesia	15.7	9.1	5.8	23.1	15.0	2.2	2.4	-12.3	-12.2	-6.2	109.1
Guam	1.9	1.0	5.3	1.2	9.0	-0.9	-11.6	-2.6	-17.6	-32.8	44.9
Kiribati	0.0	6.8	15.8	7.0	17.9	-4.2	63.7	-60.3	25.3	-28.6	21.4
Nauru	-2.3	-6.7	-2.2	3.2	-11.3	0.9	80.0	-22.2	-53.6	-30.8	0.0
New Caledonia	5.5	1.7	-11.3	22.7	1.3	1.4	23.4	30.0	-26.9	20.6	38.7
Papua New Guinea	4.9	3.1	-0.6	6.0	19.1	-6.1	8.6	8.9	-13.5	-14.6	40.4
Samoa	-3.3	12.0	5.1	-6.0	-4.7	13.6	40.0	-30.3	9.1	-11.5	9.1
Solomon Islands	0.9	2.7	2.4	1.9	19.2	-14.6	0.0	-45.2	-31.9	23.0	28.4
Tonga	2.7	-3.7	-4.8	17.4	4.3	-6.5	65.1	-28.8	-23.8	93.3	19.6
Tuvalu	–	-38.3	–	41.7	-22.7	-23.7	-28.5	-91.4	67.9	736.0	-30.2
Vanuatu	-6.3	4.3	1.3	-4.6	8.9	-4.2	-23.8	-9.5	-33.2	-1.1	34.5
SOUTH-EAST EUROPE AND CIS	**2.9**	**6.7**	**3.2**	**1.9**	**4.8**	**1.8**	**-1.1**	**32.5**	**0.2**	**6.4**	**26.2**
South-East Europe	*0.5*	*1.4*	*2.9*	*-3.5*	*-4.3*	*1.9*	*-2.7*	*16.8*	*4.0*	*14.2*	*26.5*
Albania	–	5.7	–	–	-1.9	7.1	28.8	-0.8	16.6	8.3	37.0
Bosnia and Herzegovina	–	–	–	–	–	121.1	26.2	42.7	1.4	-7.1	14.4
Bulgaria	-0.2	2.2	5.5	-12.3	3.4	-6.4	-5.5	21.3	6.4	12.4	31.1
Croatia	–	–	–	–	–	-0.8	-5.3	3.0	5.3	5.0	25.8
Macedonia, TFYR	–	–	–	–	–	1.8	-9.1	10.6	-12.5	-3.6	21.5
Romania	-4.0	8.5	1.2	-9.3	8.3	4.3	2.5	21.9	9.9	21.8	27.0
Serbia and Montenegro	–	–	–	–	–	8.8	-16.2	12.3	-18.9	19.8	19.9
Yugoslavia, SFR (former)	3.8	–	1.9	6.9	–	–	–	–	–	–	–
CIS	*3.7*	*8.2*	*3.4*	*3.7*	*7.5*	*1.7*	*-0.7*	*35.6*	*-0.5*	*5.0*	*26.2*
Armenia	–	–	–	–	–	-0.9	5.3	26.7	16.5	48.0	33.7
Belarus	–	–	–	–	–	6.5	-16.4	24.0	1.7	7.7	24.2
Georgia	–	–	–	–	–	12.8	24.2	39.1	-3.3	9.1	28.3
Kazakhstan	–	–	–	–	–	7.0	10.1	50.1	-2.0	12.4	32.9
Kyrgyzstan	–	–	–	–	–	1.6	-11.6	11.2	-5.6	2.0	19.8
Moldova, Republic of	–	–	–	–	–	-11.3	-26.7	1.7	20.9	15.7	32.6
Russian Federation	–	–	–	–	–	1.4	1.0	39.5	-2.3	3.9	25.5
Tajikistan	–	–	–	–	–	0.5	14.5	13.3	-16.4	-0.3	28.1
Turkmenistan	–	–	–	–	–	3.8	4.7	1.9	-20.7	9.0	22.3
Ukraine	–	–	–	–	–	-0.7	-8.4	25.8	11.6	10.4	28.5
USSR (former)	3.7	–	3.4	3.7	–	–	–	–	–	–	–
Uzbekistan	–	–	–	–	–	-2.9	-6.4	-2.6	1.2	-8.9	25.1

Notes: Growth rates in these tables are based on the trade figures in table 1.1 of the *UNCTAD Handbook of Statistics 2004 on CD-ROM*.

Imports - Importations (c.i.f./ c.a.f.)											Régions, pays ou zones
1980-90	1990-00	1980-85	1985-90	1990-95	1995-00	1998-99	1999-00	2000-01	2001-02	2002-03	
4.3	10.1	0.8	8.8	8.1	7.9	9.3	9.7	-2.2	12.2	25.1	Inde
2.6	2.7	-0.5	15.7	11.4	-8.6	-12.2	39.6	-7.5	-18.1	64.2	Indonésie
_	-6.6	_	_	-15.3	2.0	3.6	39.1	9.6	-7.0	1.9	Corée, Rép. populaire dém. de
11.9	7.1	6.6	19.6	12.1	-0.7	28.4	34.0	-12.1	7.8	17.6	Corée, République de
6.6	12.7	15.3	-1.3	32.5	-4.3	-5.1	2.0	-1.4	-18.3	21.6	Rép. dém. populaire lao
7.7	9.5	3.8	21.5	20.3	-1.7	12.2	25.4	-9.9	8.1	2.6	Malaisie
15.4	11.8	15.4	24.3	13.1	8.1	13.6	-3.4	1.3	-0.4	20.2	Maldives
5.5	0.8	14.1	-7.7	-13.6	7.2	1.9	19.8	2.5	7.9	14.2	Mongolie
-4.7	22.6	-7.9	-4.8	29.9	14.5	-13.8	3.4	19.8	-18.4	7.7	Myanmar
6.9	9.3	5.7	8.5	15.1	1.7	14.2	10.6	-6.4	-3.7	23.6	Népal
3.0	3.1	1.7	6.2	7.0	-2.8	9.7	6.4	-6.2	10.2	16.1	Pakistan
2.9	12.5	-8.1	21.4	18.0	2.9	3.4	13.7	-5.7	6.5	6.3	Philippines
8.0	7.8	1.6	20.4	15.6	-1.0	6.1	21.2	-13.8	0.4	9.9	Singapour
2.2	9.6	-0.8	5.8	14.9	5.3	0.9	20.4	-16.8	2.2	9.3	Sri Lanka
12.7	5.0	1.0	32.7	15.5	-5.9	17.2	23.0	0.2	4.2	17.3	Thaïlande
8.7	22.7	7.3	7.7	27.9	10.2	2.1	33.2	2.3	18.8	30.9	Viet Nam
											ECONOMIES EN DEVELOPPEMENT :
3.7	**0.3**	**-2.1**	**8.8**	**1.7**	**-2.6**	**-1.5**	**-1.5**	**2.7**	**9.2**	**17.3**	**OCEANIE**
10.7	-7.0	20.1	4.5	-7.4	-0.4	-23.9	18.1	7.7	24.7	-2.0	Samoa américaines
9.0	-3.9	-0.3	16.9	3.3	-1.5	-1.3	34.3	-6.4	-14.7	0.0	Iles Cook
0.3	2.7	-6.3	11.3	5.0	-2.7	25.1	-8.6	-3.8	3.9	19.3	Fidji
6.2	0.8	0.0	8.4	0.8	-1.0	-9.0	5.4	8.3	22.3	28.5	Polynésie française
0.7	2.5	-2.5	3.0	2.3	1.3	-30.4	20.7	21.5	-21.7	25.5	Guam
5.5	4.1	0.4	14.1	2.6	2.3	25.8	-3.5	3.2	5.3	-6.9	Kiribati
10.7	-11.7	8.4	13.1	-1.2	-7.1	18.2	107.7	-22.2	19.1	-21.0	Nauru
8.8	1.1	-6.7	18.6	0.8	-0.3	8.3	-8.1	0.7	20.0	21.8	Nouvelle-Calédonie
1.3	-1.0	-3.4	6.1	1.9	-6.9	-0.6	-6.6	-6.8	15.1	5.0	Papouasie-Nouvelle-Guinée
3.8	1.7	-3.9	11.7	1.0	2.8	19.4	-8.5	23.2	3.7	1.8	Samoa
1.9	0.7	-2.1	5.9	10.4	-10.1	-14.1	-16.4	-10.9	-41.9	47.1	Iles Salomon
4.7	1.9	1.0	9.1	4.5	-1.9	5.7	-4.5	4.7	-10.6	0.0	Tonga
_	5.2	_	8.6	21.3	2.6	-18.8	-35.7	-32.3	216.1	41.5	Tuvalu
2.4	0.7	1.1	6.6	0.5	-1.7	8.6	-9.4	17.5	-12.4	10.8	Vanuatu
4.2	**3.5**	**2.0**	**6.4**	**-0.8**	**-3.6**	**-20.8**	**14.1**	**14.7**	**11.1**	**28.5**	**EUROPE DU SUD-EST ET CEI**
1.0	*3.2*	*-1.5*	*2.0*	*-5.1*	*2.9*	*-5.3*	*9.2*	*13.8*	*14.7*	*31.7*	*Europe du Sud-Est*
_	9.5	_	_	9.9	9.8	37.5	-4.3	22.0	13.0	24.0	Albanie
_	_	_	_	_	24.4	12.1	-5.9	4.4	18.1	29.0	Bosnie-Herzégovine
-0.3	5.3	6.8	-14.0	7.5	-0.1	10.2	19.3	11.7	10.0	36.3	Bulgarie
_	8.1	_	_	8.4	0.5	-7.0	1.1	16.0	17.1	32.0	Croatie
_	_	_	_	_	3.9	-6.2	16.1	-19.6	15.0	16.2	Macédoine, LERY
-3.8	6.8	-4.5	-4.0	2.5	2.8	-12.1	25.6	19.2	14.8	34.4	Roumanie
_	_	_	_	_	0.5	-19.9	-20.3	19.2	14.9	23.3	Serbie-et-Monténégro
0.8	_	-5.5	8.7	_	_	_	_	_	_	_	Yougoslavie, RSF (anc.)
5.7	*3.6*	*3.8*	*8.1*	*1.2*	*-6.0*	*-26.5*	*16.4*	*15.1*	*9.5*	*26.9*	*CEI*
_	_	_	_	_	3.4	-11.4	10.3	-0.9	13.4	28.1	Arménie
_	_	_	_	_	6.1	-21.9	29.6	-4.2	9.7	26.5	Bélarus
_	_	_	_	_	5.9	-34.1	11.8	4.6	7.1	44.8	Géorgie
_	_	_	_	_	2.8	-15.3	37.9	27.9	2.1	26.5	Kazakhstan
_	_	_	_	_	-1.5	-28.7	-7.6	-15.7	25.6	22.2	Kirghizistan
_	_	_	_	_	-6.5	-42.7	32.4	15.6	15.7	30.2	Moldova, République de
_	_	_	_	_	-9.3	-31.9	13.5	19.8	12.6	23.3	Fédération de Russie
_	_	_	_	_	-3.2	-13.9	4.9	2.1	1.8	40.1	Tadjikistan
_	_	_	_	_	6.0	7.4	1.3	13.4	-9.8	19.8	Turkménistan
_	_	_	_	_	-5.2	-19.3	17.8	13.0	7.6	35.6	Ukraine
5.7	_	3.8	8.1	_	_	_	_	_	_	_	URSS (anc.)
_	_	_	_	_	-3.1	-7.9	7.2	1.2	-11.8	23.7	Ouzbékistan

Notes : Les taux d'accroissement ont été calculés d'après les chiffres du tableau 1.1 du *Manuel de statistiques de la CNUCED 2004 sur CD-ROM*.

1.2B Annual average growth rates of exports and imports by economic grouping
Percentage

Economic grouping	Exports (f.o.b.) - Exportations (f.a.b.)										
	1980-90	1990-00	1980-85	1985-90	1990-95	1995-00	1998-99	1999-00	2000-01	2001-02	2002-03
WORLD	**6.0**	**6.6**	**-0.7**	**12.4**	**7.6**	**3.6**	**3.8**	**12.3**	**-3.8**	**4.5**	**16.4**
DEVELOPED ECONOMIES	7.3	5.7	0.2	13.1	6.6	2.7	2.0	7.1	-2.8	3.3	15.0
DEVELOPING ECONOMIES	3.2	9.0	-3.7	12.6	10.7	5.7	8.8	23.0	-6.2	6.8	18.3
By major category											
Major petroleum exporters	-6.3	5.1	-12.5	6.7	1.5	7.2	23.7	46.1	-11.1	0.6	21.9
Other developing economies	8.9	10.0	3.6	15.0	13.2	5.4	6.3	18.4	-5.0	8.2	17.5
Major exporters of manufactures	11.5	10.7	7.2	17.3	14.8	5.8	7.2	19.8	-5.7	9.0	17.6
Remaining economies	2.5	6.4	-3.3	8.3	6.2	2.9	1.5	10.2	-0.6	3.8	16.5
America	1.3	8.1	-2.7	6.0	8.1	3.4	-1.8	10.8	-3.6	-0.8	14.0
Africa	2.6	3.4	-5.0	9.3	3.2	0.3	2.0	5.7	1.9	7.5	18.1
West Asia	0.6	5.9	-4.8	5.3	7.6	0.9	1.8	4.2	21.0	20.6	28.3
Other Asia	7.9	10.3	3.9	13.6	9.4	8.9	7.8	18.7	1.3	5.9	16.1
By income group (per capita GDP in 2000)											
High-income	2.7	8.7	-6.2	14.2	10.9	5.1	8.7	24.4	-9.6	3.5	14.6
Middle-income	4.6	7.2	1.9	10.4	9.3	3.6	8.4	16.8	-3.8	5.4	18.1
Low-income	3.1	11.3	-3.3	11.2	11.6	9.2	9.6	25.3	-0.8	14.4	24.9
MEMO ITEM:											
Least developed countries	2.2	7.2	-2.1	8.7	4.1	6.2	13.5	24.7	0.3	7.9	13.8
Heavily indebted poor countries	1.9	7.7	-2.8	8.3	4.6	6.2	9.1	19.2	1.2	10.9	16.4
Landlocked countries	3.3	12.4	-2.8	8.8	22.8	2.0	3.1	14.7	-1.3	6.8	23.9
TRADE GROUPINGS											
EUROPE											
EFTA	7.9	3.9	-0.4	14.5	4.0	1.5	5.3	12.3	-0.1	4.5	11.5
EU 25	7.5	5.4	-1.1	13.9	5.8	1.9	-0.4	2.9	1.2	6.5	19.3
EU15	7.8	5.1	-1.0	14.3	5.4	1.6	-0.5	2.5	0.7	6.1	18.7
New EU members 10	1.0	13.6	-3.2	3.0	17.9	7.7	0.1	12.5	10.9	13.7	29.0
Euro Zone	8.3	5.1	-1.2	15.3	5.7	1.6	-0.4	2.1	2.2	6.3	19.7
AMERICA											
ANCOM	-1.6	6.5	-4.7	6.2	4.7	4.7	10.8	33.7	-9.1	-4.4	8.6
CACM	-0.4	12.6	-3.8	2.5	13.8	8.7	4.2	-0.4	-10.8	0.2	11.4
CARICOM	-8.1	4.7	-11.7	-3.9	2.9	4.5	7.2	32.5	-2.7	-6.8	35.2
FTAA	5.1	8.2	0.6	11.5	8.3	6.2	5.3	14.3	-5.7	-3.3	6.5
LAIA	3.1	10.5	1.7	8.4	9.5	8.2	6.6	21.0	-3.3	0.2	9.1
MERCOSUR	4.5	7.0	3.4	8.7	9.1	2.5	-8.7	13.8	3.8	1.5	19.1
NAFTA	6.0	8.3	1.3	12.3	8.4	6.6	6.2	13.7	-6.1	-3.7	5.0
OECS	9.1	-3.7	5.4	9.6	-3.7	-2.2	-5.5	-2.7	-6.0	-2.9	-12.1
AFRICA											
CEPGL	2.6	-6.5	-0.8	5.0	-7.0	-14.0	-19.7	-17.6	23.3	21.9	3.0
COMESA	4.4	3.3	-1.2	11.0	0.3	2.4	9.4	21.6	-6.8	11.9	15.2
ECCAS	2.3	3.2	-0.7	9.9	-1.7	4.2	18.1	30.7	-2.4	8.7	14.5
ECOWAS	-4.9	3.4	-10.6	4.0	-1.6	3.1	19.2	24.5	-11.6	-0.1	31.3
MRU	4.3	-7.5	-2.2	17.7	-10.2	-7.9	-1.2	-9.2	-0.3	15.6	-27.8
SADC	2.2	2.8	-6.0	9.5	2.3	0.5	6.1	13.4	-3.9	6.4	19.3
CEMAC (UDEAC)	0.0	3.3	-2.8	9.5	0.7	3.3	10.1	20.5	9.8	1.4	16.7
UEMOA [1]	2.0	5.4	-1.4	1.7	3.9	0.5	0.3	-13.0	4.6	24.3	15.4
UMA	-3.9	2.6	-6.4	3.8	-2.4	4.9	14.6	40.5	-6.7	1.1	22.6
ASIA											
ASEAN	6.3	11.1	0.6	17.0	17.1	4.4	9.1	18.9	-9.7	5.2	11.5
Bangkok Agreement	12.8	12.2	8.2	17.7	15.4	7.8	6.9	23.8	-1.0	16.4	27.7
ECO	8.6	7.5	16.1	10.9	9.9	4.4	13.3	18.8	-1.3	11.0	33.1
GCC	-9.2	5.4	-19.5	8.4	3.1	6.8	23.1	48.7	-9.2	2.4	25.5
MSG	3.9	2.7	-3.9	9.4	13.5	-4.8	11.8	7.2	-15.4	-7.1	35.7
SAARC	7.4	9.1	2.3	14.4	11.0	5.3	4.5	16.9	0.3	9.9	14.3
INTERREGIONAL GROUPINGS											
APEC	8.1	8.5	3.2	13.5	11.7	4.7	6.4	17.1	-7.7	3.0	12.8
BSEC	3.0	17.5	5.0	-0.4	39.5	1.6	-0.5	27.4	2.1	7.2	27.8
CIS	3.7	8.2	3.4	3.7	7.5	1.7	-0.7	35.6	-0.5	5.0	26.2

Sources: Growth rates in this table are based on trade figures in table 1.1 of the *UNCTAD Handbook of Statistics 2004 on CD-ROM*.
Notes: For definition of country groupings, see "Distribution of countries and territories".

1 Formerly CEAO.

\multicolumn{11}{c}{Imports (c.i.f.) - Importations (c.a.f.)}	Groupements économiques
1980-90	1990-00	1980-85	1985-90	1990-95	1995-00	1998-99	1999-00	2000-01	2001-02	2002-03	
6.1	**6.5**	**-0.5**	**12.4**	**7.0**	**3.9**	**4.0**	**13.2**	**-3.7**	**3.6**	**16.5**	**MONDE**
6.9	6.0	-0.3	12.8	5.4	4.5	4.9	10.3	-3.7	2.8	15.5	ECONOMIES DEVELOPPEES
4.2	8.3	-1.8	12.8	12.5	3.0	3.8	20.6	-5.1	4.8	17.9	ECONOMIES EN DEVELOPPEMENT
											Par principales catégories
-3.7	2.9	-4.6	3.8	3.1	1.9	-1.5	15.8	1.1	-1.0	19.8	Principaux pays exportateurs de pétrole
6.8	9.2	-0.7	15.2	14.2	3.2	4.6	21.2	-5.8	5.5	17.7	Autres économies en developpement
9.5	9.8	1.9	18.3	15.5	3.5	7.9	24.7	-6.8	7.1	17.4	Principaux pays exportateurs d'articles manufacturés
1.6	6.9	-4.8	8.1	9.5	1.8	-7.2	7.0	-1.1	-1.4	19.1	Autres économies
-0.5	9.3	-7.5	5.7	14.8	2.4	-13.9	7.5	-3.0	-9.5	14.0	Amérique
2.8	4.3	-4.7	10.8	4.7	0.6	-4.1	2.0	-0.2	3.6	24.7	Afrique
-3.8	7.2	-4.1	0.4	15.7	-1.9	-8.9	9.1	12.1	-5.5	15.3	Asie occidentale
4.6	8.9	2.9	7.3	10.2	4.4	5.5	17.2	-1.3	7.0	19.3	Autres pays d'Asie
											Par catégories de revenus (PIB par habitant en 2000)
5.3	8.5	-2.7	16.4	13.4	3.3	5.1	21.0	-9.5	1.2	10.8	Revenu élevé
3.2	6.9	-2.1	12.2	10.9	-0.2	-3.6	16.5	-3.9	4.1	15.4	Revenu intermédiaire
3.1	9.6	0.0	7.1	12.5	5.8	9.2	23.9	3.7	12.2	32.2	Revenu faible
											POUR MEMOIRE
0.3	6.2	-4.1	4.6	5.5	4.0	3.7	4.4	7.8	2.4	19.1	Pays les moins avancés
0.2	7.9	-5.4	3.9	7.1	5.3	0.6	7.0	5.5	7.0	22.4	Pays pauvres très endettés
3.0	9.8	-1.6	6.9	17.8	0.2	-10.8	8.6	5.6	4.8	22.8	Pays enclavés
											GROUPEMENTS COMMERCIAUX
											EUROPE
8.0	3.1	-2.7	14.2	2.3	0.8	-2.9	3.5	-1.0	1.3	11.1	AELE
6.7	4.9	-2.9	14.6	3.9	2.9	1.1	5.5	-1.3	4.2	20.1	UE 25
7.0	4.4	-2.9	15.1	3.3	2.6	1.3	5.2	-1.9	3.6	19.5	UE 15
0.2	17.0	-3.6	0.9	24.4	8.0	-1.8	10.3	6.5	11.2	27.2	Nouveaux membres de l'UE 10
6.9	4.2	-3.5	15.8	3.5	2.4	1.4	5.3	-1.1	3.2	20.5	Zone Euro
											AMERIQUE
-1.5	7.9	-8.4	2.5	15.2	0.1	-21.5	12.1	11.4	-10.9	-0.9	ANCOM
1.4	12.4	-3.5	5.9	15.2	9.8	2.1	6.6	5.7	5.7	9.3	MCAC
-7.3	7.1	-12.5	-0.2	4.3	5.8	-4.4	10.3	2.9	-0.7	18.8	CARICOM
6.5	9.7	3.0	8.8	9.8	9.2	7.9	17.2	-5.6	-0.1	7.7	ZLEA
1.0	12.3	-9.2	10.5	15.3	8.4	-4.1	16.8	-2.4	-8.2	3.6	ALADI
-2.7	13.1	-13.7	7.6	22.0	1.1	-16.2	8.4	-6.3	-25.2	10.5	MERCOSUR
8.0	9.6	5.8	9.1	8.8	10.2	11.5	18.1	-6.2	1.5	7.6	ALENA
9.9	3.9	5.0	12.8	2.3	4.7	5.4	-0.1	-3.5	-5.0	14.6	OECO
											AFRIQUE
3.0	-1.6	-2.9	6.2	-10.9	-2.6	-11.7	-5.6	-21.7	20.3	32.4	CEPGL
6.4	4.7	1.8	10.7	0.5	3.0	-1.9	-5.8	1.5	2.8	19.1	COMESA
2.0	3.5	-2.1	2.9	-3.6	3.8	7.7	-2.1	9.8	10.7	27.3	CEEAC
-8.6	3.6	-12.9	0.0	3.7	1.9	-2.4	-3.6	13.5	-13.3	32.3	CEDEAO
-0.7	1.6	-9.0	8.3	5.1	-2.5	5.0	23.6	-1.7	8.3	1.4	UFM
0.3	4.5	-9.4	12.7	5.8	-0.4	-3.9	5.3	-3.9	7.5	32.0	SADC
1.9	3.6	-1.5	0.6	-0.8	0.6	-6.0	-0.6	25.5	2.8	16.2	CEMAC (UDEAC)
-0.2	3.5	-9.0	4.9	2.8	-1.5	-10.5	-8.7	6.4	7.2	31.2	UEMOA [1]
-1.1	2.5	-4.5	6.4	4.4	-0.4	-6.3	5.0	5.3	9.0	15.7	UMA
											ASIE
7.2	7.9	0.6	21.4	16.5	-2.1	6.6	23.3	-8.2	2.5	14.4	ANASE
10.5	10.1	7.6	12.1	15.0	5.1	19.5	30.8	-0.7	15.2	31.0	Accord de Bangkok
4.0	5.3	3.4	10.8	4.3	2.8	-8.9	24.4	-9.5	15.7	29.7	ECO
-3.9	5.0	-3.4	3.0	5.8	4.8	4.9	11.0	-6.1	6.6	13.9	CCG
2.8	0.6	-4.5	10.2	2.5	-4.0	7.8	-8.0	-3.2	11.1	15.0	MSG
3.8	8.8	0.9	8.1	8.9	5.4	8.9	9.9	-3.9	8.8	21.6	SAARC
											GROUPEMENTS INTERREGIONAUX
8.1	8.7	3.7	12.8	11.6	5.0	9.2	20.6	-6.3	3.6	13.6	CEAP
3.7	12.1	1.9	4.2	24.6	-1.8	-17.0	18.4	1.3	12.5	32.0	CEMN
5.7	3.6	3.8	8.1	1.2	-6.0	-26.5	16.4	15.1	9.5	26.9	CEI

Sources : Les taux d'accroissement ont été calculés d'après les chiffres du tableau 1.1 du *Manuel de statistiques de la CNUCED 2004 sur CD-ROM*.

Notes : Pour la définition des groupements, se reporter à la "Répartition des pays et territoires".

1 Anciennement CEAO.

1.3 Value of trade balance, and as percentage of imports
Millions of dollars and percentage

Region, economic grouping, country or area	Trade balance - Balance commerciale								
	1969-71	1974-76	1979-81	1984-86	1989-91	1994-96	1997-99	1999-01	2001-03
WORLD	**-12167**	**-25145**	**-32464**	**-65870**	**-116681**	**-71990**	**-108811**	**-168147**	**-165893**
DEVELOPED ECONOMIES	-11311	-55203	-112541	-88199	-112297	-15992	-126330	-311676	-344922
DEVELOPING ECONOMIES	-865	35417	80368	16228	9423	-65655	9557	105793	144625
SOUTH-EAST EUROPE AND CIS	9	-5360	-292	6102	-13807	9657	7962	37735	34405
DEVELOPED ECONOMIES:									
AMERICA	**-319**	**-8528**	**-30787**	**-127848**	**-110111**	**-166172**	**-263269**	**-400405**	**-484457**
Canada	1578	-473	3186	9210	2935	20378	13358	27560	28393
United States	-1896	-8055	-33973	-137058	-113046	-186550	-276627	-427965	-512851
DEVELOPED ECONOMIES:									
EUROPE	**-11538**	**-40524**	**-72644**	**-7471**	**-58867**	**69761**	**54149**	**13652**	**80353**
EU 25	**-9209**	**-36825**	**-69466**	**-6221**	**-59267**	**57810**	**45668**	**-5737**	**51749**
EU 15	*-8834*	*-33494*	*-66976*	*-5265*	*-59254*	*80722*	*82381*	*29787*	*88271*
Austria	-709	-2251	-5643	-3986	-8020	-9523	-5686	-4679	-2160
Belgium	..	..	..	..	..	13837	14457	12284	16014
Belgium-Luxembourg	27	-2051	-6059	-1925	-1102	..	..	..	..
Denmark	-924	-2392	-2594	-1127	3127	6239	4349	6200	7742
Finland	-270	-1500	-632	814	-99	9025	10140	10830	10868
France	-1245	-4904	-13235	-6014	-15353	2932	13711	-2639	-2505
Germany	4269	16231	9707	32204	49472	56439	69374	69831	117612
Germany (former Dem. Rep.)	-47	-1312	-1081	1349	483	_	_	_	_
Greece	-1264	-2972	-5229	-5307	-11062	-15377	-17891	-19054	-24158
Ireland	-517	-876	-2809	447	3267	10861	19386	27117	35592
Italy	-1126	-6934	-15163	-8348	-12382	31385	24081	8280	11303
Luxembourg	..	..	..	..	..	-2094	-2615	-2944	-3086
Netherlands	-2009	-1039	-1536	5111	5106	16806	14388	14821	25324
Portugal	-591	-2176	-4459	-2379	-8402	-9990	-13137	-14826	-12666
Spain	-2246	-8552	-10802	-6278	-31291	-20441	-25582	-37490	-43655
Sweden	-10	-668	-1283	3145	3697	14216	16565	14132	15142
United Kingdom	-2172	-12100	-6158	-12970	-36535	-23591	-39159	-52074	-63097
New EU members 10	*-375*	*-3331*	*-2491*	*-956*	*-13*	*-22912*	*-36713*	*-35524*	*-36522*
Cyprus	-128	-197	-610	-794	-1587	-2368	-2614	-2822	-3244
Czech Republic	_	_	_	_	_	-4726	-4417	-4335	-5516
Czechoslovakia (former)	97	-624	1331	-235	-246				
Estonia	_	_	_	_	_	-736	-1382	-1092	-1449
Hungary	-132	-666	-585	118	208	-2945	-2596	-3369	-3847
Latvia	_	_	_	_	_	-550	-1217	-1348	-1874
Lithuania	_	_	_	_	_	-824	-1899	-1749	-2217
Malta	-115	-210	-400	-357	-776	-988	-873	-863	-733
Poland	-98	-1634	-2225	313	2389	-7731	-18122	-16659	-14251
Slovakia	_	_	_	_	_	-1123	-2395	-2015	-2539
Slovenia	_	_	_	_	_	-921	-1198	-1272	-852
Other developed Europe	**-2329**	**-3699**	**-3178**	**-1250**	**400**	**11951**	**8481**	**19389**	**28604**
Faeroe Islands	-3	-26	-50	-85	81	59	26	-10	20
Iceland	-29	-144	-82	-71	-105	-65	-359	-476	-227
Norway	-1168	-2594	1341	2408	6268	10146	9016	21064	26346
Switzerland	-1129	-934	-4387	-3501	-5845	1810	-202	-1188	2466
DEVELOPED ECONOMIES:									
ASIA	**685**	**-5678**	**-7533**	**50709**	**59551**	**86952**	**91917**	**82826**	**68517**
Israel	-1210	-3641	-4281	-3759	-5188	-9965	-7333	-4591	-5759
Japan	1895	-2037	-3253	54468	64739	96918	99250	87417	74275
DEVELOPED ECONOMIES:									
OCEANIA	**-140**	**-473**	**-1576**	**-3589**	**-2871**	**-6533**	**-9128**	**-7749**	**-9335**
Australia	-207	416	-1573	-3210	-3278	-6398	-8266	-7079	-8567
New Zealand	66	-888	-3	-380	408	-135	-862	-669	-768

For sources and notes, see end of table.

1.3 Valeurs de la balance commerciale et sa part dans les importations
Millions de dollars et en pourcentage

Percentage of imports - Part dans les importations									Régions, groupements économiques, pays ou zones
1969-71	1974-76	1979-81	1984-86	1989-91	1994-96	1997-99	1999-01	2001-03	
-3.73	-2.72	-1.62	-3.15	-3.36	-1.43	-1.92	-2.68	-2.45	MONDE
-4.61	-8.14	-8.22	-6.01	-4.45	-0.46	-3.14	-7.13	-7.35	ECONOMIES DEVELOPPEES
-1.38	18.02	18.09	3.36	1.28	-4.56	0.68	5.95	7.25	ECONOMIES EN DEVELOPPEMENT
0.21	-9.88	-0.34	5.10	-9.47	8.42	7.80	31.66	21.95	EUROPE DU SUD-EST ET CEI
									ECONOMIES DEVELOPPEES :
-0.39	-5.31	-9.93	-28.84	-17.55	-18.01	-22.15	-28.58	-33.04	**AMERIQUE**
10.47	-1.33	5.03	11.50	2.39	12.09	6.35	11.88	12.19	Canada
-4.10	-6.45	-13.68	-37.95	-22.37	-24.57	-28.30	-36.57	-41.62	Etats-Unis
									ECONOMIES DEVELOPPEES :
-7.10	-9.16	-8.11	-0.97	-3.60	3.28	2.34	0.56	2.89	**EUROPE**
-6.07	-8.81	-8.21	-0.90	-3.83	2.87	2.08	-0.22	1.94	**UE 25**
-6.24	*-8.54*	*-8.29*	*-0.83*	*-3.93*	*4.23*	*3.98*	*1.37*	*3.62*	*UE 15*
-19.50	-22.25	-25.58	-17.93	-17.26	-15.31	-8.45	-6.72	-2.97	Autriche
					9.25	8.92	7.12	7.75	Belgique
0.32	-6.33	-9.26	-3.48	-0.82	..	..	..	..	Belgique-Luxembourg
-21.60	-21.62	-14.00	-5.70	9.66	14.90	9.70	13.97	15.41	Danemark
-10.06	-20.50	-4.26	5.96	-0.14	33.29	32.45	33.26	30.75	Finlande
-6.80	-8.47	-10.63	-5.40	-6.99	1.03	4.85	-0.82	-0.75	France
14.52	21.39	5.86	18.59	16.10	12.86	14.97	14.42	22.17	Allemagne
-0.95	-11.29	-5.99	5.75	4.44	–	–	–	–	Allemagne (anc. Rép. Dém. d')
-66.96	-56.20	-54.18	-51.49	-57.37	-59.21	-62.37	-65.02	-68.49	Grèce
-32.16	-22.30	-26.69	3.99	16.76	34.12	43.93	54.17	68.36	Irlande
-7.73	-16.72	-15.99	-9.47	-7.23	15.95	11.18	3.65	4.30	Italie
..	..	..	..	..	-22.56	-25.50	-26.83	-25.57	Luxembourg
-12.97	-2.54	-1.78	7.07	4.23	10.11	7.83	7.66	12.30	Pays-Bas
-38.08	-51.98	-51.53	-28.45	-35.36	-31.47	-34.63	-37.90	-32.15	Portugal
-48.54	-52.27	-34.79	-19.91	-37.43	-18.94	-18.93	-24.92	-24.89	Espagne
-0.36	-3.64	-4.05	10.62	7.26	22.90	24.50	20.66	21.22	Suède
-10.05	-22.25	-5.94	-11.20	-17.40	-9.13	-12.47	-16.05	-18.15	Royaume-Uni
-3.71	*-12.85*	*-6.40*	*-2.75*	*0.48*	*-21.94*	*-26.18*	*-22.76*	*-18.58*	*Nouveaux membres de l'UE 10*
-54.44	-51.82	-54.23	-61.45	-63.79	-66.55	-71.31	-74.30	-77.94	Chypre
					-18.10	-15.01	-12.72	-11.98	République tchèque
2.54	-7.07	10.79	-1.84	-1.15	–	–	–	–	Tchécoslovaquie (anc.)
					-28.21	-31.47	-25.96	-27.40	Estonie
-5.92	-12.92	-6.53	1.71	3.51	-19.02	-10.39	-10.82	-9.60	Hongrie
					-28.92	-41.11	-41.94	-43.79	Lettonie
					-22.02	-35.14	-31.97	-27.79	Lituanie
-73.76	-54.89	-46.80	-45.45	-42.04	-36.23	-32.57	-28.88	-24.73	Malte
-2.63	-14.30	-14.76	2.85	27.63	-25.23	-40.32	-34.62	-25.02	Pologne
					-10.51	-19.75	-14.59	-14.34	Slovaquie
					-10.24	-12.13	-12.58	-7.30	Slovénie
									Autres économies développées d'Europe
-22.68	-15.21	-6.39	-1.57	0.27	10.84	7.33	16.19	22.75	
-7.47	-22.93	-23.64	-30.74	28.95	20.74	6.96	-2.04	3.71	Iles Féroé
-16.05	-29.09	-8.31	-7.98	-6.11	-2.11	-14.86	-19.06	-8.93	Islande
-32.01	-26.46	8.26	17.88	24.34	31.27	25.60	62.43	73.87	Norvège
-17.59	-6.54	-13.30	-10.59	-9.13	2.44	-0.25	-1.41	2.76	Suisse
									ECONOMIES DEVELOPPEES :
3.06	-8.58	-5.70	36.13	24.49	25.85	27.29	22.00	17.41	**ASIE**
-59.30	-63.83	-45.00	-37.08	-30.78	-34.51	-23.59	-13.43	-16.13	Israël
10.16	-3.43	-2.83	41.87	28.54	31.29	32.44	25.53	20.80	Japon
									ECONOMIES DEVELOPPEES :
-2.31	-2.95	-4.75	-11.20	-5.34	-8.91	-11.29	-9.21	-9.27	**OCEANIE**
-4.32	3.83	-5.83	-12.35	-7.40	-10.74	-12.32	-10.13	-10.33	Australie
6.63	-26.28	0.16	-6.20	4.90	-0.81	-6.17	-4.65	-4.12	Nouvelle-Zélande

Pour les sources et les notes, se reporter à la fin du tableau.

Region, economic grouping, country or area	Trade balance - Balance commerciale								
	1969-71	1974-76	1979-81	1984-86	1989-91	1994-96	1997-99	1999-01	2001-03
DEVELOPING ECONOMIES: AMERICA	-1916	-8139	-11243	19677	6962	-30260	-51824	-35522	-12745
South America	*993*	*-1419*	*-193*	*19804*	*25055*	*-6754*	*-17832*	*6812*	*32456*
Argentina	-4	56	-567	3411	5837	-1637	-3704	1745	12827
Bolivia	17	22	46	44	110	-333	-756	-576	-311
Brazil	-287	-4912	-3392	9965	10689	-2976	-8420	-2474	11016
Chile	40	193	-1783	521	737	-1186	-1769	772	1018
Colombia	-146	31	-1017	-128	1405	-3453	-2228	626	-864
Ecuador	-91	244	312	835	600	439	123	652	-857
French Guiana	-41	-69	-226	-231	-634	-580	–	–	–
Guyana	9	-16	-38	-26	-48	-68	-80	-120	-188
Paraguay	-22	-33	-275	-265	-290	-1665	-1484	-1055	-987
Peru	269	-655	948	567	-122	-3216	-3226	-2025	-1692
Suriname	27	12	-17	16	-17	-50	-76	-5	4
Uruguay	-6	-106	-489	192	238	-853	-1054	-1097	-365
Venezuela	1228	3814	6305	4904	6551	8630	4840	10368	12854
Other America	*-2909*	*-6720*	*-11050*	*-127*	*-18092*	*-23506*	*-33992*	*-42334*	*-45201*
Antigua and Barbuda	-25	-38	-53	-151	-219	-306	-353	-357	-339
Aruba	..	..	..	-168	-442	-550	-710	-703	-690
Bahamas	-245	-262	-1120	-547	-796	-1047	-1456	-1271	-1237
Barbados	-74	-126	-317	-278	-490	-506	-772	-852	-861
Belize	-15	-24	-42	-12	-101	-97	-139	-279	-350
Bermuda	-41	-136	-286	-407	-494	-504	-588	-635	-708
Costa Rica	-88	-219	-401	-79	-374	-698	-347	-593	-1675
Cuba	-446	-278	-776	-1813	-2397	-1151	-2576	-3021	-2994
Dominica	-9	-9	-27	-24	-60	-67	-75	-88	-83
Dominican Republic	-77	-109	-501	-681	-1330	-2912	-4579	-5576	-5186
El Salvador	-4	-58	-1	-241	-721	-1636	-1813	-2359	-2817
Greenland	-39	-32	-106	-111	-14	-80	-120	-80	-11
Grenada	-15	-11	-30	-46	-83	-110	-168	-196	-212
Guadeloupe	-81	-207	-518	-588	-1385	-1529	–	–	–
Guatemala	-1	-105	-268	-61	-560	-1171	-1854	-2407	-3662
Haiti	-10	-68	-182	-240	-184	-429	-535	-716	-810
Honduras	-21	-85	-153	-99	-126	-387	-1072	-1535	-1740
Jamaica	-193	-326	-294	-457	-781	-1328	-1710	-1940	-2430
Martinique	-109	-251	-625	-574	-1301	-1591	–	–	–
Mexico	-871	-3129	-4124	8094	-4565	-5395	-10054	-15410	-15557
Montserrat	-16	-38	-11	-14	-38	-27	-20	-19	-20
Netherlands Antilles	-155	-658	-462	-281	-349	-650	-505	-607	-540
Nicaragua	-21	-104	-240	-578	-363	-586	-1036	-1221	-1307
Panama	-237	-609	-1061	-1028	-1068	-1921	-2529	-2422	-2137
Saint Kitts and Nevis	-7	-5	-20	-33	-80	-116	-118	-119	-125
Saint Lucia	-20	-28	-71	-72	-165	-213	-281	-307	-307
Saint Pierre and Miquelon	-9	-19	-7	-27	-55	-65	-64	-65	-57
Saint Vincent and the Grenadines	-12	-17	-36	-21	-60	-86	-146	-137	-148
Trinidad and Tobago	-70	232	680	298	509	611	-375	580	802
DEVELOPING ECONOMIES: AFRICA	1234	5273	11530	756	1282	-8016	-14963	3726	5305
North Africa	*1239*	*1417*	*6528*	*-4235*	*-5254*	*-9262*	*-11901*	*-1678*	*373*
Algeria	-231	11	2518	1370	2680	1093	3002	8631	9688
Egypt	-16	-1884	-3120	-7861	-9394	-8184	-11596	-10137	-8626
Libyan Arab Jamahiriya	1761	5044	11029	5559	5625	3673	2937	6584	6811
Morocco	-157	-859	-1849	-1598	-2467	-2894	-2729	-3675	-4487
Sudan	0	-389	-835	-514	-53	-772	-980	-342	-201
Tunisia	-117	-505	-1215	-1191	-1644	-2179	-2534	-2739	-2811
Other Africa	*-5*	*3857*	*5002*	*4991*	*6536*	*1246*	*-3062*	*5404*	*4932*
Angola	27	493	237	646	2028	2291	1974	3428	3503
Benin	-31	-154	-351	-195	41	-162	-307	-259	-216
Botswana	-33	-59	-235	209	31	417	191	437	685
Burkina Faso	-35	-102	-252	-253	-369	-278	-397	-416	-484
Burundi	-6	-13	-79	-69	-143	-106	-64	-87	-106
Cameroon	-13	-71	-228	-526	561	405	293	167	495
Cape Verde	-14	-33	-61	-92	-126	-223	-225	-226	-264
Central African Republic	-2	-4	9	-41	-6	5	14	31	10
Chad	-30	-62	-8	-89	-78	-82	-88	-232	-609
Comoros	-4	-11	-15	-24	-30	-48	-56	-75	-84
Congo	-36	53	304	411	508	208	723	1391	1663
Côte d'Ivoire	85	211	106	1243	751	1081	1609	1637	2291

For sources and notes, see end of table.

Percentage of imports - Part dans les importations									Régions, groupements économiques, pays ou zones
1969-71	1974-76	1979-81	1984-86	1989-91	1994-96	1997-99	1999-01	2001-03	
-9.82	**-14.28**	**-9.35**	**22.34**	**5.86**	**-12.38**	**-15.39**	**-9.80**	**-3.42**	**ECONOMIES EN DEVELOPPEMENT : AMERIQUE**
10.76	*-4.23*	*-0.22*	*47.85*	*43.61*	*-4.79*	*-10.62*	*4.50*	*24.99*	*Amérique du Sud*
0.05	3.86	-3.47	80.67	126.11	-7.48	-12.48	8.94	109.70	Argentine
10.22	8.25	8.68	11.06	18.94	-22.58	-40.47	-32.56	-17.95	Bolivie
-7.79	-35.43	-15.21	66.70	50.08	-2.91	-13.79	-4.50	21.91	Brésil
3.97	9.66	-28.14	15.99	9.59	-6.39	-8.19	4.54	5.53	Chili
-17.09	1.74	-19.91	-1.72	27.56	-26.40	-14.02	5.80	-6.51	Colombie
-30.78	31.85	16.93	48.83	30.43	11.24	9.72	22.38	-13.99	Equateur
-91.03	-96.44	-89.79	-86.06	-89.68	-81.21	_	_	_	Guyane française
6.83	-3.74	-9.57	-11.42	-16.32	-12.38	-12.61	-19.23	-22.83	Guyana
-26.57	-15.99	-47.22	-47.31	-15.40	-64.06	-60.30	-54.96	-45.19	Paraguay
42.17	-28.14	47.09	30.53	-0.22	-37.55	-33.63	-23.32	-17.85	Pérou
22.54	5.70	-2.15	5.12	-2.37	-8.65	-22.07	2.66	0.56	Suriname
-2.61	-19.81	-32.54	24.57	19.01	-28.57	-29.17	-33.28	-12.53	Uruguay
65.80	78.96	52.26	61.90	81.59	84.81	33.43	63.93	114.50	Venezuela
-34.06	*-27.01*	*-20.00*	*-0.42*	*-24.13*	*-19.93*	*-19.12*	*-19.25*	*-19.58*	*Autres économies: Amérique*
-71.14	-67.88	-58.46	-89.06	-88.95	-87.09	-90.42	-89.99	-91.24	Antigua-et-Barbuda
..	..	..	-87.63	-94.51	-97.70	-96.26	-85.95	-82.36	Aruba
-67.75	-11.86	-13.64	-15.47	-59.55	-85.62	-82.33	-72.31	-74.01	Bahamas
-65.12	-57.29	-62.30	-45.01	-70.68	-68.60	-74.29	-76.25	-79.25	Barbade
-44.22	-31.92	-28.95	-9.79	-43.95	-37.82	-43.24	-58.47	-66.05	Belize
-39.64	-77.68	-89.59	-90.72	-90.31	-90.68	-91.59	-91.45	-91.56	Bermudes
-28.38	-30.26	-28.22	-7.15	-19.90	-17.39	-6.46	-9.05	-23.55	Costa Rica
-34.33	-6.67	-12.26	-21.77	-43.99	-41.55	-61.42	-64.41	-65.17	Cuba
-56.05	-44.39	-66.22	-42.16	-53.89	-57.71	-56.75	-63.48	-66.50	Dominique
-25.15	-12.99	-32.82	-46.81	-63.44	-78.12	-83.27	-86.63	-85.34	République dominicaine
-1.57	-10.01	-0.38	-25.08	-56.43	-63.05	-58.76	-65.34	-69.43	El Salvador
-71.36	-26.07	-35.43	-36.14	-3.41	-18.72	-30.12	-21.22	-3.51	Groenland
-68.02	-48.38	-60.46	-66.56	-75.12	-83.08	-87.13	-88.26	-90.32	Grenade
-68.11	-73.04	-83.23	-86.60	-91.77	-90.70	_	_	_	Guadeloupe
-0.12	-14.19	-16.58	-4.29	-32.51	-38.43	-42.97	-48.34	-60.31	Guatemala
-17.47	-43.05	-46.24	-56.92	-53.54	-78.96	-64.83	-69.89	-72.98	Haïti
-9.99	-20.95	-16.26	-11.12	-13.17	-24.82	-42.91	-54.38	-56.66	Honduras
-38.39	-32.95	-23.09	-42.33	-41.81	-49.40	-56.60	-60.57	-66.10	Jamaïque
-76.42	-72.31	-81.57	-78.41	-85.57	-88.73	_	_	_	Martinique
-37.27	-50.12	-20.79	46.13	-9.43	-6.46	-7.47	-9.07	-8.79	Mexique
-95.70	-93.86	-88.98	-82.29	-96.01	-90.11	-82.28	-89.22	-92.45	Montserrat
-18.65	-19.13	-8.80	-16.67	-17.12	-29.56	-24.56	-23.68	-21.74	Antilles néerlandaises
-10.49	-19.25	-13.69	-64.81	-53.79	-58.37	-64.16	-67.23	-67.64	Nicaragua
-67.41	-71.40	-76.07	-76.03	-74.84	-74.94	-76.49	-73.48	-70.96	Panama
-50.72	-22.36	-48.03	-60.50	-74.02	-84.53	-78.58	-77.21	-74.39	Saint-Kitts-et-Nevis
-69.36	-61.35	-60.63	-54.83	-58.69	-69.29	-82.44	-86.53	-87.85	Sainte-Lucie
-80.75	-74.45	-84.75	-83.48	-65.76	-88.64	-92.72	-92.32	-90.41	Saint-Pierre-et-Miquelon
-76.42	-67.37	-66.80	-25.71	-44.22	-64.88	-75.14	-74.82	-78.93	Saint-Vincent-et-les Grenadines
-11.41	13.68	24.23	18.43	41.70	41.66	-12.46	17.14	19.89	Trinité-et-Tobago
9.21	**14.10**	**15.73**	**1.01**	**1.22**	**-6.78**	**-11.36**	**2.81**	**3.69**	**ECONOMIES EN DEVELOPPEMENT : AFRIQUE**
32.71	*11.43*	*22.34*	*-12.67*	*-11.68*	*-20.73*	*-23.85*	*-3.42*	*0.53*	*Afrique du Nord*
-19.13	1.71	24.13	13.24	31.65	12.48	33.76	92.30	89.87	Algérie
-0.17	-53.30	-50.85	-70.62	-62.81	-69.83	-76.25	-70.65	-64.61	Egypte
276.18	163.14	170.59	121.42	106.87	65.49	61.79	165.00	124.61	Jamahiriya arabe libyenne
-23.56	-34.01	-45.05	-41.43	-38.43	-31.09	-27.48	-33.57	-35.69	Maroc
-0.18	-46.51	-58.36	-53.99	188.84	-57.79	-58.71	-18.67	-6.89	Soudan
-38.33	-35.57	-35.98	-40.10	-32.65	-29.44	-30.68	-30.94	-28.23	Tunisie
0.86	*15.84*	*12.59*	*11.64*	*11.39*	*1.65*	*-3.75*	*6.65*	*5.69*	*Autres économies: Afrique*
7.12	105.56	16.82	50.01	142.46	136.93	76.34	110.66	89.60	Angola
-48.04	-82.75	-86.83	-56.66	16.86	-23.57	-42.36	-39.19	-32.45	Bénin
-54.49	-29.05	-31.81	32.05	3.41	23.99	8.94	21.53	34.41	Botswana
-65.62	-69.71	-75.78	-75.73	-75.87	-57.56	-59.73	-64.17	-64.71	Burkina Faso
-24.53	-23.89	-48.80	-36.16	-63.42	-56.57	-47.24	-64.18	-74.99	Burundi
-4.62	-10.88	-15.82	-37.24	44.25	34.70	20.92	10.75	25.12	Cameroun
-89.32	-94.20	-94.95	-95.18	-95.63	-96.41	-94.94	-95.50	-95.84	Cap-Vert
-6.09	-5.08	13.28	-27.14	1.00	3.53	10.24	27.33	9.62	République centrafricaine
-49.71	-55.50	-7.56	-47.97	-30.23	-26.04	-26.22	-45.75	-72.41	Tchad
-42.85	-44.68	-50.15	-61.29	-59.86	-83.23	-91.85	-90.26	-84.60	Comores
-48.16	37.84	70.46	67.80	90.65	37.94	90.43	256.24	270.62	Congo
23.49	18.62	4.01	71.28	35.72	42.02	55.43	64.54	84.68	Côte d'Ivoire

Pour les sources et les notes, se reporter à la fin du tableau.

Region, economic grouping, country or area	Trade balance - Balance commerciale								
	1969-71	1974-76	1979-81	1984-86	1989-91	1994-96	1997-99	1999-01	2001-03
Dem. Rep. of the Congo	545	772	774	640	475	480	-56	-71	113
Djibouti	-34	-109	-198	-186	-186	-171	-141	-123	-86
Equatorial Guinea	2	10	-6	-11	-14	-19	190	611	1116
Eritrea	..	..	..	..	..	-358	-407	-342	-544
Ethiopia	-49	-53	-266	-606	-526	-789	-851	-1069	-1531
Gabon	72	514	1391	930	1175	1884	1428	1604	1436
Gambia	-4	-19	-104	-57	-145	-195	-220	-159	-146
Ghana	29	-29	77	-171	-335	-435	-1073	-1328	-1068
Guinea	-20	-50	104	145	-33	-23	100	88	62
Guinea-Bissau	-24	-33	-42	-43	-62	-75	-25	5	-1
Kenya	-158	-314	-742	-429	-1080	-832	-1166	-1235	-1230
Lesotho	-29	-151	-354	-351	-627	-781	-702	-505	-454
Liberia	70	78	59	130	881	225	-92	-256	-357
Madagascar	-54	-4	-275	-36	-119	-112	-164	-120	-151
Malawi	-35	-74	-129	-6	-211	-121	-183	-162	-187
Mali	-12	-103	-224	-185	-162	-308	-137	-29	-23
Mauritania	33	25	-69	118	161	39	9	25	-24
Mauritius	-9	-42	-201	-65	-376	-503	-561	-518	-389
Mozambique	-155	-177	-452	-419	-731	-647	-651	-677	-505
Namibia	..	..	..	..	-6	-188	-402	-324	-403
Niger	-22	-15	-32	-64	-91	-104	-115	-105	-143
Nigeria	225	3526	4585	2676	4979	5546	3872	7732	8199
Reunion	-119	-322	-676	-801	-1833	-2303	–	–	–
Rwanda	-8	-35	-126	-153	-209	-158	-208	-171	-156
Sao Tome and Principe	0	1	-1	-4	-18	-22	-20	-29	-29
Senegal	-69	-126	-515	-316	-486	-366	-485	-621	-909
Seychelles	-9	-26	-72	-74	-128	-191	-259	-232	-201
Sierra Leone	-12	-67	-166	-11	-25	-97	-79	-121	-193
Somalia	-20	-69	-263	-214	36	-36	-123	-155	-165
South Africa	-404	631	4322	3794	4425	-569	-1613	436	-1045
Swaziland	12	13	-221	-142	-105	-133	-115	-114	-10
Togo	-14	-20	-245	-95	-244	-111	-162	-126	-180
Uganda	-173	-166	63	81	-94	-555	-833	-1012	-832
United Republic of Tanzania	-58	-318	-654	-514	-954	-861	-820	-937	-906
Zambia	610	299	301	15	264	292	90	-136	-295
Zimbabwe	-19	62	-67	192	-230	-435	-754	-219	-710
DEVELOPING ECONOMIES: **ASIA**	**159**	**38855**	**81316**	**-2789**	**3241**	**-26303**	**77827**	**138946**	**154179**
West Asia	*4118*	*46075*	*95204*	*3753*	*16821*	*21944*	*13695*	*59737*	*74556*
Bahrain	-19	-29	120	-230	-286	232	242	1166	1106
Iran, Islamic Republic of	1088	-1123	-5770	-1535	-3999	6327	3776	9580	8235
Iraq	683	8698	19314	115	1095	-208	2533	6752	3566
Jordan	-160	-571	-1940	-1892	-1311	-2121	-2059	-2378	-2493
Kuwait	1013	7575	11948	3837	1524	5358	3820	8387	7759
Lebanon	-458	-534	-2375	-1914	-2331	-6308	-6253	-5823	-5824
Oman	124	372	634	179	2106	2073	1663	4536	5167
Qatar	184	1510	3584	2236	1434	729	2168	6672	7618
Saudi Arabia	2013	29249	67516	2934	15431	24737	21186	35646	45198
Syrian Arab Republic	-188	-837	-2257	-1999	1127	-1649	-495	316	24
Turkey	-373	-2917	-4013	-3552	-6988	-13213	-18443	-16959	-14742
United Arab Emirates	306	5161	10069	6905	10207	6038	5473	10812	18092
Yemen	-95	-480	-1626	-1332	-1189	-51	84	1031	849
Other Asia	*-3959*	*-7220*	*-13888*	*-6542*	*-13579*	*-48247*	*64132*	*79210*	*79623*
Afghanistan	-38	-38	-105	-745	-572	-249	-214	-349	-773
Bangladesh	-180	-759	-1666	-1701	-2005	-2441	-2042	-2154	-2035
Bhutan	..	..	-41	-60	-17	-21	-37	-84	-68
Brunei Darussalam	-5	882	3240	2010	1240	218	641	1344	1424
Cambodia	-39	-79	-159	-127	-67	-338	-385	-508	-560
China	398	-212	-1286	-9378	3421	11434	37710	25295	25934
China, Hong Kong SAR	-396	-634	-2551	104	-336	-15748	-12235	-9254	-8956
China, Macao SAR	-24	-8	3	136	45	-103	137	119	-145
China, Taiwan Province of	-39	-525	886	11511	13007	9892	7756	11207	16621
India	-287	-1117	-5141	-6211	-4336	-3578	-9093	-9167	-9658
Indonesia	104	2930	10452	6807	4304	6581	19307	26236	26373
Korea, Dem. People's Republic of	..	..	..	..	-937	-535	-530	-871	-1011
Korea, Republic of	-1225	-1926	-4975	297	-4524	-12340	18180	15029	11558
Lao People's Dem. Rep.	-34	-12	-67	-129	-103	-303	-248	-205	-159
Malaysia	319	623	1872	2793	154	-1541	11309	16546	14985
Maldives	1	-4	-20	-29	-86	-212	-299	-323	-326
Mongolia	..	..	-190	-610	-173	43	-110	-162	-221
Myanmar	-42	6	91	22	-51	-398	-1329	-813	95

For sources and notes, see end of table.

Percentage of imports - Part dans les importations									Régions, groupements économiques, pays ou zones
1969-71	1974-76	1979-81	1984-86	1989-91	1994-96	1997-99	1999-01	2001-03	
330.76	267.90	242.55	52.09	28.59	54.57	-4.97	-2.82	16.01	Rép. dém. du Congo
-79.31	-86.27	-94.73	-91.98	-89.22	-92.83	-92.30	-82.18	-56.56	Djibouti
7.19	96.24	-18.68	-27.72	-22.67	33.08	51.73	111.37	193.59	Guinée équatoriale
..	..	..	..	..	-81.73	-92.78	-94.85	-93.11	Erythrée
-28.32	-16.22	-38.32	-60.09	-62.06	-65.75	-59.97	-68.68	-74.30	Ethiopie
85.83	119.22	210.45	117.65	139.04	217.08	144.05	180.21	146.66	Gabon
-19.63	-28.89	-71.66	-58.34	-78.48	-89.01	-94.15	-92.72	-94.22	Gambie
6.62	-3.45	8.14	-19.80	-29.15	-20.94	-36.75	-43.81	-36.57	Ghana
-26.08	-23.95	37.31	43.55	-4.97	-2.22	17.98	14.95	10.22	Guinée
-86.77	-85.14	-76.58	-75.92	-77.43	-60.55	-34.22	9.44	-1.87	Guinée-Bissau
-33.34	-31.87	-38.69	-28.61	-50.86	-30.39	-37.62	-40.53	-36.38	Kenya
-83.42	-90.85	-87.26	-93.32	-90.45	-82.71	-78.78	-68.75	-55.13	Lesotho
51.60	24.30	12.17	45.10	396.61	53.86	-16.30	-40.41	-60.40	Libéria
-28.36	-0.58	-41.94	-10.48	-22.78	-18.63	-23.10	-13.86	-18.10	Madagascar
-36.73	-33.34	-31.87	-1.71	-36.05	-22.64	-26.80	-27.20	-28.80	Malawi
-24.50	-59.86	-57.15	-54.45	-33.34	-43.31	-18.64	-4.67	-0.08	Mali
66.20	19.48	-25.63	53.05	69.89	9.36	4.10	8.58	-6.57	Mauritanie
-10.93	-11.86	-34.61	-12.97	-25.06	-24.56	-25.74	-24.32	-17.84	Maurice
-49.88	-45.97	-61.70	-83.22	-84.88	-77.38	-72.60	-59.78	-39.65	Mozambique
..	..	..	..	-0.52	-11.75	-24.08	-20.65	-25.60	Namibie
-41.48	-16.34	-6.12	-18.04	-24.60	-27.22	-27.87	-27.18	-31.68	Niger
21.64	96.79	37.57	38.18	88.75	81.13	42.79	83.61	84.61	Nigéria
-71.44	-81.16	-83.24	-86.52	-91.60	-92.44	–	–	–	Réunion
-28.99	-39.97	-49.98	-49.91	-67.65	-76.99	-75.24	-72.39	-70.78	Rwanda
-4.23	10.64	-8.35	-26.99	-77.53	-80.44	-77.75	-91.91	-86.32	Sao Tomé-et-Principe
-33.45	-22.00	-50.22	-34.09	-40.35	-27.82	-33.35	-38.60	-44.29	Sénégal
-77.32	-77.32	-78.13	-75.10	-73.44	-71.71	-67.13	-54.86	-45.24	Seychelles
-10.58	-35.70	-46.16	-6.53	-14.33	-56.45	-88.89	-89.19	-78.41	Sierra Leone
-37.54	-46.13	-64.11	-74.26	52.07	61.54	-38.98	-41.41	-34.78	Somalie
-9.30	8.10	41.14	30.37	23.83	-1.22	-5.26	1.53	-2.02	Afrique du Sud
20.33	10.14	-40.74	-37.54	-16.01	-13.19	-10.76	-10.67	-0.94	Swaziland
-21.91	-4.24	-49.21	-32.60	-48.31	-7.35	-27.61	-25.34	-28.06	Togo
-86.63	-83.90	36.42	25.29	-26.87	-53.45	-61.27	-67.59	-62.20	Ouganda
-16.02	-43.23	-55.35	-62.48	-72.25	-56.09	-56.08	-58.75	-49.03	République-Unie de Tanzanie
125.40	41.56	36.34	2.00	29.36	42.92	11.62	-9.45	-23.09	Zambie
-4.15	8.83	-2.11	20.02	-11.77	-16.94	-26.60	-11.85	-26.71	Zimbabwe
									ECONOMIES EN DEVELOPPEMENT :
0.08	**39.04**	**32.15**	**-0.91**	**0.69**	**-2.37**	**7.22**	**11.07**	**10.61**	**ASIE**
59.24	*140.50*	*107.77*	*3.72*	*16.15*	*16.60*	*8.62*	*34.24*	*37.83*	*Asie occidentale*
-5.86	-1.02	3.15	-7.74	-7.67	5.75	6.19	27.07	23.32	Bahreïn
62.06	0.31	-43.25	-12.16	-16.59	46.11	28.96	66.60	36.72	Iran, Rép. islamique d'
125.13	215.74	301.60	0.98	10.25	-28.84	41.84	71.61	32.95	Iraq
-81.60	-75.61	-77.47	-71.33	-53.99	-55.91	-52.96	-54.02	-47.25	Jordanie
157.76	361.93	197.15	60.46	27.43	70.02	47.68	112.40	85.37	Koweït
-69.83	-27.06	-72.02	-77.81	-81.46	-91.11	-90.37	-88.57	-83.53	Liban
664.64	67.44	34.72	4.31	79.41	48.32	34.49	86.80	84.65	Oman
261.26	383.63	245.72	195.45	90.59	32.17	79.93	209.42	177.08	Qatar
266.06	695.98	220.37	11.14	61.03	93.21	73.98	118.60	136.85	Arabie saoudite
-47.82	-45.35	-52.95	-55.05	47.57	-31.42	-12.72	7.44	1.62	République arabe syrienne
-37.70	-63.88	-55.32	-32.13	-34.56	-36.12	-40.60	-35.99	-27.92	Turquie
103.35	210.80	117.52	103.98	87.93	28.12	20.06	32.87	53.85	Emirats arabes unis
-41.95	-69.42	-71.83	-70.72	-63.83	-0.34	4.98	45.41	32.62	Yémen
-18.82	*-11.33*	*-8.00*	*-2.97*	*-2.82*	*-5.06*	*7.11*	*7.45*	*6.37*	*Autres économies: Asie*
-29.75	-10.53	-10.18	-55.89	-71.88	-59.40	-52.41	-68.35	-84.12	Afghanistan
-27.81	-66.96	-69.00	-64.39	-56.19	-41.41	-28.39	-26.55	-24.17	Bangladesh
..	..	-68.68	-71.90	-20.30	-19.02	-23.24	-43.36	-38.61	Bhoutan
2.17	375.65	617.48	323.37	121.21	11.18	42.40	97.66	91.36	Brunéi Darussalam
-50.27	-82.99	-93.85	-86.11	-42.68	-34.01	-30.39	-27.25	-23.77	Cambodge
19.56	-2.50	-7.38	-22.60	5.99	8.70	25.68	12.54	8.53	Chine
-13.36	-8.96	-11.86	0.33	-0.23	-8.42	-6.23	-4.61	-4.24	Chine, Hong Kong RAS
-35.70	-6.19	2.14	16.41	3.71	-4.87	6.85	5.61	-5.62	Chine, Macao RAS
-4.06	-8.28	5.06	51.65	23.05	10.15	7.03	9.77	14.40	Chine, Taiwan Province de
-12.54	-19.11	-36.34	-39.93	-19.95	-10.43	-20.59	-18.60	-15.85	Inde
10.64	64.28	102.76	58.99	21.89	17.69	69.87	90.05	87.07	Indonésie
..	..	..	..	-32.81	-37.10	-42.04	-54.68	-57.12	Corée, Rép. populaire dém. de
-59.69	-26.32	-22.01	0.88	-5.76	-9.12	18.67	11.32	7.27	Corée, République de
-36.58	-33.62	-73.84	-71.75	-56.00	-49.03	-41.03	-38.77	-32.02	Rép. dém. populaire lao
24.74	16.40	21.05	23.00	1.94	-2.08	18.25	22.80	19.06	Malaisie
25.87	-54.46	-74.43	-56.33	-62.72	-80.10	-81.05	-81.76	-77.89	Maldives
..	..	-29.93	-43.01	-19.05	15.29	-21.70	-27.70	-31.62	Mongolie
-25.58	3.88	25.87	9.18	-1.56	-30.38	-56.20	-33.27	5.26	Myanmar

Pour les sources et les notes, se reporter à la fin du tableau.

Region, economic grouping, country or area	Trade balance - Balance commerciale								
	1969-71	1974-76	1979-81	1984-86	1989-91	1994-96	1997-99	1999-01	2001-03
Nepal	-33	-68	-212	-300	-457	-931	-960	-775	-893
Pakistan	-290	-913	-2494	-2812	-2044	-2601	-1825	-1524	-1127
Philippines	-278	-1198	-2473	-819	-4117	-11298	-3938	1502	-1978
Singapore	-825	-2604	-4882	-3695	-6723	-6136	448	4210	10640
Sri Lanka	-51	-130	-761	-596	-839	-1471	-1229	-1424	-1370
Thailand	-529	-787	-2498	-1803	-8270	-13385	4701	6095	3959
Viet Nam	-465	-646	-990	-1207	-406	-2789	-1583	-763	-2685
DEVELOPING ECONOMIES:									
OCEANIA	**-342**	**-572**	**-1235**	**-1417**	**-2063**	**-1076**	**-1482**	**-1356**	**-2115**
American Samoa	77	16	27	-75	-55	-5	159	142	136
Cook Islands	-3	-9	-20	-20	-46	-55	-38	-38	-35
Fiji	-25	-80	-160	-117	-198	-258	-283	-264	-324
French Polynesia	-111	-264	-494	-571	-768	-743	-718	-763	-1084
Guam	-83	-240	-323	-294	-344	-401	-444	-492	-567
Kiribati	4	22	-4	-10	-22	-27	-31	-35	-37
Nauru	24	31	60	42	27	2	14	5	-12
New Caledonia	-22	2	-34	-156	-305	-414	-492	-449	-564
Papua New Guinea	-185	11	-169	-108	-135	1034	559	792	644
Samoa	-7	-22	-49	-34	-74	-85	-86	-100	-119
Solomon Islands	-4	-8	-13	-2	-29	9	10	-14	-7
Tonga	-3	-11	-29	-34	-47	-61	-62	-62	-56
Tuvalu	..	..	-4	-3	-3	-7	-8	-6	-10
Vanuatu	-3	-22	-28	-35	-64	-66	-61	-73	-79
SOUTH-EAST EUROPE AND CIS	**9**	**-5360**	**-292**	**6102**	**-13807**	**9657**	**7962**	**37735**	**34405**
South-East Europe	*-1231*	*-4666*	*-7278*	*-1728*	*-7456*	*-8774*	*-13154*	*-13454*	*-20129*
Albania	..	..	..	..	-202	-536	-669	-910	-1204
Bosnia and Herzegovina	–	–	–	–	–	-1182	-2354	-2225	-2893
Bulgaria	94	-865	322	-416	580	-291	-715	-1778	-2581
Croatia	–	–	–	–	–	-2374	-4090	-3811	-6090
Macedonia, TFYR	–	–	–	–	–	-464	-583	-631	-743
Romania	-228	-518	-1848	237	-1410	-2225	-2752	-2915	-4847
Serbia and Montenegro	–	–	–	–	–	-1700	-1990	-1184	-1772
Yugoslavia, SFR (former)	-1097	-3284	-5752	-1549	-2241	–	–	–	–
CIS	–	–	–	–	–	*18430*	*21117*	*51189*	*54533*
Armenia	–	–	–	–	–	-382	-636	-562	-536
Azerbaijan	–	–	–	–	–	-162	-197	450	506
Belarus	–	–	–	–	–	-868	-1211	-973	-1149
Georgia	–	–	–	–	–	-304	-582	-345	-454
Kazakhstan	–	–	–	–	–	928	1811	2727	3297
Kyrgyzstan	–	–	–	–	–	-141	-193	-62	-76
Moldova, Republic of	–	–	–	–	–	-154	-271	-252	-394
Russian Federation	–	–	–	–	–	20336	22797	48735	51914
Tajikistan	–	–	–	–	–	-86	-50	17	-105
Turkmenistan	–	–	–	–	–	1260	1255	1103	967
Ukraine	–	–	–	–	–	-2000	-1733	281	510
USSR (former)	1241	-694	6987	7830	-6351	–	–	–	–
Uzbekistan	–	–	–	–	–	5	126	71	53
DEVELOPING ECONOMIES									
By major category									
Major petroleum exporters	8029	66936	143811	36441	56700	73671	78296	152187	169826
Other developing economies	-8894	-31519	-63443	-20213	-47277	-139326	-68739	-46394	-25202
Major exporters of manufactures	-4393	-19339	-32576	7305	-12586	-64283	17920	26621	43822
Remaining economies	-4501	-12179	-30867	-27518	-34690	-75042	-86659	-73015	-69024
America	-1762	-3486	-10251	-3302	-5873	-30480	-37311	-27979	-21321
Africa	-584	-4366	-8534	-10836	-15712	-22711	-28900	-25643	-25994
West Asia	-619	-1104	-4315	-3806	-3642	-8428	-8312	-8201	-8316
Other Asia	-1195	-2651	-6533	-8158	-7400	-12347	-10654	-9835	-11278
By income group									
(per capita GDP in 2000)									
High-income countries	1582	41879	88844	41903	35748	2555	27140	80589	121262
Middle-income countries	-2070	-14977	-20328	-6257	-20675	-60137	-48832	-17354	-11277
Low-income countries	-377	8515	11851	-19418	-5650	-8073	31250	42558	34640
Memo item:									
LDC	-109	-2210	-8242	-7496	-6781	-9793	-12355	-9495	-9913
HIPC	-297	-1862	-7016	-4908	-2676	-7182	-10564	-7357	-8042
Land-locked countries	57	-593	-2388	-3526	-4057	-5791	-6700	-4133	-5288

Sources: Data are derived from figures reported in table 1.1 of the *UNCTAD Handbook of Statistics 2004 on CD-ROM*.
Notes: For those countries which report their imports on an f.o.b. basis, the trade balance shown is on an f.o.b./f.o.b. basis.
The regional trade balances are the sums of the reported trade balances for the relevant individual countries.
A negative sign indicates a deficit of the trade balance.

Percentage of imports - Part dans les importations									Régions, groupements économiques, pays ou zones
1969-71	1974-76	1979-81	1984-86	1989-91	1994-96	1997-99	1999-01	2001-03	
-41.06	-44.01	-65.22	-67.78	-69.15	-71.73	-65.22	-52.18	-57.41	Népal
-41.62	-44.55	-49.73	-48.94	-26.98	-23.53	-17.01	-14.57	-9.86	Pakistan
-21.79	-31.86	-31.67	-14.04	-33.21	-39.89	-9.96	4.43	-5.29	Philippines
-32.96	-30.66	-20.86	-13.69	-11.36	-5.17	0.86	3.55	8.70	Singapour
-12.55	-17.72	-41.22	-30.67	-31.38	-28.62	-20.79	-22.21	-21.86	Sri Lanka
-41.40	-23.83	-28.25	-18.32	-25.54	-20.04	11.37	10.84	5.83	Thaïlande
-98.24	-79.08	-69.50	-62.85	-15.85	-32.83	-13.69	-4.98	-12.49	Viet Nam
									ECONOMIES EN DEVELOPPEMENT :
-38.20	**-30.47**	**-35.79**	**-40.98**	**-40.86**	**-18.86**	**-27.35**	**-26.03**	**-35.82**	**OCEANIE**
423.77	33.54	77.07	-25.43	-14.74	10.82	69.33	66.54	49.82	Samoa américaines
-49.37	-73.23	-82.66	-83.69	-91.39	-92.82	-92.33	-86.38	-83.48	Iles Cook
-22.70	-29.93	-28.77	-26.44	-29.52	-28.80	-32.53	-31.33	-37.19	Fidji
-87.07	-90.91	-94.39	-93.74	-87.60	-76.74	-74.82	-77.16	-81.46	Polynésie française
-94.29	-90.72	-87.53	-83.15	-84.65	-83.03	-85.16	-87.01	-91.39	Guam
98.22	271.42	-25.77	-66.38	-85.39	-82.29	-82.57	-85.90	-90.56	Kiribati
424.60	241.78	485.00	227.24	90.21	8.43	108.47	47.51	-52.17	Nauru
-8.58	1.28	-7.80	-37.70	-35.38	-43.95	-51.54	-46.87	-50.06	Nouvelle-Calédonie
-62.20	3.45	-13.03	-10.04	-8.74	67.01	41.82	69.07	54.04	Papouasie-Nouvelle-Guinée
-51.88	-69.82	-76.16	-69.18	-88.36	-92.08	-83.90	-85.64	-88.99	Samoa
-34.57	-24.33	-15.02	-2.18	-27.55	6.09	7.92	-17.71	-5.09	Iles Salomon
-50.00	-66.46	-79.57	-83.96	-80.72	-82.22	-86.21	-87.01	-82.28	Tonga
..	..	-97.44	-83.94	-66.23	-94.37	-98.48	-99.29	-99.18	Tuvalu
-15.63	-53.41	-42.62	-53.87	-75.88	-70.39	-65.68	-76.93	-82.13	Vanuatu
0.21	**-9.88**	**-0.34**	**5.10**	**-9.47**	**8.42**	**7.80**	**31.66**	**21.95**	**EUROPE DU SUD-EST ET CEI**
-18.01	*-24.75*	*-19.83*	*-4.53*	*-21.03*	*-29.38*	*-37.85*	*-35.98*	*-39.37*	*Europe du Sud-Est*
..	..	..	..	-44.54	-74.63	-76.88	-76.66	-76.95	Albanie
					-96.57	-82.95	-69.63	-72.15	Bosnie-Herzégovine
5.00	-15.35	3.54	-2.75	10.73	-5.49	-13.55	-27.65	-29.47	Bulgarie
–	–	–	–	–	-32.97	-48.28	-45.88	-53.23	Croatie
–	–	–	–	–	-28.73	-31.88	-33.84	-37.73	Macédoine, LERY
-11.05	-8.81	-14.27	2.22	-17.58	-21.94	-24.40	-21.85	-25.24	Roumanie
–	–	–	–	–	-47.27	-45.13	-33.85	-42.43	Serbie-et-Monténégro
-38.89	-43.48	-40.14	-12.92	-12.92	–	–	–	–	Yougoslavie, RSF (anc.)
–	–	–	–	–	*20.37*	*26.18*	*62.58*	*50.42*	*CEI*
–		–	–	–	-57.05	-73.49	-66.13	-52.06	Arménie
–		–	–	–	-18.31	-18.53	33.46	34.99	Azerbaïdjan
–		–	–	–	-16.79	-14.91	-12.27	-11.75	Bélarus
–		–	–	–	-62.14	-70.77	-54.02	-54.53	Géorgie
–		–	–	–	22.67	45.12	56.50	45.47	Kazakhstan
–		–	–	–	-17.92	-26.06	-10.46	-11.41	Kirghizistan
–		–	–	–	-16.64	-28.20	-32.23	-36.04	Moldova, République de
–		–	–	–	33.96	47.12	106.18	82.98	Fédération de Russie
–		–	–	–	-12.38	-6.29	2.49	-12.16	Tadjikistan
–		–	–	–	161.38	134.77	106.57	84.57	Turkménistan
–		–	–	–	-12.51	-11.01	1.77	3.05	Ukraine
10.86	-0.75	10.65	9.34	-3.96	–	–	–	–	URSS (anc.)
–	–	–	–	–	0.69	4.44	2.39	1.60	Ouzbékistan
									ECONOMIES EN DEVELOPPEMENT
									Par principales catégories
62.40	122.34	102.55	28.88	41.23	43.38	42.68	77.12	77.79	Principaux pays exportateurs de pétrole
-17.76	-22.21	-18.79	-5.66	-6.91	-10.89	-4.76	-2.89	-1.50	Autres économies en développement
-18.59	-24.64	-16.57	3.15	-2.27	-6.22	1.82	2.24	2.96	Principaux pays exportateurs d'articles manufacturés
-17.03	-19.00	-22.08	-22.67	-21.26	-29.78	-29.80	-25.37	-22.39	Autres économies
-17.19	-13.57	-17.91	-7.51	-10.46	-29.76	-29.60	-23.64	-18.27	Amérique
-4.29	-15.31	-13.04	-20.68	-20.98	-24.09	-27.94	-25.09	-22.65	Afrique
-72.51	-46.88	-74.35	-74.44	-68.81	-78.68	-76.89	-74.84	-67.88	Asie occidentale
-42.57	-46.67	-48.82	-48.46	-32.34	-31.44	-23.40	-19.24	-18.77	Autres pays d'Asie
									Par catégories de revenus (PIB par habitant en 2000)
6.67	55.02	40.54	19.66	9.00	0.15	3.29	8.66	12.57	Pays à revenu élevé
-9.26	-20.00	-13.55	-4.50	-9.22	-15.81	-12.25	-4.34	-2.66	Pays à revenu intermédiaire
-2.13	16.33	13.60	-14.84	-3.26	-2.63	8.68	9.79	6.36	Pays à revenu faible
									Pour mémoire :
-1.86	-20.59	-36.48	-36.39	-27.84	-29.66	-31.25	-22.15	-19.92	PMA
-3.94	-12.32	-23.87	-19.35	-9.06	-16.47	-19.29	-12.52	-11.24	PPTE
2.70	-11.38	-22.34	-31.92	-27.96	-18.01	-18.43	-11.69	-12.75	Pays enclavés

Sources : Les données ont été calculées d'après les chiffres du tableau 1.1 du *Manuel de statistiques de la CNUCED 2004 sur CD-ROM.*
Notes : Lorsque les pays ont fourni leurs importations sur la base f.a.b., la balance commerciale de chaque pays est présentée sur la base f.a.b./f.a.b.
Les balances commerciales régionales sont calculées à partir des balances commerciales des pays correspondants.
Un signe négatif indique un déficit de la balance commerciale.

1.4 Intra-trade of regional and trade groups

TRADE GROUP	Value of intra-trade (exports in millions of dollars) Valeur du commerce interne au groupement (exportations en millions de dollars)						Intra-trade of groups regional exports Commerce interne des exportations régionales		
	1980	1990	1995	2000	2002	2003	1980	1990	1995
EUROPE									
EFTA	524	782	925	831	879	1072	1.4	1.1	1.1
EU (25)	483141	1022932	1385805	1618929	1732227	2063450	84.5	89.2	90.8
EU (15)	456857	981260	1259699	1420090	1491272	1767282	85.2	87.9	86.5
Euro Zone	306473	669971	860976	946891	1006699	1226917	70.2	71.7	70.6
AMERICA									
ANCOM	1161	1312	4812	5116	5070	4781	5.7	6.5	17.4
CACM	1174	667	1594	2418	2598	3288	37.2	23.2	33.0
CARICOM	599	456	877	1076	1252	1538	7.6	13.6	20.5
FTAA	167719	300700	525346	857839	797612	841264	96.4	99.0	99.4
LAIA	11192	13350	35986	44241	37154	43103	25.4	21.3	25.8
MERCOSUR	3424	4127	14199	17910	10573	13383	31.8	22.2	43.1
NAFTA	102218	226273	394472	676441	626985	651213	79.0	88.7	87.3
OECS	4	29	39	38	43	54	23.0	21.3	21.8
AFRICA									
CEPGL	2	7	8	10	12	15	3.6	6.2	6.0
COMESA	555	890	1027	1281	1465	1812	78.5	61.3	45.4
ECCAS	89	163	163	196	193	236	49.1	26.0	35.5
ECOWAS	661	1532	1875	2811	3192	3541	73.5	75.5	77.0
MRU	7	0	1	5	5	6	59.3	0.7	1.6
SADC	108	1058	4124	4453	4240	5345	54.9	86.3	82.0
CEMAC (UDEAC)	75	139	120	101	120	157	66.0	27.9	38.9
UEMOA	460	621	560	741	857	1043	52.9	49.3	47.2
UMA	109	958	1109	1112	1243	1553	33.6	69.3	66.8
ASIA									
ASEAN	12413	27365	79544	98060	91765	102281	29.0	34.0	41.9
Bangkok Agreement	783	2429	21728	37765	50901	75258	3.6	3.2	12.7
ECO	392	1243	4746	4473	4955	6696	17.1	10.9	24.8
GCC	4632	6906	6832	7218	6905	7864	7.2	14.6	12.1
MSG	11	5	18	22	27	34	2.0	0.8	1.2
SAARC	613	863	2024	2593	2998	3869	12.2	10.8	12.5
INTERREGIONAL GROUPINGS									
APEC	357697	901561	1688707	2283093	2168694	2463981	–	–	–
BSEC	1190	1229	25505	24747	27348	34668	–	–	–
CIS	-	-	31529	28760	29517	37625	–	–	–

Sources: UNCTAD secretariat computations based on International Monetary Fund, *Direction of Trade Statistics*.

Notes: For definition of country groupings, see "Distribution of countries and territories" at the beginning of this *Handbook*.

as percentage of of each group du groupement en pourcentage de chaque groupement			Intra-trade of groups as percentage of total exports of each group Commerce interne du groupement en pourcentage des exportations totales de chaque groupement						GROUPEMENTS COMMERCIAUX
2000	2002	2003	1980	1990	1995	2000	2002	2003	
									EUROPE
0.8	0.8	0.9	1.1	0.8	0.7	0.6	0.6	0.6	AELE
91.9	91.0	90.8	60.9	67.1	66.1	67.2	66.7	67.2	UE (25)
85.9	84.5	84.1	60.8	65.9	62.4	62.1	61.1	61.4	UE (15)
68.9	67.5	68.0	51.4	55.1	52.1	50.8	49.7	50.8	Zone Euro
									AMERIQUE
10.7	13.3	10.3	3.8	4.1	12.0	8.5	9.5	7.4	ANCOM
23.6	16.7	19.0	24.4	15.3	21.8	14.8	11.0	11.9	MCAC
22.3	18.4	17.2	5.4	8.0	12.2	14.4	12.5	12.5	CARICOM
99.0	99.1	99.1	43.4	46.6	52.5	60.7	60.9	59.8	ZLEA
17.0	15.2	16.5	13.9	11.6	17.3	13.1	11.4	11.8	ALADI
38.7	23.1	25.5	11.6	8.9	20.3	20.0	11.3	11.8	MERCOSUR
91.0	91.3	91.6	33.6	41.4	46.2	55.7	56.7	56.1	ALENA
22.1	22.1	27.0	9.0	8.1	12.6	10.0	3.8	6.9	OECO
									AFRIQUE
32.4	9.8	9.8	0.1	0.5	0.5	0.8	0.7	1.2	CEPGL
50.7	54.4	56.4	5.7	6.3	6.0	4.9	5.4	5.8	COMESA
53.9	36.6	33.5	1.4	1.4	1.5	1.1	1.1	1.1	CEEAC
71.6	74.8	73.0	9.6	8.0	9.0	9.5	11.5	9.8	CEDEAO
7.4	10.4	9.4	0.8	0.0	0.1	0.4	0.2	0.3	UFM
79.8	76.3	76.6	0.4	3.1	10.6	12.0	9.3	10.0	SADC
34.9	34.8	32.3	1.6	2.3	2.1	1.0	1.4	1.4	CEMAC (UDEAC)
46.7	39.2	46.0	9.6	13.0	10.3	13.1	12.1	12.8	UEMOA
73.3	67.1	67.9	0.3	2.9	3.8	2.3	2.8	2.7	UMA
									ASIE
39.1	37.8	35.1	17.4	19.0	24.6	23.0	22.7	21.2	ANASE
15.1	18.3	21.2	1.7	1.6	6.8	7.6	9.3	10.6	Accord de Bangkok
18.0	19.6	19.6	6.3	3.2	7.9	5.6	5.9	6.0	ECO
6.9	7.2	6.7	3.0	8.0	6.8	4.5	4.6	4.2	CCG
2.4	3.5	3.2	0.7	0.3	0.4	0.6	0.8	0.7	MSG
12.3	12.2	12.5	4.8	3.2	4.4	4.1	4.2	4.5	SAARC
									GROUPEMENTS INTERREGIONAUX
–	–	–	57.9	68.3	71.8	73.3	73.4	72.7	CEAP
–	–	–	5.9	4.2	18.1	14.2	14.1	14.3	CEMN
–	–	–	–	–	28.6	20.0	19.6	20.0	CEI

Sources :   Calculs du secrétariat de la CNUCED sur la base de données du Fonds monétaire international, *Direction of Trade statistics*.

Notes :   Pour la définition des groupements, se reporter à "Répartition des pays et territoires" au début du présent *Manuel*.

PART TWO

Trade and commodity price indices

DEUXIEME PARTIE

Indices du commerce et des prix des produits de base

1

2

3

4

5

6

7

8

Region and economic grouping	1980	1990	1994	1995	1996	1997	1998	1999	2001	2002	Régions et groupements économiques
WORLD	**32**	**49**	**62**	**68**	**72**	**79**	**82**	**87**	**99**	**103**	**MONDE**
DEVELOPED ECONOMIES	36	53	65	70	73	81	85	89	100	102	ECONOMIES DEVELOPPEES
DEVELOPING ECONOMIES	20	38	58	65	70	77	78	86	99	107	ECONOMIES EN DEVELOPPEMENT
By region											*Par régions*
America	**20**	**41**	**53**	**60**	**68**	**76**	**82**	**89**	**102**	**102**	**Amérique**
South America	33	57	67	71	78	85	88	93	106	107	Amérique du Sud
Other America	9	27	40	50	59	68	76	87	98	98	Autres économies : Amérique
Africa	**54**	**64**	**66**	**70**	**79**	**85**	**78**	**91**	**100**	**100**	**Afrique**
North Africa	43	68	67	69	72	80	74	84	96	101	Afrique du Nord
Other Africa	59	63	66	72	83	88	80	94	101	100	Autres économies : Afrique
Asia	**16**	**35**	**58**	**65**	**69**	**76**	**78**	**85**	**98**	**108**	**Asie**
West Asia	91	54	79	82	91	98	87	94	107	111	Asie occidentale
Other Asia	9	34	56	64	68	75	77	85	97	108	Autres économies : Asie
Oceania	**158**	**151**	**255**	**183**	**177**	**137**	**98**	**95**	**84**	**57**	**Océanie**
By major category											*Par principales catégories*
Major petroleum exporters	71	58	78	81	87	94	96	104	101	97	Principaux pays exportateurs de pétrole
Other developing economies	12	36	56	63	68	75	78	85	98	108	Autres économies en développement
Major exporters of manufactures	9	33	54	62	66	74	77	84	98	109	Principaux pays exportateurs d'articles manufacturés
Remaining economies	34	54	67	72	79	86	88	93	100	102	Autres économies
America	31	52	61	69	77	87	94	97	103	105	Amérique
Africa	45	63	71	74	81	87	84	92	106	109	Afrique
West Asia	32	63	78	84	82	85	89	92	119	144	Asie occidentale
Other Asia	17	38	67	68	75	78	78	83	72	72	Autres pays d'Asie
By income group (per capita GDP in 2000)											*Par catégories de revenus (PIB par habitant en 2000)*
High-income countries	20	38	58	66	73	79	80	87	96	100	Pays à revenu élevé
Middle-income countries	24	45	62	67	69	76	78	87	101	108	Pays à revenu intermédiaire
Low-income countries	16	34	54	62	65	73	76	85	103	119	Pays à revenu faible
MEMO ITEM:											**POUR MEMOIRE :**
LDC	14	37	49	53	62	71	69	87	82	80	PMA
HIPC	32	54	61	64	73	79	78	91	103	102	PPTE
Land-locked countries	32	57	68	70	81	87	89	100	100	116	Pays enclavés

For sources, see end of table 2.1F.

Pour les sources, se reporter à la fin du tableau 2.1F.

Region and economic grouping	1980	1990	1994	1995	1996	1997	1998	1999	2001	2002	Régions et groupements économiques
WORLD	**32**	**49**	**63**	**69**	**73**	**80**	**83**	**89**	**99**	**103**	**MONDE**
DEVELOPED ECONOMIES	36	53	62	67	71	77	84	90	100	103	ECONOMIES DEVELOPPEES
DEVELOPING ECONOMIES	19	39	64	73	78	85	81	85	97	103	ECONOMIES EN DEVELOPPEMENT
By region											*Par régions*
America	**29**	**28**	**57**	**60**	**67**	**82**	**89**	**88**	**101**	**94**	**Amérique**
South America	40	31	70	84	89	108	111	94	102	85	Amérique du Sud
Other America	23	27	48	43	52	64	74	83	100	100	Autres économies : Amérique
Africa	**69**	**70**	**73**	**82**	**84**	**91**	**96**	**97**	**106**	**107**	**Afrique**
North Africa	63	87	78	83	83	86	98	98	103	108	Afrique du Nord
Other Africa	72	61	70	82	84	94	95	97	107	106	Autres économies : Afrique
Asia	**11**	**39**	**66**	**76**	**80**	**86**	**76**	**83**	**95**	**105**	**Asie**
West Asia	15	39	44	55	70	83	84	79	79	90	Asie occidentale
Other Asia	11	39	67	77	81	86	76	83	96	106	Autres économies : Asie
Oceania	..	..	..	..	..	..	..	..	..	..	**Océanie**
By major category											*Par principales catégories*
Major petroleum exporters	79	65	79	90	91	103	91	84	107	85	Principaux pays exportateurs de pétrole
Other developing economies	16	38	64	72	77	85	80	85	97	103	Autres économies en développement
Major exporters of manufactures	12	36	62	70	75	83	77	84	97	106	Principaux pays exportateurs d'articles manufacturés
Remaining economies	44	50	73	81	86	96	99	94	95	91	Autres économies
America	47	35	74	79	86	103	110	96	100	91	Amérique
Africa	46	68	71	81	83	90	96	97	103	106	Afrique
West Asia	48	60	87	84	91	89	83	83	103	104	Asie occidentale
Other Asia	34	43	79	93	95	97	74	75	47	41	Autres pays d'Asie
By income group (per capita GDP in 2000)											*Par catégories de revenus (PIB par habitant en 2000)*
High-income countries	16	38	64	70	76	85	80	86	94	97	Pays à revenu élevé
Middle-income countries	28	46	70	84	86	94	88	88	95	100	Pays à revenu intermédiaire
Low-income countries	18	35	59	68	72	77	75	82	105	118	Pays à revenu faible
MEMO ITEM:											**POUR MEMOIRE :**
LDC	27	48	62	72	72	78	86	98	85	78	PMA
HIPC	43	56	63	70	73	80	90	100	109	102	PPTE
Land-locked countries	35	64	74	84	91	100	110	99	106	115	Pays enclavés

For sources, see end of table 2.1F.

Pour les sources, se reporter à la fin du tableau 2.1F.

2.1C Unit value indices of exports
2000 = 100

2.1C Indices de la valeur unitaire des exportations
2000 = 100

Region and economic grouping	1980	1990	1994	1995	1996	1997	1998	1999	2001	2002	Régions et groupements économiques
WORLD	**99**	**111**	**109**	**120**	**117**	**110**	**105**	**102**	**97**	**97**	**MONDE**
DEVELOPED ECONOMIES	88	114	112	123	120	112	108	106	98	98	ECONOMIES DEVELOPPEES
DEVELOPING ECONOMIES	121	103	103	111	110	107	98	95	95	94	ECONOMIES EN DEVELOPPEMENT
By region											*Par régions*
America	**131**	**94**	**97**	**105**	**104**	**104**	**96**	**93**	**94**	**95**	**Amérique**
South America	122	94	98	109	108	108	96	90	92	91	Amérique du Sud
Other America	153	94	94	100	100	100	95	96	96	98	Autres économies : Amérique
Africa	**131**	**110**	**100**	**109**	**108**	**103**	**94**	**90**	**95**	**97**	**Afrique**
North Africa	125	93	83	94	98	93	87	87	98	97	Afrique du Nord
Other Africa	132	116	106	114	112	107	97	91	94	97	Autres économies : Afrique
Asia	**115**	**105**	**105**	**112**	**111**	**108**	**99**	**96**	**95**	**94**	**Asie**
West Asia	105	95	73	82	87	83	71	78	90	93	Asie occidentale
Other Asia	123	106	108	115	114	110	101	98	96	94	Autres économies : Asie
Oceania	**31**	**37**	**49**	**69**	**68**	**75**	**86**	**97**	**103**	**128**	**Océanie**
By major category											*Par principales catégories*
Major petroleum exporters	114	89	70	78	87	82	60	65	88	92	Principaux pays exportateurs de pétrole
Other developing economies	127	106	108	115	113	110	102	99	96	95	Autres économies en développement
Major exporters of manufactures	123	106	108	114	113	110	101	99	96	95	Principaux pays exportateurs d'articles manufacturés
Remaining economies	134	109	106	118	114	112	104	98	95	96	Autres économies
America	117	92	102	115	111	110	98	93	93	92	Amérique
Africa	148	123	115	126	121	116	110	102	96	100	Afrique
West Asia	95	89	96	111	117	114	107	105	101	102	Asie occidentale
Other Asia	119	112	94	108	108	108	111	105	102	91	Autres pays d'Asie
By income group (per capita GDP in 2000)											*Par catégories de revenus (PIB par habitant en 2000)*
High-income countries	113	103	103	111	108	104	94	94	94	94	Pays à revenu élevé
Middle-income countries	125	105	108	117	120	115	104	99	97	94	Pays à revenu intermédiaire
Low-income countries	134	102	97	104	105	106	99	95	96	96	Pays à revenu faible
MEMO ITEM:											**POUR MEMOIRE :**
LDC	215	151	115	129	122	110	108	94	98	95	PMA
HIPC	162	126	109	126	121	112	109	96	99	102	PPTE
Land-locked countries	176	146	125	140	132	127	111	102	97	95	Pays enclavés

For sources, see end of table 2.1F.

Pour les sources, se reporter à la fin du tableau 2.1F.

2.1D Unit value indices of imports
2000 = 100

2.1D Indices de la valeur unitaire des importations
2000 = 100

Region and economic grouping	1980	1990	1994	1995	1996	1997	1998	1999	2001	2002	Régions et groupements économiques
WORLD	**94**	**109**	**105**	**115**	**113**	**107**	**101**	**99**	**96**	**96**	**MONDE**
DEVELOPED ECONOMIES	91	111	107	117	116	108	103	101	96	96	ECONOMIES DEVELOPPEES
DEVELOPING ECONOMIES	104	103	101	108	108	104	98	96	96	95	ECONOMIES EN DEVELOPPEMENT
By region											*Par régions*
America	**94**	**107**	**100**	**107**	**106**	**103**	**100**	**98**	**97**	**97**	**Amérique**
South America	108	120	103	108	109	105	100	96	97	95	Amérique du Sud
Other America	63	93	97	105	103	102	100	99	97	98	Autres économies : Amérique
Africa	**98**	**110**	**107**	**115**	**114**	**111**	**106**	**101**	**97**	**96**	**Afrique**
North Africa	87	102	102	110	110	107	105	102	98	98	Afrique du Nord
Other Africa	102	116	110	118	116	113	107	101	96	95	Autres économies : Afrique
Asia	**114**	**101**	**101**	**108**	**108**	**103**	**96**	**95**	**96**	**94**	**Asie**
West Asia	110	110	105	121	116	108	100	96	100	99	Asie occidentale
Other Asia	114	100	101	107	107	103	96	95	96	94	Autres économies : Asie
Oceania	..	..	..	..	..	..	..	..	..	..	**Océanie**
By major category											*Par principales catégories*
Major petroleum exporters	68	102	106	114	111	106	101	100	97	96	Principaux pays exportateurs de pétrole
Other developing economies	109	103	101	108	108	104	98	96	96	95	Autres économies en développement
Major exporters of manufactures	113	102	101	108	108	103	97	96	96	95	Principaux pays exportateurs d'articles manufacturés
Remaining economies	101	107	102	110	110	107	102	98	97	96	Autres économies
America	77	99	100	108	108	104	100	97	97	96	Amérique
Africa	117	111	109	117	116	112	107	101	97	96	Afrique
West Asia	108	95	85	96	103	101	100	98	102	105	Asie occidentale
Other Asia	102	112	84	91	93	95	89	93	96	95	Autres pays d'Asie
By income group (per capita GDP in 2000)											*Par catégories de revenus (PIB par habitant en 2000)*
High-income countries	87	98	102	109	107	103	97	95	95	93	Pays à revenu élevé
Middle-income countries	106	106	101	110	111	106	100	98	99	97	Pays à revenu intermédiaire
Low-income countries	123	108	100	105	106	103	98	98	96	95	Pays à revenu faible
MEMO ITEM:											**POUR MEMOIRE :**
LDC	148	132	107	112	123	116	112	99	100	94	PMA
HIPC	124	118	109	117	124	117	112	100	98	96	PPTE
Land-locked countries	138	121	112	119	118	116	103	100	96	94	Pays enclavés

For sources, see end of table 2.1F.

Pour les sources, se reporter à la fin du tableau 2.1F.

Region and economic grouping	1980	1990	1994	1995	1996	1997	1998	1999	2001	2002	Régions et groupements économiques
WORLD	105	102	104	104	104	103	104	103	100	101	**MONDE**
DEVELOPED ECONOMIES	97	103	105	105	104	103	105	105	101	102	ECONOMIES DEVELOPPEES
DEVELOPING ECONOMIES	117	100	102	102	102	103	100	99	99	100	ECONOMIES EN DEVELOPPEMENT
By region											*Par régions*
America	140	88	97	99	98	101	96	95	98	98	**Amérique**
South America	113	78	96	101	100	103	97	93	96	95	Amérique du Sud
Other America	242	101	97	95	96	98	95	97	99	100	Autres économies : Amérique
Africa	134	100	93	95	95	93	89	89	98	101	**Afrique**
North Africa	143	92	82	85	89	87	83	85	100	99	Afrique du Nord
Other Africa	129	100	96	97	96	94	91	90	98	102	Autres économies : Afrique
Asia	101	104	104	104	103	104	103	101	99	100	**Asie**
West Asia	96	86	69	68	75	77	70	82	90	94	Asie occidentale
Other Asia	108	106	107	107	106	107	105	103	100	100	Autres économies : Asie
Oceania	..	..	..	..	..	..	..	..	..	..	**Océanie**
By major category											*Par principales catégories*
Major petroleum exporters	168	87	66	68	79	77	60	65	91	96	Principaux pays exportateurs de pétrole
Other developing economies	117	103	107	106	105	106	104	103	100	100	Autres économies en développement
Major exporters of manufactures	109	104	107	106	105	106	105	104	100	100	Principaux pays exportateurs d'articles manufacturés
Remaining economies	133	102	104	108	104	105	102	100	99	99	Autres économies
America	153	93	102	107	103	105	98	96	97	96	Amérique
Africa	127	110	105	108	104	103	103	101	99	104	Afrique
West Asia	88	94	113	116	114	113	107	107	99	97	Asie occidentale
Other Asia	117	100	111	118	116	114	125	112	106	96	Autres pays d'Asie
By income group *(per capita GDP in 2000)*											*Par catégories de revenus* *(PIB par habitant en 2000)*
High-income countries	130	105	102	102	100	101	98	99	99	101	Pays à revenu élevé
Middle-income countries	119	98	106	107	107	108	104	102	97	97	Pays à revenu intermédiaire
Low-income countries	109	94	97	98	100	102	101	97	100	101	Pays à revenu faible
MEMO ITEM:											**POUR MEMOIRE :**
LDC	145	115	107	115	100	95	97	95	99	101	PMA
HIPC	131	107	100	108	98	96	98	96	101	106	PPTE
Land-locked countries	127	120	111	118	111	110	108	102	101	100	Pays enclavés

For sources, see end of table 2.1F.

Pour les sources, se reporter à la fin du tableau 2.1F.

2.1F Purchasing power indices of exports
2000 = 100

2.1F Indices du pouvoir d'achat des exportations
2000 = 100

Region and economic grouping	1980	1990	1994	1995	1996	1997	1998	1999	2001	2002	Régions et groupements économiques
WORLD	**33**	**50**	**64**	**70**	**74**	**81**	**85**	**90**	**100**	**105**	**MONDE**
DEVELOPED ECONOMIES	35	55	68	73	77	84	89	93	101	104	ECONOMIES DEVELOPPEES
DEVELOPING ECONOMIES	23	39	59	66	71	79	78	85	97	106	ECONOMIES EN DEVELOPPEMENT
By region											*Par régions*
America	**28**	**36**	**51**	**59**	**67**	**76**	**78**	**85**	**100**	**100**	**Amérique**
South America	37	44	65	72	77	87	85	86	101	102	Amérique du Sud
Other America	21	28	39	47	57	67	73	84	98	98	Autres économies : Amérique
Africa	**72**	**64**	**61**	**67**	**75**	**79**	**69**	**80**	**98**	**102**	**Afrique**
North Africa	61	62	55	58	64	70	61	71	96	100	Afrique du Nord
Other Africa	76	63	64	70	80	82	73	85	99	102	Autres économies : Afrique
Asia	**16**	**37**	**60**	**68**	**72**	**80**	**80**	**86**	**97**	**108**	**Asie**
West Asia	87	46	55	56	68	76	62	77	96	105	Asie occidentale
Other Asia	10	36	60	69	72	80	81	87	97	108	Autres économies : Asie
Oceania	..	..	..	..	..	..	..	..	..	..	**Océanie**
By major category											*Par principales catégories*
Major petroleum exporters	119	51	52	56	68	72	57	68	92	94	Principaux pays exportateurs de pétrole
Other developing economies	14	37	59	67	71	80	81	88	98	108	Autres économies en développement
Major exporters of manufactures	9	34	58	66	70	78	81	87	98	109	Principaux pays exportateurs d'articles manufacturés
Remaining economies	46	55	70	78	82	90	90	94	99	101	Autres économies
America	47	49	62	74	79	91	92	94	100	100	Amérique
Africa	57	69	75	80	85	90	87	94	105	113	Afrique
West Asia	28	59	89	97	93	96	95	99	118	139	Asie occidentale
Other Asia	19	38	74	80	87	90	98	94	76	68	Autres pays d'Asie
By income group (per capita GDP in 2000)											*Par catégories de revenus (PIB par habitant en 2000)*
High-income countries	25	40	59	67	73	80	78	86	95	101	Pays à revenu élevé
Middle-income countries	28	44	66	72	74	83	81	89	98	104	Pays à revenu intermédiaire
Low-income countries	18	32	52	61	65	75	77	82	103	120	Pays à revenu faible
MEMO ITEM:											**POUR MEMOIRE :**
LDC	21	42	52	61	62	67	67	82	81	81	PMA
HIPC	41	58	61	69	72	76	76	87	104	108	PPTE
Land-locked countries	41	69	76	83	91	96	96	102	101	116	Pays enclavés

Sources: UNCTAD secretariat estimates based on various national and international sources (see tables 1.1A and 8.1).

Notes:

For description of the methods used, see explanatory notes to table 8.1.

For tables 2.1C and 2.1D, regional aggregates are current period weighted.

Sources : Estimations du secrétariat de la CNUCED d'après des sources nationales et internationales (voir tableaux 1.1A et 8.1).

Notes :

Pour la description de la méthode utilisée, se reporter aux notes explicatives du tableau 8.1.

Dans les tableaux 2.1C et 2.1D, les totaux régionaux sont à coefficients de pondération correspondant à la période en cours.

2.2 Annual and quarterly indices of free-market prices of selected primary commodities
1990 = 100

Product	Level [1] Niveau [1] 1990	1980	1985	1995	1996	1997	1998	1999	2000	2001	2002	2003
ALL COMMODITIES	–	130.8	77.6	111.3	106.4	105.9	92.0	79.1	81.1	78.4	77.0	82.9
All food	–	160.5	85.2	115.8	117.1	119.3	104.3	84.2	82.9	82.5	82.5	84.8
Food and tropical beverages	–	*160.8*	*80.9*	*112.0*	*114.0*	*116.6*	*99.3*	*80.8*	*81.8*	*82.0*	*80.1*	*81.0*
Food	–	*155.2*	*65.9*	*105.2*	*111.8*	*107.1*	*92.0*	*75.3*	*79.3*	*83.3*	*79.8*	*80.0*
1. Wheat*	106.4	193.5	102.8	156.8	178.2	142.8	111.8	107.9	112.5	111.9	121.7	142.6
2. Wheat	136.8	128.7	100.8	130.7	152.3	117.6	94.6	84.2	87.1	95.0	110.7	109.9
3. Maize	107.5	..	..	115.2	145.2	106.6	94.6	87.7	80.7	81.6	89.6	95.1
4. Maize*	109.7	..	..	114.0	148.1	108.3	93.7	84.4	82.0	83.0	91.6	97.5
5. Rice	287.2	151.0	75.7	112.0	117.8	105.2	106.4	86.7	71.0	60.1	66.7	69.5
6. Sugar [2]	12.6	228.4	32.4	105.8	95.3	90.6	71.4	50.0	65.2	68.8	54.9	56.5
7. Beef [2]	115.4	109.0	84.6	74.9	70.1	72.9	67.8	72.0	76.1	83.6	83.4	83.8
8. Bananas [2]	23.5	72.1	73.4	84.7	91.1	94.9	92.0	82.8	80.9	112.3	101.5	72.3
9. Pepper	1792.4	115.7	225.2	211.4	206.3	352.9	396.4	380.8	242.2	138.1	128.5	156.6
10. Soybean meal	213.8	120.9	73.5	98.5	128.4	135.8	88.6	76.9	93.4	92.5	89.4	104.9
11. Fish meal	412.2	122.4	68.0	120.1	142.2	147.1	160.6	95.2	100.2	118.1	147.0	148.2
Tropical beverages	–	*191.0*	*162.4*	*149.3*	*125.9*	*168.5*	*138.9*	*110.6*	*95.4*	*74.9*	*81.4*	*86.0*
12 Coffee [2]	96.5	185.2	161.5	164.0	135.9	206.1	148.0	120.6	106.3	74.8	67.6	69.7
13. Coffee [2]	82.8	252.2	183.3	176.3	144.6	201.5	147.1	107.3	96.5	61.0	54.5	61.4
14. Coffee [2]	89.1	173.0	163.3	167.5	134.5	207.5	148.3	113.9	95.5	69.5	67.8	71.9
15. Coffee [2]	55.0	267.6	220.7	230.6	150.4	146.8	152.6	123.0	76.6	49.7	56.1	69.8
16. Coffee* [2]	72.1	209.1	185.2	191.5	140.6	184.4	151.1	117.4	88.3	61.9	63.3	71.1
17. Cocoa [2]	57.7	204.7	177.3	112.7	114.5	127.3	132.1	89.7	69.8	85.6	139.8	138.0
18. Tea	2039.5	109.2	97.3	80.1	87.1	109.6	113.3	..	..	..	..	..
19. Tea [3,4]	191.4	..	..	92.1	92.6	125.2	130.6	121.4	129.7	103.5	93.7	101.5
Vegetable oilseeds and oils	–	*157.8*	*135.1*	*159.9*	*152.7*	*150.9*	*162.6*	*123.7*	*96.0*	*88.4*	*110.8*	*129.7*
20. Soybeans	246.8	120.1	91.3	105.1	123.5	119.7	98.4	81.7	85.8	79.4	86.2	107.0
21. Soybean oil	447.4	133.7	127.8	139.7	123.3	126.2	139.9	95.5	75.6	79.1	101.5	123.8
22. Sunflower oil	489.3	129.3	123.1	141.7	117.7	118.8	148.8	103.7	80.1	99.0	121.4	121.3
23. Groundnut oil	963.7	89.1	93.9	102.8	93.1	104.9	94.4	81.7	74.1	70.6	71.3	129.0
24. Copra	230.7	196.4	167.3	190.1	212.0	188.0	178.2	200.1	132.1	87.6	115.4	130.0
25. Coconut oil	336.5	200.4	175.4	199.0	223.4	195.2	195.5	219.0	133.8	94.5	125.1	138.9
26. Palm kernel oil	333.9	217.3	165.1	202.9	218.0	195.2	205.6	207.8	132.8	92.3	124.5	137.4
27. Palm oil	289.8	201.5	172.7	216.8	183.2	188.3	231.5	150.4	107.0	98.6	134.6	152.9
Agricultural raw materials	–	96.4	70.3	113.4	101.6	91.4	81.7	73.2	74.8	73.2	68.1	79.8
28. Linseed oil	708.8	98.3	88.5	92.8	79.8	80.6	99.8	72.2	56.2	54.0	73.3	95.7
29. Tobacco	3397.1	67.0	76.9	77.8	89.9	104.0	98.2	91.3	88.0	88.0	80.7	77.9
30. Cotton [2]	93.9	125.1	104.9	119.4	..	96.8	87.4	75.8	89.2	84.6	70.9	79.2
31. Cotton [2]	83.8	116.9	85.1	124.6	107.0	97.4	89.7	66.5	78.2	63.3	56.7	82.8
32. Cotton [2]	79.4	107.0	80.8	127.1	108.4	98.8	90.5	69.8	72.3	57.1	55.2	76.3
33. Cotton* [2]	77.7	103.5	60.4	107.5	99.0	97.1	92.0	56.7	66.6	59.5	53.6	80.3
34. Cotton* [2]	82.6	113.4	72.4	117.9	97.4	96.0	79.0	64.3	71.7	58.1	56.0	76.8
35. Cotton [2]	511.9	60.3	62.6	..	69.3	58.0	50.9	45.2	42.4	46.0	40.0	43.8
36. Wool [5]	808.0	73.9	61.3	80.6	68.6	77.3	53.1	49.4	46.2	38.3	..	..
37. Wool [5,6]	651.6	..	..	..	..	116.6	84.8	95.0	112.6	95.7	98.9	107.7
38. Wool [5]	340.9	125.8	91.0	115.3	111.3	96.4	75.2	78.5	88.6	90.4	..	..
39. Wool [5,6]	428.9	..	..	..	..	103.2	78.4	64.5	65.5	77.5	131.9	153.7
40. Jute	408.6	76.8	139.3	89.5	111.2	73.9	63.4	67.5	68.2	80.7	66.3	59.2
41. Sisal	743.3	105.8	83.3	102.5	129.9	124.3	129.8	118.3	105.2	113.3	104.6	107.4
42. Sisal	715.0	107.0	73.5	99.4	121.4	108.7	114.9	97.3	87.9	97.8	92.3	97.7
43. Hides [5]	238.8	96.5	84.6	102.5	78.2	62.9	48.6	35.3	61.2	86.1	78.2	..
44. Hides [2]	92.2	49.8	55.5	95.6	94.7	95.7	83.2	78.2	87.0	91.7	89.0	74.1
45. Non-coniferous woods* [7]	88.6	..	..	121.6	120.6	118.9	115.6	117.4	112.9	110.6	118.9	133.2
46. Tropical logs [8]	343.5	73.3	50.6	99.2	79.3	74.9	74.0	68.6	71.2	75.7	67.8	81.4
47. Tropical sawnwood* [8]	524.3	70.1	52.6	146.3	128.9	119.7	84.6	99.2	101.4	97.1	95.6	103.6
48. Plywood* [9]	354.9	77.1	59.4	164.2	149.0	136.2	105.8	124.4	126.4	115.5	113.5	122.9
49. Rubber	865.7	164.4	87.2	184.9	162.9	116.8	82.0	71.6	77.3	66.4	88.4	125.2

For sources and notes, see end of table.

| 2001 | | 2002 | | | | 2003 | | | | 2004 | | Produit |
III	IV	I	II	III	IV	I	II	III	IV	I	II	
78.2	**73.3**	**74.7**	**76.4**	**77.3**	**79.7**	**83.1**	**79.8**	**80.2**	**88.5**	**97.4**	**97.8**	**TOTAL DES PRODUITS**
83.3	**78.1**	**79.4**	**81.0**	**82.7**	**86.9**	**88.9**	**82.3**	**80.5**	**87.6**	**94.1**	**96.3**	**Total des produits alimentaires**
82.0	*76.8*	*78.0*	*78.9*	*79.8*	*83.7*	*85.8*	*78.8*	*77.0*	*82.4*	*88.0*	*91.3*	***Produits alimentaires et boissons tropicales***
84.0	*78.2*	*78.2*	*79.0*	*79.4*	*82.7*	*84.7*	*77.6*	*75.6*	*82.1*	*87.3*	*91.7*	*Produits alimentaires*
113.3	100.5	105.6	115.8	133.0	132.2	135.6	145.7	139.7	149.3	144.4	143.8	1. Blé*
92.9	93.1	93.3	93.7	123.9	132.0	110.5	102.9	106.9	119.5	122.6	120.3	2. Blé
82.5	86.2	80.1	84.4	95.1	97.7	91.2	94.7	91.5	101.7	103.3	109.4	3. Maïs
83.3	83.8	84.1	83.4	98.3	100.5	97.6	98.0	92.9	101.5	112.2	117.4	4. Maïs*
59.4	60.4	66.6	68.5	67.2	64.7	69.2	69.3	69.4	70.0	76.6	86.9	5. Riz
65.2	59.3	55.8	49.7	52.2	61.9	67.5	57.5	52.2	48.7	48.1	52.7	6. Sucre [2]
88.8	89.1	90.4	84.9	82.4	76.1	84.0	78.8	81.7	90.7	87.8	96.4	7. Viande de boeuf [2]
126.2	96.0	97.1	118.4	93.6	97.1	96.7	63.3	57.0	72.4	92.9	108.3	8. Bananes [2]
124.9	109.5	104.1	110.4	127.4	172.2	168.0	153.1	156.5	148.8	145.0	147.8	9. Poivre
95.1	89.2	85.1	86.8	93.8	91.7	93.4	98.7	99.0	128.8	141.2	138.0	10. Farine de soja
121.1	131.4	143.0	150.8	149.7	144.5	143.5	146.5	146.9	155.9	164.2	156.9	11. Farine de poisson
71.1	*68.9*	*76.7*	*78.1*	*82.1*	*88.8*	*91.1*	*85.0*	*84.1*	*83.9*	*91.5*	*88.8*	*Boissons tropicales*
73.2	66.3	69.2	67.2	62.5	71.6	69.4	68.6	70.7	70.1	81.5	84.0	12. Café [2]
54.5	48.9	54.0	55.6	51.8	56.5	56.6	59.1	63.5	66.3	79.0	78.4	13. Café [2]
65.8	64.0	68.9	67.1	60.8	74.4	72.7	72.2	71.6	71.0	85.6	87.1	14. Café [2]
46.8	40.5	46.7	54.0	55.4	68.2	74.8	68.4	68.7	67.3	72.2	71.0	15. Café [2]
58.5	55.0	60.4	62.1	58.7	72.0	73.5	70.8	70.5	69.6	80.5	80.9	16. Café* [2]
79.2	96.0	117.1	126.7	157.1	158.4	168.3	137.8	124.9	121.1	123.2	111.7	17. Cacao [2]
..	..	..	..	..	..	..	..	..	..	..	..	18. Thé
101.9	87.6	93.7	90.3	95.9	94.7	98.7	98.9	103.0	105.4	103.3	96.2	19. Thé [3,4]
98.1	*93.7*	*96.7*	*105.5*	*116.2*	*124.7*	*125.6*	*123.6*	*121.5*	*148.2*	*164.4*	*155.1*	***Graines oléagineuses et huiles végétales***
84.0	76.3	76.5	80.0	92.0	96.3	98.3	100.0	98.8	130.9	152.8	130.9	20. Fèves de soja
90.4	86.9	82.0	89.8	109.3	125.1	116.5	119.4	118.7	140.6	151.8	140.4	21. Huile de soja
102.3	122.1	118.6	117.2	121.8	128.1	120.7	121.4	113.3	129.6	145.2	137.1	22. Huile de tournesol
69.1	69.2	69.2	67.2	68.0	80.7	106.2	135.7	149.9	124.2	124.2	124.4	23. Huile d'arachide
96.5	88.0	99.0	115.0	122.7	125.0	131.6	119.7	119.7	149.1	181.1	212.3	24. Coprah
103.3	96.7	109.4	126.5	128.6	136.0	139.9	130.8	127.9	157.0	189.3	209.0	25. Huile de coprah
102.9	92.8	105.4	126.9	128.8	137.1	140.6	125.9	122.9	160.2	185.4	207.0	26. Huile de palmiste
115.2	107.9	115.7	130.1	141.6	151.2	153.7	144.8	141.0	172.3	181.8	171.5	27. Huile de palme
74.4	**66.4**	**65.0**	**67.7**	**70.4**	**69.3**	**74.6**	**76.8**	**78.8**	**89.1**	**92.3**	**86.7**	**Matières premières d'origine agricole**
56.0	56.5	56.2	64.2	79.1	93.5	96.3	96.6	97.0	92.9	94.6	107.7	28. Huile de lin
89.4	86.2	82.1	81.2	80.1	79.6	78.2	76.5	78.4	78.5	81.7	81.5	29. Tabac
86.3	80.9	77.1	71.3	69.4	65.7	68.5	76.5	79.9	92.1	99.5	89.4	30. Coton [2]
59.2	50.6	53.2	53.0	59.6	63.2	..	..	73.8	91.9	89.7	83.6	31. Coton [2]
53.5	46.7	50.0	50.2	59.2	61.6	68.1	69.6	75.6	91.8	91.0	82.8	32. Coton [2]
54.1	46.6	49.6	48.0	55.6	61.0	69.4	76.0	..	94.2	..	..	33. Coton* [2]
52.5	47.6	51.8	50.3	58.5	63.3	71.2	71.5	74.6	89.9	89.7	82.3	34. Coton* [2]
46.7	42.8	41.6	40.9	40.2	37.3	37.9	40.1	42.3	55.1	55.6	52.6	35. Coton [2]
..	..	..	..	..	..	..	..	..	..	..	..	36. Laine [5]
90.7	72.1	93.6	94.0	91.4	116.6	118.3	108.2	103.5	100.9	110.5	107.0	37. Laine [5,6]
..	..	..	..	..	..	..	..	..	..	..	..	38. Laine [5]
79.1	81.0	115.8	123.9	128.9	159.0	166.5	155.4	154.3	138.4	140.9	128.1	39. Laine [5,6]
85.7	81.7	85.7	..	57.8	55.6	57.0	60.0	60.0	60.0	61.4	71.0	40. Jute
113.2	108.6	110.3	106.2	100.9	100.9	100.9	104.1	106.9	117.7	119.6	132.5	41. Sisal
94.8	92.7	93.7	93.7	90.9	90.9	90.9	94.3	97.2	108.4	110.4	123.8	42. Sisal
92.1	78.5	75.6	86.0	..	..	..	..	..	..	..	..	43. Peaux [5]
86.0	77.0	79.8	92.1	92.5	91.8	76.2	69.8	73.7	76.6	75.5	69.4	44. Peaux [2]
111.2	112.2	111.4	114.3	123.9	126.0	129.5	132.3	131.4	139.4	154.1	151.0	45. Bois non conifères* [7]
78.1	68.0	63.9	66.3	69.8	71.1	76.6	81.1	80.2	87.7	93.7	93.7	46. Grumes tropicales [8]
92.3	91.6	91.6	91.6	98.3	101.1	101.1	101.1	106.9	105.4	104.9	104.9	47. Grumes tropicales sciées* [8]
113.7	111.7	104.3	109.9	121.4	118.5	122.1	120.1	119.9	129.4	131.4	128.5	48. Contre-plaqué* [9]
68.2	59.2	71.7	85.5	99.5	96.8	113.8	117.2	122.0	147.8	150.8	159.2	49. Caoutchouc

Pour les sources et les notes, se reporter à la fin du tableau.

2.2 Annual and quarterly indices of free-market prices of selected primary commodities *(concluded)*
1990 = 100

Product	Level [1] Niveau [1] 1990	1980	1985	1995	1996	1997	1998	1999	2000	2001	2002	2003
Minerals, ores and metals	–	**94.9**	**67.5**	**100.7**	**88.2**	**88.7**	**74.1**	**72.9**	**81.7**	**73.9**	**72.3**	**81.0**
50. Phosphate rock	40.5	106.2	82.7	86.4	93.8	101.2	103.7	108.4	108.0	103.1	99.7	93.8
51. Manganese ore	396.3	41.3	35.0	51.5	53.4	51.9	51.4	48.1	46.9	50.1	50.1	50.1
52. Iron ore [10]	30.8	91.3	86.2	87.5	92.8	93.8	96.4	87.5	89.8	93.9	92.9	100.8
53. Iron ore* [10]	30.2	86.2	87.8	88.6	93.9	96.1	98.4	90.9	91.0	94.9	94.2	99.9
54. Aluminium	1639.5	105.4	65.9	110.1	91.8	97.6	82.8	83.0	94.5	88.1	82.3	87.3
55. Copper	2660.8	81.7	53.3	110.3	86.2	85.5	62.1	59.1	68.1	59.3	58.6	66.9
56. Copper* [2]	121.8	83.3	53.8	112.9	90.1	86.2	63.0	61.2	71.3	62.0	61.1	68.9
57. Nickel*	8864.1	73.6	55.3	92.8	84.6	78.2	52.2	67.8	97.4	67.1	76.4	108.6
58. Nickel [2]	407.3	75.6	55.6	95.8	87.7	78.7	52.7	67.5	97.7	67.4	76.0	109.2
59. Lead	810.6	111.9	48.2	77.8	95.5	77.0	65.2	62.0	56.0	58.7	55.9	63.6
60. Lead* [2]	45.1	94.2	42.3	93.1	107.9	103.3	100.4	97.0	96.7	96.8	96.7	97.1
61. Zinc	1518.9	50.1	49.7	67.9	67.5	86.7	67.4	70.9	74.3	58.3	51.3	54.5
62. Zinc* [2]	74.6	50.2	54.1	71.5	69.7	86.3	68.6	71.7	74.6	58.9	51.8	54.5
63. Tin	6235.0	269.2	193.3	99.6	98.8	90.5	88.8	86.6	87.1	71.9	65.1	78.5
64. Tin*	6084.3	269.6	196.0	100.0	100.2	90.9	88.3	87.2	88.5	72.4	66.3	80.4
65. Tungsten [11]	46.4	311.2	146.0	136.6	112.1	101.7	95.2	86.3	96.8	140.8	82.0	96.8
66. Gold* [12]	383.5	159.7	82.7	100.2	101.1	86.3	76.7	72.7	72.8	70.7	80.8	94.8
67. Silver* [13]	482.0	426.9	127.4	107.7	107.6	101.5	114.8	108.9	103.7	91.0	96.0	101.9
MEMO ITEM:												
68. Crude petroleum [14]	22.0	160.9	122.4	76.7	92.6	87.0	59.3	82.3	128.0	111.0	113.2	131.1
69. Manufactures export unit value	100.0	73.0	63.9	109.7	106.2	98.7	98.5	94.2	89.8	88.0	88.8	96.9

Sources: The prices used in the calculation of the indices shown in this table are extracted from the UNCTAD *Commodity Price Bulletin* and its *Monthly Updates*.

Notes: The group indices have been initially based on 1985 and include all commodities shown except for those with an asterisk (*).
For the group indices based on 1985, please refer to the *UNCTAD Handbook of Statistics 2004 on CD-ROM.*
The average annual indices are calculated from monthly data and may not correspond to the average from quarterly data.

1   Dollars per metric ton (if not indicated otherwise)
2   Cents per pound
3   Cents per kilogram
4   1993 level
5   Dollars per 100 kilograms
6   1996 level
7   1991 level
8   Dollars per cubic meter
9   Cents per sheet
10 Cents per Fe unit
11 Dollars per metric ton unit of WO_3
12 Dollars per troy ounce
13 Cents per troy ounce
14 Dollars per barrel

For specifications, see next page.

2001		2002				2003				2004		Produit
III	IV	I	II	III	IV	I	II	III	IV	I	II	
70.6	**68.5**	**72.1**	**73.4**	**71.2**	**72.4**	**77.1**	**76.8**	**80.6**	**89.6**	**107.7**	**108.5**	**Minéraux, minerais et métaux**
101.2	101.2	101.2	101.2	101.2	95.1	93.8	93.8	93.8	93.8	95.7	101.6	50. Phosphate brut
50.1	50.1	50.1	50.1	50.1	50.1	50.1	50.1	50.1	50.1	50.1	50.1	51. Minerai de manganèse
93.9	93.9	92.9	92.9	92.9	92.9	100.8	100.8	100.8	100.8	118.3	118.3	52. Minerai de fer [10]
95.9	95.9	95.9	93.6	93.6	93.6	93.6	102.0	102.0	102.0	102.0	121.0	53. Minerai de fer* [10]
84.1	80.4	84.2	82.7	79.9	82.5	85.2	84.2	87.6	92.3	100.6	102.3	54. Aluminium
55.3	53.6	58.5	60.5	57.0	58.4	62.5	61.6	65.9	77.4	102.6	104.8	55. Cuivre
57.7	56.3	61.5	63.1	59.2	60.6	64.7	63.7	68.0	79.1	103.4	104.5	56. Cuivre* [2]
62.0	57.0	70.0	78.4	77.1	80.1	94.1	94.4	105.7	140.3	166.2	141.0	57. Nickel*
62.8	56.6	69.1	77.8	77.1	80.0	93.5	95.2	108.6	139.3	164.3	141.6	58. Nickel [2]
58.0	59.2	60.6	56.1	53.1	53.6	56.6	56.3	63.1	78.2	104.1	100.0	59. Plomb
96.8	96.9	96.9	96.7	96.5	96.6	96.7	96.7	97.1	97.9	109.6	119.2	60. Plomb* [2]
54.4	50.2	52.3	51.5	50.4	50.9	51.7	50.9	54.1	61.2	70.5	67.6	61. Zinc
55.3	50.9	52.6	51.9	51.1	51.6	52.0	51.1	54.0	60.9	71.1	69.4	62. Zinc* [2]
63.8	63.1	61.1	66.6	64.8	67.9	72.7	74.8	77.3	89.0	111.0	147.5	63. Etain
64.2	63.6	62.7	66.9	66.9	68.6	75.0	76.9	79.1	90.7	113.7	151.9	64. Etain*
145.5	117.2	81.8	80.4	83.0	83.0	90.1	98.9	99.1	99.1	101.0	116.7	65. Tungstène [11]
71.6	72.6	75.7	81.6	81.9	84.1	91.8	90.4	94.7	102.2	106.5	102.5	66. Or* [12]
88.9	89.3	93.5	98.9	97.5	94.2	97.4	95.7	104.4	109.9	139.3	130.4	67. Argent* [13]
												POUR MEMOIRE :
113.6	87.6	94.9	114.4	122.4	120.8	142.1	120.2	128.8	133.2	145.8	161.5	68. Pétrole brut [14]
88.3	85.6	85.6	87.4	90.1	91.0	93.7	97.3	97.3	100.0	103.6	103.6	69. Valeur unitaire des exportations d'articles manufacturés

Sources : Les prix utilisés pour le calcul des indices présentés dans ce tableau sont extraits du
Bulletin des prix des produits de base de la CNUCED ainsi que de ses *mises à jour mensuelles*.

Notes : Les indices relatifs aux groupes de produits ont été initialement basés sur 1985; ils
recouvrent tous les produits présentés à l'exception de ceux munis d'un astérisque (*).
Pour les indices des groupes basés sur 1985, veuillez vous référer au
Manuel de Statistiques 2004 de la CNUCED sur CD-ROM.
Les indices moyens annuels sont calculés sur la base de données mensuelles et peuvent
ne pas correspondre aux moyennes calculées sur la base des trimestres.

1 Dollars par tonne métrique (sauf mention spéciale)
2 Cents par livre
3 Cents par kilogramme
4 Niveau 1993
5 Dollars par 100 kilogrammes
6 Niveau 1996
7 Niveau 1991
8 Dollars par mètre cube
9 Cents par feuille
10 Cents par unité de Fe
11 Dollars par tonne métrique d'unité de WO_3
12 Dollars par once "troy"
13 Cents par once "troy"
14 Dollars par baril

Pour les spécifications, se reporter à la page suivante.

Specifications

Food

1. Wheat: Argentina, Trigo Pan Upriver, f.o.b.
2. Wheat: United States, No. 2, Hard Red Winter (ordinary), f.o.b. Gulf ports.
3. Maize: Argentina, Rosario, f.o.b., 1987=100.
4. Maize: United States, No. 3 yellow, f.o.b. Gulf ports. For historical series of US No. 3, please refer to c.i.f. Rotterdam in the CD Rom.
5. Rice: Thailand, white milled, 5% broken, f.o.b. Bangkok.
6. Sugar: Caribbean ports, f.o.b. bulk basis (I.S.A.).
7. Beef: Australia and New-Zealand, frozen and boneless, 85% visible lean, f.o.b. United States ports.
8. Bananas: Central America and Ecuador, fresh, f.o.b. United States ports.
9. Pepper: White Sarawak/Muntok, spot London. Prior to January 2003, Singapore.
10. Soybean meal: Hamburg, 44/45%, f.o.b. ex-mill.
11. Fish meal: Any origin, 64/65 %, cost and freight Hamburg.

Tropical beverages

12. Coffee: Colombian mild Arabicas, ex-dock New York (I.C.A.).
13. Coffee: Brazilian and other natural Arabicas, ex-dock New York (I.C.A.).
14. Coffee: Other mild Arabicas, ex-dock New York (I.C.A.).
15. Coffee: Robustas, ex-dock New York (I.C.A.).
16. Coffee: Composite indicator price 1976 (I.C.A.).
17. Cocoa: Average of daily prices, New York/London, 3-month futures (I.C.C.A.).
18. Tea: London auction prices (all tea). London auctions ceased on 29 June 1998.
19. Tea: Mombasa auction prices, Best Pekoe Fannings 1, 1993=100.

Vegetable oils and oilseeds

20. Soybeans: United States, No. 2 yellow, c.i.f. Rotterdam.
21. Soybean oil: Any origin, crude oil, Dutch, f.o.b. ex-mill.
22. Sunflower oil: European Union, f.o.b. N.W. European ports.
23. Groundnut oil: Any origin, c.i.f. Rotterdam.
24. Copra: Philippines/Indonesia, bulk, c.i.f. N.W. European ports.
25. Coconut oil: Philippines/Indonesia, c.i.f. Rotterdam.
26. Palm kernel oil: Malaysia, c.i.f. Rotterdam.
27. Palm oil: Indonesia/Malaysia, 5%, c.i.f. N.W. European ports.

Agricultural raw materials

28. Linseed oil: Any origin, ex-tank, c.i.f. Rotterdam.
29. Tobacco: Unmanufactured tobacco, US general import price.
30. Cotton: Sudan, Barakat, X4B, c.i.f. North Europe.
31. Cotton: United States, Memphis Territory, M 1-3/32", c.i.f. North Europe.
32. Cotton: United States; New Orleans/Texas, Middling 1", c.i.f. North Europe.
33. Cotton: Pakistan, Sind/Punjab, Afzal 1-1/32", c.i.f. North Europe.
34. Cotton: Cotton Outlook Index A, Middling 1-3/32", c.i.f. North Europe.
35. Cotton: Egypt, Giza 70, good + 3/8, f.o.b. Alexandria.
36. Wool: United Kingdom and Dominions, clean: 64's (dry-combed basis).
37. Wool: Australia, 19 microns, 1996=100.
38. Wool: United Kingdom and Dominions, clean: 48's (dry-combed basis).
39. Wool: Australia, 23 microns, 1996=100.
40. Jute: Bangladesh, B.W.D., f.o.b. Chittagong-Chalna/Mongla.
41. Sisal: Tanzania/Kenya, No. 2 & 3 long, c.i.f. European ports. Prior to 1997, c.i.f. London.
42. Sisal: Tanzania/Kenya, No. 3 & UG, c.i.f. European ports. Prior to 1997, c.i.f. London.
43. Hides: East Africa, 8/12 pounds.
44. Hides: US, Chicago packer's heavy native steers, wholesale dealer's price, f.o.b. shipping point.
45. Non-coniferous woods: United Kingdom, import price index 2000 = 100, dollar equivalent.
46. Tropical logs: Sapele, loyal and marchand, UK import price. Prior to June 2000, Cameroon f.o.b.
47. Tropical sawnwood: Malaysia, Dark Red Meranti, select and better, c.i.f. French ports.
48. Plywood: Southeast Asian, Lauan, 3-ply, Extra, 182 cm x 91 cm x 4 mm, wholesale price, spot Tokyo.
49. Rubber: Singapore, No. 1 RSS, f.o.b. in bales.

Minerals, ores and metals

50. Phosphate rock: Khouribga, 70-72% BPL, f.a.s. Casablanca.
51. Manganese ore: Metallurgical 48/50% Mn content, f.o.b. United Kingdom.
52. Iron ore: Brazilian to Europe, fines, C.V.R.D., f.o.b.
53. Iron ore: Australian to Japan, fines, Hamersley, f.o.b.
54. Aluminium: London Metal Exchange, high grade, cash.
55. Copper: London Metal Exchange, grade A, cash.
56. Copper: United States producer, wire bars, f.o.b. refinery.
57. Nickel: London Metal Exchange, cash.
58. Nickel: New York dealer, 4x4 cathodes, free market.

Spécifications

Produits alimentaires

1. Blé: Argentine, Trigo Pan Upriver, f.a.b.
2. Blé: Etats-Unis, Hard Red Winter, n° 2 (ordinaire), f.a.b. ports du Golfe.
3. Maïs: Argentine, Rosario, f.a.b., 1987=100.
4. Maïs: Etats-Unis, jaune n° 3, f.a.b. ports du Golfe. Voir CD Rom pour série chronologique E-U, n° 3 , c.a.f. Rotterdam.
5. Riz: Thaïlande, blanchi, 5% brisures, f.a.b. Bangkok.
6. Sucre: Ports des Caraïbes, f.a.b. en vrac (A.I.S.).
7. Viande de boeuf: Australie et Nouvelle-Zélande, désossée et congelée, maigres à 85% visibles, f.a.b. ports des Etats-Unis.
8. Bananes: Amérique centrale et Equateur, fraîches, f.a.b. ports des Etats-Unis.
9. Poivre: Sarawak blanc/Muntok, cours du disponible à Londres. Avant janvier 2003, Singapour.
10. Farine de soja: Hambourg, 44/45%, f.a.b. départ moulin.
11. Farine de poisson: Toutes origines, 64/65 %, coût et fret Hambourg.

Boissons tropicales

12. Café: Arabicas doux colombiens, ex-dock New York (A.I.C.).
13. Café: Brésilien et autres Arabicas naturels, ex-dock New York (A.I.C.).
14. Café: Autres Arabicas doux, ex-dock New York (A.I.C.).
15. Café: Robustas, ex-dock New York (A.I.C.).
16. Café: Prix indicatif composite de 1976 (A.I.C.).
17. Cacao: Moyenne des cours quotidiens New York/Londres, 3 mois à terme (A.I.C.C.).
18. Thé: Cours aux enchères à Londres (toutes catégories de thé). Les enchères de Londres ont cessé le 29 juin 1998.
19. Thé: Cours aux enchères à Mombasa, Best Pekoe Fannings 1, 1993=100.

Huiles végétales et graines oléagineuses

20. Fèves de soja: Etats-Unis, n° 2 jaune, c.a.f. Rotterdam.
21. Huile de soja: Toutes origines, huile brute, f.a.b. Pays-Bas, départ raffinerie.
22. Huile de tournesol: Union européenne, f.a.b. ports de l'Europe du Nord-Ouest.
23. Huile d'arachide: Toutes origines, c.a.f. Rotterdam.
24. Coprah: Philippines/Indonésie, en vrac, c.a.f. ports de l'Europe du Nord-Ouest.
25. Huile de coprah: Philippines/Indonésie, c.a.f. Rotterdam.
26. Huile de palmiste: Malaisie, c.a.f. Rotterdam.
27. Huile de palme: Indonésie/Malaisie, 5 %, c.a.f. ports de l'Europe du Nord-Ouest.

Matières premières d'origine agricole

28. Huile de lin: Toutes origines, cours du disponible, c.a.f. Rotterdam.
29. Tabac: Tabac non fabriqué, prix général à l'importation aux Etats-Unis.
30. Coton: Soudan, Barakat, classe X4B, c.a.f. Europe du Nord.
31. Coton: Etats-Unis, Territoire de Memphis , M 1-3/32", c.a.f. Europe du Nord.
32. Coton: Etats-Unis, La Nouvelle-Orléans/Texas, Middling 1", c.a.f. Europe du Nord.
33. Coton: Pakistan, Sind/Punjab, Afzal 1-1/32", c.a.f. Europe du Nord.
34. Coton: Indice A de "Cotton Outlook", Middling 1-3/32", c.a.f. Europe du Nord.
35. Coton: Egypte, Giza 70, good + 3/8, f.a.b. Alexandrie.
36. Laine: Royaume-Uni et dominions, laine de 64', lavée et peignée à sec.
37. Laine: Australie, 19 microns,1996=100.
38. Laine: Royaume-Uni et dominions, laine de 48', lavée et peignée à sec.
39. Laine: Australie, 23 microns,1996=100.
40. Jute: Bangladesh, B.W.D., f.a.b. Chittagong-Chalna/Mongla.
41. Sisal: Tanzanie/Kenya, n° 2 & 3 long, c.a.f. ports européens. Avant 1997, c.a.f. Londres.
42. Sisal: Tanzanie/Kenya, n° 3 & UG, c.a.f. ports européens. Avant 1997, c.a.f. Londres.
43. Peaux: Afrique de l'Est, 8/12 livres.
44. Peaux: Etats-Unis, bouvillons abattus à Chicago, prix de gros, f.a.b. point d'expédition.
45. Bois non conifères: Royaume-Uni, indice des prix à l'importation 2000 = 100, équivalent dollar.
46. Grumes tropicales: Sapelli, loyal et marchand, prix d'importation au Royaume-Uni. Avant juin 2000, Cameroun, f.a.b.
47. Grumes tropicales sciées: Malaisie, Meranti rouge foncé, select and better, c.a.f. ports français.
48. Contre-plaqué: Asie du Sud-Est, Lauan, 3-feuilles, extra, 182 cm x 91 cm x 4 mm, prix de gros, cours du disponible à Tokyo.
49. Caoutchouc: Singapour, n° 1 RSS, f.a.b. en balles.

Minéraux, minerais et métaux

50. Phosphate brut: Khouribga, 70-72% BPL, f.a.s. Casablanca.
51. Minerai de manganèse: 48/50% teneur en Mn, f.a.b. Royaume-Uni.
52. Minerai de fer: Brésilien vers l'Europe, minerai fin, C.V.R.D., f.a.b.
53. Minerai de fer: Australien vers le Japon, minerai fin, Hamersley, f.a.b.
54. Aluminium: Bourse des métaux de Londres, haute qualité, cours au comptant.
55. Cuivre: Bourse des métaux de Londres, grade A, comptant.
56. Cuivre: Producteur Etats-Unis, barres à fil, f.a.b. sortie d'usine.
57. Nickel: Bourse des métaux de Londres, cours au comptant.
58. Nickel: Prix du négociant à New York, cathodes 4x4, marché libre.

59. Lead: London Metal Exchange, settlement and cash seller's price in warehouse, excluding duty, range main United Kingdom ports; purity 99.97% Pb.

60. Lead: North America, producer price, refined.

61. Zinc: London Metal Exchange, cash settlement.

62. Zinc: North America, high grade, daily weighted average, delivered basis.

63. Tin: London Metal Exchange, high grade, cash.

64. Tin: Ex-smelter price Kuala Lumpur market.

65. Tungsten: wolframite and sheelite, c.i.f. European ports, basis minimum 65% WO_3. Prior to April 1992, Wolfram.

66. Gold: United Kingdom, 99.5% fine, London afternoon fixing, average of daily rates.

67. Silver: Handy & Harman, 99.9% grade refined, average of daily quotations, New York.

MEMO ITEM:

68. Crude petroleum: Average of Dubai, United Kingdom Brent and West Texas crude prices, reflecting relatively equal consumption of medium, light and heavy crudes worldwide.

69. Manufactures export unit value: Developed economies, sections 5-8 of the Standard International Trade Classification (SITC), Revision 2, 1990 = 100.

59. Plomb: Bourse des métaux de Londres, prix vendeur, à terme et au comptant, à l'entrepôt, droits non acquittés, principaux ports du Royaume-Uni; pureté: 99,97% Pb.

60. Plomb: Amérique du Nord, prix des producteurs, raffiné.

61. Zinc: Bourse des métaux de Londres, cours de vente au comptant.

62. Zinc: Amérique du Nord, haute qualité, moyenne pondérée des prix journaliers à la livraison.

63. Etain: Bourse des métaux de Londres, haute qualité, cours au comptant.

64. Etain: Prix départ fonderie, marché de Kuala Lumpur.

65. Tungstène: wolframite et scheelite, c.a.f. ports européens, minimum 65% de WO_3. Avant avril 1992, Wolfram.

66. Or: Royaume-Uni, 99,5% fin, cotation de l'après-midi à Londres, moyenne des taux journaliers.

67. Argent: Handy & Harman, 99,9% raffiné, moyenne des cotations journalières à New York.

POUR MEMOIRE :

68. Pétrole brut: moyenne des prix du Dubaï, brent du Royaume-Uni et du Texas de l'Ouest, correspondant aux parts relatives de la consommation mondiale du brut moyen, léger et lourd.

69. Valeur unitaire des exportations de produits manufacturés: Economies développées, sections 5 à 8 de la Classification type pour le commerce international (CTCI), révision 2, 1990 = 100.

PART THREE

Structure of international trade by region

TROISIEME PARTIE

Structure du commerce international par régions

1

2

3

4

5

6

7

8

Origin / Origine	Year / Année	World [1] (millions of dollars) Monde [1] (millions de dollars)	Developed economies / Economies développées						South-East Europe and CIS / Europe du Sud-Est et CEI	Developing economies / Economies en développement					
			Total	Europe		USA and Canada / Etats-Unis et Canada	Japan / Japon	Other / Autres		Total	of which: dont : OPEC / OPEP	America / Amérique	Africa / Afrique	West Asia / Asie occidentale	Other Asia / Autres pays d'Asie
				Total	EU UE										
			Percentage / En pourcentage												
Afghanistan	1990	131	79.4	73.8	69.0	3.9	1.5	0.3	0.1	20.5	2.8	0.6	0.3	4.9	14.7
	1995	166	25.8	21.8	20.6	3.4	0.6	0.1	49.1	25.0	0.4	0.1	0.2	0.8	23.9
	2000	143	37.8	35.2	35.0	2.1	0.3	0.1	5.7	56.5	0.9	4.6	0.6	1.8	49.5
	2003	218	54.2	26.9	26.7	26.4	0.8	0.1	4.0	41.8	2.5	2.1	2.9	1.7	35.1
Albania - Albanie	1990	224	68.5	63.5	62.3	1.0	4.0	0.0	16.2	15.2	0.1	0.2	4.9	0.3	9.9
	1995	202	86.7	82.7	81.6	3.4	0.7	..	5.8	7.4	0.1	0.1	0.1	6.2	1.0
	2000	260	94.8	93.8	93.6	0.9	0.1	0.0	4.4	0.7	0.0	..	..	0.7	0.0
	2003	418	93.8	89.2	89.0	1.3	0.1	3.2	4.6	1.6	0.1	0.5	0.0	1.0	0.1
Algeria - Algérie	1990	11009	90.8	70.2	70.2	19.6	0.9	0.0	2.3	7.0	0.2	2.1	2.5	1.8	0.5
	1995	9357	86.8	67.1	65.7	19.1	0.7	..	2.4	10.8	0.0	2.8	2.5	3.5	2.0
	2000	20540	88.5	67.9	67.5	20.5	0.1	..	0.2	11.3	0.3	8.7	1.5	0.2	0.8
	2003	24944	85.7	59.9	59.9	25.6	0.2	0.0	0.3	14.0	1.0	4.8	2.2	4.9	2.2
American Samoa - Samoa américaines	1990	10	37.6	..	..	2.5	23.6	11.5	0.1	62.3	..	1.2	1.8	..	3.4
	1995	8	54.2	0.5	0.5	6.1	27.9	19.8	0.0	45.7	..	0.6	0.0	..	30.5
	2000	6	41.2	1.3	1.3	2.0	9.9	28.0	0.2	58.5	..	0.2	0.6	..	21.7
	2003	10	59.5	4.6	4.6	14.6	22.9	17.4	0.0	40.5	..	0.1	0.2	..	10.6
Angola	1990	3748	90.0	36.4	36.4	52.2	1.3	0.0	5.6	4.4	0.0	3.9	0.5	0.0	0.0
	1995	3412	85.9	21.6	21.6	64.0	0.4	0.0	..	14.1	0.0	3.2	0.6	0.0	10.3
	2000	7209	63.7	17.7	17.7	46.0	0.0	0.0	0.0	36.3	0.0	2.5	0.6	0.0	33.2
	2003	8522	62.5	13.5	13.5	48.1	0.9	0.0	0.0	37.5	1.0	1.7	0.8	0.0	35.1
Antigua and Barbuda - Antigua-et-Barbuda	1990	32	77.5	65.5	65.5	12.0	..	..	1.0	21.5	0.7	10.5	4.3	..	6.7
	1995	47	51.2	26.6	23.0	24.7	..	0.0	0.3	48.5	0.3	45.0	2.2	0.0	1.2
	2000	122	68.3	61.0	60.8	7.3	..	0.0	0.0	31.7	0.9	7.3	0.4	0.1	23.9
	2003	360	96.0	92.4	92.3	3.6	0.0	0.0	0.0	3.9	0.1	3.3	0.1	0.3	0.2
Argentina - Argentine	1990	12353	51.0	32.3	31.7	14.4	3.2	1.1	5.1	43.8	7.1	27.6	3.2	6.1	7.0
	1995	20363	32.9	22.5	21.4	7.7	2.1	0.6	0.5	66.0	5.5	46.6	4.4	3.5	10.1
	2000	26341	33.6	18.4	18.1	13.0	1.4	0.7	0.5	64.2	3.8	48.1	4.0	3.3	8.7
	2003	32061	33.0	20.5	20.3	10.6	1.2	0.7	0.9	65.2	3.6	40.9	4.8	3.8	15.7
Armenia - Arménie	1995	357	23.3	23.2	22.3	0.2	..	..	47.6	13.6	9.9	..	2.5	11.1	0.0
	2000	300	52.5	39.5	36.5	12.9	0.1	0.0	24.3	12.8	11.8	..	0.0	12.5	0.3
	2003	552	67.0	46.9	45.8	6.7	0.4	13.1	21.7	10.9	8.5	0.3	0.0	8.5	1.2
Aruba	1995	15	42.5	21.2	21.1	21.3	0.0	0.0	..	55.2	5.2	55.1	..	0.0	0.0
	2000	173	38.1	32.3	32.3	5.8	0.0	0.0	..	61.3	7.2	61.2	0.1	0.0	0.0
	2003	84	48.1	38.1	38.1	8.9	0.0	1.1	0.0	50.9	11.2	50.6	0.1	0.1	0.0
Australia - Australie	1990	38965	60.0	16.0	13.8	12.7	26.3	5.1	1.2	36.5	5.6	1.0	1.5	3.9	27.6
	1995	52977	50.3	11.9	11.2	8.0	23.0	7.4	0.4	47.2	5.1	1.1	1.4	2.6	39.5
	2000	63128	49.2	11.0	10.7	11.2	19.9	6.1	0.3	49.4	6.6	1.3	2.4	4.7	38.3
	2003	70783	50.4	14.1	13.8	10.2	18.1	7.6	0.4	47.7	7.2	1.3	2.2	5.3	36.8
Austria - Autriche	1990	41392	86.8	80.6	72.8	3.9	1.6	0.6	5.4	7.9	2.7	0.7	1.6	2.4	3.1
	1995	57532	88.5	82.8	76.5	3.6	1.3	0.7	3.7	7.8	1.7	1.0	1.2	1.7	3.9
	2000	67455	88.6	80.9	73.8	5.7	1.3	0.7	4.1	7.3	1.3	1.1	1.1	1.6	3.5
	2003	95784	86.7	79.2	73.7	5.6	1.1	0.8	5.8	7.2	1.4	0.8	1.0	2.0	3.4
Azerbaijan - Azerbaïdjan	1995	547	24.7	24.4	19.0	0.2	..	0.2	39.6	35.7	30.1	..	..	35.2	0.5
	2000	1745	76.3	68.0	63.1	0.5	0.0	7.7	14.8	8.9	1.2	0.4	0.6	6.9	0.9
	2003	1973	72.3	71.5	70.2	0.6	0.1	0.0	17.9	9.9	2.1	0.2	0.3	7.3	2.0
Bahamas	1990	990	96.3	41.0	29.8	53.3	1.4	0.7	0.0	3.2	0.0	2.2	0.4	..	0.5
	1995	596	80.3	50.7	40.0	28.1	0.8	0.7	1.4	17.0	2.4	3.9	3.5	0.0	9.3
	2000	864	92.1	57.9	52.2	30.4	3.3	0.5	0.4	7.3	0.0	6.4	0.3	0.2	0.4
	2003	1155	83.4	40.7	36.4	42.3	0.0	0.2	0.4	16.0	..	11.4	0.5	0.2	3.9
Bahrain - Bahreïn	1990	3836	5.4	1.6	1.6	1.9	1.8	0.0	..	11.0	5.8	0.9	0.2	5.9	3.9
	1995	4162	9.9	3.2	3.1	3.2	3.4	0.1	0.0	27.9	12.0	0.1	0.4	12.6	14.8
	2000	7574	12.8	5.3	5.0	4.2	2.8	0.5	0.0	24.0	5.6	0.1	3.0	6.4	14.5
	2003	10349	9.6	4.0	3.9	3.6	1.2	0.7	0.0	20.2	5.5	0.0	2.7	6.5	11.1

For sources and notes, see end of table 3.1B.

Pour les sources et les notes, se reporter à la fin du tableau 3.1B.

Origin / Origine	Year / Année	World[1] (millions of dollars) / Monde[1] (millions de dollars)	Developed economies / Economies développées					South-East Europe and CIS / Europe du Sud-Est et CEI	Developing economies / Economies en développement					
			Total	Europe		USA and Canada / Etats-Unis et Canada	Japan / Japon	Other / Autres		Total	of which: / dont: OPEC / OPEP	America / Amérique	Africa / Afrique	West Asia / Asie occidentale	Other Asia / Autres pays d'Asie
				Total	EU / UE										
									Percentage / En pourcentage						
Bangladesh	1990	1671	75.2	37.3	35.4	32.2	3.9	1.9	4.6	19.7	3.5	0.5	4.1	5.0	10.1
	1995	3129	83.3	45.4	44.8	34.0	3.3	0.6	1.0	15.4	2.0	0.7	2.3	3.4	9.0
	2000	5590	75.9	40.8	40.2	33.6	1.2	0.3	0.3	9.2	2.2	0.4	0.7	2.7	5.3
	2003	6324	75.7	48.1	47.4	26.6	0.9	0.2	0.1	8.7	1.4	0.4	0.9	2.1	5.3
Barbados - Barbade	1990	209	35.4	18.6	18.5	16.4	0.3	0.1	..	34.6	0.5	26.0	0.0	0.0	0.3
	1995	240	40.3	20.2	20.0	19.3	0.6	0.1	..	44.8	2.6	43.4	0.0	0.0	0.7
	2000	273	23.0	16.7	16.4	5.9	0.1	0.3	28.5	32.3	0.0	28.9	0.1	1.6	0.7
	2003	193	40.5	19.3	18.8	20.7	0.1	0.4	0.0	59.5	0.7	56.8	0.3	0.8	0.7
Belarus - Bélarus	1995	4641	30.3	28.9	28.5	1.4	0.0	0.1	63.6	6.1	0.7	0.1	2.2	1.1	2.7
	2000	7326	29.8	28.3	28.0	1.4	0.1	0.0	60.9	9.1	1.7	1.4	1.8	1.3	4.5
	2003	7802	27.4	24.4	24.3	2.9	0.1	0.0	64.7	7.2	0.6	1.5	0.8	1.3	3.4
Belgium - Belgique	2000	186596	88.8	79.0	77.1	6.3	1.2	2.3	1.0	10.2	1.3	1.3	1.9	2.1	5.0
	2003	250235	88.5	78.5	77.0	7.4	1.0	1.6	1.3	9.7	1.4	1.0	1.7	2.1	4.9
Belgium-Luxembourg - Belgique-Luxembourg	1990	117473	89.5	81.6	79.0	4.8	1.3	1.8	0.7	9.0	1.7	0.8	2.5	1.6	4.0
	1995	176563	83.7	76.7	74.6	3.8	1.2	2.0	1.0	9.5	1.3	1.3	1.9	1.5	4.8
Belize	1990	131	77.9	27.8	27.8	49.3	0.7	0.0	..	20.6	1.1	19.3	0.0	1.1	0.1
	1995	162	92.6	51.6	51.3	40.8	0.1	0.1	..	7.4	0.0	7.3	0.0	..	0.1
	2000	184	93.8	38.0	38.0	53.9	2.0	0.0	..	6.2	0.0	6.0	..	..	0.1
	2003	247	81.8	37.9	37.9	40.3	3.5	0.0	0.1	18.1	0.4	11.5	0.3	0.1	6.1
Benin - Bénin	1990	122	47.6	23.9	23.8	23.4	0.1	0.2	0.0	52.1	21.4	5.0	40.0	..	6.9
	1995	173	34.0	33.1	31.7	0.8	0.1	..	..	60.8	7.8	19.4	17.2	1.6	22.3
	2000	196	20.2	19.5	18.1	0.6	0.1	..	0.7	79.2	7.8	10.7	14.5	5.8	48.1
	2003	337	12.7	12.4	11.5	0.2	0.1	0.0	0.6	86.6	15.6	0.9	32.1	1.6	52.1
Bermuda - Bermudes	1990	60	98.7	33.2	33.2	65.5	..	..	..	0.4	..	0.4	..	..	0.0
	1995	63	55.9	6.2	6.2	49.7	..	..	..	0.0	..	0.0	..	0.0	..
	2000	800	91.3	84.4	78.5	6.2	0.1	0.6	0.1	2.4	0.4	1.0	0.5	0.3	0.6
	2003	1150	89.7	88.0	87.9	1.4	0.3	0.0	0.0	3.7	0.0	3.0	0.6	0.0	0.1
Bolivia - Bolivie	1990	923	51.6	31.2	29.1	20.0	0.3	0.0	2.2	46.2	0.4	45.3	0.0	0.1	0.5
	1995	1139	62.1	34.0	26.9	27.7	0.3	0.1	0.0	37.6	0.6	36.9	0.0	0.3	0.4
	2000	1475	53.1	28.2	17.1	24.5	0.2	0.2	0.0	45.7	3.6	44.5	0.1	0.1	1.0
	2003	1593	34.9	21.6	5.3	11.6	1.5	0.2	0.1	64.0	12.2	62.4	0.1	0.0	1.5
Bosnia and Herzegovina - Bosnie-Herzégovine	1995	52	80.1	71.8	71.2	6.4	0.0	1.9	17.4	2.4	..	1.5	0.7	0.2	0.0
	2000	669	79.8	76.6	76.3	2.7	0.1	0.4	16.0	4.2	0.3	0.1	2.5	1.1	0.6
	2003	1127	77.8	76.3	76.0	1.3	0.0	0.1	19.2	3.0	0.0	0.1	2.0	0.6	0.3
Brazil - Brésil	1990	31414	69.4	34.8	33.7	26.3	7.5	0.8	1.3	28.1	5.3	11.8	3.2	3.7	9.3
	1995	46605	56.9	29.5	28.4	19.9	6.7	0.9	1.7	40.6	4.6	23.0	3.4	3.2	10.9
	2000	59642	55.8	24.4	22.8	23.4	4.1	0.7	1.1	41.5	4.1	23.3	2.3	2.8	6.7
	2003	77113	54.8	26.5	25.4	24.2	3.4	0.7	2.6	41.0	5.4	19.1	4.0	3.8	13.6
Brunei Darussalam - Brunéi Darussalam	1990	2212	63.1	0.2	0.2	3.4	58.1	1.3	..	33.5	0.0	..	..	0.0	33.5
	1995	3388	59.4	0.8	0.8	2.1	55.6	0.9	..	40.5	0.4	..	..	..	40.5
	2000	3161	61.6	3.7	3.6	12.0	40.7	5.2	0.0	38.4	0.8	0.0	0.3	0.1	38.0
	2003	4067	64.7	2.3	2.2	10.0	40.8	11.5	..	35.3	2.6	0.0	0.5	0.1	34.7
Bulgaria - Bulgarie	1990	2032	58.4	53.6	51.6	2.8	1.6	0.4	17.6	24.0	6.0	0.7	5.4	8.6	9.3
	1995	5220	47.2	42.1	41.4	3.5	0.3	1.2	30.6	20.4	2.1	1.8	3.4	11.5	3.6
	2000	4760	61.9	50.0	48.9	4.6	0.4	0.7	18.6	16.6	1.5	0.9	1.6	12.2	1.9
	2003	7253	67.2	59.0	57.0	6.5	0.3	0.9	13.7	16.0	1.3	1.2	1.9	10.4	2.4
Burkina Faso	1990	152	53.9	52.5	41.8	0.1	1.3	..	..	45.4	0.9	..	22.6	..	22.8
	1995	164	47.9	44.2	28.5	0.4	3.2	0.0	..	51.9	5.6	1.0	33.3	0.0	17.7
	2000	167	40.2	35.7	35.6	1.8	2.7	0.0	0.5	57.4	2.1	10.0	13.5	1.9	30.7
	2003	242	22.5	18.7	18.3	0.4	3.5	0.0	0.1	75.4	1.7	5.5	17.5	1.4	49.5
Burundi	1990	75	55.6	43.2	43.0	11.8	0.5	..	..	10.2	..	..	8.7	0.9	0.7
	1995	104	49.8	49.6	38.5	0.2	0.0	..	..	13.0	0.1	..	12.6	0.3	0.1
	2000	49	66.6	60.7	35.8	0.7	0.3	..	..	17.2	0.2	..	17.0	0.2	0.0
	2003	43	69.9	54.7	52.0	14.7	0.4	0.1	1.3	25.8	0.2	0.0	19.2	0.3	6.3

For sources and notes, see end of table 3.1B.

Pour les sources et les notes, se reporter à la fin du tableau 3.1B.

Origin / Origine	Year / Année	World[1] (millions of dollars) / Monde[1] (millions de dollars)	Developed economies / Economies développées — Total	Europe Total	Europe EU / UE	USA and Canada / Etats-Unis et Canada	Japan / Japon	Other / Autres	South-East Europe and CIS / Europe du Sud-Est et CEI	Developing economies / Economies en développement — Total	of which / dont : OPEC / OPEP	America / Amérique	Africa / Afrique	West Asia / Asie occidentale	Other Asia / Autres pays d'Asie
										Percentage / En pourcentage					
Cambodia - Cambodge	1990	42	15.0	7.1	7.1	..	7.6	0.2	0.7	84.3	1.8	0.8	0.2	0.0	83.3
	1995	357	18.6	15.0	14.5	1.6	1.9	0.1	0.0	81.4	4.2	0.0	3.4	0.1	77.9
	2000	1123	88.4	21.0	20.6	66.3	1.0	0.2	0.0	10.7	0.2	0.1	0.0	0.0	10.6
	2003	2109	89.0	24.6	23.8	60.5	3.8	0.1	0.0	10.9	0.1	0.0	0.3	0.0	10.6
Cameroon - Cameroun	1990	2026	84.4	69.0	68.2	14.9	0.4	0.1	0.5	15.1	1.2	0.1	9.3	0.1	5.7
	1995	1659	79.4	76.4	76.4	2.2	0.8	0.0	0.0	18.5	0.6	0.9	8.4	0.4	8.8
	2000	1832	68.2	63.7	62.6	2.2	0.1	0.0	0.2	28.3	1.0	0.2	8.1	0.6	19.3
	2003	2240	71.6	63.9	63.9	7.6	0.1	0.0	0.2	26.3	1.4	2.7	12.8	1.0	9.8
Canada	1990	126447	91.3	9.5	8.4	75.4	5.6	0.8	0.8	7.8	1.2	1.7	0.8	0.7	4.6
	1995	190180	92.0	6.6	6.0	80.4	4.5	0.6	0.1	7.9	1.2	2.0	0.6	0.6	4.7
	2000	275183	94.9	4.9	4.6	87.4	2.2	0.4	0.1	5.0	0.8	1.5	0.4	0.4	2.7
	2003	271588	94.4	5.2	4.8	86.6	2.1	0.5	0.2	5.5	0.6	1.4	0.4	0.4	3.2
Cape Verde - Cap-Vert	1990	7	93.1	91.2	90.8	1.9	..	..	0.0	3.6	..	0.7	2.9	..	0.0
	1995	13	67.9	66.6	66.4	1.4	..	..	0.0	28.9	4.4	0.4	12.8	..	15.7
	2000	11	97.5	85.2	85.2	12.3	..	..	..	1.9	..	0.1	1.8	0.0	0.0
	2003	29	96.9	78.5	76.7	18.3	0.2	0.0	0.0	3.0	0.9	0.7	0.4	..	1.9
Central African Republic - République centrafricaine	1990	283	36.1	35.4	35.1	0.7	0.0	0.0	0.0	63.8	0.2	0.0	59.8	0.0	4.0
	1995	187	57.9	57.4	57.3	0.2	0.0	0.2	..	4.8	0.0	..	4.5	0.0	0.3
	2000	226	89.4	87.5	87.3	1.6	0.3	0.0	0.1	10.5	0.8	0.4	1.6	0.2	8.2
	2003	120	82.3	79.2	79.1	1.5	1.5	0.0	0.1	17.6	7.0	0.2	5.6	0.9	10.9
Chad - Tchad	1990	89	88.8	75.0	73.9	1.3	12.5	..	0.7	10.5	0.8	0.2	1.3	0.0	9.0
	1995	118	87.2	81.6	81.2	2.7	2.9	..	..	12.8	2.6	0.1	6.4	0.2	6.1
	2000	87	76.9	69.7	69.7	6.0	1.2	0.0	0.1	23.0	4.9	5.0	12.2	0.3	5.4
	2003	91	77.8	53.3	53.3	24.3	0.0	0.2	0.1	22.1	5.7	0.6	13.7	1.6	6.2
Chile - Chili	1990	8631	73.1	38.7	38.5	17.9	16.1	0.4	0.2	25.8	2.0	12.2	1.3	1.2	10.3
	1995	16538	61.1	28.0	27.1	15.1	17.6	0.5	0.1	36.7	2.5	18.8	0.8	0.9	16.1
	2000	19295	56.0	24.4	23.5	18.1	13.2	0.3	0.5	38.6	3.0	21.7	0.4	1.8	14.7
	2003	21464	52.5	23.3	22.8	18.1	10.5	0.6	0.5	41.0	2.0	18.2	0.5	1.4	20.8
China - Chine	1990	62760	35.7	11.0	10.7	9.2	14.7	0.8	3.7	59.8	2.5	1.2	2.1	2.2	54.1
	1995	148955	52.2	14.1	13.6	17.6	19.1	1.4	1.5	46.3	2.7	2.1	1.7	2.2	40.4
	2000	272115	58.4	16.5	16.0	24.2	15.8	1.9	1.2	40.4	3.1	2.6	1.8	2.3	33.7
	2003	438250	56.2	18.3	17.9	22.4	13.6	1.9	2.4	41.5	4.0	2.7	2.3	3.2	33.2
China, Hong Kong SAR - Chine, Hong Kong RAS	1990	82144	53.6	20.0	18.8	26.0	5.7	1.9	0.3	46.1	2.3	1.8	1.8	1.4	40.8
	1995	173556	47.4	16.1	15.3	23.3	6.1	1.8	0.2	52.3	1.9	2.8	1.5	1.4	46.6
	2000	201990	48.6	16.4	15.7	24.9	5.5	1.8	0.1	51.3	1.5	2.4	0.9	1.1	46.7
	2003	223874	41.5	14.4	13.7	20.0	5.4	1.7	0.2	58.3	1.5	1.4	0.7	1.2	54.9
China, Macao SAR - Chine, Macao RAS	1990	1690	81.0	38.6	37.4	37.8	3.1	1.6	0.1	18.9	0.2	0.3	0.4	0.2	18.1
	1995	1989	76.7	32.1	31.6	43.3	1.0	0.3	0.0	23.3	0.1	0.5	0.1	0.1	22.5
	2000	2532	79.5	28.8	28.1	49.9	0.6	0.2	0.0	19.9	0.0	0.5	0.0	0.1	19.2
	2003	2529	76.5	24.0	23.7	51.5	0.8	0.2	0.0	22.2	0.0	0.5	0.0	0.2	21.5
China, Taiwan Province of - Chine, Taiwan Province de	1990	66512	68.3	18.3	17.5	35.1	12.5	2.4	0.2	30.9	3.5	1.9	1.1	1.8	26.1
	1995	111812	52.7	13.9	13.4	25.0	11.8	2.1	0.2	46.4	3.0	2.4	1.5	1.7	40.8
	2000	148121	53.5	15.8	15.4	24.8	11.2	1.7	0.2	45.6	2.3	2.6	0.9	1.4	40.6
	2003	168198	42.8	13.9	13.6	19.4	7.7	1.7	0.4	56.1	1.5	2.8	0.8	1.4	50.9
Colombia - Colombie	1990	6753	79.5	29.6	28.9	45.6	3.8	0.5	0.6	18.2	3.3	17.2	0.1	0.2	0.7
	1995	9859	66.7	26.7	25.9	35.8	3.7	0.5	0.1	32.7	9.6	29.8	0.4	0.2	2.3
	2000	13164	67.7	14.1	13.9	51.5	1.8	0.3	0.5	30.9	10.0	29.4	0.2	0.1	1.2
	2003	13092	66.4	15.6	14.5	48.4	1.5	0.8	0.4	31.9	5.5	28.7	0.6	0.6	2.0
Comoros - Comores	1990	23	98.3	76.5	76.5	19.1	2.7	0.0	0.0	1.6	0.2	0.7	0.3	..	0.6
	1995	11	94.3	70.1	70.0	21.6	2.4	0.2	0.4	5.3	0.1	1.9	2.1	..	1.3
	2000	17	72.9	50.2	49.9	18.6	3.1	1.0	0.2	26.2	0.7	0.4	6.9	..	18.9
	2003	33	88.4	70.9	70.5	13.5	4.0	0.0	0.1	10.9	0.0	0.0	6.0	0.0	4.8

For sources and notes, see end of table 3.1B.

Pour les sources et les notes, se reporter à la fin du tableau 3.1B.

Origin / Origine	Year / Année	World (millions of dollars) / Monde (millions de dollars) [1]	Developed economies / Economies développées — Total	Europe Total	Europe EU / UE	USA and Canada / Etats-Unis et Canada	Japan / Japon	Other / Autres	South-East Europe and CIS / Europe du Sud-Est et CEI	Developing economies / Economies en développement — Total	of which: OPEC / dont: OPEP	America / Amérique	Africa / Afrique	West Asia / Asie occidentale	Other Asia / Autres pays d'Asie
Congo	1990	1209	93.7	64.2	53.7	29.5	0.1	..	0.1	2.9	0.1	0.0	2.8	0.1	0.0
	1995	842	72.1	49.2	48.4	22.6	0.4	0.0	..	24.3	0.1	0.0	3.0	0.2	21.2
	2000	2773	28.1	11.6	11.2	15.8	0.7	0.0	0.0	70.3	0.0	4.0	1.5	0.1	64.8
	2003	2732	27.8	12.2	12.1	15.2	0.4	0.0	0.0	69.8	0.1	3.2	2.9	0.1	63.6
Costa Rica	1990	1456	81.2	30.2	29.7	49.6	1.0	0.3	0.1	18.2	0.2	16.4	0.1	0.2	1.3
	1995	2702	74.7	31.8	31.0	41.4	1.0	0.5	1.2	24.0	0.6	21.0	0.2	0.2	2.4
	2000	5850	27.0	8.7	8.5	15.9	0.4	0.1	0.1	15.5	0.4	14.8	0.1	0.1	0.4
	2003	13033	49.4	21.2	20.5	26.6	1.4	0.1	0.1	22.0	0.2	13.4	0.0	0.2	8.4
Côte d'Ivoire	1990	2813	62.0	54.1	54.0	6.0	1.7	0.2	2.4	35.6	2.8	0.0	31.9	0.4	3.2
	1995	3729	68.9	63.5	63.4	4.4	0.5	0.5	2.2	28.1	3.1	0.6	22.7	0.7	4.1
	2000	3849	52.1	39.9	39.5	8.1	0.3	0.3	1.7	41.8	3.8	2.7	32.2	0.6	6.0
	2003	5486	64.7	54.1	54.0	7.3	0.2	0.4	0.0	32.2	4.9	0.9	24.8	0.8	5.5
Croatia - Croatie	1995	4632	79.8	77.3	75.9	2.1	0.0	0.4	14.0	6.2	1.0	1.0	3.3	1.0	0.9
	2000	4071	73.6	69.9	69.0	2.0	0.4	0.3	15.0	7.6	0.6	0.2	5.5	1.4	0.3
	2003	6054	72.5	67.7	66.9	2.4	1.2	0.5	18.6	4.1	0.8	0.1	2.3	0.9	0.5
Cuba	1990	1357	45.4	32.4	31.7	6.6	6.4	0.1	4.3	50.2	9.1	12.6	13.7	2.2	21.9
	1995	1499	50.5	29.1	28.5	15.6	5.7	0.2	18.7	30.8	5.7	6.5	9.2	1.4	13.7
	2000	1507	60.7	39.8	38.7	18.3	2.4	0.3	24.2	15.1	0.5	8.4	2.1	0.5	4.1
	2003	1521	59.7	40.2	38.8	17.5	1.7	0.2	14.6	25.8	3.5	10.7	3.1	3.0	8.9
Cyprus - Chypre	1990	945	56.4	53.0	51.9	1.8	0.5	1.2	6.1	27.6	8.3	0.9	4.8	20.0	1.8
	1995	1229	40.7	37.3	36.0	1.3	0.2	1.9	29.0	22.0	7.3	0.2	5.8	14.0	2.1
	2000	949	43.8	39.0	38.4	2.4	0.1	2.1	12.6	32.2	9.3	0.3	5.8	23.3	2.7
	2003	925	62.9	59.3	58.5	2.3	0.3	1.1	4.6	22.8	5.1	1.0	6.2	12.7	2.9
Czech Republic - République tchèque	1995	17178	84.4	81.3	79.4	2.1	0.5	0.4	6.5	5.8	0.6	0.6	1.1	1.5	2.6
	2000	28922	90.8	87.1	85.3	3.0	0.4	0.3	4.5	4.6	1.0	0.6	0.5	1.6	1.9
	2003	48494	91.6	88.4	86.6	2.6	0.3	0.3	4.2	4.2	1.0	0.4	0.5	1.6	1.7
Czechoslovakia (former) - Tchécoslovaquie (anc.)	1990	11654	55.9	53.6	50.9	1.2	0.8	0.4	32.4	11.7	2.4	1.5	2.1	3.4	4.7
Dem. Rep. of the Congo - Rép. dém. du Congo	1990	1353	86.5	65.4	65.2	18.7	2.4	0.0	0.3	13.2	0.0	0.2	7.7	0.4	4.8
	1995	1533	88.5	65.3	64.1	18.3	4.8	0.1	0.0	11.4	0.1	0.2	7.7	0.1	3.2
	2000	1128	97.4	76.6	76.3	19.2	1.5	0.0	0.1	2.5	0.0	0.0	1.8	0.0	0.4
	2003	1072	83.8	67.0	66.9	15.5	1.2	0.1	0.1	16.0	0.0	0.1	13.1	0.0	2.6
Denmark - Danemark	1990	34028	88.0	78.3	69.8	5.5	3.3	0.8	1.5	10.4	2.0	1.7	2.9	2.1	3.5
	1995	47493	85.9	76.4	67.7	4.6	4.0	1.0	2.2	11.9	1.8	2.5	1.9	2.0	5.4
	2000	50754	89.1	78.0	70.8	6.6	3.5	1.0	1.7	9.2	1.3	2.1	1.1	1.7	4.3
	2003	56673	86.4	73.5	64.2	7.5	3.8	1.5	2.1	11.2	1.6	2.3	1.3	2.2	5.2
Djibouti	1990	59	7.8	7.6	7.6	..	0.1	0.0	0.0	92.2	1.9	..	58.2	33.4	0.7
	1995	95	9.3	9.1	9.0	..	0.2	..	..	90.7	4.6	..	73.8	13.2	3.8
	2000	136	9.3	9.0	9.0	0.3	0.0	0.0	0.1	90.6	0.0	0.1	64.0	25.3	1.3
	2003	198	4.1	3.7	3.6	0.4	0.0	..	0.0	95.9	0.1	0.0	66.5	21.8	7.6
Dominica - Dominique	1990	55	68.0	56.9	56.9	11.0	0.0	0.0	0.2	31.8	0.0	31.0	..	..	..
	1995	47	52.7	44.8	44.8	7.8	0.0	..	..	47.3	0.0	44.8	..	..	..
	2000	54	39.6	32.1	32.1	7.5	0.0	..	..	60.3	0.0	57.1	0.0	..	0.0
	2003	62	40.1	24.6	24.6	8.9	6.6	0.1	0.5	59.1	0.3	53.7	0.1	0.0	2.5
Dominican Republic - République dominicaine	1990	744	89.0	19.4	19.4	67.6	2.0	0.0	1.0	9.1	0.1	3.5	0.5	..	4.6
	1995	3438	17.6	5.1	5.1	11.6	0.9	..	..	3.7	0.0	1.0	0.1	..	1.1
	2000	5737	94.5	6.3	6.0	88.0	0.2	0.0	0.0	5.5	0.1	4.1	0.1	0.0	1.1
	2003	4906	94.9	7.9	7.6	86.1	0.8	0.1	0.0	5.1	0.1	4.2	0.0	0.0	0.8
Ecuador - Equateur	1990	2714	62.0	10.8	10.8	48.8	1.9	0.5	0.8	36.8	0.7	17.4	0.5	..	3.5
	1995	4358	66.6	20.3	20.0	43.3	2.7	0.4	1.4	30.8	1.0	21.9	0.2	0.2	8.1
	2000	5602	62.3	16.4	16.0	41.2	4.2	0.5	3.6	33.6	2.0	25.3	0.7	0.7	7.3
	2003	6645	67.3	21.6	21.0	43.0	2.4	0.4	4.7	27.4	2.0	19.0	1.2	0.5	6.5

For sources and notes, see end of table 3.1B.

Pour les sources et les notes, se reporter à la fin du tableau 3.1B.

Destination / Origin Origine	Year Année	World [1] (millions of dollars) Monde [1] (millions de dollars)	Developed economies Economies développées — Total	Europe Total	Europe EU UE	USA and Canada Etats-Unis et Canada	Japan Japon	Other Autres	South-East Europe and CIS Europe du Sud-Est et CEI	Developing economies Economies en développement — Total	of which: dont: OPEC OPEP	America Amérique	Africa Afrique	West Asia Asie occidentale	Other Asia Autres pays d'Asie
										Percentage / En pourcentage					
Egypt - Egypte	1990	2585	61.4	43.3	42.4	8.8	2.7	6.5	18.1	18.9	7.4	0.0	3.7	8.4	6.8
	1995	3441	69.2	47.4	46.9	15.4	1.3	5.1	2.9	26.2	7.7	0.4	5.2	11.9	8.7
	2000	6287	64.3	48.5	48.3	13.3	2.1	0.5	0.9	25.1	7.4	0.9	3.3	11.4	9.5
	2003	8173	58.4	42.7	42.3	14.6	0.7	0.4	1.1	27.1	6.9	0.6	4.4	10.2	11.8
El Salvador	1990	586	64.8	28.6	28.5	35.0	1.1	0.2	..	34.9	0.1	34.7	0.0	0.0	0.2
	1995	985	51.7	31.2	30.9	19.0	1.5	0.0	0.0	48.3	1.1	47.6	0.0	0.0	0.6
	2000	1332	36.3	11.4	11.4	24.1	0.7	0.0	1.3	62.3	0.1	61.5	0.7	0.0	0.1
	2003	3285	64.1	5.3	5.1	58.4	0.4	0.0	0.7	35.1	0.1	34.0	0.0	0.0	1.0
Equatorial Guinea - Guinée équatoriale	1990	35	93.5	93.5	93.4	..	0.0	..	4.8	1.7	0.0	0.0	1.7	0.0	0.0
	1995	124	63.9	26.6	26.6	25.3	12.1	0.0	..	36.1	0.2	0.0	26.8	..	9.3
	2000	1033	76.6	59.0	59.0	13.8	3.8	..	0.0	23.4	0.0	0.8	1.9	0.1	20.7
	2003	2631	83.7	37.7	37.7	46.0	0.0	0.0	0.0	16.3	0.0	0.7	0.2	0.1	15.3
Estonia - Estonie	1995	1840	73.3	70.3	67.9	2.5	0.5	0.1	25.2	1.4	0.1	0.1	0.4	0.6	0.2
	2000	3830	86.8	84.2	81.0	2.1	0.3	0.1	9.7	3.5	0.3	0.6	0.7	0.3	1.7
	2003	5614	80.1	76.9	73.1	2.7	0.4	0.2	15.8	3.9	0.2	0.7	0.7	0.4	1.9
Ethiopia - Ethiopie	1990	294	67.4	41.2	41.2	11.2	14.9	0.1	4.2	26.1	10.2	2.5	12.7	10.2	0.7
	1995	430	71.5	51.4	50.9	6.9	12.7	0.5	0.5	27.9	9.4	..	12.6	10.1	5.1
	2000	516	60.0	40.9	40.1	5.9	10.5	2.7	0.5	38.1	8.6	0.0	16.6	7.6	13.8
	2003	605	48.7	32.9	31.9	5.8	6.8	3.2	0.5	49.0	7.6	0.0	18.1	10.5	20.3
Faeroe Islands - Iles Féroé	1990	381	98.8	94.8	93.4	4.1	..	0.0	1.1	0.0	..	0.0	0.0	..	0.0
	1995	320	99.3	97.0	90.6	2.3	..	0.0	0.0	0.6	..	0.3	0.0	..	0.3
	2000	394	98.7	93.1	87.4	5.7	..	..	0.0	1.1	0.0	0.0	0.5	0.0	0.6
	2003	493	97.5	92.9	83.5	4.6	..	..	0.4	2.0	0.0	0.0	0.5	0.0	1.4
Falkland Islands (Malvinas) - Iles Falkland (Malvinas)	1990	15	95.7	78.6	76.6	9.0	8.1	0.0	2.0	2.4	..	0.1	1.7	..	0.6
	1995	27	99.5	95.3	91.3	1.7	2.5	0.0	..	0.5	..	..	0.2	0.0	0.3
	2000	84	98.4	95.1	92.6	2.0	1.2	..	0.0	1.6	0.0	0.0	0.1	0.9	0.6
	2003	140	99.7	95.3	93.4	3.7	0.7	..	0.0	0.3	0.0	..	0.0	0.1	0.2
Fiji - Fidji	1990	498	69.2	23.3	23.3	10.6	5.9	29.3	..	5.4	..	..	..	..	5.4
	1995	618	74.4	24.5	24.5	14.7	5.9	29.3	0.0	21.9	0.0	0.0	0.0	0.0	11.4
	2000	675	71.9	16.8	16.8	21.6	4.2	29.2	0.0	21.5	0.3	0.0	0.0	0.0	8.4
	2003	720	67.1	15.3	15.3	23.8	4.8	23.2	0.0	23.4	0.3	0.0	0.0	0.0	4.8
Finland - Finlande	1990	26570	78.1	68.4	63.5	6.9	1.4	1.3	13.1	8.8	1.7	1.4	1.8	1.7	3.8
	1995	39572	78.3	66.3	61.9	7.5	2.6	2.0	5.5	15.1	2.4	2.6	1.6	1.9	9.0
	2000	45867	78.2	66.9	62.6	8.2	1.7	1.4	5.1	16.2	2.4	2.7	1.8	3.0	8.8
	2003	53000	76.1	63.6	59.9	9.3	2.1	1.1	8.6	15.8	4.1	1.9	1.6	4.8	7.5
France [2]	1990	216396	77.9	68.5	63.9	6.8	1.9	0.7	1.4	17.3	3.6	2.9	7.1	2.7	4.3
	1995	289339	77.3	68.1	63.8	6.4	1.9	0.9	1.1	19.5	3.1	3.6	6.1	2.7	6.8
	2000	323457	80.1	68.2	64.1	9.5	1.6	0.8	1.3	17.4	3.0	2.7	5.7	3.2	5.2
	2003	386394	79.2	69.1	65.4	7.5	1.6	1.0	2.0	17.5	4.1	2.3	5.6	4.0	5.0
French Guiana - Guyane française [2]	1990	85	79.9	76.1	75.5	3.2	0.6	..	..	20.1	..	19.3	0.8	..	..
	1995	158	84.3	83.2	77.6	1.1	..	..	..	15.7	..	15.5	0.3	..	..
French Polynesia - Polynésie française	1990	85	94.5	27.8	27.6	11.6	54.6	0.5	0.2	5.4	..	1.3	0.4	..	2.7
	1995	105	95.1	10.9	10.8	12.4	69.9	1.9	0.2	4.7	0.9	0.6	1.3	..	1.7
	2000	190	96.5	17.9	16.0	21.4	54.8	2.4	0.3	3.2	0.1	0.0	0.2	0.0	2.6
	2003	490	95.4	68.9	68.8	9.4	16.3	0.7	0.0	4.6	0.0	0.0	0.1	0.0	4.0
Gabon	1990	2483	82.1	47.4	45.8	29.5	4.1	1.2	0.6	16.9	0.9	9.9	4.7	..	2.4
	1995	2671	79.4	21.7	19.7	53.1	3.8	0.8	0.4	15.7	0.4	1.4	3.5	0.7	10.1
	2000	3764	76.6	23.1	23.0	52.9	0.3	0.3	0.0	18.2	0.1	2.3	1.7	0.3	13.8
	2003	3668	71.0	15.4	15.0	51.5	4.0	0.0	0.1	20.8	0.0	6.0	2.6	0.2	12.0
Gambia - Gambie	1990	172	89.4	54.8	52.5	0.0	34.6	0.0	0.7	9.3	0.1	0.1	6.8	0.0	2.5
	1995	28	62.9	59.0	58.8	3.1	0.9	..	..	37.1	0.7	0.0	26.8	0.3	10.1
	2000	39	81.0	71.1	71.1	1.4	8.4	0.0	0.9	18.1	0.1	7.3	3.9	0.1	6.8
	2003	18	48.2	46.1	45.9	0.4	1.6	0.0	1.4	50.4	0.1	0.2	8.2	0.6	41.4

For sources and notes, see end of table 3.1B.

Pour les sources et les notes, se reporter à la fin du tableau 3.1B.

Origin / Origine	Year / Année	World[1] (millions of dollars) / Monde[1] (millions de dollars)	Developed economies / Economies développées						South-East Europe and CIS / Europe du Sud-Est et CEI	Developing economies / Economies en développement					
			Total	Europe		USA and Canada / Etats-Unis et Canada	Japan / Japon	Other / Autres		Total	of which: / dont : OPEC / OPEP	America / Amérique	Africa / Afrique	West Asia / Asie occiden-tale	Other Asia / Autres pays d'Asie
				Total	EU / UE										
						Percentage / En pourcentage									
Georgia - Géorgie	1995	151	9.6	9.1	5.0	0.4	0.0	0.0	66.4	24.0	0.5	..	..	23.1	0.9
	2000	330	29.2	27.0	22.9	1.9	0.1	0.2	42.1	28.7	2.0	0.6	1.6	25.6	0.8
	2003	847	42.4	35.1	35.1	6.8	0.3	0.2	27.4	30.2	2.8	0.9	1.4	26.0	1.8
Germany - Allemagne	1990	409261	83.3	71.8	65.0	7.8	2.6	1.0	4.6	11.9	2.7	1.9	2.5	2.8	4.7
	1995	509171	80.9	69.0	62.6	8.1	2.6	1.3	3.0	16.0	2.3	2.6	2.2	2.9	8.2
	2000	548785	83.7	69.3	64.2	11.0	2.2	1.1	2.6	13.5	1.9	2.5	1.8	3.0	6.2
	2003	742020	81.7	68.8	64.1	10.0	1.8	1.1	3.9	14.2	2.1	2.0	1.8	3.3	7.1
Ghana	1990	1235	84.6	66.1	64.1	13.5	5.0	0.0	4.7	9.1	0.2	0.5	2.6	0.9	3.6
	1995	1488	77.8	60.2	58.3	13.0	4.3	0.2	1.1	16.5	4.0	0.5	7.4	1.2	7.5
	2000	1558	70.1	53.0	51.7	13.9	2.9	0.3	3.6	18.4	5.3	0.9	10.2	1.8	5.6
	2003	2009	64.1	52.7	51.4	6.0	5.2	0.2	3.9	22.6	4.7	2.7	12.1	2.4	5.4
Gibraltar	1990	49	84.7	83.8	83.3	0.6	..	0.3	0.4	14.8	0.2	0.2	1.6	0.2	12.8
	1995	86	83.8	78.3	38.2	5.2	0.0	0.3	0.7	15.5	0.4	0.5	6.6	0.4	8.1
	2000	104	89.3	86.1	64.7	1.9	1.0	0.3	7.7	3.0	0.0	1.2	1.0	0.0	0.8
	2003	291	88.5	86.7	70.4	0.9	0.0	0.9	9.9	1.6	0.0	0.6	0.5	0.1	0.3
Greece - Grèce	1990	8065	82.5	74.0	72.2	6.2	0.9	1.4	5.4	10.9	3.9	1.0	3.8	4.9	1.2
	1995	10961	75.2	69.3	67.2	3.6	0.8	1.6	12.3	12.2	2.4	1.6	2.6	5.6	2.4
	2000	10965	63.1	54.1	51.5	6.0	0.8	2.2	19.4	17.3	2.6	2.0	3.9	8.9	2.4
	2003	13193	65.6	56.3	55.0	7.1	0.6	1.6	20.1	13.5	2.8	0.7	3.2	6.8	2.7
Greenland - Groenland	1990	391	98.5	97.6	97.5	0.0	0.9	..	..	..	..	..	..	..	..
	1995	364	99.0	93.7	93.4	0.6	4.6	..	..	0.2	..	..	..	..	0.2
	2000	331	91.6	58.1	54.8	7.4	26.1	0.0	0.0	6.7	..	0.0	0.0	..	6.7
	2003	446	89.6	72.1	70.3	3.1	14.4	..	0.3	8.2	0.0	0.0	0.0	0.0	8.1
Grenada - Grenade	1990	21	68.9	56.2	56.2	9.6	3.2	0.0	..	31.1	..	30.6	..	0.5	..
	1995	23	64.1	32.9	32.9	31.1	..	..	..	35.9	..	35.4	..	0.1	0.1
	2000	77	80.5	30.3	30.3	50.2	..	..	..	19.1	..	16.2	..	..	..
	2003	47	55.9	38.2	36.8	17.2	0.4	0.1	0.1	43.1	0.0	36.9	0.3	0.0	0.7
Guadeloupe[2]	1990	122	81.6	81.4	81.3	0.2	..	..	..	18.4	0.1	18.4	0.0	..	0.0
	1995	97	80.7	79.3	79.2	1.4	..	..	..	19.0	10.4	6.5	1.8	10.4	0.3
Guam	1990	46	87.8	..	..	0.9	86.9	0.1	0.1	12.1	..	..	..	..	11.9
	1995	88	89.7	0.0	0.0	1.1	87.9	0.7	0.1	10.3	..	0.0	..	..	10.1
	2000	111	62.3	0.1	0.0	0.5	61.3	0.4	0.0	37.7	0.0	0.0	0.0	..	37.4
	2003	59	81.7	0.9	0.8	1.1	79.3	0.5	0.0	18.3	0.0	0.1	..	0.1	17.3
Guatemala	1990	1189	56.8	13.6	13.3	40.2	2.9	0.1	0.6	41.8	2.1	33.5	3.1	2.8	1.9
	1995	1936	51.6	16.2	15.9	32.4	2.8	0.2	0.0	48.0	3.1	39.8	0.7	1.7	5.5
	2000	4365	71.0	9.6	9.1	59.5	1.8	0.1	0.7	28.2	1.7	22.6	0.6	1.5	2.1
	2003	5162	64.5	5.8	5.4	57.5	1.2	0.1	1.4	33.9	1.7	25.3	0.9	1.5	4.4
Guinea - Guinée	1990	606	85.6	61.4	57.1	23.1	1.1	..	2.3	12.2	0.1	0.6	8.5	0.0	3.1
	1995	683	78.7	53.0	50.2	25.7	0.0	..	2.3	14.6	0.0	8.8	4.7	1.1	0.1
	2000	617	80.5	65.2	65.2	15.3	0.0	0.0	11.8	7.7	0.0	..	7.6	0.0	0.1
	2003	860	52.2	39.6	39.6	12.4	0.1	0.1	20.1	27.8	0.1	0.0	4.2	0.0	23.5
Guinea-Bissau - Guinée-Bissau	1990	34	56.1	55.5	55.5	0.3	0.4	0.0	2.0	41.9	0.4	..	4.4	..	37.5
	1995	94	56.4	56.0	56.0	0.0	0.5	0.0	0.4	43.1	1.4	..	1.7	..	41.5
	2000	111	4.2	3.8	3.8	0.4	0.0	..	0.0	95.8	0.0	46.6	0.8	0.0	48.4
	2003	122	10.7	9.1	9.1	1.6	0.1	..	0.0	89.3	..	23.7	1.2	..	64.5
Guyana	1990	232	83.6	48.7	48.5	28.5	6.3	0.1	2.1	14.1	2.0	13.6	0.3	0.0	0.2
	1995	525	81.5	33.7	33.6	46.1	1.4	0.3	0.1	18.2	0.5	16.5	0.3	0.0	1.3
	2000	597	76.9	29.1	29.1	46.9	0.7	0.1	4.2	18.5	0.7	14.9	0.4	0.1	3.1
	2003	584	78.7	32.2	32.1	45.9	0.5	0.1	0.4	20.4	0.7	18.2	0.6	0.1	1.6
Haiti - Haïti	1990	171	99.2	12.5	12.5	85.5	1.2	..	0.0	0.8	0.0	0.7	..	..	0.0
	1995	36	96.3	32.3	32.2	63.3	0.7	0.0	..	3.7	..	3.4	0.0	..	..
	2000	324	94.5	5.9	5.4	88.4	0.2	0.0	0.1	5.4	0.6	4.5	0.6	0.1	0.0
	2003	370	91.9	4.0	3.6	87.6	0.1	0.2	0.0	8.1	0.6	7.1	0.6	0.0	0.1

For sources and notes, see end of table 3.1B.

Pour les sources et les notes, se reporter à la fin du tableau 3.1B.

Destination / Origin / Origine	Year / Année	World[1] (millions of dollars) Monde[1] (millions de dollars)	Developed economies / Economies développées						South-East Europe and CIS / Europe du Sud-Est et CEI	Developing economies / Economies en développement					
			Total	Europe		USA and Canada / Etats-Unis et Canada	Japan / Japon	Other / Autres		Total	of which: dont : OPEC OPEP	America / Amérique	Africa / Afrique	West Asia / Asie occidentale	Other Asia / Autres pays d'Asie
				Total	EU UE										
									Percentage / En pourcentage						
Honduras	1990	812	79.6	21.8	21.8	53.1	4.8	..	..	6.4	..	3.9	..	..	..
	1995	1224	74.3	22.3	22.3	48.8	3.2	..	..	19.3	0.0	15.8	0.0	..	..
	2000	4156	82.0	8.9	8.6	70.5	2.6	0.0	0.0	12.3	0.0	7.2	0.0	0.1	0.6
	2003	4817	75.1	7.8	7.6	66.6	0.6	0.1	0.4	17.0	0.1	10.1	0.1	0.1	0.4
Hungary - Hongrie	1990	9593	58.9	53.4	51.3	3.8	1.2	0.5	27.2	9.7	2.8	0.8	1.8	3.3	3.8
	1995	12861	77.4	72.9	71.3	3.4	0.6	0.6	14.0	4.8	1.9	0.4	0.9	2.2	1.4
	2000	28087	89.0	82.8	81.4	5.4	0.6	0.3	6.9	4.1	0.4	0.6	0.4	1.2	1.9
	2003	39056	86.9	78.6	77.2	6.8	1.0	0.5	7.9	5.3	0.9	0.5	0.6	1.8	2.4
Iceland - Islande	1990	1591	94.8	78.4	71.1	10.2	6.0	0.2	2.6	2.4	0.7	0.4	0.7	0.2	1.1
	1995	1827	94.2	68.4	62.5	14.0	11.4	0.5	1.2	4.4	0.4	1.4	0.6	0.1	2.3
	2000	1896	96.0	76.4	68.7	14.0	5.3	0.3	0.6	3.4	0.8	0.4	1.1	0.1	1.9
	2003	2397	95.0	80.9	73.4	10.6	3.2	0.3	0.9	4.1	1.7	0.3	1.8	0.1	1.9
India - Inde	1990	17813	57.3	30.5	29.1	16.0	9.3	1.5	16.8	21.5	6.1	0.4	2.5	6.3	12.2
	1995	30537	55.8	28.6	27.5	18.3	7.0	1.9	3.8	36.4	8.9	1.2	4.9	8.3	22.0
	2000	42624	54.6	25.5	24.3	22.8	4.1	2.2	2.7	39.4	10.8	2.2	5.3	10.9	20.9
	2003	61559	52.0	24.5	23.6	22.0	3.2	2.4	1.7	42.9	8.2	3.0	4.8	8.4	26.5
Indonesia - Indonésie	1990	25675	70.5	12.4	12.3	13.6	42.5	1.9	0.4	29.1	2.7	0.4	0.7	2.7	25.2
	1995	45428	59.5	15.4	15.2	14.7	27.1	2.3	0.4	40.1	3.0	1.6	1.4	3.3	33.6
	2000	62103	54.7	14.6	14.3	14.3	23.2	2.6	0.3	45.0	3.0	1.7	1.8	3.3	38.1
	2003	60995	52.0	13.8	13.5	12.7	22.3	3.2	0.6	47.5	3.0	1.4	2.0	3.3	40.6
Iran, Islamic Rep. of - Iran, Rép. islamique d'	1990	19305	72.3	50.0	42.4	1.6	20.7	..	1.9	18.3	1.0	4.4	..	3.1	10.9
	1995	18360	61.7	42.0	41.2	4.6	15.1	0.1	4.0	33.9	5.0	1.5	6.0	9.3	17.1
	2000	25063	49.3	28.8	28.3	1.0	19.4	0.1	1.2	36.0	1.6	0.2	0.0	4.3	31.4
	2003	29455	48.4	24.6	24.2	0.7	23.0	0.2	1.2	34.4	1.6	0.1	1.3	5.4	27.6
Iraq	1990	10314	63.2	25.8	25.8	29.6	7.9	0.0	3.8	33.1	1.9	10.2	2.3	13.3	7.3
	1995	425	0.6	0.3	0.3	0.0	0.3	..	1.7	97.7	0.8	0.1	0.0	96.7	0.9
	2000	14426	82.2	34.3	34.3	43.2	4.2	0.5	0.6	17.2	0.2	2.1	0.4	4.3	10.3
	2003	9839	70.8	16.0	16.0	53.5	1.0	0.3	0.1	29.1	0.2	5.7	5.2	8.0	10.1
Ireland - Irlande	1990	23770	92.6	80.9	78.4	9.0	1.8	0.9	0.8	5.7	1.7	1.1	1.5	1.5	1.6
	1995	43594	89.4	76.3	73.3	9.1	3.0	0.9	1.0	7.2	1.4	1.0	1.6	1.4	3.1
	2000	76335	87.1	64.6	61.4	17.4	3.8	1.3	0.5	8.9	1.1	0.9	1.2	1.4	5.3
	2003	92822	91.0	66.2	62.3	21.1	2.6	1.1	0.5	7.8	0.8	1.0	1.0	1.0	4.8
Israel - Israël	1990	12005	77.4	39.5	36.8	29.6	7.3	1.0	0.6	13.6	0.9	2.6	1.4	0.7	8.9
	1995	19016	73.1	34.5	32.6	30.5	6.9	1.3	2.7	18.3	0.2	2.8	1.8	0.9	12.7
	2000	31910	71.3	30.2	28.5	37.7	2.6	0.8	1.2	21.4	0.3	2.8	1.7	1.5	15.3
	2003	31690	70.1	28.3	26.6	38.7	2.0	1.0	2.2	21.9	0.2	4.2	1.7	1.7	14.1
Italy - Italie	1990	170437	81.6	69.5	64.5	8.5	2.3	1.3	3.6	14.4	4.0	2.1	4.5	3.5	4.3
	1995	232915	78.2	66.0	61.7	8.2	2.3	1.7	3.3	18.4	3.3	3.5	3.5	4.1	7.2
	2000	236561	78.2	63.6	59.8	11.3	1.7	1.6	3.8	17.5	3.3	3.9	3.5	4.4	5.6
	2003	292421	76.5	63.9	59.6	9.4	1.7	1.5	5.5	17.5	4.0	2.7	3.8	5.0	5.9
Jamaica - Jamaïque	1990	1133	82.0	42.1	31.8	39.0	0.7	0.2	4.4	13.2	0.0	8.1	4.7	0.0	0.1
	1995	1813	86.2	31.7	24.1	52.4	1.8	0.2	1.7	12.2	0.1	5.5	4.0	0.0	0.5
	2000	1307	90.0	40.2	31.4	47.4	2.3	0.1	0.0	10.0	0.6	6.0	1.6	0.5	1.0
	2003	1624	83.1	39.9	32.9	41.1	1.8	0.3	3.0	14.0	0.0	5.6	1.9	0.0	6.2
Japan - Japon	1990	287678	59.1	22.1	20.7	34.0	0.0	3.0	1.0	39.9	4.7	3.4	1.9	3.2	31.1
	1995	443047	48.2	16.9	16.1	28.9	0.0	2.4	0.3	51.5	3.9	4.2	1.7	1.9	43.6
	2000	478179	51.6	17.6	16.8	31.7	0.0	2.3	0.2	48.2	3.3	3.9	1.0	2.0	41.2
	2003	473911	45.5	16.5	15.9	26.3	0.0	2.7	0.5	54.0	3.9	3.2	1.2	2.8	46.2
Jordan - Jordanie	1990	922	6.9	4.1	4.1	0.6	2.1	0.0	3.6	89.5	38.8	0.2	8.1	41.1	40.2
	1995	1442	10.3	6.4	6.4	1.5	1.5	1.0	1.3	74.2	37.7	0.4	5.7	44.8	23.3
	2000	1284	16.2	4.0	4.0	5.0	1.0	6.2	0.5	81.0	36.0	0.4	8.7	39.4	32.5
	2003	3380	28.7	5.9	5.9	19.1	2.0	1.7	0.6	59.0	33.2	(suite)	5.5	38.4	15.1
Kazakhstan	1995	5256	32.2	30.5	26.6	0.9	0.9	0.0	55.0	12.8	1.0	1.2	0.4	2.3	9.0
	2000	9876	30.1	27.7	22.9	2.2	0.1	0.1	23.7	35.8	2.3	12.7	0.2	2.9	9.1
	2003	15147	37.6	34.0	27.6	2.5	0.9	0.1	24.2	36.8	6.4	17.2	0.3	7.2	12.1

For sources and notes, see end of table 3.1B.

Pour les sources et les notes, se reporter à la fin du tableau 3.1B.

58

Destination / Origin / Origine	Year / Année	World [1] (millions of dollars) / Monde [1] (millions de dollars)	Developed economies / Economies développées					South-East Europe and CIS / Europe du Sud-Est et CEI	Developing economies / Economies en développement					
			Total	Europe		USA and Canada / Etats-Unis et Canada	Japan / Japon	Other / Autres		Total	of which: dont: OPEC / OPEP	America / Amérique	Africa / Afrique	West Asia / Asie occidentale	Other Asia / Autres pays d'Asie
				Total	EU / UE										
			Percentage / En pourcentage												
Kenya	1990	1120	43.4	38.1	37.3	3.0	1.0	1.3	1.4	47.9	1.1	..	39.0	1.2	7.8
	1995	1826	41.8	36.9	35.7	3.4	0.7	0.8	0.1	57.2	1.7	0.1	45.3	2.3	9.5
	2000	1963	43.8	35.6	34.7	5.7	1.0	1.6	0.0	54.9	2.0	0.3	39.7	2.1	12.8
	2003	2747	42.7	31.4	30.6	9.2	0.8	1.4	0.5	55.4	2.2	0.3	41.3	2.3	11.5
Kiribati	1990	3	99.0	77.7	72.3	8.9	12.2	0.2	..	1.0	0.0	0.1	..	..	0.9
	1995	13	54.0	25.9	25.9	10.5	17.0	0.5	..	46.0	0.0	0.5	..	..	36.7
	2000	21	70.5	3.2	3.2	6.1	60.0	1.2	0.0	29.5	0.0	5.4	0.0	..	24.0
	2003	32	72.7	5.1	4.9	5.5	56.6	5.7	0.0	27.2	0.0	0.1	..	0.0	27.0
Korea, Dem. People's Rep. of - Corée, Rép. populaire dém. de	1990	924	43.4	14.0	13.9	0.0	29.4	0.0	2.9	53.7	6.9	3.6	10.8	7.8	31.4
	1995	829	52.1	15.1	15.0	0.1	36.9	0.1	2.0	45.8	10.0	8.9	4.7	6.7	25.4
	2000	919	39.1	13.9	13.7	0.0	24.8	0.3	2.7	58.2	1.1	28.3	3.4	3.5	22.8
	2003	1164	20.4	6.3	6.2	0.0	13.6	0.5	1.7	77.9	1.4	25.7	4.4	3.3	44.3
Korea, Republic of - Corée, République de	1990	67812	67.1	15.7	15.0	31.2	18.6	1.6	..	24.6	4.2	3.0	1.8	3.0	16.7
	1995	131312	48.6	14.0	13.3	19.9	13.0	1.7	1.7	44.7	5.0	5.4	2.3	3.2	33.7
	2000	171826	52.4	15.0	14.4	23.4	11.9	2.1	0.9	46.7	5.6	5.3	1.9	4.1	35.0
	2003	194862	44.7	14.5	13.9	19.8	8.4	2.2	1.2	54.5	4.5	6.2	2.4	4.0	41.3
Kuwait - Koweït	1990	8182	51.0	24.0	23.9	7.0	19.0	1.0	0.5	45.0	5.4	1.9	3.0	6.9	31.2
	1995	12944	0.6	0.2	0.2	0.3	0.1	0.0	0.0	5.0	1.7	0.0	0.4	2.2	2.5
	2000	18824	52.8	13.8	13.8	14.3	24.0	0.6	0.0	47.2	4.9	0.5	1.4	2.8	42.5
	2003	18823	45.4	10.4	10.4	12.1	22.0	0.8	0.0	54.6	4.6	0.2	2.3	2.8	49.3
Kyrgyzstan - Kirghizistan	1995	483	16.8	16.4	16.4	0.5	..	..	77.9	5.3	0.7	..	..	4.7	0.6
	2000	504	44.8	44.1	37.3	0.6	0.1	..	41.4	13.8	1.7	..	0.4	3.1	10.4
	2003	582	32.1	25.6	5.4	6.4	0.0	0.0	35.2	32.7	25.2	0.0	0.0	27.2	5.5
Lao People's Dem. Rep. - Rép. dém. populaire lao	1990	64	19.8	11.1	9.9	1.6	7.1	0.1	..	80.2	0.0	0.7	1.0	0.0	78.4
	1995	311	14.5	11.1	10.9	1.7	1.7	..	0.4	59.4	..	..	..	..	59.4
	2000	390	33.5	27.9	26.3	2.6	2.8	0.1	0.0	45.4	0.4	0.0	0.1	0.2	45.1
	2003	455	31.7	28.3	27.3	1.8	1.5	0.1	0.1	40.9	0.7	0.1	0.1	0.1	40.5
Latvia - Lettonie	1995	1284	60.6	58.9	56.6	1.4	0.3	0.1	38.3	1.1	0.1	0.1	0.3	0.4	0.4
	2000	1865	87.6	82.2	80.7	4.8	0.4	0.2	8.7	3.4	1.2	0.3	2.3	0.5	0.2
	2003	3674	87.1	76.1	73.9	10.2	0.7	0.1	8.1	4.6	1.7	1.0	2.3	0.4	0.8
Lebanon - Liban	1990	456	45.9	39.0	27.7	5.5	0.9	0.5	1.4	52.8	35.6	0.1	9.4	41.3	2.0
	1995	716	34.0	28.5	25.2	3.7	1.1	0.7	5.6	58.0	35.2	0.7	8.4	45.7	3.3
	2000	714	39.3	30.1	22.9	7.9	0.8	0.5	0.6	59.3	32.8	0.6	10.8	43.3	4.6
	2003	1155	37.5	28.4	18.9	8.2	0.4	0.6	2.0	59.8	33.0	0.8	11.3	40.9	6.8
Liberia - Libéria	1990	1943	86.4	83.7	41.8	2.6	0.0	0.1	0.2	13.4	0.0	1.0	0.2	0.0	12.2
	1995	955	81.2	80.2	79.8	1.0	0.0	0.0	8.5	10.3	0.0	0.4	2.7	0.7	6.6
	2000	581	77.4	69.9	61.1	7.4	0.0	0.0	1.6	21.0	0.6	2.6	3.6	2.2	12.7
	2003	1029	85.4	79.6	76.5	5.7	0.0	0.0	0.2	14.5	0.1	0.1	2.5	2.0	10.0
Libyan Arab Jamahiriya - Jamahiriya arabe libyenne	1990	13878	84.8	84.8	84.7	0.0	0.0	..	7.6	7.6	0.2	0.1	3.3	4.0	0.2
	1995	8510	84.9	84.9	81.8	0.0	0.0	0.0	2.0	13.0	0.5	0.1	6.1	4.4	2.4
	2000	12696	88.5	88.4	85.6	0.0	0.1	..	1.5	10.0	0.1	0.3	3.2	5.9	0.6
	2003	13667	86.0	85.9	82.8	0.0	0.0	0.0	1.5	12.5	0.5	0.3	4.0	7.0	1.2
Lithuania - Lituanie	1995	2706	54.7	53.7	50.5	0.8	0.1	0.0	42.9	2.5	0.1	0.3	0.1	1.0	1.0
	2000	3810	80.2	74.6	72.1	5.2	0.3	0.1	16.5	3.2	0.1	0.5	0.1	1.8	0.7
	2003	7161	79.3	75.4	61.4	3.2	0.6	0.1	17.4	3.2	0.1	0.1	0.4	1.7	1.0
Luxembourg	2000	8245	94.8	89.0	86.5	4.7	0.7	0.5	0.6	4.5	0.6	0.8	0.9	0.9	1.9
	2003	13342	92.8	90.0	87.7	2.2	0.4	0.3	0.8	4.6	0.9	0.5	0.7	0.9	2.4
Macedonia, TFYR - Macédoine, LERY	1995	1203	48.8	45.6	42.7	3.0	0.1	0.1	44.3	6.9	0.3	0.0	1.0	3.6	2.3
	2000	986	84.7	66.6	62.6	17.6	0.2	0.3	12.5	2.5	0.9	0.1	0.7	1.6	0.2
	2003	962	80.1	73.3	72.4	6.3	0.3	0.2	15.7	4.1	0.5	0.2	0.7	1.8	1.4
Madagascar	1990	366	82.9	47.9	47.0	29.5	5.5	0.1	0.7	16.3	0.0	0.2	10.0	0.0	6.1
	1995	342	78.2	64.8	62.5	6.9	6.4	0.1	0.2	21.4	1.9	0.2	15.6	0.3	5.1
	2000	806	82.5	59.8	59.5	19.7	2.8	0.1	0.0	12.5	0.8	0.1	3.3	0.1	9.0
	2003	1041	91.0	51.8	51.6	36.3	2.8	0.1	0.0	7.7	0.1	0.0	2.7	0.1	4.9

For sources and notes, see end of table 3.1B.

Pour les sources et les notes, se reporter à la fin du tableau 3.1B.

Origin / Origine	Year / Année	World¹ (millions of dollars) Monde¹ (millions de dollars)	Developed economies / Economies développées — Total	Europe — Total	Europe — EU / UE	USA and Canada / Etats-Unis et Canada	Japan / Japon	Other / Autres	South-East Europe and CIS / Europe du Sud-Est et CEI	Developing economies / Economies en développement — Total	of which: OPEC / dont: OPEP	America / Amérique	Africa / Afrique	West Asia / Asie occidentale	Other Asia / Autres pays d'Asie
			Percentage / En pourcentage												
Malawi	1990	419	76.6	50.6	48.4	11.7	12.8	1.6	..	19.6	..	..	16.8	0.2	2.6
	1995	421	77.3	56.5	52.0	13.7	5.2	1.9	1.3	21.2	0.0	1.4	17.0	0.4	2.2
	2000	422	61.8	36.3	34.9	13.3	11.0	1.2	3.9	34.0	0.0	0.6	26.2	2.9	4.0
	2003	576	57.8	38.6	37.5	13.3	4.4	1.6	5.6	36.3	0.6	0.4	32.4	1.0	2.2
Malaysia - Malaisie	1990	29420	50.8	15.8	15.6	17.7	15.3	1.9	0.8	48.4	2.7	0.7	0.8	2.4	44.5
	1995	73724	50.4	14.6	14.4	21.6	12.5	1.8	0.2	48.9	3.1	1.6	1.1	2.4	43.8
	2000	98153	51.4	14.2	14.0	21.4	13.0	2.8	0.1	48.4	3.3	1.5	0.8	2.0	44.1
	2003	121868	46.3	13.4	13.2	20.9	9.4	2.6	0.3	53.3	2.6	2.8	1.1	2.0	47.4
Maldives	1990	52	61.5	26.5	26.2	26.3	8.5	0.2	..	38.5	..	..	..	..	38.5
	1995	50	63.7	38.7	38.4	19.3	5.7	0.0	..	36.3	0.5	..	0.0	0.5	35.8
	2000	75	66.9	17.8	17.8	44.9	4.2	0.0	..	33.1	0.0	..	..	0.0	33.1
	2003	112	58.4	15.5	15.3	32.5	10.4	..	..	41.6	4.3	0.9	..	0.0	40.7
Mali	1990	252	44.9	37.1	36.2	6.4	1.2	0.2	13.9	40.5	1.0	0.1	14.4	0.0	26.0
	1995	241	38.6	33.0	32.3	4.7	0.9	0.0	0.1	60.1	2.1	9.1	8.2	0.2	42.5
	2000	235	44.9	33.4	32.9	10.9	0.5	0.1	0.3	52.5	2.0	9.8	10.0	0.8	31.9
	2003	212	33.0	30.9	30.4	1.5	0.1	0.4	0.3	62.9	3.7	0.7	12.9	0.1	49.2
Malta - Malte	1990	1127	82.1	78.0	77.5	3.9	0.1	0.1	3.0	11.6	6.5	0.1	6.4	1.7	3.4
	1995	1913	84.1	73.1	71.6	10.1	0.9	0.1	0.3	13.3	3.2	0.3	3.0	0.8	9.2
	2000	2442	72.9	40.6	34.1	28.4	3.8	0.1	0.1	21.6	2.3	0.2	2.3	1.0	18.1
	2003	2866	51.6	37.1	36.8	12.7	1.4	0.4	0.4	41.1	2.7	1.1	3.2	2.7	34.2
Martinique²	1990	276	68.5	67.8	67.7	0.7	0.0	..	..	31.4	0.1	31.4	0.0	..	0.0
	1995	242	96.5	93.7	93.7	2.8	0.0	..	..	3.5	0.1	1.9	0.5	0.1	0.3
Mauritania - Mauritanie	1990	469	79.8	60.1	60.0	..	19.7	..	13.0	6.8	0.0	0.5	5.6	0.0	0.7
	1995	575	87.0	57.8	57.8	1.2	28.0	0.0	0.1	12.3	0.4	0.1	11.6	0.0	0.7
	2000	486	76.5	61.4	60.8	0.1	15.0	0.0	2.9	19.3	0.2	1.1	13.9	0.3	3.9
	2003	574	71.7	58.9	58.1	0.2	12.6	0.0	5.8	20.9	1.0	0.0	15.7	0.6	4.5
Mauritius - Maurice	1990	1202	94.3	80.5	79.4	13.2	0.2	0.5	0.1	5.6	0.0	0.1	4.1	0.0	1.4
	1995	1539	89.9	73.3	72.0	15.8	0.6	0.2	..	7.6	..	..	5.8	..	1.7
	2000	1488	90.4	68.7	67.4	20.9	0.5	0.3	0.0	9.6	0.2	0.3	7.6	0.1	1.4
	2003	1989	88.7	73.1	72.0	14.9	0.5	0.3	0.0	11.2	0.1	0.1	8.2	0.2	2.4
Mexico - Mexique	1990	27167	90.8	14.2	13.4	70.2	5.5	1.0	0.1	8.6	0.8	6.6	0.3	0.2	1.2
	1995	79541	92.4	5.1	4.3	86.1	1.2	0.1	0.0	7.5	0.6	5.7	0.1	0.2	1.2
	2000	166455	95.2	3.7	3.3	90.7	0.6	0.1	0.0	4.8	0.3	3.8	0.0	0.0	0.7
	2003	164922	94.1	3.6	3.5	89.4	0.7	0.2	0.0	5.8	0.4	3.5	0.1	0.1	1.4
Moldova, Republic of - Moldova, République de	1995	746	17.5	15.8	15.2	1.3	0.0	0.5	80.1	2.4	0.1	0.3	0.1	1.6	0.3
	2000	472	30.4	26.5	26.2	3.8	0.0	0.1	67.4	2.2	0.1	0.1	0.2	1.3	0.6
	2003	790	32.0	27.0	26.7	4.8	0.0	0.1	66.0	2.0	0.0	0.0	0.1	1.8	0.2
Mongolia - Mongolie	1990	91	56.0	36.4	35.9	2.0	17.6	0.0	8.8	35.2	0.1	0.4	20.7	0.1	13.9
	1995	473	46.5	31.2	15.0	5.5	9.9	0.0	30.4	23.0	0.0	..	..	0.0	23.0
	2000	536	36.9	8.6	7.7	24.5	1.5	2.3	9.0	54.0	0.0	0.1	0.0	0.2	53.7
	2003	553	39.7	4.3	4.2	34.2	1.1	0.1	7.4	52.9	0.3	0.0	..	0.6	52.2
Morocco - Maroc	1990	4572	69.0	63.0	62.0	2.1	3.6	0.3	1.2	20.9	9.2	1.3	6.7	6.0	6.5
	1995	4951	72.3	60.8	59.7	3.8	7.3	0.4	0.7	21.1	6.8	2.0	7.5	3.5	8.1
	2000	8142	75.6	64.6	63.8	6.0	3.8	1.2	1.4	15.5	2.6	2.4	2.7	2.4	8.0
	2003	9549	77.6	70.1	69.2	4.7	2.0	0.8	1.1	19.6	2.6	3.2	3.8	2.8	9.7
Mozambique	1990	381	34.1	22.3	21.9	7.5	4.0	0.3	0.1	64.5	1.0	0.7	3.1	0.4	60.3
	1995	174	62.6	41.1	41.0	7.3	14.2	0.0	0.0	35.2	0.5	0.1	30.1	0.1	4.9
	2000	364	34.7	25.5	25.5	4.9	4.3	0.0	..	45.0	0.4	0.0	36.0	0.3	8.7
	2003	1038	65.6	63.5	63.5	0.8	1.2	0.1	0.5	27.8	0.5	0.0	21.3	0.0	6.5
Myanmar	1990	409	17.6	7.6	7.0	2.5	6.9	0.7	2.7	78.7	3.8	0.0	14.3	1.5	61.1
	1995	1198	21.5	6.5	6.1	7.5	7.1	0.5	0.0	77.9	8.8	0.1	9.6	0.9	66.2
	2000	1978	47.3	16.9	16.7	24.5	5.5	0.5	0.0	52.1	1.2	0.2	8.6	0.2	42.0
	2003	2743	30.3	14.4	14.1	10.9	4.6	0.4	0.7	68.3	0.6	0.1	8.1	0.2	59.0

For sources and notes, see end of table 3.1B.

Pour les sources et les notes, se reporter à la fin du tableau 3.1B.

Destination Origin Origine	Year Année	World [1] (millions of dollars) Monde [1] (millions de dollars)	Developed economies Economies développées					South-East Europe and CIS Europe du Sud-Est et CEI	Developing economies Economies en développement					
			Total	Europe		USA and Canada Etats-Unis et Canada	Japan Japon	Other Autres		Total	of which: dont : OPEC OPEP	America Amérique	Africa Afrique	West Asia Asie occiden-tale	Other Asia Autres pays d'Asie
				Total	EU UE										
									Percentage / En pourcentage						
Nauru	1990	60	86.6	0.5	0.5	2.1	..	84.0	0.6	12.8	..	0.0	1.2	..	11.5
	1995	35	82.8	2.2	2.2	0.1	1.5	79.0	0.1	17.1	..	0.1	0.7	0.2	16.1
	2000	30	60.3	1.7	1.5	7.5	2.5	48.6	0.7	38.9	0.2	0.1	0.5	0.0	38.3
	2003	29	47.1	2.8	2.8	1.7	37.5	5.1	0.0	52.9	0.0	0.4	0.8	0.0	51.7
Nepal - Népal	1990	211	85.0	60.0	53.8	24.0	0.8	0.1	0.0	15.0	0.0	0.1	0.1	0.0	14.8
	1995	324	89.2	56.8	53.3	31.6	0.5	0.3	0.1	10.7	..	0.5	0.1	0.0	10.2
	2000	676	62.0	24.2	22.5	33.6	3.8	0.4	0.0	36.6	0.0	0.1	0.0	0.3	36.2
	2003	651	43.7	15.3	14.6	27.1	1.0	0.3	0.0	54.0	0.0	0.0	0.0	0.4	53.6
Netherlands - Pays-Bas	1990	130714	90.3	84.3	81.5	4.4	0.9	0.7	0.9	8.0	2.1	1.1	2.2	1.9	2.8
	1995	177374	87.9	82.0	79.4	4.0	1.1	0.7	1.6	9.9	1.8	1.5	1.9	1.9	4.5
	2000	229741	89.9	83.5	81.2	4.7	0.9	0.7	1.3	8.2	1.3	1.1	1.4	1.8	3.8
	2003	293335	88.9	82.5	80.1	4.8	0.8	0.7	2.0	8.4	1.7	1.1	1.7	2.1	3.4
Netherlands Antilles - Antilles néerlandaises	1990	1791	41.2	3.5	3.5	34.8	2.7	0.1	0.4	58.4	5.3	53.0	5.4	..	-0.2
	1995	1431	52.5	28.9	26.5	22.6	0.8	0.2	0.5	46.3	0.1	38.4	0.8	0.1	2.2
	2000	1973	28.6	8.7	8.6	19.8	0.1	0.0	..	70.9	12.5	62.2	2.0	0.0	3.5
	2003	2244	32.2	5.0	5.0	27.0	0.0	0.2	0.0	67.7	11.4	55.9	1.0	2.3	8.1
New Caledonia - Nouvelle-Calédonie	1990	405	89.5	55.0	55.0	6.7	25.5	2.2	..	9.0	..	..	..	..	8.1
	1995	525	88.8	44.5	44.5	8.5	28.6	7.2	0.0	11.2	0.0	0.1	0.5	..	8.8
	2000	573	75.9	37.5	37.5	5.2	27.1	6.1	..	24.1	0.1	0.0	0.0	0.0	22.6
	2003	720	66.6	36.1	36.1	1.4	21.8	7.4	..	31.8	0.2	..	3.7	..	25.7
New Zealand - Nouvelle-Zélande	1990	9430	65.6	16.6	16.3	14.8	15.8	18.3	2.0	27.5	4.2	3.2	1.6	2.7	16.1
	1995	13659	63.0	14.7	14.3	11.6	16.3	20.4	0.9	33.7	3.8	3.3	1.4	2.7	23.1
	2000	12716	65.5	15.3	15.0	16.3	13.7	20.2	0.2	32.3	4.4	3.3	1.4	2.5	22.5
	2003	16271	65.5	16.2	15.8	16.5	11.0	21.8	0.5	33.2	4.2	3.5	1.6	2.6	21.8
Nicaragua	1990	331	69.2	34.9	34.8	28.9	5.4	..	..	23.6	..	22.6	0.0	..	0.9
	1995	466	72.1	31.1	30.2	39.5	1.5	..	..	26.0	0.5	24.9	..	..	0.3
	2000	645	64.2	19.9	19.1	43.8	0.5	..	..	32.9	0.0	31.8	..	..	0.3
	2003	1249	66.9	5.6	5.4	60.6	0.4	0.2	1.5	24.6	0.2	23.7	0.0	0.0	0.2
Niger	1990	283	84.8	64.4	64.4	0.1	20.3	..	..	14.6	9.3	..	14.2	..	0.4
	1995	193	80.2	58.2	57.7	0.2	21.8	..	..	19.7	10.7	0.0	19.6	0.1	0.0
	2000	196	51.0	34.3	34.2	2.7	13.9	0.2	..	48.9	40.2	..	48.9	0.0	0.0
	2003	180	64.6	47.0	47.0	0.2	17.2	..	..	35.4	29.2	0.0	35.2	..	0.2
Nigeria - Nigéria	1990	10273	92.0	36.6	36.5	55.4	0.0	0.0	0.2	7.6	0.0	0.8	6.5	0.0	0.3
	1995	12248	76.5	34.5	33.2	41.0	1.0	0.0	0.1	23.3	1.3	4.1	8.8	0.1	9.8
	2000	21174	74.0	26.9	25.4	45.9	0.9	0.2	0.1	25.9	2.3	6.5	10.0	0.6	8.5
	2003	24068	73.7	27.5	26.3	42.7	3.4	0.2	0.0	26.2	3.3	6.3	9.4	0.7	9.4
Norway - Norvège	1990	33907	93.1	81.9	80.6	8.9	1.7	0.6	0.7	6.2	1.4	1.3	1.2	1.5	2.0
	1995	41068	93.1	80.6	79.5	10.1	1.8	0.7	0.8	6.2	0.7	1.6	0.6	0.7	3.1
	2000	57600	94.8	78.9	78.0	13.8	1.7	0.3	0.7	4.6	0.4	0.9	0.5	0.6	2.5
	2003	66980	92.3	78.1	77.2	12.0	1.7	0.4	0.9	6.9	0.4	1.8	0.6	0.8	3.5
Oman	1990	4584	18.8	13.0	12.4	3.7	2.1	0.0	0.0	81.1	62.2	0.0	4.4	65.0	11.8
	1995	5965	33.5	0.9	0.9	3.3	27.7	1.6	0.3	66.3	14.1	0.0	2.5	17.1	46.6
	2000	9046	26.8	2.0	2.0	2.9	20.4	1.5	0.1	73.1	2.9	0.0	1.3	3.7	68.1
	2003	10205	32.9	2.5	2.5	6.7	22.4	1.3	0.1	67.0	1.2	0.0	1.3	2.3	63.4
Pakistan	1990	5587	62.0	38.3	37.1	14.1	8.2	1.4	2.7	35.4	8.6	0.3	4.2	10.1	20.8
	1995	7991	56.7	31.7	31.0	16.8	6.8	1.4	1.1	41.8	11.0	1.6	4.4	12.6	23.2
	2000	8870	60.1	28.6	27.9	27.3	2.6	1.6	0.5	39.4	12.2	2.0	4.2	12.9	20.1
	2003	11767	55.5	28.9	28.4	24.3	1.1	1.2	0.5	44.0	16.5	1.6	5.4	18.4	18.6
Panama	1990	321	78.3	31.6	31.6	46.1	0.6	0.0	0.1	20.6	0.5	19.6	0.0	0.1	0.2
	1995	2062	45.8	27.8	25.6	15.3	2.6	0.1	0.6	53.4	7.0	33.1	0.1	1.3	18.4
	2000	779	70.3	17.7	17.7	45.8	1.5	0.1	0.0	29.2	0.6	24.5	0.1	0.0	3.4
	2003	1467	62.2	35.7	35.5	20.2	6.4	0.0	0.4	37.4	1.8	27.0	0.3	0.1	9.1

For sources and notes, see end of table 3.1B.

Pour les sources et les notes, se reporter à la fin du tableau 3.1B.

Origin / Origine	Year / Année	World[1] (millions of dollars) / Monde[1] (millions de dollars)	Developed economies / Economies développées					South-East Europe and CIS / Europe du Sud-Est et CEI	Developing economies / Economies en développement					
			Total	Europe Total	Europe EU / UE	USA and Canada / Etats-Unis et Canada	Japan / Japon	Other / Autres		Total	of which: / dont: OPEC / OPEP	America / Amérique	Africa / Afrique	West Asia / Asie occidentale	Other Asia / Autres pays d'Asie
								Percentage / En pourcentage							
Papua New Guinea - Papouasie-Nouvelle-Guinée	1990	1266	82.0	24.7	24.1	2.7	27.8	26.9	..	17.9	0.3	0.0	0.2	0.0	17.4
	1995	3131	68.3	16.3	16.3	1.6	21.2	29.2	0.0	17.2	0.1	0.0	0.0	..	17.0
	2000	2804	53.6	10.2	10.2	1.3	11.3	30.8	0.0	17.3	0.3	0.0	0.0	0.0	16.9
	2003	3623	47.5	10.1	10.1	1.8	7.3	28.2	0.0	18.4	3.0	0.0	0.0	0.0	18.0
Paraguay	1990	1063	37.9	33.4	28.7	3.9	0.2	0.4	0.1	62.0	0.8	48.4	0.5	0.4	4.4
	1995	919	25.1	19.8	19.4	4.9	0.1	0.3	0.0	74.7	2.8	66.3	0.6	0.1	7.4
	2000	1123	18.6	13.2	13.0	3.7	1.7	0.0	0.0	81.4	0.9	70.2	0.3	0.1	2.5
	2003	1698	23.8	18.5	18.3	3.8	1.5	0.1	0.2	76.0	1.1	61.0	0.7	2.2	2.8
Peru - Pérou	1990	3276	70.7	33.8	33.0	23.2	13.4	0.2	3.8	24.9	2.4	15.7	0.7	1.0	7.5
	1995	5513	63.7	34.2	30.5	19.9	9.1	0.5	0.8	35.6	4.3	17.1	0.7	0.8	17.0
	2000	6872	65.7	28.8	20.2	29.9	4.7	0.7	0.7	33.6	3.1	18.6	0.6	1.0	13.4
	2003	8859	67.4	32.6	24.8	28.6	4.4	0.7	0.8	31.9	1.9	17.9	0.4	0.5	13.1
Philippines	1990	8194	79.3	18.8	18.5	39.4	19.8	1.3	0.0	20.6	1.8	0.9	0.3	1.6	17.5
	1995	17371	71.6	17.9	17.7	36.9	15.8	1.0	0.0	28.3	1.8	1.1	0.2	1.2	25.6
	2000	38203	64.7	18.3	18.1	30.8	14.7	1.0	0.0	34.9	0.8	1.1	0.1	0.4	33.2
	2003	43466	52.7	15.2	15.1	21.8	14.4	1.4	0.1	47.2	0.8	1.8	0.2	0.5	44.7
Poland - Pologne	1990	13627	70.3	65.8	60.1	3.2	0.8	0.4	18.6	9.9	2.4	1.5	2.6	2.5	3.4
	1995	22895	82.2	78.8	77.2	3.0	0.2	0.2	11.0	6.7	0.9	1.3	1.3	1.0	3.0
	2000	31644	86.9	82.5	80.6	3.7	0.2	0.5	7.9	5.1	0.9	1.2	1.2	0.9	1.9
	2003	48228	85.7	81.9	79.2	3.2	0.2	0.3	9.2	5.0	0.7	1.0	1.1	1.2	1.6
Portugal	1990	16402	91.5	84.4	81.0	5.6	1.0	0.6	0.6	7.0	0.7	0.6	4.6	0.5	1.2
	1995	23177	91.0	84.3	81.3	5.1	0.8	0.8	0.4	8.0	0.6	1.7	3.8	0.8	1.6
	2000	23297	91.1	83.2	80.7	6.6	0.5	0.8	0.2	8.0	0.6	1.7	4.0	0.9	1.4
	2003	31314	90.0	82.6	80.6	6.3	0.3	0.7	0.5	8.9	0.7	1.1	4.6	1.1	2.1
Qatar	1990	3293	63.9	2.3	2.3	1.6	59.5	0.5	0.0	33.4	5.7	8.9	0.7	6.3	17.5
	1995	3681	60.9	1.3	1.3	2.5	53.6	3.5	0.0	36.1	7.1	0.0	1.1	6.9	28.1
	2000	11593	50.8	1.1	1.0	3.7	45.0	1.0	0.0	39.5	5.6	0.1	1.0	6.2	32.3
	2003	14432	50.8	6.1	6.1	2.5	41.0	1.2	0.2	38.2	2.0	0.0	1.1	2.4	34.6
Reunion - Réunion [2]	1990	183	89.4	86.2	85.8	0.0	3.1	0.0	..	10.5	..	0.7	6.2	..	3.6
	1995	208	87.4	80.7	80.4	0.6	6.1	..	..	11.9	..	0.7	6.9	..	4.1
Romania - Roumanie	1990	5871	50.8	42.4	40.8	6.3	1.6	0.5	29.7	18.6	4.1	1.9	3.7	7.8	5.2
	1995	8061	64.7	59.7	58.6	2.9	0.4	1.6	7.8	26.9	3.5	2.1	7.2	9.0	8.6
	2000	10367	76.0	71.0	69.9	4.0	0.2	0.8	8.4	15.2	2.5	0.8	3.6	8.5	2.2
	2003	17546	80.4	74.5	73.0	4.6	0.3	1.0	4.9	14.6	2.5	0.7	2.0	7.8	3.9
Russian Federation - Fédération de Russie	1995	77595	62.1	50.5	45.3	6.7	4.1	0.8	20.5	17.4	0.9	1.2	0.9	2.9	10.6
	2000	102998	69.1	57.6	52.9	7.8	2.7	1.0	15.4	15.5	1.2	1.1	1.1	4.3	9.1
	2003	133157	64.3	56.2	50.9	4.9	2.1	1.1	17.5	18.3	1.9	0.8	1.0	5.3	11.2
Rwanda	1990	100	72.7	64.4	64.3	6.4	1.9	..	..	10.4	..	..	2.0	..	8.4
	1995	63	63.8	60.9	60.6	2.8	0.1	..	0.0	6.5	0.0	0.4	2.5	0.0	3.6
	2000	94	43.3	37.6	37.1	5.3	0.4	0.0	2.6	18.2	0.1	0.0	3.2	0.6	14.4
	2003	158	13.1	11.2	11.1	1.7	0.2	0.0	4.5	50.2	37.9	0.0	2.4	0.1	47.7
Saint Helena - Sainte-Hélène	1990	6	80.6	23.1	22.9	5.6	51.9	0.0	..	19.4	..	0.0	17.9	..	1.2
	1995	4	88.5	18.4	18.4	0.2	69.9	0.1	..	11.5	5.1	0.3	3.7	5.1	2.4
	2000	7	56.8	12.2	12.2	26.7	16.5	1.4	1.0	42.3	2.0	2.8	27.8	..	11.6
	2003	20	62.0	27.4	27.2	27.7	6.9	0.1	0.0	38.0	9.4	1.6	22.3	0.0	14.1
Saint Kitts and Nevis - Saint-Kitts-et-Nevis	1990	24	96.0	34.4	34.2	61.4	0.2	..	..	4.0	..	3.7	0.0	..	0.2
	1995	40	93.4	33.4	33.1	59.8	0.2	0.0	0.8	5.8	..	5.6	0.0	..	0.1
	2000	33	88.2	21.8	21.8	66.0	0.3	..	..	11.3	..	7.8	0.0	..	0.5
	2003	74	87.4	20.1	20.1	67.2	0.1	0.0	4.3	8.0	0.0	4.8	0.1	0.0	0.1
Saint Lucia - Sainte-Lucie	1990	146	91.3	68.9	68.9	22.3	0.1	..	..	8.7	0.3	8.7	0.0	..	0.0
	1995	109	83.3	55.8	55.7	27.3	0.3	0.0	..	16.7	0.2	15.2	1.0	..	0.2
	2000	45	73.3	54.2	54.1	18.5	0.7	..	0.0	26.7	0.3	25.6	0.0	0.0	0.3
	2003	50	74.7	49.1	49.1	25.5	0.1	0.0	0.1	25.2	0.1	24.1	0.1	0.0	0.3

For sources and notes, see end of table 3.1B.

Pour les sources et les notes, se reporter à la fin du tableau 3.1B.

Origin / Origine	Year / Année	World [1] (millions of dollars) / Monde [1] (millions de dollars)	Developed economies / Economies développées — Total	Europe Total	Europe EU/UE	USA and Canada / Etats-Unis et Canada	Japan / Japon	Other / Autres	South-East Europe and CIS / Europe du Sud-Est et CEI	Developing economies / Economies en développement — Total	of which: OPEC / dont: OPEP	America / Amérique	Africa / Afrique	West Asia / Asie occidentale	Other Asia / Autres pays d'Asie
Saint Pierre and Miquelon - Saint-Pierre-et-Miquelon	1990	25	98.6	81.3	80.9	16.9	0.4	..	..	1.4	..	1.0	..	..	0.4
	1995	6	93.0	36.7	35.8	54.9	1.4	..	..	7.0	1.5	3.1	1.6	..	2.3
	2000	16	58.0	17.7	17.7	33.2	7.0	..	0.0	42.0	..	15.4	26.7	..	0.0
	2003	10	43.9	13.9	13.5	29.9	0.1	..	0.0	56.0	..	20.3	35.8	..	..
Saint Vincent and the Grenadines - Saint-Vincent-et-les Grenadines	1990	83	65.3	54.6	54.6	10.7	0.0	0.0	..	34.7	0.0	34.2	0.0	..	0.0
	1995	45	34.2	21.6	21.6	12.6	0.1	..	..	65.8	0.1	64.2	..	..	0.0
	2000	51	49.5	46.3	46.3	3.1	0.0	0.0	1.3	47.7	1.1	45.9	0.0	1.0	0.1
	2003	199	81.8	79.9	78.6	1.9	0.0	0.0	0.0	17.6	1.4	15.6	0.1	0.3	1.4
Samoa	1990	12	77.0	20.5	20.5	6.9	0.9	48.6	..	23.0	..	0.0	0.1	..	4.8
	1995	60	95.2	2.2	2.1	0.9	1.8	90.3	..	4.8	..	0.0	0.3	..	1.5
	2000	68	74.2	3.0	3.0	10.9	0.3	60.0	..	25.8	12.3	0.1	0.1	0.0	21.3
	2003	103	75.8	2.8	2.7	4.9	1.3	66.9	..	24.7	15.0	0.2	0.0	0.0	20.2
Sao Tome and Principe - Sao Tomé-et-Principe	1990	29	73.8	73.8	73.5	..	..	..	..	26.2	0.0	0.3	0.0	..	25.8
	1995	7	84.0	79.6	73.9	1.5	2.9	0.0	..	16.0	0.0	1.0	5.3	..	9.6
	2000	18	85.5	75.5	70.2	7.3	2.7	..	0.2	14.4	0.4	0.4	0.3	9.2	4.5
	2003	12	87.1	71.1	69.2	15.9	0.0	..	0.0	12.9	0.1	1.1	1.2	0.6	10.0
Saudi Arabia - Arabie saoudite	1990	44417	63.3	18.4	18.3	24.9	19.0	1.0	0.7	35.9	3.8	3.3	4.0	9.4	19.1
	1995	50005	55.7	20.4	20.4	17.7	16.2	1.4	0.0	44.2	5.3	2.3	2.9	10.9	28.2
	2000	73712	55.6	18.2	18.0	18.5	17.5	1.5	0.0	44.3	4.1	1.5	4.5	6.4	31.9
	2003	84775	54.2	16.1	15.9	21.7	15.6	0.8	0.0	45.7	4.1	1.2	5.0	7.2	32.3
Senegal - Sénégal	1990	861	49.8	47.7	47.7	0.2	1.9	..	0.0	32.9	2.0	0.0	19.1	1.6	12.1
	1995	609	34.8	33.6	33.3	0.6	0.7	0.0	0.0	56.6	5.1	0.4	25.8	2.1	28.3
	2000	693	49.4	46.3	45.3	0.6	1.2	0.1	0.0	43.7	0.7	0.5	28.2	0.4	14.5
	2003	1130	32.6	30.4	29.7	0.8	0.6	0.0	0.0	53.6	0.5	0.1	37.3	0.3	15.9
Serbia and Montenegro - Serbie-et-Monténégro	1995	66	58.9	58.6	58.3	..	0.2	0.1	0.7	40.5	29.8	2.0	31.5	6.9	0.0
	2000	1034	80.5	79.2	77.8	0.3	0.3	0.6	8.7	10.8	3.0	0.2	4.5	4.5	1.7
	2003	1692	90.1	88.5	88.3	1.0	0.1	0.5	4.6	5.3	2.4	0.0	2.8	1.4	1.0
Seychelles	1990	14	92.4	92.0	92.0	0.3	0.1	..	..	7.6	..	..	1.2	..	6.3
	1995	25	92.4	86.4	86.3	0.3	5.6	0.1	..	6.4	0.1	..	3.3	0.1	3.1
	2000	124	93.0	91.7	91.7	0.1	1.0	0.2	..	6.5	..	..	4.0	2.0	0.5
	2003	214	97.3	95.8	95.7	0.8	0.6	0.1	..	2.6	0.0	..	0.5	0.0	0.9
Sierra Leone	1990	137	92.0	66.2	66.1	25.8	..	..	..	1.0	..	..	1.0	..	..
	1995	41	50.1	45.0	45.0	5.0	0.2	..	..	25.1	..	..	25.1	..	..
	2000	124	92.8	87.8	87.7	4.6	0.4	0.0	0.2	6.7	0.2	0.2	4.4	0.0	2.1
	2003	135	92.7	86.2	86.2	6.4	0.0	0.1	0.1	6.7	0.2	0.2	4.2	0.0	2.3
Singapore - Singapour	1990	52753	50.3	16.4	15.6	22.1	8.8	3.0	0.9	48.8	2.1	1.3	2.1	2.4	41.8
	1995	118187	43.6	14.3	13.9	18.7	7.8	2.7	0.9	55.6	1.3	1.4	1.3	1.4	51.0
	2000	137932	42.5	14.5	14.0	17.7	7.5	2.8	0.1	57.4	1.4	1.9	1.2	1.5	52.2
	2003	144121	39.7	14.7	14.2	14.6	6.7	3.8	0.2	60.0	1.8	1.8	1.2	1.9	54.5
Slovakia - Slovaquie	1995	8579	86.2	84.3	83.3	1.5	0.2	0.2	8.7	5.1	0.9	0.7	0.9	1.4	2.1
	2000	11874	92.5	90.7	88.6	1.6	0.1	0.2	4.5	2.8	0.4	0.5	0.5	0.7	1.2
	2003	20541	92.8	87.2	85.9	5.1	0.3	0.1	4.8	2.3	0.2	0.1	0.3	0.9	1.0
Slovenia - Slovénie	1995	8389	77.5	73.4	72.4	3.6	0.3	0.3	19.2	3.3	0.9	0.4	0.7	1.1	1.0
	2000	8728	76.6	72.8	71.3	3.3	0.1	0.4	19.5	3.9	0.9	0.5	0.7	1.7	1.0
	2003	12752	74.5	69.9	68.1	3.8	0.2	0.5	21.7	3.8	1.2	0.3	0.7	1.7	1.1
Solomon Islands - Iles Salomon	1990	72	75.5	22.7	22.6	3.9	43.1	5.7	..	24.6	0.0	0.0	0.0	0.0	18.4
	1995	196	61.5	10.3	10.3	2.4	46.6	2.2	..	38.5	0.0	0.0	0.3	..	34.8
	2000	97	37.0	11.1	11.1	0.8	21.7	3.4	..	63.0	0.0	0.0	..	0.0	54.1
	2003	118	20.6	2.4	2.4	1.2	13.7	3.3	0.0	82.1	0.5	0.0	0.0	0.0	71.0
Somalia - Somalie	1990	150	40.4	40.1	37.6	..	0.3	0.0	0.2	59.4	38.2	0.0	1.3	56.5	1.6
	1995	172	13.0	13.0	12.9	0.0	..	0.0	0.1	86.9	68.5	..	1.3	82.3	3.3
	2000	64	3.2	2.1	1.9	0.8	0.4	0.0	0.0	96.7	39.8	0.1	4.7	87.7	4.2
	2003	95	2.9	2.3	2.3	0.1	0.5	0.0	0.0	97.1	42.8	0.1	2.8	81.6	12.6

For sources and notes, see end of table 3.1B.

Pour les sources et les notes, se reporter à la fin du tableau 3.1B.

Origin / Origine	Year / Année	World (millions of dollars) / Monde (millions de dollars) [1]	Developed economies / Economies développées						South-East Europe and CIS / Europe du Sud-Est et CEI	Developing economies / Economies en développement					
			Total	Europe Total	Europe EU / UE	USA and Canada / Etats-Unis et Canada	Japan / Japon	Other / Autres		Total	of which: OPEC / dont: OPEP	America / Amérique	Africa / Afrique	West Asia / Asie occidentale	Other Asia / Autres pays d'Asie
			Percentage / En pourcentage												
South Africa - Afrique du Sud	2000	21694	64.5	41.4	39.8	12.1	6.2	4.7	0.3	35.2	2.9	2.6	18.9	2.4	11.3
	2003	35527	66.6	41.0	39.6	13.4	9.2	3.1	0.5	32.8	2.1	1.3	14.8	2.0	14.7
South Africa (Customs Union) - Afrique du Sud (Union douanière)	1990	24701	43.9	27.8	25.2	8.0	6.7	1.4	0.1	11.8	0.0	0.7	6.0	0.4	4.6
	1995	28211	42.9	30.2	29.6	5.2	5.0	2.5	0.4	28.7	1.6	2.2	13.6	1.3	11.6
Spain - Espagne	1990	55683	82.4	74.2	71.8	6.5	1.1	0.6	0.9	13.4	3.4	3.8	4.5	2.3	2.6
	1995	91613	83.0	75.9	73.8	4.7	1.4	1.1	0.7	15.7	2.9	5.6	3.9	2.1	4.1
	2000	108185	81.1	73.5	71.6	5.5	1.0	1.1	0.9	15.6	2.5	6.0	3.4	3.3	2.7
	2003	151025	81.9	75.6	73.8	4.7	0.7	0.9	1.5	14.5	2.5	4.7	3.9	3.0	2.6
Sri Lanka	1990	1895	62.4	27.8	26.9	27.4	5.4	1.8	3.1	30.5	11.0	2.0	5.5	13.3	9.6
	1995	3801	76.9	33.1	32.4	36.9	5.3	1.6	2.6	18.5	4.0	1.2	2.4	5.8	9.0
	2000	5459	76.8	29.0	28.3	41.5	4.2	2.2	2.1	18.5	4.2	1.4	1.7	6.2	9.1
	2003	5246	74.3	27.9	27.2	34.8	3.3	2.3	2.3	21.7	5.2	1.6	1.1	8.2	10.8
Sudan - Soudan	1990	515	47.9	39.0	38.8	2.8	6.0	0.1	9.1	43.0	8.6	0.0	7.1	10.5	24.9
	1995	535	42.8	32.2	30.7	4.0	6.5	0.0	2.8	54.3	17.5	0.0	3.0	25.9	24.6
	2000	1542	29.3	11.1	11.0	0.1	18.1	0.0	0.2	70.4	6.8	0.7	8.3	10.0	50.9
	2003	1852	22.3	16.3	15.5	1.0	2.9	2.2	0.3	76.5	29.4	0.8	5.9	34.0	35.3
Suriname	1990	456	93.2	75.2	38.3	11.8	6.2	..	2.9	3.9	..	6.8	0.0	..	-2.9
	1995	482	84.8	57.2	32.6	21.5	6.0	..	1.2	14.0	0.0	13.5	0.2	..	0.3
	2000	501	87.6	51.4	28.9	32.0	4.0	0.2	0.0	12.4	0.1	9.5	2.3	0.0	0.6
	2003	591	81.2	56.3	31.2	22.8	2.1	0.0	0.5	18.3	0.1	12.5	2.7	0.0	3.1
Sweden - Suède	1990	53068	87.9	72.6	60.8	11.2	2.2	1.8	1.4	10.8	2.4	2.0	1.6	2.3	4.8
	1995	79601	83.6	69.5	59.7	9.0	2.9	2.1	1.3	12.2	1.5	1.9	1.6	1.8	6.9
	2000	87863	84.1	68.4	59.6	11.3	2.8	1.6	1.4	14.5	1.9	3.1	1.7	2.8	6.8
	2003	101889	84.2	67.9	58.1	12.8	1.9	1.5	2.3	13.2	2.6	2.0	1.8	2.8	6.6
Switzerland - Suisse	1990	63790	81.9	66.0	65.4	8.8	4.8	2.3	2.0	16.1	3.0	2.4	2.0	3.4	8.2
	1995	81353	80.1	64.6	64.0	9.5	4.0	2.1	1.1	18.8	3.2	2.5	1.8	3.8	10.6
	2000	80526	82.0	61.8	61.4	14.0	4.2	1.9	1.2	16.9	2.3	2.9	1.5	3.3	9.1
	2003	100026	78.5	62.5	62.0	11.1	3.5	1.4	1.5	20.1	2.8	3.0	1.6	4.4	10.9
Syrian Arab Republic - République arabe syrienne	1990	4210	43.4	42.4	42.0	0.9	0.1	..	33.8	21.9	9.9	0.0	2.8	18.9	0.1
	1995	3970	61.2	59.4	59.3	1.6	0.2	..	6.7	29.7	10.5	0.1	5.0	24.2	0.3
	2000	4737	67.0	63.0	63.0	3.7	0.3	0.0	1.7	28.4	8.4	0.1	2.6	24.0	1.6
	2003	6579	54.6	48.9	48.9	4.9	0.7	0.0	6.1	36.1	15.0	0.1	4.1	28.7	3.2
Tajikistan - Tadjikistan	1995	749	62.2	59.2	53.5	2.0	1.1	..	34.0	3.8	0.1	0.1	0.0	1.2	2.6
	2000	770	39.5	39.4	30.1	0.1	..	..	48.6	11.8	1.7	..	0.1	9.3	2.4
	2003	791	49.9	49.7	40.0	0.1	0.1	..	17.6	32.5	6.6	..	0.0	31.1	1.4
Thailand - Thaïlande	1990	23072	68.1	24.8	23.4	24.0	17.2	2.1	0.6	30.8	5.2	1.4	2.5	4.8	22.0
	1995	57201	54.1	17.0	16.1	18.7	16.6	1.8	0.9	45.0	5.0	1.0	1.7	4.0	35.6
	2000	68962	57.7	17.2	16.3	22.5	14.7	3.3	0.2	41.7	4.1	1.5	1.9	2.4	35.8
	2003	80521	52.4	16.4	15.1	18.2	14.2	3.7	0.5	47.0	5.5	1.5	2.1	2.9	40.4
Togo	1990	267	58.6	44.4	43.1	13.6	0.1	0.4	5.6	35.1	4.1	2.2	18.4	0.1	14.3
	1995	222	41.6	27.6	25.1	11.8	1.0	1.2	..	56.5	6.7	5.6	17.7	0.3	32.9
	2000	190	21.8	21.5	20.6	0.3	0.0	0.0	0.9	77.3	12.8	6.7	42.5	6.3	20.3
	2003	416	22.2	18.2	17.4	1.3	0.1	2.5	0.3	76.9	3.5	1.6	58.5	0.7	16.1
Tonga	1990	13	92.5	1.6	1.6	26.0	30.1	34.8	..	5.7	..	..	..	..	0.1
	1995	15	87.1	..	..	25.8	47.9	13.4	..	1.6	..	..	..	..	..
	2000	18	92.6	6.6	6.6	31.0	49.3	5.7	..	7.4	..	..	0.0	0.1	3.6
	2003	28	92.7	4.5	4.5	49.5	34.3	4.5	0.0	7.3	..	0.0	0.0	0.2	3.5
Trinidad and Tobago - Trinité-et-Tobago	1990	1986	66.9	10.3	9.0	55.4	0.8	0.5	..	31.8	2.5	25.9	0.6	0.2	0.6
	1995	3056	46.5	11.7	11.6	34.7	0.0	0.1	0.0	52.8	1.0	34.5	0.5	0.0	0.6
	2000	3041	61.4	13.4	13.4	47.9	0.1	0.0	0.0	37.5	1.2	36.3	0.6	0.0	0.4
	2003	6756	73.0	6.9	6.8	65.8	0.2	0.0	0.0	26.2	2.7	25.2	0.4	0.0	0.3
Tunisia - Tunisie	1990	3556	78.8	77.6	77.1	0.9	0.3	0.0	3.0	18.2	10.3	1.1	9.5	4.3	3.3
	1995	5785	82.7	81.2	80.2	1.2	0.3	0.0	0.2	14.1	7.6	0.8	8.1	2.1	3.2
	2000	5994	80.5	79.4	78.5	0.8	0.3	0.0	0.4	15.4	7.7	1.1	8.3	3.4	2.5
	2003	8994	82.4	81.2	78.8	0.9	0.2	0.1	0.2	13.9	7.9	0.8	8.4	2.9	1.8

For sources and notes, see end of table 3.1B.

Pour les sources et les notes, se reporter à la fin du tableau 3.1B.

3.1A Export structure by main regions of destination (continued)

3.1A Structure des exportations par principales régions de destination (suite)

Origin / Origine	Year / Année	World[1] (millions of dollars) / Monde[1] (millions de dollars)	Developed economies / Economies développées – Total	Europe Total	Europe EU / UE	USA and Canada / Etats-Unis et Canada	Japan / Japon	Other / Autres	South-East Europe and CIS / Europe du Sud-Est et CEI	Developing economies / Economies en développement – Total	of which / dont: OPEC / OPEP	America / Amérique	Africa / Afrique	West Asia / Asie occidentale	Other Asia / Autres pays d'Asie
										Percentage / En pourcentage					
Turkey - Turquie	1990	13384	69.1	59.0	56.5	7.7	1.8	0.6	6.1	22.8	13.0	0.3	5.6	12.7	4.2
	1995	21650	66.1	56.4	55.1	7.4	0.8	1.4	12.6	21.4	8.1	2.7	5.0	8.7	5.0
	2000	27769	70.8	55.5	54.3	11.9	0.5	2.8	9.2	14.5	5.7	1.0	4.9	5.6	2.9
	2003	45573	70.1	58.5	57.3	8.6	0.4	2.7	9.5	14.4	5.4	0.7	4.2	5.6	3.8
Turkmenistan - Turkménistan	1995	1881	35.0	33.2	26.7	1.7	0.0	0.0	50.0	15.0	1.5	0.2	0.0	9.4	5.3
	2000	2505	25.3	24.7	21.1	0.5	..	0.0	52.9	20.3	10.0	0.8	0.2	17.4	2.0
	2003	3442	22.3	20.6	20.0	1.7	0.0	..	42.1	27.8	17.5	1.3	0.0	24.1	2.4
Tuvalu	1990	1	29.1	12.7	12.6	..	..	16.3	70.8	0.1	..	..	..	..	0.1
	1995	1	24.4	22.7	22.7	..	0.3	1.4	..	75.6	..	3.8	53.0	..	18.1
	2000	1	78.8	77.1	63.3	..	..	1.7	0.1	21.0	..	4.7	3.2	..	0.5
	2003	1	87.1	73.3	71.7	..	..	13.8	2.5	10.4	..	0.3	1.8	..	0.0
Uganda - Ouganda	1990	181	90.5	76.1	75.5	10.3	3.5	0.5	0.7	8.8	0.3	0.0	6.9	0.7	1.2
	1995	529	94.0	87.9	86.0	3.7	1.8	0.6	0.1	5.9	0.5	0.1	2.4	0.7	2.7
	2000	312	86.8	71.2	69.3	9.3	3.6	2.7	0.8	12.4	0.6	0.3	4.3	0.5	7.3
	2003	388	82.4	68.2	65.3	9.8	2.4	2.0	1.9	15.7	1.2	0.2	5.3	0.3	9.8
Ukraine	1995	15104	22.9	18.9	18.7	2.9	0.7	0.3	51.7	16.5	0.3	0.6	1.6	5.7	8.6
	2000	14579	35.4	28.7	27.6	5.4	0.5	0.8	35.4	29.2	4.5	2.3	5.0	9.7	11.5
	2003	21516	34.9	31.9	30.9	1.6	0.5	0.9	29.2	36.0	5.7	1.9	6.2	12.6	15.3
United Arab Emirates - Emirats arabes unis	1990	21917	53.0	9.1	8.9	4.2	37.7	2.0	0.4	33.8	5.2	0.9	2.7	9.0	21.2
	1995	24089	46.1	4.0	3.9	1.8	38.4	1.9	0.7	38.5	4.4	0.1	1.6	9.6	27.2
	2000	40545	42.6	5.3	5.1	2.5	33.2	1.7	0.6	43.3	5.3	0.2	3.0	9.8	30.3
	2003	48644	38.9	7.9	7.7	2.3	26.8	1.9	0.7	44.8	6.3	0.3	2.5	11.1	30.9
United Kingdom - Royaume-Uni	1990	185101	81.5	62.0	58.3	14.4	2.5	2.6	1.0	16.7	4.5	1.7	3.5	4.6	6.9
	1995	239386	77.3	59.0	55.7	13.4	2.5	2.4	1.1	17.8	3.5	1.8	3.1	4.0	8.8
	2000	282810	84.0	62.0	59.0	17.7	2.0	2.4	0.9	14.8	2.9	1.8	2.4	3.6	7.0
	2003	306063	80.6	59.0	56.3	17.5	2.0	2.2	1.6	15.9	3.6	1.5	2.8	4.1	7.4
United Republic of Tanzania - République-Unie de Tanzanie	1990	416	53.8	42.7	40.9	7.0	3.9	0.3	0.8	42.8	2.1	0.0	8.7	1.9	32.1
	1995	697	47.2	34.6	34.0	3.5	8.4	0.6	0.2	49.6	6.7	0.0	15.8	4.9	28.9
	2000	735	59.1	51.6	50.4	2.2	4.8	0.5	0.7	40.2	2.1	0.2	19.1	1.8	19.0
	2003	911	49.0	35.4	32.6	2.8	9.9	1.0	0.9	42.5	5.0	0.2	18.9	4.0	19.5
United States - Etats-Unis	1990	393106	64.9	28.2	26.5	21.1	12.4	3.3	1.0	33.8	3.3	13.7	2.0	2.6	15.4
	1995	583451	58.6	22.9	21.6	21.6	11.0	3.1	0.8	40.5	3.3	16.5	1.7	2.5	19.8
	2000	771991	57.0	23.2	21.7	22.6	8.4	2.8	0.5	42.4	2.6	21.6	1.4	2.0	17.2
	2003	723611	56.4	22.8	21.3	23.4	7.2	3.0	0.6	43.0	2.4	20.6	1.5	2.1	18.7
Uruguay	1990	1730	41.7	27.9	27.5	11.0	1.2	1.7	5.3	51.6	4.7	39.8	1.6	4.3	5.9
	1995	2121	32.0	22.0	21.2	6.7	0.9	2.5	0.4	66.9	1.8	53.3	0.9	1.8	10.9
	2000	2295	32.6	17.2	16.3	11.0	1.5	2.9	0.3	66.1	3.1	54.3	1.8	2.1	7.9
	2003	2736	40.9	23.5	22.9	12.6	1.9	2.9	0.9	57.1	5.0	45.0	2.9	2.5	6.7
USSR (former) - URSS (anc.)	1990	45924	75.5	66.1	64.6	2.6	6.7	0.1	9.7	14.8	1.1	0.5	1.7	3.8	8.8
Uzbekistan - Ouzbékistan	1995	2718	34.3	30.0	29.8	0.6	3.7	0.0	56.6	9.0	0.1	4.1	0.0	0.7	4.2
	2000	2132	32.5	27.0	26.9	2.2	3.3	0.1	53.7	13.8	0.4	1.2	0.1	3.7	8.9
	2003	1914	29.2	20.1	19.9	4.6	4.4	0.2	41.5	29.3	2.3	0.0	0.3	7.4	21.6
Vanuatu	1990	25	89.9	57.9	54.3	3.7	20.6	7.7	0.3	9.5	0.3	0.3	0.2	0.3	2.2
	1995	29	76.6	37.9	37.9	1.1	25.1	12.5	0.4	22.5	..	0.1	7.3	..	7.0
	2000	86	35.6	5.8	5.8	9.9	18.9	1.0	0.0	64.1	20.1	0.0	0.1	..	60.5
	2003	107	15.4	3.3	3.3	1.1	7.0	4.0	..	84.2	9.0	0.1	1.0	..	79.2
Venezuela	1990	18044	71.3	14.2	14.0	54.2	2.8	0.1	0.1	27.3	0.1	14.5	0.3	0.0	1.6
	1995	19093	62.4	9.2	9.1	51.7	1.5	0.0	0.2	35.3	0.1	29.8	0.2	0.0	0.4
	2000	33358	58.9	5.1	5.0	53.1	0.7	0.0	0.1	35.7	0.2	34.6	0.0	0.2	0.7
	2002	26641	53.9	7.5	7.2	46.2	0.2	0.0	0.1	33.2	0.1	31.7	0.1	0.1	1.1
Viet Nam	1990	2525	23.9	10.0	9.8	0.1	13.5	0.3	38.2	28.4	1.7	0.5	0.2	0.9	26.8
	1995	5621	44.3	13.9	12.6	3.3	26.0	1.1	1.6	45.5	2.3	0.9	0.7	0.9	43.0
	2000	14482	54.4	21.8	20.5	5.7	17.8	9.0	1.2	43.9	4.4	0.9	1.0	2.8	39.1
	2003	21349	65.3	22.9	22.4	22.0	13.2	7.2	0.9	33.2	4.5	0.6	0.9	2.9	28.8

For sources and notes, see end of table 3.1B.

Pour les sources et les notes, se reporter à la fin du tableau 3.1B.

Destination / Origin Origine	Year Année	World [1] (millions of dollars) Monde [1] (millions de dollars)	Developed economies Economies développées					South-East Europe and CIS Europe du Sud-Est et CEI	Developing economies Economies en développement					
			Total	Europe		USA and Canada Etats-Unis et Canada	Japan Japon	Other Autres		Total	of which: dont : OPEC OPEP	America Amérique	Africa Afrique	West Asia Asie occidentale	Other Asia Autres pays d'Asie
				Total	EU UE										
			Percentage / En pourcentage												
Yemen - Yémen	1990	1561	87.5	56.7	56.6	24.1	5.2	1.5	0.4	11.6	1.8	0.0	1.4	1.9	8.3
	1995	1942	13.7	1.1	1.1	0.3	12.3	0.0	0.0	85.7	3.0	8.6	10.4	4.8	61.8
	2000	4076	12.3	2.3	1.2	6.2	2.1	1.7	1.1	83.9	4.0	1.6	2.0	4.1	76.2
	2003	4927	6.1	2.2	1.5	1.3	2.2	0.4	0.3	93.5	7.0	0.0	2.6	7.3	83.7
Yugoslavia, SFR (former) - Yougoslavie, RSF (anc.)	1990	14356	65.8	59.7	58.1	5.2	0.3	0.6	21.1	13.1	5.3	0.8	5.0	5.4	1.9
Zambia - Zambie	1990	544	64.1	31.5	30.6	1.6	31.0	0.0	..	35.9	8.7	0.0	7.8	5.4	22.7
	1995	986	42.4	16.8	16.5	9.5	16.0	0.1	0.0	56.8	9.9	0.0	12.1	8.9	35.8
	2000	757	47.8	45.9	36.4	1.6	0.0	0.2	0.0	52.2	0.1	6.7	41.8	0.1	3.6
	2003	996	24.8	17.2	17.0	1.2	6.2	0.2	0.2	75.0	0.1	7.7	48.4	0.0	18.9
Zimbabwe	1990	1491	59.3	44.1	42.1	8.4	5.5	1.4	1.0	39.4	1.1	0.7	32.1	0.4	6.2
	1995	1900	56.7	43.1	41.6	4.9	7.9	0.8	0.6	42.3	1.7	1.0	32.7	0.4	8.1
	2000	3280	27.4	19.5	17.2	3.3	4.1	0.6	1.2	27.2	1.1	0.6	17.9	1.1	7.5
	2003	2721	27.5	20.1	19.6	2.3	4.7	0.4	2.0	19.7	0.3	0.5	10.2	0.7	8.3

For sources and notes, see end of table 3.1B.

Pour les sources et les notes, se reporter à la fin du tableau 3.1B.

Origin / Origine Destination	Year Année	World[1] (millions of dollars) Monde[1] (millions de dollars)	Developed economies / Economies développées Europe Total	EU UE	USA and Canada Etats-Unis et Canada	Japan Japon	Other Autres	South-East Europe and CIS Europe du Sud-Est et CEI	Developing economies / Economies en développement Total	of which: dont: OPEC OPEP	America Amérique	Africa Afrique	West Asia Asie occidentale	Other Asia Autres pays d'Asie
			Total											
Afghanistan	1990	479	45.9	16.9	16.3	1.0	27.8	0.1	0.2	53.9	0.9	0.5	0.0	0.7	52.6
	1995	387	45.2	18.4	18.3	2.5	23.8	0.6	10.1	44.7	1.8	0.1	0.0	2.3	42.3
	2000	634	19.4	8.5	8.3	1.9	9.0	0.0	22.3	58.3	1.8	0.1	7.4	2.1	48.6
	2003	1389	30.7	17.0	16.9	5.3	8.2	0.2	14.3	55.0	1.7	0.0	4.9	2.6	47.4
Albania - Albanie	1990	423	61.8	58.7	56.6	2.7	0.3	0.0	14.7	23.5	0.1	0.2	13.7	1.5	8.1
	1995	651	81.9	81.4	80.7	0.5	0.0	0.0	12.3	5.5	0.0	0.5	0.3	4.3	0.4
	2000	1084	82.0	79.9	78.2	1.6	0.4	0.1	9.2	8.4	0.2	0.4	0.2	5.9	1.9
	2003	1821	78.6	77.3	76.4	0.7	0.1	0.4	10.5	10.9	0.4	0.8	0.6	6.6	2.6
Algeria - Algérie	1990	9679	88.3	67.6	66.3	14.9	4.6	1.1	2.7	9.1	1.0	2.6	2.6	2.5	1.4
	1995	10782	83.1	61.3	60.2	17.3	3.4	1.0	1.9	15.0	1.3	3.4	2.8	3.5	5.2
	2000	9027	78.9	59.8	59.6	15.5	3.0	0.7	5.4	15.7	1.2	2.9	2.1	4.5	6.3
	2003	14714	75.9	67.6	67.5	5.5	2.1	0.7	4.3	19.8	1.1	3.6	2.1	5.4	8.8
American Samoa - Samoa américaines	1990	68	80.4	0.0	0.0	0.4	36.6	43.5	..	19.6	..	0.1	0.5	..	16.4
	1995	73	76.8	0.8	0.7	..	24.7	51.2	0.0	23.2	..	0.0	..	..	9.1
	2000	57	83.9	0.0	0.0	1.2	12.7	69.9	..	16.1	..	0.0	..	..	12.9
	2003	112	55.8	4.7	4.7	1.0	3.7	46.4	..	44.2	..	0.1	6.0	..	35.7
Angola	1990	1723	85.0	72.9	70.3	10.1	1.9	0.1	0.2	14.8	0.1	7.3	2.3	..	5.2
	1995	1891	79.2	62.1	60.9	15.3	1.5	0.4	0.1	20.7	0.2	2.7	10.2	0.1	7.6
	2000	2184	63.5	50.8	47.1	11.3	1.3	0.1	2.0	34.5	1.0	6.0	19.5	0.5	8.5
	2003	4477	68.5	54.6	52.6	12.5	1.3	0.1	1.2	30.3	0.4	7.1	14.2	0.5	8.5
Antigua and Barbuda - Antigua-et-Barbuda	1990	176	85.2	38.3	37.5	46.7	..	0.2	0.1	14.7	..	7.4	6.5	..	0.8
	1995	298	78.8	40.9	40.2	37.7	..	0.3	0.1	21.1	0.1	15.9	1.5	0.0	3.7
	2000	917	85.5	68.2	67.5	17.2	..	0.1	0.0	14.5	0.2	8.5	0.1	0.0	5.9
	2003	605	53.4	26.7	26.2	25.5	1.1	0.2	3.3	43.3	1.7	17.5	0.2	0.9	24.6
Argentina - Argentine	1990	4078	59.6	31.9	29.4	22.1	3.3	2.3	0.6	39.8	0.5	34.8	0.5	0.3	4.2
	1995	19221	55.6	30.6	29.4	20.4	3.5	1.1	0.6	41.3	0.7	30.9	0.8	0.1	9.0
	2000	25281	49.6	24.6	23.6	20.3	4.0	0.8	0.6	47.7	1.7	34.3	1.8	0.3	11.2
	2003	12459	53.2	28.1	26.8	22.0	2.4	0.8	0.5	44.2	1.0	34.0	1.1	0.3	8.7
Armenia - Arménie	1995	696	33.9	17.4	16.3	16.5	..	..	49.8	16.2	14.9	..	0.4	15.7	0.1
	2000	885	51.2	38.5	35.9	12.2	0.4	0.0	20.5	23.0	14.0	2.4	0.0	19.3	1.3
	2003	1144	55.1	35.3	34.2	10.1	0.3	9.4	21.8	23.1	14.8	0.8	0.1	16.1	2.1
Aruba	1995	543	81.9	19.3	18.6	59.8	2.7	0.1	..	17.9	3.7	16.1	0.0	0.1	1.4
	2000	794	77.3	21.6	21.2	52.4	2.8	0.5	0.1	22.4	3.8	18.8	1.5	0.2	1.9
	2003	847	80.8	22.2	21.2	55.7	2.5	0.4	0.0	19.1	3.2	16.6	0.1	0.1	2.3
Australia - Australie	1990	43051	76.8	27.3	25.7	26.2	18.7	4.6	0.2	22.9	3.7	1.2	0.4	3.0	17.1
	1995	63226	71.4	27.1	25.6	23.8	15.4	5.0	0.1	28.3	4.0	1.2	0.6	2.4	22.2
	2000	74265	62.3	22.6	21.4	21.7	13.2	4.2	0.1	37.2	4.8	1.2	0.9	2.6	30.8
	2003	93203	59.2	24.5	23.4	17.4	12.5	4.2	0.1	40.4	4.8	1.2	1.1	2.0	34.6
Austria - Autriche	1990	49288	88.3	79.4	74.5	4.1	4.5	0.3	3.2	8.5	2.1	1.0	2.5	1.0	4.0
	1995	66263	90.0	82.7	78.6	4.7	2.5	0.2	2.6	7.4	1.4	0.8	1.5	1.0	4.1
	2000	72117	90.8	84.4	79.6	4.7	1.5	0.2	3.5	5.7	1.4	0.4	1.1	1.3	2.9
	2003	97964	89.6	85.7	80.7	2.6	1.1	0.1	4.1	6.2	1.0	0.3	1.0	1.5	3.4
Azerbaijan - Azerbaïdjan	1995	668	19.9	17.1	16.6	2.1	0.2	0.4	35.2	44.9	22.3	0.0	0.2	43.4	1.2
	2000	1172	40.5	27.6	22.3	10.4	1.4	1.2	33.4	26.0	6.7	0.6	2.1	17.8	5.4
	2003	2582	47.9	38.1	36.2	6.0	3.1	0.7	28.0	24.2	3.9	0.6	0.2	12.2	10.9
Bahamas	1990	2311	83.9	23.2	19.0	40.2	20.4	0.1	0.2	15.4	1.0	7.7	1.6	1.0	5.1
	1995	2188	73.4	34.1	32.3	34.0	5.1	0.3	10.6	15.0	2.4	9.4	0.4	0.4	4.8
	2000	3932	67.0	27.1	24.5	29.9	9.8	0.2	2.5	28.9	4.8	8.4	1.3	0.6	18.6
	2003	6564	59.7	36.1	25.7	18.5	4.9	0.2	1.0	37.9	5.1	11.5	0.1	0.9	25.4
Bahrain - Bahreïn	1990	3711	34.5	16.9	16.4	7.2	5.0	5.4	..	59.4	53.2	1.0	0.3	53.5	4.6
	1995	3716	38.7	20.9	19.5	8.6	4.0	5.1	0.2	59.1	45.2	2.1	0.6	46.1	10.3
	2000	3550	46.3	27.7	25.8	13.0	3.9	1.6	0.1	53.2	33.9	2.7	0.7	35.8	13.9
	2003	5010	47.8	27.0	23.7	11.4	7.6	1.7	0.1	51.7	34.8	2.3	1.4	36.7	11.3

For sources and notes, see end of table.

Pour les sources et les notes, se reporter à la fin du tableau.

Destination	Year / Année	World (millions of dollars) Monde [1] (millions de dollars)	Developed economies / Economies développées — Total	Europe Total	Europe EU / UE	USA and Canada Etats-Unis et Canada	Japan Japon	Other Autres	South-East Europe and CIS Europe du Sud-Est et CEI	Developing economies / Economies en développement — Total	of which / dont: OPEC OPEP	America Amérique	Africa Afrique	West Asia Asie occidentale	Other Asia Autres pays d'Asie
Bangladesh	1990	3656	44.0	20.7	18.5	8.3	13.2	1.8	1.3	41.3	6.3	1.5	0.3	5.1	34.4
	1995	6496	31.4	13.8	12.3	7.0	9.2	1.4	1.2	58.2	4.5	2.1	0.5	3.5	51.9
	2000	9001	26.3	11.3	9.7	3.5	9.4	2.0	0.9	56.0	7.0	1.5	1.0	5.3	48.1
	2003	9529	23.0	11.3	9.8	3.5	6.0	2.1	1.3	66.8	8.8	1.2	0.7	6.5	58.4
Barbados - Barbade	1990	700	68.7	22.1	21.0	39.4	5.3	1.8	0.0	31.3	4.1	27.1	0.0	0.0	3.2
	1995	765	73.0	18.7	17.3	46.0	6.8	1.6	0.0	27.0	4.0	22.9	0.1	0.1	3.8
	2000	1156	69.0	16.4	15.5	45.7	5.2	1.7	0.1	30.9	0.8	25.2	0.1	0.9	4.6
	2003	1202	65.2	17.8	16.7	41.2	4.4	1.7	0.1	34.8	0.4	29.4	0.2	0.2	5.0
Belarus - Bélarus	1995	5505	27.3	24.3	23.9	2.3	0.4	0.3	70.0	2.7	0.2	0.7	0.3	0.3	1.4
	2000	8646	24.2	21.9	21.2	1.7	0.5	0.2	70.6	4.1	0.2	1.5	0.3	0.3	2.0
	2003	12016	23.8	22.8	22.4	0.8	0.1	0.1	72.7	1.9	0.0	0.7	0.2	0.2	0.7
Belgium - Belgique	2000	175125	85.4	72.4	70.4	8.4	2.9	1.7	1.5	13.1	1.5	2.0	3.2	0.9	7.0
	2003	224950	85.8	75.0	73.3	6.4	3.2	1.2	1.7	12.4	1.8	1.9	2.6	1.2	6.7
Belgium-Luxembourg - Belgique-Luxembourg	1990	119414	88.4	80.2	77.5	5.0	2.1	1.2	1.4	10.1	2.6	1.6	4.0	1.7	2.8
	1995	158273	88.6	79.1	77.0	6.1	2.5	1.0	1.2	9.1	0.8	1.4	3.4	0.4	3.8
Belize	1990	211	77.3	15.8	15.6	60.0	1.2	0.3	0.0	22.6	0.6	18.7	0.0	0.1	3.8
	1995	259	69.7	11.0	10.7	57.2	1.3	0.2	0.0	30.3	0.2	27.8	0.0	0.0	2.4
	2000	443	66.7	11.6	11.5	52.5	2.5	0.0	0.0	33.3	1.7	31.3	..	0.1	1.9
	2003	561	57.1	14.1	13.9	39.9	3.0	0.1	0.3	42.6	0.3	35.5	0.2	0.0	6.9
Benin - Bénin	1990	265	49.4	37.4	35.5	8.9	3.1	0.0	0.8	49.8	9.1	1.8	27.8	0.4	19.6
	1995	636	60.8	51.0	50.3	6.1	3.7	0.0	0.7	38.5	7.8	0.7	18.6	1.5	17.4
	2000	562	57.7	49.8	49.5	4.5	3.4	0.0	0.9	40.9	6.0	0.5	24.2	2.3	14.0
	2003	1725	40.2	37.0	36.9	2.2	0.9	0.1	0.5	58.9	4.0	0.8	16.7	2.0	39.4
Bermuda - Bermudes	1990	595	86.5	16.9	15.7	64.2	5.2	0.3	0.0	12.1	6.8	9.6	0.0	0.0	2.4
	1995	693	91.3	11.4	10.9	76.0	3.7	0.2	0.0	8.5	1.8	6.7	0.1	0.0	1.6
	2000	4203	59.2	42.6	42.3	11.6	5.0	0.1	34.5	6.2	0.0	4.8	0.0	0.2	1.2
	2003	5839	42.0	33.5	33.2	8.2	0.4	0.1	46.7	11.2	0.0	2.0	0.0	0.0	9.2
Bolivia - Bolivie	1990	700	50.0	16.8	16.3	23.2	9.9	0.1	0.5	49.2	0.4	47.2	0.1	0.0	1.8
	1995	1449	56.1	20.0	19.3	23.3	12.4	0.4	0.3	43.5	0.9	38.9	0.2	0.0	4.4
	2000	2023	40.8	11.6	11.0	23.2	5.2	0.4	0.1	59.0	1.0	51.3	0.1	0.1	7.5
	2003	1751	23.0	8.6	8.3	11.8	1.9	0.2	0.1	73.7	1.1	69.9	0.2	0.1	3.6
Bosnia and Herzegovina - Bosnie-Herzégovine	1995	950	43.5	40.2	39.9	3.3	..	0.0	54.9	1.6	..	0.0	0.8	0.6	0.2
	2000	2644	74.6	72.3	71.4	1.9	0.2	0.2	23.9	1.5	0.0	0.1	0.0	1.1	0.3
	2003	4019	70.2	69.5	68.7	0.6	0.0	0.1	27.8	2.0	0.0	0.1	0.0	1.4	0.4
Brazil - Brésil	1990	24977	56.5	26.4	24.2	22.0	7.1	1.0	0.7	42.8	22.1	17.6	2.9	19.2	3.2
	1995	54363	61.2	30.3	28.4	23.4	6.6	0.8	1.4	37.0	6.7	20.7	2.4	3.9	10.0
	2000	61875	59.7	28.1	25.9	25.0	5.3	1.2	1.4	38.7	8.9	21.0	5.2	2.2	10.3
	2003	57744	56.8	29.3	26.8	22.5	3.6	1.4	1.1	42.0	9.8	19.1	6.5	2.9	13.5
Brunei Darussalam - Brunéi Darussalam	1990	1000	51.1	18.5	18.1	15.4	14.6	2.6	0.0	47.2	1.9	0.2	..	0.0	46.9
	1995	2960	39.1	17.2	16.4	9.2	8.8	3.9	..	59.8	2.3	0.0	..	0.3	59.6
	2000	1426	33.7	16.0	15.8	10.8	4.7	2.2	0.0	66.1	2.0	0.1	0.1	0.2	65.7
	2003	1851	40.2	30.5	30.3	2.2	5.7	1.8	..	59.6	2.0	0.0	0.1	0.2	59.2
Bulgaria - Bulgarie	1990	3462	70.3	64.7	61.6	3.4	1.7	0.5	7.0	22.7	12.0	2.6	9.0	4.5	6.5
	1995	5469	47.9	43.8	41.9	2.4	0.8	0.9	38.5	13.4	4.9	3.5	2.2	5.2	2.6
	2000	6362	56.2	50.4	49.0	3.2	1.0	0.3	32.8	10.5	0.7	2.9	0.7	3.6	3.2
	2003	10683	61.7	55.4	54.2	2.7	1.3	0.8	21.1	16.0	1.4	2.8	0.3	6.8	6.1
Burkina Faso	1990	536	58.7	46.8	46.1	7.7	4.2	..	0.1	38.7	2.2	0.5	28.2	..	9.2
	1995	481	58.4	46.0	45.2	5.1	7.1	0.2	0.2	41.1	6.7	2.3	30.4	0.2	8.0
	2000	511	50.2	44.7	44.5	3.8	1.7	0.0	0.6	43.3	6.7	0.3	38.8	0.4	3.7
	2003	863	51.4	48.4	48.2	1.7	0.9	0.4	0.6	43.0	5.9	0.4	37.3	0.4	4.9
Burundi	1990	235	55.7	47.2	46.1	1.2	7.3	0.1	0.0	32.3	12.5	..	12.0	12.5	7.5
	1995	233	62.0	51.0	50.4	5.2	5.7	0.1	0.3	36.8	1.3	..	16.4	1.3	19.0
	2000	147	46.0	24.7	24.0	3.4	5.2	0.1	0.4	51.6	12.2	..	25.9	12.2	13.1
	2003	158	37.1	31.7	31.3	3.2	2.1	0.1	0.0	61.3	19.9	0.2	29.6	13.7	17.5

For sources and notes, see end of table.

Pour les sources et les notes, se reporter à la fin du tableau.

Origin / Origine Destination	Year / Année	World [1] (millions of dollars) Monde [1] (millions de dollars)	Developed economies / Economies développées						South-East Europe and CIS Europe du Sud-Est et CEI	Developing economies / Economies en développement					
			Total	Europe		USA and Canada	Japan	Other		Total	of which: dont :	America	Africa	West Asia	Other Asia
				Total	EU UE	Etats-Unis et Canada Japon	Japon	Autres			OPEC OPEP	Amérique	Afrique	Asie occiden-tale	Autres pays d'Asie
									Percentage / En pourcentage						
Cambodia - Cambodge	1990	56	40.0	28.5	28.2	0.0	9.0	2.5	0.0	59.9	23.9	0.5	0.1	3.5	55.8
	1995	1573	15.7	7.1	7.0	2.0	5.4	1.2	0.0	84.3	5.6	0.0	0.1	0.0	84.2
	2000	1424	15.5	8.1	6.6	2.8	4.1	0.5	0.0	83.6	4.8	0.1	0.0	0.1	83.4
	2003	2932	8.8	4.1	4.0	2.2	2.0	0.5	0.2	91.0	3.0	0.1	0.0	0.1	90.9
Cameroon - Cameroun	1990	1555	81.9	69.4	67.9	6.7	5.7	0.1	0.9	17.0	0.5	1.9	8.2	0.2	6.6
	1995	1199	61.5	53.7	52.7	2.9	4.9	0.1	0.8	28.8	8.8	1.6	20.8	0.6	5.9
	2000	1490	56.8	40.4	39.8	6.4	4.9	0.2	1.3	37.7	20.3	0.9	29.3	1.6	5.9
	2003	1788	61.4	42.9	42.3	6.6	6.8	0.3	1.8	36.4	11.6	2.6	20.5	1.8	11.5
Canada	1990	131640	84.6	14.1	12.5	62.9	6.8	0.8	0.3	11.2	1.6	3.3	0.8	0.7	6.5
	1995	179617	84.6	11.7	10.2	66.7	5.4	0.8	0.3	13.3	1.2	4.1	0.8	0.4	8.0
	2000	262721	82.1	12.3	10.6	64.4	4.7	0.7	0.3	15.7	1.7	5.0	0.8	0.6	9.3
	2003	263333	79.1	13.6	11.9	60.6	4.1	0.8	0.4	19.2	2.0	5.7	1.3	0.8	11.4
Cape Verde - Cap-Vert	1990	145	83.8	79.2	78.9	4.6	..	..	3.4	9.4	..	4.4	4.1	..	0.9
	1995	260	84.3	81.2	80.8	3.0	..	0.1	0.8	11.3	0.0	5.9	3.4	..	2.0
	2000	237	85.3	75.1	74.9	4.7	5.3	0.2	1.2	12.2	0.3	2.9	2.0	2.2	5.1
	2003	361	81.6	77.8	77.6	2.8	0.9	0.0	0.4	16.7	3.1	2.2	6.2	3.8	4.4
Central African Republic - République centrafricaine	1990	184	69.5	64.4	63.6	0.8	4.3	0.0	0.2	30.1	0.1	0.8	24.4	0.2	4.7
	1995	189	76.3	49.4	49.2	2.6	24.3	0.0	0.0	13.1	0.4	0.3	11.2	0.3	1.2
	2000	126	53.7	47.8	47.7	2.0	3.5	0.4	2.0	22.5	1.4	0.2	14.9	2.8	3.7
	2003	152	44.0	36.9	36.8	5.4	1.5	0.0	0.3	29.4	1.7	0.3	20.2	3.6	4.3
Chad - Tchad	1990	167	75.0	65.9	65.4	5.3	3.8	0.0	0.1	24.9	16.6	0.2	21.3	0.2	3.1
	1995	163	74.9	64.1	63.8	7.8	2.9	0.1	..	25.1	9.7	0.1	15.5	0.8	8.8
	2000	155	66.5	58.4	57.8	6.8	1.3	0.1	0.6	32.9	17.2	..	22.9	5.6	4.4
	2003	380	65.4	45.6	45.4	19.3	0.4	0.0	5.4	29.2	10.1	0.1	22.5	4.2	2.5
Chile - Chili	1990	7227	58.5	27.7	26.1	22.1	7.9	0.8	0.8	37.5	6.2	24.1	7.8	0.2	5.0
	1995	15479	56.1	21.6	20.6	26.5	6.5	1.5	0.4	39.7	3.2	26.8	2.0	0.2	10.7
	2000	18535	42.0	16.5	15.7	20.5	3.8	1.1	0.6	46.9	3.7	32.2	2.8	0.3	11.7
	2003	19413	36.5	17.7	17.0	14.7	3.3	0.8	0.3	52.1	1.6	37.7	1.3	0.1	13.0
China - Chine	1990	53809	51.3	19.3	18.2	15.0	14.2	2.8	4.8	43.1	2.2	2.8	0.7	1.0	38.5
	1995	132163	55.7	17.2	16.3	14.2	21.9	2.3	3.9	38.7	2.5	2.2	1.1	1.6	33.7
	2000	224718	46.0	14.3	13.4	11.2	17.8	2.6	3.1	47.9	4.2	2.1	2.1	3.9	39.6
	2003	412836	43.5	14.1	13.2	9.3	18.0	2.2	3.3	47.1	4.0	3.6	2.0	3.5	38.0
China, Hong Kong SAR - Chine, Hong Kong RAS	1990	82482	38.6	12.3	10.4	8.5	16.1	1.7	0.1	61.3	1.0	0.8	0.6	0.3	59.6
	1995	192765	36.8	12.0	10.8	8.4	14.8	1.6	0.3	63.0	1.3	0.6	0.4	0.6	61.3
	2000	213319	30.8	10.0	8.8	7.5	12.0	1.4	0.2	68.9	1.2	0.6	0.3	0.5	67.5
	2003	232545	28.9	9.9	8.5	6.0	11.9	1.2	0.3	70.8	1.4	0.8	0.4	0.8	68.8
China, Macao SAR - Chine, Macao RAS	1990	1532	27.6	9.5	9.3	5.4	11.5	1.2	0.4	72.0	1.0	0.2	0.3	0.2	71.3
	1995	2049	34.6	15.0	14.6	8.4	10.4	0.8	0.3	64.4	1.0	0.1	0.4	0.6	63.2
	2000	2249	23.3	9.9	9.6	5.3	6.3	1.8	0.0	76.7	1.0	0.3	0.2	0.6	75.6
	2003	3380	16.6	7.9	7.6	2.6	4.8	1.3	0.1	83.3	0.6	8.6	0.3	0.5	74.0
China, Taiwan Province of - Chine, Taiwan Province de	1990	53753	76.1	17.7	15.3	25.0	30.0	3.6	0.2	23.5	6.6	2.4	0.5	6.1	14.5
	1995	103649	70.0	16.2	14.7	21.6	29.2	3.0	1.9	28.0	5.2	2.3	1.8	3.7	20.2
	2000	140012	61.7	12.3	11.3	18.9	27.5	3.1	1.3	36.9	6.4	1.5	2.3	4.5	28.5
	2003	138829	52.6	10.8	9.9	14.5	24.8	2.5	1.0	46.1	7.4	1.3	1.9	6.3	36.6
Colombia - Colombie	1990	5589	75.7	26.1	23.1	38.9	8.9	1.8	0.6	23.0	5.8	21.6	0.1	0.0	1.3
	1995	13859	70.5	20.8	18.7	41.7	7.5	0.5	0.2	29.0	9.9	25.2	0.1	0.0	3.3
	2000	11327	61.9	18.5	17.4	37.4	5.5	0.6	0.4	37.0	8.9	28.7	0.5	0.1	7.1
	2003	13881	54.6	17.2	15.9	31.9	4.6	0.9	0.7	39.8	5.8	27.4	0.7	0.1	11.5
Comoros - Comores	1990	86	88.2	82.5	82.4	..	5.5	0.2	..	11.8	0.1	0.1	6.7	0.1	4.9
	1995	151	70.7	68.4	68.1	0.4	1.8	0.0	0.3	29.0	0.5	0.8	22.1	0.3	5.8
	2000	63	47.6	40.2	40.2	1.4	0.4	5.5	0.0	51.3	11.6	0.3	26.3	8.1	16.7
	2003	113	58.3	43.1	42.8	0.7	14.1	0.3	0.2	40.6	7.5	0.1	23.2	6.5	10.8

For sources and notes, see end of table.   Pour les sources et les notes, se reporter à la fin du tableau.

Destination	Year / Année	World (millions of dollars) / Monde (millions de dollars)	Developed economies / Economies développées					South-East Europe and CIS / Europe du Sud-Est et CEI	Developing economies / Economies en développement					
			Total	Europe		USA and Canada / Etats-Unis et Canada	Japan / Japon	Other / Autres		Total	of which: / dont: OPEC / OPEP	America / Amérique	Africa / Afrique	West Asia / Asie occidentale	Other Asia / Autres pays d'Asie
				Total	EU / UE										
			Percentage / En pourcentage												
Congo	1990	598	76.4	66.0	65.0	6.2	4.2	0.0	0.7	9.7	1.4	1.0	4.0	1.4	3.4
	1995	463	71.5	58.5	57.7	9.7	3.2	..	0.0	11.3	0.7	0.3	7.2	0.0	3.7
	2000	908	55.9	45.4	44.8	9.8	0.7	0.0	1.0	31.9	2.1	1.2	12.3	0.4	17.9
	2003	1267	53.4	44.8	44.0	7.2	0.7	0.7	1.1	34.0	1.4	1.9	13.6	0.7	17.6
Costa Rica	1990	2026	65.6	14.9	13.9	42.0	8.4	0.2	0.2	33.6	8.0	28.2	0.0	0.0	5.4
	1995	3205	63.4	12.6	12.0	46.6	3.8	0.4	0.4	36.2	6.7	31.3	0.1	0.0	4.4
	2000	6389	38.4	9.7	9.2	24.7	3.1	0.3	0.4	26.9	5.2	22.9	0.0	0.1	3.8
	2003	11239	50.3	9.3	8.8	33.9	4.2	2.9	0.2	21.9	3.7	16.3	0.0	0.1	5.5
Côte d'Ivoire	1990	2098	59.5	51.6	50.7	5.3	2.4	0.2	0.8	37.3	24.2	2.2	29.9	0.2	5.0
	1995	3038	68.6	58.0	56.8	6.0	4.3	0.3	2.3	29.1	13.4	2.6	17.3	0.7	8.3
	2000	2734	45.8	35.6	34.8	3.6	2.7	0.3	2.6	48.3	26.5	2.8	29.1	3.0	12.3
	2003	3516	62.0	54.2	53.4	3.4	1.6	0.4	0.2	35.9	16.7	2.5	20.2	1.4	11.8
Croatia - Croatie	1995	7510	85.9	81.6	78.7	2.8	1.1	0.4	4.0	10.1	4.1	1.9	3.5	2.2	2.4
	2000	7688	78.6	71.6	69.3	3.4	1.7	0.3	10.6	9.6	3.1	1.2	2.4	2.3	3.6
	2003	14044	78.4	72.3	70.5	2.8	1.7	0.3	8.5	12.1	0.9	1.2	0.9	3.4	6.2
Cuba	1990	2956	49.1	40.6	39.4	5.1	2.7	0.7	2.7	48.1	17.3	36.1	0.7	0.0	11.4
	1995	2675	48.0	39.0	38.7	7.5	0.8	0.7	11.8	40.2	4.7	27.6	2.5	0.3	9.8
	2000	3845	44.3	37.3	37.1	6.0	0.8	0.3	3.2	52.4	26.7	41.1	1.2	0.0	10.1
	2003	3469	55.9	39.0	38.9	13.6	1.9	1.4	2.0	42.1	13.0	29.9	1.3	0.1	10.7
Cyprus - Chypre	1990	2565	81.5	61.0	59.2	7.6	11.5	1.4	4.3	14.1	4.2	0.8	1.9	3.6	7.8
	1995	3694	76.4	54.2	52.8	13.7	6.7	1.8	5.5	15.0	1.2	1.3	1.0	2.3	10.4
	2000	3846	74.7	53.9	52.6	10.7	5.8	4.3	5.8	18.3	1.7	1.3	1.7	4.2	11.1
	2003	4487	72.0	57.9	56.6	4.3	5.6	4.1	6.0	17.5	1.6	1.6	1.0	4.3	10.7
Czech Republic - République tchèque	1995	22973	82.7	76.6	73.8	4.0	1.7	0.3	10.4	5.7	0.2	0.9	0.3	0.4	4.1
	2000	34808	84.8	77.9	75.3	4.6	1.9	0.4	8.3	6.7	0.6	0.9	0.7	0.5	4.7
	2003	56128	79.9	74.0	71.5	3.4	2.3	0.3	6.6	13.6	0.5	1.1	0.5	1.1	11.0
Czechoslovakia (former) - Tchécoslovaquie (anc.)	1990	15070	64.1	62.2	57.7	0.7	0.5	0.7	26.0	10.0	0.9	2.2	0.7	1.2	5.9
Dem. Rep. of the Congo - Rép. dém. du Congo	1990	1304	70.8	58.9	57.4	7.7	4.1	0.1	0.6	28.6	2.8	0.9	11.8	0.0	15.9
	1995	1351	48.2	38.7	37.7	8.4	0.9	0.1	0.1	51.8	3.8	0.4	30.9	0.3	20.2
	2000	774	40.4	36.9	35.9	1.8	1.3	0.4	0.1	59.6	11.2	0.3	49.7	0.4	9.2
	2003	1113	48.3	43.6	42.8	3.7	0.7	0.4	0.4	51.2	11.0	0.6	43.0	0.4	7.1
Denmark - Danemark	1990	31371	88.3	77.1	69.6	6.7	4.1	0.5	1.1	10.6	1.3	3.2	0.9	1.2	5.3
	1995	42230	88.9	80.5	73.0	5.2	2.7	0.4	1.4	9.6	0.6	2.4	0.8	0.4	6.0
	2000	45530	87.7	80.9	72.2	4.9	1.5	0.4	1.1	11.0	0.7	1.9	0.4	0.8	7.9
	2003	57796	87.7	82.7	76.4	3.3	1.3	0.5	0.9	11.4	0.5	1.9	0.5	1.0	8.0
Djibouti	1990	215	58.0	49.0	47.6	3.5	5.4	0.1	0.6	36.9	7.6	0.2	12.2	10.4	14.2
	1995	440	41.4	33.8	33.3	2.8	4.8	0.0	0.0	56.7	6.7	1.5	10.8	7.3	37.2
	2000	620	36.8	30.0	29.8	3.0	3.6	0.2	0.1	60.7	21.5	0.3	11.8	20.9	27.7
	2003	764	32.3	23.8	23.7	5.0	3.4	0.0	0.1	64.8	24.5	0.8	13.4	25.5	25.0
Dominica - Dominique	1990	118	66.1	24.2	23.1	35.7	6.2	0.1	0.0	33.9	0.7	29.7	0.1	0.0	3.9
	1995	121	64.6	26.0	25.0	34.0	4.4	0.1	0.1	35.3	0.9	32.8	0.1	0.1	1.5
	2000	147	62.9	14.8	14.3	41.7	6.3	0.1	0.0	36.9	1.9	33.9	0.0	0.2	2.2
	2003	209	41.3	14.2	13.4	21.0	6.1	0.0	0.2	58.2	1.7	27.6	0.0	0.4	29.8
Dominican Republic - République dominicaine	1990	2194	66.0	12.1	11.5	43.2	10.1	0.6	0.0	34.0	13.8	30.9	0.2	0.0	2.8
	1995	5351	19.1	1.3	1.2	16.9	0.9	..	..	18.3	7.7	13.1	0.0	..	2.4
	2000	10426	72.3	8.3	8.0	60.9	3.0	0.1	0.2	27.4	10.6	21.4	0.3	0.3	5.2
	2003	9360	62.5	10.4	9.8	50.2	1.4	0.5	0.6	37.0	11.4	29.3	0.8	0.1	6.8
Ecuador - Equateur	1990	1862	69.6	26.7	23.9	33.5	9.2	0.2	0.4	30.0	5.2	25.3	0.6	..	3.4
	1995	4193	58.2	16.6	15.6	32.8	8.6	0.1	1.7	39.2	7.1	31.6	0.8	0.4	5.8
	2000	3924	51.2	14.6	13.8	30.3	5.8	0.5	1.4	46.8	7.3	37.0	1.4	0.5	7.6
	2003	6908	45.2	15.9	15.2	24.7	4.1	0.4	0.8	53.5	7.6	41.5	1.5	0.3	10.1

For sources and notes, see end of table.

Pour les sources et les notes, se reporter à la fin du tableau.

70

Origin / Origine — Destination	Year / Année	World [1] (millions of dollars) / Monde [1] (millions de dollars)	Developed economies / Economies développées — Total	Europe Total	Europe EU / UE	USA and Canada / Etats-Unis et Canada	Japan / Japon	Other / Autres	South-East Europe and CIS / Europe du Sud-Est et CEI	Developing economies / Economies en développement — Total	of which / dont: OPEC / OPEP	America / Amérique	Africa / Afrique	West Asia / Asie occidentale	Other Asia / Autres pays d'Asie
						Percentage / En pourcentage									
Egypt - Egypte	1990	9216	72.3	49.0	46.2	14.8	3.7	4.7	6.4	17.4	2.1	2.9	1.4	3.0	9.4
	1995	11739	66.6	43.0	40.2	19.4	2.7	1.5	6.4	21.5	4.0	3.2	2.4	4.4	11.5
	2000	21987	62.7	39.4	37.6	17.5	3.7	2.1	4.7	26.0	6.0	3.1	1.6	7.0	14.4
	2003	21793	56.9	37.7	35.7	14.3	3.7	1.3	5.4	31.2	7.4	5.2	3.1	8.1	14.8
El Salvador	1990	1277	61.4	14.0	12.8	43.5	3.5	0.4	0.0	35.0	6.2	33.2	0.0	0.0	1.8
	1995	2628	60.2	9.9	9.4	44.8	5.1	0.4	0.2	36.9	2.9	32.4	0.0	0.0	3.6
	2000	3765	49.4	9.5	9.0	36.1	3.3	0.6	1.1	46.8	1.8	43.4	0.1	0.1	3.1
	2003	5515	51.2	11.4	11.1	37.0	2.2	0.6	1.0	45.2	1.6	36.1	0.1	0.0	8.9
Equatorial Guinea - Guinée équatoriale	1990	102	52.9	52.6	52.0	0.1	0.2	..	2.2	45.0	..	0.2	43.1	..	1.6
	1995	139	75.7	70.9	70.3	4.3	0.3	0.2	0.2	24.0	0.1	0.0	21.6	0.0	2.4
	2000	305	84.6	47.0	45.2	33.4	4.2	0.1	0.7	14.7	0.2	1.8	10.6	0.2	2.2
	2003	1194	85.4	53.8	49.3	31.2	0.3	0.0	0.1	14.5	0.1	0.5	13.3	0.0	0.8
Estonia - Estonie	1995	2546	77.9	73.2	71.5	2.7	1.9	0.1	18.9	3.2	0.1	0.7	0.1	0.2	2.2
	2000	5334	69.8	61.9	60.0	2.4	5.3	0.1	17.0	13.3	0.2	0.4	1.3	5.6	5.9
	2003	7966	71.4	63.9	62.0	3.2	4.1	0.2	16.7	11.8	0.4	0.6	1.9	0.5	8.8
Ethiopia - Ethiopie	1990	1076	65.5	52.4	50.0	6.3	6.5	0.3	14.5	12.9	2.0	0.2	3.7	3.1	5.7
	1995	1153	62.0	40.5	39.6	13.1	8.3	0.1	0.3	33.6	12.5	0.1	6.7	12.6	14.1
	2000	1726	39.7	25.9	25.7	9.8	3.3	0.8	6.7	52.9	27.1	0.5	3.1	29.7	16.0
	2003	2704	45.7	25.4	20.4	17.3	2.6	0.3	2.4	51.3	25.7	0.7	2.5	26.7	17.1
Faeroe Islands - Iles Féroé	1990	333	97.1	93.2	67.2	1.7	2.0	0.1	1.3	1.5	0.0	0.2	..	0.1	1.1
	1995	251	98.7	98.5	75.0	0.1	..	0.1	0.1	0.8	..	0.5	..	..	0.2
	2000	455	97.5	96.6	60.1	0.8	..	0.1	0.2	1.8	1.0	0.5	0.0	0.1	1.2
	2003	591	95.1	92.4	68.1	2.5	..	0.2	3.0	1.4	0.5	0.6	..	0.1	0.7
Falkland Islands (Malvinas) - Iles Falkland (Malvinas)	1990	36	94.3	92.8	92.2	..	0.3	1.3	0.4	5.3	..	..	2.8	..	2.4
	1995	48	99.2	98.3	98.3	0.8	0.1	0.0	0.1	0.7	..	..	0.4	..	0.3
	2000	67	97.8	96.7	96.7	0.2	0.1	0.8	0.1	2.1	1.0	0.0	0.0	0.0	2.1
	2003	79	98.9	96.8	96.7	1.5	0.1	0.5	..	1.1	0.1	..	..	..	1.1
Fiji - Fidji	1990	755	74.1	5.6	5.6	13.4	11.0	44.1	..	19.7	..	..	..	..	19.7
	1995	892	75.4	5.1	4.8	10.2	7.0	53.2	0.0	24.0	1.7	0.3	0.1	0.0	23.0
	2000	764	73.0	3.7	3.6	3.7	4.0	61.6	0.0	26.0	1.7	0.3	0.1	0.0	25.3
	2003	992	62.5	2.9	2.8	2.6	4.9	52.2	0.0	36.4	1.6	0.4	0.1	0.0	35.5
Finland - Finlande	1990	26944	82.5	68.0	62.7	7.6	6.4	0.5	10.2	7.2	0.6	1.8	0.4	1.0	4.0
	1995	28113	82.7	68.4	62.7	7.2	6.2	1.0	7.6	7.9	0.2	1.6	0.4	0.2	5.6
	2000	34306	79.7	69.7	64.7	5.2	3.7	1.0	9.7	8.4	0.4	1.4	0.6	0.3	6.1
	2003	41987	79.4	71.7	68.0	4.0	2.8	0.9	12.4	8.2	0.4	1.5	0.5	0.5	5.8
France [2]	1990	234439	80.6	67.1	63.2	8.8	4.0	0.7	2.0	15.0	3.9	2.2	5.1	2.8	4.8
	1995	278251	80.3	67.9	63.9	8.3	3.4	0.7	1.7	14.8	2.8	2.0	4.1	2.1	6.5
	2000	331838	82.0	71.2	66.4	8.0	2.3	0.5	1.9	15.4	3.6	2.0	3.9	2.9	6.4
	2003	390008	81.5	73.1	69.0	6.0	1.9	0.5	2.6	15.1	3.3	1.8	4.5	2.3	6.1
French Guiana - Guyane française [2]	1990	743	87.3	81.3	81.1	3.6	2.3	0.1	0.2	11.7	0.4	9.7	0.6	0.0	1.3
	1995	783	82.7	77.5	77.0	3.7	1.4	0.2	0.4	11.0	0.9	8.5	0.2	0.1	2.2
French Polynesia - Polynésie française	1990	706	95.9	62.5	61.8	11.4	4.4	17.5	0.0	4.1	0.0	0.1	0.0	0.0	3.7
	1995	905	94.9	67.1	66.9	10.1	2.5	15.3	0.0	5.0	..	0.9	0.0	..	3.4
	2000	906	93.2	55.0	54.9	12.0	2.9	23.3	0.0	6.8	0.6	0.4	0.3	..	5.2
	2003	1728	92.7	66.8	66.7	6.3	2.1	17.5	2.0	5.3	0.4	0.5	0.0	0.0	3.5
Gabon	1990	847	83.4	71.5	70.3	7.0	4.9	0.0	0.1	16.4	0.1	1.0	10.8	0.0	4.6
	1995	930	77.3	65.8	65.4	6.6	4.8	0.0	0.0	16.8	0.6	2.0	6.4	0.4	8.1
	2000	1397	88.7	80.8	80.5	5.4	2.3	0.2	0.0	10.9	0.9	0.7	5.7	0.3	4.2
	2003	1319	81.2	73.2	72.4	5.4	2.5	0.1	0.1	18.0	1.7	1.3	11.2	0.4	5.2
Gambia - Gambie	1990	231	53.7	49.8	49.1	0.1	3.8	0.0	3.5	38.9	0.4	0.3	9.6	0.1	28.9
	1995	140	57.1	48.0	47.5	5.3	3.5	0.2	0.1	42.4	1.0	2.4	19.5	0.6	19.9
	2000	324	36.5	31.4	31.1	2.6	2.0	0.4	0.1	63.4	3.7	5.5	16.9	3.8	37.2
	2003	510	35.1	28.1	27.3	5.8	1.1	0.2	0.6	64.3	3.0	6.6	15.4	4.6	37.7

For sources and notes, see end of table.

Pour les sources et les notes, se reporter à la fin du tableau.

Origin / Origine				Developed economies / Economies développées					South-East Europe and CIS	Developing economies / Economies en développement					
		World[1] (millions of dollars)	Total	Europe		USA and Canada	Japan	Other	Europe du Sud-Est et CEI	Total	of which: dont :	America	Africa	West Asia	Other Asia
Destination	Year / Année	Monde[1] (millions de dollars)		Total	EU UE	Etats-Unis et Canada	Japon	Autres			OPEC OPEP	Amérique	Afrique	Asie occiden-tale	Autres pays d'Asie
								Percentage / En pourcentage							
Georgia - Géorgie	1995	392	22.4	17.3	16.9	3.8	0.3	1.1	55.4	22.2	0.6	0.2	0.1	21.5	0.4
	2000	704	42.6	30.9	27.6	10.2	1.0	0.5	36.3	21.1	1.5	1.0	1.6	16.8	1.3
	2003	1324	45.9	33.1	32.7	11.1	1.1	0.6	36.4	17.8	1.2	2.5	0.1	11.6	3.1
Germany - Allemagne	1990	346461	81.6	67.5	61.8	7.4	5.9	0.8	3.7	14.6	2.5	2.7	3.0	2.0	6.8
	1995	443810	81.0	67.0	60.7	7.9	5.5	0.6	3.2	15.7	1.7	2.4	2.2	1.9	9.2
	2000	500278	80.0	65.2	59.7	9.2	4.9	0.7	3.9	16.0	1.9	1.9	2.2	1.8	10.0
	2003	596449	79.4	67.5	61.3	7.8	3.6	0.5	4.0	16.5	1.4	1.9	1.8	1.9	10.9
Ghana	1990	1614	64.1	46.8	45.3	10.4	4.8	2.1	0.7	35.2	15.6	4.8	23.1	0.1	7.1
	1995	2567	57.5	44.7	43.5	7.6	4.0	1.3	0.3	41.6	15.9	6.0	22.3	0.6	12.7
	2000	3158	51.9	41.3	40.6	7.8	1.4	1.4	0.8	46.6	20.2	3.1	29.5	0.7	13.1
	2003	4091	41.6	31.4	30.8	6.8	1.9	1.5	0.7	56.8	22.7	4.3	32.7	1.0	18.7
Gibraltar	1990	599	85.8	74.0	68.5	7.7	4.1	0.0	0.0	14.1	0.1	4.9	6.6	..	2.6
	1995	767	86.1	78.6	76.3	2.7	4.3	0.5	3.8	10.1	0.4	0.1	7.6	0.6	1.9
	2000	2261	60.9	58.7	56.7	0.8	1.3	0.2	37.4	1.7	0.0	0.1	1.4	0.0	0.2
	2003	1786	81.2	75.1	74.0	1.3	4.1	0.7	11.9	6.9	0.0	0.1	1.2	3.4	2.3
Greece - Grèce	1990	19764	82.5	71.8	69.5	4.0	5.9	0.7	4.2	13.2	5.6	1.8	3.5	4.6	3.3
	1995	25944	80.5	73.6	71.6	3.6	2.7	0.6	5.6	14.0	3.9	1.8	3.1	4.0	5.0
	2000	28323	69.9	62.4	60.6	3.5	3.0	0.9	8.0	22.1	10.5	1.1	3.4	10.1	7.4
	2003	43686	67.8	57.4	55.6	5.5	4.3	0.6	10.2	21.9	6.7	1.2	2.2	7.4	11.1
Greenland - Groenland	1990	435	98.0	88.8	79.1	5.1	3.9	0.2	0.1	1.8	0.0	0.3	0.1	0.0	1.4
	1995	421	97.5	90.6	83.3	3.4	3.3	0.2	0.1	2.1	0.1	0.2	0.1	0.0	1.8
	2000	413	99.1	97.4	86.2	1.3	0.1	0.0	0.0	0.4	0.0	0.1	0.0	0.0	0.3
	2003	530	97.6	95.8	86.6	1.3	0.1	0.0	1.4	0.5	0.0	0.1	0.0	0.0	0.4
Grenada - Grenade	1990	109	66.7	22.1	21.6	35.3	7.1	2.1	0.1	33.2	1.1	28.7	0.0	0.0	4.4
	1995	130	65.1	15.8	15.4	45.4	3.3	0.6	0.1	34.8	1.3	31.7	0.0	0.1	2.9
	2000	246	66.5	14.2	14.2	47.4	4.3	0.7	..	33.5	..	25.2	..	..	1.4
	2003	256	50.4	13.8	13.3	31.0	4.2	1.3	..	49.6	1.6	38.8	0.0	0.0	1.0
Guadeloupe[2]	1990	1681	86.8	80.0	79.5	4.2	2.2	0.4	0.1	13.0	1.2	9.6	0.6	0.1	1.7
	1995	2992	57.4	54.8	54.6	2.4	..	0.2	0.0	4.7	0.1	4.2	0.1	0.0	0.4
Guam	1990	632	42.2	..	..	0.5	39.3	2.4	..	57.8	0.0	1.7	0.0	0.0	56.1
	1995	478	33.4	0.0	0.0	0.2	29.3	3.9	0.0	66.6	..	0.2	0.1	..	66.4
	2000	531	24.2	0.1	0.0	0.3	20.6	3.3	..	75.8	0.3	0.1	0.3	..	75.4
	2003	573	27.2	2.2	2.2	0.5	21.4	3.0	0.0	72.8	0.3	0.1	0.3	..	72.5
Guatemala	1990	1698	63.1	16.6	14.9	40.6	5.8	0.2	0.0	36.2	7.0	31.5	0.5	0.0	4.0
	1995	3292	61.6	11.0	10.4	46.4	3.7	0.4	0.1	37.4	4.7	33.3	0.1	0.0	3.8
	2000	5898	49.1	8.8	8.4	36.6	3.3	0.3	0.8	49.7	4.5	32.9	0.2	0.1	16.0
	2003	7502	46.8	8.2	7.8	34.6	3.3	0.6	0.7	52.0	3.7	33.2	0.3	0.1	17.8
Guinea - Guinée	1990	583	75.3	62.4	61.3	9.2	3.6	0.0	0.1	24.7	1.8	2.8	14.4	0.0	7.4
	1995	768	60.4	44.3	44.0	7.3	8.7	0.1	0.8	38.7	1.9	6.2	15.0	0.9	16.7
	2000	533	58.2	45.5	44.5	5.9	5.2	1.6	0.9	40.6	2.4	0.8	25.0	1.5	13.2
	2003	872	61.6	53.8	51.8	4.8	2.0	1.0	1.2	37.0	3.4	3.1	12.0	2.2	19.4
Guinea-Bissau - Guinée-Bissau	1990	124	73.3	61.3	61.2	1.1	10.9	..	3.2	21.5	0.3	0.8	12.8	0.0	8.0
	1995	138	55.5	48.4	48.0	0.7	6.4	0.0	0.0	41.2	0.5	1.2	4.5	..	35.5
	2000	105	47.3	44.9	43.8	0.7	1.6	0.0	0.2	44.5	0.1	2.7	13.7	0.1	28.0
	2003	144	40.7	38.7	38.3	1.0	0.9	0.2	0.5	50.3	0.0	2.9	20.5	0.2	26.7
Guyana	1990	279	63.1	24.3	23.2	33.6	5.1	0.1	0.7	36.2	1.5	31.9	0.0	1.4	2.9
	1995	517	56.5	20.2	20.0	31.2	4.0	1.0	0.1	43.4	1.9	38.7	0.0	0.0	4.6
	2000	649	42.1	11.3	11.3	27.9	2.0	0.9	0.0	57.9	1.2	52.5	0.1	0.2	5.1
	2003	654	48.0	23.4	23.0	20.8	2.5	1.3	0.0	52.0	1.4	44.2	0.1	0.5	7.2
Haiti - Haïti	1990	524	77.8	12.5	11.6	61.1	3.8	0.3	0.0	22.2	0.9	16.0	0.1	0.0	6.1
	1995	974	83.0	14.0	13.4	64.3	4.3	0.4	0.0	17.0	2.1	11.2	0.2	0.0	5.5
	2000	1256	63.1	8.9	8.6	51.4	2.3	0.5	0.1	36.9	1.7	29.7	0.2	0.7	6.1
	2003	1342	65.3	9.1	8.7	53.6	2.2	0.4	0.1	34.7	2.0	25.8	0.1	0.9	7.7

For sources and notes, see end of table.

Pour les sources et les notes, se reporter à la fin du tableau.

Destination	Year / Année	World[1] (millions of dollars) / Monde[1] (millions de dollars)	Developed economies / Economies développées Total	Europe Total	Europe EU / UE	USA and Canada / Etats-Unis et Canada	Japan / Japon	Other / Autres	South-East Europe and CIS / Europe du Sud-Est et CEI	Developing economies / Economies en développement Total	of which: OPEC / dont: OPEP	America / Amérique	Africa / Afrique	West Asia / Asie occidentale	Other Asia / Autres pays d'Asie
Honduras	1990	880	64.6	15.6	15.6	40.4	8.6	..	..	27.6	5.7	24.3	..	..	..
	1995	1643	56.9	9.7	9.7	43.6	3.6	..	..	34.9	1.3	26.9	..	..	..
	2000	5155	62.5	4.5	4.0	55.7	2.2	0.2	0.5	32.3	0.9	19.3	0.1	0.1	8.0
	2003	6009	60.8	6.3	5.9	52.4	1.8	0.2	0.5	32.8	1.8	19.5	0.0	0.0	8.0
Hungary - Hongrie	1990	8621	64.5	59.2	56.0	2.8	2.1	0.4	23.1	10.2	3.8	2.5	3.4	0.7	3.6
	1995	15483	77.1	71.1	68.5	3.4	2.2	0.3	15.7	6.5	0.6	1.4	0.6	0.3	4.1
	2000	32187	75.9	66.3	64.8	4.0	5.3	0.3	10.6	13.1	0.4	1.3	0.4	0.4	11.1
	2003	50920	76.7	71.9	70.6	2.2	2.4	0.2	9.2	14.2	0.2	0.8	0.3	0.6	12.5
Iceland - Islande	1990	1678	91.2	68.2	61.9	14.7	5.6	2.7	5.0	3.7	0.0	0.7	0.3	0.1	2.7
	1995	1768	90.3	73.4	61.9	9.3	4.4	3.2	2.4	6.8	0.2	1.0	0.2	0.1	5.4
	2000	2586	89.7	70.0	60.5	12.0	4.9	2.8	1.9	8.4	0.4	2.4	0.3	0.4	5.3
	2003	2829	86.0	72.4	63.8	8.3	3.8	1.4	3.1	11.0	0.3	2.1	0.3	0.9	7.7
India - Inde	1990	23991	58.6	35.0	34.0	12.3	7.5	3.8	6.3	34.6	16.7	2.2	3.1	18.0	11.2
	1995	34484	49.6	29.0	26.6	10.6	6.5	3.5	3.5	41.1	20.6	1.5	5.0	20.5	14.1
	2000	50336	41.6	27.3	21.2	7.0	4.0	3.2	1.6	33.4	10.4	1.5	6.4	8.3	17.2
	2003	81705	37.3	22.6	21.8	7.4	3.2	4.1	3.7	38.2	10.1	2.9	5.0	8.1	22.2
Indonesia - Indonésie	1990	22005	66.2	22.0	20.8	13.3	24.8	6.0	0.4	33.0	4.7	2.3	0.7	5.1	24.8
	1995	40629	63.4	21.6	20.4	13.7	22.7	5.5	1.3	35.1	4.3	2.6	1.5	4.0	26.8
	2000	33511	47.1	13.2	12.5	12.0	16.1	5.7	0.7	51.3	9.5	1.8	2.5	8.5	38.4
	2003	32544	39.8	11.9	11.1	9.3	13.0	5.5	1.1	58.2	10.8	1.7	4.9	8.0	43.1
Iran, Islamic Rep. of - Iran, Rép. islamique d'	1990	18722	65.9	53.1	49.9	2.5	10.3	..	3.3	21.4	6.0	3.7	..	9.7	8.0
	1995	12313	64.9	46.1	41.9	7.6	7.2	4.0	6.5	28.0	5.5	7.2	0.9	6.5	13.5
	2000	16429	44.4	34.8	33.1	3.1	3.8	2.7	8.7	35.2	7.1	5.2	1.0	7.8	21.3
	2003	28921	56.3	50.1	42.9	1.0	4.3	0.9	8.8	34.8	9.0	4.2	0.5	10.2	20.0
Iraq	1990	6526	71.3	50.0	48.3	13.6	4.6	3.1	2.7	26.0	8.8	2.3	2.1	15.7	5.9
	1995	665	27.4	26.5	19.3	0.1	0.1	0.8	0.0	72.6	1.8	0.0	0.5	60.4	11.7
	2000	3450	49.4	35.1	33.0	2.0	1.4	10.9	5.6	45.0	5.2	3.2	4.4	8.6	28.9
	2003	4684	40.5	27.4	25.4	7.5	1.8	3.8	10.1	49.3	1.6	3.3	6.6	16.5	22.9
Ireland - Irlande	1990	20830	92.9	71.8	70.3	15.1	5.5	0.3	0.5	6.0	0.3	1.0	1.3	0.3	3.5
	1995	32004	83.2	58.9	56.8	18.6	5.3	0.3	0.2	13.1	0.3	0.7	1.2	0.3	10.8
	2000	50640	81.5	59.6	57.1	17.1	4.0	0.7	0.2	12.4	0.2	0.6	0.6	0.3	10.8
	2003	53317	83.9	63.0	60.7	16.7	3.8	0.4	0.2	13.3	0.3	1.2	0.7	0.4	11.0
Israel - Israël	1990	15338	83.9	61.3	51.9	18.6	3.6	0.3	0.4	6.4	0.0	1.1	1.8	0.2	3.3
	1995	28218	82.1	58.9	52.7	19.5	3.3	0.3	1.6	9.9	0.0	0.9	1.5	0.9	6.5
	2000	36801	70.7	48.1	42.6	19.0	3.2	0.4	1.8	14.4	0.1	0.9	1.0	1.7	10.8
	2003	38328	68.0	45.0	38.4	20.2	2.4	0.4	4.3	17.8	0.0	1.3	1.0	2.8	12.8
Italy - Italie	1990	181772	77.2	68.1	63.1	5.9	2.3	0.9	4.3	18.3	7.0	2.5	8.4	3.5	4.0
	1995	205719	77.3	68.6	63.8	5.7	2.2	0.9	4.8	17.8	5.4	2.6	6.7	2.8	5.7
	2000	235279	72.6	63.0	59.4	6.0	2.5	1.0	6.2	21.2	8.1	2.5	7.8	3.9	6.9
	2003	291103	72.3	65.0	60.6	4.5	2.0	0.8	7.1	20.4	6.6	2.4	6.6	3.6	7.8
Jamaica - Jamaïque	1990	1867	73.1	12.7	11.4	54.6	4.9	0.9	0.3	24.6	5.4	21.8	0.0	0.0	2.7
	1995	2891	74.9	13.0	12.0	56.4	4.7	0.7	0.1	23.7	1.9	17.6	0.1	0.9	5.0
	2000	3308	66.2	9.0	8.2	50.2	5.8	1.2	0.1	30.8	4.0	26.0	0.1	0.8	4.0
	2003	4115	64.0	17.4	16.2	41.6	4.1	0.8	0.1	33.8	4.5	27.6	0.1	0.4	5.5
Japan - Japon	1990	235307	50.8	18.3	16.3	26.1	0.0	6.4	1.5	47.7	17.6	4.0	1.6	13.0	28.8
	1995	336027	47.5	16.3	14.7	25.8	0.0	5.5	1.5	50.9	12.7	3.4	1.4	9.1	36.6
	2000	379530	39.9	13.8	12.6	21.4	0.0	4.7	1.3	58.8	16.5	2.8	1.3	12.8	41.7
	2003	383000	36.7	14.4	13.1	17.6	0.0	4.6	1.3	62.1	17.0	2.5	1.7	13.2	44.5
Jordan - Jordanie	1990	2581	57.2	34.5	33.2	18.1	3.2	1.4	3.3	39.5	23.2	0.5	3.0	27.0	9.0
	1995	3713	50.5	35.6	34.0	9.6	3.9	1.4	2.8	45.0	18.5	2.9	2.3	25.2	14.6
	2000	4597	50.6	32.8	31.6	10.5	3.9	3.3	3.5	43.3	21.3	2.7	1.9	24.4	14.3
	2003	7062	48.3	33.6	32.4	8.0	3.1	3.7	2.3	47.3	18.7	2.4	2.5	22.1	20.4
Kazakhstan	1995	3807	20.5	17.9	16.4	1.9	0.2	0.5	70.0	9.5	0.5	1.0	0.0	3.7	4.7
	2000	5048	33.1	23.9	22.8	6.0	2.1	0.5	54.5	12.4	0.8	2.0	0.5	3.6	6.1
	2003	9355	32.5	28.1	27.3	2.3	1.2	0.4	41.4	26.1	0.8	1.6	0.3	3.1	21.1

For sources and notes, see end of table.

Pour les sources et les notes, se reporter à la fin du tableau.

Origin / Origine — Destination	Year / Année	World (millions of dollars) / Monde (millions de dollars)	Developed economies / Economies développées — Total	Europe — Total	Europe — EU / UE	USA and Canada / Etats-Unis et Canada	Japan / Japon	Other / Autres	South-East Europe and CIS / Europe du Sud-Est et CEI	Developing economies / Economies en développement — Total	of which: OPEC / dont: OPEP	America / Amérique	Africa / Afrique	West Asia / Asie occidentale	Other Asia / Autres pays d'Asie
									Percentage / En pourcentage					
Kenya	1990	2041	67.2	45.5	44.3	9.0	11.9	0.8	0.3	24.5	11.2	0.7	4.7	11.5	7.3
	1995	3249	54.5	39.9	38.7	4.2	9.1	1.2	0.4	45.0	10.2	1.1	10.9	10.8	22.2
	2000	3310	46.8	29.6	28.8	9.8	4.4	2.9	0.9	51.7	21.3	2.1	10.5	23.6	15.6
	2003	4182	36.6	24.8	23.9	5.4	4.9	1.4	0.8	61.9	24.3	1.1	12.4	27.1	21.4
Kiribati	1990	43	96.6	6.0	5.9	48.7	11.6	30.4	..	3.4	..	0.1	..	..	3.3
	1995	80	88.5	61.1	61.0	3.2	2.2	22.1	0.1	11.4	..	0.0	..	..	2.9
	2000	51	74.9	7.2	7.1	9.4	19.3	38.9	..	25.1	0.7	0.1	..	..	6.8
	2003	53	61.2	4.6	4.5	3.4	5.6	47.7	..	38.8	0.3	1.0	..	..	12.7
Korea, Dem. People's Rep. of - Corée, Rép. populaire dém. de	1990	1326	39.5	17.4	16.9	0.0	14.6	7.4	0.4	60.1	13.2	0.9	1.4	10.4	47.4
	1995	1549	35.4	16.4	16.1	0.4	18.2	0.4	10.0	54.6	0.6	3.6	0.2	0.5	49.9
	2000	1905	23.5	10.5	10.2	1.0	11.8	0.2	2.9	73.6	11.8	8.4	5.0	5.1	55.1
	2003	2327	18.9	13.1	12.3	1.4	4.3	0.1	5.0	76.1	13.6	7.6	7.2	6.0	55.2
Korea, Republic of - Corée, République de	1990	74405	66.9	13.1	12.2	24.7	25.0	4.1	..	20.7	7.1	2.3	0.8	7.0	10.3
	1995	135110	67.9	14.9	13.7	24.4	24.1	4.4	1.8	29.6	10.0	2.9	1.7	8.4	16.4
	2000	160479	54.8	10.9	10.1	19.6	19.8	4.4	1.6	43.6	17.3	2.0	2.0	15.6	23.9
	2003	186782	51.2	12.1	11.0	15.0	20.5	3.6	1.2	47.6	14.7	2.4	1.4	13.7	30.1
Kuwait - Koweït	1990	4049	62.0	37.9	36.4	11.7	11.4	1.0	3.2	21.4	1.1	1.0	0.2	2.8	17.0
	1995	7771	68.2	40.0	38.7	17.5	9.4	1.3	0.5	31.2	10.7	1.6	1.3	14.1	14.2
	2000	7388	58.2	34.1	32.7	12.5	8.7	2.9	0.2	41.6	15.6	1.5	1.5	19.9	18.6
	2003	11075	66.2	36.3	34.6	15.5	10.4	3.9	0.5	33.4	10.7	1.1	0.8	15.0	16.5
Kyrgyzstan - Kirghizistan	1995	392	3.7	1.6	1.6	1.6	0.5	..	68.8	27.5	1.0	0.7	..	2.0	24.8
	2000	555	28.2	14.6	13.7	11.7	1.8	0.1	54.1	17.7	2.9	0.1	..	7.7	9.8
	2003	712	23.4	13.7	13.1	7.9	1.7	0.1	57.8	18.8	2.0	0.2	0.1	5.6	12.9
Lao People's Dem. Rep. - Rép. dém. populaire lao	1990	149	25.9	9.7	9.0	0.8	14.5	0.9	0.0	73.7	0.1	0.2	0.1	0.1	73.3
	1995	589	9.8	1.2	1.2	0.3	8.3	0.1	0.5	62.4	..	..	..	..	62.4
	2000	686	11.7	6.6	6.5	0.7	3.4	0.9	0.2	86.5	0.1	0.0	0.0	0.0	86.4
	2003	841	8.7	5.4	5.0	0.6	1.8	1.0	0.3	89.2	0.1	0.0	0.0	0.2	89.0
Latvia - Lettonie	1995	1810	69.9	66.0	64.3	2.1	0.6	1.2	28.3	1.8	0.1	0.6	0.1	0.2	0.9
	2000	3184	79.9	77.0	74.0	2.2	0.1	0.5	17.3	2.4	0.1	0.2	0.1	0.5	1.6
	2003	6902	76.7	73.9	71.7	2.2	0.3	0.3	19.1	3.7	0.1	0.3	0.1	0.5	2.9
Lebanon - Liban	1990	2515	62.9	54.4	50.5	4.6	3.9	0.1	4.3	32.8	3.9	1.5	1.4	18.0	12.0
	1995	6769	69.4	55.7	49.6	10.6	2.9	0.2	5.3	23.8	3.5	2.5	2.2	8.2	10.9
	2000	6228	64.4	52.7	45.7	7.8	3.4	0.5	6.3	27.9	5.5	1.9	2.8	12.5	10.7
	2003	7849	63.5	56.5	54.3	4.7	2.0	0.3	5.1	29.8	5.7	1.5	2.0	14.8	11.5
Liberia - Libéria	1990	4259	68.1	38.9	33.5	1.2	28.0	0.0	5.7	26.2	0.2	1.0	0.7	0.0	24.6
	1995	5683	67.5	32.9	31.9	0.8	33.7	0.0	3.0	29.4	0.3	0.8	0.9	0.2	27.5
	2000	5447	58.0	42.2	41.0	1.0	14.8	0.0	4.3	37.7	0.3	1.0	3.0	0.2	33.5
	2003	4375	37.2	20.5	18.4	0.9	15.9	0.0	3.3	59.5	0.1	0.5	1.4	0.3	57.2
Libyan Arab Jamahiriya - Jamahiriya arabe libyenne	1990	5663	77.5	70.8	66.8	2.2	4.3	0.2	1.5	21.0	0.4	2.7	5.3	5.9	7.1
	1995	5147	72.4	67.2	65.6	1.0	4.1	0.2	0.2	27.4	0.8	1.9	8.9	7.8	8.8
	2000	4092	69.6	65.6	63.9	0.9	2.5	0.5	1.8	28.7	1.5	2.8	11.6	6.2	8.0
	2003	6267	69.0	64.9	63.1	0.5	3.5	0.1	2.1	29.0	1.2	1.0	10.2	5.9	11.9
Lithuania - Lituanie	1995	3649	55.4	52.6	50.2	2.3	0.2	0.3	42.4	2.2	0.2	0.9	0.2	0.4	0.6
	2000	5457	60.5	55.8	54.0	2.7	1.9	0.2	32.0	6.0	0.2	0.9	0.3	0.6	4.1
	2003	9803	64.1	58.5	56.4	3.1	2.2	0.2	25.6	9.0	0.2	1.0	0.5	0.9	6.6
Luxembourg	2000	11386	91.9	86.6	84.1	3.7	1.6	0.0	0.2	7.3	0.3	0.6	0.2	0.2	6.4
	2003	16306	81.5	77.7	76.8	2.7	1.1	0.0	0.2	17.4	0.3	0.1	0.2	0.2	17.0
Macedonia, TFYR - Macédoine, LERY	1995	1712	56.6	51.2	50.1	3.7	0.9	0.9	35.1	8.3	0.8	1.5	0.4	4.2	2.2
	2000	2085	55.5	50.0	48.6	4.1	1.1	0.4	36.7	7.8	0.4	1.8	0.6	3.0	2.2
	2003	2256	67.3	65.7	64.3	1.3	0.1	0.1	22.9	9.8	0.3	0.6	0.3	6.3	2.4
Madagascar	1990	608	56.9	48.5	46.9	2.3	6.0	0.1	0.7	25.2	3.3	0.9	5.3	3.1	14.3
	1995	525	64.0	53.4	52.0	4.1	6.1	0.4	0.7	35.2	12.0	1.4	7.9	11.9	14.1
	2000	906	73.4	53.2	52.9	17.5	2.5	0.1	0.0	22.1	0.7	0.1	3.0	0.1	8.0
	2003	949	59.8	51.1	50.9	5.5	2.3	0.9	0.0	38.8	4.1	0.1	4.0	2.8	31.9

For sources and notes, see end of table.

Pour les sources et les notes, se reporter à la fin du tableau.

Destination	Year / Année	World [1] (millions of dollars) / Monde [1] (millions de dollars)	Developed economies / Economies développées						South-East Europe and CIS / Europe du Sud-Est et CEI	Developing economies / Economies en développement					
			Total	Europe		USA and Canada / Etats-Unis et Canada	Japan / Japon	Other / Autres		Total	of which: dont: OPEC / OPEP	America / Amérique	Africa / Afrique	West Asia / Asie occidentale	Other Asia / Autres pays d'Asie
				Total	EU / UE										
			Percentage / En pourcentage												
Malawi	1990	627	48.9	38.9	37.6	2.4	7.0	0.6	0.0	48.1	0.0	..	42.1	0.0	5.9
	1995	500	41.7	32.8	32.0	3.4	5.0	0.4	0.4	57.9	1.0	0.9	45.3	0.6	11.2
	2000	568	16.3	10.7	10.4	2.9	2.2	0.4	0.2	83.5	0.1	1.1	73.3	0.0	9.0
	2003	680	16.6	10.3	9.9	3.0	3.1	0.2	0.0	83.3	0.2	0.3	73.2	0.0	9.9
Malaysia - Malaisie	1990	29170	63.8	17.5	16.1	17.9	24.2	4.1	0.4	35.7	2.2	1.8	0.5	1.2	32.0
	1995	77620	64.5	17.3	15.3	16.8	27.3	3.1	0.4	34.4	2.1	1.2	0.5	0.8	31.8
	2000	82195	52.7	12.3	11.0	17.1	21.1	2.3	0.3	45.1	4.2	0.8	0.5	2.0	41.8
	2003	98909	38.5	11.6	10.6	12.5	12.5	1.8	0.6	59.6	3.6	0.9	0.4	1.8	56.4
Maldives	1990	138	17.4	13.3	13.0	0.5	3.3	0.3	0.0	82.6	0.7	0.0	..	0.5	82.0
	1995	357	21.0	15.4	14.7	0.6	3.8	1.2	0.0	78.9	28.4	0.0	0.3	28.5	50.1
	2000	388	20.6	10.5	9.6	3.7	3.4	2.9	0.0	79.4	11.7	0.1	0.4	8.9	70.1
	2003	470	20.8	12.0	11.2	2.7	2.2	3.9	0.0	79.1	10.3	0.1	2.9	8.0	68.0
Mali	1990	714	45.2	41.7	41.0	2.0	1.4	0.2	0.7	50.3	2.4	0.2	43.8	2.4	4.0
	1995	990	39.8	34.8	34.3	3.4	1.5	0.2	0.0	54.8	0.2	0.5	45.4	0.4	8.6
	2000	1270	30.9	26.9	26.8	3.3	0.5	0.2	0.2	61.5	0.9	0.4	52.7	0.3	8.1
	2003	1510	32.6	29.1	28.9	2.5	0.4	0.6	0.6	57.8	0.5	1.2	50.1	0.3	6.2
Malta - Malte	1990	1951	87.1	79.5	78.5	3.5	3.7	0.3	2.1	10.7	3.4	1.2	3.6	0.8	5.1
	1995	2942	83.5	74.4	73.3	6.1	2.5	0.4	0.6	15.9	3.1	0.8	3.6	0.8	10.6
	2000	3400	75.8	62.3	60.5	10.9	2.0	0.6	0.5	23.7	1.6	0.5	1.6	1.5	20.1
	2003	5923	65.4	55.4	54.1	3.9	5.2	0.9	6.2	28.4	1.7	0.3	2.1	3.7	22.3
Martinique [2]	1990	1740	86.8	81.5	80.6	2.9	2.1	0.3	0.1	12.1	6.2	4.1	0.7	5.2	1.4
	1995	1970	84.3	78.5	77.8	3.1	2.2	0.4	0.0	13.2	2.7	4.6	3.0	2.0	2.8
Mauritania - Mauritanie	1990	388	78.0	69.1	68.3	6.5	2.3	0.0	0.6	17.0	5.4	1.0	6.7	0.4	8.9
	1995	654	69.0	56.4	56.0	7.7	4.9	0.1	0.1	26.0	5.7	0.5	10.6	0.5	14.3
	2000	635	65.7	60.1	59.9	3.0	2.5	0.1	2.8	22.5	5.8	0.6	6.8	1.6	13.6
	2003	1044	60.6	52.2	49.8	3.8	4.0	0.7	5.6	25.8	2.8	4.1	8.6	2.5	10.6
Mauritius - Maurice	1990	1620	54.1	39.0	37.1	4.9	5.9	4.3	0.1	45.8	3.0	1.1	12.9	5.7	26.1
	1995	1976	47.4	35.1	32.8	2.8	4.8	4.7	..	49.9	4.2	1.9	14.4	4.0	29.7
	2000	2088	40.6	28.9	27.3	3.1	4.1	4.5	0.3	59.1	4.9	1.4	18.6	5.4	33.7
	2003	2982	50.5	44.0	42.7	1.2	2.1	3.2	0.2	49.3	6.1	1.8	14.3	6.8	26.5
Mexico - Mexique	1990	33016	91.7	19.2	17.8	67.4	4.3	0.8	0.1	7.6	0.6	4.4	0.3	0.1	2.8
	1995	79697	91.6	9.9	9.4	76.4	5.0	0.3	0.1	8.0	0.5	2.7	0.2	0.0	5.1
	2000	191904	88.6	8.8	8.3	75.4	3.7	0.4	0.3	10.9	0.8	2.6	0.3	0.2	7.6
	2003	187600	80.3	10.7	10.2	64.2	4.5	0.6	0.3	18.8	0.8	4.5	0.1	0.2	13.8
Moldova, Republic of - Moldova, République de	1995	841	20.0	17.8	16.7	1.3	0.2	0.7	78.8	1.2	0.0	0.1	0.0	0.8	0.3
	2000	776	43.9	36.8	36.1	6.3	0.3	0.4	51.0	5.1	0.3	0.2	0.3	2.4	2.2
	2003	1403	40.2	36.5	36.0	2.5	0.8	0.3	51.8	8.0	0.1	0.6	0.2	3.5	3.6
Mongolia - Mongolie	1990	144	67.8	57.1	54.3	..	10.7	0.1	8.9	23.2	0.0	0.1	0.7	0.0	22.5
	1995	415	28.8	13.8	12.3	4.0	10.9	0.1	50.9	20.4	0.0	..	..	0.1	20.3
	2000	614	29.9	12.7	12.1	4.8	11.9	0.6	36.4	33.7	0.4	0.0	0.0	0.2	33.5
	2003	867	24.8	14.2	13.6	2.8	5.7	2.1	36.6	38.6	0.5	0.1	..	0.2	38.3
Morocco - Maroc	1990	7913	62.0	52.9	51.4	7.6	1.6	..	3.0	23.0	12.6	2.3	6.9	10.6	3.1
	1995	9502	62.3	53.2	51.9	7.6	1.3	0.3	3.3	21.4	9.9	3.7	5.2	8.6	3.9
	2000	12536	71.4	63.9	63.0	6.0	1.1	0.3	1.6	15.8	6.0	2.3	3.7	4.1	5.6
	2003	16532	67.5	62.4	61.6	3.8	1.2	0.1	2.2	26.8	12.1	3.1	4.5	11.3	7.9
Mozambique	1990	913	57.7	43.8	42.5	8.6	4.8	0.6	0.0	42.2	11.9	1.6	11.1	11.6	17.9
	1995	747	46.0	32.5	31.3	8.3	4.9	0.3	..	46.4	0.8	1.3	35.6	0.7	8.7
	2000	1046	26.5	16.9	16.7	4.5	4.6	0.5	..	61.2	0.5	0.6	51.8	0.6	8.2
	2003	1756	30.2	15.0	14.4	4.6	1.3	9.3	0.0	41.0	2.2	0.4	27.8	0.9	11.9
Myanmar	1990	668	42.9	19.6	16.4	3.1	16.6	3.7	3.8	53.2	0.5	0.1	0.5	0.0	52.6
	1995	2342	16.7	7.9	7.6	0.8	7.4	0.6	0.8	82.4	2.9	0.0	0.1	0.0	82.3
	2000	3053	12.3	4.0	3.9	0.6	7.1	0.7	0.6	86.9	2.5	0.0	0.1	0.2	86.7
	2003	3448	6.9	2.3	2.1	0.2	4.0	0.4	1.9	91.1	1.7	0.0	0.1	0.2	90.7

For sources and notes, see end of table.

Pour les sources et les notes, se reporter à la fin du tableau.

Destination	Year / Année	World [1] (millions of dollars) / Monde [1] (millions de dollars)	Developed economies / Economies développées — Total	Europe Total	Europe EU / UE	USA and Canada / Etats-Unis et Canada	Japan / Japon	Other / Autres	South-East Europe and CIS / Europe du Sud-Est et CEI	Developing economies / Economies en développement — Total	of which: / dont: OPEC / OPEP	America / Amérique	Africa / Afrique	West Asia / Asie occidentale	Other Asia / Autres pays d'Asie
Nauru	1990	38	66.8	7.3	7.1	0.6	0.5	58.5	0.1	33.1	..	0.0	2.4	..	30.7
	1995	35	89.1	9.9	9.8	2.2	4.6	72.6	0.1	10.8	..	0.0	0.2	0.3	7.6
	2000	32	87.3	16.0	16.0	20.7	0.3	50.3	..	12.7	6.9	..	0.1	..	11.7
	2003	30	77.9	5.6	5.2	7.1	0.3	64.9	0.4	21.7	10.2	..	0.0	..	20.2
Nepal - Népal	1990	587	46.6	19.3	18.2	2.8	18.7	5.8	0.8	52.6	0.0	0.5	0.2	0.0	51.9
	1995	767	27.1	11.3	9.8	1.9	8.7	5.3	..	72.9	0.4	0.5	0.0	1.9	70.5
	2000	1060	17.6	8.9	8.6	3.1	3.2	2.3	0.5	79.4	15.8	0.0	0.0	15.0	64.3
	2003	995	16.9	10.9	10.4	2.1	1.5	2.6	1.2	78.2	23.5	0.1	0.1	23.4	54.6
Netherlands - Pays-Bas	1990	123382	83.6	71.0	68.1	8.6	3.3	0.8	1.6	14.8	5.7	2.8	2.8	4.1	5.1
	1995	157681	81.4	67.6	64.2	9.5	3.7	0.7	1.3	17.3	4.2	3.1	2.2	3.0	9.0
	2000	215716	71.7	55.3	52.9	10.7	4.7	0.9	2.1	24.0	4.6	3.2	2.1	3.4	15.2
	2003	261256	71.4	58.0	54.5	8.6	3.9	0.9	2.9	25.1	3.7	3.4	2.4	2.9	16.4
Netherlands Antilles - Antilles néerlandaises	1990	2135	25.0	9.1	8.9	13.6	2.2	0.1	0.6	74.1	61.4	71.0	0.0	1.9	0.6
	1995	1853	71.7	37.0	30.0	31.1	3.3	0.2	0.0	26.6	1.1	18.9	0.0	0.0	7.7
	2000	2812	22.9	8.5	8.4	13.3	1.0	0.1	0.0	76.6	72.5	71.1	0.9	3.5	0.7
	2003	4183	33.2	11.6	11.5	20.1	1.5	0.1	2.4	63.9	46.2	57.3	0.1	4.6	1.8
New Caledonia - Nouvelle-Calédonie	1990	749	88.4	65.5	65.1	6.2	4.9	11.9	0.1	9.3	0.2	0.1	0.8	..	7.2
	1995	957	87.1	59.5	59.2	4.5	4.3	18.7	0.1	12.2	0.7	0.4	0.4	0.1	10.6
	2000	924	83.7	54.7	54.0	3.9	3.3	21.8	0.0	15.5	0.7	0.5	0.3	0.1	14.1
	2003	1541	80.7	60.5	60.0	3.8	2.6	13.8	0.1	17.8	0.6	0.5	0.4	0.1	16.4
New Zealand - Nouvelle-Zélande	1990	9564	80.5	24.9	23.1	19.8	15.4	20.4	0.1	18.8	5.3	1.2	0.3	5.2	11.0
	1995	13794	79.0	22.8	21.7	20.4	13.9	21.8	0.0	20.6	3.1	1.1	0.6	2.3	15.7
	2000	13951	71.0	18.5	17.6	19.0	11.3	22.3	0.1	28.4	5.9	1.8	1.2	5.6	19.3
	2003	18466	68.7	20.9	19.8	13.7	11.8	22.4	0.3	31.4	4.9	1.0	1.4	4.2	24.2
Nicaragua	1990	667	41.8	20.3	19.1	14.8	6.7	..	..	45.2	9.4	36.5	0.6	..	7.2
	1995	975	46.3	9.8	9.0	31.4	5.2	..	..	50.7	6.0	45.5	..	..	4.2
	2000	1800	37.1	4.9	4.7	26.2	6.0	..	..	60.9	11.0	55.1	..	..	3.6
	2003	2446	32.4	6.4	5.9	23.0	2.4	0.5	0.6	64.0	7.6	44.6	..	0.1	17.5
Niger	1990	389	57.7	44.5	44.1	7.2	6.0	0.0	0.0	35.4	15.3	0.1	27.8	0.5	7.0
	1995	300	50.7	38.4	38.1	5.8	6.5	0.0	0.2	36.0	12.7	0.7	27.3	0.3	7.4
	2000	774	16.0	11.7	11.6	1.9	2.1	0.3	0.3	83.2	67.9	0.2	13.7	64.4	4.9
	2003	494	38.5	26.1	25.9	5.5	4.9	0.4	1.3	60.0	9.6	4.2	37.7	2.5	15.5
Nigeria - Nigéria	1990	4317	80.1	64.1	60.8	9.1	6.0	1.0	1.4	17.0	0.3	4.4	0.8	0.2	11.7
	1995	5814	67.7	52.2	50.2	11.7	3.3	0.5	1.0	31.1	1.3	4.9	5.0	0.4	20.8
	2000	8974	58.7	45.2	44.2	9.3	3.5	0.6	3.2	38.0	3.4	3.9	5.0	0.9	28.1
	2003	14633	56.1	44.7	43.3	8.1	2.7	0.6	1.8	42.1	2.1	5.6	4.3	0.7	31.4
Norway - Norvège	1990	26748	84.5	69.6	68.0	10.1	4.4	0.4	1.9	13.6	0.4	4.7	4.5	0.4	4.0
	1995	32525	88.1	74.9	73.3	8.9	3.8	0.4	2.0	9.9	0.3	2.6	0.9	0.4	6.1
	2000	31811	84.5	70.8	69.3	9.6	3.7	0.4	3.0	12.5	0.4	2.8	0.9	0.5	7.9
	2003	41755	88.3	80.2	78.6	5.6	2.1	0.4	1.6	10.1	0.2	1.9	0.8	0.5	6.7
Oman	1990	2726	60.2	31.4	29.1	9.4	16.7	2.7	0.5	37.7	25.8	0.4	0.5	27.0	9.8
	1995	4253	54.9	29.2	28.2	7.0	15.8	3.0	0.3	44.7	30.5	1.0	0.4	30.0	13.3
	2000	5346	45.2	23.2	21.5	4.3	15.3	2.5	0.1	54.6	37.7	1.5	0.7	39.2	13.2
	2003	6333	52.3	26.4	25.4	6.2	16.8	2.8	0.1	47.6	32.4	1.6	0.5	34.2	11.3
Pakistan	1990	7383	56.1	27.8	24.9	14.1	11.9	2.4	1.5	42.4	18.5	1.0	2.6	19.5	19.2
	1995	11461	50.4	27.7	24.5	10.4	10.7	1.5	1.7	47.9	18.7	1.7	2.7	20.0	23.5
	2000	10721	33.4	18.1	15.4	6.9	5.7	2.8	1.0	65.6	38.0	1.2	3.0	38.8	22.5
	2003	15492	33.9	18.5	17.2	7.3	6.3	1.9	0.7	65.4	32.5	0.7	2.8	32.6	29.3
Panama	1990	1510	48.9	8.3	7.7	35.2	4.9	0.5	0.2	40.2	2.4	26.3	0.1	0.0	4.4
	1995	2530	56.4	8.8	8.3	41.8	5.2	0.6	0.1	42.7	3.2	23.4	0.0	0.1	4.9
	2000	3405	49.4	8.9	8.5	34.1	5.5	0.6	0.1	49.9	6.7	32.6	0.1	0.2	5.1
	2003	15864	62.7	12.0	11.9	13.1	37.4	0.2	0.5	33.0	1.3	10.0	0.0	0.0	23.4

For sources and notes, see end of table.

Pour les sources et les notes, se reporter à la fin du tableau.

Origin / Origine Destination	Year / Année	World [1] (millions of dollars) Monde [1] (millions de dollars)	Developed economies / Economies développées						South-East Europe and CIS Europe du Sud-Est et CEI	Developing economies / Economies en développement					
			Total	Europe		USA and Canada Etats-Unis et Canada	Japan Japon	Other Autres		Total	of which: dont : OPEC OPEP	America Amérique	Africa Afrique	West Asia Asie occidentale	Other Asia Autres pays d'Asie
				Total	EU UE										
			Percentage / En pourcentage												
Papua New Guinea - Papouasie-Nouvelle-Guinée	1990	1315	82.0	6.9	6.7	11.5	13.3	50.2	0.1	17.7	1.0	0.5	0.3	0.0	16.8
	1995	1451	73.5	5.2	5.2	4.2	9.2	54.9	..	26.0	1.8	0.3	0.4	0.0	25.0
	2000	1239	62.1	2.9	2.8	2.3	4.0	52.9	0.1	36.6	3.0	0.2	0.9	0.1	35.1
	2003	1359	61.0	3.0	2.8	2.6	3.5	51.9	0.3	37.2	2.8	0.2	0.1	0.0	36.4
Paraguay	1990	1341	44.1	16.0	15.3	12.6	15.4	0.1	0.2	55.7	4.5	34.9	4.8	0.0	14.1
	1995	3077	33.2	11.7	11.2	12.9	8.5	0.1	0.1	66.5	0.8	45.9	0.9	0.0	19.7
	2000	3010	28.8	10.0	9.6	16.6	2.0	0.2	0.0	71.1	0.2	57.6	0.2	0.0	13.2
	2003	2568	29.8	7.2	6.8	21.0	1.3	0.3	0.1	69.8	0.3	55.9	0.3	0.0	13.5
Peru - Pérou	1990	3172	56.1	22.8	17.4	28.6	2.3	2.6	0.3	29.9	1.5	27.6	0.3	0.0	2.0
	1995	8291	53.5	19.2	18.3	28.4	5.1	0.9	0.6	45.9	4.8	37.6	0.3	0.3	7.7
	2000	7956	59.2	21.5	20.1	31.7	4.3	0.9	0.3	40.5	5.1	32.5	0.3	0.1	7.3
	2003	9047	56.5	23.1	20.4	29.6	2.1	0.7	0.4	43.0	2.9	32.0	0.6	0.1	9.7
Philippines	1990	12993	56.5	12.8	12.1	21.0	18.4	4.3	0.4	43.1	12.7	2.6	0.7	11.4	27.9
	1995	28282	57.2	11.5	10.8	19.4	22.3	4.0	0.3	39.8	9.7	1.7	0.6	7.9	29.1
	2000	34489	52.2	9.8	9.2	19.2	18.9	4.3	0.3	46.8	10.5	0.8	0.2	9.1	36.5
	2003	47041	49.6	8.8	8.4	18.5	20.0	2.3	0.5	49.1	8.1	1.1	0.2	6.7	41.0
Poland - Pologne	1990	8976	68.4	63.8	55.9	1.7	2.3	0.5	22.8	8.2	3.2	0.9	0.5	3.6	3.1
	1995	29050	80.4	74.1	71.0	4.3	1.6	0.4	9.7	9.9	1.4	1.4	1.6	0.9	5.9
	2000	48940	78.3	70.9	68.7	4.8	2.2	0.5	11.5	10.2	0.5	1.3	0.6	0.5	7.7
	2003	70077	80.8	78.3	75.9	1.4	0.9	0.2	9.4	9.8	0.3	1.2	0.8	1.1	6.6
Portugal	1990	25104	82.9	75.3	71.9	4.6	2.6	0.4	0.2	16.7	7.1	3.6	7.4	3.2	2.5
	1995	33309	84.0	78.0	75.1	3.6	2.2	0.3	1.0	14.9	4.8	3.3	5.1	2.4	4.0
	2000	38224	84.6	78.4	75.4	3.4	2.6	0.3	1.0	14.5	5.0	2.8	4.6	3.0	3.9
	2003	45033	85.1	80.7	78.4	2.4	1.7	0.3	1.7	13.2	4.4	3.3	4.8	1.9	3.2
Qatar	1990	1695	71.8	44.8	43.3	9.7	14.7	2.6	0.6	27.0	8.2	2.1	0.6	12.5	11.8
	1995	1929	62.5	35.9	33.7	11.1	13.4	2.1	0.0	35.9	14.6	1.8	0.8	17.8	15.1
	2000	3252	61.5	37.3	35.4	11.2	11.0	2.0	0.1	37.8	14.7	1.5	0.6	17.6	18.1
	2003	5340	74.0	53.5	51.7	8.9	9.8	1.8	0.1	24.6	9.2	1.0	0.6	11.0	11.7
Reunion - Réunion [2]	1990	2075	82.4	79.7	79.7	0.5	2.2	..	..	14.8	0.3	0.3	5.7	5.7	3.0
	1995	2717	83.6	80.4	80.2	0.6	2.1	0.5	0.0	16.3	1.0	1.1	6.0	3.9	5.3
Romania - Roumanie	1990	10293	40.5	33.5	31.4	4.8	0.8	1.4	28.3	30.6	19.7	2.1	6.6	18.3	3.7
	1995	10388	65.6	58.5	56.3	4.5	0.7	1.9	16.5	17.8	3.1	2.2	4.6	5.5	5.5
	2000	13054	72.5	66.5	65.1	3.4	1.3	1.4	14.3	9.5	0.5	2.3	0.6	2.3	4.3
	2003	24116	76.3	72.7	71.7	2.4	0.5	0.7	12.0	11.3	0.4	1.3	0.7	3.3	6.0
Russian Federation - Fédération de Russie	1995	46399	59.0	50.1	48.2	6.2	1.6	1.1	30.8	10.1	0.6	2.3	0.4	1.5	6.0
	2000	33853	51.5	40.3	39.0	8.6	1.7	0.9	35.4	13.1	0.6	3.5	1.1	1.3	7.1
	2003	63031	59.7	51.3	50.0	5.0	2.8	0.6	21.1	19.2	0.5	4.0	0.9	1.6	12.7
Rwanda	1990	288	61.0	52.2	50.7	1.8	6.9	0.1	0.2	33.2	1.2	0.3	21.1	1.2	10.6
	1995	284	53.0	30.0	29.5	15.9	6.6	0.5	0.0	35.6	1.2	0.0	31.2	1.3	3.1
	2000	251	34.5	22.4	22.3	8.2	3.8	0.1	1.6	40.8	2.7	0.0	34.1	2.6	4.0
	2003	350	33.5	26.7	26.5	2.8	2.3	1.6	0.9	41.8	2.7	0.0	35.3	2.7	3.6
Saint Helena - Sainte-Hélène	1990	21	99.8	99.4	99.2	..	0.4	..	..	0.2	..	0.2	..	..	0.0
	1995	25	84.7	82.7	82.6	1.5	0.5	..	..	15.3	..	0.2	14.2	..	0.9
	2000	43	64.3	62.5	62.5	1.3	0.1	0.3	..	35.7	3.2	1.7	29.7	1.1	3.3
	2003	39	61.2	55.2	55.2	5.7	0.2	0.1	0.1	38.7	3.7	0.5	33.3	1.8	3.2
Saint Kitts and Nevis - Saint-Kitts-et-Nevis	1990	108	87.5	26.1	25.4	57.2	3.8	0.4	..	12.5	..	11.7	..	..	0.8
	1995	176	59.1	16.1	15.8	39.4	3.5	0.2	0.0	40.9	..	17.3	23.1	..	0.4
	2000	196	77.4	9.0	8.8	64.6	3.7	0.1	0.0	22.5	0.4	21.0	0.1	0.0	0.8
	2003	248	75.1	32.0	31.6	40.1	2.9	0.1	0.4	24.5	0.2	22.8	0.1	0.1	0.8
Saint Lucia - Sainte-Lucie	1990	200	83.4	26.3	25.7	49.1	7.6	0.5	0.0	16.6	1.1	13.5	..	..	3.1
	1995	307	67.0	19.5	19.3	41.9	4.7	0.9	0.1	32.8	0.8	25.8	2.5	0.1	4.5
	2000	350	68.4	17.9	17.7	44.8	4.5	1.2	0.0	31.5	0.7	26.3	0.1	0.1	4.9
	2003	691	30.4	8.3	8.0	20.2	1.4	0.5	0.0	69.6	3.7	68.0	0.1	0.1	1.4

For sources and notes, see end of table.

Pour les sources et les notes, se reporter à la fin du tableau.

Origin / Origine — Destination	Year / Année	World[1] (millions of dollars) / Monde[1] (millions de dollars)	Developed economies / Economies développées — Total	Europe — Total	Europe — EU / UE	USA and Canada / Etats-Unis et Canada	Japan / Japon	Other / Autres	South-East Europe and CIS / Europe du Sud-Est et CEI	Developing economies / Economies en développement — Total	of which: OPEC / dont: OPEP	America / Amérique	Africa / Afrique	West Asia / Asie occidentale	Other Asia / Autres pays d'Asie
Saint Pierre and Miquelon - Saint-Pierre-et-Miquelon	1990	72	99.8	50.3	50.2	48.1	1.4	..	..	0.2	..	0.2	..	..	0.0
	1995	47	99.2	70.6	70.1	28.6	0.1	..	..	0.8	..	0.2	..	..	0.6
	2000	108	48.7	27.9	27.8	15.1	5.5	0.1	..	51.3	..	0.0	51.1	0.1	0.1
	2003	130	38.8	26.8	26.8	12.0	..	0.0	..	61.2	..	0.0	61.2	..	..
Saint Vincent and the Grenadines - Saint-Vincent-et-les Grenadines	1990	136	70.7	27.0	26.5	40.3	3.3	0.1	0.0	29.2	0.7	25.3	0.0	0.0	3.8
	1995	136	64.4	21.7	21.4	40.3	2.2	0.2	0.0	35.5	0.9	31.9	0.1	0.0	3.4
	2000	162	62.1	16.1	15.8	41.2	3.7	1.1	0.0	37.8	1.1	35.9	0.0	0.0	1.8
	2003	494	69.4	56.2	55.1	-11.2	1.6	0.4	0.8	29.8	0.3	15.9	0.2	1.4	12.3
Samoa	1990	83	70.1	9.1	9.0	9.9	8.8	42.4	0.1	29.8	..	0.0	..	..	7.0
	1995	144	82.6	1.8	1.8	5.7	20.8	54.3	..	17.1	..	0.0	0.0	..	9.4
	2000	271	77.5	1.1	1.1	26.3	8.8	41.3	..	22.3	1.7	1.1	0.0	0.1	8.6
	2003	236	59.4	3.4	3.2	5.3	12.8	38.0	..	40.2	3.2	2.6	0.0	0.2	16.6
Sao Tome and Principe - Sao Tomé-et-Principe	1990	51	99.2	65.4	59.7	29.6	4.1	0.1	..	0.8	..	0.2	0.2	..	0.3
	1995	44	87.0	80.6	80.6	4.5	1.6	0.3	..	13.0	..	2.9	4.7	..	5.4
	2000	40	87.8	82.2	81.6	2.6	3.0	..	2.3	9.9	1.5	1.3	6.5	0.1	2.0
	2003	61	91.6	87.5	87.0	3.5	0.5	0.0	0.6	7.8	0.9	0.6	3.9	0.1	3.2
Saudi Arabia - Arabie saoudite	1990	24081	77.8	43.5	36.9	17.4	15.3	1.6	0.6	21.3	2.2	1.6	2.0	4.6	13.1
	1995	27449	72.6	41.3	36.1	22.5	7.7	1.1	1.1	26.0	3.5	2.4	3.0	5.8	14.8
	2000	30298	66.8	33.3	30.1	20.2	10.4	2.9	..	29.1	3.8	2.4	2.4	6.0	17.0
	2003	53208	54.0	33.4	31.6	10.1	7.7	2.8	1.1	42.3	2.2	1.9	3.9	6.3	27.1
Senegal - Sénégal	1990	1387	65.9	55.6	55.0	7.4	2.9	0.0	0.5	32.4	7.1	1.9	21.1	0.6	8.9
	1995	1256	63.5	52.8	52.2	6.7	3.6	0.3	0.3	34.8	6.6	6.1	14.1	0.4	14.3
	2000	1463	60.0	48.7	48.1	5.3	2.7	0.2	0.1	38.3	14.9	1.7	20.9	1.2	14.5
	2003	2358	54.2	44.6	44.2	4.3	2.2	0.3	0.9	43.0	13.8	5.0	21.1	2.6	14.3
Serbia and Montenegro - Serbie-et-Monténégro	1995	383	82.6	82.3	75.0	0.0	0.2	0.1	9.1	8.3	2.6	0.1	2.6	5.6	..
	2000	3310	72.6	70.3	67.5	1.1	1.1	0.1	17.3	10.2	4.7	0.1	4.8	3.3	2.0
	2003	5738	82.8	81.2	81.0	1.0	0.4	0.2	6.8	10.5	3.8	0.3	3.8	3.1	3.2
Seychelles	1990	186	47.6	38.0	37.7	1.9	6.1	1.6	0.1	52.1	8.9	0.2	17.9	17.0	17.0
	1995	240	44.7	33.6	33.2	4.0	5.6	1.4	..	55.3	0.8	0.1	19.8	12.2	23.3
	2000	338	44.0	39.4	38.9	2.0	1.1	1.6	..	55.8	23.3	0.1	15.1	23.0	17.5
	2003	414	44.1	40.2	39.5	1.1	1.1	1.7	..	44.9	18.1	0.2	14.2	17.3	13.2
Sierra Leone	1990	197	65.4	50.5	49.4	9.6	5.2	0.2	0.5	32.4	19.7	0.5	24.5	0.0	7.3
	1995	247	61.5	52.0	50.0	8.2	0.9	0.4	1.0	35.0	3.8	1.1	16.3	0.4	17.3
	2000	328	73.7	65.4	65.1	6.3	1.9	0.1	0.1	22.8	4.4	0.6	10.1	0.8	11.3
	2003	577	69.3	62.4	62.1	5.9	0.9	0.2	1.9	26.1	4.1	0.9	14.7	0.8	9.6
Singapore - Singapour	1990	60954	54.6	15.5	14.0	16.7	20.1	2.3	0.3	45.0	9.8	1.2	0.8	10.8	32.3
	1995	124394	53.6	15.2	13.7	15.5	21.1	1.8	0.4	46.0	5.8	0.9	0.6	6.4	38.1
	2000	134630	48.5	13.8	11.9	15.4	17.2	2.1	0.3	50.7	7.4	0.7	0.5	7.9	41.6
	2003	127996	43.6	15.0	13.2	14.5	12.0	2.1	0.6	55.7	7.9	0.9	0.6	8.4	45.7
Slovakia - Slovaquie	1995	9648	74.5	70.0	68.1	2.7	1.5	0.3	19.5	5.4	0.3	1.1	0.7	0.4	3.3
	2000	14054	75.0	70.9	69.5	2.2	1.7	0.2	19.4	4.8	0.3	0.5	0.3	0.3	3.7
	2003	23163	81.5	80.5	79.1	0.6	0.3	0.1	13.6	4.1	0.1	0.5	0.2	0.5	3.0
Slovenia - Slovénie	1995	9645	84.1	78.5	76.0	3.5	1.6	0.4	10.4	5.5	0.9	0.9	1.2	0.4	3.0
	2000	10089	84.0	78.0	76.0	3.6	1.6	0.8	9.5	6.6	1.1	0.8	1.0	0.6	4.1
	2003	14879	86.2	83.9	82.4	1.2	0.7	0.3	7.7	6.1	0.7	1.0	0.8	0.8	3.5
Solomon Islands - Iles Salomon	1990	98	75.0	5.8	5.8	6.1	21.1	42.0	..	24.6	..	0.0	0.1	..	20.9
	1995	155	66.1	2.9	2.9	1.9	10.2	51.1	0.1	33.3	..	0.0	0.2	..	29.7
	2000	123	46.3	2.6	2.3	5.3	5.4	33.1	..	52.5	0.8	0.1	0.5	..	44.1
	2003	126	42.7	2.8	2.8	1.7	3.1	35.1	..	55.6	1.6	0.0	0.7	0.0	44.0
Somalia - Somalie	1990	394	68.8	62.6	53.6	3.9	2.3	0.0	0.3	28.2	6.2	0.3	11.3	6.3	10.2
	1995	245	16.1	11.6	11.5	4.1	0.4	..	0.0	75.6	12.8	7.1	36.8	17.5	14.2
	2000	314	15.5	13.4	13.3	1.9	0.2	0.0	0.2	72.8	7.9	6.6	41.2	9.4	15.7
	2003	391	7.2	5.1	5.0	2.0	0.0	0.1	0.0	79.4	6.9	10.7	47.5	10.0	11.2

For sources and notes, see end of table.

Pour les sources et les notes, se reporter à la fin du tableau.

Destination	Year / Année	World[1] (millions of dollars) / Monde[1] (millions de dollars)	Developed economies / Economies développées — Total	Europe Total	Europe EU / UE	USA and Canada / Etats-Unis et Canada	Japan / Japon	Other / Autres	South-East Europe and CIS / Europe du Sud-Est et CEI	Developing economies / Economies en développement — Total	of which: OPEC / dont: OPEP	America / Amérique	Africa / Afrique	West Asia / Asie occidentale	Other Asia / Autres pays d'Asie
South Africa - Afrique du Sud	2000	28763	66.7	43.0	41.5	12.5	7.2	4.0	0.2	33.0	11.0	2.5	4.1	9.8	16.6
	2003	37173	65.0	46.6	45.4	9.0	6.0	3.3	0.1	34.7	12.2	3.4	3.9	11.1	16.3
South Africa (Customs Union) - Afrique du Sud (Union douanière)	1990	19136	71.8	47.1	44.4	13.4	9.7	1.6	0.1	9.5	0.1	1.9	2.6	0.1	4.9
	1995	29504	73.5	48.0	45.4	12.9	10.2	2.5	0.3	24.5	6.5	2.5	2.7	6.6	12.7
Spain - Espagne	1990	87800	78.9	65.2	63.2	8.8	4.4	0.5	1.8	18.6	7.2	4.6	6.6	2.9	4.5
	1995	115501	79.0	68.1	66.0	6.9	3.3	0.7	1.7	18.7	5.4	4.3	5.7	2.4	6.3
	2000	144679	75.6	67.6	65.9	5.0	2.3	0.7	2.0	22.5	8.5	4.2	7.7	3.3	7.2
	2003	201262	76.5	70.4	68.1	3.4	2.1	0.6	2.2	21.2	6.3	3.9	6.7	2.9	7.4
Sri Lanka	1990	2636	40.9	17.0	16.2	8.6	12.3	3.0	1.0	58.0	12.1	1.2	4.4	12.0	40.4
	1995	4481	40.3	21.3	19.2	4.2	11.1	3.7	0.8	58.7	7.9	2.9	1.8	7.2	46.8
	2000	6688	34.4	16.2	14.4	4.5	9.7	4.0	0.1	65.3	10.0	0.5	0.6	8.5	55.7
	2003	7563	31.3	16.9	15.4	2.7	5.5	3.5	0.1	68.4	14.7	0.6	0.6	14.1	53.0
Sudan - Soudan	1990	1305	51.1	42.8	41.3	4.1	3.9	0.3	3.5	45.4	27.7	0.1	16.2	19.5	9.5
	1995	1263	40.3	33.5	32.0	3.9	2.6	0.2	3.7	56.0	30.6	0.1	22.1	16.3	17.4
	2000	1485	41.1	32.5	31.1	2.5	2.3	3.8	1.6	57.3	12.5	1.5	6.9	18.4	30.5
	2003	2020	41.1	31.9	30.8	2.5	2.7	4.0	2.9	56.0	10.4	1.1	6.0	13.1	35.8
Suriname	1990	484	73.5	30.6	30.3	40.2	2.8	..	0.1	25.2	0.5	22.1	0.0	..	3.0
	1995	586	70.0	25.0	24.1	42.8	2.1	0.0	0.0	30.0	3.1	23.6	0.6	0.0	5.7
	2000	480	65.5	26.7	26.3	31.0	7.4	0.4	0.0	34.5	5.7	23.2	4.2	0.1	7.1
	2003	694	66.9	29.3	29.1	31.2	6.2	0.1	0.0	33.1	0.6	22.7	0.1	0.2	10.1
Sweden - Suède	1990	49355	88.7	72.5	62.0	10.1	5.6	0.5	2.2	9.1	1.3	2.0	0.6	1.1	5.4
	1995	64568	87.1	78.0	68.7	5.8	2.9	0.4	0.9	7.2	1.2	1.3	0.5	0.9	4.4
	2000	72952	90.1	79.7	70.2	7.1	2.9	0.4	1.1	8.8	1.1	1.2	0.5	1.0	6.1
	2003	83259	89.0	82.2	72.9	4.3	2.2	0.4	1.9	9.1	1.2	1.1	0.3	1.5	6.2
Switzerland - Suisse	1990	69705	90.8	79.5	78.8	6.4	4.4	0.5	0.7	8.5	1.2	2.0	1.7	1.1	3.7
	1995	80050	91.6	81.1	80.7	6.8	3.2	0.5	0.7	7.7	1.3	1.1	1.3	0.9	4.4
	2000	82542	88.0	76.3	76.0	8.3	2.8	0.6	3.0	9.1	1.6	1.3	1.7	0.8	5.2
	2003	117762	86.7	75.9	75.6	8.4	1.8	0.5	4.7	8.6	1.2	1.7	1.5	0.7	4.6
Syrian Arab Republic - République arabe syrienne	1990	2392	63.3	48.8	48.0	11.1	3.3	..	7.0	21.7	4.1	2.9	2.7	13.2	3.0
	1995	4709	47.2	35.8	35.2	7.0	4.4	..	16.1	21.6	3.1	2.5	2.8	11.1	5.3
	2000	5419	43.6	36.5	35.5	4.5	2.4	0.3	7.6	30.5	6.1	2.2	2.6	9.4	16.3
	2003	8488	39.9	34.3	32.7	3.0	2.4	0.2	9.0	34.2	5.1	3.5	2.1	9.9	18.7
Tajikistan - Tadjikistan	1995	810	38.8	35.0	27.6	3.8	..	..	59.0	2.2	0.1	0.0	1.0	0.6	0.6
	2000	671	6.0	5.7	5.7	0.1	0.0	0.1	89.6	4.4	1.6	..	0.1	2.2	2.2
	2003	881	10.3	9.5	9.1	0.7	0.1	0.1	72.7	17.0	7.3	4.4	0.9	10.7	0.9
Thailand - Thaïlande	1990	33408	63.7	19.0	16.9	11.9	30.4	2.4	0.7	34.9	4.0	2.0	0.9	3.8	28.1
	1995	73692	61.0	17.1	15.4	12.2	29.3	2.4	1.8	37.2	3.1	1.5	0.9	3.4	26.7
	2000	61924	51.4	11.7	10.4	12.3	24.7	2.7	1.0	45.5	8.9	1.3	1.3	9.7	33.1
	2003	75809	48.5	11.4	10.3	10.0	24.1	3.0	1.1	48.5	8.4	2.0	1.3	9.3	35.7
Togo	1990	581	69.8	59.0	57.2	6.4	4.3	..	0.2	29.5	2.3	0.8	20.3	0.2	8.1
	1995	384	67.8	55.7	54.5	8.3	3.8	0.0	1.0	31.0	3.4	1.6	20.8	0.7	7.9
	2000	324	58.4	50.3	49.9	4.4	3.2	0.6	4.0	35.0	3.4	0.4	22.7	1.8	9.7
	2003	563	56.3	51.6	51.2	2.9	1.5	0.3	3.3	38.1	5.0	2.0	20.5	3.3	12.3
Tonga	1990	67	68.1	1.8	1.7	10.3	6.0	50.0	0.0	24.3	0.1	0.1	..	..	11.7
	1995	77	82.1	0.1	0.1	10.4	5.8	65.8	..	7.5	..	..	..	..	..
	2000	83	64.4	4.7	4.6	10.3	15.2	34.3	..	35.6	1.2	0.2	..	..	16.9
	2003	100	68.9	6.1	6.1	6.7	2.0	54.1	0.5	30.6	1.0	0.7	0.1	0.0	7.6
Trinidad and Tobago - Trinité-et-Tobago	1990	1230	69.5	17.4	16.9	46.8	3.6	1.6	0.0	30.4	8.9	21.4	3.4	0.2	4.2
	1995	1968	70.9	18.3	17.3	49.1	2.8	0.7	0.3	28.6	6.0	19.9	0.9	0.1	5.0
	2000	2353	53.3	11.5	11.0	37.1	3.5	1.2	0.5	46.1	19.7	37.3	3.9	0.1	4.9
	2003	3678	60.7	20.3	19.5	34.5	4.3	1.6	0.8	38.4	13.7	28.6	4.5	0.1	5.2
Tunisia - Tunisie	1990	6127	76.1	68.0	66.8	5.7	1.6	0.8	2.5	17.6	4.2	2.5	5.7	4.6	4.5
	1995	8032	80.6	72.8	71.3	5.9	1.8	0.1	1.1	12.9	4.4	1.4	6.2	2.7	2.6
	2000	8601	79.4	72.4	71.4	4.8	2.0	0.1	2.8	16.4	6.4	1.6	6.5	3.6	4.7
	2003	12440	77.7	73.8	72.6	2.7	1.2	0.1	4.4	16.0	6.0	2.0	6.0	3.6	4.5

For sources and notes, see end of table.

Pour les sources et les notes, se reporter à la fin du tableau.

Origin / Origine — Destination	Year / Année	World[1] (millions of dollars) / Monde[1] (millions de dollars)	Developed economies / Economies développées — Total	Europe — Total	Europe — EU UE	USA and Canada / Etats-Unis et Canada	Japan / Japon	Other / Autres	South-East Europe and CIS / Europe du Sud-Est et CEI	Developing economies / Economies en développement — Total	of which / dont: OPEC OPEP	America / Amérique	Africa / Afrique	West Asia / Asie occidentale	Other Asia / Autres pays d'Asie
Turkey - Turquie	1990	23147	63.9	47.5	44.9	10.6	4.8	0.9	8.2	27.2	15.2	2.4	5.8	13.2	5.8
	1995	35760	67.4	50.8	48.3	11.2	3.9	1.4	11.6	21.0	9.0	2.9	3.9	7.1	7.2
	2000	54502	64.5	52.4	50.3	7.7	3.0	1.5	12.7	19.7	8.0	1.2	5.0	4.8	8.7
	2003	68724	64.2	56.1	51.5	4.8	2.2	1.1	13.0	20.1	7.7	1.3	4.8	4.6	9.3
Turkmenistan - Turkménistan	1995	1364	26.7	20.3	19.6	3.9	0.6	2.0	55.1	18.2	3.6	0.0	0.0	15.7	2.4
	2000	1788	25.7	14.1	13.7	3.5	8.1	0.1	38.2	30.2	13.3	0.1	..	27.5	2.2
	2003	2504	17.5	15.2	12.2	1.9	0.1	0.3	49.3	27.3	12.3	0.1	..	21.7	5.5
Tuvalu	1990	4	88.8	32.7	32.7	..	21.3	34.8	0.3	11.0	..	0.5	..	..	10.5
	1995	9	53.4	11.3	11.3	3.7	2.3	36.1	..	46.6	..	4.9	..	..	2.3
	2000	13	37.6	11.9	11.9	..	1.1	24.6	..	62.4	0.1	..	..	..	1.9
	2003	23	48.5	18.8	12.2	..	8.5	21.3	..	51.5	0.1	..	..	..	1.7
Uganda - Ouganda	1990	582	50.0	39.9	39.1	5.4	4.6	0.1	0.4	49.6	1.7	0.2	38.8	1.8	8.7
	1995	872	41.8	31.2	30.6	3.8	6.6	0.2	0.1	58.2	2.9	0.1	40.3	2.8	14.9
	2000	879	31.2	23.9	23.2	3.6	3.5	0.2	0.7	68.1	3.0	0.3	54.9	2.8	10.1
	2003	1259	28.9	21.6	21.1	4.1	3.1	0.2	1.1	70.0	2.9	0.2	53.6	2.8	13.5
Ukraine	1995	20077	28.2	26.2	25.7	1.4	0.2	0.3	47.5	3.5	0.1	0.3	0.5	1.1	1.6
	2000	13955	34.4	30.1	28.2	2.8	0.7	0.8	58.6	7.0	0.3	1.3	1.0	1.3	3.3
	2003	23476	44.4	42.0	40.9	1.2	0.7	0.5	44.3	11.3	0.4	1.0	0.9	1.3	7.0
United Arab Emirates - Emirats arabes unis	1990	11472	60.7	34.9	33.0	9.4	14.2	2.1	0.7	35.1	8.0	1.0	0.7	10.1	23.4
	1995	20984	55.3	34.9	33.3	9.0	9.9	1.5	0.4	44.4	8.2	1.0	1.7	8.2	33.4
	2000	25464	59.5	38.8	37.2	8.8	9.6	2.3	0.6	39.9	7.7	0.7	1.5	8.1	29.7
	2003	50947	59.3	40.6	38.1	8.1	7.9	2.8	1.2	39.5	5.2	0.6	1.4	5.8	31.6
United Kingdom - Royaume-Uni	1990	223040	85.1	65.2	58.3	13.0	5.4	1.6	1.0	13.3	2.0	1.8	2.4	1.8	7.2
	1995	262507	79.4	58.5	52.6	13.7	5.8	1.4	0.8	15.9	1.8	1.9	2.1	1.4	10.4
	2000	334967	78.5	57.0	51.5	15.3	4.7	1.4	1.0	20.2	1.9	1.9	2.6	1.7	13.9
	2003	383671	75.6	58.9	54.2	11.8	3.5	1.4	1.6	20.7	1.6	1.8	3.0	2.2	13.5
United Republic of Tanzania - République-Unie de Tanzanie	1990	1022	73.1	61.0	58.7	3.5	7.7	0.8	0.8	23.7	12.1	0.9	4.3	12.1	6.2
	1995	1879	36.3	25.1	24.3	4.4	6.3	0.5	0.1	61.0	10.2	0.4	26.5	13.6	20.4
	2000	1520	45.3	23.5	22.4	6.0	9.3	6.4	0.7	53.9	10.4	2.0	20.6	11.2	20.1
	2003	2136	35.9	25.4	23.8	4.4	4.0	2.1	0.6	59.2	12.7	0.7	18.5	13.5	26.5
United States - Etats-Unis	1990	517020	59.7	21.7	20.2	18.1	18.0	1.9	0.4	39.8	7.4	13.0	3.3	3.4	20.1
	1995	770972	56.7	19.6	18.1	19.2	16.5	1.4	0.7	42.5	4.7	14.0	2.1	1.8	24.6
	2000	1238200	52.3	19.9	18.6	18.5	12.1	1.8	0.9	46.9	5.5	17.0	2.3	2.4	25.1
	2003	1305250	49.7	21.2	19.9	17.4	9.3	1.7	0.9	49.4	5.6	17.1	2.6	2.7	27.0
Uruguay	1990	1317	35.7	20.5	19.7	11.4	3.3	0.5	3.4	59.2	5.1	50.1	1.0	4.1	4.0
	1995	2867	36.0	22.1	21.1	10.5	2.6	0.7	0.8	62.8	4.1	52.2	1.5	2.1	7.0
	2000	3466	32.5	19.6	18.8	10.5	1.7	0.7	3.3	63.8	6.8	51.7	3.8	0.8	7.4
	2003	3247	31.0	17.5	15.4	11.4	1.4	0.7	8.0	60.9	3.3	47.9	3.0	0.5	9.6
USSR (former) - URSS (anc.)	1990	58559	73.2	59.9	58.1	7.6	4.8	0.9	7.9	18.9	1.1	1.9	2.1	3.8	11.1
Uzbekistan - Ouzbékistan	1995	3030	28.9	23.3	22.8	2.3	3.0	0.3	53.0	18.1	2.5	0.2	0.0	5.1	12.8
	2000	2067	40.8	30.1	29.4	8.9	1.3	0.5	39.0	20.1	0.1	0.1	0.0	4.4	15.6
	2003	2452	38.8	23.2	21.9	11.6	1.9	2.1	37.3	23.9	0.1	0.1	0.0	5.5	18.3
Vanuatu	1990	286	96.6	21.9	21.8	2.3	60.9	11.5	0.0	3.2	0.0	0.3	..	0.0	1.9
	1995	151	76.9	7.6	7.5	0.8	40.9	27.6	0.0	22.3	..	0.1	1.1	0.0	14.9
	2000	124	59.0	6.7	6.4	1.2	19.1	32.0	..	39.2	0.3	0.4	0.2	..	28.2
	2003	161	47.1	3.8	3.6	1.0	14.2	28.1	..	50.9	0.3	0.2	0.2	0.0	36.3
Venezuela	1990	6682	83.4	28.7	27.1	49.6	3.9	1.3	0.1	16.5	0.1	13.2	0.4	0.1	2.2
	1995	10791	71.0	19.1	18.1	46.8	4.4	0.7	0.2	28.8	0.2	24.2	0.3	0.2	3.7
	2000	20323	51.1	15.1	14.6	32.9	2.5	0.5	0.2	34.0	0.6	19.9	0.5	0.1	9.5
	2002	13506	58.5	20.3	19.3	34.0	3.4	0.8	0.4	36.2	0.1	29.5	0.2	0.1	5.5
Viet Nam	1990	2842	20.0	13.5	13.1	0.2	5.9	0.4	7.7	29.9	0.3	0.2	0.1	0.0	29.6
	1995	8359	24.2	10.1	9.2	1.9	11.0	1.3	1.9	64.9	2.6	0.2	0.1	0.3	64.3
	2000	15636	29.2	9.6	8.7	2.6	14.7	2.3	2.4	67.7	3.3	0.4	0.3	1.2	65.8
	2003	25705	29.3	10.6	9.9	5.9	11.2	1.7	3.2	66.8	3.3	0.7	0.3	1.4	64.3

For sources and notes, see end of table.

Pour les sources et les notes, se reporter à la fin du tableau.

Origin / Origine	Year / Année	World [1] (millions of dollars) / Monde [1] (millions de dollars)	Developed economies / Economies développées						South-East Europe and CIS / Europe du Sud-Est et CEI	Developing economies / Economies en développement					
			Total	Europe		USA and Canada / Etats-Unis et Canada	Japan / Japon	Other / Autres		Total	of which: dont: OPEC / OPEP	America / Amérique	Africa / Afrique	West Asia / Asie occidentale	Other Asia / Autres pays d'Asie
Destination				Total	EU / UE										
			Percentage / En pourcentage												
Yemen - Yémen	1990	2385	47.1	31.1	30.6	5.8	4.2	6.0	10.3	42.5	14.0	0.8	5.4	20.7	15.6
	1995	1578	36.3	23.9	23.6	8.0	4.0	0.4	1.1	61.8	29.0	3.7	4.6	33.0	20.6
	2000	2323	33.8	23.3	18.6	4.7	3.2	2.6	0.3	63.4	29.9	3.6	5.7	35.2	18.9
	2003	4147	32.5	21.8	19.5	5.8	3.1	1.8	0.9	65.8	30.6	4.7	3.7	35.6	21.9
Yugoslavia, SFR (former) - Yougoslavie, RSF (anc.)	1990	19227	70.9	63.1	60.7	4.9	2.2	0.7	14.3	14.7	4.4	2.5	3.9	3.6	4.6
Zambia - Zambie	1990	1218	57.8	40.1	38.9	10.8	6.7	0.3	0.2	42.0	7.7	0.2	31.5	6.0	4.3
	1995	782	34.0	21.5	20.3	6.7	5.8	0.1	0.0	66.0	16.6	0.4	44.6	16.5	4.4
	2000	1101	23.5	14.3	13.4	5.7	3.2	0.3	0.0	75.7	1.8	0.6	69.1	1.6	4.5
	2003	1402	14.1	10.6	10.3	2.2	1.2	0.2	0.1	84.9	2.2	0.5	76.2	1.8	6.4
Zimbabwe	1990	1849	48.8	32.6	30.6	8.0	4.5	3.6	0.5	39.4	0.2	1.4	32.9	0.1	4.9
	1995	2726	40.9	27.3	25.5	5.5	7.3	0.8	0.2	52.5	0.8	2.4	42.8	0.7	6.5
	2000	1810	29.4	17.9	16.7	6.2	4.1	1.2	0.2	59.2	1.4	1.1	49.0	1.1	8.0
	2003	2069	14.9	10.6	10.2	2.5	0.9	0.8	0.0	71.9	1.4	0.2	65.3	1.2	5.2

Sources: UNCTAD secretariat computations based on International Monetary Fund, *Direction of Trade Statistics* data and UN/DESA/Statistics Division's data.

Notes:

1 Includes unspecified destinations.

2 From 1996, France data include trade of French Guiana, Guadeloupe, Martinique and Reunion.

Sources : Calculs du secrétariat de la CNUCED sur la base de données du Fonds monétaire international, *Direction of Trade Statistics* et de données de ONU/DAES/Division de statistique.

Notes :

1 Y compris des destinations non spécifiées.

2 A partir de 1996, les données de la France incluent celles de la Guadeloupe, la Guyane française, la Martinique et la Réunion.

3.2.1A Export structure by destination and by major commodity groups
World

Destination	Year / Année	World [1] / Monde [1]	Developed economies / Economies développées							South-East Europe and CIS / Europe du Sud-Est et CEI
			Total	Europe		USA / Etats-Unis	Canada	Japan / Japon	Australia, New Zealand / Australie Nouvelle-Zélande	
Commodity groups				Total	EU / UE					

				Millions of dollars						
All products	1999	5571175	3911311	2341497	2216244	990868	210153	267202	72789	93619
	2000	6287738	4257111	2428003	2301280	1166220	231010	324326	75761	110279
	2001	6065269	4143062	2438725	2313536	1086380	216409	301658	70948	126808
	2002	6306330	4275149	2537010	2408499	1116681	217444	295878	80144	138073

				Share by destination (percentage)						
All products	1999	100.0	70.2	42.0	39.8	17.8	3.8	4.8	1.3	1.7
	2000	100.0	67.7	38.6	36.6	18.5	3.7	5.2	1.2	1.8
	2001	100.0	68.3	40.2	38.1	17.9	3.6	5.0	1.2	2.1
	2002	100.0	67.8	40.2	38.2	17.7	3.4	4.7	1.3	2.2
All food items	1999	100.0	70.3	47.5	45.9	10.2	2.6	8.7	0.9	3.4
(SITC 0 + 1 + 22 + 4)	2000	100.0	68.5	44.3	42.8	10.9	2.8	9.2	0.9	3.3
	2001	100.0	67.8	44.6	43.1	10.7	2.8	8.4	0.8	3.9
	2002	100.0	68.1	45.3	43.8	10.8	2.9	7.8	0.9	3.9
Agricultural raw materials	1999	100.0	68.8	40.4	38.9	15.7	2.7	9.0	0.8	1.4
(SITC 2 - 22 - 27 - 28)	2000	100.0	66.3	38.9	37.5	14.6	2.8	8.9	0.8	1.6
	2001	100.0	65.9	39.8	38.3	14.4	2.7	8.1	0.6	1.8
	2002	100.0	65.2	40.2	38.7	14.0	2.7	7.4	0.7	1.8
Ores and metals	1999	100.0	70.0	44.4	41.5	12.6	3.2	8.8	0.7	1.6
(SITC 27 + 28 + 68)	2000	100.0	67.5	42.4	39.9	12.4	3.2	8.6	0.6	1.9
	2001	100.0	66.8	43.1	40.4	12.4	3.0	7.4	0.5	2.1
	2002	100.0	64.8	42.7	40.0	11.2	2.9	7.0	0.5	2.1
Fuels (SITC 3)	1999	100.0	61.5	31.5	29.8	18.2	1.6	9.2	0.9	2.2
	2000	100.0	62.9	31.4	30.1	20.4	1.5	8.4	0.9	1.9
	2001	100.0	63.6	31.8	30.7	20.2	1.7	8.7	0.9	2.4
	2002	100.0	63.3	32.5	31.1	19.5	1.5	8.7	1.1	2.3
Manufactured goods	1999	100.0	71.4	42.6	40.4	18.8	4.2	3.8	1.4	1.4
(SITC 5 to 8 less 68)	2000	100.0	69.1	39.5	37.4	19.4	4.1	4.2	1.3	1.5
	2001	100.0	69.4	41.0	38.9	18.7	3.9	4.1	1.3	1.9
	2002	100.0	68.8	40.9	38.9	18.5	3.8	3.8	1.4	2.1

				Share by major commodity groups (percentage)						
All food items	1999	7.7	7.7	8.7	8.9	4.4	5.3	14.0	5.1	15.4
(SITC 0 + 1 + 22 + 4)	2000	6.7	6.8	7.7	7.9	3.9	5.1	12.0	5.1	12.8
	2001	7.2	7.1	8.0	8.1	4.3	5.7	12.2	5.2	13.5
	2002	7.3	7.3	8.2	8.4	4.5	6.1	12.1	5.1	13.0
Agricultural raw materials	1999	1.9	1.8	1.8	1.8	1.7	1.3	3.5	1.1	1.6
(SITC 2 - 22 - 27 - 28)	2000	1.8	1.8	1.8	1.9	1.4	1.4	3.1	1.2	1.6
	2001	1.8	1.7	1.8	1.8	1.4	1.4	2.9	1.0	1.6
	2002	1.8	1.7	1.8	1.8	1.4	1.4	2.8	1.0	1.4
Ores and metals	1999	2.8	2.8	2.9	2.9	2.0	2.4	5.1	1.4	2.6
(SITC 27 + 28 + 68)	2000	2.8	2.8	3.1	3.1	1.9	2.4	4.7	1.3	3.1
	2001	2.8	2.7	3.0	2.9	1.9	2.3	4.1	1.2	2.8
	2002	2.7	2.5	2.8	2.8	1.7	2.3	4.0	1.1	2.5
Fuels (SITC 3)	1999	7.5	6.6	5.6	5.6	7.6	3.1	14.4	5.3	9.8
	2000	10.5	9.8	8.6	8.7	11.6	4.3	17.1	7.7	11.4
	2001	9.8	9.1	7.8	7.9	11.1	4.6	17.2	7.6	11.1
	2002	9.4	8.8	7.6	7.7	10.4	4.1	17.4	7.9	10.1
Manufactured goods	1999	77.2	78.5	78.2	78.3	81.6	85.6	61.6	83.5	64.7
(SITC 5 to 8 less 68)	2000	75.2	76.8	76.8	76.9	78.7	84.4	61.9	81.7	65.1
	2001	75.4	76.6	76.8	76.8	78.6	82.4	62.4	81.1	69.6
	2002	75.8	77.0	77.2	77.2	79.1	83.0	61.8	80.9	71.9

Sources: UNCTAD secretariat computations based on UN/DESA/Statistics Division's data.

For notes, see end of table 3.2.2J.

3.2.1A Structure des exportations par destination et par principaux groupes de produits
Monde

| | Developing economies / Economies en développement | | | | | | | | | Destination | |
Total	Major petroleum exporters / Principaux exportateurs de pétrole	Major exporters of manufactures / Principaux exportateurs d'articles manufacturés	America / Amérique	Africa / Afrique	West Asia / Asie occidentale	Other Asia / Autres économies d'Asie — Total	China / Chine	Oceania / Océanie	Year / Année	Groupes de produits
				Millions de dollars						
1452431	163033	1013977	307226	118423	141322	880240	160363	5219	1999	**Total tous produits**
1745042	184868	1257823	362854	125856	162021	1089059	207439	5252	2000	
1655204	204126	1154466	349175	129912	164597	1005857	215905	5663	2001	
1769792	216694	1253573	326168	136978	184180	1115893	261378	6574	2002	
				Parts par destinations (en pourcentage)						
26.1	2.9	18.2	5.5	2.1	2.5	15.8	2.9	0.1	1999	**Total tous produits**
27.8	2.9	20.0	5.8	2.0	2.6	17.3	3.3	0.1	2000	
27.3	3.4	19.0	5.8	2.1	2.7	16.6	3.6	0.1	2001	
28.1	3.4	19.9	5.2	2.2	2.9	17.7	4.1	0.1	2002	
25.1	5.4	12.3	5.7	3.8	4.1	11.3	1.7	0.2	1999	Produits alimentaires
26.8	5.9	13.4	6.1	4.0	4.5	12.1	2.2	0.1	2000	(CTCI 0 + 1 + 22 + 4)
27.1	6.1	13.1	6.2	4.2	4.3	12.2	2.2	0.1	2001	
26.7	6.1	13.2	5.7	4.3	4.3	12.3	2.2	0.1	2002	
29.2	2.9	21.5	4.1	2.4	2.1	20.5	6.4	0.0	1999	Matières premières
31.5	3.1	23.8	4.4	2.2	2.5	22.4	7.8	0.0	2000	d'origine agricole
31.5	2.9	23.8	4.2	2.2	2.3	22.7	8.5	0.1	2001	(CTCI 2 - 22 - 27 - 28)
32.3	2.9	24.6	4.1	2.2	2.7	23.3	9.4	0.1	2002	
25.6	2.0	21.1	3.5	1.1	1.9	19.0	4.4	0.0	1999	Minerais et métaux
27.4	2.0	22.7	3.7	1.2	2.1	20.3	5.4	0.0	2000	(CTCI 27 + 28 + 68)
27.9	2.3	23.0	3.5	1.2	2.4	20.8	6.2	0.0	2001	
30.1	2.5	24.9	3.3	1.3	2.7	22.7	7.0	0.0	2002	
25.3	2.1	17.6	5.3	1.9	1.8	16.2	1.9	0.1	1999	Combustibles (CTCI 3)
24.6	2.0	17.0	5.4	1.8	1.7	15.5	2.4	0.1	2000	
23.7	2.0	16.4	5.0	1.6	1.8	15.2	2.1	0.1	2001	
25.0	2.0	17.3	5.0	1.7	1.8	16.4	2.2	0.1	2002	
26.4	2.8	18.8	5.6	2.0	2.5	16.1	3.0	0.1	1999	Articles manufacturés
28.5	2.9	21.0	5.9	1.9	2.6	18.0	3.4	0.1	2000	(CTCI 5 à 8 moins 68)
27.8	3.3	19.8	5.9	2.1	2.7	17.0	3.7	0.1	2001	
28.5	3.4	20.6	5.2	2.1	3.0	18.1	4.4	0.1	2002	
				Parts par principaux groupes de produits (en pourcentage)						
7.4	14.3	5.2	8.0	13.8	12.6	5.5	4.6	12.6	1999	Produits alimentaires
6.5	13.4	4.5	7.0	13.5	11.6	4.7	4.4	11.8	2000	(CTCI 0 + 1 + 22 + 4)
7.1	13.1	4.9	7.8	14.0	11.4	5.3	4.4	11.0	2001	
7.0	12.9	4.9	8.0	14.6	10.7	5.1	3.9	10.4	2002	
2.1	1.9	2.2	1.4	2.1	1.6	2.4	4.2	1.0	1999	Matières premières
2.1	1.9	2.2	1.4	2.0	1.8	2.3	4.3	0.9	2000	d'origine agricole
2.1	1.5	2.2	1.3	1.8	1.5	2.4	4.3	1.0	2001	(CTCI 2 - 22 - 27 - 28)
2.0	1.5	2.2	1.4	1.8	1.7	2.3	4.0	0.9	2002	
2.7	1.9	3.2	1.8	1.4	2.1	3.3	4.2	0.5	1999	Minerais et métaux
2.8	1.9	3.2	1.8	1.8	2.3	3.3	4.7	0.6	2000	(CTCI 27 + 28 + 68)
2.8	1.8	3.3	1.7	1.5	2.4	3.5	4.8	0.5	2001	
2.8	1.9	3.3	1.7	1.6	2.5	3.4	4.5	0.4	2002	
7.3	5.2	7.3	7.2	6.5	5.3	7.7	4.8	9.1	1999	Combustibles (CTCI 3)
9.3	7.2	9.0	9.8	9.6	6.9	9.4	7.8	15.7	2000	
8.5	5.9	8.5	8.6	7.1	6.4	9.0	5.7	11.8	2001	
8.4	5.4	8.2	9.1	7.3	5.9	8.7	5.0	10.7	2002	
78.1	74.2	79.6	78.8	73.6	76.1	78.8	80.4	72.2	1999	Articles manufacturés
77.3	73.8	79.1	77.5	71.6	75.5	78.3	77.7	66.8	2000	(CTCI 5 à 8 moins 68)
76.8	75.0	78.5	77.7	72.7	75.0	77.4	79.3	71.3	2001	
76.9	75.9	78.5	76.7	72.5	76.7	77.6	80.7	73.6	2002	

Sources: Calculs du secrétariat de la CNUCED basés sur des données de ONU/DAES/Division de statistique.

Pour les notes, se reporter à la fin du tableau 3.2.2J.

3.2.1B Export structure by destination and by major commodity groups
Developed economies

Destination / Commodity groups	Year Année	World Monde [1]	Developed economies / Economies développées — Total	Europe Total	EU UE	USA Etats-Unis	Canada	Japan Japon	Australia, New Zealand / Australie Nouvelle-Zélande	South-East Europe and CIS / Europe du Sud-Est et CEI
Millions of dollars										
All products	1999	3819296	2898493	1967780	1859684	552007	190957	115796	48834	53490
	2000	4106163	3015225	1977899	1870283	628792	206640	129051	48229	59828
	2001	4005470	2995280	2016544	1906516	597164	193905	119343	45810	75070
	2002	4120322	3076758	2093106	1982090	604065	193427	113382	51519	84959
Share by destination (percentage)										
All products	1999	100.0	75.9	51.5	48.7	14.5	5.0	3.0	1.3	1.4
	2000	100.0	73.4	48.2	45.5	15.3	5.0	3.1	1.2	1.5
	2001	100.0	74.8	50.3	47.6	14.9	4.8	3.0	1.1	1.9
	2002	100.0	74.7	50.8	48.1	14.7	4.7	2.8	1.3	2.1
All food items	1999	100.0	77.2	57.8	55.9	7.6	3.4	7.2	0.8	2.7
(SITC 0 + 1 + 22 + 4)	2000	100.0	75.6	54.6	52.8	8.2	3.7	7.8	0.9	2.7
	2001	100.0	75.6	55.1	53.2	8.6	3.7	7.0	0.8	3.0
	2002	100.0	76.7	56.4	54.5	8.9	3.8	6.4	0.9	3.0
Agricultural raw materials	1999	100.0	76.7	46.1	44.4	17.5	3.7	8.2	0.8	0.8
(SITC 2 - 22 - 27 - 28)	2000	100.0	73.4	44.2	42.6	16.2	4.0	7.9	0.8	1.0
	2001	100.0	72.8	45.6	43.7	15.6	3.7	7.0	0.6	1.2
	2002	100.0	72.2	46.5	44.6	14.7	3.6	6.4	0.7	1.4
Ores and metals	1999	100.0	75.9	51.6	48.8	12.7	4.5	6.0	0.7	0.8
(SITC 27 + 28 + 68)	2000	100.0	74.3	49.7	47.1	13.3	4.4	6.1	0.5	0.9
	2001	100.0	73.9	51.0	48.0	12.9	4.1	5.2	0.5	1.0
	2002	100.0	72.7	51.5	48.3	11.5	4.0	4.9	0.5	1.1
Fuels (SITC 3)	1999	100.0	82.9	55.3	52.1	19.6	3.6	3.7	0.5	0.9
	2000	100.0	84.6	52.5	49.8	25.4	3.3	2.6	0.5	0.6
	2001	100.0	85.0	52.3	49.9	25.7	3.8	2.6	0.5	0.6
	2002	100.0	83.6	52.7	50.1	24.3	3.2	2.8	0.5	0.6
Manufactured goods	1999	100.0	76.0	51.4	48.5	14.8	5.3	2.5	1.4	1.3
(SITC 5 to 8 less 68)	2000	100.0	73.7	48.4	45.8	15.3	5.4	2.6	1.3	1.5
	2001	100.0	74.5	50.4	47.6	14.7	5.0	2.5	1.2	1.9
	2002	100.0	74.5	50.9	48.1	14.5	4.9	2.3	1.3	2.2
Share by major commodity groups (percentage)										
All food items	1999	7.6	7.7	8.5	8.7	4.0	5.1	18.1	4.8	14.4
(SITC 0 + 1 + 22 + 4)	2000	6.8	7.0	7.7	7.9	3.7	5.0	16.9	5.1	12.4
	2001	7.2	7.3	7.9	8.1	4.1	5.6	17.0	5.2	11.7
	2002	7.4	7.6	8.2	8.4	4.5	6.0	17.1	5.3	10.7
Agricultural raw materials	1999	1.8	1.9	1.6	1.7	2.2	1.4	5.0	1.1	1.1
(SITC 2 - 22 - 27 - 28)	2000	1.9	1.9	1.7	1.7	2.0	1.5	4.7	1.3	1.3
	2001	1.8	1.8	1.6	1.7	1.9	1.4	4.3	1.0	1.1
	2002	1.8	1.8	1.7	1.7	1.8	1.4	4.3	1.1	1.2
Ores and metals	1999	2.4	2.4	2.4	2.4	2.1	2.2	4.8	1.3	1.4
(SITC 27 + 28 + 68)	2000	2.6	2.6	2.7	2.7	2.3	2.3	5.1	1.1	1.5
	2001	2.5	2.5	2.6	2.6	2.2	2.1	4.4	1.0	1.4
	2002	2.5	2.4	2.5	2.5	1.9	2.1	4.4	1.0	1.3
Fuels (SITC 3)	1999	3.2	3.5	3.5	3.4	4.4	2.3	3.9	1.4	2.1
	2000	4.7	5.5	5.2	5.2	7.9	3.1	4.0	1.8	2.0
	2001	4.6	5.2	4.8	4.8	7.9	3.6	4.0	1.8	1.5
	2002	4.4	4.9	4.5	4.6	7.3	3.0	4.5	1.7	1.3
Manufactured goods	1999	81.4	81.5	81.2	81.1	83.2	86.7	66.1	87.5	78.4
(SITC 5 to 8 less 68)	2000	80.3	80.6	80.8	80.7	80.3	85.7	67.5	87.0	81.5
	2001	80.1	79.8	80.1	80.1	79.2	83.5	68.1	87.0	82.3
	2002	80.6	80.5	80.7	80.7	80.0	84.0	67.2	86.9	84.2

Sources: UNCTAD secretariat computations based on UN/DESA/Statistics Division's data.

For notes, see end of table 3.2.2J.

Total	of which dont		America Amérique	Africa Afrique	West Asia Asie occidentale	Other Asia Autres économies d'Asie		Oceania Océanie	Year Année	Destination
	Major petroleum exporters Principaux exportateurs de pétrole	Major exporters of manufactures Principaux exportateurs d'articles manufacturés				Total	China Chine			Groupes de produits

Developing economies / Economies en développement

Millions de dollars

803212	97476	550821	221129	76667	89212	412150	62340	4054	1999	Total tous produits
928673	102517	668436	253393	78040	95844	497913	75705	3483	2000	
875024	114304	606401	241890	81469	94423	453433	85275	3810	2001	
899015	120569	627688	225286	83165	106391	479954	102424	4220	2002	

Parts par destinations (en pourcentage)

21.0	2.6	14.4	5.8	2.0	2.3	10.8	1.6	0.1	1999	Total tous produits
22.6	2.5	16.3	6.2	1.9	2.3	12.1	1.8	0.1	2000	
21.8	2.9	15.1	6.0	2.0	2.4	11.3	2.1	0.1	2001	
21.8	2.9	15.2	5.5	2.0	2.6	11.6	2.5	0.1	2002	
18.6	4.1	9.2	4.9	3.3	3.0	7.3	0.9	0.2	1999	Produits alimentaires
20.2	4.5	10.4	5.3	3.5	3.2	8.0	1.2	0.2	2000	(CTCI 0 + 1 + 22 + 4)
20.0	4.3	10.1	5.6	3.4	2.7	8.1	1.1	0.2	2001	
18.7	4.0	9.8	5.2	3.4	2.5	7.4	1.1	0.2	2002	
21.9	2.5	16.0	4.1	1.9	1.6	14.3	3.5	0.1	1999	Matières premières
24.8	2.7	18.7	4.7	1.7	2.0	16.4	4.6	0.1	2000	d'origine agricole
25.1	2.5	19.1	4.4	1.8	1.9	17.0	5.3	0.1	2001	(CTCI 2 - 22 - 27 - 28)
25.6	2.5	19.7	4.3	1.8	2.3	17.2	6.0	0.1	2002	
19.5	1.4	16.4	3.1	1.0	1.3	14.2	2.8	0.0	1999	Minerais et métaux
20.7	1.3	17.8	3.0	1.0	1.2	15.5	3.6	0.0	2000	(CTCI 27 + 28 + 68)
20.9	1.5	18.0	2.8	0.9	1.3	15.9	4.5	0.0	2001	
22.2	1.7	19.1	2.8	0.9	1.7	16.8	4.7	0.0	2002	
11.5	0.9	8.1	3.8	1.3	0.9	5.2	1.0	0.2	1999	Combustibles (CTCI 3)
10.5	0.9	7.3	3.8	1.4	0.9	4.2	0.5	0.2	2000	
9.6	0.8	6.7	3.3	1.2	0.6	4.2	0.6	0.2	2001	
10.5	0.8	7.3	3.6	1.4	0.7	4.7	0.8	0.1	2002	
21.7	2.5	15.0	6.0	2.0	2.4	11.1	1.6	0.1	1999	Articles manufacturés
23.7	2.5	17.3	6.5	1.9	2.4	12.8	1.9	0.1	2000	(CTCI 5 à 8 moins 68)
22.6	2.9	15.8	6.4	2.0	2.5	11.7	2.2	0.1	2001	
22.5	3.0	15.9	5.7	2.0	2.7	12.1	2.6	0.1	2002	

Parts par principaux groupes de produits (en pourcentage)

6.7	12.1	4.9	6.4	12.5	9.7	5.1	4.2	13.4	1999	Produits alimentaires
6.1	12.2	4.4	5.9	12.7	9.2	4.5	4.4	14.7	2000	(CTCI 0 + 1 + 22 + 4)
6.6	11.0	4.8	6.6	12.0	8.3	5.2	3.9	13.7	2001	
6.3	10.1	4.7	7.0	12.4	7.2	4.7	3.2	13.2	2002	
1.9	1.8	2.0	1.3	1.7	1.2	2.4	4.0	1.1	1999	Matières premières
2.0	2.0	2.1	1.4	1.7	1.6	2.5	4.6	1.2	2000	d'origine agricole
2.1	1.6	2.3	1.3	1.6	1.5	2.7	4.5	1.0	2001	(CTCI 2 - 22 - 27 - 28)
2.1	1.6	2.4	1.4	1.6	1.6	2.7	4.4	1.0	2002	
2.2	1.4	2.7	1.3	1.2	1.3	3.2	4.2	0.5	1999	Minerais et métaux
2.4	1.4	2.8	1.3	1.4	1.3	3.3	5.1	0.6	2000	(CTCI 27 + 28 + 68)
2.4	1.3	3.0	1.2	1.1	1.4	3.6	5.4	0.5	2001	
2.5	1.4	3.1	1.3	1.1	1.6	3.5	4.6	0.5	2002	
1.8	1.1	1.8	2.1	2.1	1.3	1.5	2.0	7.4	1999	Combustibles (CTCI 3)
2.2	1.6	2.1	2.9	3.4	1.8	1.6	1.2	10.8	2000	
2.0	1.4	2.0	2.5	2.8	1.2	1.7	1.4	8.5	2001	
2.1	1.2	2.1	2.9	2.9	1.2	1.8	1.5	6.2	2002	
83.8	80.6	84.8	84.8	79.9	83.9	84.1	82.0	72.0	1999	Articles manufacturés
84.3	80.8	85.3	85.1	79.2	84.2	84.8	83.0	66.6	2000	(CTCI 5 à 8 moins 68)
83.0	81.1	83.8	84.7	79.3	83.6	82.7	81.7	72.2	2001	
83.3	82.6	84.0	83.6	79.7	85.4	83.4	83.1	74.6	2002	

Sources: Calculs du secrétariat de la CNUCED basés sur des données de ONU/DAES/Division de statistique.

Pour les notes, se reporter à la fin du tableau 3.2.2J.

Destination / Commodity groups	Year Année	World [1] Monde [1]	Developed economies Economies développées							South-East Europe and CIS Europe du Sud-Est et CEI
			Total	Europe		USA Etats-Unis	Canada	Japan Japon	Australia, New Zealand Australie Nouvelle-Zélande	
				Total	EU UE					
Millions of dollars										
All products	1999	126015	71935	62274	56851	6162	244	2323	73	27632
	2000	167450	99088	87660	81522	6693	280	3009	33	36387
	2001	172010	93549	85116	81569	4963	270	2277	44	34612
	2002	173897	96422	87855	82904	5144	276	2057	39	33547
Share by destination (percentage)										
All products	1999	100.0	57.1	49.4	45.1	4.9	0.2	1.8	0.1	21.9
	2000	100.0	59.2	52.4	48.7	4.0	0.2	1.8	0.0	21.7
	2001	100.0	54.4	49.5	47.4	2.9	0.2	1.3	0.0	20.1
	2002	100.0	55.4	50.5	47.7	3.0	0.2	1.2	0.0	19.3
All food items	1999	100.0	33.4	26.9	25.4	2.1	0.2	1.7	0.4	52.3
(SITC 0 + 1 + 22 + 4)	2000	100.0	32.4	26.8	25.1	1.5	0.2	2.7	0.2	53.7
	2001	100.0	34.4	28.2	26.6	1.8	0.3	2.5	0.2	48.7
	2002	100.0	34.9	28.8	27.3	1.6	0.3	2.6	0.1	44.4
Agricultural raw materials	1999	100.0	58.2	48.9	46.4	0.8	0.0	8.1	0.0	13.2
(SITC 2 - 22 - 27 - 28)	2000	100.0	58.5	49.0	46.3	0.6	0.0	8.5	0.0	14.0
	2001	100.0	55.6	47.3	45.3	0.7	0.1	7.3	0.0	15.2
	2002	100.0	53.9	46.9	45.1	0.7	0.1	5.9	0.0	11.7
Ores and metals	1999	100.0	79.7	63.1	57.1	7.8	0.1	8.4	0.0	9.4
(SITC 27 + 28 + 68)	2000	100.0	72.9	57.4	53.5	7.9	0.2	7.2	0.0	12.1
	2001	100.0	72.0	52.4	48.6	11.2	0.2	8.0	0.0	13.1
	2002	100.0	70.2	53.1	49.8	10.9	0.2	5.7	0.0	12.9
Fuels (SITC 3)	1999	100.0	65.7	64.5	58.6	0.4	0.0	0.4	–	20.1
	2000	100.0	68.7	67.1	63.0	0.4	0.0	0.5	–	16.4
	2001	100.0	65.9	64.4	62.0	0.5	0.0	0.3	–	18.0
	2002	100.0	69.3	66.5	62.4	1.5	0.0	0.5	0.0	17.4
Manufactured goods	1999	100.0	50.3	43.5	42.2	5.5	0.4	0.4	0.1	22.3
(SITC 5 to 8 less 68)	2000	100.0	50.4	43.7	42.4	5.6	0.4	0.4	0.0	23.3
	2001	100.0	50.2	44.6	43.1	4.5	0.3	0.3	0.0	24.9
	2002	100.0	47.9	43.0	41.2	3.8	0.3	0.3	0.0	23.1
Share by major commodity groups (percentage)										
All food items	1999	4.7	2.7	2.5	2.6	2.0	5.9	4.4	31.2	11.1
(SITC 0 + 1 + 22 + 4)	2000	3.8	2.1	1.9	1.9	1.4	4.3	5.6	40.0	9.3
	2001	4.4	2.8	2.5	2.5	2.8	8.8	8.4	33.9	10.7
	2002	4.9	3.1	2.8	2.8	2.6	10.6	10.7	25.8	11.3
Agricultural raw materials	1999	4.8	4.9	4.8	5.0	0.8	0.7	21.1	1.1	2.9
(SITC 2 - 22 - 27 - 28)	2000	4.0	4.0	3.8	3.8	0.6	1.0	18.9	4.5	2.6
	2001	3.7	3.8	3.5	3.5	0.9	1.8	20.4	3.0	2.8
	2002	3.9	3.8	3.6	3.7	0.9	3.0	19.2	1.9	2.4
Ores and metals	1999	10.5	14.7	13.4	13.3	16.9	7.5	48.2	0.5	4.5
(SITC 27 + 28 + 68)	2000	9.7	11.9	10.6	10.7	19.2	9.9	39.1	4.0	5.4
	2001	8.4	11.2	8.9	8.6	32.7	11.0	51.0	9.4	5.5
	2002	8.0	10.1	8.4	8.4	29.4	9.0	38.7	16.3	5.3
Fuels (SITC 3)	1999	30.5	35.1	39.8	39.5	2.6	4.9	6.8	–	27.9
	2000	39.4	45.7	50.5	51.0	3.5	0.2	10.0	–	29.7
.	2001	39.3	47.6	51.2	51.4	6.3	1.1	8.8	–	35.3
	2002	40.7	50.9	53.6	53.3	20.0	3.5	16.8	0.0	36.8
Manufactured goods	1999	38.3	33.7	33.7	35.8	42.9	80.3	7.9	64.1	39.0
(SITC 5 to 8 less 68)	2000	34.6	29.5	28.9	30.1	48.6	82.0	6.9	50.7	37.2
	2001	36.4	33.6	32.8	33.1	57.2	76.8	8.7	53.1	45.0
	2002	36.1	31.2	30.7	31.2	46.5	73.5	9.2	55.5	43.2

Sources: UNCTAD secretariat computations based on UN/DESA/Statistics Division's data.   For notes, see end of table 3.2.2J.

3.2.1C Structure des exportations par destination et par principaux groupes de produits
Europe du Sud-Est et CEI

	Developing economies / Economies en développement								Destination	
	of which / dont					Other Asia / Autres économies d'Asie				
Total	Major petroleum exporters / Principaux exportateurs de pétrole	Major exporters of manufactures / Principaux exportateurs d'articles manufacturés	America / Amérique	Africa / Afrique	West Asia / Asie occidentale	Total	China / Chine	Oceania / Océanie	Year / Année	Groupes de produits
Millions de dollars										
24345	3002	13824	4974	2652	5850	10858	5013	11	1999	**Total tous produits**
31907	3544	18219	7520	2727	8727	12927	6820	6	2000	
30334	5006	16156	6533	2612	10330	10812	5345	47	2001	
34310	5200	19645	5997	3146	10659	14475	7262	33	2002	
Parts par destinations (en pourcentage)										
19.3	2.4	11.0	3.9	2.1	4.6	8.6	4.0	0.0	1999	**Total tous produits**
19.1	2.1	10.9	4.5	1.6	5.2	7.7	4.1	0.0	2000	
17.6	2.9	9.4	3.8	1.5	6.0	6.3	3.1	0.0	2001	
19.7	3.0	11.3	3.4	1.8	6.1	8.3	4.2	0.0	2002	
14.1	2.4	7.4	0.8	2.7	6.0	4.6	0.7	0.0	1999	Produits alimentaires
13.6	3.4	5.8	0.3	2.8	6.1	4.4	1.2	0.0	2000	(CTCI 0 + 1 + 22 + 4)
16.1	5.6	5.6	0.3	4.1	6.6	5.1	1.3	0.0	2001	
20.0	7.0	5.0	0.5	7.6	7.3	4.6	0.9	0.0	2002	
28.6	3.8	18.7	0.7	3.2	7.4	17.2	8.2	0.0	1999	Matières premières
27.5	3.1	19.9	0.7	3.5	7.8	15.5	10.1	0.0	2000	d'origine agricole
29.1	2.9	22.2	0.2	2.9	6.5	19.5	14.0	0.0	2001	(CTCI 2 - 22 - 27 - 28)
34.3	3.3	26.8	0.1	3.0	7.0	24.3	18.9	0.0	2002	
10.9	0.6	9.3	0.5	0.5	4.4	5.5	2.7	0.0	1999	Minerais et métaux
15.0	0.5	13.2	0.7	0.7	5.0	8.7	5.5	0.0	2000	(CTCI 27 + 28 + 68)
14.9	0.5	13.3	0.5	0.6	6.8	7.0	4.5	0.0	2001	
16.9	0.8	14.8	0.5	0.9	7.1	8.4	5.2	0.0	2002	
14.2	0.5	3.7	9.5	0.1	2.8	1.8	0.7	0.0	1999	Combustibles (CTCI 3)
14.9	0.5	4.7	9.1	0.2	3.7	1.8	0.7	0.0	2000	
13.4	0.8	4.4	7.4	0.4	3.9	1.8	0.8	0.0	2001	
13.3	0.8	5.5	6.5	0.2	3.7	2.8	1.3	0.0	2002	
27.4	3.8	18.2	2.4	3.4	6.3	15.3	7.7	0.0	1999	Articles manufacturés
26.3	4.1	17.4	2.4	3.1	7.3	13.6	6.8	0.0	2000	(CTCI 5 à 8 moins 68)
24.8	5.8	14.5	2.3	2.8	8.6	11.1	5.0	0.1	2001	
28.9	5.7	18.0	2.0	3.1	9.0	14.7	6.8	0.0	2002	
Parts par principaux groupes de produits (en pourcentage)										
3.4	4.7	3.1	0.9	6.0	6.1	2.5	0.8	19.5	1999	Produits alimentaires
2.7	6.1	2.0	0.2	6.4	4.4	2.2	1.1	9.5	2000	(CTCI 0 + 1 + 22 + 4)
4.0	8.4	2.6	0.4	12.0	4.9	3.6	1.9	2.0	2001	
5.0	11.5	2.2	0.8	20.7	5.9	2.7	1.1	1.4	2002	
7.1	7.7	8.2	0.9	7.4	7.7	9.6	10.0	2.0	1999	Matières premières
5.8	5.9	7.3	0.6	8.7	6.0	8.1	10.0	3.6	2000	d'origine agricole
6.1	3.7	8.8	0.2	7.1	4.0	11.5	16.7	0.4	2001	(CTCI 2 - 22 - 27 - 28)
6.7	4.2	9.2	0.1	6.3	4.4	11.3	17.5	0.3	2002	
5.9	2.6	8.9	1.3	2.4	10.0	6.7	7.1	0.5	1999	Minerais et métaux
7.7	2.1	11.7	1.4	4.3	9.3	10.9	13.0	4.7	2000	(CTCI 27 + 28 + 68)
7.1	1.6	12.0	1.1	3.4	9.5	9.3	12.1	0.0	2001	
6.9	2.0	10.5	1.1	4.1	9.3	8.1	9.9	0.5	2002	
22.3	6.0	10.3	73.2	1.6	18.3	6.3	5.0	8.9	1999	Combustibles (CTCI 3)
30.7	9.7	17.0	79.3	5.2	28.3	9.4	6.7	22.0	2000	
29.8	11.2	18.3	76.4	9.3	25.4	11.0	10.7	1.2	2001	
27.5	11.2	19.7	77.3	5.2	24.7	13.8	12.5	4.1	2002	
54.3	60.5	63.7	23.1	62.4	51.8	68.0	74.4	68.5	1999	Articles manufacturés
47.8	66.8	55.4	18.1	65.7	48.2	60.9	58.0	49.6	2000	(CTCI 5 à 8 moins 68)
51.3	72.9	56.2	21.8	66.8	52.2	64.3	58.7	96.2	2001	
52.9	68.9	57.4	20.5	62.5	53.2	63.8	58.9	93.6	2002	

Sources: Calculs du secrétariat de la CNUCED basés sur des données de ONU/DAES/Division de statistique.

Pour les notes, se reporter à la fin du tableau 3.2.2J.

3.2.1D Export structure by destination and by major commodity groups
Developing economies

Destination Commodity groups	Year Année	World [1] Monde [1]	Developed economies Economies développées							South-East Europe and CIS Europe du Sud-Est et CEI
			Total	Europe		USA Etats-Unis	Canada	Japan Japon	Australia, New Zealand Australie Nouvelle-Zélande	
				Total	EU UE					
			Millions of dollars							
All products	1999	1625864	940883	311443	299709	432699	18952	149083	23882	12496
	2000	2014125	1142798	362443	349475	530735	24090	192266	27500	14063
	2001	1887789	1054232	337065	325452	484253	22235	180038	25094	17127
	2002	2012111	1101969	356050	343505	507471	23741	180439	28585	19568
			Share by destination (percentage)							
All products	1999	100.0	57.9	19.2	18.4	26.6	1.2	9.2	1.5	0.8
	2000	100.0	56.7	18.0	17.4	26.4	1.2	9.5	1.4	0.7
	2001	100.0	55.8	17.9	17.2	25.7	1.2	9.5	1.3	0.9
	2002	100.0	54.8	17.7	17.1	25.2	1.2	9.0	1.4	1.0
All food items	1999	100.0	57.1	26.3	25.5	16.2	1.1	12.2	1.0	2.7
(SITC 0 + 1 + 22 + 4)	2000	100.0	55.5	23.9	23.1	16.7	1.2	12.5	1.0	2.4
	2001	100.0	53.3	23.8	23.1	15.5	1.1	11.6	0.9	3.3
	2002	100.0	52.2	23.5	22.9	15.5	1.1	11.0	0.9	3.4
Agricultural raw materials	1999	100.0	51.5	24.1	23.3	14.5	0.6	11.3	0.8	0.3
(SITC 2 - 22 - 27 - 28)	2000	100.0	50.8	24.1	23.3	13.7	0.6	11.4	0.8	0.4
	2001	100.0	50.5	23.5	22.8	14.3	0.7	11.2	0.8	0.5
	2002	100.0	50.2	22.9	22.3	15.1	0.9	10.4	0.8	0.5
Ores and metals	1999	100.0	56.3	25.8	23.4	13.5	1.5	14.2	0.8	1.0
(SITC 27 + 28 + 68)	2000	100.0	52.3	23.4	21.4	11.9	1.7	13.9	0.9	1.0
	2001	100.0	51.0	24.6	22.8	11.7	1.7	11.7	0.8	1.1
	2002	100.0	48.1	23.2	21.5	10.8	1.5	11.4	0.8	1.2
Fuels (SITC 3)	1999	100.0	50.6	15.0	14.8	20.2	0.8	13.2	1.2	0.1
	2000	100.0	51.4	15.4	15.2	21.3	0.9	12.5	1.2	0.1
	2001	100.0	51.6	14.4	14.2	21.2	0.9	13.7	1.3	0.2
	2002	100.0	51.5	14.9	14.7	20.6	0.9	13.4	1.6	0.1
Manufactured goods	1999	100.0	59.9	18.6	18.1	30.4	1.3	7.7	1.6	0.7
(SITC 5 to 8 less 68)	2000	100.0	58.9	17.7	17.1	29.9	1.3	8.3	1.4	0.7
	2001	100.0	57.8	17.6	17.1	29.1	1.3	8.2	1.4	0.8
	2002	100.0	56.3	17.2	16.8	28.4	1.3	7.6	1.4	0.9
			Share by major commodity groups (percentage)							
All food items	1999	8.3	8.2	11.4	11.5	5.1	7.6	11.1	5.6	29.5
(SITC 0 + 1 + 22 + 4)	2000	6.7	6.6	8.9	9.0	4.3	6.5	8.8	5.0	23.4
	2001	7.4	7.1	9.9	9.9	4.5	7.1	9.0	5.0	27.3
	2002	7.4	7.0	9.8	9.9	4.5	6.7	9.0	4.8	25.8
Agricultural raw materials	1999	1.7	1.5	2.2	2.2	0.9	0.9	2.1	1.0	0.7
(SITC 2 - 22 - 27 - 28)	2000	1.6	1.4	2.1	2.1	0.8	0.8	1.9	1.0	0.8
	2001	1.5	1.4	2.0	2.0	0.8	0.8	1.8	0.9	0.9
	2002	1.5	1.4	1.9	1.9	0.9	1.1	1.7	0.8	0.8
Ores and metals	1999	3.0	2.9	4.0	3.8	1.5	3.9	4.7	1.6	3.8
(SITC 27 + 28 + 68)	2000	2.7	2.5	3.5	3.3	1.2	3.8	3.9	1.7	4.0
	2001	2.7	2.5	3.7	3.6	1.2	3.9	3.3	1.7	3.4
	2002	2.6	2.3	3.4	3.3	1.1	3.3	3.3	1.5	3.1
Fuels (SITC 3)	1999	15.7	13.7	12.3	12.6	11.9	11.0	22.6	13.2	2.6
	2000	19.9	18.0	17.0	17.4	16.1	14.6	26.0	18.0	3.6
	2001	18.1	16.8	14.6	14.9	15.0	13.7	26.1	18.1	4.2
	2002	17.1	16.1	14.4	14.7	14.0	12.9	25.6	19.1	2.3
Manufactured goods	1999	70.2	72.6	68.3	69.0	80.1	75.3	59.0	75.4	63.1
(SITC 5 to 8 less 68)	2000	68.1	70.7	67.1	67.3	77.2	73.3	59.0	72.3	67.7
	2001	68.9	71.3	68.0	68.3	78.0	73.3	59.3	70.4	63.9
	2002	69.5	71.4	67.7	68.2	78.3	74.6	59.0	70.1	67.7

Sources: UNCTAD secretariat computations based on UN/DESA/Statistics Division's data.   For notes, see end of table 3.2.2J.

3.2.1D Structure des exportations par destination et par principaux groupes de produits
Economies en développement

		of which dont					Other Asia Autres économies d'Asie				Destination
Total	Major petroleum exporters Principaux exportateurs de pétrole	Major exporters of manufactures Principaux exportateurs d'articles manufacturés	America Amérique	Africa Afrique	West Asia Asie occidentale	Total	China Chine	Oceania Océanie	Year Année	Groupes de produits

Total	Major petroleum exporters	Major exporters of manufactures	America	Africa	West Asia	Other Asia Total	China	Oceania	Year	Groupes de produits
					Millions de dollars					
624873	62555	449332	81123	39104	46261	457232	93010	1154	1999	Total tous produits
784462	78807	571168	101941	45088	57450	578219	124914	1764	2000	
749845	84815	531908	100752	45831	59843	541612	125285	1807	2001	
836467	90925	606240	94886	50667	67130	621463	151692	2321	2002	
			Parts par destinations (en pourcentage)							
38.4	3.8	27.6	5.0	2.4	2.8	28.1	5.7	0.1	1999	Total tous produits
38.9	3.9	28.4	5.1	2.2	2.9	28.7	6.2	0.1	2000	
39.7	4.5	28.2	5.3	2.4	3.2	28.7	6.6	0.1	2001	
41.6	4.5	30.1	4.7	2.5	3.3	30.9	7.5	0.1	2002	
39.3	8.4	19.1	7.5	4.9	6.5	20.4	3.5	0.1	1999	Produits alimentaires
41.1	8.9	19.9	7.8	5.1	7.1	21.0	4.2	0.1	2000	(CTCI 0 + 1 + 22 + 4)
42.3	9.9	19.5	7.9	5.7	7.5	21.1	4.3	0.1	2001	
43.6	10.2	20.7	7.0	6.1	7.7	22.8	4.7	0.1	2002	
47.6	3.8	36.0	4.9	3.4	2.3	37.0	13.3	0.0	1999	Matières premières
48.6	4.0	36.9	4.6	3.1	2.6	38.2	14.9	0.0	2000	d'origine agricole
48.5	3.9	36.3	4.8	3.0	2.6	38.1	15.6	0.1	2001	(CTCI 2 - 22 - 27 - 28)
48.9	3.9	36.6	4.6	2.9	2.8	38.5	15.9	0.1	2002	
41.0	3.3	33.2	5.2	1.4	2.5	31.8	7.9	0.0	1999	Minerais et métaux
44.4	3.9	35.2	5.9	1.8	3.2	33.5	9.1	0.0	2000	(CTCI 27 + 28 + 68)
45.5	4.3	35.8	5.8	1.9	3.3	34.6	10.2	0.0	2001	
48.7	4.6	38.8	4.9	2.2	3.6	38.0	12.0	0.0	2002	
33.6	2.8	24.3	5.4	2.4	2.1	23.7	2.4	0.1	1999	Combustibles (CTCI 3)
33.0	2.8	23.8	5.5	2.3	1.8	23.3	3.7	0.1	2000	
33.4	2.9	24.1	5.5	2.0	2.0	23.8	3.1	0.1	2001	
35.0	2.8	24.9	5.4	2.2	2.0	25.3	3.1	0.1	2002	
39.2	3.6	29.1	4.7	2.1	2.6	29.7	6.5	0.1	1999	Articles manufacturés
40.2	3.7	30.2	4.7	1.9	2.7	30.8	6.9	0.1	2000	(CTCI 5 à 8 moins 68)
40.8	4.4	29.9	5.0	2.2	3.0	30.5	7.6	0.1	2001	
42.5	4.4	31.9	4.3	2.2	3.2	32.6	8.7	0.1	2002	
			Parts par principaux groupes de produits (en pourcentage)							
8.5	18.1	5.7	12.5	16.8	19.0	6.0	5.1	9.7	1999	Produits alimentaires
7.1	15.3	4.7	10.4	15.4	16.7	4.9	4.6	6.1	2000	(CTCI 0 + 1 + 22 + 4)
7.9	16.3	5.1	11.0	17.5	17.5	5.4	4.8	5.5	2001	
7.7	16.7	5.1	10.9	17.8	17.0	5.4	4.6	5.3	2002	
2.1	1.7	2.2	1.7	2.5	1.4	2.3	4.0	0.5	1999	Matières premières
2.0	1.6	2.0	1.4	2.2	1.4	2.1	3.8	0.4	2000	d'origine agricole
1.8	1.3	1.9	1.3	1.8	1.2	2.0	3.5	1.1	2001	(CTCI 2 - 22 - 27 - 28)
1.7	1.3	1.8	1.4	1.7	1.3	1.8	3.1	0.7	2002	
3.2	2.6	3.6	3.1	1.8	2.7	3.4	4.1	0.5	1999	Minerais et métaux
3.1	2.7	3.3	3.1	2.2	3.0	3.1	3.9	0.4	2000	(CTCI 27 + 28 + 68)
3.1	2.6	3.4	2.9	2.1	2.8	3.3	4.1	0.6	2001	
3.0	2.6	3.3	2.7	2.3	2.8	3.2	4.2	0.2	2002	
13.7	11.6	13.8	16.9	15.5	11.4	13.2	6.7	15.3	1999	Combustibles (CTCI 3)
16.9	14.3	16.7	21.8	20.4	12.3	16.1	11.8	25.4	2000	
15.2	11.7	15.5	18.7	14.7	11.4	15.1	8.5	19.1	2001	
14.4	10.6	14.2	19.5	14.7	10.3	14.0	7.1	18.9	2002	
71.6	64.9	73.8	65.6	62.1	64.1	74.2	79.6	73.0	1999	Articles manufacturés
70.3	65.0	72.5	63.1	58.8	65.0	73.0	75.6	67.2	2000	(CTCI 5 à 8 moins 68)
70.7	66.8	73.1	64.4	61.2	65.4	73.2	78.6	68.9	2001	
71.0	67.3	73.6	63.7	61.2	66.7	73.4	80.2	71.4	2002	

Sources: Calculs du secrétariat de la CNUCED basés sur des données de ONU/DAES/Division de statistique.

Pour les notes, se reporter à la fin du tableau 3.2.2J.

3.2.1E Export structure by destination and by major commodity groups
Major petroleum exporters

Commodity groups	Year / Année	World / Monde [1]	Developed economies / Economies développées Total	Europe Total	Europe EU / UE (Total)	USA / Etats-Unis	Canada	Japan / Japon	Australia, New Zealand / Australie Nouvelle-Zélande	South-East Europe and CIS / Europe du Sud-Est et CEI
Millions of dollars										
All products	1999	264791	130758	45534	44858	46734	2350	33578	2545	1496
	2000	388586	197395	68478	67631	74549	3775	47202	3380	1820
	2001	340955	173849	56893	55875	65593	3351	44520	3483	2229
	2002	344231	173059	58353	57299	62668	3379	44424	4220	1902
Share by destination (percentage)										
All products	1999	100.0	49.4	17.2	16.9	17.6	0.9	12.7	1.0	0.6
	2000	100.0	50.8	17.6	17.4	19.2	1.0	12.1	0.9	0.5
	2001	100.0	51.0	16.7	16.4	19.2	1.0	13.1	1.0	0.7
	2002	100.0	50.3	17.0	16.6	18.2	1.0	12.9	1.2	0.6
All food items	1999	100.0	40.3	18.9	18.7	11.1	0.4	9.3	0.6	3.5
(SITC 0 + 1 + 22 + 4)	2000	100.0	37.3	16.2	16.0	10.1	0.5	9.9	0.6	3.2
	2001	100.0	32.5	14.0	13.8	8.6	0.4	8.9	0.6	2.7
	2002	100.0	31.4	15.4	15.3	7.8	0.3	7.2	0.5	2.7
Agricultural raw materials	1999	100.0	49.6	23.7	23.1	16.1	1.4	6.7	1.4	0.5
(SITC 2 - 22 - 27 - 28)	2000	100.0	46.5	23.8	23.1	12.4	1.3	7.2	1.6	0.6
	2001	100.0	42.6	22.8	22.2	10.3	1.0	7.0	1.3	0.8
	2002	100.0	43.8	20.7	20.4	12.1	1.3	8.4	1.1	0.5
Ores and metals	1999	100.0	50.0	16.4	15.7	7.3	0.2	25.7	0.5	0.9
(SITC 27 + 28 + 68)	2000	100.0	50.7	17.2	16.3	6.5	0.4	26.0	0.5	1.5
	2001	100.0	44.6	17.3	16.8	6.7	0.6	19.4	0.6	2.8
	2002	100.0	44.3	18.0	17.6	7.1	0.2	18.2	0.8	1.4
Fuels (SITC 3)	1999	100.0	50.8	16.7	16.5	18.6	0.9	13.9	0.7	0.1
	2000	100.0	52.3	17.5	17.4	20.3	1.0	12.8	0.7	0.1
	2001	100.0	53.6	16.5	16.3	20.7	1.0	14.5	0.9	0.2
	2002	100.0	53.2	16.9	16.7	19.5	1.0	14.7	1.1	0.1
Manufactured goods	1999	100.0	45.5	18.5	18.0	16.8	1.0	7.4	1.9	2.0
(SITC 5 to 8 less 68)	2000	100.0	45.9	18.1	17.7	17.0	1.0	8.1	1.7	1.7
	2001	100.0	44.7	17.6	17.0	17.1	0.9	7.4	1.7	2.0
	2002	100.0	43.2	17.1	16.6	16.7	1.1	6.7	1.7	1.9
Share by major commodity groups (percentage)										
All food items	1999	3.7	3.0	4.1	4.1	2.3	1.7	2.7	2.3	22.9
(SITC 0 + 1 + 22 + 4)	2000	2.6	1.9	2.4	2.4	1.4	1.3	2.1	1.9	17.8
	2001	3.0	1.9	2.5	2.5	1.3	1.2	2.1	1.9	12.5
	2002	3.6	2.2	3.2	3.3	1.5	1.2	2.0	1.5	17.5
Agricultural raw materials	1999	1.0	1.0	1.4	1.4	0.9	1.6	0.5	1.5	0.9
(SITC 2 - 22 - 27 - 28)	2000	0.8	0.8	1.1	1.1	0.5	1.2	0.5	1.5	1.0
	2001	0.9	0.7	1.2	1.2	0.5	1.0	0.5	1.2	1.1
	2002	1.0	0.9	1.3	1.3	0.7	1.3	0.7	0.9	0.9
Ores and metals	1999	2.0	2.1	1.9	1.9	0.8	0.6	4.1	1.0	3.3
(SITC 27 + 28 + 68)	2000	1.8	1.8	1.7	1.7	0.6	0.8	3.8	1.0	5.6
	2001	2.0	1.8	2.1	2.1	0.7	1.3	3.0	1.1	8.6
	2002	2.0	1.7	2.1	2.1	0.8	0.4	2.8	1.3	5.1
Fuels (SITC 3)	1999	74.4	76.6	72.2	72.6	78.2	74.9	81.8	57.9	9.4
	2000	79.0	81.4	78.6	78.9	83.7	81.0	83.1	63.9	17.9
	2001	75.9	79.8	75.1	75.7	81.8	79.9	84.3	63.6	23.8
	2002	75.0	79.3	74.6	75.1	80.4	77.5	85.3	67.1	14.8
Manufactured goods	1999	18.0	16.6	19.3	19.1	17.2	20.0	10.5	35.3	62.9
(SITC 5 to 8 less 68)	2000	15.6	14.1	16.0	15.8	13.8	15.7	10.4	31.2	56.3
	2001	17.7	15.5	18.7	18.3	15.7	16.5	10.1	29.1	53.6
	2002	18.0	15.5	18.2	17.9	16.6	19.5	9.3	24.6	61.2

Sources: UNCTAD secretariat computations based on UN/DESA/Statistics Division's data.

For notes, see end of table 3.2.2J.

| Total | of which dont | | America | Africa | West Asia | Other Asia | | Oceania | Year | Destination |
| | Major petroleum exporters | Major exporters of manufactures | Amérique | Afrique | Asie occidentale | Autres économies d'Asie | | Océanie | Année | |
	Principaux exportateurs de pétrole	Principaux exportateurs d'articles manufacturés				Total	China Chine			Groupes de produits
Millions de dollars										
94515	15162	62628	11597	8141	14488	60215	5074	75	1999	**Total tous produits**
132653	20227	89726	16654	10990	18658	86223	11600	128	2000	
118912	20731	77754	14728	8879	19843	75366	8305	96	2001	
125797	21060	80751	14944	10334	20103	80324	9116	92	2002	
Parts par destinations (en pourcentage)										
35.7	5.7	23.7	4.4	3.1	5.5	22.7	1.9	0.0	1999	**Total tous produits**
34.1	5.2	23.1	4.3	2.8	4.8	22.2	3.0	0.0	2000	
34.9	6.1	22.8	4.3	2.6	5.8	22.1	2.4	0.0	2001	
36.5	6.1	23.5	4.3	3.0	5.8	23.3	2.6	0.0	2002	
55.5	19.1	25.4	5.1	3.4	21.1	25.8	3.4	0.0	1999	Produits alimentaires
58.9	23.8	24.3	4.6	3.6	25.5	25.1	2.3	0.1	2000	(CTCI 0 + 1 + 22 + 4)
64.3	29.7	21.7	5.1	5.3	30.6	23.2	1.8	0.1	2001	
65.5	27.0	24.8	5.6	5.5	27.8	26.6	2.2	0.1	2002	
49.5	3.5	39.6	3.2	3.5	5.5	37.3	14.1	0.0	1999	Matières premières
52.6	3.3	43.6	3.2	2.7	5.9	40.7	18.5	0.1	2000	d'origine agricole
56.2	3.6	44.3	2.9	3.8	5.1	44.3	19.7	0.1	2001	(CTCI 2 - 22 - 27 - 28)
55.4	3.7	43.5	3.0	3.9	5.6	42.9	20.8	0.0	2002	
48.7	9.5	35.0	4.1	1.7	10.0	32.9	1.7	0.0	1999	Minerais et métaux
47.7	9.4	33.8	3.8	1.5	9.8	32.4	2.3	0.0	2000	(CTCI 27 + 28 + 68)
52.4	11.1	36.4	3.8	1.8	10.5	36.3	3.3	0.0	2001	
53.9	12.3	36.3	4.4	2.3	11.4	35.8	4.1	0.0	2002	
30.0	2.8	22.5	4.4	2.3	2.4	20.9	1.6	0.0	1999	Combustibles (CTCI 3)
29.2	2.6	21.9	4.3	2.3	2.1	20.5	3.0	0.0	2000	
28.6	2.4	21.7	4.2	1.7	2.3	20.5	2.1	0.0	2001	
30.0	2.1	22.3	4.1	2.1	1.9	21.8	2.2	0.0	2002	
52.0	14.2	25.5	4.5	6.3	13.9	27.1	2.3	0.1	1999	Articles manufacturés
52.0	15.0	26.4	4.5	5.3	14.6	27.5	2.6	0.1	2000	(CTCI 5 à 8 moins 68)
52.7	16.9	24.9	5.1	5.9	15.8	25.8	3.0	0.1	2001	
54.3	17.6	25.4	5.2	6.1	16.7	26.3	3.6	0.1	2002	
Parts par principaux groupes de produits (en pourcentage)										
5.8	12.4	4.0	4.4	4.2	14.4	4.2	6.6	5.7	1999	Produits alimentaires
4.4	11.7	2.7	2.7	3.3	13.6	2.9	2.0	8.8	2000	(CTCI 0 + 1 + 22 + 4)
5.5	14.7	2.9	3.5	6.1	15.8	3.1	2.2	7.0	2001	
6.4	15.6	3.8	4.6	6.5	16.9	4.0	3.0	9.6	2002	
1.4	0.6	1.7	0.8	1.2	1.0	1.7	7.6	0.8	1999	Matières premières
1.3	0.5	1.6	0.6	0.8	1.0	1.5	5.2	1.5	2000	d'origine agricole
1.4	0.5	1.7	0.6	1.3	0.8	1.8	7.2	3.5	2001	(CTCI 2 - 22 - 27 - 28)
1.6	0.6	1.9	0.7	1.3	1.0	1.9	8.1	1.2	2002	
2.8	3.4	3.0	1.9	1.1	3.7	2.9	1.8	1.6	1999	Minerais et métaux
2.5	3.2	2.6	1.6	0.9	3.6	2.6	1.4	1.3	2000	(CTCI 27 + 28 + 68)
3.0	3.7	3.2	1.8	1.4	3.7	3.3	2.7	0.4	2001	
2.9	4.0	3.0	2.0	1.5	3.8	3.0	3.0	0.4	2002	
62.6	37.0	70.8	74.1	55.7	33.2	68.4	61.8	11.0	1999	Combustibles (CTCI 3)
67.7	39.0	74.9	78.7	65.6	33.9	73.1	78.1	25.1	2000	
62.4	30.5	72.3	73.2	50.1	29.9	70.3	66.2	24.0	2001	
61.6	26.3	71.4	71.2	53.5	24.8	70.2	61.5	17.2	2002	
26.2	44.8	19.4	18.7	37.0	45.6	21.5	22.0	77.6	1999	Articles manufacturés
23.7	45.0	17.8	16.3	29.1	47.3	19.3	13.4	63.2	2000	(CTCI 5 à 8 moins 68)
26.7	49.1	19.3	20.8	40.4	48.1	20.6	21.6	65.2	2001	
26.8	51.8	19.5	21.4	36.5	51.6	20.3	24.3	71.5	2002	

Developing economies / Economies en développement — Other Asia / Autres économies d'Asie

Sources: Calculs du secrétariat de la CNUCED basés sur des données de ONU/DAES/Division de statistique.

Pour les notes, se reporter à la fin du tableau 3.2.2J.

3.2.1F Export structure by destination and by major commodity groups
Major exporters of manufactures

Commodity groups	Year Année	World [1] Monde [1]	Developed economies — Economies développées								South-East Europe and CIS Europe du Sud-Est et CEI
			Total	Europe		USA Etats-Unis	Canada	Japan Japon	Australia, New Zealand Australie Nouvelle-Zélande		
				Total	EU UE						

					Millions of dollars						
All products	**1999**	**1172601**	**695004**	**203209**	**194964**	**349362**	**14327**	**105380**	**19040**		**9240**
	2000	**1409990**	**820083**	**226736**	**218374**	**415369**	**17748**	**134425**	**21259**		**10459**
	2001	**1329773**	**761791**	**215036**	**207420**	**381179**	**16282**	**125767**	**19197**		**12733**
	2002	**1452292**	**804640**	**228313**	**220691**	**406068**	**17867**	**126142**	**21644**		**15425**

					Share by destination (percentage)						
All products	**1999**	**100.0**	**59.3**	**17.3**	**16.6**	**29.8**	**1.2**	**9.0**	**1.6**		**0.8**
	2000	**100.0**	**58.2**	**16.1**	**15.5**	**29.5**	**1.3**	**9.5**	**1.5**		**0.7**
	2001	**100.0**	**57.3**	**16.2**	**15.6**	**28.7**	**1.2**	**9.5**	**1.4**		**1.0**
	2002	**100.0**	**55.4**	**15.7**	**15.2**	**28.0**	**1.2**	**8.7**	**1.5**		**1.1**
All food items	1999	100.0	58.1	20.5	19.8	17.9	1.1	17.0	1.3		3.1
(SITC 0 + 1 + 22 + 4)	2000	100.0	58.1	18.9	18.2	18.9	1.1	17.5	1.4		2.5
	2001	100.0	56.0	19.8	19.1	17.4	1.2	16.2	1.2		3.8
	2002	100.0	54.2	18.7	18.2	17.6	1.2	15.2	1.2		3.9
Agricultural raw materials	1999	100.0	49.6	19.5	19.2	14.0	0.6	14.3	1.0		0.3
(SITC 2 - 22 - 27 - 28)	2000	100.0	49.4	19.4	19.0	13.9	0.6	14.4	1.0		0.2
	2001	100.0	48.8	18.7	18.3	14.3	0.7	14.0	0.9		0.3
	2002	100.0	48.4	18.5	18.1	14.6	0.9	13.2	1.0		0.3
Ores and metals	1999	100.0	46.4	17.4	16.2	13.6	0.7	12.8	1.0		0.8
(SITC 27 + 28 + 68)	2000	100.0	45.3	16.7	15.4	13.2	0.7	12.8	1.0		0.9
	2001	100.0	42.7	16.3	15.3	12.6	0.6	11.3	1.1		0.8
	2002	100.0	39.7	15.1	14.0	11.5	0.7	10.7	1.0		1.3
Fuels (SITC 3)	1999	100.0	47.0	5.6	5.1	23.3	0.7	14.9	2.4		0.4
	2000	100.0	47.5	5.2	5.0	23.7	0.6	15.4	2.4		0.3
	2001	100.0	45.3	4.4	4.2	22.2	0.5	15.6	2.5		0.3
	2002	100.0	45.3	5.3	5.2	23.7	0.4	13.1	2.7		0.2
Manufactured goods	1999	100.0	60.3	17.4	16.9	31.7	1.3	8.1	1.6		0.7
(SITC 5 to 8 less 68)	2000	100.0	59.2	16.4	15.8	31.1	1.3	8.6	1.5		0.7
	2001	100.0	58.5	16.4	15.9	30.5	1.3	8.7	1.4		0.8
	2002	100.0	56.6	15.9	15.5	29.6	1.3	8.0	1.4		0.9

					Share by major commodity groups (percentage)						
All food items	1999	6.1	6.0	7.3	7.3	3.7	5.6	11.6	5.1		23.8
(SITC 0 + 1 + 22 + 4)	2000	5.1	5.1	6.0	6.0	3.3	4.7	9.4	4.7		17.0
	2001	5.7	5.5	6.9	6.9	3.4	5.3	9.7	4.7		22.3
	2002	5.6	5.4	6.6	6.6	3.5	5.4	9.7	4.5		20.3
Agricultural raw materials	1999	1.4	1.2	1.5	1.6	0.6	0.7	2.2	0.9		0.4
(SITC 2 - 22 - 27 - 28)	2000	1.3	1.1	1.6	1.6	0.6	0.6	2.0	0.8		0.4
	2001	1.2	1.0	1.4	1.4	0.6	0.6	1.8	0.8		0.4
	2002	1.1	1.0	1.3	1.4	0.6	0.8	1.7	0.8		0.3
Ores and metals	1999	1.9	1.5	1.9	1.8	0.8	1.1	2.6	1.1		2.0
(SITC 27 + 28 + 68)	2000	1.8	1.4	1.9	1.8	0.8	1.0	2.4	1.2		2.2
	2001	1.7	1.3	1.8	1.7	0.8	0.8	2.1	1.3		1.5
	2002	1.7	1.2	1.6	1.6	0.7	1.0	2.1	1.1		2.1
Fuels (SITC 3)	1999	3.3	2.6	1.1	1.0	2.6	1.8	5.5	4.9		1.6
	2000	4.6	3.7	1.5	1.5	3.7	2.2	7.4	7.4		1.5
	2001	4.2	3.3	1.1	1.1	3.3	1.6	6.9	7.4		1.2
	2002	4.0	3.3	1.4	1.4	3.4	1.3	6.1	7.2		0.7
Manufactured goods	1999	86.4	87.9	86.7	87.6	91.8	90.4	77.7	84.6		72.0
(SITC 5 to 8 less 68)	2000	86.5	88.1	88.1	88.5	91.2	91.1	78.5	83.5		78.6
	2001	86.1	88.0	87.3	87.8	91.5	91.1	79.0	81.4		74.2
	2002	85.5	87.3	86.6	87.0	90.5	90.6	78.6	82.7		76.0

Sources: UNCTAD secretariat computations based on UN/DESA/Statistics Division's data.   For notes, see end of table 3.2.2J.

3.2.1F Structure des exportations par destinations et par principaux groupes de produits
Principaux pays exportateurs d'articles manufacturés

| Total | of which dont | | America | Africa | West Asia | Other Asia | | Oceania | Year | Destination |
| | Major petroleum exporters | Major exporters of manufactures | | | | Autres économies d'Asie | | | Année | |
	Principaux exportateurs de pétrole	Principaux exportateurs d'articles manufacturés	Amérique	Afrique	Asie occi- dentale	Total	China Chine	Océanie		
										Groupes de produits
	Millions de dollars									
463738	38562	356138	42099	19215	26253	375203	84231	967	1999	**Total tous produits**
572800	47613	444536	52605	20431	31771	466453	106662	1541	2000	
548263	51653	416724	51817	22813	32426	439624	109434	1583	2001	
627291	57114	487588	49666	24696	38520	512320	134354	2089	2002	
	Parts par destinations (en pourcentage)									
39.5	**3.3**	**30.4**	**3.6**	**1.6**	**2.2**	**32.0**	**7.2**	**0.1**	**1999**	**Total tous produits**
40.6	**3.4**	**31.5**	**3.7**	**1.4**	**2.3**	**33.1**	**7.6**	**0.1**	**2000**	
41.2	**3.9**	**31.3**	**3.9**	**1.7**	**2.4**	**33.1**	**8.2**	**0.1**	**2001**	
43.2	**3.9**	**33.6**	**3.4**	**1.7**	**2.7**	**35.3**	**9.3**	**0.1**	**2002**	
38.5	7.7	21.5	2.5	3.8	5.3	26.8	4.6	0.1	1999	Produits alimentaires
38.9	7.2	22.1	2.7	3.5	5.1	27.5	5.1	0.1	2000	(CTCI 0 + 1 + 22 + 4)
39.6	7.9	21.6	2.8	4.2	5.3	27.2	5.0	0.1	2001	
41.6	8.4	23.3	2.3	4.6	5.3	29.3	5.6	0.1	2002	
50.0	3.7	40.7	3.0	1.0	1.8	44.2	17.6	0.0	1999	Matières premières
50.1	3.9	40.7	2.8	1.1	2.2	44.0	18.3	0.0	2000	d'origine agricole
50.5	3.8	40.7	2.9	1.2	2.2	44.1	19.2	0.0	2001	(CTCI 2 - 22 - 27 - 28)
50.9	3.7	41.1	2.8	1.2	2.4	44.4	19.2	0.0	2002	
52.6	3.5	44.2	3.0	1.1	2.2	46.3	13.8	0.0	1999	Minerais et métaux
53.6	3.8	44.4	3.2	1.2	2.5	46.7	14.1	0.0	2000	(CTCI 27 + 28 + 68)
56.2	4.5	46.1	3.1	1.4	2.8	48.9	15.5	0.0	2001	
58.9	4.5	49.4	2.6	1.2	2.9	52.1	17.4	0.0	2002	
50.3	3.3	37.5	4.4	1.0	0.9	43.6	6.4	0.4	1999	Combustibles (CTCI 3)
47.1	4.0	34.0	4.9	0.7	0.7	40.2	6.0	0.6	2000	
48.4	5.1	35.0	4.3	0.5	1.0	41.9	5.7	0.6	2001	
52.6	6.2	37.2	4.6	0.8	2.9	43.6	5.4	0.7	2002	
38.9	3.0	30.3	3.7	1.5	2.1	31.5	7.1	0.1	1999	Articles manufacturés
40.0	3.1	31.6	3.8	1.4	2.1	32.6	7.5	0.1	2000	(CTCI 5 à 8 moins 68)
40.5	3.5	31.4	3.9	1.6	2.3	32.6	8.3	0.1	2001	
42.3	3.6	33.5	3.4	1.6	2.5	34.7	9.5	0.1	2002	
	Parts par principaux groupes de produits (en pourcentage)									
6.0	14.3	4.3	4.2	14.1	14.6	5.1	3.9	6.1	1999	Produits alimentaires
4.9	11.0	3.6	3.7	12.3	11.7	4.3	3.5	3.6	2000	(CTCI 0 + 1 + 22 + 4)
5.5	11.6	3.9	4.1	14.0	12.4	4.7	3.4	3.2	2001	
5.4	11.8	3.9	3.7	14.9	11.2	4.6	3.4	2.9	2002	
1.7	1.6	1.8	1.1	0.8	1.1	1.9	3.4	0.2	1999	Matières premières
1.6	1.5	1.7	1.0	1.0	1.3	1.7	3.2	0.1	2000	d'origine agricole
1.5	1.2	1.5	0.9	0.8	1.1	1.6	2.8	0.2	2001	(CTCI 2 - 22 - 27 - 28)
1.3	1.1	1.4	0.9	0.8	1.0	1.4	2.4	0.1	2002	
2.5	2.0	2.7	1.5	1.3	1.8	2.7	3.6	0.3	1999	Minerais et métaux
2.4	2.0	2.5	1.5	1.5	2.0	2.5	3.3	0.3	2000	(CTCI 27 + 28 + 68)
2.4	2.0	2.5	1.4	1.4	2.0	2.6	3.3	0.7	2001	
2.3	1.9	2.5	1.3	1.2	1.9	2.5	3.2	0.2	2002	
4.2	3.3	4.1	4.0	2.0	1.3	4.5	2.9	17.1	1999	Combustibles (CTCI 3)
5.3	5.4	4.9	5.9	2.1	1.4	5.5	3.6	26.9	2000	
4.9	5.5	4.7	4.7	1.3	1.8	5.3	2.9	20.1	2001	
4.9	6.3	4.4	5.4	2.0	4.3	5.0	2.3	19.8	2002	
84.8	77.8	86.2	88.9	81.1	79.9	85.0	85.7	75.5	1999	Articles manufacturés
85.1	78.6	86.5	87.7	82.6	81.6	85.2	86.1	68.6	2000	(CTCI 5 à 8 moins 68)
84.5	78.4	86.3	86.6	79.1	80.9	84.8	87.1	70.5	2001	
83.7	77.2	85.4	85.5	78.3	79.7	84.1	87.7	73.1	2002	

Sources: Calculs du secrétariat de la CNUCED basés sur des données de ONU/DAES/Division de statistique.

Pour les notes, se reporter à la fin du tableau 3.2.2J.

Commodity groups	Year Année	World¹ Monde¹	Developed economies / Economies développées — Total	Europe Total	EU UE	USA Etats-Unis	Canada	Japan Japon	Australia, New Zealand Australie Nouvelle-Zélande	South-East Europe and CIS Europe du Sud-Est et CEI
						Millions of dollars				
All products	1999	293885	222986	42022	39802	167890	4944	7158	623	1818
	2000	352869	266687	44432	41684	207535	6023	7601	775	1573
	2001	341450	251320	43489	41020	194397	5882	6542	593	2694
	2002	343327	255675	44241	41507	198846	5548	5978	669	2721
					Share by destination (percentage)					
All products	1999	100.0	75.9	14.3	13.5	57.1	1.7	2.4	0.2	0.6
	2000	100.0	75.6	12.6	11.8	58.8	1.7	2.2	0.2	0.4
	2001	100.0	73.6	12.7	12.0	56.9	1.7	1.9	0.2	0.8
	2002	100.0	74.5	12.9	12.1	57.9	1.6	1.7	0.2	0.8
All food items	1999	100.0	65.5	32.0	31.1	26.7	1.2	4.9	0.4	2.8
(SITC 0 + 1 + 22 + 4)	2000	100.0	63.8	29.5	28.6	27.6	1.4	4.4	0.6	2.4
	2001	100.0	59.7	29.0	28.1	24.5	1.3	4.1	0.4	4.2
	2002	100.0	60.3	29.7	28.9	24.7	1.2	4.0	0.3	4.1
Agricultural raw materials	1999	100.0	71.0	26.6	25.6	35.4	0.7	8.0	0.3	0.3
(SITC 2 - 22 - 27 - 28)	2000	100.0	71.8	30.2	29.0	32.5	0.6	8.3	0.3	0.2
	2001	100.0	68.3	25.8	24.9	33.4	0.8	7.9	0.3	0.4
	2002	100.0	69.7	25.6	24.6	36.3	1.2	6.2	0.4	0.5
Ores and metals	1999	100.0	71.8	34.0	30.9	21.6	3.1	13.1	0.1	1.0
(SITC 27 + 28 + 68)	2000	100.0	68.7	31.3	27.9	20.7	3.3	13.2	0.2	0.9
	2001	100.0	68.8	32.6	29.2	21.1	3.4	11.5	0.1	0.8
	2002	100.0	66.4	31.7	28.7	21.0	3.1	10.3	0.2	0.9
Fuels (SITC 3)	1999	100.0	71.5	6.4	6.2	61.6	2.2	1.0	0.1	0.0
	2000	100.0	70.9	6.6	6.5	62.3	1.3	0.6	0.1	0.0
	2001	100.0	67.4	7.1	7.0	58.1	1.4	0.7	0.0	0.1
	2002	100.0	68.7	7.9	7.9	59.0	1.0	0.5	0.0	0.0
Manufactured goods	1999	100.0	81.2	7.2	7.0	71.7	1.6	0.6	0.2	0.0
(SITC 5 to 8 less 68)	2000	100.0	81.4	6.6	6.3	72.2	1.7	0.6	0.2	0.0
	2001	100.0	80.3	6.4	6.0	71.6	1.7	0.4	0.2	0.0
	2002	100.0	81.5	6.2	5.8	72.9	1.7	0.4	0.2	0.0
					Share by major commodity groups (percentage)					
All food items	1999	18.5	16.0	41.4	42.5	8.6	13.4	37.1	34.1	85.0
(SITC 0 + 1 + 22 + 4)	2000	15.3	12.9	35.8	37.0	7.2	12.2	31.4	39.6	81.4
	2001	16.7	13.6	38.0	39.1	7.2	12.7	35.9	37.6	88.7
	2002	16.8	13.6	38.7	40.2	7.2	12.6	38.4	26.9	87.9
Agricultural raw materials	1999	2.3	2.2	4.4	4.4	1.5	0.9	7.7	3.7	1.0
(SITC 2 - 22 - 27 - 28)	2000	2.2	2.1	5.3	5.5	1.2	0.8	8.5	2.9	1.1
	2001	2.3	2.1	4.6	4.7	1.3	1.1	9.4	3.6	1.2
	2002	2.2	2.1	4.4	4.5	1.4	1.6	7.9	4.1	1.4
Ores and metals	1999	6.6	6.3	15.7	15.1	2.5	12.0	35.5	2.4	10.3
(SITC 27 + 28 + 68)	2000	6.4	5.8	15.9	15.1	2.2	12.2	39.2	5.4	13.6
	2001	6.1	5.7	15.6	14.8	2.3	12.2	36.6	4.5	6.3
	2002	6.0	5.3	14.8	14.2	2.2	11.7	35.5	5.1	6.7
Fuels (SITC 3)	1999	13.4	12.6	6.0	6.1	14.5	17.4	5.5	5.0	0.4
	2000	17.8	16.7	9.3	9.8	18.9	13.5	4.7	8.4	0.5
	2001	15.6	14.3	8.7	9.1	15.9	13.0	5.3	0.2	1.5
	2002	15.9	14.7	9.8	10.4	16.2	9.6	4.2	1.2	0.4
Manufactured goods	1999	57.7	61.8	29.0	29.6	72.4	53.2	14.0	54.7	3.2
(SITC 5 to 8 less 68)	2000	57.1	61.5	30.1	30.4	70.1	58.4	16.0	43.7	3.3
	2001	57.9	63.2	29.0	28.9	72.9	58.2	12.2	53.9	2.2
	2002	57.7	63.1	27.8	27.6	72.6	61.5	13.6	61.5	3.6

Sources: UNCTAD secretariat computations based on UN/DESA/Statistics Division's data.

For notes, see end of table 3.2.2J.

						Developing economies Economies en développement					
Total	of which dont		America Amérique	Africa Afrique	West Asia Asie occidentale	Other Asia Autres économies d'Asie		Oceania Océanie	Year Année	Destination	Groupes de produits
	Major petroleum exporters Principaux exportateurs de pétrole	Major exporters of manufactures Principaux exportateurs d'articles manufacturés				Total	China Chine				
Millions de dollars											
65863	8883	21922	49352	2822	2760	10916	2134	13	1999		Total tous produits
80603	11289	27696	61721	2910	3117	12846	3776	10	2000		
83808	13233	29007	61437	3706	3686	14968	5189	11	2001		
81923	11861	30633	56058	4081	4187	17585	6298	12	2002		
Parts par destinations (en pourcentage)											
22.4	3.0	7.5	16.8	1.0	0.9	3.7	0.7	0.0	1999		Total tous produits
22.8	3.2	7.8	17.5	0.8	0.9	3.6	1.1	0.0	2000		
24.5	3.9	8.5	18.0	1.1	1.1	4.4	1.5	0.0	2001		
23.9	3.5	8.9	16.3	1.2	1.2	5.1	1.8	0.0	2002		
31.3	5.4	11.8	17.5	3.1	3.6	7.2	1.7	0.0	1999		Produits alimentaires
33.0	5.5	13.2	18.5	2.9	3.6	8.0	3.0	0.0	2000		(CTCI 0 + 1 + 22 + 4)
35.6	7.0	13.4	18.2	3.8	4.4	9.2	3.5	0.0	2001		
35.3	7.0	14.0	16.5	4.2	4.6	10.1	4.2	0.0	2002		
27.5	3.6	15.1	14.0	0.8	1.0	11.8	2.4	0.0	1999		Matières premières
27.8	3.5	15.9	13.5	0.8	1.2	12.4	4.5	0.0	2000		d'origine agricole
31.1	3.3	18.2	13.5	0.7	1.0	15.9	7.6	0.0	2001		(CTCI 2 - 22 - 27 - 28)
29.7	3.2	17.2	13.8	0.6	1.2	14.1	7.0	0.0	2002		
27.0	2.4	18.2	11.5	1.0	1.5	13.0	3.2	0.0	1999		Minerais et métaux
30.1	3.1	20.4	12.6	1.1	2.3	14.2	4.9	0.0	2000		(CTCI 27 + 28 + 68)
30.2	2.7	20.7	12.8	1.2	1.8	14.5	6.8	0.0	2001		
32.5	2.8	24.1	11.1	1.1	2.0	18.4	8.8	0.0	2002		
25.0	6.7	4.9	24.0	0.2	0.1	0.7	0.0	0.0	1999		Combustibles (CTCI 3)
26.5	6.2	6.2	24.9	0.1	0.1	1.3	0.1	0.0	2000		
29.7	7.1	6.9	26.6	0.2	0.2	2.7	0.2	0.0	2001		
29.3	6.1	7.0	24.7	0.4	0.6	3.5	0.1	0.0	2002		
18.7	1.5	5.3	16.0	0.4	0.3	2.0	0.2	0.0	1999		Articles manufacturés
18.4	1.7	5.4	15.9	0.5	0.3	1.8	0.3	0.0	2000		(CTCI 5 à 8 moins 68)
19.6	2.3	6.0	16.7	0.5	0.3	2.0	0.5	0.0	2001		
18.4	1.9	6.3	14.9	0.6	0.4	2.5	0.8	0.0	2002		
Parts par principaux groupes de produits (en pourcentage)											
25.9	33.3	29.2	19.2	59.0	70.0	35.9	43.8	62.2	1999		Produits alimentaires
22.1	26.0	25.8	16.1	54.2	62.4	33.4	43.2	62.2	2000		(CTCI 0 + 1 + 22 + 4)
24.3	30.2	26.4	16.9	57.9	68.5	35.1	38.0	42.9	2001		
24.9	33.9	26.3	17.0	58.9	62.8	33.0	38.3	38.9	2002		
2.9	2.8	4.7	2.0	1.9	2.4	7.5	7.7	0.2	1999		Matières premières
2.7	2.4	4.5	1.7	2.1	2.9	7.6	9.5	0.5	2000		d'origine agricole
2.9	1.9	4.9	1.7	1.5	2.1	8.2	11.4	9.3	2001		(CTCI 2 - 22 - 27 - 28)
2.8	2.0	4.3	1.9	1.2	2.2	6.2	8.6	2.8	2002		
8.0	5.3	16.2	4.5	7.1	10.7	23.2	28.9	0.2	1999		Minerais et métaux
8.4	6.2	16.6	4.6	8.4	16.5	24.9	29.1	0.3	2000		(CTCI 27 + 28 + 68)
7.5	4.3	14.9	4.3	6.9	9.9	20.1	27.4	3.2	2001		
8.2	4.8	16.2	4.1	5.5	9.9	21.5	28.6	0.2	2002		
15.0	29.9	8.9	19.2	2.5	1.3	2.4	0.2	0.3	1999		Combustibles (CTCI 3)
20.6	34.7	14.0	25.4	2.9	1.3	6.5	1.3	0.9	2000		
18.9	28.7	12.7	23.1	3.5	3.6	9.5	2.3	6.2	2001		
19.5	28.0	12.6	24.0	5.9	8.2	10.9	0.5	3.9	2002		
48.1	28.6	40.9	54.9	26.3	15.5	30.9	19.3	36.8	1999		Articles manufacturés
46.0	30.4	39.0	52.0	31.2	16.3	27.6	16.9	35.8	2000		(CTCI 5 à 8 moins 68)
46.2	34.6	41.1	53.8	28.7	15.4	27.0	20.9	38.2	2001		
44.5	31.2	40.6	52.8	27.6	16.9	28.4	24.0	54.0	2002		

Sources: Calculs du secrétariat de la CNUCED basés sur des données de ONU/DAES/Division de statistique.

Pour les notes, se reporter à la fin du tableau 3.2.2J.

3.2.1H Export structure by destination and by major commodity groups
Developing Africa

| Commodity groups | Year / Année | World / Monde ¹ | Developed economies / Economies développées | | | | | | | South-East Europe and CIS / Europe du Sud-Est et CEI |
| | | | Total | Europe | | USA / Etats-Unis | Canada | Japan / Japon | Australia, New Zealand / Australie Nouvelle-Zélande | |
				Total	EU / UE					
Millions of dollars										
All products	1999	106275	73676	51580	50274	16491	1148	3024	693	543
	2000	141662	96643	66265	63865	24466	1791	2467	785	554
	2001	125498	81512	57089	55247	19332	1310	2222	766	551
	2002	123461	85490	61506	59009	18287	1280	2910	862	587
Share by destination (percentage)										
All products	1999	100.0	69.3	48.5	47.3	15.5	1.1	2.8	0.7	0.5
	2000	100.0	68.2	46.8	45.1	17.3	1.3	1.7	0.6	0.4
	2001	100.0	65.0	45.5	44.0	15.4	1.0	1.8	0.6	0.4
	2002	100.0	69.2	49.8	47.8	14.8	1.0	2.4	0.7	0.5
All food items	1999	100.0	66.4	54.2	53.1	4.7	0.8	5.6	0.6	2.0
(SITC 0 + 1 + 22 + 4)	2000	100.0	61.9	50.1	48.4	4.3	0.7	5.7	0.6	1.6
	2001	100.0	62.6	51.2	49.5	4.7	0.6	5.1	0.5	2.0
	2002	100.0	62.7	51.3	49.9	5.3	0.6	4.6	0.5	2.4
Agricultural raw materials	1999	100.0	55.8	46.9	44.3	2.8	0.2	5.1	0.3	0.3
(SITC 2 - 22 - 27 - 28)	2000	100.0	55.3	45.7	43.5	3.6	0.2	5.3	0.2	0.2
	2001	100.0	56.8	47.9	45.9	2.5	0.2	5.6	0.3	0.4
	2002	100.0	55.5	46.1	45.1	2.9	0.2	5.7	0.3	0.4
Ores and metals	1999	100.0	78.0	43.7	38.7	17.1	0.7	15.4	0.6	1.1
(SITC 27 + 28 + 68)	2000	100.0	65.1	45.1	41.5	8.6	1.1	8.8	0.8	1.4
	2001	100.0	65.2	46.7	44.2	8.4	0.7	7.7	0.9	1.1
	2002	100.0	63.1	44.0	41.1	5.9	0.7	10.9	1.0	0.9
Fuels (SITC 3)	1999	100.0	70.6	43.3	42.6	24.2	1.6	0.7	0.3	0.2
	2000	100.0	71.9	42.9	42.3	26.0	1.8	0.4	0.2	0.2
	2001	100.0	71.9	42.9	42.2	26.0	1.7	0.4	0.3	0.2
	2002	100.0	73.1	46.3	45.3	23.5	1.7	1.0	0.3	0.1
Manufactured goods	1999	100.0	68.9	56.2	55.6	8.0	0.6	1.6	1.4	0.3
(SITC 5 to 8 less 68)	2000	100.0	71.2	57.8	55.5	8.7	0.5	1.8	1.3	0.3
	2001	100.0	61.3	50.2	49.4	7.0	0.5	1.5	1.3	0.3
	2002	100.0	68.5	54.8	53.8	8.9	0.4	1.9	1.5	0.3
Share by major commodity groups (percentage)										
All food items	1999	12.9	12.4	14.4	14.5	3.9	9.5	25.7	12.1	49.9
(SITC 0 + 1 + 22 + 4)	2000	9.5	8.6	10.2	10.2	2.4	5.5	31.0	10.0	39.6
	2001	10.5	10.1	11.8	11.8	3.2	6.5	30.2	9.4	47.9
	2002	11.5	10.4	11.9	12.0	4.1	6.5	22.3	8.3	58.7
Agricultural raw materials	1999	4.2	3.4	4.0	3.9	0.8	0.8	7.5	1.8	2.2
(SITC 2 - 22 - 27 - 28)	2000	3.2	2.6	3.2	3.1	0.7	0.5	9.8	1.1	1.9
	2001	3.3	2.9	3.5	3.5	0.6	0.5	10.6	1.5	2.9
	2002	3.6	2.9	3.3	3.4	0.7	0.5	8.6	1.3	3.0
Ores and metals	1999	7.5	8.4	6.7	6.1	8.2	4.7	40.4	7.4	16.0
(SITC 27 + 28 + 68)	2000	4.4	4.2	4.2	4.0	2.2	3.9	22.1	6.1	15.4
	2001	5.1	5.1	5.2	5.1	2.8	3.3	22.1	7.9	12.5
	2002	5.4	5.0	4.8	4.7	2.2	3.8	25.0	7.7	10.3
Fuels (SITC 3)	1999	46.3	47.2	41.3	41.7	72.3	69.6	10.8	18.4	14.8
	2000	54.6	57.5	50.1	51.2	82.2	79.6	11.7	22.9	23.7
	2001	47.4	52.4	44.7	45.4	80.0	76.9	11.5	20.7	16.4
	2002	47.1	49.8	43.8	44.7	74.9	76.9	20.1	17.9	9.5
Manufactured goods	1999	28.3	28.1	32.8	33.3	14.7	15.4	15.5	60.0	15.9
(SITC 5 to 8 less 68)	2000	24.8	25.9	30.7	30.5	12.5	10.5	25.4	59.9	19.3
	2001	29.4	27.8	32.5	33.0	13.4	12.7	25.6	60.4	20.3
	2002	30.0	29.7	33.1	33.8	18.0	12.2	24.0	64.7	18.3

Sources: UNCTAD secretariat computations based on UN/DESA/Statistics Division's data.

For notes, see end of table 3.2.2J.

| Developing economies / Economies en développement | | | | | | | | | Year | Destination |
| Total | of which / dont | | America | Africa | West Asia | Other Asia / Autres économies d'Asie | | Oceania | Année | |
	Major petroleum exporters / Principaux exportateurs de pétrole	Major exporters of manufactures / Principaux exportateurs d'articles manufacturés	Amérique	Afrique	Asie occidentale	Total	China / Chine	Océanie		Groupes de produits
				Millions de dollars						
30550	3270	15394	3557	11905	2982	12082	1632	25	1999	Total tous produits
39012	4703	19676	4623	14123	4470	15757	3652	39	2000	
33440	4239	15765	3523	13554	3734	12584	3194	46	2001	
34791	5204	15454	3223	14922	4113	12489	3446	44	2002	
			Parts par destinations (en pourcentage)							
28.7	3.1	14.5	3.3	11.2	2.8	11.4	1.5	0.0	1999	Total tous produits
27.5	3.3	13.9	3.3	10.0	3.2	11.1	2.6	0.0	2000	
26.6	3.4	12.6	2.8	10.8	3.0	10.0	2.5	0.0	2001	
28.2	4.2	12.5	2.6	12.1	3.3	10.1	2.8	0.0	2002	
30.8	8.7	6.6	0.8	16.9	6.2	6.8	0.9	0.1	1999	Produits alimentaires
35.7	11.4	5.5	0.7	20.9	7.9	6.2	0.9	0.0	2000	(CTCI 0 + 1 + 22 + 4)
34.0	9.7	5.5	0.7	21.8	5.8	5.7	1.0	0.0	2001	
33.8	10.8	4.7	0.6	22.1	6.3	4.7	0.4	0.1	2002	
43.5	4.6	22.3	2.6	15.6	3.1	22.2	4.9	0.0	1999	Matières premières
43.7	4.6	23.3	1.7	14.6	3.1	24.3	5.7	0.0	2000	d'origine agricole
41.8	4.7	23.4	1.3	12.3	3.2	25.0	6.4	0.0	2001	(CTCI 2 - 22 - 27 - 28)
43.4	4.6	24.3	0.9	11.5	3.4	27.5	7.6	0.0	2002	
20.8	1.8	15.2	1.7	3.6	1.4	14.1	2.3	0.0	1999	Minerais et métaux
30.2	2.4	19.3	3.2	7.9	2.0	17.2	3.6	0.0	2000	(CTCI 27 + 28 + 68)
27.6	2.1	18.6	2.3	7.0	1.6	16.8	4.8	0.0	2001	
30.3	2.5	18.1	2.4	9.1	1.7	17.2	5.2	0.0	2002	
27.2	0.6	19.3	5.0	6.4	2.3	13.6	2.0	0.0	1999	Combustibles (CTCI 3)
26.1	1.6	18.1	4.7	5.2	2.8	13.4	3.7	0.0	2000	
26.2	1.6	17.4	4.5	6.3	2.9	12.6	3.7	0.0	2001	
24.6	1.6	16.8	4.1	5.4	3.1	12.0	4.0	0.0	2002	
30.1	4.7	9.2	2.5	17.3	2.5	7.8	0.5	0.0	1999	Articles manufacturés
27.8	4.5	7.5	1.7	16.6	2.8	6.7	0.6	0.0	2000	(CTCI 5 à 8 moins 68)
25.7	4.5	6.9	1.6	15.4	2.7	6.0	0.8	0.1	2001	
30.5	6.1	7.4	1.6	19.4	2.9	6.6	1.0	0.0	2002	
			Parts par principaux groupes de produits (en pourcentage)							
13.9	36.5	5.9	3.2	19.5	28.4	7.8	7.9	46.8	1999	Produits alimentaires
12.3	32.7	3.7	2.1	19.9	23.7	5.3	3.2	16.1	2000	(CTCI 0 + 1 + 22 + 4)
13.4	30.1	4.6	2.5	21.2	20.5	6.0	4.3	7.3	2001	
13.8	29.5	4.4	2.7	21.1	21.9	5.4	1.7	25.4	2002	
6.3	6.3	6.4	3.2	5.8	4.6	8.1	13.2	1.1	1999	Matières premières
5.2	4.5	5.5	1.7	4.7	3.2	7.1	7.2	1.7	2000	d'origine agricole
5.2	4.7	6.2	1.5	3.8	3.6	8.3	8.4	1.7	2001	(CTCI 2 - 22 - 27 - 28)
5.5	3.9	6.9	1.3	3.4	3.6	9.7	9.8	2.3	2002	
5.4	4.5	7.8	3.7	2.4	3.8	9.3	11.2	4.0	1999	Minerais et métaux
4.8	3.2	6.1	4.3	3.5	2.8	6.8	6.1	0.4	2000	(CTCI 27 + 28 + 68)
5.3	3.2	7.5	4.2	3.3	2.7	8.5	9.6	0.0	2001	
5.8	3.3	7.9	4.9	4.1	2.8	9.2	10.1	0.6	2002	
43.9	9.2	61.8	68.6	26.5	37.4	55.2	59.0	31.9	1999	Combustibles (CTCI 3)
51.8	25.8	71.3	79.0	28.4	47.6	65.8	77.4	71.5	2000	
46.5	22.3	65.4	75.5	27.4	45.9	59.3	68.8	38.9	2001	
41.1	18.3	63.1	73.2	20.9	44.0	56.0	67.6	39.6	2002	
29.7	43.4	18.0	21.2	43.7	25.6	19.5	8.7	16.0	1999	Articles manufacturés
25.1	33.5	13.4	12.9	41.3	22.4	14.9	6.2	10.1	2000	(CTCI 5 à 8 moins 68)
28.4	39.0	16.1	16.3	41.9	26.5	17.7	8.9	52.0	2001	
32.5	43.8	17.7	17.9	48.1	26.2	19.6	10.9	31.9	2002	

Sources: Calculs du secrétariat de la CNUCED basés sur des données de ONU/DAES/Division de statistique.

Pour les notes, se reporter à la fin du tableau 3.2.2J.

3.2.1I Export structure by destination and by major commodity groups
Developing West Asia

Destination / Commodity groups	Year / Année	World[1] / Monde[1]	Developed economies / Economies développées							South-East Europe and CIS / Europe du Sud-Est et CEI
			Total	Europe		USA / Etats-Unis	Canada	Japan / Japon	Australia, New Zealand / Australie Nouvelle-Zélande	
				Total	EU / UE					
			Millions of dollars							
All products	1999	173166	73291	32073	31496	17530	716	21344	935	3627
	2000	247030	105508	41759	41209	28519	1606	31171	1738	4014
	2001	233011	103247	40389	39705	28969	1591	30088	1293	4853
	2002	237123	105012	43301	42454	28267	1934	29124	1397	5221
			Share by destination (percentage)							
All products	1999	100.0	42.3	18.5	18.2	10.1	0.4	12.3	0.5	2.1
	2000	100.0	42.7	16.9	16.7	11.5	0.7	12.6	0.7	1.6
	2001	100.0	44.3	17.3	17.0	12.4	0.7	12.9	0.6	2.1
	2002	100.0	44.3	18.3	17.9	11.9	0.8	12.3	0.6	2.2
All food items	1999	100.0	40.3	31.5	30.2	5.7	0.4	1.2	0.6	10.5
(SITC 0 + 1 + 22 + 4)	2000	100.0	33.8	27.0	25.8	3.6	0.5	1.4	0.6	10.3
	2001	100.0	31.7	25.1	24.2	3.9	0.4	1.0	0.5	8.6
	2002	100.0	30.5	24.5	23.7	3.4	0.4	1.0	0.5	8.3
Agricultural raw materials	1999	100.0	50.3	45.6	44.3	1.6	0.2	1.5	0.1	2.0
(SITC 2 - 22 - 27 - 28)	2000	100.0	48.3	44.2	43.0	1.3	0.1	1.9	0.1	3.1
	2001	100.0	44.0	40.5	39.2	1.6	0.1	1.0	0.0	3.2
	2002	100.0	44.5	41.3	39.9	1.0	0.1	1.1	0.1	2.2
Ores and metals	1999	100.0	37.5	22.9	21.6	4.3	0.1	8.6	0.4	3.0
(SITC 27 + 28 + 68)	2000	100.0	37.7	21.5	20.7	5.4	0.3	8.9	0.5	3.7
	2001	100.0	29.7	18.3	17.7	3.6	0.1	6.2	0.4	4.9
	2002	100.0	29.9	18.6	18.2	3.8	0.1	6.1	0.2	3.5
Fuels (SITC 3)	1999	100.0	39.6	10.9	10.9	10.9	0.3	17.0	0.6	0.1
	2000	100.0	41.1	11.8	11.8	12.1	0.6	15.9	0.7	0.1
	2001	100.0	44.2	11.3	11.2	14.1	0.7	17.5	0.6	0.3
	2002	100.0	43.6	11.3	11.2	13.6	0.9	17.2	0.7	0.2
Manufactured goods	1999	100.0	51.7	38.9	38.1	9.3	0.8	0.8	0.5	6.7
(SITC 5 to 8 less 68)	2000	100.0	50.8	36.8	35.9	10.4	0.8	0.8	0.6	6.5
	2001	100.0	48.7	35.7	35.0	9.6	0.6	0.7	0.5	6.8
	2002	100.0	49.4	37.1	36.2	9.1	0.7	0.5	0.4	7.2
			Share by major commodity groups (percentage)							
All food items	1999	4.4	4.2	7.5	7.4	2.5	4.3	0.4	4.6	22.2
(SITC 0 + 1 + 22 + 4)	2000	3.0	2.4	4.8	4.6	0.9	2.3	0.3	2.6	19.0
	2001	3.8	2.7	5.5	5.4	1.2	2.2	0.3	3.6	15.7
	2002	3.7	2.6	5.0	5.0	1.1	1.8	0.3	3.3	14.1
Agricultural raw materials	1999	0.5	0.5	1.1	1.1	0.1	0.3	0.1	0.0	0.5
(SITC 2 - 22 - 27 - 28)	2000	0.3	0.4	0.9	0.8	0.0	0.1	0.0	0.0	0.6
	2001	0.4	0.4	0.9	0.9	0.1	0.1	0.0	0.0	0.6
	2002	0.4	0.4	0.8	0.8	0.0	0.1	0.0	0.0	0.4
Ores and metals	1999	1.9	1.7	2.3	2.2	0.8	0.5	1.3	1.5	2.7
(SITC 27 + 28 + 68)	2000	1.4	1.3	1.8	1.8	0.7	0.6	1.0	1.0	3.2
	2001	1.6	1.1	1.7	1.7	0.5	0.3	0.8	1.2	3.8
	2002	1.6	1.1	1.6	1.6	0.5	0.2	0.8	0.7	2.5
Fuels (SITC 3)	1999	70.4	65.9	41.3	42.0	75.9	52.9	96.8	72.9	2.8
	2000	77.3	74.4	53.8	54.5	80.9	74.4	97.5	80.2	6.0
	2001	72.0	71.8	46.8	47.5	81.5	78.5	97.8	75.3	9.3
	2002	70.0	68.9	43.1	43.8	79.9	77.9	97.8	78.3	5.3
Manufactured goods	1999	22.4	27.4	47.2	47.0	20.6	41.1	1.4	20.9	71.6
(SITC 5 to 8 less 68)	2000	17.5	20.8	38.1	37.7	15.8	22.3	1.1	16.0	70.4
	2001	21.4	23.6	44.2	44.0	16.6	18.7	1.1	19.7	70.0
	2002	23.4	26.1	47.6	47.4	17.9	19.8	1.0	17.6	77.1

Sources: UNCTAD secretariat computations based on UN/DESA/Statistics Division's data.

For notes, see end of table 3.2.2J.

Total	of which dont		America	Africa	West Asia	Other Asia Autres économies d'Asie		Oceania	Year	Destination
	Major petroleum exporters	Major exporters of manufactures					China		Année	
	Principaux exportateurs de pétrole	Principaux exportateurs d'articles manufacturés	Amérique	Afrique	Asie occidentale	Total	Chine	Océanie		Groupes de produits

Developing economies / Economies en développement

Millions de dollars

Total	Major petroleum	Major manuf.	America	Africa	West Asia	Other Total	China	Oceania	Year	
58175	13783	35367	1265	6554	14030	36324	2258	1	1999	**Total tous produits**
80630	16995	52124	1790	8582	16965	53291	6920	1	2000	
78202	19100	47456	2205	7399	19737	48846	5045	16	2001	
82252	19969	47884	2062	8983	20166	51022	4696	19	2002	

Parts par destinations (en pourcentage)

33.6	8.0	20.4	0.7	3.8	8.1	21.0	1.3	0.0	1999	**Total tous produits**
32.6	6.9	21.1	0.7	3.5	6.9	21.6	2.8	0.0	2000	
33.6	8.2	20.4	0.9	3.2	8.5	21.0	2.2	0.0	2001	
34.7	8.4	20.2	0.9	3.8	8.5	21.5	2.0	0.0	2002	
46.4	30.8	6.4	0.9	4.8	33.8	6.9	0.2	0.0	1999	Produits alimentaires
52.8	36.9	5.6	0.8	5.6	40.1	6.3	0.2	0.0	2000	(CTCI 0 + 1 + 22 + 4)
55.7	40.1	5.2	0.8	6.7	42.2	6.0	0.2	0.0	2001	
58.8	43.6	5.5	0.7	5.9	45.2	6.9	0.3	0.0	2002	
43.2	12.9	19.7	1.1	7.5	18.3	16.3	1.6	_	1999	Matières premières
42.9	13.6	19.9	0.3	7.8	20.5	14.3	1.7	_	2000	d'origine agricole
46.2	13.3	16.4	0.2	9.5	16.2	19.3	2.9	1.1	2001	(CTCI 2 - 22 - 27 - 28)
46.2	12.0	16.6	0.1	9.5	16.3	19.3	1.7	1.0	2002	
58.1	17.6	35.1	0.2	3.5	18.3	36.1	2.9	0.0	1999	Minerais et métaux
57.2	19.8	31.4	0.3	3.5	21.0	32.4	2.8	0.0	2000	(CTCI 27 + 28 + 68)
63.4	22.3	35.2	0.2	3.4	20.9	38.9	5.1	_	2001	
64.9	23.7	34.6	0.1	4.6	22.0	38.2	6.1	0.0	2002	
30.6	2.9	24.4	0.7	2.1	3.1	24.7	1.5	_	1999	Combustibles (CTCI 3)
29.9	2.3	24.2	0.7	2.5	2.3	24.4	3.3	_	2000	
29.2	2.0	24.0	0.8	1.6	2.6	24.1	2.3	0.0	2001	
30.9	1.7	24.4	1.0	2.3	2.1	25.5	2.0	0.0	2002	
37.9	18.1	9.9	0.7	8.9	17.2	11.1	0.9	0.0	1999	Articles manufacturés
39.0	20.6	9.7	0.7	7.5	19.7	11.1	1.3	0.0	2000	(CTCI 5 à 8 moins 68)
40.6	21.8	10.1	0.8	7.7	20.5	11.6	2.0	0.0	2001	
39.2	21.5	9.3	0.6	7.7	20.2	10.7	2.1	0.0	2002	

Parts par principaux groupes de produits (en pourcentage)

6.1	17.1	1.4	5.4	5.6	18.5	1.5	0.7	13.2	1999	Produits alimentaires
4.8	16.0	0.8	3.3	4.8	17.4	0.9	0.3	5.9	2000	(CTCI 0 + 1 + 22 + 4)
6.3	18.6	1.0	3.4	8.0	18.9	1.1	0.4	2.3	2001	
6.3	19.4	1.0	3.2	5.8	19.9	1.2	0.5	15.7	2002	
0.6	0.8	0.4	0.7	0.9	1.0	0.4	0.6	_	1999	Matières premières
0.4	0.6	0.3	0.1	0.7	1.0	0.2	0.2	_	2000	d'origine agricole
0.6	0.7	0.3	0.1	1.2	0.8	0.4	0.5	64.5	2001	(CTCI 2 - 22 - 27 - 28)
0.5	0.5	0.3	0.1	0.9	0.7	0.3	0.3	47.1	2002	
3.3	4.2	3.3	0.5	1.7	4.3	3.3	4.2	3.4	1999	Minerais et métaux
2.5	4.1	2.1	0.5	1.4	4.3	2.1	1.4	0.8	2000	(CTCI 27 + 28 + 68)
3.1	4.4	2.8	0.3	1.7	4.0	3.0	3.8	_	2001	
3.0	4.5	2.7	0.1	1.9	4.1	2.8	4.9	1.4	2002	
64.1	25.4	83.9	70.7	38.2	27.1	82.8	79.7	_	1999	Combustibles (CTCI 3)
70.9	25.9	88.5	79.6	54.8	25.8	87.6	90.0	_	2000	
62.7	17.5	84.9	62.8	36.4	22.5	83.0	75.7	1.2	2001	
62.3	13.9	84.4	80.7	42.5	17.0	82.9	69.4	2.2	2002	
25.3	51.1	10.8	22.7	52.9	47.5	11.9	14.9	83.4	1999	Articles manufacturés
20.9	52.6	8.1	16.5	37.7	50.3	9.0	8.1	93.3	2000	(CTCI 5 à 8 moins 68)
25.9	57.1	10.6	18.1	51.8	51.9	11.9	19.4	30.2	2001	
26.5	59.9	10.8	15.8	47.8	55.6	11.7	24.5	23.0	2002	

Sources: Calculs du secrétariat de la CNUCED basés sur des données de ONU/DAES/Division de statistique.

Pour les notes, se reporter à la fin du tableau 3.2.2J.

3.2.1J Export structure by destination and by major commodity groups
Other developing Asia

Commodity groups	Year / Année	World [1] / Monde [1]	Developed economies / Economies développées — Total	Europe — Total	Europe — EU / UE	USA / Etats-Unis	Canada	Japan / Japon	Australia, New Zealand / Australie Nouvelle-Zélande	South-East Europe and CIS / Europe du Sud-Est et CEI
		Millions of dollars								
All products	1999	1047798	568619	184956	177334	230536	12137	116712	21234	6505
	2000	1267255	671741	209358	202094	269968	14663	150079	23813	7912
	2001	1183441	616414	195568	188958	241321	13448	140503	22153	9023
	2002	1304097	654174	206527	200063	261892	14976	141773	25350	11034
		Share by destination (percentage)								
All products	1999	100.0	54.3	17.7	16.9	22.0	1.2	11.1	2.0	0.6
	2000	100.0	53.0	16.5	15.9	21.3	1.2	11.8	1.9	0.6
	2001	100.0	52.1	16.5	16.0	20.4	1.1	11.9	1.9	0.8
	2002	100.0	50.2	15.8	15.3	20.1	1.1	10.9	1.9	0.8
All food items	1999	100.0	49.4	13.9	13.2	10.6	1.1	22.0	1.6	1.8
(SITC 0 + 1 + 22 + 4)	2000	100.0	49.4	12.6	12.1	11.4	1.2	22.6	1.5	1.7
	2001	100.0	48.3	12.6	12.2	11.1	1.2	21.8	1.5	2.1
	2002	100.0	45.9	12.2	11.9	11.3	1.1	19.7	1.5	2.4
Agricultural raw materials	1999	100.0	41.8	15.6	15.5	9.4	0.8	14.8	1.2	0.3
(SITC 2 - 22 - 27 - 28)	2000	100.0	40.7	15.2	15.1	8.7	0.8	14.6	1.2	0.4
	2001	100.0	40.4	14.8	14.6	8.7	0.8	14.8	1.2	0.4
	2002	100.0	40.3	14.6	14.5	9.4	1.0	14.0	1.2	0.4
Ores and metals	1999	100.0	34.5	9.8	9.2	5.2	0.5	16.7	1.3	0.6
(SITC 27 + 28 + 68)	2000	100.0	34.8	9.5	9.1	5.1	0.5	17.4	1.3	0.7
	2001	100.0	32.6	10.4	10.2	4.6	0.5	14.7	1.4	0.8
	2002	100.0	29.5	9.1	8.9	3.8	0.4	14.0	1.4	1.1
Fuels (SITC 3)	1999	100.0	40.5	2.9	2.7	4.4	0.1	27.9	5.2	0.3
	2000	100.0	39.5	2.7	2.5	4.5	0.1	27.4	4.8	0.2
	2001	100.0	39.0	1.7	1.6	4.2	0.1	27.5	5.5	0.2
	2002	100.0	38.2	2.0	1.9	4.0	0.1	25.8	6.3	0.1
Manufactured goods	1999	100.0	55.9	18.6	18.1	24.3	1.2	9.5	1.9	0.6
(SITC 5 to 8 less 68)	2000	100.0	54.7	17.7	17.2	23.5	1.2	10.2	1.7	0.6
	2001	100.0	53.8	17.7	17.2	22.5	1.2	10.3	1.6	0.7
	2002	100.0	51.8	17.0	16.5	22.1	1.2	9.4	1.7	0.8
		Share by major commodity groups (percentage)								
All food items	1999	5.6	5.1	4.4	4.4	2.7	5.2	11.0	4.5	16.3
(SITC 0 + 1 + 22 + 4)	2000	4.7	4.4	3.6	3.6	2.5	4.8	9.0	3.8	13.0
	2001	5.1	4.7	3.8	3.9	2.8	5.3	9.3	4.0	13.9
	2002	5.1	4.7	3.9	4.0	2.9	5.1	9.3	4.1	14.3
Agricultural raw materials	1999	1.5	1.2	1.3	1.4	0.6	1.0	2.0	0.9	0.7
(SITC 2 - 22 - 27 - 28)	2000	1.4	1.1	1.3	1.3	0.6	1.0	1.8	0.9	0.8
	2001	1.3	1.0	1.2	1.2	0.6	0.9	1.6	0.8	0.8
	2002	1.3	1.0	1.2	1.2	0.6	1.1	1.6	0.8	0.7
Ores and metals	1999	1.6	1.0	0.9	0.9	0.4	0.7	2.4	1.0	1.5
(SITC 27 + 28 + 68)	2000	1.6	1.1	0.9	0.9	0.4	0.7	2.3	1.1	1.7
	2001	1.6	1.0	1.0	1.0	0.4	0.7	2.0	1.2	1.6
	2002	1.6	0.9	0.9	0.9	0.3	0.6	2.0	1.1	2.1
Fuels (SITC 3)	1999	4.2	3.2	0.7	0.7	0.8	0.4	10.6	10.9	2.1
	2000	5.5	4.1	0.9	0.9	1.1	0.6	12.6	13.8	1.7
	2001	5.2	3.9	0.5	0.5	1.1	0.3	12.0	15.4	1.4
	2002	5.0	3.8	0.6	0.6	1.0	0.3	11.9	16.3	0.9
Manufactured goods	1999	86.0	88.5	90.8	91.9	95.0	92.0	73.4	79.4	79.1
(SITC 5 to 8 less 68)	2000	86.0	88.7	92.3	92.6	94.9	92.6	73.8	78.0	82.5
	2001	85.7	88.5	91.9	92.4	94.8	92.3	74.6	74.3	81.8
	2002	84.8	87.4	90.8	91.2	93.3	91.9	73.6	73.8	81.6

Sources: UNCTAD secretariat computations based on UN/DESA/Statistics Division's data.   For notes, see end of table 3.2.2J.

Total	of which dont		America Amérique	Africa Afrique	West Asia Asie occi- dentale	Other Asia Autres économies d'Asie		Oceania Océanie	Year Année	Destination
	Major petroleum exporters Principaux exportateurs de pétrole	Major exporters of manufactures Principaux exportateurs d'articles manufacturés				Total	China Chine			Groupes de produits
Millions de dollars										
469401	36615	375879	26774	17807	26487	397294	86961	1039	1999	Total tous produits
583030	45800	470597	33418	19453	32896	495614	110534	1648	2000	
553165	48223	438568	33005	21154	32684	464653	111835	1669	2001	
636236	53881	511123	33135	22663	38661	539611	137222	2165	2002	
Parts par destinations (en pourcentage)										
44.8	3.5	35.9	2.6	1.7	2.5	37.9	8.3	0.1	1999	Total tous produits
46.0	3.6	37.1	2.6	1.5	2.6	39.1	8.7	0.1	2000	
46.7	4.1	37.1	2.8	1.8	2.8	39.3	9.5	0.1	2001	
48.8	4.1	39.2	2.5	1.7	3.0	41.4	10.5	0.2	2002	
48.1	8.2	30.6	0.8	3.8	5.8	37.6	6.3	0.1	1999	Produits alimentaires
48.4	8.1	30.9	0.9	3.5	6.1	37.8	6.6	0.1	2000	(CTCI 0 + 1 + 22 + 4)
48.8	8.3	30.6	0.9	4.0	5.8	38.1	6.5	0.1	2001	
51.1	8.5	32.0	1.0	4.4	5.7	39.9	6.6	0.1	2002	
57.8	3.2	49.8	1.7	1.0	1.8	53.3	21.0	0.0	1999	Matières premières
59.0	3.7	50.0	1.6	1.1	2.4	53.8	22.3	0.0	2000	d'origine agricole
59.1	3.5	50.1	1.6	1.2	2.4	53.9	22.9	0.0	2001	(CTCI 2 - 22 - 27 - 28)
59.2	3.6	49.7	1.6	1.4	2.8	53.4	22.9	0.0	2002	
64.9	2.6	59.6	0.9	0.6	1.4	62.1	17.4	0.0	1999	Minerais et métaux
64.5	2.9	58.6	0.6	0.6	1.7	61.5	17.2	0.0	2000	(CTCI 27 + 28 + 68)
66.6	3.4	59.5	0.6	0.7	2.2	63.0	17.3	0.1	2001	
69.4	3.8	62.1	0.6	0.7	2.4	65.7	19.2	0.0	2002	
56.9	1.8	47.4	2.0	0.8	0.7	53.0	7.8	0.4	1999	Combustibles (CTCI 3)
55.4	2.5	45.3	2.2	0.6	0.8	51.2	8.2	0.6	2000	
55.1	3.0	45.8	1.0	0.3	0.9	52.3	7.4	0.5	2001	
59.7	4.0	48.9	1.5	0.4	2.1	55.0	7.8	0.6	2002	
43.5	3.3	35.0	2.8	1.6	2.4	36.5	8.1	0.1	1999	Articles manufacturés
44.7	3.4	36.3	2.8	1.5	2.5	37.7	8.5	0.1	2000	(CTCI 5 à 8 moins 68)
45.4	3.9	36.3	3.0	1.7	2.7	37.9	9.5	0.1	2001	
47.4	3.9	38.4	2.7	1.7	2.9	40.0	10.7	0.1	2002	
Parts par principaux groupes de produits (en pourcentage)										
6.0	13.1	4.8	1.8	12.5	12.9	5.5	4.2	6.4	1999	Produits alimentaires
5.0	10.7	3.9	1.6	10.9	11.1	4.6	3.6	4.3	2000	(CTCI 0 + 1 + 22 + 4)
5.3	10.3	4.2	1.6	11.3	10.6	4.9	3.5	3.9	2001	
5.4	10.6	4.2	2.0	13.1	9.9	4.9	3.2	3.5	2002	
1.9	1.4	2.1	1.0	0.9	1.1	2.1	3.8	0.2	1999	Matières premières
1.8	1.5	1.9	0.9	1.0	1.3	2.0	3.7	0.2	2000	d'origine agricole
1.6	1.1	1.8	0.7	0.8	1.1	1.8	3.1	0.4	2001	(CTCI 2 - 22 - 27 - 28)
1.6	1.1	1.6	0.8	1.0	1.2	1.7	2.8	0.2	2002	
2.3	1.2	2.7	0.5	0.5	0.9	2.6	3.4	0.4	1999	Minerais et métaux
2.2	1.3	2.5	0.4	0.6	1.1	2.5	3.2	0.4	2000	(CTCI 27 + 28 + 68)
2.3	1.3	2.6	0.4	0.7	1.3	2.6	2.9	0.6	2001	
2.2	1.4	2.5	0.4	0.6	1.3	2.5	2.9	0.2	2002	
5.4	2.2	5.6	3.3	1.9	1.2	5.9	4.0	16.0	1999	Combustibles (CTCI 3)
6.6	3.8	6.7	4.5	2.1	1.6	7.1	5.1	25.5	2000	
6.1	3.8	6.4	1.8	1.0	1.7	6.9	4.0	19.4	2001	
6.1	4.8	6.2	2.9	1.2	3.5	6.6	3.7	19.1	2002	
83.4	80.8	84.0	93.1	83.4	82.3	82.9	84.1	75.9	1999	Articles manufacturés
83.5	81.3	84.1	92.5	85.0	82.9	82.9	84.1	69.1	2000	(CTCI 5 à 8 moins 68)
83.3	82.0	84.1	91.8	82.6	83.6	82.7	85.9	70.6	2001	
82.3	80.3	83.1	89.2	81.3	82.2	82.0	86.4	73.4	2002	

Sources: Calculs du secrétariat de la CNUCED basés sur des données de
ONU/DAES/Division de statistique.

Pour les notes, se reporter à la fin du tableau 3.2.2J.

Origin Commodity groups	Year Année	World [1] Monde [1]	Developed economies Economies développées							South-East Europe and CIS Europe du Sud-Est et CEI
			Total	Europe		USA Etats-Unis	Canada	Japan Japon	Australia, New Zealand Australie Nouvelle- Zélande	
				Total	EU UE					
				Millions of dollars						
All products	1999	5571175	3819296	2377276	2248874	692784	238778	417610	67008	126015
	2000	6287738	4106163	2462910	2318968	780332	277113	479248	75153	167450
	2001	6065269	4005470	2507207	2363426	731006	259903	403364	74929	172010
	2002	6306330	4120322	2647706	2497873	693222	252418	416715	80748	173897
				Share by origin (percentage)						
All products	1999	100.0	68.6	42.7	40.4	12.4	4.3	7.5	1.2	2.3
	2000	100.0	65.3	39.2	36.9	12.4	4.4	7.6	1.2	2.7
	2001	100.0	66.0	41.3	39.0	12.1	4.3	6.7	1.2	2.8
	2002	100.0	65.3	42.0	39.6	11.0	4.0	6.6	1.3	2.8
All food items	1999	100.0	67.3	46.6	44.7	12.1	3.8	0.5	4.1	1.4
(SITC 0 + 1 + 22 + 4)	2000	100.0	66.4	44.2	42.4	12.9	4.2	0.5	4.4	1.5
	2001	100.0	66.2	44.1	42.4	12.4	4.4	0.7	4.4	1.7
	2002	100.0	66.0	45.3	43.6	11.5	4.1	0.5	4.4	1.9
Agricultural raw materials	1999	100.0	67.4	31.5	30.6	13.4	15.4	2.0	4.9	5.8
(SITC 2 - 22 - 27 - 28)	2000	100.0	66.5	29.4	28.5	14.9	15.0	1.9	5.0	5.9
	2001	100.0	67.7	32.1	31.3	14.8	13.4	1.9	5.2	5.9
	2002	100.0	67.4	33.7	32.9	14.0	12.3	2.0	5.0	6.0
Ores and metals	1999	100.0	59.8	34.5	30.0	7.8	6.9	3.3	7.0	8.6
(SITC 27 + 28 + 68)	2000	100.0	60.4	34.6	29.7	8.1	6.8	3.3	7.4	9.2
	2001	100.0	60.9	34.9	30.5	8.2	6.7	3.3	7.7	8.7
	2002	100.0	60.4	35.1	30.6	7.8	6.7	3.2	7.4	8.3
Fuels (SITC 3)	1999	100.0	29.5	19.6	14.2	2.4	4.9	0.3	2.3	9.2
	2000	100.0	29.4	19.5	13.7	2.0	5.5	0.2	2.1	10.0
	2001	100.0	31.0	20.1	13.9	2.2	6.2	0.3	2.3	11.4
	2002	100.0	30.3	20.4	14.3	2.0	5.4	0.2	2.3	11.9
Manufactured goods	1999	100.0	72.3	45.0	43.0	13.5	3.7	9.1	0.4	1.1
(SITC 5 to 8 less 68)	2000	100.0	69.8	41.7	39.9	13.8	3.7	9.5	0.4	1.2
	2001	100.0	70.2	44.2	42.3	13.2	3.5	8.2	0.4	1.4
	2002	100.0	69.5	45.1	43.1	12.0	3.3	8.1	0.4	1.3
				Share by major commodity groups (percentage)						
All food items	1999	7.7	7.6	8.4	8.6	7.5	6.9	0.5	26.2	4.7
(SITC 0 + 1 + 22 + 4)	2000	6.7	6.8	7.6	7.7	7.0	6.4	0.5	24.5	3.8
	2001	7.2	7.2	7.7	7.8	7.4	7.4	0.8	25.7	4.4
	2002	7.3	7.4	7.9	8.1	7.7	7.4	0.5	25.0	4.9
Agricultural raw materials	1999	1.9	1.8	1.4	1.4	2.0	6.7	0.5	7.6	4.8
(SITC 2 - 22 - 27 - 28)	2000	1.8	1.9	1.4	1.4	2.2	6.2	0.5	7.6	4.0
	2001	1.8	1.8	1.4	1.4	2.2	5.5	0.5	7.5	3.7
	2002	1.8	1.8	1.4	1.5	2.3	5.5	0.5	6.9	3.9
Ores and metals	1999	2.8	2.4	2.2	2.1	1.7	4.4	1.2	16.2	10.5
(SITC 27 + 28 + 68)	2000	2.8	2.6	2.5	2.3	1.8	4.3	1.2	17.5	9.7
	2001	2.8	2.5	2.3	2.2	1.9	4.3	1.4	17.1	8.4
	2002	2.7	2.5	2.2	2.1	1.9	4.4	1.3	15.4	8.0
Fuels (SITC 3)	1999	7.5	3.2	3.4	2.6	1.4	8.5	0.3	14.3	30.5
	2000	10.5	4.7	5.2	3.9	1.7	13.1	0.3	18.2	39.4
	2001	9.8	4.6	4.8	3.5	1.8	14.1	0.4	17.9	39.3
	2002	9.4	4.4	4.6	3.4	1.7	12.6	0.3	17.0	40.7
Manufactured goods	1999	77.2	81.4	81.4	82.2	83.5	66.7	94.2	28.2	38.3
(SITC 5 to 8 less 68)	2000	75.2	80.3	80.1	81.3	83.5	63.4	93.9	25.5	34.6
	2001	75.4	80.1	80.6	81.7	82.8	62.0	92.8	25.0	36.4
	2002	75.8	80.6	81.5	82.5	82.4	63.0	93.0	24.6	36.1

Sources: UNCTAD secretariat computations based on UN/DESA/Statistics Division's data.

For notes, see end of table 3.2.2J.

| Developing economies / Economies en développement | | | | | | | | | | Origine |
| Total | of which / dont | | America / Amérique | Africa / Afrique | West Asia / Asie occidentale | Other Asia / Autres économies d'Asie | | Oceania / Océanie | Year / Année | |
	Major petroleum exporters / Principaux exportateurs de pétole	Major exporters of manufactures / Principaux exportateurs d'articles manufacturés				Total	China			Groupes de produits
				Millions de dollars						
1625864	264791	1172601	293885	106275	173166	1047798	194931	4739	1999	Total tous produits
2014125	388586	1409990	352869	141662	247030	1267255	249203	5309	2000	
1887789	340955	1329773	341450	125498	233011	1183441	266098	4389	2001	
2012111	344231	1452292	343327	123461	237123	1304097	325596	4103	2002	
			Parts par origines (en pourcentage)							
29.2	4.8	21.0	5.3	1.9	3.1	18.8	3.5	0.1	1999	Total tous produits
32.0	6.2	22.4	5.6	2.3	3.9	20.2	4.0	0.1	2000	
31.1	5.6	21.9	5.6	2.1	3.8	19.5	4.4	0.1	2001	
31.9	5.5	23.0	5.4	2.0	3.8	20.7	5.2	0.1	2002	
31.4	2.3	16.7	12.6	3.2	1.8	13.6	2.7	0.2	1999	Produits alimentaires
32.1	2.4	17.2	12.8	3.2	1.7	14.3	3.2	0.2	2000	(CTCI 0 + 1 + 22 + 4)
32.0	2.3	17.3	13.1	3.0	2.0	13.7	3.3	0.2	2001	
32.2	2.6	17.5	12.5	3.1	1.9	14.5	3.5	0.1	2002	
26.8	2.6	15.5	6.6	4.2	0.8	15.0	2.4	0.1	1999	Matières premières
27.6	2.8	16.0	6.9	4.0	0.7	15.8	2.5	0.1	2000	d'origine agricole
26.4	2.8	14.6	7.2	3.9	0.9	14.3	2.2	0.1	2001	(CTCI 2 - 22 - 27 - 28)
26.6	3.2	14.7	6.8	3.9	0.8	14.9	2.4	0.1	2002	
31.6	3.5	14.2	12.6	5.1	2.1	10.9	2.5	0.8	1999	Minerais et métaux
30.5	3.9	14.3	12.7	3.5	2.0	11.4	2.6	0.9	2000	(CTCI 27 + 28 + 68)
30.4	4.1	13.8	12.4	3.8	2.3	11.3	2.8	0.7	2001	
31.3	4.0	14.8	12.3	4.0	2.3	12.2	3.1	0.5	2002	
61.3	47.2	9.3	9.5	11.8	29.2	10.6	1.1	0.1	1999	Combustibles (CTCI 3)
60.6	46.5	9.7	9.5	11.7	28.9	10.5	1.2	0.1	2000	
57.7	43.6	9.4	9.0	10.0	28.2	10.3	1.4	0.1	2001	
57.8	43.3	9.8	9.2	9.8	27.9	10.9	1.4	0.1	2002	
26.5	1.1	23.6	3.9	0.7	0.9	21.0	4.0	0.0	1999	Articles manufacturés
29.0	1.3	25.8	4.3	0.7	0.9	23.1	4.7	0.0	2000	(CTCI 5 à 8 moins 68)
28.5	1.3	25.0	4.3	0.8	1.1	22.2	5.2	0.0	2001	
29.2	1.3	26.0	4.1	0.8	1.2	23.1	6.1	0.0	2002	
			Parts par principaux groupes de produits (en pourcentage)							
8.3	3.7	6.1	18.5	12.9	4.4	5.6	6.0	16.0	1999	Produits alimentaires
6.7	2.6	5.1	15.3	9.5	3.0	4.7	5.4	14.2	2000	(CTCI 0 + 1 + 22 + 4)
7.4	3.0	5.7	16.7	10.5	3.8	5.1	5.3	16.4	2001	
7.4	3.6	5.6	16.8	11.5	3.7	5.1	5.0	15.1	2002	
1.7	1.0	1.4	2.3	4.2	0.5	1.5	1.3	3.1	1999	Matières premières
1.6	0.8	1.3	2.2	3.2	0.3	1.4	1.1	3.2	2000	d'origine agricole
1.5	0.9	1.2	2.3	3.3	0.4	1.3	0.9	3.4	2001	(CTCI 2 - 22 - 27 - 28)
1.5	1.0	1.1	2.2	3.6	0.4	1.3	0.8	3.1	2002	
3.0	2.0	1.9	6.6	7.5	1.9	1.6	2.0	26.0	1999	Minerais et métaux
2.7	1.8	1.8	6.4	4.4	1.4	1.6	1.8	29.4	2000	(CTCI 27 + 28 + 68)
2.7	2.0	1.7	6.1	5.1	1.6	1.6	1.7	24.9	2001	
2.6	2.0	1.7	6.0	5.4	1.6	1.6	1.6	22.2	2002	
15.7	74.4	3.3	13.4	46.3	70.4	4.2	2.4	11.8	1999	Combustibles (CTCI 3)
19.9	79.0	4.6	17.8	54.6	77.3	5.5	3.2	13.2	2000	
18.1	75.9	4.2	15.6	47.4	72.0	5.2	3.2	12.0	2001	
17.1	75.0	4.0	15.9	47.1	70.0	5.0	2.6	13.1	2002	
70.2	18.0	86.4	57.7	28.3	22.4	86.0	88.3	36.4	1999	Articles manufacturés
68.1	15.6	86.5	57.1	24.8	17.5	86.0	88.2	34.5	2000	(CTCI 5 à 8 moins 68)
68.9	17.7	86.1	57.9	29.4	21.4	85.7	88.6	37.2	2001	
69.5	18.0	85.5	57.7	30.0	23.4	84.8	89.9	39.7	2002	

Sources: Calculs du secrétariat de la CNUCED basés sur des données de
ONU/DAES/Division de statistique.

Pour les notes, se reporter à la fin du tableau 3.2.2J.

3.2.2B Import structure by origin and by major commodity groups
Developed economies

| Commodity groups | Year / Année | World [1] / Monde [1] | Developed economies / Economies développées | | | | | | | South-East Europe and CIS / Europe du Sud-Est et CEI |
			Total	Europe Total	EU / UE	USA / Etats-Unis	Canada	Japan / Japon	Australia, New Zealand / Australie Nouvelle-Zélande	
						Millions of dollars				
All products	1999	3911311	2898493	1984707	1872926	407908	226137	227877	32594	71935
	2000	4257111	3015225	2005317	1879413	443723	262644	246651	34131	99088
	2001	4143062	2995280	2069384	1945394	416438	245792	208342	34326	93549
	2002	4275149	3076758	2184838	2057363	390641	238879	204489	36595	96422
						Share by origin (percentage)				
All products	1999	100.0	74.1	50.7	47.9	10.4	5.8	5.8	0.8	1.8
	2000	100.0	70.8	47.1	44.1	10.4	6.2	5.8	0.8	2.3
	2001	100.0	72.3	49.9	47.0	10.1	5.9	5.0	0.8	2.3
	2002	100.0	72.0	51.1	48.1	9.1	5.6	4.8	0.9	2.3
All food items (SITC 0 + 1 + 22 + 4)	1999	100.0	73.9	56.9	54.5	9.4	4.3	0.2	2.8	0.6
	2000	100.0	73.2	54.8	52.5	10.1	4.8	0.2	3.1	0.7
	2001	100.0	73.9	55.6	53.4	9.6	5.2	0.2	3.1	0.9
	2002	100.0	74.4	56.9	54.9	8.8	5.0	0.2	3.1	1.0
Agricultural raw materials (SITC 2 - 22 - 27 - 28)	1999	100.0	75.1	39.2	38.0	11.1	20.1	0.8	3.4	4.9
	2000	100.0	73.7	37.3	36.2	11.9	20.1	0.7	3.2	5.2
	2001	100.0	74.8	41.4	40.3	11.0	18.1	0.7	3.2	5.0
	2002	100.0	74.5	43.6	42.5	10.1	16.5	0.7	3.2	5.0
Ores and metals (SITC 27 + 28 + 68)	1999	100.0	64.8	43.6	37.6	7.2	9.2	0.9	3.7	9.8
	2000	100.0	66.5	44.7	38.1	7.5	9.2	1.0	3.9	9.9
	2001	100.0	67.4	45.2	39.5	7.7	9.2	1.0	4.1	9.3
	2002	100.0	67.7	46.1	40.3	7.4	9.3	0.7	4.0	9.0
Fuels (SITC 3)	1999	100.0	39.8	28.2	19.6	1.9	7.7	0.1	1.8	9.8
	2000	100.0	39.5	28.0	18.8	1.4	8.6	0.1	1.4	10.9
	2001	100.0	41.4	28.4	18.9	1.7	9.6	0.1	1.6	11.8
	2002	100.0	40.0	28.5	19.2	1.3	8.3	0.1	1.7	13.0
Manufactured goods (SITC 5 to 8 less 68)	1999	100.0	77.0	52.7	50.4	11.2	5.0	7.1	0.4	0.8
	2000	100.0	74.4	49.6	47.5	11.4	5.2	7.2	0.3	0.9
	2001	100.0	75.3	52.4	50.1	10.9	4.9	6.2	0.3	1.0
	2002	100.0	75.2	53.8	51.5	9.9	4.6	5.9	0.4	0.9
						Share by major commodity groups (percentage)				
All food items (SITC 0 + 1 + 22 + 4)	1999	7.7	7.7	8.7	8.8	7.0	5.8	0.3	25.6	2.7
	2000	6.8	7.0	7.9	8.1	6.6	5.3	0.3	25.9	2.1
	2001	7.1	7.3	7.9	8.1	6.8	6.2	0.3	26.9	2.8
	2002	7.3	7.6	8.2	8.4	7.1	6.6	0.3	26.8	3.1
Agricultural raw materials (SITC 2 - 22 - 27 - 28)	1999	1.8	1.9	1.4	1.5	2.0	6.4	0.3	7.5	4.9
	2000	1.8	1.9	1.4	1.5	2.0	5.8	0.2	7.0	4.0
	2001	1.7	1.8	1.4	1.5	1.9	5.2	0.2	6.6	3.8
	2002	1.7	1.8	1.5	1.5	1.9	5.0	0.3	6.5	3.8
Ores and metals (SITC 27 + 28 + 68)	1999	2.8	2.4	2.4	2.2	1.9	4.4	0.4	12.3	14.7
	2000	2.8	2.6	2.7	2.4	2.0	4.2	0.5	13.6	11.9
	2001	2.7	2.5	2.4	2.3	2.1	4.2	0.5	13.3	11.2
	2002	2.5	2.4	2.3	2.1	2.1	4.2	0.4	11.7	10.1
Fuels (SITC 3)	1999	6.6	3.5	3.6	2.7	1.2	8.7	0.2	14.3	35.1
	2000	9.8	5.5	5.8	4.2	1.3	13.7	0.2	17.5	45.7
	2001	9.1	5.2	5.2	3.7	1.5	14.8	0.2	17.7	47.6
	2002	8.8	4.9	4.9	3.5	1.3	13.2	0.2	17.4	50.9
Manufactured goods (SITC 5 to 8 less 68)	1999	78.5	81.5	81.6	82.6	84.0	67.7	95.6	35.5	33.7
	2000	76.8	80.6	80.8	82.5	84.1	64.2	95.1	32.4	29.5
	2001	76.6	79.8	80.3	81.7	83.3	62.7	94.6	31.3	33.6
	2002	77.0	80.5	81.1	82.4	83.6	63.6	94.8	32.3	31.2

Sources: UNCTAD secretariat computations based on UN/DESA/Statistics Division's data.

For notes, see end of table 3.2.2J.

Total	of which dont — Major petroleum exporters / Principaux exportateurs de pétole	Major exporters of manufactures / Principaux exportateurs d'articles manufacturés	America / Amérique	Africa / Afrique	West Asia / Asie occidentale	Other Asia Total	Other Asia China	Oceania / Océanie	Year Année	Origine / Groupes de produits
— Millions de dollars										
940883	130758	695004	222986	73676	73291	568619	113483	2312	1999	Total tous produits
1142798	197395	820083	266687	96643	105508	671741	143582	2218	2000	
1054232	173849	761791	251320	81512	103247	616414	152795	1739	2001	
1101969	173059	804640	255675	85490	105012	654174	182561	1618	2002	
— Parts par origines (en pourcentage)										
24.1	3.3	17.8	5.7	1.9	1.9	14.5	2.9	0.1	1999	Total tous produits
26.8	4.6	19.3	6.3	2.3	2.5	15.8	3.4	0.1	2000	
25.4	4.2	18.4	6.1	2.0	2.5	14.9	3.7	0.0	2001	
25.8	4.0	18.8	6.0	2.0	2.5	15.3	4.3	0.0	2002	
25.5	1.3	13.8	11.8	3.0	1.0	9.5	2.2	0.1	1999	Produits alimentaires
26.1	1.3	14.5	11.9	2.9	0.9	10.3	2.6	0.1	2000	(CTCI 0 + 1 + 22 + 4)
25.2	1.1	14.3	11.5	2.8	1.0	9.8	2.8	0.1	2001	
24.7	1.2	13.9	11.1	2.8	0.9	9.8	2.7	0.1	2002	
20.0	1.9	11.1	6.8	3.4	0.6	9.1	2.1	0.1	1999	Matières premières
21.1	2.0	12.0	7.5	3.4	0.5	9.7	2.3	0.1	2000	d'origine agricole
20.2	1.8	10.8	7.5	3.4	0.6	8.7	2.2	0.1	2001	(CTCI 2 - 22 - 27 - 28)
20.5	2.1	10.9	7.3	3.4	0.5	9.2	2.2	0.1	2002	
25.4	2.5	9.4	12.9	5.7	1.1	5.4	1.7	0.2	1999	Minerais et métaux
23.6	2.9	9.6	12.9	3.4	1.1	5.9	1.8	0.3	2000	(CTCI 27 + 28 + 68)
23.2	2.8	8.8	12.8	3.7	1.0	5.5	1.8	0.2	2001	
23.2	2.8	9.1	12.6	3.9	1.0	5.5	1.7	0.2	2002	
50.4	39.0	7.1	11.0	13.6	18.8	7.0	0.7	0.0	1999	Combustibles (CTCI 3)
49.6	38.7	7.3	10.7	13.4	18.9	6.6	0.8	0.0	2000	
46.8	36.7	6.7	9.5	11.3	19.6	6.3	0.8	0.0	2001	
47.0	36.4	7.0	9.9	11.3	19.2	6.6	0.8	0.0	2002	
22.3	0.7	19.9	4.5	0.7	0.7	16.4	3.3	0.0	1999	Articles manufacturés
24.7	0.9	22.1	5.0	0.8	0.7	18.2	3.9	0.0	2000	(CTCI 5 à 8 moins 68)
23.7	0.8	21.1	5.0	0.7	0.8	17.2	4.3	0.0	2001	
23.9	0.8	21.3	4.9	0.8	0.8	17.4	5.1	0.0	2002	
— Parts par principaux groupes de produits (en pourcentage)										
8.2	3.0	6.0	16.0	12.4	4.2	5.1	5.8	18.0	1999	Produits alimentaires
6.6	1.9	5.1	12.9	8.6	2.4	4.4	5.2	16.9	2000	(CTCI 0 + 1 + 22 + 4)
7.1	1.9	5.5	13.6	10.1	2.7	4.7	5.4	22.3	2001	
7.0	2.2	5.4	13.6	10.4	2.6	4.7	4.6	22.1	2002	
1.5	1.0	1.2	2.2	3.4	0.5	1.2	1.3	3.1	1999	Matières premières
1.4	0.8	1.1	2.1	2.6	0.4	1.1	1.2	3.0	2000	d'origine agricole
1.4	0.7	1.0	2.1	2.9	0.4	1.0	1.0	3.5	2001	(CTCI 2 - 22 - 27 - 28)
1.4	0.9	1.0	2.1	2.9	0.4	1.0	0.9	2.8	2002	
2.9	2.1	1.5	6.3	8.4	1.7	1.0	1.6	11.2	1999	Minerais et métaux
2.5	1.8	1.4	5.8	4.2	1.3	1.1	1.5	16.8	2000	(CTCI 27 + 28 + 68)
2.5	1.8	1.3	5.7	5.1	1.1	1.0	1.3	12.3	2001	
2.3	1.7	1.2	5.3	5.0	1.1	0.9	1.0	10.1	2002	
13.7	76.6	2.6	12.6	47.2	65.9	3.2	1.5	0.1	1999	Combustibles (CTCI 3)
18.0	81.4	3.7	16.7	57.5	74.4	4.1	2.3	0.2	2000	
16.8	79.8	3.3	14.3	52.4	71.8	3.9	2.0	0.1	2001	
16.1	79.3	3.3	14.7	49.8	68.9	3.8	1.6	4.8	2002	
72.6	16.6	87.9	61.8	28.1	27.4	88.5	89.8	56.4	1999	Articles manufacturés
70.7	14.1	88.1	61.5	25.9	20.8	88.7	89.8	51.3	2000	(CTCI 5 à 8 moins 68)
71.3	15.5	88.0	63.2	27.8	23.6	88.5	90.3	46.6	2001	
71.4	15.5	87.3	63.1	29.7	26.1	87.4	91.8	47.5	2002	

Sources: Calculs du secrétariat de la CNUCED basés sur des données de ONU/DAES/Division de statistique.

Pour les notes, se reporter à la fin du tableau 3.2.2J.

Commodity groups	Year / Année	World [1] / Monde [1]	Developed economies / Economies développées — Total	Europe — Total	Europe — EU / UE	USA / Etats-Unis	Canada	Japan / Japon	Australia, New Zealand / Australie Nouvelle-Zélande	South-East Europe and CIS / Europe du Sud-Est et CEI
						Millions of dollars				
All products	1999	93619	53490	48540	47479	3414	239	860	121	27632
	2000	110279	59828	54241	52865	3923	262	911	101	36387
	2001	126808	75070	68555	66892	4577	297	1021	138	34612
	2002	138073	84959	78298	76359	4409	271	1217	171	33547
						Share by origin (percentage)				
All products	1999	100.0	57.1	51.8	50.7	3.6	0.3	0.9	0.1	29.5
	2000	100.0	54.3	49.2	47.9	3.6	0.2	0.8	0.1	33.0
	2001	100.0	59.2	54.1	52.8	3.6	0.2	0.8	0.1	27.3
	2002	100.0	61.5	56.7	55.3	3.2	0.2	0.9	0.1	24.3
All food items	1999	100.0	53.3	47.0	45.9	5.2	0.2	0.1	0.5	21.2
(SITC 0 + 1 + 22 + 4)	2000	100.0	52.7	44.2	42.6	7.6	0.2	0.1	0.3	24.0
	2001	100.0	51.3	42.9	41.0	7.2	0.4	0.1	0.3	21.6
	2002	100.0	50.6	44.7	42.4	4.8	0.4	0.1	0.5	21.2
Agricultural raw materials	1999	100.0	39.6	37.1	36.8	1.1	0.4	0.5	0.3	54.2
(SITC 2 - 22 - 27 - 28)	2000	100.0	41.5	38.5	38.0	1.4	0.3	0.3	0.6	52.0
	2001	100.0	43.4	40.8	40.5	1.1	0.1	0.4	0.8	49.1
	2002	100.0	52.7	50.2	49.9	0.9	0.2	0.4	0.7	39.8
Ores and metals	1999	100.0	29.5	28.4	28.1	0.4	0.2	0.1	0.3	51.1
(SITC 27 + 28 + 68)	2000	100.0	26.6	24.6	23.8	0.6	0.1	0.6	0.6	57.0
	2001	100.0	29.7	27.7	27.4	0.7	0.2	0.3	0.6	53.9
	2002	100.0	30.9	29.5	29.1	0.4	0.0	0.8	0.1	51.7
Fuels (SITC 3)	1999	100.0	12.3	11.3	11.2	0.5	0.1	0.2	0.3	84.2
	2000	100.0	9.7	9.0	8.7	0.6	0.1	0.1	0.0	86.2
	2001	100.0	8.2	7.6	7.6	0.4	0.0	0.1	0.1	86.7
	2002	100.0	8.1	7.6	7.6	0.3	0.0	0.0	0.2	88.7
Manufactured goods	1999	100.0	69.2	63.2	61.8	3.9	0.3	1.3	0.0	17.8
(SITC 5 to 8 less 68)	2000	100.0	67.9	62.5	61.0	3.5	0.3	1.2	0.0	18.8
	2001	100.0	70.0	64.7	63.3	3.4	0.2	1.1	0.0	17.6
	2002	100.0	72.1	66.8	65.3	3.3	0.2	1.2	0.1	14.6
						Share by major commodity groups (percentage)				
All food items	1999	15.4	14.4	14.0	14.0	22.1	14.8	1.6	57.1	11.1
(SITC 0 + 1 + 22 + 4)	2000	12.8	12.4	11.5	11.4	27.2	13.2	1.0	47.5	9.3
	2001	13.5	11.7	10.8	10.5	26.9	24.4	1.7	41.1	10.7
	2002	13.0	10.7	10.2	10.0	19.6	23.5	1.1	47.2	11.3
Agricultural raw materials	1999	1.6	1.1	1.1	1.2	0.5	2.3	0.9	4.1	2.9
(SITC 2 - 22 - 27 - 28)	2000	1.6	1.3	1.3	1.3	0.7	2.2	0.6	10.3	2.6
	2001	1.6	1.1	1.2	1.2	0.5	0.6	0.7	11.9	2.8
	2002	1.4	1.2	1.3	1.3	0.4	1.4	0.6	8.6	2.4
Ores and metals	1999	2.6	1.4	1.4	1.4	0.3	2.2	0.2	6.9	4.5
(SITC 27 + 28 + 68)	2000	3.1	1.5	1.6	1.6	0.6	1.6	2.1	20.9	5.4
	2001	2.8	1.4	1.4	1.4	0.5	2.7	1.2	16.1	5.5
	2002	2.5	1.3	1.3	1.3	0.3	0.1	2.3	1.4	5.3
Fuels (SITC 3)	1999	9.8	2.1	2.1	2.2	1.4	3.1	1.6	21.9	27.9
	2000	11.4	2.0	2.1	2.1	1.8	4.5	0.8	0.1	29.7
	2001	11.1	1.5	1.6	1.6	1.1	1.3	0.8	11.3	35.3
	2002	10.1	1.3	1.4	1.4	0.9	0.3	0.3	12.9	36.8
Manufactured goods	1999	64.7	78.4	78.9	78.9	69.4	71.5	94.3	8.9	39.0
(SITC 5 to 8 less 68)	2000	65.1	81.5	82.7	82.8	63.6	72.9	93.0	20.5	37.2
	2001	69.6	82.3	83.4	83.5	66.0	67.9	94.3	19.0	45.0
	2002	71.9	84.2	84.7	84.9	74.0	71.4	94.5	29.1	43.2

Sources: UNCTAD secretariat computations based on UN/DESA/Statistics Division's data.

For notes, see end of table 3.2.2J.

	Developing economies / Economies en développement								Origine	
Total	of which / dont		America Amérique	Africa Afrique	West Asia Asie occidentale	Other Asia / Autres économies d'Asie		Oceania Océanie	Year Année	
	Major petroleum exporters Principaux exportateurs de pétrole	Major exporters of manufactures Principaux exportateurs d'articles manufacturés				Total	China			Groupes de produits
Millions de dollars										
12496	1496	9240	1818	543	3627	6505	2525	3	1999	**Total tous produits**
14063	1820	10459	1573	554	4014	7912	3619	10	2000	
17127	2229	12733	2694	551	4853	9023	4074	5	2001	
19568	1902	15425	2721	587	5221	11034	5799	4	2002	
Parts par origines (en pourcentage)										
13.3	1.6	9.9	1.9	0.6	3.9	6.9	2.7	0.0	1999	**Total tous produits**
12.8	1.7	9.5	1.4	0.5	3.6	7.2	3.3	0.0	2000	
13.5	1.8	10.0	2.1	0.4	3.8	7.1	3.2	0.0	2001	
14.2	1.4	11.2	2.0	0.4	3.8	8.0	4.2	0.0	2002	
25.5	2.4	15.2	10.7	1.9	5.6	7.3	1.6	0.0	1999	Produits alimentaires
23.3	2.3	12.6	9.1	1.6	5.4	7.3	1.7	0.0	2000	(CTCI 0 + 1 + 22 + 4)
27.2	1.6	16.5	13.9	1.5	4.4	7.3	1.9	0.0	2001	
28.2	1.9	17.5	13.3	1.9	4.1	8.8	3.1	0.0	2002	
6.2	0.9	2.7	1.2	0.8	1.1	3.1	0.7	0.0	1999	Matières premières
6.5	1.0	2.5	1.0	0.6	1.4	3.6	0.4	0.0	2000	d'origine agricole
7.5	1.2	2.6	1.6	0.8	1.5	3.5	0.4	0.0	2001	(CTCI 2 - 22 - 27 - 28)
7.5	0.9	2.4	1.9	0.9	1.0	3.7	0.4	0.0	2002	
19.4	2.0	7.5	7.7	3.6	4.1	4.0	1.2	0.1	1999	Minerais et métaux
16.4	3.0	6.6	6.2	2.5	3.7	3.9	1.2	0.1	2000	(CTCI 27 + 28 + 68)
16.3	5.5	5.4	4.8	2.0	5.3	4.2	1.2	0.1	2001	
17.4	2.8	9.5	5.2	1.7	3.8	6.6	1.4	0.0	2002	
3.5	1.5	1.7	0.1	0.9	1.1	1.5	0.9	0.0	1999	Combustibles (CTCI 3)
4.1	2.6	1.3	0.1	1.0	1.9	1.1	0.6	0.0	2000	
5.1	3.8	1.1	0.3	0.6	3.2	0.9	0.6	0.0	2001	
3.2	2.0	0.8	0.1	0.4	2.0	0.7	0.4	0.0	2002	
13.0	1.6	11.0	0.1	0.1	4.3	8.5	3.6	0.0	1999	Articles manufacturés
13.3	1.4	11.4	0.1	0.1	3.9	9.1	4.5	0.0	2000	(CTCI 5 à 8 moins 68)
12.4	1.4	10.7	0.1	0.1	3.9	8.4	4.1	0.0	2001	
13.3	1.2	11.8	0.1	0.1	4.1	9.1	5.2	0.0	2002	
Parts par principaux groupes de produits (en pourcentage)										
29.5	22.9	23.8	85.0	49.9	22.2	16.3	9.3	1.2	1999	Produits alimentaires
23.4	17.8	17.0	81.4	39.6	19.0	13.0	6.6	6.3	2000	(CTCI 0 + 1 + 22 + 4)
27.3	12.5	22.3	88.7	47.9	15.7	13.9	8.0	15.0	2001	
25.8	17.5	20.3	87.9	58.7	14.1	14.3	9.7	32.8	2002	
0.7	0.9	0.4	1.0	2.2	0.5	0.7	0.4	7.0	1999	Matières premières
0.8	1.0	0.4	1.1	1.9	0.6	0.8	0.2	1.0	2000	d'origine agricole
0.9	1.1	0.4	1.2	2.9	0.6	0.8	0.2	1.4	2001	(CTCI 2 - 22 - 27 - 28)
0.8	0.9	0.3	1.4	3.0	0.4	0.7	0.2	0.3	2002	
3.8	3.3	2.0	10.3	16.0	2.7	1.5	1.1	61.8	1999	Minerais et métaux
4.0	5.6	2.2	13.6	15.4	3.2	1.7	1.1	27.2	2000	(CTCI 27 + 28 + 68)
3.4	8.6	1.5	6.3	12.5	3.8	1.6	1.0	55.9	2001	
3.1	5.1	2.1	6.7	10.3	2.5	2.1	0.8	39.1	2002	
2.6	9.4	1.6	0.4	14.8	2.8	2.1	3.2	0.3	1999	Combustibles (CTCI 3)
3.6	17.9	1.5	0.5	23.7	6.0	1.7	2.2	0.0	2000	
4.2	23.8	1.2	1.5	16.4	9.3	1.4	2.2	0.0	2001	
2.3	14.8	0.7	0.4	9.5	5.3	0.9	1.0	1.3	2002	
63.1	62.9	72.0	3.2	15.9	71.6	79.1	85.7	29.5	1999	Articles manufacturés
67.7	56.3	78.6	3.3	19.3	70.4	82.5	89.8	65.4	2000	(CTCI 5 à 8 moins 68)
63.9	53.6	74.2	2.2	20.3	70.0	81.8	88.5	27.0	2001	
67.7	61.2	76.0	3.6	18.3	77.1	81.6	88.3	25.6	2002	

Sources: Calculs du secrétariat de la CNUCED basés sur des données de ONU/DAES/Division de statistique.

Pour les notes, se reporter à la fin du tableau 3.2.2J.

Origin / Commodity groups	Year Année	World [1] Monde [1]	Developed economies Economies développées Total	Europe Total	Europe EU UE	USA Etats-Unis	Canada	Japan Japon	Australia, New Zealand Australie Nouvelle-Zélande	South-East Europe and CIS Europe du Sud-Est et CEI
Millions of dollars										
All products	1999	1452431	803212	290405	274852	281082	12397	188757	25800	24345
	2000	1745042	928673	313361	296710	332377	14205	231579	30421	31907
	2001	1655204	875024	321123	303009	309728	13810	193870	30378	30334
	2002	1769792	899015	339620	319213	297907	13264	210916	31272	34310
Share by origin (percentage)										
All products	1999	100.0	55.3	20.0	18.9	19.4	0.9	13.0	1.8	1.7
	2000	100.0	53.2	18.0	17.0	19.0	0.8	13.3	1.7	1.8
	2001	100.0	52.9	19.4	18.3	18.7	0.8	11.7	1.8	1.8
	2002	100.0	50.8	19.2	18.0	16.8	0.7	11.9	1.8	1.9
All food items	1999	100.0	50.0	19.0	18.4	20.6	3.2	1.4	5.8	0.8
(SITC 0 + 1 + 22 + 4)	2000	100.0	50.0	18.3	17.6	21.0	3.3	1.3	6.1	0.8
	2001	100.0	48.9	16.6	16.0	20.7	3.3	2.0	6.2	1.0
	2002	100.0	46.2	16.4	15.7	19.8	2.4	1.2	6.3	1.4
Agricultural raw materials	1999	100.0	50.6	12.6	12.4	19.7	5.1	4.8	8.2	5.7
(SITC 2 - 22 - 27 - 28)	2000	100.0	52.4	11.9	11.8	22.2	5.3	4.6	8.1	5.1
	2001	100.0	54.0	12.0	11.8	23.8	4.4	4.7	8.9	5.5
	2002	100.0	53.4	12.5	12.3	22.9	4.9	4.7	8.3	6.4
Ores and metals	1999	100.0	45.6	12.3	11.0	10.8	1.8	10.5	10.1	3.7
(SITC 27 + 28 + 68)	2000	100.0	45.6	12.8	11.3	11.1	2.0	9.8	9.8	5.0
	2001	100.0	45.7	13.0	11.2	10.8	1.9	9.4	10.4	4.6
	2002	100.0	44.7	13.4	11.2	9.7	2.1	9.3	9.9	4.7
Fuels (SITC 3)	1999	100.0	13.4	4.1	3.5	4.8	0.5	0.8	3.3	5.2
	2000	100.0	12.5	3.6	3.3	4.7	0.2	0.6	3.4	6.0
	2001	100.0	12.5	3.3	2.6	4.5	0.3	0.8	3.7	6.4
	2002	100.0	12.7	3.7	2.9	4.5	0.3	0.7	3.5	6.3
Manufactured goods	1999	100.0	59.4	21.9	20.7	20.6	0.5	15.4	0.6	1.2
(SITC 5 to 8 less 68)	2000	100.0	58.0	20.2	19.1	20.4	0.5	15.9	0.5	1.1
	2001	100.0	57.1	21.6	20.4	20.1	0.5	13.9	0.6	1.2
	2002	100.0	55.0	21.6	20.4	17.8	0.5	14.2	0.6	1.3
Share by major commodity groups (percentage)										
All food items	1999	7.4	6.7	7.1	7.2	7.9	27.5	0.8	24.3	3.4
(SITC 0 + 1 + 22 + 4)	2000	6.5	6.1	6.6	6.7	7.2	26.3	0.6	22.6	2.7
	2001	7.1	6.6	6.1	6.2	7.9	27.9	1.2	24.2	4.0
	2002	7.0	6.3	5.9	6.1	8.2	22.1	0.7	24.7	5.0
Agricultural raw materials	1999	2.1	1.9	1.3	1.4	2.1	12.6	0.8	9.7	7.1
(SITC 2 - 22 - 27 - 28)	2000	2.1	2.0	1.4	1.4	2.4	13.4	0.7	9.6	5.8
	2001	2.1	2.1	1.3	1.3	2.6	10.9	0.8	10.0	6.1
	2002	2.0	2.1	1.3	1.4	2.8	13.3	0.8	9.6	6.7
Ores and metals	1999	2.7	2.2	1.7	1.6	1.5	5.6	2.2	15.4	5.9
(SITC 27 + 28 + 68)	2000	2.8	2.4	2.0	1.9	1.6	6.7	2.1	15.6	7.7
	2001	2.8	2.4	1.9	1.7	1.6	6.5	2.3	16.0	7.1
	2002	2.8	2.5	2.0	1.8	1.6	8.2	2.2	16.0	6.9
Fuels (SITC 3)	1999	7.3	1.8	1.5	1.3	1.8	3.8	0.4	13.3	22.3
	2000	9.3	2.2	1.9	1.8	2.3	2.8	0.4	18.2	30.7
	2001	8.5	2.0	1.4	1.2	2.1	2.9	0.6	17.0	29.8
	2002	8.4	2.1	1.6	1.4	2.2	3.1	0.5	16.7	27.5
Manufactured goods	1999	78.1	83.8	85.5	85.5	82.9	47.4	92.5	26.0	54.3
(SITC 5 to 8 less 68)	2000	77.3	84.3	86.8	86.9	83.0	49.0	92.6	23.4	47.8
	2001	76.8	83.0	85.6	85.7	82.4	49.7	90.9	23.5	51.3
	2002	76.9	83.3	86.8	87.0	81.1	51.3	91.3	24.0	52.9

Sources: UNCTAD secretariat computations based on UN/DESA/Statistics Division's data.

For notes, see end of table 3.2.2J.

	of which dont					Other Asia / Autres économies d'Asie				
Total	Major petroleum exporters / Principaux exportateurs de pétole	Major exporters of manufactures / Principaux exportateurs d'articles manufacturés	America Amérique	Africa Afrique	West Asia Asie occi-dentale	Total	China	Oceania Océanie	Year Année	Groupes de produits

Developing economies / Economies en développement

Millions de dollars

Total	Major petroleum exporters	Major exporters of manufactures	America	Africa	West Asia	Other Asia Total	China	Oceania	Year	Groupes de produits
624873	94515	463738	65863	30550	58175	469401	78918	883	1999	**Total tous produits**
784462	132653	572800	80603	39012	80630	583030	101991	1187	2000	
749845	118912	548263	83808	33440	78202	553165	109222	1230	2001	
836467	125797	627291	81923	34791	82252	636236	137220	1266	2002	

Parts par origines (en pourcentage)

Total	Major petroleum exporters	Major exporters of manufactures	America	Africa	West Asia	Other Asia Total	China	Oceania	Year	Groupes de produits
43.0	**6.5**	**31.9**	**4.5**	**2.1**	**4.0**	**32.3**	**5.4**	**0.1**	1999	**Total tous produits**
45.0	**7.6**	**32.8**	**4.6**	**2.2**	**4.6**	**33.4**	**5.8**	**0.1**	2000	
45.3	**7.2**	**33.1**	**5.1**	**2.0**	**4.7**	**33.4**	**6.6**	**0.1**	2001	
47.3	**7.1**	**35.4**	**4.6**	**2.0**	**4.6**	**35.9**	**7.8**	**0.1**	2002	
49.2	5.1	25.6	15.8	3.9	3.3	26.1	4.6	0.1	1999	Produits alimentaires
49.2	5.2	24.9	15.7	4.2	3.4	25.7	5.1	0.1	2000	(CTCI 0 + 1 + 22 + 4)
50.1	5.6	25.3	17.2	3.8	4.2	24.8	4.8	0.1	2001	
52.4	6.5	27.2	16.5	3.9	4.2	27.7	5.8	0.1	2002	
43.7	4.4	26.5	6.2	6.3	1.1	29.7	3.1	0.2	1999	Matières premières
42.5	4.7	25.5	6.1	5.6	1.0	29.6	3.0	0.3	2000	d'origine agricole
40.6	5.1	23.4	7.1	5.2	1.3	26.8	2.4	0.3	2001	(CTCI 2 - 22 - 27 - 28)
40.2	5.4	23.2	6.3	5.3	1.1	27.3	2.8	0.2	2002	
50.7	6.7	29.1	13.4	4.2	4.8	27.7	5.0	0.6	1999	Minerais et métaux
49.4	6.8	27.9	14.0	3.9	4.1	26.9	5.0	0.5	2000	(CTCI 27 + 28 + 68)
49.7	7.8	27.8	13.5	3.8	5.1	26.9	5.5	0.4	2001	
50.6	7.2	29.0	13.3	4.0	4.9	28.1	6.3	0.3	2002	
81.4	56.2	18.5	9.4	12.7	35.4	24.0	2.7	0.0	1999	Combustibles (CTCI 3)
81.4	55.3	18.6	10.2	12.4	35.2	23.6	2.8	0.0	2000	
81.1	52.6	19.2	11.3	11.0	34.8	24.0	3.7	0.0	2001	
80.9	52.1	20.6	10.7	9.6	34.4	26.1	3.7	0.0	2002	
39.5	2.2	34.7	2.8	0.8	1.3	34.5	6.0	0.0	1999	Articles manufacturés
40.9	2.3	36.1	2.7	0.7	1.3	36.1	6.5	0.0	2000	(CTCI 5 à 8 moins 68)
41.7	2.5	36.4	3.0	0.7	1.6	36.2	7.4	0.1	2001	
43.6	2.5	38.5	2.7	0.8	1.6	38.5	8.8	0.1	2002	

Parts par principaux groupes de produits (en pourcentage)

Total	Major petroleum exporters	Major exporters of manufactures	America	Africa	West Asia	Other Asia Total	China	Oceania	Year	Groupes de produits
8.5	5.8	6.0	25.9	13.9	6.1	6.0	6.3	17.8	1999	Produits alimentaires
7.1	4.4	4.9	22.1	12.3	4.8	5.0	5.7	12.6	2000	(CTCI 0 + 1 + 22 + 4)
7.9	5.5	5.5	24.3	13.4	6.3	5.3	5.2	12.2	2001	
7.7	6.4	5.4	24.9	13.8	6.3	5.4	5.2	8.3	2002	
2.1	1.4	1.7	2.9	6.3	0.6	1.9	1.2	8.6	1999	Matières premières
2.0	1.3	1.6	2.7	5.2	0.4	1.8	1.1	8.5	2000	d'origine agricole
1.8	1.4	1.5	2.9	5.2	0.6	1.6	0.8	7.2	2001	(CTCI 2 - 22 - 27 - 28)
1.7	1.6	1.3	2.8	5.5	0.5	1.6	0.7	6.5	2002	
3.2	2.8	2.5	8.0	5.4	3.3	2.3	2.5	26.1	1999	Minerais et métaux
3.1	2.5	2.4	8.4	4.8	2.5	2.2	2.4	21.9	2000	(CTCI 27 + 28 + 68)
3.1	3.0	2.4	7.5	5.3	3.1	2.3	2.4	14.4	2001	
3.0	2.9	2.3	8.2	5.8	3.0	2.2	2.3	11.6	2002	
13.7	62.6	4.2	15.0	43.9	64.1	5.4	3.6	0.3	1999	Combustibles (CTCI 3)
16.9	67.7	5.3	20.6	51.8	70.9	6.6	4.5	0.4	2000	
15.2	62.4	4.9	18.9	46.5	62.7	6.1	4.8	0.4	2001	
14.4	61.6	4.9	19.5	41.1	62.3	6.1	4.0	0.7	2002	
71.6	26.2	84.8	48.1	29.7	25.3	83.4	86.2	45.5	1999	Articles manufacturés
70.3	23.7	85.1	46.0	25.1	20.9	83.5	86.0	56.5	2000	(CTCI 5 à 8 moins 68)
70.7	26.7	84.5	46.2	28.4	25.9	83.3	86.4	65.7	2001	
71.0	26.8	83.7	44.5	32.5	26.5	82.3	87.4	67.1	2002	

Sources: Calculs du secrétariat de la CNUCED basés sur des données de
ONU/DAES/Division de statistique.

Pour les notes, se reporter à la fin du tableau 3.2.2J.

3.2.2E   Import structure by origin and by major commodity groups
Major petroleum exporters

Commodity groups	Year / Année	World [1] / Monde [1]	Developed economies / Economies développées							South-East Europe and CIS / Europe du Sud-Est et CEI
			Total	Europe		USA / Etats-Unis	Canada	Japan / Japon	Australia, New Zealand / Australie Nouvelle-Zélande	
				Total	EU / UE					
Millions of dollars										
All products	1999	163033	97476	55140	52870	22789	2027	14447	3007	3002
	2000	184868	102517	56930	54442	22597	2339	17076	3482	3544
	2001	204126	114304	66764	63930	23704	2019	17487	4210	5006
	2002	216694	120569	73468	70171	22565	1789	18330	4324	5200
Share by origin (percentage)										
All products	1999	100.0	59.8	33.8	32.4	14.0	1.2	8.9	1.8	1.8
	2000	100.0	55.5	30.8	29.4	12.2	1.3	9.2	1.9	1.9
	2001	100.0	56.0	32.7	31.3	11.6	1.0	8.6	2.1	2.5
	2002	100.0	55.6	33.9	32.4	10.4	0.8	8.5	2.0	2.4
All food items (SITC 0 + 1 + 22 + 4)	1999	100.0	50.8	29.9	29.4	11.8	4.3	0.4	4.4	0.6
	2000	100.0	50.4	28.6	28.1	12.0	4.5	0.2	5.0	0.9
	2001	100.0	46.8	26.2	25.7	11.5	3.2	0.2	5.7	1.6
	2002	100.0	43.7	24.7	24.1	10.4	2.2	0.2	6.2	2.1
Agricultural raw materials (SITC 2 - 22 - 27 - 28)	1999	100.0	57.9	17.4	17.2	15.7	6.6	5.5	12.7	7.5
	2000	100.0	58.4	16.0	15.8	18.2	8.2	5.2	10.7	5.9
	2001	100.0	58.6	18.8	18.6	19.1	4.0	5.3	11.5	5.8
	2002	100.0	58.1	20.8	20.6	18.6	4.6	4.7	9.4	6.7
Ores and metals (SITC 27 + 28 + 68)	1999	100.0	43.7	23.1	22.6	7.3	1.2	5.4	6.8	2.6
	2000	100.0	38.7	21.2	20.8	5.9	1.1	4.4	6.0	2.1
	2001	100.0	39.6	21.9	21.4	5.8	2.2	4.3	5.3	2.1
	2002	100.0	40.2	23.1	22.8	4.8	1.5	4.7	6.1	2.5
Fuels (SITC 3)	1999	100.0	13.1	8.5	8.4	2.8	0.0	0.4	1.4	2.1
	2000	100.0	12.7	8.9	8.9	3.0	0.0	0.3	0.5	2.6
	2001	100.0	12.9	8.6	8.5	3.1	0.0	0.3	0.9	4.6
	2002	100.0	12.7	8.5	8.4	2.9	0.0	0.4	0.9	5.0
Manufactured goods (SITC 5 to 8 less 68)	1999	100.0	65.0	37.0	35.2	15.0	0.6	11.3	1.0	1.5
	2000	100.0	60.7	34.1	32.5	12.7	0.6	12.1	1.1	1.7
	2001	100.0	60.6	35.7	34.0	12.1	0.6	10.9	1.1	2.4
	2002	100.0	60.6	37.8	35.9	10.5	0.5	10.7	1.1	2.2
Share by major commodity groups (percentage)										
All food items (SITC 0 + 1 + 22 + 4)	1999	14.3	12.1	12.6	12.9	12.0	49.3	0.7	34.0	4.7
	2000	13.4	12.2	12.5	12.8	13.2	48.1	0.3	35.6	6.1
	2001	13.1	11.0	10.5	10.7	13.0	42.2	0.3	36.5	8.4
	2002	12.9	10.1	9.4	9.6	12.9	35.0	0.3	39.9	11.5
Agricultural raw materials (SITC 2 - 22 - 27 - 28)	1999	1.9	1.8	1.0	1.0	2.1	9.9	1.2	13.0	7.7
	2000	1.9	2.0	1.0	1.0	2.9	12.4	1.1	10.9	5.9
	2001	1.5	1.6	0.9	0.9	2.5	6.2	0.9	8.6	3.7
	2002	1.5	1.6	0.9	1.0	2.7	8.5	0.8	7.1	4.2
Ores and metals (SITC 27 + 28 + 68)	1999	1.9	1.4	1.3	1.3	1.0	1.7	1.1	6.8	2.6
	2000	1.9	1.4	1.3	1.4	0.9	1.6	0.9	6.2	2.1
	2001	1.8	1.3	1.2	1.3	0.9	4.2	0.9	4.8	1.6
	2002	1.9	1.4	1.3	1.4	0.9	3.5	1.1	5.9	2.0
Fuels (SITC 3)	1999	5.2	1.1	1.3	1.4	1.1	0.0	0.2	4.0	6.0
	2000	7.2	1.6	2.1	2.2	1.8	0.1	0.2	2.1	9.7
	2001	5.9	1.4	1.5	1.6	1.6	0.2	0.2	2.7	11.2
	2002	5.4	1.2	1.4	1.4	1.5	0.1	0.3	2.5	11.2
Manufactured goods (SITC 5 to 8 less 68)	1999	74.2	80.6	81.1	80.6	79.7	37.2	94.9	39.6	60.5
	2000	73.8	80.8	81.8	81.4	76.9	36.7	96.4	42.3	66.8
	2001	75.0	81.1	81.9	81.5	78.1	44.9	95.5	40.7	72.9
	2002	75.9	82.6	84.5	84.1	76.1	50.1	95.7	41.0	68.9

Sources: UNCTAD secretariat computations based on UN/DESA/Statistics Division's data.

For notes, see end of table 3.2.2J.

3.2.2E Structure des importations par origine et par principaux groupes de produits
Principaux pays exportateurs de pétrole

						Developing economies / Economies en développement				Origine
	of which / dont						Other Asia / Autres économies d'Asie			
Total	Major petroleum exporters / Principaux exportateurs de pétole	Major exporters of manufactures / Principaux exportateurs d'articles manufacturés	America / Amérique	Africa / Afrique	West Asia / Asie occidentale	Total	China	Oceania / Océanie	Year / Année	Groupes de produits

Millions de dollars

Total	Major petroleum exp.	Major exp. manuf.	America	Africa	West Asia	Other Asia Total	China	Oceania	Year	Groupes de produits
62555	15162	38562	8883	3270	13783	36615	6389	5	1999	Total tous produits
78807	20227	47613	11289	4703	16995	45800	9294	20	2000	
84815	20731	51653	13233	4239	19100	48223	10440	20	2001	
90925	21060	57114	11861	5204	19969	53881	13510	11	2002	

Parts par origines (en pourcentage)

Total	Major petroleum exp.	Major exp. manuf.	America	Africa	West Asia	Other Asia Total	China	Oceania	Year	Groupes de produits
38.4	9.3	23.7	5.4	2.0	8.5	22.5	3.9	0.0	1999	Total tous produits
42.6	10.9	25.8	6.1	2.5	9.2	24.8	5.0	0.0	2000	
41.6	10.2	25.3	6.5	2.1	9.4	23.6	5.1	0.0	2001	
42.0	9.7	26.4	5.5	2.4	9.2	24.9	6.2	0.0	2002	
48.6	8.1	23.7	12.7	5.1	10.2	20.6	2.4	0.0	1999	Produits alimentaires
48.8	9.6	21.1	11.9	6.2	11.0	19.7	2.4	0.0	2000	(CTCI 0 + 1 + 22 + 4)
51.6	11.4	22.4	14.9	4.8	13.3	18.6	2.0	0.0	2001	
54.2	11.8	24.2	14.4	5.5	13.8	20.5	3.0	0.0	2002	
34.5	3.1	19.6	8.2	6.7	3.4	16.3	2.5	0.0	1999	Matières premières
35.6	3.0	20.4	7.8	5.9	3.1	18.8	3.0	0.0	2000	d'origine agricole
35.6	3.5	19.2	8.1	6.3	4.0	17.2	1.4	0.0	2001	(CTCI 2 - 22 - 27 - 28)
35.1	4.0	18.7	7.4	6.2	3.2	18.3	2.1	0.0	2002	
53.7	16.9	25.0	15.6	4.8	19.1	14.2	2.4	_	1999	Minerais et métaux
59.2	18.0	27.0	19.4	4.2	19.4	16.3	2.4	0.0	2000	(CTCI 27 + 28 + 68)
58.3	20.5	27.3	15.0	3.6	22.3	17.2	3.1	0.2	2001	
57.3	19.8	26.3	13.6	4.1	21.3	18.3	3.5	0.0	2002	
84.8	65.6	14.8	31.1	3.5	40.9	9.4	1.2	_	1999	Combustibles (CTCI 3)
84.7	59.4	19.2	29.5	9.1	33.1	12.9	2.7	_	2000	
82.5	52.5	23.7	31.6	7.9	27.8	15.2	3.8	_	2001	
82.3	47.3	30.9	28.3	8.1	23.7	22.1	3.3	_	2002	
33.5	5.6	24.8	2.1	1.2	5.8	24.5	4.6	0.0	1999	Articles manufacturés
37.5	6.7	27.4	2.5	1.2	6.5	27.3	5.8	0.0	2000	(CTCI 5 à 8 moins 68)
37.1	6.7	26.5	3.0	1.1	7.1	25.9	6.0	0.0	2001	
37.2	6.6	26.8	2.2	1.4	7.3	26.3	7.3	0.0	2002	

Parts par principaux groupes de produits (en pourcentage)

Total	Major petroleum exp.	Major exp. manuf.	America	Africa	West Asia	Other Asia Total	China	Oceania	Year	Groupes de produits
18.1	12.4	14.3	33.3	36.5	17.1	13.1	8.8	38.7	1999	Produits alimentaires
15.3	11.7	11.0	26.0	32.7	16.0	10.7	6.5	42.4	2000	(CTCI 0 + 1 + 22 + 4)
16.3	14.7	11.6	30.2	30.1	18.6	10.3	5.2	29.5	2001	
16.7	15.6	11.8	33.9	29.5	19.4	10.6	6.2	42.2	2002	
1.7	0.6	1.6	2.8	6.3	0.8	1.4	1.2	1.2	1999	Matières premières
1.6	0.5	1.5	2.4	4.5	0.6	1.5	1.2	1.0	2000	d'origine agricole
1.3	0.5	1.2	1.9	4.7	0.7	1.1	0.4	2.3	2001	(CTCI 2 - 22 - 27 - 28)
1.3	0.6	1.1	2.0	3.9	0.5	1.1	0.5	2.8	2002	
2.6	3.4	2.0	5.3	4.5	4.2	1.2	1.1	_	1999	Minerais et métaux
2.7	3.2	2.0	6.2	3.2	4.1	1.3	0.9	3.2	2000	(CTCI 27 + 28 + 68)
2.6	3.7	2.0	4.3	3.2	4.4	1.3	1.1	29.8	2001	
2.6	4.0	1.9	4.8	3.3	4.5	1.4	1.1	0.1	2002	
11.6	37.0	3.3	29.9	9.2	25.4	2.2	1.6	_	1999	Combustibles (CTCI 3)
14.3	39.0	5.4	34.7	25.8	25.9	3.8	3.9	_	2000	
11.7	30.5	5.5	28.7	22.3	17.5	3.8	4.4	_	2001	
10.6	26.3	6.3	28.0	18.3	13.9	4.8	2.9	_	2002	
64.9	44.8	77.8	28.6	43.4	51.1	80.8	86.6	58.4	1999	Articles manufacturés
65.0	45.0	78.6	30.4	33.5	52.6	81.3	85.6	53.0	2000	(CTCI 5 à 8 moins 68)
66.8	49.1	78.4	34.6	39.0	57.1	82.0	88.2	38.1	2001	
67.3	51.8	77.2	31.2	43.8	59.9	80.3	88.7	53.9	2002	

Sources: Calculs du secrétariat de la CNUCED basés sur des données de ONU/DAES/Division de statistique.

Pour les notes, se reporter à la fin du tableau 3.2.2J.

Origin / Commodity groups	Year / Année	World [1] / Monde [1]	Developed economies / Economies développées							South-East Europe and CIS / Europe du Sud-Est et CEI
			Total	Europe		USA / Etats-Unis	Canada	Japan / Japon	Australia, New Zealand / Australie Nouvelle-Zélande	
				Total	EU / UE					
Millions of dollars										
All products	1999	1013977	550821	153410	143368	212565	7785	154226	18982	13824
	2000	1257823	668436	174149	163034	261867	9283	194227	23128	18219
	2001	1154466	606401	172386	160872	238690	9276	158823	22159	16156
	2002	1253573	627688	183933	170514	231494	9141	175189	22892	19645
Share by origin (percentage)										
All products	1999	100.0	54.3	15.1	14.1	21.0	0.8	15.2	1.9	1.4
	2000	100.0	53.1	13.8	13.0	20.8	0.7	15.4	1.8	1.4
	2001	100.0	52.5	14.9	13.9	20.7	0.8	13.8	1.9	1.4
	2002	100.0	50.1	14.7	13.6	18.5	0.7	14.0	1.8	1.6
All food items	1999	100.0	50.5	12.1	11.4	25.5	2.9	2.5	7.4	0.8
(SITC 0 + 1 + 22 + 4)	2000	100.0	51.6	11.5	10.8	27.2	3.0	2.4	7.5	0.7
	2001	100.0	51.4	10.5	9.8	27.7	3.4	2.4	7.4	0.7
	2002	100.0	48.8	10.5	9.8	26.0	2.4	2.3	7.5	0.7
Agricultural raw materials	1999	100.0	50.1	10.0	9.8	20.4	5.6	5.3	8.6	5.1
(SITC 2 - 22 - 27 - 28)	2000	100.0	52.4	9.9	9.7	23.0	5.6	5.0	8.7	4.9
	2001	100.0	54.2	9.6	9.4	24.7	5.1	5.1	9.6	5.5
	2002	100.0	53.8	9.9	9.8	23.8	5.5	5.2	9.2	6.6
Ores and metals	1999	100.0	46.5	10.1	8.7	11.3	1.7	12.0	11.2	3.8
(SITC 27 + 28 + 68)	2000	100.0	47.3	11.1	9.4	11.8	2.1	11.2	10.9	5.3
	2001	100.0	47.7	11.1	9.0	11.9	1.9	10.8	11.8	5.0
	2002	100.0	46.3	11.7	9.1	10.7	2.3	10.5	10.9	4.9
Fuels (SITC 3)	1999	100.0	13.5	2.7	1.9	5.2	0.6	1.1	4.0	1.9
	2000	100.0	12.6	1.9	1.5	5.1	0.3	0.8	4.4	2.8
	2001	100.0	12.6	1.7	0.9	4.8	0.4	1.1	4.7	3.0
	2002	100.0	12.8	2.3	1.4	4.6	0.3	1.0	4.5	3.8
Manufactured goods	1999	100.0	57.8	16.6	15.6	22.3	0.5	17.5	0.5	1.1
(SITC 5 to 8 less 68)	2000	100.0	57.3	15.7	14.7	22.3	0.5	17.9	0.4	1.0
	2001	100.0	56.1	16.7	15.7	22.1	0.5	15.8	0.4	1.0
	2002	100.0	53.5	16.6	15.5	19.5	0.5	16.1	0.4	1.1
Share by major commodity groups (percentage)										
All food items	1999	5.2	4.9	4.2	4.2	6.4	19.6	0.8	20.7	3.1
(SITC 0 + 1 + 22 + 4)	2000	4.5	4.4	3.7	3.7	5.9	18.1	0.7	18.3	2.0
	2001	4.9	4.8	3.5	3.5	6.6	21.0	0.8	19.0	2.6
	2002	4.9	4.7	3.5	3.5	6.8	15.9	0.8	19.9	2.2
Agricultural raw materials	1999	2.2	2.0	1.5	1.5	2.2	16.2	0.8	10.1	8.2
(SITC 2 - 22 - 27 - 28)	2000	2.2	2.1	1.5	1.6	2.4	16.4	0.7	10.3	7.3
	2001	2.2	2.3	1.4	1.5	2.7	14.0	0.8	11.1	8.8
	2002	2.2	2.4	1.5	1.6	2.8	16.6	0.8	11.0	9.2
Ores and metals	1999	3.2	2.7	2.1	2.0	1.7	7.1	2.5	19.2	8.9
(SITC 27 + 28 + 68)	2000	3.2	2.8	2.6	2.3	1.8	9.0	2.3	19.0	11.7
	2001	3.3	3.0	2.5	2.2	1.9	7.9	2.6	20.5	12.0
	2002	3.3	3.1	2.6	2.2	1.9	10.3	2.5	19.9	10.5
Fuels (SITC 3)	1999	7.3	1.8	1.3	1.0	1.8	5.3	0.5	15.3	10.3
	2000	9.0	2.1	1.2	1.1	2.2	3.6	0.5	21.3	17.0
	2001	8.5	2.0	1.0	0.6	2.0	3.8	0.6	20.6	18.3
	2002	8.2	2.1	1.3	0.8	2.1	3.7	0.6	20.3	19.7
Manufactured goods	1999	79.6	84.8	87.5	87.9	84.7	49.1	91.7	20.9	63.7
(SITC 5 to 8 less 68)	2000	79.1	85.3	89.5	89.9	84.6	51.5	91.9	18.5	55.4
	2001	78.5	83.8	87.7	88.2	83.8	51.9	90.3	18.0	56.2
	2002	78.5	84.0	88.7	89.5	82.9	52.1	90.3	18.0	57.4

Sources: UNCTAD secretariat computations based on UN/DESA/Statistics Division's data.

For notes, see end of table 3.2.2J.

Total	Major petroleum exporters / Principaux exportateurs de pétole	Major exporters of manufactures / Principaux exportateurs d'articles manufacturés	America / Amérique	Africa / Afrique	West Asia / Asie occidentale	Other Asia - Autres économies d'Asie Total	China	Oceania / Océanie	Year / Année	Groupes de produits
				Millions de dollars						
449332	62628	356138	21922	15394	35367	375879	61077	770	1999	Total tous produits
571168	89726	444536	27696	19676	52124	470597	78081	1075	2000	
531908	77754	416724	29007	15765	47456	438568	82740	1112	2001	
606240	80751	487588	30633	15454	47884	511123	105632	1146	2002	
				Parts par origines (en pourcentage)						
44.3	6.2	35.1	2.2	1.5	3.5	37.1	6.0	0.1	1999	Total tous produits
45.4	7.1	35.3	2.2	1.6	4.1	37.4	6.2	0.1	2000	
46.1	6.7	36.1	2.5	1.4	4.1	38.0	7.2	0.1	2001	
48.4	6.4	38.9	2.4	1.2	3.8	40.8	8.4	0.1	2002	
48.7	4.7	29.1	12.1	1.7	0.9	33.8	6.8	0.2	1999	Produits alimentaires
47.7	4.3	28.4	12.6	1.3	0.7	32.9	7.6	0.2	2000	(CTCI 0 + 1 + 22 + 4)
47.9	3.9	28.6	13.4	1.3	0.8	32.2	7.4	0.2	2001	
50.5	5.0	30.8	13.2	1.1	0.8	35.2	8.6	0.1	2002	
44.8	4.8	29.3	4.6	4.4	0.7	34.8	3.6	0.3	1999	Matières premières
42.7	5.2	27.4	4.6	3.9	0.6	33.2	3.4	0.3	2000	d'origine agricole
40.3	5.3	25.1	5.5	3.8	0.6	30.0	2.8	0.3	2001	(CTCI 2 - 22 - 27 - 28)
39.6	5.6	24.6	4.8	3.9	0.5	30.1	3.0	0.3	2002	
49.7	5.8	29.6	10.9	3.7	3.5	30.9	5.6	0.7	1999	Minerais et métaux
47.3	5.8	28.0	11.4	3.0	2.7	29.6	5.5	0.6	2000	(CTCI 27 + 28 + 68)
47.3	6.5	27.6	11.2	3.1	3.4	29.1	6.1	0.4	2001	
48.8	5.9	29.4	11.9	2.9	3.1	30.5	7.0	0.3	2002	
84.6	60.3	19.8	2.7	12.9	40.3	28.6	3.2	0.0	1999	Combustibles (CTCI 3)
84.7	59.7	19.4	3.4	12.5	41.0	27.8	3.2	0.0	2000	
84.4	57.5	20.0	3.8	10.6	41.2	28.8	4.2	0.0	2001	
83.4	56.0	21.1	3.7	9.5	39.3	31.0	4.1	0.0	2002	
41.1	1.5	38.0	1.1	0.3	0.5	39.1	6.5	0.0	1999	Articles manufacturés
41.6	1.6	38.7	1.1	0.3	0.4	39.8	6.7	0.1	2000	(CTCI 5 à 8 moins 68)
42.9	1.7	39.7	1.3	0.3	0.6	40.7	7.9	0.1	2001	
45.3	1.6	42.3	1.3	0.3	0.5	43.2	9.4	0.1	2002	
			Parts par principaux groupes de produits (en pourcentage)							
5.7	4.0	4.3	29.2	5.9	1.4	4.8	5.9	14.8	1999	Produits alimentaires
4.7	2.7	3.6	25.8	3.7	0.8	3.9	5.5	9.8	2000	(CTCI 0 + 1 + 22 + 4)
5.1	2.9	3.9	26.4	4.6	1.0	4.2	5.1	9.3	2001	
5.1	3.8	3.9	26.3	4.4	1.0	4.2	5.0	5.3	2002	
2.2	1.7	1.8	4.7	6.4	0.4	2.1	1.3	9.4	1999	Matières premières
2.0	1.6	1.7	4.5	5.5	0.3	1.9	1.2	8.9	2000	d'origine agricole
1.9	1.7	1.5	4.9	6.2	0.3	1.8	0.9	7.4	2001	(CTCI 2 - 22 - 27 - 28)
1.8	1.9	1.4	4.3	6.9	0.3	1.6	0.8	6.7	2002	
3.6	3.0	2.7	16.2	7.8	3.3	2.7	3.0	29.3	1999	Minerais et métaux
3.3	2.6	2.5	16.6	6.1	2.1	2.5	2.9	23.5	2000	(CTCI 27 + 28 + 68)
3.4	3.2	2.5	14.9	7.5	2.8	2.6	2.8	15.0	2001	
3.3	3.0	2.5	16.2	7.9	2.7	2.5	2.8	12.5	2002	
13.8	70.8	4.1	8.9	61.8	83.9	5.6	3.9	0.0	1999	Combustibles (CTCI 3)
16.7	74.9	4.9	14.0	71.3	88.5	6.7	4.6	0.3	2000	
15.5	72.3	4.7	12.7	65.4	84.9	6.4	5.0	0.1	2001	
14.2	71.4	4.4	12.6	63.1	84.4	6.2	4.0	0.2	2002	
73.8	19.4	86.2	40.9	18.0	10.8	84.0	85.8	44.7	1999	Articles manufacturés
72.5	17.8	86.5	39.0	13.4	8.1	84.1	85.7	57.4	2000	(CTCI 5 à 8 moins 68)
73.1	19.3	86.3	41.1	16.1	10.6	84.1	86.1	68.2	2001	
73.6	19.5	85.4	40.6	17.7	10.8	83.1	87.5	69.0	2002	

Sources: Calculs du secrétariat de la CNUCED basés sur des données de ONU/DAES/Division de statistique.

Pour les notes, se reporter à la fin du tableau 3.2.2J.

Origin	Year	World [1]	Developed economies								South-East Europe and CIS
				Europe							
	Année	Monde [1]	Total	Total	EU	USA	Canada	Japan	Australia, New Zealand	
Commodity groups											
					UE	Etats-Unis		Japon	Australie Nouvelle-Zélande	Europe du Sud-Est et CEI

Commodity groups	Year	World [1]	Total	Total	EU/UE	USA	Canada	Japan	Australia NZ	SE Europe CIS
		Millions of dollars								
All products	1999	307226	221129	55517	52618	141950	3884	17891	1119	4974
	2000	362854	253393	56730	53744	170806	4261	19477	1223	7520
	2001	349175	241890	58847	55125	159696	4537	16418	1332	6533
	2002	326168	225286	55485	51973	148849	3894	14782	1253	5997
		Share by origin (percentage)								
All products	1999	100.0	72.0	18.1	17.1	46.2	1.3	5.8	0.4	1.6
	2000	100.0	69.8	15.6	14.8	47.1	1.2	5.4	0.3	2.1
	2001	100.0	69.3	16.9	15.8	45.7	1.3	4.7	0.4	1.9
	2002	100.0	69.1	17.0	15.9	45.6	1.2	4.5	0.4	1.8
All food items	1999	100.0	58.2	13.2	12.4	38.5	4.6	0.1	1.8	0.2
(SITC 0 + 1 + 22 + 4)	2000	100.0	58.3	13.1	12.4	38.3	4.8	0.1	1.9	0.1
	2001	100.0	59.1	11.9	11.2	39.4	5.1	0.1	2.6	0.1
	2002	100.0	60.3	11.9	11.3	41.7	4.4	0.0	2.1	0.2
Agricultural raw materials	1999	100.0	67.4	6.6	6.4	56.8	1.7	0.8	1.0	1.1
(SITC 2 - 22 - 27 - 28)	2000	100.0	70.4	6.4	6.3	60.2	1.7	0.6	1.1	0.9
	2001	100.0	70.2	5.9	5.8	60.3	1.9	0.8	1.0	0.2
	2002	100.0	70.0	6.3	6.1	60.1	1.9	0.7	0.7	0.2
Ores and metals	1999	100.0	52.1	10.1	9.6	38.6	2.1	0.5	0.3	1.2
(SITC 27 + 28 + 68)	2000	100.0	49.6	10.9	10.5	34.9	2.5	0.5	0.4	1.7
	2001	100.0	49.2	12.9	12.7	32.6	2.6	0.4	0.3	1.2
	2002	100.0	52.2	11.8	11.6	35.9	3.6	0.3	0.1	1.2
Fuels (SITC 3)	1999	100.0	21.4	3.7	3.4	15.8	0.6	0.1	1.2	16.5
	2000	100.0	20.8	2.4	2.1	17.3	0.2	0.1	0.8	16.8
	2001	100.0	20.4	2.4	1.7	16.6	0.4	0.1	0.9	16.7
	2002	100.0	22.0	3.2	2.4	17.3	0.4	0.1	1.0	15.7
Manufactured goods	1999	100.0	77.5	20.2	19.1	48.7	1.0	7.3	0.1	0.5
(SITC 5 to 8 less 68)	2000	100.0	76.6	18.0	17.1	50.4	0.9	6.8	0.1	0.5
	2001	100.0	75.5	19.3	18.1	48.8	1.0	5.9	0.1	0.5
	2002	100.0	75.3	19.8	18.6	48.3	0.9	5.8	0.1	0.5
		Share by major commodity groups (percentage)								
All food items	1999	8.0	6.4	5.8	5.7	6.6	28.7	0.1	39.7	0.9
(SITC 0 + 1 + 22 + 4)	2000	7.0	5.9	5.9	5.9	5.7	28.6	0.1	39.3	0.2
	2001	7.8	6.6	5.5	5.5	6.7	30.6	0.1	52.1	0.4
	2002	8.0	7.0	5.6	5.7	7.3	29.4	0.1	44.4	0.8
Agricultural raw materials	1999	1.4	1.3	0.5	0.5	1.7	1.9	0.2	3.9	0.9
(SITC 2 - 22 - 27 - 28)	2000	1.4	1.4	0.6	0.6	1.8	2.0	0.2	4.4	0.6
	2001	1.3	1.3	0.5	0.5	1.7	1.9	0.2	3.5	0.2
	2002	1.4	1.4	0.5	0.5	1.9	2.3	0.2	2.5	0.1
Ores and metals	1999	1.8	1.3	1.0	1.0	1.5	3.0	0.2	1.4	1.3
(SITC 27 + 28 + 68)	2000	1.8	1.3	1.3	1.3	1.3	3.8	0.2	2.1	1.4
	2001	1.7	1.2	1.3	1.4	1.2	3.4	0.2	1.2	1.1
	2002	1.7	1.3	1.2	1.2	1.3	5.0	0.1	0.6	1.1
Fuels (SITC 3)	1999	7.2	2.1	1.5	1.4	2.5	3.5	0.2	23.1	73.2
	2000	9.8	2.9	1.5	1.4	3.6	2.1	0.2	22.4	79.3
	2001	8.6	2.5	1.2	0.9	3.1	2.3	0.2	20.7	76.4
	2002	9.1	2.9	1.7	1.4	3.4	2.7	0.3	23.6	77.3
Manufactured goods	1999	78.8	84.8	88.1	88.0	83.0	59.6	98.2	31.7	23.1
(SITC 5 to 8 less 68)	2000	77.5	85.1	89.4	89.6	83.1	61.1	98.2	31.2	18.1
	2001	77.7	84.7	89.0	89.1	82.9	59.2	98.1	22.0	21.8
	2002	76.7	83.6	89.1	89.3	81.2	57.9	98.3	27.8	20.5

Sources: UNCTAD secretariat computations based on UN/DESA/Statistics Division's data.   For notes, see end of table 3.2.2J.

Total	of which dont		America Amérique	Africa Afrique	West Asia Asie occidentale	Other Asia Autres économies d'Asie		Oceania Océanie	Year Année	Origine
	Major petroleum exporters Principaux exportateurs de pétole	Major exporters of manufactures Principaux exportateurs d'articles manufacturés				Total	China			Groupes de produits
Millions de dollars										
81123	11597	42099	49352	3557	1265	26774	5219	175	1999	**Total tous produits**
101941	16654	52605	61721	4623	1790	33418	7141	388	2000	
100752	14728	51817	61437	3523	2205	33005	8168	582	2001	
94886	14944	49666	56058	3223	2062	33135	9399	408	2002	
Parts par origines (en pourcentage)										
26.4	3.8	13.7	16.1	1.2	0.4	8.7	1.7	0.1	1999	**Total tous produits**
28.1	4.6	14.5	17.0	1.3	0.5	9.2	2.0	0.1	2000	
28.9	4.2	14.8	17.6	1.0	0.6	9.5	2.3	0.2	2001	
29.1	4.6	15.2	17.2	1.0	0.6	10.2	2.9	0.1	2002	
41.6	2.1	7.3	38.9	0.5	0.3	2.0	0.5	0.0	1999	Produits alimentaires
41.7	1.8	7.7	39.0	0.4	0.2	2.1	0.6	0.0	2000	(CTCI 0 + 1 + 22 + 4)
40.8	1.9	7.8	38.3	0.3	0.3	1.9	0.6	0.0	2001	
39.6	2.6	7.0	36.5	0.3	0.2	2.5	0.8	0.0	2002	
31.5	2.0	11.1	22.4	2.7	0.2	6.3	0.9	0.0	1999	Matières premières
28.7	2.0	10.1	21.1	1.6	0.0	5.9	0.5	0.0	2000	d'origine agricole
29.5	2.0	10.1	22.9	1.2	0.0	5.4	0.4	0.0	2001	(CTCI 2 - 22 - 27 - 28)
29.8	2.3	10.2	22.9	0.9	0.0	6.0	0.5	0.0	2002	
46.6	4.1	12.1	41.3	2.4	0.1	2.7	0.6	_	1999	Minerais et métaux
48.7	4.1	12.4	43.6	3.0	0.1	1.9	0.5	_	2000	(CTCI 27 + 28 + 68)
49.6	4.4	11.9	45.0	2.5	0.1	2.0	0.7	_	2001	
46.6	5.5	12.0	41.5	2.9	0.0	2.1	0.7	_	2002	
62.1	38.9	7.7	43.0	11.1	4.1	4.0	0.6	_	1999	Combustibles (CTCI 3)
62.4	36.8	8.8	44.0	10.3	4.0	4.2	0.6	_	2000	
62.9	36.1	8.1	47.4	8.9	4.6	2.0	1.0	0.0	2001	
62.3	35.9	9.0	45.4	8.0	5.6	3.3	1.6	_	2002	
22.0	0.9	15.5	11.2	0.3	0.1	10.3	2.0	0.1	1999	Articles manufacturés
22.9	1.0	16.4	11.4	0.2	0.1	11.0	2.4	0.1	2000	(CTCI 5 à 8 moins 68)
23.9	1.1	16.5	12.2	0.2	0.1	11.2	2.8	0.2	2001	
24.2	1.3	17.0	11.8	0.2	0.1	11.8	3.5	0.2	2002	
Parts par principaux groupes de produits (en pourcentage)										
12.5	4.4	4.2	19.2	3.2	5.4	1.8	2.2	0.3	1999	Produits alimentaires
10.4	2.7	3.7	16.1	2.1	3.3	1.6	2.1	0.0	2000	(CTCI 0 + 1 + 22 + 4)
11.0	3.5	4.1	16.9	2.5	3.4	1.6	2.0	0.0	2001	
10.9	4.6	3.7	17.0	2.7	3.2	2.0	2.1	0.0	2002	
1.7	0.8	1.1	2.0	3.2	0.7	1.0	0.7	0.0	1999	Matières premières
1.4	0.6	1.0	1.7	1.7	0.1	0.9	0.3	0.0	2000	d'origine agricole
1.3	0.6	0.9	1.7	1.5	0.1	0.7	0.2	0.0	2001	(CTCI 2 - 22 - 27 - 28)
1.4	0.7	0.9	1.9	1.3	0.1	0.8	0.3	0.0	2002	
3.1	1.9	1.5	4.5	3.7	0.5	0.5	0.7	_	1999	Minerais et métaux
3.1	1.6	1.5	4.6	4.3	0.5	0.4	0.5	_	2000	(CTCI 27 + 28 + 68)
2.9	1.8	1.4	4.3	4.2	0.3	0.4	0.5	_	2001	
2.7	2.0	1.3	4.1	4.9	0.1	0.4	0.4	_	2002	
16.9	74.1	4.0	19.2	68.6	70.7	3.3	2.4	_	1999	Combustibles (CTCI 3)
21.8	78.7	5.9	25.4	79.0	79.6	4.5	2.9	_	2000	
18.7	73.2	4.7	23.1	75.5	62.8	1.8	3.8	0.0	2001	
19.5	71.2	5.4	24.0	73.2	80.7	2.9	4.9	_	2002	
65.6	18.7	88.9	54.9	21.2	22.7	93.1	93.9	99.7	1999	Articles manufacturés
63.1	16.3	87.7	52.0	12.9	16.5	92.5	94.1	99.9	2000	(CTCI 5 à 8 moins 68)
64.4	20.8	86.6	53.8	16.3	18.1	91.8	93.4	99.9	2001	
63.7	21.4	85.5	52.8	17.9	15.8	89.2	92.0	99.9	2002	

Developing economies / Economies en développement

Other Asia / Autres économies d'Asie

Origin Commodity groups	Year Année	World [1] Monde [1]	Developed economies Economies développées							South-East Europe and CIS Europe du Sud-Est et CEI
			Total	Europe		USA Etats-Unis	Canada	Japan Japon	Australia, New Zealand Australie Nouvelle-Zélande	
				Total	EU UE					
				Millions of dollars						
All products	1999	118423	76667	58999	57286	9905	1086	5294	951	2652
	2000	125856	78040	59733	58133	10955	1050	4908	925	2727
	2001	129912	81469	62409	60594	12366	996	4311	1020	2612
	2002	136978	83165	65203	63366	10655	1049	4817	1100	3146
				Share by origin (percentage)						
All products	1999	100.0	64.7	49.8	48.4	8.4	0.9	4.5	0.8	2.2
	2000	100.0	62.0	47.5	46.2	8.7	0.8	3.9	0.7	2.2
	2001	100.0	62.7	48.0	46.6	9.5	0.8	3.3	0.8	2.0
	2002	100.0	60.7	47.6	46.3	7.8	0.8	3.5	0.8	2.3
All food items	1999	100.0	58.8	38.6	38.0	13.9	3.3	0.1	3.0	1.0
(SITC 0 + 1 + 22 + 4)	2000	100.0	58.2	38.2	37.2	13.6	3.5	0.1	2.7	1.0
	2001	100.0	54.1	36.5	35.5	11.5	3.2	0.1	2.7	1.7
	2002	100.0	51.6	34.8	33.8	11.3	3.0	0.1	2.4	3.2
Agricultural raw materials	1999	100.0	53.6	40.1	39.9	8.0	2.5	1.7	1.2	7.8
(SITC 2 - 22 - 27 - 28)	2000	100.0	51.4	37.8	37.4	8.3	1.8	1.7	1.4	9.4
	2001	100.0	56.0	41.7	41.5	8.9	1.8	1.9	1.4	8.0
	2002	100.0	56.0	43.4	42.9	7.0	2.0	1.9	1.6	8.2
Ores and metals	1999	100.0	55.4	40.1	39.3	8.0	3.2	1.0	2.8	3.7
(SITC 27 + 28 + 68)	2000	100.0	50.3	35.4	35.0	10.5	1.6	0.8	1.7	5.3
	2001	100.0	45.4	38.2	37.8	3.4	1.9	0.4	1.2	4.6
	2002	100.0	41.9	35.2	34.9	2.4	1.7	0.3	2.2	5.9
Fuels (SITC 3)	1999	100.0	20.8	17.7	17.6	2.3	0.3	0.0	0.4	0.6
	2000	100.0	22.3	19.8	19.6	1.8	0.1	0.0	0.6	1.2
	2001	100.0	24.5	20.8	20.5	2.3	0.1	0.0	1.3	2.6
	2002	100.0	24.2	20.3	20.1	2.2	0.2	0.0	1.5	1.6
Manufactured goods	1999	100.0	70.3	55.2	53.4	7.8	0.5	5.9	0.4	1.9
(SITC 5 to 8 less 68)	2000	100.0	68.6	53.7	52.2	8.5	0.4	5.3	0.3	2.0
	2001	100.0	68.4	53.1	51.4	9.9	0.3	4.4	0.4	1.8
	2002	100.0	66.8	53.4	51.8	7.6	0.3	4.7	0.4	2.0
				Share by major commodity groups (percentage)						
All food items	1999	13.8	12.5	10.7	10.8	22.9	49.0	0.2	51.6	6.0
(SITC 0 + 1 + 22 + 4)	2000	13.5	12.7	10.9	10.9	21.2	56.6	0.4	49.8	6.4
	2001	14.0	12.0	10.6	10.6	16.8	58.4	0.5	48.6	12.0
	2002	14.6	12.4	10.7	10.7	21.2	57.3	0.3	44.3	20.7
Agricultural raw materials	1999	2.1	1.7	1.7	1.7	2.0	5.7	0.8	3.1	7.4
(SITC 2 - 22 - 27 - 28)	2000	2.0	1.7	1.6	1.6	1.9	4.4	0.9	3.8	8.7
	2001	1.8	1.6	1.6	1.6	1.7	4.2	1.0	3.2	7.1
	2002	1.8	1.6	1.6	1.6	1.6	4.5	1.0	3.5	6.3
Ores and metals	1999	1.4	1.2	1.2	1.2	1.4	5.1	0.3	5.0	2.4
(SITC 27 + 28 + 68)	2000	1.8	1.4	1.3	1.3	2.1	3.4	0.4	4.0	4.3
	2001	1.5	1.1	1.2	1.2	0.5	3.8	0.2	2.2	3.4
	2002	1.6	1.1	1.2	1.2	0.5	3.5	0.1	4.4	4.1
Fuels (SITC 3)	1999	6.5	2.1	2.3	2.4	1.8	1.8	0.0	3.2	1.6
	2000	9.6	3.4	4.0	4.1	2.0	1.7	0.0	7.4	5.2
	2001	7.1	2.8	3.1	3.1	1.7	1.3	0.0	11.5	9.3
	2002	7.3	2.9	3.1	3.2	2.1	1.6	0.1	13.6	5.2
Manufactured goods	1999	73.6	79.9	81.6	81.3	68.8	36.3	97.3	36.7	62.4
(SITC 5 to 8 less 68)	2000	71.6	79.2	81.0	80.9	69.7	31.8	96.6	33.8	65.7
	2001	72.7	79.3	80.3	80.2	75.8	29.9	96.5	33.1	66.8
	2002	72.5	79.7	81.3	81.2	70.8	30.8	97.4	32.2	62.5

Sources: UNCTAD secretariat computations based on UN/DESA/Statistics Division's data.

For notes, see end of table 3.2.2J.

| | Developing economies / Economies en développement | | | | | | | | | Origine |
| | of which / dont | | | | | | Other Asia / Autres économies d'Asie | | | |
Total	Major petroleum exporters / Principaux exportateurs de pétole	Major exporters of manufactures / Principaux exportateurs d'articles manufacturés	America / Amérique	Africa / Afrique	West Asia / Asie occidentale	Total	China	Oceania / Océanie	Year / Année	Groupes de produits
				Millions de dollars						
39104	8141	19215	2822	11905	6554	17807	4082	16	1999	**Total tous produits**
45088	10990	20431	2910	14123	8582	19453	5007	19	2000	
45831	8879	22813	3706	13554	7399	21154	5962	19	2001	
50667	10334	24696	4081	14922	8983	22663	6919	18	2002	
			Parts par origines (en pourcentage)							
33.0	6.9	16.2	2.4	10.1	5.5	15.0	3.4	0.0	1999	**Total tous produits**
35.8	8.7	16.2	2.3	11.2	6.8	15.5	4.0	0.0	2000	
35.3	6.8	17.6	2.9	10.4	5.7	16.3	4.6	0.0	2001	
37.0	7.5	18.0	3.0	10.9	6.6	16.5	5.1	0.0	2002	
40.2	2.1	16.6	10.2	14.2	2.3	13.6	2.5	0.0	1999	Produits alimentaires
40.7	2.1	14.8	9.3	16.6	2.4	12.4	2.6	0.0	2000	(CTCI 0 + 1 + 22 + 4)
44.2	3.0	17.6	11.8	15.9	3.3	13.2	2.3	0.0	2001	
45.1	3.4	18.4	12.0	15.7	2.6	14.8	2.1	0.0	2002	
38.5	3.8	6.5	2.2	27.8	2.4	6.2	0.3	0.0	1999	Matières premières
39.2	3.5	8.0	2.4	26.6	2.5	7.7	0.3	0.0	2000	d'origine agricole
36.0	4.9	8.0	2.4	22.1	3.9	7.7	0.6	0.0	2001	(CTCI 2 - 22 - 27 - 28)
35.8	5.7	8.4	2.0	20.9	3.5	9.4	0.8	0.0	2002	
41.0	5.4	14.3	11.7	16.7	6.7	5.6	1.9	0.3	1999	Minerais et métaux
44.4	4.7	13.9	11.0	22.1	5.5	5.5	1.7	0.3	2000	(CTCI 27 + 28 + 68)
50.0	6.5	16.4	13.1	22.9	6.6	7.1	2.3	0.2	2001	
52.1	7.2	14.0	10.1	27.7	8.0	6.2	2.1	0.2	2002	
78.7	58.7	4.9	0.9	40.9	32.4	4.5	0.7	0.0	1999	Combustibles (CTCI 3)
76.5	59.9	3.6	0.7	33.3	39.1	3.4	0.5	_	2000	
72.9	48.0	3.2	1.4	40.1	29.1	2.3	1.2	0.0	2001	
74.1	55.0	4.9	2.4	31.0	38.0	2.8	0.7	_	2002	
27.8	3.5	17.9	0.9	6.0	4.0	17.0	4.1	0.0	1999	Articles manufacturés
29.4	3.5	18.7	1.0	6.5	3.6	18.3	4.9	0.0	2000	(CTCI 5 à 8 moins 68)
29.7	3.8	19.1	1.1	6.0	4.1	18.5	5.5	0.0	2001	
31.3	3.8	19.5	1.1	7.2	4.3	18.6	6.2	0.0	2002	
		Parts par principaux groupes de produits (en pourcentage)								
16.8	4.2	14.1	59.0	19.5	5.6	12.5	9.9	6.3	1999	Produits alimentaires
15.4	3.3	12.3	54.2	19.9	4.8	10.9	9.0	33.1	2000	(CTCI 0 + 1 + 22 + 4)
17.5	6.1	14.0	57.9	21.2	8.0	11.3	6.9	26.8	2001	
17.8	6.5	14.9	58.9	21.1	5.8	13.1	6.2	24.5	2002	
2.5	1.2	0.8	1.9	5.8	0.9	0.9	0.2	1.7	1999	Matières premières
2.2	0.8	1.0	2.1	4.7	0.7	1.0	0.2	0.9	2000	d'origine agricole
1.8	1.3	0.8	1.5	3.8	1.2	0.8	0.2	1.3	2001	(CTCI 2 - 22 - 27 - 28)
1.7	1.3	0.8	1.2	3.4	0.9	1.0	0.3	1.2	2002	
1.8	1.1	1.3	7.1	2.4	1.7	0.5	0.8	29.7	1999	Minerais et métaux
2.2	0.9	1.5	8.4	3.5	1.4	0.6	0.7	30.7	2000	(CTCI 27 + 28 + 68)
2.1	1.4	1.4	6.9	3.3	1.7	0.7	0.7	23.2	2001	
2.3	1.5	1.2	5.5	4.1	1.9	0.6	0.7	20.8	2002	
15.5	55.7	2.0	2.5	26.5	38.2	1.9	1.4	0.0	1999	Combustibles (CTCI 3)
20.4	65.6	2.1	2.9	28.4	54.8	2.1	1.3	_	2000	
14.7	50.1	1.3	3.5	27.4	36.4	1.0	1.9	0.5	2001	
14.7	53.5	2.0	5.9	20.9	42.5	1.2	1.0	_	2002	
62.1	37.0	81.1	26.3	43.7	52.9	83.4	86.5	61.3	1999	Articles manufacturés
58.8	29.1	82.6	31.2	41.3	37.7	85.0	88.4	34.7	2000	(CTCI 5 à 8 moins 68)
61.2	40.4	79.1	28.7	41.9	51.8	82.6	87.7	47.8	2001	
61.2	36.5	78.3	27.6	48.1	47.8	81.3	89.3	53.0	2002	

Sources: Calculs du secrétariat de la CNUCED basés sur des données de
ONU/DAES/Division de statistique.

Pour les notes, se reporter à la fin du tableau 3.2.2J.

3.2.2I Import structure by origin and by major commodity groups
Developing West Asia

Origin / Commodity groups	Year Année	World [1] Monde [1]	Developed economies Economies développées							South-East Europe and CIS Europe du Sud-Est et CEI
			Total	Europe		USA Etats-Unis	Canada	Japan Japon	Australia, New Zealand Australie Nouvelle-Zélande	
				Total	EU UE					
		Millions of dollars								
All products	1999	141322	89212	60108	57334	16422	977	9618	1726	5850
	2000	162021	95844	67477	64406	15003	1158	9644	2088	8727
	2001	164597	94423	65209	62130	14927	939	10315	2660	10330
	2002	184180	106391	75745	71758	15010	866	11495	2819	10659
		Share by origin (percentage)								
All products	1999	100.0	63.1	42.5	40.6	11.6	0.7	6.8	1.2	4.1
	2000	100.0	59.2	41.6	39.8	9.3	0.7	6.0	1.3	5.4
	2001	100.0	57.4	39.6	37.7	9.1	0.6	6.3	1.6	6.3
	2002	100.0	57.8	41.1	39.0	8.1	0.5	6.2	1.5	5.8
All food items	1999	100.0	48.5	30.2	29.5	11.5	2.6	0.2	4.0	2.0
(SITC 0 + 1 + 22 + 4)	2000	100.0	46.9	27.7	27.0	11.7	3.2	0.1	4.2	2.0
	2001	100.0	41.6	23.6	23.0	11.0	2.0	0.1	4.9	2.7
	2002	100.0	39.0	22.8	22.2	9.4	0.5	0.1	5.7	3.2
Agricultural raw materials	1999	100.0	50.6	30.0	29.8	11.1	2.3	2.3	3.3	20.5
(SITC 2 - 22 - 27 - 28)	2000	100.0	52.4	27.5	27.3	16.3	1.9	1.3	4.2	18.4
	2001	100.0	54.5	29.8	29.4	17.4	1.3	1.5	4.2	16.5
	2002	100.0	56.8	32.8	32.4	16.8	1.4	1.5	3.9	15.4
Ores and metals	1999	100.0	38.7	29.6	27.8	4.2	0.3	2.9	1.3	19.7
(SITC 27 + 28 + 68)	2000	100.0	33.1	26.4	25.5	2.9	0.5	1.9	1.1	21.4
	2001	100.0	33.1	25.9	24.8	3.7	0.5	1.6	1.3	24.9
	2002	100.0	37.4	29.3	28.1	3.7	0.8	1.3	2.2	21.8
Fuels (SITC 3)	1999	100.0	15.0	11.6	11.0	1.5	0.4	0.1	1.4	14.3
	2000	100.0	15.2	12.7	11.7	1.5	0.3	0.0	0.6	22.0
	2001	100.0	10.7	8.2	7.0	1.2	0.4	0.0	0.9	24.8
	2002	100.0	11.5	8.8	7.1	1.2	0.5	0.0	0.9	24.4
Manufactured goods	1999	100.0	69.6	47.3	45.0	12.2	0.4	8.7	0.7	2.8
(SITC 5 to 8 less 68)	2000	100.0	66.0	47.6	45.3	9.3	0.4	7.7	0.8	3.4
	2001	100.0	63.9	45.0	42.7	9.3	0.4	8.0	1.0	4.4
	2002	100.0	64.3	46.6	44.1	8.2	0.4	7.9	0.9	4.0
		Share by major commodity groups (percentage)								
All food items	1999	12.6	9.7	8.9	9.1	12.5	48.0	0.3	41.4	6.1
(SITC 0 + 1 + 22 + 4)	2000	11.6	9.2	7.7	7.9	14.7	52.1	0.3	38.1	4.4
	2001	11.4	8.3	6.8	7.0	13.8	40.3	0.3	34.7	4.9
	2002	10.7	7.2	5.9	6.1	12.4	12.2	0.2	39.5	5.9
Agricultural raw materials	1999	1.6	1.2	1.1	1.1	1.5	5.1	0.5	4.2	7.7
(SITC 2 - 22 - 27 - 28)	2000	1.8	1.6	1.2	1.2	3.1	4.7	0.4	5.7	6.0
	2001	1.5	1.5	1.2	1.2	2.9	3.4	0.4	4.0	4.0
	2002	1.7	1.6	1.3	1.4	3.4	5.0	0.4	4.2	4.4
Ores and metals	1999	2.1	1.3	1.5	1.4	0.8	1.0	0.9	2.2	10.0
(SITC 27 + 28 + 68)	2000	2.3	1.3	1.5	1.5	0.7	1.6	0.8	1.9	9.3
	2001	2.4	1.4	1.6	1.6	1.0	1.9	0.6	2.0	9.5
	2002	2.5	1.6	1.8	1.8	1.1	4.2	0.5	3.5	9.3
Fuels (SITC 3)	1999	5.3	1.3	1.4	1.4	0.7	3.4	0.1	5.9	18.3
	2000	6.9	1.8	2.1	2.0	1.1	3.2	0.0	3.5	28.3
	2001	6.4	1.2	1.3	1.2	0.8	4.0	0.1	3.7	25.4
	2002	5.9	1.2	1.3	' 1.1	0.9	6.4	0.0	3.4	24.7
Manufactured goods	1999	76.1	83.9	84.7	84.4	80.2	39.9	97.4	42.4	51.8
(SITC 5 to 8 less 68)	2000	75.5	84.2	86.2	86.0	75.5	37.0	97.5	46.9	48.2
	2001	75.0	83.6	85.1	84.9	77.0	46.3	96.3	45.8	52.2
	2002	76.7	85.4	87.0	86.8	77.3	67.7	97.1	44.5	53.2

Sources: UNCTAD secretariat computations based on UN/DESA/Statistics Division's data.

For notes, see end of table 3.2.2J.

3.2.2I Structure des importations par origine et par principaux groupes de produits
Asie occidentale en développement

| Total | of which dont | | America Amérique | Africa Afrique | West Asia Asie occi-dentale | Other Asia Autres économies d'Asie | | Oceania Océanie | Year Année | Origine |
	Major petroleum exporters Principaux exportateurs de pétole	Major exporters of manufactures Principaux exportateurs d'articles manufacturés				Total	China			Groupes de produits
										Millions de dollars
46261	14488	26253	2760	2982	14030	26487	4696	1	1999	**Total tous produits**
57450	18658	31771	3117	4470	16965	32896	6525	2	2000	
59843	19843	32426	3686	3734	19737	32684	6931	3	2001	
67130	20103	38520	4187	4113	20166	38661	9704	3	2002	
										Parts par origines (en pourcentage)
32.7	10.3	18.6	2.0	2.1	9.9	18.7	3.3	0.0	1999	**Total tous produits**
35.5	11.5	19.6	1.9	2.8	10.5	20.3	4.0	0.0	2000	
36.4	12.1	19.7	2.2	2.3	12.0	19.9	4.2	0.0	2001	
36.4	10.9	20.9	2.3	2.2	10.9	21.0	5.3	0.0	2002	
49.5	11.7	21.5	10.9	4.8	14.6	19.2	1.2	0.0	1999	Produits alimentaires
51.0	13.5	19.7	10.3	5.6	15.7	19.4	1.4	0.0	2000	(CTCI 0 + 1 + 22 + 4)
55.7	16.6	21.3	13.4	4.1	19.8	18.4	1.4	0.0	2001	
57.8	17.2	21.9	13.3	4.6	20.3	19.5	1.6	0.0	2002	
28.9	6.8	13.0	3.0	6.2	6.7	13.0	0.4	_	1999	Matières premières
29.1	6.7	14.1	3.2	5.0	5.8	15.1	0.7	_	2000	d'origine agricole
29.0	6.1	13.9	3.1	5.4	6.0	14.5	0.5	0.0	2001	(CTCI 2 - 22 - 27 - 28)
27.8	6.5	12.9	3.0	4.9	4.7	15.2	1.3	0.0	2002	
41.6	18.1	15.9	9.9	3.8	20.1	7.7	1.1	_	1999	Minerais et métaux
45.6	17.9	16.5	13.5	3.3	19.5	9.3	1.3	_	2000	(CTCI 27 + 28 + 68)
42.0	18.3	16.5	9.2	2.6	19.9	10.3	1.5	_	2001	
40.8	16.8	15.7	9.1	2.5	18.3	10.9	1.7	_	2002	
70.6	64.4	4.6	0.5	14.9	50.9	4.3	1.1	_	1999	Combustibles (CTCI 3)
62.8	56.2	3.9	0.4	19.0	38.9	4.6	0.8	_	2000	
64.5	56.0	5.5	1.2	16.2	41.9	5.1	1.0	_	2001	
64.1	46.1	15.4	3.2	16.7	31.8	12.4	1.1	_	2002	
27.6	6.1	19.5	0.4	0.7	6.2	20.3	4.0	0.0	1999	Articles manufacturés
30.5	7.2	21.2	0.4	0.8	7.0	22.3	4.8	0.0	2000	(CTCI 5 à 8 moins 68)
31.7	7.7	21.2	0.5	0.8	8.3	22.1	5.2	0.0	2001	
31.7	7.3	21.7	0.5	0.8	7.9	22.5	6.4	0.0	2002	
										Parts par principaux groupes de produits (en pourcentage)
19.0	14.4	14.6	70.0	28.4	18.5	12.9	4.4	54.7	1999	Produits alimentaires
16.7	13.6	11.7	62.4	23.7	17.4	11.1	4.0	49.6	2000	(CTCI 0 + 1 + 22 + 4)
17.5	15.8	12.4	68.5	20.5	18.9	10.6	3.7	24.4	2001	
17.0	16.9	11.2	62.8	21.9	19.9	9.9	3.2	16.3	2002	
1.4	1.0	1.1	2.4	4.6	1.0	1.1	0.2	_	1999	Matières premières
1.4	1.0	1.3	2.9	3.2	1.0	1.3	0.3	_	2000	d'origine agricole
1.2	0.8	1.1	2.1	3.6	0.8	1.1	0.2	4.1	2001	(CTCI 2 - 22 - 27 - 28)
1.3	1.0	1.0	2.2	3.6	0.7	1.2	0.4	1.2	2002	
2.7	3.7	1.8	10.7	3.8	4.3	0.9	0.7	_	1999	Minerais et métaux
3.0	3.6	2.0	16.5	2.8	4.3	1.1	0.8	_	2000	(CTCI 27 + 28 + 68)
2.8	3.7	2.0	9.9	2.7	4.0	1.3	0.8	_	2001	
2.8	3.8	1.9	9.9	2.8	4.1	1.3	0.8	_	2002	
11.4	33.2	1.3	1.3	37.4	27.1	1.2	1.7	_	1999	Combustibles (CTCI 3)
12.3	33.9	1.4	1.3	47.6	25.8	1.6	1.4	_	2000	
11.4	29.9	1.8	3.6	45.9	22.5	1.7	1.5	_	2001	
10.3	24.8	4.3	8.2	44.0	17.0	3.5	1.3	_	2002	
64.1	45.6	79.9	15.5	25.6	47.5	82.3	92.3	45.3	1999	Articles manufacturés
65.0	47.3	81.6	16.3	22.4	50.3	82.9	90.2	50.4	2000	(CTCI 5 à 8 moins 68)
65.4	48.1	80.9	15.4	26.5	51.9	83.6	92.6	71.5	2001	
66.7	51.6	79.7	16.9	26.2	55.6	82.2	93.5	80.8	2002	

Sources: Calculs du secrétariat de la CNUCED basés sur des données de
ONU/DAES/Division de statistique.

Pour les notes, se reporter à la fin du tableau 3.2.2J.

Origin Commodity groups	Year Année	World [1] Monde [1]	Developed economies / Economies développées							South-East Europe and CIS Europe du Sud-Est et CEI
			Total	Europe		USA Etats-Unis	Canada	Japan Japon	Australia, New Zealand Australie Nouvelle-Zélande	
				Total	EU UE					
All products					Millions of dollars					
All products	1999	880240	412150	114393	106231	112384	6433	155408	20323	10858
	2000	1089059	497913	128250	119265	135235	7725	197197	24617	12927
	2001	1005857	453433	133026	123576	122401	7326	162502	23864	10812
	2002	1115893	479954	141261	130249	123109	7441	179442	24485	14475
					Share by origin (percentage)					
All products	1999	100.0	46.8	13.0	12.1	12.8	0.7	17.7	2.3	1.2
	2000	100.0	45.7	11.8	11.0	12.4	0.7	18.1	2.3	1.2
	2001	100.0	45.1	13.2	12.3	12.2	0.7	16.2	2.4	1.1
	2002	100.0	43.0	12.7	11.7	11.0	0.7	16.1	2.2	1.3
All food items	1999	100.0	43.1	11.3	10.7	17.4	2.6	2.9	8.9	0.5
(SITC 0 + 1 + 22 + 4)	2000	100.0	43.9	10.7	10.2	18.4	2.6	2.7	9.4	0.5
	2001	100.0	44.0	9.8	9.3	17.8	2.8	4.3	9.2	0.7
	2002	100.0	39.8	9.6	9.0	16.5	1.9	2.6	9.2	0.7
Agricultural raw materials	1999	100.0	46.8	8.8	8.6	14.4	6.4	6.2	10.9	4.9
(SITC 2 - 22 - 27 - 28)	2000	100.0	48.8	8.8	8.6	16.7	6.7	6.0	10.6	4.1
	2001	100.0	50.6	8.5	8.3	19.0	5.5	6.1	11.5	5.1
	2002	100.0	49.7	8.3	8.2	18.5	6.1	6.1	10.7	6.3
Ores and metals	1999	100.0	44.5	9.3	7.9	6.5	1.8	13.7	13.2	2.5
(SITC 27 + 28 + 68)	2000	100.0	45.9	10.4	8.5	7.7	2.1	12.8	12.9	3.9
	2001	100.0	46.6	10.1	7.9	8.3	2.0	12.3	13.7	2.9
	2002	100.0	44.6	10.5	7.8	7.1	2.1	12.1	12.7	3.1
Fuels (SITC 3)	1999	100.0	9.4	1.9	1.0	1.8	0.4	1.2	4.1	1.0
	2000	100.0	8.0	1.1	0.8	1.1	0.2	0.9	4.6	1.2
	2001	100.0	8.6	1.2	0.6	1.2	0.3	1.1	4.8	1.3
	2002	100.0	8.7	1.6	0.8	1.2	0.2	1.1	4.5	2.0
Manufactured goods	1999	100.0	50.0	14.3	13.4	13.7	0.4	20.5	0.6	1.1
(SITC 5 to 8 less 68)	2000	100.0	49.6	13.3	12.5	13.5	0.4	21.2	0.6	0.9
	2001	100.0	48.2	14.8	13.9	13.1	0.4	18.7	0.6	0.9
	2002	100.0	46.3	14.4	13.4	11.7	0.4	18.7	0.5	1.1
					Share by major commodity groups (percentage)					
All food items	1999	5.5	5.1	4.8	4.9	7.6	20.1	0.9	21.3	2.5
(SITC 0 + 1 + 22 + 4)	2000	4.7	4.5	4.3	4.4	7.0	17.1	0.7	19.7	2.2
	2001	5.3	5.2	3.9	4.0	7.8	20.6	1.4	20.7	3.6
	2002	5.1	4.7	3.9	3.9	7.6	14.5	0.8	21.4	2.7
Agricultural raw materials	1999	2.4	2.4	1.7	1.7	2.8	21.4	0.9	11.5	9.6
(SITC 2 - 22 - 27 - 28)	2000	2.3	2.5	1.7	1.8	3.2	22.1	0.8	11.0	8.1
	2001	2.4	2.7	1.6	1.6	3.8	18.4	0.9	11.8	11.5
	2002	2.3	2.7	1.5	1.6	3.9	21.3	0.9	11.4	11.3
Ores and metals	1999	3.3	3.2	2.4	2.2	1.7	8.0	2.6	19.0	6.7
(SITC 27 + 28 + 68)	2000	3.3	3.3	2.9	2.6	2.0	9.6	2.3	18.9	10.9
	2001	3.5	3.6	2.7	2.2	2.4	9.4	2.6	20.0	9.3
	2002	3.4	3.5	2.8	2.3	2.2	10.9	2.6	19.7	8.1
Fuels (SITC 3)	1999	7.7	1.5	1.1	0.7	1.1	4.5	0.5	13.5	6.3
	2000	9.4	1.6	0.9	0.7	0.8	3.2	0.5	19.3	9.4
	2001	9.0	1.7	0.8	0.4	0.9	3.4	0.6	18.3	11.0
	2002	8.7	1.8	1.1	0.6	1.0	3.1	0.6	18.1	13.8
Manufactured goods	1999	78.8	84.1	86.8	87.2	84.6	42.9	91.4	21.7	68.0
(SITC 5 to 8 less 68)	2000	78.3	84.8	88.6	89.0	84.9	46.5	91.7	19.2	60.9
	2001	77.4	82.7	86.8	87.3	83.0	47.0	89.7	19.0	64.3
	2002	77.6	83.4	88.2	89.1	82.5	48.8	90.2	19.1	63.8

Sources: UNCTAD secretariat computations based on UN/DESA/Statistics Division's data.

For notes, see next page.

Structure des importations par origine et par principaux groupes de produits
Autres pays d'Asie en développement

Total	of which dont		America	Africa	West Asia	Other Asia		Oceania	Year	Origine
	Major petroleum exporters	Major exporters of manufactures	Amérique	Afrique	Asie occi-dentale	Autres économies d'Asie		Océanie	Année	
	Principaux exportateurs de pétole	Principaux exportateurs d'articles manufacturés				Total	China			Groupes de produits

Total	Major petroleum exporters	Major exporters of manufactures	America	Africa	West Asia	Total	China	Oceania	Year	Origine
				Millions de dollars						
457232	60215	375203	10916	12082	36324	397294	64857	617	1999	**Total tous produits**
578219	86223	466453	12846	15757	53291	495614	83258	712	2000	
541612	75366	439624	14968	12584	48846	464653	88097	561	2001	
621463	80324	512320	17585	12489	51022	539611	111097	757	2002	
			Parts par origines (en pourcentage)							
51.9	6.8	42.6	1.2	1.4	4.1	45.1	7.4	0.1	1999	**Total tous produits**
53.1	7.9	42.8	1.2	1.4	4.9	45.5	7.6	0.1	2000	
53.8	7.5	43.7	1.5	1.3	4.9	46.2	8.8	0.1	2001	
55.7	7.2	45.9	1.6	1.1	4.6	48.4	10.0	0.1	2002	
56.4	5.2	39.4	8.0	1.9	1.1	45.1	8.7	0.3	1999	Produits alimentaires
55.5	4.9	38.9	8.4	1.6	0.9	44.4	9.6	0.2	2000	(CTCI 0 + 1 + 22 + 4)
55.3	4.5	38.5	9.9	1.4	1.0	42.8	9.2	0.2	2001	
59.5	5.7	41.6	10.2	1.2	1.1	46.9	10.9	0.1	2002	
48.3	4.8	33.3	3.8	4.6	0.6	38.9	4.2	0.3	1999	Matières premières
47.1	5.1	31.6	3.8	4.4	0.5	38.1	4.1	0.4	2000	d'origine agricole
44.3	5.5	28.4	5.0	4.3	0.7	33.9	3.2	0.4	2001	(CTCI 2 - 22 - 27 - 28)
44.0	5.8	28.1	4.2	4.7	0.7	34.2	3.5	0.3	2002	
53.0	6.1	34.5	8.6	3.8	4.0	35.7	6.4	0.8	1999	Minerais et métaux
50.2	6.2	32.8	8.8	3.0	3.1	34.6	6.4	0.7	2000	(CTCI 27 + 28 + 68)
50.5	7.2	32.4	8.6	3.1	4.2	34.1	7.0	0.5	2001	
52.3	6.3	33.9	9.9	3.0	3.8	35.2	8.0	0.4	2002	
89.6	61.0	25.1	0.4	9.9	44.5	34.8	3.8	0.0	1999	Combustibles (CTCI 3)
90.8	61.4	25.2	0.8	10.1	45.4	34.5	4.1	0.0	2000	
90.1	58.6	25.9	1.6	8.2	44.8	35.5	5.2	0.0	2001	
89.3	57.7	26.1	2.0	7.2	43.4	36.7	4.9	0.0	2002	
49.0	1.9	46.0	0.5	0.3	0.6	47.5	8.0	0.0	1999	Articles manufacturés
49.5	2.0	46.6	0.4	0.3	0.6	48.2	8.3	0.0	2000	(CTCI 5 à 8 moins 68)
50.9	2.0	47.9	0.5	0.3	0.7	49.4	9.6	0.0	2001	
52.7	1.9	49.7	0.6	0.3	0.7	51.1	11.1	0.0	2002	
			Parts par principaux groupes de produits (en pourcentage)							
6.0	4.2	5.1	35.9	7.8	1.5	5.5	6.5	21.0	1999	Produits alimentaires
4.9	2.9	4.3	33.4	5.3	0.9	4.6	5.9	16.8	2000	(CTCI 0 + 1 + 22 + 4)
5.4	3.1	4.7	35.1	6.0	1.1	4.9	5.5	21.1	2001	
5.4	4.0	4.6	33.0	5.4	1.2	4.9	5.6	9.6	2002	
2.3	1.7	1.9	7.5	8.1	0.4	2.1	1.4	11.8	1999	Matières premières
2.1	1.5	1.7	7.6	7.1	0.2	2.0	1.3	13.8	2000	d'origine agricole
2.0	1.8	1.6	8.2	8.3	0.4	1.8	0.9	15.4	2001	(CTCI 2 - 22 - 27 - 28)
1.8	1.9	1.4	6.2	9.7	0.3	1.7	0.8	10.6	2002	
3.4	2.9	2.7	23.2	9.3	3.3	2.6	2.9	36.6	1999	Minerais et métaux
3.1	2.6	2.5	24.9	6.8	2.1	2.5	2.8	35.6	2000	(CTCI 27 + 28 + 68)
3.3	3.3	2.6	20.1	8.5	3.0	2.6	2.8	30.8	2001	
3.2	3.0	2.5	21.5	9.2	2.8	2.5	2.7	19.0	2002	
13.2	68.4	4.5	2.4	55.2	82.8	5.9	4.0	0.1	1999	Combustibles (CTCI 3)
16.1	73.1	5.5	6.5	65.8	87.6	7.1	5.0	0.5	2000	
15.1	70.3	5.3	9.5	59.3	83.0	6.9	5.4	0.1	2001	
14.0	70.2	5.0	10.9	56.0	82.9	6.6	4.3	0.4	2002	
74.2	21.5	85.0	30.9	19.5	11.9	82.9	85.1	28.2	1999	Articles manufacturés
73.0	19.3	85.2	27.6	14.9	9.0	82.9	84.8	33.2	2000	(CTCI 5 à 8 moins 68)
73.2	20.6	84.8	27.0	17.7	11.9	82.7	85.1	32.5	2001	
73.4	20.3	84.1	28.4	19.6	11.7	82.0	86.3	51.0	2002	

Sources: Calculs du secrétariat de la CNUCED basés sur des données de ONU/DAES/Division de statistique.

Pour les notes, se reporter à la page suivante.

Structure of international trade by region

Structure du commerce international par région

Sources: UNCTAD secretariat computations based on UN/DESA/Statistics Division's data.

General note:

Data in this table are not strictly comparable with the export and import data in table 1.1, mainly owing to more frequent revisions of the latter table.
Furthermore, certain adjustments made for total exports are not reflected in this table as it is not possible to distribute them by destination and commodity group.

The commodity classification is in accordance with the United Nations Standard International Trade Classification (SITC).

Data shown in these tables are based on official export figures converted to US dollars. Where official figures were not available, estimates have been based on imports reported by partner countries and on other subsidiary data.

The data have been adjusted: (a) to include estimates for countries and territories for which either no official data are available, or data are not classified according to the SITC; (b) to approximate calendar years; (c) where possible, to include ships' stores and bunkers in total exports. Except for a few countries, figures are in accordance with the Special Trade System.

It should be noted that while data in these tables show exports by destination, these data may differ considerably from data on imports as reported by countries of destination. The differences are accounted for by a variety of factors, of which the following may be of particular importance:

(1) Most import data are reported on a c.i.f. rather than an f.o.b. basis.

(2) Imports arrive at destination and are registered with some time-lag from the date they were recorded as exports.

(3) There may be considerable differences between the recorded destination of exports and the actual destination as shown in import statistics. Similarly, the SITC classification used by the exporting country may differ from the one assigned by the importing country.

(4) Both exports and imports may, for various reasons, be over- or under-invoiced (to avoid taxes or controls or to facilitate capital flight).

Despite efforts to allocate trade flows by destination, origin and commodity group, a margin of unallocated trade flows remains.

Footnotes:

1 Includes special category exports, ships' stores and bunkers and other exports of minor importance whose destination could not be determined.

Sources : Calculs du secrétariat de la CNUCED basés sur des données de ONU/DAES/Division de statistique.

Remarques générales :

Les données présentées dans ce tableau ne sont pas strictement comparables à celles des exportations et importations du tableau 1.1, principalement en raison de la révision plus fréquente de ces dernières. De plus, certains ajustements apportés au total des exportations n'apparaissent pas dans le présent tableau du fait qu'il n'est pas possible de les répartir par destination et groupe de produits.

La classification par produits utilisée est la Classification type pour le commerce international (CTCI) des Nations Unies.

Les données présentées dans ce tableau sont fondées essentiellement sur des chiffres officiels d'exportation, convertis en dollars des Etats-Unis. Quand les chiffres officiels n'étaient pas disponibles, on a eu recours à des estimations basées sur les importations déclarées par les pays partenaires ou sur d'autres données subsidiaires.

Les données ont été ajustées pour : a) que soient incluses les estimations faites pour les pays ne fournissant pas de données officielles ou dont les données ne sont pas ventilées selon la CTCI; b) qu'elles correspondent aux années civiles; c) que les exportations de combustibles de soute et avitaillement des navires et aéronefs étrangers soient, dans la mesure du possible, comprises dans les totaux. À l'exception de quelques pays, les chiffres correspondent au commerce spécial.

Il faut relever que les données se rapportant aux exportations ventilées par destination présentées dans ces tableaux peuvent accuser un écart considérable par rapport aux données des importations déclarées par les pays destinataires. Cet écart est dû à divers facteurs dont les suivants sont d'une importance particulière :

1. Les importations sont déclarées en principe "valeur c.a.f." plutôt que "valeur f.a.b".

2. Les importations de marchandises peuvent arriver à destination et être enregistrées bien après la date de leur enregistrement à l'exportation.

3. D'importantes différences peuvent exister entre la destination des exportations déclarée par les pays exportateurs et la destination réelle telle qu' indiquée dans les statistiques d'importation. De même, une version différente de la CTCI peut avoir été utilisée par le pays exportateur et le pays importateur.

4. Les exportations et les importations peuvent, pour différentes raisons, avoir été sous-évaluées ou surévaluées (pour éviter le paiement de taxes, éviter leur contrôle ou faciliter la fuite de capitaux).

En dépit des efforts déployés pour répartir les flux commerciaux par destination, origine et groupes de produits, il subsiste encore une marge d'exportations et d'importations non distribuées.

Notes :

1 Y compris les exportations de catégorie spéciale, combustibles de soute et avitaillement des navires et aéronefs et autres exportations de moindre importance dont la destination n'a pas pu être déterminée.

PART FOUR

Structure of international trade by product

QUATRIEME PARTIE

Structure du commerce international par produits

1

2

3

4

5

6

7

8

4.1A   Structure des exportations par principales catégories

Country or area / Pays ou zones	Year / Année	Total value (millions of dollars) / Valeur totale (millions de dollars)	By main categories of exports (percentage) / Par principales catégories de produits exportés (en pourcentage)					of which: / dont:			
			All food items / Produits alimentaires	Agricultural raw materials / Matières premières d'origine agricole	Fuels / Combustibles	Ores and metals / Minéraux et métaux	Manufactured goods / Produits manufacturés	Chemical products / Produits chimiques	Other manufactured goods / Articles manufacturés divers	Machinery and transport equipment / Machines et matériel de transport	Un-allocated / Non distribué
SITC / CTCI			0+1+22+4	2 less (22+27+28)	3	27+28+68	5 to 8 less 68	5	(6+8) less 68	7	
Albania - Albanie	2000	261	6.6	6.0	1.9	3.7	81.6	. 0.7	79.0	1.9	0.3
	2003	447	5.6	5.1	1.0	4.1	84.1	0.6	80.0	3.6	0.0
Algeria - Algérie	1990	11011	0.5	0.0	96.5	0.4	2.6	0.6	1.2	0.9	0.0
	1995	9357	1.2	0.1	95.2	0.5	3.0	1.2	1.4	0.4	0.0
	2000	22031	0.2	0.1	98.1	0.3	1.4	0.7	0.5	0.2	0.0
	2003	24612	0.2	0.0	98.0	0.4	1.3	0.9	0.4	0.1	0.0
Andorra - Andorre	1995	48	6.5	1.6	0.2	2.3	89.4	3.6	52.0	33.8	0.1
	2000	45	8.2	1.3	0.1	2.2	85.6	8.2	52.1	25.4	2.5
	2002	63	4.0	0.8	0.0	2.2	90.7	7.1	43.0	40.5	2.4
Angola	1990	3910	0.2	0.0	93.5	6.2	0.1	0.0	0.1	0.0	0.0
Anguilla	2003	4	28.6	0.0	0.2	0.0	71.1	0.4	22.3	48.4	0.0
Argentina - Argentine	1990	12352	56.3	3.9	8.0	2.4	29.3	6.0	17.5	5.8	0.1
	1995	20963	49.8	4.0	10.4	1.6	34.1	6.3	16.2	11.6	0.0
	2000	26410	43.4	1.5	17.8	3.3	32.3	7.1	11.8	13.5	1.7
	2002	25709	45.7	1.2	17.1	3.9	30.7	7.6	12.0	11.1	1.5
Armenia - Arménie	2000	294	9.4	3.4	7.0	17.9	59.2	1.2	47.5	10.5	3.2
	2003	668	11.8	0.7	2.0	13.5	63.8	0.4	59.8	3.5	8.1
Aruba	1995	15	35.7	1.9	0.0	0.0	62.4	3.8	39.8	18.8	0.0
	2003	84	50.6	1.1	0.0	0.1	42.8	29.1	7.2	6.5	5.4
Australia - Australie	1990	38781	20.5	9.8	19.3	24.5	18.6	2.6	7.8	8.2	7.3
	1995	53001	19.6	7.5	16.8	19.3	27.6	4.0	10.8	12.8	9.3
	2000	61881	20.3	5.8	21.5	21.1	25.0	4.3	9.0	11.6	6.3
	2003	70300	18.2	4.8	19.8	19.6	24.7	4.7	8.4	11.6	12.9
Austria - Autriche	1990	41881	3.3	4.4	1.0	3.2	87.9	8.2	42.2	37.5	0.1
	1995	57583	3.8	3.3	1.0	3.3	87.8	9.0	39.6	39.2	0.6
	2000	58603	5.2	3.0	1.4	2.6	86.7	9.0	34.6	43.1	1.0
	2003	88685	6.0	2.6	2.6	2.6	81.3	9.3	32.4	39.6	4.9
Azerbaijan - Azerbaïdjan	2000	1745	3.2	2.4	85.1	2.9	6.5	2.0	0.9	3.6	0.0
	2003	2592	4.8	1.5	86.0	2.3	5.2	2.0	1.8	1.4	0.1
Bahamas	1995	176	38.8	5.1	0.0	12.6	43.2	9.5	7.1	26.6	0.1
	2000	555	22.0	2.2	15.1	3.2	57.5	21.1	10.5	25.9	0.0
	2001	376	32.4	1.6	18.3	5.8	41.9	26.0	3.9	12.0	0.0
Bahrain - Bahreïn	1995	3475	2.8	0.1	52.3	25.9	18.9	6.1	11.2	1.7	0.1
	2000	6195	0.9	0.1	72.5	16.0	10.6	2.4	7.1	1.0	0.0
	2003	6610	1.0	0.1	70.8	16.8	11.4	3.0	6.1	2.2	0.0
Bangladesh	1990	1556	14.3	6.8	1.3	0.0	77.5	1.1	75.5	0.9	0.1
	1995	3407	10.4	2.7	0.5	0.0	85.2	3.0	80.5	1.6	1.3
	2003	4788	7.7	2.1	0.6	0.0	89.5	0.3	88.9	0.4	0.0
Barbados - Barbade	1990	213	27.3	0.1	27.5	0.1	43.3	11.9	19.3	12.1	1.7
	1995	238	28.8	0.9	14.4	1.5	54.1	13.5	20.8	19.8	0.3
	2000	273	27.3	0.1	22.1	0.2	48.7	13.7	21.1	13.9	1.5
	2003	250	26.6	0.5	26.2	0.2	45.2	12.8	20.9	11.5	1.4
Belarus - Bélarus	2000	7331	6.8	3.6	19.8	0.8	66.5	12.9	29.7	23.9	2.5
	2003	9964	8.5	3.7	22.0	1.1	63.8	11.8	29.2	22.8	1.0
Belgium - Belgique	2000	184851	9.1	1.5	4.4	3.0	80.8	20.3	30.9	29.6	1.2
	2003	255301	9.0	1.2	5.3	2.2	81.3	27.3	26.5	27.5	0.9
Belgium-Luxembourg - Belgique-Luxembourg	1990	118296	9.4	1.5	3.5	4.2	77.2	13.7	36.3	27.3	4.2
	1995	168154	10.3	1.2	2.7	3.6	76.4	16.0	33.1	27.3	5.8

For sources and notes, see end of table 4.1B.   Pour les sources et les notes, se reporter à la fin du tableau 4.1B.

Country or area Pays ou zones	Year Année	Total value (millions of dollars) Valeur totale (millions de dollars)	By main categories of exports (percentage) Par principales catégories de produits exportés (en pourcentage)								
			All food items Produits alimentaires	Agricultural raw materials Matières premières d'origine agricole	Fuels Combustibles	Ores and metals Minéraux et métaux	Manufactured goods Produits manufacturés	of which: / dont:			Unallocated Non distribué
								Chemical products Produits chimiques	Other manufactured goods Articles manufacturés divers	Machinery and transport equipment Machines et matériel de transport	
SITC / CTCI			0+1+22+4	2 less (22+27+28)	3	27+28+68	5 to 8 less 68	5	(6+8) less 68	7	
Belize	1995	162	79.7	1.3	3.2	0.2	15.7	1.2	11.6	3.0	0.0
	2000	200	81.7	1.3	2.0	0.0	14.6	0.3	12.9	1.3	0.3
	2002	164	39.3	0.9	0.0	0.0	0.7	0.1	0.3	0.3	59.1
Benin - Bénin	1995	333	11.8	38.9	2.8	38.9	6.6	0.2	4.9	1.5	1.1
	2000	188	20.1	69.7	0.0	0.1	7.1	0.7	5.1	1.3	3.1
	2002	304	37.2	45.1	0.4	0.1	8.5	0.7	6.5	1.2	8.7
Bolivia - Bolivie	1990	923	18.9	7.6	24.6	44.1	4.7	0.6	4.1	0.0	0.1
	1995	1181	19.1	8.7	12.9	31.5	16.5	1.1	12.2	3.2	11.3
	2000	1457	28.4	3.0	12.2	23.1	27.1	0.8	12.9	13.4	6.2
	2003	1651	29.6	2.0	30.1	17.7	16.1	1.2	11.0	3.9	4.5
Bosnia and Herzegovina - Bosnie-Herzégovine	2003	1028	4.8	13.6	6.1	19.3	56.2	2.2	36.5	17.5	0.0
Botswana	2000	2763	2.8	0.3	0.1	7.0	89.5	0.9	85.1	3.5	0.3
	2001	2533	3.1	0.5	0.1	5.5	90.6	1.2	86.5	2.9	0.3
Brazil - Brésil	1990	31411	27.7	3.3	2.2	13.7	51.8	5.9	27.4	18.5	1.3
	1995	46505	28.5	5.1	0.9	10.3	53.1	6.6	27.5	19.0	2.1
	2000	55282	23.2	4.8	1.6	10.1	57.7	6.4	23.2	28.0	2.6
	2003	73084	28.6	4.5	5.2	8.5	51.0	5.9	21.8	23.2	2.1
Brunei Darussalam - Brunéi Darussalam	1990	2213	0.7	0.0	96.5	0.1	2.7	0.1	1.3	1.4	0.0
Bulgaria - Bulgarie	2000	4822	9.8	2.7	11.7	12.7	56.8	10.0	37.2	9.6	6.4
	2003	7540	10.2	2.2	5.8	10.3	65.9	7.5	45.4	13.0	5.7
Burkina Faso	1995	171	22.1	59.1	1.6	0.3	8.6	0.4	5.0	3.1	8.3
	2000	184	18.8	58.0	3.2	0.0	18.1	1.7	11.8	4.6	1.9
	2002	171	19.4	61.5	0.0	0.1	18.3	0.6	12.3	5.5	0.7
Burundi	1995	179	59.8	2.7	0.0	0.7	2.2	0.5	1.6	0.1	34.5
	2000	43	85.8	7.1	0.0	0.7	0.5	0.0	0.2	0.3	5.9
	2002	27	81.4	1.3	0.0	3.0	1.7	0.0	1.2	0.4	12.6
Cameroon - Cameroun	1990	2081	20.4	14.3	49.9	6.9	8.5	1.5	4.7	2.3	0.0
	1995	1539	27.0	27.5	29.2	8.4	7.9	1.0	5.8	1.1	0.0
	2000	1833	14.9	21.0	54.2	5.6	4.3	0.4	3.3	0.5	0.0
	2003	2246	19.9	19.5	49.4	4.2	6.9	0.9	4.8	1.2	0.0
Canada	1990	126899	8.6	9.0	10.0	8.5	57.8	5.2	15.4	37.2	6.2
	1995	191118	7.6	9.2	9.1	6.7	61.9	5.8	17.6	38.5	5.5
	2000	277113	6.3	6.2	13.1	4.3	63.4	5.3	17.9	40.2	6.6
	2003	272045	7.3	5.1	16.1	4.5	60.6	6.2	18.4	35.9	6.5
Cape Verde - Cap-Vert	1995	32	6.1	0.3	34.1	0.1	59.4	0.8	20.2	38.3	0.0
	2000	49	4.0	0.1	48.5	0.0	47.4	0.5	21.9	25.1	0.0
	2001	10	3.5	0.0	0.0	0.0	95.7	0.3	93.2	2.2	0.8
Central African Republic - République centrafricaine	1995	120	4.2	19.8	0.8	30.1	44.5	0.4	35.3	8.8	0.6
	2000	79	10.6	13.1	0.5	7.6	68.2	0.1	65.6	2.5	0.0
	2001	74	2.7	27.9	0.1	20.2	49.0	0.8	46.6	1.6	0.1
Chile - Chili	1990	8522	23.1	9.5	0.5	53.1	9.8	3.4	5.3	1.1	4.0
	1995	15901	23.7	13.5	0.3	47.1	11.8	3.4	6.5	1.8	3.7
	2000	18214	24.3	10.8	1.1	44.5	15.4	5.6	7.1	2.7	3.9
	2003	20077	27.8	9.3	2.2	41.0	15.6	6.7	7.0	1.9	4.1
China - Chine	1990	62091	12.7	3.5	8.4	2.1	71.4	6.0	47.9	17.4	1.9
	1995	148779	8.2	1.8	3.6	2.1	84.0	6.1	56.9	21.1	0.3
	2000	249202	5.4	1.1	3.2	1.8	88.2	4.8	50.3	33.1	0.2
	2003	438228	4.4	0.7	2.5	1.6	90.6	4.4	43.3	42.8	0.2

For sources and notes, see end of table 4.1B.   Pour les sources et les notes, se reporter à la fin du tableau 4.1B.

Country or area / Pays ou zones	Year / Année	Total value (millions of dollars) / Valeur totale (millions de dollars)	By main categories of exports (percentage) / Par principales catégories de produits exportés (en pourcentage)					of which: / dont:			Un-allo-cated / Non distri-bué
			All food items / Produits alimentaires	Agricultural raw materials / Matières premières d'origine agricole	Fuels / Combustibles	Ores and metals / Minéraux et métaux	Manufactured goods / Produits manufacturés	Chemical products / Produits chimiques	Other manufactured goods / Articles manufacturés divers	Machinery and transport equipment / Machines et matériel de transport	
SITC / CTCI			0+1+22+4	2 less (22+27+28)	3	27+28+68	5 to 8 less 68	5	(6+8) less 68	7	
China, Hong Kong SAR - Chine, Hong Kong RAS	1990	82390	4.1	1.4	0.7	1.1	91.8	5.3	60.8	25.7	0.9
	1995	173871	3.0	1.3	1.0	1.7	92.5	6.2	54.0	32.3	0.6
	2000	202683	1.8	1.0	0.3	1.4	95.0	5.1	51.5	38.3	0.5
	2003	228654	1.2	0.8	0.2	1.2	94.2	4.7	43.5	46.0	2.3
China, Macao SAR - Chine, Macao RAS	1990	1701	1.0	0.8	0.0	0.1	98.2	1.3	95.1	1.8	0.0
	1995	2025	1.7	2.4	0.0	0.0	95.9	1.0	90.5	4.4	0.0
	2000	2547	1.0	0.6	0.7	0.1	97.6	0.9	91.1	5.7	0.0
	2003	2581	1.1	1.2	1.3	0.3	96.1	1.0	90.2	4.9	0.0
China, Taiwan Province of - Chine, Taiwan Province de	1990	67025	4.0	1.5	0.6	1.2	92.6	4.0	49.5	39.1	0.1
	1995	111343	3.4	1.5	0.7	1.4	92.8	6.5	38.2	48.0	0.1
	2000	148727	1.2	1.1	1.2	1.2	95.1	6.0	30.7	58.4	0.2
	2003	150600	1.3	1.2	2.3	1.3	93.7	7.8	30.3	55.6	0.3
Colombia - Colombie	1990	6765	32.8	4.3	36.9	0.2	25.1	3.4	20.5	1.3	0.7
	1995	10201	30.8	5.4	27.2	0.6	34.2	7.9	23.8	2.6	1.7
	2000	13158	19.0	4.7	43.1	0.7	32.5	10.1	18.1	4.3	0.1
	2003	13092	17.4	5.5	37.2	1.0	34.3	9.2	21.9	3.3	4.5
Comoros - Comores	1995	11	76.4	0.0	0.0	0.0	23.2	21.2	0.3	1.8	0.4
	2000	7	88.7	0.0	0.0	0.0	8.2	5.9	0.3	2.1	3.1
Congo	1995	1090	1.0	8.3	87.6	0.3	2.7	0.3	2.1	0.4	0.0
Cook Islands - Iles Cook	2000	7	4.5	0.3	0.0	0.0	95.2	0.0	95.2	0.0	0.0
	2003	9	74.9	1.1	0.0	0.0	24.0	0.0	24.0	0.0	0.0
Costa Rica	1990	1456	58.2	5.5	1.0	0.9	26.8	4.9	18.7	3.3	7.6
	1995	2702	63.4	5.0	0.8	1.1	25.1	6.3	15.6	3.2	4.7
	2000	5487	30.0	3.0	0.6	0.8	65.5	5.2	20.9	39.4	0.1
	2003	5800	30.1	3.1	0.5	0.7	65.4	7.0	24.7	33.7	0.2
Côte d'Ivoire	1995	3737	58.7	16.0	9.8	0.2	14.2	4.2	8.6	1.4	1.1
	2000	3628	49.8	13.8	20.3	0.2	14.4	4.1	9.2	1.0	1.5
	2003	5493	55.6	9.2	12.8	0.2	20.0	4.0	6.2	9.7	2.2
Croatia - Croatie	1995	4633	10.8	4.6	8.6	2.3	73.7	17.3	39.7	16.8	0.1
	2000	4432	8.9	4.5	11.0	3.0	72.5	12.4	33.2	27.0	0.1
	2003	6164	12.2	4.2	9.6	2.3	71.4	9.5	32.7	29.2	0.3
Cuba	2000	1676	49.9	0.2	3.1	37.3	9.4	2.5	6.2	0.7	0.1
	2001	1665	59.0	0.2	1.5	29.2	10.1	3.3	5.6	1.2	0.0
Cyprus - Chypre	1990	949	33.6	0.4	6.5	1.0	58.4	5.1	38.6	14.7	0.0
	1995	1231	50.5	0.4	3.7	1.2	44.1	6.3	25.7	12.1	0.0
	2000	954	43.5	0.6	10.7	3.1	42.1	7.3	18.9	16.0	0.1
	2003	923	28.5	0.6	9.3	3.4	57.9	11.3	16.4	30.3	0.2
Czech Republic - République tchèque	1995	21686	5.9	3.7	4.3	2.8	81.6	9.1	43.2	29.3	1.7
	2000	29053	4.1	2.3	3.1	1.9	88.4	7.0	37.0	44.4	0.3
	2003	48720	3.4	1.8	2.9	1.7	90.1	5.7	34.3	50.1	0.2
Czechoslovakia (former) - Tchécoslovaquie (anc.)	1990	15745	6.1	2.1	3.5	1.2	86.8	8.4	32.5	45.9	0.2
Denmark - Danemark	1990	34843	27.1	3.4	3.4	1.2	60.1	8.3	25.4	26.4	4.8
	1995	48789	24.0	2.9	2.6	1.2	59.8	9.5	25.1	25.1	9.6
	2000	49210	19.7	2.5	7.0	1.0	64.1	10.8	27.0	26.4	5.6
	2003	65346	19.3	2.6	6.5	1.3	66.2	13.2	25.4	27.6	4.1
Djibouti	1990	25	39.1	4.7	0.0	0.2	7.8	0.2	1.5	6.2	48.1
Dominica - Dominique	1990	55	64.4	0.9	0.0	0.1	34.6	24.1	9.5	0.9	0.0
	1995	45	50.3	0.3	0.0	1.3	48.1	42.7	2.7	2.7	0.0
	2000	54	37.7	0.1	0.0	4.0	58.2	52.1	2.7	3.4	0.0
	2003	39	35.4	0.1	0.0	4.2	60.3	58.5	0.8	1.0	0.0

For sources and notes, see end of table 4.1B.

Pour les sources et les notes, se reporter à la fin du tableau 4.1B.

4.1A Export structure by main categories (continued)
4.1A Structure des exportations par principales catégories (suite)

Country or area / Pays ou zones	Year / Année	Total value (millions of dollars) / Valeur totale (millions de dollars)	All food items / Produits alimentaires	Agricultural raw materials / Matières premières d'origine agricole	Fuels / Combustibles	Ores and metals / Minéraux et métaux	Manufactured goods / Produits manufacturés	Chemical products / Produits chimiques	Other manufactured goods / Articles manufacturés divers	Machinery and transport equipment / Machines et matériel de transport	Un-allocated / Non distribué
SITC / CTCI			0+1+22+4	2 less (22+27+28)	3	27+28+68	5 to 8 less 68	5	(6+8) less 68	7	
Dominican Republic - République dominicaine	1995	2603	18.7	0.4	0.1	0.3	76.2	2.8	64.6	8.8	4.4
	2001	814	40.8	1.6	15.8	1.7	34.2	6.1	26.7	1.4	5.9
Ecuador - Equateur	1990	2714	44.1	1.4	51.9	0.2	2.3	0.4	1.7	0.3	0.1
	1995	4361	51.8	3.0	35.1	0.3	7.6	1.2	4.4	2.0	2.2
	2000	4822	36.5	3.9	50.7	0.2	8.6	1.6	5.1	1.9	0.2
	2003	6038	40.7	5.6	43.2	0.2	10.1	1.9	5.0	3.1	0.2
Egypt - Egypte	1990	2582	9.7	9.5	29.5	8.9	42.4	4.8	37.0	0.7	0.0
	1995	3444	9.8	6.1	37.3	6.4	40.3	5.8	33.8	0.6	0.1
	2000	4639	8.5	1.2	63.6	5.8	21.0	7.6	13.4	0.0	0.0
	2003	6161	8.4	6.8	43.1	3.1	30.5	7.4	22.1	0.9	8.1
El Salvador	1990	409	57.2	0.8	1.5	2.7	37.7	9.3	25.8	2.7	0.0
	1995	985	57.0	1.2	0.1	2.9	38.8	11.4	24.6	2.8	0.1
	2000	1341	42.4	0.6	5.0	2.4	48.4	13.0	31.5	3.9	1.3
	2003	1255	33.8	0.7	5.0	3.3	57.1	13.7	39.5	3.9	0.1
Eritrea - Erythrée	2000	19	67.4	6.0	0.0	5.2	21.3	3.2	16.2	1.8	0.2
	2002	52	76.3	7.7	0.0	1.4	14.7	1.1	12.1	1.5	0.0
Estonia - Estonie	1995	1840	16.1	9.6	7.1	3.1	64.1	8.2	36.0	19.9	0.0
	2000	3830	8.0	9.6	4.5	5.5	72.4	5.6	30.8	36.0	0.0
	2003	5623	10.6	8.7	4.2	2.4	74.0	6.2	38.3	29.5	0.0
Ethiopia - Ethiopie	1995	422	72.5	13.4	2.9	0.1	11.2	0.3	10.8	0.0	0.0
	2000	482	66.5	17.6	0.0	0.9	9.2	0.0	9.1	0.1	5.7
	2003	513	62.0	25.9	0.0	0.7	11.4	0.0	11.3	0.0	0.1
Ethiopia (former) - Ethiopie (anc.)	1990	294	63.3	25.1	6.2	0.0	5.3	2.0	3.2	0.0	0.1
Faeroe Islands - Iles Féroé	1990	400	92.3	0.9	0.0	0.0	6.8	0.1	0.0	6.7	0.0
	2003	483	93.4	2.9	0.0	0.0	3.7	0.1	0.0	3.6	0.0
Fiji - Fidji	1990	496	43.6	5.0	10.9	0.3	29.2	0.8	23.2	5.3	11.0
	2000	469	34.9	4.6	0.0	0.2	46.1	0.7	45.1	0.2	14.2
	2003	503	47.9	3.8	0.0	0.4	39.1	1.4	37.2	0.6	8.8
Finland - Finlande	1990	26650	2.4	9.6	1.5	3.6	82.8	6.3	45.7	30.8	0.1
	1995	40409	2.3	8.4	1.9	3.1	83.3	5.9	42.1	35.3	1.0
	2000	45475	1.6	6.3	3.5	3.1	84.8	5.8	33.7	45.2	0.6
	2003	52503	1.9	6.3	4.0	2.8	84.1	6.9	34.9	42.2	0.9
France [1]	1990	209996	15.8	1.7	2.4	2.8	76.9	13.3	26.4	37.3	0.4
	1995	284046	14.4	1.3	2.4	2.5	79.1	14.6	24.8	39.6	0.2
	2000	302248	11.1	1.1	2.9	2.0	82.7	15.1	22.7	44.9	0.1
	2003	358099	11.8	1.0	2.7	1.8	82.3	16.7	22.9	42.8	0.2
French Guiana - Guyane française [1]	1990	90	63.5	4.3	0.0	0.3	26.4	1.7	6.0	18.7	5.5
	1995	158	32.2	1.5	0.2	0.1	50.2	1.4	15.8	33.0	15.9
French Polynesia - Polynésie française	2000	244	5.9	0.8	0.0	0.2	90.3	0.6	75.6	14.1	2.7
	2003	151	14.5	2.2	0.0	0.1	83.2	1.6	69.1	12.5	0.0
Gabon	2000	2600	0.8	11.8	83.3	1.7	2.3	0.1	1.8	0.4	0.0
Gambia - Gambie	1995	19	58.8	0.5	0.2	1.0	36.8	2.4	27.5	7.0	2.7
	2000	16	80.8	1.2	0.1	0.2	17.0	9.6	2.6	4.7	0.7
Georgia - Géorgie	2000	330	27.4	3.0	8.4	28.2	32.4	10.4	9.1	12.9	0.6
	2003	475	34.2	2.8	4.9	24.3	29.6	6.1	10.7	12.8	4.3

For sources and notes, see end of table 4.1B.　　Pour les sources et les notes, se reporter à la fin du tableau 4.1B.

Country or area Pays ou zones	Year Année	Total value (millions of dollars) Valeur totale (millions de dollars)	By main categories of exports (percentage) Par principales catégories de produits exportés (en pourcentage)					of which: / dont:			
			All food items Produits alimen-taires	Agricul-tural raw materials Matières premières d'origine agricole	Fuels Combus-tibles	Ores and metals Minéraux et métaux	Manu-factured goods Produits manu-facturés	Chemical products Produits chimi-ques	Other manu-factured goods Articles manu-facturés divers	Machinery and transport equipment Machines et matériel de transport	Un-allo-cated Non distri-bué
SITC / CTCI			0+1+22+4	2 less (22+27+28)	3	27+28+68	5 to 8 less 68	5	(6+8) less 68	7	
Germany - Allemagne	1995	523697	5.1	1.0	1.0	2.6	84.4	13.0	24.5	46.9	5.7
	2000	549637	4.2	0.9	1.5	2.5	83.9	12.4	21.7	49.8	7.1
	2003	748531	4.3	0.8	1.6	2.1	84.4	12.6	21.5	50.2	6.8
Germany (former Dem. Rep. of) - Allemagne (anc. Rép. Dém. d')	1990	23600	3.6	1.2	2.2	1.6	90.0	10.4	26.4	53.2	1.3
Germany (former Federal Rep. of) - Allemagne (anc. Rép. fédérale d')	1990	398381	4.8	1.1	1.4	2.5	88.9	12.4	27.2	49.3	1.3
Ghana	2000	1671	30.7	6.5	4.9	11.9	9.3	0.6	7.5	1.2	36.7
Greece - Grèce	1990	8060	29.5	2.6	7.3	7.7	52.8	4.1	44.5	4.2	0.1
	1995	10955	29.5	4.4	6.5	7.9	49.3	4.8	36.6	8.0	2.3
	2000	10964	21.8	3.3	14.7	7.7	49.4	7.9	29.6	11.9	3.1
	2002	10766	24.0	2.7	8.5	8.6	54.8	9.7	32.0	13.2	1.5
Greenland - Groenland	1990	391	96.1	0.1	0.9	0.0	1.5	0.0	1.0	0.5	1.4
	1995	364	95.1	0.6	0.8	0.0	1.5	0.0	1.2	0.3	2.0
	2000	263	95.4	0.4	0.0	0.0	1.6	0.0	0.6	1.0	2.5
	2002	263	90.0	0.5	0.0	0.0	5.1	0.0	1.1	4.0	4.4
Grenada - Grenade	1990	26	66.1	0.3	0.0	0.0	33.5	3.6	24.4	5.5	0.0
	1995	22	79.5	0.1	0.0	0.2	20.3	2.6	13.8	3.8	0.0
	2000	76	33.1	0.0	0.0	0.1	66.8	1.4	6.9	58.6	0.0
	2003	38	54.0	0.0	0.1	0.1	45.7	2.5	14.0	29.3	0.0
Guadeloupe [1]	1990	122	77.2	0.3	0.0	0.9	21.5	3.5	5.5	12.6	0.0
	1995	162	52.2	0.1	0.0	0.7	47.0	1.2	9.3	36.5	0.1
Guatemala	1990	1163	66.9	6.2	2.1	0.3	24.5	9.6	13.8	1.1	0.0
	1995	1936	65.2	4.1	2.1	0.5	28.2	10.8	15.5	1.8	0.0
	2000	2699	56.2	3.8	6.0	1.9	32.0	11.6	18.1	2.4	0.0
	2003	2635	47.0	4.0	8.2	0.4	40.3	16.5	19.8	4.0	0.0
Guinea - Guinée	1995	702	7.4	1.1	0.5	63.7	24.9	18.2	4.6	2.1	2.3
	2000	522	2.5	2.4	0.0	51.7	24.7	10.9	12.9	0.9	18.7
	2002	525	1.5	0.6	0.1	53.9	19.0	17.1	1.8	0.1	24.9
Guinea-Bissau - Guinée-Bissau	1995	14	89.1	10.7	0.0	0.0	0.2	0.0	0.0	0.1	0.0
Guyana	2000	520	43.3	2.9	0.0	15.2	11.9	0.7	9.4	1.8	26.6
	2003	472	50.1	3.2	0.0	5.2	21.2	1.5	16.1	3.6	20.2
Haiti - Haïti	1990	171	13.9	0.5	0.0	0.1	85.3	0.4	72.6	12.3	0.1
	1995	35	37.5	0.3	0.0	0.0	62.2	7.1	53.6	1.4	0.0
Honduras	1990	555	81.6	3.9	0.8	4.2	9.3	1.5	7.6	0.2	0.2
	1995	656	86.9	3.3	0.0	0.5	9.1	1.7	6.7	0.7	0.2
	2000	1076	67.8	4.9	2.3	5.8	19.2	6.5	12.1	0.6	0.1
	2002	1627	49.5	13.6	0.2	4.2	32.6	5.0	26.7	0.8	0.0
Hungary - Hongrie	1990	9588	22.8	2.8	3.1	5.9	62.8	12.4	24.7	25.6	2.6
	1995	12452	21.4	2.3	3.1	5.0	68.1	11.5	30.5	26.1	0.1
	2000	28092	7.3	1.0	1.6	2.2	86.1	6.1	20.4	59.6	1.7
	2003	42309	7.2	0.8	1.6	1.9	88.5	6.7	19.8	62.0	0.0
Iceland - Islande	1990	1586	79.8	0.5	0.0	11.1	8.0	0.1	5.9	2.1	0.6
	1995	1803	75.5	0.5	0.0	12.0	11.6	0.7	5.8	5.1	0.3
	2000	1901	65.2	0.9	0.4	19.3	13.3	1.4	6.4	5.5	0.9
	2003	2381	64.1	1.0	0.2	19.3	14.5	3.6	7.0	4.0	0.8
India - Inde	1990	17940	15.5	4.0	2.9	5.7	69.8	7.4	55.0	7.4	2.0
	1995	31699	18.7	1.3	1.7	3.6	73.2	8.1	57.6	7.5	1.6
	2000	45250	12.9	1.2	4.3	2.9	76.4	10.4	58.1	7.9	2.2
	2002	52471	12.3	1.1	5.2	4.3	74.8	11.2	55.2	8.4	2.4

For sources and notes, see end of table 4.1B.

Pour les sources et les notes, se reporter à la fin du tableau 4.1B.

Country or area / Pays ou zones	Year / Année	Total value (millions of dollars) / Valeur totale (millions de dollars)	By main categories of exports (percentage) / Par principales catégories de produits exportés (en pourcentage)					of which: / dont:			Un-allo-cated / Non distri-bué
			All food items / Produits alimen-taires	Agricul-tural raw materials / Matières premières d'origine agricole	Fuels / Combus-tibles	Ores and metals / Minéraux et métaux	Manu-factured goods / Produits manu-facturés	Chemical products / Produits chimi-ques	Other manu-factured goods / Articles manu-facturés divers	Machinery and transport equipment / Machines et matériel de transport	
SITC / CTCI			0+1+22+4	2 less (22+27+28)	3	27+28+68	5 to 8 less 68	5	(6+8) less 68	7	
Indonesia - Indonésie	1990	25675	11.1	5.1	43.8	4.4	35.2	2.4	31.4	1.4	0.5
	1995	45418	11.4	6.7	25.3	6.0	50.5	3.3	38.8	8.4	0.1
	2000	62124	8.9	3.6	25.2	4.9	56.7	5.0	34.4	17.3	0.6
	2003	61058	11.3	5.0	25.7	5.7	51.8	5.5	30.3	16.0	0.5
Iran, Islamic Rep. of - Iran, Rép. islamique d'	2000	27771	2.9	0.4	88.6	0.8	7.1	1.2	5.5	0.5	0.1
	2003	33788	4.2	0.4	85.6	1.1	8.7	2.2	5.5	1.0	0.0
Ireland - Irlande	1990	23799	22.3	1.7	0.7	2.0	69.0	15.5	22.3	31.3	4.3
	1995	43789	19.4	1.1	0.4	1.1	71.1	18.4	18.1	34.5	6.9
	2000	76288	8.3	0.5	0.3	0.8	85.9	32.8	12.9	40.2	4.3
	2002	88483	7.2	0.4	0.4	0.5	87.7	41.8	10.7	35.1	3.7
Israel - Israël	1990	12052	8.5	2.5	0.7	1.6	86.6	13.7	48.6	24.3	0.2
	1995	19047	5.3	1.7	0.0	1.4	89.1	13.9	48.5	26.7	2.4
	2000	31407	2.6	1.1	0.7	1.2	94.2	12.2	46.5	35.5	0.2
	2003	31783	4.5	1.0	0.4	1.3	92.6	14.0	52.2	26.4	0.2
Italy - Italie	1990	168554	6.3	0.7	2.3	1.4	88.0	6.2	44.3	37.5	1.3
	1995	230441	6.6	0.7	1.3	1.4	89.2	7.8	43.8	37.6	0.9
	2000	240516	6.1	0.7	2.0	1.4	88.5	9.2	41.0	38.3	1.4
	2003	292347	6.8	0.6	2.2	1.3	86.6	10.1	39.2	37.2	2.4
Jamaica - Jamaïque	1990	1143	18.9	0.4	1.4	64.2	15.2	2.1	10.4	2.7	0.0
	1995	1424	21.7	0.3	0.5	. 49.4	28.1	2.6	22.4	3.1	0.0
	2000	1308	22.0	0.2	0.3	56.9	20.6	5.4	13.2	2.1	0.0
	2002	1104	22.7	0.2	2.6	64.7	9.9	5.4	3.5	1.0	0.0
Japan - Japon	1990	286947	0.6	0.6	0.5	0.9	95.9	5.4	19.6	70.9	1.6
	1995	442937	0.5	0.6	0.6	1.0	95.1	6.7	18.2	70.3	2.1
	2000	479248	0.5	0.5	0.4	1.2	93.8	7.2	18.0	68.7	3.7
	2003	471996	0.5	0.5	0.4	1.3	92.9	8.0	18.0	66.9	4.3
Jordan - Jordanie	1990	1063	9.9	0.5	0.0	33.2	55.8	27.2	16.8	11.8	0.6
	1995	1769	22.3	1.8	0.0	19.8	54.9	26.6	15.4	13.0	1.2
	2000	1293	14.0	0.6	0.0	11.1	73.8	21.4	33.2	19.1	0.5
	2003	3082	14.1	0.3	0.2	12.6	65.9	19.6	35.6	10.7	6.9
Kazakhstan	2000	8789	6.8	1.4	52.0	19.9	17.9	2.5	13.2	2.1	2.0
	2003	12927	6.0	1.3	61.2	14.1	16.4	2.0	12.6	1.8	1.1
Kenya	1990	1028	48.8	5.5	13.1	2.9	29.7	4.2	14.9	10.6	0.0
	1995	1826	56.1	7.3	6.1	2.8	27.6	6.5	19.5	1.6	0.1
	2000	1571	59.0	8.6	8.1	3.2	20.7	5.5	14.6	0.5	0.5
	2003	2551	42.4	10.8	19.2	3.0	24.0	4.8	16.1	3.1	0.6
Kiribati	1990	3	54.9	19.7	0.0	1.2	0.8	0.0	0.8	0.0	23.5
	1995	7	85.1	1.7	0.0	0.1	1.1	0.0	1.0	0.0	12.0
Korea, Republic of - Corée, République de	1990	65016	3.3	1.3	1.1	0.8	93.2	3.8	50.1	39.3	0.3
	1995	125056	2.3	1.3	2.0	1.0	91.5	7.1	31.9	52.5	2.0
	2000	172267	1.5	0.9	5.5	1.2	89.9	7.9	23.9	58.1	0.9
	2002	162466	1.6	0.9	4.1	1.3	91.6	8.4	22.0	61.3	0.6
Kuwait - Koweït	1990	6935	0.7	0.1	92.3	0.2	6.4	1.8	2.3	2.3	0.4
	1995	12944	0.3	0.0	94.7	0.3	4.7	2.0	1.3	1.4	0.0
	2000	19401	0.3	0.1	93.5	0.2	5.9	4.3	0.8	0.8	0.0
	2001	16164	0.4	0.1	92.4	0.2	6.8	5.0	1.0	0.8	0.2
Kyrgyzstan - Kirghizistan	1995	412	22.8	12.7	11.1	11.7	41.1	11.8	20.0	9.3	0.8
	2003	582	8.8	9.6	11.6	3.1	21.6	1.3	13.0	7.3	45.3
Latvia - Lettonie	1995	1305	14.4	22.9	1.8	0.9	58.3	6.9	36.4	15.0	1.8
	2000	1869	5.7	30.0	2.5	6.0	55.5	6.4	42.5	6.6	0.3
	2003	2894	8.8	27.1	1.4	4.0	58.5	6.1	43.6	8.8	0.3

For sources and notes, see end of table 4.1B.

Pour les sources et les notes, se reporter à la fin du tableau 4.1B.

Country or area Pays ou zones	Year Année	Total value (millions of dollars) Valeur totale (millions de dollars)	By main categories of exports (percentage) Par principales catégories de produits exportés (en pourcentage)								
			All food items Produits alimentaires	Agricultural raw materials Matières premières d'origine agricole	Fuels Combustibles	Ores and metals Minéraux et métaux	Manufactured goods Produits manufacturés	of which: / dont:			Unallocated Non distribué
								Chemical products Produits chimiques	Other manufactured goods Articles manufacturés divers	Machinery and transport equipment Machines et matériel de transport	
SITC / CTCI			0+1+22+4	2 less (22+27+28)	3	27+28+68	5 to 8 less 68	5	(6+8) less 68	7	
Lebanon - Liban	2000	714	18.4	1.8	0.2	6.9	66.0	13.2	40.5	12.2	6.8
	2003	1524	14.9	1.4	0.2	7.4	52.2	8.5	30.9	12.8	23.8
Lesotho	2000	336	4.7	0.1	0.0	0.0	94.9	0.3	86.9	7.7	0.3
	2002	358	7.1	5.1	0.0	0.1	87.4	0.6	81.7	5.1	0.3
Libyan Arab Jamahiriya - Jamahiriya arabe libyenne	1990	13877	0.4	0.2	94.4	0.3	4.7	3.8	0.9	0.0	0.0
Lithuania - Lituanie	1995	2706	18.1	7.8	11.4	5.0	57.7	14.2	27.8	15.7	0.0
	2000	3809	11.6	5.2	20.9	2.1	60.0	9.5	33.3	17.3	0.2
	2003	7162	11.5	4.3	19.4	1.5	62.9	7.5	29.0	26.4	0.2
Luxembourg	2000	7466	7.0	0.6	0.1	5.3	85.4	6.3	50.9	28.1	1.6
	2002	8591	7.1	0.7	0.6	4.7	85.0	6.2	51.1	27.7	1.8
Macedonia, TFYR - Macédoine, LERY	1995	1204	18.3	5.2	0.4	17.7	58.2	5.5	39.8	12.9	0.1
	2000	1323	15.0	1.7	4.8	8.8	69.4	4.5	58.7	6.3	0.3
	2003	1363	16.8	1.2	5.4	4.7	71.7	5.1	60.8	5.9	0.2
Madagascar	1990	292	72.8	3.7	0.5	7.7	14.4	1.5	11.1	1.8	0.9
	1995	360	67.3	5.8	4.0	6.8	14.1	2.1	11.1	0.9	2.0
	2000	378	64.2	5.0	7.1	3.8	18.8	1.8	15.9	1.2	1.0
	2001	486	71.5	5.8	2.6	2.1	16.2	1.9	13.2	1.1	1.9
Malawi	1990	412	90.8	1.9	0.0	0.0	7.1	0.4	3.8	2.8	0.2
	1995	433	88.0	2.1	0.1	0.1	9.7	0.4	7.3	2.0	0.0
	2000	369	89.4	3.0	0.2	0.2	7.1	0.7	5.5	1.0	0.0
	2002	377	85.1	2.7	0.0	0.3	11.8	0.9	10.9	0.1	0.0
Malaysia - Malaisie	1990	29453	11.7	13.7	18.3	2.1	53.9	1.6	16.5	35.7	0.4
	1995	73778	9.5	6.1	7.0	1.3	74.7	3.0	16.6	55.1	1.3
	2000	98230	5.5	2.6	9.6	1.0	80.4	3.8	14.0	62.5	0.8
	2003	104969	8.6	2.4	10.1	0.9	76.7	5.1	14.8	56.8	1.4
Maldives	1995	50	73.8	0.7	0.0	0.2	25.3	0.0	25.3	0.0	0.0
	2000	76	53.7	0.0	0.0	0.1	46.2	0.0	46.1	0.0	0.0
	2003	113	67.7	0.0	0.0	0.3	32.0	0.0	32.0	0.0	0.0
Mali	1990	330	36.1	62.3	0.0	0.0	1.6	0.0	0.6	0.9	0.1
	2000	473	1.7	34.4	1.0	0.2	4.8	0.5	1.5	2.8	57.8
	2001	519	1.6	3.7	1.9	0.1	9.2	0.6	1.9	6.7	83.5
Malta - Malte	1990	1126	3.3	0.1	2.1	1.4	92.5	1.6	39.3	51.6	0.6
	1995	1913	2.1	0.1	1.6	0.5	95.6	2.1	27.1	66.3	0.1
	2000	2438	2.6	0.1	4.4	0.3	92.5	1.6	20.0	70.9	0.1
	2001	1959	3.9	0.1	5.5	0.3	90.1	2.3	24.7	63.2	0.1
Martinique [1]	1990	276	60.6	0.6	15.9	0.4	22.5	3.3	7.9	11.4	0.0
	1995	242	62.0	0.3	17.8	1.0	18.8	2.1	3.7	13.0	0.0
	1995	509	52.9	0.1	3.9	38.4	1.9	0.0	0.5	1.3	2.9
Mauritius - Maurice	1990	1221	31.9	0.5	1.4	0.2	65.8	0.9	63.5	1.4	0.2
	1995	1538	28.6	0.7	0.0	0.2	70.2	0.8	67.1	2.3	0.4
	2000	1490	17.8	0.5	0.0	0.2	80.8	0.9	78.6	1.3	0.7
	2003	1839	24.8	0.4	0.1	0.3	73.6	1.7	67.5	4.3	0.8
Mexico - Mexique	1990	26345	11.6	1.6	37.5	5.7	43.3	6.7	11.0	25.6	0.4
	1995	79541	7.7	1.3	10.3	2.9	77.5	5.0	20.1	52.5	0.3
	2000	166192	4.9	0.6	9.7	1.3	83.4	3.2	21.2	59.1	0.1
	2003	165395	5.5	0.5	11.2	1.2	81.4	3.5	21.0	56.9	0.1
Moldova, Republic of - Moldova, République de	1995	746	71.7	1.8	0.9	3.0	22.7	1.4	13.5	7.9	0.0
	2000	472	59.8	3.1	0.1	1.8	34.9	1.8	26.8	6.2	0.4
	2003	790	58.3	5.0	0.6	2.8	33.3	1.2	26.8	5.2	0.2

For sources and notes, see end of table 4.1B.

Pour les sources et les notes, se reporter à la fin du tableau 4.1B.

Country or area / Pays ou zones	Year / Année	Total value (millions of dollars) / Valeur totale (millions de dollars)	By main categories of exports (percentage) / Par principales catégories de produits exportés (en pourcentage)					of which: / dont:			
			All food items / Produits alimentaires	Agricultural raw materials / Matières premières d'origine agricole	Fuels / Combustibles	Ores and metals / Minéraux et métaux	Manufactured goods / Produits manufacturés	Chemical products / Produits chimiques	Other manufactured goods / Articles manufacturés divers	Machinery and transport equipment / Machines et matériel de transport	Unallocated / Non distribué
SITC / CTCI			0+1+22+4	2 less (22+27+28)	3	27+28+68	5 to 8 less 68	5	(6+8) less 68	7	
Mongolia - Mongolie	2000	466	3.8	27.9	0.5	40.9	25.6	0.3	24.9	0.4	1.4
	2003	616	2.4	9.8	2.3	33.3	29.3	0.1	28.3	0.9	23.0
Montserrat	2000	1	0.6	0.0	0.0	0.0	99.3	0.3	48.9	50.1	0.1
	2003	2	0.1	0.2	40.6	0.0	51.4	0.0	24.1	27.3	7.6
Morocco - Maroc	1990	4231	26.1	2.9	3.6	15.1	52.3	19.4	27.8	5.0	0.0
	1995	4719	31.4	3.4	2.2	11.5	51.4	20.8	27.4	3.2	0.0
	2000	7432	21.5	2.0	3.7	8.7	64.1	12.0	41.0	11.0	0.0
	2002	7850	21.4	1.6	3.7	8.2	64.8	11.2	41.0	12.6	0.4
Namibia - Namibie	2000	1327	28.5	1.0	2.1	10.9	54.7	0.7	50.9	3.1	2.9
	2001	1404	35.7	0.9	0.7	9.2	50.8	0.5	46.4	3.9	2.7
Nepal - Népal	1990	180	13.2	3.0	0.0	0.3	83.3	0.5	82.8	0.0	0.3
	1995	359	7.8	1.1	0.0	0.1	83.7	1.2	82.4	0.1	7.2
	2000	709	9.9	0.5	0.0	0.2	66.7	8.5	57.7	0.5	22.7
Netherlands - Pays-Bas	1990	131507	19.9	4.2	9.8	2.8	59.1	15.0	20.8	23.4	4.1
	1995	177626	19.8	3.9	7.2	2.7	62.3	16.2	19.6	26.6	4.0
	2000	180072	15.0	3.2	10.0	2.2	69.3	13.7	19.1	36.6	0.2
	2002	175385	17.6	3.6	7.1	2.2	69.2	17.4	19.6	32.2	0.3
New Caledonia - Nouvelle-Calédonie	2000	635	4.0	0.1	0.9	34.4	60.6	0.2	58.9	1.5	0.1
	2003	740	3.9	0.1	1.2	24.7	69.3	0.2	66.9	2.2	0.9
New Zealand - Nouvelle-Zélande	1990	9470	44.9	17.9	3.8	5.4	25.2	5.2	13.0	7.1	2.7
	1995	13745	42.4	18.0	1.6	4.8	30.6	7.6	14.4	8.6	2.6
	2000	13272	43.9	13.7	2.6	4.7	30.0	6.8	12.8	10.4	5.1
	2003	16231	47.2	11.9	1.4	3.6	31.5	6.2	14.2	11.1	4.4
Nicaragua	1990	340	73.6	13.1	0.3	0.7	7.9	3.4	4.4	0.1	4.4
	1995	509	73.3	2.9	0.6	0.8	20.3	1.2	13.0	6.1	2.0
	2000	629	84.8	2.0	1.7	0.4	7.3	1.9	4.8	0.7	3.7
	2003	585	78.2	1.8	1.3	0.7	11.9	3.6	7.3	1.1	6.1
Niger	1995	273	26.3	2.4	0.6	55.4	14.4	0.6	7.9	5.9	0.8
	2000	330	37.7	2.8	1.1	27.7	29.7	1.1	15.9	12.8	1.0
	2003	206	30.4	3.6	1.6	55.0	7.9	0.4	6.2	1.2	1.5
Nigeria - Nigéria	2000	27055	0.1	0.0	99.6	0.0	0.2	0.0	0.1	0.1	0.0
Norway - Norvège	1990	33948	7.0	2.1	48.0	10.2	32.5	6.3	12.2	14.0	0.3
	1995	41740	8.3	1.5	47.3	8.7	26.7	3.1	10.3	13.3	7.4
	2000	59899	6.4	0.7	63.9	6.1	18.4	2.6	6.7	9.2	4.5
	2003	67122	5.9	0.7	61.2	6.6	21.0	3.1	6.6	11.3	4.6
Oman	1990	5504	1.5	0.0	91.9	1.0	5.2	0.3	1.4	3.5	0.5
	1995	5917	4.8	0.0	78.6	1.8	13.9	0.4	3.9	9.6	0.9
	2000	10852	3.6	0.0	82.5	0.9	12.4	0.8	3.3	8.3	0.7
	2003	10115	5.5	0.0	77.1	0.8	15.5	1.2	5.1	9.2	1.1
Pakistan	1990	5573	9.2	10.1	1.3	0.3	78.8	0.4	77.4	1.0	0.2
	1995	8158	11.7	3.8	1.0	0.2	83.0	0.7	81.8	0.5	0.3
	2000	9201	10.5	2.9	1.4	0.2	84.8	1.6	82.2	1.0	0.2
	2003	11930	10.7	1.6	2.3	0.2	85.0	2.4	81.4	1.3	0.2
Panama	1990	341	74.6	1.3	0.1	1.3	20.4	4.7	12.8	2.9	2.3
	1995	577	74.3	0.5	3.2	1.1	20.2	5.1	14.9	0.2	0.8
	2000	772	73.7	1.5	6.8	2.1	15.9	5.0	10.8	0.1	0.0
	2003	799	85.0	0.9	0.7	2.0	11.1	2.9	8.2	0.1	0.3
Papua New Guinea - Papouasie-Nouvelle-Guinée	1990	1262	17.7	7.8	0.1	47.4	7.3	0.1	1.5	5.7	19.7
	2000	2407	15.3	2.3	28.8	51.3	2.2	0.0	0.2	2.0	0.1
	2003	2052	21.2	2.9	22.4	40.8	5.5	0.1	2.1	3.3	7.2

For sources and notes, see end of table 4.1B.

Pour les sources et les notes, se reporter à la fin du tableau 4.1B.

Country or area / Pays ou zones	Year / Année	Total value (millions of dollars) / Valeur totale (millions de dollars)	All food items / Produits alimentaires	Agricultural raw materials / Matières premières d'origine agricole	Fuels / Combustibles	Ores and metals / Minéraux et métaux	Manufactured goods / Produits manufacturés	Chemical products / Produits chimiques	Other manufactured goods / Articles manufacturés divers	Machinery and transport equipment / Machines et matériel de transport	Un-allocated / Non distribué
SITC / CTCI			0+1+22+4	2 less (22+27+28)	3	27+28+68	5 to 8 less 68	5	(6+8) less 68	7	
Paraguay	1990	959	52.4	37.6	0.0	0.1	9.9	3.2	6.6	0.1	0.0
	1995	919	43.9	36.4	0.2	0.3	19.3	2.6	15.9	0.8	0.0
	2000	871	64.8	15.5	0.1	0.4	19.3	2.6	16.2	0.5	0.0
	2003	1242	76.9	8.9	0.0	0.4	13.7	3.2	10.0	0.5	0.0
Peru - Pérou	1990	3313	21.2	3.3	10.0	47.0	18.4	2.1	15.3	1.0	0.0
	1995	5440	28.8	2.5	4.9	41.7	13.6	2.2	10.8	0.6	8.5
	2000	6866	25.3	2.5	5.9	32.7	16.9	2.4	13.5	1.1	16.7
	2003	8749	20.7	2.1	7.6	29.4	17.0	2.7	13.5	0.9	23.1
Philippines	1990	8186	18.7	1.8	2.2	8.1	37.8	3.2	22.1	12.5	31.3
	1995	17447	12.8	1.2	1.5	4.3	40.8	1.9	16.8	22.2	39.3
	2000	38078	4.8	0.6	1.3	1.6	91.3	0.9	14.3	76.1	0.4
	2002	35208	5.2	0.5	1.2	1.4	91.4	1.0	14.3	76.1	0.3
Poland - Pologne	1990	12600	12.0	2.8	11.5	10.0	58.2	8.8	24.8	24.6	5.5
	1995	22862	10.4	2.8	8.2	7.3	71.0	7.7	42.2	21.0	0.4
	2000	31613	7.9	1.8	5.1	4.9	80.2	6.7	39.3	34.1	0.1
	2003	53539	7.8	1.5	4.3	3.7	81.1	6.3	37.5	37.3	1.6
Portugal	1990	16426	7.1	6.3	3.6	2.9	79.7	5.2	55.3	19.3	0.3
	1995	23370	7.2	4.6	3.2	1.8	82.9	4.8	51.6	26.5	0.2
	2000	24365	6.8	3.5	2.6	1.9	85.0	5.6	45.3	34.1	0.3
	2002	26485	7.5	2.4	1.9	1.6	86.3	5.6	45.1	35.5	0.3
Qatar	1990	3641	0.1	0.0	81.5	0.2	18.1	10.0	6.1	2.0	0.1
	1995	3557	0.4	0.0	80.2	0.2	19.1	11.2	6.6	1.3	0.0
	2000	8847	0.1	0.0	89.5	0.1	10.2	5.3	3.7	1.2	0.0
	2002	8231	0.1	0.0	87.1	0.1	12.6	6.1	4.7	1.8	0.1
Reunion - Réunion [1]	1990	186	82.4	0.5	0.2	0.4	16.6	2.5	5.6	8.5	0.0
	1995	209	78.1	0.5	0.2	0.5	20.7	1.7	6.3	12.7	0.0
Romania - Roumanie	1990	5847	1.1	2.4	17.8	4.1	72.9	6.5	36.4	29.9	1.7
	1995	7910	6.5	3.3	7.9	3.5	77.5	10.7	53.5	13.3	1.3
	2000	10367	3.1	4.9	7.2	7.5	76.7	5.8	51.7	19.2	0.7
	2003	17618	3.2	3.1	6.5	4.3	82.3	4.8	55.8	21.8	0.6
Russian Federation - Fédération de Russie	2000	103008	1.2	3.1	51.3	9.1	22.2	4.8	11.5	5.9	13.0
	2003	133717	2.0	3.2	53.0	6.8	21.2	4.4	9.9	7.0	13.8
Rwanda	2003	51	52.3	7.3	6.8	23.3	10.3	0.5	3.2	6.7	0.0
Saint Kitts and Nevis - Saint-Kitts-et-Nevis	1995	19	54.2	0.3	0.2	0.1	45.1	0.7	7.7	36.6	0.1
	2000	33	24.4	0.0	0.0	0.0	75.4	0.2	8.9	66.3	0.1
	2001	31	24.9	0.0	0.1	0.0	74.8	0.2	9.3	65.4	0.1
Saint Lucia - Sainte-Lucie	1990	127	67.7	0.5	0.0	0.0	31.8	0.4	23.4	8.0	0.0
	1995	109	58.5	0.4	0.0	0.0	40.9	0.8	29.0	11.1	0.1
	2000	43	72.3	0.4	0.0	0.0	26.8	1.3	14.2	11.4	0.5
	2003	62	46.5	0.2	9.6	0.6	41.8	1.5	18.2	22.1	1.3
Saint Vincent and the Grenadines - Saint-Vincent-et-les Grenadines	1995	59	81.0	0.2	0.0	0.1	18.8	0.9	13.8	4.0	0.0
	2000	51	74.6	0.2	0.0	0.1	25.2	1.9	9.6	13.7	0.0
	2003	38	73.3	0.1	0.1	0.0	26.4	0.5	12.3	13.6	0.0
	1990	9	89.0	0.1	0.9	0.0	10.0	0.1	8.7	1.2	0.0
	2002	71	25.3	0.5	0.7	0.0	73.4	0.2	7.0	66.2	0.0
Sao Tome and Principe - Sao Tomé-et-Principe	2000	3	96.9	0.1	0.0	0.0	3.0	0.4	0.8	1.7	0.0
	2003	7	94.8	0.1	0.0	0.0	5.0	0.0	0.7	4.3	0.0
Saudi Arabia - Arabie saoudite	1990	44416	0.8	0.1	90.3	0.5	8.2	5.7	1.5	1.1	0.0
	1995	49030	0.9	0.1	86.8	0.6	11.6	8.4	2.2	1.0	0.0
	2000	77711	0.6	0.1	91.5	0.1	7.7	5.4	1.5	0.8	0.0
	2002	61932	0.9	0.2	86.0	0.3	12.6	8.2	2.7	1.6	0.1

For sources and notes, see end of table 4.1B.

Pour les sources et les notes, se reporter à la fin du tableau 4.1B.

Country or area / Pays ou zones	Year / Année	Total value (millions of dollars) / Valeur totale (millions de dollars)	By main categories of exports (percentage) / Par principales catégories de produits exportés (en pourcentage)					of which: / dont:			Un-allocated / Non distribué
			All food items / Produits alimentaires	Agricultural raw materials / Matières premières d'origine agricole	Fuels / Combustibles	Ores and metals / Minéraux et métaux	Manufactured goods / Produits manufacturés	Chemical products / Produits chimiques	Other manufactured goods / Articles manufacturés divers	Machinery and transport equipment / Machines et matériel de transport	
SITC / CTCI			0+1+22+4	2 less (22+27+28)	3	27+28+68	5 to 8 less 68	5	(6+8) less 68	7	
Senegal - Sénégal	1990	783	53.2	2.7	12.4	9.3	22.5	14.9	5.2	2.4	0.0
	1995	531	15.4	8.5	15.1	10.6	49.4	39.5	7.4	2.5	1.0
	2000	693	52.4	1.7	14.0	4.8	26.9	17.3	6.1	3.5	0.1
	2002	696	16.8	3.3	22.7	5.8	51.3	38.4	9.4	3.5	0.1
Serbia and Montenegro - Serbie-et-Monténégro	2000	1711	17.0	5.7	0.3	15.6	61.4	8.4	40.5	12.5	0.0
	2002	2275	23.1	4.0	3.4	12.1	57.3	7.3	38.8	11.1	0.0
Seychelles	1990	57	24.5	0.0	49.4	0.1	26.0	0.1	1.1	24.8	0.0
	1995	53	45.9	0.0	46.7	0.1	7.3	0.5	3.9	3.0	0.0
	2002	38	51.7	0.0	40.0	0.1	8.2	0.1	2.6	5.5	0.1
Sierra Leone	2002	41	91.6	0.8	0.0	0.1	7.5	0.9	4.3	2.3	0.0
Singapore - Singapour	1990	52716	5.2	2.6	18.2	1.5	71.1	6.2	14.7	50.1	1.4
	1995	118263	3.9	1.1	6.9	2.0	83.7	5.9	12.2	65.6	2.4
	2000	137806	2.2	0.5	9.7	1.1	85.4	6.9	11.1	67.4	1.1
	2003	143561	1.9	0.3	8.5	1.1	84.2	11.7	11.4	61.1	4.0
Slovakia - Slovaquie	1995	8374	6.2	3.6	4.3	3.6	81.6	12.5	50.1	18.9	0.8
	2000	11885	3.2	2.2	7.0	3.4	83.6	7.9	36.2	39.5	0.6
	2003	21547	3.1	1.6	5.2	2.4	87.6	5.2	35.1	47.4	0.2
Slovenia - Slovénie	1995	8316	3.9	1.8	1.2	3.4	89.5	10.4	47.7	31.4	0.2
	2000	8732	3.7	1.6	0.7	4.2	89.7	10.9	42.9	35.9	0.2
	2003	12767	3.5	1.2	1.4	3.8	89.9	13.5	39.9	36.5	0.2
South Africa - Afrique du Sud	2000	26075	8.5	3.8	10.2	10.7	53.9	7.8	28.6	17.5	12.8
	2003	30897	9.9	3.3	9.8	19.0	57.3	7.5	29.1	20.7	0.7
South Africa (Customs Union) - Afrique du Sud (Union douanière)	1995	28226	7.9	4.1	8.9	8.0	43.1	7.0	27.4	8.8	28.0
Spain - Espagne	1990	55632	14.7	2.1	4.8	2.5	74.4	7.8	27.8	38.8	1.5
	1995	89616	15.4	1.6	1.8	2.4	77.9	8.4	27.1	42.4	1.0
	2000	113343	13.5	1.3	3.7	2.3	77.5	9.3	25.8	42.4	1.7
	2002	125872	15.0	1.2	2.7	2.0	77.5	10.8	26.5	40.2	1.6
Sri Lanka	1990	1913	33.9	5.7	1.5	1.6	53.2	1.0	49.3	2.8	4.2
	2002	4723	20.8	1.7	0.3	1.9	74.1	0.7	68.4	5.0	1.3
Sudan - Soudan	1995	685	43.3	46.1	0.3	0.4	6.2	0.0	6.1	0.0	3.8
	2000	1631	16.6	4.7	66.7	0.5	7.6	0.1	2.1	5.4	3.9
	2002	1617	17.4	5.3	69.2	0.3	3.2	0.2	1.4	1.6	4.6
Suriname	1990	475	15.9	0.0	1.5	81.8	0.7	0.0	0.4	0.3	0.1
	1995	483	17.9	0.3	2.2	74.0	2.0	0.0	0.9	1.1	3.6
	2000	514	14.1	0.7	6.7	62.1	4.5	0.9	1.0	2.6	11.9
Swaziland	2000	891	33.6	10.7	0.7	0.4	54.3	20.1	24.5	9.7	0.2
	2002	974	14.6	7.9	0.7	0.2	76.4	47.8	25.0	3.6	0.2
Sweden - Suède	1990	57292	2.2	7.3	3.1	3.4	82.6	7.3	31.9	43.4	1.6
	1995	77436	2.2	6.5	1.9	2.9	78.6	6.5	30.0	42.1	7.9
	2000	77262	2.5	1.0	3.1	2.7	84.9	9.9	28.5	46.5	5.8
	2003	101572	3.3	4.5	3.0	2.3	81.2	11.4	27.7	42.1	5.6
Switzerland - Suisse	1990	63794	2.7	0.7	0.1	2.6	93.4	21.3	40.6	31.5	0.3
	1995	81641	3.0	0.7	0.2	2.5	93.2	25.7	36.1	31.4	0.4
	2000	81534	2.5	0.6	0.4	5.6	90.6	27.0	33.0	30.6	0.2
	2003	99390	2.6	0.5	0.4	3.2	93.1	33.9	32.3	26.9	0.3
Syrian Arab Republic - République arabe syrienne	1990	4214	13.7	4.5	45.2	1.0	35.7	12.8	22.7	0.2	0.0
	1995	3970	12.3	7.0	62.5	0.8	17.4	0.6	16.0	0.8	0.0
	2000	4633	8.8	4.6	76.4	0.7	7.8	0.3	7.4	0.1	1.8
	2002	6230	13.0	3.4	72.2	0.8	7.4	0.4	6.6	0.4	3.1

For sources and notes, see end of table 4.1B.

Pour les sources et les notes, se reporter à la fin du tableau 4.1B.

Country or area Pays ou zones	Year Année	Total value (millions of dollars) Valeur totale (millions de dollars)	By main categories of exports (percentage) Par principales catégories de produits exportés (en pourcentage)								
			All food items Produits alimentaires	Agricultural raw materials Matières premières d'origine agricole	Fuels Combustibles	Ores and metals Minéraux et métaux	Manufactured goods Produits manufacturés	of which: / dont:			Unallocated Non distribué
								Chemical products Produits chimiques	Other manufactured goods Articles manufacturés divers	Machinery and transport equipment Machines et matériel de transport	
SITC / CTCI			0+1+22+4	2 less (22+27+28)	3	27+28+68	5 to 8 less 68	5	(6+8) less 68	7	
Thailand - Thaïlande	1990	23069	28.7	5.1	0.8	1.0	63.2	2.0	39.2	22.0	1.2
	1995	56439	19.3	5.3	0.7	0.6	73.1	3.8	35.7	33.6	1.0
	2000	68787	14.4	3.3	3.2	1.3	75.3	5.9	25.7	43.6	2.5
	2003	80331	14.1	4.6	2.7	1.0	74.8	6.5	24.5	43.8	2.8
Togo	1990	268	23.0	21.5	0.0	44.7	9.1	0.4	8.0	0.7	1.8
	1995	383	14.1	24.7	18.7	17.7	15.2	0.9	9.3	4.9	9.6
	2000	192	19.6	23.4	0.6	25.5	30.8	0.6	26.3	3.9	0.0
	2002	251	23.2	16.3	0.5	16.7	43.2	1.3	39.6	2.4	0.0
Trinidad and Tobago - Trinité-et-Tobago	1990	2080	5.5	0.1	67.1	0.5	26.7	14.1	10.6	1.9	0.1
	1995	2467	8.4	0.2	47.9	0.2	43.3	24.9	16.2	2.3	0.0
	2000	4273	5.7	0.1	65.3	0.1	28.8	17.3	10.3	1.2	0.0
	2001	5113	5.1	0.1	51.9	0.2	42.7	16.2	10.5	16.0	0.1
Tunisia - Tunisie	1990	3498	11.0	1.0	17.3	1.6	69.1	14.5	46.8	7.8	0.0
	1995	5475	9.8	0.6	8.5	1.7	79.4	11.9	58.0	9.5	0.0
	2000	5850	8.7	0.7	12.1	1.5	77.0	10.4	53.4	13.2	0.0
	2003	7354	7.6	0.9	8.6	1.5	81.4	9.4	55.8	16.3	0.1
Turkey - Turquie	1990	12959	22.4	3.0	2.3	4.5	67.7	5.7	55.4	6.6	0.1
	1995	21599	19.6	1.5	1.3	3.3	74.3	4.1	59.4	10.8	0.1
	2000	27485	12.8	1.1	1.1	3.0	82.0	4.4	57.1	20.5	0.0
	2003	47253	10.0	1.1	2.1	2.2	84.3	3.8	54.0	26.5	0.3
Turkmenistan - Turkménistan	2000	2506	0.3	9.9	81.0	0.4	6.9	0.4	5.8	0.6	1.5
Uganda - Ouganda	1995	575	86.0	4.4	0.1	0.6	4.2	1.0	2.0	1.2	4.7
	2000	402	60.1	12.5	7.1	4.1	5.3	1.1	1.8	2.5	10.8
	2003	165	62.8	22.0	0.1	0.2	8.8	2.0	3.9	3.0	6.0
Ukraine	2000	14573	9.2	1.7	5.6	14.1	67.0	9.0	45.1	12.9	2.4
	2002	17927	13.1	1.8	9.2	8.6	66.2	7.6	44.5	14.1	1.1
United Arab Emirates - Emirats arabes unis	1990	3945	16.7	2.3	1.5	11.8	60.8	4.7	36.0	20.1	6.9
United Kingdom - Royaume-Uni	1990	185500	7.0	1.0	7.6	3.1	79.2	12.5	26.4	40.3	2.1
	1995	234372	7.6	0.7	6.2	2.7	81.5	12.2	25.6	43.7	1.3
	2000	276438	5.5	0.5	8.7	2.4	82.1	12.4	22.1	47.7	1.0
	2003	320057	5.7	0.6	8.1	2.2	83.0	16.2	22.4	44.4	0.5
United Republic of Tanzania - République-Unie de Tanzanie	2000	656	54.7	11.1	0.1	0.4	16.2	0.8	14.4	1.0	17.5
	2003	1222	37.8	7.5	1.3	5.9	11.6	1.2	8.8	1.6	36.0
United States - Etats-Unis	1990	392866	10.8	4.3	3.2	3.0	74.0	9.8	17.7	46.5	4.8
	1995	582965	10.1	3.7	1.8	2.5	77.3	10.4	18.6	48.3	4.6
	2000	780332	7.0	2.2	1.8	1.8	83.1	10.4	20.0	52.8	4.1
	2003	723609	8.1	2.4	2.0	2.0	81.4	12.8	20.0	48.6	4.1
Uruguay	1990	1708	39.2	20.8	0.0	0.4	38.5	7.7	28.8	2.0	1.0
	1995	2106	44.2	5.3	1.1	0.7	48.2	5.6	36.7	6.0	0.5
	2000	2299	46.3	4.5	1.5	0.5	46.3	6.2	31.6	8.5	0.9
	2003	2198	52.5	5.8	1.6	0.5	38.7	5.5	30.5	2.7	0.9
Vanuatu	1990	14	79.1	8.2	0.0	0.1	12.6	1.8	8.3	2.5	0.0
Venezuela	1990	18044	1.9	0.4	80.1	7.4	10.2	1.8	6.7	1.7	0.0
	1995	19087	2.8	0.1	76.3	6.6	13.7	4.1	6.8	2.8	0.5
	2000	30948	1.5	0.2	86.1	3.3	8.8	2.8	4.9	1.1	0.1
	2003	24974	1.1	0.2	82.2	4.1	12.3	3.1	6.5	2.7	0.2

For sources and notes, see end of table 4.1B.

Pour les sources et les notes, se reporter à la fin du tableau 4.1B.

Country or area Pays ou zones	Year Année	Total value (millions of dollars) Valeur totale (millions de dollars)	By main categories of exports (percentage) Par principales catégories de produits exportés (en pourcentage)								
			All food items Produits alimentaires	Agricultural raw materials Matières premières d'origine agricole	Fuels Combustibles	Ores and metals Minéraux et métaux	Manufactured goods Produits manufacturés	of which: / dont:			Un-allocated Non distribué
								Chemical products Produits chimiques	Other manufactured goods Articles manufacturés divers	Machinery and transport equipment Machines et matériel de transport	
SITC / CTCI			0+1+22+4	2 less (22+27+28)	3	27+28+68	5 to 8 less 68	5	(6+8) less 68	7	
Viet Nam	2000	14483	25.3	2.0	26.4	0.4	42.6	0.9	33.0	8.7	3.2
	2002	16706	25.4	2.3	21.2	0.5	49.9	1.5	40.4	7.9	0.7
Yemen - Yémen	1995	1917	2.7	0.6	94.3	0.5	1.9	0.1	0.8	0.9	0.0
	2000	4078	2.1	0.4	96.5	0.1	0.9	0.3	0.3	0.3	0.0
Yugoslavia, SFR (former) - Yougoslavie, RSF (anc.)	1990	14307	7.3	4.3	2.5	8.9	76.7	9.6	37.2	29.9	0.3
Zambia - Zambie	1995	1055	2.7	0.6	3.3	86.5	6.9	0.2	5.2	1.5	0.0
	2000	666	10.2	3.6	1.6	55.5	27.7	0.5	23.7	3.4	1.4
	2002	930	9.2	2.8	2.1	63.6	19.2	1.0	13.3	4.9	3.1
Zimbabwe	1990	1470	44.0	7.3	0.7	15.9	30.8	1.7	25.5	3.7	1.3
	1995	1846	43.2	6.8	1.3	11.6	36.9	2.6	31.6	2.7	0.3
	2000	1925	47.1	12.5	1.1	10.9	28.0	2.8	22.9	2.4	0.3
	2002	2327	25.0	10.6	1.1	19.0	34.8	4.1	25.9	4.8	9.5

For sources and notes, see end of table 4.1B.

Pour les sources et les notes, se reporter à la fin du tableau 4.1B.

Country or area Pays ou zones	Year Année	Total value (millions of dollars) Valeur totale (millions de dollars)	By main categories of imports (percentage) Par principales catégories de produits importés (en pourcentage)								
			All food items Produits alimen-taires	Agricul-tural raw materials Matières premières d'origine agricole	Fuels Combus-tibles	Ores and metals Minéraux et métaux	Manu-factured goods Produits manu-facturés	of which: / dont:			Un-allo-cated Non distri-bué
								Chemical products Produits chimi-ques	Other manu-factured goods Articles manu-facturés divers	Machinery and transport equipment Machines et matériel de transport	
SITC / CTCI			0+1+22+4	2 less (22+27+28)	3	27+28+68	5 to 8 less 68	5	(6+8) less 68	7	
Albania - Albanie	2000	1089	21.8	0.9	9.1	1.5	66.5	6.7	38.0	21.8	0.1
	2003	1864	19.6	1.0	8.6	1.7	69.0	7.2	40.1	21.7	0.0
Algeria - Algérie	1990	9736	23.7	4.7	1.1	2.0	68.4	8.2	21.2	39.0	0.0
	1995	10782	29.5	3.2	1.1	1.6	64.6	11.2	22.4	31.1	0.1
	2000	9152	28.2	2.6	1.4	1.2	66.6	11.5	20.0	35.1	0.0
	2003	13533	22.4	2.4	0.8	1.2	73.2	12.0	22.3	38.8	0.0
Andorra - Andorre	1995	1025	29.7	0.7	3.6	0.7	65.2	9.1	36.0	20.0	0.2
	2000	1011	19.9	0.5	4.4	0.8	74.0	10.2	40.7	23.1	0.4
	2002	1198	19.3	0.4	4.5	0.6	74.8	10.0	39.0	25.8	0.3
Anguilla	2003	77	27.6	1.8	10.4	1.4	58.7	5.4	28.3	25.0	0.1
Argentina - Argentine	1990	4077	4.0	4.0	8.3	7.5	75.9	27.6	16.3	32.0	0.4
	1995	20122	5.5	2.0	4.3	2.7	85.4	17.5	23.4	44.5	0.1
	2000	23851	4.9	1.5	3.7	2.4	87.1	18.1	23.9	45.0	0.5
	2002	8990	4.6	2.4	5.0	4.5	82.8	31.0	20.4	31.4	0.7
Armenia - Arménie	2000	840	25.0	0.9	20.8	0.9	51.0	10.7	25.5	14.7	1.4
	2003	1212	17.5	1.0	14.0	3.1	60.5	7.7	38.6	14.3	3.9
Aruba	1995	571	23.0	3.4	0.0	1.4	72.3	10.3	35.5	26.5	0.0
	2003	793	20.2	2.8	0.1	2.6	73.3	13.0	34.5	25.9	1.1
Australia - Australie	1990	38633	5.0	2.0	5.7	1.4	83.8	10.2	28.6	45.1	2.0
	1995	57423	4.9	1.7	5.1	1.3	85.6	10.9	27.8	47.0	1.4
	2000	71178	4.6	1.4	8.3	1.1	83.0	11.3	25.6	46.1	1.6
	2003	84493	5.0	1.1	7.8	1.2	82.0	11.3	25.2	45.5	2.9
Austria - Autriche	1990	50018	5.2	3.1	6.3	3.8	81.4	9.6	34.0	37.9	0.2
	1995	66406	5.7	3.2	4.5	3.9	81.6	10.4	34.5	36.7	1.2
	2000	64039	5.8	2.8	5.8	2.9	82.4	10.0	31.3	41.0	0.3
	2003	92424	6.0	2.3	8.0	3.1	74.1	10.1	27.9	36.1	6.6
Azerbaijan - Azerbaïdjan	2000	1172	18.6	1.7	4.9	3.6	71.2	7.8	22.3	41.1	0.0
	2003	2626	11.7	1.0	11.3	1.9	74.0	5.3	28.6	40.1	0.1
Bahamas	1995	1243	18.8	1.9	12.6	0.5	64.5	8.1	30.6	25.8	1.7
	2000	2002	16.7	2.7	10.4	0.6	67.8	8.6	32.9	26.2	1.8
	2001	1927	17.5	2.1	15.2	0.6	63.2	7.3	29.7	26.3	1.5
Bahrain - Bahreïn	1995	3679	12.3	1.0	36.7	4.7	44.7	5.4	22.5	16.8	0.7
	2000	4633	9.7	0.8	45.5	6.8	37.2	4.6	16.5	16.1	0.0
	2003	5402	9.4	0.8	39.4	6.6	43.8	4.7	16.5	22.5	0.0
Bangladesh	1990	3432	19.0	5.4	16.5	3.1	55.8	8.2	29.1	18.6	0.2
	1995	5438	17.3	3.4	7.8	2.3	69.1	10.1	44.4	14.7	0.2
	2003	7070	19.8	7.3	8.0	2.3	62.6	10.9	32.0	19.6	0.0
Barbados - Barbade	1990	698	17.4	2.5	14.3	1.6	61.8	10.1	27.5	24.2	2.4
	1995	766	18.3	2.4	8.5	1.1	69.5	11.8	30.9	26.8	0.3
	2000	1156	15.4	2.3	11.5	1.0	69.4	9.3	32.3	27.9	0.3
	2003	1195	17.0	1.9	15.4	0.8	64.5	10.1	28.8	25.6	0.3
Belarus - Bélarus	2000	8492	12.1	2.3	30.6	3.6	49.8	11.7	21.3	16.8	1.6
	2003	11505	11.5	2.1	26.5	3.6	54.9	10.3	22.3	22.2	1.4
Belgium - Belgique	2000	171366	8.6	1.9	8.8	3.7	76.8	16.7	29.9	30.2	0.2
	2003	235366	8.9	1.4	8.9	3.2	77.2	23.1	25.4	28.7	0.2
	1990	120068	9.8	2.4	8.1	5.5	68.1	11.2	31.4	25.5	6.2
	1995	153388	11.2	2.1	6.2	4.8	70.5	13.6	30.7	26.2	5.2
Belize	1995	259	19.1	0.3	11.5	0.7	68.4	10.4	32.3	25.7	0.1
	2000	447	14.0	0.6	17.0	0.5	67.4	9.7	29.0	28.7	0.5
	2002	527	11.4	0.5	11.0	0.5	47.6	7.8	20.1	19.7	29.0

For sources, see end of table.

Pour les sources, se reporter à la fin du tableau.

Country or area Pays ou zones	Year Année	Total value (millions of dollars) Valeur totale (millions de dollars)	By main categories of imports (percentage) Par principales catégories de produits importés (en pourcentage)								
			All food items Produits alimentaires	Agricultural raw materials Matières premières d'origine agricole	Fuels Combustibles	Ores and metals Minéraux et métaux	Manufactured goods Produits manufacturés	of which: / dont:			Unallocated Non distribué
								Chemical products Produits chimiques	Other manufactured goods Articles manufacturés divers	Machinery and transport equipment Machines et matériel de transport	
SITC / CTCI			0+1+22+4	2 less (22+27+28)	3	27+28+68	5 to 8 less 68	5	(6+8) less 68	7	
Benin - Bénin	1995	719	27.3	2.7	9.4	1.0	59.4	13.7	27.7	18.0	0.2
	2000	547	21.9	5.3	19.2	1.0	52.6	10.2	27.4	15.1	0.0
	2002	727	23.9	5.3	17.4	0.8	52.6	13.3	25.8	13.4	0.0
Bermuda - Bermudes	1995	633	20.7	1.4	6.4	0.2	67.1	8.4	31.7	27.0	4.2
Bolivia - Bolivie	1990	703	11.4	2.1	0.6	0.7	83.9	11.0	27.0	45.9	1.3
	1995	1396	9.5	1.7	4.6	2.6	81.0	13.4	21.1	46.4	0.7
	2000	1849	13.5	1.6	4.9	0.6	78.7	14.1	26.7	37.9	0.7
	2003	1684	13.2	1.5	7.3	0.7	76.6	17.5	27.4	31.7	0.7
Bosnia and Herzegovina - Bosnie-Herzégovine	2003	3312	20.3	0.9	7.8	2.8	68.2	11.0	31.9	25.3	0.0
Botswana	2000	2072	14.0	0.8	4.9	2.2	73.1	6.4	32.1	34.6	5.0
	2001	1811	13.9	0.8	6.7	2.0	71.4	6.8	32.6	31.9	5.2
Brazil - Brésil	1990	22459	9.4	2.6	27.0	4.9	56.2	15.3	12.5	28.3	0.0
	1995	53734	10.7	2.7	12.1	3.4	71.0	15.1	16.8	39.1	0.0
	2000	58931	6.8	2.0	15.1	3.1	72.9	17.7	14.1	41.1	0.1
	2003	50824	7.1	1.7	15.9	3.2	72.0	21.5	13.8	36.8	0.0
Brunei Darussalam - Brunéi Darussalam	1990	1001	19.2	0.4	0.9	1.3	77.9	6.7	36.7	34.4	0.3
Bulgaria - Bulgarie	2000	6505	5.2	1.3	25.9	5.7	59.0	9.1	25.0	24.9	3.0
	2003	10901	5.4	1.4	4.0	5.4	68.3	9.7	29.9	28.6	15.6
Burkina Faso	1995	484	21.2	1.5	14.0	1.2	62.0	14.5	27.9	19.6	0.0
	2000	724	12.6	0.6	25.3	0.9	60.6	8.4	15.4	36.9	0.0
	2002	583	21.3	0.7	16.9	0.9	60.2	15.6	21.5	23.1	0.0
Burundi	1995	270	20.9	1.9	11.4	1.2	64.1	13.9	20.9	29.3	0.5
	2000	150	22.9	2.4	11.9	2.2	59.9	13.1	23.9	22.9	0.6
	2002	129	11.2	2.5	12.9	1.8	71.0	18.0	30.1	22.9	0.7
Cameroon - Cameroun	1990	1656	18.5	0.5	1.5	4.4	75.1	14.1	33.2	27.8	0.0
	1995	1079	17.4	2.5	2.5	5.6	71.9	16.4	24.6	30.9	0.0
	2000	1489	18.2	1.6	23.2	3.6	53.5	11.8	18.5	23.2	0.0
	2003	2021	18.8	1.7	12.4	3.3	63.8	14.3	21.7	27.8	0.0
Canada	1990	116509	6.1	1.6	6.3	3.1	79.8	6.6	23.0	50.2	3.1
	1995	164371	5.7	1.7	3.7	3.3	82.6	7.9	23.1	51.5	3.1
	2000	240091	5.0	1.3	5.2	2.5	83.6	8.2	23.5	51.9	2.3
	2003	239699	6.1	1.4	6.3	2.4	81.6	10.1	23.9	47.6	2.2
Cape Verde - Cap-Vert	1995	327	31.1	2.6	14.3	0.2	51.6	5.4	23.4	22.8	0.2
	2000	237	31.0	2.2	6.1	0.3	60.5	6.0	26.0	28.5	0.0
	2001	248	33.7	2.5	5.6	0.4	57.7	5.9	24.0	27.7	0.1
Central African Republic - République centrafricaine	1995	265	15.6	9.8	8.7	1.6	64.2	7.9	14.1	42.2	0.0
	2000	70	29.3	4.3	7.5	4.5	54.3	12.8	18.3	23.2	0.0
	2001	68	27.0	4.1	5.1	3.0	60.9	13.7	18.7	28.5	0.0
Chad - Tchad	1995	215	24.3	0.6	17.9	0.6	56.1	7.3	24.9	23.9	0.5
Chile - Chili	1990	7022	4.4	2.1	15.7	1.1	75.4	11.9	20.0	43.6	1.3
	1995	14903	6.7	1.6	9.0	2.2	79.2	12.0	25.1	42.1	1.3
	2000	16620	7.4	1.1	18.2	1.1	71.4	12.5	24.1	34.8	0.9
	2003	17376	8.3	1.1	19.1	1.4	69.7	13.0	22.7	34.0	0.4
China - Chine	1990	53345	8.7	5.8	2.4	2.9	79.7	12.5	26.8	40.3	0.5
	1995	132083	7.0	5.0	3.9	4.4	79.0	13.0	26.0	40.0	0.7
	2000	225094	4.0	4.5	9.2	5.9	75.6	13.3	21.4	40.9	0.8
	2003	412760	3.6	3.7	7.1	5.6	79.6	11.7	21.1	46.8	0.3

For sources, see end of table.

Pour les sources, se reporter à la fin du tableau.

Country or area Pays ou zones	Year Année	Total value (millions of dollars) Valeur totale (millions de dollars)	By main categories of imports (percentage) Par principales catégories de produits importés (en pourcentage)					of which: / dont:			
			All food items Produits alimen-taires	Agricul-tural raw materials Matières premières d'origine agricole	Fuels Combus-tibles	Ores and metals Minéraux et métaux	Manu-factured goods Produits manu-facturés	Chemical products Produits chimi-ques	Other manu-factured goods Articles manu-facturés divers	Machinery and transport equipment Machines et matériel de transport	Un-allo-cated Non distri-bué
SITC / CTCI			0+1+22+4	2 less (22+27+28)	3	27+28+68	5 to 8 less 68	5	(6+8) less 68	7	
China, Hong Kong SAR - Chine, Hong Kong RAS	1990	84725	7.7	2.1	2.4	1.5	83.3	7.2	48.8	27.2	3.1
	1995	196072	5.4	1.6	1.9	2.1	87.0	7.3	43.2	36.5	2.0
	2000	214042	4.3	1.2	2.1	1.7	90.0	6.2	41.4	42.4	0.7
	2003	233194	3.6	1.0	2.0	1.7	91.0	5.7	37.1	48.1	0.7
China, Macao SAR - Chine, Macao RAS	1990	1533	11.8	3.4	4.7	1.1	78.6	5.8	57.5	15.2	0.5
	1995	2025	13.9	2.6	5.2	0.6	77.3	4.4	54.0	18.8	0.4
	2000	2261	11.4	1.1	7.7	0.4	79.2	3.8	59.6	15.8	0.3
	2003	2755	13.0	1.3	7.2	0.4	78.1	4.0	52.7	21.3	0.1
China, Taiwan Province of - Chine, Taiwan Province de	1990	54696	6.4	4.9	11.0	5.8	67.2	12.5	17.8	36.9	4.7
	1995	103506	5.4	4.2	7.0	6.0	74.2	13.0	21.0	40.2	3.2
	2000	140244	3.6	2.0	9.4	4.5	78.8	10.9	17.8	50.2	1.7
	2003	127243	4.3	1.9	12.1	5.0	75.1	12.1	18.7	44.3	1.6
Colombia - Colombie	1990	5589	7.1	3.4	6.0	3.4	76.7	22.6	17.9	36.2	3.3
	1995	13883	9.4	2.5	2.9	2.5	77.6	18.0	22.1	37.5	5.1
	2000	11757	11.9	2.8	2.1	2.4	80.4	23.1	24.4	32.9	0.4
	2003	13881	11.2	2.4	1.8	2.1	81.3	21.9	21.4	38.0	1.2
Comoros - Comores	1995	62	48.5	0.9	12.7	0.7	36.7	3.1	19.2	14.3	0.5
	2000	72	21.9	0.4	4.1	0.2	72.5	2.3	60.2	10.1	1.0
Congo	1995	556	20.8	0.9	19.6	0.8	58.0	13.9	23.9	20.2	0.0
Cook Islands - Iles Cook	2003	71	23.4	3.1	4.5	0.8	68.1	5.6	30.4	32.1	0.0
Costa Rica	1990	2282	7.6	1.6	9.6	2.0	65.6	16.3	26.1	23.2	13.6
	1995	3205	10.2	1.2	8.5	2.0	77.4	19.7	31.1	26.5	0.7
	2000	6029	7.4	0.8	8.1	1.8	81.5	14.5	29.2	37.8	0.3
	2003	7388	7.7	0.9	7.7	1.3	82.1	14.7	26.1	41.3	0.3
Côte d'Ivoire	1995	2472	20.9	0.9	19.2	1.5	56.6	12.9	19.3	24.4	0.9
	2000	2482	17.2	1.1	33.8	1.4	46.2	14.2	15.5	16.4	0.4
	2003	3536	21.7	0.6	17.1	1.2	48.5	14.2	12.9	21.5	10.8
Croatia - Croatie	1995	7509	11.8	1.7	11.6	2.5	66.6	10.6	29.5	26.6	5.8
	2000	7886	8.3	1.5	14.6	2.3	73.3	12.5	28.2	32.5	0.0
	2003	14153	8.5	1.5	11.0	1.7	77.1	10.8	29.2	37.1	0.3
Cuba	2000	4843	15.8	1.3	24.0	1.2	57.7	8.5	24.0	25.2	0.0
	2001	5251	18.4	1.1	19.7	1.2	59.5	10.0	24.4	25.1	0.0
Cyprus - Chypre	1990	2564	14.3	1.4	10.6	1.6	70.8	7.9	32.5	30.5	1.2
	1995	3694	20.4	1.3	7.8	1.2	65.3	8.6	29.1	27.6	4.0
	2000	3846	18.6	1.0	12.8	1.2	64.9	8.5	28.4	28.0	1.6
	2003	4466	12.1	1.3	9.9	1.1	71.5	10.3	32.4	28.8	4.2
Czech Republic - République tchèque	1995	25303	6.7	2.6	7.9	4.2	77.4	11.6	29.8	36.0	1.2
	2000	32243	4.9	1.9	9.7	3.6	79.8	10.9	28.9	40.0	0.1
	2003	51239	4.8	1.7	7.5	3.3	82.7	11.1	28.8	42.7	0.0
Czechoslovakia (former) - Tchécoslovaquie (anc.)	1990	17006	8.3	6.0	11.2	5.9	68.6	10.1	14.0	44.5	0.0
Denmark - Danemark	1990	31576	11.9	3.3	7.0	2.3	73.1	11.2	30.3	31.5	2.4
	1995	43142	12.0	3.0	3.4	2.0	72.7	11.0	29.7	32.0	6.9
	2000	44587	11.4	2.7	5.7	1.7	75.9	9.6	30.4	35.9	2.7
	2003	56167	12.4	2.8	4.2	1.7	77.0	10.8	30.5	35.6	2.0
Djibouti	1990	215	29.9	11.4	7.0	0.8	47.7	5.7	24.3	17.7	3.2
Dominica - Dominique	1990	118	23.6	1.6	6.1	0.6	68.1	11.1	30.9	26.1	0.0
	1995	117	26.2	2.0	5.6	0.4	65.7	13.4	28.4	23.8	0.0
	2000	148	21.0	2.2	9.6	0.3	66.9	11.7	29.0	26.1	0.0
	2003	127	23.7	1.5	10.9	0.3	63.5	11.1	29.9	22.5	0.1

For sources, see end of table.

Pour les sources, se reporter à la fin du tableau.

Country or area Pays ou zones	Year Année	Total value (millions of dollars) Valeur totale (millions de dollars)	By main categories of imports (percentage) Par principales catégories de produits importés (en pourcentage)								
			All food items Produits alimentaires	Agricultural raw materials Matières premières d'origine agricole	Fuels Combustibles	Ores and metals Minéraux et métaux	Manufactured goods Produits manufacturés	of which: / dont:			Unallocated Non distribué
								Chemical products Produits chimiques	Other manufactured goods Articles manufacturés divers	Machinery and transport equipment Machines et matériel de transport	
SITC / CTCI			0+1+22+4	2 less (22+27+28)	3	27+28+68	5 to 8 less 68	5	(6+8) less 68	7	
Dominican Republic - République dominicaine	2001	5497	12.1	2.0	22.6	1.0	62.2	10.9	21.9	29.4	0.1
Ecuador - Equateur	1990	1804	8.7	2.8	2.1	2.5	83.8	22.6	24.6	36.6	0.1
	1995	4195	7.6	2.8	5.9	1.9	81.8	17.5	23.8	40.5	0.0
	2000	3446	9.0	3.3	8.2	1.8	76.4	23.7	25.9	26.9	1.4
	2003	6534	9.2	1.5	10.3	1.0	78.0	16.7	23.8	37.4	0.0
Egypt - Egypte	1990	9202	31.5	7.1	2.7	2.4	56.3	12.6	20.9	22.8	0.0
	1995	11739	28.4	7.1	1.2	2.7	60.6	13.1	22.3	25.2	0.0
	2003	10893	24.9	4.6	5.2	2.8	48.4	12.0	17.5	18.9	14.1
El Salvador	1990	902	14.2	3.3	15.5	3.8	63.2	19.2	23.4	20.5	0.0
	1995	2628	14.8	2.0	9.3	1.5	72.3	17.0	25.3	30.1	0.1
	2000	3795	16.2	2.1	15.7	1.2	64.8	14.8	23.5	26.4	0.2
	2003	4382	17.7	2.1	14.2	1.1	64.4	15.4	25.6	23.4	0.4
Eritrea - Erythrée	2000	328	37.4	1.2	1.5	0.9	58.4	6.7	28.6	23.1	0.5
	2002	538	30.9	1.5	1.1	1.1	65.0	6.6	29.5	29.0	0.3
Estonia - Estonie	1995	2546	13.8	2.9	11.0	1.4	70.8	9.4	31.7	29.7	0.1
	2000	5052	9.8	3.3	7.3	3.5	76.1	9.0	26.0	41.1	0.0
	2003	7967	11.2	3.1	6.0	1.7	77.8	9.3	27.4	41.1	0.3
Ethiopia - Ethiopie	1995	1141	13.8	1.9	11.1	0.8	72.4	14.0	22.9	35.5	0.0
	2000	1260	7.0	1.2	20.1	0.7	70.9	11.4	27.6	32.0	0.1
	2003	2686	21.5	0.7	12.0	1.5	64.0	8.8	24.8	30.5	0.3
Ethiopia (former) - Ethiopie (anc.)	1990	1076	14.9	2.3	11.9	1.2	69.7	10.1	19.9	39.7	0.0
Faeroe Islands - Iles Féroé	1990	333	20.9	2.2	12.1	1.3	54.1	6.0	23.6	24.4	9.5
	2003	564	15.9	2.7	9.8	1.0	70.7	6.3	22.7	41.7	0.0
Fiji - Fidji	1990	755	14.6	0.3	14.1	0.8	69.0	7.1	31.2	30.7	1.2
	2000	776	13.7	0.6	6.8	0.8	70.9	6.7	43.8	20.4	7.1
	2003	1087	18.2	0.3	12.2	0.9	68.0	7.9	32.2	27.8	0.3
Finland - Finlande	1990	27004	4.9	2.3	11.8	4.5	75.9	10.6	26.7	38.6	0.7
	1995	29520	6.0	3.6	8.8	5.7	74.1	12.1	23.3	38.7	1.9
	2000	33886	5.2	2.4	11.9	5.6	72.4	10.3	20.1	42.0	2.4
	2003	41572	6.0	2.8	12.3	5.5	70.9	11.6	21.0	38.3	2.5
France [1]	1990	233163	9.8	2.6	9.6	3.8	73.8	10.5	29.3	34.1	0.4
	1995	273387	10.7	2.5	6.8	3.5	76.1	12.4	28.3	35.4	0.3
	2000	310897	7.9	1.9	9.9	2.9	77.2	12.1	26.0	39.1	0.1
	2003	362503	8.8	1.7	9.7	2.4	77.4	13.4	27.2	36.8	0.1
French Guiana - Guyane française [1]	1990	743	15.2	0.2	7.7	0.6	75.0	5.1	29.7	40.3	1.4
	1995	783	18.7	0.1	5.4	0.3	73.5	7.8	23.6	42.1	2.1
French Polynesia - Polynésie française	2000	1072	20.0	1.9	7.3	0.8	69.6	8.3	28.0	33.3	0.5
	2003	1568	17.4	1.3	6.4	0.7	74.1	7.2	23.6	43.3	0.1
Gabon	2000	956	18.5	0.5	4.2	1.0	75.4	8.3	18.6	48.5	0.4
Gambia - Gambie	1995	215	36.4	0.7	14.2	0.3	45.8	5.6	18.2	22.0	2.6
	2000	189	34.5	0.7	12.0	0.8	51.2	5.4	23.8	21.9	0.9
Georgia - Géorgie	2000	651	22.6	0.6	21.2	0.7	54.8	10.0	18.1	26.7	0.1
	2003	1135	18.2	0.4	17.7	0.7	62.7	11.5	25.4	25.8	0.4
Germany - Allemagne	1995	464145	9.8	2.6	6.2	4.0	70.0	9.0	29.2	31.7	7.4
	2000	500814	6.6	1.7	8.7	3.5	67.4	8.8	22.8	35.7	12.1
	2003	601761	7.3	1.6	8.7	3.0	70.4	10.4	23.0	37.1	8.9

For sources, see end of table.

Pour les sources, se reporter à la fin du tableau.

Country or area Pays ou zones	Year Année	Total value (millions of dollars) Valeur totale (millions de dollars)	By main categories of imports (percentage) Par principales catégories de produits importés (en pourcentage)					of which: / dont:			
			All food items Produits alimentaires	Agricultural raw materials Matières premières d'origine agricole	Fuels Combustibles	Ores and metals Minéraux et métaux	Manufactured goods Produits manufacturés	Chemical products Produits chimiques	Other manufactured goods Articles manufacturés divers	Machinery and transport equipment Machines et matériel de transport	Unallocated Non distribué
SITC / CTCI			0+1+22+4	2 less (22+27+28)	3	27+28+68	5 to 8 less 68	5	(6+8) less 68	7	
Germany (former Dem. Rep. of) - Allemagne (anc. Rép. Dém. d')	1990	14220	7.3	4.6	24.3	6.5	53.8	5.9	18.8	29.1	3.5
Germany (former Federal Rep. of) - Allemagne (anc. Rép. fédérale d')	1990	342483	10.1	3.1	8.3	4.5	71.6	8.8	30.4	32.4	2.4
Ghana	2000	2933	12.8	2.4	21.5	2.9	59.5	9.7	19.4	30.3	1.0
Greece - Grèce	1990	19777	15.3	3.4	7.7	2.9	70.4	10.4	29.0	31.0	0.2
	1995	25927	16.0	2.4	7.3	3.0	71.0	13.0	30.6	27.4	0.3
	2000	29816	11.3	1.5	13.5	2.7	70.8	11.5	24.7	34.6	0.2
	2002	32519	12.9	1.6	13.9	2.6	68.0	10.8	24.3	32.9	1.0
Greenland - Groenland	1990	435	16.6	0.9	12.0	0.8	56.1	3.9	27.9	24.3	13.4
	1995	421	14.2	1.2	5.8	0.4	59.2	4.2	30.5	24.6	19.2
	2000	347	15.3	0.8	18.9	0.5	52.3	3.4	22.1	26.8	12.2
	2002	355	17.2	1.5	9.0	0.5	61.6	4.2	33.3	24.0	10.3
Grenada - Grenade	1990	109	28.0	3.5	6.8	0.3	61.3	9.0	29.8	22.4	0.1
	1995	129	27.5	2.5	7.8	0.4	61.8	8.5	32.1	21.1	0.0
	2000	239	18.4	2.2	8.8	0.8	69.9	6.3	30.8	32.8	0.0
	2003	253	17.9	2.3	6.9	0.6	72.2	6.6	35.3	30.3	0.0
Guadeloupe [1]	1990	1681	19.2	1.9	5.5	0.7	70.4	7.7	31.6	31.1	2.4
	1995	1901	21.0	1.6	5.8	0.8	69.0	9.3	27.8	31.9	1.8
Guatemala	1990	1649	10.2	1.6	16.9	1.8	69.0	20.0	22.6	26.4	0.4
	1995	3292	11.9	1.5	12.5	1.2	72.9	17.1	24.4	31.4	0.1
	2000	4882	12.1	1.7	12.7	1.3	72.1	16.2	23.5	32.5	0.1
	2003	6719	12.6	1.2	13.8	1.1	71.2	17.6	26.2	27.4	0.1
Guinea - Guinée	1995	819	31.0	1.0	19.1	0.8	47.3	6.4	20.0	20.9	0.8
	2000	612	24.2	1.2	25.0	0.7	48.7	8.6	21.1	19.0	0.3
	2002	666	23.1	1.2	21.7	0.8	53.0	12.6	21.3	19.1	0.3
Guinea-Bissau - Guinée-Bissau	1995	57	43.6	0.5	16.2	0.2	39.6	4.9	11.8	22.9	0.0
Guyana	2000	573	13.9	0.5	22.3	0.4	62.6	11.1	24.6	26.9	0.2
	2003	557	15.6	0.5	24.5	0.5	58.8	11.0	25.0	22.8	0.2
Honduras	1990	942	10.2	1.2	16.2	1.4	70.7	20.0	27.0	23.7	0.3
	1995	1728	12.6	1.1	11.5	1.2	73.5	17.1	27.3	29.1	0.0
	2000	2482	22.2	2.4	18.3	1.0	50.1	20.7	23.1	6.3	6.1
	2002	3033	22.0	1.2	20.4	1.1	55.3	20.0	24.8	10.5	0.0
Hungary - Hongrie	1990	8647	7.6	3.6	14.2	3.8	70.4	14.9	20.8	34.6	0.4
	1995	15186	5.7	3.0	11.9	4.3	75.1	14.3	30.8	30.0	0.0
	2000	32079	2.9	1.5	4.8	2.7	83.9	8.6	24.3	50.9	4.3
	2003	46394	3.4	1.3	5.8	2.3	86.7	9.5	24.5	52.7	0.5
Iceland - Islande	1990	1659	9.3	1.7	9.9	4.0	75.0	7.8	32.2	35.0	0.1
	1995	1751	11.8	1.6	7.3	4.6	74.6	9.1	33.3	32.2	0.2
	2000	2380	9.1	1.2	9.4	4.8	75.4	7.7	28.1	39.6	0.1
	2003	2826	10.4	1.8	7.8	5.4	74.5	10.1	29.1	35.3	0.1
India - Inde	1990	23799	3.2	4.0	27.3	8.0	51.2	12.9	20.3	18.0	6.2
	1995	36592	4.2	3.9	23.7	6.8	52.8	15.3	17.3	20.2	8.5
	2000	51377	4.4	3.2	34.8	4.7	42.8	8.9	18.9	15.1	10.1
	2002	61118	5.4	2.9	32.1	4.2	47.9	9.1	19.9	18.8	7.4
Indonesia - Indonésie	1990	21837	5.1	4.7	9.0	5.0	76.1	15.4	17.3	43.4	0.2
	1995	40629	8.8	6.1	7.6	4.6	72.6	15.1	17.3	40.2	0.2
	2000	33515	10.0	7.1	18.4	3.6	60.8	17.2	16.0	27.6	0.1
	2003	32551	11.4	5.3	24.0	3.1	56.1	15.8	13.8	26.4	0.1
Iran, Islamic Rep. of - Iran, Rép. islamique d'	2000	13626	19.0	2.6	2.4	2.5	73.2	14.3	23.3	35.6	0.4
	2003	25638	10.5	2.0	5.8	2.3	79.2	12.3	20.9	46.0	0.1

For sources, see end of table.

Pour les sources, se reporter à la fin du tableau.

Country or area / Pays ou zones	Year / Année	Total value (millions of dollars) / Valeur totale (millions de dollars)	By main categories of imports (percentage) / Par principales catégories de produits importés (en pourcentage)								
			All food items / Produits alimentaires	Agricultural raw materials / Matières premières d'origine agricole	Fuels / Combustibles	Ores and metals / Minéraux et métaux	Manufactured goods / Produits manufacturés	of which: / dont:			Un-allocated / Non distribué
								Chemical products / Produits chimiques	Other manufactured goods / Articles manufacturés divers	Machinery and transport equipment / Machines et matériel de transport	
SITC / CTCI			0+1+22+4	2 less (22+27+28)	3	27+28+68	5 to 8 less 68	5	(6+8) less 68	7	
Ireland - Irlande	1990	20728	10.6	1.7	6.5	2.4	76.0	12.1	28.0	35.9	2.9
	1995	32321	8.5	1.2	3.3	2.1	75.7	12.7	20.8	42.2	9.2
	2000	50689	6.3	0.9	4.1	1.2	81.8	10.9	17.9	53.0	5.7
	2002	52204	7.3	0.8	3.3	1.3	81.3	12.5	18.2	50.6	6.0
Israel - Israël	1990	15324	7.8	2.4	8.9	2.6	76.2	9.6	40.2	26.4	2.2
	1995	28344	6.6	1.5	5.9	2.2	81.7	9.2	38.6	33.9	2.0
	2000	35742	5.4	1.0	10.1	1.8	81.2	8.8	37.7	34.8	0.5
	2003	34211	6.1	1.1	11.0	1.8	79.4	10.3	40.3	28.8	0.5
Italy - Italie	1990	180057	12.0	5.2	10.5	4.7	63.0	10.9	22.0	30.1	4.6
	1995	200320	11.4	5.4	7.4	5.0	67.0	13.0	24.3	29.7	3.8
	2000	238257	8.5	3.9	9.7	4.4	68.1	12.0	22.9	33.2	5.4
	2003	290793	9.3	3.0	9.2	3.5	68.7	12.9	23.3	32.5	6.2
Jamaica - Jamaïque	1990	1919	15.1	1.2	19.8	1.0	61.0	11.8	23.8	25.5	1.8
	1995	2773	14.3	1.6	12.7	0.9	67.6	9.5	30.6	27.4	3.0
	2000	3192	15.5	1.5	18.4	0.6	61.2	10.5	27.6	23.2	2.8
	2002	3543	15.2	1.4	17.8	0.6	63.3	10.0	24.0	29.4	1.7
Japan - Japon	1990	234799	14.5	7.0	24.2	8.9	42.8	6.5	21.0	15.4	2.6
	1995	336094	16.0	6.1	16.1	6.5	53.0	7.1	23.3	22.5	2.2
	2000	379663	12.8	3.6	20.4	5.5	56.0	6.8	21.3	27.9	1.7
	2003	383452	12.3	2.9	21.2	4.9	57.0	7.6	21.9	27.5	1.7
Jordan - Jordanie	1990	2603	25.8	1.4	18.1	1.5	51.6	11.0	21.5	19.0	1.7
	1995	3696	20.6	2.1	12.9	2.5	60.5	12.1	24.0	24.5	1.4
	2000	4013	21.2	2.3	4.8	2.5	65.9	11.8	21.8	32.3	3.3
	2003	5653	17.6	1.6	16.5	2.0	58.8	11.0	24.9	22.9	3.4
Kazakhstan	2000	5033	9.1	0.9	11.4	3.1	75.1	11.4	24.3	39.4	0.4
	2003	8409	8.0	0.9	11.1	1.6	78.3	12.1	25.5	40.7	0.1
Kenya	1990	2133	9.3	2.9	19.9	2.1	65.5	11.0	14.3	40.2	0.3
	1995	2818	10.1	1.9	14.7	2.0	71.2	15.2	22.5	33.5	0.1
	2000	2891	14.0	2.5	22.2	1.5	59.6	14.6	17.2	27.8	0.3
	2003	3475	12.2	2.1	23.1	1.5	61.0	15.2	18.6	27.3	0.2
Kiribati	1990	27	31.4	2.6	10.7	0.2	54.5	4.6	30.8	19.1	0.6
	1995	34	39.4	1.3	10.1	0.5	48.1	7.0	26.4	14.7	0.6
Korea, Republic of - Corée, République de	1990	69839	5.6	7.9	15.9	6.6	63.2	10.5	18.4	34.3	0.8
	1995	135113	5.4	5.3	14.2	6.3	66.5	9.5	20.4	36.6	2.3
	2000	160479	4.8	3.1	23.8	5.5	61.1	8.2	16.1	36.8	1.6
	2002	152124	5.9	2.9	21.4	5.4	63.0	9.1	18.9	35.0	1.3
Kuwait - Koweït	1990	3352	16.7	0.8	0.7	1.8	77.8	7.2	37.8	32.8	2.2
	1995	7790	15.5	1.1	0.5	1.7	80.8	7.1	32.5	41.2	0.4
	2000	7157	17.4	0.9	0.6	2.2	77.5	8.1	31.8	37.6	1.3
	2001	7869	15.3	0.7	0.5	2.5	74.6	7.4	30.3	36.9	6.4
Kyrgyzstan - Kirghizistan	1995	522	18.3	2.7	36.1	2.5	40.4	6.1	16.0	18.3	0.0
	2003	717	12.8	1.7	25.3	2.9	57.2	14.3	23.0	19.9	0.2
Latvia - Lettonie	1995	1818	10.5	1.7	21.2	1.0	65.4	12.5	27.6	25.3	0.1
	2000	3191	12.3	2.0	12.4	2.0	71.3	12.2	31.0	28.1	0.1
	2003	5244	11.7	2.7	9.5	1.8	74.1	12.1	31.1	30.9	0.2
Lebanon - Liban	2000	6227	17.8	1.7	16.5	2.1	56.0	10.0	24.2	21.8	6.0
	2003	7167	18.1	1.5	15.7	2.3	60.1	11.7	26.5	21.9	2.3
Lesotho	2000	613	17.5	0.8	18.9	2.3	48.4	5.9	34.8	7.7	12.0
	2002	800	23.1	0.8	7.7	0.8	62.4	12.3	37.8	12.3	5.1
Libyan Arab Jamahiriya - Jamahiriya arabe libyenne	1990	5599	22.9	1.6	0.3	1.2	73.8	6.8	32.4	34.6	0.3

For sources, see end of table.

Country or area Pays ou zones	Year Année	Total value (millions of dollars) Valeur totale (millions de dollars)	By main categories of imports (percentage) Par principales catégories de produits importés (en pourcentage)									
			All food items Produits alimentaires	Agricultural raw materials Matières premières d'origine agricole	Fuels Combustibles	Ores and metals Minéraux et métaux	Manufactured goods Produits manufacturés	of which: / dont:				Unallocated Non distribué
								Chemical products Produits chimiques	Other manufactured goods Articles manufacturés divers	Machinery and transport equipment Machines et matériel de transport	
SITC / CTCI			0+1+22+4	2 less (22+27+28)	3	27+28+68	5 to 8 less 68	5	(6+8) less 68	7	
Lithuania - Lituanie	1995	3649	13.1	3.8	19.4	3.9	57.9	12.4	23.8	21.7	1.8
	2000	5456	9.7	2.9	21.8	2.2	60.7	12.1	24.4	24.3	2.7
	2003	9803	8.0	2.3	16.8	1.7	69.4	11.4	23.9	34.2	1.6
Luxembourg	2000	10051	10.3	1.2	7.1	5.5	75.7	9.4	28.6	37.7	0.2
	2002	11527	10.7	1.2	8.2	5.4	74.2	9.0	29.4	35.7	0.2
Macedonia, TFYR - Macédoine, LERY	1995	1719	17.4	3.3	11.7	3.0	64.4	11.8	33.1	19.5	0.3
	2000	2094	12.1	1.8	13.9	1.9	45.1	8.9	16.7	19.5	25.3
	2003	2300	14.1	1.6	14.1	1.7	49.0	11.0	19.2	18.8	19.6
Madagascar	1990	569	11.2	1.4	17.2	0.6	68.9	12.8	23.1	33.0	0.7
	1995	550	16.3	1.8	14.0	0.6	65.0	12.8	26.6	25.6	2.2
	2000	708	18.2	0.4	31.1	0.4	49.3	10.2	20.2	18.8	0.6
	2001	729	14.4	0.3	27.9	0.6	55.8	11.1	21.5	23.2	1.0
Malawi	1990	580	8.7	0.8	10.7	1.5	77.8	17.7	24.4	35.7	0.5
	1995	500	13.9	0.6	11.1	0.9	73.4	22.5	23.3	27.6	0.1
	2000	544	10.4	1.6	15.3	0.7	71.9	12.6	27.4	31.9	0.1
	2002	695	23.5	1.1	11.1	0.9	63.4	17.1	22.8	23.5	0.1
Malaysia - Malaisie	1990	29246	6.9	1.3	5.1	3.5	78.2	8.4	19.5	50.3	5.0
	1995	77046	4.8	1.2	2.3	3.2	83.6	7.0	16.7	59.8	4.9
	2000	81290	4.3	1.3	4.9	3.0	83.8	7.1	14.1	62.7	2.7
	2003	82741	5.1	1.1	5.6	2.9	82.1	7.0	13.8	61.3	3.2
Maldives	1995	268	24.0	2.1	11.4	1.9	60.7	5.5	28.8	26.4	0.0
	2000	389	23.6	1.8	11.7	1.9	61.0	5.2	30.7	25.1	0.0
	2003	471	20.9	2.2	11.8	2.0	63.0	5.3	30.5	27.2	0.0
Mali	1990	602	25.5	0.6	19.5	1.1	52.7	10.7	19.8	22.2	0.6
	2000	806	15.1	0.9	23.6	0.7	59.4	13.6	20.7	25.1	0.3
	2001	1013	16.2	0.7	21.9	0.7	60.3	12.3	21.8	26.2	0.2
Malta - Malte	1990	1953	10.2	1.0	5.2	1.7	80.0	6.6	27.6	45.8	1.9
	1995	2942	10.1	0.8	4.0	1.0	83.3	6.8	24.6	51.9	0.8
	2000	3399	8.4	0.5	7.2	0.7	82.5	6.1	19.2	57.1	0.7
	2001	2727	10.9	0.7	8.3	0.9	78.3	7.2	21.9	49.3	0.9
Martinique [1]	1990	1740	17.9	1.2	9.9	0.5	68.4	9.1	27.7	31.6	2.1
	1995	1970	19.3	1.1	7.5	0.5	69.5	10.0	27.1	32.3	2.0
Mauritania - Mauritanie	1995	455	23.6	0.6	22.0	0.3	53.3	4.3	15.8	33.3	0.0
Mauritius - Maurice	1990	1696	12.4	2.6	7.8	0.8	75.6	6.3	41.2	28.1	0.8
	1995	2000	16.6	3.0	6.9	0.8	71.9	7.5	45.3	19.1	0.8
	2000	2081	14.2	2.3	11.8	1.1	70.4	7.5	40.4	22.5	0.2
	2003	2360	17.4	2.0	10.9	0.9	68.5	8.4	37.8	22.3	0.3
Mexico - Mexique	1990	29560	14.6	3.5	3.8	3.1	64.0	10.2	20.6	33.3	10.9
	1995	72453	6.3	2.3	2.1	2.2	80.1	9.6	27.4	43.1	6.9
	2000	174412	4.9	1.4	3.1	2.0	85.9	8.4	26.4	51.1	2.8
	2003	171291	6.5	1.5	3.4	2.0	85.8	10.3	26.3	49.2	0.7
Moldova, Republic of - Moldova, République de	1995	841	8.1	2.6	46.0	1.5	41.6	9.1	17.3	15.2	0.2
	2000	777	13.1	2.4	32.4	1.1	50.9	11.1	25.7	14.1	0.1
	2003	1399	13.5	4.1	20.6	1.0	60.7	11.7	29.4	19.7	0.1
Mongolia - Mongolie	2000	615	16.6	0.6	19.1	0.4	63.4	4.6	25.2	33.6	0.0
	2003	801	14.4	0.6	19.9	0.5	64.5	5.6	26.9	32.0	0.0
Montserrat	2000	22	21.1	2.3	11.6	2.2	62.0	5.6	25.9	30.5	0.9
	2003	28	16.5	1.8	15.4	1.5	64.3	4.2	27.7	32.5	0.5

For sources, see end of table.

Pour les sources, se reporter à la fin du tableau.

Country or area Pays ou zones	Year Année	Total value (millions of dollars) Valeur totale (millions de dollars)	By main categories of imports (percentage) Par principales catégories de produits importés (en pourcentage)								
			All food items Produits alimen-taires	Agricul-tural raw materials Matières premières d'origine agricole	Fuels Combus-tibles	Ores and metals Minéraux et métaux	Manu-factured goods Produits manu-facturés	of which: / dont:			Un-allo-cated Non distri-bué
								Chemical products Produits chimi-ques	Other manu-factured goods Articles manu-facturés divers	Machinery and transport equipment Machines et matériel de transport	
SITC / CTCI			0+1+22+4	2 less (22+27+28)	3	27+28+68	5 to 8 less 68	5	(6+8) less 68	7	
Morocco - Maroc	1990	6922	9.8	6.0	16.9	6.2	61.0	10.6	21.1	29.3	0.0
	1995	8540	19.5	6.3	13.8	4.0	56.4	11.8	21.5	23.1	0.0
	2000	11533	13.7	3.1	17.7	2.5	62.9	8.5	26.9	27.4	0.1
	2002	11878	14.0	3.2	15.5	2.5	64.6	9.6	29.4	25.6	0.2
Namibia - Namibie	2000	1435	16.8	0.7	3.2	0.9	78.0	8.2	32.2	37.6	0.4
	2001	1553	13.1	0.6	10.4	1.8	73.8	10.5	29.0	34.3	0.3
Nepal - Népal	1990	611	13.9	6.6	8.3	1.9	63.4	16.8	28.5	18.0	5.9
	1995	1292	9.8	2.3	9.5	2.6	36.9	8.6	13.3	15.0	38.8
	2000	1558	11.7	3.5	15.2	2.8	45.6	10.6	17.7	17.2	21.3
Netherlands - Pays-Bas	1990	125980	12.6	2.4	10.5	3.1	70.6	10.1	29.6	30.9	0.7
	1995	157929	13.9	2.4	7.7	3.5	71.8	12.9	26.0	32.9	0.7
	2000	174671	9.8	2.0	11.5	2.9	73.7	10.4	22.0	41.3	0.1
	2002	163367	11.6	2.0	11.9	2.7	71.7	12.5	23.2	36.1	0.1
New Caledonia - Nouvelle-Calédonie	2000	1017	15.1	1.0	14.8	0.8	68.2	8.8	26.3	33.1	0.2
	2003	1594	12.1	0.8	10.5	0.8	72.9	7.5	21.2	44.2	2.9
New Zealand - Nouvelle-Zélande	1990	9483	6.8	1.2	7.7	4.2	79.8	11.3	26.8	41.6	0.3
	1995	13958	7.4	1.2	5.4	3.5	82.4	12.8	27.5	42.1	0.1
	2000	13904	7.7	0.9	10.5	3.1	77.7	12.0	26.4	39.3	0.1
	2003	18199	8.1	0.9	9.4	2.4	78.4	11.3	26.2	40.9	0.8
Nicaragua	1990	635	19.3	1.1	19.0	1.3	59.3	12.8	15.5	31.0	0.0
	1995	1009	17.9	0.9	17.9	0.6	62.6	17.4	22.2	23.0	0.0
	2000	1721	15.9	0.6	17.8	0.8	64.8	14.6	25.4	24.8	0.1
	2003	1836	17.4	0.5	15.6	0.5	65.9	17.6	25.4	22.9	0.1
Niger	1995	345	32.4	0.7	12.9	3.1	50.8	11.1	22.4	17.3	0.2
	2000	385	35.1	3.6	21.4	1.7	38.2	9.5	15.7	13.0	0.0
	2003	551	33.5	4.3	16.9	1.2	44.0	8.0	16.4	19.6	0.0
Nigeria - Nigéria	2000	5805	19.9	0.9	1.8	2.4	75.0	20.1	21.3	33.5	0.0
Norway - Norvège	1990	26862	5.9	1.9	4.4	7.5	79.7	7.9	30.8	41.0	0.6
	1995	32706	6.8	2.7	2.9	6.7	79.4	9.4	32.0	38.0	1.5
	2000	34358	6.5	2.1	3.5	6.7	80.0	8.6	26.9	44.6	1.2
	2003	39379	7.6	2.0	4.5	6.5	78.6	9.5	30.4	38.7	0.8
Oman	1990	2681	18.0	0.8	4.1	0.7	67.2	6.3	24.4	36.5	9.3
	1995	4249	19.7	0.8	1.5	2.4	68.2	6.6	21.8	39.7	7.4
	2000	5039	22.2	0.7	1.7	3.0	68.7	6.1	18.8	43.8	3.8
	2003	6572	17.4	0.6	3.3	4.8	70.6	6.8	20.1	43.7	3.3
Pakistan	1990	7356	17.4	4.0	20.9	3.6	54.1	16.3	12.3	25.6	0.1
	1995	11704	17.5	5.5	16.2	2.6	56.6	16.8	10.9	28.9	1.6
	2000	11070	13.8	3.2	32.6	2.1	45.9	17.9	9.5	18.5	2.4
	2003	13038	11.3	4.9	23.7	2.6	55.3	17.9	12.7	24.7	2.2
Panama	1990	1489	11.9	0.7	16.4	1.1	69.6	15.3	33.9	20.4	0.4
	1995	2511	10.7	0.8	13.7	1.4	73.1	13.3	30.8	29.0	0.4
	2000	3378	11.7	0.5	18.6	0.9	68.3	11.4	27.5	29.4	0.0
	2003	3124	14.4	0.6	11.8	0.9	72.3	13.9	29.2	29.2	0.0
Papua New Guinea - Papouasie-Nouvelle-Guinée	1990	1233	18.4	0.4	6.8	0.7	72.7	7.0	27.5	38.3	1.0
	2000	1035	18.3	0.7	22.1	0.9	57.6	7.0	21.2	29.5	0.3
	2003	1302	16.5	0.7	13.3	0.5	68.7	8.2	25.7	34.8	0.3
Paraguay	1990	1349	8.0	0.1	14.3	0.7	76.8	8.1	24.3	44.4	0.1
	1995	3136	18.5	0.2	6.6	0.7	73.7	8.9	22.6	42.2	0.3
	2000	2193	17.2	0.5	13.6	0.7	67.9	14.1	24.7	29.1	0.0
	2002	1672	12.3	1.1	16.7	1.2	68.7	17.6	23.4	27.7	0.0

For sources, see end of table.

Pour les sources, se reporter à la fin du tableau.

Country or area / Pays ou zones	Year / Année	Total value (millions of dollars) / Valeur totale (millions de dollars)	By main categories of imports (percentage) / Par principales catégories de produits importés (en pourcentage)								
			All food items / Produits alimentaires	Agricultural raw materials / Matières premières d'origine agricole	Fuels / Combustibles	Ores and metals / Minéraux et métaux	Manufactured goods / Produits manufacturés	of which: / dont:			Unallocated / Non distribué
								Chemical products / Produits chimiques	Other manufactured goods / Articles manufacturés divers	Machinery and transport equipment / Machines et matériel de transport	
SITC / CTCI			0+1+22+4	2 less (22+27+28)	3	27+28+68	5 to 8 less 68	5	(6+8) less 68	7	
Peru - Pérou	1990	2634	23.6	1.7	12.5	1.0	61.2	14.6	13.9	32.7	0.0
	1995	7584	13.5	1.8	8.8	0.8	75.0	13.0	23.0	39.1	0.0
	2000	7415	11.6	1.7	15.6	0.6	70.4	15.3	22.5	32.6	0.0
	2003	8414	12.6	1.8	17.4	0.7	67.5	16.4	22.7	28.4	0.0
Philippines	1990	13042	10.3	2.4	14.9	3.4	53.1	11.3	15.9	25.9	15.8
	1995	28487	8.3	2.2	9.2	3.2	57.8	9.0	16.4	32.4	19.2
	2000	33807	7.7	1.5	12.1	2.7	75.8	8.6	14.8	52.4	0.2
	2002	35426	7.6	1.0	9.3	2.2	79.8	7.3	12.2	60.3	0.2
Poland - Pologne	1990	7449	7.7	3.3	24.0	4.9	60.0	8.1	17.8	34.1	0.1
	1995	29019	9.5	3.1	9.2	3.3	74.4	14.6	29.9	29.9	0.5
	2000	48834	6.1	1.9	10.9	2.9	78.2	13.7	27.4	37.0	0.0
	2003	67976	5.3	1.8	9.2	2.7	79.6	14.3	27.6	37.7	1.3
Portugal	1990	25411	11.5	3.8	10.8	2.2	71.3	9.0	25.5	36.8	0.4
	1995	33565	13.6	3.4	8.2	2.1	72.0	10.2	28.1	33.7	0.6
	2000	39947	11.2	2.5	10.3	2.4	73.1	9.2	26.6	37.3	0.5
	2002	39983	12.5	2.2	9.7	2.3	73.0	10.8	28.1	34.1	0.4
Qatar	1990	1695	17.3	0.7	0.7	3.1	78.0	5.5	27.7	44.8	0.2
	1995	3398	9.3	0.6	0.5	2.3	86.9	4.7	34.0	48.3	0.3
	2000	3252	11.7	0.6	0.4	2.6	84.4	6.1	32.8	45.5	0.2
	2002	4052	11.9	0.8	0.7	2.5	83.5	6.8	29.1	47.7	0.6
Reunion - Réunion [1]	1990	2074	18.3	1.6	6.3	0.5	71.0	9.2	31.1	30.6	2.4
	1995	2711	19.9	1.6	4.7	0.9	71.0	10.6	30.7	29.7	1.9
Romania - Roumanie	1990	9089	11.9	4.3	38.3	6.2	38.9	7.4	9.4	22.1	0.4
	1995	10278	8.5	2.3	21.4	3.6	63.1	10.5	28.0	24.7	1.2
	2000	13054	7.0	1.3	12.2	3.8	75.3	9.7	36.4	29.1	0.4
	2003	24003	7.0	1.1	11.0	2.5	78.2	10.0	38.8	29.4	0.2
Russian Federation - Fédération de Russie	2000	45453	15.1	1.6	3.3	4.8	40.0	8.3	14.4	17.2	35.3
	2003	57415	19.3	1.2	2.3	3.4	64.6	12.2	20.7	31.7	9.3
Rwanda	2003	265	11.7	4.0	15.6	2.0	66.7	11.8	26.2	28.7	0.0
Saint Kitts and Nevis - Saint-Kitts-et-Nevis	1995	132	21.1	2.5	4.4	0.9	71.2	7.6	35.8	27.7	0.0
	2000	196	19.0	2.5	7.6	0.7	70.1	7.0	35.1	28.0	0.0
	2001	189	17.4	2.0	7.5	1.3	71.8	7.6	36.8	27.4	0.0
Saint Lucia - Sainte-Lucie	1990	272	23.2	2.4	7.5	0.9	66.0	9.8	34.8	21.4	0.1
	1995	306	26.7	2.4	7.6	1.0	62.2	9.1	34.1	19.0	0.1
	2000	355	23.6	2.4	9.4	0.9	63.8	7.9	31.5	24.4	0.0
	2003	393	23.1	1.7	10.7	0.7	63.8	7.1	30.6	26.2	0.0
Saint Vincent and the Grenadines - Saint-Vincent-et-les Grenadines	1995	134	22.5	2.6	6.1	0.5	68.3	12.5	38.1	17.7	0.0
	2000	162	26.7	2.4	9.7	0.7	60.5	9.7	32.1	18.7	0.0
	2003	201	21.6	2.7	9.8	0.5	65.2	8.4	32.1	24.7	0.0
	1990	82	27.1	1.9	11.4	0.8	58.8	4.7	25.2	28.9	0.0
	2002	132	27.2	1.5	13.0	0.6	57.8	6.0	29.1	22.7	0.0
Sao Tome and Principe - Sao Tomé-et-Principe	2000	30	30.9	0.4	10.7	0.7	57.3	3.1	23.6	30.7	0.0
	2003	42	38.5	1.0	10.6	0.3	49.6	5.0	20.6	23.9	0.1
Saudi Arabia - Arabie saoudite	1990	24069	13.8	0.7	0.2	2.7	75.7	9.2	29.1	37.4	6.9
	1995	28085	16.1	1.2	0.2	3.5	73.6	9.3	28.7	35.5	5.5
	2000	30237	17.7	1.0	0.2	3.0	73.2	9.4	24.6	39.2	4.9
	2003	36965	16.0	0.9	0.3	2.5	78.5	10.5	25.3	42.6	1.8
Senegal - Sénégal	1990	1620	28.7	1.8	16.0	2.3	51.2	9.7	20.2	21.3	0.0
	1995	1224	32.5	2.2	10.0	1.6	53.2	13.9	21.3	18.1	0.4
	2000	1553	23.3	2.1	22.6	1.3	50.7	10.4	17.5	22.8	0.0
	2002	2780	22.1	1.3	36.1	1.6	39.0	8.9	13.0	17.1	0.0

For sources, see end of table.

Pour les sources, se reporter à la fin du tableau.

Country or area Pays ou zones	Year Année	Total value (millions of dollars) Valeur totale (millions de dollars)	By main categories of imports (percentage) Par principales catégories de produits importés (en pourcentage)								
			All food items Produits alimen-taires	Agricul-tural raw materials Matières premières d'origine agricole	Fuels Combus-tibles	Ores and metals Minéraux et métaux	Manu-factured goods Produits manu-facturés	of which: / dont:			Un-allo-cated Non distri-bué
								Chemical products Produits chimi-ques	Other manu-factured goods Articles manu-facturés divers	Machinery and transport equipment Machines et matériel de transport	
SITC / CTCI			0+1+22+4	2 less (22+27+28)	3	27+28+68	5 to 8 less 68	5	(6+8) less 68	7	
Serbia and Montenegro - Serbie-et-Monténégro	2000	3711	9.3	3.6	20.1	3.6	63.3	14.8	26.4	22.1	0.0
	2002	6320	11.4	2.0	17.0	2.7	66.9	13.3	27.8	25.7	0.0
Seychelles	1990	187	18.9	1.8	19.3	1.2	58.7	5.4	26.8	26.5	0.1
	1995	255	21.2	1.5	17.4	0.7	59.1	6.3	25.8	27.0	0.2
	2002	246	24.8	1.0	16.5	0.6	57.0	5.4	23.4	28.1	0.1
Sierra Leone	2002	352	22.5	7.6	39.7	0.8	29.3	4.6	12.9	11.8	0.1
Singapore - Singapour	1990	60790	6.1	1.7	15.9	2.1	72.9	7.6	20.5	44.8	1.4
	1995	124503	4.6	0.9	8.1	2.3	83.0	6.4	18.7	57.9	1.2
	2000	134546	3.2	0.4	12.1	1.6	81.6	5.6	15.3	60.7	1.1
	2003	127381	3.4	0.4	13.6	1.1	80.1	6.6	14.5	59.0	1.5
Slovakia - Slovaquie	1995	8162	8.9	2.8	12.8	5.9	69.4	14.3	25.0	30.1	0.2
	2000	12774	5.6	1.8	17.6	3.7	71.2	10.7	24.9	35.6	0.1
	2003	22171	4.6	1.5	12.1	3.0	78.7	9.5	28.1	41.0	0.0
Slovenia - Slovénie	1995	9492	7.8	4.5	6.7	4.3	73.8	11.9	28.3	33.7	2.9
	2000	10115	6.0	3.6	9.2	5.2	75.9	12.2	29.6	34.1	0.2
	2003	13850	5.9	3.0	7.8	4.7	78.4	13.1	30.9	34.4	0.2
South Africa - Afrique du Sud	2000	26607	4.7	1.5	14.4	2.7	68.6	11.6	20.1	36.9	8.1
	2003	33590	5.0	1.4	11.9	2.7	69.6	10.9	19.4	39.3	9.4
South Africa (Customs Union) - Afrique du Sud (Union douanière)	1995	26745	6.7	2.3	8.4	2.4	77.8	12.3	20.7	44.8	2.5
Spain - Espagne	1990	87703	10.8	3.2	11.7	3.7	70.3	9.8	22.4	38.1	0.4
	1995	113399	13.6	3.0	8.4	3.9	70.8	12.0	23.3	35.5	0.4
	2000	152898	9.1	1.9	12.2	3.1	72.8	10.6	21.6	40.7	0.8
	2002	165920	10.3	1.7	10.9	2.9	73.4	12.4	23.0	37.9	0.9
Sri Lanka	1990	2634	19.1	1.8	12.7	1.5	64.8	11.8	33.9	19.2	0.2
	2002	6039	14.1	1.2	13.9	2.0	67.5	8.6	40.5	18.3	1.4
Sudan - Soudan	1995	1185	24.4	1.8	13.9	0.5	59.4	10.6	21.0	27.8	0.0
	2000	1657	21.7	1.0	7.4	0.9	69.0	11.7	23.3	34.0	0.0
	2002	2493	18.7	0.9	4.8	0.9	74.4	10.2	26.3	37.9	0.3
Suriname	1990	469	11.3	0.2	17.9	1.8	68.5	21.7	21.5	25.3	0.3
	1995	583	14.0	0.1	11.8	1.2	73.0	15.9	21.6	35.5	0.0
	2000	526	18.1	0.4	6.7	0.9	73.3	10.2	26.9	36.2	0.6
Swaziland	2000	1099	18.7	2.3	12.6	0.8	64.2	11.0	26.0	27.2	1.4
	2002	891	18.2	2.2	12.7	1.0	64.4	11.4	30.4	22.6	1.6
Sweden - Suède	1990	54488	6.1	2.0	9.0	3.5	78.5	9.2	30.8	38.5	0.9
	1995	61647	6.7	2.2	5.9	3.8	79.9	10.6	27.7	41.7	1.5
	2000	67741	6.2	1.1	9.0	3.3	75.1	9.4	24.4	41.3	5.3
	2003	83380	7.8	1.8	9.5	2.8	75.2	10.4	25.3	39.5	2.9
Switzerland - Suisse	1990	69691	6.3	2.1	4.6	2.9	83.5	11.4	40.5	31.5	0.7
	1995	80152	6.4	1.9	2.9	3.0	85.3	14.4	37.5	33.4	0.4
	2000	83584	5.5	1.4	4.6	5.7	82.6	16.2	33.2	33.2	0.2
	2003	95204	6.2	1.3	4.4	3.9	83.8	21.7	32.0	30.1	0.4
Syrian Arab Republic - République arabe syrienne	1990	2400	31.1	1.9	3.0	1.4	61.7	13.5	28.4	19.8	1.0
	1995	4709	16.7	3.3	1.1	1.3	75.6	10.2	33.9	31.6	2.0
	2000	3815	19.0	3.3	3.7	1.8	64.7	12.9	30.9	20.9	7.4
	2002	4277	16.3	3.8	3.0	2.7	64.0	13.1	26.3	24.6	10.2
Thailand - Thaïlande	1990	33371	5.0	4.7	9.3	3.6	74.4	10.2	23.1	41.0	3.1
	1995	70781	3.8	4.1	6.8	3.2	80.1	10.2	22.5	47.4	2.0
	2000	61451	4.3	2.9	12.4	3.1	75.7	10.7	20.4	44.6	1.6
	2003	75805	4.9	2.7	12.0	3.3	75.1	10.8	20.8	43.5	2.0

For sources, see end of table.

Pour les sources, se reporter à la fin du tableau.

Country or area Pays ou zones	Year Année	Total value (millions of dollars) Valeur totale (millions de dollars)	By main categories of imports (percentage) Par principales catégories de produits importés (en pourcentage)					of which: / dont:			
			All food items Produits alimen-taires	Agricul-tural raw materials Matières premières d'origine agricole	Fuels Combus-tibles	Ores and metals Minéraux et métaux	Manu-factured goods Produits manu-facturés	Chemical products Produits chimi-ques	Other manu-factured goods Articles manu-facturés divers	Machinery and transport equipment Machines et matériel de transport	Un-allo-cated Non distri-bué
SITC / CTCI			0+1+22+4	2 less (22+27+28)	3	27+28+68	5 to 8 less 68	5	(6+8) less 68	7	
Togo	1990	581	22.4	1.2	8.3	0.9	66.7	12.4	31.8	22.6	0.5
	1995	556	18.4	1.9	29.9	1.3	48.5	8.4	23.0	17.1	0.0
	2000	324	18.4	1.7	18.8	1.6	59.5	10.5	30.4	18.5	0.0
	2002	405	22.1	1.2	15.1	1.9	59.8	10.5	30.0	19.3	0.0
Trinidad and Tobago - Trinité-et-Tobago	1990	1262	19.4	1.1	11.4	5.6	62.1	13.9	25.5	22.7	0.3
	1995	1724	15.7	0.7	0.5	5.7	76.0	12.9	26.5	36.7	0.5
	2000	3308	8.3	1.0	32.3	2.0	56.1	7.7	17.7	30.6	0.3
	2001	3932	8.8	0.7	23.5	1.1	64.9	7.4	17.1	40.5	1.0
Tunisia - Tunisie	1990	5476	10.6	4.3	9.0	4.5	71.3	8.7	34.3	28.3	0.1
	1995	7903	12.5	4.2	7.3	3.0	72.7	8.9	37.8	26.0	0.3
	2000	8566	8.2	3.0	10.6	2.5	75.4	8.6	34.5	32.2	0.2
	2003	10147	9.1	3.0	6.9	2.7	78.1	10.2	37.6	30.4	0.3
Turkey - Turquie	1990	22301	8.3	4.2	20.8	5.5	61.1	12.7	16.9	31.5	0.1
	1995	35707	7.0	5.5	13.0	5.9	68.4	14.8	21.5	32.1	0.2
	2000	54150	3.9	3.7	17.6	4.0	70.6	13.4	19.5	37.6	0.2
	2003	69340	4.0	3.5	16.8	5.3	66.1	14.8	20.3	31.0	4.3
Turkmenistan - Turkménistan	2000	1786	11.7	0.4	1.2	1.0	79.8	8.7	26.8	44.3	5.9
Uganda - Ouganda	1995	1038	15.8	2.6	1.8	2.0	77.8	10.4	32.5	34.8	0.1
	2000	936	14.1	2.2	17.5	1.5	64.6	11.3	26.2	27.1	0.1
	2003	1375	16.2	2.0	13.7	1.3	66.7	13.0	28.8	24.9	0.1
Ukraine	2000	13956	6.3	1.5	43.0	5.4	41.0	8.6	14.8	17.6	2.7
	2002	16976	6.4	1.3	39.3	3.4	48.3	10.4	17.0	20.9	1.3
United Arab Emirates - Emirats arabes unis	1990	11580	14.4	0.9	3.2	4.3	76.6	7.2	37.5	31.9	0.7
United Kingdom - Royaume-Uni	1990	224771	10.3	2.9	6.3	3.8	75.5	8.4	29.7	37.4	1.3
	1995	261456	10.1	2.4	3.6	3.4	79.7	10.2	28.2	41.2	0.9
	2000	330197	7.9	1.7	4.5	2.8	82.2	9.1	27.1	46.0	0.8
	2003	399478	8.9	1.6	4.6	2.2	82.1	11.1	27.5	43.6	0.7
United Republic of Tanzania - République-Unie de Tanzanie	1995	1653	10.0	1.2	0.5	3.8	84.4	19.5	26.6	38.3	0.0
	2000	1586	14.6	2.5	18.6	1.2	63.1	10.0	20.3	32.8	0.0
	2003	2193	13.2	1.8	18.5	0.9	65.5	12.2	21.4	31.8	0.0
United States - Etats-Unis	1990	517524	5.8	1.9	13.3	3.0	72.6	4.5	26.8	41.3	3.4
	1995	770821	4.8	2.1	8.2	2.7	78.9	5.4	27.1	46.4	3.4
	2000	1258080	4.1	1.4	11.1	2.2	77.0	6.0	26.2	44.8	4.2
	2003	1305092	4.6	1.3	12.5	1.7	75.9	7.9	27.1	40.9	4.0
Uruguay	1990	1415	6.9	3.8	18.1	2.0	69.1	20.4	18.6	30.2	0.0
	1995	2866	10.4	4.0	10.2	1.2	74.3	15.0	24.8	34.5	0.0
	2000	3466	11.5	2.6	15.4	1.1	69.3	16.6	24.9	27.9	0.0
	2003	2190	12.6	4.8	22.2	1.5	58.9	22.1	20.9	15.9	0.0
Venezuela	1990	6601	11.2	3.7	3.3	4.4	76.6	15.4	19.7	41.4	0.8
	1995	10791	14.3	4.5	1.2	3.7	76.4	16.2	22.5	37.7	0.0
	2000	14584	11.7	1.8	3.7	1.8	81.0	14.0	24.8	42.2	0.1
	2003	8358	17.3	2.0	2.0	1.7	76.8	20.5	20.2	36.1	0.2
Viet Nam	2000	15637	5.2	2.9	13.5	2.3	72.8	15.2	27.5	30.0	3.3
	2002	19746	6.2	3.1	11.0	2.8	76.1	14.6	32.5	28.9	0.9
Wallis and Futuna Islands - Iles Wallis et Futuna	2003	39	28.6	1.1	9.5	0.2	59.0	7.9	24.1	27.1	1.6
Yemen - Yémen	1995	1817	28.9	2.4	7.9	1.4	59.4	8.2	28.1	23.1	0.0
	2000	2326	35.6	1.5	12.0	1.1	48.7	9.7	18.2	20.8	1.0
Yugoslavia, SFR (former) - Yougoslavie, RSF (anc.)	1990	18869	12.0	4.7	17.0	3.6	62.3	12.5	23.2	26.6	0.4

For sources, see end of table.

Pour les sources, se reporter à la fin du tableau.

Country or area / Pays ou zones	Year / Année	Total value (millions of dollars) / Valeur totale (millions de dollars)	By main categories of imports (percentage) / Par principales catégories de produits importés (en pourcentage)								
			All food items / Produits alimentaires	Agricultural raw materials / Matières premières d'origine agricole	Fuels / Combustibles	Ores and metals / Minéraux et métaux	Manufactured goods / Produits manufacturés	of which: / dont:			Unallocated / Non distribué
								Chemical products / Produits chimiques	Other manufactured goods / Articles manufacturés divers	Machinery and transport equipment / Machines et matériel de transport	
SITC / CTCI			0+1+22+4	2 less (22+27+28)	3	27+28+68	5 to 8 less 68	5	(6+8) less 68	7	
Zambia - Zambie	1995	708	9.9	2.3	13.2	2.1	72.3	13.4	21.0	37.9	0.2
	2000	993	7.3	2.4	18.0	2.5	69.2	13.5	25.3	30.4	0.6
	2002	1253	13.9	1.6	7.1	1.6	75.0	15.1	28.8	31.1	0.7
Zimbabwe	1990	1852	3.7	2.6	15.6	2.5	72.7	15.4	20.0	37.4	3.0
	1995	2659	6.0	1.9	9.0	2.1	77.9	13.7	21.9	42.3	3.1
	2002	2467	11.1	1.9	8.3	2.3	75.9	18.5	23.1	34.2	0.5

Sources: UNCTAD secretariat computations based on UN/DESA/Statistics Division's data.

Sources: Calculs du secrétariat de la CNUCED sur la base de données de ONU/DAES/Division de statistique.

Notes:

1   From 1996, France data include trade of French Guiana, Guadeloupe, Martinique and Reunion.

Notes :

1   A partir de 1996, les données de la France incluent celles de la Guadeloupe, la Guyane française, la Martinique et la Réunion.

4.2A Export structure at the SITC Revision 2 group (3-digit) level (ranked by average 2001-2002 values)
World

4.2A Structure des exportations au niveau des groupes (position à trois chiffres) de la CTCI révision 2 (classées d'après la moyenne des valeurs de 2001-2002)
Monde

SITC group / Groupes de la CTCI	1990-1991			2001-2002			Growth rates (percentage) / Taux d'accroissement (en pourcentage) (1990-2002)	
	Value (millions of dollars) / Valeur (millions de dollars)	Percentage of the grouping total / En pourcentage du total du groupement	Percentage of world / En pourcentage du monde	Value (millions of dollars) / Valeur (millions de dollars)	Percentage of the grouping total / En pourcentage du total du groupement	Percentage of world / En pourcentage du monde	Value / Valeur	Difference from world / Différence par rapport au monde
	1	2	3	4	5	6	7	8
All commodity groups	3407618	100.00	100.00	6144369	100.00	100.00	5.8	0.0
781 Passengr motor vehicl, exc bus	170783	5.01	100.00	325072	5.29	100.00	6.2	0.0
333 Crude petroleum	182154	5.35	100.00	319256	5.20	100.00	5.6	0.0
776 Transistors, valves, etc	67559	1.98	100.00	246838	4.02	100.00	13.7	0.0
764 Telecom equip, parts, acces	62548	1.84	100.00	207779	3.38	100.00	12.3	0.0
752 Automatic data processing equip	71974	2.11	100.00	182433	2.97	100.00	9.9	0.0
759 Office, adp machy parts, acces	52867	1.55	100.00	149741	2.44	100.00	10.8	0.0
541 Medicinal, pharmaceutical prdts	39338	1.15	100.00	149005	2.43	100.00	12.2	0.0
334 Petroleum products, refined	84532	2.48	100.00	146717	2.39	100.00	5.6	0.0
784 Motor vehicl parts, acces nes	85038	2.50	100.00	144635	2.35	100.00	5.5	0.0
931 Special transactions	62175	1.82	100.00	129568	2.11	100.00	6.7	0.0
792 Aircraft, etc	72394	2.12	100.00	116057	1.89	100.00	5.1	0.0
778 Electrical machinery nes	39075	1.15	100.00	91922	1.50	100.00	8.4	0.0
772 Switchgear etc, parts nes	37295	1.09	100.00	87625	1.43	100.00	8.8	0.0
583 Polymerization, etc, prdts	48101	1.41	100.00	84126	1.37	100.00	5.7	0.0
341 Gas, natural and manufactured	34405	1.01	100.00	80241	1.31	100.00	8.6	0.0
874 Measuring, controlg instruments	37950	1.11	100.00	74025	1.20	100.00	6.8	0.0
641 Paper and paperboard	50242	1.47	100.00	73461	1.20	100.00	4.1	0.0
713 Intern combust piston engines	36707	1.08	100.00	68745	1.12	100.00	6.3	0.0
749 Non-electr machy parts, acces	37371	1.10	100.00	67758	1.10	100.00	5.8	0.0
821 Furniture and parts thereof	30474	0.89	100.00	64001	1.04	100.00	7.4	0.0
728 Oth machy for spec industries	39641	1.16	100.00	63657	1.04	100.00	5.3	0.0
893 Articles of plastic nes	29160	0.86	100.00	59117	0.96	100.00	6.8	0.0
782 Lorries, spec motor vehicl nes	37339	1.10	100.00	57882	0.94	100.00	4.6	0.0
667 Pearl, prec, semi-prec stones	25416	0.75	100.00	55315	0.90	100.00	7.1	0.0
714 Engines and motors nes	23016	0.68	100.00	53721	0.87	100.00	8.7	0.0
699 Base metal manufactures nes	24917	0.73	100.00	51047	0.83	100.00	7.1	0.0
845 Outer garments knit nonelastic	27918	0.82	100.00	50008	0.81	100.00	5.8	0.0
674 Iron, steel univ, plate, sheet	36648	1.08	100.00	49220	0.80	100.00	3.1	0.0
843 Women's outwear non-knit	28682	0.84	100.00	49194	0.80	100.00	4.7	0.0
894 Toys, sporting goods, etc	25399	0.75	100.00	47978	0.78	100.00	5.9	0.0
684 Aluminium	28271	0.83	100.00	47967	0.78	100.00	5.5	0.0
598 Miscel chemical prdts nes	21636	0.63	100.00	45532	0.74	100.00	7.2	0.0
515 Organo-inorgan compounds, etc	13773	0.40	100.00	45416	0.74	100.00	12.1	0.0
793 Ships, boats, etc	26413	0.78	100.00	44605	0.73	100.00	4.6	0.0
851 Footwear	30303	0.89	100.00	42917	0.70	100.00	3.0	0.0
775 Household type equip nes	22536	0.66	100.00	41979	0.68	100.00	5.6	0.0
743 Pumps nes, centrifuges, etc	20437	0.60	100.00	40884	0.67	100.00	6.6	0.0
741 Heating, cooling equipment	24052	0.71	100.00	40884	0.67	100.00	5.0	0.0
582 Prdts of condensation, etc	17920	0.53	100.00	39512	0.64	100.00	7.8	0.0
011 Meat, fresh, chilled, frozen	28982	0.85	100.00	38794	0.63	100.00	2.2	0.0
723 Civil engineering equip, etc	21638	0.64	100.00	37880	0.62	100.00	5.5	0.0
773 Electricity distributing equip	14042	0.41	100.00	37659	0.61	100.00	9.5	0.0
842 Men's outwear non-knit	18942	0.56	100.00	34750	0.57	100.00	5.6	0.0
898 Musical instruments and parts	19863	0.58	100.00	33381	0.54	100.00	4.9	0.0
846 Under garments knitted	13854	0.41	100.00	33105	0.54	100.00	8.7	0.0
771 Electric power machinery nes	11514	0.34	100.00	32748	0.53	100.00	10.8	0.0
716 Rotating electric plant	14357	0.42	100.00	32635	0.53	100.00	7.5	0.0
651 Textile yarn	25057	0.74	100.00	32515	0.53	100.00	2.7	0.0
892 Printed matter	19331	0.57	100.00	31419	0.51	100.00	4.6	0.0
112 Alcoholic beverages	19610	0.58	100.00	31221	0.51	100.00	4.3	0.0
761 Television receivers	17657	0.52	100.00	30552	0.50	100.00	4.9	0.0
744 Mechanical handling equipment	22390	0.66	100.00	29777	0.48	100.00	3.2	0.0
763 Sound recorders, phonographs	16303	0.48	100.00	29710	0.48	100.00	5.0	0.0
872 Medical instruments nes	11034	0.32	100.00	29687	0.48	100.00	9.3	0.0

For sources and notes, see end of table 4.2E.

Pour les sources et les notes, se reporter à la fin du tableau 4.2E.

148

4.2A Export structure at the SITC Revision 2 group (3-digit) level (ranked by average 2001-2002 values)
World (continued)

4.2A Structure des exportations au niveau des groupes (position à trois chiffres) de la CTCI révision 2 (classées d'après la moyenne des valeurs de 2001-2002)
Monde (suite)

SITC group / Groupes de la CTCI	1990-1991			2001-2002			Growth rates (percentage) Taux d'accroissement (en pourcentage) (1990-2002)	
	Value (millions of dollars) Valeur (millions de dollars)	Percentage of the grouping total En pourcentage du total du groupement	Percentage of world En pourcentage du monde	Value (millions of dollars) Valeur (millions de dollars)	Percentage of the grouping total En pourcentage du total du groupement	Percentage of world En pourcentage du monde	Value Valeur	Difference from world Différence par rapport au monde
	1	2	3	4	5	6	7	8
653 Woven man-made fib fabric	24990	0.73	100.00	29492	0.48	100.00	1.6	0.0
682 Copper	23535	0.69	100.00	29414	0.48	100.00	2.6	0.0
642 Paper and paperboard, cut	14198	0.42	100.00	29274	0.48	100.00	6.8	0.0
057 Fruit, nuts, fresh, dried	20170	0.59	100.00	28784	0.47	100.00	3.4	0.0
736 Metal working machy, tools	23874	0.70	100.00	28597	0.47	100.00	3.0	0.0
553 Perfumery, cosmetics, etc	10710	0.31	100.00	26896	0.44	100.00	8.5	0.0
514 Nitrogen-function compounds	16322	0.48	100.00	26028	0.42	100.00	3.8	0.0
672 Iron, steel primary forms	19081	0.56	100.00	25986	0.42	100.00	3.0	0.0
899 Other manufactured goods	12414	0.36	100.00	25685	0.42	100.00	6.5	0.0
625 Rubber tyres,tubes, etc	15825	0.46	100.00	25168	0.41	100.00	4.6	0.0
248 Wood, shaped, rail sleepers	18121	0.53	100.00	24980	0.41	100.00	2.7	0.0
897 Gold, silver ware, jewellery	13804	0.41	100.00	24804	0.40	100.00	5.1	0.0
054 Vegtb etc fresh, simply prsrvd	17422	0.51	100.00	24521	0.40	100.00	3.0	0.0
745 Non-electr machy, tools nes	16413	0.48	100.00	24461	0.40	100.00	3.9	0.0
533 Pigments, paints, varnishes etc	11912	0.35	100.00	24452	0.40	100.00	7.1	0.0
652 Cotton fabrics, woven	16318	0.48	100.00	23377	0.38	100.00	3.4	0.0
678 Iron, steel tubes, pipes, etc	18290	0.54	100.00	22996	0.37	100.00	2.5	0.0
673 Iron, steel shapes, etc	18712	0.55	100.00	22900	0.37	100.00	1.6	0.0
034 Fish, fresh, chilled, frozen	15113	0.44	100.00	22788	0.37	100.00	3.7	0.0
081 Feeding stuff for animals	16097	0.47	100.00	22382	0.36	100.00	2.5	0.0
884 Optical goods nes	5879	0.17	100.00	21413	0.35	100.00	13.0	0.0
322 Coal, lignite and peat	18440	0.54	100.00	21010	0.34	100.00	0.8	0.0
511 Hydrocarbons nes, derivtives	15069	0.44	100.00	20785	0.34	100.00	3.5	0.0
695 Tools	12542	0.37	100.00	20766	0.34	100.00	5.2	0.0
785 Cycles, etc, motorized or not	11170	0.33	100.00	20434	0.33	100.00	5.2	0.0
742 Pumps for liquids, etc	11665	0.34	100.00	20291	0.33	100.00	5.3	0.0
657 Spec textile fabrics, products	11618	0.34	100.00	20105	0.33	100.00	5.2	0.0
724 Textile, leather machinery	21895	0.64	100.00	19424	0.32	100.00	-1.5	0.0
812 Plumbg, heatg, lightg equip	9589	0.28	100.00	19037	0.31	100.00	6.4	0.0
287 Base metals ores, conc nes	16758	0.49	100.00	19000	0.31	100.00	2.1	0.0
098 Edible products, preps nes	8497	0.25	100.00	18983	0.31	100.00	6.8	0.0
251 Pulp and waste paper	16472	0.48	100.00	18889	0.31	100.00	2.0	0.0
048 Cereal etc preparations	9965	0.29	100.00	18665	0.30	100.00	5.6	0.0
885 Watches and clocks	16071	0.47	100.00	18283	0.30	100.00	1.0	0.0
658 Textile articles nes	9126	0.27	100.00	18260	0.30	100.00	6.6	0.0
635 Wood manufactures nes	8709	0.26	100.00	17435	0.28	100.00	6.9	0.0
664 Glass	9367	0.27	100.00	17275	0.28	100.00	5.9	0.0
611 Leather	9528	0.28	100.00	17241	0.28	100.00	5.3	0.0
513 Carboxylic acids, etc	9802	0.29	100.00	17160	0.28	100.00	5.1	0.0
762 Radio-broadcast receivers	14034	0.41	100.00	16870	0.27	100.00	1.4	0.0
036 Shell fish fresh, frozen	11865	0.35	100.00	16803	0.27	100.00	3.0	0.0
882 Photogr and cinema supplies	12770	0.37	100.00	16544	0.27	100.00	2.8	0.0
522 Inorg chem elmnt, oxides, etc	12477	0.37	100.00	16400	0.27	100.00	2.9	0.0
774 Electro-medical, xray equip	8430	0.25	100.00	16377	0.27	100.00	6.0	0.0
831 Travel goods, handbags, etc	8652	0.25	100.00	16227	0.26	100.00	5.6	0.0
881 Photogr apparatus, equip nes	8011	0.24	100.00	15793	0.26	100.00	7.2	0.0
783 Road motor vehicles nes	7152	0.21	100.00	15558	0.25	100.00	7.6	0.0
655 Knitted, etc, fabric	7215	0.21	100.00	15452	0.25	100.00	7.5	0.0
122 Tobacco, manufactured	13045	0.38	100.00	15433	0.25	100.00	1.4	0.0
292 Crude vegetb materials nes	11733	0.34	100.00	15348	0.25	100.00	2.4	0.0
041 Wheat etc, unmilled	14494	0.43	100.00	15030	0.24	100.00	0.0	0.0
848 Headgear, non-textile clothing	10404	0.31	100.00	14898	0.24	100.00	2.8	0.0
691 Structures and parts nes	9680	0.28	100.00	14772	0.24	100.00	3.9	0.0
562 Fertilizers, manufactured	14490	0.43	100.00	14712	0.24	100.00	0.6	0.0
222 Seeds for soft fixed oils	10074	0.30	100.00	14594	0.24	100.00	3.8	0.0

For sources and notes, see end of table 4.2E.

Pour les sources et les notes, se reporter à la fin du tableau 4.2E.

4.2A Export structure at the SITC Revision 2 group (3-digit) level (ranked by average 2001-2002 values)
World (continued)

4.2A Structure des exportations au niveau des groupes (position à trois chiffres) de la CTCI révision 2 (classées d'après la moyenne des valeurs de 2001-2002)
Monde (suite)

SITC group Groupes de la CTCI	1990-1991			2001-2002			Growth rates (percentage) Taux d'accroissement (en pourcentage) (1990-2002)	
	Value (millions of dollars) Valeur (millions de dollars)	Percentage of the grouping total En pourcentage du total du groupement	Percentage of world En pourcentage du monde	Value (millions of dollars) Valeur (millions de dollars)	Percentage of the grouping total En pourcentage du total du groupement	Percentage of world En pourcentage du monde	Value Valeur	Difference from world Différence par rapport au monde
	1	2	3	4	5	6	7	8
512 Alcohols, phenols, etc	8016	0.24	100.00	14524	0.24	100.00	5.7	0.0
554 Soap, cleansing, etc preps	7135	0.21	100.00	14446	0.24	100.00	6.5	0.0
516 Other organic chemicals	7030	0.21	100.00	14020	0.23	100.00	6.9	0.0
697 Base metal household equip	6806	0.20	100.00	13721	0.22	100.00	6.4	0.0
726 Print and bookbind machy, parts	10809	0.32	100.00	13712	0.22	100.00	2.6	0.0
634 Veneers, plywood, etc	9551	0.28	100.00	13580	0.22	100.00	3.0	0.0
663 Mineral manufactures nes	8684	0.25	100.00	13454	0.22	100.00	4.4	0.0
022 Milk and cream	8880	0.26	100.00	13335	0.22	100.00	3.1	0.0
058 Fruit prsrvd, preprd	8952	0.26	100.00	12714	0.21	100.00	3.3	0.0
061 Sugar and honey	11843	0.35	100.00	12574	0.20	100.00	0.2	0.0
751 Office machines	11868	0.35	100.00	12571	0.20	100.00	0.9	0.0
871 Optical instruments	3540	0.10	100.00	12469	0.20	100.00	14.3	0.0
523 Other inorganic chemicals	7957	0.23	100.00	12183	0.20	100.00	4.0	0.0
721 Agricult machinry exc tractor	8724	0.26	100.00	11714	0.19	100.00	3.3	0.0
694 Stell, copper nails, nuts, etc	6535	0.19	100.00	11691	0.19	100.00	6.0	0.0
628 Rubber articles nes	5018	0.15	100.00	11690	0.19	100.00	8.1	0.0
661 Lime, cement and building prdts	7537	0.22	100.00	11397	0.19	100.00	3.8	0.0
844 Under garments non-knit	7730	0.23	100.00	11114	0.18	100.00	3.0	0.0
024 Cheese and curd	8035	0.24	100.00	11043	0.18	100.00	2.4	0.0
591 Pesticides, disinfectants	7307	0.21	100.00	10794	0.18	100.00	4.3	0.0
665 Glassware	7051	0.21	100.00	10776	0.18	100.00	4.0	0.0
662 Clay, refractory building prdts	7436	0.22	100.00	10709	0.17	100.00	3.2	0.0
786 Trailers, non-motor vehicl nes	7169	0.21	100.00	10707	0.17	100.00	4.3	0.0
681 Silver, platinum, etc	5764	0.17	100.00	10687	0.17	100.00	8.0	0.0
037 Fish etc prepd, prsrvd nes	6518	0.19	100.00	9719	0.16	100.00	3.7	0.0
592 Starch, inulin, gluten, etc	4995	0.15	100.00	9676	0.16	100.00	6.2	0.0
281 Iron ore and concentrates	8361	0.25	100.00	9569	0.16	100.00	1.7	0.0
847 Textile clothing accessoris nes	5334	0.16	100.00	9543	0.16	100.00	5.8	0.0
044 Maize (corn), unmilled	9193	0.27	100.00	9413	0.15	100.00	-0.1	0.0
896 Works of art, etc	11357	0.33	100.00	9401	0.15	100.00	-0.3	0.0
551 Essential oils, perfume, etc	3785	0.11	100.00	9259	0.15	100.00	8.9	0.0
423 Fixed vegetable oils, soft	6298	0.18	100.00	9070	0.15	100.00	4.0	0.0
335 Residual petroleum prdts nes	5038	0.15	100.00	8990	0.15	100.00	6.5	0.0
791 Railway vehicles	5003	0.15	100.00	8934	0.15	100.00	5.2	0.0
001 Live animals for food	9440	0.28	100.00	8823	0.14	100.00	-0.7	0.0
531 Synth dye, natrl indigo, lakes	7697	0.23	100.00	8751	0.14	100.00	1.3	0.0
659 Floor coverings, etc	8982	0.26	100.00	8696	0.14	100.00	-0.2	0.0
071 Coffee and substitutes	8648	0.25	100.00	8693	0.14	100.00	1.8	0.0
654 Other woven textile fabric	8706	0.26	100.00	8617	0.14	100.00	-0.1	0.0
737 Metal working machinery nes	7039	0.21	100.00	8523	0.14	100.00	2.7	0.0
621 Materials of rubber	4083	0.12	100.00	8356	0.14	100.00	6.9	0.0
671 Pig iron, etc	6475	0.19	100.00	8254	0.13	100.00	2.6	0.0
282 Iron and steel scrap	5006	0.15	100.00	8012	0.13	100.00	4.1	0.0
722 Tractors non-road	6785	0.20	100.00	8012	0.13	100.00	2.6	0.0
056 Vegtb etc prsrvd, preprd	5336	0.16	100.00	7882	0.13	100.00	3.4	0.0
073 Chocolate and products	4327	0.13	100.00	7859	0.13	100.00	4.9	0.0
288 Non-ferrous metal scrap nes	5770	0.17	100.00	7828	0.13	100.00	3.4	0.0
895 Office supplies nes	4642	0.14	100.00	7683	0.13	100.00	5.1	0.0
424 Other fixed vegetable oils	3769	0.11	100.00	7531	0.12	100.00	6.6	0.0
263 Cotton	8847	0.26	100.00	7329	0.12	100.00	-1.9	0.0
247 Other wood rough, squared	7687	0.23	100.00	7187	0.12	100.00	-0.9	0.0
278 Other crude minerals	6781	0.20	100.00	7026	0.11	100.00	0.9	0.0
692 Metal tanks, boxes, etc	5013	0.15	100.00	6984	0.11	100.00	3.2	0.0
612 Leather, etc, manufactures	4337	0.13	100.00	6896	0.11	100.00	3.7	0.0
042 Rice	4307	0.13	100.00	6813	0.11	100.00	4.6	0.0

For sources and notes, see end of table 4.2E.

Pour les sources et les notes, se reporter à la fin du tableau 4.2E.

4.2A Export structure at the SITC Revision 2 group (3-digit) level (ranked by average 2001-2002 values)
World *(concluded)*

4.2A Structure des exportations au niveau des groupes (position à trois chiffres) de la CTCI révision 2 (classées d'après la moyenne des valeurs de 2001-2002)
Monde *(fin)*

SITC group / Groupes de la CTCI	1990-1991			2001-2002			Growth rates (percentage) Taux d'accroissement (en pourcentage) (1990-2002)	
	Value (millions of dollars) Valeur (millions de dollars)	Percentage of the grouping total En pourcentage du total du groupement	Percentage of world En pourcentage du monde	Value (millions of dollars) Valeur (millions de dollars)	Percentage of the grouping total En pourcentage du total du groupement	Percentage of world En pourcentage du monde	Value Valeur	Difference from world Différence par rapport au monde
	1	2	3	4	5	6	7	8
725 Paper etc mill machinery	6887	0.20	100.00	6550	0.11	100.00	0.7	0.0
683 Nickel	3518	0.10	100.00	6535	0.11	100.00	7.0	0.0
718 Oth power generating machinery	3676	0.11	100.00	6391	0.10	100.00	5.9	0.0
014 Meat prepd, prsrvd nes, etc	4226	0.12	100.00	6380	0.10	100.00	3.4	0.0
233 Rubber, synthetic, reclaimed	5304	0.16	100.00	6288	0.10	100.00	2.5	0.0
111 Non alcoholic beverages nes	2550	0.07	100.00	6125	0.10	100.00	7.7	0.0
727 Food machinery, non-demestic	5293	0.16	100.00	5910	0.10	100.00	1.0	0.0
211 Hides skins, exc furs, raw	5024	0.15	100.00	5597	0.09	100.00	0.4	0.0
121 Tobacco, unmanufactd, refuse	5256	0.15	100.00	5569	0.09	100.00	0.9	0.0
696 Cutlery	2872	0.08	100.00	5412	0.09	100.00	6.0	0.0
524 Radioactive etc materials	5095	0.15	100.00	5358	0.09	100.00	-0.5	0.0
656 Lace, ribbon, tulle, etc	3048	0.09	100.00	5295	0.09	100.00	5.2	0.0
072 Cocoa	4009	0.12	100.00	5292	0.09	100.00	2.3	0.0
666 Pottery	4485	0.13	100.00	4985	0.08	100.00	1.2	0.0
693 Wire products, non-electric	3474	0.10	100.00	4842	0.08	100.00	3.5	0.0
679 Iron, steel castings unworked	2573	0.08	100.00	4671	0.08	100.00	6.4	0.0
686 Zinc	4095	0.12	100.00	4477	0.07	100.00	2.2	0.0
951 War firearms, ammunition	5402	0.16	100.00	4464	0.07	100.00	-1.4	0.0
062 Sugar preps non-chocolate	2213	0.06	100.00	4270	0.07	100.00	5.8	0.0
266 Synthetic fibres for spinning	3936	0.12	100.00	4237	0.07	100.00	0.9	0.0
273 Stone, sand and gravel	2653	0.08	100.00	3927	0.06	100.00	3.5	0.0
677 Iron, steel wire, exc w rod	3150	0.09	100.00	3671	0.06	100.00	1.6	0.0
232 Natural rubber, gums	4151	0.12	100.00	3651	0.06	100.00	-1.6	0.0
431 Procesd animl and veg oil, etc	2029	0.06	100.00	3565	0.06	100.00	4.5	0.0
689 Non-fer base metals nes	1794	0.05	100.00	3457	0.06	100.00	7.2	0.0
291 Crude animal materials nes	2678	0.08	100.00	3402	0.06	100.00	2.4	0.0
289 Prec metal ores, waste nes	1180	0.03	100.00	3220	0.05	100.00	11.1	0.0
268 Wool (exc tops), animal hair	5679	0.17	100.00	3196	0.05	100.00	-5.3	0.0
712 Steam engines, turbines	2823	0.08	100.00	3047	0.05	100.00	1.0	0.0
873 Meters and counters nes	1393	0.04	100.00	2942	0.05	100.00	6.9	0.0
584 Cellulose, derivatives, etc	1948	0.06	100.00	2794	0.05	100.00	3.1	0.0
035 Fish salted, dried, smoked	2287	0.07	100.00	2774	0.05	100.00	1.8	0.0

For sources and notes, see end of table 4.2E.

Pour les sources et les notes, se reporter à la fin du tableau 4.2E.

SITC group / Groupes de la CTCI	1990-1991			2001-2002			Growth rates (percentage) Taux d'accroissement (en pourcentage) (1990-2002)	
	Value (millions of dollars) Valeur (millions de dollars)	Percentage of the grouping total En pourcentage du total du groupement	Percentage of world En pourcentage du monde	Value (millions of dollars) Valeur (millions de dollars)	Percentage of the grouping total En pourcentage du total du groupement	Percentage of world En pourcentage du monde	Value Valeur	Difference from world Différence par rapport au monde
	1	2	3	4	5	6	7	8
All commodity groups	2495591	100.00	73.24	4032905	100.00	65.64	4.8	-1.0
781 Passengr motor vehicl, exc bus	162543	6.51	95.17	288609	7.16	88.78	5.5	-0.7
541 Medicinal, pharmaceutical prdts	35568	1.43	90.42	138916	3.44	93.23	12.5	0.2
764 Telecom equip, parts, acces	47696	1.91	76.25	126816	3.14	61.03	10.6	-1.7
784 Motor vehicl parts, acces nes	76699	3.07	90.19	125801	3.12	86.98	5.0	-0.4
776 Transistors, valves, etc	45185	1.81	66.88	125779	3.12	50.96	10.7	-3.0
792 Aircraft, etc	69301	2.78	95.73	107997	2.68	93.06	4.9	-0.3
931 Special transactions	47250	1.89	75.99	101607	2.52	78.42	7.5	0.8
752 Automatic data processing equip	55912	2.24	77.68	98878	2.45	54.20	6.3	-3.5
759 Office, adp machy parts, acces	42163	1.69	79.75	73908	1.83	49.36	6.1	-4.8
641 Paper and paperboard	46592	1.87	92.73	63888	1.58	86.97	3.5	-0.6
334 Petroleum products, refined	43033	1.72	50.91	63825	1.58	43.50	3.8	-1.8
874 Measuring, controlg instruments	35805	1.43	94.35	63773	1.58	86.15	5.9	-0.8
778 Electrical machinery nes	33400	1.34	85.48	61586	1.53	67.00	6.4	-2.0
583 Polymerization, etc, prdts	40379	1.62	83.95	61322	1.52	72.89	4.4	-1.2
713 Intern combust piston engines	32961	1.32	89.80	60423	1.50	87.90	6.1	-0.2
333 Crude petroleum	28247	1.13	15.51	58847	1.46	18.43	7.0	1.4
772 Switchgear etc, parts nes	32755	1.31	87.83	58676	1.45	66.96	6.3	-2.6
728 Oth machy for spec industries	35083	1.41	88.50	55032	1.36	86.45	5.0	-0.2
749 Non-electr machy parts, acces	33782	1.35	90.40	54999	1.36	81.17	4.8	-1.0
714 Engines and motors nes	22097	0.89	96.01	50593	1.25	94.18	8.6	-0.1
782 Lorries, spec motor vehicl nes	35547	1.42	95.20	46051	1.14	79.56	2.9	-1.6
821 Furniture and parts thereof	24848	1.00	81.54	44347	1.10	69.29	5.9	-1.4
515 Organo-inorgan compounds, etc	12226	0.49	88.77	40926	1.01	90.11	12.3	0.2
893 Articles of plastic nes	23088	0.93	79.18	40502	1.00	68.51	5.6	-1.2
598 Miscel chemical prdts nes	19804	0.79	91.53	39284	0.97	86.28	6.6	-0.6
699 Base metal manufactures nes	20525	0.82	82.37	37625	0.93	73.71	6.3	-0.9
667 Pearl, prec, semi-prec stones	18925	0.76	74.46	36224	0.90	65.49	6.4	-0.8
674 Iron, steel univ, plate, sheet	31328	1.26	85.48	34676	0.86	70.45	1.3	-1.8
743 Pumps nes, centrifuges, etc	18731	0.75	91.65	33903	0.84	82.93	5.8	-0.8
341 Gas, natural and manufactured	12383	0.50	35.99	33698	0.84	42.00	9.5	0.9
684 Aluminium	22374	0.90	79.14	32669	0.81	68.11	4.2	-1.3
011 Meat, fresh, chilled, frozen	24905	1.00	85.93	31839	0.79	82.07	1.8	-0.4
723 Civil engineering equip, etc	19366	0.78	89.50	31509	0.78	83.18	4.8	-0.7
741 Heating, cooling equipment	21955	0.88	91.28	31172	0.77	76.25	3.6	-1.4
582 Prdts of condensation, etc	16077	0.64	89.72	30677	0.76	77.64	6.5	-1.4
793 Ships, boats, etc	19923	0.80	75.43	27978	0.69	62.72	2.7	-1.9
744 Mechanical handling equipment	20718	0.83	92.53	26629	0.66	89.43	3.0	-0.3
112 Alcoholic beverages	17970	0.72	91.64	26327	0.65	84.33	3.6	-0.7
892 Printed matter	17405	0.70	90.04	26025	0.65	82.83	3.8	-0.8
872 Medical instruments nes	10199	0.41	92.44	24600	0.61	82.86	8.4	-0.9
736 Metal working machy, tools	21428	0.86	89.75	24422	0.61	85.40	2.5	-0.4
775 Household type equip nes	17015	0.68	75.50	24054	0.60	57.30	3.3	-2.4
898 Musical instruments and parts	16580	0.66	83.47	24040	0.60	72.02	3.7	-1.2
553 Perfumery, cosmetics, etc	9334	0.37	87.15	22910	0.57	85.18	8.2	-0.3
642 Paper and paperboard, cut	12320	0.49	86.77	22634	0.56	77.32	5.8	-1.1
773 Electricity distributing equip	11210	0.45	79.83	22229	0.55	59.03	7.0	-2.5
514 Nitrogen-function compounds	14896	0.60	91.26	22215	0.55	85.35	3.0	-0.8
716 Rotating electric plant	11954	0.48	83.26	21840	0.54	66.92	5.3	-2.2
745 Non-electr machy, tools nes	15600	0.63	95.04	21539	0.53	88.06	3.3	-0.7
533 Pigments, paints, varnishes etc	10824	0.43	90.86	20198	0.50	82.60	6.2	-0.9
894 Toys, sporting goods, etc	11399	0.46	44.88	19968	0.50	41.62	5.4	-0.5
248 Wood, shaped, rail sleepers	13303	0.53	73.42	18538	0.46	74.21	2.9	0.1
625 Rubber tyres,tubes, etc	13296	0.53	84.02	18237	0.45	72.46	3.3	-1.3
742 Pumps for liquids, etc	11143	0.45	95.52	18128	0.45	89.34	4.7	-0.6

For sources and notes, see end of table 4.2E.

Pour les sources et les notes, se reporter à la fin du tableau 4.2E.

4.2B Export structure at the SITC Revision 2 group (3-digit) level (ranked by average 2001-2002 values)
Developed economies
(continued)

4.2B Structure des exportations au niveau des groupes (position à trois chiffres) de la CTCI révision 2 (classées d'après la moyenne des valeurs de 2001-2002)
Economies développées
(suite)

SITC group / Groupes de la CTCI	1990-1991			2001-2002			Growth rates (percentage) Taux d'accroissement (en pourcentage) (1990-2002)	
	Value (millions of dollars) Valeur (millions de dollars)	Percentage of the grouping total En pourcentage du total du groupement	Percentage of world En pourcentage du monde	Value (millions of dollars) Valeur (millions de dollars)	Percentage of the grouping total En pourcentage du total du groupement	Percentage of world En pourcentage du monde	Value Valeur	Difference from world Différence par rapport au monde
	1	2	3	4	5	6	7	8
851 Footwear	13859	0.56	45.73	18061	0.45	42.08	2.5	-0.5
678 Iron, steel tubes, pipes, etc	15497	0.62	84.73	17014	0.42	73.99	1.3	-1.2
771 Electric power machinery nes	8189	0.33	71.12	16941	0.42	51.73	7.9	-2.9
054 Vegtb etc fresh, simply prsrvd	12324	0.49	70.74	16657	0.41	67.93	2.8	-0.3
899 Other manufactured goods	7257	0.29	58.46	16516	0.41	64.30	7.6	1.0
843 Women's outwear non-knit	13295	0.53	46.35	16317	0.40	33.17	1.9	-2.9
884 Optical goods nes	4828	0.19	82.13	16316	0.40	76.20	12.4	-0.6
057 Fruit, nuts, fresh, dried	11671	0.47	57.87	16286	0.40	56.58	3.2	-0.2
048 Cereal etc preparations	9099	0.36	91.30	16008	0.40	85.77	5.1	-0.6
673 Iron, steel shapes, etc	14678	0.59	78.44	15694	0.39	68.53	0.7	-0.8
845 Outer garments knit nonelastic	11372	0.46	40.73	15372	0.38	30.74	3.1	-2.7
774 Electro-medical, xray equip	8230	0.33	97.63	15197	0.38	92.79	5.5	-0.5
724 Textile, leather machinery	18871	0.76	86.19	15094	0.37	77.71	-2.4	-0.8
695 Tools	10600	0.42	84.51	15056	0.37	72.50	3.9	-1.4
682 Copper	13557	0.54	57.60	14883	0.37	50.60	1.2	-1.4
897 Gold, silver ware, jewellery	9886	0.40	71.62	14838	0.37	59.82	3.4	-1.7
511 Hydrocarbons nes, derivtives	13147	0.53	87.25	14817	0.37	71.29	1.6	-1.9
098 Edible products, preps nes	7173	0.29	84.42	14807	0.37	78.00	5.9	-0.9
651 Textile yarn	15160	0.61	60.50	14652	0.36	45.06	0.2	-2.5
251 Pulp and waste paper	14308	0.57	86.86	14566	0.36	77.11	0.8	-1.1
763 Sound recorders, phonographs	11416	0.46	70.03	14325	0.36	48.22	2.5	-2.5
882 Photogr and cinema supplies	11890	0.48	93.11	13907	0.34	84.06	1.8	-1.0
081 Feeding stuff for animals	9800	0.39	60.88	13811	0.34	61.71	2.8	0.3
672 Iron, steel primary forms	12916	0.52	67.69	13718	0.34	52.79	0.8	-2.3
657 Spec textile fabrics, products	8749	0.35	75.31	13580	0.34	67.54	4.2	-1.0
761 Television receivers	10377	0.42	58.77	13565	0.34	44.40	3.7	-1.2
785 Cycles, etc, motorized or not	7839	0.31	70.17	13541	0.34	66.27	4.8	-0.3
034 Fish, fresh, chilled, frozen	10107	0.41	66.87	13368	0.33	58.66	2.8	-0.9
783 Road motor vehicles nes	6771	0.27	94.67	13290	0.33	85.42	6.8	-0.8
664 Glass	8281	0.33	88.40	13249	0.33	76.70	4.6	-1.3
653 Woven man-made fib fabric	13222	0.53	52.91	12743	0.32	43.21	-0.1	-1.7
726 Print and bookbind machy, parts	10506	0.42	97.19	12588	0.31	91.80	2.3	-0.4
812 Plumbg, heatg, lightg equip	7542	0.30	78.65	12137	0.30	63.76	4.6	-1.8
635 Wood manufactures nes	6343	0.25	72.84	11988	0.30	68.76	6.5	-0.4
322 Coal, lignite and peat	13776	0.55	74.71	11971	0.30	56.98	-1.3	-2.2
846 Under garments knitted	5897	0.24	42.57	11697	0.29	35.33	6.8	-1.9
041 Wheat etc, unmilled	13372	0.54	92.26	11658	0.29	77.56	-1.5	-1.5
513 Carboxylic acids, etc	8579	0.34	87.53	11614	0.29	67.68	2.9	-2.3
022 Milk and cream	8502	0.34	95.75	11541	0.29	86.54	2.2	-0.9
842 Men's outwear non-knit	8399	0.34	44.34	11500	0.29	33.09	3.0	-2.6
691 Structures and parts nes	8545	0.34	88.27	11453	0.28	77.53	2.9	-1.0
554 Soap, cleansing, etc preps	6144	0.25	86.10	11452	0.28	79.27	5.6	-0.9
663 Mineral manufactures nes	7717	0.31	88.86	11315	0.28	84.10	4.0	-0.4
122 Tobacco, manufactured	10374	0.42	79.52	11298	0.28	73.21	1.0	-0.4
292 Crude vegetb materials nes	8735	0.35	74.45	11175	0.28	72.81	2.3	-0.2
721 Agricult machinry exc tractor	8098	0.32	92.82	10936	0.27	93.36	3.3	0.0
024 Cheese and curd	7925	0.32	98.63	10648	0.26	96.43	2.2	-0.2
516 Other organic chemicals	6245	0.25	88.83	10543	0.26	75.20	5.2	-1.7
652 Cotton fabrics, woven	8495	0.34	52.06	10408	0.26	44.52	2.1	-1.3
885 Watches and clocks	9579	0.38	59.60	10246	0.25	56.04	0.4	-0.7
522 Inorg chem elmnt, oxides, etc	8825	0.35	70.73	9775	0.24	59.60	1.6	-1.4
881 Photogr apparatus, equip nes	6296	0.25	78.60	9661	0.24	61.17	5.1	-2.2
628 Rubber articles nes	4351	0.17	86.70	9538	0.24	81.59	7.5	-0.6
896 Works of art, etc	10868	0.44	95.69	9102	0.23	96.82	-0.1	0.2
681 Silver, platinum, etc	4412	0.18	76.54	8872	0.22	83.02	8.6	0.6

For sources and notes, see end of table 4.2E.

Pour les sources et les notes, se reporter à la fin du tableau 4.2E.

4.2B Export structure at the SITC Revision 2 group (3-digit) level (ranked by average 2001-2002 values)
Developed economies
(continued)

4.2B Structure des exportations au niveau des groupes (position à trois chiffres) de la CTCI révision 2 (classées d'après la moyenne des valeurs de 2001-2002)
Economies développées
(suite)

SITC group / Groupes de la CTCI	1990-1991			2001-2002			Growth rates (percentage) / Taux d'accroissement (en pourcentage) (1990-2002)	
	Value (millions of dollars) / Valeur (millions de dollars)	Percentage of the grouping total / En pourcentage du total du groupement	Percentage of world / En pourcentage du monde	Value (millions of dollars) / Valeur (millions de dollars)	Percentage of the grouping total / En pourcentage du total du groupement	Percentage of world / En pourcentage du monde	Value / Valeur	Difference from world / Différence par rapport au monde
	1	2	3	4	5	6	7	8
512 Alcohols, phenols, etc	6003	0.24	74.89	8836	0.22	60.83	4.3	-1.3
222 Seeds for soft fixed oils	6624	0.27	65.75	8760	0.22	60.02	2.9	-0.9
562 Fertilizers, manufactured	8967	0.36	61.88	8682	0.22	59.01	0.7	0.1
523 Other inorganic chemicals	6438	0.26	80.91	8659	0.21	71.08	3.0	-1.0
662 Clay, refractory building prdts	6797	0.27	91.41	8580	0.21	80.12	2.1	-1.2
591 Pesticides, disinfectants	6567	0.26	89.88	8562	0.21	79.33	3.1	-1.2
694 Stell, copper nails, nuts, etc	5084	0.20	77.80	8276	0.21	70.79	5.2	-0.8
611 Leather	5662	0.23	59.43	8036	0.20	46.61	3.2	-2.1
287 Base metals ores, conc nes	9086	0.36	54.22	8007	0.20	42.14	0.0	-2.0
665 Glassware	5846	0.23	82.91	7980	0.20	74.06	3.0	-0.9
634 Veneers, plywood, etc	4740	0.19	49.63	7966	0.20	58.66	5.5	2.5
551 Essential oils, perfume, etc	3177	0.13	83.93	7818	0.19	84.44	9.0	0.1
592 Starch, inulin, gluten, etc	4450	0.18	89.09	7818	0.19	80.80	5.3	-0.9
791 Railway vehicles	4155	0.17	83.07	7545	0.19	84.45	4.9	-0.3
058 Fruit prsrvd, preprd	5205	0.21	58.15	7457	0.18	58.65	3.2	-0.1
871 Optical instruments	3069	0.12	86.70	7383	0.18	59.21	9.8	-4.4
737 Metal working machinery nes	6360	0.25	90.36	7347	0.18	86.20	2.2	-0.5
751 Office machines	9786	0.39	82.45	7275	0.18	57.87	-1.9	-2.8
786 Trailers, non-motor vehicl nes	5012	0.20	69.91	7246	0.18	67.67	4.1	-0.2
722 Tractors non-road	6000	0.24	88.43	7225	0.18	90.18	2.7	0.1
001 Live animals for food	6392	0.26	67.72	7187	0.18	81.46	0.7	1.4
621 Materials of rubber	3666	0.15	89.79	7133	0.18	85.37	6.4	-0.5
697 Base metal household equip	4540	0.18	66.71	7047	0.17	51.36	4.0	-2.4
073 Chocolate and products	4072	0.16	94.13	6933	0.17	88.23	4.3	-0.6
044 Maize (corn), unmilled	7685	0.31	83.60	6644	0.16	70.58	-1.3	-1.2
658 Textile articles nes	4106	0.16	44.99	6362	0.16	34.84	4.6	-2.1
661 Lime, cement and building prdts	5337	0.21	70.81	6282	0.16	55.12	1.4	-2.4
288 Non-ferrous metal scrap nes	4994	0.20	86.55	6221	0.15	79.48	2.6	-0.9
335 Residual petroleum prdts nes	3924	0.16	77.89	6144	0.15	68.34	4.6	-1.9
725 Paper etc mill machinery	6445	0.26	93.59	6061	0.15	92.54	0.7	0.0
282 Iron and steel scrap	4359	0.17	87.09	6059	0.15	75.62	2.2	-1.9
531 Synth dye, natrl indigo, lakes	6384	0.26	82.95	6053	0.15	69.17	-0.2	-1.6
654 Other woven textile fabric	5824	0.23	66.90	5798	0.14	67.28	0.0	0.0
831 Travel goods, handbags, etc	3156	0.13	36.48	5579	0.14	34.38	5.3	-0.3
692 Metal tanks, boxes, etc	4416	0.18	88.10	5527	0.14	79.14	2.3	-0.9
036 Shell fish fresh, frozen	3673	0.15	30.95	5489	0.14	32.67	3.7	0.7
659 Floor coverings, etc	5878	0.24	65.45	5476	0.14	62.96	-0.3	-0.1
655 Knitted, etc, fabric	3426	0.14	47.48	5453	0.14	35.29	5.0	-2.5
423 Fixed vegetable oils, soft	4054	0.16	64.37	5391	0.13	59.44	3.0	-1.0
727 Food machinery, non-demestic	4945	0.20	93.43	5375	0.13	90.94	0.8	-0.2
762 Radio-broadcast receivers	5077	0.20	36.18	5337	0.13	31.64	0.6	-0.8
056 Vegtb etc prsrvd, preprd	3200	0.13	59.97	5183	0.13	65.76	4.3	0.8
718 Oth power generating machinery	3146	0.13	85.59	5174	0.13	80.96	5.0	-0.9
895 Office supplies nes	3768	0.15	81.17	5079	0.13	66.11	3.3	-1.8
061 Sugar and honey	5067	0.20	42.79	4974	0.12	39.56	-0.5	-0.7
111 Non alcoholic beverages nes	2007	0.08	78.70	4834	0.12	78.92	7.8	0.1
847 Textile clothing accessoris nes	2869	0.11	53.79	4736	0.12	49.63	5.2	-0.7
524 Radioactive etc materials	4690	0.19	92.04	4734	0.12	88.34	-0.7	-0.2
278 Other crude minerals	4287	0.17	63.23	4635	0.11	65.96	0.9	0.0
848 Headgear, non-textile clothing	3305	0.13	31.76	4531	0.11	30.41	2.8	0.0
683 Nickel	2695	0.11	76.60	4524	0.11	69.22	5.8	-1.1
014 Meat prepd, prsrvd nes, etc	3141	0.13	74.33	4517	0.11	70.81	2.9	-0.5
233 Rubber, synthetic, reclaimed	3820	0.15	72.02	4503	0.11	71.61	1.7	-0.8
211 Hides skins, exc furs, raw	4153	0.17	82.67	4417	0.11	78.91	0.0	-0.4
951 War firearms, ammunition	5062	0.20	93.71	4249	0.11	95.18	-1.9	-0.5

For sources and notes, see end of table 4.2E.

Pour les sources et les notes, se reporter à la fin du tableau 4.2E.

4.2B **Export structure at the SITC Revision 2 group (3-digit) level (ranked by average 2001-2002 values)**
Developed economies
(concluded)

4.2B **Structure des exportations au niveau des groupes (position à trois chiffres) de la CTCI révision 2 (classées d'après la moyenne des valeurs de 2001-2002)**
Economies développées
(fin)

SITC group Groupes de la CTCI	1990-1991			2001-2002			Growth rates (percentage) Taux d'accroissement (en pourcentage) (1990-2002)	
	Value (millions of dollars) Valeur (millions de dollars)	Percentage of the grouping total En pourcentage du total du groupement	Percentage of world En pourcentage du monde	Value (millions of dollars) Valeur (millions de dollars)	Percentage of the grouping total En pourcentage du total du groupement	Percentage of world En pourcentage du monde	Value Valeur	Difference from world Différence par rapport au monde
	1	2	3	4	5	6	7	8
281 Iron ore and concentrates	3466	0.14	41.46	4052	0.10	42.34	1.8	0.1
037 Fish etc prepd, prsrvd nes	2904	0.12	44.56	3826	0.09	39.37	2.5	-1.2
247 Other wood rough, squared	4186	0.17	54.45	3776	0.09	52.54	-1.4	-0.5
263 Cotton	3829	0.15	43.28	3532	0.09	48.19	-0.2	1.7
693 Wire products, non-electric	2711	0.11	78.02	3205	0.08	66.19	1.9	-1.6
679 Iron, steel castings unworked	2025	0.08	78.72	3197	0.08	68.44	5.0	-1.4
612 Leather, etc, manufactures	1578	0.06	36.39	3167	0.08	45.93	6.6	2.9
696 Cutlery	1825	0.07	63.53	3090	0.08	57.11	4.9	-1.0
071 Coffee and substitutes	1846	0.07	21.34	3058	0.08	35.17	5.4	3.6
062 Sugar preps non-chocolate	1824	0.07	82.43	2870	0.07	67.22	3.8	-2.0
712 Steam engines, turbines	1907	0.08	67.57	2676	0.07	87.82	2.3	1.3
273 Stone, sand and gravel	2016	0.08	76.01	2669	0.07	67.96	2.6	-0.9
656 Lace, ribbon, tulle, etc	1978	0.08	64.91	2654	0.07	50.12	3.1	-2.2
677 Iron, steel wire, exc w rod	2580	0.10	81.93	2565	0.06	69.88	0.1	-1.5
686 Zinc	2795	0.11	68.25	2561	0.06	57.20	0.0	-2.2
666 Pottery	3069	0.12	68.43	2557	0.06	51.29	-1.4	-2.6
023 Butter	3141	0.13	97.97	2522	0.06	93.13	-2.1	-0.4
584 Cellulose, derivatives, etc	1786	0.07	91.68	2504	0.06	89.63	2.8	-0.3
268 Wool (exc tops), animal hair	4022	0.16	70.82	2478	0.06	77.55	-4.7	0.6
121 Tobacco, unmanufactd, refuse	2397	0.10	45.61	2349	0.06	42.19	0.0	-0.9
671 Pig iron, etc	2839	0.11	43.84	2317	0.06	28.07	-0.7	-3.3
873 Meters and counters nes	1273	0.05	91.37	2232	0.06	75.86	5.1	-1.8
689 Non-fer base metals nes	1297	0.05	72.32	2212	0.05	64.01	6.4	-0.7
042 Rice	1752	0.07	40.68	2086	0.05	30.62	1.2	-3.4
291 Crude animal materials nes	1531	0.06	57.17	2082	0.05	61.22	2.9	0.6
431 Procesd animl and veg oil, etc	1154	0.05	56.88	2082	0.05	58.42	4.5	0.1
844 Under garments non-knit	1879	0.08	24.31	2077	0.05	18.69	0.9	-2.1
035 Fish salted, dried, smoked	1912	0.08	83.61	2009	0.05	72.44	0.7	-1.1
266 Synthetic fibres for spinning	2688	0.11	68.30	1939	0.05	45.77	-2.5	-3.4
267 Other man-made fibres	1970	0.08	78.74	1931	0.05	81.18	-0.6	-0.1
043 Barley, unmilled	2918	0.12	97.74	1896	0.05	76.61	-3.0	-1.7
289 Prec metal ores, waste nes	871	0.03	73.86	1892	0.05	58.76	8.4	-2.7

For sources and notes, see end of table 4.2E.

Pour les sources et les notes, se reporter à la fin du tableau 4.2E.

4.2C   **Export structure at the SITC Revision 2 group (3-digit) level (ranked by average 2001-2002 values)**   Developing economies

4.2C   **Structure des exportations au niveau des groupes (position à trois chiffres) de la CTCI révision 2 (classées d'après la moyenne des valeurs de 2001-2002)**   Economies en développement

SITC group Groupes de la CTCI	1990-1991			2001-2002			Growth rates (percentage) Taux d'accroissement (en pourcentage) (1990-2002)	
	Value (millions of dollars) Valeur (millions de dollars)	Percentage of the grouping total En pourcentage du total du groupement	Percentage of world En pourcentage du monde	Value (millions of dollars) Valeur (millions de dollars)	Percentage of the grouping total En pourcentage du total du groupement	Percentage of world En pourcentage du monde	Value Valeur	Difference from world Différence par rapport au monde
	1	2	3	4	5	6	7	8
All commodity groups	811239	100.00	23.81	1940125	100.00	31.58	8.4	2.6
333 Crude petroleum	140887	17.37	77.35	227959	11.75	71.40	4.9	-0.6
776 Transistors, valves, etc	22255	2.74	32.94	120816	6.23	48.95	18.2	4.5
752 Automatic data processing equip	15972	1.97	22.19	83448	4.30	45.74	17.3	7.4
764 Telecom equip, parts, acces	14054	1.73	22.47	80172	4.13	38.59	16.4	4.2
759 Office, adp machy parts, acces	10605	1.31	20.06	75760	3.90	50.59	20.3	9.4
334 Petroleum products, refined	32699	4.03	38.68	67691	3.49	46.14	7.7	2.1
781 Passengr motor vehicl, exc bus	6628	0.82	3.88	35960	1.85	11.06	16.8	10.6
845 Outer garments knit nonelastic	16359	2.02	58.60	33600	1.73	67.19	7.1	1.4
843 Women's outwear non-knit	15215	1.88	53.05	30507	1.57	62.01	6.1	1.4
778 Electrical machinery nes	5448	0.67	13.94	29609	1.53	32.21	15.5	7.1
772 Switchgear etc, parts nes	4383	0.54	11.75	28520	1.47	32.55	18.5	9.6
341 Gas, natural and manufactured	12713	1.57	36.95	28224	1.45	35.17	8.4	-0.2
894 Toys, sporting goods, etc	13845	1.71	54.51	27796	1.43	57.93	6.3	0.4
851 Footwear	15023	1.85	49.58	23644	1.22	55.09	3.6	0.6
583 Polymerization, etc, prdts	7402	0.91	15.39	21752	1.12	25.86	10.3	4.6
842 Men's outwear non-knit	10263	1.27	54.18	21694	1.12	62.43	6.8	1.2
846 Under garments knitted	7894	0.97	56.98	20578	1.06	62.16	9.6	0.9
667 Pearl, prec, semi-prec stones	6120	0.75	24.08	18957	0.98	34.27	9.6	2.5
821 Furniture and parts thereof	4251	0.52	13.95	18460	0.95	28.84	13.7	6.4
893 Articles of plastic nes	5999	0.74	20.57	18332	0.94	31.01	10.1	3.3
784 Motor vehicl parts, acces nes	7178	0.88	8.44	18188	0.94	12.58	10.2	4.8
775 Household type equip nes	4979	0.61	22.09	17477	0.90	41.63	11.2	5.6
651 Textile yarn	9724	1.20	38.81	17174	0.89	52.82	5.4	2.7
761 Television receivers	7002	0.86	39.65	16866	0.87	55.20	6.6	1.7
653 Woven man-made fib fabric	11656	1.44	46.64	16585	0.85	56.24	3.1	1.6
931 Special transactions	14823	1.83	23.84	15853	0.82	12.23	-1.1	-7.8
771 Electric power machinery nes	3160	0.39	27.45	15520	0.80	47.39	15.8	4.9
763 Sound recorders, phonographs	4837	0.60	29.67	15379	0.79	51.76	9.0	4.0
793 Ships, boats, etc	5488	0.68	20.78	15095	0.78	33.84	9.6	5.0
773 Electricity distributing equip	2554	0.31	18.18	14650	0.76	38.90	15.8	6.3
699 Base metal manufactures nes	4253	0.52	17.07	12689	0.65	24.86	10.0	2.9
652 Cotton fabrics, woven	7543	0.93	46.23	12652	0.65	54.12	4.7	1.3
057 Fruit, nuts, fresh, dried	8453	1.04	41.91	12226	0.63	42.48	3.5	0.1
682 Copper	7644	0.94	32.48	12112	0.62	41.18	4.9	2.3
749 Non-electr machy parts, acces	3140	0.39	8.40	11718	0.60	17.29	12.4	6.6
658 Textile articles nes	4623	0.57	50.65	11618	0.60	63.62	8.4	1.8
762 Radio-broadcast receivers	8930	1.10	63.63	11531	0.59	68.35	1.8	0.4
036 Shell fish fresh, frozen	7938	0.98	66.90	11243	0.58	66.91	3.0	0.0
674 Iron, steel univ, plate, sheet	4803	0.59	13.11	11080	0.57	22.51	8.4	5.3
782 Lorries, spec motor vehicl nes	1091	0.13	2.92	10979	0.57	18.97	22.7	18.1
831 Travel goods, handbags, etc	5485	0.68	63.40	10543	0.54	64.97	5.8	0.1
716 Rotating electric plant	2118	0.26	14.75	10400	0.54	31.87	15.1	7.5
848 Headgear, non-textile clothing	7009	0.86	67.37	10244	0.53	68.76	2.8	0.0
287 Base metals ores, conc nes	7272	0.90	43.40	10192	0.53	53.64	3.7	1.6
655 Knitted, etc, fabric	3761	0.46	52.13	9950	0.51	64.40	9.3	1.8
897 Gold, silver ware, jewellery	3896	0.48	28.22	9941	0.51	40.08	8.4	3.3
684 Aluminium	4503	0.56	15.93	9926	0.51	20.69	7.5	2.0
541 Medicinal, pharmaceutical prdts	3247	0.40	8.26	9488	0.49	6.37	10.3	-2.0
741 Heating, cooling equipment	1945	0.24	8.09	9373	0.48	22.93	13.3	8.3
874 Measuring, controlg instruments	1867	0.23	4.92	9295	0.48	12.56	15.2	8.5
898 Musical instruments and parts	3248	0.40	16.35	9179	0.47	27.50	9.4	4.4
899 Other manufactured goods	5105	0.63	41.12	9093	0.47	35.40	5.0	-1.5
034 Fish, fresh, chilled, frozen	4465	0.55	29.55	9013	0.46	39.55	6.4	2.7
611 Leather	3576	0.44	37.53	8924	0.46	51.76	8.0	2.7

For sources and notes, see end of table 4.2E.

Pour les sources et les notes, se reporter à la fin du tableau 4.2E.

4.2C   Export structure at the SITC Revision 2
        group (3-digit) level (ranked by average
        2001-2002 values)
        Developing economies
        (continued)

4.2C   Structure des exportations au niveau des groupes (position
        à trois chiffres) de la CTCI révision 2 (classées d'après la
        moyenne des valeurs de 2001-2002)
        Economies en développement
        (suite)

SITC group / Groupes de la CTCI	1990-1991			2001-2002			Growth rates (percentage) Taux d'accroissement (en pourcentage) (1990-2002)	
	Value (millions of dollars) Valeur (millions de dollars)	Percentage of the grouping total En pourcentage du total du groupement	Percentage of world En pourcentage du monde	Value (millions of dollars) Valeur (millions de dollars)	Percentage of the grouping total En pourcentage du total du groupement	Percentage of world En pourcentage du monde	Value Valeur	Difference from world Différence par rapport au monde
	1	2	3	4	5	6	7	8
582 Prdts of condensation, etc	1795	0.22	10.02	8692	0.45	22.00	15.7	7.8
844 Under garments non-knit	5801	0.72	75.05	8620	0.44	77.56	3.2	0.2
081 Feeding stuff for animals	6131	0.76	38.09	8374	0.43	37.41	2.0	-0.5
728 Oth machy for spec industries	3924	0.48	9.90	8313	0.43	13.06	7.9	2.7
641 Paper and paperboard	3099	0.38	6.17	8173	0.42	11.13	9.8	5.7
885 Watches and clocks	6386	0.79	39.73	8011	0.41	43.82	2.0	1.0
713 Intern combust piston engines	3362	0.41	9.16	8005	0.41	11.64	8.6	2.3
054 Vegtb etc fresh, simply prsrvd	4990	0.62	28.64	7601	0.39	31.00	3.5	0.5
322 Coal, lignite and peat	3161	0.39	17.14	7506	0.39	35.72	7.3	6.4
792 Aircraft, etc	2068	0.25	2.86	7446	0.38	6.42	12.9	7.8
061 Sugar and honey	6684	0.82	56.44	7232	0.37	57.52	0.6	0.4
785 Cycles, etc, motorized or not	3250	0.40	29.10	6830	0.35	33.42	6.0	0.8
672 Iron, steel primary forms	4423	0.55	23.18	6745	0.35	25.96	3.9	0.8
812 Plumbg, heatg, lightg equip	1975	0.24	20.60	6673	0.34	35.05	10.9	4.6
011 Meat, fresh, chilled, frozen	3908	0.48	13.48	6599	0.34	17.01	4.4	2.2
743 Pumps nes, centrifuges, etc	1608	0.20	7.87	6596	0.34	16.13	12.3	5.7
697 Base metal household equip	2166	0.27	31.82	6496	0.33	47.34	9.9	3.6
642 Paper and paperboard, cut	1795	0.22	12.64	6417	0.33	21.92	11.9	5.0
625 Rubber tyres,tubes, etc	2358	0.29	14.90	6380	0.33	25.35	9.3	4.6
657 Spec textile fabrics, products	2819	0.35	24.27	6352	0.33	31.60	7.5	2.3
424 Other fixed vegetable oils	3130	0.39	83.04	6299	0.32	83.63	6.5	-0.1
881 Photogr apparatus, equip nes	1665	0.21	20.79	6105	0.31	38.66	12.6	5.4
598 Miscel chemical prdts nes	1727	0.21	7.98	5981	0.31	13.14	11.9	4.7
037 Fish etc prepd, prsrvd nes	3277	0.40	50.27	5792	0.30	59.59	5.3	1.6
522 Inorg chem elmnt, oxides, etc	2938	0.36	23.55	5730	0.30	34.94	6.5	3.6
723 Civil engineering equip, etc	1472	0.18	6.80	5684	0.29	15.01	12.4	7.0
071 Coffee and substitutes	6802	0.84	78.65	5623	0.29	64.68	0.5	-1.3
222 Seeds for soft fixed oils	3158	0.39	31.34	5612	0.29	38.45	5.8	2.0
511 Hydrocarbons nes, derivtives	1772	0.22	11.76	5474	0.28	26.34	11.2	7.7
513 Carboxylic acids, etc	1171	0.14	11.94	5358	0.28	31.22	14.3	9.2
751 Office machines	2023	0.25	17.05	5282	0.27	42.02	8.5	7.6
512 Alcohols, phenols, etc	1780	0.22	22.20	5251	0.27	36.15	9.1	3.5
634 Veneers, plywood, etc	4550	0.56	47.64	5119	0.26	37.70	-0.2	-3.1
635 Wood manufactures nes	2183	0.27	25.06	5119	0.26	29.36	7.8	0.9
884 Optical goods nes	1046	0.13	17.79	5042	0.26	23.55	15.2	2.2
678 Iron, steel tubes, pipes, etc	2522	0.31	13.79	5011	0.26	21.79	7.0	4.5
872 Medical instruments nes	798	0.10	7.24	5006	0.26	16.86	16.4	7.1
871 Optical instruments	458	0.06	12.95	4980	0.26	39.94	27.0	12.7
058 Fruit prsrvd, preprd	3600	0.44	40.21	4979	0.26	39.16	3.4	0.1
673 Iron, steel shapes, etc	3624	0.45	19.37	4938	0.25	21.56	2.0	0.4
892 Printed matter	1629	0.20	8.42	4934	0.25	15.70	10.2	5.6
695 Tools	1795	0.22	14.31	4932	0.25	23.75	9.3	4.1
281 Iron ore and concentrates	4367	0.54	52.23	4870	0.25	50.89	1.7	0.0
661 Lime, cement and building prdts	2059	0.25	27.31	4769	0.25	41.85	8.3	4.5
042 Rice	2522	0.31	58.57	4722	0.24	69.31	6.4	1.8
248 Wood, shaped, rail sleepers	3315	0.41	18.29	4714	0.24	18.87	2.4	-0.4
847 Textile clothing accessoris nes	2443	0.30	45.80	4705	0.24	49.30	6.5	0.6
671 Pig iron, etc	2449	0.30	37.82	4376	0.23	53.02	5.5	3.0
112 Alcoholic beverages	1444	0.18	7.36	4295	0.22	13.76	10.3	6.0
724 Textile, leather machinery	2687	0.33	12.27	4254	0.22	21.90	3.0	4.5
515 Organo-inorgan compounds, etc	1487	0.18	10.79	4150	0.21	9.14	9.7	-2.3
292 Crude vegetb materials nes	2864	0.35	24.41	4078	0.21	26.57	3.1	0.6
533 Pigments, paints, varnishes etc	1019	0.13	8.56	4017	0.21	16.43	13.1	6.0
098 Edible products, preps nes	1101	0.14	12.96	3974	0.20	20.94	12.3	5.4
664 Glass	1021	0.13	10.90	3862	0.20	22.36	12.8	6.9

For sources and notes, see end of table 4.2E.

Pour les sources et les notes, se reporter à la fin du tableau 4.2E.

4.2C Export structure at the SITC Revision 2 group (3-digit) level (ranked by average 2001-2002 values)
Developing economies
(continued)

4.2C Structure des exportations au niveau des groupes (position à trois chiffres) de la CTCI révision 2 (classées d'après la moyenne des valeurs de 2001-2002)
Economies en développement
(suite)

SITC group / Groupes de la CTCI	1990-1991			2001-2002			Growth rates (percentage) Taux d'accroissement (en pourcentage) (1990-2002)	
	Value (millions of dollars) Valeur (millions de dollars)	Percentage of the grouping total En pourcentage du total du groupement	Percentage of world En pourcentage du monde	Value (millions of dollars) Valeur (millions de dollars)	Percentage of the grouping total En pourcentage du total du groupement	Percentage of world En pourcentage du monde	Value Valeur	Difference from world Différence par rapport au monde
	1	2	3	4	5	6	7	8
736 Metal working machy, tools	1671	0.21	7.00	3858	0.20	13.49	8.3	5.3
122 Tobacco, manufactured	2643	0.33	20.26	3849	0.20	24.94	2.1	0.7
553 Perfumery, cosmetics, etc	1344	0.17	12.55	3793	0.20	14.10	10.6	2.1
251 Pulp and waste paper	1582	0.20	9.60	3730	0.19	19.75	8.6	6.6
514 Nitrogen-function compounds	1342	0.17	8.22	3674	0.19	14.11	9.8	6.0
232 Natural rubber, gums	4006	0.49	96.52	3480	0.18	95.34	-1.8	-0.2
072 Cocoa	2852	0.35	71.15	3434	0.18	64.90	1.2	-1.1
516 Other organic chemicals	765	0.09	10.88	3331	0.17	23.76	15.3	8.4
786 Trailers, non-motor vehicl nes	2039	0.25	28.45	3318	0.17	30.99	4.9	0.6
694 Stell, copper nails, nuts, etc	1408	0.17	21.54	3313	0.17	28.34	8.5	2.4
423 Fixed vegetable oils, soft	2180	0.27	34.61	3271	0.17	36.06	4.9	0.9
659 Floor coverings, etc	2973	0.37	33.10	3128	0.16	35.97	0.0	0.3
562 Fertilizers, manufactured	2329	0.29	16.07	3092	0.16	21.01	3.1	2.4
523 Other inorganic chemicals	1316	0.16	16.53	3088	0.16	25.35	7.7	3.7
612 Leather, etc, manufactures	2616	0.32	60.31	3055	0.16	44.30	0.4	-3.3
121 Tobacco, unmanufactd, refuse	2822	0.35	53.69	3017	0.16	54.17	1.5	0.6
691 Structures and parts nes	951	0.12	9.83	2972	0.15	20.12	9.4	5.4
744 Mechanical handling equipment	1358	0.17	6.06	2881	0.15	9.68	6.9	3.6
745 Non-electr machy, tools nes	765	0.09	4.66	2826	0.15	11.55	11.7	7.8
554 Soap, cleansing, etc preps	952	0.12	13.34	2821	0.15	19.53	10.9	4.3
531 Synth dye, natrl indigo, lakes	1292	0.16	16.79	2662	0.14	30.42	6.5	5.2
044 Maize (corn), unmilled	1469	0.18	15.98	2658	0.14	28.24	4.3	4.4
654 Other woven textile fabric	2736	0.34	31.43	2633	0.14	30.56	-0.4	-0.4
656 Lace, ribbon, tulle, etc	1068	0.13	35.05	2619	0.14	49.46	8.1	2.9
882 Photogr and cinema supplies	863	0.11	6.75	2606	0.13	15.75	11.0	8.2
895 Office supplies nes	862	0.11	18.57	2588	0.13	33.69	10.3	5.3
056 Vegtb etc prsrvd, preprd	2098	0.26	39.32	2584	0.13	32.78	1.8	-1.7
335 Residual petroleum prdts nes	907	0.11	18.00	2577	0.13	28.66	12.3	5.8
665 Glassware	1112	0.14	15.77	2565	0.13	23.80	7.2	3.3
048 Cereal etc preparations	855	0.11	8.58	2449	0.13	13.12	9.7	4.1
263 Cotton	3882	0.48	43.88	2439	0.13	33.29	-3.5	-1.6
666 Pottery	1384	0.17	30.86	2344	0.12	47.03	5.0	3.8
714 Engines and motors nes	863	0.11	3.75	2320	0.12	4.32	7.4	-1.2
696 Cutlery	1041	0.13	36.25	2296	0.12	42.42	7.4	1.5
591 Pesticides, disinfectants	694	0.09	9.50	2193	0.11	20.32	12.0	7.7
266 Synthetic fibres for spinning	1171	0.14	29.75	2143	0.11	50.59	5.7	4.8
074 Tea and mate	2198	0.27	84.35	2112	0.11	81.26	1.3	-0.1
278 Other crude minerals	1682	0.21	24.80	2085	0.11	29.67	2.4	1.5
628 Rubber articles nes	626	0.08	12.47	2037	0.11	17.42	11.8	3.7
783 Road motor vehicles nes	322	0.04	4.50	2010	0.10	12.92	16.0	8.4
663 Mineral manufactures nes	878	0.11	10.11	1983	0.10	14.74	7.0	2.6
041 Wheat etc, unmilled	999	0.12	6.89	1941	0.10	12.92	5.7	5.7
742 Pumps for liquids, etc	438	0.05	3.75	1916	0.10	9.44	13.8	8.5
662 Clay, refractory building prdts	584	0.07	7.86	1891	0.10	17.65	10.7	7.5
075 Spices	1075	0.13	78.65	1864	0.10	75.81	6.6	0.0
014 Meat prepd, prsrvd nes, etc	988	0.12	23.38	1770	0.09	27.74	5.1	1.7
247 Other wood rough, squared	2683	0.33	34.91	1736	0.09	24.15	-3.6	-2.7
592 Starch, inulin, gluten, etc	469	0.06	9.40	1674	0.09	17.30	12.0	5.8
681 Silver, platinum, etc	575	0.07	9.98	1642	0.08	15.37	12.5	4.5
022 Milk and cream	354	0.04	3.99	1556	0.08	11.67	13.9	10.8
001 Live animals for food	1719	0.21	18.22	1502	0.08	17.03	-1.7	-1.0
431 Procesd animl and veg oil, etc	866	0.11	42.67	1465	0.08	41.10	4.3	-0.1
693 Wire products, non-electric	684	0.08	19.69	1464	0.08	30.23	7.4	3.9
686 Zinc	777	0.10	18.97	1457	0.08	32.53	8.2	6.0
551 Essential oils, perfume, etc	591	0.07	15.60	1410	0.07	15.23	8.2	-0.7

For sources and notes, see end of table 4.2E.

Pour les sources et les notes, se reporter à la fin du tableau 4.2E.

4.2C Export structure at the SITC Revision 2 group (3-digit) level (ranked by average 2001-2002 values) Developing economies *(concluded)*

4.2C Structure des exportations au niveau des groupes (position à trois chiffres) de la CTCI révision 2 (classées d'après la moyenne des valeurs de 2001-2002) Economies en développement *(fin)*

SITC group / Groupes de la CTCI	1990-1991			2001-2002			Growth rates (percentage) Taux d'accroissement (en pourcentage) (1990-2002)	
	Value (millions of dollars) Valeur (millions de dollars)	Percentage of the grouping total En pourcen-tage du total du groupement	Percentage of world En pourcentage du monde	Value (millions of dollars) Valeur (millions de dollars)	Percentage of the grouping total En pourcentage du total du groupement	Percentage of world En pourcentage du monde	Value Valeur	Difference from world Différence par rapport au monde
	1	2	3	4	5	6	7	8
233 Rubber, synthetic, reclaimed	352	0.04	6.64	1400	0.07	22.27	13.6	11.1
679 Iron, steel castings unworked	453	0.06	17.61	1388	0.07	29.71	11.6	5.2
288 Non-ferrous metal scrap nes	703	0.09	12.19	1382	0.07	17.66	6.8	3.4
692 Metal tanks, boxes, etc	570	0.07	11.37	1355	0.07	19.41	7.8	4.6
289 Prec metal ores, waste nes	306	0.04	25.90	1289	0.07	40.03	16.2	5.1
062 Sugar preps non-chocolate	374	0.05	16.90	1287	0.07	30.15	11.3	5.5
291 Crude animal materials nes	1073	0.13	40.07	1273	0.07	37.41	2.0	-0.4
111 Non alcoholic beverages nes	539	0.07	21.14	1218	0.06	19.89	6.8	-1.0
273 Stone, sand and gravel	619	0.08	23.34	1161	0.06	29.57	5.6	2.0
621 Materials of rubber	374	0.05	9.15	1147	0.06	13.72	10.7	3.8
774 Electro-medical, xray equip	190	0.02	2.25	1139	0.06	6.95	17.6	11.6
271 Fertilizers, crude	1161	0.14	45.56	1082	0.06	78.88	0.2	2.7
323 Briquettes, coke and semi-coke	150	0.02	7.69	1045	0.05	43.32	20.9	18.7
726 Print and bookbind machy, parts	283	0.03	2.62	1037	0.05	7.56	10.1	7.5
687 Tin	1129	0.14	83.69	1023	0.05	81.26	0.3	-0.3
737 Metal working machinery nes	341	0.04	4.84	1005	0.05	11.79	10.0	7.3
677 Iron, steel wire, exc w rod	492	0.06	15.62	961	0.05	26.17	6.4	4.8
211 Hides skins, exc furs, raw	689	0.08	13.71	901	0.05	16.10	1.6	1.2
689 Non-fer base metals nes	421	0.05	23.49	873	0.05	25.25	7.7	0.5
791 Railway vehicles	185	0.02	3.70	860	0.04	9.62	18.4	13.2
282 Iron and steel scrap	442	0.05	8.82	817	0.04	10.20	6.3	2.2
035 Fish salted, dried, smoked	367	0.05	16.06	750	0.04	27.03	5.9	4.1
711 Steam boilers and auxil parts	148	0.02	7.11	724	0.04	27.31	14.5	12.4
268 Wool (exc tops), animal hair	1452	0.18	25.56	685	0.04	21.43	-6.4	-1.1
873 Meters and counters nes	92	0.01	6.59	681	0.04	23.16	19.5	12.6
073 Chocolate and products	236	0.03	5.44	676	0.03	8.60	9.9	5.0
246 Pulpwood, chips, woodwaste	254	0.03	15.27	602	0.03	34.10	8.2	6.8
721 Agricult machinry exc tractor	275	0.03	3.16	594	0.03	5.07	7.4	4.1
683 Nickel	326	0.04	9.27	571	0.03	8.74	5.0	-1.9
046 Wheat etc, meal or flour	251	0.03	14.37	538	0.03	29.61	7.2	7.4
685 Lead	279	0.03	21.11	498	0.03	35.07	6.4	4.2
722 Tractors non-road	129	0.02	1.90	492	0.03	6.15	13.0	10.4

For sources and notes, see end of table 4.2E.

Pour les sources et les notes, se reporter à la fin du tableau 4.2E.

4.2D   Export structure at the SITC Revision 2 group (3-digit) level (ranked by average 2001-2002 values)
Individual countries and territories

4.2D   Structure des exportations au niveau des groupes (position à trois chiffres) de la CTCI révision 2 (classées d'après la moyenne des valeurs de 2001-2002)
Pays et territoires individuels

SITC group / Groupes de la CTCI	2001-2002			
	Value (thousands of dollars) Valeur (milliers de dollars)	As percentage En pourcentage		
		of country total du total du pays	of ** des **	of world du monde
	1	2	3	4

Albania - Albanie (** = South-East Europe & CIS)

	1	2	3	4
All commodity groups	309120	100.00	0.18	0.01
612 Leather, etc, manufactures	82995	26.85	12.32	1.20
842 Men's outwear non-knit	30657	9.92	1.97	0.09
845 Outer garments knit nonelastic	22890	7.40	2.21	0.05
843 Women's outwear non-knit	21191	6.86	0.89	0.04
846 Under garments knitted	19697	6.37	2.37	0.06
844 Under garments non-knit	18659	6.04	4.48	0.17
292 Crude vegetb materials nes	10299	3.33	10.87	0.07
699 Base metal manufactures nes	9964	3.22	1.36	0.02
611 Leather	7984	2.58	2.84	0.05
851 Footwear	7708	2.49	0.64	0.02
Remainder	77075	24.93		

Algeria - Algérie (** = developing)

	1	2	3	4
All commodity groups	16250074	100.00	0.84	0.26
333 Crude petroleum	6644393	40.89	2.91	2.08
341 Gas, natural and manufactured	6620227	40.74	23.46	8.25
334 Petroleum products, refined	2456072	15.11	3.63	1.67
335 Residual petroleum prdts nes	160043	0.98	6.21	1.78
522 Inorg chem elmnt, oxides, etc	64749	0.40	1.13	0.39
511 Hydrocarbons nes, derivtives	40129	0.25	0.73	0.19
562 Fertilizers, manufactured	27984	0.17	0.91	0.19
672 Iron, steel primary forms	26846	0.17	0.40	0.10
271 Fertilizers, crude	15219	0.09	1.41	1.11
611 Leather	14806	0.09	0.17	0.09
Remainder	179605	1.11		

Andorra - Andorre (** = developed)

	1	2	3	4
All commodity groups	57805	100.00	0.00	0.00
781 Passengr motor vehicl, exc bus	12216	21.13	0.00	0.00
881 Photogr apparatus, equip nes	6017	10.41	0.06	0.04
898 Musical instruments and parts	4586	7.93	0.02	0.01
553 Perfumery, cosmetics, etc	3504	6.06	0.02	0.01
894 Toys, sporting goods, etc	2912	5.04	0.01	0.01
892 Printed matter	2827	4.89	0.01	0.01
899 Other manufactured goods	2265	3.92	0.01	0.01
744 Mechanical handling equipment	1682	2.91	0.01	0.01
872 Medical instruments nes	1023	1.77	0.00	0.00
657 Spec textile fabrics, products	965	1.67	0.01	0.00
Remainder	19807	34.26		

Argentina - Argentine (** = developing)

	1	2	3	4
All commodity groups	26159692	100.00	1.35	0.43
081 Feeding stuff for animals	2704894	10.34	32.30	12.09
333 Crude petroleum	2309001	8.83	1.01	0.72
423 Fixed vegetable oils, soft	1737484	6.64	53.12	19.16
334 Petroleum products, refined	1342485	5.13	1.98	0.92
222 Seeds for soft fixed oils	1334323	5.10	23.78	9.14
041 Wheat etc, unmilled	1199433	4.59	61.79	7.98
044 Maize (corn), unmilled	956839	3.66	36.00	10.16
781 Passengr motor vehicl, exc bus	775976	2.97	2.16	0.24
611 Leather	731325	2.80	8.20	4.24
341 Gas, natural and manufactured	623336	2.38	2.21	0.78
Remainder	12444599	47.57		

Armenia - Arménie (** = South-East Europe & CIS)

	1	2	3	4
All commodity groups	359322	100.00	0.21	0.01
667 Pearl, prec, semi-prec stones	126692	35.26	94.54	0.23
112 Alcoholic beverages	41122	11.44	6.87	0.13
971 Gold, non-monetary nes	26137	7.27	4.63	0.12
287 Base metals ores, conc nes	24091	6.70	3.01	0.13
351 Electric current	15030	4.18	1.75	0.14
288 Non-ferrous metal scrap nes	12327	3.43	5.50	0.16
897 Gold, silver ware, jewellery	11428	3.18	46.57	0.05
682 Copper	9739	2.71	0.40	0.03
233 Rubber, synthetic, reclaimed	8688	2.42	2.26	0.14
671 Pig iron, etc	7719	2.15	0.49	0.09
Remainder	76348	21.25		

Aruba (** = developing)

	1	2	3	4
All commodity groups	138631	100.00	0.01	0.00
334 Petroleum products, refined	110000	79.35	0.16	0.07
335 Residual petroleum prdts nes	13388	9.66	0.52	0.15
073 Chocolate and products	2276	1.64	0.34	0.03
931 Special transactions	1626	1.17	0.01	0.00
971 Gold, non-monetary nes	1550	1.12	0.02	0.01
061 Sugar and honey	1393	1.00	0.02	0.01
042 Rice	999	0.72	0.02	0.01
667 Pearl, prec, semi-prec stones	851	0.61	0.00	0.00
333 Crude petroleum	815	0.59	0.00	0.00
098 Edible products, preps nes	699	0.50	0.02	0.00
Remainder	5035	3.63		

Australia - Australie (** = developed)

	1	2	3	4
All commodity groups	63171714	100.00	1.57	1.03
322 Coal, lignite and peat	6725742	10.65	56.18	32.01
287 Base metals ores, conc nes	3728274	5.90	46.56	19.62
333 Crude petroleum	3357401	5.31	5.71	1.05
011 Meat, fresh, chilled, frozen	3214838	5.09	10.10	8.29
931 Special transactions	2953354	4.68	2.91	2.28
971 Gold, non-monetary nes	2777485	4.40	23.80	13.18
281 Iron ore and concentrates	2766573	4.38	68.28	28.91
684 Aluminium	2373516	3.76	7.27	4.95
041 Wheat etc, unmilled	2244900	3.55	19.26	14.94
341 Gas, natural and manufactured	1830885	2.90	5.43	2.28
Remainder	31198746	49.39		

Austria - Autriche (** = developed)

	1	2	3	4
All commodity groups	61830244	100.00	1.53	1.01
781 Passengr motor vehicl, exc bus	3024707	4.89	1.05	0.93
713 Intern combust piston engines	2723169	4.40	4.51	3.96
641 Paper and paperboard	2520656	4.08	3.95	3.43
541 Medicinal, pharmaceutical prdts	2034122	3.29	1.46	1.37
784 Motor vehicl parts, acces nes	1999553	3.23	1.59	1.38
728 Oth machy for spec industries	1407868	2.28	2.56	2.21
699 Base metal manufactures nes	1357721	2.20	3.61	2.66
772 Switchgear etc, parts nes	1299468	2.10	2.21	1.48
674 Iron, steel univ, plate, sheet	1294518	2.09	3.73	2.63
776 Transistors, valves, etc	1267580	2.05	1.01	0.51
Remainder	42900882	69.38		

For sources and notes, see end of table 4.2E.

Pour les sources et les notes, se reporter à la fin du tableau 4.2E.

4.2D Export structure at the SITC Revision 2 group (3-digit) level (ranked by average 2001-2002 values) Individual countries and territories *(continued)*

4.2D Structure des exportations au niveau des groupes (position à trois chiffres) de la CTCI révision 2 (classées d'après la moyenne des valeurs de 2001-2002) Pays et territoires individuels *(suite)*

SITC group / Groupes de la CTCI	2001-2002 Value (thousands of dollars) / Valeur (milliers de dollars)	As percentage / En pourcentage of country total / du total du pays	of ** / des **	of world / du monde
	1	2	3	4
Azerbaijan - Azerbaïdjan (= South-East Europe & CIS)**				
All commodity groups	2240890	100.00	1.31	0.04
333 Crude petroleum	1600873	71.44	4.93	0.50
334 Petroleum products, refined	403142	17.99	2.65	0.27
263 Cotton	18884	0.84	1.39	0.26
723 Civil engineering equip, etc	18381	0.82	2.68	0.05
057 Fruit, nuts, fresh, dried	17478	0.78	6.44	0.06
583 Polymerization, etc, prdts	17015	0.76	1.62	0.02
931 Special transactions	14044	0.63	0.12	0.01
122 Tobacco, manufactured	12908	0.58	4.51	0.08
287 Base metals ores, conc nes	12766	0.57	1.59	0.07
351 Electric current	11695	0.52	1.36	0.11
Remainder	113703	5.07		
Bahamas (= developing)**				
All commodity groups	496191	100.00	0.03	0.01
583 Polymerization, etc, prdts	94670	19.08	0.44	0.11
036 Shell fish fresh, frozen	94650	19.08	0.84	0.56
334 Petroleum products, refined	90855	18.31	0.13	0.06
112 Alcoholic beverages	52350	10.55	1.22	0.17
278 Other crude minerals	19836	4.00	0.95	0.28
744 Mechanical handling equipment	13595	2.74	0.47	0.05
515 Organo-inorgan compounds, etc	12805	2.58	0.31	0.03
553 Perfumery, cosmetics, etc	12327	2.48	0.33	0.05
057 Fruit, nuts, fresh, dried	9971	2.01	0.08	0.03
764 Telecom equip, parts, acces	7524	1.52	0.01	0.00
Remainder	87608	17.66		
Bahrain - Bahreïn (= developing)**				
All commodity groups	5669437	100.00	0.29	0.09
334 Petroleum products, refined	3803838	67.09	5.62	2.59
684 Aluminium	798631	14.09	8.05	1.66
843 Women's outwear non-knit	289594	5.11	0.95	0.59
281 Iron ore and concentrates	219075	3.86	4.50	2.29
562 Fertilizers, manufactured	65015	1.15	2.10	0.44
652 Cotton fabrics, woven	60567	1.07	0.48	0.26
842 Men's outwear non-knit	44749	0.79	0.21	0.13
512 Alcohols, phenols, etc	44381	0.78	0.85	0.31
931 Special transactions	37500	0.66	0.24	0.03
741 Heating, cooling equipment	30200	0.53	0.32	0.07
Remainder	275887	4.87		
Bangladesh (= developing)**				
All commodity groups	5123638	100.00	0.26	0.08
842 Men's outwear non-knit	1130023	22.06	5.21	3.25
844 Under garments non-knit	765567	14.94	8.88	6.89
843 Women's outwear non-knit	749838	14.63	2.46	1.52
846 Under garments knitted	603230	11.77	2.93	1.82
845 Outer garments knit nonelastic	542308	10.58	1.61	1.08
036 Shell fish fresh, frozen	301230	5.88	2.68	1.79
611 Leather	224606	4.38	2.52	1.30
658 Textile articles nes	165205	3.22	1.42	0.90
654 Other woven textile fabric	83936	1.64	3.19	0.97
651 Textile yarn	61312	1.20	0.36	0.19
Remainder	496384	9.69		
Barbados - Barbade (= developing)**				
All commodity groups	237399	100.00	0.01	0.00
334 Petroleum products, refined	36562	15.40	0.05	0.02
112 Alcoholic beverages	20584	8.67	0.48	0.07
061 Sugar and honey	20446	8.61	0.28	0.16
541 Medicinal, pharmaceutical prdts	15693	6.61	0.17	0.01
098 Edible products, preps nes	14098	5.94	0.35	0.07
772 Switchgear etc, parts nes	12783	5.38	0.04	0.01
661 Lime, cement and building prdts	10190	4.29	0.21	0.09
591 Pesticides, disinfectants	9745	4.11	0.44	0.09
892 Printed matter	5992	2.52	0.12	0.02
692 Metal tanks, boxes, etc	5395	2.27	0.40	0.08
Remainder	85910	36.19		
Belarus - Bélarus (= South-East Europe & CIS)**				
All commodity groups	7656024	100.00	4.47	0.12
334 Petroleum products, refined	1344716	17.56	8.85	0.92
562 Fertilizers, manufactured	539336	7.04	18.35	3.67
782 Lorries, spec motor vehicl nes	372551	4.87	43.70	0.64
722 Tractors non-road	206186	2.69	70.05	2.57
775 Household type equip nes	202422	2.64	45.16	0.48
821 Furniture and parts thereof	160364	2.09	13.44	0.25
673 Iron, steel shapes, etc	154093	2.01	6.79	0.67
783 Road motor vehicles nes	142263	1.86	55.15	0.91
651 Textile yarn	141256	1.85	20.51	0.43
784 Motor vehicl parts, acces nes	134288	1.75	20.82	0.09
Remainder	4258548	55.62		
Belgium - Belgique (= developed)**				
All commodity groups	198257287	100.00	4.92	3.23
781 Passengr motor vehicl, exc bus	20070073	10.12	6.95	6.17
541 Medicinal, pharmaceutical prdts	15579875	7.86	11.22	10.46
667 Pearl, prec, semi-prec stones	12510669	6.31	34.54	22.62
583 Polymerization, etc, prdts	7638841	3.85	12.46	9.08
334 Petroleum products, refined	6649927	3.35	10.42	4.53
674 Iron, steel univ, plate, sheet	3980535	2.01	11.48	8.09
784 Motor vehicl parts, acces nes	3836044	1.93	3.05	2.65
515 Organo-inorgan compounds, etc	3687767	1.86	9.01	8.12
514 Nitrogen-function compounds	2953980	1.49	13.30	11.35
752 Automatic data processing equip	2929621	1.48	2.96	1.61
Remainder	118419956	59.73		
Belize (= developing)**				
All commodity groups	173187	100.00	0.01	0.00
931 Special transactions	106797	61.67	0.67	0.08
061 Sugar and honey	31421	18.14	0.43	0.25
057 Fruit, nuts, fresh, dried	15156	8.75	0.12	0.05
036 Shell fish fresh, frozen	10184	5.88	0.09	0.06
054 Vegtb etc fresh, simply prsrvd	2870	1.66	0.04	0.01
058 Fruit prsrvd, preprd	2279	1.32	0.05	0.02
248 Wood, shaped, rail sleepers	1210	0.70	0.03	0.00
034 Fish, fresh, chilled, frozen	575	0.33	0.01	0.00
793 Ships, boats, etc	425	0.25	0.00	0.00
081 Feeding stuff for animals	410	0.24	0.00	0.00
Remainder	1859	1.07		

For sources and notes, see end of table 4.2E.

Pour les sources et les notes, se reporter à la fin du tableau 4.2E.

4.2D **Export structure at the SITC Revision 2 group (3-digit) level (ranked by average 2001-2002 values)**
Individual countries and territories
(continued)

4.2D **Structure des exportations au niveau des groupes (position à trois chiffres) de la CTCI révision 2 (classées d'après la moyenne des valeurs de 2001-2002)**
Pays et territoires individuels
(suite)

SITC group / Groupes de la CTCI	2001-2002				SITC group / Groupes de la CTCI	2001-2002			
	Value (thousands of dollars) / Valeur (milliers de dollars)	As percentage / En pourcentage				Value (thousands of dollars) / Valeur (milliers de dollars)	As percentage / En pourcentage		
		of country total / du total du pays	of ** / des **	of world / du monde			of country total / du total du pays	of ** / des **	of world / du monde
	1	2	3	4		1	2	3	4
Benin - Bénin (= developing)**					**Brazil - Brésil (** = developing)**				
All commodity groups	242911	100.00	0.01	0.00	All commodity groups	59292185	100.00	3.06	0.96
263 Cotton	123493	50.84	5.06	1.68	792 Aircraft, etc	3176100	5.36	42.66	2.74
011 Meat, fresh, chilled, frozen	38054	15.67	0.58	0.10	281 Iron ore and concentrates	2990196	5.04	61.40	31.25
971 Gold, non-monetary nes	18365	7.56	0.21	0.09	222 Seeds for soft fixed oils	2883713	4.86	51.39	19.76
057 Fruit, nuts, fresh, dried	14789	6.09	0.12	0.05	011 Meat, fresh, chilled, frozen	2641785	4.46	40.03	6.81
652 Cotton fabrics, woven	7047	2.90	0.06	0.03	081 Feeding stuff for animals	2233474	3.77	26.67	9.98
248 Wood, shaped, rail sleepers	5627	2.32	0.12	0.02	061 Sugar and honey	2211731	3.73	30.58	17.59
081 Feeding stuff for animals	4531	1.87	0.05	0.02	781 Passengr motor vehicl, exc bus	1978770	3.34	5.50	0.61
222 Seeds for soft fixed oils	4046	1.67	0.07	0.03	784 Motor vehicl parts, acces nes	1555717	2.62	8.55	1.08
122 Tobacco, manufactured	3009	1.24	0.08	0.02	851 Footwear	1532119	2.58	6.48	3.57
056 Vegtb etc prsrvd, preprd	3009	1.24	0.12	0.04	764 Telecom equip, parts, acces	1453897	2.45	1.81	0.70
Remainder	20940	8.62			Remainder	36634683	61.79		
Bolivia - Bolivie (= developing)**					**Bulgaria - Bulgarie (** = South-East Europe & CIS)**				
All commodity groups	1362270	100.00	0.07	0.02	All commodity groups	5431357	100.00	3.17	0.09
341 Gas, natural and manufactured	255796	18.78	0.91	0.32	931 Special transactions	412778	7.60	3.41	0.32
081 Feeding stuff for animals	203213	14.92	2.43	0.91	334 Petroleum products, refined	395271	7.28	2.60	0.27
287 Base metals ores, conc nes	131977	9.69	1.29	0.69	843 Women's outwear non-knit	316221	5.82	13.34	0.64
423 Fixed vegetable oils, soft	100295	7.36	3.07	1.11	682 Copper	297509	5.48	12.30	1.01
971 Gold, non-monetary nes	90895	6.67	1.03	0.43	845 Outer garments knit nonelastic	250435	4.61	24.16	0.50
289 Prec metal ores, waste nes	56597	4.15	4.39	1.76	842 Men's outwear non-knit	204814	3.77	13.16	0.59
897 Gold, silver ware, jewellery	55296	4.06	0.56	0.22	846 Under garments knitted	166678	3.07	20.08	0.50
333 Crude petroleum	54720	4.02	0.02	0.02	672 Iron, steel primary forms	163367	3.01	2.96	0.63
687 Tin	49891	3.66	4.88	3.96	674 Iron, steel univ, plate, sheet	133567	2.46	3.86	0.27
723 Civil engineering equip, etc	34036	2.50	0.60	0.09	541 Medicinal, pharmaceutical prdts	90810	1.67	15.12	0.06
Remainder	329554	24.19			Remainder	2999907	55.23		
Bosnia and Herzegovina - Bosnie-Herzégovine (= South-East Europe & CIS)**					**Burkina Faso (** = developing)**				
All commodity groups	1027835	100.00	0.60	0.02	All commodity groups	171576	100.00	0.01	0.00
684 Aluminium	152753	14.86	2.84	0.32	263 Cotton	104433	60.87	4.28	1.42
248 Wood, shaped, rail sleepers	133669	13.00	7.74	0.54	001 Live animals for food	10894	6.35	0.73	0.12
821 Furniture and parts thereof	69220	6.73	5.80	0.11	222 Seeds for soft fixed oils	6755	3.94	0.12	0.05
851 Footwear	60923	5.93	5.03	0.14	611 Leather	5687	3.31	0.06	0.03
842 Men's outwear non-knit	42435	4.13	2.73	0.12	651 Textile yarn	4870	2.84	0.03	0.01
843 Women's outwear non-knit	38443	3.74	1.62	0.08	423 Fixed vegetable oils, soft	3733	2.18	0.11	0.04
612 Leather, etc, manufactures	29121	2.83	4.32	0.42	223 Seeds for other fixed oils	3372	1.97	1.23	0.37
334 Petroleum products, refined	28811	2.80	0.19	0.02	723 Civil engineering equip, etc	2626	1.53	0.05	0.01
211 Hides skins, exc furs, raw	27219	2.65	9.75	0.49	061 Sugar and honey	2624	1.53	0.04	0.02
351 Electric current	21741	2.12	2.53	0.20	122 Tobacco, manufactured	2306	1.34	0.06	0.01
Remainder	423502	41.20			Remainder	24277	14.15		
Botswana (= developing)**					**Cambodia - Cambodge (** = developing)**				
All commodity groups	2520922	100.00	0.13	0.04	All commodity groups	1225937	100.00	0.06	0.02
667 Pearl, prec, semi-prec stones	2112065	83.78	11.14	3.82	845 Outer garments knit nonelastic	390183	31.83	1.16	0.78
287 Base metals ores, conc nes	103073	4.09	1.01	0.54	843 Women's outwear non-knit	251645	20.53	0.82	0.51
011 Meat, fresh, chilled, frozen	62444	2.48	0.95	0.16	842 Men's outwear non-knit	159943	13.05	0.74	0.46
783 Road motor vehicles nes	32311	1.28	1.61	0.21	846 Under garments knitted	131845	10.75	0.64	0.40
277 Natural abrasives nes	27271	1.08	6.95	2.97	851 Footwear	97314	7.94	0.41	0.23
523 Other inorganic chemicals	22363	0.89	0.72	0.18	844 Under garments non-knit	83598	6.82	0.97	0.75
781 Passengr motor vehicl, exc bus	12575	0.50	0.03	0.00	232 Natural rubber, gums	18111	1.48	0.52	0.50
211 Hides skins, exc furs, raw	10531	0.42	1.17	0.19	634 Veneers, plywood, etc	16928	1.38	0.33	0.12
845 Outer garments knit nonelastic	9669	0.38	0.03	0.02	848 Headgear, non-textile clothing	11885	0.97	0.12	0.08
846 Under garments knitted	8370	0.33	0.04	0.03	658 Textile articles nes	8958	0.73	0.08	0.05
Remainder	120250	4.77			Remainder	55529	4.53		

For sources and notes, see end of table 4.2E.

Pour les sources et les notes, se reporter à la fin du tableau 4.2E.

4.2D **Export structure at the SITC Revision 2 group (3-digit) level (ranked by average 2001-2002 values)**
Individual countries and territories
(continued)

4.2D **Structure des exportations au niveau des groupes (position à trois chiffres) de la CTCI révision 2 (classées d'après la moyenne des valeurs de 2001-2002)**
Pays et territoires individuels
(suite)

SITC group / Groupes de la CTCI	Value (thousands of dollars) Valeur (milliers de dollars)	2001-2002 As percentage En pourcentage		
		of country total du total du pays	of ** des **	of world du monde
	1	2	3	4

Cameroon - Cameroun (= developing)**

All commodity groups	1775572	100.00	0.09	0.03
333 Crude petroleum	817058	46.02	0.36	0.26
248 Wood, shaped, rail sleepers	215257	12.12	4.57	0.86
072 Cocoa	189532	10.67	5.52	3.58
263 Cotton	95989	5.41	3.93	1.31
684 Aluminium	85202	4.80	0.86	0.18
334 Petroleum products, refined	79902	4.50	0.12	0.05
071 Coffee and substitutes	63595	3.58	1.13	0.73
057 Fruit, nuts, fresh, dried	46387	2.61	0.38	0.16
634 Veneers, plywood, etc	38226	2.15	0.75	0.28
247 Other wood rough, squared	25991	1.46	1.50	0.36
Remainder	118434	6.67		

Canada (= developed)**

All commodity groups	256160534	100.00	6.35	4.17
781 Passengr motor vehicl, exc bus	31952345	12.47	11.07	9.83
931 Special transactions	15982727	6.24	15.73	12.34
341 Gas, natural and manufactured	15535589	6.06	46.10	19.36
333 Crude petroleum	10936874	4.27	18.59	3.43
784 Motor vehicl parts, acces nes	10550769	4.12	8.39	7.29
641 Paper and paperboard	9651834	3.77	15.11	13.14
782 Lorries, spec motor vehicl nes	9145087	3.57	19.86	15.80
792 Aircraft, etc	7973563	3.11	7.38	6.87
248 Wood, shaped, rail sleepers	7541949	2.94	40.68	30.19
764 Telecom equip, parts, acces	5302098	2.07	4.18	2.55
Remainder	131587699	51.37		

Central African Republic - République centrafricaine (= developing)**

All commodity groups	65047	100.00	0.00	0.00
667 Pearl, prec, semi-prec stones	34869	53.61	0.18	0.06
247 Other wood rough, squared	9748	14.99	0.56	0.14
277 Natural abrasives nes	7501	11.53	1.91	0.82
263 Cotton	5694	8.75	0.23	0.08
248 Wood, shaped, rail sleepers	2668	4.10	0.06	0.01
071 Coffee and substitutes	1271	1.95	0.02	0.01
652 Cotton fabrics, woven	357	0.55	0.00	0.00
541 Medicinal, pharmaceutical prdts	233	0.36	0.00	0.00
782 Lorries, spec motor vehicl nes	199	0.31	0.00	0.00
771 Electric power machinery nes	190	0.29	0.00	0.00
Remainder	2318	3.56		

Chile - Chili (= developing)**

All commodity groups	18084239	100.00	0.93	0.29
682 Copper	4732844	26.17	39.08	16.09
287 Base metals ores, conc nes	2166981	11.98	21.26	11.40
057 Fruit, nuts, fresh, dried	1273124	7.04	10.41	4.42
034 Fish, fresh, chilled, frozen	1227458	6.79	13.62	5.39
251 Pulp and waste paper	945565	5.23	25.35	5.01
112 Alcoholic beverages	634980	3.51	14.78	2.03
248 Wood, shaped, rail sleepers	577138	3.19	12.24	2.31
931 Special transactions	478922	2.65	3.02	0.37
641 Paper and paperboard	359226	1.99	4.40	0.49
512 Alcohols, phenols, etc	341777	1.89	6.51	2.35
Remainder	5346324	29.56		

China - Chine (= developing)**

All commodity groups	295846981	100.00	15.25	4.81
764 Telecom equip, parts, acces	17756611	6.00	22.15	8.55
752 Automatic data processing equip	16613033	5.62	19.91	9.11
759 Office, adp machy parts, acces	11336623	3.83	14.96	7.57
894 Toys, sporting goods, etc	11223675	3.79	40.38	23.39
851 Footwear	10178539	3.44	43.05	23.72
845 Outer garments knit nonelastic	10090081	3.41	30.03	20.18
843 Women's outwear non-knit	9225477	3.12	30.24	18.75
778 Electrical machinery nes	7206628	2.44	24.34	7.84
842 Men's outwear non-knit	6888648	2.33	31.75	19.82
776 Transistors, valves, etc	6104366	2.06	5.05	2.47
Remainder	189223299	63.96		

China, Hong Kong SAR - Chine, Hong Kong RAS (= developing)**

All commodity groups	196496929	100.00	10.13	3.20
776 Transistors, valves, etc	14982822	7.62	12.40	6.07
764 Telecom equip, parts, acces	14782103	7.52	18.44	7.11
759 Office, adp machy parts, acces	12162220	6.19	16.05	8.12
894 Toys, sporting goods, etc	11035937	5.62	39.70	23.00
845 Outer garments knit nonelastic	8461951	4.31	25.18	16.92
843 Women's outwear non-knit	5984485	3.05	19.62	12.17
851 Footwear	5520652	2.81	23.35	12.86
752 Automatic data processing equip	5488924	2.79	6.58	3.01
885 Watches and clocks	4755404	2.42	59.36	26.01
772 Switchgear etc, parts nes	4389293	2.23	15.39	5.01
Remainder	108933139	55.44		

China, Macao SAR - Chine, Macao RAS (= developing)**

All commodity groups	2328630	100.00	0.12	0.04
845 Outer garments knit nonelastic	730659	31.38	2.17	1.46
843 Women's outwear non-knit	374563	16.09	1.23	0.76
846 Under garments knitted	284002	12.20	1.38	0.86
842 Men's outwear non-knit	163641	7.03	0.75	0.47
651 Textile yarn	107628	4.62	0.63	0.33
844 Under garments non-knit	84777	3.64	0.98	0.76
851 Footwear	82094	3.53	0.35	0.19
652 Cotton fabrics, woven	72414	3.11	0.57	0.31
655 Knitted, etc, fabric	67672	2.91	0.68	0.44
653 Woven man-made fib fabric	34146	1.47	0.21	0.12
Remainder	327034	14.04		

China, Taiwan Province of - Chine, Taiwan Province de (= developing)**

All commodity groups	126734085	100.00	6.53	2.06
776 Transistors, valves, etc	16266073	12.83	13.46	6.59
752 Automatic data processing equip	12041015	9.50	14.43	6.60
759 Office, adp machy parts, acces	11351498	8.96	14.98	7.58
764 Telecom equip, parts, acces	5552019	4.38	6.93	2.67
772 Switchgear etc, parts nes	4231474	3.34	14.84	4.83
778 Electrical machinery nes	3975759	3.14	13.43	4.33
583 Polymerization, etc, prdts	3193746	2.52	14.68	3.80
674 Iron, steel univ, plate, sheet	2551035	2.01	23.02	5.18
653 Woven man-made fib fabric	2548592	2.01	15.37	8.64
699 Base metal manufactures nes	2270329	1.79	17.89	4.45
Remainder	62752545	49.52		

For sources and notes, see end of table 4.2E.

Pour les sources et les notes, se reporter à la fin du tableau 4.2E.

4.2D **Export structure at the SITC Revision 2 group (3-digit) level (ranked by average 2001-2002 values)** Individual countries and territories *(continued)*

4.2D **Structure des exportations au niveau des groupes (position à trois chiffres) de la CTCI révision 2 (classées d'après la moyenne des valeurs de 2001-2002)** Pays et territoires individuels *(suite)*

SITC group / Groupes de la CTCI	2001-2002 Value (thousands of dollars) Valeur (milliers de dollars)	As percentage / En pourcentage of country total du total du pays	of ** des **	of world du monde
	1	2	3	4
Colombia - Colombie (= developing)**				
All commodity groups	12099474	100.00	0.62	0.20
333 Crude petroleum	2584131	21.36	1.13	0.81
322 Coal, lignite and peat	1065678	8.81	14.20	5.07
071 Coffee and substitutes	861864	7.12	15.33	9.91
334 Petroleum products, refined	678713	5.61	1.00	0.46
292 Crude vegetb materials nes	645119	5.33	15.82	4.20
057 Fruit, nuts, fresh, dried	439628	3.63	3.60	1.53
533 Pigments, paints, varnishes etc	263184	2.18	6.55	1.08
583 Polymerization, etc, prdts	260752	2.16	1.20	0.31
541 Medicinal, pharmaceutical prdts	256492	2.12	2.70	0.17
671 Pig iron, etc	254173	2.10	5.81	3.08
Remainder	4789740	39.59		
Congo (= developing)**				
All commodity groups	1612419	100.00	0.08	0.03
333 Crude petroleum	1157839	71.81	0.51	0.36
334 Petroleum products, refined	99452	6.17	0.15	0.07
247 Other wood rough, squared	97952	6.07	5.64	1.36
341 Gas, natural and manufactured	84724	5.25	0.30	0.11
667 Pearl, prec, semi-prec stones	40786	2.53	0.22	0.07
287 Base metals ores, conc nes	26702	1.66	0.26	0.14
248 Wood, shaped, rail sleepers	25569	1.59	0.54	0.10
689 Non-fer base metals nes	15670	0.97	1.80	0.45
061 Sugar and honey	10853	0.67	0.15	0.09
071 Coffee and substitutes	7120	0.44	0.13	0.08
Remainder	45755	2.84		
Costa Rica (= developing)**				
All commodity groups	4833080	100.00	0.25	0.08
759 Office, adp machy parts, acces	843381	17.45	1.11	0.56
057 Fruit, nuts, fresh, dried	715585	14.81	5.85	2.49
872 Medical instruments nes	315537	6.53	6.30	1.06
846 Under garments knitted	179726	3.72	0.87	0.54
071 Coffee and substitutes	169587	3.51	3.02	1.95
541 Medicinal, pharmaceutical prdts	169471	3.51	1.79	0.11
292 Crude vegetb materials nes	156470	3.24	3.84	1.02
098 Edible products, preps nes	137266	2.84	3.45	0.72
058 Fruit prsrvd, preprd	106007	2.19	2.13	0.83
772 Switchgear etc, parts nes	104759	2.17	0.37	0.12
Remainder	1935292	40.04		
Côte d'Ivoire (= developing)**				
All commodity groups	4463992	100.00	0.23	0.07
072 Cocoa	1656547	37.11	48.24	31.31
334 Petroleum products, refined	580275	13.00	0.86	0.40
071 Coffee and substitutes	224888	5.04	4.00	2.59
248 Wood, shaped, rail sleepers	211238	4.73	4.48	0.85
793 Ships, boats, etc	205126	4.60	1.36	0.46
057 Fruit, nuts, fresh, dried	183374	4.11	1.50	0.64
263 Cotton	147851	3.31	6.06	2.02
037 Fish etc prepd, prsrvd nes	133558	2.99	2.31	1.37
232 Natural rubber, gums	85629	1.92	2.46	2.35
333 Crude petroleum	83442	1.87	0.04	0.03
Remainder	952064	21.33		

SITC group / Groupes de la CTCI	2001-2002 Value (thousands of dollars) Valeur (milliers de dollars)	As percentage / En pourcentage of country total du total du pays	of ** des **	of world du monde
	1	2	3	4
Croatia - Croatie (= South-East Europe & CIS)**				
All commodity groups	4778981	100.00	2.79	0.08
793 Ships, boats, etc	659189	13.79	43.04	1.48
334 Petroleum products, refined	316804	6.63	2.08	0.22
541 Medicinal, pharmaceutical prdts	182966	3.83	30.46	0.12
845 Outer garments knit nonelastic	140648	2.94	13.57	0.28
821 Furniture and parts thereof	135487	2.84	11.35	0.21
842 Men's outwear non-knit	129385	2.71	8.31	0.37
341 Gas, natural and manufactured	123595	2.59	0.67	0.15
248 Wood, shaped, rail sleepers	123097	2.58	7.13	0.49
843 Women's outwear non-knit	118725	2.48	5.01	0.24
583 Polymerization, etc, prdts	115547	2.42	10.98	0.14
Remainder	2733538	57.20		
Cuba (= developing)**				
All commodity groups	1549769	100.00	0.08	0.03
061 Sugar and honey	513574	33.14	7.10	4.08
287 Base metals ores, conc nes	432147	27.88	4.24	2.27
122 Tobacco, manufactured	224740	14.50	5.84	1.46
036 Shell fish fresh, frozen	71765	4.63	0.64	0.43
058 Fruit prsrvd, preprd	46433	3.00	0.93	0.37
541 Medicinal, pharmaceutical prdts	38027	2.45	0.40	0.03
661 Lime, cement and building prdts	31835	2.05	0.67	0.28
672 Iron, steel primary forms	26429	1.71	0.39	0.10
334 Petroleum products, refined	23044	1.49	0.03	0.02
121 Tobacco, unmanufactd, refuse	20469	1.32	0.68	0.37
Remainder	121305	7.83		
Cyprus - Chypre (= developed)**				
All commodity groups	905906	100.00	0.02	0.01
122 Tobacco, manufactured	185352	20.46	1.64	1.20
781 Passengr motor vehicl, exc bus	85795	9.47	0.03	0.03
334 Petroleum products, refined	78305	8.64	0.12	0.05
541 Medicinal, pharmaceutical prdts	66630	7.36	0.05	0.04
782 Lorries, spec motor vehicl nes	55947	6.18	0.12	0.10
054 Vegtb etc fresh, simply prsrvd	30893	3.41	0.19	0.13
057 Fruit, nuts, fresh, dried	28917	3.19	0.18	0.10
653 Woven man-made fib fabric	18803	2.08	0.15	0.06
112 Alcoholic beverages	18062	1.99	0.07	0.06
024 Cheese and curd	16565	1.83	0.16	0.15
Remainder	320637	35.39		
Czech Republic - République tchèque (= developed)**				
All commodity groups	38823846	100.00	0.96	0.63
781 Passengr motor vehicl, exc bus	3868262	9.96	1.34	1.19
784 Motor vehicl parts, acces nes	2404752	6.19	1.91	1.66
752 Automatic data processing equip	1709266	4.40	1.73	0.94
778 Electrical machinery nes	1208761	3.11	1.96	1.31
821 Furniture and parts thereof	1015932	2.62	2.29	1.59
699 Base metal manufactures nes	907655	2.34	2.41	1.78
772 Switchgear etc, parts nes	895340	2.31	1.53	1.02
773 Electricity distributing equip	763949	1.97	3.44	2.03
893 Articles of plastic nes	684503	1.76	1.69	1.16
764 Telecom equip, parts, acces	646826	1.67	0.51	0.31
Remainder	24718602	63.67		

For sources and notes, see end of table 4.2E.

Pour les sources et les notes, se reporter à la fin du tableau 4.2E.

4.2D Export structure at the SITC Revision 2 group (3-digit) level (ranked by average 2001-2002 values)
Individual countries and territories
(continued)

4.2D Structure des exportations au niveau des groupes (position à trois chiffres) de la CTCI révision 2 (classées d'après la moyenne des valeurs de 2001-2002)
Pays et territoires individuels
(suite)

SITC group / Groupes de la CTCI	2001-2002			
	Value (thousands of dollars) / Valeur (milliers de dollars)	As percentage / En pourcentage		
		of country total / du total du pays	of ** / des **	of world / du monde
	1	2	3	4

Denmark - Danemark (** = developed)

SITC group	1	2	3	4
All commodity groups	53331516	100.00	1.32	0.87
541 Medicinal, pharmaceutical prdts	3596898	6.74	2.59	2.41
011 Meat, fresh, chilled, frozen	2812432	5.27	8.83	7.25
931 Special transactions	2484147	4.66	2.44	1.92
764 Telecom equip, parts, acces	2275654	4.27	1.79	1.10
333 Crude petroleum	2209260	4.14	3.75	0.69
821 Furniture and parts thereof	1995440	3.74	4.50	3.12
716 Rotating electric plant	1498174	2.81	6.86	4.59
893 Articles of plastic nes	1017764	1.91	2.51	1.72
034 Fish, fresh, chilled, frozen	984335	1.85	7.36	4.32
741 Heating, cooling equipment	910541	1.71	2.92	2.23
Remainder	33546872	62.90		

Dominica - Dominique (** = developing)

SITC group	1	2	3	4
All commodity groups	42713	100.00	0.00	0.00
554 Soap, cleansing, etc preps	12521	29.31	0.44	0.09
057 Fruit, nuts, fresh, dried	12190	28.54	0.10	0.04
553 Perfumery, cosmetics, etc	6089	14.26	0.16	0.02
054 Vegtb etc fresh, simply prsrvd	1651	3.86	0.02	0.01
273 Stone, sand and gravel	1602	3.75	0.14	0.04
591 Pesticides, disinfectants	1591	3.72	0.07	0.01
533 Pigments, paints, varnishes etc	1191	2.79	0.03	0.00
098 Edible products, preps nes	1174	2.75	0.03	0.01
551 Essential oils, perfume, etc	1032	2.42	0.07	0.01
716 Rotating electric plant	349	0.82	0.00	0.00
Remainder	3325	7.78		

Dominican Republic - République dominicaine (** = developing)

SITC group	1	2	3	4
All commodity groups	824041	100.00	0.04	0.01
671 Pig iron, etc	80258	9.74	1.83	0.97
842 Men's outwear non-knit	75196	9.13	0.35	0.22
334 Petroleum products, refined	64192	7.79	0.09	0.04
846 Under garments knitted	57376	6.96	0.28	0.17
057 Fruit, nuts, fresh, dried	41567	5.04	0.34	0.14
061 Sugar and honey	41079	4.99	0.57	0.33
931 Special transactions	34395	4.17	0.22	0.03
872 Medical instruments nes	33483	4.06	0.67	0.11
122 Tobacco, manufactured	30402	3.69	0.79	0.20
843 Women's outwear non-knit	27408	3.33	0.09	0.06
Remainder	338688	41.10		

Ecuador - Equateur (** = developing)

SITC group	1	2	3	4
All commodity groups	4844490	100.00	0.25	0.08
333 Crude petroleum	1780414	36.75	0.78	0.56
057 Fruit, nuts, fresh, dried	932834	19.26	7.63	3.24
037 Fish etc prepd, prsrvd nes	305763	6.31	5.28	3.15
036 Shell fish fresh, frozen	269410	5.56	2.40	1.60
292 Crude vegtb materials nes	263584	5.44	6.46	1.72
334 Petroleum products, refined	152866	3.16	0.23	0.10
072 Cocoa	100359	2.07	2.92	1.90
034 Fish, fresh, chilled, frozen	90970	1.88	1.01	0.40
781 Passengr motor vehicl, exc bus	69327	1.43	0.19	0.02
058 Fruit prsrvd, preprd	49773	1.03	1.00	0.39
Remainder	829190	17.12		

Egypt - Egypte (** = developing)

SITC group	1	2	3	4
All commodity groups	4426578	100.00	0.23	0.07
334 Petroleum products, refined	1218352	27.52	1.80	0.83
931 Special transactions	363434	8.21	2.29	0.28
333 Crude petroleum	307178	6.94	0.13	0.10
263 Cotton	259140	5.85	10.62	3.54
684 Aluminium	125017	2.82	1.26	0.26
042 Rice	124537	2.81	2.64	1.83
651 Textile yarn	119273	2.69	0.69	0.37
661 Lime, cement and building prdts	115923	2.62	2.43	1.02
658 Textile articles nes	108337	2.45	0.93	0.59
054 Vegtb etc fresh, simply prsrvd	102678	2.32	1.35	0.42
Remainder	1582709	35.75		

El Salvador (** = developing)

SITC group	1	2	3	4
All commodity groups	1225791	100.00	0.06	0.02
071 Coffee and substitutes	113937	9.30	2.03	1.31
642 Paper and paperboard, cut	88164	7.19	1.37	0.30
334 Petroleum products, refined	69492	5.67	0.10	0.05
061 Sugar and honey	68079	5.55	0.94	0.54
541 Medicinal, pharmaceutical prdts	54309	4.43	0.57	0.04
554 Soap, cleansing, etc preps	49401	4.03	1.75	0.34
098 Edible products, preps nes	46491	3.79	1.17	0.24
846 Under garments knitted	41044	3.35	0.20	0.12
674 Iron, steel univ, plate, sheet	39694	3.24	0.36	0.08
048 Cereal etc preparations	31952	2.61	1.30	0.17
Remainder	623227	50.84		

Equatorial Guinea - Guinée équatoriale (** = developing)

SITC group	1	2	3	4
All commodity groups	1171442	100.00	0.06	0.02
333 Crude petroleum	1027040	87.67	0.45	0.32
247 Other wood rough, squared	57295	4.89	3.30	0.80
512 Alcohols, phenols, etc	40503	3.46	0.77	0.28
334 Petroleum products, refined	13515	1.15	0.02	0.01
341 Gas, natural and manufactured	10615	0.91	0.04	0.01
634 Veneers, plywood, etc	5865	0.50	0.11	0.04
931 Special transactions	4660	0.40	0.03	0.00
034 Fish, fresh, chilled, frozen	3626	0.31	0.04	0.02
072 Cocoa	1979	0.17	0.06	0.04
874 Measuring, controlg instruments	1596	0.14	0.02	0.00
Remainder	4749	0.41		

Estonia - Estonie (** = developed)

SITC group	1	2	3	4
All commodity groups	4175459	100.00	0.10	0.07
764 Telecom equip, parts, acces	682755	16.35	0.54	0.33
821 Furniture and parts thereof	213326	5.11	0.48	0.33
248 Wood, shaped, rail sleepers	183738	4.40	0.99	0.74
691 Structures and parts nes	145372	3.48	1.27	0.98
635 Wood manufactures nes	136016	3.26	1.13	0.78
334 Petroleum products, refined	131694	3.15	0.21	0.09
072 Cocoa	111625	2.67	6.03	2.11
247 Other wood rough, squared	103995	2.49	2.75	1.45
781 Passengr motor vehicl, exc bus	87656	2.10	0.03	0.03
641 Paper and paperboard	86985	2.08	0.14	0.12
Remainder	2292297	54.90		

For sources and notes, see end of table 4.2E.

Pour les sources et les notes, se reporter à la fin du tableau 4.2E.

4.2D Export structure at the SITC Revision 2 group (3-digit) level (ranked by average 2001-2002 values)
Individual countries and territories
(continued)

4.2D Structure des exportations au niveau des groupes (position à trois chiffres) de la CTCI révision 2 (classées d'après la moyenne des valeurs de 2001-2002)
Pays et territoires individuels
(suite)

Left table

SITC group / Groupes de la CTCI	Value (thousands of dollars) / Valeur (milliers de dollars) 1	of country total / du total du pays 2	of ** / des ** 3	of world / du monde 4
Ethiopia - Ethiopie (= developing)**				
All commodity groups	408734	100.00	0.02	0.01
071 Coffee and substitutes	152515	37.31	2.71	1.75
292 Crude vegetb materials nes	51569	12.62	1.26	0.34
611 Leather	50029	12.24	0.56	0.29
054 Vegtb etc fresh, simply prsrvd	33487	8.19	0.44	0.14
222 Seeds for soft fixed oils	28474	6.97	0.51	0.20
211 Hides skins, exc furs, raw	18312	4.48	2.03	0.33
045 Cereals nes, unmilled	15048	3.68	11.53	1.04
061 Sugar and honey	11248	2.75	0.16	0.09
223 Seeds for other fixed oils	10397	2.54	3.78	1.15
287 Base metals ores, conc nes	7520	1.84	0.07	0.04
Remainder	30137	7.37		
Faeroe Islands - Iles Féroé (= developed)**				
All commodity groups	518760	100.00	0.01	0.01
034 Fish, fresh, chilled, frozen	346677	66.83	2.59	1.52
035 Fish salted, dried, smoked	83159	16.03	4.14	3.00
036 Shell fish fresh, frozen	23744	4.58	0.43	0.14
081 Feeding stuff for animals	20654	3.98	0.15	0.09
037 Fish etc prepd, prsrvd nes	17863	3.44	0.47	0.18
793 Ships, boats, etc	13430	2.59	0.05	0.03
291 Crude animal materials nes	7411	1.43	0.36	0.22
892 Printed matter	2112	0.41	0.01	0.01
411 Animal oils and fats	1101	0.21	0.09	0.08
894 Toys, sporting goods, etc	799	0.15	0.00	0.00
Remainder	1811	0.35		
Fiji - Fidji (= developing)**				
All commodity groups	491396	100.00	0.03	0.01
061 Sugar and honey	116334	23.67	1.61	0.93
843 Women's outwear non-knit	62485	12.72	0.20	0.13
334 Petroleum products, refined	43487	8.85	0.06	0.03
842 Men's outwear non-knit	42481	8.64	0.20	0.12
971 Gold, non-monetary nes	35120	7.15	0.40	0.17
034 Fish, fresh, chilled, frozen	29939	6.09	0.33	0.13
111 Non alcoholic beverages nes	13056	2.66	1.07	0.21
246 Pulpwood, chips, woodwaste	10813	2.20	1.80	0.61
851 Footwear	9736	1.98	0.04	0.02
054 Vegtb etc fresh, simply prsrvd	8985	1.83	0.12	0.04
Remainder	118960	24.21		
Finland - Finlande (= developed)**				
All commodity groups	44408841	100.00	1.10	0.72
764 Telecom equip, parts, acces	8104530	18.25	6.39	3.90
641 Paper and paperboard	7769609	17.50	12.16	10.58
793 Ships, boats, etc	1520594	3.42	5.43	3.41
334 Petroleum products, refined	1402397	3.16	2.20	0.96
248 Wood, shaped, rail sleepers	1389791	3.13	7.50	5.56
674 Iron, steel univ, plate, sheet	1133548	2.55	3.27	2.30
781 Passengr motor vehicl, exc bus	978623	2.20	0.34	0.30
251 Pulp and waste paper	842225	1.90	5.78	4.46
728 Oth machy for spec industries	738870	1.66	1.34	1.16
725 Paper etc mill machinery	711392	1.60	11.74	10.86
Remainder	19817262	44.62		

Right table

SITC group / Groupes de la CTCI	Value (thousands of dollars) / Valeur (milliers de dollars) 1	of country total / du total du pays 2	of ** / des ** 3	of world / du monde 4
France (= developed)**				
All commodity groups	292083904	100.00	7.24	4.75
781 Passengr motor vehicl, exc bus	22973001	7.87	7.96	7.07
792 Aircraft, etc	17189647	5.89	15.92	14.81
541 Medicinal, pharmaceutical prdts	13788700	4.72	9.93	9.25
784 Motor vehicl parts, acces nes	11716310	4.01	9.31	8.10
764 Telecom equip, parts, acces	8654208	2.96	6.82	4.17
112 Alcoholic beverages	7179048	2.46	27.27	22.99
776 Transistors, valves, etc	6378676	2.18	5.07	2.58
553 Perfumery, cosmetics, etc	6357744	2.18	27.75	23.64
772 Switchgear etc, parts nes	5019110	1.72	8.55	5.73
714 Engines and motors nes	4955406	1.70	9.79	9.22
Remainder	187872055	64.32		
French Polynesia - Polynésie française (= developing)**				
All commodity groups	175418	100.00	0.01	0.00
667 Pearl, prec, semi-prec stones	117235	66.83	0.62	0.21
792 Aircraft, etc	14882	8.48	0.20	0.01
034 Fish, fresh, chilled, frozen	9935	5.66	0.11	0.04
058 Fruit prsrvd, preprd	7208	4.11	0.14	0.06
793 Ships, boats, etc	5394	3.07	0.04	0.01
897 Gold, silver ware, jewellery	2840	1.62	0.03	0.01
424 Other fixed vegetable oils	2112	1.20	0.03	0.01
714 Engines and motors nes	2025	1.15	0.09	0.00
075 Spices	1540	0.88	0.08	0.06
291 Crude animal materials nes	1431	0.82	0.11	0.04
Remainder	10815	6.17		
Gabon (= developing)**				
All commodity groups	2684539	100.00	0.14	0.04
333 Crude petroleum	2185792	81.42	0.96	0.68
247 Other wood rough, squared	301232	11.22	17.36	4.19
334 Petroleum products, refined	50906	1.90	0.08	0.03
287 Base metals ores, conc nes	45834	1.71	0.45	0.24
634 Veneers, plywood, etc	36785	1.37	0.72	0.27
248 Wood, shaped, rail sleepers	14749	0.55	0.31	0.06
036 Shell fish fresh, frozen	11648	0.43	0.10	0.07
122 Tobacco, manufactured	7764	0.29	0.20	0.05
842 Men's outwear non-knit	2721	0.10	0.01	0.01
782 Lorries, spec motor vehicl nes	2056	0.08	0.02	0.00
Remainder	25056	0.93		
Georgia - Géorgie (= South-East Europe & CIS)**				
All commodity groups	246516	100.00	0.14	0.00
112 Alcoholic beverages	28068	11.39	4.69	0.09
792 Aircraft, etc	27795	11.27	4.53	0.02
282 Iron and steel scrap	25362	10.29	2.23	0.32
288 Non-ferrous metal scrap nes	17747	7.20	7.91	0.23
671 Pig iron, etc	13479	5.47	0.86	0.16
111 Non alcoholic beverages nes	11708	4.75	16.00	0.19
287 Base metals ores, conc nes	10986	4.46	1.37	0.06
971 Gold, non-monetary nes	9606	3.90	1.70	0.05
057 Fruit, nuts, fresh, dried	8963	3.64	3.30	0.03
351 Electric current	8527	3.46	0.99	0.08
Remainder	84276	34.19		

For sources and notes, see end of table 4.2E.

Pour les sources et les notes, se reporter à la fin du tableau 4.2E.

4.2D Export structure at the SITC Revision 2 group (3-digit) level (ranked by average 2001-2002 values)
Individual countries and territories
(continued)

4.2D Structure des exportations au niveau des groupes (position à trois chiffres) de la CTCI révision 2 (classées d'après la moyenne des valeurs de 2001-2002)
Pays et territoires individuels
(suite)

SITC group / Groupes de la CTCI	2001-2002				SITC group / Groupes de la CTCI	2001-2002			
	Value (thousands of dollars) / Valeur (milliers de dollars)	of country total / du total du pays	of ** / des **	of world / du monde		Value (thousands of dollars) / Valeur (milliers de dollars)	of country total / du total du pays	of ** / des **	of world / du monde
	1	2	3	4		1	2	3	4
Germany - Allemagne (= developed)**					**Grenada - Grenade (** = developing)**				
All commodity groups	579135830	100.00	14.36	9.43	All commodity groups	48450	100.00	0.00	0.00
781 Passengr motor vehicl, exc bus	70735809	12.21	24.51	21.76	075 Spices	14267	29.45	0.77	0.58
931 Special transactions	18972850	3.28	18.67	14.64	046 Wheat etc, meal or flour	4421	9.13	0.82	0.24
784 Motor vehicl parts, acces nes	18520183	3.20	14.72	12.80	759 Office, adp machy parts, acces	4218	8.71	0.01	0.00
541 Medicinal, pharmaceutical prdts	17442369	3.01	12.56	11.71	773 Electricity distributing equip	4202	8.67	0.03	0.01
792 Aircraft, etc	16743888	2.89	15.50	14.43	772 Switchgear etc, parts nes	4198	8.67	0.01	0.00
764 Telecom equip, parts, acces	15518212	2.68	12.24	7.47	034 Fish, fresh, chilled, frozen	3892	8.03	0.04	0.02
583 Polymerization, etc, prdts	12555703	2.17	20.48	14.92	642 Paper and paperboard, cut	1874	3.87	0.03	0.01
749 Non-electr machy parts, acces	11965788	2.07	21.76	17.66	551 Essential oils, perfume, etc	1776	3.67	0.13	0.02
772 Switchgear etc, parts nes	11306284	1.95	19.27	12.90	072 Cocoa	1299	2.68	0.04	0.02
776 Transistors, valves, etc	11240777	1.94	8.94	4.55	723 Civil engineering equip, etc	1063	2.19	0.02	0.00
Remainder	374133968	64.60			Remainder	7238	14.94		
Ghana (= developing)**					**Guatemala (** = developing)**				
All commodity groups	2197456	100.00	0.11	0.04	All commodity groups	2235393	100.00	0.12	0.04
971 Gold, non-monetary nes	805782	36.67	9.11	3.82	071 Coffee and substitutes	284515	12.73	5.06	3.27
072 Cocoa	401584	18.27	11.69	7.59	057 Fruit, nuts, fresh, dried	237695	10.63	1.94	0.83
684 Aluminium	199921	9.10	2.01	0.42	061 Sugar and honey	234463	10.49	3.24	1.86
248 Wood, shaped, rail sleepers	108233	4.93	2.30	0.43	333 Crude petroleum	125076	5.60	0.05	0.04
334 Petroleum products, refined	79577	3.62	0.12	0.05	075 Spices	95762	4.28	5.14	3.89
037 Fish etc prepd, prsrvd nes	75219	3.42	1.30	0.77	541 Medicinal, pharmaceutical prdts	85572	3.83	0.90	0.06
634 Veneers, plywood, etc	67465	3.07	1.32	0.50	048 Cereal etc preparations	69383	3.10	2.83	0.37
058 Fruit prsrvd, preprd	60742	2.76	1.22	0.48	054 Vegtb etc fresh, simply prsrvd	48751	2.18	0.64	0.20
057 Fruit, nuts, fresh, dried	42903	1.95	0.35	0.15	553 Perfumery, cosmetics, etc	46682	2.09	1.23	0.17
287 Base metals ores, conc nes	39470	1.80	0.39	0.21	292 Crude vegetb materials nes	45707	2.04	1.12	0.30
Remainder	316564	14.41			Remainder	961788	43.03		
Greece - Grèce (= developed)**					**Guinea - Guinée (** = developing)**				
All commodity groups	10521801	100.00	0.26	0.17	All commodity groups	550148	100.00	0.03	0.01
334 Petroleum products, refined	920883	8.75	1.44	0.63	287 Base metals ores, conc nes	283532	51.54	2.78	1.49
845 Outer garments knit nonelastic	592868	5.63	3.86	1.19	971 Gold, non-monetary nes	124256	22.59	1.41	0.59
684 Aluminium	523281	4.97	1.60	1.09	522 Inorg chem elmnt, oxides, etc	94194	17.12	1.64	0.57
057 Fruit, nuts, fresh, dried	438049	4.16	2.69	1.52	892 Printed matter	11407	2.07	0.23	0.04
846 Under garments knitted	408186	3.88	3.49	1.23	277 Natural abrasives nes	8212	1.49	2.09	0.89
058 Fruit prsrvd, preprd	301039	2.86	4.04	2.37	681 Silver, platinum, etc	4427	0.80	0.27	0.04
541 Medicinal, pharmaceutical prdts	290713	2.76	0.21	0.20	071 Coffee and substitutes	3690	0.67	0.07	0.04
263 Cotton	248132	2.36	7.03	3.39	334 Petroleum products, refined	2341	0.43	0.00	0.00
121 Tobacco, unmanufactd, refuse	233127	2.22	9.92	4.19	723 Civil engineering equip, etc	1711	0.31	0.03	0.00
056 Vegtb etc prsrvd, preprd	227097	2.16	4.38	2.88	232 Natural rubber, gums	1151	0.21	0.03	0.03
Remainder	6338426	60.24			Remainder	15226	2.77		
Greenland - Groenland (= developing)**					**Guyana (** = developing)**				
All commodity groups	269885	100.00	0.01	0.00	All commodity groups	463870	100.00	0.02	0.01
036 Shell fish fresh, frozen	120180	44.53	1.07	0.72	971 Gold, non-monetary nes	103006	22.21	1.16	0.49
037 Fish etc prepd, prsrvd nes	64232	23.80	1.11	0.66	061 Sugar and honey	91877	19.81	1.27	0.73
034 Fish, fresh, chilled, frozen	47518	17.61	0.53	0.21	287 Base metals ores, conc nes	53893	11.62	0.53	0.28
931 Special transactions	15789	5.85	0.10	0.01	042 Rice	42394	9.14	0.90	0.62
035 Fish salted, dried, smoked	8101	3.00	1.08	0.29	036 Shell fish fresh, frozen	38963	8.40	0.35	0.23
793 Ships, boats, etc	3963	1.47	0.03	0.01	034 Fish, fresh, chilled, frozen	17911	3.86	0.20	0.08
792 Aircraft, etc	3636	1.35	0.05	0.00	634 Veneers, plywood, etc	17703	3.82	0.35	0.13
212 Furskins, raw	1039	0.39	0.34	0.07	667 Pearl, prec, semi-prec stones	16382	3.53	0.09	0.03
896 Works of art, etc	850	0.32	0.30	0.01	248 Wood, shaped, rail sleepers	16349	3.52	0.35	0.07
848 Headgear, non-textile clothing	555	0.21	0.01	0.00	112 Alcoholic beverages	10350	2.23	0.24	0.03
Remainder	4020	1.49			Remainder	55042	11.87		

For sources and notes, see end of table 4.2E.

Pour les sources et les notes, se reporter à la fin du tableau 4.2E.

4.2D   Export structure at the SITC Revision 2
        group (3-digit) level (ranked by average
        2001-2002 values)
        Individual countries and territories
        (continued)

4.2D   Structure des exportations au niveau des groupes
        (position à trois chiffres) de la CTCI révision 2
        (classées d'après la moyenne des valeurs de 2001-2002)
        Pays et territoires individuels
        (suite)

SITC group / Groupes de la CTCI	2001-2002				SITC group / Groupes de la CTCI	2001-2002			
	Value (thousands of dollars) Valeur (milliers de dollars)	As percentage / En pourcentage				Value (thousands of dollars) Valeur (milliers de dollars)	As percentage / En pourcentage		
		of country total du total du pays	of ** des **	of world du monde			of country total du total du pays	of ** des **	of world du monde
	1	2	3	4		1	2	3	4
Haiti - Haïti (= developing)**					**India - Inde (** = developing)**				
All commodity groups	277096	100.00	0.01	0.00	All commodity groups	48388969	100.00	2.49	0.79
846 Under garments knitted	106602	38.47	0.52	0.32	667 Pearl, prec, semi-prec stones	6890201	14.24	36.35	12.46
845 Outer garments knit nonelastic	70229	25.34	0.21	0.14	334 Petroleum products, refined	2322600	4.80	3.43	1.58
842 Men's outwear non-knit	16929	6.11	0.08	0.05	843 Women's outwear non-knit	1880585	3.89	6.16	3.82
843 Women's outwear non-knit	8766	3.16	0.03	0.02	651 Textile yarn	1720177	3.55	10.02	5.29
844 Under garments non-knit	8581	3.10	0.10	0.08	541 Medicinal, pharmaceutical prdts	1554115	3.21	16.38	1.04
847 Textile clothing accessoris nes	8115	2.93	0.17	0.09	846 Under garments knitted	1384716	2.86	6.73	4.18
071 Coffee and substitutes	7322	2.64	0.13	0.08	897 Gold, silver ware, jewellery	1325023	2.74	13.33	5.34
057 Fruit, nuts, fresh, dried	6313	2.28	0.05	0.02	931 Special transactions	1261578	2.61	7.96	0.97
551 Essential oils, perfume, etc	4710	1.70	0.33	0.05	658 Textile articles nes	1179941	2.44	10.16	6.46
072 Cocoa	4273	1.54	0.12	0.08	036 Shell fish fresh, frozen	1020619	2.11	9.08	6.07
Remainder	35258	12.72			Remainder	27849415	57.55		
Honduras (= developing)**					**Indonesia - Indonésie (** = developing)**				
All commodity groups	1477447	100.00	0.08	0.02	All commodity groups	56737774	100.00	2.92	0.92
057 Fruit, nuts, fresh, dried	277349	18.77	2.27	0.96	341 Gas, natural and manufactured	5654899	9.97	20.04	7.05
061 Sugar and honey	168083	11.38	2.32	1.34	333 Crude petroleum	5471146	9.64	2.40	1.71
071 Coffee and substitutes	155082	10.50	2.76	1.78	634 Veneers, plywood, etc	2048381	3.61	40.01	15.08
248 Wood, shaped, rail sleepers	132024	8.94	2.80	0.53	287 Base metals ores, conc nes	1938250	3.42	19.02	10.20
054 Vegtb etc fresh, simply prsrvd	90977	6.16	1.20	0.37	424 Other fixed vegetable oils	1926222	3.39	30.58	25.58
846 Under garments knitted	67821	4.59	0.33	0.20	322 Coal, lignite and peat	1690052	2.98	22.52	8.04
424 Other fixed vegetable oils	58346	3.95	0.93	0.77	821 Furniture and parts thereof	1476135	2.60	8.00	2.31
554 Soap, cleansing, etc preps	46629	3.16	1.65	0.32	764 Telecom equip, parts, acces	1342779	2.37	1.67	0.65
282 Iron and steel scrap	41320	2.80	5.05	0.52	641 Paper and paperboard	1337834	2.36	16.37	1.82
058 Fruit prsrvd, preprd	30051	2.03	0.60	0.24	851 Footwear	1294589	2.28	5.48	3.02
Remainder	409767	27.73			Remainder	32557487	57.38		
Hungary - Hongrie (= developed)**					**Iran, Islamic Rep. of - Iran, Rép. islamique d' (** = developing)**				
All commodity groups	32417160	100.00	0.80	0.53	All commodity groups	25824061	100.00	1.33	0.42
764 Telecom equip, parts, acces	3152367	9.72	2.49	1.52	333 Crude petroleum	21458382	83.09	9.41	6.72
713 Intern combust piston engines	2962367	9.14	4.90	4.31	659 Floor coverings, etc	615329	2.38	19.67	7.08
752 Automatic data processing equip	1732457	5.34	1.75	0.95	057 Fruit, nuts, fresh, dried	569992	2.21	4.66	1.98
781 Passengr motor vehicl, exc bus	1473873	4.55	0.51	0.45	341 Gas, natural and manufactured	365992	1.42	1.30	0.46
778 Electrical machinery nes	1042821	3.22	1.69	1.13	335 Residual petroleum prdts nes	169972	0.66	6.60	1.89
784 Motor vehicl parts, acces nes	1037914	3.20	0.83	0.72	672 Iron, steel primary forms	166340	0.64	2.47	0.64
772 Switchgear etc, parts nes	878933	2.71	1.50	1.00	334 Petroleum products, refined	140466	0.54	0.21	0.10
773 Electricity distributing equip	863778	2.66	3.89	2.29	511 Hydrocarbons nes, derivtives	114985	0.45	2.10	0.55
759 Office, adp machy parts, acces	760702	2.35	1.03	0.51	054 Vegtb etc fresh, simply prsrvd	104858	0.41	1.38	0.43
931 Special transactions	747230	2.31	0.74	0.58	851 Footwear	84343	0.33	0.36	0.20
Remainder	17764718	54.80			Remainder	2033402	7.87		
Iceland - Islande (= developed)**					**Ireland - Irlande (** = developed)**				
All commodity groups	2124212	100.00	0.05	0.03	All commodity groups	85725025	100.00	2.13	1.40
034 Fish, fresh, chilled, frozen	677802	31.91	5.07	2.97	515 Organo-inorgan compounds, etc	12724057	14.84	31.09	28.02
684 Aluminium	412929	19.44	1.26	0.86	541 Medicinal, pharmaceutical prdts	11394882	13.29	8.20	7.65
035 Fish salted, dried, smoked	290681	13.68	14.47	10.48	752 Automatic data processing equip	9300784	10.85	9.41	5.10
081 Feeding stuff for animals	166431	7.83	1.21	0.74	759 Office, adp machy parts, acces	8874149	10.35	12.01	5.93
037 Fish etc prepd, prsrvd nes	138323	6.51	3.61	1.42	776 Transistors, valves, etc	6607579	7.71	5.25	2.68
671 Pig iron, etc	52850	2.49	2.28	0.64	931 Special transactions	3302700	3.85	3.25	2.55
541 Medicinal, pharmaceutical prdts	51649	2.43	0.04	0.03	514 Nitrogen-function compounds	2933377	3.42	13.20	11.27
411 Animal oils and fats	41186	1.94	3.37	2.94	764 Telecom equip, parts, acces	2728714	3.18	2.15	1.31
036 Shell fish fresh, frozen	32572	1.53	0.59	0.19	898 Musical instruments and parts	2724453	3.18	11.33	8.16
793 Ships, boats, etc	31854	1.50	0.11	0.07	551 Essential oils, perfume, etc	2306227	2.69	29.50	24.91
Remainder	227935	10.73			Remainder	22828104	26.63		

For sources and notes, see end of table 4.2E.

Pour les sources et les notes, se reporter à la fin du tableau 4.2E.

168

4.2D Export structure at the SITC Revision 2 group (3-digit) level (ranked by average 2001-2002 values)
Individual countries and territories
(continued)

4.2D Structure des exportations au niveau des groupes (position à trois chiffres) de la CTCI révision 2 (classées d'après la moyenne des valeurs de 2001-2002)
Pays et territoires individuels
(suite)

SITC group / Groupes de la CTCI	2001-2002 Value (thousands of dollars) / Valeur (milliers de dollars) 1	As percentage / En pourcentage — of country total / du total du pays 2	of ** / des ** 3	of world / du monde 4	SITC group / Groupes de la CTCI	2001-2002 Value (thousands of dollars) / Valeur (milliers de dollars) 1	As percentage / En pourcentage — of country total / du total du pays 2	of ** / des ** 3	of world / du monde 4
Israel - Israël (= developed)**					**Jordan - Jordanie (** = developing)**				
All commodity groups	29286582	100.00	0.73	0.48	All commodity groups	2532225	100.00	0.13	0.04
667 Pearl, prec, semi-prec stones	9545851	32.59	26.35	17.26	271 Fertilizers, crude	325884	12.87	30.11	23.75
764 Telecom equip, parts, acces	2827560	9.65	2.23	1.36	842 Men's outwear non-knit	224110	8.85	1.03	0.64
776 Transistors, valves, etc	1375382	4.70	1.09	0.56	541 Medicinal, pharmaceutical prdts	205559	8.12	2.17	0.14
792 Aircraft, etc	1009182	3.45	0.93	0.87	054 Vegtb etc fresh, simply prsrvd	122578	4.84	1.61	0.50
541 Medicinal, pharmaceutical prdts	782923	2.67	0.56	0.53	971 Gold, non-monetary nes	92716	3.66	1.05	0.44
893 Articles of plastic nes	719850	2.46	1.78	1.22	844 Under garments non-knit	91263	3.60	1.06	0.82
874 Measuring, controlg instruments	642842	2.20	1.01	0.87	562 Fertilizers, manufactured	88350	3.49	2.86	0.60
774 Electro-medical, xray equip	551900	1.88	3.63	3.37	431 Procesd animl and veg oil, etc	75288	2.97	5.14	2.11
778 Electrical machinery nes	525748	1.80	0.85	0.57	522 Inorg chem elmnt, oxides, etc	74567	2.94	1.30	0.45
759 Office, adp machy parts, acces	429216	1.47	0.58	0.29	554 Soap, cleansing, etc preps	54817	2.16	1.94	0.38
Remainder	10876127	37.14			Remainder	1177095	46.48		
Italy - Italie (= developed)**					**Kazakhstan (** = South-East Europe & CIS)**				
All commodity groups	249341097	100.00	6.18	4.06	All commodity groups	9164377	100.00	5.35	0.15
821 Furniture and parts thereof	8727344	3.50	19.68	13.64	333 Crude petroleum	4537802	49.52	13.98	1.42
541 Medicinal, pharmaceutical prdts	8153500	3.27	5.87	5.47	682 Copper	748406	8.17	30.93	2.54
728 Oth machy for spec industries	7503316	3.01	13.63	11.79	674 Iron, steel univ, plate, sheet	497009	5.42	14.35	1.01
784 Motor vehicl parts, acces nes	7334569	2.94	5.83	5.07	041 Wheat etc, unmilled	339361	3.70	23.71	2.26
781 Passengr motor vehicl, exc bus	6660310	2.67	2.31	2.05	287 Base metals ores, conc nes	339311	3.70	42.34	1.79
851 Footwear	6519103	2.61	36.10	15.19	671 Pig iron, etc	336074	3.67	21.53	4.07
749 Non-electr machy parts, acces	6055409	2.43	11.01	8.94	322 Coal, lignite and peat	238138	2.60	15.53	1.13
775 Household type equip nes	5651573	2.27	23.49	13.46	686 Zinc	167696	1.83	36.49	3.75
897 Gold, silver ware, jewellery	4927072	1.98	33.21	19.86	681 Silver, platinum, etc	144981	1.58	83.81	1.36
699 Base metal manufactures nes	4403396	1.77	11.70	8.63	672 Iron, steel primary forms	143533	1.57	2.60	0.55
Remainder	183405503	73.56			Remainder	1672065	18.25		
Jamaica - Jamaïque (= developing)**					**Korea, Republic of - Corée, République de (** = developing)**				
All commodity groups	1162179	100.00	0.06	0.02	All commodity groups	156450265	100.00	8.06	2.55
287 Base metals ores, conc nes	698723	60.12	6.86	3.68	776 Transistors, valves, etc	15388069	9.84	12.74	6.23
846 Under garments knitted	67038	5.77	0.33	0.20	764 Telecom equip, parts, acces	14039250	8.97	17.51	6.76
061 Sugar and honey	66013	5.68	0.91	0.52	781 Passengr motor vehicl, exc bus	12748108	8.15	35.45	3.92
112 Alcoholic beverages	46537	4.00	1.08	0.15	793 Ships, boats, etc	10185662	6.51	67.48	22.84
512 Alcohols, phenols, etc	35465	3.05	0.68	0.24	752 Automatic data processing equip	7863223	5.03	9.42	4.31
071 Coffee and substitutes	31795	2.74	0.57	0.37	334 Petroleum products, refined	7006973	4.48	10.35	4.78
057 Fruit, nuts, fresh, dried	28296	2.43	0.23	0.10	759 Office, adp machy parts, acces	6830220	4.37	9.02	4.56
054 Vegtb etc fresh, simply prsrvd	16845	1.45	0.22	0.07	583 Polymerization, etc, prdts	4003905	2.56	18.41	4.76
334 Petroleum products, refined	16396	1.41	0.02	0.01	653 Woven man-made fib fabric	3414758	2.18	20.59	11.58
098 Edible products, preps nes	15140	1.30	0.38	0.08	674 Iron, steel univ, plate, sheet	3030692	1.94	27.35	6.16
Remainder	139930	12.04			Remainder	71939405	45.98		
Japan - Japon (= developed)**					**Kuwait - Koweït (** = developing)**				
All commodity groups	410039435	100.00	10.17	6.67	All commodity groups	15794954	100.00	0.81	0.26
781 Passengr motor vehicl, exc bus	57845797	14.11	20.04	17.79	333 Crude petroleum	9154703	57.96	4.02	2.87
776 Transistors, valves, etc	30482275	7.43	24.23	12.35	334 Petroleum products, refined	4611923	29.20	6.81	3.14
931 Special transactions	16564883	4.04	16.30	12.78	341 Gas, natural and manufactured	778510	4.93	2.76	0.97
784 Motor vehicl parts, acces nes	16366349	3.99	13.01	11.32	583 Polymerization, etc, prdts	504006	3.19	2.32	0.60
778 Electrical machinery nes	14203744	3.46	23.06	15.45	512 Alcohols, phenols, etc	97384	0.62	1.85	0.67
759 Office, adp machy parts, acces	13563876	3.31	18.35	9.06	335 Residual petroleum prdts nes	88550	0.56	3.44	0.98
752 Automatic data processing equip	11892002	2.90	12.03	6.52	931 Special transactions	62819	0.40	0.40	0.05
764 Telecom equip, parts, acces	11414420	2.78	9.00	5.49	562 Fertilizers, manufactured	45733	0.29	1.48	0.31
713 Intern combust piston engines	10501303	2.56	17.38	15.28	714 Engines and motors nes	34622	0.22	1.49	0.06
772 Switchgear etc, parts nes	9960400	2.43	16.98	11.37	522 Inorg chem elmnt, oxides, etc	26056	0.16	0.45	0.16
Remainder	217244385	52.98			Remainder	390648	2.47		

For sources and notes, see end of table 4.2E.

Pour les sources et les notes, se reporter à la fin du tableau 4.2E.

169

**4.2D   Export structure at the SITC Revision 2
group (3-digit) level (ranked by average
2001-2002 values)**
Individual countries and territories
(continued)

**4.2D   Structure des exportations au niveau des groupes
(position à trois chiffres) de la CTCI révision 2
(classées d'après la moyenne des valeurs de 2001-2002)**
Pays et territoires individuels
(suite)

SITC group / Groupes de la CTCI	2001-2002				SITC group / Groupes de la CTCI	2001-2002			
	Value (thousands of dollars) / Valeur (milliers de dollars)	As percentage / En pourcentage				Value (thousands of dollars) / Valeur (milliers de dollars)	As percentage / En pourcentage		
		of country total / du total du pays	of ** / des **	of world / du monde			of country total / du total du pays	of ** / des **	of world / du monde
	1	2	3	4		1	2	3	4
Kyrgyzstan - Kirghizistan (= South-East Europe & CIS)**					**Lesotho (** = developing)**				
All commodity groups	470310	100.00	0.27	0.01	All commodity groups	318774	100.00	0.02	0.01
971 Gold, non-monetary nes	166296	35.36	29.44	0.79	844 Under garments non-knit	58799	18.45	0.68	0.53
263 Cotton	46308	9.85	3.41	0.63	845 Outer garments knit nonelastic	58488	18.35	0.17	0.12
334 Petroleum products, refined	36118	7.68	0.24	0.02	842 Men's outwear non-knit	46865	14.70	0.22	0.13
351 Electric current	22518	4.79	2.62	0.21	851 Footwear	29281	9.19	0.12	0.07
121 Tobacco, unmanufactd, refuse	20189	4.29	9.96	0.36	846 Under garments knitted	22165	6.95	0.11	0.07
211 Hides skins, exc furs, raw	19551	4.16	7.00	0.35	761 Television receivers	21755	6.82	0.13	0.07
778 Electrical machinery nes	14298	3.04	1.97	0.02	111 Non alcoholic beverages nes	20270	6.36	1.66	0.33
783 Road motor vehicles nes	11521	2.45	4.47	0.07	652 Cotton fabrics, woven	12638	3.96	0.10	0.05
054 Vegtb etc fresh, simply prsrvd	10754	2.29	4.09	0.04	211 Hides skins, exc furs, raw	7237	2.27	0.80	0.13
784 Motor vehicl parts, acces nes	7478	1.59	1.16	0.01	268 Wool (exc tops), animal hair	5810	1.82	0.85	0.18
Remainder	115278	24.51			Remainder	35468	11.13		
Lao People's Dem. Rep. - Rép. dém. populaire lao (= developing)**					**Libyan Arab Jamahiriya - Jamahiriya arabe libyenne (** = developing)**				
All commodity groups	174675	100.00	0.01	0.00	All commodity groups	9719870	100.00	0.50	0.16
248 Wood, shaped, rail sleepers	40731	23.32	0.86	0.16	333 Crude petroleum	7802398	80.27	3.42	2.44
842 Men's outwear non-knit	24365	13.95	0.11	0.07	334 Petroleum products, refined	1259342	12.96	1.86	0.86
845 Outer garments knit nonelastic	21231	12.15	0.06	0.04	341 Gas, natural and manufactured	182621	1.88	0.65	0.23
846 Under garments knitted	15988	9.15	0.08	0.05	512 Alcohols, phenols, etc	83966	0.86	1.60	0.58
843 Women's outwear non-knit	14963	8.57	0.05	0.03	511 Hydrocarbons nes, derivtives	74235	0.76	1.36	0.36
247 Other wood rough, squared	13793	7.90	0.79	0.19	562 Fertilizers, manufactured	60713	0.62	1.96	0.41
844 Under garments non-knit	11232	6.43	0.13	0.10	672 Iron, steel primary forms	57639	0.59	0.85	0.22
071 Coffee and substitutes	7847	4.49	0.14	0.09	583 Polymerization, etc, prdts	33155	0.34	0.15	0.04
001 Live animals for food	3619	2.07	0.24	0.04	673 Iron, steel shapes, etc	25674	0.26	0.52	0.11
287 Base metals ores, conc nes	3274	1.87	0.03	0.02	335 Residual petroleum prdts nes	24899	0.26	0.97	0.28
Remainder	17634	10.10			Remainder	115231	1.19		
Latvia - Lettonie (= developed)**					**Lithuania - Lituanie (** = developed)**				
All commodity groups	2142565	100.00	0.05	0.03	All commodity groups	5068149	100.00	0.13	0.08
248 Wood, shaped, rail sleepers	382181	17.84	2.06	1.53	334 Petroleum products, refined	974035	19.22	1.53	0.66
247 Other wood rough, squared	110943	5.18	2.94	1.54	781 Passengr motor vehicl, exc bus	269047	5.31	0.09	0.08
673 Iron, steel shapes, etc	108084	5.04	0.69	0.47	843 Women's outwear non-knit	253974	5.01	1.56	0.52
635 Wood manufactures nes	105871	4.94	0.88	0.61	562 Fertilizers, manufactured	190067	3.75	2.19	1.29
821 Furniture and parts thereof	101736	4.75	0.23	0.16	821 Furniture and parts thereof	177118	3.49	0.40	0.28
634 Veneers, plywood, etc	92267	4.31	1.16	0.68	776 Transistors, valves, etc	148860	2.94	0.12	0.06
684 Aluminium	75857	3.54	0.23	0.16	842 Men's outwear non-knit	127127	2.51	1.11	0.37
541 Medicinal, pharmaceutical prdts	60325	2.82	0.04	0.04	248 Wood, shaped, rail sleepers	121932	2.41	0.66	0.49
843 Women's outwear non-knit	56186	2.62	0.34	0.11	845 Outer garments knit nonelastic	100687	1.99	0.66	0.20
651 Textile yarn	53875	2.51	0.37	0.17	024 Cheese and curd	95576	1.89	0.90	0.87
Remainder	995241	46.45			Remainder	2609727	51.49		
Lebanon - Liban (= developing)**					**Luxembourg (** = developed)**				
All commodity groups	967384	100.00	0.05	0.02	All commodity groups	8393059	100.00	0.21	0.14
971 Gold, non-monetary nes	94165	9.73	1.06	0.45	673 Iron, steel shapes, etc	1004974	11.97	6.40	4.39
897 Gold, silver ware, jewellery	69694	7.20	0.70	0.28	764 Telecom equip, parts, acces	654486	7.80	0.52	0.31
522 Inorg chem elmnt, oxides, etc	40839	4.22	0.71	0.25	674 Iron, steel univ, plate, sheet	448789	5.35	1.29	0.91
892 Printed matter	39273	4.06	0.80	0.12	898 Musical instruments and parts	411532	4.90	1.71	1.23
661 Lime, cement and building prdts	37751	3.90	0.79	0.33	893 Articles of plastic nes	336532	4.01	0.83	0.57
716 Rotating electric plant	33131	3.42	0.32	0.10	749 Non-electr machy parts, acces	331525	3.95	0.60	0.49
057 Fruit, nuts, fresh, dried	29025	3.00	0.24	0.10	772 Switchgear etc, parts nes	268642	3.20	0.46	0.31
121 Tobacco, unmanufactd, refuse	25559	2.64	0.85	0.46	684 Aluminium	259746	3.09	0.80	0.54
642 Paper and paperboard, cut	25044	2.59	0.39	0.09	641 Paper and paperboard	247092	2.94	0.39	0.34
269 Waste of textile fabrics	21146	2.19	5.09	1.31	781 Passengr motor vehicl, exc bus	238091	2.84	0.08	0.07
Remainder	551757	57.04			Remainder	4191650	49.94		

For sources and notes, see end of table 4.2E.

Pour les sources et les notes, se reporter à la fin du tableau 4.2E.

4.2D Export structure at the SITC Revision 2 group (3-digit) level (ranked by average 2001-2002 values)
Individual countries and territories
(continued)

4.2D Structure des exportations au niveau des groupes (position à trois chiffres) de la CTCI révision 2 (classées d'après la moyenne des valeurs de 2001-2002)
Pays et territoires individuels
(suite)

SITC group / Groupes de la CTCI	Value (thousands of dollars) / Valeur (milliers de dollars)	As percentage / En pourcentage — of country total / du total du pays	of ** / des **	of world / du monde
	1	2	3	4
Macedonia, TFYR - Macédoine, LERY (= South-East Europe & CIS)**				
All commodity groups	1135293	100.00	0.66	0.02
843 Women's outwear non-knit	144863	12.76	6.11	0.29
674 Iron, steel univ, plate, sheet	115594	10.18	3.34	0.23
844 Under garments non-knit	66194	5.83	15.88	0.60
842 Men's outwear non-knit	59782	5.27	3.84	0.17
121 Tobacco, unmanufactd, refuse	53380	4.70	26.35	0.96
686 Zinc	45551	4.01	9.91	1.02
671 Pig iron, etc	31479	2.77	2.02	0.38
334 Petroleum products, refined	31435	2.77	0.21	0.02
112 Alcoholic beverages	31132	2.74	5.20	0.10
851 Footwear	29879	2.63	2.47	0.07
Remainder	526004	46.33		
Madagascar (= developing)**				
All commodity groups	385699	100.00	0.02	0.01
075 Spices	156826	40.66	8.41	6.38
036 Shell fish fresh, frozen	58971	15.29	0.52	0.35
845 Outer garments knit nonelastic	16561	4.29	0.05	0.03
892 Printed matter	9045	2.35	0.18	0.03
843 Women's outwear non-knit	7850	2.04	0.03	0.02
652 Cotton fabrics, woven	7617	1.97	0.06	0.03
334 Petroleum products, refined	7585	1.97	0.01	0.01
842 Men's outwear non-knit	7337	1.90	0.03	0.02
292 Crude vegetb materials nes	7255	1.88	0.18	0.05
057 Fruit, nuts, fresh, dried	7216	1.87	0.06	0.03
Remainder	99434	25.78		
Malawi (= developing)**				
All commodity groups	413398	100.00	0.02	0.01
121 Tobacco, unmanufactd, refuse	246961	59.74	8.19	4.43
061 Sugar and honey	49696	12.02	0.69	0.40
074 Tea and mate	35712	8.64	1.69	1.37
842 Men's outwear non-knit	11502	2.78	0.05	0.03
844 Under garments non-knit	7998	1.93	0.09	0.07
263 Cotton	5414	1.31	0.22	0.07
057 Fruit, nuts, fresh, dried	4546	1.10	0.04	0.02
071 Coffee and substitutes	4491	1.09	0.08	0.05
846 Under garments knitted	4480	1.08	0.02	0.01
845 Outer garments knit nonelastic	4334	1.05	0.01	0.01
Remainder	38265	9.26		
Malaysia - Malaisie (= developing)**				
All commodity groups	91031388	100.00	4.69	1.48
776 Transistors, valves, etc	17568495	19.30	14.54	7.12
759 Office, adp machy parts, acces	9319184	10.24	12.30	6.22
752 Automatic data processing equip	7886908	8.66	9.45	4.32
764 Telecom equip, parts, acces	5515980	6.06	6.88	2.65
341 Gas, natural and manufactured	3317148	3.64	11.75	4.13
424 Other fixed vegetable oils	3094414	3.40	49.13	41.09
333 Crude petroleum	3056667	3.36	1.34	0.96
772 Switchgear etc, parts nes	2550839	2.80	8.94	2.91
763 Sound recorders, phonographs	2105251	2.31	13.69	7.09
761 Television receivers	2036863	2.24	12.08	6.67
Remainder	34579638	37.99		
Maldives (= developing)**				
All commodity groups	83722	100.00	0.00	0.00
034 Fish, fresh, chilled, frozen	24262	28.98	0.27	0.11
846 Under garments knitted	21295	25.43	0.10	0.06
035 Fish salted, dried, smoked	11852	14.16	1.58	0.43
037 Fish etc prepd, prsrvd nes	9952	11.89	0.17	0.10
842 Men's outwear non-knit	7118	8.50	0.03	0.02
036 Shell fish fresh, frozen	2891	3.45	0.03	0.02
843 Women's outwear non-knit	2459	2.94	0.01	0.00
845 Outer garments knit nonelastic	2405	2.87	0.01	0.00
081 Feeding stuff for animals	1003	1.20	0.01	0.00
844 Under garments non-knit	281	0.34	0.00	0.00
Remainder	206	0.25		
Mali (= developing)**				
All commodity groups	718823	100.00	0.04	0.01
263 Cotton	343144	47.74	14.07	4.68
971 Gold, non-monetary nes	218150	30.35	2.47	1.04
611 Leather	12689	1.77	0.14	0.07
334 Petroleum products, refined	8600	1.20	0.01	0.01
723 Civil engineering equip, etc	8495	1.18	0.15	0.02
776 Transistors, valves, etc	8441	1.17	0.01	0.00
778 Electrical machinery nes	7127	0.99	0.02	0.01
752 Automatic data processing equip	7003	0.97	0.01	0.00
896 Works of art, etc	5706	0.79	2.00	0.06
211 Hides skins, exc furs, raw	5675	0.79	0.63	0.10
Remainder	93793	13.05		
Malta - Malte (= developed)**				
All commodity groups	2044902	100.00	0.05	0.03
776 Transistors, valves, etc	1047062	51.20	0.83	0.42
842 Men's outwear non-knit	134963	6.60	1.17	0.39
334 Petroleum products, refined	112011	5.48	0.18	0.08
772 Switchgear etc, parts nes	84750	4.14	0.14	0.10
894 Toys, sporting goods, etc	46901	2.29	0.23	0.10
892 Printed matter	43794	2.14	0.17	0.14
628 Rubber articles nes	42910	2.10	0.45	0.37
897 Gold, silver ware, jewellery	34736	1.70	0.23	0.14
872 Medical instruments nes	34398	1.68	0.14	0.12
612 Leather, etc, manufactures	31706	1.55	1.00	0.46
Remainder	431672	21.11		
Mauritania - Mauritanie (= developing)**				
All commodity groups	447862	100.00	0.02	0.01
281 Iron ore and concentrates	192921	43.08	3.96	2.02
034 Fish, fresh, chilled, frozen	122015	27.24	1.35	0.54
036 Shell fish fresh, frozen	100178	22.37	0.89	0.60
081 Feeding stuff for animals	8915	1.99	0.11	0.04
035 Fish salted, dried, smoked	2306	0.51	0.31	0.08
562 Fertilizers, manufactured	2248	0.50	0.07	0.02
842 Men's outwear non-knit	2089	0.47	0.01	0.01
682 Copper	1531	0.34	0.01	0.01
112 Alcoholic beverages	832	0.19	0.02	0.00
793 Ships, boats, etc	795	0.18	0.01	0.00
Remainder	14034	3.13		

For sources and notes, see end of table 4.2E.

Pour les sources et les notes, se reporter à la fin du tableau 4.2E.

171

4.2D Export structure at the SITC Revision 2 group (3-digit) level (ranked by average 2001-2002 values)
Individual countries and territories
(continued)

4.2D Structure des exportations au niveau des groupes (position à trois chiffres) de la CTCI révision 2 (classées d'après la moyenne des valeurs de 2001-2002)
Pays et territoires individuels
(suite)

SITC group / Groupes de la CTCI	2001-2002 Value (thousands of dollars) / Valeur (milliers de dollars)	As percentage / En pourcentage of country total / du total du pays	of ** / des **	of world / du monde
	1	2	3	4
Mauritius - Maurice (= developing)**				
All commodity groups	1638125	100.00	0.08	0.03
846 Under garments knitted	337878	20.63	1.64	1.02
061 Sugar and honey	285411	17.42	3.95	2.27
845 Outer garments knit nonelastic	169424	10.34	0.50	0.34
842 Men's outwear non-knit	146352	8.93	0.67	0.42
843 Women's outwear non-knit	136135	8.31	0.45	0.28
844 Under garments non-knit	111905	6.83	1.30	1.01
037 Fish etc prepd, prsrvd nes	65094	3.97	1.12	0.67
652 Cotton fabrics, woven	42978	2.62	0.34	0.18
034 Fish, fresh, chilled, frozen	34125	2.08	0.38	0.15
667 Pearl, prec, semi-prec stones	33526	2.05	0.18	0.06
Remainder	275298	16.81		
Mexico - Mexique (= developing)**				
All commodity groups	159546676	100.00	8.22	2.60
781 Passengr motor vehicl, exc bus	14623202	9.17	40.66	4.50
333 Crude petroleum	12350500	7.74	5.42	3.87
764 Telecom equip, parts, acces	10131799	6.35	12.64	4.88
752 Automatic data processing equip	9477750	5.94	11.36	5.20
761 Television receivers	6469545	4.05	38.36	21.18
782 Lorries, spec motor vehicl nes	6404268	4.01	58.33	11.06
784 Motor vehicl parts, acces nes	6094154	3.82	33.51	4.21
773 Electricity distributing equip	5919360	3.71	40.40	15.72
778 Electrical machinery nes	5155696	3.23	17.41	5.61
772 Switchgear etc, parts nes	4883710	3.06	17.12	5.57
Remainder	78036692	48.91		
Moldova, Republic of - Moldova, République de (= South-East Europe & CIS)**				
All commodity groups	606013	100.00	0.66	0.01
112 Alcoholic beverages	184982	30.52	6.11	0.59
843 Women's outwear non-knit	34441	5.68	3.34	0.07
057 Fruit, nuts, fresh, dried	27976	4.62	15.88	0.10
842 Men's outwear non-knit	25958	4.28	3.84	0.07
058 Fruit prsrvd, preprd	22824	3.77	26.35	0.18
121 Tobacco, unmanufactd, refuse	19435	3.21	9.91	0.35
845 Outer garments knit nonelastic	17840	2.94	2.02	0.04
222 Seeds for soft fixed oils	17309	2.86	0.21	0.12
846 Under garments knitted	15137	2.50	5.20	0.05
041 Wheat etc, unmilled	14922	2.46	2.47	0.10
Remainder	225188	37.16		
Mongolia - Mongolie (= developing)**				
All commodity groups	464463	100.00	0.02	0.01
287 Base metals ores, conc nes	151780	32.68	1.49	0.80
268 Wool (exc tops), animal hair	55351	11.92	8.08	1.73
971 Gold, non-monetary nes	38480	8.28	0.44	0.18
611 Leather	37330	8.04	0.42	0.22
845 Outer garments knit nonelastic	28666	6.17	0.09	0.06
843 Women's outwear non-knit	25502	5.49	0.08	0.05
842 Men's outwear non-knit	25077	5.40	0.12	0.07
278 Other crude minerals	19672	4.24	0.94	0.28
011 Meat, fresh, chilled, frozen	18925	4.07	0.29	0.05
844 Under garments non-knit	15584	3.36	0.18	0.14
Remainder	48097	10.36		
Morocco - Maroc (= developing)**				
All commodity groups	7497164	100.00	0.39	0.12
843 Women's outwear non-knit	844487	11.26	2.77	1.72
842 Men's outwear non-knit	570167	7.61	2.63	1.64
036 Shell fish fresh, frozen	498963	6.66	4.44	2.97
522 Inorg chem elmnt, oxides, etc	461625	6.16	8.06	2.81
776 Transistors, valves, etc	444184	5.92	0.37	0.18
846 Under garments knitted	436445	5.82	2.12	1.32
271 Fertilizers, crude	368660	4.92	34.07	26.87
845 Outer garments knit nonelastic	366966	4.89	1.09	0.73
562 Fertilizers, manufactured	340512	4.54	11.01	2.31
773 Electricity distributing equip	270954	3.61	1.85	0.72
Remainder	2894201	38.60		
Mozambique (= developing)**				
All commodity groups	691534	100.00	0.04	0.01
684 Aluminium	376777	54.48	3.80	0.79
036 Shell fish fresh, frozen	92895	13.43	0.83	0.55
351 Electric current	56402	8.16	5.20	0.52
081 Feeding stuff for animals	15946	2.31	0.19	0.07
263 Cotton	15856	2.29	0.65	0.22
057 Fruit, nuts, fresh, dried	13663	1.98	0.11	0.05
121 Tobacco, unmanufactd, refuse	8949	1.29	0.30	0.16
334 Petroleum products, refined	8036	1.16	0.01	0.01
061 Sugar and honey	7903	1.14	0.11	0.06
247 Other wood rough, squared	7611	1.10	0.44	0.11
Remainder	87499	12.65		
Myanmar (= developing)**				
All commodity groups	2713961	100.00	0.14	0.04
341 Gas, natural and manufactured	664353	24.48	2.35	0.83
845 Outer garments knit nonelastic	337575	12.44	1.00	0.68
054 Vegtb etc fresh, simply prsrvd	308928	11.38	4.06	1.26
247 Other wood rough, squared	266396	9.82	15.35	3.71
842 Men's outwear non-knit	143931	5.30	0.66	0.41
036 Shell fish fresh, frozen	133354	4.91	1.19	0.79
843 Women's outwear non-knit	113089	4.17	0.37	0.23
846 Under garments knitted	111952	4.13	0.54	0.34
248 Wood, shaped, rail sleepers	107184	3.95	2.27	0.43
042 Rice	71545	2.64	1.52	1.05
Remainder	455657	16.79		
Namibia - Namibie (= developing)**				
All commodity groups	953530	100.00	0.05	0.02
667 Pearl, prec, semi-prec stones	304250	31.91	1.60	0.55
034 Fish, fresh, chilled, frozen	199486	20.92	2.21	0.88
892 Printed matter	105123	11.02	2.13	0.33
286 Uranium, thorium ores, conc	69386	7.28	43.96	17.56
112 Alcoholic beverages	33281	3.49	0.77	0.11
001 Live animals for food	30312	3.18	2.02	0.34
011 Meat, fresh, chilled, frozen	22627	2.37	0.34	0.06
971 Gold, non-monetary nes	16726	1.75	0.19	0.07
111 Non alcoholic beverages nes	11183	1.17	0.92	0.18
081 Feeding stuff for animals	9861	1.03	0.12	0.04
Remainder	151295	15.87		

For sources and notes, see end of table 4.2E.

Pour les sources et les notes, se reporter à la fin du tableau 4.2E.

4.2D **Export structure at the SITC Revision 2 group (3-digit) level (ranked by average 2001-2002 values)**
Individual countries and territories
(continued)

4.2D **Structure des exportations au niveau des groupes (position à trois chiffres) de la CTCI révision 2 (classées d'après la moyenne des valeurs de 2001-2002)**
Pays et territoires individuels
(suite)

SITC group / Groupes de la CTCI	2001-2002 Value (thousands of dollars) / Valeur (milliers de dollars)	As percentage / En pourcentage of country total / du total du pays	of ** / des **	of world / du monde
	1	2	3	4
Nepal - Népal (= developing)**				
All commodity groups	652457	100.00	0.03	0.01
931 Special transactions	147441	22.60	0.93	0.11
659 Floor coverings, etc	134727	20.65	4.31	1.55
843 Women's outwear non-knit	70400	10.79	0.23	0.14
844 Under garments non-knit	44526	6.82	0.52	0.40
847 Textile clothing accessoris nes	38634	5.92	0.82	0.40
023 Butter	35282	5.41	36.80	1.30
553 Perfumery, cosmetics, etc	29881	4.58	0.79	0.11
842 Men's outwear non-knit	24229	3.71	0.11	0.07
554 Soap, cleansing, etc preps	14034	2.15	0.50	0.10
658 Textile articles nes	13635	2.09	0.12	0.07
Remainder	99670	15.28		
Netherlands - Pays-Bas (= developed)**				
All commodity groups	172432536	100.00	4.28	2.81
752 Automatic data processing equip	15331706	8.89	15.51	8.40
334 Petroleum products, refined	11229194	6.51	17.59	7.65
759 Office, adp machy parts, acces	7717434	4.48	10.44	5.15
541 Medicinal, pharmaceutical prdts	5654532	3.28	4.07	3.79
292 Crude vegetb materials nes	4734858	2.75	42.37	30.85
583 Polymerization, etc, prdts	4246574	2.46	6.93	5.05
764 Telecom equip, parts, acces	4173533	2.42	3.29	2.01
054 Vegtb etc fresh, simply prsrvd	3581159	2.08	21.50	14.60
781 Passengr motor vehicl, exc bus	3460440	2.01	1.20	1.06
011 Meat, fresh, chilled, frozen	3279500	1.90	10.30	8.45
Remainder	109023606	63.23		
New Caledonia - Nouvelle-Calédonie (= developing)**				
All commodity groups	431848	100.00	0.02	0.01
671 Pig iron, etc	268320	62.13	6.13	3.25
287 Base metals ores, conc nes	110623	25.62	1.09	0.58
036 Shell fish fresh, frozen	17559	4.07	0.16	0.10
034 Fish, fresh, chilled, frozen	5348	1.24	0.06	0.02
334 Petroleum products, refined	5017	1.16	0.01	0.00
792 Aircraft, etc	3590	0.83	0.05	0.00
684 Aluminium	2800	0.65	0.03	0.01
697 Base metal household equip	1972	0.46	0.03	0.01
054 Vegtb etc fresh, simply prsrvd	1158	0.27	0.02	0.00
764 Telecom equip, parts, acces	973	0.23	0.00	0.00
Remainder	14488	3.35		
New Zealand - Nouvelle-Zélande (= developed)**				
All commodity groups	14055502	100.00	0.35	0.23
011 Meat, fresh, chilled, frozen	1898108	13.50	5.96	4.89
022 Milk and cream	1494312	10.63	12.95	11.21
592 Starch, inulin, gluten, etc	602535	4.29	7.71	6.23
024 Cheese and curd	575859	4.10	5.41	5.21
931 Special transactions	514071	3.66	0.51	0.40
684 Aluminium	471510	3.35	1.44	0.98
023 Butter	462148	3.29	18.32	17.06
057 Fruit, nuts, fresh, dried	461560	3.28	2.83	1.60
248 Wood, shaped, rail sleepers	427585	3.04	2.31	1.71
034 Fish, fresh, chilled, frozen	404322	2.88	3.02	1.77
Remainder	6743491	47.98		

SITC group / Groupes de la CTCI	2001-2002 Value (thousands of dollars) / Valeur (milliers de dollars)	As percentage / En pourcentage of country total / du total du pays	of ** / des **	of world / du monde
	1	2	3	4
Nicaragua (= developing)**				
All commodity groups	583515	100.00	0.03	0.01
071 Coffee and substitutes	91537	15.69	1.63	1.05
011 Meat, fresh, chilled, frozen	79681	13.66	1.21	0.21
061 Sugar and honey	38581	6.61	0.53	0.31
036 Shell fish fresh, frozen	34467	5.91	0.31	0.21
971 Gold, non-monetary nes	30828	5.28	0.35	0.15
222 Seeds for soft fixed oils	30083	5.16	0.54	0.21
001 Live animals for food	24125	4.13	1.61	0.27
054 Vegtb etc fresh, simply prsrvd	20476	3.51	0.27	0.08
057 Fruit, nuts, fresh, dried	17085	2.93	0.14	0.06
024 Cheese and curd	15292	2.62	6.18	0.14
Remainder	201361	34.51		
Niger (= developing)**				
All commodity groups	177448	100.00	0.01	0.00
286 Uranium, thorium ores, conc	88208	49.71	55.88	22.33
001 Live animals for food	38277	21.57	2.55	0.43
054 Vegtb etc fresh, simply prsrvd	17617	9.93	0.23	0.07
652 Cotton fabrics, woven	5995	3.38	0.05	0.03
035 Fish salted, dried, smoked	4875	2.75	0.65	0.18
122 Tobacco, manufactured	4844	2.73	0.13	0.03
269 Waste of textile fabrics	3254	1.83	0.78	0.20
941 Zoo animals, pets, etc	3087	1.74	2.53	0.79
334 Petroleum products, refined	1392	0.78	0.00	0.00
728 Oth machy for spec industries	810	0.46	0.01	0.00
Remainder	9088	5.12		
Nigeria - Nigéria (= developing)**				
All commodity groups	16451824	100.00	0.85	0.27
333 Crude petroleum	16391574	99.63	7.19	5.13
223 Seeds for other fixed oils	10841	0.07	3.95	1.20
793 Ships, boats, etc	10730	0.07	0.07	0.02
222 Seeds for soft fixed oils	6109	0.04	0.11	0.04
653 Woven man-made fib fabric	4223	0.03	0.03	0.01
723 Civil engineering equip, etc	2801	0.02	0.05	0.01
661 Lime, cement and building prdts	2130	0.01	0.04	0.02
697 Base metal household equip	1565	0.01	0.02	0.01
691 Structures and parts nes	1418	0.01	0.05	0.01
072 Cocoa	1262	0.01	0.04	0.02
Remainder	19173	0.12		
Norway - Norvège (= developed)**				
All commodity groups	59265495	100.00	1.47	0.96
333 Crude petroleum	26283869	44.35	44.66	8.23
341 Gas, natural and manufactured	7960912	13.43	23.62	9.92
034 Fish, fresh, chilled, frozen	2539390	4.28	19.00	11.14
931 Special transactions	2536340	4.28	2.50	1.96
684 Aluminium	2368161	4.00	7.25	4.94
334 Petroleum products, refined	1698973	2.87	2.66	1.16
793 Ships, boats, etc	1571220	2.65	5.62	3.52
641 Paper and paperboard	701053	1.18	1.10	0.95
035 Fish salted, dried, smoked	607053	1.02	30.21	21.88
792 Aircraft, etc	560416	0.95	0.52	0.48
Remainder	12438108	20.99		

For sources and notes, see end of table 4.2E.

Pour les sources et les notes, se reporter à la fin du tableau 4.2E.

4.2D Export structure at the SITC Revision 2 group (3-digit) level (ranked by average 2001-2002 values)
Individual countries and territories
(continued)

4.2D Structure des exportations au niveau des groupes (position à trois chiffres) de la CTCI révision 2 (classées d'après la moyenne des valeurs de 2001-2002)
Pays et territoires individuels
(suite)

SITC group / Groupes de la CTCI	Value (thousands of dollars) / Valeur (milliers de dollars)	2001-2002 As percentage / En pourcentage			SITC group / Groupes de la CTCI	Value (thousands of dollars) / Valeur (milliers de dollars)	2001-2002 As percentage / En pourcentage		
		of country total / du total du pays	of ** / des **	of world / du monde			of country total / du total du pays	of ** / des **	of world / du monde
	1	2	3	4		1	2	3	4
Oman (= developing)**					**Paraguay (** = developing)**				
All commodity groups	11136523	100.00	0.57	0.18	All commodity groups	970402	100.00	0.05	0.02
333 Crude petroleum	7583082	68.09	3.33	2.38	222 Seeds for soft fixed oils	356969	36.79	6.36	2.45
341 Gas, natural and manufactured	1157477	10.39	4.10	1.44	011 Meat, fresh, chilled, frozen	75603	7.79	1.15	0.19
122 Tobacco, manufactured	379004	3.40	9.85	2.46	081 Feeding stuff for animals	73036	7.53	0.87	0.33
781 Passengr motor vehicl, exc bus	359812	3.23	1.00	0.11	263 Cotton	60475	6.23	2.48	0.83
784 Motor vehicl parts, acces nes	210508	1.89	1.16	0.15	423 Fixed vegetable oils, soft	58892	6.07	1.80	0.65
782 Lorries, spec motor vehicl nes	98154	0.88	0.89	0.17	611 Leather	53498	5.51	0.60	0.31
653 Woven man-made fib fabric	70708	0.63	0.43	0.24	121 Tobacco, unmanufactd, refuse	44743	4.61	1.48	0.80
022 Milk and cream	63424	0.57	4.08	0.48	248 Wood, shaped, rail sleepers	43715	4.50	0.93	0.18
723 Civil engineering equip, etc	56492	0.51	0.99	0.15	044 Maize (corn), unmilled	33797	3.48	1.27	0.36
931 Special transactions	54639	0.49	0.34	0.04	122 Tobacco, manufactured	15244	1.57	0.40	0.10
Remainder	1103222	9.91			Remainder	154430	15.91		
Pakistan (= developing)**					**Peru - Pérou (** = developing)**				
All commodity groups	9573074	100.00	0.49	0.16	All commodity groups	7158008	100.00	0.37	0.12
658 Textile articles nes	1629446	17.02	14.02	8.92	971 Gold, non-monetary nes	1316748	18.40	14.89	6.25
652 Cotton fabrics, woven	1143086	11.94	9.03	4.89	081 Feeding stuff for animals	853457	11.92	10.19	3.81
651 Textile yarn	1035233	10.81	6.03	3.18	287 Base metals ores, conc nes	842075	11.76	8.26	4.43
846 Under garments knitted	529266	5.53	2.57	1.60	682 Copper	814990	11.39	6.73	2.77
042 Rice	492046	5.14	10.42	7.22	846 Under garments knitted	311560	4.35	1.51	0.94
653 Woven man-made fib fabric	468103	4.89	2.82	1.59	334 Petroleum products, refined	301339	4.21	0.45	0.21
848 Headgear, non-textile clothing	419180	4.38	4.09	2.81	071 Coffee and substitutes	184436	2.58	3.28	2.12
842 Men's outwear non-knit	382673	4.00	1.76	1.10	681 Silver, platinum, etc	168212	2.35	10.24	1.57
845 Outer garments knit nonelastic	331634	3.46	0.99	0.66	845 Outer garments knit nonelastic	157325	2.20	0.47	0.31
659 Floor coverings, etc	254446	2.66	8.14	2.93	686 Zinc	156094	2.18	10.72	3.49
Remainder	2887961	30.17			Remainder	2051772	28.66		
Panama (= developing)**					**Philippines (** = developing)**				
All commodity groups	828013	100.00	0.04	0.01	All commodity groups	33679001	100.00	1.74	0.55
034 Fish, fresh, chilled, frozen	196243	23.70	2.18	0.86	776 Transistors, valves, etc	13732863	40.78	11.37	5.56
057 Fruit, nuts, fresh, dried	150320	18.15	1.23	0.52	752 Automatic data processing equip	4410375	13.10	5.29	2.42
036 Shell fish fresh, frozen	85436	10.32	0.76	0.51	759 Office, adp machy parts, acces	2699283	8.01	3.56	1.80
334 Petroleum products, refined	51087	6.17	0.08	0.03	772 Switchgear etc, parts nes	962507	2.86	3.37	1.10
001 Live animals for food	25369	3.06	1.69	0.29	764 Telecom equip, parts, acces	931387	2.77	1.16	0.45
541 Medicinal, pharmaceutical prdts	20495	2.48	0.22	0.01	843 Women's outwear non-knit	873486	2.59	2.86	1.78
037 Fish etc prepd, prsrvd nes	18586	2.24	0.32	0.19	784 Motor vehicl parts, acces nes	689988	2.05	3.79	0.48
035 Fish salted, dried, smoked	18524	2.24	2.47	0.67	773 Electricity distributing equip	563027	1.67	3.84	1.50
011 Meat, fresh, chilled, frozen	17394	2.10	0.26	0.04	845 Outer garments knit nonelastic	516619	1.53	1.54	1.03
061 Sugar and honey	14520	1.75	0.20	0.12	057 Fruit, nuts, fresh, dried	451398	1.34	3.69	1.57
Remainder	230039	27.78			Remainder	7848068	23.30		
Papua New Guinea - Papouasie-Nouvelle-Guinée (= developing)**					**Poland - Pologne (** = developed)**				
All commodity groups	1680688	100.00	0.09	0.03	All commodity groups	38153848	100.00	0.95	0.62
289 Prec metal ores, waste nes	711802	42.35	55.22	22.10	821 Furniture and parts thereof	2698515	7.07	6.08	4.22
333 Crude petroleum	483202	28.75	0.21	0.15	793 Ships, boats, etc	2104787	5.52	7.52	4.72
287 Base metals ores, conc nes	149710	8.91	1.47	0.79	713 Intern combust piston engines	1669694	4.38	2.76	2.43
424 Other fixed vegetable oils	103330	6.15	1.64	1.37	781 Passengr motor vehicl, exc bus	1402058	3.67	0.49	0.43
071 Coffee and substitutes	102252	6.08	1.82	1.18	784 Motor vehicl parts, acces nes	1266569	3.32	1.01	0.88
247 Other wood rough, squared	30487	1.81	1.76	0.42	761 Television receivers	996118	2.61	7.34	3.26
793 Ships, boats, etc	14330	0.85	0.09	0.03	322 Coal, lignite and peat	867785	2.27	7.25	4.13
035 Fish salted, dried, smoked	10311	0.61	1.38	0.37	773 Electricity distributing equip	819729	2.15	3.69	2.18
072 Cocoa	8640	0.51	0.25	0.16	843 Women's outwear non-knit	807331	2.12	4.95	1.64
036 Shell fish fresh, frozen	8246	0.49	0.07	0.05	641 Paper and paperboard	760455	1.99	1.19	1.04
Remainder	58380	3.47			Remainder	24760807	64.90		

For sources and notes, see end of table 4.2E.

Pour les sources et les notes, se reporter à la fin du tableau 4.2E.

4.2D Export structure at the SITC Revision 2 group (3-digit) level (ranked by average 2001-2002 values)
Individual countries and territories
(continued)

4.2D Structure des exportations au niveau des groupes (position à trois chiffres) de la CTCI révision 2 (classées d'après la moyenne des valeurs de 2001-2002)
Pays et territoires individuels
(suite)

SITC group / Groupes de la CTCI	2001-2002 Value (thousands of dollars) / Valeur (milliers de dollars)	As percentage En pourcentage of country total / du total du pays	of ** / des **	of world / du monde	SITC group / Groupes de la CTCI	2001-2002 Value (thousands of dollars) / Valeur (milliers de dollars)	As percentage En pourcentage of country total / du total du pays	of ** / des **	of world / du monde
	1	2	3	4		1	2	3	4
Portugal (= developed)**					**Rwanda (** = developing)**				
All commodity groups	25466474	100.00	0.63	0.41	All commodity groups	50754	100.00	0.00	0.00
781 Passengr motor vehicl, exc bus	2789730	10.95	0.97	0.86	287 Base metals ores, conc nes	18614	36.68	0.18	0.10
851 Footwear	1424262	5.59	7.89	3.32	071 Coffee and substitutes	14514	28.60	0.26	0.17
773 Electricity distributing equip	875295	3.44	3.94	2.32	074 Tea and mate	14173	27.93	0.67	0.55
845 Outer garments knit nonelastic	843906	3.31	5.49	1.69	211 Hides skins, exc furs, raw	1508	2.97	0.17	0.03
846 Under garments knitted	800704	3.14	6.85	2.42	653 Woven man-made fib fabric	600	1.18	0.00	0.00
658 Textile articles nes	776454	3.05	12.20	4.25	292 Crude vegetb materials nes	566	1.12	0.01	0.00
633 Cork manufactures	771346	3.03	66.47	63.40	651 Textile yarn	117	0.23	0.00	0.00
784 Motor vehicl parts, acces nes	723464	2.84	0.58	0.50	553 Perfumery, cosmetics, etc	93	0.18	0.00	0.00
641 Paper and paperboard	702847	2.76	1.10	0.96	523 Other inorganic chemicals	57	0.11	0.00	0.00
762 Radio-broadcast receivers	651646	2.56	12.21	3.86	611 Leather	52	0.10	0.00	0.00
Remainder	15106820	59.32			Remainder	459	0.90		
Qatar (= developing)**					**Samoa (** = developing)**				
All commodity groups	9468387	100.00	0.49	0.15	All commodity groups	67069	100.00	0.00	0.00
333 Crude petroleum	4245951	44.84	1.86	1.33	773 Electricity distributing equip	40746	60.75	0.28	0.11
341 Gas, natural and manufactured	3917726	41.38	13.88	4.88	034 Fish, fresh, chilled, frozen	13849	20.65	0.15	0.06
334 Petroleum products, refined	366953	3.88	0.54	0.25	112 Alcoholic beverages	1372	2.05	0.03	0.00
583 Polymerization, etc, prdts	238149	2.52	1.09	0.28	424 Other fixed vegetable oils	1139	1.70	0.02	0.02
562 Fertilizers, manufactured	180056	1.90	5.82	1.22	793 Ships, boats, etc	1133	1.69	0.01	0.00
673 Iron, steel shapes, etc	168686	1.78	3.42	0.74	677 Iron, steel wire, exc w rod	1132	1.69	0.12	0.03
843 Women's outwear non-knit	56192	0.59	0.18	0.11	845 Outer garments knit nonelastic	821	1.22	0.00	0.00
522 Inorg chem elmnt, oxides, etc	55894	0.59	0.98	0.34	057 Fruit, nuts, fresh, dried	679	1.01	0.01	0.00
842 Men's outwear non-knit	44768	0.47	0.21	0.13	054 Vegtb etc fresh, simply prsrvd	538	0.80	0.01	0.00
691 Structures and parts nes	31682	0.33	1.07	0.21	723 Civil engineering equip, etc	456	0.68	0.01	0.00
Remainder	162330	1.71			Remainder	5203	7.76		
Romania - Roumanie (= South-East Europe & CIS)**					**Saudi Arabia - Arabie saoudite (** = developing)**				
All commodity groups	12630043	100.00	7.37	0.21	All commodity groups	67667491	100.00	3.49	1.10
843 Women's outwear non-knit	1177137	9.32	49.66	2.39	333 Crude petroleum	54280618	80.22	23.81	17.00
334 Petroleum products, refined	784117	6.21	5.16	0.53	334 Petroleum products, refined	4960910	7.33	7.33	3.38
842 Men's outwear non-knit	769760	6.09	49.47	2.22	583 Polymerization, etc, prdts	1443927	2.13	6.64	1.72
851 Footwear	698960	5.53	57.67	1.63	512 Alcohols, phenols, etc	1184545	1.75	22.56	8.16
821 Furniture and parts thereof	557538	4.41	46.71	0.87	511 Hydrocarbons nes, derivtives	860788	1.27	15.72	4.14
845 Outer garments knit nonelastic	425759	3.37	41.07	0.85	516 Other organic chemicals	683891	1.01	20.53	4.88
773 Electricity distributing equip	399588	3.16	51.25	1.06	562 Fertilizers, manufactured	319200	0.47	10.32	2.17
764 Telecom equip, parts, acces	380223	3.01	48.10	0.18	792 Aircraft, etc	313414	0.46	4.21	0.27
612 Leather, etc, manufactures	372958	2.95	55.35	5.41	522 Inorg chem elmnt, oxides, etc	227094	0.34	3.96	1.38
248 Wood, shaped, rail sleepers	357815	2.83	20.71	1.43	642 Paper and paperboard, cut	183474	0.27	2.86	0.63
Remainder	6706188	53.10			Remainder	3209631	4.74		
Russian Federation - Fédération de Russie (= South-East Europe & CIS)**					**Senegal - Sénégal (** = developing)**				
All commodity groups	100508457	100.00	58.66	1.64	All commodity groups	740535	100.00	0.04	0.01
333 Crude petroleum	26003955	25.87	80.13	8.15	334 Petroleum products, refined	127779	17.25	0.19	0.09
341 Gas, natural and manufactured	16677179	16.59	91.04	20.78	522 Inorg chem elmnt, oxides, etc	123142	16.63	2.15	0.75
931 Special transactions	11241081	11.18	92.83	8.68	034 Fish, fresh, chilled, frozen	63153	8.53	0.70	0.28
334 Petroleum products, refined	10278397	10.23	67.62	7.01	423 Fixed vegetable oils, soft	62279	8.41	1.90	0.69
684 Aluminium	3881333	3.86	72.24	8.09	036 Shell fish fresh, frozen	47286	6.39	0.42	0.28
672 Iron, steel primary forms	2824249	2.81	51.14	10.87	562 Fertilizers, manufactured	28820	3.89	0.93	0.20
562 Fertilizers, manufactured	1654585	1.65	56.30	11.25	081 Feeding stuff for animals	22498	3.04	0.27	0.10
247 Other wood rough, squared	1518002	1.51	90.63	21.12	333 Crude petroleum	18872	2.55	0.01	0.01
683 Nickel	1432787	1.43	99.47	21.92	271 Fertilizers, crude	17764	2.40	1.64	1.29
674 Iron, steel univ, plate, sheet	1314550	1.31	37.94	2.67	553 Perfumery, cosmetics, etc	17083	2.31	0.45	0.06
Remainder	23682340	23.56			Remainder	211859	28.61		

For sources and notes, see end of table 4.2E.

Pour les sources et les notes, se reporter à la fin du tableau 4.2E.

4.2D Export structure at the SITC Revision 2 group (3-digit) level (ranked by average 2001-2002 values)
Individual countries and territories
(continued)

4.2D Structure des exportations au niveau des groupes (position à trois chiffres) de la CTCI révision 2 (classées d'après la moyenne des valeurs de 2001-2002)
Pays et territoires individuels
(suite)

SITC group / Groupes de la CTCI	2001-2002				SITC group / Groupes de la CTCI	2001-2002			
	Value (thousands of dollars) / Valeur (milliers de dollars)	As percentage / En pourcentage				Value (thousands of dollars) / Valeur (milliers de dollars)	As percentage / En pourcentage		
		of country total / du total du pays	of ** / des **	of world / du monde			of country total / du total du pays	of ** / des **	of world / du monde
	1	2	3	4		1	2	3	4

Serbia and Montenegro - Serbie-et-Monténégro (** = South-East Europe & CIS)

SITC group	1	2	3	4
All commodity groups	2040239	100.00	1.19	0.03
684 Aluminium	171226	8.39	3.19	0.36
058 Fruit prsrvd, preprd	104914	5.14	37.69	0.83
625 Rubber tyres,tubes, etc	71759	3.52	13.01	0.29
682 Copper	67611	3.31	2.79	0.23
061 Sugar and honey	65405	3.21	17.79	0.52
583 Polymerization, etc, prdts	55460	2.72	5.27	0.07
674 Iron, steel univ, plate, sheet	52945	2.60	1.53	0.11
842 Men's outwear non-knit	51944	2.55	3.34	0.15
851 Footwear	47680	2.34	3.93	0.11
893 Articles of plastic nes	47416	2.32	16.79	0.08
Remainder	1303878	63.91		

South Africa - Afrique du Sud (** = developing)

SITC group	1	2	3	4
All commodity groups	25495995	100.00	1.31	0.41
667 Pearl, prec, semi-prec stones	3377890	13.25	9.33	6.11
931 Special transactions	1684926	6.61	1.66	1.30
322 Coal, lignite and peat	1639813	6.43	13.70	7.80
781 Passengr motor vehicl, exc bus	1243423	4.88	0.43	0.38
671 Pig iron, etc	1016247	3.99	43.86	12.31
743 Pumps nes, centrifuges, etc	877616	3.44	2.59	2.15
684 Aluminium	854418	3.35	2.62	1.78
334 Petroleum products, refined	787843	3.09	1.23	0.54
287 Base metals ores, conc nes	573923	2.25	7.17	3.02
057 Fruit, nuts, fresh, dried	560459	2.20	3.44	1.95
Remainder	12879437	50.52		

Singapore - Singapour (** = developing)

SITC group	1	2	3	4
All commodity groups	123465385	100.00	6.36	2.01
776 Transistors, valves, etc	28339768	22.95	23.46	11.48
752 Automatic data processing equip	16051368	13.00	19.24	8.80
759 Office, adp machy parts, acces	10087861	8.17	13.32	6.74
334 Petroleum products, refined	8898610	7.21	13.15	6.07
764 Telecom equip, parts, acces	5218039	4.23	6.51	2.51
931 Special transactions	4626171	3.75	29.18	3.57
772 Switchgear etc, parts nes	2827967	2.29	9.92	3.23
778 Electrical machinery nes	2657566	2.15	8.98	2.89
898 Musical instruments and parts	2171409	1.76	23.66	6.51
515 Organo-inorgan compounds, etc	2016991	1.63	48.60	4.44
Remainder	40569635	32.86		

Spain - Espagne (** = developed)

SITC group	1	2	3	4
All commodity groups	121010481	100.00	3.00	1.97
781 Passengr motor vehicl, exc bus	17304564	14.30	6.00	5.32
784 Motor vehicl parts, acces nes	6510692	5.38	5.18	4.50
057 Fruit, nuts, fresh, dried	3676990	3.04	22.58	12.77
541 Medicinal, pharmaceutical prdts	3054109	2.52	2.20	2.05
054 Vegtb etc fresh, simply prsrvd	2915259	2.41	17.50	11.89
782 Lorries, spec motor vehicl nes	2752405	2.27	5.98	4.76
334 Petroleum products, refined	2645450	2.19	4.14	1.80
662 Clay, refractory building prdts	1985951	1.64	23.15	18.54
851 Footwear	1959734	1.62	10.85	4.57
931 Special transactions	1881741	1.56	1.85	1.45
Remainder	76323585	63.07		

Slovakia - Slovaquie (** = developed)

SITC group	1	2	3	4
All commodity groups	13555835	100.00	0.34	0.22
781 Passengr motor vehicl, exc bus	1960011	14.46	0.68	0.60
334 Petroleum products, refined	736941	5.44	1.15	0.50
674 Iron, steel univ, plate, sheet	627822	4.63	1.81	1.28
784 Motor vehicl parts, acces nes	551925	4.07	0.44	0.38
821 Furniture and parts thereof	418888	3.09	0.94	0.65
773 Electricity distributing equip	416109	3.07	1.87	1.10
749 Non-electr machy parts, acces	332502	2.45	0.60	0.49
641 Paper and paperboard	292036	2.15	0.46	0.40
672 Iron, steel primary forms	283108	2.09	2.06	1.09
684 Aluminium	280792	2.07	0.86	0.59
Remainder	7655701	56.48		

Sri Lanka (** = developing)

SITC group	1	2	3	4
All commodity groups	4697485	100.00	0.24	0.08
843 Women's outwear non-knit	743537	15.83	2.44	1.51
074 Tea and mate	665217	14.16	31.50	25.60
846 Under garments knitted	478219	10.18	2.32	1.44
842 Men's outwear non-knit	388125	8.26	1.79	1.12
845 Outer garments knit nonelastic	362616	7.72	1.08	0.73
844 Under garments non-knit	235847	5.02	2.74	2.12
667 Pearl, prec, semi-prec stones	226884	4.83	1.20	0.41
848 Headgear, non-textile clothing	107011	2.28	1.04	0.72
792 Aircraft, etc	87355	1.86	1.17	0.08
625 Rubber tyres,tubes, etc	85418	1.82	1.34	0.34
Remainder	1317256	28.04		

Slovenia - Slovénie (** = developed)

SITC group	1	2	3	4
All commodity groups	9804312	100.00	0.24	0.16
781 Passengr motor vehicl, exc bus	787801	8.04	0.27	0.24
821 Furniture and parts thereof	680293	6.94	1.53	1.06
775 Household type equip nes	595403	6.07	2.48	1.42
541 Medicinal, pharmaceutical prdts	535586	5.46	0.39	0.36
684 Aluminium	303079	3.09	0.93	0.63
641 Paper and paperboard	295983	3.02	0.46	0.40
778 Electrical machinery nes	254109	2.59	0.41	0.28
784 Motor vehicl parts, acces nes	238597	2.43	0.19	0.16
699 Base metal manufactures nes	199295	2.03	0.53	0.39
716 Rotating electric plant	198793	2.03	0.91	0.61
Remainder	5715373	58.29		

Sudan - Soudan (** = developing)

SITC group	1	2	3	4
All commodity groups	1659080	100.00	0.09	0.03
334 Petroleum products, refined	1146604	69.11	1.69	0.78
222 Seeds for soft fixed oils	87276	5.26	1.56	0.60
971 Gold, non-monetary nes	70295	4.24	0.80	0.33
333 Crude petroleum	64434	3.88	0.03	0.02
001 Live animals for food	61413	3.70	4.09	0.70
263 Cotton	48187	2.90	1.98	0.66
292 Crude vegetb materials nes	23051	1.39	0.57	0.15
611 Leather	21733	1.31	0.24	0.13
341 Gas, natural and manufactured	18989	1.14	0.07	0.02
061 Sugar and honey	18077	1.09	0.25	0.14
Remainder	99021	5.97		

For sources and notes, see end of table 4.2E.

Pour les sources et les notes, se reporter à la fin du tableau 4.2E.

4.2D **Export structure at the SITC Revision 2 group (3-digit) level (ranked by average 2001-2002 values)**
Individual countries and territories
(continued)

4.2D **Structure des exportations au niveau des groupes (position à trois chiffres) de la CTCI révision 2 (classées d'après la moyenne des valeurs de 2001-2002)**
Pays et territoires individuels
(suite)

SITC group / Groupes de la CTCI	2001-2002				SITC group / Groupes de la CTCI	2001-2002			
	Value (thousands of dollars) / Valeur (milliers de dollars)	As percentage / En pourcentage				Value (thousands of dollars) / Valeur (milliers de dollars)	As percentage / En pourcentage		
		of country total / du total du pays	of ** / des **	of world / du monde			of country total / du total du pays	of ** / des **	of world / du monde
	1	2	3	4		1	2	3	4
Suriname (** = developing)					Syrian Arab Republic - République arabe syrienne (** = developing)				
All commodity groups	504443	100.00	0.03	0.01	All commodity groups	5742091	100.00	0.30	0.09
287 Base metals ores, conc nes	313123	62.07	3.07	1.65	333 Crude petroleum	3838402	66.85	1.68	1.20
971 Gold, non-monetary nes	57369	11.37	0.65	0.27	334 Petroleum products, refined	407752	7.10	0.60	0.28
036 Shell fish fresh, frozen	35359	7.01	0.31	0.21	001 Live animals for food	221775	3.86	14.76	2.51
333 Crude petroleum	21902	4.34	0.01	0.01	263 Cotton	210108	3.66	8.61	2.87
334 Petroleum products, refined	11772	2.33	0.02	0.01	931 Special transactions	141875	2.47	0.89	0.11
042 Rice	10950	2.17	0.23	0.16	054 Vegtb etc fresh, simply prsrvd	122381	2.13	1.61	0.50
057 Fruit, nuts, fresh, dried	9470	1.88	0.08	0.03	057 Fruit, nuts, fresh, dried	99528	1.73	0.81	0.35
034 Fish, fresh, chilled, frozen	4063	0.81	0.05	0.02	651 Textile yarn	87530	1.52	0.51	0.27
744 Mechanical handling equipment	3887	0.77	0.13	0.01	075 Spices	63907	1.11	3.43	2.60
122 Tobacco, manufactured	2840	0.56	0.07	0.02	041 Wheat etc, unmilled	55809	0.97	2.87	0.37
Remainder	33710	6.68			Remainder	493023	8.59		
Swaziland (** = developing)					Tajikistan - Tadjikistan (** = South-East Europe & CIS)				
All commodity groups	826052	100.00	0.04	0.01	All commodity groups	705429	100.00	0.41	0.01
551 Essential oils, perfume, etc	293771	35.56	20.83	3.17	684 Aluminium	378488	53.65	7.04	0.79
846 Under garments knitted	70524	8.54	0.34	0.21	351 Electric current	93669	13.28	10.90	0.86
061 Sugar and honey	68102	8.24	0.94	0.54	263 Cotton	84650	12.00	6.24	1.16
098 Edible products, preps nes	63550	7.69	1.60	0.33	792 Aircraft, etc	37348	5.29	6.08	0.03
251 Pulp and waste paper	58475	7.08	1.57	0.31	971 Gold, non-monetary nes	24625	3.49	4.36	0.12
845 Outer garments knit nonelastic	34004	4.12	0.10	0.07	057 Fruit, nuts, fresh, dried	14938	2.12	5.51	0.05
062 Sugar preps non-chocolate	17487	2.12	1.36	0.41	716 Rotating electric plant	11434	1.62	2.90	0.04
058 Fruit prsrvd, preprd	14691	1.78	0.30	0.12	652 Cotton fabrics, woven	10785	1.53	3.41	0.05
899 Other manufactured goods	14621	1.77	0.16	0.06	572 Explosives, pyrotechnic prdts	8363	1.19	12.57	0.65
892 Printed matter	9737	1.18	0.20	0.03	651 Textile yarn	7044	1.00	1.02	0.02
Remainder	181090	21.92			Remainder	34086	4.83		
Sweden - Suède (** = developed)					Thailand - Thaïlande (** = developing)				
All commodity groups	79627777	100.00	1.97	1.30	All commodity groups	66940603	100.00	3.45	1.09
764 Telecom equip, parts, acces	6981172	8.77	5.50	3.36	759 Office, adp machy parts, acces	6171301	9.22	8.15	4.12
641 Paper and paperboard	5892661	7.40	9.22	8.02	776 Transistors, valves, etc	4831810	7.22	4.00	1.96
781 Passengr motor vehicl, exc bus	4517736	5.67	1.57	1.39	931 Special transactions	2312834	3.46	14.59	1.79
541 Medicinal, pharmaceutical prdts	4387569	5.51	3.16	2.94	037 Fish etc prepd, prsrvd nes	2068366	3.09	35.71	21.28
931 Special transactions	3853617	4.84	3.79	2.97	764 Telecom equip, parts, acces	1968336	2.94	2.46	0.95
784 Motor vehicl parts, acces nes	3359361	4.22	2.67	2.32	752 Automatic data processing equip	1835307	2.74	2.20	1.01
248 Wood, shaped, rail sleepers	2040812	2.56	11.01	8.17	036 Shell fish fresh, frozen	1649141	2.46	14.67	9.81
334 Petroleum products, refined	2005296	2.52	3.14	1.37	042 Rice	1622471	2.42	34.36	23.81
674 Iron, steel univ, plate, sheet	1547390	1.94	4.46	3.14	772 Switchgear etc, parts nes	1526159	2.28	5.35	1.74
251 Pulp and waste paper	1506542	1.89	10.34	7.98	583 Polymerization, etc, prdts	1440107	2.15	6.62	1.71
Remainder	43535620	54.67			Remainder	41514771	62.02		
Switzerland - Suisse (** = developed)					Togo (** = developing)				
All commodity groups	85009977	100.00	2.11	1.38	All commodity groups	235425	100.00	0.01	0.00
541 Medicinal, pharmaceutical prdts	14665134	17.25	10.56	9.84	661 Lime, cement and building prdts	65592	27.86	1.38	0.58
885 Watches and clocks	6450278	7.59	62.95	35.28	271 Fertilizers, crude	42568	18.08	3.93	3.10
515 Organo-inorgan compounds, etc	2927572	3.44	7.15	6.45	263 Cotton	31098	13.21	1.27	0.42
728 Oth machy for spec industries	2572599	3.03	4.67	4.04	046 Wheat etc, meal or flour	9444	4.01	1.75	0.52
514 Nitrogen-function compounds	2191431	2.58	9.86	8.42	673 Iron, steel shapes, etc	8975	3.81	0.18	0.04
874 Measuring, controlg instruments	2070439	2.44	3.25	2.80	034 Fish, fresh, chilled, frozen	7634	3.24	0.08	0.03
681 Silver, platinum, etc	2036164	2.40	22.95	19.05	674 Iron, steel univ, plate, sheet	7260	3.08	0.07	0.01
736 Metal working machy, tools	1972857	2.32	8.08	6.90	072 Cocoa	5890	2.50	0.17	0.11
772 Switchgear etc, parts nes	1903537	2.24	3.24	2.17	424 Other fixed vegetable oils	4585	1.95	0.07	0.06
899 Other manufactured goods	1903080	2.24	11.52	7.41	071 Coffee and substitutes	3944	1.68	0.07	0.05
Remainder	46316885	54.48			Remainder	48436	20.57		

For sources and notes, see end of table 4.2E.

Pour les sources et les notes, se reporter à la fin du tableau 4.2E.

4.2D   Export structure at the SITC Revision 2 group (3-digit) level (ranked by average 2001-2002 values)
Individual countries and territories
(continued)

4.2D   Structure des exportations au niveau des groupes (position à trois chiffres) de la CTCI révision 2 (classées d'après la moyenne des valeurs de 2001-2002)
Pays et territoires individuels
(suite)

SITC group / Groupes de la CTCI	2001-2002				SITC group / Groupes de la CTCI	2001-2002			
	Value (thousands of dollars) / Valeur (milliers de dollars)	of country total / du total du pays	of ** / des **	of world / du monde		Value (thousands of dollars) / Valeur (milliers de dollars)	of country total / du total du pays	of ** / des **	of world / du monde
	1	2	3	4		1	2	3	4
Trinidad and Tobago - Trinité-et-Tobago (= developing)**					**Uganda - Ouganda (** = developing)**				
All commodity groups	4496976	100.00	0.23	0.07	All commodity groups	458952	100.00	0.02	0.01
334 Petroleum products, refined	1323018	29.42	1.95	0.90	071 Coffee and substitutes	97139	21.17	1.73	1.12
793 Ships, boats, etc	588280	13.08	3.90	1.32	034 Fish, fresh, chilled, frozen	80193	17.47	0.89	0.35
341 Gas, natural and manufactured	453300	10.08	1.61	0.56	971 Gold, non-monetary nes	54973	11.98	0.62	0.26
333 Crude petroleum	419808	9.34	0.18	0.13	121 Tobacco, unmanufactd, refuse	37975	8.27	1.26	0.68
522 Inorg chem elmnt, oxides, etc	386535	8.60	6.75	2.36	074 Tea and mate	30777	6.71	1.46	1.18
512 Alcohols, phenols, etc	226086	5.03	4.31	1.56	292 Crude vegetb materials nes	17804	3.88	0.44	0.12
673 Iron, steel shapes, etc	149308	3.32	3.02	0.65	211 Hides skins, exc furs, raw	17289	3.77	1.92	0.31
335 Residual petroleum prdts nes	137441	3.06	5.33	1.53	351 Electric current	13100	2.85	1.21	0.12
671 Pig iron, etc	95831	2.13	2.19	1.16	263 Cotton	12301	2.68	0.50	0.17
562 Fertilizers, manufactured	57734	1.28	1.87	0.39	334 Petroleum products, refined	11481	2.50	0.02	0.01
Remainder	659635	14.67			Remainder	85919	18.72		
Tunisia - Tunisie (= developing)**					**Ukraine (** = South-East Europe & CIS)**				
All commodity groups	6741611	100.00	0.35	0.11	All commodity groups	17096068	100.00	9.98	0.28
842 Men's outwear non-knit	1135394	16.84	5.23	3.27	672 Iron, steel primary forms	2042178	11.95	36.98	7.86
843 Women's outwear non-knit	696500	10.33	2.28	1.42	673 Iron, steel shapes, etc	1288506	7.54	56.81	5.63
333 Crude petroleum	494637	7.34	0.22	0.15	674 Iron, steel univ, plate, sheet	977818	5.72	28.22	1.99
846 Under garments knitted	361423	5.36	1.76	1.09	334 Petroleum products, refined	933740	5.46	6.14	0.64
845 Outer garments knit nonelastic	307796	4.57	0.92	0.62	671 Pig iron, etc	498842	2.92	31.96	6.04
562 Fertilizers, manufactured	289196	4.29	9.35	1.97	695 Tools	489815	2.87	62.96	2.36
773 Electricity distributing equip	270527	4.01	1.85	0.72	041 Wheat etc, unmilled	457872	2.68	31.99	3.05
772 Switchgear etc, parts nes	220081	3.26	0.77	0.25	678 Iron, steel tubes, pipes, etc	392831	2.30	40.44	1.71
851 Footwear	183234	2.72	0.77	0.43	562 Fertilizers, manufactured	382547	2.24	13.02	2.60
612 Leather, etc, manufactures	159476	2.37	5.22	2.31	281 Iron ore and concentrates	353623	2.07	54.61	3.70
Remainder	2623346	38.91			Remainder	9278295	54.27		
Turkey - Turquie (= developing)**					**United Arab Emirates - Emirats arabes unis (** = developing)**				
All commodity groups	33244095	100.00	1.71	0.54	All commodity groups	33347772	100.00	1.72	0.54
845 Outer garments knit nonelastic	1919928	5.78	5.71	3.84	333 Crude petroleum	16952587	50.84	7.44	5.31
843 Women's outwear non-knit	1830295	5.51	6.00	3.72	334 Petroleum products, refined	3864745	11.59	5.71	2.63
846 Under garments knitted	1828837	5.50	8.89	5.52	341 Gas, natural and manufactured	1792096	5.37	6.35	2.23
673 Iron, steel shapes, etc	1227200	3.69	24.85	5.36	684 Aluminium	819137	2.46	8.25	1.71
057 Fruit, nuts, fresh, dried	1161666	3.49	9.50	4.04	653 Woven man-made fib fabric	725660	2.18	4.38	2.46
761 Television receivers	1159298	3.49	6.87	3.79	764 Telecom equip, parts, acces	636684	1.91	0.79	0.31
781 Passengr motor vehicl, exc bus	1135140	3.41	3.16	0.35	971 Gold, non-monetary nes	531630	1.59	6.01	2.52
658 Textile articles nes	1132081	3.41	9.74	6.20	122 Tobacco, manufactured	516252	1.55	13.41	3.35
842 Men's outwear non-knit	792529	2.38	3.65	2.28	667 Pearl, prec, semi-prec stones	365095	1.09	1.93	0.66
651 Textile yarn	738182	2.22	4.30	2.27	553 Perfumery, cosmetics, etc	333330	1.00	8.79	1.24
Remainder	20318938	61.12			Remainder	6810559	20.42		
Turkmenistan - Turkménistan (= South-East Europe & CIS)**					**United Kingdom - Royaume-Uni (** = developed)**				
All commodity groups	1846294	100.00	1.08	0.03	All commodity groups	272353113	100.00	6.75	4.43
341 Gas, natural and manufactured	920278	49.84	5.02	1.15	764 Telecom equip, parts, acces	17260337	6.34	13.61	8.31
334 Petroleum products, refined	378095	20.48	2.49	0.26	333 Crude petroleum	14865829	5.46	25.26	4.66
333 Crude petroleum	178272	9.66	0.55	0.06	541 Medicinal, pharmaceutical prdts	13964154	5.13	10.05	9.37
263 Cotton	172017	9.32	12.67	2.35	781 Passengr motor vehicl, exc bus	13746153	5.05	4.76	4.23
651 Textile yarn	40216	2.18	5.84	0.12	714 Engines and motors nes	11053128	4.06	21.85	20.58
931 Special transactions	28024	1.52	0.23	0.02	752 Automatic data processing equip	10823901	3.97	10.95	5.93
652 Cotton fabrics, woven	21713	1.18	6.86	0.09	776 Transistors, valves, etc	9786110	3.59	7.78	3.96
846 Under garments knitted	14430	0.78	1.74	0.04	792 Aircraft, etc	8976586	3.30	8.31	7.73
351 Electric current	12115	0.66	1.41	0.11	667 Pearl, prec, semi-prec stones	6686722	2.46	18.46	12.09
655 Knitted, etc, fabric	11012	0.60	22.70	0.07	874 Measuring, controlg instruments	6482567	2.38	10.17	8.76
Remainder	70124	3.80			Remainder	158707625	58.27		

For sources and notes, see end of table 4.2E.   Pour les sources et les notes, se reporter à la fin du tableau 4.2E.

178

4.2D   Export structure at the SITC Revision 2 group (3-digit) level (ranked by average 2001-2002 values)
Individual countries and territories
(concluded)

4.2D   Structure des exportations au niveau des groupes (position à trois chiffres) de la CTCI révision 2 (classées d'après la moyenne des valeurs de 2001-2002)
Pays et territoires individuels
(fin)

SITC group / Groupes de la CTCI	Value (thousands of dollars) Valeur (milliers de dollars)	As percentage En pourcentage			SITC group / Groupes de la CTCI	Value (thousands of dollars) Valeur (milliers de dollars)	As percentage En pourcentage		
		of country total du total du pays	of ** des **	of world du monde			of country total du total du pays	of ** des **	of world du monde
	1	2	3	4		1	2	3	4
United Republic of Tanzania - République-Unie de Tanzanie (= developing)**					**Venezuela (** = developing)**				
All commodity groups	832114	100.00	0.04	0.01	All commodity groups	24645753	100.00	1.27	0.40
971 Gold, non-monetary nes	237269	28.51	2.68	1.13	333 Crude petroleum	16539323	67.11	7.26	5.18
034 Fish, fresh, chilled, frozen	94029	11.30	1.04	0.41	334 Petroleum products, refined	3267800	13.26	4.83	2.23
289 Prec metal ores, waste nes	60382	7.26	4.68	1.88	684 Aluminium	753653	3.06	7.59	1.57
057 Fruit, nuts, fresh, dried	53202	6.39	0.44	0.18	671 Pig iron, etc	355873	1.44	8.13	4.31
071 Coffee and substitutes	45933	5.52	0.82	0.53	322 Coal, lignite and peat	264895	1.07	3.53	1.26
667 Pearl, prec, semi-prec stones	44134	5.30	0.23	0.08	674 Iron, steel univ, plate, sheet	220399	0.89	1.99	0.45
121 Tobacco, unmanufactd, refuse	42862	5.15	1.42	0.77	672 Iron, steel primary forms	206145	0.84	3.06	0.79
263 Cotton	33174	3.99	1.36	0.45	516 Other organic chemicals	181056	0.73	5.44	1.29
074 Tea and mate	28903	3.47	1.37	1.11	583 Polymerization, etc, prdts	167866	0.68	0.77	0.20
054 Vegtb etc fresh, simply prsrvd	19557	2.35	0.26	0.08	784 Motor vehicl parts, acces nes	151933	0.62	0.84	0.11
Remainder	172669	20.75			Remainder	2536808	10.29		
United States - Etats-Unis (= developed)**					**Viet Nam (** = developing)**				
All commodity groups	712114069	100.00	17.66	11.59	All commodity groups	14583169	100.00	0.75	0.24
776 Transistors, valves, etc	46070176	6.47	36.63	18.66	333 Crude petroleum	3197788	21.93	1.40	1.00
792 Aircraft, etc	44282509	6.22	41.00	38.16	851 Footwear	1771599	12.15	7.49	4.13
784 Motor vehicl parts, acces nes	29207050	4.10	23.22	20.19	036 Shell fish fresh, frozen	1457182	9.99	12.96	8.67
752 Automatic data processing equip	24599195	3.45	24.88	13.48	842 Men's outwear non-knit	852617	5.85	3.93	2.45
764 Telecom equip, parts, acces	23860328	3.35	18.81	11.48	042 Rice	674881	4.63	14.29	9.91
931 Special transactions	23521042	3.30	23.15	18.15	759 Office, adp machy parts, acces	377136	2.59	0.50	0.25
874 Measuring, controlg instruments	19784907	2.78	31.02	26.73	071 Coffee and substitutes	361641	2.48	6.43	4.16
781 Passengr motor vehicl, exc bus	19735109	2.77	6.84	6.07	821 Furniture and parts thereof	351000	2.41	1.90	0.55
759 Office, adp machy parts, acces	19021789	2.67	25.74	12.70	057 Fruit, nuts, fresh, dried	347472	2.38	2.84	1.21
714 Engines and motors nes	16979730	2.38	33.56	31.61	034 Fish, fresh, chilled, frozen	296347	2.03	3.29	1.30
Remainder	445052233	62.50			Remainder	4895507	33.57		
Uruguay (= developing)**					**Zambia - Zambie (** = developing)**				
All commodity groups	1959306	100.00	0.10	0.03	All commodity groups	957067	100.00	0.05	0.02
011 Meat, fresh, chilled, frozen	270823	13.82	4.10	0.70	682 Copper	510862	53.38	4.22	1.74
611 Leather	219133	11.18	2.46	1.27	689 Non-fer base metals nes	90781	9.49	10.40	2.63
042 Rice	154044	7.86	3.26	2.26	699 Base metal manufactures nes	60652	6.34	0.48	0.12
651 Textile yarn	130608	6.67	0.76	0.40	061 Sugar and honey	38831	4.06	0.54	0.31
034 Fish, fresh, chilled, frozen	78314	4.00	0.87	0.34	651 Textile yarn	27394	2.86	0.16	0.08
022 Milk and cream	71796	3.66	4.61	0.54	667 Pearl, prec, semi-prec stones	20258	2.12	0.11	0.04
048 Cereal etc preparations	63967	3.26	2.61	0.34	971 Gold, non-monetary nes	19365	2.02	0.22	0.09
781 Passengr motor vehicl, exc bus	52643	2.69	0.15	0.02	723 Civil engineering equip, etc	15055	1.57	0.26	0.04
122 Tobacco, manufactured	45074	2.30	1.17	0.29	263 Cotton	13184	1.38	0.54	0.18
057 Fruit, nuts, fresh, dried	44276	2.26	0.36	0.15	121 Tobacco, unmanufactd, refuse	13086	1.37	0.43	0.23
Remainder	828627	42.29			Remainder	147601	15.42		
Uzbekistan - Ouzbékistan (= South-East Europe & CIS)**					**Zimbabwe (** = developing)**				
All commodity groups	3086651	100.00	1.80	0.05	All commodity groups	1767087	100.00	0.09	0.03
263 Cotton	941115	30.49	69.33	12.84	121 Tobacco, unmanufactd, refuse	379150	21.46	12.57	6.81
341 Gas, natural and manufactured	295663	9.58	1.61	0.37	683 Nickel	160037	9.06	28.01	2.45
351 Electric current	255424	8.28	29.72	2.34	671 Pig iron, etc	143213	8.10	3.27	1.74
971 Gold, non-monetary nes	229188	7.43	40.57	1.09	263 Cotton	115137	6.52	4.72	1.57
651 Textile yarn	186284	6.04	27.05	0.57	971 Gold, non-monetary nes	110383	6.25	1.25	0.52
682 Copper	125739	4.07	5.20	0.43	287 Base metals ores, conc nes	76633	4.34	0.75	0.40
781 Passengr motor vehicl, exc bus	90749	2.94	18.06	0.03	278 Other crude minerals	59561	3.37	2.86	0.85
057 Fruit, nuts, fresh, dried	88803	2.88	32.73	0.31	061 Sugar and honey	57845	3.27	0.80	0.46
334 Petroleum products, refined	88457	2.87	0.58	0.06	292 Crude vegetb materials nes	36023	2.04	0.88	0.23
652 Cotton fabrics, woven	81881	2.65	25.85	0.35	122 Tobacco, manufactured	35116	1.99	0.91	0.23
Remainder	703350	22.79			Remainder	593988	33.61		

For sources and notes, see end of table 4.2E.

Pour les sources et les notes, se reporter à la fin du tableau 4.2E.

179

4.2E Major exporters for 70 leading products among developing economies, at the SITC Revision 2 group (3-digit) level (ranked by average 2001-2002 values)

4.2E Principaux exportateurs de 70 produits majeurs parmi les économies en développement, au niveau des groupes (position à trois chiffres) de la CTCI révision 2 (classés d'après la moyenne des valeurs de 2001-2002)

Country / Pays	2001-2002 Value (thousands of dollars) Valeur (milliers de dollars)	As percentage / En pourcentage of country total du total du pays	of developing countries des pays en dévelop- pement	of world du monde	Country / Pays	2001-2002 Value (thousands of dollars) Valeur (milliers de dollars)	As percentage / En pourcentage of country total du total du pays	of developing countries des pays en dévelop- pement	of world du monde
	1	2	3	4		1	2	3	4
011 MEAT, FRESH, CHILLED, FROZEN					**057 FRUIT, NUTS, FRESH, DRIED**				
World	38793781	0.63	_	100.00	World	28783566	0.47	_	100.00
Developed countries	31839457	0.79	_	82.07	Developed countries	16286094	0.40	_	56.58
Developing countries	6599457	0.34	100.00	17.01	Developing countries	12226166	0.63	100.00	42.48
Brazil	2641785	4.46	40.03	6.81	Chile	1273124	7.04	10.41	4.42
China	743433	0.25	11.27	1.92	Turkey	1161666	3.49	9.50	4.04
China, Hong Kong SAR	714594	0.36	10.83	1.84	Ecuador	932834	19.26	7.63	3.24
Thailand	612696	0.92	9.28	1.58	Mexico	731202	0.46	5.98	2.54
Argentina	331456	1.27	5.02	0.85	Costa Rica	715585	14.81	5.85	2.49
Uruguay	270823	13.82	4.10	0.70	Iran, Islamic Republic of	569992	2.21	4.66	1.98
India	264153	0.55	4.00	0.68	South Africa	560459	2.20	4.58	1.95
Mexico	204031	0.13	3.09	0.53	India	494677	1.02	4.05	1.72
Chile	142168	0.79	2.15	0.37	Argentina	481661	1.84	3.94	1.67
Nicaragua	79681	13.66	1.21	0.21	Philippines	451398	1.34	3.69	1.57
034 FISH, FRESH, CHILLED, FROZEN					**061 SUGAR AND HONEY**				
World	22788306	0.37	_	100.00	World	12574061	0.20	_	100.00
Developed countries	13367668	0.33	_	58.66	Developed countries	4974002	0.12	_	39.56
Developing countries	9013342	0.46	100.00	39.55	Developing countries	7232455	0.37	100.00	57.52
China	1679304	0.57	18.63	7.37	Brazil	2211731	3.73	30.58	17.59
Chile	1227458	6.79	13.62	5.39	Thailand	786657	1.18	10.88	6.26
China, Taiwan Province of	982659	0.78	10.90	4.31	Cuba	513574	33.14	7.10	4.08
Korea, Republic of	549785	0.35	6.10	2.41	India	388731	0.80	5.37	3.09
Thailand	394083	0.59	4.37	1.73	Mauritius	285411	17.42	3.95	2.27
Indonesia	353310	0.62	3.92	1.55	South Africa	272194	1.07	3.76	2.16
Argentina	335739	1.28	3.72	1.47	Guatemala	234463	10.49	3.24	1.86
Viet Nam	296347	2.03	3.29	1.30	Colombia	225891	1.87	3.12	1.80
India	283204	0.59	3.14	1.24	China	172967	0.06	2.39	1.38
Singapore	209484	0.17	2.32	0.92	Honduras	168083	11.38	2.32	1.34
036 SHELL FISH FRESH, FROZEN					**081 FEEDING STUFF FOR ANIMALS**				
World	16803282	0.27	_	100.00	World	22382172	0.36	_	100.00
Developed countries	5489098	0.14	_	32.67	Developed countries	13811149	0.34	_	61.71
Developing countries	11242990	0.58	100.00	66.91	Developing countries	8374088	0.43	100.00	37.41
Thailand	1649141	2.46	14.67	9.81	Argentina	2704894	10.34	32.30	12.09
Viet Nam	1457182	9.99	12.96	8.67	Brazil	2233474	3.77	26.67	9.98
India	1020619	2.11	9.08	6.07	Peru	853457	11.92	10.19	3.81
Indonesia	994247	1.75	8.84	5.92	India	412844	0.85	4.93	1.84
China	936387	0.32	8.33	5.57	China	384353	0.13	4.59	1.72
Morocco	498963	6.66	4.44	2.97	Chile	335550	1.86	4.01	1.50
Argentina	473559	1.81	4.21	2.82	Thailand	279718	0.42	3.34	1.25
Mexico	436003	0.27	3.88	2.59	Bolivia	203213	14.92	2.43	0.91
Bangladesh	301230	5.88	2.68	1.79	Malaysia	124289	0.14	1.48	0.56
Korea, Republic of	271990	0.17	2.42	1.62	Indonesia	96474	0.17	1.15	0.43
054 VEGTB ETC FRESH, SIMPLY PRSRVD					**287 BASE METALS ORES, CONC NES**				
World	24520576	0.40	_	100.00	World	19000464	0.31	_	100.00
Developed countries	16657161	0.41	_	67.93	Developed countries	8006645	0.20	_	42.14
Developing countries	7600729	0.39	100.00	31.00	Developing countries	10192374	0.53	100.00	53.64
Mexico	2279483	1.43	29.99	9.30	Chile	2166981	11.98	21.26	11.40
China	1617008	0.55	21.27	6.59	Indonesia	1938250	3.42	19.02	10.20
Thailand	399263	0.60	5.25	1.63	Peru	842075	11.76	8.26	4.43
Turkey	340257	1.02	4.48	1.39	Jamaica	698723	60.12	6.86	3.68
Myanmar	308928	11.38	4.06	1.26	South Africa	573923	2.25	5.63	3.02
Argentina	253282	0.97	3.33	1.03	Argentina	481453	1.84	4.72	2.53
India	231398	0.48	3.04	0.94	Cuba	432147	27.88	4.24	2.27
Morocco	197237	2.63	2.59	0.80	Brazil	380421	0.64	3.73	2.00
Peru	130965	1.83	1.72	0.53	Suriname	313123	62.07	3.07	1.65
Jordan	122578	4.84	1.61	0.50	Guinea	283532	51.54	2.78	1.49

For sources and notes, see end of table.

Pour les sources et les notes, se reporter à la fin du tableau.

4.2E Major exporters for 70 leading products among developing economies, at the SITC Revision 2 group (3-digit) level (ranked by average 2001-2002 values) *(continued)*

4.2E Principaux exportateurs de 70 produits majeurs parmi les économies en développement, au niveau des groupes (position à trois chiffres) de la CTCI révision 2 (classés d'après la moyenne des valeurs de 2001-2002) *(suite)*

Country / Pays	Value (thousands of dollars) / Valeur (milliers de dollars)	2001-2002 As percentage / En pourcentage — of country total / du total du pays	of developing countries / des pays en développement	of world / du monde	Country / Pays	Value (thousands of dollars) / Valeur (milliers de dollars)	2001-2002 As percentage / En pourcentage — of country total / du total du pays	of developing countries / des pays en développement	of world / du monde
	1	2	3	4		1	2	3	4
322 COAL, LIGNITE AND PEAT					**541 MEDICINAL, PHARMACEUTICAL PRDTS**				
World	21010202	0.34	_	100.00	World	149004836	2.43	_	100.00
Developed countries	11971280	0.30	_	56.98	Developed countries	138916450	3.44	_	93.23
Developing countries	7505580	0.39	100.00	35.72	Developing countries	9487677	0.49	100.00	6.37
China	2601185	0.88	34.66	12.38	China	2151034	0.73	22.67	1.44
Indonesia	1690052	2.98	22.52	8.04	India	1554115	3.21	16.38	1.04
South Africa	1639813	6.43	21.85	7.80	Mexico	1128592	0.71	11.90	0.76
Colombia	1065678	8.81	14.20	5.07	Singapore	1024928	0.83	10.80	0.69
Venezuela	264895	1.07	3.53	1.26	China, Hong Kong SAR	687428	0.35	7.25	0.46
Viet Nam	133784	0.92	1.78	0.64	Korea, Republic of	340346	0.22	3.59	0.23
India	57342	0.12	0.76	0.27	Argentina	324693	1.24	3.42	0.22
Myanmar	17455	0.64	0.23	0.08	Brazil	281449	0.47	2.97	0.19
Korea, Dem. People's Republic of	10972	1.50	0.15	0.05	Colombia	256492	2.12	2.70	0.17
Swaziland	6227	0.75	0.08	0.03	Jordan	205559	8.12	2.17	0.14
333 CRUDE PETROLEUM					**582 PRDTS OF CONDENSATION, ETC**				
World	319256198	5.20	_	100.00	World	39512043	0.64	_	100.00
Developed countries	58846702	1.46	_	18.43	Developed countries	30677176	0.76	_	77.64
Developing countries	227958779	11.75	100.00	71.40	Developing countries	8691747	0.45	100.00	22.00
Saudi Arabia	54280618	80.22	23.81	17.00	Korea, Republic of	1987749	1.27	22.87	5.03
Iran, Islamic Republic of	21458382	83.09	9.41	6.72	China, Taiwan Province of	1535788	1.21	17.67	3.89
United Arab Emirates	16952587	50.84	7.44	5.31	China, Hong Kong SAR	1141825	0.58	13.14	2.89
Venezuela	16539323	67.11	7.26	5.18	Singapore	930533	0.75	10.71	2.36
Nigeria	16391574	99.63	7.19	5.13	Thailand	509455	0.76	5.86	1.29
Iraq	14347231	98.10	6.29	4.49	China	490159	0.17	5.64	1.24
Mexico	12350500	7.74	5.42	3.87	Malaysia	454823	0.50	5.23	1.15
Kuwait	9154703	57.96	4.02	2.87	Indonesia	399890	0.70	4.60	1.01
Libyan Arab Jamahiriya	7802398	80.27	3.42	2.44	Mexico	284394	0.18	3.27	0.72
Oman	7583082	68.09	3.33	2.38	India	203453	0.42	2.34	0.51
334 PETROLEUM PRODUCTS, REFINED					**583 POLYMERIZATION, ETC, PRDTS**				
World	146716961	2.39	_	100.00	World	84125894	1.37	_	100.00
Developed countries	63824679	1.58	_	43.50	Developed countries	61321561	1.52	_	72.89
Developing countries	67691255	3.49	100.00	46.14	Developing countries	21752015	1.12	100.00	25.86
Singapore	8898610	7.21	13.15	6.07	China, Hong Kong SAR	4029918	2.05	18.53	4.79
Korea, Republic of	7006973	4.48	10.35	4.78	Korea, Republic of	4003905	2.56	18.41	4.76
Saudi Arabia	4960910	7.33	7.33	3.38	China, Taiwan Province of	3193746	2.52	14.68	3.80
Kuwait	4611923	29.20	6.81	3.14	Singapore	1502204	1.22	6.91	1.79
United Arab Emirates	3864745	11.59	5.71	2.63	Saudi Arabia	1443927	2.13	6.64	1.72
Bahrain	3803838	67.09	5.62	2.59	Thailand	1440107	2.15	6.62	1.71
Venezuela	3267800	13.26	4.83	2.23	Mexico	826857	0.52	3.80	0.98
Algeria	2456072	15.11	3.63	1.67	Malaysia	775017	0.85	3.56	0.92
India	2322600	4.80	3.43	1.58	China	598941	0.20	2.75	0.71
China	2264800	0.77	3.35	1.54	Kuwait	504006	3.19	2.32	0.60
341 GAS, NATURAL AND MANUFACTURED					**611 LEATHER**				
World	80241142	1.31	_	100.00	World	17241055	0.28	_	100.00
Developed countries	33697955	0.84	_	42.00	Developed countries	8035792	0.20	_	46.61
Developing countries	28223689	1.45	100.00	35.17	Developing countries	8924009	0.46	100.00	51.76
Algeria	6620227	40.74	23.46	8.25	China, Hong Kong SAR	1845563	0.94	20.68	10.70
Indonesia	5654899	9.97	20.04	7.05	Korea, Republic of	1178534	0.75	13.21	6.84
Qatar	3917726	41.38	13.88	4.88	China	926574	0.31	10.38	5.37
Malaysia	3317148	3.64	11.75	4.13	Brazil	914142	1.54	10.24	5.30
United Arab Emirates	1792096	5.37	6.35	2.23	China, Taiwan Province of	789640	0.62	8.85	4.58
Oman	1157477	10.39	4.10	1.44	Argentina	731325	2.80	8.20	4.24
Brunei Darussalam	1110455	41.50	3.93	1.38	India	485351	1.00	5.44	2.82
Kuwait	778510	4.93	2.76	0.97	Thailand	262153	0.39	2.94	1.52
Myanmar	664353	24.48	2.35	0.83	Pakistan	243106	2.54	2.72	1.41
Argentina	623336	2.38	2.21	0.78	Bangladesh	224606	4.38	2.52	1.30

For sources and notes, see end of table.

Pour les sources et les notes, se reporter à la fin du tableau.

4.2E   Major exporters for 70 leading products among developing economies, at the SITC Revision 2 group (3-digit) level (ranked by average 2001-2002 values) *(continued)*

4.2E   Principaux exportateurs de 70 produits majeurs parmi les économies en développement, au niveau des groupes (position à trois chiffres) de la CTCI révision 2 (classés d'après la moyenne des valeurs de 2001-2002) *(suite)*

Country / Pays	Value (thousands of dollars) / Valeur (milliers de dollars)	As percentage / En pourcentage			Country / Pays	Value (thousands of dollars) / Valeur (milliers de dollars)	As percentage / En pourcentage		
		of country total / du total du pays	of developing countries / des pays en développement	of world / du monde			of country total / du total du pays	of developing countries / des pays en développement	of world / du monde
	1	2	3	4		1	2	3	4
641 PAPER AND PAPERBOARD					**655 KNITTED, ETC, FABRIC**				
World	73460548	1.20	_	100.00	World	15452091	0.25	_	100.00
Developed countries	63888153	1.58	_	86.97	Developed countries	5453156	0.14	_	35.29
Developing countries	8173023	0.42	100.00	11.13	Developing countries	9950419	0.51	100.00	64.40
Indonesia	1337834	2.36	16.37	1.82	Korea, Republic of	2589639	1.66	26.03	16.76
Korea, Republic of	1335816	0.85	16.34	1.82	China, Hong Kong SAR	2276206	1.16	22.88	14.73
China, Hong Kong SAR	996871	0.51	12.20	1.36	China, Taiwan Province of	2202177	1.74	22.13	14.25
Brazil	699744	1.18	8.56	0.95	China	1684949	0.57	16.93	10.90
China	562290	0.19	6.88	0.77	Turkey	251325	0.76	2.53	1.63
China, Taiwan Province of	464230	0.37	5.68	0.63	Singapore	137375	0.11	1.38	0.89
Thailand	451613	0.67	5.53	0.61	Malaysia	117476	0.13	1.18	0.76
Chile	359226	1.99	4.40	0.49	Mexico	98383	0.06	0.99	0.64
South Africa	345164	1.35	4.22	0.47	Thailand	78612	0.12	0.79	0.51
Malaysia	340917	0.37	4.17	0.46	Pakistan	69715	0.73	0.70	0.45
651 TEXTILE YARN					**658 TEXTILE ARTICLES NES**				
World	32515015	0.53	_	100.00	World	18260482	0.30	_	100.00
Developed countries	14652052	0.36	_	45.06	Developed countries	6362491	0.16	_	34.84
Developing countries	17174401	0.89	100.00	52.82	Developing countries	11618198	0.60	100.00	63.62
China, Hong Kong SAR	3144417	1.60	18.31	9.67	China	4031016	1.36	34.70	22.08
China	2929688	0.99	17.06	9.01	Pakistan	1629446	17.02	14.02	8.92
China, Taiwan Province of	1759400	1.39	10.24	5.41	India	1179941	2.44	10.16	6.46
India	1720177	3.55	10.02	5.29	Turkey	1132081	3.41	9.74	6.20
Korea, Republic of	1365861	0.87	7.95	4.20	Mexico	764260	0.48	6.58	4.19
Indonesia	1237086	2.18	7.20	3.80	China, Hong Kong SAR	466078	0.24	4.01	2.55
Pakistan	1035233	10.81	6.03	3.18	Korea, Republic of	385448	0.25	3.32	2.11
Turkey	738182	2.22	4.30	2.27	Brazil	277058	0.47	2.38	1.52
Thailand	518616	0.77	3.02	1.60	China, Taiwan Province of	258498	0.20	2.22	1.42
Malaysia	464896	0.51	2.71	1.43	Indonesia	217951	0.38	1.88	1.19
652 COTTON FABRICS, WOVEN					**667 PEARL, PREC, SEMI-PREC STONES**				
World	23376942	0.38	_	100.00	World	55314691	0.90	_	100.00
Developed countries	10408399	0.26	_	44.52	Developed countries	36224014	0.90	_	65.49
Developing countries	12651817	0.65	100.00	54.12	Developing countries	18956670	0.98	100.00	34.27
China	3765807	1.27	29.76	16.11	India	6890201	14.24	36.35	12.46
China, Hong Kong SAR	2937014	1.49	23.21	12.56	South Africa	3377890	13.25	17.82	6.11
Pakistan	1143086	11.94	9.03	4.89	China, Hong Kong SAR	2656135	1.35	14.01	4.80
India	992414	2.05	7.84	4.25	Botswana	2112065	83.78	11.14	3.82
Korea, Republic of	662030	0.42	5.23	2.83	China	729814	0.25	3.85	1.32
China, Taiwan Province of	580762	0.46	4.59	2.48	Thailand	575149	0.86	3.03	1.04
Turkey	559094	1.68	4.42	2.39	Angola	465972	8.57	2.46	0.84
Indonesia	403846	0.71	3.19	1.73	United Arab Emirates	365095	1.09	1.93	0.66
Thailand	288210	0.43	2.28	1.23	Dem. Rep. of the Congo (ex Zaire)	361217	64.85	1.91	0.65
Mexico	219930	0.14	1.74	0.94	Namibia	304250	31.91	1.60	0.55
653 WOVEN MAN-MADE FIB FABRIC					**672 IRON, STEEL PRIMARY FORMS**				
World	29492180	0.48	_	100.00	World	25986056	0.42	_	100.00
Developed countries	12742935	0.32	_	43.21	Developed countries	13717875	0.34	_	52.79
Developing countries	16585378	0.85	100.00	56.24	Developing countries	6745067	0.35	100.00	25.96
China	3629529	1.23	21.88	12.31	Brazil	1418365	2.39	21.03	5.46
Korea, Republic of	3414758	2.18	20.59	11.58	Korea, Republic of	1084171	0.69	16.07	4.17
China, Taiwan Province of	2548592	2.01	15.37	8.64	China, Taiwan Province of	776768	0.61	11.52	2.99
China, Hong Kong SAR	1705769	0.87	10.28	5.78	Turkey	610181	1.84	9.05	2.35
Indonesia	981237	1.73	5.92	3.33	China	556030	0.19	8.24	2.14
United Arab Emirates	725660	2.18	4.38	2.46	South Africa	553122	2.17	8.20	2.13
Turkey	720434	2.17	4.34	2.44	Mexico	420270	0.26	6.23	1.62
India	706512	1.46	4.26	2.40	India	330002	0.68	4.89	1.27
Thailand	495714	0.74	2.99	1.68	Venezuela	206145	0.84	3.06	0.79
Pakistan	468103	4.89	2.82	1.59	Iran, Islamic Republic of	166340	0.64	2.47	0.64

For sources and notes, see end of table.

Pour les sources et les notes, se reporter à la fin du tableau.

4.2E   Major exporters for 70 leading products among developing economies, at the SITC Revision 2 group (3-digit) level (ranked by average 2001-2002 values) *(continued)*

4.2E   Principaux exportateurs de 70 produits majeurs parmi les économies en développement, au niveau des groupes (position à trois chiffres) de la CTCI révision 2 (classés d'après la moyenne des valeurs de 2001-2002) *(suite)*

Country / Pays	2001-2002 Value (thousands of dollars) / Valeur (milliers de dollars)	As percentage / En pourcentage — of country total / du total du pays	of developing countries / des pays en développement	of world / du monde	Country / Pays	2001-2002 Value (thousands of dollars) / Valeur (milliers de dollars)	As percentage / En pourcentage — of country total / du total du pays	of developing countries / des pays en développement	of world / du monde
	1	2	3	4		1	2	3	4
674 IRON, STEEL UNIV, PLATE, SHEET					**713 INTERN COMBUST PISTON ENGINES**				
World	49220241	0.80	_	100.00	World	68744801	1.12	_	100.00
Developed countries	34675814	0.86	_	70.45	Developed countries	60423370	1.50	_	87.90
Developing countries	11079816	0.57	100.00	22.51	Developing countries	8005207	0.41	100.00	11.64
Korea, Republic of	3030692	1.94	27.35	6.16	Mexico	3284371	2.06	41.03	4.78
China, Taiwan Province of	2551035	2.01	23.02	5.18	Brazil	1246943	2.10	15.58	1.81
China, Hong Kong SAR	1233965	0.63	11.14	2.51	China	630491	0.21	7.88	0.92
India	709740	1.47	6.41	1.44	Korea, Republic of	457031	0.29	5.71	0.66
Brazil	544633	0.92	4.92	1.11	Turkey	421500	1.27	5.27	0.61
Mexico	408166	0.26	3.68	0.83	Singapore	363481	0.29	4.54	0.53
China	384615	0.13	3.47	0.78	Thailand	293820	0.44	3.67	0.43
South Africa	355940	1.40	3.21	0.72	Malaysia	186717	0.21	2.33	0.27
Thailand	289870	0.43	2.62	0.59	South Africa	177234	0.70	2.21	0.26
Argentina	275051	1.05	2.48	0.56	China, Hong Kong SAR	172766	0.09	2.16	0.25
682 COPPER					**716 ROTATING ELECTRIC PLANT**				
World	29413703	0.48	_	100.00	World	32634601	0.53	_	100.00
Developed countries	14882758	0.37	_	50.60	Developed countries	21839891	0.54	_	66.92
Developing countries	12111522	0.62	100.00	41.18	Developing countries	10399865	0.54	100.00	31.87
Chile	4732844	26.17	39.08	16.09	China	2369463	0.80	22.78	7.26
China, Taiwan Province of	928045	0.73	7.66	3.16	Mexico	2026943	1.27	19.49	6.21
China, Hong Kong SAR	883005	0.45	7.29	3.00	China, Hong Kong SAR	1784209	0.91	17.16	5.47
Korea, Republic of	831370	0.53	6.86	2.83	Thailand	854480	1.28	8.22	2.62
Peru	814990	11.39	6.73	2.77	Singapore	850863	0.69	8.18	2.61
China	571058	0.19	4.72	1.94	Korea, Republic of	601219	0.38	5.78	1.84
Zambia	510862	53.38	4.22	1.74	China, Taiwan Province of	440304	0.35	4.23	1.35
Mexico	497122	0.31	4.10	1.69	Malaysia	374192	0.41	3.60	1.15
Indonesia	426506	0.75	3.52	1.45	Brazil	327362	0.55	3.15	1.00
Malaysia	379901	0.42	3.14	1.29	Indonesia	276404	0.49	2.66	0.85
684 ALUMINIUM					**728 OTH MACHY FOR SPEC INDUSTRIES**				
World	47967057	0.78	_	100.00	World	63657223	1.04	_	100.00
Developed countries	32668946	0.81	_	68.11	Developed countries	55031534	1.36	_	86.45
Developing countries	9925626	0.51	100.00	20.69	Developing countries	8313043	0.43	100.00	13.06
China	1242451	0.42	12.52	2.59	China, Taiwan Province of	1990276	1.57	23.94	3.13
Brazil	1159605	1.96	11.68	2.42	Korea, Republic of	1410847	0.90	16.97	2.22
South Africa	854418	3.35	8.61	1.78	China, Hong Kong SAR	1082896	0.55	13.03	1.70
United Arab Emirates	819137	2.46	8.25	1.71	Singapore	1010391	0.82	12.15	1.59
Bahrain	798631	14.09	8.05	1.66	China	854552	0.29	10.28	1.34
Venezuela	753653	3.06	7.59	1.57	Mexico	461894	0.29	5.56	0.73
Korea, Republic of	591899	0.38	5.96	1.23	Malaysia	405740	0.45	4.88	0.64
China, Hong Kong SAR	448761	0.23	4.52	0.94	India	178462	0.37	2.15	0.28
China, Taiwan Province of	420881	0.33	4.24	0.88	Brazil	151456	0.26	1.82	0.24
Mozambique	376777	54.48	3.80	0.79	South Africa	150400	0.59	1.81	0.24
699 BASE METAL MANUFACTURES NES					**741 HEATING, COOLING EQUIPMENT**				
World	51047058	0.83	_	100.00	World	40883632	0.67	_	100.00
Developed countries	37625179	0.93	_	73.71	Developed countries	31172161	0.77	_	76.25
Developing countries	12689067	0.65	100.00	24.86	Developing countries	9373012	0.48	100.00	22.93
China	3274360	1.11	25.80	6.41	China	1889211	0.64	20.16	4.62
Mexico	2521496	1.58	19.87	4.94	Korea, Republic of	1849937	1.18	19.74	4.52
China, Taiwan Province of	2270329	1.79	17.89	4.45	Thailand	1287846	1.92	13.74	3.15
China, Hong Kong SAR	1248849	0.64	9.84	2.45	Mexico	1154394	0.72	12.32	2.82
Korea, Republic of	804905	0.51	6.34	1.58	China, Taiwan Province of	626417	0.49	6.68	1.53
Singapore	369505	0.30	2.91	0.72	China, Hong Kong SAR	567863	0.29	6.06	1.39
Malaysia	369336	0.41	2.91	0.72	Malaysia	551203	0.61	5.88	1.35
Thailand	326520	0.49	2.57	0.64	Singapore	367359	0.30	3.92	0.90
India	321218	0.66	2.53	0.63	Brazil	141769	0.24	1.51	0.35
Brazil	213246	0.36	1.68	0.42	Turkey	141124	0.42	1.51	0.35

For sources and notes, see end of table.

Pour les sources et les notes, se reporter à la fin du tableau.

4.2E Major exporters for 70 leading products among developing economies, at the SITC Revision 2 group (3-digit) level (ranked by average 2001-2002 values) *(continued)*

4.2E Principaux exportateurs de 70 produits majeurs parmi les économies en développement, au niveau des groupes (position à trois chiffres) de la CTCI révision 2 (classés d'après la moyenne des valeurs de 2001-2002) *(suite)*

Country / Pays	Value (thousands of dollars) Valeur (milliers de dollars)	As percentage / En pourcentage			Country / Pays	Value (thousands of dollars) Valeur (milliers de dollars)	As percentage / En pourcentage		
		of country total du total du pays	of developing countries des pays en dévelop-pement	of world du monde			of country total du total du pays	of developing countries des pays en dévelop-pement	of world du monde
	1	2	3	4		1	2	3	4
743 PUMPS NES, CENTRIFUGES, ETC					**761 TELEVISION RECEIVERS**				
World	40884177	0.67	_	100.00	World	30552459	0.50	_	100.00
Developed countries	33903482	0.84	_	82.93	Developed countries	13564822	0.34	_	44.40
Developing countries	6595981	0.34	100.00	16.13	Developing countries	16866349	0.87	100.00	55.20
Mexico	1084191	0.68	16.44	2.65	Mexico	6469545	4.05	38.36	21.18
South Africa	877616	3.44	13.31	2.15	Malaysia	2036863	2.24	12.08	6.67
Korea, Republic of	768473	0.49	11.65	1.88	China	1993622	0.67	11.82	6.53
China, Taiwan Province of	680508	0.54	10.32	1.66	Korea, Republic of	1831110	1.17	10.86	5.99
China	560489	0.19	8.50	1.37	Turkey	1159298	3.49	6.87	3.79
Brazil	543204	0.92	8.24	1.33	Thailand	941109	1.41	5.58	3.08
China, Hong Kong SAR	515976	0.26	7.82	1.26	China, Taiwan Province of	605362	0.48	3.59	1.98
Singapore	486955	0.39	7.38	1.19	Singapore	573570	0.46	3.40	1.88
Thailand	308249	0.46	4.67	0.75	China, Hong Kong SAR	410651	0.21	2.43	1.34
Malaysia	254903	0.28	3.86	0.62	Indonesia	323660	0.57	1.92	1.06
749 NON-ELECTR MACHY PARTS, ACCES					**762 RADIO-BROADCAST RECEIVERS**				
World	67757601	1.10	_	100.00	World	16869668	0.27	_	100.00
Developed countries	54999317	1.36	_	81.17	Developed countries	5337069	0.13	_	31.64
Developing countries	11718312	0.60	100.00	17.29	Developing countries	11530696	0.59	100.00	68.35
China	2815467	0.95	24.03	4.16	China	2837566	0.96	24.61	16.82
Mexico	1980919	1.24	16.90	2.92	China, Hong Kong SAR	2714928	1.38	23.55	16.09
China, Taiwan Province of	1474602	1.16	12.58	2.18	Malaysia	1742340	1.91	15.11	10.33
Singapore	1281332	1.04	10.93	1.89	Mexico	1627752	1.02	14.12	9.65
Korea, Republic of	1216101	0.78	10.38	1.79	Singapore	769693	0.62	6.68	4.56
China, Hong Kong SAR	820000	0.42	7.00	1.21	Indonesia	597191	1.05	5.18	3.54
Brazil	423557	0.71	3.61	0.63	Korea, Republic of	391733	0.25	3.40	2.32
Thailand	410671	0.61	3.50	0.61	Thailand	374393	0.56	3.25	2.22
Malaysia	280675	0.31	2.40	0.41	Brazil	147638	0.25	1.28	0.88
India	227784	0.47	1.94	0.34	Philippines	125905	0.37	1.09	0.75
752 AUTOMATIC DATA PROCESSING EQUIP					**763 SOUND RECORDERS, PHONOGRAPHS**				
World	182432630	2.97	_	100.00	World	29710371	0.48	_	100.00
Developed countries	98877723	2.45	_	54.20	Developed countries	14325286	0.36	_	48.22
Developing countries	83448176	4.30	100.00	45.74	Developing countries	15378725	0.79	100.00	51.76
China	16613033	5.62	19.91	9.11	China	5299969	1.79	34.46	17.84
Singapore	16051368	13.00	19.24	8.80	China, Hong Kong SAR	2879462	1.47	18.72	9.69
China, Taiwan Province of	12041015	9.50	14.43	6.60	Malaysia	2105251	2.31	13.69	7.09
Mexico	9477750	5.94	11.36	5.20	Korea, Republic of	1784755	1.14	11.61	6.01
Malaysia	7886908	8.66	9.45	4.32	Indonesia	1092935	1.93	7.11	3.68
Korea, Republic of	7863223	5.03	9.42	4.31	Singapore	959115	0.78	6.24	3.23
China, Hong Kong SAR	5488924	2.79	6.58	3.01	Mexico	427105	0.27	2.78	1.44
Philippines	4410375	13.10	5.29	2.42	China, Taiwan Province of	361892	0.29	2.35	1.22
Thailand	1835307	2.74	2.20	1.01	Thailand	325114	0.49	2.11	1.09
Indonesia	1173112	2.07	1.41	0.64	United Arab Emirates	84520	0.25	0.55	0.28
759 OFFICE, ADP MACHY PARTS, ACCES					**764 TELECOM EQUIP, PARTS, ACCES**				
World	149741013	2.44	_	100.00	World	207778564	3.38	_	100.00
Developed countries	73908007	1.83	_	49.36	Developed countries	126816234	3.14	_	61.03
Developing countries	75760443	3.90	100.00	50.59	Developing countries	80171790	4.13	100.00	38.59
China, Hong Kong SAR	12162220	6.19	16.05	8.12	China	17756611	6.00	22.15	8.55
China, Taiwan Province of	11351498	8.96	14.98	7.58	China, Hong Kong SAR	14782103	7.52	18.44	7.11
China	11336623	3.83	14.96	7.57	Korea, Republic of	14039250	8.97	17.51	6.76
Singapore	10087861	8.17	13.32	6.74	Mexico	10131799	6.35	12.64	4.88
Malaysia	9319184	10.24	12.30	6.22	China, Taiwan Province of	5552019	4.38	6.93	2.67
Korea, Republic of	6830220	4.37	9.02	4.56	Malaysia	5515980	6.06	6.88	2.65
Thailand	6171301	9.22	8.15	4.12	Singapore	5218039	4.23	6.51	2.51
Mexico	2934634	1.84	3.87	1.96	Thailand	1968336	2.94	2.46	0.95
Philippines	2699283	8.01	3.56	1.80	Brazil	1453897	2.45	1.81	0.70
Indonesia	940753	1.66	1.24	0.63	Indonesia	1342779	2.37	1.67	0.65

For sources and notes, see end of table.

Pour les sources et les notes, se reporter à la fin du tableau.

4.2E   Major exporters for 70 leading products
among developing economies, at the
SITC Revision 2 group (3-digit) level
(ranked by average 2001-2002 values)
(continued)

4.2E   Principaux exportateurs de 70 produits majeurs
parmi les économies en développement, au niveau des
groupes (position à trois chiffres) de la CTCI révision 2
(classés d'après la moyenne des valeurs de
2001-2002) (suite)

Country / Pays	2001-2002				Country / Pays	2001-2002			
	Value (thousands of dollars) / Valeur (milliers de dollars)	As percentage / En pourcentage				Value (thousands of dollars) / Valeur (milliers de dollars)	As percentage / En pourcentage		
		of country total / du total du pays	of developing countries / des pays en développement	of world / du monde			of country total / du total du pays	of developing countries / des pays en développement	of world / du monde
	1	2	3	4		1	2	3	4
771 ELECTRIC POWER MACHINERY NES					**776 TRANSISTORS, VALVES, ETC**				
World	32747979	0.53	_	100.00	World	246837528	4.02	_	100.00
Developed countries	16941170	0.42	_	51.73	Developed countries	125778795	3.12	_	50.96
Developing countries	15520391	0.80	100.00	47.39	Developing countries	120815840	6.23	100.00	48.95
China	3926862	1.33	25.30	11.99	Singapore	28339768	22.95	23.46	11.48
China, Hong Kong SAR	3748696	1.91	24.15	11.45	Malaysia	17568495	19.30	14.54	7.12
Mexico	2348760	1.47	15.13	7.17	China, Taiwan Province of	16266073	12.83	13.46	6.59
China, Taiwan Province of	1511782	1.19	9.74	4.62	Korea, Republic of	15388069	9.84	12.74	6.23
Singapore	829479	0.67	5.34	2.53	China, Hong Kong SAR	14982822	7.62	12.40	6.07
Thailand	818212	1.22	5.27	2.50	Philippines	13732863	40.78	11.37	5.56
Korea, Republic of	705081	0.45	4.54	2.15	China	6104366	2.06	5.05	2.47
Malaysia	515376	0.57	3.32	1.57	Thailand	4831810	7.22	4.00	1.96
Indonesia	255739	0.45	1.65	0.78	Mexico	1968362	1.23	1.63	0.80
Turkey	156769	0.47	1.01	0.48	Indonesia	539639	0.95	0.45	0.22
772 SWITCHGEAR ETC, PARTS NES					**778 ELECTRICAL MACHINERY NES**				
World	87625217	1.43	_	100.00	World	91921552	1.50	_	100.00
Developed countries	58675845	1.45	_	66.96	Developed countries	61586219	1.53	_	67.00
Developing countries	28519616	1.47	100.00	32.55	Developing countries	29608569	1.53	100.00	32.21
Mexico	4883710	3.06	17.12	5.57	China	7206628	2.44	24.34	7.84
China, Hong Kong SAR	4389293	2.23	15.39	5.01	Mexico	5155696	3.23	17.41	5.61
China, Taiwan Province of	4231474	3.34	14.84	4.83	China, Hong Kong SAR	4266623	2.17	14.41	4.64
China	3903793	1.32	13.69	4.46	China, Taiwan Province of	3975759	3.14	13.43	4.33
Singapore	2827967	2.29	9.92	3.23	Singapore	2657566	2.15	8.98	2.89
Malaysia	2550839	2.80	8.94	2.91	Korea, Republic of	1751724	1.12	5.92	1.91
Thailand	1526159	2.28	5.35	1.74	Malaysia	1238974	1.36	4.18	1.35
Korea, Republic of	1380038	0.88	4.84	1.57	Thailand	974676	1.46	3.29	1.06
Philippines	962507	2.86	3.37	1.10	Indonesia	606396	1.07	2.05	0.66
Indonesia	529765	0.93	1.86	0.60	Brazil	348279	0.59	1.18	0.38
773 ELECTRICITY DISTRIBUTING EQUIP					**781 PASSENGR MOTOR VEHICL, EXC BUS**				
World	37658707	0.61	_	100.00	World	325072257	5.29	_	100.00
Developed countries	22228605	0.55	_	59.03	Developed countries	288609248	7.16	_	88.78
Developing countries	14650385	0.76	100.00	38.90	Developing countries	35960418	1.85	100.00	11.06
Mexico	5919360	3.71	40.40	15.72	Mexico	14623202	9.17	40.66	4.50
China	1996913	0.67	13.63	5.30	Korea, Republic of	12748108	8.15	35.45	3.92
China, Hong Kong SAR	1438163	0.73	9.82	3.82	Brazil	1978770	3.34	5.50	0.61
Korea, Republic of	664357	0.42	4.53	1.76	South Africa	1243423	4.88	3.46	0.38
China, Taiwan Province of	595576	0.47	4.07	1.58	Turkey	1135140	3.41	3.16	0.35
Philippines	563027	1.67	3.84	1.50	China, Hong Kong SAR	844599	0.43	2.35	0.26
Turkey	477159	1.44	3.26	1.27	Argentina	775976	2.97	2.16	0.24
Thailand	427300	0.64	2.92	1.13	Thailand	693136	1.04	1.93	0.21
Malaysia	369492	0.41	2.52	0.98	Oman	359812	3.23	1.00	0.11
Singapore	360824	0.29	2.46	0.96	United Arab Emirates	321742	0.96	0.89	0.10
775 HOUSEHOLD TYPE EQUIP NES					**782 LORRIES, SPEC MOTOR VEHICL NES**				
World	41979323	0.68	_	100.00	World	57882099	0.94	_	100.00
Developed countries	24054487	0.60	_	57.30	Developed countries	46050505	1.14	_	79.56
Developing countries	17476586	0.90	100.00	41.63	Developing countries	10978978	0.57	100.00	18.97
China	6084281	2.06	34.81	14.49	Mexico	6404268	4.01	58.33	11.06
China, Hong Kong SAR	3328989	1.69	19.05	7.93	Thailand	1279056	1.91	11.65	2.21
Korea, Republic of	2418511	1.55	13.84	5.76	Korea, Republic of	656892	0.42	5.98	1.13
Mexico	1964043	1.23	11.24	4.68	Turkey	552408	1.66	5.03	0.95
Thailand	943682	1.41	5.40	2.25	Argentina	506597	1.94	4.61	0.88
Turkey	596030	1.79	3.41	1.42	Brazil	467205	0.79	4.26	0.81
Singapore	499529	0.40	2.86	1.19	South Africa	212177	0.83	1.93	0.37
China, Taiwan Province of	445324	0.35	2.55	1.06	China	131102	0.04	1.19	0.23
Malaysia	360937	0.40	2.07	0.86	Colombia	124021	1.03	1.13	0.21
United Arab Emirates	153373	0.46	0.88	0.37	Oman	98154	0.88	0.89	0.17

For sources and notes, see end of table.

Pour les sources et les notes, se reporter à la fin du tableau.

4.2E Major exporters for 70 leading products among developing economies, at the SITC Revision 2 group (3-digit) level (ranked by average 2001-2002 values) *(continued)*

4.2E Principaux exportateurs de 70 produits majeurs parmi les économies en développement, au niveau des groupes (position à trois chiffres) de la CTCI révision 2 (classés d'après la moyenne des valeurs de 2001-2002) *(suite)*

Country / Pays	2001-2002 Value (thousands of dollars) / Valeur (milliers de dollars)	As percentage / En pourcentage — of country total / du total du pays	of developing countries / des pays en développement	of world / du monde
	1	2	3	4
784 MOTOR VEHICL PARTS, ACCES NES				
World	144634802	2.35	_	100.00
Developed countries	125801340	3.12	_	86.98
Developing countries	18188403	0.94	100.00	12.58
Mexico	6094154	3.82	33.51	4.21
Korea, Republic of	2111329	1.35	11.61	1.46
China, Taiwan Province of	1696874	1.34	9.33	1.17
China	1609684	0.54	8.85	1.11
Brazil	1555717	2.62	8.55	1.08
Philippines	689988	2.05	3.79	0.48
Turkey	622739	1.87	3.42	0.43
Thailand	514555	0.77	2.83	0.36
Singapore	479741	0.39	2.64	0.33
Argentina	429017	1.64	2.36	0.30
785 CYCLES, ETC, MOTORIZED OR NOT				
World	20434275	0.33	_	100.00
Developed countries	13541067	0.34	_	66.27
Developing countries	6829748	0.35	100.00	33.42
China	2727568	0.92	39.94	13.35
China, Taiwan Province of	1979904	1.56	28.99	9.69
Thailand	331688	0.50	4.86	1.62
India	323383	0.67	4.73	1.58
China, Hong Kong SAR	312619	0.16	4.58	1.53
Singapore	227086	0.18	3.32	1.11
Indonesia	183112	0.32	2.68	0.90
Korea, Republic of	141274	0.09	2.07	0.69
Viet Nam	135161	0.93	1.98	0.66
Malaysia	128330	0.14	1.88	0.63
792 AIRCRAFT, ETC				
World	116056799	1.89	_	100.00
Developed countries	107997053	2.68	_	93.06
Developing countries	7445822	0.38	100.00	6.42
Brazil	3176100	5.36	42.66	2.74
Singapore	893507	0.72	12.00	0.77
China	416839	0.14	5.60	0.36
Mexico	391822	0.25	5.26	0.34
Korea, Republic of	347514	0.22	4.67	0.30
Turkey	325725	0.98	4.37	0.28
Saudi Arabia	313414	0.46	4.21	0.27
Malaysia	237026	0.26	3.18	0.20
South Africa	157974	0.62	2.12	0.14
Argentina	136367	0.52	1.83	0.12
793 SHIPS, BOATS, ETC				
World	44605176	0.73	_	100.00
Developed countries	27978385	0.69	_	62.72
Developing countries	15095057	0.78	100.00	33.84
Korea, Republic of	10185662	6.51	67.48	22.84
China	1926098	0.65	12.76	4.32
Trinidad and Tobago	588280	13.08	3.90	1.32
China, Taiwan Province of	534622	0.42	3.54	1.20
Singapore	482977	0.39	3.20	1.08
Turkey	299360	0.90	1.98	0.67
Côte d'Ivoire	205126	4.60	1.36	0.46
United Arab Emirates	99994	0.30	0.66	0.22
Malaysia	86229	0.09	0.57	0.19
India	74910	0.15	0.50	0.17

Country / Pays	2001-2002 Value (thousands of dollars) / Valeur (milliers de dollars)	As percentage / En pourcentage — of country total / du total du pays	of developing countries / des pays en développement	of world / du monde
	1	2	3	4
812 PLUMBG, HEATG, LIGHTG EQUIP				
World	19036664	0.31	_	100.00
Developed countries	12137164	0.30	_	63.76
Developing countries	6672507	0.34	100.00	35.05
China	2689131	0.91	40.30	14.13
China, Hong Kong SAR	1432877	0.73	21.47	7.53
Mexico	1108530	0.69	16.61	5.82
China, Taiwan Province of	339455	0.27	5.09	1.78
Turkey	210557	0.63	3.16	1.11
Thailand	143772	0.21	2.15	0.76
Malaysia	82870	0.09	1.24	0.44
Korea, Republic of	73801	0.05	1.11	0.39
Indonesia	68995	0.12	1.03	0.36
Singapore	68368	0.06	1.02	0.36
821 FURNITURE AND PARTS THEREOF				
World	64001223	1.04	_	100.00
Developed countries	44347334	1.10	_	69.29
Developing countries	18460316	0.95	100.00	28.84
China	5883631	1.99	31.87	9.19
Mexico	3351289	2.10	18.15	5.24
Indonesia	1476135	2.60	8.00	2.31
Malaysia	1437285	1.58	7.79	2.25
China, Taiwan Province of	1256085	0.99	6.80	1.96
China, Hong Kong SAR	1087239	0.55	5.89	1.70
Thailand	889973	1.33	4.82	1.39
Brazil	523678	0.88	2.84	0.82
South Africa	422489	1.66	2.29	0.66
Viet Nam	351000	2.41	1.90	0.55
831 TRAVEL GOODS, HANDBAGS, ETC				
World	16226520	0.26	_	100.00
Developed countries	5579418	0.14	_	34.38
Developing countries	10542993	0.54	100.00	64.97
China, Hong Kong SAR	4235042	2.16	40.17	26.10
China	4165322	1.41	39.51	25.67
Thailand	452951	0.68	4.30	2.79
India	329773	0.68	3.13	2.03
Philippines	213112	0.63	2.02	1.31
Korea, Republic of	186765	0.12	1.77	1.15
Viet Nam	183574	1.26	1.74	1.13
Indonesia	151850	0.27	1.44	0.94
Mexico	123420	0.08	1.17	0.76
China, Taiwan Province of	110515	0.09	1.05	0.68
842 MEN'S OUTWEAR NON-KNIT				
World	34750313	0.57	_	100.00
Developed countries	11500244	0.29	_	33.09
Developing countries	21693929	1.12	100.00	62.43
China	6888648	2.33	31.75	19.82
China, Hong Kong SAR	2267008	1.15	10.45	6.52
Mexico	2167781	1.36	9.99	6.24
Tunisia	1135394	16.84	5.23	3.27
Bangladesh	1130023	22.06	5.21	3.25
Viet Nam	852617	5.85	3.93	2.45
Indonesia	824762	1.45	3.80	2.37
Turkey	792529	2.38	3.65	2.28
Morocco	570167	7.61	2.63	1.64
Thailand	514941	0.77	2.37	1.48

For sources and notes, see end of table.

Pour les sources et les notes, se reporter à la fin du tableau.

4.2E   Major exporters for 70 leading products
among developing economies, at the
SITC Revision 2 group (3-digit) level
(ranked by average 2001-2002 values)
(continued)

4.2E   Principaux exportateurs de 70 produits majeurs
parmi les économies en développement, au niveau des
groupes (position à trois chiffres) de la CTCI révision 2
(classés d'après la moyenne des valeurs de
2001-2002) (suite)

Country / Pays	Value (thousands of dollars) / Valeur (milliers de dollars)	As percentage / En pourcentage			Country / Pays	Value (thousands of dollars) / Valeur (milliers de dollars)	As percentage / En pourcentage		
		of country total / du total du pays	of developing countries / des pays en dévelop-pement	of world / du monde			of country total / du total du pays	of developing countries / des pays en dévelop-pement	of world / du monde
	1	2	3	4		1	2	3	4
843 WOMEN'S OUTWEAR NON-KNIT					**848 HEADGEAR, NON-TEXTILE CLOTHING**				
World	49194007	0.80	_	100.00	World	14897755	0.24	_	100.00
Developed countries	16316942	0.40	_	33.17	Developed countries	4531072	0.11	_	30.41
Developing countries	30506532	1.57	100.00	62.01	Developing countries	10244013	0.53	100.00	68.76
China	9225477	3.12	30.24	18.75	China	4585394	1.55	44.76	30.78
China, Hong Kong SAR	5984485	3.05	19.62	12.17	China, Hong Kong SAR	1519402	0.77	14.83	10.20
India	1880585	3.89	6.16	3.82	Malaysia	876993	0.96	8.56	5.89
Mexico	1875368	1.18	6.15	3.81	Thailand	464663	0.69	4.54	3.12
Turkey	1830295	5.51	6.00	3.72	Pakistan	419180	4.38	4.09	2.81
Indonesia	1194820	2.11	3.92	2.43	Turkey	388461	1.17	3.79	2.61
Philippines	873486	2.59	2.86	1.78	India	385255	0.80	3.76	2.59
Morocco	844487	11.26	2.77	1.72	Korea, Republic of	365357	0.23	3.57	2.45
Bangladesh	749838	14.63	2.46	1.52	China, Taiwan Province of	301902	0.24	2.95	2.03
Sri Lanka	743537	15.83	2.44	1.51	Indonesia	225994	0.40	2.21	1.52
844 UNDER GARMENTS NON-KNIT					**851 FOOTWEAR**				
World	11114496	0.18	_	100.00	World	42917005	0.70	_	100.00
Developed countries	2077336	0.05	_	18.69	Developed countries	18060551	0.45	_	42.08
Developing countries	8620442	0.44	100.00	77.56	Developing countries	23644369	1.22	100.00	55.09
China	2385283	0.81	27.67	21.46	China	10178539	3.44	43.05	23.72
China, Hong Kong SAR	1143828	0.58	13.27	10.29	China, Hong Kong SAR	5520652	2.81	23.35	12.86
India	770424	1.59	8.94	6.93	Viet Nam	1771599	12.15	7.49	4.13
Bangladesh	765567	14.94	8.88	6.89	Brazil	1532119	2.58	6.48	3.57
Indonesia	415011	0.73	4.81	3.73	Indonesia	1294589	2.28	5.48	3.02
Korea, Republic of	333979	0.21	3.87	3.00	Thailand	806550	1.20	3.41	1.88
Northern Mariana Islands	270000	23.88	3.13	2.43	India	420192	0.87	1.78	0.98
Turkey	245256	0.74	2.85	2.21	Korea, Republic of	301258	0.19	1.27	0.70
Sri Lanka	235847	5.02	2.74	2.12	Mexico	269944	0.17	1.14	0.63
Philippines	216386	0.64	2.51	1.95	Tunisia	183234	2.72	0.77	0.43
845 OUTER GARMENTS KNIT NONELASTIC					**874 MEASURING, CONTROLG INSTRUMENTS**				
World	50008350	0.81	_	100.00	World	74024951	1.20	_	100.00
Developed countries	15372016	0.38	_	30.74	Developed countries	63773102	1.58	_	86.15
Developing countries	33599634	1.73	100.00	67.19	Developing countries	9294614	0.48	100.00	12.56
China	10090081	3.41	30.03	20.18	Mexico	2179711	1.37	23.45	2.94
China, Hong Kong SAR	8461951	4.31	25.18	16.92	Singapore	1570195	1.27	16.89	2.12
Turkey	1919928	5.78	5.71	3.84	China, Hong Kong SAR	1512136	0.77	16.27	2.04
Mexico	1685796	1.06	5.02	3.37	China	1175462	0.40	12.65	1.59
Korea, Republic of	1185560	0.76	3.53	2.37	Malaysia	916070	1.01	9.86	1.24
Thailand	1087838	1.63	3.24	2.18	China, Taiwan Province of	585844	0.46	6.30	0.79
China, Taiwan Province of	921873	0.73	2.74	1.84	Korea, Republic of	378995	0.24	4.08	0.51
Singapore	837464	0.68	2.49	1.67	Brazil	181250	0.31	1.95	0.24
Indonesia	806981	1.42	2.40	1.61	Thailand	144883	0.22	1.56	0.20
China, Macao SAR	730659	31.38	2.17	1.46	Philippines	100977	0.30	1.09	0.14
846 UNDER GARMENTS KNITTED					**885 WATCHES AND CLOCKS**				
World	33104928	0.54	_	100.00	World	18282967	0.30	_	100.00
Developed countries	11697093	0.29	_	35.33	Developed countries	10246314	0.25	_	56.04
Developing countries	20577624	1.06	100.00	62.16	Developing countries	8011229	0.41	100.00	43.82
China	4269997	1.44	20.75	12.90	China, Hong Kong SAR	4755404	2.42	59.36	26.01
China, Hong Kong SAR	3302625	1.68	16.05	9.98	China	1559934	0.53	19.47	8.53
Turkey	1828837	5.50	8.89	5.52	Singapore	531296	0.43	6.63	2.91
Mexico	1606432	1.01	7.81	4.85	Thailand	279930	0.42	3.49	1.53
India	1384716	2.86	6.73	4.18	Korea, Republic of	162813	0.10	2.03	0.89
Indonesia	737669	1.30	3.58	2.23	Philippines	151728	0.45	1.89	0.83
Thailand	734026	1.10	3.57	2.22	Malaysia	136501	0.15	1.70	0.75
Bangladesh	603230	11.77	2.93	1.82	Mexico	119142	0.07	1.49	0.65
Korea, Republic of	558722	0.36	2.72	1.69	China, Taiwan Province of	103629	0.08	1.29	0.57
Pakistan	529266	5.53	2.57	1.60	United Arab Emirates	79187	0.24	0.99	0.43

For sources and notes, see end of table.

Pour les sources et les notes, se reporter à la fin du tableau.

4.2E Major exporters for 70 leading products among developing economies, at the SITC Revision 2 group (3-digit) level (ranked by average 2001-2002 values) *(concluded)*

4.2E Principaux exportateurs de 70 produits majeurs parmi les économies en développement, au niveau des groupes (position à trois chiffres) de la CTCI révision 2 (classés d'après la moyenne des valeurs de 2001-2002) *(fin)*

Country / Pays	Value (thousands of dollars) / Valeur (milliers de dollars)	As percentage / En pourcentage		
		of country total / du total du pays	of developing countries / des pays en développement	of world / du monde
	1	2	3	4

893 ARTICLES OF PLASTIC NES

Country	Value	2	3	4
World	59116501	0.96	_	100.00
Developed countries	40502409	1.00	_	68.51
Developing countries	18331722	0.94	100.00	31.01
China	5642392	1.91	30.78	9.54
China, Hong Kong SAR	3440099	1.75	18.77	5.82
China, Taiwan Province of	2211151	1.74	12.06	3.74
Mexico	1772139	1.11	9.67	3.00
Korea, Republic of	839675	0.54	4.58	1.42
Malaysia	684592	0.75	3.73	1.16
Thailand	631325	0.94	3.44	1.07
Singapore	616019	0.50	3.36	1.04
Turkey	291204	0.88	1.59	0.49
Indonesia	273774	0.48	1.49	0.46

894 TOYS, SPORTING GOODS, ETC

Country	Value	2	3	4
World	47978381	0.78	_	100.00
Developed countries	19967824	0.50	_	41.62
Developing countries	27795750	1.43	100.00	57.93
China	11223675	3.79	40.38	23.39
China, Hong Kong SAR	11035937	5.62	39.70	23.00
China, Taiwan Province of	1782215	1.41	6.41	3.71
Mexico	1077599	0.68	3.88	2.25
Thailand	555648	0.83	2.00	1.16
Korea, Republic of	516113	0.33	1.86	1.08
Malaysia	249169	0.27	0.90	0.52
Pakistan	234292	2.45	0.84	0.49
Indonesia	183901	0.32	0.66	0.38
Singapore	169945	0.14	0.61	0.35

897 GOLD, SILVER WARE, JEWELLERY

Country	Value	2	3	4
World	24803929	0.40	_	100.00
Developed countries	14838093	0.37	_	59.82
Developing countries	9941296	0.51	100.00	40.08
China, Hong Kong SAR	2476408	1.26	24.91	9.98
China	1633974	0.55	16.44	6.59
India	1325023	2.74	13.33	5.34
Thailand	1103696	1.65	11.10	4.45
Korea, Republic of	621040	0.40	6.25	2.50
Turkey	503337	1.51	5.06	2.03
Malaysia	473351	0.52	4.76	1.91
Mexico	353925	0.22	3.56	1.43
Singapore	286487	0.23	2.88	1.16
United Arab Emirates	221816	0.67	2.23	0.89

898 MUSICAL INSTRUMENTS AND PARTS

Country	Value	2	3	4
World	33380555	0.54	_	100.00
Developed countries	24040264	0.60	_	72.02
Developing countries	9179139	0.47	100.00	27.50
Singapore	2171409	1.76	23.66	6.51
China, Taiwan Province of	1962193	1.55	21.38	5.88
China	1014929	0.34	11.06	3.04
China, Hong Kong SAR	984617	0.50	10.73	2.95
Korea, Republic of	960164	0.61	10.46	2.88
Mexico	605809	0.38	6.60	1.81
Malaysia	420126	0.46	4.58	1.26
Indonesia	281767	0.50	3.07	0.84
India	247030	0.51	2.69	0.74
Thailand	244928	0.37	2.67	0.73

899 OTHER MANUFACTURED GOODS

Country	Value	2	3	4
World	25685075	0.42	_	100.00
Developed countries	16516082	0.41	_	64.30
Developing countries	9092911	0.47	100.00	35.40
China	3566404	1.21	39.22	13.89
China, Hong Kong SAR	2500009	1.27	27.49	9.73
China, Taiwan Province of	478753	0.38	5.27	1.86
Korea, Republic of	407170	0.26	4.48	1.59
Mexico	405298	0.25	4.46	1.58
Indonesia	226278	0.40	2.49	0.88
Thailand	214444	0.32	2.36	0.83
Singapore	209361	0.17	2.30	0.82
Philippines	147848	0.44	1.63	0.58
Viet Nam	141307	0.97	1.55	0.55

931 SPECIAL TRANSACTIONS

Country	Value	2	3	4
World	129568453	2.11	_	100.00
Developed countries	101606505	2.52	_	78.42
Developing countries	15852627	0.82	100.00	12.23
Singapore	4626171	3.75	29.18	3.57
Thailand	2312834	3.46	14.59	1.79
South Africa	1684926	6.61	10.63	1.30
India	1261578	2.61	7.96	0.97
Brazil	1115157	1.88	7.03	0.86
Malaysia	947732	1.04	5.98	0.73
China	609779	0.21	3.85	0.47
Chile	478822	2.65	3.02	0.37
Egypt	363434	8.21	2.29	0.28
Palestinian territory	350000	87.33	2.21	0.27

For sources and notes, see next page.

Pour les sources et les notes, se reporter à la page suivante.

Source: UNCTAD secretariat computations based on UN/DESA/Statistics Division's data.

In the case of tables 4.2A, B and C, columns (1) and (4) show export values f.o.b. in millions of dollars. Columns (2) and (5) show the percentage share of each commodity in the grouping total (i.e. "World" in table 4.2A, "Developed economies" in table 4.2B, and "Developing economies" in table 4.2C).

Columns (3) and (6) refer to the percentage share which the indicated value (for a particular commodity in a particular country grouping) represents in world total exports of that commodity. For the purpose of these tables, the world total for each commodity represents the sum of the exports of that commodity for each of the individual countries, adjusted to include estimates where data for 1990, 1991, 2001 or 2002 were not available.

Column (7) shows compound annual average growth rates, based on the values for the period 1990-2002.

Column (8) shows the amount by which the growth rate in column (7) differs from the corresponding average world growth for the particular commodity (as shown in table 4.2A).

In the case of tables 4.2D and 4.2E, column (1) shows export values f.o.b. in thousands of dollars. Column (2) shows, for each commodity presented, its percentage share in the individual country's export total.

In table 4.2D column (3) shows the relative importance of each commodity shown, expressed as a percentage share of the relevant grouping total for that commodity (i.e. "developed", which refers to developed economies; "developing", which refers to developing economies; or "South-East Europe & CIS", which refers to countries in South-East Europe and CIS. The symbol ** is defined for each country shown and indicates the grouping total to which the percentage share shown applies.

In the case of table 4.2E, column (3) refers only to the share of individual developing countries in the particular commodity total for all developing countries.

Column (4) refers to the percentage share which the value indicated (for a particular commodity in a particular country or country grouping) represents in world total exports of that commodity. The world total for each commodity, for the purpose of these tables, represents the sum of the exports of that commodity for each of the individual countries, adjusted to include estimates where data for 2001 and 2002 were not available.

While the groupings and world totals for each commodity (shown in tables 4.2A, B and C) are based on the most complete data available for each of the individual countries, the data actually shown in table 4.2 D have been limited to the 10 most important commodity exports for each country in cases where sufficient data were available. The value shown under "All commodity groups" correspond to the sum of all SITC 3-digit commodity groups' exports. In some instances, it may therefore be lower than the total value of exports shown in table 4.1A.

Source : Calculs du secrétariat de la CNUCED fondés sur des données de ONU/DAES/Division de statistique.

Dans le cas des tableaux 4.2A, B et C, les colonnes (1) et (4) présentent la valeur des exportations f.a.b. en millions de dollars. Les colonnes (2) et (5) présentent la part en pourcentage de chaque produit dans le total du groupement, c'est-à-dire «Monde» dans le tableau 4.2A, «Economies développées» dans le tableau 4.2B et «Economies en développement» dans le tableau 4.2C.

Les colonnes (3) et (6) se réfèrent à la part en pourcentage que la valeur indiquée (pour un produit déterminé dans un pays ou groupement de pays déterminés) représente dans le total des exportations mondiales de ce produit. Dans ces tableaux, le total mondial pour chaque produit représente la somme des exportations de ce produit pour chaque pays, ajustée pour y inclure des estimations lorsque les données de 1990, 1991, 2001 ou 2002 n'étaient pas disponibles.

La colonne (7) présente les taux d'accroissement annuel moyen, calculés d'après les valeurs pour la période 1990-2002.

La colonne (8) présente la différence en points entre le taux d'accroissement dans la colonne (7) et le taux d'accroissement moyen mondial pour le produit déterminé (comme indiqué dans le tableau 4.2A).

Dans le cas des tableaux 4.2D et 4.2E, la colonne (1) présente la valeur des exportations f.a.b. en milliers de dollars. La colonne (2) montre, pour chaque produit indiqué, sa part en pourcentage dans le total des exportations du pays concerné.

Dans le tableau 4.2D la colonne (3) présente l'importance relative de chaque produit indiqué, présenté en termes de pourcentage du total du groupement auquel le pays appartient *(«developed»* se réfère aux économies dévelopées, «*developing*» aux économies en développement, et "*South-East Europe & CIS*" aux pays de l'Europe du Sud-Est et CEI). Le symbole ** est défini pour chaque pays inclus et se réfère au groupement auquel la part en pourcentage donnée correspond.

Dans le cas du tableau 4.2E, la colonne (3) se rapporte seulement à la part de chaque pays en développement dans le total des exportations des pays en développement du produit déterminé.

La colonne (4) se réfère à la part en pourcentage que la valeur indiquée (pour un produit déterminé dans un pays ou groupement de pays déterminé) représente dans le total des exportations mondiales de ce produit. Dans ces tableaux, le total mondial pour chaque produit représente la somme des exportations de ce produit pour chaque pays, ajustée pour inclure des estimations lorsque les données de 2001 et 2002 n'étaient pas disponibles.

Les totaux du monde ou des groupements de pays pour chaque produit (figurant dans les tableaux 4.2A, B et C) sont fondés sur toutes les données disponibles pour chaque pays, alors que les chiffres présentés dans le tableau 4.2 D ont été limités aux 10 produits majeurs exportés pour chaque pays, lorsque les données étaient disponibles. La valeur indiquée sous l'intitulé "All commodity groups" (Tous groupes de produits) correspond à la somme des exportations disponibles au niveau des groupes de produits à 3 chiffres de la CTCI. Dans certains cas cette valeur peut, par conséquent, être inférieure à la valeur totale des exportations indiquée dans le tableau 4.1A.

Export structure
Explanatory notes for table 4.2
(concluded)

Structure des exportations
Notes explicatives du tableau 4.2
(fin)

For convenience, the "remainder" (i.e. all commodities other than the ones explicitly shown in the table) is given in table 4.2D. The relatively large size of this remainder in the case of the developed economies, the more advanced developing economies and the countries in South-East Europe and CIS results from the higher degree of diversification of exports.

In the case of some of the developing economies and some of the countries in South-East Europe and CIS, a high remainder may indicate incomplete data on the commodity structure, with a relatively large "unallocated" share. (See also table 4.1A.)

Table 4.2E shows 10 leading developing exporting countries for each of the 70 commodity groups, selected on the basis of ranking by value presented in table 4.2C. In addition, the sub-table on each commodity group shows the world total, the total exports from developed market economy countries and developing countries and territories.

Special transactions and commodities not classified according to kind falling within SITC Rev. 2 group 931 may include confidential data.

The French equivalent of the country names shown in table 4.2E can be found in table 4.2D. The French equivalent for the 3-digit SITC classification shown in the series of tables 4.2 may be found in the *English/French Glossary of 3-digit SITC Commodity Groups,* included after these *Explanatory Notes.*

Note for tables in part 4:

The figures shown refer in general to special or national trade. They may therefore differ from those in table 1.1A.

Pour plus de commodité, le «*remainder*» (reste) est indiqué dans le tableau 4.2D (il représente l'ensemble des produits autres que ceux explicitement inscrits au tableau). La relative importance de ce reste dans le cas des économies développées, des pays les plus avancés parmi les économies en développement ainsi que des pays de l'Europe du Sud-Est et de la CEI, résulte du très haut degré de diversification de leurs exportations.

Dans le cas de certains pays en développement et de pays de l'Europe du Sud-Est et CEI, un reste élevé peut indiquer des données incomplètes sur la structure des produits, avec une part «non distribuée» relativement élevé. (Voir également le tableau 4.1A.)

Le tableau 4.2E présente les 10 principaux pays en développement exportateurs pour chacun des 70 groupes de produits, sélectionnés sur la base du classement par valeur présenté dans le tableau 4.2C. De plus, le sous-tableau de chaque groupe de produits fait apparaître le total mondial, le total des exportations des pays développés à économie de marché et des pays et territoires en développement.

Les transactions spéciales et articles non classés par catégories inscrites au groupe 931 de la CTCI Rev. 2 peuvent inclure des données confidentielles.

Pour la traduction des noms des pays présentés dans le tableau 4.2E, se reporter au tableau 4.2D. Pour la traduction des groupes de la CTCI (position à trois chiffres) présentés dans la série de tableaux 4.2, se reporter au *Glossaire anglais/français de la CTCI au niveau des groupes de produits (position à trois chiffres)*, qui apparaît après ces *Notes explicatives.*

Note relative aux tableaux de la partie 4 :

Les données présentées correspondent en général au commerce spécial ou national. Elles peuvent, par conséquent, dans certains cas, être différentes de celles présentées dans le tableau 1.1A.

English/French Glossary of 3-digit Standard International Trade Classification (SITC), Revision 2 Groups

Glossaire anglais/français de la Classification type pour le commerce international (CTCI), révision 2 au niveau des groupes (position à 3 chiffres)

Section 0 Food and live animals.

001 Live animals chiefly for food.

011 Meat and edible meat offals, fresh, chilled or frozen.
012 Meat and edible meat offals (except poultry liver), salted, in brine, dried or smoked.
014 Meat and edible meat offals, prepared or preserved, n.e.s.; fish extracts.

022 Milk and cream.
023 Butter.
024 Cheese and curd.
025 Eggs and yolks, fresh, dried or otherwise preserved, sweetened or not.

034 Fish, fresh (live or dead), chilled or frozen.
035 Fish, dried, salted or in brine; smoked fish.
036 Crustaceans and molluscs, fresh, chilled, frozen, salted, in brine or dried.
037 Fish, crustaceans and molluscs, prepared or preserved, n.e.s.

041 Wheat (including spelt) and meslin, unmilled.
042 Rice.
043 Barley, unmilled.
044 Maize (corn), unmilled.
045 Cereals, unmilled (other than wheat, rice, barley and maize).
046 Meal and flour of wheat and flour of meslin.
047 Other cereal meals and flours.
048 Cereal preparations and preparations of flour or starch of fruits or vegetables.

054 Vegetables, fresh, chilled, frozen or simply preserved; roots, tubers.
056 Vegetables, roots and tubers, prepared or preserved, n.e.s.
057 Fruit and nuts (not including oil nuts), fresh or dried.
058 Fruit, preserved, and fruit preparations.

061 Sugar and honey.
062 Sugar confectionery and other sugar preparations.

071 Coffee and coffee substitutes.
072 Cocoa.
073 Chocolate and other food preparations with cocoa.
074 Tea and maté.
075 Spices.

081 Feed stuff for animals (not including unmilled cereals).

091 Margarine and shortening.
098 Edible products and preparations, n.e.s.

Section 1 Beverages and tobacco.

111 Non-alcoholic beverages, n.e.s.
112 Alcoholic beverages.

121 Tobacco, unmanufactured; tobacco refuse.
122 Tobacco, manufactured.

Section 0 Produits alimentaires et animaux vivants.

001 Animaux vivants destinés à l'alimentation humaine.

011 Viandes et abats comestibles, frais, réfrigérés ou congelés.
012 Viandes et abats comestibles (sauf foies de volailles), salés, séchés ou fumés.
014 Préparations ou conserves de viandes, n.d.a.; extraits de poisson.

022 Lait et crème de lait.
023 Beurre.
024 Fromage et caillebotte.
025 Oeufs et jaunes d'oeufs, frais, séchés ou autrement conservés, sucrés ou non.

034 Poissons frais (vivants ou morts), réfrigérés ou congelés.
035 Poissons séchés, salés ou en saumure; poissons fumés.
036 Crustacés, mollusques et coquillages, frais, réfrigérés, congelés ou séchés.
037 Poissons, crustacés et mollusques, préparés ou conservés, n.d.a.

041 Froment (y compris l'épeautre) et méteil non moulus.
042 Riz.
043 Orge non mondée.
044 Maïs non moulu.
045 Céréales non moulues autres que froment, riz, orge et maïs.
046 Semoule et farine de froment et farine de méteil.
047 Autres semoules et farines de céréales.
048 Préparations à base de céréales, farines et fécules de fruits ou de légumes.

054 Légumes, frais, congelés, racines et tubercules.
056 Légumes, racines et tubercules, préparés ou conservés, n.d.a.
057 Fruits (sauf fruits oléagineux), frais ou secs.
058 Préparations et conserves de fruits.

061 Sucres et miel.
062 Sucreries et autres préparations, non compris la confiserie au chocolat.

071 Café et succédanés du café.
072 Cacao.
073 Chocolat et autres préparations contenant du cacao.
074 Thé et maté.
075 Épices.

081 Nourriture pour animaux (sauf céréales non moulues).

091 Margarine et graisses culinaires.
098 Produits et préparations alimentaires, n.d.a.

Section 1 Boissons et tabacs.

111 Boissons non alcooliques, n.d.a.
112 Boissons alcooliques.

121 Tabacs, non fabriqués; déchets de tabac.
122 Tabacs fabriqués.

English/French Glossary of 3-digit Standard International Trade Classification (SITC), Revision 2 Groups *(continued)*

Glossaire anglais/français de la Classification type pour le commerce international (CTCI), révision 2 au niveau des groupes (position à 3 chiffres)*(suite)*

Section 2 Crude materials, inedible, except fuels.

Section 2 Matières brutes non comestibles, carburants non compris.

211 Hides and skins (except fur skins), raw.
212 Fur skins, raw (including astrakhan, caracul and similar skins).

222 Oil-seeds and oleaginous fruit, whole or broken (excluding flours and meals).
223 Oil-seeds and oleaginous fruit, whole or broken (non-defatted flours and meals).

232 Natural rubber latex; natural rubber and similar natural gums.
233 Synthetic rubber latex; synthetic rubber and reclaimed rubber; waste and scrap.

244 Cork, natural, raw and waste (including in blocks or sheets).
245 Fuel wood (excluding wood waste) and wood charcoal.
246 Pulpwood (including chips and wood waste).
247 Other wood in the rough or roughly squared.
248 Wood, simply worked, and railway sleepers of wood.

251 Pulp and waste paper.

261 Silk.
263 Cotton.
264 Jute and other textile bast fibres, n.e.s., raw or processed.
265 Vegetable textile fibres and waste of such fibres.
266 Synthetic fibres suitable for spinning.
267 Other man-made fibres suitable for spinning and waste.
268 Wool and other animal hair (excluding wool tops).
269 Old clothing and other old textile articles; rags.

271 Fertilizers, crude.
273 Stone, sand and gravel.
274 Sulphur and unroasted iron pyrites.
277 Natural abrasives, n.e.s (including industrial diamonds).
278 Other crude minerals.

281 Iron ore and concentrates.
282 Waste and scrap metal of iron or steel.
286 Ores and concentrates of uranium and thorium.
287 Ores and concentrates of base metals, n.e.s.
288 Non-ferrous base metal waste and scrap, n.e.s.
289 Ores and concentrates of precious metals; waste and scrap.

291 Crude animal materials, n.e.s.
292 Crude vegetable materials, n.e.s.

211 Cuirs et peaux (non compris les pelleteries), bruts.
212 Pelleteries brutes (y compris astrakan, caracul et peaux similaires).

222 Graines et fruits oléagineux (non compris les farines).
223 Graines et fruits oléagineux (y compris les farines).

232 Latex de caoutchouc naturel; caoutchouc et gommes naturelles.
233 Latex de caoutchouc synthétique et régénéré; déchets et débris.

244 Liège naturel brut et déchets (y compris en bloc ou en feuilles).
245 Bois de chauffage (non compris les déchets) et charbon de bois.
246 Bois de trituration (y compris les plaquettes et déchets).
247 Autres bois bruts ou simplement équarris.
248 Bois, simplement travaillés, et traverses pour voies ferrées.

251 Pâtes à papier et déchets de papier.

261 Soie.
263 Coton.
264 Jute et autres fibres textiles libériennes, n.d.a., bruts ou autrement traités.
265 Fibres végétales, autres que le coton et le jute.
266 Fibres synthétiques de longueur suffisante pour être filées.
267 Autres fibres textiles synthétiques de longueur suffisante pour être filées.
268 Laines et poils fins ou grossiers (non compris les rubans).
269 Friperie, drilles et chiffons.

271 Engrais bruts.
273 Pierres, sables et graviers.
274 Soufre et pyrites de fer non grillées.
277 Abrasifs naturels, n.d.a. (y compris les diamants industriels).
278 Autres minéraux bruts.

281 Minerais de fer et concentrés.
282 Ferrailles, déchets et débris de fonte, de fer ou d'acier.
286 Minerais d'uranium et de thorium, même enrichis.
287 Minerais de métaux communs, même enrichis, n.d.a.
288 Déchets et débris de métaux communs non ferreux, n.d.a.
289 Minerais de métaux précieux; cendres d'orfèvre.

291 Matières brutes d'origine animale, n.d.a.
292 Matières brutes d'origine végétale, n.d.a.

**English/French Glossary of 3-digit Standard
International Trade Classification (SITC),
Revision 2 Groups** *(continued)*

**Glossaire anglais/français de la Classification type
pour le commerce international (CTCI), révision 2
au niveau des groupes (position à 3 chiffres)***(suite)*

Section 3 Mineral fuels, lubricants and related materials.

322 Coal, lignite and peat.
323 Briquettes; coke and semi-coke of coal, lignite or peat.

333 Petroleum oils, crude, and crude oils obtained from bituminous minerals.
334 Petroleum products, refined.
335 Residual petroleum products, n.e.s., and related materials.

341 Gas, natural and manufactured.
351 Electric current.

Section 4 Animal and vegetable oils and fats.

411 Animal oils and fats.

423 Fixed vegetable oils, soft, crude, refined or purified.
424 Other fixed vegetable oils, fluid or solid, crude, refined or purified.

431 Animal and vegetable oils and fats, processed and waxes.

Section 5 Chemicals.

511 Hydrocarbons, n.e.s., and their halogenated, sulphonated, nitrated or nitrosated derivatives.
512 Alcohols, phenols, and their derivatives.
513 Carboxylic acids, and their anhydrides, halides, and derivatives.
514 Nitrogen-function compounds.
515 Organo-inorganic and heterocyclic compounds.
516 Other organic chemicals.

522 Inorganic chemical elements, oxides and halogen salts.
523 Other inorganic chemicals.
524 Radioactive and associated materials.

531 Synthetic organic dyestuffs, etc., natural indigo and colour lakes.
532 Dyeing and tanning extracts; synthetic tanning materials.
533 Pigments, paints, varnishes and related materials.

541 Medicinal and pharmaceutical products.

551 Essential oils, perfume and flavour materials.
553 Perfumery, cosmetics and toilet preparations.
554 Soap, cleansing and polishing preparations.

562 Fertilizers, manufactured.

572 Explosives and pyrotechnic products.

Section 3 Combustibles minéraux, lubrifiants et produits connexes.

322 Houilles, lignites et tourbe.
323 Briquettes; cokes et semi-cokes de houille, lignite et tourbe.

333 Huiles brutes de pétrole ou de minéraux bitumineux.
334 Produits raffinés du pétrole.
335 Produits résiduels du pétrole, n.d.a., et produits connexes.

341 Gaz naturel et gaz manufacturé.
351 Energie électrique.

Section 4 Huiles et graisses d'origine animale ou végétale.

411 Huiles et graisses d'origine animale.

423 Huiles végétales fixes, douces, brutes, épurées ou raffinées.
424 Autres huiles végétales fixes.

431 Huiles et graisses animales et végétales, préparées et cires.

Section 5 Produits chimiques.

511 Hydrocarbures, n.d.a., et leurs dérivés halogénés, sulfonés, nitrés et nitrosés.
512 Alcools, phénols, et leurs dérivés halogénés.
513 Acides carboxyliques, leurs anhydrides, halogénures et dérivés.
514 Composés à fonctions azotées.
515 Composés organo-minéraux et composés hétérocycliques
516 Autres produits chimiques organiques.

522 Produits chimiques inorganiques; oxydes et sels halogénés.
523 Autres produits chimiques inorganiques.
524 Matières radioactives et produits associés.

531 Matières colorantes organiques synthétiques, etc., indigo naturel et laques colorantes.
532 Extraits utilisés pour la teinture et le tannage.
533 Pigments, peintures, vernis et produits connexes.

541 Produits médicinaux et pharmaceutiques.

551 Huiles essentielles, produits utilisés en parfumerie et confiserie.
553 Produits de parfumerie ou de toilette préparés et cosmétiques.
554 Savons, produits détersifs et d'entretien.

562 Engrais manufacturés.

572 Explosifs et articles de pyrotechnie.

English/French Glossary of 3-digit Standard
International Trade Classification (SITC),
Revision 2 Groups *(continued)*

Glossaire anglais/français de la Classification type
pour le commerce international (CTCI), révision 2
au niveau des groupes (position à 3 chiffres)*(suite)*

Section 5 Chemicals *(continued)*.

582 Condensation, polycondensation and polyaddition products.
583 Polymerization and copolymerization products.
584 Regenerated cellulose; cellulose nitrate and other cellulose esters.
585 Other artificial resins and plastic materials.

591 Disinfectants, insecticides, fungicides, weedkillers.
592 Starches, inulin and wheat gluten, albuminoidal substances.
598 Miscellaneous chemical products, n.e.s.

Section 6 Manufactured goods classified chiefly by material.

611 Leather.
612 Manufactures of leather or composition leather, n.e.s.
613 Fur skins, tanned or dressed, pieces or cuttings of fur skin.

621 Materials of rubber (pastes, plates, sheets).
625 Rubber tyres, tyre cases, for wheels of all kinds.
628 Articles of rubber, n.e.s.

633 Cork manufactures.
634 Veneers, plywood, improved or reconstituted wood.
635 Wood manufactures, n.e.s.

641 Paper and paperboard.
642 Paper and paperboard, cut to size or shape.

651 Textile yarn.
652 Cotton fabrics, woven.
653 Fabrics, woven, of man-made fibres.
654 Textile fabrics, woven, other than cotton man-made fibres.
655 Knitted or crocheted fabrics.
656 Tulle, lace, embroidery, and small wares.
657 Special textile fabrics and related products.
658 Made-up articles wholly or chiefly of textile materials.
659 Floor coverings.

661 Lime, cement, and fabricated construction materials.
662 Clay construction materials and refractory construction materials.
663 Mineral manufactures, n.e.s.
664 Glass
665 Glassware
666 Pottery
667 Pearls, precious and semi-precious stones, unworked or worked.

671 Pig iron, spiegeleisen, sponge iron, iron or steel.
672 Ingots and other primary forms of iron or steel.
673 Iron and steel bars, rods, angles, shapes and sections.
674 Universals, plates and sheets, of iron or steel.
675 Hoop and strip, of iron or steel, hot-rolled or cold-rolled.
676 Rails and railway track construction material.
677 Iron or steel wire, whether or not coated.
678 Tubes, pipes and fittings, of iron or steel.
679 Iron and steel castings, forgings and stampings; rough.

Section 5 Produits chimiques *(suite)*.

582 Produits de condensation, polycondensation et poly-addition.
583 Produits de polymérisation et copolymérisation.
584 Cellulose régénérée; nitrates, acétates et autres esters.
585 Autres résines artificielles et matières plastiques.

591 Désinfectants, insecticides, fongicides, herbicides.
592 Amidons, inuline, gluten de froment, matières albuminoïdes.
598 Produits divers des industries chimiques, n.d.a.

Section 6 Articles manufacturés classés principalement d'après la matière première.

611 Cuirs et peaux.
612 Ouvrages en cuir, articles de bourrellerie, n.d.a.
613 Pelleteries tannées ou apprêtées, déchets et chutes.

621 Produits en caoutchouc (pâtes, plaques, tubes).
625 Bandages, pneumatiques en caoutchouc vulcanisé, pour roues de tous genres.
628 Ouvrages en caoutchouc, n.d.a.

633 Ouvrages en liège.
634 Placages, contreplaqués et autres bois façonnés.
635 Articles manufacturés en bois, n.d.a.

641 Papiers et cartons.
642 Papiers et cartons découpés.

651 Fils textiles.
652 Tissus de coton.
653 Tissus de fibres textiles synthétiques.
654 Tissus autres que le coton, matières textiles synthétiques et artificielles.
655 Etoffes de bonneterie.
656 Tulles, dentelles, broderie, articles de mercerie.
657 Tissus spéciaux et produits connexes.
658 Articles façonnés entièrement en matières textiles.
659 Couvre-parquets.

661 Chaux, ciments et matériaux de construction fabriqués.
662 Matériaux de construction en argile et réfractaires.
663 Articles minéraux manufacturés, n.d.a.
664 Verre.
665 Ouvrages en verre.
666 Poterie.
667 Perles fines, pierres gemmes et similaires brutes ou travaillées.

671 Fonte, fonte spiegel, fer spongieux, poudres de fer.
672 Lingots et formes primaires en fer ou en acier.
673 Barres et profilés en fer ou en acier.
674 Larges plats et tôles, en fer ou en acier.
675 Feuillards en fer ou en acier, laminés à chaud ou à froid.
676 Rails et autres éléments de voies ferrées, en fonte.
677 Fils de fer ou d'acier, nus ou revêtus.
678 Tubes, tuyaux et accessoires, en fonte, fer ou acier.
679 Ouvrages en fonte, fer ou acier, à l'état brut

English/French Glossary of 3-digit Standard International Trade Classification (SITC), Revision 2 Groups *(continued)*

Glossaire anglais/français de la Classification type pour le commerce international (CTCI), révision 2 au niveau des groupes (position à 3 chiffres)*(suite)*

Section 6 Manufactured goods classified chiefly by material *(continued).*

681 Silver, platinum and other metals of the platinum group.
682 Copper.
683 Nickel.
684 Aluminium.
685 Lead.
686 Zinc.
687 Tin.
688 Uranium depleted in U235, thorium and alloys.
689 Miscellaneous non-ferrous base metals, metallurgy.

691 Structures and parts of structures; iron, steel and aluminium.
692 Metal containers for storage and transport.
693 Wire products and fencing grills.
694 Nails, screws, nuts and bolts of iron, steel or copper.
695 Tools for use in hand or in machines.
696 Cutlery.
697 Household equipment of base metal, n.e.s.
699 Manufactures of base metal, n.e.s.

Section 7 Machinery and transport equipment.

711 Steam and other vapour generating boilers, and parts.
712 Steam and other vapour power units, steam engines.
713 Internal combustion piston engines, and parts.
714 Engines and motors, non-electric.
716 Rotating electric plant and parts.
718 Other power generating machinery and parts.

721 Agricultural machinery and parts.
722 Tractors whether or not fitted with power take-offs.
723 Civil engineering and contractors plant and parts.
724 Textile and leather machinery and parts.
725 Paper and pulp mill machinery, machinery for manufacture of paper.
726 Printing and bookbinding machinery, and parts.
727 Food processing machines and parts.
728 Machinery and equipment specialized for particular industries.

736 Machine tools for working metal or metal carbides, and parts.
737 Metalworking machinery, and parts.

741 Heating and cooling equipment, and parts.
742 Pumps for liquids, liquid elevators, and parts.
743 Pumps, compressors, fans and blowers.
744 Mechanical handling equipment, and parts.
745 Other non-electrical machinery, tools, apparatus, and parts.
749 Non-electric accessories of machinery.

751 Office machines.
752 Automatic data processing machines and units thereof.
759 Parts of and accessories suitable for 751, 752.

Section 6 Articles manufacturés classés principalement d'après la matière première *(suite).*

681 Argent, platine et autres métaux de la mine du platine.
682 Cuivre.
683 Nickel.
684 Aluminium.
685 Plomb.
686 Zinc.
687 Etain.
688 Uranium appauvri en U235, thorium et alliages.
689 Autres métaux communs non ferreux, et cermets.

691 Constructions et parties de constructions, en fer, acier et aluminium.
692 Récipients métalliques pour le stockage et le transport.
693 Ouvrages en fils métalliques et grillages.
694 Clous, vis, écrous, rivets et similaires en fer, acier et cuivre.
695 Outils à main et outils pour machines.
696 Coutellerie.
697 Articles de ménage et domestiques en métaux communs.
699 Articles manufacturés en métaux communs, n.d.a

Section 7 Machines et matériel de transport.

711 Générateurs de vapeur d'eau et appareils auxiliaires.
712 Machines à vapeur d'eau, locomotives et pièces.
713 Moteurs à explosion, combustion interne et pièces.
714 Moteurs et machines motrices, non électriques.
716 Machines et appareils électriques rotatifs et pièces.
718 Autres moteurs et machines motrices et parties.

721 Machines agricoles et leurs parties détachées.
722 Tracteurs (y compris les tracteurs-treuils).
723 Appareils et matériels de génie civil et de construction.
724 Machines et appareils pour l'industrie textile, cuirs, et pièces.
725 Machines et appareils pour fabrication de pâte à papier et du papier.
726 Machines et appareils pour l'imprimerie, brochage, et pièces.
727 Machines et appareils pour l'industrie alimentaire, et pièces.
728 Autres machines et appareils pour l'industrie particulière, et pièces.

736 Machines-outils pour le travail des métaux et carbures métalliques.
737 Machines et appareils pour le travail des métaux, et pièces.

741 Machines et appareils de chauffage, réfrigération, et pièces.
742 Pompes, motopompes et turbopompes pour liquides.
743 Pompes, compresseurs et ventilateurs.
744 Equipement mécanique de manutention, et pièces.
745 Autres machines, appareils et outils, non électriques, et pièces.
749 Pièces détachées de machines non électriques.

751 Machines et appareils de bureau.
752 Machines automatiques de traitement de l'information.
759 Pièces détachées et accessoires pour machines des groupes 751 et 752.

English/French Glossary of 3-digit Standard
International Trade Classification (SITC),
Revision 2 Groups *(continued)*

Glossaire anglais/français de la Classification type
pour le commerce international (CTCI), révision 2
au niveau des groupes (position à 3 chiffres)*(suite)*

Section 7   Machinery and transport equipment *(continued)*.

  761 Television receivers.
  762 Radio-broadcast receivers.
  763 Gramophones, dictating and sound recorders.
  764 Telecommunications equipment, and parts.

  771 Electric power machinery, and parts thereof.
  772 Electrical apparatus such as switches, relays, fuses and plugs.
  773 Equipment for distributing electricity.
  774 Electric and radiological apparatus, for medical purposes.
  775 Household type, electrical and non-electrical equipment.
  776 Thermionic, cold and photo-cathode valves, tubes, and parts.
  778 Electrical machinery and apparatus, n.e.s.

  781 Passenger motor cars for transport of passengers and goods.
  782 Motor vehicles for transport of goods materials.
  783 Road motor vehicles, n.e.s.
  784 Parts and accessories of 722, 781, 782, 783.
  785 Motorcycles, motor scooters and invalid carriages.
  786 Trailers and other vehicles, not motorized.

  791 Railway vehicles and associated equipment.
  792 Aircraft and associated equipment and parts.
  793 Ships, boats and floating structures.

Section 8   Miscellaneous manufactured articles.

  812 Sanitary, plumbing, heating and lighting fixtures.

  821 Furniture and parts thereof.

  831 Travel goods, handbags, briefcases, purses and sheaths.
  842 Outergarments, men's, of textile fabrics.
  843 Outergarments, women's, of textile fabrics.
  844 Undergarments of textile fabrics.
  845 Outergarments and other articles, knitted.
  846 Undergarments, knitted or crocheted.
  847 Clothing accessories of textile fabrics.
  848 Articles of apparel and clothing accessories, non-textile.

  851 Footwear.

  871 Optical instruments and apparatus.
  872 Medical instruments and appliances.
  873 Meters and counters, n.e.s.
  874 Measuring, checking, analysing instruments.

  881 Photographic apparatus and equipment, n.e.s.
  882 Photographic and cinematographic supplies.
  883 Cinematography film, exposed and developed, negative or positive.
  884 Optical goods, n.e.s.
  885 Watches and clocks.

Section 7   Machines et matériel de transport *(suite)*.

  761 Récepteurs de télévision.
  762 Récepteurs de radiodiffusion et combinés.
  763 Phonographes, machines à dicter et appareils d'enregistrement.
  764 Équipement de télécommunication, et pièces.

  771 Machines et appareils pour la production et la transformation de l'électricité.
  772 Appareillage pour la coupure, le sectionnement et la protection des circuits électriques.
  773 Équipement pour la distribution d'électricité.
  774 Appareils d'électricité médicale et de radiologie.
  775 Machines et appareils, électriques ou non, à usage domestique.
  776 Lampes, tubes, valves électroniques à vide et à vapeur.
  778 Autres machines et appareils électriques, n.d.a.

  781 Voitures automobiles pour le transport des personnes.
  782 Voitures automobiles pour le transport des marchandises.
  783 Véhicules automobiles routiers, n.d.a.
  784 Pièces détachées et accessoires pour 722, 781, 782, 783.
  785 Motocycles, scooters et véhicules similaires pour le transport des malades.
  786 Remorques et autres véhicules non motorisés.

  791 Véhicules et matériel pour chemins de fer.
  792 Appareils de navigation aérienne, matériel connexe, et pièces.
  793 Navires, bateaux et engins flottants.

Section 8   Articles manufacturés divers.

  812 Appareils sanitaires, de plomberie, de chauffage et d'éclairage.

  821 Meubles et leur parties et pièces détachées.

  831 Articles de voyage, malles, sacs et serviettes.

  842 Vêtements de dessus pour homme, en matières textiles.
  843 Vêtements de dessus pour femmes en matières textiles.
  844 Vêtements de dessous en matières textiles.
  845 Vêtements de dessus et accessoires de bonneterie.
  846 Sous-vêtements de bonneterie.
  847 Accessoires du vêtement en matières textiles.
  848 Vêtements et accessoires du vêtement en matières autres que les textiles.

  851 Chaussures.

  871 Appareils et instruments d'optique.
  872 Instruments et appareils médico-chirurgicaux.
  873 Compteurs et instruments de mesures, n.d.a.
  874 Instruments de mesure, vérification et analyse.

  881 Appareils et équipement photographiques, n.d.a.
  882 Produits photographiques et cinématographiques.
  883 Films cinématographiques, impressionnés et développés, négatifs ou positifs.
  884 Éléments d'optique, n.d.a.
  885 Horlogerie

English/French Glossary of 3-digit Standard International Trade Classification (SITC), Revision 2 Groups *(concluded)*

Glossaire anglais/français de la Classification type pour le commerce international (CTCI), révision 2 au niveau des groupes (position à 3 chiffres) *(fin)*

Section 8   Miscellaneous manufactured articles *(continued)*.

892 Printed matter.

893 Articles of materials described in division 58.

894 Baby carriages and toys.

895 Office and stationery supplies, n.e.s.

896 Works of art, collectors' pieces and antiques.

897 Jewellery, goldsmith wares and other articles of precious materials.

898 Musical instruments, parts and accessories.

899 Other miscellaneous manufactured articles.

Section 9   Commodities and transactions not classified according to kind.

911 Postal packages not classified according to kind.

931 Special transactions and commodities, not classified according to kind.

941 Animals, live, n.e.s., including zoo-animals.

951 Armoured fighting vehicles, arms of war and ammunition.

961 Coins (other than gold), not being legal tender.

971 Gold, non-monetary.

Section 8   Articles manufacturés divers *(suite)*.

892 Imprimés.

893 Ouvrages, en matières de la division 58.

894 Voitures pour le transport des enfants et jouets.

895 Articles de papeterie et fournitures de bureau, n.d.a.

896 Objets d'art, de collection ou d'antiquité.

897 Bijouterie, orfèvrerie, autres ouvrages en métaux précieux.

898 Instruments de musique et pièces détachées.

899 Autres articles manufacturés divers, n.d.a.

Section 9   Articles et transactions non classés par catégories.

911 Colis postaux, non classés par catégories.

931 Transactions spéciales et articles non classés par catégories.

941 Animaux vivants, n.d.a., y compris les animaux de zoo.

951 Véhicules blindés de combat, armes de guerre et munitions.

961 Monnaies n'ayant pas cours légal.

971 Or, non monétaire.

PART FIVE

International trade in services

CINQUIEME PARTIE

Commerce international des services

1

2

3

4

5

6

7

8

Region, economic grouping, country or area	Exports - Exportations (f.o.b. / f.a.b.)								
	1985	1990	1995	1998	1999	2000	2001	2002	2003
WORLD	**407476**	**830172**	**1239719**	**1401978**	**1445730**	**1528032**	**1538402**	**1634521**	**1860351**
DEVELOPED ECONOMIES	320313	668495	930372	1055117	1093155	1143254	1147447	1228154	1409325
DEVELOPING ECONOMIES	82119	153824	288537	318470	328208	358005	360414	370787	406798
SOUTH-EAST EUROPE AND CIS	5044	7853	20810	28391	24367	26773	30541	35579	44228
DEVELOPED ECONOMIES: AMERICA	**82920**	**165670**	**243481**	**294963**	**316287**	**336577**	**324036**	**331345**	**347026**
Canada	9827	19210	26128	33836	36117	40230	39225	40748	42934
United States	73093	146460	217353	261127	280170	296347	284811	290597	304092
DEVELOPED ECONOMIES: EUROPE	**206916**	**444178**	**593192**	**668308**	**686838**	**704009**	**728619**	**799250**	**946807**
EU 25	**190248**	**411958**	**552802**	**625082**	**641571**	**656821**	**682233**	**750119**	**888696**
EU 15	*184226*	*400446*	*519729*	*589026*	*609156*	*620901*	*644854*	*710920*	*843557*
Austria	9697	23279	32211	29759	31306	31342	33352	35198	43668
Belgium	..	..	..	..	..	..	..	37776	44742
Belgium-Luxembourg	10796	28417	35466	38081	45292	49789	50314	..	..
Denmark	5487	12830	15307	15212	20090	24107	25367	27182	32104
Finland	2429	4649	7415	6698	6522	6177	5832	6490	7775
France	35558	76457	84090	84958	82387	80917	82298	86564	99732
Germany	30663	62661	80231	84496	83887	83095	88360	104635	123000
Greece	2600	6560	9605	..	16506	19239	19456	20223	24286
Ireland	1302	3445	5017	16735	15688	18538	23465	28600	38008
Italy	19818	49666	61620	67549	58788	56556	57676	60251	73855
Luxembourg	..	..	..	..	..	..	..	20415	25451
Netherlands	13796	29302	45917	49760	49210	49318	51211	56011	65033
Portugal	1931	5096	8236	8829	8680	8490	8840	9755	11866
Spain	12723	27937	40209	49308	53418	53540	58201	62682	76881
Sweden	6121	13726	15622	17952	19904	20252	21997	24009	30654
United Kingdom	31306	56422	78783	109776	117479	119542	118485	131129	146501
New EU members 10	*6023*	*11512*	*33073*	*36056*	*32415*	*35920*	*37378*	*39199*	*45139*
Cyprus	738	2004	2991	2955	3190	4068	4340	4512	5214
Czech Republic	–	–	6725	7665	7048	6839	7092	7083	7789
Czechoslovakia (former)	2285	2673	–	–	–	–	–	–	–
Estonia	–	–	877	1480	1490	1499	1649	1713	2234
Hungary	622	2884	5146	5401	5213	5611	6645	6893	7974
Latvia	–	–	720	1108	1024	1212	1189	1252	1527
Lithuania	–	–	485	1109	1092	1059	1157	1464	1878
Malta	274	752	1048	1181	1220	1105	1106	1144	1269
Poland	2104	3200	10675	10840	8363	10398	9753	10035	11166
Slovakia	–	–	2378	2292	1899	2241	..	2812	3297
Slovenia	–	–	2027	2025	1875	1888	1960	2292	2791
Other developed Europe	**16668**	**32219**	**40390**	**43227**	**45267**	**47188**	**46386**	**49130**	**58112**
Iceland	394	560	691	953	930	1044	1086	1154	1372
Norway	7456	12765	13672	15542	15878	17263	17603	18598	21789
Switzerland	8817	18895	26027	26731	28459	28881	27697	29378	34950
DEVELOPED ECONOMIES: ASIA	*24800*	*45953*	*73062*	*71902*	*68245*	*79577*	*73721*	*74492*	*87848*
Israel	3152	4569	7788	9490	7246	10339	9205	8780	10227
Japan	21648	41384	65274	62412	60998	69238	64516	65712	77621
DEVELOPED ECONOMIES: OCEANIA	*5677*	*12695*	*20637*	*19944*	*21785*	*23092*	*21070*	*23066*	*27644*
Australia	4219	10201	16156	16181	17399	18677	16698	17906	21204
New Zealand	1458	2494	4481	3763	4386	4415	4373	5161	6440

For sources and notes, see end of table.

5.1 Valeur des exportations et des importations de services par régions et par pays
Millions de dollars

				Imports - Importations (c.i.f. / c.a.f.)					Régions, groupements économiques, pays ou zones
1985	1990	1995	1998	1999	2000	2001	2002	2003	
430444	859980	1240732	1377108	1431853	1518712	1524949	1622426	1835460	MONDE
302536	660009	887917	995664	1042466	1086318	1092238	1166641	1339505	ECONOMIES DEVELOPEES
123282	183543	323724	352198	363827	401732	395267	412428	444935	ECONOMIES EN DEVELOPPEMENT
4626	16428	29090	29246	25561	30662	37444	43358	51020	EUROPE DU SUD-EST ET CEI
									ECONOMIES DEVELOPEES : AMERIQUE
85942	145353	174764	219405	240303	269026	267297	278057	306961	
13912	28303	33473	38156	40573	44118	43880	45129	50662	Canada
72030	117050	141291	181249	199730	224908	223417	232928	256299	Etats-Unis
									ECONOMIES DEVELOPEES : EUROPE
173447	408357	560322	633019	655951	667793	685976	748821	884461	
160727	384241	531497	602148	624155	636590	653321	714064	846322	UE 25
155915	*375334*	*509344*	*577340*	*599303*	*609704*	*625315*	*682775*	*808245*	*UE 15*
6389	14197	27703	27398	29422	29653	31437	34498	42893	Autriche
..	..	..	..	..	..	..	35727	42823	Belgique
9941	26581	33134	34411	39167	41868	43316	..	..	Belgique-Luxembourg
4794	10218	14040	15779	18517	21488	22485	25116	28293	Danemark
2920	7627	9584	7767	7615	8440	8105	8009	9743	Finlande
25891	61052	66117	67728	64449	61044	56861	69291	84799	France
36220	85125	132523	135120	141003	137253	141931	147332	172477	Allemagne
1401	3000	4368	..	9251	11286	11589	10677	11254	Grèce
1547	5178	11303	29626	26534	31272	35339	41964	52314	Irlande
16406	46795	55050	63379	57707	55601	57753	63542	75237	Italie
..	..	..	..	..	..	..	13640	16916	Luxembourg
14948	29708	44770	47285	49471	51337	53717	57190	66219	Pays-Bas
1269	4005	6611	6903	6814	6605	6343	6733	7930	Portugal
4551	16055	21510	27421	30532	31283	33988	37365	45959	Espagne
6681	17058	17216	21721	22617	23440	23020	23958	28771	Suède
22957	48737	65415	87740	96205	99134	99435	107736	122620	Royaume-Uni
4812	*8907*	*22153*	*24808*	*24852*	*26886*	*28006*	*31289*	*38076*	*Nouveaux membres de l'UE 10*
302	674	1106	1133	1147	1585	1615	1764	2278	Chypre
		4882	5750	5850	5436	5567	6439	7320	République tchèque
1723	2472	–	–	–	–	–	–	–	Tchécoslovaquie (anc.)
–	–	498	910	918	936	1069	1126	1383	Estonie
723	2400	3839	4198	4360	4510	5199	6322	8171	Hongrie
–	–	246	806	689	770	693	708	944	Lettonie
–	–	498	868	786	679	700	915	1264	Lituanie
218	514	664	720	755	733	738	740	834	Malte
1846	2847	7138	6624	6982	8993	8960	9186	10647	Pologne
–	–	1838	2276	1844	1805	..	2351	3056	Slovaquie
–	–	1444	1524	1522	1438	1458	1736	2181	Slovénie
									Autres économies développées d'Europe
12720	24116	28825	30871	31796	31203	32655	34757	38140	
363	556	642	965	1027	1164	1074	1132	1477	Islande
7515	12358	13147	14820	14882	14465	15104	16520	19545	Norvège
4842	11202	15037	15085	15888	15573	16477	17106	17117	Suisse
									ECONOMIES DEVELOPEES : ASIE
33656.4	89203	131027	121469	123300	126566	117731	116892	120933	
2404	4921	8401	9636	8142	9702	9482	8952	9404	Israël
31252	84281	122626	111833	115158	116864	108249	107940	111529	Japon
									ECONOMIES DEVELOPEES : OCEANIE
9490.49	17096	21804	21771	22911	22932	21234	22871	27151	
7677	13772	17110	17272	18330	18388	16948	18107	21514	Australie
1814	3324	4694	4499	4581	4544	4287	4763	5637	Nouvelle-Zélande

Pour les sources et les notes, se reporter à la fin du tableau.

5.1 Value of exports and imports of services by region and country
(continued)
Millions of dollars

Region, economic grouping, country or area	Exports - Exportations (f.o.b. / f.a.b.)								
	1985	1990	1995	1998	1999	2000	2001	2002	2003
DEVELOPING ECONOMIES: AMERICA	19054	30982	45689	54871	55995	62146	60378	59114	62669
South America	7953	13242	20888	24579	23613	26451	25984	24104	26441
Argentina	1651	2446	3817	4756	4617	4808	4440	3039	3989
Bolivia	97	146	192	251	259	224	236	257	306
Brazil	2086	3762	6135	7631	7189	9498	9322	9551	10483
Chile	693	1848	3333	3952	3869	4083	4138	4332	4805
Colombia	855	1600	1701	1955	1941	2049	2190	1866	1792
Ecuador	397	538	728	678	730	849	862	923	898
Guyana	48	..	133	142	147	169	172	172	186
Paraguay	153	418	584	626	575	619	555	568	590
Peru	695	798	1131	1775	1594	1604	1510	1544	1679
Suriname	79	37	104	72	79	91	59	39	59
Uruguay	404	466	1359	1319	1262	1276	1123	754	778
Venezuela	797	1183	1671	1423	1352	1182	1376	1060	877
Other America	11101	17741	24800	30292	32382	35695	34395	35010	36228
Anguilla	..	41	56	79	69	65	70	66	..
Antigua and Barbuda	150	312	348	429	439	416	403	392	..
Aruba	..	411	645	892	990	1032	..	1073	..
Bahamas	1122	1500	1542	1533	1811	2037	1890	..	..
Barbados	439	654	867	1024	1029	1090	1069	1041	..
Belize	38	115	133	140	162	172	175	184	..
Costa Rica	275	609	969	1343	1666	1936	1901	1870	2027
Cuba	..	..	1419	2128	2667	2642	2571	2636	..
Dominica	10	33	61	88	101	90	76	..	..
Dominican Republic	584	1097	1951	2502	2850	3228	3110	3071	3435
El Salvador	224	329	389	588	640	698	704	782	824
Grenada	31	64	99	120	144	153	133	133	..
Guatemala	101	356	666	640	700	777	1045	1140	..
Haiti	114	52	104	180	..	..	..	..	..
Honduras	104	137	258	377	474	479	487	530	576
Jamaica	610	1027	1598	1770	1978	2026	1897	1920	..
Mexico	4808	8094	9780	11661	11734	13756	12701	12740	12712
Montserrat	..	18	25	13	20	16	14	14	..
Netherlands Antilles	674	1161	1492	1509	1519	1613	1649	1716	..
Nicaragua	39	60	117	184	214	221	223	226	249
Panama	1180	1092	1519	1892	1848	1994	2005	2252	2557
Saint Kitts and Nevis	23	54	82	101	101	99	99	91	..
Saint Lucia	70	151	265	320	306	321	283	258	..
Saint Vincent and the Grenadines	19	45	74	107	126	126	131	137	..
Trinidad and Tobago	264	329	343	672	603	554	574	..	..
DEVELOPING ECONOMIES: AFRICA	12152	21473	27584	29604	32492	32569	33450	34473	40750
North Africa	5940	10455	14221	14828	16870	17236	17646	18207	21369
Algeria	531	497	..	..	..	..	..	..	..
Egypt	3024	5971	8590	8141	9494	9803	9042	9320	11073
Libyan Arab Jamahiriya	63	117	31	40	59	..	..	..	..
Morocco	983	2009	2173	2827	3115	3034	4029	4360	5412
Sudan	374	173	125	16	82	27	15	132	137
Tunisia	965	1688	2509	2757	2920	2767	2912	2681	2937
Other Africa	6212	11018	13363	14776	15622	15334	15804	16266	19381
Angola	129	109	113	122	153	267	203	207	..
Benin	38	126	194	142	177	136	147	..	..
Botswana	76	210	260	255	373	..	..	..	..
Burkina Faso	27	69	..	..	..	31	37	..	..
Burundi	13	17	16	4	4	4	5	6	6
Cameroon	499	382	304	..	..	..	..	..	..
Cape Verde	25	35	67	86	105	108	130	153	224
Central African Republic	47	69	..	..	..	..	..	..	..
Chad	33	41	..	..	..	..	..	..	..
Comoros	4	17	35	..	..	..	..	..	..
Congo	75	99	87	118	146	137	144	165	..
Côte d'Ivoire	399	590	531	615	586	482	578	585	713
Dem. Rep. of the Congo	126	230	132	60	70	69	69	71	..
Djibouti	..	..	151	..	..	..	..	..	..
Equatorial Guinea	..	5	4	..	..	..	..	..	..

For sources and notes, see end of table.

5.1 Valeur des exportations et des importations de services par régions et par pays
(suite)
Millions de dollars

Imports - Importations (c.i.f. / c.a.f.)									Régions, groupements économiques, pays ou zones
1985	1990	1995	1998	1999	2000	2001	2002	2003	
23210	36440	56589	68403	67021	74222	74297	68107	70903	**ECONOMIES EN DEVELOPPEMENT : AMERIQUE**
13109	*20280*	*37531*	*43758*	*40392*	*44160*	*44529*	*37284*	*39371*	*Amérique du Sud*
2187	3120	7234	9246	8768	9130	8384	4697	5530	Argentine
246	311	350	441	450	468	399	433	486	Bolivie
3790	7523	13630	16676	14172	16660	17081	14509	15559	Brésil
1081	2076	3657	4404	4606	4802	4983	4988	5571	Chili
1427	1750	2885	3416	3144	3328	3618	3332	3343	Colombie
636	804	1173	1241	1181	1269	1434	1632	1590	Equateur
104	..	172	174	178	193	192	196	205	Guyana
180	434	711	576	493	436	390	350	348	Paraguay
934	1164	1864	2432	2256	2341	2391	2530	2609	Pérou
141	171	161	197	151	216	174	166	195	Suriname
340	393	858	884	802	882	801	600	615	Uruguay
2043	2534	4836	4072	4191	4435	4681	3852	3319	Venezuela
10102	*16160*	*19058*	*24645*	*26629*	*30062*	*29767*	*30823*	*31532*	*Autres économies : Amérique*
..	15	28	38	38	41	39	39	..	Anguilla
38	105	148	169	177	154	172	175	..	Antigua-et-Barbuda
..	135	245	553	713	679	..	644	..	Aruba
383	573	639	991	954	1007	939	..	..	Bahamas
156	250	363	432	458	487	499	495	..	Barbade
28	60	95	99	108	120	122	131	..	Belize
282	550	913	1110	1195	1273	1169	1182	1188	Costa Rica
..	..	574	468	551	303	265	273	..	Cuba
12	30	44	55	59	53	52	..	..	Dominique
275	440	966	1320	1248	1373	1284	1314	1216	République dominicaine
291	315	510	737	823	933	954	1022	994	El Salvador
21	33	38	70	80	87	82	88	..	Grenade
180	384	695	792	791	825	928	1044	..	Guatemala
212	72	285	381	..	..	..	..	..	Haïti
195	220	334	447	502	598	627	602	653	Honduras
415	697	1104	1294	1323	1423	1514	1649	..	Jamaïque
5524	10323	9715	13008	14471	17360	17194	17660	18233	Mexique
..	12	15	21	22	19	24	23	..	Montserrat
452	518	563	611	662	734	767	770	..	Antilles néerlandaises
130	112	221	268	335	343	353	336	372	Nicaragua
657	689	1088	1253	1146	1141	1106	1273	1294	Panama
10	35	55	62	85	76	75	80	..	Saint-Kitts-et-Nevis
38	81	124	132	136	124	113	125	..	Sainte-Lucie
18	32	55	79	66	60	60	60	..	Saint-Vincent-et-les Grenadines
725	479	242	255	274	388	370	..	..	Trinité-et-Tobago
22689	29959	37115	39740	38437	39312	40063	40312	43726	**ECONOMIES EN DEVELOPPEMENT : AFRIQUE**
9318	*9013*	*10249*	*12131*	*12219*	*13554*	*13704*	*13975*	*14533*	*Afrique du Nord*
2565	1321	..	..	..	..	..	..	..	Algérie
3190	3788	4873	6492	6452	7513	7037	6629	6474	Egypte
1775	1385	597	877	989	..	..	..	..	Jamahiriya arabe libyenne
829	1445	1890	1963	2003	1892	2118	2413	2874	Maroc
346	228	172	204	275	648	660	818	686	Soudan
612	846	1352	1257	1234	1218	1425	1450	1612	Tunisie
13371	*20946*	*26866*	*27609*	*26218*	*25758*	*26360*	*26337*	*29194*	*Autres économies : Afrique*
641	1807	2051	2635	2595	2699	3518	3322	..	Angola
111	131	272	191	215	192	192	..	..	Bénin
130	376	444	522	516	..	..	..	..	Botswana
129	216	..	..	..	140	141	..	..	Burkina Faso
89	129	83	42	25	43	38	43	45	Burundi
936	1045	499	..	..	..	..	..	..	Cameroun
9	28	60	91	116	100	119	142	203	Cap-Vert
108	169	..	..	..	..	..	..	..	République centrafricaine
154	228	..	..	..	..	..	..	..	Tchad
36	44	50	..	..	..	..	..	..	Comores
526	769	692	857	869	738	852	927	..	Congo
763	1626	1376	1524	1459	1227	1271	1545	1728	Côte d'Ivoire
597	758	474	139	65	189	207	225	..	Rép. dém. du Congo
..	..	87	..	..	..	..	..	..	Djibouti
..	36	76	..	..	..	..	..	..	Guinée équatoriale

Pour les sources et les notes, se reporter à la fin du tableau.

5.1 Value of exports and imports of services by region and country
(continued)
Millions of dollars

Region, economic grouping, country or area	Exports - Exportations (f.o.b. / f.a.b.)								
	1985	1990	1995	1998	1999	2000	2001	2002	2003
Eritrea	–	–	49	82	48	61	..	..	..
Ethiopia	289	305	345	392	474	506	523	585	..
Gabon	138	242	217	220	281	..	..	..	..
Gambia	24	57	54	..	..	..	..	..	..
Ghana	38	86	151	441	468	504	532	555	630
Guinea	..	157	117	111	113	68	103	90	134
Guinea-Bissau	7	7	6	..	..	..	..	..	..
Kenya	577	1138	1025	830	935	993	1089	1018	1153
Lesotho	18	41	39	54	44	43	40	35	..
Liberia	35	..	..	..	..	..	..	..	..
Madagascar	59	153	242	291	326	364	351	224	..
Malawi	26	37	24	32	49	34	44	49	..
Mali	57	85	88	79	104	94	151	169	..
Mauritania	27	27	28	34	..	..	..	..	..
Mauritius	121	484	778	917	1036	1070	1222	1135	..
Mozambique	66	103	242	286	295	325	250	339	304
Namibia	..	132	315	327	324	184	257	237	360
Niger	39	44	33	..	..	..	..	..	..
Nigeria	316	965	608	884	980	..	..	..	..
Rwanda	35	42	18	48	51	59	66	65	..
Sao Tome and Principe	2	4	..	7	12	14	13	13	..
Senegal	276	515	512	425	416	387	398	456	..
Seychelles	112	172	279	247	277	294	296	307	..
Sierra Leone	24	61	87	19	22	42	52	38	..
Somalia	36	..	..	..	..	..	..	..	..
South Africa	1734	3406	4619	5396	5210	5046	4653	4672	6602
Swaziland	28	108	152	91	69	214	121	117	..
Togo	87	149	87	76	68	62	72	..	..
Uganda	23	..	104	176	196	213	221	233	290
United Republic of Tanzania	106	131	583	555	600	627	679	666	..
Zambia	68	107	..	102	107	114	..	..	..
Zimbabwe	295	264	..	..	..	..	..	..	..
DEVELOPING ECONOMIES: ASIA	**50498**	**100591**	**214178**	**232919**	**238697**	**262399**	**265670**	**276241**	**302343**
West Asia	*15899*	*22102*	*34888*	*52207*	*47040*	*46064*	*46046*	*34422*	*40731*
Bahrain	911	359	683	725	859	933	950	1068	1068
Iran, Islamic Republic of	370	436	593	1793	1216	1382	2012	3488	5025
Iraq	4959	6487	10050	12990	14633	10148	14062	2166	1809
Jordan	1167	1447	1709	1825	1702	1637	1482	1513	1493
Kuwait	1137	1279	1401	1762	1560	1822	1663	1648	1916
Oman	14	68	13	369	401	424	349	..	..
Palestinian territory	..	..	274	394	475	393	108	..	..
Qatar	..	..	..	..	..	..	..	..	..
Saudi Arabia	3561	3031	3480	4730	5380	4785	5014	5184	5346
Syrian Arab Republic	656	874	1899	1666	1651	1699	1781	1559	..
Turkey	2864	8016	14606	23879	16881	20429	16059	14785	19086
United Arab Emirates	..	..	..	1900	2100	2200	2400	2400	2800
Yemen	–	106	179	174	183	211	166	166	318
Yemen Arab Republic (former)	156	–	–	–	–	–	–	–	–
Yemen, Democratic (former)	102	–	–	–	–	–	–	–	–
Other Asia	*34599*	*78489*	*179290*	*180712*	*191657*	*216335*	*219624*	*241819*	*261612*
Afghanistan	40	..	..	..	..	..	..	..	..
Bangladesh	238	392	698	724	778	815	752	849	979
Bhutan	17	28	15	21	22	30	30	33	..
Brunei Darussalam	..	..	545	282	316	198	199	217	..
Cambodia	..	..	114	177	294	428	525	604	526
China	3055	5855	19130	23895	26248	30431	33334	39745	46734
China, Hong Kong SAR	..	..	..	33235	34226	38736	39450	43008	44624
China, Macao SAR	..	..	..	..	..	..	..	4467	..
China, Taiwan Province of	2559	7008	15016	16768	17161	20010	19547	21635	23102
India	3384	4625	6775	11691	14509	19175	20886	24859	27616
Indonesia	844	2488	5469	4479	4599	5213	5500	6661	..
Korea, Republic of	3823	9637	22827	25565	26529	30534	29055	28388	32702
Lao People's Dem. Rep.	21	24	97	145	130	176	166	..	..
Malaysia	1934	3859	11602	11517	11919	13941	14455	14878	13578
Maldives	66	101	233	331	343	348	354	355	..
Mongolia	70	48	57	78	76	78	114	184	..

For sources and notes, see end of table.

5.1 Valeur des exportations et des importations de services par régions et par pays
(suite)
Millions de dollars

1985	1990	1995	1998	1999	2000	2001	2002	2003	Régions, groupements économiques, pays ou zones
					Imports - Importations (c.i.f. / c.a.f.)				
–	–	45	187	105	28	..	..	..	Erythrée
271	359	353	456	466	491	526	583	..	Ethiopie
1058	1007	892	991	867	..	..	..	..	Gabon
19	52	69	..	..	..	..	..	..	Gambie
168	301	432	659	646	584	606	621	904	Ghana
..	367	389	383	364	285	319	331	307	Guinée
25	20	30	..	..	..	..	..	..	Guinée-Bissau
360	700	868	695	570	719	766	646	671	Kenya
36	81	61	52	50	43	49	56	..	Lesotho
80	..	..	..	..	..	..	..	..	Libéria
167	242	359	436	456	522	511	398	..	Madagascar
143	268	151	162	185	167	171	222	..	Malawi
264	374	435	304	365	312	421	387	..	Mali
202	137	217	153	..	..	..	..	..	Mauritanie
130	421	641	718	728	763	810	787	..	Maurice
100	206	350	396	406	446	618	550	548	Mozambique
..	354	551	457	446	333	276	224	249	Namibie
127	227	152	..	..	..	..	..	..	Niger
1656	1976	4619	4166	3476	..	..	..	..	Nigéria
114	129	155	190	193	200	189	202	..	Rwanda
9	9	..	10	12	11	12	13	..	Sao Tomé-et-Principe
367	676	578	443	430	405	414	474	..	Sénégal
59	80	103	132	156	175	169	201	..	Seychelles
43	74	92	39	101	113	111	81	..	Sierra Leone
97	..	..	..	..	..	..	..	..	Somalie
2227	3737	5971	5658	5759	5823	5251	5340	7554	Afrique du Sud
62	179	209	268	192	291	186	142	..	Swaziland
132	244	164	149	131	118	130	..	..	Togo
130	195	563	728	419	459	523	519	509	Ouganda
209	288	799	988	795	682	689	713	..	République-Unie de Tanzanie
254	386	..	282	306	340	..	..	..	Zambie
462	496	..	..	..	..	..	..	..	Zimbabwe
									ECONOMIES EN DEVELOPPEMENT : ASIE
76861	116314	228795	242738	257037	286855	279714	302958	329349	
38893	*37428*	*38094*	*50658*	*50866*	*57396*	*51447*	*55039*	*64090*	*Asie occidentale*
489	474	634	652	700	738	748	927	871	Bahreïn
3308	3962	2339	2760	2457	2296	3497	3983	8528	Iran, Rép. islamique d'
445	586	265	392	230	229	429	260	470	Iraq
1287	1268	1615	1784	1698	1723	1725	1790	1753	Jordanie
4086	3359	5381	5542	5171	4920	5354	5837	6557	Koweït
713	719	985	1683	1511	1566	1678	..	..	Oman
..	..	391	508	520	524	740	..	..	Territoire palestinien
..	..	..	..	..	..	..	..	..	Qatar
25822	22414	19283	16881	18855	25262	19307	20006	20800	Arabie saoudite
975	892	1537	1491	1612	1667	1694	1883	..	République arabe syrienne
1333	3071	5024	10373	9394	9061	6929	6905	8581	Turquie
..	..	..	7900	8000	8600	8500	9800	10300	Emirats arabes unis
–	683	639	693	719	809	848	935	1004	Yémen
230	–	–	–	–	–	–	–	–	Rép. arabe du Yémen (anc.)
206	–	–	–	–	–	–	–	–	Yémen dém. (anc.)
37968	*78885*	*190701*	*192080*	*206171*	*229459*	*228266*	*247919*	*265258*	*Autres économies : Asie*
154	..	..	..	..	..	..	..	..	Afghanistan
478	700	1531	1237	1397	1620	1522	1406	1710	Bangladesh
39	28	27	64	82	107	106	114	..	Bhoutan
..	..	517	847	818	768	761	819	..	Brunéi Darussalam
..	..	188	221	292	328	347	374	394	Cambodge
2524	4352	25223	26672	31589	36031	39267	46528	55306	Chine
..	..	..	24991	23726	24584	24677	25603	25185	Chine, Hong Kong RAS
..	..	..	..	..	..	..	1050	..	Chine, Macao RAS
5433	14658	24053	24169	24362	26647	24465	24719	25635	Chine, Taiwan Province de
3903	6090	10268	14540	17271	16654	16254	18691	16932	Inde
5135	6056	13540	11961	11573	15011	15880	17054	..	Indonésie
3364	10252	25806	24541	27180	33381	32927	36585	40313	Corée, République de
43	26	122	96	52	43	32	..	..	Rép. dém. populaire lao
3927	5485	14981	13127	14735	16747	16657	16448	17532	Malaisie
27	38	77	99	108	110	109	111	..	Maldives
40	155	95	147	146	163	205	266	..	Mongolie

Pour les sources et les notes, se reporter à la fin du tableau.

5.1 Value of exports and imports of services by region and country
(concluded)
Millions of dollars

Region, economic grouping, country or area	Exports - Exportations (f.o.b. / f.a.b.)								
	1985	1990	1995	1998	1999	2000	2001	2002	2003
Myanmar	67	94	365	633	512	478	424	..	..
Nepal	157	204	679	565	655	506	413	..	..
Pakistan	849	1429	1857	1404	1373	1380	1459	2429	2977
Philippines	2235	3244	9348	7477	4803	3972	3148	3055	2970
Singapore	4688	12811	29160	22192	26362	29099	28855	29977	30706
Sri Lanka	245	440	819	917	964	939	1355	1268	..
Thailand	2041	6419	14845	13156	14635	13868	13024	15391	15774
Viet Nam	..	..	..	2616	2493	2702	2810	2948	..
DEVELOPING ECONOMIES: OCEANIA	**415**	**778**	**1087**	**1076**	**1025**	**890**	**916**	**959**	**1036**
Fiji	273	417	564	503	525	..	..	..	..
Kiribati	5	8	..	..	..	..	..	..	..
Papua New Guinea	64	206	321	318	248	243	285	..	..
Samoa	10	36	56	63	61	..	..	..	..
Solomon Islands	9	25	42	55	56	..	..	..	..
Tonga	16	26	..	..	..	..	20	23	..
Vanuatu	38	60	82	114	115	130	119	..	..
SOUTH-EAST EUROPE AND CIS	**5044**	**7853**	**20810**	**28391**	**24367**	**26773**	**30541**	**35579**	**44228**
South-East Europe	*5044*	*7853*	*5615*	*8533*	*8284*	*9766*	*10945*	*12338*	*17353*
Albania	15	32	99	87	269	448	534	585	720
Bosnia and Herzegovina	–	–	..	420	394	360	376	382	487
Bulgaria	1047	837	1431	1788	1788	2175	2123	2365	3163
Croatia	–	–	2223	3949	3723	4096	4876	5567	8621
Macedonia, TFYR	–	–	..	149	273	317	245	253	326
Romania	746	610	1494	1226	1365	1747	2032	2347	3028
Serbia and Montenegro	–	–	..	914	471	624	759	839	1007
Yugoslavia, SFR (former)	3236	6374	–	–	–	–	–	–	–
CIS	*..*	*..*	*15195*	*19859*	*16083*	*17007*	*19596*	*23241*	*26875*
Armenia	–	–	29	130	136	137	187	184	207
Azerbaijan	–	–	172	332	257	260	290	362	432
Belarus	–	–	466	925	753	1016	1102	1300	1500
Georgia	–	–	..	365	217	206	314	392	442
Kazakhstan	–	–	535	904	933	1133	1307	1588	1701
Kyrgyzstan	–	–	39	63	65	62	80	138	..
Moldova, Republic of	–	–	145	152	136	164	171	215	251
Russian Federation	–	–	10568	12375	9071	9565	11442	13611	16030
Tajikistan	–	–	..	..	..	..	..	69	89
Turkmenistan	–	–	..	..	..	..	..	..	..
Ukraine	–	–	2846	3922	3869	3800	3995	4682	5214
Uzbekistan	–	–	191	310	308	345	417	495	..
DEVELOPING ECONOMIES	**82119**	**153824**	**288537**	**318470**	**328208**	**358005**	**360414**	**370787**	**406798**
By major category									
Major petroleum exporters	15699	19828	29666	36903	39190	35653	41065	31914	35471
Other developing economies	66420	133996	258871	281567	289018	322352	319349	338873	371327
Major exporters of manufactures	41208	91458	193561	208666	212196	243446	239837	258010	280086
Remaining economies	25212	42539	65310	72901	76822	78905	79512	80863	91242
America	10425	16453	26269	31975	33598	35543	34756	33452	36275
Africa	10900	19445	25735	27174	29673	29282	30081	30902	36926
West Asia	1167	1447	1983	2220	2176	2030	1589	1542	1501
Other Asia	2305	4415	10235	10456	10350	11160	12171	14007	15504
By income group (per capita GDP in 2000)									
High-income countries	36480	72812	136649	140460	147805	164903	162683	168148	179386
Middle-income countries	24468	48480	86316	101517	98788	107207	102676	106308	118562
Low-income countries	21171	32532	65572	76492	81616	85895	95055	96332	108850
MEMO ITEM:									
LDC	3219	4042	6357	6629	7239	7415	7421	7782	8196
HIPC	4352	5877	8970	10108	10566	10899	11261	11677	12652
Land-locked countries	1629	2305	4697	6069	6433	6463	6816	7724	8848
Developing economies excluding China	79064	147969	269407	294575	301960	327574	327080	331043	360064
Sub-Saharan Africa	6586	11190	13488	14792	15704	15361	15819	16398	19518

For sources and notes, see next page.

5.1 Valeur des exportations et des importations de services par régions et par pays
(fin)
Millions de dollars

Imports - Importations (c.i.f. / c.a.f.)									Régions, groupements économiques, pays ou zones
1985	1990	1995	1998	1999	2000	2001	2002	2003	
83	73	246	369	291	328	380	..	..	Myanmar
116	167	313	196	212	200	215	..	..	Népal
1184	2073	2938	2261	2146	2252	2330	2241	3288	Pakistan
867	1761	6926	10107	7515	6402	5198	4072	4197	Philippines
3554	8642	20587	19320	23937	26938	26886	29729	29569	Singapour
457	639	1199	1362	1414	1621	1180	997	..	Sri Lanka
1815	6309	18804	11998	13583	15460	14610	16720	18503	Thaïlande
..	..	..	3146	3040	3252	3382	3698	..	Viet Nam
									ECONOMIES EN DEVELOPPEMENT :
521	**830**	**1226**	**1316**	**1332**	**1343**	**1193**	**1052**	**957**	**OCEANIE**
131	257	399	352	390	..	..	..	..	Fidji
11	19	..	..	..	..	..	..	..	Kiribati
288	403	642	794	728	772	662	..	..	Papouasie-Nouvelle-Guinée
11	25	35	29	25	..	..	..	..	Samoa
43	79	77	55	87	..	...	..	..	Iles Salomon
16	23	..	..	..	..	28	32	..	Tonga
20	24	35	57	72	70	73	..	..	Vanuatu
4626	**16428**	**29090**	**29246**	**25561**	**30662**	**37444**	**43358**	**51020**	**EUROPE DU SUD-EST ET CEI**
4626	*16428*	*5047*	*6097*	*6220*	*6678*	*7056*	*8312*	*10647*	*Europe du Sud-Est*
18	29	157	129	163	429	444	590	803	Albanie
–	–	..	207	226	197	203	241	297	Bosnie-Herzégovine
654	600	1278	1415	1474	1670	1721	1883	2563	Bulgarie
–	–	1361	1887	2098	1828	1948	2413	2980	Croatie
–	–	..	209	231	268	264	275	329	Macédoine, LERY
524	787	1819	1829	1785	1993	2153	2338	2958	Roumanie
–	–	..	421	243	293	323	572	718	Serbie-et-Monténégro
3430	15012	–	–	–	–	–	–	–	Yougoslavie, RSF (anc.)
..	..	*24043*	*23149*	*19340*	*23984*	*30388*	*35046*	*40373*	*CEI*
–	–	52	209	198	193	204	225	276	Arménie
–	–	305	701	485	485	665	1298	2047	Azerbaïdjan
–	–	284	443	439	563	841	908	944	Bélarus
–	–	..	345	224	216	237	357	389	Géorgie
–	–	776	1154	1104	2004	2825	3667	4066	Kazakhstan
–	–	195	176	154	149	125	145	..	Kirghizistan
–	–	196	199	178	202	203	246	290	Moldova, République de
–	–	20206	16456	13352	16229	20712	23497	27122	Fédération de Russie
–	–	..	..	..	..	..	105	122	Tadjikistan
–	–	..	..	..	..	..	..	..	Turkménistan
–	–	1334	2545	2292	3004	3580	3535	3657	Ukraine
–	–	193	164	270	380	506	709	..	Ouzbékistan
123282	**183543**	**323724**	**352198**	**363827**	**401732**	**395267**	**412428**	**444935**	**ECONOMIES EN DEVELOPPEMENT**
									Par principales catégories
52850	50942	60978	66605	66834	76900	74450	77626	85101	Principaux pays exportateurs de pétrole
70432	132601	262747	285593	296993	324832	320817	334801	359833	Autres économies en développement
40728	89483	195812	209521	221935	245926	242146	258169	275545	Principaux pays exportateurs d'articles manufacturés
29704	43118	66934	76072	75058	78906	78671	76632	84289	Autres économies
10676	15063	27602	33780	33251	34646	34203	30963	32642	Amérique
14468	21694	26900	28876	28375	29835	30125	30833	34574	Afrique
1287	1268	2006	2291	2218	2247	2465	2833	3226	Asie occidentale
2752	4264	9201	9808	9882	10836	10684	10951	12891	Autres pays d'Asie
									Par catégories de revenus (PIB par habitant en 2000)
63179	93921	147986	163095	172545	195910	187384	193920	202090	Pays à revenu élevé
33212	50244	90416	94862	93783	101479	99760	100540	113944	Pays à revenu intermédiaire
26891	39377	85323	94241	97499	104343	108124	117968	128901	Pays à revenu faible
									POUR MEMOIRE :
6853	10043	12613	13229	13146	14239	15680	16053	16747	PMA
9087	13955	16640	19134	18467	19281	21180	22131	23480	PPTE
3293	4933	8012	9476	8675	9694	11010	13092	15163	Pays enclavés
120758	179191	298501	325526	332238	365701	356000	365900	389628	Economies en développement Chine non comprise
13718	21174	27038	27813	26493	26406	27020	27155	29880	Afrique subsaharienne

Pour les sources et les notes, se reporter à la page suivante.

5.1 Value of exports and imports of services by region and country

5.1 Valeur des exportations et des importations des services par régions et par pays

Sources: UNCTAD secretariat calculations based on IMF, *Balance of Payments Statistics* on CD-ROM, and national sources.

Notes:

The table shows values of exports (credits) and imports (debits) of services that were derived from statistics on international service transactions as presented in the IMF's *Balance of Payments Statistics*. Services are defined as the economic output of intangible commodities that may be produced, transferred and consumed at the same time.

However, services cover a heterogeneous range of intangible products and activities that are difficult to capture within a single definition and are sometimes hard to separate from goods. Services are outputs produced to order, and they typically include changes in the condition of the consumers realized through the activities of the producers at the demand of customers. Ownership rights over services cannot be established. By the time production of a service is completed, it must have been provided to a consumer.

Services figures shown here comprise 11 principal services categories according to the concepts and definitions of the IMF *Balance of Payments Manual* (1993, BPM 5). The aggregate data from table 5.1 include the UNCTAD secretariat's estimates of missing values that are not shown separately.

The 11 principal BPM 5 service components included in the figures are transport, travel, communications, construction, insurance, financial services, computer and information services, royalties and license fees, other business services, personal, cultural and recreational services, and government services n.i.e. For more detailed explanations of each of these categories, as well as of certain inconsistencies that may arise in methods of reporting by different countries, please refer to the IMF Balance of Payments Manual. Given the general difficulties involved in statistically capturing certain aspects of the trade in services, the balance-of-payments figures presented here may be somewhat downward-biased as compared with the actual value of the international trade in services.

Sources :   Calculs du Secrétariat de la CNUCED, basés sur *Balance of Payments Statistics* sur CD-ROM et des sources nationales.

Notes :

Le tableau inclut les valeurs des exportations (crédits) et des importations (débits) des services qui proviennent des statistiques sur les transactions internationales de services, telles qu'elles sont présentées dans *Balance of Payments Statistics* du FMI. Les services sont définis comme rendements économiques de produits intangibles qui peuvent être produits, transférés et consommés au même moment.

Cependant, les services recouvrent un groupe large et hétérogène de produits et d'activités que l'on peut difficilement englober dans une définition. Parfois, la démarcation entre les services et les marchandises n'est pas aisée. Les services sont produits sur commande et ils ont généralement pour résultat un changement des conditions des consommateurs qui ont demandé ces services. Pour que la production d'un service soit terminée, il doit être fourni au consommateur.

Les chiffres présentés comprennent 11 catégories principales de services conformément aux concepts et définitions *du Manuel de la balance des paiements* du FMI (1993, MBP 5). Les agrégats inclus dans le tableau 5.1 comprennent les valeurs manquantes estimées par le secrétariat de la CNUCED et qui ne sont pas présentées séparément.

Les 11 catégories principales des services du MBP 5, incluses dans les chiffres présentés, comprennent : transports, voyages, communications, services de bâtiment et travaux publics, assurances, services financiers, services d'informatique et d'information, redevances et droits de licence, autres services aux entreprises, services personnels, culturels et relatifs aux loisirs et les services fournis ou reçus par les administrations publiques. Pour une explication plus détaillée de chacune de ces catégories, ainsi que pour des indications supplémentaires sur certaines incohérences qui peuvent exister dans les méthodes statistiques employées par différents pays, veuillez vous référer au Manuel de la balance des paiements du FMI. De manière générale, les difficultés à mesurer statistiquement la valeur du commerce des services persistent et les données de la balance des paiements sur les services peuvent être inférieures à la valeur des transactions réelles.

5.2A Leading exporters of services among developing economies by main category of services (ranked by 2002 values)

5.2A Principaux exportateurs de services parmi les économies en développement par catégories de services (classés d'après les valeurs de 2002)

Country or area / Pays ou zones	2001			2002			2003		
	Millions of dollars / Millions de dollars	As % of country's total [1] / En % du total du pays [1]	Annual change in % / Variation annuelle en %	Millions of dollars / Millions de dollars	As % of country's total [1] / En % du total du pays [1]	Annual change in % / Variation annuelle en %	Millions of dollars / Millions de dollars	As % of country's total [1] / En % du total du pays [1]	Annual change in % / Variation annuelle en %
TRANSPORT - TRANSPORTS [2]									
Korea, Republic of - Corée, République de	13180	45.4	-4	13216	46.6	0	16996	52.0	29
Singapore - Singapour	11180	38.7	-6	11437	38.5	2	..	..	..
China - Chine	4635	13.9	26	5720	14.4	23	7906	16.9	38
China, Taiwan Province of - Chine, Taiwan Province de	3581	18.3	-13	3750	17.3	5	4387	19.0	17
Thailand - Thaïlande	3057	23.5	-6	3265	21.2	7	3499	22.2	7
Malaysia - Malaisie	2748	19.0	-2	2855	19.2	4	..	..	..
Egypt - Egypte	2738	30.3	4	2797	30.0	2	3299	29.8	18
Turkey - Turquie	2854	17.8	-3	2795	18.9	-2	2184	11.4	-22
India - Inde	1991	9.5	2	2530	10.2	27	..	..	..
Chile - Chili	2294	55.4	5	2205	50.9	-4	2672	55.6	21
Brazil - Brésil	1422	15.3	1	1536	16.1	8	1858	17.7	21
Panama	1134	56.6	-2	1216	54.0	7	1409	55.1	16
Mexico - Mexique	1282	10.1	-6	1143	9.0	-11	1113	8.8	-3
Kuwait - Koweït	1203	72.4	-13	1129	68.5	-6	1366	71.3	21
Indonesia - Indonésie	..	..	..	1058	15.9	..	..	..	..
South Africa - Afrique du Sud	1166	25.1	-1	1023	21.9	-12	1263	19.1	23
Pakistan	818	56.1	-3	792	32.6	-3	845	28.4	7
Morocco - Maroc	660	16.4	36	780	17.9	18	908	16.8	16
Argentina - Argentine	850	19.2	-23	715	23.5	-16	867	21.7	21
Philippines	659	20.9	-26	630	20.6	-4	581	19.6	-8
TRAVEL - VOYAGES [3]									
China - Chine	17792	53.4	10	20385	51.3	15	17406	37.2	-15
Mexico - Mexique	8401	66.1	1	8858	69.5	5	9457	74.4	7
Turkey - Turquie	8090	50.4	6	8481	57.4	5	13203	69.2	56
Thailand - Thaïlande	7075	54.3	-5	7901	51.3	12	7822	49.6	-1
Malaysia - Malaisie	6863	47.5	37	7118	47.8	4	..	..	..
Korea, Republic of - Corée, République de	6384	22.0	-7	5936	20.9	-7	5256	16.1	-11
Indonesia - Indonésie	5276	95.9	6	5285	79.3	0	..	..	..
China, Taiwan Province of - Chine, Taiwan Province de	3990	20.4	7	4583	21.2	15	2913	12.6	-36
Singapore - Singapour	4586	15.9	-12	4381	14.7	-4	..	..	..
China, Macao SAR - Chine, Macao RAS	..	..	..	4018	90.0	..	..	..	..
Egypt - Egypte	3800	42.0	-13	3764	40.4	-1	4584	41.4	22
India - Inde	2940	14.1	-9	3013	12.1	2	..	..	..
South Africa - Afrique du Sud	2569	55.2	-4	2923	62.6	14	4270	64.7	46
Dominican Republic - République dominicaine	2798	90.0	-2	2730	88.9	-2	3110	90.5	14
Morocco - Maroc	2583	64.1	27	2646	60.7	2	3214	59.4	21
Brazil - Brésil	1731	18.6	-4	1998	20.9	15	2479	23.6	24
Philippines	1723	54.7	-19	1740	57.0	1	1464	49.3	-16
Argentina - Argentine	2642	59.5	-9	1535	50.5	-42	2097	52.6	37
Tunisia - Tunisie	1751	60.1	4	1523	56.8	-13	1583	53.9	4
Jamaica - Jamaïque	1232	65.0	-8	1209	63.0	-2	..	..	..

For sources and notes, see end of table 5.2B.

Pour les sources et les notes, se reporter à la fin du tableau 5.2B.

5.2A   Leading exporters of services among developing economies by main category of services (ranked by 2002 values) (continued)

5.2A   Principaux exportateurs de services parmi les économies en développement par catégories de services (classés d'après les valeurs de 2002) (suite)

Country or area / Pays ou zones	2001			2002			2003		
	Millions of dollars / Millions de dollars	As % of country's total [1] / En % du total du pays [1]	Annual change in % / Variation annuelle en %	Millions of dollars / Millions de dollars	As % of country's total [1] / En % du total du pays [1]	Annual change in % / Variation annuelle en %	Millions of dollars / Millions de dollars	As % of country's total [1] / En % du total du pays [1]	Annual change in % / Variation annuelle en %
COMMUNICATIONS [4]									
Mexico - Mexique	787	6.2	-35	557	4.4	-29	423	3.3	-24
China - Chine	271	0.8	-80	550	1.4	103	638	1.4	16
Korea, Republic of - Corée, République de	398	1.4	3	378	1.3	-5	343	1.0	-9
Pakistan	202	13.8	6	332	13.7	64	190	6.4	-43
Philippines	328	10.4	80	310	10.1	-5	475	16.0	53
China, Taiwan Province of - Chine, Taiwan Province de	264	1.4	-10	283	1.3	7	338	1.5	19
Malaysia - Malaisie	242	1.7	34	235	1.6	-3	..	..	..
Morocco - Maroc	169	4.2	49	231	5.3	37	249	4.6	7
Egypt - Egypte	232	2.6	-24	221	2.4	-5	309	2.8	40
Jamaica - Jamaïque	165	8.7	-21	178	9.3	8	..	..	..
Indonesia - Indonésie	85	1.5	-1	174	2.6	104	..	..	..
Chile - Chili	125	3.0	-40	162	3.7	30	166	3.5	3
Colombia - Colombie	182	8.3	0	145	7.8	-20	130	7.3	-10
Argentina - Argentine	175	3.9	14	143	4.7	-18	142	3.6	-1
Brazil - Brésil	242	2.6	577	135	1.4	-44	449	4.3	232
Thailand - Thaïlande	109	0.8	-18	130	0.8	19	145	0.9	12
Dominican Republic - République dominicaine	99	3.2	-29	103	3.3	4	104	3.0	2
Ecuador - Equateur	96	11.1	57	98	10.6	2	103	11.4	5
El Salvador	109	15.5	26	93	11.9	-14	123	14.9	32
Peru - Pérou	84	5.6	0	89	5.7	5	93	5.6	5
CONSTRUCTION - BATIMENTS ET TRAVAUX PUBLICS									
China - Chine	830	2.5	38	1246	3.1	50	1290	2.8	3
Turkey - Turquie	685	4.3	-34	849	5.7	24	743	3.9	-12
Malaysia - Malaisie	338	2.3	8	427	2.9	26	..	..	..
Thailand - Thaïlande	296	2.3	29	244	1.6	-17	182	1.2	-26
Egypt - Egypte	141	1.6	52	172	1.8	22	222	2.0	29
China, Taiwan Province of - Chine, Taiwan Province de	99	0.5	-17	100	0.5	1	118	0.5	18
Tunisia - Tunisie	71	2.4	41	89	3.3	26	122	4.1	36
Netherlands Antilles - Antilles néerlandaises	50	3.0	47	48	2.8	-5	..	..	..
Korea, Republic of - Corée, République de	82	0.3	181	39	0.1	-52	37	0.1	-6
Sri Lanka	41	3.0	..	34	2.7	-16	..	..	..
Mozambique	2	0.7	796	31	9.0	1608	12	3.9	-61
Guinea - Guinée	13	12.5	214	29	31.9	124	42	31.4	46
Philippines	64	2.0	-34	28	0.9	-56	50	1.7	79
Guatemala	3	0.3	..	23	2.0	741	..	..	..
El Salvador	16	2.2	11	22	2.8	41	10	1.2	-55
Côte d'Ivoire	17	2.9	62	18	3.0	5	..	..	..
Argentina - Argentine	..	..	..	16	0.5	..	41	1.0	150
Brazil - Brésil	18	0.2	-92	12	0.1	-32	10	0.1	-16
Madagascar	18	5.0	-13	10	4.3	-44	..	..	..
Senegal - Sénégal	11	2.7	-48	9	2.1	-11	..	..	..

For sources and notes, see end of table 5.2B.

Pour les sources et les notes, se reporter à la fin du tableau 5.2B.

5.2A **Leading exporters of services among developing economies by main category of services (ranked by 2002 values)** *(continued)*

5.2A **Principaux exportateurs de services parmi les économies en développement par catégories de services (classés d'après les valeurs de 2002)** *(suite)*

Country or area Pays ou zones	2001			2002			2003		
	Millions of dollars Millions de dollars	As % of country's total [1] En % du total du pays [1]	Annual change in % Variation annuelle en %	Millions of dollars Millions de dollars	As % of country's total [1] En % du total du pays [1]	Annual change in % Variation annuelle en %	Millions of dollars Millions de dollars	As % of country's total [1] En % du total du pays [1]	Annual change in % Variation annuelle en %
COMPUTER AND INFORMATION SERVICES - INFORMATIQUE ET INFORMATION									
China - Chine	461	1.4	30	638	1.6	38	1102	2.4	73
Malaysia - Malaisie	176	1.2	116	182	1.2	3	..	..	..
Costa Rica	125	6.6	109	153	8.2	23	167	8.2	9
China, Taiwan Province of - Chine, Taiwan Province de	154	0.8	32	115	0.5	-25	110	0.5	-4
Argentina - Argentine	181	4.1	31	96	3.2	-47	124	3.1	29
Chile - Chili	43	1.0	28	56	1.3	30	55	1.1	-1
Sri Lanka	66	4.9	..	50	3.9	-24	..	..	..
Brazil - Brésil	27	0.3	-21	36	0.4	35	29	0.3	-20
Jamaica - Jamaïque	37	1.9	-9	34	1.8	-7	..	..	..
Egypt - Egypte	22	0.2	-3	27	0.3	23	23	0.2	-17
Philippines	22	0.7	-71	21	0.7	-5	25	0.8	19
Pakistan	19	1.3	-14	21	0.9	11	34	1.1	62
Korea, Republic of - Corée, République de	16	0.1	52	20	0.1	21	30	0.1	52
Tunisia - Tunisie	21	0.7	6	18	0.7	-12	19	0.7	6
Dominican Republic - République dominicaine	..	..	..	18	0.6	..	18	0.5	-1
Barbados - Barbade	17	1.6	1	18	1.7	1	..	..	..
Uruguay	14	1.3	44	14	1.8	-6	14	1.9	6
Venezuela	7	0.5	0	8	0.8	14	4	0.5	-50
Guatemala	5	0.5	30	7	0.6	50	..	..	..
Mauritius - Maurice	6	0.5	116	6	0.5	2	..	..	..
INSURANCE - ASSURANCE									
Mexico - Mexique	1352	10.6	-25	1212	9.5	-10	1163	9.1	-4
Singapore - Singapour	632	2.2	41	752	2.5	19	..	..	..
China, Taiwan Province of - Chine, Taiwan Province de	404	2.1	-33	563	2.6	39	451	2.0	-20
India - Inde	271	1.3	4	368	1.5	36	..	..	..
South Africa - Afrique du Sud	323	6.9	-28	239	5.1	-26	324	4.9	35
China - Chine	227	0.7	111	209	0.5	-8	313	0.7	50
Brazil - Brésil	180	1.9	-42	206	2.2	15	124	1.2	-40
Malaysia - Malaisie	265	1.8	70	156	1.0	-41	..	..	..
Chile - Chili	71	1.7	-7	138	3.2	95	136	2.8	-1
Kuwait - Koweït	72	4.3	0	109	6.6	51	84	4.4	-23
Peru - Pérou	116	7.7	3	94	6.1	-19	88	5.3	-6
Thailand - Thaïlande	88	0.7	8	92	0.6	5	129	0.8	40
Barbados - Barbade	85	7.9	7	87	8.4	3	..	..	..
Guatemala	30	2.9	61	49	4.3	64	..	..	..
Sri Lanka	423	31.2	942	45	3.6	-89	..	..	..
Korea, Republic of - Corée, République de	60	0.2	-12	37	0.1	-39	71	0.2	93
Philippines	48	1.5	-27	35	1.1	-27	54	1.8	54
Bolivia - Bolivie	35	15.0	-14	34	13.1	-5	42	13.6	24
El Salvador	27	3.8	-58	30	3.9	13	58	7.1	92
Morocco - Maroc	29	0.7	-2	28	0.7	-3	76	1.4	167

For sources and notes, see end of table 5.2B.

Pour les sources et les notes, se reporter à la fin du tableau 5.2B.

5.2A   Leading exporters of services among developing economies by main category of services (ranked by 2002 values) *(continued)*

5.2A   Principaux exportateurs de services parmi les économies en développement par catégories de services (classés d'après les valeurs de 2002) *(suite)*

Country or area / Pays ou zones	2001			2002			2003		
	Millions of dollars / Millions de dollars	As % of country's total [1] / En % du total du pays [1]	Annual change in % / Variation annuelle en %	Millions of dollars / Millions de dollars	As % of country's total [1] / En % du total du pays [1]	Annual change in % / Variation annuelle en %	Millions of dollars / Millions de dollars	As % of country's total [1] / En % du total du pays [1]	Annual change in % / Variation annuelle en %
FINANCIAL SERVICES - SERVICES FINANCIERS									
China, Taiwan Province of - Chine, Taiwan Province de	514	2.6	-36	757	3.5	47	863	3.7	14
Korea, Republic of - Corée, République de	533	1.8	-24	695	2.4	30	696	2.1	0
Brazil - Brésil	317	3.4	-16	390	4.1	23	363	3.5	-7
Panama	127	6.3	-10	259	11.5	105	295	11.5	14
Turkey - Turquie	331	2.1	-10	221	1.5	-33	291	1.5	32
Egypt - Egypte	70	0.8	35	85	0.9	21	80	0.7	-6
Barbados - Barbade	71	6.6	-6	70	6.7	-1	..	..	..
Uruguay	72	6.4	16	54	7.2	-25	58	7.5	7
China - Chine	99	0.3	27	51	0.1	-48	152	0.3	198
Malaysia - Malaisie	110	0.8	-31	51	0.3	-54	..	..	..
Tunisia - Tunisie	38	1.3	14	42	1.6	10	55	1.9	31
Côte d'Ivoire	47	8.1	66	39	6.6	-17	..	..	..
Guyana	23	13.3	22	38	21.8	64	63	34.0	68
Colombia - Colombie	53	2.4	-28	36	1.9	-33	36	2.0	0
Philippines	33	1.0	-59	32	1.0	-3	58	2.0	81
Chile - Chili	34	0.8	-9	25	0.6	-28	27	0.6	10
Jamaica - Jamaïque	16	0.8	25	22	1.2	42	..	..	..
Pakistan	11	0.8	10	17	0.7	55	13	0.4	-24
Mauritius - Maurice	68	5.6	218	17	1.5	-75	..	..	..
China, Macao SAR - Chine, Macao RAS	..	..	..	17	0.4	..	..	..	..
ROYALTIES AND LICENSE FEES - REDEVANCES ET DROITS DE LICENCE									
Korea, Republic of - Corée, République de	924	3.2	34	835	2.9	-10	1325	4.1	59
China, Taiwan Province of - Chine, Taiwan Province de	339	1.7	-9	255	1.2	-25	215	0.9	-16
Paraguay	180	32.4	-11	187	32.9	4	193	32.8	3
China - Chine	110	0.3	37	133	0.3	21	107	0.2	-19
Brazil - Brésil	112	1.2	-10	100	1.0	-11	108	1.0	8
Mexico - Mexique	41	0.3	-5	48	0.4	18	84	0.7	74
Chile - Chili	25	0.6	149	41	0.9	65	45	0.9	10
Egypt - Egypte	46	0.5	-22	38	0.4	-19	121	1.1	221
South Africa - Afrique du Sud	42	0.9	-15	34	0.7	-18	49	0.7	43
Guyana	23	13.4	56	34	20.0	49	32	17.3	-7
Argentina - Argentine	44	1.0	34	25	0.8	-43	32	0.8	30
Tunisia - Tunisie	15	0.5	5	16	0.6	6	18	0.6	10
India - Inde	85	0.4	35	12	0.0	-85	..	..	..
Malaysia - Malaisie	21	0.1	14	12	0.1	-42	..	..	..
Morocco - Maroc	15	0.4	-32	11	0.3	-26	25	0.5	128
Lesotho	11	28.4	-2	11	29.8	-8	..	..	..
Kenya	5	0.5	-29	10	1.0	98	12	1.0	17
Thailand - Thaïlande	9	0.1	2	7	0.0	-17	7	0.0	-10
Jamaica - Jamaïque	6	0.3	-8	6	0.3	3	..	..	..
Pakistan	2	0.1	..	6	0.2	200	8	0.3	33

For sources and notes, see end of table 5.2B.

Pour les sources et les notes, se reporter à la fin du tableau 5.2B.

5.2A Leading exporters of services among developing economies by main category of services (ranked by 2002 values) *(concluded)*

5.2A Principaux exportateurs de services parmi les économies en développement par catégories de services (classés d'après les valeurs de 2002) *(fin)*

Country or area / Pays ou zones	2001			2002			2003		
	Millions of dollars / Millions de dollars	As % of country's total [1] / En % du total du pays [1]	Annual change in % / Variation annuelle en %	Millions of dollars / Millions de dollars	As % of country's total [1] / En % du total du pays [1]	Annual change in % / Variation annuelle en %	Millions of dollars / Millions de dollars	As % of country's total [1] / En % du total du pays [1]	Annual change in % / Variation annuelle en %
OTHER BUSINESS SERVICES - AUTRES SERVICES AUX ENTREPRISES [5]									
India - Inde	15126	72.4	16	18630	74.9	23	..	..	..
Singapore - Singapour	12357	42.8	8	13030	43.9	5	..	..	..
China, Taiwan Province of - Chine, Taiwan Province de	10034	51.3	4	11048	51.1	10	13529	58.6	22
China - Chine	8448	25.3	10	10419	26.2	23	17427	37.3	67
Korea, Republic of - Corée, République de	6388	22.0	-11	6006	21.2	-6	6672	20.4	11
Saudi Arabia - Arabie saoudite	5014	100.0	5	5184	100.0	3	5346	100.0	3
Brazil - Brésil	4613	49.5	1	4319	45.2	-6	4133	39.4	-4
Thailand - Thaïlande	2298	17.6	-12	3665	23.8	59	3885	24.6	6
Malaysia - Malaisie	3537	24.5	-30	2153	14.5	-39	..	..	..
Egypt - Egypte	1737	19.2	-18	1948	20.9	12	2092	18.9	7
Turkey - Turquie	2856	17.8	-49	1012	6.8	-65	1352	7.1	34
Chile - Chili	652	15.8	8	699	16.1	7	725	15.1	4
Netherlands Antilles - Antilles néerlandaises	591	35.8	-1	659	38.4	11	..	..	..
Morocco - Maroc	331	8.2	102	401	9.2	21	609	11.2	52
Jordan - Jordanie	434	29.3	-25	399	26.4	-8	344	23.0	-14
Argentina - Argentine	349	7.9	30	354	11.6	1	508	12.7	44
South Africa - Afrique du Sud	383	8.2	-19	315	6.7	-18	453	6.9	44
Tunisia - Tunisie	256	8.8	0	267	10.0	4	283	9.6	6
Mexico - Mexique	369	2.9	-29	255	2.0	-31	41	0.3	-84
Costa Rica	241	12.7	24	243	13.0	1	261	12.9	7
PERSONAL, CULTURAL AND RECREATIONAL SERVICES - SERVICES PERSONNELS, CULTURELS ET RELATIFS AUX LOISIRS									
Malaysia - Malaisie	29	0.2	-11	1566	10.5	5261	..	..	..
Turkey - Turquie	1072	6.7	-59	1338	9.0	25	781	4.1	-42
Mexico - Mexique	318	2.5	-3	400	3.1	26	293	2.3	-27
Korea, Republic of - Corée, République de	138	0.5	1	185	0.7	34	76	0.2	-59
Argentina - Argentine	38	0.8	108	79	2.6	111	97	2.4	22
Brazil - Brésil	58	0.6	-9	58	0.6	1	54	0.5	-7
Egypt - Egypte	19	0.2	25	54	0.6	186	72	0.7	34
China, Taiwan Province of - Chine, Taiwan Province de	36	0.2	38	47	0.2	31	40	0.2	-15
Chile - Chili	29	0.7	34	39	0.9	33	41	0.9	7
Ecuador - Equateur	24	2.8	-38	32	3.4	32	34	3.8	7
China - Chine	28	0.1	148	30	0.1	6	33	0.1	13
Colombia - Colombie	25	1.2	9	27	1.5	6	29	1.6	5
Congo	17	11.6	34	21	13.0	28	..	..	..
Jamaica - Jamaïque	9	0.5	-6	9	0.5	2	..	..	..
Philippines	15	0.5	-65	7	0.2	-53	10	0.3	43
Mauritius - Maurice	3	0.2	40	5	0.4	80	..	..	..
Venezuela	6	0.4	0	5	0.5	-17	5	0.6	0
Ethiopia - Ethiopie	1	0.3	-7	3	0.6	147	..	..	..
United Republic of Tanzania - République-Unie de Tanzanie	0	0.0	0	3	0.5	3000	..	..	..
Tunisia - Tunisie	4	0.1	43	3	0.1	-33	5	0.2	93

For sources and notes, see end of table 5.2B

Pour les sources et les notes, se reporter à la fin du tableau 5.2B.

5.2B   Leading importers of services among developing economies by main category of services (ranked by 2002 values)

5.2B   Principaux importateurs de services parmi les économies en développement par catégories de services (classés d'après les valeurs de 2002)

Country or area Pays ou zones	2001			2002			2003		
	Millions of dollars Millions de dollars	As % of country's total [1] En % du total du pays [1]	Annual change in % Variation annuelle en %	Millions of dollars Millions de dollars	As % of country's total [1] En % du total du pays [1]	Annual change in % Variation annuelle en %	Millions of dollars Millions de dollars	As % of country's total [1] En % du total du pays [1]	Annual change in % Variation annuelle en %
TRANSPORT - TRANSPORTS [2]									
China - Chine	11325	28.8	9	13612	29.3	20	18233	33.0	34
Singapore - Singapour	11358	42.2	-9	11561	42.4	2	..	..	..
Korea, Republic of - Corée, République de	11043	33.5	0	11301	30.9	2	13475	33.4	19
Thailand - Thaïlande	6830	46.7	1	7121	42.6	4	8357	45.2	17
China, Taiwan Province of - Chine, Taiwan Province de	6105	25.0	-2	5967	24.1	-2	6714	26.2	13
Malaysia - Malaisie	5736	34.4	-3	5892	35.8	3	..	..	..
Indonesia - Indonésie	3876	24.4	-3	5150	30.2	33	..	..	..
Brazil - Brésil	4388	25.7	2	3494	24.1	-20	3592	23.1	3
India - Inde	2406	14.8	-25	2537	13.6	5	..	..	..
Saudi Arabia - Arabie saoudite	2320	12.0	3	2403	12.0	4	2747	13.2	14
South Africa - Afrique du Sud	2185	41.6	-10	2341	43.8	7	3381	44.8	44
Chile - Chili	2260	45.4	3	2207	44.2	-2	2483	44.6	13
Philippines	2417	46.5	-19	2000	49.1	-17	2236	53.3	12
Mexico - Mexique	2105	12.2	6	1990	11.3	-5	1930	10.6	-3
Turkey - Turquie	2021	29.2	-18	1934	28.0	-4	2707	31.5	40
Egypt - Egypte	2037	29.0	-8	1782	26.9	-13	2013	31.1	13
Kuwait - Koweït	1575	29.4	3	1747	29.9	11	2000	30.5	14
Venezuela	1967	42.0	9	1550	40.2	-21	1320	39.8	-15
Pakistan	1553	66.7	2	1388	61.9	-11	1581	48.1	14
Colombia - Colombie	1414	39.1	8	1202	36.1	-15	1260	37.7	5
TRAVEL - VOYAGES [3]									
China - Chine	13909	35.4	6	15398	33.1	11	15187	27.5	-1
Korea, Republic of - Corée, République de	7617	23.1	7	10465	28.6	37	9988	24.8	-5
China, Taiwan Province of - Chine, Taiwan Province de	7319	29.9	-10	6956	28.1	-5	6480	25.3	-7
Mexico - Mexique	5702	33.2	4	6060	34.3	6	6253	34.3	3
Singapore - Singapour	5604	20.8	23	5213	19.1	-7	..	..	..
India - Inde	2306	14.2	-21	3449	18.5	50	..	..	..
Thailand - Thaïlande	2924	20.0	5	3303	19.8	13	3495	18.9	6
Indonesia - Indonésie	3406	21.4	7	3289	19.3	-3	..	..	..
Kuwait - Koweït	2843	53.1	14	3021	51.7	6	3349	51.1	11
Malaysia - Malaisie	2614	15.7	26	2618	15.9	0	..	..	..
Brazil - Brésil	3199	18.7	-18	2396	16.5	-25	2261	14.5	-6
Argentina - Argentine	3893	46.4	-12	2328	49.6	-40	2575	46.6	11
Turkey - Turquie	1738	25.1	1	1881	27.2	8	2113	24.6	12
South Africa - Afrique du Sud	1878	35.8	-10	1811	33.9	-4	2452	32.5	35
Egypt - Egypte	1132	16.1	6	1266	19.1	12	1321	20.4	4
Colombia - Colombie	1164	32.2	10	1075	32.3	-8	1026	30.7	-5
Venezuela	1108	23.7	5	981	25.5	-11	810	24.4	-17
Philippines	1229	23.6	22	871	21.4	-29	632	15.1	-27
Syrian Arab Republic - République arabe syrienne	670	39.6	0	760	40.4	13	..	..	..
Chile - Chili	708	14.2	14	633	12.7	-11	768	13.8	21

For sources and notes, see end of table.

Pour les sources et les notes, se reporter à la fin du tableau.

5.2B Leading importers of services among developing economies by main category of services (ranked by 2002 values) *(continued)*

5.2B Principaux importateurs de services parmi les économies en développement par catégories de services (classés d'après les valeurs de 2002) *(suite)*

Country or area / Pays ou zones	2001			2002			2003		
	Millions of dollars / Millions de dollars	As % of country's total [1] / En % du total du pays [1]	Annual change in % / Variation annuelle en %	Millions of dollars / Millions de dollars	As % of country's total [1] / En % du total du pays [1]	Annual change in % / Variation annuelle en %	Millions of dollars / Millions de dollars	As % of country's total [1] / En % du total du pays [1]	Annual change in % / Variation annuelle en %
COMMUNICATIONS [4]									
Korea, Republic of - Corée, République de	742	2.3	19	685	1.9	-8	650	1.6	-5
China, Taiwan Province of - Chine, Taiwan Province de	441	1.8	-16	473	1.9	7	460	1.8	-3
China - Chine	326	0.8	35	470	1.0	44	427	0.8	-9
Malaysia - Malaisie	285	1.7	23	232	1.4	-19	..	..	..
Argentina - Argentine	218	2.6	30	202	4.3	-7	207	3.7	2
Mexico - Mexique	331	1.9	-10	197	1.1	-40	310	1.7	58
Indonesia - Indonésie	51	0.3	4	171	1.0	236	..	..	..
Chile - Chili	95	1.9	-14	137	2.8	44	146	2.6	6
Egypt - Egypte	128	1.8	25	125	1.9	-2	148	2.3	18
Brazil - Brésil	213	1.2	564	122	0.8	-43	366	2.4	201
Colombia - Colombie	114	3.2	-8	113	3.4	-1	115	3.4	1
Jamaica - Jamaïque	50	3.3	58	104	6.3	107	..	..	..
Thailand - Thaïlande	145	1.0	271	86	0.5	-40	180	1.0	108
Philippines	215	4.1	-18	86	2.1	-60	82	2.0	-5
Turkey - Turquie	102	1.5	21	72	1.0	-29	231	2.7	221
Guatemala	11	1.2	1269	67	6.4	513	..	..	..
Peru - Pérou	63	2.6	0	66	2.6	5	69	2.6	5
Venezuela	78	1.7	-7	62	1.6	-21	57	1.7	-8
South Africa - Afrique du Sud	70	1.3	-16	60	1.1	-14	86	1.1	43
United Republic of Tanzania - République-Unie de Tanzanie	10	1.5	61	52	7.3	419	..	..	..
CONSTRUCTION - BATIMENTS ET TRAVAUX PUBLICS									
China - Chine	847	2.2	-15	964	2.1	14	1183	2.1	23
Angola	..	..	..	555	16.7	..	..	..	..
China, Taiwan Province of - Chine, Taiwan Province de	414	1.7	-6	485	2.0	17	457	1.8	-6
Malaysia - Malaisie	757	4.5	-31	476	2.9	-37	..	..	..
Tunisia - Tunisie	135	9.5	21	160	11.0	18	160	9.9	0
Egypt - Egypte	..	..	..	124	1.9	..	108	1.7	-14
Philippines	299	5.8	141	123	3.0	-59	65	1.5	-47
Mozambique	40	6.4	41	91	16.6	130	61	11.1	-33
Ethiopia - Ethiopie	30	5.6	186	81	13.9	173	..	..	..
Thailand - Thaïlande	110	0.8	5	72	0.4	-35	152	0.8	110
Netherlands Antilles - Antilles néerlandaises	55	7.2	74	47	6.1	-15	..	..	..
Madagascar	47	9.2	28	41	10.2	-13	..	..	..
Honduras	35	5.6	-13	35	5.8	0	58	8.9	66
Mali	10	2.4	848	32	8.2	208	..	..	..
Sri Lanka	38	3.3	..	32	3.2	-18	..	..	..
Yemen - Yémen	39	4.6	-24	30	3.2	-23	34	3.4	15
Seychelles	36	21.0	3	26	13.0	-27	..	..	..
Korea, Republic of - Corée, République de	15	0.0	-4	24	0.1	56	16	0.0	-31
Cambodia - Cambodge	30	8.7	-19	22	5.8	-28	16	4.0	-28
Mauritius - Maurice	6	0.7	1303	19	2.4	216	..	..	..

For sources and notes, see end of table.

Pour les sources et les notes, se reporter à la fin du tableau.

5.2B   Leading importers of services among developing economies by main category of services (ranked by 2002 values) (continued)

5.2B   Principaux importateurs de services parmi les économies en développement par catégories de services (classés d'après les valeurs de 2002) (suite)

Country or area / Pays ou zones	2001			2002			2003		
	Millions of dollars / Millions de dollars	As % of country's total [1] / En % du total du pays [1]	Annual change in % / Variation annuelle en %	Millions of dollars / Millions de dollars	As % of country's total [1] / En % du total du pays [1]	Annual change in % / Variation annuelle en %	Millions of dollars / Millions de dollars	As % of country's total [1] / En % du total du pays [1]	Annual change in % / Variation annuelle en %
COMPUTER AND INFORMATION SERVICES - INFORMATIQUE ET INFORMATION									
Brazil - Brésil	1133	6.6	-1	1155	8.0	2	1063	6.8	-8
China - Chine	345	0.9	30	1133	2.4	228	1036	1.9	-9
China, Taiwan Province of - Chine, Taiwan Province de	254	1.0	17	305	1.2	20	248	1.0	-19
Malaysia - Malaisie	215	1.3	7	172	1.0	-20	..	..	..
Korea, Republic of - Corée, République de	104	0.3	13	124	0.3	20	134	0.3	7
Argentina - Argentine	180	2.1	33	96	2.0	-47	101	1.8	5
Venezuela	71	1.5	6	65	1.7	-8	58	1.7	-11
Philippines	83	1.6	-12	46	1.1	-45	41	1.0	-11
Chile - Chili	47	0.9	-41	41	0.8	-12	42	0.8	3
Colombia - Colombie	40	1.1	-12	28	0.9	-30	70	2.1	147
China, Macao SAR - Chine, Macao RAS	..	..	..	15	1.4	..	..	..	..
Costa Rica	14	1.2	53	15	1.2	3	10	0.9	-31
Egypt - Egypte	13	0.2	-37	14	0.2	9	27	0.4	94
Jamaica - Jamaïque	14	0.9	94	12	0.7	-16	..	..	..
El Salvador	10	1.0	-32	9	0.9	-7	3	0.3	-65
Namibia - Namibie	13	4.8	-6	9	3.9	-34	12	4.9	40
Mauritius - Maurice	9	1.1	66	8	1.1	-6	..	..	..
Netherlands Antilles - Antilles néerlandaises	5	0.7	-63	7	1.0	47	..	..	..
Côte d'Ivoire	7	0.6	-3	7	0.5	4	..	..	..
Tunisia - Tunisie	8	0.5	31	7	0.5	-8	7	0.4	-1
INSURANCE - ASSURANCE									
Mexico - Mexique	6488	37.7	3	6520	36.9	1	6755	37.0	4
China - Chine	2711	6.9	10	3246	7.0	20	4564	8.3	41
Singapore - Singapour	1148	4.3	-7	1177	4.3	2	..	..	..
Thailand - Thaïlande	804	5.5	0	973	5.8	21	1122	6.1	15
China, Taiwan Province of - Chine, Taiwan Province de	736	3.0	25	953	3.9	29	1236	4.8	30
Brazil - Brésil	455	2.7	44	626	4.3	38	560	3.6	-11
Korea, Republic of - Corée, République de	374	1.1	156	571	1.6	53	410	1.0	-28
South Africa - Afrique du Sud	434	8.3	14	502	9.4	16	646	8.6	29
Malaysia - Malaisie	340	2.0	18	434	2.6	28	..	..	..
Egypt - Egypte	411	5.8	-9	398	6.0	-3	423	6.5	6
Turkey - Turquie	282	4.1	-18	372	5.4	32	622	7.2	67
Chile - Chili	211	4.2	10	349	7.0	66	383	6.9	10
India - Inde	256	1.6	105	311	1.7	21	..	..	..
Philippines	123	2.4	-24	282	6.9	129	306	7.3	9
Colombia - Colombie	239	6.6	19	282	8.5	18	238	7.1	-16
Saudi Arabia - Arabie saoudite	258	1.3	3	267	1.3	4	305	1.5	14
Peru - Pérou	188	7.9	14	243	9.6	29	263	10.1	8
Indonesia - Indonésie	286	1.8	-11	183	1.1	-36	..	..	..
Venezuela	193	4.1	7	171	4.4	-11	137	4.1	-20
Ecuador - Equateur	65	4.6	97	131	8.0	100	91	5.7	-30

For sources and notes, see end of table.

Pour les sources et les notes, se reporter à la fin du tableau.

5.2B Leading importers of services among developing economies by main category of services (ranked by 2002 values) *(continued)*

5.2B Principaux importateurs de services parmi les économies en développement par catégories de services (classés d'après les valeurs de 2002) *(suite)*

Country or area Pays ou zones	2001			2002			2003		
	Millions of dollars Millions de dollars	As % of country's total [1] En % du total du pays [1]	Annual change in % Variation annuelle en %	Millions of dollars Millions de dollars	As % of country's total [1] En % du total du pays [1]	Annual change in % Variation annuelle en %	Millions of dollars Millions de dollars	As % of country's total [1] En % du total du pays [1]	Annual change in % Variation annuelle en %
FINANCIAL SERVICES - SERVICES FINANCIERS									
China, Taiwan Province of - Chine, Taiwan Province de	708	2.9	-32	856	3.5	21	1112	4.3	30
Brazil - Brésil	624	3.7	-7	623	4.3	0	745	4.8	20
Turkey - Turquie	722	10.4	8	621	9.0	-14	374	4.4	-40
Chile - Chili	203	4.1	-8	230	4.6	13	249	4.5	8
Mexico - Mexique	557	3.2	-39	200	1.1	-64	500	2.7	150
Panama	59	5.4	63	173	13.6	192	177	13.7	2
Colombia - Colombie	156	4.3	13	143	4.3	-9	160	4.8	12
Venezuela	70	1.5	52	117	3.0	67	122	3.7	4
Malaysia - Malaisie	197	1.2	12	102	0.6	-48	..	..	..
Côte d'Ivoire	84	6.6	-4	90	5.8	7	..	..	..
China - Chine	77	0.2	-21	90	0.2	17	233	0.4	159
Korea, Republic of - Corée, République de	83	0.3	-57	70	0.2	-16	110	0.3	58
Pakistan	46	2.0	2	53	2.4	15	73	2.2	38
Argentina - Argentine	185	2.2	9	53	1.1	-71	122	2.2	131
Philippines	75	1.4	-84	45	1.1	-40	54	1.3	20
Guyana	27	13.9	34	39	19.7	44	59	28.5	52
Tunisia - Tunisie	41	2.9	15	34	2.3	-18	35	2.2	3
Angola	..	..	..	34	1.0	..	..	..	..
Egypt - Egypte	27	0.4	30	28	0.4	4	26	0.4	-10
Kenya	24	3.2	51	28	4.3	13	32	4.7	15
ROYALTIES AND LICENSE FEES - REDEVANCES ET DROITS DE LICENCE									
China - Chine	1938	4.9	51	3114	6.7	61	3548	6.4	14
Korea, Republic of - Corée, République de	3053	9.3	-5	3002	8.2	-2	3597	8.9	20
China, Taiwan Province of - Chine, Taiwan Province de	1499	6.1	-18	1720	7.0	15	1689	6.6	-2
Brazil - Brésil	1244	7.3	-12	1229	8.5	-1	1228	7.9	0
Thailand - Thaïlande	823	5.6	16	1104	6.6	34	1256	6.8	14
Mexico - Mexique	419	2.4	3	720	4.1	72	608	3.3	-16
Malaysia - Malaisie	751	4.5	38	628	3.8	-16	..	..	..
India - Inde	567	3.5	8	350	1.9	-38	..	..	..
Argentina - Argentine	532	6.3	-5	293	6.2	-45	342	6.2	17
Chile - Chili	269	5.4	-10	250	5.0	-7	266	4.8	6
Philippines	159	3.1	-19	230	5.6	45	273	6.5	19
Egypt - Egypte	361	5.1	-10	171	2.6	-53	165	2.5	-4
South Africa - Afrique du Sud	176	3.4	-28	152	2.9	-14	266	3.5	75
Turkey - Turquie	119	1.7	-31	107	1.5	-10	167	1.9	56
Colombia - Colombie	72	2.0	0	85	2.6	19	72	2.1	-16
Peru - Pérou	61	2.6	-2	65	2.6	6	65	2.5	0
Venezuela	260	5.6	41	58	1.5	-78	48	1.4	-17
Costa Rica	49	4.2	-2	51	4.3	4	64	5.4	25
Swaziland	43	23.0	22	46	32.1	7	..	..	..
Ecuador - Equateur	52	3.6	-16	44	2.7	-16	43	2.7	-2

For sources and notes, see end of table.

Pour les sources et les notes, se reporter à la fin du tableau.

5.2B   Leading importers of services among developing economies by main category of services (ranked by 2002 values) *(concluded)*

5.2B   Principaux importateurs de services parmi les économies en développement par catégories de services (classés d'après les valeurs de 2002) *(fin)*

Country or area / Pays ou zones	2001			2002			2003		
	Millions of dollars / Millions de dollars	As % of country's total[1] / En % du total du pays[1]	Annual change in % / Variation annuelle en %	Millions of dollars / Millions de dollars	As % of country's total[1] / En % du total du pays[1]	Annual change in % / Variation annuelle en %	Millions of dollars / Millions de dollars	As % of country's total[1] / En % du total du pays[1]	Annual change in % / Variation annuelle en %
OTHER BUSINESS SERVICES - AUTRES SERVICES AUX ENTREPRISES[5]									
India - Inde	10444	64.3	10	11817	63.2	13	..	..	..
Korea, Republic of - Corée, République de	9237	28.1	-11	9607	26.3	4	11221	27.8	17
Singapore - Singapour	8638	32.1	1	9204	33.7	7	..	..	..
Indonesia - Indonésie	7976	50.2	11	7986	46.8	0	..	..	..
China - Chine	7504	19.1	8	7957	17.1	6	10371	18.8	30
China, Taiwan Province of - Chine, Taiwan Province de	5769	23.6	-9	5920	23.9	3	6201	24.2	5
Saudi Arabia - Arabie saoudite	4586	23.8	-46	4492	22.5	-2	4809	23.1	7
Thailand - Thaïlande	2839	19.4	-31	3913	23.4	38	3771	20.4	-4
Brazil - Brésil	4203	24.6	22	3543	24.4	-16	4379	28.1	24
Malaysia - Malaisie	5539	33.3	-8	2906	17.7	-48	..	..	..
Egypt - Egypte	2225	31.6	-22	2090	31.5	-6	1793	27.7	-14
Angola	2623	74.6	50	1994	60.0	-24	..	..	..
Mexico - Mexique	721	4.2	-28	1085	6.1	50	1094	6.0	1
Turkey - Turquie	1163	16.8	-21	1080	15.6	-7	1377	16.0	28
Chile - Chili	1019	20.5	12	972	19.5	-5	1055	18.9	9
Venezuela	691	14.8	-6	694	18.0	0	453	13.6	-35
Congo	606	71.1	10	674	72.7	11	..	..	..
Morocco - Maroc	443	20.9	8	496	20.5	12	602	20.9	21
Peru - Pérou	438	18.3	-16	466	18.4	6	480	18.4	3
Jamaica - Jamaïque	427	28.2	8	436	26.5	2	..	..	..
PERSONAL, CULTURAL AND RECREATIONAL SERVICES - SERVICES PERSONNELS, CULTURELS ET RELATIFS AUX LOISIRS									
Malaysia - Malaisie	106	0.6	52	2790	17.0	2531	..	..	..
Brazil - Brésil	365	2.1	1	309	2.1	-15	337	2.2	9
Korea, Republic of - Corée, République de	206	0.6	29	283	0.8	37	261	0.6	-8
Mexico - Mexique	198	1.2	-19	260	1.5	31	221	1.2	-15
China, Taiwan Province of - Chine, Taiwan Province de	190	0.8	17	217	0.9	14	206	0.8	-5
Turkey - Turquie	286	4.1	-81	188	2.7	-34	117	1.4	-38
Argentina - Argentine	228	2.7	33	98	2.1	-57	112	2.0	15
China - Chine	50	0.1	34	96	0.2	92	70	0.1	-28
Ecuador - Equateur	71	5.0	37	86	5.3	21	92	5.8	7
Venezuela	71	1.5	-1	69	1.8	-3	72	2.2	4
Chile - Chili	36	0.7	-17	35	0.7	-3	38	0.7	8
Colombia - Colombie	27	0.7	3	28	0.8	3	29	0.9	5
Uruguay	16	2.0	30	18	3.0	9	10	1.6	-44
Philippines	57	1.1	-56	17	0.4	-70	15	0.4	-12
Angola	..	..	..	15	0.5	..	..	..	..
Egypt - Egypte	22	0.3	7	14	0.2	-39	15	0.2	12
Mauritius - Maurice	5	0.6	12	9	1.2	98	..	..	..
Malawi	5	3.2	-9	9	4.1	67	..	..	..
Honduras	8	1.3	2	9	1.4	4	9	1.4	6
Congo	5	0.6	8	5	0.6	10	..	..	..

For sources and notes, see next page.

Pour les sources et les notes, se reporter à la page suivante.

5.2 Leading exporters and importers of services among developing economies by main category of services (ranked by 2002 values)

5.2 Principaux exportateurs et importateurs de services parmi les économies en développement par catégories de services (classés d'après les valeurs de 2002)

Sources: International Monetary Fund (IMF), *Balance of Payments,* CD-ROM.

Sources : Fonds monétaire international (FMI), *Balance des paiements,* CD-ROM.

Notes:

Notes :

1 As percentage of country's total exports (total imports) of services.

1 En pourcentage du total des exportations (importations) de services du pays.

2 Excludes freight insurance, which is included with insurance services.

2 Non-compris l'assurance du fret, incluse dans la rubrique des services d'assurance.

3 Includes goods and services acquired from an economy by non-resident travellers during visits shorter than one year.

3 Comprend les biens et services acquis dans une économie par les voyageurs non résidents, au cours d'un séjour inférieur à un an.

4 Postal, courier and telecommunications services between residents and non-residents.

4 Services postaux (y compris les messageries) et les services de télécommunication, entre résidents et non résidents.

5 Includes merchanting and other trade-related services, operational leasing services, and miscellaneous business, professional and technical services.

5 Y compris le négoce international et les autres services liés au commerce, la location-exploitation et divers services aux entreprises, spécialisés et techniques.

	1990	1995	1998	1999	2000	2001	2002	2003
Afghanistan								
Tourism expenditures (millions of dollars)	1	1	1	..	..	..	..	..
Tourists' overnight stays (thousands)	..	..	..	..	..	..	..	..
Arrivals of tourists (thousands)	8	4	4	..	..	..	..	..
Average length of stay (days)	..	..	..	..	..	..	..	..
Albania - Albanie								
Dépenses des touristes (millions de dollars)	4	65	54	211	389	446	487	..
Nuitées des touristes (milliers)	..	..	..	..	..	..	..	..
Arrivées des touristes (milliers)	30	40	28	26	32	34	..	..
Durée moyenne de séjour (jours)	..	..	3	4	3	3	..	..
Algeria - Algérie								
Tourism expenditures (millions of dollars)	64	32	74	80	96	100	133	161
Tourists' overnight stays (thousands)	..	..	..	..	..	..	..	..
Arrivals of tourists (thousands)	1137	520	678	749	866	901	988	1166
Average length of stay (days)	..	..	..	..	..	..	..	..
American Samoa - Samoa américaines								
Dépenses des touristes (millions de dollars)	10	10	10	..	..	..	..	..
Nuitées des touristes (milliers)	..	..	..	..	..	..	..	..
Arrivées des touristes (milliers)	26	34	36	41	44	36	..	..
Durée moyenne de séjour (jours)	..	..	..	..	..	..	..	..
Andorra - Andorre								
Tourism expenditures (millions of dollars)	..	..	..	..	..	..	..	..
Tourists' overnight stays (thousands)	..	..	..	6491	8628	9809	9737	..
Arrivals of tourists (thousands)	..	..	..	2347	2949	3516	3387	..
Average length of stay (days)	..	..	..	3	3	3	3	..
Angola								
Dépenses des touristes (millions de dollars)	13	10	8	13	18	22	60	71
Nuitées des touristes (milliers)	..	..	95	48	77	112	207	217
Arrivées des touristes (milliers)	67	9	52	45	51	67	91	107
Durée moyenne de séjour (jours)	..	..	..	..	..	..	..	..
Anguilla								
Tourism expenditures (millions of dollars)	35	49	58	56	55	61	55	62
Tourists' overnight stays (thousands)	..	366	404	400	377	411	369	399
Arrivals of tourists (thousands)	31	39	44	47	44	48	44	47
Average length of stay (days)	11	10	9	9	9	9	8	9
Antigua and Barbuda - Antigua-et-Barbuda								
Dépenses des touristes (millions de dollars)	298	247	256	290	290	272	274	301
Nuitées des touristes (milliers)	..	..	..	..	..	..	..	..
Arrivées des touristes (milliers)	206	220	234	240	237	..	..	..
Durée moyenne de séjour (jours)	..	..	..	..	..	..	..	..
Argentina - Argentine								
Tourism expenditures (millions of dollars)	1131	2144	2936	2813	2817	2547	1476	2037
Tourists' overnight stays (thousands)	..	..	..	..	..	..	..	..
Arrivals of tourists (thousands)	1930	2289	3012	2898	2909	2620	2820	3374
Average length of stay (days)	..	..	10	10	10	10	10	10
Armenia - Arménie								
Dépenses des touristes (millions de dollars)	–	5	10	27	45	123	162	206
Nuitées des touristes (milliers)	–	78	..	..	151	200	202	343
Arrivées des touristes (milliers)	–	12	32	41	45	123	162	206
Durée moyenne de séjour (jours)	–	6	7	..	..	7	7	10
Aruba								
Tourism expenditures (millions of dollars)	350	521	732	778	815	825	832	852
Tourists' overnight stays (thousands)	3380	4473	4890	5142	5248	5145	4863	5098
Arrivals of tourists (thousands)	433	619	647	683	721	691	643	642
Average length of stay (days)	8	7	9	9	9	8	8	8

For sources and notes, see end of table.   Pour les sources et les notes, se reporter à la fin du tableau.

	1990	1995	1998	1999	2000	2001	2002	2003
				Australia - Australie				
Dépenses des touristes (millions de dollars)	4088	7857	7335	8028	8451	7624	8087	7112
Nuitées des touristes (milliers)	22950	26645	62356	63402	74433	77834	84098	83093
Arrivées des touristes (milliers)	2215	3726	3825	4109	4530	4435	4420	4354
Durée moyenne de séjour (jours)	..	23	25	24	26	27	27	27
				Austria - Autriche				
Tourism expenditures (millions of dollars)	13417	12927	11276	11035	9931	10236	11400	13567
Tourists' overnight stays (thousands)	94788	63840	63195	63831	64468	65523	67346	..
Arrivals of tourists (thousands)	19011	17173	17352	17467	17982	18180	18611	19078
Average length of stay (days)	..	..	5	5	5	5	5	..
				Azerbaijan - Azerbaïdjan				
Dépenses des touristes (millions de dollars)	–	70	125	81	63	43	51	..
Nuitées des touristes (milliers)	–	..	..	..	..	..	..	..
Arrivées des touristes (milliers)	–	93	483	602	681	767	834	..
Durée moyenne de séjour (jours)	–	..	..	..	..	..	..	..
				Bahamas				
Tourism expenditures (millions of dollars)	1332	1346	1354	1583	1737	1650	1763	1759
Tourists' overnight stays (thousands)	8963	9031	..	..	9048	8973	8704	8948
Arrivals of tourists (thousands)	1562	1598	1528	1577	1544	1538	1513	1510
Average length of stay (days)	6	6	6	5	6	6	6	6
				Bahrain - Bahreïn				
Dépenses des touristes (millions de dollars)	135	247	366	518	573	630	741	..
Nuitées des touristes (milliers)	..	..	..	..	..	..	..	..
Arrivées des touristes (milliers)	1376	1396	1640	2019	2420	2789	3167	..
Durée moyenne de séjour (jours)	..	..	2	2	2	2	2	..
				Bangladesh				
Tourism expenditures (millions of dollars)	11	25	52	50	50	48	57	..
Tourists' overnight stays (thousands)	..	..	..	..	..	..	..	..
Arrivals of tourists (thousands)	115	156	172	173	199	207	207	..
Average length of stay (days)	..	10	9	7	7	6	..	..
				Barbados - Barbade				
Dépenses des touristes (millions de dollars)	494	612	703	666	711	687	648	..
Nuitées des touristes (milliers)	2337	2488	2303	..	2695	..	..	..
Arrivées des touristes (milliers)	432	442	512	515	545	507	498	531
Durée moyenne de séjour (jours)	11	11	11	10	10	10	11	..
				Belarus - Bélarus				
Tourism expenditures (millions of dollars)	–	23	22	12	93	171	193	..
Tourists' overnight stays (thousands)	–	..	..	..	..	..	..	..
Arrivals of tourists (thousands)	–	161	355	75	60	61	..	..
Average length of stay (days)	–	..	..	..	..	..	..	..
				Belgium - Belgique				
Dépenses des touristes (millions de dollars)	3721	4548	4623	6472	6592	6903	6892	8288
Nuitées des touristes (milliers)	12886	13878	14838	15366	15526	15373	15895	15929
Arrivées des touristes (milliers)	5147	5560	6179	6369	6457	6452	6724	6690
Durée moyenne de séjour (jours)	..	..	..	..	..	..	..	..
				Belize				
Tourism expenditures (millions of dollars)	44	77	108	111	120	121	133	156
Tourists' overnight stays (thousands)	..	..	..	..	..	..	..	..
Arrivals of tourists (thousands)	88	131	176	181	196	196	200	221
Average length of stay (days)	..	9	7	7	8	8	8	7
				Benin - Bénin				
Dépenses des touristes (millions de dollars)	55	85	64	94	77	73	60	..
Nuitées des touristes (milliers)	406	314	525	212	200	190	144	..
Arrivées des touristes (milliers)	110	138	152	80	96	88	72	..
Durée moyenne de séjour (jours)	4	..	..	2	2	..	..	..

For sources and notes, see end of table.　　　　　　　　　　Pour les sources et les notes, se reporter à la fin du tableau.

	1990	1995	1998	1999	2000	2001	2002	2003
Bermuda - Bermudes								
Tourism expenditures (millions of dollars)	490	488	487	479	431	351	379	370
Tourists' overnight stays (thousands)	2739	2421	2274	2145	1966	1775	1822	1598
Arrivals of tourists (thousands)	435	387	370	355	332	278	284	257
Average length of stay (days)	6	6	6	6	6	6	6	6
Bhutan - Bhoutan								
Dépenses des touristes (millions de dollars)	2	5	8	9	10	9	8	8
Nuitées des touristes (milliers)	..	..	..	..	..	..	..	..
Arrivées des touristes (milliers)	2	5	6	7	8	6	6	6
Durée moyenne de séjour (jours)	..	..	..	..	7	7	7	7
Bolivia - Bolivie								
Tourism expenditures (millions of dollars)	91	139	200	174	160	163	164	172
Tourists' overnight stays (thousands)	..	..	..	..	..	..	..	..
Arrivals of tourists (thousands)	254	284	387	342	306	322	334	352
Average length of stay (days)	..	11	10	10	10	..	..	..
Bosnia and Herzegovina - Bosnie-Herzégovine								
Dépenses des touristes (millions de dollars)	–	..	210	188	165	175	190	234
Nuitées des touristes (milliers)	–	..	355	346	389	330	392	419
Arrivées des touristes (milliers)	–	..	148	147	171	139	160	165
Durée moyenne de séjour (jours)	–	..	..	..	..	..	..	..
Botswana								
Tourism expenditures (millions of dollars)	117	162	175	234	313	300	309	..
Tourists' overnight stays (thousands)	..	..	..	..	..	..	..	..
Arrivals of tourists (thousands)	543	521	750	843	1104	1049	1037	..
Average length of stay (days)	..	..	..	..	..	..	..	..
Brazil - Brésil								
Dépenses des touristes (millions de dollars)	1444	2097	3678	3994	4228	3701	3120	..
Nuitées des touristes (milliers)	..	..	..	..	..	..	..	..
Arrivées des touristes (milliers)	1091	1991	4818	5107	5313	4773	3783	..
Durée moyenne de séjour (jours)	14	13	13	14	12	12	14	..
British Virgin Islands - Iles Vierges britanniques								
Tourism expenditures (millions of dollars)	132	211	255	300	316	337	342	..
Tourists' overnight stays (thousands)	..	..	..	..	..	..	..	..
Arrivals of tourists (thousands)	160	219	279	286	281	296	285	..
Average length of stay (days)	9	9	9	9	9	10	9	..
Brunei Darussalam - Brunéi Darussalam								
Dépenses des touristes (millions de dollars)	35	37	37	..	..	..	..	..
Nuitées des touristes (milliers)	..	..	..	..	..	..	..	..
Arrivées des touristes (milliers)	377	498	964	967	984	840	..	..
Durée moyenne de séjour (jours)	..	4	..	..	..	..	..	..
Bulgaria - Bulgarie								
Tourism expenditures (millions of dollars)	320	473	966	932	1074	1201	1344	1623
Tourists' overnight stays (thousands)	12759	5438	5197	4382	5170	6190	7055	9142
Arrivals of tourists (thousands)	1586	3466	2667	2472	2785	3186	3433	4048
Average length of stay (days)	6	7	8	8	8	8	9	9
Burkina Faso								
Dépenses des touristes (millions de dollars)	11	25	42	..	..	35	39	..
Nuitées des touristes (milliers)	..	..	..	..	..	..	..	..
Arrivées des touristes (milliers)	74	124	160	117	126	128	150	163
Durée moyenne de séjour (jours)	3	2	4	3	4	3	3	..
Burundi								
Tourism expenditures (millions of dollars)	4	1	1	1	1	1	1	..
Tourists' overnight stays (thousands)	..	..	..	..	..	..	..	..
Arrivals of tourists (thousands)	109	34	15	26	29	36	..	..
Average length of stay (days)	..	..	..	..	..	..	..	..

For sources and notes, see end of table.   Pour les sources et les notes, se reporter à la fin du tableau.

	1990	1995	1998	1999	2000	2001	2002	2003
				Cambodia - Cambodge				
Dépenses des touristes (millions de dollars)	..	100	166	190	228	304	379	..
Nuitées des touristes (milliers)	..	..	..	..	..	..	..	..
Arrivées des touristes (milliers)	17	220	286	368	466	605	787	701
Durée moyenne de séjour (jours)	..	8	5	6	6	6	6	..
				Cameroon - Cameroun				
Tourism expenditures (millions of dollars)	53	36	40	..	39	..	..	..
Tourists' overnight stays (thousands)	..	..	..	..	..	..	..	..
Arrivals of tourists (thousands)	89	100	247	262	277	221	226	..
Average length of stay (days)	..	..	..	..	..	..	..	..
				Canada				
Dépenses des touristes (millions de dollars)	6339	7882	9452	10190	10839	10774	9700	9301
Nuitées des touristes (milliers)	82177	91983	98283	105720	119381	125022	122150	106225
Arrivées des touristes (milliers)	15209	16932	18870	19411	19627	19679	20057	17498
Durée moyenne de séjour (jours)	5	5	5	..	..	..	..	..
				Cape Verde - Cap-Vert				
Tourism expenditures (millions of dollars)	6	10	20	28	41	54	66	..
Tourists' overnight stays (thousands)	..	..	..	..	..	..	..	..
Arrivals of tourists (thousands)	24	28	52	67	83	115	126	..
Average length of stay (days)	..	..	7	..	..	..	..	..
				Cayman Islands - Iles Caïmanes				
Dépenses des touristes (millions de dollars)	236	394	534	525	559	585	607	..
Nuitées des touristes (milliers)	..	..	..	..	..	..	..	..
Arrivées des touristes (milliers)	253	361	404	395	354	334	303	294
Durée moyenne de séjour (jours)	5	7	7	7	7	6	6	..
				Central African Republic - République centrafricaine				
Tourism expenditures (millions of dollars)	3	4	4	8	5	5	3	..
Tourists' overnight stays (thousands)	..	..	..	..	..	..	..	..
Arrivals of tourists (thousands)	6	26	7	10	..	..	..	..
Average length of stay (days)	..	..	..	..	..	..	..	..
				Chad - Tchad				
Dépenses des touristes (millions de dollars)	8	43	15	..	..	23	..	..
Nuitées des touristes (milliers)	..	..	..	..	..	..	..	..
Arrivées des touristes (milliers)	9	19	41	47	43	57	32	..
Durée moyenne de séjour (jours)	..	..	..	..	..	..	..	..
				Chile - Chili				
Tourism expenditures (millions of dollars)	540	911	1105	911	819	799	898	860
Tourists' overnight stays (thousands)	..	..	..	..	..	..	..	..
Arrivals of tourists (thousands)	943	1540	1759	1632	1742	1723	1412	1614
Average length of stay (days)	12	12	12	10	10	10	13	12
				China - Chine				
Dépenses des touristes (millions de dollars)	2218	8733	12602	14099	16224	17792	20385	17406
Nuitées des touristes (milliers)	..	..	..	..	..	..	..	..
Arrivées des touristes (milliers)	10484	20034	25073	27047	31229	33167	36803	32970
Durée moyenne de séjour (jours)	..	..	..	..	..	..	..	..
				China, Hong Kong SAR - Chine, Hong Kong RAS				
Tourism expenditures (millions of dollars)	5032	9604	7496	7210	7886	8241	..	..
Tourists' overnight stays (thousands)	..	..	..	..	..	..	..	..
Arrivals of tourists (thousands)	6581	10200	10160	11328	13059	13725	16566	15537
Average length of stay (days)	3	4	3	3	3	3	..	..
				China, Macao SAR - Chine, Macao RAS				
Dépenses des touristes (millions de dollars)	1473	3233	2648	2598	3205	3745	4440	5303
Nuitées des touristes (milliers)	..	..	..	..	..	..	..	..
Arrivées des touristes (milliers)	2513	4202	4517	5050	5197	5842	6565	6309
Durée moyenne de séjour (jours)	..	..	..	..	..	..	..	..

For sources and notes, see end of table.

Pour les sources et les notes, se reporter à la fin du tableau.

	1990	1995	1998	1999	2000	2001	2002	2003
China, Taiwan Province of - Chine, Taiwan Province								
Tourism expenditures (millions of dollars)	1740	3286	3372	3571	3738	3991	4584	2976
Tourists' overnight stays (thousands)	12494	14834	15058	15966	16487	16987	16856	14461
Arrivals of tourists (thousands)	1934	2332	2299	2411	2624	2617	2978	2248
Average length of stay (days)	7	7	8	8	7	7	8	8
Colombia - Colombie								
Dépenses des touristes (millions de dollars)	406	657	928	927	1026	1209	962	..
Nuitées des touristes (milliers)	..	..	..	..	..	..	..	..
Arrivées des touristes (milliers)	813	1399	674	546	557	616	541	..
Durée moyenne de séjour (jours)	13	3	..	..	..	..	..	..
Comoros - Comores								
Tourism expenditures (millions of dollars)	2	21	16	19	15	9	11	..
Tourists' overnight stays (thousands)	..	181	206	184	161	135	133	..
Arrivals of tourists (thousands)	8	23	27	24	24	19	19	..
Average length of stay (days)	..	7	..	..	..	..	..	..
Congo								
Dépenses des touristes (millions de dollars)	8	14	9	12	12	22	25	..
Nuitées des touristes (milliers)	..	..	..	..	..	..	..	..
Arrivées des touristes (milliers)	33	37	20	14	19	28	..	..
Durée moyenne de séjour (jours)	..	..	..	..	..	..	..	..
Cook Islands - Iles Cook								
Tourism expenditures (millions of dollars)	16	28	34	39	36	38	46	..
Tourists' overnight stays (thousands)	..	..	..	..	..	..	..	..
Arrivals of tourists (thousands)	34	48	49	56	73	75	73	78
Average length of stay (days)	7	9	10	10	11	11	11	11
Costa Rica								
Dépenses des touristes (millions de dollars)	275	660	884	1036	1229	1096	1078	..
Nuitées des touristes (milliers)	..	..	..	..	..	..	..	..
Arrivées des touristes (milliers)	435	785	943	1032	1088	1131	1113	..
Durée moyenne de séjour (jours)	9	10	10	11	11	13	11	..
Côte d'Ivoire								
Tourism expenditures (millions of dollars)	51	89	98	100	49	53	50	..
Tourists' overnight stays (thousands)	..	..	..	..	..	..	..	..
Arrivals of tourists (thousands)	196	188	301	..	..	..	..	..
Average length of stay (days)	..	4	..	..	..	..	..	..
Croatia - Croatie								
Dépenses des touristes (millions de dollars)	–	1349	2733	2493	2758	3335	3811	6376
Nuitées des touristes (milliers)	–	8763	26545	21885	34045	38384	..	..
Arrivées des touristes (milliers)	–	1485	4499	3805	5831	6544	6944	7409
Durée moyenne de séjour (jours)	–	..	..	..	6	6	6	6
Cuba								
Tourism expenditures (millions of dollars)	243	963	1556	1695	1737	1692	1633	..
Tourists' overnight stays (thousands)	3703	6394	10095	10976	11557	11250	..	..
Arrivals of tourists (thousands)	327	742	1390	1561	1741	1736	1656	..
Average length of stay (days)	9	..	11	10	11	11	11	..
Cyprus - Chypre								
Dépenses des touristes (millions de dollars)	1258	1788	1696	1888	1918	1986	1860	1977
Nuitées des touristes (milliers)	9426	14222	14456	16731	17419	18826	..	..
Arrivées des touristes (milliers)	1561	2100	2223	2434	2686	2697	2418	2303
Durée moyenne de séjour (jours)	15	12	11	11	10	10	11	11
Czech Republic - République tchèque								
Tourism expenditures (millions of dollars)	–	2875	3871	3154	2982	3106	2941	3554
Tourists' overnight stays (thousands)	–	10327	16218	16125	15831	16564	..	..
Arrivals of tourists (thousands)	–	3381	5482	5610	4666	5194	4579	5076
Average length of stay (days)	–	..	3	3	4	3	3	3

For sources and notes, see end of table.

Pour les sources et les notes, se reporter à la fin du tableau.

	1990	1995	1998	1999	2000	2001	2002	2003
				Dem. Rep. of the Congo - Rép. dém. du Congo				
Dépenses des touristes (millions de dollars)	7	5	2	..	..	..	..	..
Nuitées des touristes (milliers)	..	..	..	..	..	..	..	..
Arrivées des touristes (milliers)	55	35	53	80	103	..	..	..
Durée moyenne de séjour (jours)	5	15	..	..	..	..	..	..
				Denmark - Danemark				
Tourism expenditures (millions of dollars)	3322	3728	3313	3836	4038	4600	5785	..
Tourists' overnight stays (thousands)	9338	10790	10288	9966	10008	9748	..	..
Arrivals of tourists (thousands)	1838	2124	2073	2023	2088	2028	2010	2016
Average length of stay (days)	..	..	..	..	..	..	..	..
				Djibouti				
Dépenses des touristes (millions de dollars)	6	4	4	..	..	..	..	..
Nuitées des touristes (milliers)	..	..	..	..	..	..	..	..
Arrivées des touristes (milliers)	33	21	21	..	..	..	..	..
Durée moyenne de séjour (jours)	..	..	..	..	..	..	..	..
				Dominica - Dominique				
Tourism expenditures (millions of dollars)	20	34	47	51	48	46	46	51
Tourists' overnight stays (thousands)	..	..	..	..	..	..	..	..
Arrivals of tourists (thousands)	45	60	66	74	70	66	69	..
Average length of stay (days)	11	11	..	9	9	8	9	..
				Dominican Republic - République dominicaine				
Dépenses des touristes (millions de dollars)	900	1568	2153	2483	2860	2798	2736	3110
Nuitées des touristes (milliers)	..	..	..	..	..	..	..	..
Arrivées des touristes (milliers)	1305	1776	2309	2649	2978	2882	2811	3282
Durée moyenne de séjour (jours)	9	11	10	11	10	10	10	10
				Ecuador - Equateur				
Tourism expenditures (millions of dollars)	188	255	291	343	402	430	447	406
Tourists' overnight stays (thousands)	..	..	..	..	..	..	..	..
Arrivals of tourists (thousands)	362	440	511	518	627	641	683	760
Average length of stay (days)	..	..	..	..	..	..	..	..
				Egypt - Egypte				
Dépenses des touristes (millions de dollars)	1100	2684	2565	3903	4345	3800	3764	4584
Nuitées des touristes (milliers)	..	..	..	..	..	..	..	..
Arrivées des touristes (milliers)	2411	2871	3213	4490	5116	4357	4906	5746
Durée moyenne de séjour (jours)	8	7	6	7	6	6	6	9
				El Salvador				
Tourism expenditures (millions of dollars)	18	41	125	211	254	235	342	..
Tourists' overnight stays (thousands)	..	..	..	..	..	..	..	..
Arrivals of tourists (thousands)	194	235	542	658	795	735	951	..
Average length of stay (days)	..	2	3	4	4	4	4	..
				Equatorial Guinea - Guinée équatoriale				
Dépenses des touristes (millions de dollars)	1	1	0	10	5	14	..	..
Nuitées des touristes (milliers)	..	..	..	..	..	..	..	..
Arrivées des touristes (milliers)	..	..	..	..	..	..	..	..
Durée moyenne de séjour (jours)	..	..	..	..	..	..	..	..
				Eritrea - Erythrée				
Tourism expenditures (millions of dollars)	–	58	34	28	36	74	73	..
Tourists' overnight stays (thousands)	–	..	..	..	..	..	..	..
Arrivals of tourists (thousands)	–	315	188	57	70	113	101	80
Average length of stay (days)	–	..	22	24	17	24	28	..
				Estonia - Estonie				
Dépenses des touristes (millions de dollars)	–	353	534	560	506	507	555	682
Nuitées des touristes (milliers)	–	789	1185	1230	1598	1911	1998	2268
Arrivées des touristes (milliers)	–	530	825	950	1220	1320	1362	1462
Durée moyenne de séjour (jours)	–	5	6	6	5	6	5	5

For sources and notes, see end of table. Pour les sources et les notes, se reporter à la fin du tableau.

	1990	1995	1998	1999	2000	2001	2002	2003
				Ethiopia - Ethiopie				
Tourism expenditures (millions of dollars)	25	26	16	16	68	75	77	..
Tourists' overnight stays (thousands)	..	..	..	..	..	..	..	..
Arrivals of tourists (thousands)	79	103	112	115	136	148	156	..
Average length of stay (days)	..	..	..	..	..	5	..	..
				Fiji - Fidji				
Dépenses des touristes (millions de dollars)	202	283	244	282	181	217	261	349
Nuitées des touristes (milliers)	..	..	..	..	..	..	..	..
Arrivées des touristes (milliers)	279	318	371	410	294	348	398	431
Durée moyenne de séjour (jours)	..	..	9	8	9	9	9	9
				Finland - Finlande				
Tourism expenditures (millions of dollars)	1167	1570	1643	1528	1412	1441	1573	1873
Tourists' overnight stays (thousands)	2830	3292	3700	3774	4066	4183	4290	4331
Arrivals of tourists (thousands)	1572	1779	2644	2454	2714	2826	2875	2601
Average length of stay (days)	..	..	6	4	6	6	7	7
				France				
Dépenses des touristes (millions de dollars)	20184	27527	29931	31507	30754	29979	32329	36347
Nuitées des touristes (milliers)	387205	490877	518142	550018	585443	581037	588430	567006
Arrivées des touristes (milliers)	52497	60033	70109	73147	77190	75202	77012	75048
Durée moyenne de séjour (jours)	7	8	7	7	7	7	8	8
				French Guiana - Guyane française				
Tourism expenditures (millions of dollars)	..	..	51	50	..	42	45	..
Tourists' overnight stays (thousands)	..	..	..	..	..	..	..	..
Arrivals of tourists (thousands)	..	..	68	70	..	65	65	..
Average length of stay (days)	..	..	..	..	..	..	..	..
				French Polynesia - Polynésie française				
Dépenses des touristes (millions de dollars)	171	326	354	394	..	..	..	..
Nuitées des touristes (milliers)	1399	2067	2217	2493	..	2875	2592	2888
Arrivées des touristes (milliers)	132	172	189	211	252	228	189	213
Durée moyenne de séjour (jours)	11	12	12	12	12	13	14	14
				Gabon				
Tourism expenditures (millions of dollars)	3	17	23	15	..	17	..	..
Tourists' overnight stays (thousands)	..	..	..	..	..	..	..	..
Arrivals of tourists (thousands)	109	125	195	177	155	169	208	222
Average length of stay (days)	..	..	..	..	..	..	..	..
				Gambia - Gambie				
Dépenses des touristes (millions de dollars)	26	23	49	..	..	..	..	..
Nuitées des touristes (milliers)	..	..	..	..	..	..	..	..
Arrivées des touristes (milliers)	100	45	91	96	79	57	79	..
Durée moyenne de séjour (jours)	13	13	..	..	..	..	..	..
				Georgia - Géorgie				
Tourism expenditures (millions of dollars)	–	..	423	400	413	442	472	..
Tourists' overnight stays (thousands)	–	..	1585	2667	2730	2417	2387	..
Arrivals of tourists (thousands)	–	85	317	384	387	302	298	..
Average length of stay (days)	–	..	..	..	7	8	8	..
				Germany - Allemagne				
Dépenses des touristes (millions de dollars)	14288	17243	17911	17225	18479	18422	19158	22829
Nuitées des touristes (milliers)	39146	35481	37260	38655	42629	40798	40655	41746
Arrivées des touristes (milliers)	17045	14847	16511	17116	18983	17861	17969	18399
Durée moyenne de séjour (jours)	..	..	..	..	..	..	..	..
				Ghana				
Tourism expenditures (millions of dollars)	81	233	284	304	335	351	358	..
Tourists' overnight stays (thousands)	..	2906	3601	..	..	..	..	..
Arrivals of tourists (thousands)	146	286	348	373	399	439	483	..
Average length of stay (days)	..	10	10	10	..	..	..	..

For sources and notes, see end of table.　　　　　　　　　　　　　　Pour les sources et les notes, se reporter à la fin du tableau.

	1990	1995	1998	1999	2000	2001	2002	2003
				Greece - Grèce				
Dépenses des touristes (millions de dollars)	2587	4136	6188	8783	9221	9447	9703	10629
Nuitées des touristes (milliers)	..	..	..	..	..	..	..	..
Arrivées des touristes (milliers)	8873	10130	10916	12164	13096	14057	14180	..
Durée moyenne de séjour (jours)	..	..	..	..	..	..	..	..
				Grenada - Grenade				
Tourism expenditures (millions of dollars)	38	54	83	88	93	83	91	104
Tourists' overnight stays (thousands)	..	..	..	..	626	..	..	..
Arrivals of tourists (thousands)	76	108	116	125	129	123	132	142
Average length of stay (days)	..	..	7	7	7	7	..	..
				Guadeloupe				
Dépenses des touristes (millions de dollars)	197	458	466	375	418	..	..	..
Nuitées des touristes (milliers)	2016	3840	4158	..	..	..	..	..
Arrivées des touristes (milliers)	331	640	580	561	603	521	..	..
Durée moyenne de séjour (jours)	..	..	..	..	..	..	..	..
				Guam				
Tourism expenditures (millions of dollars)	936	1275	2361	1908	..	..	..	..
Tourists' overnight stays (thousands)	..	..	..	..	..	..	..	..
Arrivals of tourists (thousands)	780	1362	1137	1162	1287	1160	1059	910
Average length of stay (days)	..	..	..	..	..	..	..	..
				Guatemala				
Dépenses des touristes (millions de dollars)	185	277	323	399	535	493	612	599
Nuitées des touristes (milliers)	3201	3674	..	..	..	..	..	..
Arrivées des touristes (milliers)	509	563	636	823	826	835	884	880
Durée moyenne de séjour (jours)	6	7	..	..	..	..	..	..
				Guinea - Guinée				
Tourism expenditures (millions of dollars)	30	1	1	7	12	14	43	..
Tourists' overnight stays (thousands)	..	..	..	..	698	526	600	928
Arrivals of tourists (thousands)	..	..	23	27	33	38	43	44
Average length of stay (days)	..	..	..	..	3	3	3	..
				Guyana				
Dépenses des touristes (millions de dollars)	27	33	108	106	75	61	49	..
Nuitées des touristes (milliers)	..	..	..	..	..	..	..	..
Arrivées des touristes (milliers)	64	106	66	75	105	99	104	..
Durée moyenne de séjour (jours)	..	..	19	..	..	..	..	..
				Haiti - Haïti				
Tourism expenditures (millions of dollars)	46	56	56	55	54	54	..	..
Tourists' overnight stays (thousands)	1150	968	..	..	..	..	..	..
Arrivals of tourists (thousands)	144	145	147	143	140	142	..	..
Average length of stay (days)	..	..	..	..	..	..	..	..
				Honduras				
Dépenses des touristes (millions de dollars)	29	107	168	195	260	275	342	..
Nuitées des touristes (milliers)	..	..	..	..	..	..	..	..
Arrivées des touristes (milliers)	290	271	321	371	471	518	550	..
Durée moyenne de séjour (jours)	..	..	8	9	10	11	11	..
				Hungary - Hongrie				
Tourism expenditures (millions of dollars)	824	2929	3644	3563	3445	3770	3273	..
Tourists' overnight stays (thousands)	13618	9998	10138	9943	10514	10894	10361	..
Arrivals of tourists (thousands)	3693	2878	2871	2789	2992	3070	3013	..
Average length of stay (days)	..	6	..	..	..	..	..	..
				Iceland - Islande				
Dépenses des touristes (millions de dollars)	139	186	206	223	228	235	250	319
Nuitées des touristes (milliers)	..	815	1017	1102	1142	1184	1257	1377
Arrivées des touristes (milliers)	142	190	565	601	634	672	705	771
Durée moyenne de séjour (jours)	..	..	..	..	..	..	..	..

For sources and notes, see end of table.   Pour les sources et les notes, se reporter à la fin du tableau.

	1990	1995	1998	1999	2000	2001	2002	2003
India - Inde								
Tourism expenditures (millions of dollars)	1513	2583	2948	3009	3168	3042	2923	..
Tourists' overnight stays (thousands)	..	..	..	..	..	..	..	..
Arrivals of tourists (thousands)	1707	2124	2359	2482	2649	2537	2384	2750
Average length of stay (days)	29	30	31	..	..	..	..	..
Indonesia - Indonésie								
Dépenses des touristes (millions de dollars)	2105	5229	4331	4710	5749	5396	4306	..
Nuitées des touristes (milliers)	..	44151	42287	49686	62087	54062	..	..
Arrivées des touristes (milliers)	2178	4324	4606	4728	5064	5154	5033	4467
Durée moyenne de séjour (jours)	12	10	9	11	12	10	10	..
Iran, Islamic Rep. of - Iran, Rép. islamique d'								
Tourism expenditures (millions of dollars)	61	205	490	403	467	891	1249	..
Tourists' overnight stays (thousands)	..	..	..	..	..	..	..	..
Arrivals of tourists (thousands)	154	489	1008	1321	1342	1402	1585	..
Average length of stay (days)	..	..	5	5	5	5	5	..
Iraq								
Dépenses des touristes (millions de dollars)	55	13	13	..	..	..	..	..
Nuitées des touristes (milliers)	..	..	..	..	..	..	..	..
Arrivées des touristes (milliers)	748	61	45	30	78	127	..	..
Durée moyenne de séjour (jours)	..	..	..	..	..	..	..	..
Ireland - Irlande								
Tourism expenditures (millions of dollars)	1459	2211	3247	3320	3359	3513	3768	..
Tourists' overnight stays (thousands)	36183	13902	18326	18861	21516	18332	17677	..
Arrivals of tourists (thousands)	3666	4818	6064	6403	6646	6353	6476	..
Average length of stay (days)	10	8	8	7	7	8	7	..
Israel - Israël								
Dépenses des touristes (millions de dollars)	1396	2964	2808	3659	3338	1570	1197	..
Nuitées des touristes (milliers)	6167	10084	9385	9598	10352	4637	2745	..
Arrivées des touristes (milliers)	1063	2215	1942	2312	2417	1196	862	1063
Durée moyenne de séjour (jours)	18	16	16	15	15	22	22	..
Italy - Italie								
Tourism expenditures (millions of dollars)	16458	28729	29866	28359	27500	25796	26915	31286
Tourists' overnight stays (thousands)	84720	113001	121242	126668	140357	146672	145560	138941
Arrivals of tourists (thousands)	26679	31052	34933	36516	41181	39563	39799	39604
Average length of stay (days)	..	..	..	..	..	..	..	..
Jamaica - Jamaïque								
Dépenses des touristes (millions de dollars)	740	1069	1197	1280	1333	1233	1209	1336
Nuitées des touristes (milliers)	9194	11107	12354	11816	12327	12109	12038	12844
Arrivées des touristes (milliers)	989	1147	1225	1248	1323	1277	1266	1350
Durée moyenne de séjour (jours)	11	11	11	10	10	10	10	..
Japan - Japon								
Tourism expenditures (millions of dollars)	3578	3226	3742	3428	3373	3301	3499	8846
Tourists' overnight stays (thousands)	..	..	..	..	..	..	..	..
Arrivals of tourists (thousands)	3236	3345	4106	4438	4757	4772	5239	5212
Average length of stay (days)	13	9	9	8	8	9	8	9
Jordan - Jordanie								
Dépenses des touristes (millions de dollars)	512	652	773	795	722	700	786	815
Nuitées des touristes (milliers)	..	..	..	..	..	..	..	..
Arrivées des touristes (milliers)	572	1074	1256	1358	1427	1478	1622	1573
Durée moyenne de séjour (jours)	5	4	4	4	4	5	4	4
Kazakhstan								
Tourism expenditures (millions of dollars)	–	122	407	363	356	396	621	564
Tourists' overnight stays (thousands)	–	..	..	..	..	..	..	..
Arrivals of tourists (thousands)	–	..	..	..	1471	1845	2832	..
Average length of stay (days)	–	..	..	..	..	..	..	..

For sources and notes, see end of table.

Pour les sources et les notes, se reporter à la fin du tableau.

	1990	1995	1998	1999	2000	2001	2002	2003
Kenya								
Dépenses des touristes (millions de dollars)	443	486	290	304	276	308	297	..
Nuitées des touristes (milliers)	..	..	..	..	..	..	..	..
Arrivées des touristes (milliers)	814	896	792	862	899	841	838	..
Durée moyenne de séjour (jours)	..	..	..	..	..	..	..	..
Kiribati								
Tourism expenditures (millions of dollars)	1	2	3	3	3	3	..	..
Tourists' overnight stays (thousands)	..	..	..	..	..	..	..	..
Arrivals of tourists (thousands)	3	4	6	5	5	5	5	..
Average length of stay (days)	..	..	..	..	..	..	..	..
Korea, Dem. People's Rep. of - Corée, Rép. populaire dém. de								
Dépenses des touristes (millions de dollars)	..	..	..	..	..	..	..	..
Nuitées des touristes (milliers)	..	..	..	..	..	..	..	..
Arrivées des touristes (milliers)	115	128	130	..	..	..	..	..
Durée moyenne de séjour (jours)	..	..	..	..	..	..	..	..
Korea, Republic of - Corée, République de								
Tourism expenditures (millions of dollars)	3559	5587	6865	6802	6811	6373	5919	5241
Tourists' overnight stays (thousands)	9952	8768	..	..	..	..	..	..
Arrivals of tourists (thousands)	2959	3753	4250	4660	5322	5147	5347	4754
Average length of stay (days)	6	5	5	5	5	5	5	6
Kuwait - Koweït								
Dépenses des touristes (millions de dollars)	132	121	207	92	98	104	119	..
Nuitées des touristes (milliers)	..	..	..	..	..	..	..	..
Arrivées des touristes (milliers)	15	72	77	84	78	73	..	..
Durée moyenne de séjour (jours)	..	..	..	4	3	..	..	..
Kyrgyzstan - Kirghizistan								
Tourism expenditures (millions of dollars)	–	5	8	14	15	24	36	..
Tourists' overnight stays (thousands)	..	..	..	..	..	..	..	..
Arrivals of tourists (thousands)	–	36	59	48	59	99	140	..
Average length of stay (days)	–	..	..	..	..	..	..	..
Lao People's Dem. Rep. - Rép. dém. populaire lao								
Dépenses des touristes (millions de dollars)	3	25	80	97	114	104	113	..
Nuitées des touristes (milliers)	..	..	..	..	..	..	..	..
Arrivées des touristes (milliers)	14	60	200	259	191	173	215	..
Durée moyenne de séjour (jours)	..	4	5	6	6	8	..	..
Latvia - Lettonie								
Tourism expenditures (millions of dollars)	–	20	182	117	131	120	161	222
Tourists' overnight stays (thousands)	–	668	733	724	697	847	871	983
Arrivals of tourists (thousands)	–	539	576	544	509	591	848	971
Average length of stay (days)	–	..	6	6	6	6	5	4
Lebanon - Liban								
Dépenses des touristes (millions de dollars)	..	710	1221	673	742	837	956	..
Nuitées des touristes (milliers)	..	..	..	..	..	..	..	..
Arrivées des touristes (milliers)	..	450	631	673	742	837	956	..
Durée moyenne de séjour (jours)	..	..	..	4	3	3	3	..
Lesotho								
Tourism expenditures (millions of dollars)	17	27	24	23	24	23	20	..
Tourists' overnight stays (thousands)	359	..	336	417	..	..	..	..
Arrivals of tourists (thousands)	171	87	150	186	63	38	124	..
Average length of stay (days)	..	..	..	..	..	..	..	..
Libyan Arab Jamahiriya - Jamahiriya arabe libyenne								
Dépenses des touristes (millions de dollars)	6	6	18	28	97	94	75	79
Nuitées des touristes (milliers)	..	..	269	339	..	..	..	..
Arrivées des touristes (milliers)	96	56	32	178	174	169	135	142
Durée moyenne de séjour (jours)	..	..	7	7	7	7	7	7

For sources and notes, see end of table.

Pour les sources et les notes, se reporter à la fin du tableau.

	1990	1995	1998	1999	2000	2001	2002	2003
				Liechtenstein				
Tourism expenditures (millions of dollars)	..	..	..	..	..	..	..	..
Tourists' overnight stays (thousands)	..	..	..	..	..	..	..	..
Arrivals of tourists (thousands)	78	59	59	60	62	56	49	49
Average length of stay (days)	2	2	2	2	2	2	2	2
				Lithuania - Lituanie				
Dépenses des touristes (millions de dollars)	–	77	460	550	391	383	513	568
Nuitées des touristes (milliers)	–	762	1034	998	966	1073	1149	1170
Arrivées des touristes (milliers)	–	650	1416	1422	1083	1271	1428	1491
Durée moyenne de séjour (jours)	–	9	9	9	6	7	7	10
				Luxembourg				
Tourism expenditures (millions of dollars)	..	1721	1763	1817	1794	1909	2179	2779
Tourists' overnight stays (thousands)	2430	2378	2327	2500	2405	2422	2469	2541
Arrivals of tourists (thousands)	820	768	789	863	852	836	885	867
Average length of stay (days)	..	..	3	3	3	3	3	3
				Macedonia, TFYR - Macédoine, LERY				
Dépenses des touristes (millions de dollars)	–	19	15	37	37	25	39	57
Nuitées des touristes (milliers)	–	276	360	474	494	213	275	346
Arrivées des touristes (milliers)	–	147	157	181	224	99	123	158
Durée moyenne de séjour (jours)	–	..	..	..	..	..	..	..
				Madagascar				
Tourism expenditures (millions of dollars)	40	58	92	100	121	115	36	..
Tourists' overnight stays (thousands)	..	..	..	..	..	..	..	..
Arrivals of tourists (thousands)	53	75	121	138	160	170	62	..
Average length of stay (days)	12	17	20	20	20	20	9	..
				Malawi				
Dépenses des touristes (millions de dollars)	16	9	15	20	27	28	69	72
Nuitées des touristes (milliers)	1178	1345	1236	1013	1325	2029	2893	3259
Arrivées des touristes (milliers)	130	192	220	254	228	266	383	421
Durée moyenne de séjour (jours)	9	8	8	8	7	..	8	8
				Malaysia - Malaisie				
Tourism expenditures (millions of dollars)	1667	3909	2189	3242	4562	6374	6785	..
Tourists' overnight stays (thousands)	..	..	..	..	..	..	..	..
Arrivals of tourists (thousands)	7446	7469	5551	7931	10222	12775	13292	10577
Average length of stay (days)	5	5	6	6	6	6	..	..
				Maldives				
Dépenses des touristes (millions de dollars)	89	211	303	314	321	327	318	388
Nuitées des touristes (milliers)	..	..	..	..	..	..	..	..
Arrivées des touristes (milliers)	195	315	396	430	467	461	485	564
Durée moyenne de séjour (jours)	..	..	..	..	..	..	..	..
				Mali				
Tourism expenditures (millions of dollars)	47	25	89	77	71	..	..	..
Tourists' overnight stays (thousands)	..	..	..	..	..	..	..	..
Arrivals of tourists (thousands)	44	42	83	82	86	89	96	70
Average length of stay (days)	..	..	..	..	..	..	..	..
				Malta - Malte				
Dépenses des touristes (millions de dollars)	496	659	656	679	614	579	568	..
Nuitées des touristes (milliers)	9604	10919	11326	11658	10266	11067	10599	..
Arrivées des touristes (milliers)	872	1116	1182	1214	1216	1180	1134	..
Durée moyenne de séjour (jours)	9	10	10	10	8	9	..	..
				Marshall Islands - Iles Marshall				
Tourism expenditures (millions of dollars)	..	3	3	4	4	4	4	..
Tourists' overnight stays (thousands)	..	..	..	..	..	..	..	..
Arrivals of tourists (thousands)	5	6	6	5	5	5	6	7
Average length of stay (days)	..	5	..	..	..	..	..	..

For sources and notes, see end of table.   Pour les sources et les notes, se reporter à la fin du tableau.

	1990	1995	1998	1999	2000	2001	2002	2003
Martinique								
Dépenses des touristes (millions de dollars)	240	384	415	404	302	245	237	..
Nuitées des touristes (milliers)	4290	6970	8133	7497	6956	5556	6022	..
Arrivées des touristes (milliers)	282	457	549	564	526	460	447	..
Durée moyenne de séjour (jours)	15	15	14	13	13	12	14	..
Mauritania - Mauritanie								
Tourism expenditures (millions of dollars)	9	11	20	28	..	..	..	..
Tourists' overnight stays (thousands)	..	..	..	..	..	..	..	..
Arrivals of tourists (thousands)	..	..	..	24	30	..	..	..
Average length of stay (days)	..	..	..	..	5	..	..	..
Mauritius - Maurice								
Dépenses des touristes (millions de dollars)	244	430	503	543	542	624	612	695
Nuitées des touristes (milliers)	..	..	..	..	..	..	..	..
Arrivées des touristes (milliers)	292	422	558	578	656	660	682	702
Durée moyenne de séjour (jours)	12	11	10	10	10	10	11	..
Mexico - Mexique								
Tourism expenditures (millions of dollars)	5467	6179	7493	7223	8295	8401	8858	9457
Tourists' overnight stays (thousands)	..	..	..	..	..	..	..	..
Arrivals of tourists (thousands)	17176	20241	19392	19043	20641	19810	19667	18665
Average length of stay (days)	11	11	10	10	10	10	10	10
Micronesia, Federated States of - Micronésie, Etats fédérés de								
Dépenses des touristes (millions de dollars)	..	..	11	12	15	13	..	..
Nuitées des touristes (milliers)	..	..	..	..	..	..	..	..
Arrivées des touristes (milliers)	..	..	13	16	21	15	19	..
Durée moyenne de séjour (jours)	..	..	..	..	..	..	..	..
Moldova, Republic of - Moldova, République de								
Tourism expenditures (millions of dollars)	–	57	40	34	39	37	47	58
Tourists' overnight stays (thousands)	–	..	..	..	..	..	..	..
Arrivals of tourists (thousands)	–	32	19	14	18	16	18	21
Average length of stay (days)	–	..	..	..	..	..	..	..
Monaco								
Dépenses des touristes (millions de dollars)	..	..	..	..	..	..	..	..
Nuitées des touristes (milliers)	..	..	..	..	..	..	..	..
Arrivées des touristes (milliers)	245	233	278	278	300	270	263	..
Durée moyenne de séjour (jours)	..	..	..	..	..	..	..	..
Mongolia - Mongolie								
Tourism expenditures (millions of dollars)	5	21	32	28	27	103	167	149
Tourists' overnight stays (thousands)	..	..	..	..	..	..	..	..
Arrivals of tourists (thousands)	147	108	165	138	137	166	229	201
Average length of stay (days)	..	..	..	..	..	..	..	..
Montserrat								
Dépenses des touristes (millions de dollars)	7	20	6	8	9	8	9	7
Nuitées des touristes (milliers)	..	..	..	..	..	..	..	..
Arrivées des touristes (milliers)	13	19	7	10	10	10	10	..
Durée moyenne de séjour (jours)	..	..	..	..	..	..	..	..
Morocco - Maroc								
Tourism expenditures (millions of dollars)	1259	1304	1712	1880	2039	2583	2646	2846
Tourists' overnight stays (thousands)	18720	18436	21021	22486	21152	20349	18478	18190
Arrivals of tourists (thousands)	4024	2602	3095	3817	4240	4342	4303	4552
Average length of stay (days)	9	12	10	10	9	9	8	8
Mozambique								
Dépenses des touristes (millions de dollars)	..	..	146	156	186	134	144	..
Nuitées des touristes (milliers)	..	..	..	..	..	..	..	..
Arrivées des touristes (milliers)	..	..	..	..	..	..	943	..
Durée moyenne de séjour (jours)	..	..	..	..	..	..	..	..

For sources and notes, see end of table.

Pour les sources et les notes, se reporter à la fin du tableau.

	1990	1995	1998	1999	2000	2001	2002	2003
				Myanmar				
Tourism expenditures (millions of dollars)	9	38	35	35	42	45	..	..
Tourists' overnight stays (thousands)	..	..	..	..	..	..	..	..
Arrivals of tourists (thousands)	21	117	201	198	208	205	217	206
Average length of stay (days)	7	7	7	7	7	7	7	..
				Namibia - Namibie				
Dépenses des touristes (millions de dollars)	85	278	288	287	208	197	219	..
Nuitées des touristes (milliers)	..	700	925	650	619	800	1006	..
Arrivées des touristes (milliers)	..	399	614	..	..	670	757	844
Durée moyenne de séjour (jours)	..	..	..	..	..	18	19	..
				Nepal - Népal				
Tourism expenditures (millions of dollars)	64	117	153	168	167	140	107	..
Tourists' overnight stays (thousands)	..	..	..	..	..	..	..	..
Arrivals of tourists (thousands)	255	363	464	492	464	361	275	..
Average length of stay (days)	12	11	11	12	12	12	8	..
				Netherlands - Pays-Bas				
Dépenses des touristes (millions de dollars)	4155	6252	6850	6996	7217	6723	7706	9228
Nuitées des touristes (milliers)	16459	19741	24967	27433	27261	25502	26368	25342
Arrivées des touristes (milliers)	5795	6574	9312	9874	10003	9500	9595	9181
Durée moyenne de séjour (jours)	..	..	3	3	3	3	3	3
				New Caledonia - Nouvelle-Calédonie				
Tourism expenditures (millions of dollars)	94	108	110	112	110	93	..	..
Tourists' overnight stays (thousands)	..	..	..	..	..	..	..	..
Arrivals of tourists (thousands)	87	86	104	100	110	101	104	102
Average length of stay (days)	..	18	16	16	16	14	16	16
				New Zealand - Nouvelle-Zélande				
Dépenses des touristes (millions de dollars)	1030	1488	1835	2237	2249	2336	2933	3806
Nuitées des touristes (milliers)	20654	..	7470	8230	9115	10452	11625	11683
Arrivées des touristes (milliers)	976	1409	1485	1607	1787	1909	2045	2104
Durée moyenne de séjour (jours)	21	19	20	20	20	21	22	22
				Nicaragua				
Tourism expenditures (millions of dollars)	12	50	90	107	111	109	116	152
Tourists' overnight stays (thousands)	88	210	335	301	375	339	423	412
Arrivals of tourists (thousands)	106	281	406	468	486	483	472	526
Average length of stay (days)	..	..	..	3	3	3	3	4
				Niger				
Dépenses des touristes (millions de dollars)	17	15	25	26	28	32	28	..
Nuitées des touristes (milliers)	105	200	198	208	215	218	199	..
Arrivées des touristes (milliers)	21	35	42	44	50	53	58	..
Durée moyenne de séjour (jours)	13	16	10	10	7	7	7	..
				Nigeria - Nigéria				
Tourism expenditures (millions of dollars)	25	54	142	171	200	232	263	..
Tourists' overnight stays (thousands)	..	..	..	..	..	..	..	..
Arrivals of tourists (thousands)	190	656	739	776	813	850	887	..
Average length of stay (days)	..	..	..	..	..	..	..	..
				Niue - Nioué				
Dépenses des touristes (millions de dollars)	..	2	1	..	..	..	..	..
Nuitées des touristes (milliers)	..	..	..	..	..	..	..	..
Arrivées des touristes (milliers)	1	2	2	2	2	1	2	3
Durée moyenne de séjour (jours)	..	..	..	..	..	..	..	..
				Northern Mariana Islands - Iles Mariannes du Nord				
Tourism expenditures (millions of dollars)	455	655	647	..	..	..	..	..
Tourists' overnight stays (thousands)	..	..	..	..	..	..	..	..
Arrivals of tourists (thousands)	426	669	481	493	517	438	466	452
Average length of stay (days)	..	..	..	..	..	..	..	..

For sources and notes, see end of table.

Pour les sources et les notes, se reporter à la fin du tableau.

	1990	1995	1998	1999	2000	2001	2002	2003
Norway - Norvège								
Dépenses des touristes (millions de dollars)	1570	2362	2230	2335	1992	1961	2161	2548
Nuitées des touristes (milliers)	5840	7060	7869	7815	7469	7322	7275	6956
Arrivées des touristes (milliers)	1955	2880	3256	3223	3104	3073	3111	3146
Durée moyenne de séjour (jours)	..	..	..	..	..	..	..	..
Oman								
Tourism expenditures (millions of dollars)	69	92	208	208	224	145	208	..
Tourists' overnight stays (thousands)	..	..	..	..	..	3815	3965	..
Arrivals of tourists (thousands)	149	279	424	503	571	829	817	..
Average length of stay (days)	..	..	..	..	..	5	5	..
Pakistan								
Dépenses des touristes (millions de dollars)	156	114	69	76	85	100	92	136
Nuitées des touristes (milliers)	..	..	..	..	..	..	..	..
Arrivées des touristes (milliers)	424	378	429	432	557	500	498	479
Durée moyenne de séjour (jours)	30	30	30	25	25	25	25	25
Palau - Palaos								
Tourism expenditures (millions of dollars)	..	..	58	54	53	59	59	..
Tourists' overnight stays (thousands)	..	..	..	..	..	..	..	..
Arrivals of tourists (thousands)	33	53	64	55	58	54	59	68
Average length of stay (days)	..	..	..	..	..	..	..	..
Palestinian territory - Territoire palestinien								
Dépenses des touristes (millions de dollars)	..	..	114	132	155	9	..	..
Nuitées des touristes (milliers)	..	..	675	907	1106	217	204	239
Arrivées des touristes (milliers)	..	..	201	271	330	7	..	..
Durée moyenne de séjour (jours)	..	..	3	3	4	3	3	3
Panama								
Tourism expenditures (millions of dollars)	179	367	494	538	576	626	679	805
Tourists' overnight stays (thousands)	..	..	..	..	..	..	..	..
Arrivals of tourists (thousands)	214	345	431	457	484	519	534	566
Average length of stay (days)	10	10	11	10	10	11	10	11
Papua New Guinea - Papouasie-Nouvelle-Guinée								
Dépenses des touristes (millions de dollars)	41	60	75	76	92	101	..	..
Nuitées des touristes (milliers)	..	..	..	..	..	..	..	..
Arrivées des touristes (milliers)	41	42	67	67	58	54	54	56
Durée moyenne de séjour (jours)	..	..	..	8	10	9	..	..
Paraguay								
Tourism expenditures (millions of dollars)	128	137	111	81	73	69	62	..
Tourists' overnight stays (thousands)	..	..	..	..	..	..	..	..
Arrivals of tourists (thousands)	280	438	350	269	289	279	250	..
Average length of stay (days)	4	3	4	4	2	2	..	..
Peru - Pérou								
Dépenses des touristes (millions de dollars)	217	428	845	890	911	788	801	832
Nuitées des touristes (milliers)	..	..	..	..	..	..	..	..
Arrivées des touristes (milliers)	317	444	723	691	796	797	862	931
Durée moyenne de séjour (jours)	13	17	9	10	10	10	11	..
Philippines								
Tourism expenditures (millions of dollars)	1306	2454	2413	2531	2134	1723	1741	1523
Tourists' overnight stays (thousands)	..	..	..	..	..	..	..	..
Arrivals of tourists (thousands)	1025	1760	2149	2171	1992	1797	1933	1907
Average length of stay (days)	12	10	9	9	9	10	9	9
Poland - Pologne								
Dépenses des touristes (millions de dollars)	358	6614	7946	6100	6100	4815	4500	4100
Nuitées des touristes (milliers)	5350	5480	7230	7182	6891	6991	7085	7828
Arrivées des touristes (milliers)	3400	19215	18780	17950	17400	15000	13980	13720
Durée moyenne de séjour (jours)	..	5	5	5	5	..	..	..

For sources and notes, see end of table.

Pour les sources et les notes, se reporter à la fin du tableau.

	1990	1995	1998	1999	2000	2001	2002	2003
Portugal								
Tourism expenditures (millions of dollars)	3555	4339	5302	5261	5282	5485	5720	6927
Tourists' overnight stays (thousands)	19349	22241	25273	25080	25785	25229	24574	24369
Arrivals of tourists (thousands)	8020	9511	11295	11632	12097	12167	11644	..
Average length of stay (days)	7	7	7	7	7	7	5	5
Puerto Rico - Porto Rico								
Dépenses des touristes (millions de dollars)	1366	1828	2233	2139	2388	2728	2486	2677
Nuitées des touristes (milliers)	..	..	..	..	..	..	..	..
Arrivées des touristes (milliers)	2560	3131	3396	3024	3341	3551	3087	3238
Durée moyenne de séjour (jours)	..	..	..	..	..	..	..	..
Qatar								
Tourism expenditures (millions of dollars)	..	..	..	..	..	..	..	..
Tourists' overnight stays (thousands)	795	427	403	..	..	..	..	..
Arrivals of tourists (thousands)	136	294	46	51	67	76	..	..
Average length of stay (days)	..	..	..	..	..	..	..	..
Reunion - Réunion								
Dépenses des touristes (millions de dollars)	..	216	271	259	255	244	284	351
Nuitées des touristes (milliers)	..	..	..	..	..	..	..	..
Arrivées des touristes (milliers)	200	304	400	394	430	424	426	432
Durée moyenne de séjour (jours)	17	16	16	16	16	16	16	17
Romania - Roumanie								
Tourism expenditures (millions of dollars)	106	590	260	254	359	500	612	..
Tourists' overnight stays (thousands)	4238	2381	2207	1981	2149	2391	2534	..
Arrivals of tourists (thousands)	3009	2757	2966	3209	3274	3300	3204	..
Average length of stay (days)	..	..	3	2	2	3	3	..
Russian Federation - Fédération de Russie								
Dépenses des touristes (millions de dollars)	–	4312	6508	3723	3429	3572	4167	4502
Nuitées des touristes (milliers)	–	..	..	..	..	..	..	..
Arrivées des touristes (milliers)	–	10290	16188	18820	7030	7400	7943	..
Durée moyenne de séjour (jours)	–	..	..	..	..	..	..	..
Rwanda								
Tourism expenditures (millions of dollars)	10	2	19	17	23	25	31	..
Tourists' overnight stays (thousands)	..	..	..	..	..	..	..	..
Arrivals of tourists (thousands)	..	..	..	..	104	113	..	..
Average length of stay (days)	..	..	..	..	..	..	..	..
Saint Kitts and Nevis - Saint-Kitts-et-Nevis								
Dépenses des touristes (millions de dollars)	58	65	76	68	58	62	56	61
Nuitées des touristes (milliers)	..	..	..	..	..	..	..	..
Arrivées des touristes (milliers)	73	79	93	84	73	71	68	..
Durée moyenne de séjour (jours)	9	9	9	9	..	..	..	..
Saint Lucia - Sainte-Lucie								
Tourism expenditures (millions of dollars)	154	268	291	311	279	233	210	282
Tourists' overnight stays (thousands)	..	..	..	..	..	..	..	..
Arrivals of tourists (thousands)	141	231	252	264	270	250	253	277
Average length of stay (days)	..	..	..	..	..	..	..	..
Saint Vincent and the Grenadines - Saint-Vincent-et-les Grenadines								
Dépenses des touristes (millions de dollars)	56	41	73	76	75	80	83	85
Nuitées des touristes (milliers)	..	..	..	..	..	..	33	..
Arrivées des touristes (milliers)	54	60	67	68	73	71	78	79
Durée moyenne de séjour (jours)	10	12	11	11	..	..	12	7
Samoa								
Tourism sexpenditures (millions of dollars)	20	34	39	42	41	40	45	53
Tourists' overnight stays (thousands)	..	..	..	..	..	..	..	..
Arrivals of tourists (thousands)	48	68	78	85	88	88	89	92
Average length of stay (days)	..	..	..	..	..	..	..	..

For sources and notes, see end of table.

Pour les sources et les notes, se reporter à la fin du tableau.

	1990	1995	1998	1999	2000	2001	2002	2003
Sao Tome and Principe - Sao Tomé-et-Principe								
Dépenses des touristes (millions de dollars)	2	2	4	9	10	10	10	..
Nuitées des touristes (milliers)	..	..	..	..	..	..	..	..
Arrivées des touristes (milliers)	4	6	6	6	7	8	..	..
Durée moyenne de séjour (jours)	..	..	..	..	..	..	..	..
Saudi Arabia - Arabie saoudite								
Tourism expenditures (millions of dollars)	1884	..	..	..	..	3420	3420	..
Tourists' overnight stays (thousands)	..	..	..	..	..	..	..	..
Arrivals of tourists (thousands)	2209	3325	..	..	6585	6727	7511	7332
Average length of stay (days)	..	..	..	..	..	..	..	..
Senegal - Sénégal								
Dépenses des touristes (millions de dollars)	167	161	178	166	140	172	181	184
Nuitées des touristes (milliers)	1068	1139	1449	1469	1401	1499	1569	1451
Arrivées des touristes (milliers)	246	280	352	369	389	396	427	354
Durée moyenne de séjour (jours)	..	..	..	4	4	4	4	4
Serbia and Montenegro - Serbie-et-Monténégro								
Tourism expenditures (millions of dollars)	–	42	40	18	28	43	77	..
Tourists' overnight stays (thousands)	–	776	990	498	865	1281	1650	1707
Arrivals of tourists (thousands)	–	228	283	152	239	351	448	481
Average length of stay (days)	–	..	..	..	..	..	..	..
Seychelles								
Dépenses des touristes (millions de dollars)	126	98	111	112	105	111	129	126
Nuitées des touristes (milliers)	1048	1147	..	..	..	..	..	..
Arrivées des touristes (milliers)	104	121	128	125	130	130	132	122
Durée moyenne de séjour (jours)	10	10	11	10	10	10	10	10
Sierra Leone								
Tourism expenditures (millions of dollars)	19	6	14	4	22	29	33	52
Tourists' overnight stays (thousands)	..	..	..	..	..	..	..	..
Arrivals of tourists (thousands)	98	38	13	11	16	24	28	37
Average length of stay (days)	..	..	15	3	13	11	10	16
Singapore - Singapour								
Dépenses des touristes (millions de dollars)	4937	7646	4596	5073	5202	4586	4381	..
Nuitées des touristes (milliers)	..	..	..	..	..	..	..	..
Arrivées des touristes (milliers)	4842	6422	5631	6258	6917	6725	6997	5705
Durée moyenne de séjour (jours)	3	4	3	3	3	3	3	3
Slovakia - Slovaquie								
Tourism expenditures (millions of dollars)	–	620	489	461	432	639	724	863
Tourists' overnight stays (thousands)	–	3069	3311	3524	3743	4378	5043	4964
Arrivals of tourists (thousands)	–	903	896	975	1053	1219	1399	1387
Average length of stay (days)	–	..	4	4	4	4	4	4
Slovenia - Slovénie								
Dépenses des touristes (millions de dollars)	–	1084	1088	958	961	987	1086	1338
Nuitées des touristes (milliers)	–	2322	2934	2627	3277	3653	3847	4175
Arrivées des touristes (milliers)	–	732	977	884	1090	1219	1302	1373
Durée moyenne de séjour (jours)	–	..	3	3	3	3	3	3
Solomon Islands - Iles Salomon								
Tourism expenditures (millions of dollars)	7	16	7	6	4	5	1	..
Tourists' overnight stays (thousands)	..	..	..	..	..	..	..	..
Arrivals of tourists (thousands)	9	12	13	21	..	..	..	..
Average length of stay (days)	..	..	..	..	..	..	..	..
South Africa - Afrique du Sud								
Dépenses des touristes (millions de dollars)	992	2126	2717	2637	2513	2428	2728	..
Nuitées des touristes (milliers)	..	..	..	..	..	..	..	..
Arrivées des touristes (milliers)	1029	4488	5732	5890	5872	5787	6430	6505
Durée moyenne de séjour (jours)	..	..	..	..	..	..	..	..

For sources and notes, see end of table. Pour les sources et les notes, se reporter à la fin du tableau.

	1990	1995	1998	1999	2000	2001	2002	2003
				Spain - Espagne				
Tourism expenditures (millions of dollars)	18593	25388	29839	32497	31454	32873	33609	41708
Tourists' overnight stays (thousands)	68630	107787	122486	160424	233897	232035	220707	218756
Arrivals of tourists (thousands)	34085	34920	43396	46776	47898	50094	52327	52478
Average length of stay (days)	11	12	13	..	..	..	..	..
				Sri Lanka				
Dépenses des touristes (millions de dollars)	132	225	231	275	253	211	253	340
Nuitées des touristes (milliers)	3225	4024	3944	4479	4056	3342	3989	5093
Arrivées des touristes (milliers)	298	403	381	436	400	337	393	501
Durée moyenne de séjour (jours)	11	10	10	10	10	10	10	10
				Sudan - Soudan				
Tourism expenditures (millions of dollars)	21	19	21	22	30	56	62	..
Tourists' overnight stays (thousands)	..	..	..	..	..	..	..	..
Arrivals of tourists (thousands)	33	29	38	39	38	50	55	..
Average length of stay (days)	..	..	..	..	..	..	..	..
				Suriname				
Dépenses des touristes (millions de dollars)	11	21	2	9	16	14	3	..
Nuitées des touristes (milliers)	..	..	..	..	..	..	..	..
Arrivées des touristes (milliers)	46	43	55	63	58	..	..	..
Durée moyenne de séjour (jours)	..	..	..	..	..	..	..	..
				Swaziland				
Tourism expenditures (millions of dollars)	30	48	47	34	37	29	26	..
Tourists' overnight stays (thousands)	..	..	..	..	..	..	..	..
Arrivals of tourists (thousands)	263	300	284	289	281	283	256	..
Average length of stay (days)	..	..	1	1	1	1	1	..
				Sweden - Suède				
Dépenses des touristes (millions de dollars)	2906	3434	4124	4151	4079	4275	4701	5290
Nuitées des touristes (milliers)	6575	7861	8029	8601	8654	9133	9768	9715
Arrivées des touristes (milliers)	1900	2310	2573	2595	2746	7431	7458	7450
Durée moyenne de séjour (jours)	..	..	..	..	..	..	..	..
				Switzerland - Suisse				
Tourism expenditures (millions of dollars)	7411	9365	7973	7769	7581	7310	7628	..
Tourists' overnight stays (thousands)	36889	33984	32237	31863	32844	32111	29641	28569
Arrivals of tourists (thousands)	13200	11500	10900	10700	11000	10800	10000	..
Average length of stay (days)	..	..	..	..	..	..	..	..
			Syrian Arab Republic - République arabe syrienne					
Dépenses des touristes (millions de dollars)	320	1338	1017	1031	1082	..	1424	1408
Nuitées des touristes (milliers)	..	3160	4454	5130	5997	..	21695	20687
Arrivées des touristes (milliers)	562	815	1267	1386	1416	1318	2870	2788
Durée moyenne de séjour (jours)	3	2	4	4	5	3	10	10
				Tajikistan - Tadjikistan				
Tourism expenditures (millions of dollars)	–	..	..	..	..	..	2	..
Tourists' overnight stays (thousands)	–	..	..	..	..	..	..	..
Arrivals of tourists (thousands)	–	..	..	2	4	4	..	..
Average length of stay (days)	–	..	..	..	..	..	..	..
				Thailand - Thaïlande				
Dépenses des touristes (millions de dollars)	4326	8043	6202	7040	7489	7077	7902	7821
Nuitées des touristes (milliers)	..	..	..	..	..	..	..	..
Arrivées des touristes (milliers)	5299	6952	7843	8651	9579	10133	10873	10082
Durée moyenne de séjour (jours)	7	7	8	8	8	8	8	8
				Togo				
Tourism expenditures (millions of dollars)	58	13	13	9	5	11	9	..
Tourists' overnight stays (thousands)	..	..	..	..	..	..	..	..
Arrivals of tourists (thousands)	103	53	69	70	60	57	58	61
Average length of stay (days)	..	..	..	..	..	..	..	..

For sources and notes, see end of table.   Pour les sources et les notes, se reporter à la fin du tableau.

	1990	1995	1998	1999	2000	2001	2002	2003
Tonga								
Dépenses des touristes (millions de dollars)	9	10	8	9	7	7	9	..
Nuitées des touristes (milliers)	328	488	..	..	..	..	..	..
Arrivées des touristes (milliers)	21	29	27	31	35	32	37	40
Durée moyenne de séjour (jours)	..	..	..	..	..	..	..	..
Trinidad and Tobago - Trinité-et-Tobago								
Tourism expenditures (millions of dollars)	95	73	201	210	213	201	224	..
Tourists' overnight stays (thousands)	..	..	..	..	..	..	..	..
Arrivals of tourists (thousands)	195	260	334	358	399	383	384	..
Average length of stay (days)	..	..	..	..	..	..	17	..
Tunisia - Tunisie								
Dépenses des touristes (millions de dollars)	948	1393	1504	1647	1529	1627	1422	1475
Nuitées des touristes (milliers)	..	..	..	..	..	..	..	..
Arrivées des touristes (milliers)	3204	4120	4718	4832	5058	5387	5064	5114
Durée moyenne de séjour (jours)	6	6	6	7	7	6	5	5
Turkey - Turquie								
Tourism expenditures (millions of dollars)	3225	4957	7809	5203	7636	10067	11901	13203
Tourists' overnight stays (thousands)	13271	18477	30433	20435	28511	36368	43312	..
Arrivals of tourists (thousands)	4799	7083	8960	6893	9586	10783	12790	13341
Average length of stay (days)	8	9	9	..	..	10	..	..
Turkmenistan - Turkménistan								
Dépenses des touristes (millions de dollars)	–	..	192	..	..	..	..	..
Nuitées des touristes (milliers)	–	..	..	..	..	..	..	..
Arrivées des touristes (milliers)	–	218	300	..	..	..	..	..
Durée moyenne de séjour (jours)	–	..	..	..	..	..	..	..
Turks and Caicos Islands - Iles Turques et Caïques								
Tourism expenditures (millions of dollars)	37	53	157	238	285	311	292	..
Tourists' overnight stays (thousands)	..	600	831	906	1142	1239	1172	..
Arrivals of tourists (thousands)	49	79	111	121	152	165	157	..
Average length of stay (days)	..	8	7	..	..	8	8	..
Tuvalu								
Dépenses des touristes (millions de dollars)	..	..	..	..	..	..	..	..
Nuitées des touristes (milliers)	..	..	..	..	..	..	..	..
Arrivées des touristes (milliers)	1	1	1	1	1	1	1	..
Durée moyenne de séjour (jours)	..	..	..	..	..	..	..	..
Uganda - Ouganda								
Tourism expenditures (millions of dollars)	10	78	95	102	113	163	185	..
Tourists' overnight stays (thousands)	..	640	780	756	772	820	1016	..
Arrivals of tourists (thousands)	69	160	195	189	193	205	254	..
Average length of stay (days)	..	..	..	..	..	..	..	..
Ukraine								
Dépenses des touristes (millions de dollars)	–	3865	3317	2124	2207	2725	2992	..
Nuitées des touristes (milliers)	–	5332	5357	3601	5053	5177	4757	..
Arrivées des touristes (milliers)	–	3716	6208	4232	4406	5791	6326	..
Durée moyenne de séjour (jours)	–	3	6	7	5	5	5	..
United Arab Emirates - Emirats arabes unis								
Tourism expenditures (millions of dollars)	169	632	859	893	1012	1064	1328	1477
Tourists' overnight stays (thousands)	..	..	..	..	..	..	..	..
Arrivals of tourists (thousands)	633	2315	2991	3393	3907	4134	5445	5871
Average length of stay (days)	..	..	..	..	..	..	..	..
United Kingdom - Royaume-Uni								
Dépenses des touristes (millions de dollars)	13762	18554	20985	20221	19374	16276	17591	19511
Nuitées des touristes (milliers)	196100	220300	230777	211735	203759	189516	199285	204286
Arrivées des touristes (milliers)	18013	23537	25745	25394	25209	22835	24180	24785
Durée moyenne de séjour (jours)	11	9	9	8	8	8	8	8

For sources and notes, see end of table.

Pour les sources et les notes, se reporter à la fin du tableau.

5.3 Selected indicators of tourism
(concluded)

5.3 Sélection d'indicateurs du tourisme
(fin)

	1990	1995	1998	1999	2000	2001	2002	2003
United Republic of Tanzania - République-Unie de Tanzanie								
Tourism expenditures (millions of dollars)	65	259	570	733	739	725	730	731
Tourists' overnight stays (thousands)	1265	417	2534	1695	1957	2015	2100	2200
Arrivals of tourists (thousands)	153	285	450	564	459	501	550	552
Average length of stay (days)	..	..	..	..	..	..	..	..
United States - Etats-Unis								
Dépenses des touristes (millions de dollars)	43007	63395	71325	74801	82400	71893	66547	65054
Nuitées des touristes (milliers)	..	..	..	..	..	..	..	..
Arrivées des touristes (milliers)	39362	43318	46396	48492	50945	44898	41892	40356
Durée moyenne de séjour (jours)	..	..	..	..	..	..	..	..
United States Virgin Islands - Iles Vierges américaines								
Tourism expenditures (millions of dollars)	697	822	940	955	1206	1323	1195	1271
Tourists' overnight stays (thousands)	..	1049	914	966	1060	1040	1057	1051
Arrivals of tourists (thousands)	463	454	422	484	607	592	553	538
Average length of stay (days)	..	..	..	..	..	..	..	..
Uruguay								
Dépenses des touristes (millions de dollars)	262	611	695	653	652	561	315	318
Nuitées des touristes (milliers)	..	..	3478	3488	3319	2992	2927	3531
Arrivées des touristes (milliers)	1267	2022	2163	2073	1968	1892	1258	1420
Durée moyenne de séjour (jours)	10	8	7	..	7	7	7	7
Uzbekistan - Ouzbékistan								
Tourism expenditures (millions of dollars)	–	..	167	102	63	72	68	48
Tourists' overnight stays (thousands)	–	1315	1748	1033	918	1082	1069	935
Arrivals of tourists (thousands)	–	92	811	487	302	345	332	231
Average length of stay (days)	–	..	2	2	3	3	3	3
Vanuatu								
Dépenses des touristes (millions de dollars)	39	58	52	56	58	46	..	..
Nuitées des touristes (milliers)	..	..	..	..	..	..	..	..
Arrivées des touristes (milliers)	35	44	52	51	58	53	49	50
Durée moyenne de séjour (jours)	15	9	8	7	8	8	9	10
Venezuela								
Tourism expenditures (millions of dollars)	496	951	961	673	634	682	468	314
Tourists' overnight stays (thousands)	..	..	12821	9126	8456	10512	9126	9819
Arrivals of tourists (thousands)	525	700	685	587	469	584	432	337
Average length of stay (days)	..	19	18	13	14	13	15	14
Viet Nam								
Dépenses des touristes (millions de dollars)	85	86	86	..	..	..	..	..
Nuitées des touristes (milliers)	..	..	..	..	..	..	..	..
Arrivées des touristes (milliers)	250	1351	978	1211	1383	1599	..	..
Durée moyenne de séjour (jours)	..	5	6	6	6	6	..	..
Yemen - Yémen								
Tourism expenditures (millions of dollars)	20	50	84	61	73	38	38	..
Tourists' overnight stays (thousands)	..	..	..	..	..	..	..	..
Arrivals of tourists (thousands)	52	61	88	58	73	76	..	..
Average length of stay (days)	4	6	6	6	7	3	..	..
Zambia - Zambie								
Dépenses des touristes (millions de dollars)	41	47	75	85	111	117	134	149
Nuitées des touristes (milliers)	..	..	2820	3046	..	..	..	..
Arrivées des touristes (milliers)	141	163	362	404	457	492	565	578
Durée moyenne de séjour (jours)	11	8	8	8	6	9	8	8
Zimbabwe								
Tourism expenditures (millions of dollars)	60	145	158	202	125	81	76	44
Tourists' overnight stays (thousands)	..	6270	..	..	..	..	..	..
Arrivals of tourists (thousands)	605	1363	1986	2101	1868	2068	..	..
Average length of stay (days)	6	5	3	..	..	..	..	..

For sources and notes, see next page.

Pour les sources et les notes, se reporter à la page suivante.

Sources:

World Tourism Organization (WTO), Database.

Notes:

All indicators refer to non-resident tourists or international visitors. This includes all persons who arrive in an economy to stay for less than a year for business purposes or personal reasons. Tourists are those who stay at least one night in a collective or private accommodation in a country visited. Same-day visitors are persons who do not stay overnight in a country visited.

Tourism expenditures correspond to the item "Travel receipts" in IMF balance of payments data. It refers to expenditures of non-resident tourists and visitors within the territory of a reporting economy. Transport expenditures are not included.

Tourists' overnight stays refer to the number of nights spent by non-resident tourists in a reporting country and concern all types of tourism accommodation.

Arrivals of tourists represent the total number of non-resident tourists and visitors who arrived in a reporting economy during a given year. When the same person visits a country several times in a year, the total number of arrivals is counted. Similarly, when a person travels to several countries during one trip, her/his arrival in each country is recorded separately.

Countries differ in the way in which they count arrivals: some take into account all arrivals of non-resident visitors at national borders, while others count arrivals at hotels and other types of tourism accommodation. For more information refer to the World Tourism Organization's *Compendium of Tourism Statistics 2004*.

Average length-of-stay figures refer to the average number of days spent by a non-resident tourist in a reporting country.

Sources :

Organisation mondiale du toursime (OMT), Base de données.

Notes :

Tous les indicateurs se réfèrent aux touristes non-résidents ou aux visiteurs internationaux. Cela inclut des personnes qui arrivent sur le territoire d'une économie pour y rester moins d'une année pour affaires ou pour des raisons personnelles. Les touristes sont ceux qui séjournent dans le pays visité au moins une nuit dans un logement collectif ou privé. Les visiteurs d'une journée sont des personnes qui ne passent pas la nuit dans le pays visité.

Les dépenses dans le tourisme correspondent à la rubrique "Revenus des voyages" de la balance des paiements du FMI. Elles se réfèrent aux dépenses des touristes et des visiteurs non résidents sur le territoire de l'économie déclarante. Les dépenses pour le transport n'y sont pas incluses.

Les nuitées des touristes se réfèrent au nombre de nuits (nuitées) que les touristes non résidents ont passées dans le pays déclarant et concernent tout type d'établissement touristique.

Les arrivées des touristes représentent le nombre total de touristes et de visiteurs qui sont arrivés dans l'économie déclarante durant une année. Quand une personne visite un pays plusieurs fois par an, chaque visite est comptée séparément. De même, si quelqu'un se rend dans plusieurs pays durant un voyage, son arrivée dans chaque pays est prise en compte.

Les pays déclarent les arrivées des visiteurs de manières différentes: certains prennent en compte toutes les arrivées aux frontières nationales et d' autres comptent les arrivées dans des hôtels et autres types de logements touristiques. Pour plus d'informations se référer au *Compendium des statistiques du tourisme 2004* de l'Organisation mondiale du tourisme.

Les chiffres sur la durée moyenne de séjour se réfèrent au nombre moyen de jours qu'un visiteur non résident a passés dans le pays déclarant.

PART SIX

International finance

SIXIEME PARTIE

Flux financiers internationaux

Country or area / Pays ou zones	Year / Année	Goods and services / Biens et services			Income / Revenu				Current transfers (net) / Transferts courants (nets)	Current account balance / Solde du compte des transactions courantes
		Exports / Exportations	Imports / Importations	Balance on goods and services / Balance des biens et services	Debit / Débit		Credit / Crédit			
					Total	of which: / dont : Direct investment income / Revenu d'investissement direct	Total	of which: / dont : Direct investment income / Revenu d'investissement direct		
		(1)	(2)	(3) = (1)+(2)	(4)	(5)	(6)	(7)	(8)	(9)
Albania - Albanie	1990	354	-485	-131	-2	..	..	..	15	-118
	2000	704	-1499	-796	-9	0	116	..	533	-156
	2002	915	-2076	-1160	-21	-1	148	..	625	-408
	2003	1167	-2586	-1419	-24	-1	195	..	842	-407
Algeria - Algérie	1990	13462	-10107	3355	-2341	-151	73	5	333	1420
Angola	1990	3992	-3386	607	-776	-314	11	..	-77	-236
	1995	3836	-3519	317	-783	-386	16	..	156	-295
	2000	8188	-5739	2449	-1715	-929	34	..	28	796
	2001	6737	-6697	40	-1584	-927	23	..	91	-1431
Anguilla	1990	41	-43	-2	-8	-7	2	..	0	-9
	2000	69	-124	-55	-7	-4	4	0	3	-54
	2001	74	-108	-34	-5	-4	2	..	1	-36
	2002	70	-100	-30	-7	-6	2	..	0	-35
Antigua and Barbuda - Antigua-et-Barbuda	1990	345	-341	5	-48	-19	2	..	10	-31
	2000	466	-497	-31	-60	-22	16	..	9	-66
	2001	441	-493	-52	-40	-23	19	..	9	-64
	2002	437	-510	-74	-47	-22	13	..	6	-103
Argentina - Argentine	1990	14800	-6846	7954	-6254	-637	1854	2	998	4552
	2000	31149	-33020	-1871	-14968	-3086	7446	978	403	-8989
	2002	28748	-13170	15578	-10061	-540	3052	349	572	9142
	2003	33555	-18649	14906	-10866	-1480	3197	457	601	7838
Armenia - Arménie	1995	300	-726	-427	-15	..	55	..	168	-218
	2000	447	-966	-519	-51	-22	104	..	188	-278
	2002	698	-1107	-409	-48	-13	137	..	173	-148
	2003	894	-1397	-503	-72	-35	163	..	225	-186
Aruba	1990	566	-716	-149	-23	..	15	..	-1	-158
	1995	1992	-2018	-26	-25	-6	16	..	34	0
	2000	3614	-3289	325	-54	..	47	..	-36	282
	2002	2589	-2694	-105	-106	-60	34	1	-66	-244
Australia - Australie	1990	49843	-53056	-3213	-16404	-4488	3228	760	439	-15950
	2000	82729	-87253	-4524	-19893	-7332	8984	5490	-47	-15481
	2002	83005	-88637	-5632	-19823	-8218	8154	4747	-64	-17365
	2003	91799	-107364	-15565	-24490	-11502	9579	5598	-77	-30554
Austria - Autriche	1990	63694	-61580	2114	-10087	-933	9145	313	-6	1166
	2000	96026	-97074	-1048	-14456	-2598	11992	1279	-1352	-4864
	2002	108865	-104594	4272	-15255	-3299	13173	2022	-1615	575
	2003	132769	-130063	2706	-18136	-4546	15358	2794	-2320	-2392
Azerbaijan - Azerbaïdjan	1995	785	-1290	-505	-16	0	10	0	111	-401
	2000	2118	-2024	95	-391	-317	56	..	73	-168
	2002	2667	-3121	-454	-422	-356	37	..	70	-768
	2003	3057	-4770	-1713	-495	-422	53	0	134	-2021
Bahamas	1990	1784	-1653	131	-405	..	232	..	6	-37
	1995	1768	-1796	-28	-211	..	75	..	18	-146
	2000	2842	-3184	-342	-385	..	212	..	43	-471
	2001	2504	-2704	-200	-284	..	94	..	42	-348
Bahrain - Bahreïn	1990	4119	-3999	120	-5275	-112	5497	83	-272	70
	2000	7176	-5132	2044	-6552	-881	6328	209	-990	830
	2002	6955	-5624	1332	-2204	-934	1679	235	-1320	-513
	2003	7758	-5950	1808	-1743	-944	1207	258	-1340	-68

For sources and notes, see end of table.

Pour les sources et les notes, se reporter à la fin du tableau.

Country or area Pays ou zones	Year Année	Goods and services Biens et services			Income Revenu				Current transfers (net) Transferts courants (nets)	Current account balance Solde du compte des transactions courantes
		Exports Exportations	Imports Importations	Balance on goods and services Balance des biens et services	Debit / Débit		Credit / Crédit			
					Total	of which: / dont : Direct investment income Revenu d'investissement direct	Total	of which: / dont : Direct investment income Revenu d'investissement direct		
		(1)	(2)	(3) = (1)+(2)	(4)	(5)	(6)	(7)	(8)	(9)
Bangladesh	1990	2064	-3960	-1896	-180	..	64	..	1613	-398
	2000	7214	-9673	-2459	-345	-149	78	2	2420	-306
	2001	6837	-9655	-2818	-362	-175	77	2	2568	-535
	2002	6951	-9186	-2235	-322	-129	57	1	3239	739
Barbados - Barbade	1990	873	-878	-5	-76	-9	30	1	43	-8
	2000	1377	-1518	-141	-152	-17	70	6	78	-145
	2001	1340	-1451	-111	-166	-18	73	6	94	-111
	2002	1294	-1450	-156	-174	-19	72	6	86	-171
Belarus - Bélarus	1995	5269	-5752	-483	-53	..	2	..	76	-458
	2000	7656	-8087	-431	-72	-5	26	0	155	-323
	2002	9264	-9787	-523	-73	-17	45	1	174	-378
	2003	11592	-12270	-678	-94	-26	66	1	200	-505
Belgium - Belgique	2002	205968	-195186	10783	-29003	-10211	35845	6168	-4321	13305
	2003	248041	-236590	11451	-30335	-11627	37165	7171	-6658	11623
Belgium-Luxembourg - Belgique-Luxembourg	1990	138605	-135098	3507	-63228	..	65544	..	-2197	3627
	1995	190685	-178798	11887	-67990	-10772	74798	6161	-4463	14232
	2000	214466	-203954	10512	-70625	-11488	75673	5138	-4179	11381
	2001	213812	-203106	10705	-75999	-13739	78906	6909	-4220	9392
Belize	1990	245	-248	-4	-21	-7	11	..	29	15
	2000	385	-523	-139	-59	-28	5	..	62	-131
	2001	450	-611	-161	-83	-33	11	..	48	-185
	2002	494	-631	-137	-79	-33	7	..	46	-163
Benin - Bénin	1990	364	-454	-90	-38	0	12	..	97	-18
	1995	614	-895	-280	-25	..	24	1	121	-160
	2000	528	-708	-179	-40	-4	28	5	111	-81
	2001	521	-745	-224	-43	-7	29	8	163	-75
Bolivia - Bolivie	1990	977	-1086	-110	-267	-17	19	..	159	-199
	2000	1470	-2078	-608	-365	-148	140	3	387	-446
	2002	1555	-2072	-517	-308	-183	103	3	369	-352
	2003	1879	-2005	-126	-373	-234	72	3	446	19
Bosnia and Herzegovina - Bosnie-Herzégovine	2000	1533	-3993	-2460	-73	..	392	..	1260	-881
	2001	1510	-4295	-2784	-81	-2	396	..	1252	-1217
	2002	1492	-4690	-3198	-86	-5	339	..	1195	-1751
	2003	1985	-5723	-3737	-107	-10	349	..	1399	-2096
Botswana	1990	2005	-1987	18	-522	-407	416	30	69	-19
	1995	2421	-2050	371	-516	-416	483	58	-39	300
Brazil - Brésil	1990	35170	-28184	6986	-12765	-1892	1157	27	799	-3823
	2000	64584	-72444	-7860	-21507	-4238	3621	999	1521	-24225
	2002	69913	-61749	8164	-21486	-5950	3295	967	2390	-7637
	2003	83567	-63818	19749	-21891	-5984	3339	886	2867	4063
Bulgaria - Bulgarie	1990	6950	-8027	-1077	-878	..	120	..	125	-1710
	2000	7000	-7670	-670	-644	-107	321	-2	290	-704
	2002	8057	-9170	-1113	-581	-228	320	1	547	-827
	2003	10602	-12475	-1873	-813	-388	328	1	692	-1666
Burkina Faso	1990	349	-758	-409	-18	-6	18	..	332	-77
	2000	237	-658	-421	-34	-3	14	0	122	-319
	2001	260	-650	-390	-40	-5	15	0	124	-291
Burundi	1990	89	-318	-229	-23	-3	8	..	174	-69
	2000	53	-151	-98	-14	-12	2	2	59	-50
	2002	37	-148	-111	-13	-10	1	1	117	-5
	2003	43	-175	-132	-19	-15	1	1	124	-25

For sources and notes, see end of table.

Pour les sources et les notes, se reporter à la fin du tableau.

Country or area / Pays ou zones	Year / Année	Goods and services / Biens et services			Income / Revenu				Current transfers (net) / Transferts courants (nets)	Current account balance / Solde du compte des transactions courantes
		Exports / Exportations	Imports / Importations	Balance on goods and services / Balance des biens et services	Debit / Débit		Credit / Crédit			
					Total	of which: / dont : Direct investment income / Revenu d'investissement direct	Total	of which: / dont : Direct investment income / Revenu d'investissement direct		
		(1)	(2)	(3) = (1)+(2)	(4)	(5)	(6)	(7)	(8)	(9)
Cambodia - Cambodge	1995	969	-1375	-406	-67	4	10	..	277	-186
	2000	1830	-2267	-438	-190	-122	67	5	425	-135
	2001	2096	-2441	-346	-193	-134	58	5	396	-86
	2002	2350	-2693	-343	-219	-151	51	6	447	-64
Cameroon - Cameroun	1990	2508	-2475	32	-566	-138	8	2	-26	-551
	1995	2040	-1608	433	-425	-21	12	5	69	90
Canada	1990	149538	-149118	419	-34460	-5730	15072	3890	-796	-19764
	2000	329252	-288093	41159	-47036	-16468	24746	10164	754	19622
	2002	304502	-272447	32055	-38133	-13174	19881	8687	645	14447
	2003	328728	-294943	33786	-40238	-14851	23500	11899	221	17268
Cape Verde - Cap-Vert	1990	57	-149	-92	-4	0	6	0	86	-4
	2000	146	-326	-180	-18	-5	5	2	135	-58
	2002	195	-420	-226	-18	-4	6	4	166	-72
	2003	277	-547	-270	-30	-2	13	5	210	-77
Central African Republic - République centrafricaine	1990	220	-410	-191	-22	-2	1	..	123	-89
Chad - Tchad	1990	271	-488	-216	-24	..	3	..	192	-46
Chile - Chili	1990	10221	-9166	1055	-2222	-387	484	2	198	-485
	2000	23293	-21893	1400	-4453	-2539	1598	568	558	-898
	2002	22509	-20909	1600	-3960	-2447	1046	289	430	-885
	2003	25851	-23602	2249	-4394	-3010	1114	397	438	-594
China - Chine	1990	57374	-46706	10668	-1962	-46	3017	..	274	11997
	2000	279562	-250688	28874	-27216	-20198	12550	62	6311	20518
	2001	299409	-271325	28084	-28563	-21489	9388	146	8492	17401
	2002	365396	-328012	37383	-23290	-17823	8344	126	12984	35422
China, Hong Kong SAR - Chine, Hong Kong RAS	2000	241434	-235475	5958	-50699	-34183	53494	19748	-1670	7083
	2001	230376	-223934	6441	-44036	-31395	49315	21606	-1780	9941
	2002	243308	-230956	12352	-41083	-32663	43223	22953	-1896	12596
	2003	269280	-255620	13659	-37813	-30647	42198	23538	-1889	16155
Colombia - Colombie	1990	8679	-6858	1821	-2652	-964	347	20	1026	542
	2000	15771	-14417	1354	-3337	-655	1051	31	1673	740
	2002	14182	-15409	-1227	-3559	-1033	711	88	2624	-1451
	2003	15376	-16601	-1225	-3995	-1558	548	120	3216	-1456
Comoros - Comores	1990	35	-89	-54	-4	-1	3	0	45	-10
	1995	46	-103	-58	-2	0	3	..	38	-19
Congo	1990	1488	-1282	206	-475	..	15	..	3	-251
	2000	2628	-1194	1435	-819	-466	14	0	19	648
	2001	2199	-1534	666	-694	-369	15	0	-15	-28
	2002	2454	-1618	836	-866	-572	6	..	-10	-34
Costa Rica	1990	1963	-2346	-383	-363	-60	130	3	192	-424
	2000	7750	-7297	452	-1495	-1141	243	11	93	-707
	2002	7140	-7719	-579	-835	-506	318	179	181	-916
	2003	8152	-8483	-331	-1062	-710	213	86	213	-967
Côte d'Ivoire	1990	3503	-3445	58	-1149	-75	58	..	-181	-1214
	2000	4370	-3629	742	-794	-284	142	3	-330	-241
	2002	5860	-4000	1860	-771	-284	141	2	-462	768
	2003	6557	-5048	1509	-854	..	167	..	-469	353
Croatia - Croatie	1995	6741	-9106	-2365	-248	-6	219	7	802	-1592
	2000	8663	-9599	-936	-754	-162	346	9	883	-461
	2002	10571	-13065	-2494	-930	-344	428	23	1076	-1920
	2003	14907	-17186	-2279	-1700	-985	487	29	1394	-2099

For sources and notes, see end of table.

Pour les sources et les notes, se reporter à la fin du tableau.

Country or area Pays ou zones	Year Année	Goods and services Biens et services			Income Revenu				Current transfers (net) Transferts courants (nets)	Current account balance Solde du compte des transactions courantes
		Exports Exportations	Imports Importations	Balance on goods and services Balance des biens et services	Debit / Débit		Credit / Crédit			
					Total	of which: / dont : Direct investment income Revenu d' investissement direct	Total	of which: / dont : Direct investment income Revenu d' investissement direct		
		(1)	(2)	(3) = (1)+(2)	(4)	(5)	(6)	(7)	(8)	(9)
Cyprus - Chypre	1990	2955	-3178	-223	-217	-4	159	..	127	-154
	2000	4157	-4717	-559	-531	-44	509	72	126	-456
	2002	5325	-5968	-643	-452	-138	512	154	66	-517
	2003	6585	-6937	-352	-532	-268	451	129	151	-282
Czech Republic - République tchèque	1995	28202	-30044	-1842	-1301	-66	1197	19	572	-1374
	2000	35858	-37550	-1692	-3323	-1379	1952	-11	373	-2690
	2002	45562	-47159	-1597	-5632	-3207	2052	-70	912	-4265
	2003	56526	-58561	-2035	-6809	-3990	2643	-73	541	-5661
Czechoslovakia (former) - Tchécoslovaquie (anc.)	1990	14307	-15529	-1222	-709	..	498	..	206	-1227
Denmark - Danemark	1990	48902	-41415	7487	-11719	..	6011	..	-408	1372
	2000	74291	-64931	9360	-15749	..	11815	..	-3015	2412
	2002	82768	-72394	10374	-15040	..	12270	..	-2612	4991
	2003	97306	-83353	13952	-13238	-3792	9257	2619	-3833	6139
Djibouti	1995	185	-292	-107	-9	-5	26	..	67	-23
Dominica - Dominique	1990	89	-134	-45	-9	-5	4	0	6	-44
	1995	112	-147	-35	-17	-12	3	0	8	-41
	2000	144	-183	-39	-38	-26	5	0	18	-54
	2001	120	-167	-47	-23	-14	4	0	17	-49
Dominican Republic - République dominicaine	1990	1832	-2233	-402	-335	-90	86	..	371	-280
	2000	8964	-10852	-1888	-1341	-1068	300	..	1902	-1027
	2002	8236	-10151	-1915	-1452	-1153	300	..	2269	-798
	2003	8875	-9100	-225	-1587	-1244	344	..	2336	867
Ecuador - Equateur	1990	3262	-2519	743	-1235	-125	25	..	107	-360
	2000	5987	-5012	975	-1476	-280	70	..	1352	921
	2002	6121	-7828	-1707	-1335	-302	30	..	1654	-1359
	2003	7095	-7858	-763	-1492	-367	27	..	1772	-455
Egypt - Egypte	1990	9895	-14091	-4196	-1879	-14	857	247	7545	2327
	2000	16864	-22895	-6031	-983	-92	1871	71	4172	-971
	2002	16438	-19508	-3071	-965	-89	698	56	3960	622
	2003	20060	-19662	398	-832	-47	578	76	3599	3743
El Salvador	1990	973	-1624	-651	-161	-31	29	..	631	-152
	2000	3662	-5636	-1975	-394	-60	141	..	1797	-431
	2002	3803	-5914	-2111	-483	-89	159	2	2023	-412
	2003	3987	-6430	-2443	-548	-77	140	8	2117	-734
Equatorial Guinea - Guinée équatoriale	1990	42	-89	-47	-10	..	..	..	38	-19
	1995	94	-196	-102	-25	..	0	..	4	-123
Estonia - Estonie	1995	2573	-2860	-287	-61	-26	64	1	126	-158
	2000	4810	-5016	-205	-322	-205	118	13	116	-294
	2002	5245	-5747	-503	-530	-397	203	52	113	-717
	2003	6837	-7566	-729	-822	-651	245	92	106	-1199
Ethiopia - Ethiopie	1990	597	-1271	-674	-78	..	9	..	449	-294
	2000	992	-1622	-630	-52	-9	16	..	680	15
	2001	978	-2151	-1173	-48	-12	16	0	751	-454
	2002	1066	-2038	-972	-37	-11	14	0	845	-150
Fiji - Fidji	1990	833	-899	-67	-75	-49	49	10	-1	-94
	1995	1084	-1160	-76	-95	-84	55	5	3	-113
Finland - Finlande	1990	31180	-33456	-2276	-7239	-277	3505	-340	-952	-6962
	2000	51880	-40459	11421	-8989	-2837	7265	3825	-723	8975
	2002	51346	-39983	11363	-9259	-2773	8657	4447	-612	10148
	2003	60262	-48840	11423	-10408	-2676	9293	4318	-1012	9295

For sources and notes, see end of table.

Pour les sources et les notes, se reporter à la fin du tableau.

Country or area / Pays ou zones	Year / Année	Goods and services / Biens et services			Income / Revenu				Current transfers (net) / Transferts courants (nets)	Current account balance / Solde du compte des transactions courantes
		Exports / Exportations	Imports / Importations	Balance on goods and services / Balance des biens et services	Debit / Débit		Credit / Crédit			
					Total	of which: / dont : Direct investment income / Revenu d'investissement direct	Total	of which: / dont : Direct investment income / Revenu d'investissement direct		
		(1)	(2)	(3) = (1)+(2)	(4)	(5)	(6)	(7)	(8)	(9)
France	1990	285389	-283238	2152	-59632	-2698	55736	2267	-8199	-9944
	2000	379115	-362861	16255	-56809	-5400	72392	14749	-13256	18581
	2002	394224	-370034	24191	-60856	261	64836	4660	-14382	13789
	2003	461600	-445625	15976	-80976	-5787	88571	18783	-19187	4384
Gabon	1990	2730	-1812	919	-637	-116	20	13	-134	168
	1995	2945	-1772	1172	-700	-236	35	3	-42	465
Gambia - Gambie	1990	168	-192	-24	-13	..	2	..	59	23
	1995	177	-232	-55	-10	..	4	..	52	-8
Georgia - Géorgie	2000	665	-1187	-521	-61	0	179	..	135	-269
	2001	810	-1283	-472	-65	-11	98	..	228	-212
	2002	993	-1441	-448	-127	-53	166	4	200	-209
	2003	1273	-1856	-583	-145	-69	179	4	158	-391
Germany - Allemagne	1990	473670	-427621	46049	-45300	-6749	65892	6063	-21954	44688
	2000	632923	-629630	3294	-100874	-10255	98399	16449	-26035	-25216
	2002	722138	-636628	85510	-106088	-10698	90392	1552	-26371	43443
	2003	873318	-773427	99891	-124396	-18337	110547	10248	-32529	53514
Ghana	1990	983	-1506	-522	-77	-7	-34	..	411	-223
	2000	2441	-3350	-910	-123	..	16	..	631	-387
	2002	2570	-3328	-758	-189	..	15	..	900	-32
	2003	3192	-4180	-987	-178	..	21	..	1399	255
Greece - Grèce	1990	13018	-19564	-6546	-2024	-78	315	19	4718	-3537
	2000	29440	-41727	-12286	-3692	-319	2807	48	3352	-9820
	2002	30091	-41997	-11906	-3487	-368	1530	67	3458	-10405
	2003	36864	-49437	-12573	-4693	-604	1769	115	4272	-11225
Grenada - Grenade	1990	93	-139	-46	-14	-8	3	0	11	-46
	2000	236	-308	-73	-37	-28	5	0	20	-84
	2001	197	-279	-82	-42	-34	4	0	22	-99
	2002	175	-270	-95	-49	-32	4	0	23	-116
Guatemala	1990	1568	-1812	-244	-217	-37	21	1	227	-213
	2000	3862	-5567	-1705	-424	-248	214	78	865	-1050
	2001	3905	-6070	-2165	-402	-205	317	80	997	-1253
	2002	3769	-6622	-2854	-449	-257	151	79	1958	-1193
Guinea - Guinée	1990	829	-953	-124	-162	-61	13	..	70	-203
	2000	734	-872	-138	-101	-8	23	..	75	-140
	2001	834	-881	-47	-114	-46	11	0	90	-60
	2002	976	-999	-23	-75	-1	6	0	46	-46
Guinea-Bissau - Guinée-Bissau	1990	26	-88	-62	-22	..	..	..	39	-45
	1995	30	-89	-60	-21	..	..	..	46	-35
Guyana	1995	629	-708	-79	-130	..	12	..	62	-135
	2000	674	-779	-104	-70	-6	12	..	47	-115
	2001	662	-777	-114	-74	-5	10	..	44	-134
	2002	667	-759	-92	-67	-4	8	..	40	-111
Haiti - Haïti	1990	318	-515	-197	-25	..	7	7	193	-22
	1995	192	-802	-609	-31	-4	..	..	553	-87
Honduras	1990	1033	-1127	-94	-258	-72	21	..	280	-51
	2000	2491	-3267	-777	-257	-70	110	..	648	-276
	2002	2504	-3411	-907	-250	-108	67	..	848	-242
	2003	2654	-3719	-1064	-240	-110	57	..	968	-279

For sources and notes, see end of table.

Pour les sources et les notes, se reporter à la fin du tableau.

6.1A   Balance of payments: current account summaries
(continued)
Millions of dollars

6.1A   Balance des paiements : sommaires des
comptes des transactions courantes *(suite)*
Millions de dollars

Country or area Pays ou zones	Year Année	Goods and services Biens et services			Income Revenu				Current transfers (net) Transferts courants (nets)	Current account balance Solde du compte des transactions courantes
		Exports Exportations	Imports Importations	Balance on goods and services Balance des biens et services	Debit / Débit		Credit / Crédit			
					Total	of which: / dont : Direct investment income Revenu d' investissement direct	Total	of which: / dont : Direct investment income Revenu d' investissement direct		
		(1)	(2)	(3) = (1)+(2)	(4)	(5)	(6)	(7)	(8)	(9)
Hungary - Hongrie	1990	12035	-11017	1019	-1707	-37	280	27	787	379
	2000	34808	-36600	-1793	-2549	-832	1123	32	318	-2900
	2002	42599	-44104	-1506	-2801	-1113	1215	52	447	-2644
	2003	51203	-54766	-3562	-5785	-3856	1330	115	653	-7364
Iceland - Islande	1990	2149	-2065	83	-297	-8	83	6	-4	-134
	2000	2946	-3540	-595	-390	-16	147	13	-10	-847
	2002	3394	-3222	172	-398	-14	190	44	14	-22
	2003	3758	-4073	-315	-467	-42	225	57	-15	-572
India - Inde	1990	22911	-29527	-6616	-3693	..	436	..	2837	-7036
	2000	64811	-76922	-12111	-6290	..	2405	..	13356	-2640
	2001	66285	-74485	-8200	-5461	..	2777	..	12644	1761
	2002	77602	-83850	-6248	-6184	..	2298	..	14790	4656
Indonesia - Indonésie	1990	29295	-27511	1784	-5599	-2192	409	..	418	-2988
	2000	70619	-55377	15242	-11529	-3574	2456	..	1816	7985
	2001	62864	-50549	12315	-8940	-3158	2004	..	1520	6899
	2002	65826	-52706	13120	-8366	-3215	1318	..	1751	7823
Iran, Islamic Rep. of - Iran, Rép. islamique d'	1990	19741	-22292	-2551	-78	..	456	..	2500	327
	1995	18953	-15113	3840	-794	..	316	..	-4	3358
	2000	29727	-17503	12224	-604	..	404	..	621	12645
Ireland - Irlande	1990	26786	-24576	2211	-8235	-4350	3280	395	2384	-361
	2000	92068	-79792	12276	-41160	-21707	27613	3061	915	-356
	2002	112816	-92732	20084	-49464	-29249	27281	3728	701	-1399
	2003	127578	-104077	23501	-58333	-35688	32191	4614	536	-2105
Israel - Israël	1990	17312	-20228	-2916	-3571	-162	1590	17	5061	163
	2000	41351	-43748	-2397	-10740	-2502	3683	728	6483	-2972
	2002	36106	-40171	-4065	-6485	-776	2464	414	6766	-1320
	2003	40382	-41736	-1354	-6573	-1362	2214	728	6378	665
Italy - Italie	1990	219970	-218573	1397	-33709	-613	18997	264	-3164	-16479
	2000	297029	-286526	10504	-50680	-3535	38671	1936	-4276	-5781
	2002	313931	-300689	13243	-57854	-4957	43304	5205	-5434	-6741
	2003	367119	-358802	8319	-74921	-5385	52819	5513	-8158	-21942
Jamaica - Jamaïque	1990	2217	-2390	-173	-538	-189	108	1	291	-312
	2000	3589	-4427	-838	-543	-290	193	9	821	-367
	2001	3351	-4587	-1235	-656	-301	218	6	914	-759
	2002	3229	-4828	-1600	-826	-435	221	17	1086	-1119
Japan - Japon	1990	323692	-297306	26386	-100152	..	122644	..	-4800	44078
	2000	528751	-459661	69091	-36799	-2615	97199	8241	-9831	119660
	2002	461293	-409691	51601	-25709	-5320	91478	16692	-4923	112447
	2003	526740	-454252	72487	-23971	-5041	95211	13110	-7512	136215
Jordan - Jordanie	1990	2511	-3569	-1058	-282	..	67	..	1045	-227
	2000	3536	-5796	-2260	-535	-1	670	..	2184	59
	2002	4283	-6240	-1958	-372	-1	484	..	2264	418
	2003	4575	-6750	-2175	-371	-2	493	..	3140	1088
Kazakhstan	1995	5975	-6102	-127	-190	-74	45	..	59	-213
	2000	10421	-8853	1569	-1281	-934	139	..	249	676
	2002	11615	-11394	222	-1265	-919	234	-8	113	-696
	2003	14933	-13210	1723	-1998	-1424	257	-16	-165	-183
Kenya	1990	2228	-2705	-477	-423	-132	5	..	368	-527
	2000	2776	-3763	-987	-178	-29	45	..	921	-199
	2001	2981	-4004	-1023	-167	-48	46	..	805	-340
	2002	3181	-3805	-624	-178	-75	35	..	631	-137
Kiribati	1990	11	-46	-35	-2	-2	19	..	9	-9

For sources and notes, see end of table.

Pour les sources et les notes, se reporter à la fin du tableau.

Country or area / Pays ou zones	Year / Année	Goods and services / Biens et services			Income / Revenu				Current transfers (net) / Transferts courants (nets)	Current account balance / Solde du compte des transactions courantes
		Exports / Exportations	Imports / Importations	Balance on goods and services / Balance des biens et services	Debit / Débit		Credit / Crédit			
					Total	of which: / dont : Direct investment income / Revenu d' investissement direct	Total	of which: / dont : Direct investment income / Revenu d' investissement direct		
		(1)	(2)	(3) = (1)+(2)	(4)	(5)	(6)	(7)	(8)	(9)
Korea, Republic of - Corée, République de	1990	73295	-76361	-3065	-2982	-266	2895	374	1150	-2003
	2000	206482	-192499	13982	-8797	-1194	6375	449	680	12241
	2001	180317	-170653	9664	-7848	-1661	6650	503	-227	8239
	2002	190697	-183977	6719	-6356	-1812	6807	592	-1079	6092
Kuwait - Koweït	1990	8268	-7169	1099	-846	..	8584	..	-4951	3886
	2000	21301	-11372	9929	-616	..	7315	..	-1956	14672
	2002	17015	-13961	3053	-365	..	3708	..	-2145	4251
	2003	22875	-16254	6621	-285	..	3611	..	-2379	7567
Kyrgyzstan - Kirghizistan	1995	448	-726	-278	-39	..	4	..	79	-235
	2000	573	-655	-82	-101	-39	17	..	87	-79
	2001	561	-565	-4	-77	-27	12	..	51	-19
	2002	636	-697	-61	-66	-17	6	..	86	-35
Lao People's Dem. Rep. - Rép. dém. populaire lao	1990	102	-212	-110	-3	..	2	..	56	-55
	1995	408	-748	-341	-13	-6	7	..	110	-237
	2000	506	-578	-72	-60	..	7	..	116	-8
	2001	477	-560	-82	-40	..	6	..	34	-82
Latvia - Lettonie	1995	2088	-2193	-106	-53	0	71	0	71	-16
	2000	3270	-3886	-616	-191	-84	215	1	97	-495
	2002	3828	-4728	-900	-296	-155	289	0	260	-647
	2003	4698	-6112	-1414	-424	-246	365	3	517	-956
Lesotho	1990	100	-754	-654	-22	-13	455	..	286	65
	2000	254	-770	-516	-63	-15	289	..	139	-151
	2001	319	-728	-408	-57	-16	235	..	135	-95
	2002	390	-792	-401	-16	..	178	-12	121	-119
Libyan Arab Jamahiriya - Jamahiriya arabe libyenne	1990	11468	-8960	2508	-493	-436	666	18	-481	2201
	1995	7513	-5777	1736	-302	-253	435	13	-220	1650
Lithuania - Lituanie	1995	3191	-3902	-711	-64	-8	51	0	109	-614
	2000	5109	-5833	-724	-379	-123	186	15	243	-675
	2002	7492	-8258	-766	-375	-124	192	7	229	-721
	2003	9536	-10626	-1090	-717	-401	235	8	294	-1278
Luxembourg	1995	19198	-17787	1410	-47209	..	48798	..	-573	2426
	2000	28936	-24636	4300	-51678	..	50400	..	-461	2562
	2002	30083	-25381	4702	-52206	-6250	49841	1665	-702	1636
	2003	36684	-30612	6073	-55117	-7607	52092	2482	-556	2492
Macedonia, TFYR - Macédoine, LERY	2000	1637	-2279	-642	-87	-7	42	0	615	-72
	2001	1400	-1946	-546	-93	-13	53	0	343	-244
	2002	1364	-2156	-792	-82	-24	51	0	498	-325
Madagascar	1990	471	-809	-338	-176	-1	15	..	234	-265
	2000	1188	-1520	-332	-64	-4	22	..	113	-260
	2001	1279	-1466	-187	-106	-38	24	..	129	-140
	2002	710	-1001	-291	-101	-37	26	..	96	-270
Malawi	1990	443	-549	-106	-89	-5	9	..	99	-86
	2000	437	-629	-192	-51	-15	33	..	135	-73
	2001	472	-644	-172	-43	-14	12	..	143	-60
	2002	472	-795	-323	-45	-22	6	..	161	-201
Malaysia - Malaisie	1990	32665	-31765	900	-3721	-1926	1849	63	102	-870
	2000	112370	-94350	18020	-9594	-7173	1986	-222	-1924	8488
	2001	102436	-86254	16182	-8590	-5933	1847	-65	-2152	7287
	2002	108261	-91696	16565	-8734	-6121	2139	177	-2781	7190

For sources and notes, see end of table.

Pour les sources et les notes, se reporter à la fin du tableau.

Country or area / Pays ou zones	Year / Année	Goods and services / Biens et services			Income / Revenu				Current transfers (net) / Transferts courants (nets)	Current account balance / Solde du compte des transactions courantes
		Exports / Exportations	Imports / Importations	Balance on goods and services / Balance des biens et services	Debit / Débit		Credit / Crédit			
					Total	of which: / dont : Direct investment income / Revenu d'investissement direct	Total	of which: / dont : Direct investment income / Revenu d'investissement direct		
		(1)	(2)	(3) = (1)+(2)	(4)	(5)	(6)	(7)	(8)	(9)
Maldives	1990	179	-159	20	-18	-14	5	..	4	10
	2000	457	-452	6	-40	-34	10	..	-27	-51
	2001	464	-455	9	-45	-40	7	..	-28	-57
	2002	489	-456	33	-41	-35	4	..	-41	-44
Mali	1990	420	-830	-410	-59	-4	23	..	225	-221
	2000	639	-904	-265	-119	-76	21	1	126	-237
	2001	876	-1156	-280	-188	-141	22	1	136	-310
	2002	1045	-1099	-55	-276	-227	36	0	146	-149
Malta - Malte	1990	1950	-2283	-333	-79	-74	269	248	87	-56
	2000	3584	-3965	-382	-1009	-998	895	885	25	-470
	2002	3399	-3408	-10	-832	-823	834	826	-38	-46
	2003	3774	-4028	-254	-843	-833	880	868	-54	-271
Mauritania - Mauritanie	1990	471	-520	-49	-50	-1	4	..	86	-10
	1995	504	-510	-5	-49	-4	1	..	76	22
Mauritius - Maurice	1990	1722	-1916	-194	-79	-22	56	2	97	-119
	2000	2622	-2707	-85	-65	-8	49	1	64	-37
	2001	2850	-2656	194	-61	-5	75	2	68	276
	2002	2965	-2805	160	-65	-9	75	0	89	259
Mexico - Mexique	1990	48805	-51915	-3110	-11589	-2304	3273	..	3975	-7451
	2000	180211	-191818	-11608	-19622	-5923	6048	..	6994	-18188
	2002	173503	-186339	-12836	-15565	-3528	4050	..	10269	-14082
	2003	177634	-188779	-11144	-15486	-3755	3672	..	13728	-9231
Moldova, Republic of - Moldova, République de	1995	884	-1006	-122	-32	0	14	..	56	-85
	2000	641	-972	-331	-123	-11	173	..	166	-115
	2002	875	-1284	-409	-109	-29	216	..	251	-51
	2003	1057	-1719	-662	-111	-28	326	..	305	-142
Mongolia - Mongolie	1990	493	-1096	-603	-49	..	5	..	7	-640
	2000	614	-771	-158	-20	-9	13	..	94	-70
	2001	637	-829	-193	-17	-6	15	..	132	-62
	2002	708	-946	-238	-19	-5	14	..	138	-105
Montserrat	1990	19	-55	-36	-3	-2	2	..	14	-23
	2000	17	-38	-21	-4	-3	1	..	17	-7
	2001	15	-41	-26	-2	-1	1	..	21	-6
	2002	16	-46	-30	-5	-3	1	..	25	-8
Morocco - Maroc	1990	6239	-7783	-1544	-1071	-69	83	..	2336	-196
	2000	10453	-12546	-2093	-1140	-268	276	13	2483	-475
	2002	12199	-13314	-1115	-1115	-482	377	9	3330	1477
	2003	14140	-15913	-1773	-1157	-585	428	13	4123	1622
Mozambique	1990	229	-996	-766	-168	..	70	..	448	-415
	2000	689	-1492	-802	-271	0	79	..	231	-764
	2002	1019	-1765	-747	-655	-28	52	..	638	-712
	2003	1184	-1776	-592	-221	-42	56	..	242	-516
Myanmar	1990	319	-603	-283	-194	-147	2	..	39	-436
	1995	1307	-2020	-713	-125	..	16	..	562	-261
	2000	2139	-2493	-354	-169	-137	35	..	276	-212
	2001	2741	-2968	-228	-403	-381	36	..	286	-309
Namibia - Namibie	1990	1220	-1584	-364	-146	-67	183	3	354	28
	2000	1494	-1643	-149	-226	-194	247	0	436	309
	2002	1308	-1506	-198	-134	-95	171	-1	275	113
	2003	1621	-1975	-355	-54	3	280	0	465	337

For sources and notes, see end of table.   Pour les sources et les notes, se reporter à la fin du tableau.

Country or area / Pays ou zones	Year / Année	Goods and services / Biens et services			Income / Revenu				Current transfers (net) / Transferts courants (nets)	Current account balance / Solde du compte des transactions courantes
		Exports / Exportations	Imports / Importations	Balance on goods and services / Balance des biens et services	Debit / Débit		Credit / Crédit			
					Total	of which: / dont : Direct investment income / Revenu d' investissement direct	Total	of which: / dont : Direct investment income / Revenu d' investissement direct		
		(1)	(2)	(3) = (1)+(2)	(4)	(5)	(6)	(7)	(8)	(9)
Nepal - Népal	1990	422	-834	-412	-11	..	25	..	109	-289
	1995	1029	-1624	-595	-35	..	44	..	230	-356
	2000	1282	-1790	-508	-35	..	72	..	340	-131
	2001	1134	-1700	-567	-59	..	70	..	390	-165
Netherlands - Pays-Bas	1990	159304	-147652	11652	-26869	-7053	26249	6334	-2943	8089
	2000	253728	-238320	15408	-47869	-16210	45497	20245	-6219	6817
	2002	262898	-244133	18765	-42495	-7569	40054	13883	-6208	10116
	2003	318069	-292506	25563	-49641	-12020	48288	14700	-7743	16467
Netherlands Antilles - Antilles néerlandaises	1990	1464	-1631	-166	-110	-73	126	15	106	-44
	2000	2290	-2395	-106	-103	-4	126	2	32	-51
	2001	2288	-2519	-232	-84	-4	104	6	6	-206
	2002	2292	-2372	-80	-90	-10	91	2	112	32
New Zealand - Nouvelle-Zélande	1990	11683	-11699	-15	-2295	-129	719	305	138	-1453
	2000	17945	-17394	551	-3959	-1873	710	101	236	-2462
	2002	19678	-18777	901	-4037	-2039	1077	204	120	-1938
	2003	23268	-22856	412	-5274	-2963	1379	462	145	-3337
Nicaragua	1990	392	-682	-290	-229	..	12	..	202	-305
	2000	1102	-2145	-1043	-233	-69	31	..	453	-792
	2002	1143	-2189	-1046	-210	-71	9	..	462	-784
	2003	1298	-2393	-1095	-210	-77	7	..	519	-780
Niger	1990	533	-728	-196	-74	-23	20	0	14	-236
	1995	321	-457	-136	-53	-4	6	0	31	-152
Nigeria - Nigéria	1990	14550	-6909	7642	-2949	-135	211	..	85	4988
	1995	12342	-12841	-499	-2979	-1330	101	..	799	-2578
Norway - Norvège	1990	47078	-38911	8168	-6596	-798	3896	86	-1476	3992
	2000	77726	-48953	28773	-8278	-2418	6641	1479	-1285	25851
	2002	78515	-52098	26416	-7986	-2145	8733	1481	-2394	24769
	2003	90861	-60707	30154	-9130	-2530	10497	1997	-3076	28444
Oman	1990	5577	-3342	2235	-629	-390	375	..	-874	1106
	1995	6078	-5035	1043	-699	-507	325	..	-1469	-801
	2000	11743	-6159	5584	-1001	-674	291	..	-1451	3423
	2001	11423	-6988	4434	-897	-614	309	..	-1532	2315
Pakistan	1990	6835	-10205	-3371	-1181	-53	96	..	2794	-1661
	2000	10119	-12148	-2029	-2336	-429	118	2	4162	-85
	2002	12261	-12669	-408	-2414	-576	128	2	6548	3854
	2003	14846	-15257	-411	-2397	-893	180	3	6225	3597
Panama	1990	4438	-4193	245	-1395	-196	1139	..	219	209
	2000	7820	-8099	-279	-2193	-615	1579	..	177	-716
	2002	7567	-7625	-58	-1221	-277	937	..	250	-92
	2003	7608	-7437	171	-1589	-712	770	..	241	-408
Papua New Guinea - Papouasie-Nouvelle-Guinée	1990	1381	-1509	-128	-210	-158	107	..	156	-76
	1995	2992	-1905	1087	-511	-409	23	4	75	674
	2000	2337	-1771	566	-242	-198	32	1	-5	351
	2001	2098	-1594	504	-250	-206	20	2	13	286
Paraguay	1990	2514	-2169	345	-115	-17	116	..	43	390
	2000	2844	-3340	-496	-219	-84	248	12	177	-291
	2002	2426	-2488	-61	-175	-38	193	30	116	73
	2003	2850	-2869	-18	-165	-49	165	23	165	146
Peru - Pérou	1990	4120	-4087	33	-1928	-15	195	..	281	-1419
	2000	8559	-9707	-1148	-2146	-344	737	..	999	-1559
	2002	9267	-9946	-680	-1827	-479	337	..	1043	-1127
	2003	10664	-10864	-200	-2364	-1007	282	..	1221	-1061

For sources and notes, see end of table.

Pour les sources et les notes, se reporter à la fin du tableau.

Country or area Pays ou zones	Year Année	Goods and services Biens et services			Income Revenu				Current transfers (net) Transferts courants (nets)	Current account balance Solde du compte des transactions courantes
		Exports Expor- tations	Imports Impor- tations	Balance on goods and services Balance des biens et services	Debit / Débit		Credit / Crédit			
					Total	of which: / dont : Direct investment income Revenu d' investissement direct	Total	of which: / dont : Direct investment income Revenu d' investissement direct		
		(1)	(2)	(3) = (1)+(2)	(4)	(5)	(6)	(7)	(8)	(9)
Philippines	1990	11430	-13967	-2537	-2470	-311	1598	17	714	-2695
	2000	41267	-39883	1384	-3367	-179	7804	57	437	6258
	2002	37432	-38042	-610	-3456	-909	7946	15	503	4383
	2003	37812	-40292	-2480	-3200	-612	8415	13	612	3347
Poland - Pologne	1990	19037	-15095	3942	-3989	-20	603	..	2511	3067
	2000	46300	-57202	-10902	-3709	-700	2251	24	2380	-9980
	2002	56777	-63177	-6400	-3837	-770	1950	-53	3280	-5007
	2003	72173	-77379	-5206	-5237	-1591	2125	22	4233	-4085
Portugal	1990	21554	-27146	-5592	-1457	-102	1360	1	5507	-181
	2000	33715	-45683	-11967	-7101	-1717	4570	494	3385	-11114
	2002	37113	-45973	-8860	-7250	-1061	5205	586	2787	-8118
	2003	45399	-53907	-8508	-7993	-1221	5544	765	3408	-7549
Romania - Roumanie	1990	6380	-9901	-3521	-14	..	175	1	106	-3254
	2000	12113	-14043	-1930	-610	-72	325	8	860	-1355
	2002	16223	-18825	-2602	-872	-197	413	11	1536	-1525
	2003	20646	-25113	-4467	-1077	-254	372	11	1861	-3311
Russian Federation - Fédération de Russie	1995	92987	-82809	10178	-7650	-197	4281	100	156	6965
	2000	114599	-61091	53508	-11491	-887	4752	61	71	46840
	2002	120912	-84463	36449	-12260	-2969	5677	695	-750	29116
	2003	151959	-102558	49401	-24228	-12521	11057	6338	-385	35845
Rwanda	1990	143	-354	-211	-21	-6	4	..	143	-85
	2000	128	-423	-296	-28	-3	14	..	216	-94
	2001	159	-434	-275	-34	-3	14	..	193	-102
	2002	132	-435	-302	-27	0	8	..	195	-126
Saint Kitts and Nevis - Saint-Kitts-et-Nevis	1990	82	-132	-50	-8	-5	3	..	7	-47
	2000	150	-249	-99	-36	-21	6	..	63	-66
	2001	154	-241	-87	-39	-23	5	..	16	-106
	2002	155	-257	-102	-44	-23	6	0	16	-124
Saint Lucia - Sainte-Lucie	1990	282	-320	-38	-32	-26	6	..	8	-57
	2000	384	-437	-52	-48	-31	4	..	18	-79
	2001	338	-385	-48	-44	-28	3	..	14	-75
	2002	328	-402	-73	-46	-28	3	..	13	-104
Saint Vincent and the Grenadines - Saint-Vincent-et-les Grenadines	1990	130	-152	-22	-16	-13	5	0	10	-24
	2000	178	-204	-26	-22	-13	3	..	16	-29
	2001	174	-212	-37	-19	-11	2	..	13	-41
	2002	177	-217	-40	-17	-11	3	..	12	-42
Samoa	1990	45	-95	-50	-2	..	7	..	54	9
	1995	64	-115	-51	-4	..	5	..	60	9
Sao Tome and Principe - Sao Tomé-et-Principe	1990	8	-22	-14	0	..	0	..	2	-12
	2000	16	-36	-20	-4	..	..	..	4	-19
	2001	16	-36	-20	-5	..	..	..	4	-21
	2002	19	-41	-23	-5	..	..	..	5	-23
Saudi Arabia - Arabie saoudite	1990	47445	-43939	3506	-1220	-1220	9199	..	-15637	-4152
	2000	82369	-53003	29367	-2869	-2869	3349	..	-15511	14336
	2002	77745	-49670	28075	-3930	-3930	3719	..	-15975	11889
	2003	100715	-54713	46002	-4283	-4283	2998	..	-15016	29702
Senegal - Sénégal	1990	1453	-1840	-387	-213	-60	84	31	153	-363
	2000	1307	-1742	-435	-197	-84	85	11	214	-332
	2001	1401	-1842	-441	-172	-73	67	7	300	-245
	2002	1523	-2078	-556	-197	-93	67	3	369	-317

For sources and notes, see end of table.

Pour les sources et les notes, se reporter à la fin du tableau.

6.1A Balance of payments: current account summaries (continued)
Millions of dollars

6.1A Balance des paiements : sommaires des comptes des transactions courantes (suite)
Millions de dollars

Country or area / Pays ou zones	Year / Année	Goods and services / Biens et services			Income / Revenu				Current transfers (net) / Transferts courants (nets)	Current account balance / Solde du compte des transactions courantes
		Exports / Exportations	Imports / Importations	Balance on goods and services / Balance des biens et services	Debit / Débit		Credit / Crédit			
					Total	of which: / dont : Direct investment income / Revenu d' investissement direct	Total	of which: / dont : Direct investment income / Revenu d' investissement direct		
		(1)	(2)	(3) = (1)+(2)	(4)	(5)	(6)	(7)	(8)	(9)
Seychelles	1990	229	-247	-18	-18	-8	5	1	18	-13
	2000	489	-486	3	-58	-12	9	3	5	-41
	2001	513	-591	-78	-52	-28	8	3	4	-118
	2002	543	-578	-34	-100	-74	7	2	3	-124
Sierra Leone	1990	210	-215	-5	-72	-51	1	1	7	-69
	2000	55	-250	-195	-13	-2	7	1	88	-112
	2001	81	-276	-195	-15	-1	4	1	107	-98
	2002	98	-336	-238	-21	-2	18	0	167	-73
Singapore - Singapour	1990	67489	-64953	2537	-5502	..	6508	..	-421	3122
	2000	168960	-154501	14459	-16349	..	16291	..	-1121	13280
	2001	153298	-136561	16737	-15021	..	15566	..	-1146	16137
	2002	158076	-137123	20953	-15512	..	14367	..	-1105	18704
Slovakia - Slovaquie	1995	10969	-10658	311	-263	0	250	0	93	390
	2000	14137	-14596	-459	-623	-43	268	27	120	-694
Slovenia - Slovénie	1995	10377	-10748	-371	-204	4	406	-1	95	-75
	2000	10696	-11385	-689	-408	-90	434	23	115	-548
	2002	12764	-12452	312	-559	-115	488	5	134	375
	2003	15719	-15733	-14	-670	-118	592	13	106	15
Solomon Islands - Iles Salomon	1990	95	-156	-61	-8	-2	2	..	38	-28
	1995	210	-231	-21	-8	-7	1	0	36	8
South Africa - Afrique du Sud	1990	27742	-21016	6726	-4929	-962	657	353	-321	2134
	2000	36891	-33075	3816	-5696	-2329	2511	878	-926	-295
	2002	36095	-32132	3963	-4975	-2365	2179	637	-556	610
	2003	45304	-42556	2748	-6137	-3014	2751	769	-819	-1456
Spain - Espagne	1990	83595	-100870	-17275	-11350	-2455	7817	357	2799	-18009
	2000	169745	-182308	-12564	-23268	-4064	15017	1931	1578	-19237
	2002	190631	-198155	-7524	-30922	-6728	20234	5467	2168	-16044
	2003	236426	-248427	-12001	-36573	-7253	24654	8005	244	-23676
Sri Lanka	1990	2293	-2965	-672	-260	-25	93	0	541	-298
	2000	6378	-8105	-1727	-449	-109	149	2	983	-1044
	2001	6172	-7154	-982	-375	-104	108	3	1005	-243
	2002	5967	-7103	-1135	-327	-100	75	2	1123	-264
Sudan - Soudan	1990	499	-877	-378	-148	..	12	..	141	-372
	2000	1834	-2014	-180	-580	..	5	..	237	-518
	2002	2081	-3112	-1031	-638	-633	29	..	666	-974
	2003	2491	-3337	-846	-592	-531	10	..	718	-710
Suriname	1990	869	-840	29	-19	-3	4	..	53	67
	2000	490	-462	28	-7	..	13	..	-2	32
	2002	408	-488	-80	-51	..	8	..	-9	-131
	2003	547	-653	-106	-60	..	12	..	-5	-159
Swaziland	1990	658	-768	-110	-103	-85	162	9	102	51
	2000	1119	-1332	-213	-113	-81	154	1	107	-65
	2001	1160	-1302	-142	-106	-90	160	1	34	-53
	2002	1072	-1177	-105	-93	-77	141	2	10	-46
Sweden - Suède	1990	70561	-70490	70	-14164	-473	9691	3690	-1936	-6339
	2000	107683	-95656	12027	-22137	-8867	20074	12880	-3348	6617
	2002	108181	-91499	16682	-19044	-6523	18018	11800	-2872	12784
	2003	132734	-111918	20816	-22638	-8547	22934	14696	1732	22844
Switzerland - Suisse	1990	96927	-96388	539	-19939	-1286	28686	2829	-2329	6955
	2000	123723	-108311	15412	-39682	-10516	61612	26114	-2926	34417
	2001	123523	-110740	12783	-38049	-7606	53147	18684	-3983	23898
	2002	129853	-111149	18705	-29944	-5350	41429	12103	-4179	26011

For sources and notes, see end of table.

Pour les sources et les notes, se reporter à la fin du tableau.

Country or area / Pays ou zones	Year / Année	Goods and services / Biens et services — Exports / Exportations (1)	Imports / Importations (2)	Balance on goods and services / Balance des biens et services (3) = (1)+(2)	Income / Revenu — Debit / Débit — Total (4)	of which / dont : Direct investment income / Revenu d' investissement direct (5)	Credit / Crédit — Total (6)	of which / dont : Direct investment income / Revenu d' investissement direct (7)	Current transfers (net) / Transferts courants (nets) (8)	Current account balance / Solde du compte des transactions courantes (9)
Syrian Arab Republic - République arabe syrienne	1990	5030	-2955	2075	-831	..	430	..	88	1762
	2000	6845	-5390	1455	-1224	..	345	..	485	1061
	2001	7487	-5976	1511	-1162	..	379	..	493	1221
	2002	8227	-6341	1886	-1175	..	250	..	479	1440
Tajikistan - Tadjikistan	2002	768	-928	-160	-42	0	1	..	186	-15
	2003	995	-1147	-153	-71	-1	1	..	218	-5
Thailand - Thaïlande	1990	29230	-35870	-6641	-2913	-312	2059	1	213	-7281
	2000	81762	-71653	10109	-5616	..	4235	..	586	9313
	2002	81480	-73729	7751	-4696	..	3356	..	603	7014
	2003	94171	-85293	8877	-4790	..	2988	..	890	7965
Togo	1990	663	-847	-184	-65	-15	33	..	132	-84
	1995	465	-671	-206	-42	-1	9	7	118	-122
	2000	424	-602	-179	-62	-17	33	2	68	-140
	2001	429	-646	-217	-55	-25	26	1	77	-169
Tonga	1990	38	-74	-36	-1	0	5	0	37	6
	2001	24	-91	-67	-2	..	6	..	51	-13
Trinidad and Tobago - Trinité-et-Tobago	1990	2289	-1427	862	-436	-197	40	..	-6	459
	1995	2799	-2110	688	-467	-187	77	..	-4	294
	2000	4844	-3709	1135	-709	..	81	..	38	544
	2001	4878	-3956	922	-648	..	109	..	33	416
Tunisia - Tunisie	1990	5203	-6039	-836	-552	-97	97	1	828	-463
	2000	8607	-9311	-705	-1036	-468	94	3	825	-821
	2002	9538	-10431	-893	-1056	-473	72	6	1131	-746
	2003	10964	-11909	-945	-1174	-537	81	9	1307	-730
Turkey - Turquie	1990	21042	-25652	-4610	-3425	-161	917	..	4493	-2625
	2000	51150	-62192	-11042	-6838	-279	2836	368	5225	-9819
	2002	54909	-55366	-457	-7040	-379	2486	293	3490	-1521
	2003	70292	-73821	-3529	-7673	-471	2246	203	2106	-6850
Uganda - Ouganda	1990	178	-686	-509	-48	..	..	..	293	-263
	2000	663	-1409	-745	-166	-19	53	..	499	-359
	2001	673	-1550	-877	-178	-17	37	..	584	-433
	2002	720	-1643	-923	-160	-18	24	..	707	-353
Ukraine	1995	17090	-18280	-1190	-681	..	247	..	472	-1152
	2000	19522	-17947	1575	-1085	-43	143	..	848	1481
	2002	23351	-21494	1857	-769	-105	165	..	1921	3174
	2003	28953	-27665	1288	-835	-90	254	..	2184	2891
United Kingdom - Royaume-Uni	1990	239226	-264090	-24863	-144991	-13960	139837	29032	-8794	-38811
	2000	403920	-433362	-29442	-196780	-41460	204717	68029	-14714	-36219
	2002	410984	-457806	-46821	-156037	-28290	188647	79384	-12844	-27055
	2003	453503	-506919	-53415	-170357	-39564	206361	90931	-16046	-33457
United Republic of Tanzania - République-Unie de Tanzanie	1990	538	-1474	-936	-191	..	6	..	562	-559
	2000	1291	-2050	-759	-180	-13	50	..	391	-499
	2001	1456	-2250	-794	-141	-1	55	..	399	-480
	2002	1568	-2224	-656	-91	-2	74	..	420	-251
United States - Etats-Unis	1990	535260	-616120	-80860	-143190	-3450	171750	65980	-26660	-78960
	2000	1070979	-1449328	-378345	-329863	-56910	350449	151839	-55684	-413442
	2002	975940	-1397678	-421736	-259625	-46459	266798	147291	-59381	-473943
	2003	1020503	-1517009	-496507	-261104	-68655	294385	187522	-67439	-530664
Uruguay	1990	2158	-1659	499	-580	..	258	..	8	186
	2000	3660	-4193	-533	-842	-89	782	1	28	-566
	2002	2676	-2474	202	-405	202	453	0	72	322
	2003	3051	-2707	344	-602	-10	238	..	72	52

For sources and notes, see end of table.

Pour les sources et les notes, se reporter à la fin du tableau.

Country or area Pays ou zones	Year Année	Goods and services Biens et services			Income Revenu				Current transfers (net) Transferts courants (nets)	Current account balance Solde du compte des transactions courantes
		Exports Exportations	Imports Importations	Balance on goods and services Balance des biens et services	Debit / Débit		Credit / Crédit			
					Total	of which: / dont : Direct investment income Revenu d'investissement direct	Total	of which: / dont : Direct investment income Revenu d'investissement direct		
		(1)	(2)	(3) = (1)+(2)	(4)	(5)	(6)	(7)	(8)	(9)
Vanuatu	1990	74	-103	-29	-33	-15	32	..	25	-6
	1995	110	-115	-5	-50	-36	13	..	23	-18
	2000	157	-147	10	-32	-22	19	..	8	5
	2001	139	-151	-12	-21	-14	17	..	18	2
Venezuela	1990	18806	-9451	9355	-3432	-224	2658	231	-302	8279
	2000	34711	-21300	13411	-4437	-1424	3049	296	-170	11853
	2002	27716	-17474	10242	-4241	-1913	1587	286	-165	7423
	2003	26627	-14026	12601	-4096	-1681	1121	219	-2	9624
Viet Nam	2000	17150	-17325	-175	-782	..	331	..	1732	1106
	2001	17837	-17928	-91	-795	..	318	..	1250	682
	2002	19654	-21458	-1804	-888	..	167	..	1921	-604
Yemen - Yémen	1990	1490	-2170	-680	-409	-283	38	..	1790	739
	2000	4008	-3294	714	-927	-855	150	..	1399	1337
	2002	3787	-3867	-80	-901	-840	135	..	1384	538
	2003	4252	-4561	-309	-1008	-945	99	..	1367	149
Yugoslavia, SFR (former) - Yougoslavie, RSF (anc.)	1990	20682	-31996	-11314	-1667	..	789	..	9828	-2364
Zambia - Zambie	1990	1360	-1897	-537	-439	-115	2	..	380	-594
	2000	871	-1318	-447	-166	..	46	..	14	-553
Zimbabwe	1990	2012	-2001	11	-286	-92	23	1	112	-140

Sources: IMF, *Balance of Payments Statistics* on CD-ROM.

Notes: See following pages.

Sources : FMI, *Balance of Payments Statistics* sur CD-ROM.

Notes : Se reporter aux pages suivantes.

Balance of payments:	Balance des paiements :
current account	compte courant
General notes for table 6.1A	Notes générales du tableau 6.1A

The countries presented in table 6.1A are those covered in the IMF *Balance of Payments Statistics* on CD-ROM.

The following explanatory notes are intended to provide a brief description of the balance-of-payments categories presented in table 6.1A. There are many exceptions to the definitions of categories, and for these the reader should refer to the country notes in the IMF *Balance of Payments Statistics Yearbook* or the corresponding CD-ROM. For further information on the concepts and definitions used, see the IMF *Balance of Payments Manual* (1993, BPM 5).

Balance of payments current account data cover all transactions between residents and non-residents involving economic values and mainly concerning goods, services, income and current transfers, recorded as gross debits and gross credits.

Column 1. Exports of goods (f.o.b.) and services

According to the definition in BPM 5, the goods component in the figures presented in table 6.1A includes general merchandise, goods for processing (gross value of goods before and after processing), repairs on goods (value of repairs only), goods procured in ports and non-monetary gold. The services component in those figures comprises 11 main BPM 5 categories: transportation, travel, communications, construction, insurance, financial services, computer and information services, royalties and licence fees, other business services, personal-cultural-recreational services, and government services n.i.e. Figures on trade in services are provided separately in table 5.1.

The components of export figures related to goods in table 6.1A differ from those reported in the trade returns in table 1.1 because of adjustments for coverage, valuation, timing, inland freight, etc. Such adjustments are necessary to make the trade statistics compatible with the concepts used in the balance of payments. Further adjustments are applied in cases in which the market price for goods differs from the price used for customs purposes. The valuation problem is probably more important for imports than for exports and is likely to be a factor whenever there is a long delay between the date of sale and the date on which the import duty becomes payable. For additional information on adjustments required for valuation, timing, etc., see the IMF *Balance of Payments Manual* and the United Nations *International Trade Statistics Concepts and Definitions*, Statistical Papers (Series M, No. 52).

Column 2. Imports of goods (f.o.b.) and services

Adjustments for coverage, valuation, timing, etc., are made to imports reported in trade returns, as described in the notes for column 1. In addition, an adjustment is made to convert imports from a c.i.f. to an f.o.b. basis for those countries reporting imports c.i.f.

Les pays présentés dans le tableau 6.1A sont ceux analysés dans la *Balance of Payments Statistics* sur CD-ROM du FMI.

L'objet des notes explicatives qui suivent est de fournir une description brève des rubriques des balances des paiements présentées dans le tableau 6.1A. En fait, les définitions des catégories comportent plusieurs exceptions, et pour celles-ci le lecteur doit se référer aux notes par pays du FMI *Balance of Payments Statistics Yearbook* ou du CD-ROM correspondant. Pour des détails sur les concepts et les définitions utilisés, voir le *Manuel de la balance des paiements* du FMI (1993, MBP 5).

Les données du compte des transactions courantes de la balance des paiements recouvrent toutes les transactions, entre entités résidentes et non résidentes, portant sur des valeurs économiques, principalement concernant les biens, les services, les revenus et les transferts courants et faisant apparaître les crédits ou les débits bruts.

Colonne 1. Exportations de biens (f.a.b.) et services

Conformément à la définition du MBP 5, la partie relative aux biens, présentée dans le tableau 6.1A, comprend les marchandises générales, les biens importés ou exportés pour subir une transformation (valeur brut des biens avant et après transformation), la valeur des réparations de biens (seulement la valeur des réparations), les biens achetés dans les ports et l'or non monétaire. La partie relative aux services comprend 11 principales catégories du MBP 5 : transports, voyages, communications, services de bâtiment et travaux publics, assurances, services financiers, services d'informatique et d'information, redevances et droits de licence, autres services aux entreprises, services personnels, culturels et relatifs aux loisirs et services fournis ou reçus par les administrations publiques, n.c.a. Les données sur le commerce des services sont présentées séparément dans le tableau 5.1.

La partie des données relative aux exportations de biens dans le tableau 6.1A est différente des données présentées dans le tableau 1.1 relatif au commerce mondial. Ces différences sont dues principalement aux ajustements effectués sur la couverture, l'évaluation, la date d'enregistrement des transactions, le fret terrestre, etc. Les ajustements des données relatives aux importations et aux exportations sont nécessaires, car ils permettent de rendre les données du commerce extérieur compatibles avec les concepts employés dans les statistiques de balance des paiements. Les ajustements d'évaluation sont requis, en particulier dans les cas où les prix du marché auxquels les marchandises ont été vendues diffèrent des prix utilisés par les autorités douanières. Ce problème d'évaluation est probablement plus important pour les importations que pour les exportations et devient un sérieux facteur lorsque s'écoule une longue période entre la date de vente et la date à laquelle les importations sont soumises aux droits de douane. Pour de plus amples détails sur les ajustements d'évaluation, de date d'enregistrement des transactions, etc., se référer aux publications suivantes : FMI *Manuel de la balance des paiements*, et ONU *Statistiques du commerce international – Concepts et définitions*, Etudes statistiques (Série M, No. 52).

Colonne 2. Importations de biens (f.a.b.) et services

Les ajustements au titre de la couverture, de l'évaluation, de la date d'enregistrement des transactions, etc. sont également effectués sur les données présentant des importations, comme décrit ci-dessus dans les notes portant sur la colonne 1. Par ailleurs, les importations déclarées sur la base c.a.f. sont converties sur la base f.a.b. pour les pays qui reportent c.a.f.

Balance of payments:
current account
General notes for table 6.1A *(concluded)*

Balance des paiements :
compte courant
Notes générales du tableau 6.1A *(fin)*

Column 3. Balance on goods and services

The figures presented show the balance of trade in goods (f.o.b./f.o.b. basis) and services.

Column 4. Income, total debit

Income figures shown on the debit side comprise compensation of non-resident employees and investment income payments on external financial assets and liabilities. Included in the investment income are payments on direct investment (column 5), and portfolio and other investments. Column 4 presents total payments for income.

Column 5. Direct investment income, debit

The heading includes two categories: income on equity and income on debt, as income accruing to a direct investor residing in one economy from the ownership of direct investment capital in another economy. Income on direct investment is presented on a net basis for both direct investment abroad and in the reporting economy (i.e. receipts of income on equity and income on debt less payments on income on equity and income on debt for each).

Column 6. Income, total credit

This is a counterpart to column 4. Column 6 presents total receipts for income.

Column 7. Direct investment income, credit

This is a counterpart to column 5.

Column 8. Current transfers, net

Transfers are defined as economic values exchanged without *quid pro quo* (without reciprocity). BPM 5 distinguishes current and capital transfers. Current transfers comprise two main categories: general government and other transfers. General government transfers include transfers – in cash or in kind – between governments of different economies or between governments and international organizations (international cooperation). Other transfers occur between other sectors of the economy and non-residents of that economy and can take place between individuals, non-governmental institutions, organizations and groups. Workers' remittances also fall into this category.

Column 9. Current account balance

Balance of payments current account data cover all transactions between residents and non-residents involving economic values and concerning goods, services, income and current transfers, recorded as gross debits and gross credits.

Colonne 3. Balance des biens et services

Les chiffres inclus présentent la balance du commerce de biens (f.a.b./f.a.b.) et services.

Colonne 4. Revenu, débit total

Les chiffres relatifs au revenu et présentés comme débit comprennent la rémunération des salariés non résidents et les paiements du revenu des investissements afférents aux avoirs ou engagements financiers extérieurs. Le revenu des investissements se subdivise en paiements provenant d'investissement direct (colonne 5), d'investissement de portefeuille et d'autres investissements. La colonne 4 montre les paiements totaux du revenu.

Colonne 5. Revenu d'investissement direct, débit

Deux catégories figurent sous cette rubrique : titres de participation et titres de créance. Ils recouvrent les revenus qui rapportent à un investisseur direct, résidant dans une économie, des capitaux d'investissement direct qu'il possède dans une entreprise située dans une autre économie. Aussi bien pour les investissements directs à l'étranger que pour ceux de l'étranger, c'est le montant net des revenus que l'on reporte (autrement dit : dans chaque cas, les revenus perçus moins les revenus versés).

Colonne 6. Revenu, crédit total

Voir la description de la colonne 4. La colonne 6 présente les recettes totales des revenus.

Colonne 7. Revenu d'investissement direct, crédit

Voir la description de la colonne 5.

Colonne 8. Transferts courants, nets

Les transferts sont définis comme des valeurs économiques échangées sans *quid pro quo* (sans réciprocité). MBP 5 distingue les transferts courants et les transferts de capitaux. Les transferts courants se répartissent en deux grandes catégories sectorielles : les administrations publiques et les autres secteurs. Parmi les transferts courants des administrations publiques, on trouve les transferts – en espèces ou en nature – entre les administrations publiques de différentes économies ou entre les administrations publiques et les organisations internationales (coopération internationale). Les transferts d'autres secteurs s'opèrent entre tous les autres secteurs d'une économie et les non résidents de celle-ci. Ils peuvent avoir lieu entre les particuliers, les institutions non gouvernementales, les organisations et les groupes. Les envois de fonds des travailleurs sont également inclus sous cette rubrique.

Colonne 9. Solde du compte des transactions courantes

Les données du compte des transactions courantes de la balance des paiements recouvrent toutes les transactions, entre entités résidentes et non résidentes, portant sur des valeurs économiques et principalement concernant les biens, les services, les revenus et les transferts courants, faisant apparaître les crédits ou débits bruts.

6.1B   Balance of payments: capital and financial
          account summaries
          Millions of dollars

6.1B   Balance des paiements : sommaires des
          comptes de capital et d'opérations financières
          Millions de dollars

Country or area / Pays ou zones	Year / Année	Capital account, net / Compte de capital, net	Direct investment / Investissement direct		Portfolio investment / Investissement de portefeuille		Other investment / Autres investissements		Reserve assets / Avoirs de réserve	Financial account, net / Compte financier, net	Capital and financial account, net / Compte de capital et compte financier, net
			Abroad / A l'étranger	In reporting economy / Dans l'économie déclarante	Assets / Avoirs	Liabilities / Engagements	Assets / Avoirs	Liabilities / Engagements			
		(1)	(2)	(3)	(4)	(5)	(6)	(7)	(8)	(9)	(10) = (1) + (9)
Albania - Albanie	1990	..	..	..	..	..	..	88	32	120	120
	2000	78	..	143	-25	..	-40	123	-132	69	147
	2002	121	..	135	-37	..	-3	111	-29	178	299
	2003	157	..	178	-22	..	-72	118	-100	103	259
Algeria - Algérie	1990	..	-5	0	..	..	-229	-712	-138	-1084	-1084
Angola	1990	..	-1	-335	..	..	-349	941	-2	255	255
	2000	18	..	879	..	..	-702	-309	-631	-763	-745
	2001	4	..	2145	..	..	-517	-360	466	1736	1740
Anguilla	1990	3	..	11	..	..	10	1	-3	19	23
	2000	10	..	38	..	..	-1	4	0	41	50
	2001	9	..	33	..	1	-3	-10	-4	16	25
	2002	7	..	37	-1	0	-1	-18	-2	16	22
Antigua and Barbuda - Antigua-et-Barbuda	1990	5	..	61	..	..	-2	2	1	61	66
	2000	39	..	28	0	2	0	12	6	48	88
	2001	12	..	44	0	-2	-4	22	-16	44	56
	2002	14	..	48	-3	1	-11	50	-8	77	91
Argentina - Argentine	1990	..	..	1836	-241	-1068	661	-3333	-3121	-5267	-5267
	2000	106	-901	10418	-1252	-1331	-1368	3060	403	9029	9135
	2002	406	627	1093	477	-6886	-8896	1440	4526	-7618	-7212
	2003	70	-774	1020	-95	-8064	-4448	9679	-3497	-6179	-6109
Armenia - Arménie	1995	8	..	25	..	..	-9	257	-76	198	206
	2000	28	..	104	-19	0	-9	177	-20	233	261
	2002	68	..	111	3	-2	-89	142	-83	83	151
	2003	93	0	121	0	0	-79	88	-60	70	163
Aruba	1990	..	..	131	9	-15	-10	58	-12	161	161
	2000	10	-12	-228	-43	2	-98	63	16	-299	-289
	2002	19	-6	239	14	22	-43	38	-33	230	250
Australia - Australie	1990	1516	-1013	8111	380	6971	-2735	4521	-1740	14495	16011
	2000	615	-829	12884	-12465	15588	-4347	2815	1365	14136	14751
	2002	443	-7393	16141	-16400	17007	-2955	10705	-122	17185	17628
	2003	764	-17115	8601	-8911	50692	-6295	9173	-6877	29361	30124
Austria - Autriche	1990	8	-1701	653	-1608	3239	-1433	831	15	-4	4
	2000	-432	-5599	8523	-27145	30360	-16334	13790	746	4153	3721
	2002	-571	-5501	886	-22964	18599	11239	-6733	1723	-3227	-3798
	2003	-127	-7139	6916	-17604	23516	-14575	11301	2036	3683	3556
Azerbaijan - Azerbaïdjan	1995	-2	..	330	-2	0	-22	198	-162	342	341
	2000	..	-1	130	..	..	-114	427	-274	168	168
	2002	-29	-326	1392	0	..	-303	115	5	884	856
	2003	-23	-933	3285	0	..	-169	55	-82	2156	2133
Bahamas	1990	-8	0	-17	..	..	2283	-2199	-12	55	47
	1995	-13	0	107	..	..	7437	-7439	3	107	95
	2000	-16	..	250	..	..	-19067	19247	61	490	474
	2001	-20	..	101	..	..	-25412	25591	30	310	289
Bahrain - Bahreïn	1990	457	-25	-183	698	..	10769	-10102	-796	361	818
	2000	50	-10	364	-88	282	-3834	3256	-200	-230	-180
	2002	102	-190	217	-5140	915	33425	-30462	-35	-1269	-1167
	2003	50	-741	517	-3064	688	-20787	23134	-44	-297	-247
Bangladesh	1990	..	..	3	..	0	-208	757	-79	474	474
	2000	249	..	280	..	1	-1247	619	121	-225	23
	2001	235	..	79	0	-3	-434	557	208	406	641
	2002	364	-3	52	-1	-1	-560	171	-412	-754	-390
Barbados - Barbade	1990	..	-1	11	-3	-22	-22	76	48	86	86
	2000	2	-1	19	-29	100	53	147	-178	111	113
	2001	1	-1	19	-31	150	-57	204	-223	62	63
	2002	..	0	17	-36	-9	-253	316	24	59	59

For sources and notes, see end of table.

Pour les sources et les notes, se reporter à la fin du tableau.

257

6.1B Balance of payments: capital and financial account summaries
(continued)
Millions of dollars

6.1B Balance des paiements : sommaires des comptes de capital et d'opérations financières
(suite)
Millions de dollars

Country or area / Pays ou zones	Year / Année	Capital account, net / Compte de capital, net	Direct investment / Investissement direct — Abroad / A l'étranger	Direct investment — In reporting economy / Dans l'économie déclarante	Portfolio investment / Investissement de portefeuille — Assets / Avoirs	Portfolio — Liabilities / Engagements	Other investment / Autres investissements — Assets / Avoirs	Other — Liabilities / Engagements	Reserve assets / Avoirs de réserve	Financial account, net / Compte financier, net	Capital and financial account, net / Compte de capital et compte financier, net
		(1)	(2)	(3)	(4)	(5)	(6)	(7)	(8)	(9)	(10) = (1) + (9)
Belarus - Bélarus	1995	7	..	15	..	..	-155	707	-284	282	290
	2000	69	0	119	-6	50	42	-114	-76	15	84
	2002	53	206	247	-2	-7	-309	351	-101	385	438
	2003	69	-2	171	1	5	-61	184	14	312	381
Belgium - Belgique	2002	-661	-11442	13772	-5007	19683	-44556	15636	32	-13825	-14486
	2003	-968	-23302	33768	-3190	5739	-80013	71572	1723	2449	1481
Belgium-Luxembourg - Belgique-Luxembourg	1990	..	-6314	8047	-9443	7946	-64422	62536	-404	-2055	-2055
	1995	378	-11603	10689	-29472	4650	-23445	34426	-243	-13155	-12777
	2000	-213	-207472	214941	-122814	132547	-39033	14999	959	-8274	-8487
	2001	26	-86091	73635	-125068	140588	-70053	63158	-1442	-9420	-9395
Belize	1990	..	..	17	..	..	..	5	-12	10	10
	2000	1	..	18	..	113	-39	83	-52	123	124
	2001	1	..	60	..	-15	-2	129	3	175	175
	2002	10	..	25	..	110	-1	9	5	149	159
Benin - Bénin	1990	125	..	62	-5	..	-6	-111	-58	-118	7
	1995	89	-1	7	-64	0	-62	109	82	72	161
	2000	73	-8	64	6	-2	25	3	-87	1	74
	2001	70	-2	44	3	-4	-34	143	-147	1	71
Bolivia - Bolivie	1990	7	-1	27	..	..	-32	214	-5	203	210
	2000	..	-3	736	55	..	-146	-180	39	501	501
	2002	..	-3	677	-19	..	-194	228	303	992	992
	2003	..	-3	171	-68	..	-178	490	-152	261	261
Bosnia and Herzegovina - Bosnie-Herzégovine	2000	525	..	146	..	..	-417	396	-77	48	573
	2001	383	..	118	..	..	906	345	-762	608	991
	2002	392	..	268	..	..	315	503	110	1195	1587
	2003	479	..	382	..	..	136	881	-197	1202	1681
Botswana	1990	65	-7	96	..	1	-137	130	-307	-225	-160
	1995	14	-41	70	-36	6	-89	56	-207	-240	-226
Brazil - Brésil	1990	35	-665	989	-67	579	-2864	6587	-474	4084	4119
	2000	273	-2282	32779	-1696	8651	-2989	-15131	2260	21395	21667
	2002	433	-2482	16590	-321	-4797	-3211	2250	-314	7358	7790
	2003	498	-249	10144	179	5129	-9483	-859	-8479	-3770	-3272
Bulgaria - Bulgarie	1990	..	..	4	..	..	384	374	878	1640	1640
	2000	25	-3	1002	-62	-115	-332	566	-409	644	669
	2002	0	-28	905	218	-302	283	539	-586	1035	1035
	2003	0	-22	1419	-72	-135	148	716	-932	1121	1121
Burkina Faso	1990	..	..	..	..	..	-7	89	-7	75	75
	2000	186	0	23	6	0	-10	77	31	127	314
	2001	197	-1	9	10	2	6	95	-31	90	288
Burundi	1990	-1	0	1	..	..	4	72	4	81	81
	2000	0	..	12	..	..	7	65	1	84	84
	2002	0	..	..	..	..	-4	53	-47	2	1
	2003	-1	..	0	..	..	-20	69	-10	39	38
Cambodia - Cambodge	1995	92	..	151	..	..	-103	108	-73	82	174
	2000	36	-7	149	-7	..	-184	241	-109	83	119
	2001	45	-7	148	-8	..	-118	140	-90	65	110
	2002	13	-6	54	-8	..	-12	260	-188	101	114
Cameroon - Cameroun	1990	3	-15	-113	56	..	482	160	65	634	637
	1995	20	-1	7	-26	..	-147	180	14	28	48
Canada	1990	5331	-5229	7581	-2239	15964	-8442	9648	-1139	16144	21475
	2000	3581	-44487	66144	-42975	10259	-4195	754	-3720	-18220	-14639
	2002	3177	-26461	20940	-15928	13365	-8531	5009	185	-11421	-8243
	2003	2836	-22241	6273	-9139	13160	-20555	10910	3255	-18337	-15501

For sources and notes, see end of table.

Pour les sources et les notes, se reporter à la fin du tableau.

6.1B Balance of payments: capital and financial account summaries
(continued)
Millions of dollars

6.1B Balance des paiements : sommaires des comptes de capital et d'opérations financières
(suite)
Millions de dollars

Country or area Pays ou zones	Year Année	Capital account, net Compte de capital, net	Direct investment Investissement direct		Portfolio investment Investissement de portefeuille		Other investment Autres investissements		Reserve assets, Avoirs de réserve	Financial account, net Compte financier, net	Capital and financial account, net Compte de capital et compte financier, net
			Abroad A l'étranger	In reporting economy Dans l'économie déclarante	Assets Avoirs	Liabilities Engagements	Assets Avoirs	Liabilities Engagements			
		(1)	(2)	(3)	(4)	(5)	(6)	(7)	(8)	(9)	(10) = (1) + (9)
Cape Verde - Cap-Vert	1990	2	0	0	..	..	-29	4	12	-12	-11
	2000	11	-1	33	0	..	-22	39	10	59	70
	2002	9	..	15	..	..	-2	58	0	71	79
	2003	21	..	15	..	..	-7	44	10	62	83
Central African Republic - République centrafricaine	1990	..	-4	1	..	..	-16	98	9	88	88
Chad - Tchad	1990	..	..	..	..	..	..	75	4	79	79
Chile - Chili	1990	..	-8	661	..	361	355	1287	-2121	535	535
	2000	..	-3987	4860	766	-127	-2065	1338	-317	471	471
	2002	..	-294	1888	-3083	999	1624	1087	-185	1912	1912
	2003	..	-1395	2982	-5327	1701	-387	1678	357	-273	-273
China - Chine	1990	..	-830	3487	-241	..	-231	578	-11555	-8792	-8792
	2000	-35	-916	38399	-11308	7317	-43864	12329	-10693	-8735	-8770
	2001	-54	-6884	44241	-20654	1249	20813	-3933	-47447	-12615	-12669
	2002	-50	-2518	49308	-12095	1752	-3077	-1029	-75217	-42876	-42926
China, Hong Kong SAR - Chine, Hong Kong RAS	2000	-1546	-59352	61924	-22022	46508	18279	-41376	-10044	-5878	-7424
	2001	-1174	-11345	23776	-40133	-1161	59137	-41985	-4684	-11310	-12484
	2002	-2011	-17463	9682	-37702	-1084	46617	-26412	2377	-17373	-19385
	2003	-1016	-3747	13539	-31458	991	-22181	15193	-994	-18447	-19463
Colombia - Colombie	1990	..	-16	500	..	-4	-102	-380	-610	-612	-612
	2000	..	-325	2395	-1173	1453	-551	-1623	-862	-791	-791
	2002	..	-857	2115	2029	-933	283	-1246	-139	1170	1170
	2003	..	-923	1746	-1741	130	1651	59	188	1065	1065
Comoros - Comores	1990	..	-1	0	..	..	1	14	5	19	19
	1995	..	..	1	..	..	-2	18	3	21	21
Congo	1990	..	..	..	..	..	-68	473	-113	292	292
	2000	17	-4	166	-4	0	-74	-488	-184	-588	-571
	2001	19	-6	77	-12	..	-41	-141	144	21	40
	2002	14	-4	331	-7	..	-25	-146	91	240	254
Costa Rica	1990	..	-2	163	..	-28	-125	176	197	381	381
	2000	18	-5	409	-18	-50	-344	154	153	298	316
	2002	6	-34	662	28	74	217	97	-163	882	888
	2003	28	-27	577	-92	96	171	485	-339	871	899
Côte d'Ivoire	1990	..	..	48	4	..	-92	1347	16	1324	1324
	2000	8	..	235	-13	5	-182	293	-89	246	254
	2002	8	..	213	-21	50	-439	34	-584	-754	-746
	2003	5	..	180	-35	52	-413	-108	-17	-341	-336
Croatia - Croatie	1995	..	-6	114	0	5	420	1005	-443	1095	1095
	2000	21	-4	1089	-23	730	-966	971	-582	1216	1237
	2002	443	-533	1124	-627	397	359	2236	-697	2259	2703
	2003	84	-80	1956	155	854	-2521	4249	-1392	3221	3305
Cyprus - Chypre	1990	..	-5	127	..	-38	-115	467	-294	142	142
	2000	..	-202	163	-293	89	-1389	1895	8	272	272
	2002	-5	-299	614	-636	161	2161	-1100	-389	462	456
	2003	23	-345	838	-664	807	-2550	1962	188	253	276
Czech Republic - République tchèque	1995	7	-37	2568	-325	1695	-2492	6816	-7453	771	778
	2000	-5	-43	4987	-2236	482	984	-300	-844	2991	2986
	2002	-4	-211	8497	-2373	814	4015	9	-6618	4003	3999
	2003	-3	-242	2514	-3006	1753	2279	2414	-442	5413	5410
Czechoslovakia (former) - Tchécoslovaquie (anc.)	1990	..	-20	207	..	..	-711	1166	1127	1770	1770
Denmark - Danemark	1990	..	-1482	1132	-1168	4068	-5442	7312	-3385	1035	1035
	2000	-14	-28355	35847	-23723	5783	-2143	8435	5649	1819	1805
	2002	101	-5152	6410	-4362	4843	-6307	6476	-5615	-3090	-2990
	2003	-45	-1314	2908	-21938	6012	-9983	19832	-4674	-9169	-9214

For sources and notes, see end of table.

Pour les sources et les notes, se reporter à la fin du tableau.

259

Country or area / Pays ou zones	Year / Année	Capital account, net / Compte de capital, net	Direct investment / Investissement direct Abroad / A l'étranger	Direct investment / Investissement direct In reporting economy / Dans l'économie déclarante	Portfolio investment / Investissement de portefeuille Assets / Avoirs	Portfolio investment / Investissement de portefeuille Liabilities / Engagements	Other investment / Autres investissements Assets / Avoirs	Other investment / Autres investissements Liabilities / Engagements	Reserve assets / Avoirs de réserve	Financial account, net / Compte financier, net	Capital and financial account, net / Compte de capital et compte financier, net
		(1)	(2)	(3)	(4)	(5)	(6)	(7)	(8)	(9)	(10) = (1) + (9)
Djibouti	1995	18	..	3	..	..	..	-7	7	4	22
Dominica - Dominique	1990	14	..	13	..	0	11	5	-4	24	38
	1995	25	..	54	-8	..	-4	-1	-7	34	58
	2000	8	..	11	0	14	-10	32	0	46	54
	2001	18	..	12	0	0	-5	21	-5	23	41
Dominican Republic - République dominicaine	1990	..	..	133	..	..	89	129	49	400	400
	2000	2	..	953	268	-4	-165	521	70	1643	1645
	2002	7	..	917	-14	-12	-1402	915	526	930	937
	2003	6	..	310	-20	553	-1535	-64	352	-405	-399
Ecuador - Equateur	1990	..	..	126	..	..	..	369	-261	234	234
	2000	1977	..	720	..	-1725	-1274	-297	-307	-2883	-906
	2002	31	..	1275	..	0	-1394	1382	68	1332	1362
	2003	78	..	1555	..	8	-904	-316	-150	193	271
Egypt - Egypte	1990	10610	-12	734	15	..	-1921	-9875	-2508	-13567	-2957
	2000	..	-51	1235	-3	269	-2991	619	1306	384	384
	2002	..	-28	647	-6	-672	-2943	530	-57	-2529	-2529
	2003	..	-21	237	-25	-18	-4651	-446	-395	-5318	-5318
El Salvador	1990	..	..	2	..	..	-21	36	-165	-148	-148
	2000	109	5	173	-9	-17	-245	380	46	333	442
	2002	209	26	470	-289	555	-225	150	124	810	1019
	2003	113	-19	104	-264	453	20	796	-316	773	886
Equatorial Guinea - Guinée équatoriale	1990	..	..	11	..	..	..	10	-3	17	17
	1995	53	..	127	..	..	..	-58	-9	60	113
Estonia - Estonie	1995	-1	-2	201	-33	11	-99	185	-113	150	149
	2000	17	-63	387	16	76	-167	139	-122	265	282
	2002	19	-132	285	-192	345	51	385	-55	682	701
	2003	40	-148	891	-394	558	-127	560	-169	1168	1208
Ethiopia - Ethiopie	1990	..	..	..	..	..	87	307	35	428	428
	2000	..	..	..	..	..	116	187	-84	218	218
	2001	..	..	..	..	..	25	454	117	596	596
	2002	..	..	..	..	..	-4	573	439	1008	1008
Fiji - Fidji	1990	48	-13	92	..	..	-18	-10	-34	17	65
	1995	87	3	70	..	..	12	-12	-77	-5	82
Finland - Finlande	1990	..	-2782	812	-469	5696	720	8428	-3931	8474	8474
	2000	103	-23898	9125	-18920	17116	-5636	14002	-351	-9192	-9089
	2002	89	-7801	8156	-13432	8899	-1328	-2773	113	-8490	-8402
	2003	108	7538	2899	-9872	8943	-16164	-1389	507	-5821	-5713
France	1990	-4133	-34824	13183	-8409	43219	-61543	73137	-10947	13817	9684
	2000	1392	-174320	42370	-97435	132332	632	59088	2433	-30116	-28724
	2002	-194	-49675	49442	-84653	67887	-36414	24268	3965	-19871	-20064
	2003	-8238	-57423	47753	-147532	136159	-20007	47420	-1274	-1964	-10202
Gabon	1990	..	-29	73	..	..	-285	330	-219	-130	-130
	1995	5	-35	-315	-30	80	-40	8	42	-288	-284
Gambia - Gambie	1990	..	..	..	..	..	-1	-8	-3	-12	-12
	1995	..	..	8	..	..	-4	15	4	24	24
Georgia - Géorgie	2000	-5	1	131	3	..	-8	-60	20	86	82
	2001	-5	0	110	0	..	-25	144	-47	182	177
	2002	18	-4	167	0	..	-73	132	-38	185	203
	2003	20	-4	338	0	..	-6	30	6	364	384
Germany - Allemagne	1990	-3113	-24484	3005	-13991	12290	-74670	43340	-7253	-61795	-64907
	2000	6188	-59744	210086	-191545	40882	-80175	120926	5222	34216	40404
	2002	-226	-9289	35547	-60355	101755	-164474	27693	1979	-68223	-68449
	2003	358	-1523	11268	-37588	103515	-153361	15677	684	-62032	-61675

For sources and notes, see end of table.

Pour les sources et les notes, se reporter à la fin du tableau.

6.1B Balance of payments: capital and financial account summaries
(continued)
Millions of dollars

6.1B Balance des paiements : sommaires des comptes de capital et d'opérations financières
(suite)
Millions de dollars

Country or area / Pays ou zones	Year / Année	Capital account, net / Compte de capital, net	Direct investment / Investissement direct Abroad / A l'étranger	Direct investment / Investissement direct In reporting economy / Dans l'économie déclarante	Portfolio investment / Investissement de portefeuille Assets / Avoirs	Portfolio investment / Investissement de portefeuille Liabilities / Engagements	Other investment / Autres investissements Assets / Avoirs	Other investment / Autres investissements Liabilities / Engagements	Reserve assets / Avoirs de réserve	Financial account, net / Compte financier, net	Capital and financial account, net / Compte de capital et compte financier, net
		(1)	(2)	(3)	(4)	(5)	(6)	(7)	(8)	(9)	(10) = (1) + (9)
Ghana	1990	-1	..	15	..	..	-94	242	26	189	188
	2000	..	..	166	..	..	70	158	161	555	555
	2002	..	..	59	..	..	95	-23	-294	-163	-163
	2003	..	..	137	..	..	68	372	-785	-208	-208
Greece - Grèce	1990	..	..	1005	..	..	..	2757	-40	3722	3722
	2000	2112	-2099	1083	-1184	9262	6970	-3551	-2573	8257	10370
	2002	1522	-669	53	-1893	12315	-6953	8896	-1863	9711	11233
	2003	1411	-9	717	-9807	23456	-4413	-3887	4723	10890	12301
Grenada - Grenade	1990	22	..	13	..	0	-11	17	-2	16	38
	2000	32	..	37	0	20	-11	18	-7	57	89
	2001	42	..	59	0	0	-5	-6	-6	41	84
	2002	32	..	58	-2	109	-14	-43	-31	77	109
Guatemala	1990	..	..	48	-2	-15	-78	182	42	177	177
	2000	86	..	230	-36	79	213	1035	-643	878	964
	2001	93	..	456	-45	175	157	804	-474	1072	1166
	2002	130	..	110	-38	-108	196	1012	-21	1151	1281
Guinea - Guinée	1990	7	..	18	..	..	-53	182	-3	144	151
	2000	..	..	10	9	..	-17	4	50	56	56
	2001	..	..	2	5	..	12	48	-4	62	62
	2002	31	..	..	5	..	-4	82	-76	6	37
Guinea-Bissau - Guinée-Bissau	1990	29	..	..	..	..	..	23	-5	18	47
	1995	49	..	..	..	..	..	1	-4	-3	46
Guyana	1995	10	..	74	..	3	-9	44	1	113	124
	2000	16	..	67	-3	-2	66	-30	-24	74	91
	2001	32	..	56	10	-3	66	-42	-10	76	108
	2002	34	..	44	18	8	45	-34	-6	75	108
Haiti - Haïti	1990	..	8	..	..	..	-23	44	39	68	68
	1995	50	..	7	..	..	-11	91	-176	-89	-39
Honduras	1990	..	..	44	0	..	-40	175	-20	159	159
	2000	129	..	282	-59	-1	-204	43	-32	28	157
	2002	80	..	176	-4	..	24	-2	-92	102	182
	2003	27	..	198	-4	..	-78	-41	100	176	203
Hungary - Hongrie	1990	..	..	..	..	..	-524	-423	558	-388	-388
	2000	270	-547	1694	831	-187	-193	2204	-1052	2810	3080
	2002	179	-264	854	-47	1838	-1574	-473	1792	1920	2099
	2003	-77	-1598	2506	35	2900	-2606	6039	-336	6975	6898
Iceland - Islande	1990	2	-12	22	..	25	-49	251	-74	163	165
	2000	-3	-375	155	-667	1142	-79	671	74	920	917
	2002	-1	-228	124	-337	577	-336	373	-61	111	109
	2003	-5	-169	147	-593	3696	-1978	-345	-307	451	446
India - Inde	1990	..	..	..	..	..	-611	5281	2798	7468	7468
	2000	-296	-424	2657	-173	2774	-1519	6024	-5928	3411	3115
	2001	162	-697	4334	-70	2041	2205	1566	-11897	-2519	-2357
	2002	3480	-453	3030	-36	967	4790	-234	-16868	-8803	-5323
Indonesia - Indonésie	1990	..	..	1093	..	-93	..	3332	-2088	2244	2244
	2000	..	..	-4550	..	-1909	-150	-162	-4851	-11622	-11622
	2001	..	..	-3278	..	-243	-125	-5324	1370	-7599	-7599
	2002	..	..	145	..	1222	-500	-2988	-4010	-6131	-6131
Iran, Islamic Rep. of - Iran, Rép. islamique d'	1990	..	..	..	..	..	-1510	1805	325	620	620
	1995	..	..	17	..	..	-419	-372	-2786	-3560	-3560
	2000	..	..	39	..	..	-8257	-1971	-1083	-11273	-11273
Ireland - Irlande	1990	387	-365	627	-465	266	-5284	3212	-626	-2635	-2248
	2000	1074	-4641	25501	-83075	77906	-37036	28883	-121	7791	8865
	2002	512	-8524	29131	-105302	68812	-33267	49038	292	2158	2669
	2003	442	-3528	26599	-161319	106389	-48864	84028	1890	2841	3283

For sources and notes, see end of table.

Pour les sources et les notes, se reporter à la fin du tableau.

Country or area / Pays ou zones	Year / Année	Capital account, net / Compte de capital, net	Direct investment / Investissement direct		Portfolio investment / Investissement de portefeuille		Other investment / Autres investissements		Reserve assets / Avoirs de réserve	Financial account, net / Compte financier, net	Capital and financial account, net / Compte de capital et compte financier, net
			Abroad / A l'étranger	In reporting economy / Dans l'économie déclarante	Assets / Avoirs	Liabilities / Engagements	Assets / Avoirs	Liabilities / Engagements			
		(1)	(2)	(3)	(4)	(5)	(6)	(7)	(8)	(9)	(10) = (1) + (9)
Israel - Israël	1990	728	-199	151	-368	-171	-632	1677	-511	-53	675
	2000	455	-3465	5012	-2805	5032	-2126	1478	-33	3757	4212
	2002	151	-1116	1723	-2686	748	-1063	982	-190	-1409	-1259
	2003	458	-1773	3672	-3078	2293	-1634	-438	-74	-692	-233
Italy - Italie	1990	759	-7394	6411	-19325	19216	-13894	57542	-11623	31016	31775
	2000	2879	-12078	13176	-80263	57020	242	27074	-3247	4257	7136
	2002	736	-17247	14699	-15265	32928	4164	-5383	-3169	8022	8759
	2003	3110	-9871	17285	-58515	61388	-29790	44310	-1115	18262	21371
Jamaica - Jamaïque	1990	-16	..	138	..	..	-3	229	-65	299	283
	2000	2	-74	468	-70	6	-96	600	-499	336	338
	2001	-22	-89	614	-39	70	-216	1302	-847	796	773
	2002	-17	-74	481	-351	156	-185	821	255	1103	1086
Japan - Japon	1990	-1062	-50497	1777	-37798	46680	..	9120	9085	-30710	-31772
	2000	-9259	-31534	8227	-83362	47387	-4148	-10211	-48955	-127268	-136526
	2002	-3321	-32017	9087	-85931	-20044	36407	26634	-46134	-109514	-112836
	2003	-3998	-28766	6238	-176291	81181	149892	34095	-187153	-115229	-119227
Jordan - Jordanie	1990	..	31	38	..	..	222	272	-412	152	152
	2000	65	-5	787	..	-141	146	589	-1815	-439	-374
	2002	68	-25	56	-192	-52	11	656	-943	-489	-420
	2003	94	..	376	-119	-349	283	-539	-1248	-1596	-1502
Kazakhstan	1995	-381	0	964	..	7	-657	990	-440	864	483
	2000	-291	-4	1283	-86	31	44	-400	-129	738	447
	2002	-120	-426	2583	-1078	-183	-1098	1559	-535	822	702
	2003	-29	120	2068	-2073	212	-873	3259	-1534	1195	1167
Kenya	1990	7	..	57	..	..	73	265	59	453	460
	2000	50	..	111	-11	-4	-56	343	-107	277	327
	2001	51	..	5	-7	5	-86	388	-168	138	190
	2002	81	-7	28	-10	5	-133	-39	-2	-158	-76
Kiribati	1990	12	..	0	-8	..	..	3	7	2	14
Korea, Republic of - Corée, République de	1990	-331	-1052	788	-500	662	-2425	5500	1208	4103	3772
	2000	-615	-4999	9283	-520	12697	-2289	-1268	-23790	-11065	-11680
	2001	-731	-2420	3528	-5521	12227	7099	-17341	-7586	-10137	-10868
	2002	-1091	-2674	1972	-5036	4940	-2404	5538	-11770	-9156	-10247
Kuwait - Koweït	1990	..	-239	..	-919	537	829	205	897	1310	1310
	2000	2217	303	16	-12923	254	-1108	-316	-2268	-16042	-13825
	2002	1672	155	7	-3425	161	-3754	1695	973	-4190	-2518
	2003	1429	4990	-67	-13379	336	-2812	-399	1824	-9508	-8078
Kyrgyzstan - Kirghizistan	1995	-29	..	96	0	2	12	231	0	341	312
	2000	-11	-5	-2	-2	0	-27	112	-21	80	69
	2001	-32	-6	5	1	..	-4	35	-18	31	-1
	2002	-28	..	5	-3	-10	21	88	-43	55	27
Lao People's Dem. Rep. - Rép. dém. populaire lao	1990	11	..	6	..	..	-5	83	-1	84	95
	1995	13	..	95	..	..	-2	111	-73	131	144
	2000	..	..	34	..	..	19	66	-36	83	83
	2001	..	..	24	..	..	25	83	7	140	140
Latvia - Lettonie	1995	..	65	180	-37	..	-31	456	36	669	669
	2000	30	-9	410	-346	25	-361	763	7	491	521
	2002	18	-8	382	-220	-10	-476	1007	-2	687	704
	2003	34	-32	359	-286	62	-666	1463	-69	837	871
Lesotho	1990	..	..	17	..	..	-110	51	-21	-62	-62
	2000	22	..	118	..	..	-19	-19	-13	67	89
	2001	17	..	117	..	..	-20	-4	-170	-77	-60
	2002	23	0	81	..	..	1	9	120	211	234
Libyan Arab Jamahiriya - Jamahiriya arabe libyenne	1990	..	-105	159	-115	..	-715	-230	-1158	-2164	-2164
	1995	..	-69	-88	-106	..	-1363	1419	-1701	-1908	-1908

For sources and notes, see end of table.

Pour les sources et les notes, se reporter à la fin du tableau.

262

6.1B   Balance of payments: capital and financial
account summaries
(continued)
Millions of dollars

6.1B   Balance des paiements : sommaires des
comptes de capital et d'opérations financières
(suite)
Millions de dollars

Country or area / Pays ou zones	Year / Année	Capital account, net / Compte de capital, net	Direct investment / Investissement direct		Portfolio investment / Investissement de portefeuille		Other investment / Autres investissements		Reserve assets / Avoirs de réserve	Financial account, net / Compte financier, net	Capital and financial account, net / Compte de capital et compte financier, net
			Abroad / A l'étranger	In reporting economy / Dans l'économie déclarante	Assets / Avoirs	Liabilities / Engagements	Assets / Avoirs	Liabilities / Engagements			
		(1)	(2)	(3)	(4)	(5)	(6)	(7)	(8)	(9)	(10) = (1) + (9)
Lithuania - Lituanie	1995	-39	-1	73	-10	27	-36	546	-231	366	327
	2000	2	-4	379	-141	406	40	-5	-131	544	547
	2002	56	-18	712	-125	149	155	137	-422	586	642
	2003	68	-37	179	30	222	-101	1296	-531	1030	1097
Luxembourg	2002	-166	-154425	130051	7478	63289	-19494	-27134	-35	-310	-476
	2003	-176	-96428	87871	-78423	99152	-30035	9236	-108	-1898	-2074
Macedonia, TFYR - Macédoine, LERY	2000	0	1	175	-1	0	-78	178	-264	11	11
	2001	1	-1	442	3	0	-98	-28	-78	240	241
	2002	8	0	77	1	0	245	-125	131	329	338
Madagascar	1990	3	..	22	..	..	-7	78	167	260	263
	2000	115	..	83	..	..	-87	142	-30	107	222
	2001	113	..	93	..	..	-128	102	18	84	197
	2002	58	..	8	..	..	42	143	8	201	259
Malawi	1990	..	..	..	..	1	34	100	-34	100	100
	2000	..	..	26	..	..	..	162	-91	97	97
	2001	..	..	19	..	..	..	187	75	281	281
	2002	..	..	6	..	..	..	144	-105	44	44
Malaysia - Malaisie	1990	-48	..	2332	..	-255	-205	-89	-1951	-167	-215
	2000	..	-2026	3788	-387	-2145	-5565	..	1009	-5267	-5267
	2001	..	-267	554	254	-666	-2702	-829	-1000	-4893	-4893
	2002	..	-1905	3203	-563	-836	-4597	1868	-3657	-6799	-6799
Maldives	1990	..	..	6	..	..	-2	5	0	8	8
	2000	..	..	13	..	..	23	4	4	45	45
	2001	..	..	12	..	..	21	2	30	65	65
	2002	..	..	12	..	..	36	31	-8	71	71
Mali	1990	117	..	6	..	..	-30	192	-55	112	229
	2000	105	-4	82	15	1	-87	185	-58	135	240
	2001	139	-17	122	-1	12	-88	65	14	108	247
	2002	144	-2	244	-1	54	-248	123	-159	11	155
Malta - Malte	1990	..	..	46	-2	..	-243	156	96	53	53
	2000	19	-26	604	-745	-9	-929	1260	222	378	397
	2002	7	3	-416	-411	-2	-543	1573	-288	-84	-77
	2003	6	-24	395	-1554	-12	-24	1451	-144	113	119
Mauritania - Mauritanie	1990	..	..	7	..	..	206	-181	41	72	72
	1995	..	..	7	..	0	211	-179	-43	-4	-4
Mauritius - Maurice	1990	-1	-1	41	-2	..	-7	64	-188	-93	-94
	2000	-1	-13	266	-19	-120	-308	452	-231	27	27
	2001	-1	-3	-28	-18	-2	-337	139	52	-196	-197
	2002	-2	-1	28	-18	1	-440	555	-341	-218	-220
Mexico - Mexique	1990	..	..	2634	-7354	3369	-1345	12180	-3261	6223	6223
	2000	..	..	16586	1290	-1134	5809	-4091	-2862	15598	15598
	2002	..	-930	14774	1134	-632	11601	-3377	-7376	15194	15194
	2003	..	-1390	10784	91	3864	8266	-3931	-9833	7850	7850
Moldova, Republic of - Moldova, République de	1995	0	-1	67	..	0	-116	231	-77	103	103
	2000	-12	0	136	..	117	-29	-43	-47	134	122
	2002	-15	0	117	-1	-26	-58	71	-27	75	59
	2003	-13	0	58	2	-24	-50	93	-14	65	53
Mongolia - Mongolie	1990	..	..	..	..	..	-2	543	102	643	643
	2000	..	..	54	..	..	-44	82	-2	89	89
	2001	..	..	43	..	..	-5	72	-16	94	94
	2002	..	..	78	..	..	-32	103	-58	91	91
Montserrat	1990	5	..	10	..	..	15	-1	-3	21	26
	2000	4	..	3	..	1	-5	4	4	7	12
	2001	8	..	1	..	-1	-1	-3	-2	-5	2
	2002	13	..	2	..	0	0	-2	-2	-2	11

For sources and notes, see end of table.   Pour les sources et les notes, se reporter à la fin du tableau.

6.1B Balance of payments: capital and financial account summaries *(continued)* Millions of dollars

6.1B Balance des paiements : sommaires des comptes de capital et d'opérations financières *(suite)* Millions de dollars

Country or area / Pays ou zones	Year / Année	Capital account, net / Compte de capital, net (1)	Direct investment / Investissement direct — Abroad / A l'étranger (2)	Direct investment — In reporting economy / Dans l'économie déclarante (3)	Portfolio investment / Investissement de portefeuille — Assets / Avoirs (4)	Portfolio investment — Liabilities / Engagements (5)	Other investment / Autres investissements — Assets / Avoirs (6)	Other investment — Liabilities / Engagements (7)	Reserve assets / Avoirs de réserve (8)	Financial account, net / Compte financier, net (9)	Capital and financial account, net / Compte de capital et compte financier, net (10) = (1) + (9)
Morocco - Maroc	1990	-5	..	165	..	..	-267	1830	-1537	191	186
	2000	-6	-59	427	..	18	..	-435	416	367	361
	2002	-6	-28	480	..	-8	..	-1089	-644	-1289	-1295
	2003	-10	-12	2279	..	6	-776	-1072	-1660	-1235	-1245
Mozambique	1990	22	..	9	..	..	..	301	-18	293	315
	2000	306	..	139	..	..	-145	503	-77	420	726
	2002	1169	..	348	32	..	-208	-315	-98	-240	929
	2003	284	..	337	5	..	-77	241	-181	324	608
Myanmar	1990	235	..	163	..	..	..	22	-6	179	414
	1995	..	..	280	..	..	..	-35	32	277	277
	2000	..	..	258	..	..	..	-45	23	236	236
	2001	..	..	210	..	..	..	189	-180	219	219
Namibia - Namibie	1990	42	-1	30	-5	15	-328	86	-37	-240	-197
	2000	113	-2	186	-118	-20	-502	109	-11	-358	-246
	2002	111	5	174	-144	-45	-247	105	-18	-171	-59
	2003	57	11	146	-217	-81	-451	104	95	-394	-337
Nepal - Népal	1990	..	..	..	..	..	116	176	-8	284	284
	2000	..	..	0	..	..	129	148	-291	-15	-15
	2001	..	..	..	..	..	11	-98	-5	-92	-92
Netherlands - Pays-Bas	1990	-301	-13718	10676	-3547	-1367	-25277	28376	-268	-5190	-5491
	2000	-97	-74489	63229	-65634	55242	-28390	46538	-219	-7703	-7801
	2002	-545	-33951	28534	-64293	49954	-40263	54313	132	-12418	-12964
	2003	-2028	-36619	19197	-56769	81272	-64038	33983	920	-22509	-24537
Netherlands Antilles - Antilles néerlandaises	1990	-2	-2	8	-50	1	-249	302	30	39	38
	2000	30	2	-63	-38	0	-41	99	48	7	37
	2001	37	0	-5	-32	0	84	327	-232	142	179
	2002	28	-1	8	-38	1	0	55	-75	-51	-23
New Zealand - Nouvelle-Zélande	1990	213	-1594	1735	-111	282	-81	1479	-1014	696	909
	2000	-180	-1300	3370	-2318	1536	-476	431	143	1386	1207
	2002	765	-185	738	-935	2401	-1086	-103	-1086	-256	509
	2003	508	-299	2438	-856	2184	318	-379	-782	2624	3132
Nicaragua	1990	..	..	..	..	..	..	447	7	454	454
	2000	334	..	267	..	35	80	95	17	493	827
	2002	884	..	204	..	1	3	-372	-71	-236	649
	2003	516	..	201	..	0	-16	97	-45	237	753
Niger	1990	202	0	41	..	..	-2	23	-10	52	254
	1995	65	-7	7	..	..	-18	16	-26	-28	37
Nigeria - Nigéria	1990	..	..	588	..	-197	-2886	-250	-2478	-5223	-5223
	1995	-66	..	1079	..	-82	-3295	4808	217	2727	2661
Norway - Norvège	1990	31	-1470	1003	-987	1548	-1502	648	-414	-1175	-1144
	2000	-91	-8511	5806	-25143	9843	-14100	19171	-3686	-17081	-17171
	2002	-75	-3680	502	-22988	5412	-10205	27975	-5723	-13534	-13609
	2003	680	-2226	1958	-19290	12629	-23171	10106	-297	-20418	-19738
Oman	1990	..	..	142	..	..	-270	-369	-135	-633	-633
	1995	..	..	46	..	..	-52	-13	432	413	413
	2000	8	..	70	..	-36	-356	-172	-2262	-2757	-2749
	2001	-10	..	42	..	13	229	-1170	-1034	-1920	-1931
Pakistan	1990	8	-2	245	..	87	-365	1321	471	1758	1766
	2000	..	-11	308	..	9	-437	-348	7	-472	-472
	2002	40	-28	823	..	-722	-64	-352	-4525	-4868	-4828
	2003	1131	-19	534	-2	-274	-395	-1375	-3089	-4620	-3489
Panama	1990	..	..	136	-200	-36	-1422	1806	-356	-72	-72
	2000	2	..	603	-100	184	355	-834	108	316	317
	2002	..	..	78	10	102	3146	-3420	-221	-306	-306
	2003	..	..	792	-59	140	464	-1316	164	184	184

For sources and notes, see end of table.

Pour les sources et les notes, se reporter à la fin du tableau.

6.1B Balance of payments: capital and financial account summaries (continued)
Millions of dollars

6.1B Balance des paiements : sommaires des comptes de capital et d'opérations financières (suite)
Millions de dollars

Country or area / Pays ou zones	Year / Année	Capital account, net / Compte de capital, net	Direct investment / Investissement direct — Abroad / A l'étranger	Direct investment / Investissement direct — In reporting economy / Dans l'économie déclarante	Portfolio investment / Investissement de portefeuille — Assets / Avoirs	Portfolio investment / Investissement de portefeuille — Liabilities / Engagements	Other investment / Autres investissements — Assets / Avoirs	Other investment / Autres investissements — Liabilities / Engagements	Reserve assets / Avoirs de réserve	Financial account, net / Compte financier, net	Capital and financial account, net / Compte de capital et compte financier, net
		(1)	(2)	(3)	(4)	(5)	(6)	(7)	(8)	(9)	(10) = (1) + (9)
Papua New Guinea - Papouasie-Nouvelle-Guinée	1990	-37	0	155	..	..	..	113	-75	193	155
	1995	..	..	455	-49	..	-284	-532	-177	-587	-587
	2000	..	..	96	-124	..	-41	-167	-128	-364	-364
	2001	..	..	63	-73	..	-67	-4	-204	-285	-285
Paraguay	1990	13	..	77	..	..	-50	-71	-220	-264	-252
	2000	3	-6	119	2	1	-209	250	210	367	370
	2002	4	-6	9	..	0	-10	101	86	181	185
	2003	15	-6	91	..	0	202	1	-303	-15	0
Peru - Pérou	1990	-25	..	41	-48	..	468	1384	-287	1558	1533
	2000	-67	..	810	-538	75	248	221	329	1145	1079
	2002	-82	..	2156	-280	1724	5	-1754	-851	1001	919
	2003	-30	-60	1377	-1435	1211	328	-471	-515	435	406
Philippines	1990	..	..	530	..	-50	..	1234	388	2102	2102
	2000	38	108	1345	-812	1019	-15313	9914	73	-3666	-3628
	2002	-19	-59	1792	-449	1571	-13165	7622	399	-2288	-2307
	2003	21	-158	319	-1586	880	-13307	8043	360	-5449	-5428
Poland - Pologne	1990	..	..	89	..	..	-4504	3603	-2418	-3229	-3229
	2000	34	-16	9343	-84	3423	-3870	1156	-624	9597	9631
	2002	-7	-230	4131	-1157	2826	1887	396	-648	6307	6300
	2003	-46	-386	4225	-1296	3740	-1700	4347	-1206	6855	6809
Portugal	1990	..	-163	2610	..	961	-2442	1598	-3542	-979	-979
	2000	1512	-7655	6836	-4583	2792	-10873	23888	-371	10358	11869
	2002	1917	-3462	1790	-7539	10173	-1726	8113	-1017	6326	8243
	2003	3081	-125	969	-19272	15430	-10676	12156	6455	5011	8091
Romania - Roumanie	1990	..	-18	..	..	..	562	1069	1494	3107	3107
	2000	36	11	1037	28	73	-407	1380	-928	1194	1230
	2002	93	-16	1144	..	382	692	1888	-1802	2288	2381
	2003	213	-39	1844	9	569	72	2066	-1134	3387	3600
Russian Federation - Fédération de Russie	1995	-348	-605	2065	-1704	-739	-150	14013	-10382	2498	2150
	2000	10954	-3177	2713	-411	-9923	-17662	-4167	-16009	-48636	-37682
	2002	-12388	-3533	3461	-796	3756	2120	-3873	-11375	-10226	-22614
	2003	-993	-9727	6725	-2543	-2338	-16472	22656	-26365	-27422	-28415
Rwanda	1990	-1	..	8	0	..	8	39	1	55	55
	2000	63	..	8	0	..	23	31	78	141	204
	2001	62	..	5	..	..	0	-1	11	14	77
	2002	66	..	3	..	..	8	65	20	96	162
Saint Kitts and Nevis - Saint-Kitts-et-Nevis	1990	2	..	49	..	..	-1	3	0	51	53
	2000	6	..	96	0	5	-11	-20	4	75	81
	2001	10	0	88	-1	36	-8	-11	-12	92	103
	2002	15	..	80	..	31	1	-7	-9	97	112
Saint Lucia - Sainte-Lucie	1990	4	..	45	..	0	2	5	-6	45	49
	2000	14	..	55	-1	29	-15	3	-5	66	80
	2001	26	..	24	-4	17	-17	25	-12	32	58
	2002	21	..	48	-17	35	-16	18	-5	63	85
Saint Vincent and the Grenadines - Saint-Vincent-et-les Grenadines	1990	19	..	8	..	..	-11	5	-5	-3	15
	2000	6	..	38	-1	2	-9	-6	-14	11	16
	2001	9	..	21	0	3	-11	36	-9	41	49
	2002	11	..	32	-5	6	-8	-13	6	19	29
Samoa	1990	..	..	..	..	..	..	0	9	-12	-3	-3
	1995	..	..	..	..	..	..	-6	-2	-8	-8
Sao Tome and Principe - Sao Tomé-et-Principe	1990	..	..	..	..	..	..	14	1	15	15
	2000	12	..	4	..	..	-5	11	-2	9	21
	2001	18	..	3	..	..	-5	6	-4	1	18
	2002	15	..	3	..	..	0	7	-2	8	23

For sources and notes, see end of table.

Pour les sources et les notes, se reporter à la fin du tableau.

Country or area / Pays ou zones	Year / Année	Capital account, net / Compte de capital, net	Direct investment / Investissement direct — Abroad / A l'étranger	Direct investment — In reporting economy / Dans l'économie déclarante	Portfolio investment / Investissement de portefeuille — Assets / Avoirs	Portfolio investment — Liabilities / Engagements	Other investment / Autres investissements — Assets / Avoirs	Other investment — Liabilities / Engagements	Reserve assets / Avoirs de réserve	Financial account, net / Compte financier, net	Capital and financial account, net / Compte de capital et compte financier, net
		(1)	(2)	(3)	(4)	(5)	(6)	(7)	(8)	(9)	(10) = (1) + (9)
Saudi Arabia - Arabie saoudite	1990	..	..	1864	-3342	..	1437	-1183	5376	4152	4152
	2000	..	..	-1884	-9394	..	-3942	3549	-2665	-14336	-14336
	2002	..	..	-615	7558	..	-11660	-4437	-2736	-11889	-11889
	2003	..	..	-587	-18765	..	-7957	-784	-1608	-29702	-29702
Senegal - Sénégal	1990	172	10	57	-1	2	58	58	10	193	364
	2000	83	-10	72	11	12	-4	191	-14	258	341
	2001	146	1	38	16	-8	-4	139	-90	92	238
	2002	127	-36	80	-25	-13	12	236	-93	159	286
Seychelles	1990	..	-1	20	2	0	-3	5	-4	19	19
	2000	1	-7	24	0	1	-15	76	-19	60	61
	2001	9	-9	59	0	1	-9	40	10	94	103
	2002	5	-9	61	0	1	-10	101	-26	119	124
Sierra Leone	1990	0	..	32	..	..	-20	13	-5	20	20
	2000	..	..	39	..	..	44	30	2	115	115
	2001	0	..	10	..	..	-3	8	-14	0	1
	2002	51	..	2	0	..	8	74	-32	51	102
Singapore - Singapour	1990	-22	-2034	5575	-1610	573	-220	1664	-5431	-1484	-1506
	2000	-163	-6061	12463	-11482	-2036	-8452	13642	-6806	-8731	-8894
	2001	-161	-9548	10949	-11284	187	-11183	5490	861	-14528	-14689
	2002	-160	-4082	6097	-11374	-1272	-289	-4735	-1342	-16997	-17157
Slovakia - Slovaquie	1995	46	-10	236	157	53	-116	689	-1590	-580	-534
	2000	91	-22	2052	-195	1016	-973	-533	-794	553	644
Slovenia - Slovénie	1995	-7	10	150	-29	15	-243	609	-237	276	269
	2000	4	-65	136	-58	246	-519	941	-178	502	506
	2002	2	-117	1865	-94	27	-887	663	-1867	-410	-408
	2003	4	-306	180	-221	-31	-1090	1732	-342	-77	-73
Solomon Islands - Iles Salomon	1990	0	..	10	..	..	-1	18	9	37	36
	1995	1	..	2	..	..	..	-10	1	-8	-7
South Africa - Afrique du Sud	1990	-56	-28	-76	-332	338	129	-1650	-355	-1974	-2030
	2000	-52	-277	969	-3672	1807	59	1354	-464	-365	-417
	2002	-15	402	735	-875	457	1761	-1884	-1659	-1062	-1077
	2003	2	-721	820	-132	893	3216	2214	-7762	-1473	-1471
Spain - Espagne	1990	1451	-3522	13984	-1357	10382	-13175	16665	-7188	15782	17232
	2000	4792	-53866	36931	-59320	58146	-18640	51666	2881	19823	24616
	2002	7309	-32410	36727	-28983	34849	-22610	34623	-3690	13793	21102
	2003	9982	-23350	25513	-91061	40908	-14437	70570	15487	19931	29913
Sri Lanka	1990	..	-1	43	..	..	-116	619	-132	413	413
	2000	49	..	173	19	-63	-244	477	447	808	857
	2001	50	..	172	..	-11	183	48	-291	101	151
	2002	55	-11	242	..	25	104	140	-394	105	161
Sudan - Soudan	1990	..	..	..	..	..	-29	385	5	361	361
	2000	-119	..	392	..	..	-53	38	-108	269	149
	2002	..	..	713	15	..	-148	202	-300	481	481
	2003	..	..	1349	35	..	297	-317	-423	941	941
Suriname	1990	-5	..	-77	..	1	28	21	-18	-45	-50
	2000	2	..	-148	..	..	25	-16	-10	-149	-147
	2002	6	..	-74	..	..	24	12	19	-19	-13
	2003	9	..	-76	..	..	47	-7	-7	-44	-35
Swaziland	1990	2	-8	30	-1	-2	-39	-20	-11	-50	-48
	2000	0	-17	90	-4	1	-98	40	6	18	19
	2001	0	18	50	-4	-3	-156	49	57	12	11
	2002	0	9	45	1	0	-50	-6	29	27	27

For sources and notes, see end of table.

Pour les sources et les notes, se reporter à la fin du tableau.

6.1B Balance of payments: capital and financial
account summaries
(continued)
Millions of dollars

6.1B Balance des paiements : sommaires des
comptes de capital et d'opérations financières
(suite)
Millions de dollars

Country or area / Pays ou zones	Year / Année	Capital account, net / Compte de capital, net	Direct investment / Investissement direct		Portfolio investment / Investissement de portefeuille		Other investment / Autres investissements		Reserve assets / Avoirs de réserve	Financial account, net / Compte financier, net	Capital and financial account, net / Compte de capital et compte financier, net
			Abroad / A l'étranger	In reporting economy / Dans l'économie déclarante	Assets / Avoirs	Liabilities / Engagements	Assets / Avoirs	Liabilities / Engagements			
		(1)	(2)	(3)	(4)	(5)	(6)	(7)	(8)	(9)	(10) = (1) + (9)
Sweden - Suède	1990	-353	-14629	1982	-3644	6112	-9618	39074	-7552	11726	11373
	2000	384	-39962	22125	-12772	9017	-16000	34609	-170	-3467	-3083
	2002	-79	-10673	11709	-4038	-6691	-998	155	-665	-11369	-11448
	2003	-46	-17341	3268	-13701	4134	-8349	10744	-2076	-22240	-22286
Switzerland - Suisse	1990	..	-7176	5987	-746	-551	-28677	19920	-1169	-12411	-12411
	2000	-3539	-44673	19878	-22309	10548	-93277	99604	4005	-26224	-29763
	2001	1522	-18299	9529	-42841	1896	23059	-10382	-638	-37676	-36154
	2002	-1133	-10069	3599	-29914	7323	-43832	39200	-2402	-36094	-37227
Syrian Arab Republic - République arabe syrienne	1990	..	..	..	..	..	-2008	172	-36	-1872	-1872
	2000	63	..	270	..	..	1206	-1615	-814	-953	-890
	2001	17	..	110	..	..	1136	-1490	-1020	-1264	-1247
	2002	20	..	115	..	..	1180	-1545	-1050	-1300	-1280
Tajikistan - Tadjikistan	2002	45	..	36	..	2	-23	11	0	25	71
	2003	14	..	32	..	0	-16	45	-40	21	35
Thailand - Thaïlande	1990	-1	-140	2444	..	-38	-164	6722	-2961	5863	5862
	2000	..	23	3366	-160	-546	-2203	-10716	1608	-8628	-8628
	2002	..	-106	953	-913	-694	4135	-7603	-4197	-8424	-8424
	2003	..	-558	1866	-937	302	-416	-8837	-122	-8701	-8701
Togo	1990	..	..	18	-2	4	25	87	-29	104	104
	1995	3	6	26	5	..	12	96	-27	139	141
	2000	9	0	42	1	6	9	96	-28	126	135
	2001	21	7	64	5	6	8	56	7	153	175
Tonga	1990	0	0	0	0	-8	5	1	-6	-8	-8
	2001	9	..	..	..	..	..	1	-2	-1	8
Trinidad and Tobago - Trinité-et-Tobago	1990	-19	..	109	..	..	63	-303	-198	-328	-347
	1995	-12	..	299	-8	17	-57	-509	-40	-298	-310
	2000	..	-25	680	..	-30	398	-848	-441	-267	-267
	2001	..	-150	835	..	-206	285	-442	-502	-181	-181
Tunisia - Tunisie	1990	-7	1	76	-1	3	-343	476	-220	-7	-14
	2000	3	-1	752	..	-20	-624	500	245	851	854
	2002	75	-1	795	..	6	-886	942	-139	717	793
	2003	59	-2	541	..	14	-428	985	-380	730	789
Turkey - Turquie	1990	..	16	684	-134	681	-409	3151	-895	3094	3094
	2000	..	-870	982	-593	1615	-1939	13705	-383	12518	12518
	2002	..	-176	1038	-2096	1503	-777	8226	-6177	1542	1542
	2003	..	-499	1562	-1386	3955	-986	4256	-4030	2872	2872
Uganda - Ouganda	1990	..	..	..	..	..	..	249	5	254	254
	2000	70	..	161	..	..	-1	134	-45	249	318
	2001	71	..	145	..	..	-15	344	-175	298	369
	2002	16	..	150	..	..	-18	82	114	329	345
Ukraine	1995	6	-10	267	-12	16	-1574	2679	-469	898	904
	2000	-8	-1	595	-4	-197	-449	-868	-401	-1325	-1333
	2002	17	5	693	2	-1718	-781	551	-1047	-2296	-2279
	2003	-17	-13	1424	1	-923	-940	587	-2045	-1909	-1926
United Kingdom - Royaume-Uni	1990	888	-20124	33504	-29952	23846	-94789	114100	-131	26454	27341
	2000	2309	-245375	122157	-97086	255647	-417549	423218	-5300	37975	40284
	2002	1324	-34199	29179	1166	76571	-150485	91135	635	15353	16677
	2003	2056	-51171	15526	-56265	149318	-432300	410446	2592	29651	31708
United Republic of Tanzania - République-Unie de Tanzanie	1990	338	..	..	..	..	..	324	-141	183	521
	2000	420	..	463	..	..	-134	364	-199	494	914
	2001	1079	..	327	..	..	-77	-683	-183	-615	464
	2002	1168	..	240	..	..	3	-705	-371	-833	335

For sources and notes, see end of table.

Pour les sources et les notes, se reporter à la fin du tableau.

6.1B Balance of payments: capital and financial
account summaries
(concluded)
Millions of dollars

6.1B Balance des paiements : sommaires des
comptes de capital et d'opérations financières
(fin)
Millions de dollars

Country or area Pays ou zones	Year Année	Capital account, net Compte de capital, net	Direct investment Investissement direct		Portfolio investment Investissement de portefeuille		Other investment Autres investissements		Reserve assets Avoirs de réserve	Financial account, net Compte financier, net	Capital and financial account, net Compte de capital et compte financier, net
			Abroad A l'étranger	In reporting economy Dans l'économie déclarante	Assets Avoirs	Liabilities Engagements	Assets Avoirs	Liabilities Engagements			
		(1)	(2)	(3)	(4)	(5)	(6)	(7)	(8)	(9)	(10) = (1) + (9)
United States - Etats-Unis	1990	-6578	-37200	48490	-28771	22010	-13140	71047	-2233	60203	53625
	2000	-808	-159212	321274	-121908	436573	-288388	289049	-295	477093	476285
	2002	-1259	-134836	72410	15889	427883	-75387	267952	-3693	570219	568959
	2003	-3079	-173798	39889	-72337	544488	-38801	244795	1529	545765	542687
Uruguay	1990	..	..	..	..	108	-632	343	-40	-222	-222
	2000	..	1	274	-98	290	-690	1004	-166	613	613
	2002	..	-54	175	95	205	1825	-2608	2331	1970	1970
	2003	..	-4	275	-522	23	-1253	1561	-1380	-1301	-1301
Vanuatu	1990	16	..	13	..	..	-1	2	-5	9	26
	1995	32	..	31	..	..	-2	-4	-5	20	52
	2000	-24	..	20	1	..	-14	11	1	19	-4
	2001	-16	..	18	-4	..	-11	4	1	7	-9
Venezuela	1990	..	-375	451	-1952	17928	-2305	-15908	-4376	-6537	-6537
	2000	..	-521	4701	-954	-2180	-4839	316	-5449	-8927	-8927
	2002	..	-1020	779	-1347	-957	-7407	584	4428	-4940	-4940
	2003	..	-1143	2531	-175	-885	-1977	-1511	-5454	-8614	-8614
Viet Nam	2000	..	..	1298	..	..	-2089	454	-89	-426	-426
	2001	..	..	1300	..	..	-1197	329	-267	165	165
	2002	..	..	1400	..	..	624	53	-435	1642	1642
Yemen - Yémen	1995	..	..	-218	-3	..	159	-45	-263	-370	-370
	2000	339	..	6	0	..	-178	-370	-1429	-1971	-1632
	2002	..	..	114	-6	..	-125	-9	-557	-582	-582
	2003	86	..	-89	0	..	-32	56	-326	-391	-305
Yugoslavia, SFR (former) - Yougoslavie, RSF (anc.)	1990	..	..	..	..	..	496	2742	-1102	2136	2136
Zambia - Zambie	1990	-3	..	203	..	..	-275	467	-119	275	272
	2000	153	..	122	..	-1	-85	270	-90	215	368
Zimbabwe	1990	-7	..	-12	10	-32	..	254	-63	157	150

For sources and notes, see following pages.

Pour les sources et les notes, se reporter aux pages suivantes.

Balance of payments:
capital and financial account
General notes for table 6.1B

Balance des paiements :
comptes de capital et d'opérations financières
Notes générales du tableau 6.1B

The countries presented in table 6.1B are those covered in the IMF *Balance of Payments Statistics* on CD-ROM.

The following explanatory notes are intended to provide a brief description of the balance-of-payments categories presented in table 6.1B. There are many exceptions to the definitions of categories and for these the reader should refer to the country notes in the IMF *Balance of Payments Statistics Yearbook* or the corresponding CD-ROM. For further information on the concepts and definitions used, see the IMF *Balance of Payments Manual* (1993, BPM 5).

The capital account and the financial account are two major components of the capital and financial account. They cover transactions in foreign assets and liabilities. All valuation changes or other non-transaction modifications of net foreign assets are not reflected in these accounts, but are accounted for in International investment position. Assets represent claims on non-residents, while liabilities are indebtedness to non-residents of the reporting economy. In some instances, both parties to a transaction could be residents or non-residents.

Column 1. Capital account, net

The capital account consists of capital transfers and of acquisition or disposal of non-produced, non-financial assets. Transfers refer to transactions exchanged without *quid-pro-quo* (without reciprocity). Capital transfers include transfers of ownership of fixed assets or of funds linked to acquisition or disposal of fixed assets. They further incorporate cancellations of liabilities by creditors, where the later receive no counterpart value. Acquisitions/disposals of non-produced, non-financial assets mainly refer to intangibles, such as patents, leases, and goodwill. Items are entered in capital account as net credits or debits. Column 1, as presented here, shows the total net amounts (net credits less net debits).

Column 2. Direct investment abroad

Within the financial account, direct investment is firstly split according to its direction into direct investment abroad and direct investment in reporting economy (column 3). Further subdivisions include: direct investment in equity capital, reinvested earnings and other direct investment capital (inter-company transactions.) Direct investment is defined as investment that reflects a lasting interest of a resident entity of one economy (direct investor) in an entity resident in another economy (direct investment enterprise). It covers all the transactions between direct investors and direct investment enterprises. Direct investment implies a significant degree of influence by the investor on the management of the direct investment enterprise.

Column 3. Direct investment in reporting economy

This is a counterpart to column 2.

Column 4. Portfolio investment assets

Within portfolio investment the distinction is being made between assets and liabilities (column 5). Assets are viewed as claims on the rest of the world and liabilities as indebtedness to the rest of the world. Portfolio investment covers transactions in equity securities and debt securities. The later are subdivided into bonds, notes, money market instruments and financial derivatives (when the derivatives generate financial claims or liabilities).

Les pays présentés dans le tableau 6.1B sont ceux analysés dans la *Balance of Payments Statistics* sur CD-ROM du FMI.

Les notes explicatives suivantes fournissent une description brève des rubriques des balances des paiements présentées dans le tableau 6.1B. En fait, les définitions des catégories comportent plusieurs exceptions, et pour celles-ci le lecteur doit se référer aux notes par pays du FMI *Balance of Payments Statistics Yearbook* ou du CD-ROM correspondant. Pour des détails sur les concepts et les définitions utilisés, voir le *Manuel de la balance des paiements* du FMI (1993, MBP 5).

Le compte de capital et le compte financier sont les deux principaux composants du compte de capital et d'opérations financières. Ils couvrent les transactions en avoirs (actifs) et engagements (passifs) étrangers. Toutes les réévaluations et autres variations d'avoirs et d'engagements qui ne reflètent pas des transactions, sont exclues du compte de capital et d'opérations financières ; elles apparaissent dans la position extérieure globale. Les avoirs représentent des créances sur les non-résidents et les engagements des dettes envers les non-résidents. Dans certains cas, il peut s'agir de deux résidents ou de deux non résidents.

Colonne 1. Compte de capital, net

Le compte de capital est subdivisé en transferts de capital et en acquisitions ou cessions d'avoirs non financiers non produits. Les transferts sont les transactions échangées sans *quid-pro-quo* (sans réciprocité.) Les transferts de capitaux comprennent les transferts de propriété d'un actif fixe ou les transferts de fonds liés à l'acquisition ou à la cession d'un actif fixe. De plus, ils incorporent la remise d'une dette par un créancier, sans que celui-ci ne reçoive une valeur équivalente. Les acquisitions ou cession d'avoirs non financiers non produits se réfèrent aux avoirs incorporels tels que les brevets, les contrats de location et marques. Les éléments du compte de capital sont reportés comme les crédits ou les débits nets. La colonne 1 présente les totaux (crédits nets moins débits nets).

Colonne 2. Investissement direct à l'étranger

Dans le Compte financier, l'investissement direct est d'abord divisé en fonction du sens des mouvements de capitaux entre investissement de l'économie déclarante à l'étranger et celui en provenance de l'étranger investi dans l'économie déclarante (colonne 3). Les subdivisions suivantes incluent : capital social, bénéfices réinvestis et autres transactions. L'investissement direct étranger est accompagné d'un intérêt durable de la part d'une entité résidente d'une économie (l'investisseur direct) pour une entité résidente d'une autre économie (l'entreprise d'investissement direct.) Il recouvre toutes les transactions entre les investisseurs directs et les entreprises d'investissement direct. L'investissement direct donne à l'investisseur le privilège d'exercer une influence significative sur la gestion de l'entreprise dans laquelle il a investi.

Colonne 3. Investissement direct dans l'économie déclarante

Voir la description de la colonne 2.

Colonne 4. Investissement de portefeuille, avoirs

En investissement de portefeuille on distingue les avoirs et les engagements (colonne 5). Les avoirs représentent les créances sur les non-résidents et les engagements les endettements envers les non-résidents. Les investissements de portefeuille couvrent les transactions portant sur les titres de participation et les titres de créances, ces dernières étant subdivisées en trois catégories : obligations et autres titres d'emprunt, instruments du marché monétaire et produits financiers dérivés (lorsque les dérivés résultent en créances ou en engagements financiers).

Balance of payments:
capital and financial account
General notes for table 6.1B *(concluded)*

Balance des paiements :
comptes de capital et d'opérations financières
Notes générales du tableau 6.1B *(fin)*

Column 5. Portfolio investment liabilities

This is a counterpart to column 4.

Column 6. Other investment assets

Other investment is a residual category that covers all financial transaction not included under direct investment, portfolio investment or reserve assets. Assets and liabilities (column 7) in this category are classified primarily on an instrument bases, such as trade credits, loans, currency and deposits.

Column 7. Other investment liabilities

This is a counterpart to column 6.

Column 8. Reserve assets

Includes: monetary gold, special drawing rights, reserve position in the IMF, foreign exchange and other claims.

Column 9. Financial account, net

The financial account constituents are classified according to the type of investment or by a functional breakdown into four main components: direct investment, portfolio investment, other investment and reserve assets. Each component is further divided into relevant subcomponents. The sum of figures in columns 2 to 8 is equal to column 9 (financial account balance). Where the financial account subcomponents do not add up to the total net financial account, the difference can be attributed to financial derivatives that are not shown within this table.

Column 10. Capital and financial account, net

The capital account and the financial account are two major components of the capital and financial account. Balance of the later corresponds to the sum of the net capital account and net financial account. Where the financial account subcomponents do not add up to the sum represented by net financial account, the difference can be attributed to financial derivatives (see notes for column 9).

Colonne 5. Investissement de portefeuille, engagements

Voir la description de la colonne 4.

Colonne 6. Autres investissements, avoirs

Les autres investissements constituent une catégorie résiduelle qui comprend toutes les opérations sur actifs et passifs financiers qui ne figurent pas parmi les investissements directs, les investissements de portefeuille ou les avoirs de réserve. Les avoirs et les engagements (colonne 7) sont repartis par instruments tels que les crédits commerciaux, les prêts, la monnaie fiduciaire et les dépôts.

Colonne 7. Autres investissements, engagements

Voir la description de la colonne 6.

Colonne 8. Avoirs de réserve

Comprend : l'or monétaire, droits de tirage spéciaux, position de réserve dans le FMI, devises et autres créances.

Colonne 9. Compte financier, net

Les éléments qui constituent le compte financier se divisent selon le type d'investissement ou selon une ventilation fonctionnelle en quatre principaux composants : investissements directs, investissements de portefeuille, autres investissements et avoirs de réserve. Chaque composant comprend plusieurs sous-groupes. La somme de tous les chiffres des colonnes 2 à 8 est égale à la colonne 9 (balance du compte financier). Dans le cas où la somme des éléments du compte financier ne correspond pas au total, la différence peut être attribuée aux instruments financiers dérivés, qui ne sont pas présentés dans ce tableau.

Colonne 10. Compte de capital et d'opérations financières, net

Le compte de capital et le compte financier sont les deux principaux composants du compte de capital et d'opérations financières. La balance de ce dernier correspond à la somme du compte de capital net et du compte financier net. Dans le cas où la somme des éléments composants du compte financier ne correspond pas au total, la différence peut être attribuée aux instruments financiers dérivés (voir les notes de la colonne 9).

Region, country or area	Inward flows - Flux entrants								
	1980	1990	1995	1998	1999	2000	2001	2002	2003
WORLD	**54986**	**208646**	**335734**	**690905**	**1086750**	**1387953**	**817574**	**678751**	**560115**
DEVELOPED ECONOMIES	46626	171805	216705	489489	847601	1129119	590527	513109	379401
DEVELOPING ECONOMIES	8336	36766	114226	190778	228685	249764	215542	152495	165130
SOUTH-EAST EUROPE AND CIS	24	75	4802	10638	10465	9069	11505	13147	15584
DEVELOPED ECONOMIES: AMERICA	**22725**	**56004**	**68027**	**197243**	**308119**	**380798**	**186948**	**83900**	**36352**
Canada	5807	7582	9255	22809	24743	66791	27487	21030	6580
United States	16918	48422	58772	174434	283376	314007	159461	62870	29772
DEVELOPED ECONOMIES: EUROPE	**21523**	**104060**	**131428**	**279960**	**519294**	**718569**	**387872**	**403447**	**323063**
EU 25	**21439**	**97516**	**126971**	**267142**	**499443**	**693172**	**376766**	**396774**	**308362**
EU 15	*21317*	*96774*	*114560*	*249931*	*479372*	*671417*	*357441*	*374000*	*295694*
Austria	239	653	1904	4533	2975	8840	5919	952	6855
Belgium-Luxembourg	1545	8047	10689	22691	119693	88739	88203	131743	117041
Denmark	52	1132	4177	7730	16700	33818	11525	6637	2608
Finland	28	787	1063	2040	4581	8015	3732	7920	2765
France	3283	15614	23676	30984	46545	43250	50476	48906	46981
Germany	333	2962	12025	24593	56077	198276	21138	36014	12866
Greece	672	1005	1053	85	571	1089	1560	51	586
Ireland	286	622	1443	8579	18218	25843	9659	24486	25497
Italy	577	6411	4842	2635	6911	13375	14871	14545	16421
Netherlands	2278	10514	12301	36964	41205	63854	51927	25571	19674
Portugal	157	2610	685	3144	1234	6787	5892	1844	962
Spain	1493	13984	6285	11797	15758	37523	28005	35908	25625
Sweden	251	1971	14448	19835	60926	23242	11910	11647	3296
United Kingdom	10123	30461	19969	74321	87979	118764	52623	27776	14515
New EU members 10 [1]	*123*	*742*	*12411*	*17211*	*20071*	*21755*	*19325*	*22774*	*12669*
Cyprus	85	127	86	264	685	804	652	614	830
Czech Republic	–	–	2568	3700	6310	4984	5639	8483	2583
Estonia	–	–	202	581	305	387	542	284	891
Hungary	1	311	5103	3828	3312	2764	3936	2845	2470
Latvia	–	–	180	357	347	411	163	384	360
Lithuania	–	–	73	926	486	379	446	732	179
Malta	27	46	132	267	822	622	281	-428	380
Poland	10	89	3659	6365	7270	9341	5713	4131	4225
Slovakia	–	–	258	707	428	1925	1584	4123	571
Slovenia	–	–	152	218	106	137	369	1606	181
Other developed Europe	**84**	**6545**	**4457**	**12819**	**19851**	**25397**	**11106**	**6673**	**14700**
Gibraltar	2	36	11	-162	17	138	12	27	20
Iceland	22	22	-9	146	69	175	176	126	147
Norway	60	1003	2231	3893	8046	5829	2062	872	2372
Switzerland	..	5484	2223	8941	11719	19255	8856	5648	12161
DEVELOPED ECONOMIES: ASIA	**329**	**1878**	**1622**	**5079**	**15852**	**13334**	**9790**	**10960**	**10069**
Israel	51	125	1581	1887	3111	5011	3549	1721	3745
Japan	278	1753	41	3192	12741	8323	6241	9239	6324
DEVELOPED ECONOMIES: OCEANIA	**2048**	**9863**	**15628**	**7206**	**4336**	**16418**	**5917**	**14801**	**9917**
Australia	1870	8128	11970	6015	2924	13071	4006	13978	7900
New Zealand	178	1735	3659	1191	1412	3347	1911	823	2017

For sources and notes, see end of table.

6.2 Investissement direct étranger : flux entrants et sortants
Millions de dollars

Outward flows - Flux sortants									Régions, pays ou zones
1980	1990	1995	1998	1999	2000	2001	2002	2003	
53683	242057	358235	687240	1092279	1186838	721501	596487	611662	**MONDE**
50364	225796	304908	632514	1014634	1084931	659153	548869	572125	ECONOMIES DEVELOPPEES
3319	16243	52691	53190	74982	98710	59494	42937	34423	ECONOMIES EN DEVELOPPEMENT
..	18	636	1537	2663	3197	2854	4681	5114	EUROPE DU SUD-EST ET CEI
23328	36219	103536	165362	226638	187301	160986	141749	173426	**ECONOMIES DEVELOPPEES : AMERIQUE**
4098	5237	11462	34358	17247	44675	36113	26409	21542	Canada
19230	30982	92074	131004	209391	142626	124873	115340	151884	Etats-Unis
24086	138708	175228	437556	764170	860479	448092	365773	352829	**ECONOMIES DEVELOPPEES : EUROPE**
23833	130520	159855	416412	724660	807223	430242	352443	339566	**UE 25**
23812	*130480*	*159716*	*415362*	*724312*	*806151*	*429159*	*351181*	*336454*	*UE 15*
101	1701	1131	2745	3301	5740	3137	5252	7083	Autriche
196	6314	11603	28845	122304	86362	100646	138471	132638	Belgique-Luxembourg
94	1482	3070	4477	16943	26558	13374	5686	1158	Danemark
137	2708	1497	18647	6605	22572	8362	7622	-7370	Finlande
3095	36233	15755	48611	126856	177449	86767	49434	57279	France
4702	24235	39049	88823	108692	56557	36855	8622	2560	Allemagne
..	11	42	262	539	2102	616	655	47	Grèce
..	364	821	3906	6111	4640	4069	3099	1911	Irlande
740	7394	7024	12407	6722	12316	21472	17123	9121	Italie
5918	13658	20182	36669	57610	75635	47968	34554	36092	Pays-Bas
14	163	688	3847	3168	7512	7564	3289	95	Portugal
311	3522	4076	18936	42084	54675	33093	31512	23373	Espagne
625	14746	11215	24370	21928	40662	6380	10683	17375	Suède
7881	17948	43562	122816	201451	233371	58855	35180	55093	Royaume-Uni
21	*40*	*139*	*1050*	*347*	*1073*	*1083*	*1261*	*3111*	*Nouveaux membres de l'UE 10* [1]
..	5	28	69	146	202	218	299	345	Chypre
–	–	37	125	90	43	165	206	232	République tchèque
–	–	3	6	83	63	200	132	148	Estonie
..	..	59	319	250	620	368	275	1581	Hongrie
–	–	-66	54	17	10	12	8	32	Lettonie
–	–	1	4	9	4	7	18	37	Lituanie
..	..	5	15	45	26	24	-4	24	Malte
21	16	42	316	31	17	-90	230	386	Pologne
–	–	41	147	-371	21	35	5	22	Slovaquie
–	–	-10	-5	48	66	144	93	304	Slovénie
253	8188	15373	21144	39510	53256	17850	13330	13264	**Autres économies développées d'Europe**
..	..	..	..	..	..	..	..	..	Gibraltar
..	10	24	71	121	390	344	215	168	Islande
253	1470	3140	2306	6113	8193	-734	5537	2176	Norvège
..	6707	12210	18767	33276	44673	18240	7578	10919	Suisse
2382	48281	23197	25315	23710	35023	38963	33396	30574	**ECONOMIES DEVELOPPEES : ASIE**
-3	257	567	1163	967	3465	630	1115	1774	Israël
2385	48024	22630	24152	22743	31558	38333	32281	28800	Japon
568	2588	2947	4280	115	2129	11112	7952	15295	**ECONOMIES DEVELOPPEES : OCEANIE**
461	994	3284	3352	-688	829	12228	7576	15108	Australie
107	1594	-337	928	803	1300	-1116	376	188	Nouvelle-Zélande

Pour les sources et les notes, se reporter à la fin du tableau.

Region, country or area	Inward flows - Flux entrants								
	1980	1990	1995	1998	1999	2000	2001	2002	2003
DEVOLOPING ECONOMIES: AMERICA	7494	9615	30280	82491	107406	97537	88139	51358	49722
South America	*3634*	*4902*	*18622*	*52715*	*69677*	*57852*	*38771*	*26788*	*21268*
Argentina	678	1836	5609	7291	23988	10418	2166	785	478
Bolivia	50	101	374	1023	1010	822	832	1044	160
Brazil	1910	989	4405	28856	28578	32779	22457	16590	10144
Chile	287	661	2956	4628	8761	4860	4200	1888	2982
Colombia	157	500	968	2829	1508	2395	2525	2115	1762
Ecuador	70	126	452	870	648	720	1330	1275	1555
Guyana	..	8	74	47	48	67	56	44	26
Paraguay	30	71	103	342	95	104	85	11	82
Peru	63	41	2557	1644	1940	810	1144	2156	1377
Suriname	18	77	-21	38	-24	-97	-27	-74	-92
Uruguay	290	42	157	164	235	273	320	175	263
Venezuela	80	451	985	4985	2890	4701	3683	779	2531
Other America	*3861*	*4713*	*11658*	*29776*	*37729*	*39684*	*49367*	*24570*	*28454*
Anguilla	..	11	18	28	38	38	33	37	28
Antigua and Barbuda	20	61	32	23	31	28	44	48	57
Aruba	..	131	1	84	-425	117	-261	289	165
Bahamas	4	-17	107	147	149	250	101	200	145
Barbados	3	11	12	16	17	19	19	17	121
Belize	..	19	21	19	60	30	60	25	40
Bermuda	940	819	641	5399	9470	10627	13346	2711	8500
British Virgin Islands	-1	18	-577	1362	3648	830	222	132	400
Cayman Islands	20	49	50	4354	6569	6922	4356	2509	4600
Costa Rica	53	162	337	612	620	409	454	662	587
Cuba	..	1	5	15	9	-10	4	3	3
Dominica	..	13	54	7	18	11	12	14	17
Dominican Republic	93	133	414	700	1338	953	1079	917	310
El Salvador	6	2	38	1104	216	173	279	208	157
Grenada	..	13	20	49	42	37	59	58	59
Guatemala	111	59	75	673	155	230	456	110	104
Haiti	13	8	-2	11	30	13	4	6	8
Honduras	6	44	76	99	237	282	193	176	198
Jamaica	28	175	147	369	524	469	614	479	520
Mexico	2090	2633	9655	12332	13206	16586	26776	14745	10783
Montserrat	..	10	3	3	8	3	..	2	2
Netherlands Antilles	35	8	-150	-53	-22	-63	-5	8	-81
Nicaragua	7	..	75	195	300	267	150	204	201
Panama	219	136	223	1296	652	603	405	78	792
Saint Kitts and Nevis	1	49	21	32	58	96	88	82	53
Saint Lucia	31	49	33	83	83	55	22	31	32
Saint Vincent and the Grenadines	1	8	31	89	56	29	21	32	38
Trinidad and Tobago	185	109	299	730	643	680	835	791	616
DEVELOPING ECONOMIES: AFRICA	400	2427	5392	9114	11590	8728	19616	11780	15033
North Africa	*152*	*1157*	*1173*	*2904*	*3032*	*2918*	*5490*	*3631*	*5784*
Algeria	349	40	..	501	507	438	1196	1065	634
Egypt	548	734	595	1076	1065	1235	510	647	237
Libyan Arab Jamahiriya	-1089	159	-88	-128	-128	-142	-101	-96	700
Morocco	89	165	332	417	850	215	2825	481	2279
Sudan	9	-31	12	371	371	392	574	713	1349
Tunisia	246	90	323	668	368	779	486	821	584
Other Africa	*248*	*1270*	*4219*	*6209*	*8558*	*5810*	*14126*	*8149*	*9250*
Angola	37	-335	472	1114	2471	879	2146	1643	1415
Benin	4	62	8	33	38	56	41	41	51
Botswana	112	96	70	96	37	57	31	405	86
Burkina Faso	..	..	10	4	8	23	8	9	11
Burundi	5	1	2	2	..	12	..	..	..
Cameroon	130	-113	7	50	40	31	75	176	215
Cape Verde	..	..	26	9	53	34	9	12	14
Central African Republic	5	..	6	8	4	..	5	6	4

For sources and notes, see end of table.

			Outward flows - Flux sortants						Régions, pays ou zones
1980	1990	1995	1998	1999	2000	2001	2002	2003	
1129	**3210**	**7494**	**19865**	**31279**	**13738**	**11971**	**6009**	**10666**	**ECONOMIES EN DEVELOPPEMENT : AMERIQUE**
411	*1138*	*3780*	*8497*	*7097*	*8026*	*-178*	*4080*	*4559*	*Amérique du Sud*
-110	63	1497	2325	1730	901	161	-627	774	Argentine
..	1	2	3	3	3	3	3	3	Bolivie
367	625	1096	2854	1690	2282	-2258	2482	249	Brésil
44	8	752	1483	2558	3987	1610	294	1395	Chili
106	16	256	796	116	325	16	857	926	Colombie
3	3	73	-84	..	..	..	..	..	Equateur
..	..	..	..	-2	2	..	..	..	Guyana
2	..	5	6	6	6	6	-2	5	Paraguay
..	50	8	62	128	..	74	..	60	Pérou
..	..	..	..	..	..	..	..	..	Suriname
..	..	..	9	-3	..	6	54	3	Uruguay
..	375	91	1043	872	521	204	1020	1143	Venezuela
717	*2072*	*3714*	*11368*	*24182*	*5712*	*12149*	*1929*	*6107*	*Autres économies : Amérique*
..	..	..	1	1	1	1	1	1	Anguilla
..	..	-2	-1	..	1	..	..	..	Antigua-et-Barbuda
..	..	2	1	4	13	-15	3	12	Aruba
115	..	..	1	..	..	..	..	..	Bahamas
..	1	3	1	1	1	1	..	..	Barbade
..	2	3	6	..	6	..	..	2	Belize
273	768	608	2980	18137	2426	-5407	-1823	-1601	Bermudes
..	..	2444	-830	1500	1141	8333	-209	3088	Iles Vierges britanniques
5	372	183	4452	2187	1795	2811	967	1858	Iles Caïmanes
5	2	6	5	5	9	9	34	47	Costa Rica
..	..	..	..	..	..	..	..	..	Cuba
..	..	..	..	..	..	..	..	..	Dominique
..	..	15	2	6	61	-33	..	..	République dominicaine
..	..	..	1	54	-5	-10	-26	19	El Salvador
..	..	..	..	..	..	..	..	..	Grenade
..	..	-24	8	-3	16	1	5	7	Guatemala
..	-8	1	1	-1	1	..	..	..	Haïti
..	..	..	..	..	..	..	..	..	Honduras
..	37	66	82	95	74	89	74	79	Jamaïque
1	223	-263	1363	1475	984	4404	930	1390	Mexique
..	..	..	..	..	..	..	..	..	Montserrat
..	2	1	-2	-1	-2	..	1	..	Antilles néerlandaises
..	..	..	7	3	4	5	4	4	Nicaragua
318	669	671	3289	356	-839	1902	1861	975	Panama
..	..	..	..	..	..	..	..	..	Saint-Kitts-et-Nevis
..	..	..	..	..	..	..	..	..	Sainte-Lucie
..	..	..	..	..	..	..	..	..	Saint-Vincent-et-les Grenadines
..	1	..	1	364	25	58	106	225	Trinité-et-Tobago
1128	**2098**	**2976**	**1982**	**2564**	**1319**	**-2535**	**115**	**1288**	**ECONOMIES EN DEVELOPPEMENT : AFRIQUE**
126	*135*	*137*	*367*	*313*	*227*	*202*	*266*	*148*	*Afrique du Nord*
34	5	4	1	47	18	9	100	14	Algérie
7	12	34	46	38	51	12	28	21	Egypte
47	105	83	299	208	98	84	110	100	Jamahiriya arabe libyenne
39	13	12	20	18	58	97	28	12	Maroc
..	..	..	..	..	..	..	..	..	Soudan
..	..	3	2	3	2	..	..	1	Tunisie
1002	*1962*	*2839*	*1614*	*2252*	*1092*	*-2738*	*-152*	*1140*	*Autres économies : Afrique*
..	..	..	..	..	..	..	..	..	Angola
..	..	..	2	23	8	2	..	3	Bénin
2	7	41	4	1	2	381	43	40	Botswana
..	..	..	5	5	..	..	1	..	Burkina Faso
..	..	..	..	..	..	..	..	..	Burundi
-8	15	..	..	3	4	3	3	3	Cameroun
..	..	..	..	..	1	..	..	..	Cap-Vert
..	4	1	..	..	..	..	1	..	République centrafricaine

Pour les sources et les notes, se reporter à la fin du tableau.

Region, country or area	Inward flows - Flux entrants								
	1980	1990	1995	1998	1999	2000	2001	2002	2003
Chad	..	9	33	22	25	116	453	1030	837
Comoros	..	..	..	..	..	..	1	..	1
Congo	40	23	124	34	491	168	76	152	386
Côte d'Ivoire	95	48	212	380	324	235	273	230	389
Dem. Rep. of the Congo	110	-14	-22	61	11	23	82	117	158
Djibouti	..	..	3	3	4	3	3	4	11
Equatorial Guinea	..	11	65	306	238	109	931	323	1431
Eritrea	–	–	..	149	83	28	12	20	22
Ethiopia	1	12	14	261	70	135	20	75	60
Gabon	32	73	-323	104	-205	-43	-88	251	53
Gambia	..	14	15	24	49	44	35	43	60
Ghana	16	15	107	56	267	115	89	59	137
Guinea	..	18	..	18	63	10	2	30	8
Guinea-Bissau	..	2	..	4	9	..	..	1	2
Kenya	79	57	33	11	14	111	5	28	82
Lesotho	4	16	23	27	33	31	28	27	42
Madagascar	..	22	10	16	58	69	84	8	50
Malawi	9	23	6	12	59	26	19	6	23
Mali	2	6	111	9	1	78	104	102	129
Mauritania	27	7	7	..	..	40	92	118	214
Mauritius	1	41	19	12	49	277	32	33	70
Mozambique	4	9	45	235	382	139	255	155	337
Namibia	..	30	153	77	20	186	365	181	84
Niger	49	41	14	-1	..	9	26	8	31
Nigeria	-739	588	1079	1051	1005	930	1104	1281	1200
Rwanda	16	8	2	7	2	8	4	7	5
Sao Tome and Principe	..	..	..	4	3	4	3	3	10
Senegal	14	57	35	60	142	62	39	54	78
Seychelles	10	20	40	55	60	56	65	48	58
Sierra Leone	-19	32	-2	-10	6	5	2	4	8
Somalia	..	6	1	..	..	..	..	..	1
South Africa	-10	-78	1241	561	1502	888	6789	757	762
Swaziland	26	28	43	109	100	91	51	47	44
Togo	43	23	32	19	29	41	71	53	20
Uganda	4	-6	125	210	222	275	229	249	283
United Republic of Tanzania	5	..	150	172	542	282	467	240	248
Zambia	62	203	97	198	163	122	72	82	100
Zimbabwe	2	-12	118	444	59	23	4	26	20
DEVELOPING ECONOMIES: ASIA	**322**	**24179**	**77862**	**98932**	**109392**	**143372**	**107675**	**89267**	**100217**
West Asia	*-3247*	*2025*	*40*	*6796*	*276*	*690*	*5447*	*2940*	*3302*
Bahrain	-418	-183	431	180	454	364	81	217	517
Iran, Islamic Republic of	81	-362	17	24	35	39	55	276	120
Iraq	2	..	2	7	-7	-3	-6	-2	..
Jordan	34	38	13	310	158	787	100	56	379
Kuwait	..	6	7	59	72	16	-147	7	67
Lebanon	-12	6	35	200	250	298	249	257	358
Oman	98	142	29	101	39	16	83	23	138
Palestinian territory	..	..	123	218	189	62	20	..	..
Qatar	11	5	94	347	113	252	296	631	400
Saudi Arabia	-3192	1864	-1877	4289	-780	-1884	20	-615	208
Syrian Arab Republic	..	71	100	82	263	270	110	115	150
Turkey	18	684	885	940	783	982	3266	1038	575
United Arab Emirates	98	-116	400	258	-985	-515	1184	834	480
Yemen	34	-131	-218	-219	-308	6	136	102	-89
Other Asia	*3569*	*22154*	*77822*	*92136*	*109115*	*142683*	*102228*	*86326*	*96915*
Afghanistan	9	..	..	..	6	..	..	..	..
Bangladesh	9	3	2	190	180	280	79	52	121
Bhutan	..	2	..	..	..	..	..	..	..
Brunei Darussalam	-20	3	583	573	748	549	526	1035	2009
Cambodia	1	..	151	243	230	149	149	145	87
China	57	3487	37521	45463	40319	40715	46878	52743	53505
China, Hong Kong SAR	710	3275	6213	14766	24580	61939	23775	9682	13561
China, Macao SAR	..	..	2	-18	9	..	160	382	350
China, Taiwan Province of	166	1330	1559	222	2926	4928	4109	1445	453

For sources and notes, see end of table.

Outward flows - Flux sortants									Régions, pays ou zones
1980	1990	1995	1998	1999	2000	2001	2002	2003	
..	11	-3	..	-2	..	..	..	..	Tchad
..	1	..	..	..	..	..	..	..	Comores
..	3	-2	-9	2	4	6	7	..	Congo
..	31	56	36	57	..	2	2	2	Côte d'Ivoire
..	..	..	..	..	..	..	..	..	Rép. dém. du Congo
..	..	..	..	..	..	..	..	..	Djibouti
..	..	..	..	2	-4	4	..	..	Guinée équatoriale
–	–	..	..	..	..	..	..	..	Erythrée
..	..	..	254	-46	-1	69	7	25	Ethiopie
8	29	33	-15	12	26	4	..	..	Gabon
..	3	7	6	4	5	5	5	7	Gambie
..	..	..	30	77	52	53	61	55	Ghana
..	..	..	..	3	2	2	2	2	Guinée
..	..	..	..	..	..	..	..	..	Guinée-Bissau
1	..	13	..	..	..	..	7	2	Kenya
..	..	..	..	..	..	..	..	..	Lesotho
..	1	..	1	..	1	..	..	..	Madagascar
..	..	..	6	3	3	4	3	3	Malawi
..	..	..	27	50	4	17	19	13	Mali
..	..	..	..	..	..	..	..	..	Mauritanie
..	..	4	14	6	13	3	9	41	Maurice
..	..	..	..	..	..	..	..	..	Mozambique
..	1	-4	-1	..	3	-13	-5	-6	Namibie
-4	..	2	10	..	..	-4	..	-1	Niger
3	1824	104	107	92	85	94	101	93	Nigéria
..	..	..	..	..	..	..	..	..	Rwanda
..	..	..	..	..	..	..	..	..	Sao Tomé-et-Principe
2	-10	-3	10	6	..	-7	39	11	Sénégal
4	1	16	3	9	7	9	9	8	Seychelles
..	..	..	..	..	..	..	..	..	Sierra Leone
..	..	..	..	..	..	..	..	..	Somalie
755	27	2498	1779	1580	271	-3180	-399	720	Afrique du Sud
9	3	30	23	12	17	-18	-9	..	Swaziland
..	5	6	22	41	..	-7	..	-2	Togo
..	-12	119	20	-8	-28	-5	-14	-15	Ouganda
..	..	..	..	..	1	..	..	..	République-Unie de Tanzanie
..	..	..	..	..	..	..	..	..	Zambie
..	17	13	9	9	8	4	3	5	Zimbabwe
									ECONOMIES EN DEVELOPPEMENT :
1044	**10931**	**42238**	**31398**	**41162**	**83585**	**49942**	**36813**	**22440**	**ASIE**
586	*-979*	*-703*	*-1089*	*1946*	*3555*	*4879*	*2161*	*-1047*	*Asie occidentale*
..	25	-16	181	163	10	216	190	741	Bahreïn
..	..	2	10	738	348	2812	1299	1486	Iran, Rép. islamique d'
..	..	..	..	..	..	..	..	..	Iraq
3	-31	-27	2	5	5	9	25	3	Jordanie
407	-239	-1022	-1867	23	-303	365	-155	-4989	Koweït
..	-16	6	-1	5	125	92	74	97	Liban
..	..	11	-5	3	-2	-1	..	-1	Oman
..	..	129	160	169	213	380	..	..	Territoire palestinien
..	..	30	20	30	41	112	61	71	Qatar
178	-642	63	74	50	155	-44	50	54	Arabie saoudite
..	..	..	..	..	..	..	..	..	République arabe syrienne
..	-16	113	367	645	870	497	175	499	Turquie
-2	-59	7	-30	115	2094	441	442	992	Emirats arabes unis
..	..	..	..	..	..	..	..	..	Yémen
458	*11910*	*42941*	*32487*	*39216*	*80031*	*45063*	*34652*	*23487*	*Autres économies : Asie*
..	..	..	..	..	..	..	..	..	Afghanistan
..	..	2	3	..	2	21	4	8	Bangladesh
..	..	..	..	..	..	..	..	..	Bhoutan
..	..	20	10	20	-3	9	8	5	Brunéi Darussalam
..	..	..	20	9	7	7	6	10	Cambodge
..	830	2000	2634	1775	916	6884	2518	1800	Chine
82	2448	25000	16985	19358	59375	11345	17463	3769	Chine, Hong Kong RAS
..	..	..	..	..	..	11	62	24	Chine, Macao RAS
42	5243	2983	3836	4420	6701	5480	4886	5679	Chine, Taiwan Province de

Pour les sources et les notes, se reporter à la fin du tableau.

6.2 Foreign direct investment: inward and outward flows (concluded)
Millions of dollars

Region, country or area	Inward flows - Flux entrants								
	1980	1990	1995	1998	1999	2000	2001	2002	2003
India	79	237	2151	2633	2168	2319	3403	3449	4269
Indonesia	180	1092	4346	-241	-1866	-4550	-2977	145	-597
Korea, Dem. People's Republic of	..	-61	..	31	-15	5	-4	-15	-5
Korea, Republic of	17	759	1249	5039	9436	8572	3683	2941	3752
Lao People's Dem. Rep.	..	6	88	45	52	34	24	25	19
Malaysia	934	2611	5815	2714	3895	3788	554	3203	2474
Maldives	..	6	7	12	12	13	12	12	12
Mongolia	..	..	10	19	30	54	43	78	132
Myanmar	..	225	318	684	304	208	192	191	128
Nepal	..	6	8	12	4	..	21	2	30
Pakistan	64	250	719	507	530	305	385	823	1405
Philippines	-106	550	1574	2212	1725	1345	982	1792	319
Singapore	1236	5575	11591	7690	16067	17217	15038	5730	11409
Sri Lanka	43	43	65	150	201	175	82	197	229
Thailand	189	2575	2070	7491	6091	3350	3813	1068	1802
Viet Nam	..	180	1780	1700	1484	1289	1300	1200	1450
DEVELOPING ECONOMIES:									
OCEANIA	**119**	**544**	**692**	**240**	**297**	**128**	**113**	**91**	**158**
Fiji	36	84	57	103	-4	-16	42	26	20
Kiribati	..	..	..	..	..	..	..	..	..
New Caledonia	2	31	..	..	4	22	-1	2	8
Papua New Guinea	76	398	595	110	296	96	63	21	101
Samoa	..	7	3	3	2	-2	1	..	..
Solomon Islands	2	10	2	2	-19	1	-12	-1	-2
Tonga	..	..	2	2	2	5	1	2	3
Tuvalu	..	..	..	..	..	..	..	26	9
Vanuatu	3	13	31	20	13	20	18	15	19
SOUTH-EAST EUROPE AND CIS	**24**	**75**	**4802**	**10638**	**10465**	**9069**	**11505**	**13147**	**15584**
South-East Europe	*24*	*71*	*748*	*3842*	*3667*	*3617*	*4475*	*4126*	*6714*
Albania	..	..	70	45	41	143	207	135	180
Bosnia and Herzegovina	–	–	..	56	154	147	130	265	381
Bulgaria	..	4	90	537	819	1002	813	905	1419
Croatia	–	–	114	932	1467	1089	1561	1124	1713
Macedonia, TFYR	–	–	9	128	33	175	442	78	95
Romania	..	..	419	2031	1041	1037	1157	1144	1566
Serbia and Montenegro	–	–	45	113	112	25	165	475	1360
Yugoslavia, SFR (former)	24	67	–	–	–	–	–	–	–
CIS	–	–	*4054*	*6795*	*6798*	*5452*	*7030*	*9021*	*8870*
Armenia	–	–	25	237	135	124	88	150	155
Azerbaijan	–	–	330	1023	510	130	227	1392	3285
Belarus	–	–	15	203	444	119	96	247	171
Georgia	–	–	6	265	82	131	110	165	338
Kazakhstan	–	–	964	1151	1472	1283	2835	2590	2068
Kyrgyzstan	–	–	96	109	44	-2	5	5	25
Moldova, Republic of	–	–	67	76	38	134	146	117	58
Russian Federation	–	–	2065	2761	3309	2714	2469	3461	1144
Tajikistan	–	–	10	25	21	24	9	36	32
Turkmenistan	–	–	233	62	125	126	170	100	100
Ukraine	–	–	267	743	496	595	792	693	1424
Uzbekistan	–	–	-24	140	121	75	83	65	70
MEMO ITEM:									
LDC	536	578	1698	4541	5675	3802	6454	5763	7356
Land-locked countries	387	615	2970	5800	4479	4087	6064	7772	7987
Developing economies excluding China	8279	33279	76706	145315	188366	209050	168665	99752	111625

Sources: International Monetary Fund (IMF), *International Financial Statistics (IFS)* and *Balance of Payments Statistics* on CD-ROM;
UNCTAD, *World Investment Report 2004: The Shift Towards Services*.

Notes: For details, see "Definitions and sources" in annex B of
UNCTAD, *World Investment Report 2004: The Shift Towards Services.*

1 Prior to 1993, data for this group include figures for former Czechoslovakia that are not shown separately.

6.2 Investissement direct étranger : flux entrants et sortants *(fin)*
Millions de dollars

Outward flows - Flux sortants									Régions, pays ou zones
1980	1990	1995	1998	1999	2000	2001	2002	2003	
4	6	119	47	80	509	1397	1107	913	Inde
6	-11	1319	44	72	150	125	116	130	Indonésie
..	..	..	..	..	..	..	..	..	Corée, Rép. populaire dém. de
26	1052	3552	4740	4198	4999	2420	2617	3429	Corée, République de
..	..	..	..	..	168	3	57	76	Rép. dém. populaire lao
201	129	2488	863	1422	2026	267	1904	1370	Malaisie
..	..	..	..	..	..	..	..	..	Maldives
..	..	..	..	..	..	..	..	..	Mongolie
..	..	..	..	..	..	..	..	..	Myanmar
..	..	..	..	..	..	..	..	..	Népal
-5	2	..	5	1	11	31	28	19	Pakistan
1	22	98	160	-29	-108	-160	59	158	Philippines
98	2034	4467	2996	7517	5298	17063	3699	5536	Singapour
..	..	6	13	24	2	..	11	4	Sri Lanka
3	154	887	132	349	-22	162	106	557	Thaïlande
..	..	..	..	..	..	..	..	..	Viet Nam
									ECONOMIES EN DEVELOPPEMENT : OCEANIE
18	4	-16	-56	-24	67	116	..	29	
2	-4	-17	-56	-58	69	7	..	25	Fidji
..	..	..	..	..	..	..	..	..	Kiribati
..	..	..	..	..	..	..	..	..	Nouvelle-Calédonie
16	8	..	..	35	-2	109	..	3	Papouasie-Nouvelle-Guinée
..	..	..	..	..	..	..	..	..	Samoa
..	..	..	..	..	..	..	..	..	Iles Salomon
..	..	..	..	..	..	..	..	..	Tonga
..	..	..	..	..	..	..	..	..	Tuvalu
..	..	..	..	..	..	..	..	..	Vanuatu
..	18	636	1537	2663	3197	2854	4681	5114	**EUROPE DU SUD-EST ET CEI**
..	18	19	90	88	2	148	587	144	*Europe du Sud-Est*
..	..	12	1	7	6	..	4	3	Albanie
–	–	8	..	..	..	..	..	..	Bosnie-Herzégovine
..	..	-8	..	17	3	10	28	22	Bulgarie
–	–	5	98	47	4	155	533	62	Croatie
–	–	..	..	..	..	..	..	..	Macédoine, LERY
..	18	2	-9	16	-11	-17	16	56	Roumanie
–	–	..	..	..	..	..	5	..	Serbie-et-Monténégro
..	..	–	–	–	–	–	–	–	Yougoslavie, RSF (anc.)
–	–	617	1447	2576	3196	2706	4095	4970	*CEI*
–	–	..	12	13	8	11	11	..	Arménie
–	–	..	137	336	..	158	326	933	Azerbaïdjan
–	–	..	2	..	..	..	-206	2	Bélarus
–	–	..	..	1	..	..	4	4	Géorgie
–	–	..	8	4	4	-26	426	-120	Kazakhstan
–	–	..	23	6	5	6	6	5	Kirghizistan
–	–	..	..	..	..	..	..	..	Moldova, République de
–	–	606	1270	2208	3177	2533	3533	4133	Fédération de Russie
–	–	..	..	..	..	..	..	..	Tadjikistan
–	–	..	..	..	..	..	..	..	Turkménistan
–	–	10	-4	7	1	23	-5	13	Ukraine
–	–	..	..	..	..	..	..	..	Ouzbékistan
									POUR MEMOIRE :
228	-6	38	-342	400	780	-53	83	273	PMA
10	31	213	544	394	199	611	883	974	Pays enclavés
3319	15413	50691	50556	73207	97794	52610	40419	32623	Economies en développement Chine non comprise

Sources : Fonds monétaire international (FMI), *International Financial Statistics (IFS)* and *Balance of Payments Statistics* sur CD-ROM; *World Investment Report 2004: The Shift Towards Services* de la CNUCED.

Notes : Pour plus de détails concernant les sources, voir "Definitions and sources" dans l'annexe B du *World Investment Report 2004: The Shift Towards Services* de la CNUCED.

1 Avant 1993, les données incluent les chiffres de l'ancienne Tchécoslovaquie qui ne sont pas présentés séparément.

| Country or area [1] | Total amount (millions of dollars) | | | | | | As percentage of exports of goods and services | | | | | |
| Pays ou zones [1] | Montant total (millions de dollars) | | | | | | En pourcentage des exportations de biens et services | | | | | |
	1990	1995	2000	2001	2002	2003	1990	1995	2000	2001	2002	2003
Mexico - Mexique	3098	4368	7596	9919	11029	14595	6.3	4.9	4.2	5.8	6.4	8.2
India - Inde	2384	6223	8482	8245	8411	..	10.4	16.4	13.1	12.4	10.8	..
Philippines	1465	5360	6212	6164	7381	7880	12.8	20.0	15.1	17.9	19.7	20.8
Morocco - Maroc	2006	1970	2161	3261	2877	3628	32.2	21.8	20.7	29.2	23.6	25.7
Egypt - Egypte	4284	3226	2852	2911	2893	2961	43.3	24.3	16.9	18.1	17.6	14.8
Turkey - Turquie	3246	3327	4560	2786	1936	729	15.4	9.1	8.9	5.5	3.5	1.0
Bangladesh	779	1202	1968	2105	2858	..	37.7	27.1	27.3	30.8	41.1	..
Colombia - Colombie	495	815	1610	2056	2480	3076	5.7	6.6	10.2	13.7	17.5	20.0
Jordan - Jordanie	499	1441	1845	2011	2135	2201	19.9	41.4	52.2	53.3	49.9	48.1
Dominican Republic - République dominicaine	315	839	1839	1982	2194	2325	17.2	14.6	20.5	23.6	26.6	26.2
El Salvador	366	1064	1765	1926	1954	2122	37.6	52.2	48.2	53.6	51.4	53.2
Brazil - Brésil	573	3315	1649	1775	2449	2821	1.6	6.3	2.6	2.6	3.5	3.4
Pakistan	2006	1712	1075	1461	3554	3964	29.4	16.8	10.6	13.8	29.0	26.7
Ecuador - Equateur	51	386	1322	1421	1438	1545	1.6	7.4	22.1	25.2	23.5	21.8
Yemen - Yémen	1498	1081	1288	1295	1294	1270	100.6	50.0	32.1	36.6	34.2	29.9
Thailand - Thaïlande	973	1695	1697	1252	1380	1601	3.3	2.4	2.1	1.6	1.7	1.7
China - Chine	124	350	758	1209	2353	..	0.2	0.2	0.3	0.4	0.6	..
Sri Lanka	401	809	1166	1185	1309	..	17.5	17.5	18.3	19.2	21.9	..
Jamaica - Jamaïque	229	653	892	1058	1259	..	10.3	19.2	24.8	31.6	39.0	..
Indonesia - Indonésie	166	651	1190	1046	1259	..	0.6	1.2	1.7	1.7	1.9	..
Tunisia - Tunisie	551	680	796	927	1071	1250	10.6	8.5	9.2	9.7	11.2	11.4
Peru - Pérou	87	599	718	753	705	860	2.1	9.0	8.4	8.8	7.6	8.1
Sudan - Soudan	62	346	641	740	978	1224	12.4	50.8	34.9	43.2	47.0	49.1
Korea, Republic of - Corée, République de	1037	1080	735	652	581	..	1.4	0.7	0.4	0.4	0.3	..
Guatemala	119	358	596	634	1600	..	7.6	12.7	15.4	16.2	42.5	..
Honduras	63	124	416	540	718	867	6.1	7.6	16.7	22.3	28.7	32.7
Uganda - Ouganda	..	..	238	483	365	..	..	..	35.9	71.8	50.7	..
Malaysia - Malaisie [2]	185	116	342	367	435	..	0.6	0.1	0.3	0.4	0.4	..
Nicaragua	..	75	320	336	377	439	..	11.3	29.0	29.6	32.9	33.8
Senegal - Sénégal	142	146	233	305	344	..	9.8	9.7	17.9	21.7	22.6	..
South Africa - Afrique du Sud	136	105	344	297	288	436	0.5	0.3	0.9	0.8	0.8	1.0
China, Taiwan Province of - Chine, Taiwan Province	39	142	274	275	273	..	..	..	..	..	..	..
Paraguay	34	287	265	264	202	222	1.3	6.0	9.3	10.8	8.3	7.8
Lesotho	428	411	252	209	184	..	427.6	206.3	99.4	65.6	47.1	..
Costa Rica	12	123	136	198	251	321	0.6	2.8	1.8	2.9	3.5	3.9
Argentina - Argentine	..	56	86	190	187	253	..	0.2	0.3	0.6	0.7	0.8
Syrian Arab Republic - République arabe syrienne	385	339	180	170	135	..	7.7	5.9	2.6	2.3	1.6	..
Nepal - Népal	..	57	111	147	..	..	..	5.5	8.7	13.0	..	..
Bolivia - Bolivie	5	7	127	135	113	126	0.5	0.6	8.6	8.9	7.3	6.7
Barbados - Barbade	38	53	102	118	109	..	4.3	4.7	7.4	8.8	8.4	..
Myanmar	6	81	104	117	..	..	1.9	6.2	4.8	4.3	..	..
Côte d'Ivoire	44	151	119	116	120	141	1.3	3.5	2.7	2.6	2.0	2.2
Cambodia - Cambodge	..	12	103	113	123	..	..	1.2	5.6	5.4	5.2	..
Mali	107	112	73	88	138	..	25.5	21.2	11.4	10.1	13.2	..
Benin - Bénin	101	100	87	84	..	..	27.8	16.3	16.5	16.1	..	..
Cape Verde - Cap-Vert	59	106	87	81	85	92	104.1	126.8	59.6	48.5	43.7	33.3
Swaziland	113	83	74	74	62	..	17.1	8.1	6.6	6.4	5.8	..
Panama	110	112	16	73	85	85	2.5	1.5	0.2	0.9	1.1	1.1
Togo	27	15	34	69	..	..	4.1	3.2	8.1	16.0	..	..
Vanuatu	8	14	35	53	..	..	11.1	12.3	22.1	37.9	..	..

For sources and notes, see end of table 6.3B.

Pour les sources et les notes, se reporter à la fin du tableau 6.3B.

Country or area [1] Pays ou zones [1]	Total amount (millions of dollars) Montant total (millions de dollars)						As percentage of imports of goods and services En pourcentage des importations de biens et services					
	1990	1995	2000	2001	2002	2003	1990	1995	2000	2001	2001	2003
Saudi Arabia - Arabie saoudite	11236	16616	15411	15140	15875	14916	25.6	37.0	29.1	31.6	32.0	27.3
Kuwait - Koweït	770	1354	1734	1784	1925	2144	10.7	10.7	15.3	14.4	13.8	13.2
Oman	856	1537	1451	1532	..	..	25.6	30.5	23.6	21.9	..	..
China, Taiwan Province of - Chine, Taiwan Province	221	1595	1831	1466	1269	..	..	..	..	..	..	..
Bahrain - Bahreïn	332	500	1013	1287	1334	1340	8.3	12.1	19.7	26.8	23.7	22.5
Korea, Republic of - Corée, République de	364	635	972	1014	1398	..	0.5	0.4	0.5	0.6	0.8	..
China - Chine	5	..	790	990	1223	..	0.0	..	0.3	0.4	0.4	..
Brazil - Brésil	12	347	366	709	361	333	0.0	0.5	0.5	1.0	0.6	0.5
Malaysia - Malaisie [2]	230	1329	599	634	3826	..	0.7	1.5	0.6	0.7	4.2	..
South Africa - Afrique du Sud	1199	629	685	568	541	749	5.7	1.9	2.1	1.8	1.7	1.8
Uganda - Ouganda	..	..	353	409	302	..	..	..	25.1	26.4	18.4	..
Venezuela	701	203	331	406	384	210	7.4	1.2	1.6	1.7	2.2	1.5
Côte d'Ivoire	471	457	390	380	574	590	13.7	12.0	10.7	10.3	14.3	11.7
Argentina - Argentine	..	190	268	256	88	110	..	0.7	0.8	0.9	0.7	0.6
Jamaica - Jamaïque	27	74	179	217	279	..	1.1	2.0	4.1	4.7	5.8	..
Angola	150	210	266	216	..	..	4.4	6.0	4.6	3.2	..	..
Colombia - Colombie	44	150	219	204	158	65	0.6	0.9	1.5	1.3	1.0	0.4
Sri Lanka	..	16	20	194	210	..	..	0.3	0.2	2.7	3.0	..
Jordan - Jordanie	71	107	197	193	194	192	2.0	2.2	3.4	3.2	3.1	2.8
Costa Rica	..	36	142	140	148	192	..	0.8	2.0	2.0	1.9	2.3
Peru - Pérou	75	34	91	100	110	105	1.8	0.4	0.9	1.0	1.1	1.0
Swaziland	4	4	21	79	21	..	0.5	0.3	1.6	6.1	1.8	..
Vanuatu	12	18	73	78	..	..	12.1	15.8	49.4	51.8	..	..
Bahamas	46	44	73	72	..	..	2.8	2.5	2.3	2.7	..	..
Mozambique	25	21	156	64	50	30	2.6	2.0	10.5	4.0	2.8	1.7
Yemen - Yémen	106	61	61	64	64	60	4.9	2.5	1.8	1.8	1.7	1.3
Philippines	5	151	93	56	58	37	0.0	0.5	0.2	0.2	0.2	0.1
Cambodia - Cambodge	..	52	60	52	63	..	..	3.8	2.6	2.1	2.3	..
Senegal - Sénégal	79	76	55	51	39	..	4.3	4.2	3.2	2.8	1.9	..
Maldives	8	27	46	50	51	..	5.2	8.6	10.3	11.0	11.1	..
India - Inde	106	419	55	48	198	..	0.4	0.9	0.1	0.1	0.2	..
Burkina Faso	81	..	45	44	..	..	10.7	..	6.8	6.8	..	..
Netherlands Antilles - Antilles néerlandaises	11	11	47	44	55	..	0.7	0.5	2.0	1.7	2.3	..
Panama	22	20	22	42	45	53	0.5	0.3	0.3	0.5	0.6	0.7
Guyana	..	12	27	41	47	..	..	1.7	3.5	5.2	6.2	..
Guinea - Guinée	20	10	27	37	18	..	2.1	1.0	3.1	4.2	1.8	..
Bolivia - Bolivie	8	9	37	36	38	39	0.7	0.6	1.8	1.8	1.8	1.9
Morocco - Maroc	16	20	29	36	36	44	0.2	0.2	0.2	0.3	0.3	0.3
Egypt - Egypte	27	223	32	35	14	79	0.2	1.3	0.1	0.2	0.1	0.4
Rwanda	21	1	28	33	32	..	6.1	0.3	6.6	7.5	7.4	..
Guatemala	14	8	56	32	82	..	0.7	0.2	1.0	0.5	1.2	..
Congo	55	27	37	32	35	..	4.3	2.0	3.1	2.1	2.2	..
Syrian Arab Republic - République arabe syrienne	..	15	29	30	35	..	..	0.3	0.5	0.5	0.6	..
El Salvador	3	..	20	26	22	25	0.2	..	0.3	0.5	0.4	0.4
Lesotho	..	75	28	25	21	..	..	7.2	3.6	3.4	2.7	..
Nepal - Népal	..	9	17	24	..	..	..	0.6	0.9	1.4	..	..
Tunisia - Tunisie	13	36	27	24	20	24	0.2	0.4	0.3	0.2	0.2	0.2
Mali	45	42	26	23	30	..	5.5	4.3	2.9	2.0	2.8	..
United Republic of Tanzania - République-Unie de Tanzanie	..	1	20	22	21	..	..	0.0	1.0	1.0	0.9	..
Dominican Republic - République dominicaine	..	7	19	22	23	23	..	0.1	0.2	0.2	0.2	0.3

For sources and notes, see next page.

Pour les sources et les notes, se reporter à la page suivante.

6.3 Workers' remittances

6.3 Envois de fonds des travailleurs

Sources: IMF, *Balance of Payments Statistics* on CD-ROM.

Notes:

According to the definition of the IMF *Balance of Payments Manual (1993, BPM 5)*, workers' remittances are goods and financial instruments transferred by migrants living and working (being residents) in a new economy to residents of the economy in which the migrants formerly resided. A migrant must live and work in the new economy for more than one year to be considered a resident there.

The IMF *Balance of Payments Manual (BPM 5)* classifies workers' remittances separately from compensation of employees and from migrants' capital transfers. **Table 6.3 includes all three categories in the values shown, in order to present a clearer picture of the flows that enter or exit economies via transfers by migrant workers.**

1 Fifty developing countries and territories selected and ranked according to the 2001 values for each flow of workers' remittances.

2 For 1999, 2000 and 2001 data include compensation of employees only. Workers' remittances were not available.

Sources : FMI, *Balance of Payments Statistics* sur CD-ROM.

Notes :

Selon la définition du *Manuel de la balance des paiements* du FMI (1993, MBP 5), les envois de fonds des travailleurs sont les transferts de biens ou d'actifs financiers effectués par les migrants qui vivent et travaillent (sont considérés résidents) dans une économie en faveur des résidents de leur ancien pays de résidence. Un migrant doit vivre et travailler dans une nouvelle économie durant plus d'une année pour y être considéré résident.

Le Manuel de la balance des paiements du FMI (MBP 5) distingue séparément les envois de fonds des travailleurs, la rémunération des salariés et les transferts de capital des migrants. **Les valeurs dans le tableau 6.3 incluent les trois catégories mentionnées, afin d'offrir une présentation plus exhaustive des flux entrants ou sortants d'une économie à travers les transferts réalisés par les travailleurs migrants.**

1 Cinquante pays et territoires en développement choisis et classés d'après les valeurs de 2001 des envois de fonds des travailleurs.

2 Pour 1999, 2000 et 2001 les données comprennent seulement la rémunération des salariés. Les envois de fonds des travailleurs ne sont pas disponibles.

Region, economic grouping, country or area	Total reserves minus gold (end-of-year data) (millions of dollars) Réserves totales moins l'or (données de fin d'année) (en millions de dollars)								
	1980	1990	1995	1998	1999	2000	2001	2002	2003
DEVELOPING ECONOMIES	164089.7	321959.9	665414.6	881604.8	965692.8	1043504.1	1135494.7	1344070.4	1693620.7
DEVELOPING ECONOMIES: AMERICA	38876.5	47447.6	129173.0	160972.7	153768.7	156575.2	158854.0	160931.4	195631.0
South America	*31493.3*	*34329.2*	*105921.7*	*119226.7*	*110663.5*	*108531.7*	*98679.8*	*95156.5*	*120661.2*
Argentina	6719.5	4592.3	14287.8	24752.2	26252.0	25146.9	14553.1	10489.3	14153.4
Bolivia	106.1	166.8	660.0	948.5	974.9	926.4	886.4	580.5	716.8
Brazil	5769.3	7440.6	49708.1	42579.8	34796.0	32488.3	35739.4	37683.5	49110.7
Chile	3123.2	6068.5	14139.8	15869.3	14616.6	15034.9	14379.0	15341.1	15839.6
Colombia	4830.8	4627.5	8348.7	8651.1	8007.9	8916.0	10153.7	10732.4	10783.9
Ecuador	1013.0	838.5	1627.6	1619.7	1642.4	946.9	839.8	714.6	812.6
Guyana	12.7	28.7	268.9	276.6	268.3	305.0	287.3	284.5	276.4
Paraguay	761.9	661.4	1092.9	864.7	978.1	762.8	713.5	629.2	967.4
Peru	1979.8	1039.8	8221.8	9565.5	8730.5	8374.0	8671.9	9339.1	9776.8
Suriname	189.3	21.1	132.9	106.1	38.5	63.0	119.3	106.2	105.8
Uruguay	383.8	523.5	1150.1	2073.2	2081.2	2478.9	3097.1	769.2	2083.2
Venezuela	6604.0	8320.5	6283.1	11919.9	12277.3	13088.5	9239.5	8487.1	16034.7
Other America	*7383.2*	*13118.4*	*23251.3*	*41746.0*	*43105.2*	*48043.5*	*60174.2*	*65774.9*	*74969.9*
Anguilla	..	7.2	12.8	18.2	19.9	20.3	24.2	26.2	33.3
Antigua and Barbuda	7.8	27.5	59.4	59.4	69.7	63.6	79.7	87.7	113.8
Aruba	..	97.9	216.7	222.2	219.9	208.0	293.7	339.7	295.2
Bahamas	92.3	158.2	179.2	346.5	410.5	349.7	319.3	380.7	491.1
Barbados	78.9	117.5	219.1	366.0	301.9	472.7	690.4	668.5	737.0
Belize	12.7	69.8	37.6	44.1	71.3	122.9	112.0	114.5	84.7
Costa Rica	145.6	520.6	1046.6	1063.4	1460.4	1317.8	1329.8	1496.6	1836.3
Dominica	5.1	14.5	22.1	27.7	31.6	29.4	31.2	45.5	47.7
Dominican Republic	201.8	61.6	365.6	501.9	694.0	627.2	1099.5	468.4	253.2
El Salvador	77.7	414.8	758.3	1613.1	2003.8	1922.4	1741.0	1622.8	1942.9
Grenada	12.9	17.6	36.7	46.8	50.8	57.7	63.9	87.8	83.2
Guatemala	444.7	282.0	702.0	1335.1	1189.2	1746.4	2292.2	2299.1	2833.2
Haiti	16.2	3.2	191.6	258.2	264.0	182.2	141.4	81.7	62.0
Honduras	149.8	40.4	261.5	818.1	1257.6	1313.0	1415.6	1524.0	1430.0
Jamaica	105.0	168.2	681.3	709.5	554.5	1053.7	1900.5	1645.1	1194.9
Mexico	2959.9	9862.9	16846.8	31799.1	31782.3	35508.9	44740.7	50594.4	58955.7
Montserrat	..	10.0	8.8	24.8	14.0	10.4	12.5	14.4	15.2
Netherlands Antilles	94.6	215.0	203.0	248.0	265.0	261.0	301.0	406.3	372.2
Nicaragua	64.5	106.6	136.2	350.4	509.7	488.5	379.9	448.1	502.1
Panama	117.4	343.5	781.4	954.5	822.9	722.6	1091.8	1182.8	1011.0
Saint Kitts and Nevis	..	16.3	33.5	46.8	49.6	45.2	56.4	65.8	64.8
Saint Lucia	8.3	44.6	63.1	70.6	74.5	78.8	88.9	93.9	108.1
Saint Vincent and the Grenadines	7.3	26.5	29.8	38.8	42.6	55.2	61.4	53.2	51.2
Trinidad and Tobago	2780.8	492.0	358.2	783.1	945.4	1386.3	1907.1	2027.7	2451.1
DEVELOPING ECONOMIES: AFRICA	33207.6	25253.3	41875.2	66130.1	63328.5	79333.2	91744.3	99190.0	124426.0
North Africa	*18946.6*	*12120.3*	*23556.1*	*38614.8*	*34429.1*	*44483.8*	*56388.8*	*63651.2*	*83942.1*
Algeria	3772.6	724.8	2005.2	6845.6	4525.7	12023.9	18081.5	23237.5	33125.2
Egypt	1046.0	2683.6	16181.2	18123.9	14484.1	13117.6	12925.9	13242.4	13588.7
Libyan Arab Jamahiriya	13090.6	5839.2	..	7269.7	7279.7	12460.8	14800.5	14307.5	19584.0
Morocco	398.6	2066.5	3601.1	4435.0	5689.4	4823.2	8473.9	10132.7	13851.1
Sudan	48.7	11.4	163.4	90.6	188.7	247.3	117.9	440.9	847.5
Tunisia	590.1	794.8	1605.3	1850.1	2261.5	1811.0	1989.2	2290.3	2945.4
Other Africa	*14261.0*	*13133.0*	*18319.1*	*27515.3*	*28899.4*	*34849.4*	*35355.5*	*35538.8*	*40484.0*
Angola	..	..	212.8	203.5	496.1	1198.2	731.9	375.6	638.4
Benin	8.2	64.9	198.0	261.5	400.1	458.1	578.1	615.7	509.8
Botswana	334.0	3331.5	4695.5	5940.7	6298.7	6318.2	5897.3	5473.9	..
Burkina Faso	68.2	300.5	347.4	373.3	295.0	243.6	260.5	313.4	434.8
Burundi	94.5	105.0	209.5	65.5	48.0	32.9	17.7	58.8	67.0
Cameroon	188.9	25.5	3.8	1.3	4.4	212.0	331.8	629.7	639.6
Cape Verde	42.4	77.0	36.9	8.3	42.6	28.3	45.4	79.8	93.6
Central African Republic	55.0	118.6	233.6	145.7	136.3	133.3	118.8	123.2	132.4

For sources and notes, see end of table.

Annual change in reserves (millions of dollars) Variations annuelles des réserves (en millions de dollars)					Number of months of imports [1] Nombre de mois d'importations [1]								Régions, groupements économiques, pays ou zones
1998-99	1999-00	2000-01	2001-02	2002-03	1980	1990	1995	1999	2000	2001	2002	2003	
84088.0	77811.3	91990.6	208575.8	349550.3	4.2	4.8	5.3	6.8	6.9	7.6	8.1	9.4	**ECONOMIES EN DEVELOPPEMENT**
													ECONOMIES EN DEVELOPPEMENT : AMERIQUE
-7204.0	2806.5	2278.8	2077.4	34699.7	3.9	4.4	6.0	5.2	5.0	5.3	5.5	6.5	
-8563.2	*-2131.9*	*-9851.9*	*-3523.3*	*25504.7*	*5.6*	*6.7*	*9.0*	*9.2*	*8.7*	*8.7*	*9.0*	*11.0*	*Amérique du Sud*
1499.8	-1105.1	-10593.9	-4063.7	3664.1	8.1	9.0	7.8	12.4	13.3	11.9	11.0	12.3	Argentine
26.4	-48.5	-40.0	-306.0	136.3	1.6	2.4	5.2	6.5	6.3	6.1	4.1	5.3	Bolivie
-7783.8	-2307.7	3251.1	1944.1	11427.3	2.8	3.9	10.8	7.6	6.7	8.0	9.0	11.6	Brésil
-1252.8	418.4	-655.9	962.1	498.5	5.8	9.1	9.7	10.2	9.9	9.9	10.1	9.8	Chili
-643.2	908.1	1237.7	578.7	51.5	11.7	10.6	7.3	8.7	8.8	9.5	9.7	9.3	Colombie
22.7	-695.5	-107.2	-125.1	98.0	5.4	4.7	4.8	5.9	2.5	1.7	1.3	1.5	Equateur
-8.3	36.7	-17.7	-2.8	-8.1	0.4	1.1	5.7	5.1	5.9	6.0	4.3	3.3	Guyana
113.3	-215.2	-49.3	-84.3	338.2	15.1	5.6	4.7	6.2	4.5	4.2	3.3	4.6	Paraguay
-835.0	-356.5	297.9	667.2	437.8	7.9	3.3	10.5	12.3	11.2	11.5	11.4	11.2	Pérou
-67.7	24.5	56.3	-13.1	-0.4	4.2	0.5	2.9	1.7	1.9	2.7	2.2	2.1	Suriname
8.0	397.7	618.2	-2327.9	1314.0	2.8	4.2	4.5	7.3	9.1	14.8	4.4	11.4	Uruguay
357.4	811.2	-3849.0	-752.4	7547.6	6.4	10.8	6.7	9.7	9.2	7.4	9.8	21.5	Venezuela
1359.2	*4938.3*	*12130.7*	*5600.7*	*9194.9*	*1.7*	*2.3*	*2.4*	*2.5*	*2.6*	*3.2*	*3.5*	*3.9*	*Autres économies : Amérique*
1.8	0.4	3.9	2.0	7.1	..	..	..	..	..	..	..	..	Anguilla
10.4	-6.2	16.2	7.9	26.1	1.0	1.2	2.0	2.1	2.0	2.6	2.8	3.7	Antigua-et-Barbuda
-2.3	-11.9	85.7	46.0	-44.5	..	2.3	4.5	3.3	3.0	4.2	4.9	4.3	Aruba
64.0	-60.9	-30.4	61.4	110.5	0.2	1.7	1.7	2.8	2.4	2.4	2.8	3.4	Bahamas
-64.0	170.8	217.7	-21.9	68.5	1.7	2.0	3.3	3.2	5.1	7.8	7.4	7.8	Barbade
27.2	51.6	-10.9	2.5	-29.8	1.0	3.6	1.8	1.9	2.8	2.6	2.6	1.8	Belize
397.0	-142.7	12.1	166.7	339.7	1.3	3.2	3.0	2.8	2.4	2.3	2.4	2.9	Costa Rica
3.9	-2.2	1.9	14.3	2.2	1.3	1.5	2.2	2.7	2.5	3.0	4.5	4.6	Dominique
192.1	-66.8	472.3	-631.1	-215.3	1.5	0.4	1.1	1.3	1.1	2.2	0.9	0.5	République dominicaine
390.7	-81.4	-181.4	-118.2	320.2	1.0	3.7	3.3	6.9	6.0	5.4	4.7	5.3	El Salvador
4.0	6.8	6.3	23.9	-4.6	3.0	1.8	3.2	2.7	3.0	3.5	4.3	3.7	Grenade
-145.9	557.2	545.8	7.0	534.1	3.3	1.9	2.6	3.1	4.0	4.7	4.4	5.2	Guatemala
5.8	-81.9	-40.7	-59.7	-19.7	0.5	0.1	3.5	3.1	2.1	1.6	0.9	0.6	Haïti
439.5	55.5	102.5	108.4	-94.0	1.8	0.5	1.8	5.5	5.4	5.7	5.9	5.2	Honduras
-154.9	499.2	846.9	-255.4	-450.2	1.0	1.1	2.8	2.1	3.8	6.6	5.2	3.5	Jamaïque
-16.8	3726.6	9231.9	5853.7	8361.3	1.4	2.5	2.4	2.3	2.4	3.0	3.4	4.0	Mexique
-10.8	-3.6	2.1	1.9	0.8	..	2.9	3.5	7.5	5.9	7.1	7.5	8.0	Montserrat
17.0	-4.0	40.0	105.3	-34.1	0.2	1.2	1.1	1.3	1.1	1.4	2.0	1.7	Antilles néerlandaises
159.3	-21.3	-108.5	68.2	53.9	0.8	1.8	1.5	3.3	3.3	2.6	2.7	2.7	Nicaragua
-131.6	-100.3	369.2	91.1	-171.9	0.9	2.6	3.5	2.9	2.7	4.4	4.7	3.9	Panama
2.8	-4.4	11.2	9.3	-1.0	..	1.8	2.9	3.9	3.5	4.4	4.6	4.0	Saint-Kitts-et-Nevis
3.9	4.3	10.1	5.0	14.2	0.8	1.9	2.4	2.5	2.7	3.2	3.3	3.4	Sainte-Lucie
3.8	12.6	6.3	-8.2	-2.0	1.5	2.3	2.7	2.8	3.8	4.1	3.4	3.1	Saint-Vincent-et-les Grenadines
162.3	440.9	520.8	120.6	423.4	10.6	4.3	2.2	3.8	4.8	6.4	6.1	6.7	Trinité-et-Tobago
													ECONOMIES EN DEVELOPPEMENT : AFRIQUE
-2801.6	16004.7	12411.1	7445.7	25236.0	4.0	3.2	4.2	5.9	7.3	8.2	7.8	8.9	
-4185.7	*10054.7*	*11904.9*	*7262.4*	*20290.9*	*6.5*	*3.7*	*6.9*	*8.5*	*10.9*	*13.2*	*13.4*	*16.6*	*Afrique du Nord*
-2319.9	7498.2	6057.6	5156.0	9887.8	4.1	1.0	2.5	5.9	15.3	21.2	24.6	33.3	Algérie
-3639.8	-1366.5	-191.7	316.6	346.3	1.8	2.6	15.7	11.6	11.8	12.3	11.6	11.0	Egypte
10.1	5181.1	2339.7	-493.1	5276.6	20.7	13.1	..	23.0	36.4	35.0	28.2	36.4	Jamahiriya arabe libyenne
1254.3	-866.2	3650.7	1658.8	3718.5	1.1	3.6	4.4	6.4	5.1	8.9	9.2	11.4	Maroc
98.1	58.6	-129.5	323.1	406.6	0.4	0.2	1.4	1.5	1.5	0.6	2.3	4.9	Soudan
411.4	-450.5	178.2	301.1	655.1	1.9	1.8	2.5	3.2	2.4	2.5	2.7	3.2	Tunisie
1384.1	*5950.0*	*506.1*	*183.3*	*4945.2*	*2.7*	*2.9*	*2.8*	*4.4*	*5.1*	*5.1*	*4.5*	*4.5*	*Autres économies : Afrique*
292.7	702.1	-466.4	-356.3	262.8	..	..	1.5	1.9	4.6	2.5	1.0	1.4	Angola
138.6	58.1	120.0	37.7	-106.0	0.2	3.1	3.4	7.1	9.1	10.8	10.4	8.2	Bénin
358.1	19.5	-421.0	-423.3	..	5.3	20.6	31.0	32.3	35.4	37.7	31.8	..	Botswana
-78.3	-51.4	16.9	52.9	121.4	2.4	6.8	7.6	5.5	4.6	4.5	4.7	6.1	Burkina Faso
-17.5	-15.1	-15.2	41.1	8.2	6.9	5.2	13.9	4.3	2.8	1.6	4.9	5.1	Burundi
3.1	207.6	119.8	297.8	10.0	1.5	0.2	0.0	0.0	1.5	2.2	3.8	3.6	Cameroun
34.3	-14.4	17.2	34.4	13.8	7.3	6.6	1.8	2.2	1.5	2.1	3.2	3.5	Cap-Vert
-9.4	-3.0	-14.5	4.5	9.2	7.5	11.5	17.8	13.2	14.3	12.5	12.5	13.6	République centrafricaine

Pour les sources et les notes, se reporter à la fin du tableau.

Region, economic grouping, country or area	Total reserves minus gold (end-of-year data) (millions of dollars) Réserves totales moins l'or (données de fin d'année) (en millions de dollars)								
	1980	1990	1995	1998	1999	2000	2001	2002	2003
Chad	5.1	127.8	142.5	120.1	95.0	110.7	122.4	218.7	187.1
Comoros	6.4	29.7	44.5	39.1	37.2	43.2	62.3	79.9	94.3
Congo	85.9	5.9	59.3	0.8	39.4	222.0	68.9	31.6	34.8
Côte d'Ivoire	19.7	4.0	529.0	855.5	630.4	667.9	1019.0	1863.3	2230.5
Dem. Rep. of the Congo	204.1	219.1	146.6	..	..	..	..	..	..
Djibouti	..	93.6	72.2	66.5	70.6	67.8	70.3	73.7	100.1
Equatorial Guinea	..	0.7	0.0	0.8	3.4	23.0	70.9	88.5	237.7
Eritrea	–	–	40.5	23.1	34.2	25.5	39.8	30.3	24.7
Ethiopia	80.1	20.2	771.5	511.1	458.5	306.3	433.2	881.8	955.6
Gabon	107.5	273.8	148.1	15.4	18.0	190.1	9.9	139.7	196.6
Gambia	5.7	55.4	106.2	106.4	111.3	109.4	106.0	106.9	
Ghana	180.4	218.8	697.5	377.0	453.8	232.1	298.2	539.8	1352.8
Guinea	..	..	86.8	236.7	199.7	147.9	200.2	171.4	..
Guinea-Bissau	..	18.2	20.3	35.8	35.3	66.7	69.5	102.7	164.4
Kenya	491.7	205.4	353.4	783.1	791.6	897.7	1064.9	1068.0	1481.9
Lesotho	50.3	72.4	456.7	575.1	499.6	417.9	386.5	406.4	460.3
Liberia	5.5	..	28.1	0.6	0.4	0.3	0.5	3.3	..
Madagascar	9.1	92.1	109.0	171.4	227.2	285.2	398.4	363.3	414.3
Malawi	68.4	137.2	110.0	269.7	250.6	246.9	206.7	165.2	126.0
Mali	14.5	190.5	323.0	402.9	349.7	381.3	348.9	594.5	908.7
Mauritania	139.9	54.1	85.5	202.9	224.3	279.9	284.5	396.2	415.3
Mauritius	90.7	737.6	863.3	559.0	731.0	897.4	835.6	1227.4	1577.3
Mozambique	..	232.6	195.3	608.5	651.6	725.1	715.6	819.2	998.5
Namibia	..	..	221.0	260.3	305.5	260.0	234.3	323.1	325.2
Niger	125.9	222.2	94.7	53.1	39.2	80.4	107.0	133.9	114.1
Nigeria	10234.8	3864.3	1443.4	7100.8	5450.3	9910.9	10456.7	7331.3	7128.4
Rwanda	196.1	44.4	99.1	168.8	174.2	190.6	212.1	243.7	214.7
Sao Tome and Principe	..	..	5.1	9.7	10.9	11.6	15.5	17.4	25.5
Senegal	8.1	11.0	271.8	430.8	403.0	384.0	447.3	637.4	794.5
Seychelles	18.4	16.6	27.1	21.6	30.4	43.8	37.1	69.8	67.4
Sierra Leone	30.6	5.4	34.6	43.9	39.5	49.2	51.3	84.7	66.6
Somalia	14.0	..	..	..	..	..	..	..	..
South Africa	725.8	1008.3	2819.9	4356.9	6353.1	6082.8	6045.3	5904.3	6495.5
Swaziland	158.7	216.5	298.2	358.6	375.9	351.8	271.8	275.8	277.5
Togo	77.6	353.2	130.4	117.8	122.1	152.3	126.4	205.1	182.5
Uganda	3.0	44.0	458.9	725.4	763.1	808.0	983.4	934.0	1080.3
United Republic of Tanzania	20.3	192.8	270.2	599.2	775.5	974.2	1156.6	1528.8	2038.4
Zambia	78.2	193.1	222.7	69.4	45.4	244.8	183.5	535.1	247.7
Zimbabwe	213.5	149.2	595.5	130.8	268.0	193.1	64.7	83.4	..
DEVELOPING ECONOMIES: ASIA	**91368.5**	**248439.4**	**493538.3**	**653638.0**	**747681.6**	**806622.4**	**883869.3**	**1083006.4**	**1372358.0**
West Asia	*54140.5*	*43484.5*	*61860.0*	*72544.4*	*86618.2*	*93625.4*	*91271.5*	*108349.7*	*125740.9*
Bahrain	953.4	1234.9	1279.9	1079.2	1369.0	1564.1	1684.0	1725.8	1778.4
Iran, Islamic Republic of	10222.9	..	..	..	..	..	..	..	..
Jordan	1142.8	848.8	1972.9	1750.4	2629.1	3331.3	3062.2	3975.9	5194.3
Kuwait	3928.5	1951.7	3560.8	3947.1	4823.7	7082.4	9897.3	9208.1	7577.0
Lebanon	1588.2	659.9	4533.3	6556.3	7775.6	5943.7	5013.8	7243.8	12519.5
Oman	581.4	1672.4	1830.7	1937.7	2767.5	2379.9	2364.9	3173.5	3593.5
Qatar	343.5	631.1	743.9	1043.4	1304.2	1158.0	1312.7	1566.8	2944.2
Saudi Arabia [2]	23436.7	11667.7	8621.6	14220.1	16996.9	19585.5	17595.7	20610.5	22620.0
Syrian Arab Republic	336.5	..	..	..	..	..	..	..	..
Turkey	1077.0	6049.5	12441.9	19488.8	23345.9	22488.5	18879.2	27068.6	33991.0
United Arab Emirates	2014.7	4583.9	7470.9	9077.1	10675.1	13522.6	14146.4	15219.4	15087.8
Yemen	–	422.2	619.0	995.5	1471.5	2900.3	3658.1	4410.5	4987.0
Yemen Arab Republic (former)	1282.6	–	–	–	–	–	–	–	–
Yemen, Democratic (former)	233.8	–	–	–	–	–	–	–	–
West Asia unspecified	6998.6	13762.5	18785.0	12448.8	13459.9	13669.2	13657.1	14146.8	15448.3

For sources and notes, see end of table.

Annual change in reserves (millions of dollars) / Variations annuelles des réserves (en millions de dollars)					Number of months of imports [1] / Nombre de mois d'importations [1]								Régions, groupements économiques, pays ou zones
1998-99	1999-00	2000-01	2001-02	2002-03	1980	1990	1995	1999	2000	2001	2002	2003	
-25.1	15.7	11.7	96.3	-31.6	0.7	5.7	4.9	3.6	2.7	1.8	2.9	2.7	Tchad
-2.0	6.1	19.1	17.6	14.4	2.5	6.5	9.0	5.9	6.1	8.2	9.8	10.1	Comores
38.5	182.7	-153.1	-37.3	3.2	2.0	0.1	0.6	0.7	5.1	1.4	0.6	0.6	Congo
-225.1	37.5	351.2	844.3	367.2	0.1	0.0	2.2	2.9	3.3	5.0	7.7	8.1	Côte d'Ivoire
..	..	..	..	..	1.7	1.7	1.4	..	..	..	..	..	Rép. dém. du Congo
4.2	-2.8	2.5	3.4	26.4	..	5.2	4.9	5.6	5.5	5.5	5.6	7.8	Djibouti
2.6	19.7	47.8	17.7	149.2	..	0.1	0.0	0.1	0.5	1.5	1.7	3.4	Guinée équatoriale
11.2	-8.7	14.2	-9.5	-5.6	_	_	1.1	1.3	0.8	1.0	0.6	0.4	Erythrée
-52.6	-152.2	126.9	448.5	73.9	1.3	0.3	7.3	3.9	2.4	3.0	4.9	4.3	Ethiopie
2.5	172.1	-180.2	129.8	56.9	1.7	3.8	1.9	0.2	2.5	0.1	1.6	2.0	Gabon
4.9	-1.8	-3.4	0.9		0.5	3.4	5.8	7.0	8.2	9.0	7.8	..	Gambie
76.8	-221.7	66.2	241.5	813.1	1.9	2.3	4.2	1.7	1.0	1.4	2.1	4.7	Ghana
-37.0	-51.8	52.3	-28.8	..	..	..	1.4	4.1	2.9	3.8	3.1	..	Guinée
-0.5	31.5	2.7	33.2	61.7	..	2.7	2.2	8.4	14.4	13.9	19.4	28.7	Guinée-Bissau
8.5	106.2	167.1	3.1	413.9	2.9	1.2	1.4	3.2	3.4	4.0	3.7	4.8	Kenya
-75.5	-81.7	-31.4	19.9	54.0	1.4	1.2	5.5	8.0	7.1	6.3	5.4	5.4	Lesotho
-0.2	-0.2	0.2	2.8	..	0.1	..	0.6	0.0	0.0	0.0	0.1	..	Libéria
55.8	58.0	113.2	-35.1	51.0	0.2	2.2	2.1	3.1	3.5	6.1	5.6	5.2	Madagascar
-19.1	-3.7	-40.2	-41.6	-39.2	2.1	2.6	2.4	5.0	5.4	3.9	3.0	2.3	Malawi
-53.2	31.6	-32.4	245.6	314.2	0.4	4.3	5.0	7.0	6.9	5.7	7.6	9.7	Mali
21.4	55.6	4.6	111.7	19.1	6.1	2.1	2.1	8.6	9.6	9.4	13.4	14.1	Mauritanie
172.0	166.5	-61.8	391.8	349.9	1.9	5.6	4.9	4.0	5.3	4.8	6.5	8.0	Maurice
43.1	73.5	-9.5	103.6	179.3	..	3.1	3.2	6.8	7.8	7.1	7.2	8.8	Mozambique
45.2	-45.5	-25.8	88.9	2.1	..	..	1.6	2.3	2.0	1.9	2.5	2.3	Namibie
-13.8	41.2	26.6	26.9	-19.9	2.7	7.2	2.8	1.2	2.5	3.3	3.4	2.5	Niger
-1650.5	4460.6	545.8	-3125.3	-202.9	6.5	6.4	2.4	7.6	11.7	13.1	9.6	7.9	Nigéria
5.4	16.5	21.5	31.6	-29.0	8.8	1.8	4.8	9.1	9.9	11.3	14.2	12.3	Rwanda
1.2	0.8	3.8	1.9	8.1	..	..	2.4	3.9	4.8	6.2	5.7	7.3	Sao Tomé-et-Principe
-27.8	-19.0	63.3	190.1	157.2	0.1	0.1	2.3	3.1	2.8	2.9	3.5	3.9	Sénégal
8.8	13.4	-6.6	32.7	-2.4	2.3	1.1	1.1	0.9	1.3	1.0	2.0	1.9	Seychelles
-4.4	9.7	2.1	33.4	-18.1	1.0	0.4	2.4	4.1	3.6	2.8	3.6	2.6	Sierra Leone
..	..	..	..	..	0.4	..	..	..	..	..	..	..	Somalie
1996.3	-270.3	-37.5	-141.0	591.3	0.4	0.7	1.1	2.7	2.5	2.5	2.0	1.9	Afrique du Sud
17.3	-24.1	-80.0	4.1	1.7	3.1	3.8	3.5	4.3	3.9	3.1	3.2	3.1	Swaziland
4.3	30.3	-25.9	78.7	-22.6	1.9	8.3	2.5	3.0	3.7	2.8	3.5	2.6	Togo
37.7	44.9	175.3	-49.4	146.3	0.1	2.2	4.9	6.4	6.2	8.7	9.5	10.4	Ouganda
176.3	198.8	182.4	372.2	509.6	0.2	1.6	2.1	6.0	7.2	8.2	9.5	11.2	République-Unie de Tanzanie
-24.0	199.4	-61.4	351.7	-287.4	0.9	2.3	3.5	0.6	2.6	1.7	5.1	2.4	Zambie
137.2	-74.8	-128.4	18.7	..	1.6	0.9	2.6	1.6	1.3	0.3	0.3	..	Zimbabwe
													ECONOMIES EN DEVELOPPEMENT : ASIE
94043.6	58940.7	77247.0	199137.1	289351.6	4.4	5.2	5.3	7.4	7.5	8.1	8.7	10.1	
14073.9	*7007.2*	*-2353.9*	*17078.1*	*17391.2*	*7.3*	*6.4*	*6.1*	*7.2*	*7.6*	*7.5*	*7.8*	*8.3*	*Asie occidentale*
289.8	195.1	119.8	41.8	52.6	3.0	3.8	3.9	3.9	4.2	4.4	4.1	4.2	Bahreïn
..	..	..	..	..	9.1	..	..	..	..	..	..	..	Iran, Rép. islamique d'
878.7	702.2	-269.0	913.7	1218.4	4.9	4.0	5.9	7.6	8.5	7.5	8.6	10.3	Jordanie
876.6	2258.7	2815.0	-689.2	-1631.1	7.0	5.4	5.3	7.8	11.3	14.1	11.2	8.4	Koweït
1219.4	-1832.0	-929.9	2230.0	5275.6	5.3	2.5	7.3	15.0	10.6	8.8	12.8	21.0	Liban
829.7	-387.6	-14.9	808.5	420.0	3.5	6.8	5.0	6.8	5.3	4.8	6.1	6.6	Oman
260.8	-146.2	154.7	254.1	1377.4	2.8	4.4	2.9	5.4	4.0	4.0	4.1	6.8	Qatar
2776.8	2588.6	-1989.8	3014.7	2009.6	8.6	5.3	3.7	7.0	7.7	6.7	7.4	7.8	Arabie saoudite [2]
..	..	..	..	..	0.9	..	..	..	..	..	..	..	République arabe syrienne
3857.0	-857.4	-3609.3	8189.4	6922.4	1.5	3.4	3.8	5.9	5.6	5.0	5.6	6.2	Turquie
1598.0	2847.6	623.7	1073.0	-131.6	2.6	4.4	4.1	3.6	4.8	5.5	5.2	4.7	Emirats arabes unis
475.9	1428.8	757.9	752.4	576.4	_	2.8	4.1	8.2	15.0	17.9	18.7	19.7	Yémen
_	_	_	_	_	..	_	_	_	_	_	_	_	Rép. arabe du Yémen (anc.)
_	_	_	_	_	..	_	_	_	_	_	_	_	Yémen dém. (anc.)
1011.1	209.4	-12.2	489.7	1301.5	..	..	..	..	..	..	..	..	Asie occidentale non spécifiée

Pour les sources et les notes, se reporter à la fin du tableau.

Region, economic grouping, country or area	Total reserves minus gold (end-of-year data) (millions of dollars) Réserves totales moins l'or (données de fin d'année) (en millions de dollars)								
	1980	1990	1995	1998	1999	2000	2001	2002	2003
Other Asia	*37228.0*	*204954.9*	*431678.3*	*581093.6*	*661063.4*	*712997.0*	*792597.8*	*974656.8*	*1246617.2*
Afghanistan	371.2	266.4	..	..	..	..	..	..	..
Bangladesh	299.7	628.7	2339.7	1905.4	1603.6	1486.0	1275.0	1683.2	2577.9
Bhutan	..	86.0	124.3	249.6	274.4	295.4	284.6	320.6	315.8
Cambodia	..	..	192.0	324.4	393.2	501.7	586.8	776.2	815.5
China	2545.7	29586.2	75376.6	149187.8	157727.5	168277.3	215604.6	291127.6	408151.4
China, Hong Kong SAR	..	24568.1	55398.1	89650.1	96236.0	107542.1	111155.0	111896.0	118360.0
China, Macao SAR	..	520.6	2256.6	2462.6	2857.4	3323.0	3508.4	3800.4	4343.4
China, Taiwan Province of	2205.0	72441.0	90310.1	90341.0	106200.0	106741.9	122211.0	161656.4	206631.6
India	6943.9	1521.0	17921.9	27340.7	32666.7	37902.3	45870.5	67665.5	98938.0
Indonesia	5391.7	7459.1	13708.3	22713.4	26445.0	28501.8	27246.2	30968.9	34962.4
Korea, Republic of	2924.9	14793.0	32677.8	51974.5	73987.4	96130.5	102753.3	121345.2	155283.9
Lao People's Dem. Rep.	..	1.8	92.1	112.2	101.2	139.0	130.9	191.6	208.6
Malaysia	4387.4	9754.1	23774.5	25559.4	30588.2	29522.6	30474.5	34221.6	44515.1
Maldives	1.0	24.4	48.0	118.5	127.1	122.8	93.1	133.1	159.5
Mongolia	..	..	117.0	94.1	136.5	178.8	205.7	349.7	236.1
Myanmar	260.6	312.8	561.2	314.9	265.5	223.0	400.5	470.0	550.2
Nepal	182.8	295.3	586.4	756.3	845.1	945.4	1037.7	1017.6	1222.5
Pakistan	495.8	295.9	1732.8	1028.0	1511.4	1513.3	3640.0	8078.3	10941.0
Philippines	2846.1	924.4	6372.4	9225.6	13229.7	13046.6	13429.0	13135.5	13457.4
Singapore	6566.8	27748.4	68695.3	74928.0	76843.1	80132.1	75374.9	82021.1	95746.0
Sri Lanka	245.5	422.9	2087.7	1979.8	1635.6	1039.0	1286.8	1631.0	..
Thailand	1560.2	13305.1	35982.0	28825.1	34062.8	32015.9	32354.8	38046.4	41077.0
Viet Nam	..	..	1323.7	2002.3	3326.2	3416.5	3674.6	4121.0	6224.2
DEVELOPING ECONOMIES: OCEANIA	**637.1**	**819.5**	**828.1**	**863.9**	**914.0**	**973.3**	**1027.1**	**942.7**	**1205.7**
Fiji	167.5	260.8	349.0	385.7	428.7	411.8	366.4	358.8	423.6
Micronesia, Federated States of	..	..	69.5	101.6	92.7	113.1	98.3	117.4	89.6
Papua New Guinea	423.4	403.0	261.4	192.9	205.1	286.9	422.7	321.5	485.3
Samoa	2.8	69.1	55.3	61.4	68.2	63.7	56.6	62.5	83.9
Solomon Islands	29.6	17.6	15.9	49.0	51.1	32.0	19.3	18.3	36.8
Tonga	13.8	31.3	28.7	28.7	26.8	27.0	26.1	27.7	42.6
Vanuatu	..	37.7	48.3	44.7	41.4	38.9	37.7	36.5	43.8
DEVELOPING ECONOMIES	**164089.7**	**321959.9**	**665414.6**	**881604.8**	**965692.8**	**1043504.1**	**1135494.7**	**1344070.4**	**1693620.7**
By major category									
Major petroleum exporters	92494.9	63120.8	67333.3	101849.1	110609.5	141105.5	147159.2	157374.4	188563.9
Other developing economies	71594.8	258839.1	598081.4	779755.7	855083.3	902398.6	988335.5	1186696.0	1505056.8
Major exporters of manufactures	39786.1	217994.1	485505.4	640899.9	711465.5	761797.0	848586.8	1036461.7	1324217.6
Remaining economies	31808.7	40844.9	112576.0	138855.8	143617.8	140601.6	139748.6	150234.3	180839.2
America	20668.0	21116.6	55773.8	73642.8	73702.7	73842.2	66926.3	61732.4	68706.6
Africa	5916.3	14545.4	38006.4	44694.4	45519.4	43327.3	47595.0	53766.9	63718.6
West Asia	2731.0	1508.8	6506.3	8306.6	10404.7	9275.0	8076.1	11219.7	17713.7
Other Asia	1856.4	2854.7	11461.4	11348.1	13077.0	13183.8	16124.1	22572.6	29494.7
By income group (per capita GDP in 2000)									
High-income countries	80517.9	198900.0	331504.2	443154.4	498576.6	551822.0	571701.6	643723.8	777968.1
Middle-income countries	48944.2	72755.4	200247.4	202190.8	207997.8	207807.0	220770.0	249324.0	301621.8
Low-income countries	34627.7	50304.5	133663.1	236259.5	259118.4	283875.1	343023.2	451022.6	614030.8
MEMO ITEM:									
LDC	4139.7	5252.0	10601.3	12034.5	12844.1	15547.1	16559.8	20220.6	24181.0
HIPC	4443.7	4382.3	10686.7	14006.7	16781.7	19997.7	21841.3	26502.6	32835.9
Land-locked countries	2967.4	6750.6	13683.0	15835.1	16778.3	16883.5	17417.7	18602.0	22523.7
Developing economies excluding China	161544.0	292373.7	590038.0	732417.0	807965.3	875226.7	919890.1	1052942.8	1285469.3
Sub-Saharan Africa	14309.7	13144.4	18482.5	27605.9	29088.1	35096.7	35473.4	35979.7	41331.5

For sources and notes, see next page.

1998-99	1999-00	2000-01	2001-02	2002-03	1980	1990	1995	1999	2000	2001	2002	2003	Régions, groupements économiques, pays ou zones
79969.8	*51933.6*	*79600.8*	*182059.0*	*271960.4*	*2.8*	*5.0*	*5.2*	*7.4*	*7.4*	*8.2*	*8.8*	*10.3*	*Autres économies : Asie*
..	..	..	..	..	5.2	4.1	..	..	..	..	..	..	Afghanistan
-301.8	-117.7	-210.9	408.2	894.7	1.4	2.2	4.3	2.4	2.1	1.9	2.4	3.4	Bangladesh
24.8	20.9	-10.8	36.0	-4.8	..	12.6	12.4	17.1	18.0	19.2	22.9	22.1	Bhoutan
68.8	108.5	85.1	189.3	39.4	..	..	2.0	2.7	3.0	3.2	3.7	3.6	Cambodge
8539.7	10549.9	47327.3	75523.0	117023.8	1.5	6.1	6.7	9.7	8.6	9.6	9.9	11.9	Chine
6585.9	11306.1	3612.9	741.0	6464.1	..	3.2	3.4	5.9	6.2	6.5	6.1	6.1	Chine, Hong Kong RAS
394.8	465.6	185.4	291.9	543.0	..	3.7	13.4	16.0	17.2	17.1	17.3	18.9	Chine, Macao RAS
15859.0	541.9	15469.0	39445.5	44975.1	1.3	14.8	10.6	10.2	10.4	13.3	16.2	19.5	Chine, Taiwan Province de
5326.0	5235.6	7968.2	21795.0	31272.5	5.5	0.8	5.9	8.0	8.9	10.3	12.8	16.8	Inde
3731.6	2056.8	-1255.7	3722.8	3993.4	5.4	3.8	3.9	11.0	10.6	11.6	11.1	10.1	Indonésie
22012.9	22143.2	6622.7	18591.9	33938.7	1.5	2.4	2.8	6.3	7.7	8.4	8.8	10.4	Corée, République de
-11.0	37.8	-8.0	60.7	17.0	..	0.1	1.7	2.3	3.1	3.3	4.8	4.8	Rép. dém. populaire lao
5028.8	-1065.5	951.8	3747.1	10293.5	4.7	3.6	3.7	5.0	4.6	4.8	5.1	6.5	Malaisie
8.6	-4.3	-29.7	40.1	26.4	0.4	2.0	2.0	3.9	3.8	2.8	3.7	4.1	Maldives
42.4	42.3	26.9	144.0	-113.6	..	..	3.2	2.9	3.5	3.8	5.8	3.7	Mongolie
-49.5	-42.5	177.5	69.5	80.2	8.5	8.1	5.0	1.4	1.0	1.8	2.3	2.6	Myanmar
88.8	100.3	92.3	-20.1	204.9	6.2	5.0	5.2	6.8	7.5	8.6	7.7	8.4	Népal
483.4	2.0	2126.7	4438.3	2862.7	1.1	0.5	1.8	1.7	1.7	4.1	8.0	10.1	Pakistan
4004.2	-183.2	382.5	-293.6	322.0	4.1	0.9	2.5	4.6	4.4	4.5	4.1	4.1	Philippines
1915.1	3289.0	-4757.2	6646.2	13724.9	3.1	5.3	6.4	7.5	7.7	7.8	8.1	9.0	Singapour
-344.2	-596.6	247.8	344.1	..	1.5	1.8	4.7	3.0	1.9	2.6	3.1	..	Sri Lanka
5237.8	-2046.9	338.9	5691.7	3030.5	2.0	4.5	6.0	7.3	6.2	6.1	6.5	6.5	Thaïlande
1323.9	90.4	258.1	446.5	2103.1	..	..	1.7	2.9	2.6	2.5	2.3	3.0	Viet Nam
													ECONOMIES EN DEVELOPPEMENT : OCEANIE
50.0	**59.4**	**53.8**	**-84.4**	**263.0**	**3.7**	**4.0**	**3.4**	**4.5**	**5.1**	**5.3**	**4.5**	**5.5**	
43.0	-16.9	-45.4	-7.6	64.8	3.4	4.5	4.5	6.0	6.1	5.4	4.8	5.2	Fidji
-8.9	20.4	-14.7	19.1	-27.8	..	..	..	..	..	..	..	..	Micronésie, Etats fédérés de
12.3	81.7	135.8	-101.1	163.8	4.2	3.5	2.0	2.1	3.1	4.4	3.1	4.5	Papouasie-Nouvelle-Guinée
6.8	-4.5	-7.0	5.9	21.4	0.6	9.5	6.8	7.4	6.5	5.1	5.5	7.3	Samoa
2.1	-19.1	-12.7	-1.1	18.5	4.0	2.1	1.3	6.1	4.4	3.6	3.7	6.3	Iles Salomon
-1.9	0.2	-0.9	1.6	14.9	4.2	6.2	4.5	4.5	4.6	4.6	5.1	7.9	Tonga
-3.3	-2.4	-1.3	-1.1	7.3	..	5.1	6.0	5.5	5.0	4.7	4.7	5.3	Vanuatu
													ECONOMIES EN DEVELOPPEMENT
84088.0	**77811.3**	**91990.6**	**208575.8**	**349550.3**	**4.2**	**4.8**	**5.3**	**6.8**	**6.9**	**7.6**	**8.1**	**9.4**	
													Par principales catégories
8760.4	30496.0	6053.7	10215.2	31189.5	7.6	6.7	5.4	8.2	9.9	10.6	10.5	11.4	Principaux pays exportateurs de pétrole
75327.6	47315.3	85936.9	198360.6	318360.8	2.6	4.5	5.3	6.7	6.6	7.3	7.8	9.2	Autres économies en développement
70565.6	50331.5	86789.8	187874.8	287755.9	2.5	4.8	5.3	6.8	6.8	7.5	8.2	9.7	Principaux pays exportateurs d'articles manufacturés
4762.0	-3016.2	-853.0	10485.7	30604.9	2.9	3.4	5.3	6.3	6.0	6.0	5.9	6.6	Autres économies
60.0	139.5	-6915.9	-5193.9	6974.2	5.0	5.5	6.5	7.9	7.7	7.5	6.8	7.1	Amérique
825.0	-2192.1	4267.8	6171.9	9951.7	1.2	2.5	4.6	5.4	5.1	5.5	5.4	5.8	Afrique
2098.1	-1129.8	-1198.9	3143.7	6494.0	5.2	3.2	6.8	12.0	9.7	8.2	10.9	16.1	Asie occidentale
1729.0	106.8	2940.3	6448.5	6922.0	1.9	1.9	3.4	3.3	3.1	3.7	4.5	5.4	Autres pays d'Asie
													Par catégories de revenus (PIB par habitant en 2000)
55422.2	53245.4	19879.5	72022.2	134244.3	4.6	5.5	5.0	6.5	6.9	7.5	8.0	9.2	Pays à revenu élevé
5807.0	-190.9	12963.0	28554.1	52297.8	4.0	4.4	6.3	6.7	6.4	6.8	7.1	8.0	Pays à revenu intermédiaire
22858.9	24756.7	59148.0	107999.5	163008.2	3.6	3.5	4.8	7.6	7.4	8.3	8.9	10.6	Pays à revenu faible
													POUR MEMOIRE :
809.5	2703.0	1012.7	3660.9	3960.4	2.7	2.7	3.6	3.8	4.3	4.4	4.9	5.4	PMA
2775.0	3216.0	1843.6	4661.4	6333.3	2.2	2.0	2.7	3.5	4.0	4.1	4.3	4.8	PPTE
943.2	105.2	534.3	1184.2	3921.8	3.4	5.7	8.3	10.4	10.2	10.1	9.7	10.9	Pays enclavés
75548.4	67261.4	44663.3	133052.8	232526.5	4.3	4.7	5.2	6.5	6.7	7.2	7.7	8.8	Economies en développement Chine non comprise
1482.2	6008.6	376.7	506.3	5351.8	2.6	2.9	2.8	4.3	5.0	5.0	4.4	4.5	Afrique subsaharienne

Column group headers:
- Annual change in reserves (millions of dollars) / Variations annuelles des réserves (en millions de dollars): 1998-99, 1999-00, 2000-01, 2001-02, 2002-03
- Number of months of imports[1] / Nombre de mois d'importations[1]: 1980, 1990, 1995, 1999, 2000, 2001, 2002, 2003

Pour les sources et les notes, se reporter à la page suivante.

6.4 International reserves of developing economies

6.4 Réserves internationales des économies en développement

Sources: IMF, *International Financial Statistics* on CD-ROM.

Notes: International reserves refer to Total reserves minus gold. According to the IMF definition, Total reserves minus gold consists of the sum of the country's Foreign exchange, their Reserve position in the IMF and the US dollar value of SDR holdings by their monetary authorities.
(SDR - Special drawing rights)

1 Reserve stock of the year divided by the average monthly imports of the current and following year. Data on imports are based on figures shown in table 1.1 of this *Handbook*. Data for year 2003 have been calculated on the basis of monthly imports of the current year.

2 Reserves data have been revised starting with 1996 because national financial authorities have modified their methodology for classification of foreign assets. For details, please refer to the source.

Sources : FMI, *International Financial Statistics* sur CD-ROM.

Notes : Les réserves internationales se réfèrent aux Réserves totales moins l'or. Selon la définition du FMI, les réserves totales moins l'or représentent la somme des avoirs du pays en devises, leur position des réserves au FMI et la valeur en dollars E.U. des avoirs en DTS de leurs autorités monétaires.
(DTS - Droits de tirage speciaux)

1 Montant des réserves de l'année, divisé par la moyenne mensuelle des importations de l'année en cours et de l'année suivante. Les données des importations se basent sur les chiffres présentés dans le tableau 1.1 de ce *Manuel*. Les chiffres pour l'année 2003 ont été calculés sur la base des importations mensuelles de l'année en cours.

2 Les données des réserves ont été revisées à partir de 1996, en raison d'une modification par les autorités financières nationales, de leur méthodologie de classification des avoirs extérieurs. Pour plus de détails, se reporter à la source.

6.5 Official financial flows from bilateral and multilateral sources to developing economies
Millions of dollars

6.5 Flux financiers publics bilatéraux et multilatéraux à destination des économies en développement
En millions de dollars

Region, economic grouping, country or area / Régions, groupements économiques, pays ou zones	Year / Année	Total flows / Flux totaux	ODA / OA [1] APD / AP [1] Total [3]	of which DAC [4] dont CAD [4] Bilateral Bilatéraux	of which DAC [4] dont CAD [4] Multilateral [5] Multilatéraux [5]	OOF [2] AASP [2] Total [3]	of which DAC [4] dont CAD [4] Bilateral Bilatéraux	of which DAC [4] dont CAD [4] Multilateral [5] Multilatéraux [5]
DEVELOPING ECONOMIES - ECONOMIES EN DEVELOPPEMENT	1990	74209.1	56033.6	36903.9	13260.1	18178.9	8060.6	10136.7
	1995	68114.2	56300.7	38532.9	17068.0	11797.1	8875.4	2897.8
	2000	49726.5	46495.5	34086.2	11754.3	3230.9	-4946.4	8141.1
	2002	50704.1	56208.2	37150.0	16497.9	-5485.2	901.7	-6344.5
DEVELOPING ECONOMIES: AMERICA - ECONOMIES EN DEVELOPPEMENT : AMERIQUE	1990	13630.8	5287.6	4188.4	1088.1	8343.5	3709.3	4634.3
	1995	8124.3	6459.2	4807.3	1618.0	1665.1	78.1	1557.5
	2000	11299.2	5161.2	4034.1	1076.5	6138.0	-457.2	6551.4
	2002	5210.7	5217.8	4003.7	1149.9	11.7	-160.2	189.7
South America - Amérique du Sud	*1990*	*5262.7*	*2047.5*	*1569.5*	*476.6*	*3215.5*	*1601.7*	*1613.8*
	1995	*3613.3*	*2479.8*	*1910.0*	*567.7*	*1133.5*	*862.2*	*271.4*
	2000	*7024.9*	*1974.7*	*1562.0*	*396.8*	*5050.3*	*-185.3*	*5235.5*
	2002	*1942.9*	*2386.1*	*1953.4*	*390.2*	*-443.2*	*-73.5*	*-369.7*
Argentina - Argentine	1990	905.0	169.9	166.2	3.7	735.1	411.9	323.2
	1995	2530.4	143.5	110.3	33.2	2386.9	719.7	1667.1
	2000	700.9	76.3	43.5	25.3	624.6	-553.4	1178.0
	2002	-1694.2	0.1	51.9	-83.2	-1694.2	-162.3	-1532.0
Bolivia - Bolivie	1990	578.1	547.3	364.7	182.6	30.8	10.4	20.4
	1995	719.7	718.8	518.0	200.5	0.9	-18.8	19.7
	2000	438.8	474.6	336.1	138.3	-35.8	-25.4	-10.4
	2002	616.6	681.0	482.2	198.2	-64.4	0.2	-64.6
Brazil - Brésil	1990	530.6	155.5	142.1	13.4	375.5	709.9	-334.5
	1995	-38.5	273.1	204.1	72.4	-311.6	-33.0	-278.6
	2000	4188.7	322.4	222.5	98.4	3866.3	430.9	3435.4
	2002	1800.7	375.9	197.6	177.3	1424.8	262.4	1162.4
Chile - Chili	1990	787.6	103.9	83.3	20.6	683.7	207.9	475.8
	1995	-1626.5	157.4	143.3	14.1	-1783.9	-98.2	-1685.8
	2000	-207.2	49.3	41.0	7.7	-256.5	-175.6	-80.8
	2002	-355.7	-22.6	-13.8	-9.3	-333.1	-88.0	-245.1
Colombia - Colombie	1990	-0.5	89.5	86.6	2.9	-90.0	-93.2	3.2
	1995	73.7	171.1	160.7	10.1	-97.4	131.3	-228.7
	2000	-23.9	186.9	178.5	7.8	-210.9	-276.9	66.0
	2002	214.8	441.0	426.1	13.7	-226.2	-69.3	-156.9
Ecuador - Equateur	1990	354.2	160.9	122.2	38.3	193.3	112.7	80.6
	1995	637.2	227.1	160.7	65.6	410.1	85.3	324.8
	2000	227.1	146.8	137.4	8.6	80.3	-28.4	108.7
	2002	348.2	216.0	205.1	10.3	132.1	160.5	-28.4
Falkland Islands (Malvinas) - Iles Falkland (Malvinas)	1990	1.8	1.8	1.8	..	..	..	..
	1995	1.7	1.7	0.1	1.6	..	..	..
	2000	0.7	-0.2	..	-0.2	1.0	-0.4	1.4
	2002	-0.4	-0.3	..	-0.3	-0.1	0.0	-0.1
Guyana	1990	222.0	168.8	35.8	132.9	53.2	72.0	-18.8
	1995	81.5	86.0	23.2	62.7	-4.6	11.3	-15.8
	2000	95.3	107.3	51.9	55.4	-11.9	-0.7	-11.2
	2002	60.9	64.8	34.0	30.8	-3.9	-0.8	-3.1
Paraguay	1990	29.8	57.5	47.6	9.0	-27.8	1.6	-29.4
	1995	153.7	139.6	105.8	30.3	14.1	-20.1	34.2
	2000	202.3	81.8	72.9	8.5	120.5	8.3	112.2
	2002	84.6	56.7	50.8	5.1	28.0	11.0	16.9
Peru - Pérou	1990	401.4	400.2	350.4	49.8	1.2	-2.0	3.2
	1995	819.7	372.9	327.0	45.5	446.9	65.4	381.5
	2000	1116.2	401.1	372.7	26.0	715.1	513.2	201.9
	2002	520.4	491.3	463.0	26.0	29.1	-147.9	177.0
Suriname	1990	64.8	61.7	51.2	10.5	3.1	-0.9	4.0
	1995	75.3	77.1	70.3	6.7	-1.8	-1.1	-0.7
	2000	36.2	34.4	29.1	5.2	1.8	0.0	1.8
	2002	11.4	11.6	7.7	3.9	-0.2	0.0	-0.2

For sources and notes, see end of table.

Pour les sources et les notes, se reporter à la fin du tableau.

6.5 Official financial flows from bilateral and multilateral sources to developing economies (continued)
Millions of dollars

6.5 Flux financiers publics bilatéraux et multilatéraux à destination des économies en développement (suite)
En millions de dollars

Region, economic grouping, country or area / Régions, groupements économiques, pays ou zones	Year / Année	Total flows / Flux totaux	ODA / OA [1] APD / AP [1] Total [3]	of which DAC [4] dont CAD [4] Bilateral / Bilatéraux	of which DAC [4] dont CAD [4] Multilateral [5] / Multilatéraux [5]	OOF [2] AASP [2] Total [3]	of which DAC [4] dont CAD [4] Bilateral / Bilatéraux	of which DAC [4] dont CAD [4] Multilateral [5] / Multilatéraux [5]
Uruguay	1990	87.3	53.1	41.7	11.3	34.2	1.1	33.1
	1995	54.7	67.8	57.5	10.2	-13.0	-2.6	-10.4
	2000	198.7	17.5	15.3	1.4	181.3	2.0	179.2
	2002	442.9	13.4	6.8	3.2	429.5	-14.4	443.9
Venezuela	1990	1300.7	77.5	75.7	1.8	1223.2	170.3	1052.9
	1995	130.8	43.8	29.0	14.9	86.9	22.9	64.0
	2000	51.1	76.6	61.3	14.6	-25.5	-78.8	53.3
	2002	-107.3	57.1	42.0	14.6	-164.4	-25.0	-139.4
Other America - Autres économies d'Amérique	*1990*	*7693.5*	*2704.3*	*2266.2*	*428.5*	*4989.2*	*2107.8*	*2881.4*
	1995	*3850.7*	*3369.6*	*2409.2*	*929.5*	*481.2*	*-912.0*	*1363.7*
	2000	*3117.0*	*2066.5*	*1469.3*	*562.3*	*1050.6*	*-273.5*	*1280.2*
	2002	*2692.3*	*2302.0*	*1658.2*	*633.9*	*409.2*	*-95.5*	*522.5*
Anguilla	1990	3.9	3.8	2.4	1.4	0.1	0.0	0.1
	1995	3.5	3.4	2.5	0.8	0.1	0.0	0.1
	2000	7.7	3.5	3.8	-0.3	4.2	0.0	4.2
	2002	5.3	0.7	1.8	-1.1	4.5	5.0	-0.5
Antigua and Barbuda - Antigua-et-Barbuda	1990	-2.6	4.7	2.9	1.7	-7.3	-7.3	0.0
	1995	-0.8	2.3	0.8	0.7	-3.1	-3.1	0.0
	2000	9.9	9.8	3.7	1.1	0.1	0.0	0.1
	2002	12.6	14.0	11.1	4.1	-1.3	-2.2	0.9
Aruba	1990	30.0	30.0	28.9	1.1	0.0	0.0	0.0
	1995	29.7	25.8	18.0	7.9	3.9	4.0	0.0
	2000	10.0	11.5	10.7	0.8	-1.5	-1.5	0.0
	2002	9.6	10.5	10.2	0.3	-0.9	-0.9	0.0
Bahamas	1990	30.9	3.5	0.4	2.2	27.4	-0.5	28.0
	1995	6.9	4.6	1.3	2.5	2.4	-4.6	7.0
	2000	10.2	5.5	5.2	0.3	4.7	-3.6	8.3
	2002	11.2	5.3	6.9	-1.7	7.0	4.8	2.2
Barbados - Barbade	1990	21.7	2.9	1.4	1.5	18.8	10.7	8.1
	1995	8.6	-0.7	0.1	-0.9	9.4	-3.0	12.3
	2000	16.1	0.3	1.0	-0.8	15.9	3.1	12.8
	2002	10.0	3.4	2.8	0.5	6.6	-0.8	7.4
Belize	1990	38.6	30.4	18.8	11.4	8.1	4.1	4.1
	1995	23.7	18.6	8.8	6.6	5.2	-2.0	7.2
	2000	31.8	14.7	2.9	11.2	17.2	3.5	13.7
	2002	28.9	22.2	9.0	9.3	6.7	-11.8	18.5
Bermuda - Bermudes	1990	51.0	42.2	42.1	0.1	8.8	8.8	0.0
	1995	27.4	-2.1	-2.1	..	29.5	..	..
	2000	43.9	0.1	0.1	..	43.9	..	..
	2002	-17.7	0.0	0.0	..	-17.7	..	..
British Virgin Islands - Iles Vierges britanniques	1990	9.4	5.6	3.0	2.5	3.9	1.6	2.3
	1995	2.6	1.4	0.3	1.1	1.2	0.0	1.2
	2000	8.5	4.8	1.2	3.6	3.7	5.0	-1.3
Cayman Islands - Iles Caïmanes	1990	11.9	3.0	2.1	0.9	8.9	2.4	6.5
	1995	-0.1	-0.6	-0.6	0.0	0.5	0.8	-0.3
	2000	550.0	-3.6	-3.2	-0.5	553.6	553.1	0.5
	2002	-10.6	-1.9	0.0	-1.9	-9.9	-9.5	-0.3
Costa Rica	1990	240.3	229.5	206.6	21.7	10.8	21.1	-10.3
	1995	84.1	34.2	16.6	4.6	49.9	-28.2	78.1
	2000	-37.4	11.8	17.2	-6.2	-49.2	-26.9	-22.3
	2002	-17.8	5.3	4.5	-0.1	-23.1	-0.4	-22.7
Cuba	1990	59.3	51.0	33.6	17.4	8.3	8.3	0.0
	1995	56.5	63.6	33.7	29.8	-7.1	-7.1	0.0
	2000	47.5	44.0	30.8	12.9	3.5	3.5	0.0
	2002	37.0	61.0	49.6	11.0	-24.0	-24.0	0.0

For sources and notes, see end of table.

Pour les sources et les notes, se reporter à la fin du tableau.

6.5 Official financial flows from bilateral and multilateral sources to developing economies
(continued)
Millions of dollars

6.5 Flux financiers publics bilatéraux et multilatéraux à destination des économies en développement
(suite)
En millions de dollars

Region, economic grouping, country or area / Régions, groupements économiques, pays ou zones	Year / Année	Total flows / Flux totaux	ODA / OA [1] APD / AP [1]			OOF [2] AASP [2]		
			Total [3]	of which DAC [4] dont CAD [4]		Total [3]	of which DAC [4] dont CAD [4]	
				Bilateral Bilatéraux	Multilateral [5] Multilatéraux [5]		Bilateral Bilatéraux	Multilateral [5] Multilatéraux [5]
Dominica - Dominique	1990	19.5	19.7	10.8	8.5	-0.3	-0.4	0.1
	1995	24.3	25.1	9.5	14.5	-0.8	-1.2	0.4
	2000	18.5	15.2	5.9	6.5	3.3	-0.1	3.4
	2002	51.9	29.9	14.0	15.9	22.0	16.8	5.1
Dominican Republic - République dominicaine	1990	136.7	102.0	72.7	28.2	34.7	1.4	33.3
	1995	165.8	119.8	81.2	37.2	46.0	-12.1	58.1
	2000	79.3	62.4	44.6	17.8	16.9	-36.3	53.1
	2002	316.7	156.7	138.2	18.3	160.0	-22.7	182.7
El Salvador	1990	308.7	347.7	312.0	34.7	-39.0	-0.9	-38.1
	1995	382.9	297.2	243.7	52.4	85.7	0.0	85.6
	2000	283.7	180.0	172.3	7.1	103.7	-13.5	117.2
	2002	353.0	233.5	217.9	14.5	119.5	-13.2	132.7
Grenada - Grenade	1990	13.0	13.8	5.0	8.7	-0.9	-1.1	0.2
	1995	8.4	10.9	5.6	4.5	-2.5	-0.6	-1.9
	2000	19.9	16.5	9.9	3.2	3.4	-0.2	3.6
	2002	12.6	9.5	2.2	8.8	3.1	-0.1	3.2
Guatemala	1990	222.3	202.1	149.5	51.3	20.1	6.2	13.9
	1995	207.4	209.8	161.4	46.6	-2.4	11.6	-14.0
	2000	321.7	263.6	230.3	32.8	58.0	6.7	51.4
	2002	381.6	248.7	199.6	48.6	132.8	-41.0	173.8
Haiti - Haïti	1990	168.0	168.5	117.1	51.2	-0.5	-0.1	-0.4
	1995	719.9	725.9	510.0	215.8	-6.0	-6.0	0.0
	2000	207.2	208.3	153.9	54.4	-1.1	-1.1	0.0
	2002	154.7	155.7	125.4	30.0	-1.0	-1.0	0.0
Honduras	1990	434.0	449.2	383.5	64.7	-15.2	-0.7	-14.6
	1995	397.1	405.6	232.9	171.3	-8.4	25.4	-33.9
	2000	397.8	450.0	310.6	134.8	-52.2	19.5	-71.7
	2002	384.3	434.9	297.9	136.5	-50.6	-6.8	-43.8
Jamaica - Jamaïque	1990	325.7	271.0	251.9	19.3	54.7	37.5	17.3
	1995	88.3	108.5	67.5	41.2	-20.1	-8.7	-11.5
	2000	130.2	10.0	-26.4	30.0	120.2	-19.9	140.1
	2002	82.5	24.3	-3.6	28.3	58.2	-23.5	81.7
Mexico - Mexique	1990	5027.3	159.3	144.7	14.5	4868.0	2030.1	2837.9
	1995	408.8	385.1	365.1	20.0	23.7	-990.9	1014.6
	2000	77.8	-54.1	-68.4	13.7	131.9	-710.7	842.6
	2002	86.2	135.5	92.6	42.5	-49.3	-38.8	-10.5
Montserrat	1990	8.3	8.4	7.8	0.5	-0.1	0.0	-0.1
	1995	9.8	9.5	9.1	0.4	0.3	0.0	0.3
	2000	30.9	30.9	30.9	0.1	-0.1	0.0	-0.1
	2002	41.6	43.5	45.3	-1.8	-2.0	0.0	-2.0
Netherlands Antilles - Antilles néerlandaises	1990	50.2	58.1	53.0	5.1	-7.9	-10.9	3.0
	1995	97.0	98.4	94.0	4.4	-1.4	0.0	-1.4
	2000	178.5	177.0	173.8	3.1	1.5	2.4	-0.9
	2002	149.1	92.6	94.2	-1.7	56.5	56.5	0.0
Nicaragua	1990	329.5	332.4	288.5	43.9	-2.9	-1.8	-1.1
	1995	826.8	652.9	492.1	159.7	173.9	165.1	8.8
	2000	553.3	561.5	325.9	235.3	-8.3	-6.2	-2.0
	2002	506.7	517.5	287.2	227.9	-10.8	1.9	-12.6
Panama	1990	23.7	99.6	96.0	2.6	-75.8	-35.0	-40.8
	1995	64.0	39.9	33.5	5.2	24.2	-17.2	41.3
	2000	105.2	16.5	11.7	-3.3	88.7	-12.4	101.1
	2002	70.6	35.3	23.3	11.4	35.3	-4.9	40.2
Saint Kitts and Nevis - Saint-Kitts-et-Nevis	1990	8.2	8.1	5.0	2.9	0.1	0.0	0.1
	1995	5.6	3.9	1.7	0.7	1.7	0.2	1.5
	2000	6.0	3.9	0.1	4.1	2.1	-1.3	3.3

For sources and notes, see end of table.

Pour les sources et les notes, se reporter à la fin du tableau.

293

6.5 Official financial flows from bilateral and multilateral sources to developing economies *(continued)* Millions of dollars

6.5 Flux financiers publics bilatéraux et multilatéraux à destination des économies en développement *(suite)* En millions de dollars

Region, economic grouping, country or area / Régions, groupements économiques, pays ou zones	Year / Année	Total flows / Flux totaux	ODA / OA [1] APD / AP [1] Total [3]	of which DAC [4] dont CAD [4] Bilateral Bilatéraux	of which DAC [4] dont CAD [4] Multilateral [5] Multilatéraux [5]	OOF [2] AASP [2] Total [3]	of which DAC [4] dont CAD [4] Bilateral Bilatéraux	of which DAC [4] dont CAD [4] Multilateral [5] Multilatéraux [5]
Saint Lucia - Sainte-Lucie	1990	15.9	12.4	6.2	5.9	3.5	-0.4	3.9
	1995	52.9	48.3	12.7	34.6	4.6	0.1	4.5
	2000	13.5	11.0	7.1	4.4	2.5	0.0	2.5
	2002	42.0	33.5	12.5	21.2	8.5	0.0	8.5
Saint Vincent and the Grenadines - Saint-Vincent-et-les Grenadines	1990	15.4	15.4	5.2	9.7	..	..	0.0
	1995	48.3	47.7	6.3	40.7	0.6	0.4	0.2
	2000	9.7	6.2	3.8	1.1	3.5	0.0	3.5
	2002	7.7	4.8	1.1	4.2	3.0	0.0	3.0
Trinidad and Tobago - Trinité-et-Tobago	1990	81.2	18.2	6.1	12.1	63.0	34.8	28.2
	1995	95.6	25.4	-1.8	27.1	70.2	-35.1	105.4
	2000	-21.6	-1.5	4.4	-5.9	-20.1	-36.7	16.5
	2002	-52.6	-7.2	5.7	-13.1	-45.3	1.4	-46.7
Turks and Caicos Islands - Iles Turques et Caïques	1990	11.8	11.8	8.9	3.0	0.0	0.0	0.0
	1995	5.7	5.6	5.5	0.1	0.1	0.0	0.1
	2000	7.3	6.7	5.6	1.1	0.6	0.0	0.6
	2002	5.3	4.4	2.6	1.8	0.9	0.0	0.9
Unspecified - Non spécifiée	*1990*	*674.6*	*535.8*	*352.8*	*183.0*	*138.8*	*-0.2*	*139.1*
	1995	*660.2*	*609.9*	*488.1*	*120.9*	*50.4*	*127.9*	*-77.6*
	2000	*1157.3*	*1120.1*	*1002.7*	*117.4*	*37.2*	*1.5*	*35.7*
	2002	*575.4*	*529.7*	*392.1*	*125.8*	*45.7*	*8.8*	*36.9*
DEVELOPING ECONOMIES: AFRICA - ECONOMIES EN DEVELOPPEMENT : AFRIQUE	**1990**	**28257.9**	**25311.0**	**15817.3**	**6361.1**	**2949.9**	**999.6**	**1950.2**
	1995	**25328.5**	**21958.7**	**13223.1**	**8588.2**	**3372.9**	**3576.5**	**-203.7**
	2000	**14516.5**	**15790.7**	**10384.4**	**5106.0**	**-1274.2**	**-343.5**	**-930.8**
	2002	**24173.0**	**22295.6**	**13368.7**	**8225.7**	**1877.5**	**3447.7**	**-1570.2**
North Africa - Afrique du Nord	*1990*	*8019.0*	*7842.8*	*4501.3*	*678.9*	*176.2*	*-801.1*	*977.3*
	1995	*6323.7*	*3133.0*	*2504.2*	*522.9*	*3190.7*	*2708.8*	*481.9*
	2000	*2042.3*	*2412.3*	*1750.0*	*440.7*	*-370.0*	*91.4*	*-461.4*
	2002	*2631.3*	*3119.5*	*1846.9*	*869.1*	*-488.2*	*298.7*	*-786.9*
Algeria - Algérie	1990	675.9	132.0	102.2	21.8	543.9	260.7	283.3
	1995	1989.8	297.7	275.3	34.4	1692.2	1325.6	366.6
	2000	-40.4	201.0	65.7	64.1	-241.4	-143.4	-98.0
	2002	118.8	361.0	122.8	95.4	-242.3	-75.2	-167.1
Egypt - Egypte	1990	4157.0	5428.8	3163.1	80.0	-1271.8	-1234.3	-37.6
	1995	2654.3	2016.3	1691.2	208.2	638.0	775.7	-137.7
	2000	1368.3	1328.4	1138.9	135.6	39.9	220.0	-180.0
	2002	1373.8	1286.1	1124.2	131.4	87.7	166.1	-78.4
Libyan Arab Jamahiriya - Jamahiriya arabe libyenne	1990	19.5	19.5	7.6	11.8	..	..	..
	1995	6.3	6.3	3.2	3.0	..	..	..
	2000	15.4	15.4	11.9	3.1	..	..	..
	2002	10.4	10.4	4.4	4.6	..	..	..
Morocco - Maroc	1990	1696.9	1048.8	595.4	92.4	648.1	161.9	486.2
	1995	488.3	495.2	347.4	127.9	-6.9	-163.6	156.7
	2000	276.3	419.3	293.1	130.4	-143.0	-47.3	-95.7
	2002	343.7	636.2	218.7	282.7	-292.5	235.3	-527.8
Sudan - Soudan	1990	819.7	822.3	420.0	394.4	-2.6	2.7	-5.2
	1995	256.1	242.4	130.6	108.2	13.7	-4.3	18.1
	2000	216.0	225.4	90.3	35.7	-9.5	-9.1	-0.4
	2002	350.9	350.9	232.3	67.5	0.0	0.0	0.0
Tunisia - Tunisie	1990	649.9	391.4	212.9	78.5	258.5	7.9	250.7
	1995	929.0	75.2	56.5	41.2	853.7	775.4	78.3
	2000	206.7	222.8	150.3	71.9	-16.0	71.2	-87.2
	2002	433.8	475.0	144.6	287.5	-41.1	-27.5	-13.6
Other Africa - Autres économies d'Afrique	*1990*	*19227.8*	*16473.6*	*10475.7*	*5537.3*	*2757.2*	*1794.9*	*962.3*
	1995	*17904.0*	*17759.3*	*9896.3*	*7821.4*	*147.8*	*836.8*	*-689.0*
	2000	*11217.3*	*12123.2*	*7786.7*	*4270.7*	*-905.9*	*-441.7*	*-464.3*
	2002	*19631.6*	*17295.3*	*10319.2*	*6717.0*	*2336.3*	*3118.2*	*-781.9*

For sources and notes, see end of table.

Pour les sources et les notes, se reporter à la fin du tableau.

6.5 **Official financial flows from bilateral and multilateral sources to developing economies** *(continued)* Millions of dollars

6.5 **Flux financiers publics bilatéraux et multilatéraux à destination des économies en développement** *(suite)* En millions de dollars

Region, economic grouping, country or area / Régions, groupements économiques, pays ou zones	Year / Année	Total flows / Flux totaux	ODA / OA [1] APD / AP [1]			OOF [2] AASP [2]		
			Total [3]	of which DAC [4] dont CAD [4]		Total [3]	of which DAC [4] dont CAD [4]	
				Bilateral Bilatéraux	Multilateral [5] Multilatéraux [5]		Bilateral Bilatéraux	Multilateral [5] Multilatéraux [5]
Angola	1990	345.9	268.3	163.2	103.3	77.7	76.2	1.5
	1995	491.1	417.9	241.7	176.1	73.1	73.1	0.0
	2000	260.8	306.7	189.1	111.5	-45.9	-23.3	-22.6
	2002	468.2	421.4	286.4	136.4	46.9	49.7	-2.8
Benin - Bénin	1990	295.9	268.0	125.7	142.6	27.9	26.2	1.7
	1995	282.6	280.5	177.4	96.3	2.2	2.9	-0.8
	2000	227.6	238.6	190.5	49.2	-11.0	-11.0	0.0
	2002	217.7	220.3	140.1	77.9	-2.6	-2.3	-0.4
Botswana	1990	169.0	146.8	121.2	27.4	22.2	4.6	17.6
	1995	69.2	90.1	54.5	35.2	-20.9	18.5	-39.4
	2000	34.3	30.7	23.5	8.1	3.6	23.1	-19.5
	2002	21.2	37.6	36.7	2.6	-16.4	0.0	-16.4
Burkina Faso	1990	332.4	331.0	238.7	81.0	1.4	1.3	0.1
	1995	488.6	491.0	252.3	230.9	-2.4	0.1	-2.5
	2000	330.5	336.0	227.8	104.5	-5.5	-3.5	-2.0
	2002	463.6	472.7	229.9	198.2	-9.2	-7.2	-1.9
Burundi	1990	260.7	264.1	157.6	106.3	-3.4	0.9	-4.4
	1995	286.0	287.7	108.4	182.1	-1.8	0.2	-2.0
	2000	92.7	92.7	40.9	51.7	..	..	..
	2002	172.1	172.1	84.7	87.4	..	..	..
Cameroon - Cameroun	1990	608.5	445.7	339.1	109.2	162.8	75.1	87.7
	1995	579.2	443.8	345.5	96.8	135.4	235.2	-99.8
	2000	309.3	379.9	213.5	169.1	-70.6	9.4	-80.0
	2002	822.9	631.9	436.2	195.2	191.0	223.7	-32.7
Cape Verde - Cap-Vert	1990	106.5	107.9	75.9	31.6	-1.4	-0.2	-1.1
	1995	117.3	117.3	76.9	40.2	0.1	0.4	-0.3
	2000	92.5	94.1	69.7	24.7	-1.6	-0.1	-1.4
	2002	91.9	92.2	43.2	50.4	-0.3	-0.1	-0.2
Central African Republic - République centrafricaine	1990	250.1	250.4	99.9	148.2	2.8	3.9	-1.1
	1995	167.8	168.6	122.4	42.8	2.2	2.2	0.0
	2000	74.1	75.4	53.1	22.5	-1.3	-1.3	0.0
	2002	59.2	59.8	39.6	20.2	-0.6	-0.4	-0.2
Chad - Tchad	1990	313.7	313.8	183.3	128.2	-0.1	-0.1	0.0
	1995	238.6	236.4	127.0	108.8	2.2	2.2	0.0
	2000	129.8	130.8	53.3	76.7	-0.9	-0.9	0.0
	2002	235.9	233.0	67.0	164.0	2.9	-1.4	4.3
Comoros - Comores	1990	45.4	45.3	30.6	14.5	0.1	0.1	0.0
	1995	41.6	41.8	21.7	20.0	-0.1	-0.1	0.0
	2000	18.7	18.8	10.8	7.8	0.0	0.0	0.0
	2002	31.9	32.5	11.0	16.6	-0.6	-0.6	0.0
Congo	1990	227.2	218.1	202.0	16.1	9.1	13.2	-4.1
	1995	394.6	125.4	105.0	20.4	269.2	287.2	-18.0
	2000	17.7	33.3	23.0	10.2	-15.6	-12.4	-3.2
	2002	386.1	419.8	41.4	378.3	-33.7	-27.2	-6.5
Côte d'Ivoire	1990	1123.2	687.7	530.6	157.1	435.5	134.2	301.3
	1995	1148.4	1212.9	726.6	485.8	-64.5	31.6	-96.1
	2000	276.9	351.8	250.1	101.2	-74.9	17.8	-92.7
	2002	1187.9	1068.8	831.1	237.2	119.2	330.9	-211.7
Dem. Rep. of the Congo - Rép. dém. du Congo	1990	1421.0	897.1	632.7	187.2	523.9	380.6	143.3
	1995	189.4	195.7	117.7	77.9	-6.3	-5.1	-1.2
	2000	180.1	183.5	102.7	80.7	-3.4	0.0	-3.4
	2002	722.3	806.7	351.0	455.5	-84.5	0.0	-84.5
Djibouti	1990	193.7	193.8	88.3	17.4	-0.1	-0.1	0.0
	1995	105.3	105.1	79.6	22.3	0.2	0.2	0.0
	2000	71.4	71.4	42.1	19.7	0.0	0.0	0.0
	2002	77.8	77.8	36.9	38.8	..	..	..

For sources and notes, see end of table.

Pour les sources et les notes, se reporter à la fin du tableau.

6.5 Official financial flows from bilateral and multilateral sources to developing economies
(continued)
Millions of dollars

6.5 Flux financiers publics bilatéraux et multilatéraux à destination des économies en développement
(suite)
En millions de dollars

Region, economic grouping, country or area / Régions, groupements économiques, pays ou zones	Year / Année	Total flows / Flux totaux	ODA / OA [1] APD / AP [1] Total [3]	of which DAC [4] dont CAD [4] Bilateral / Bilatéraux	of which DAC [4] dont CAD [4] Multilateral [5] / Multilatéraux [5]	OOF [2] AASP [2] Total [3]	of which DAC [4] dont CAD [4] Bilateral / Bilatéraux	of which DAC [4] dont CAD [4] Multilateral [5] / Multilatéraux [5]
Equatorial Guinea - Guinée équatoriale	1990	61.3	60.8	43.6	17.1	0.6	0.0	0.6
	1995	35.3	33.6	21.7	11.9	1.8	1.8	0.0
	2000	20.3	21.3	18.2	3.3	-1.1	-0.7	-0.4
	2002	19.2	20.2	13.7	6.7	-1.1	-0.7	-0.4
Eritrea - Erythrée	1995	149.0	149.0	94.6	49.1	..	..	0.0
	2000	176.0	176.0	111.9	54.9	0.0	0.0	0.0
	2002	230.5	230.4	120.7	96.9	0.0	0.0	0.0
Ethiopia - Ethiopie	1990	1013.5	1015.6	509.7	438.1	-2.0	-2.3	0.3
	1995	905.7	883.2	525.5	357.1	22.5	5.5	17.1
	2000	674.2	693.0	379.5	298.4	-18.8	-1.0	-17.9
	2002	1272.8	1306.7	489.2	783.6	-34.0	-13.3	-20.6
Gabon	1990	318.6	132.4	126.9	5.5	186.3	129.7	56.5
	1995	285.3	144.0	135.6	9.2	141.4	99.7	41.7
	2000	-42.0	11.8	-11.7	23.4	-53.7	-23.2	-30.5
	2002	72.4	71.9	49.5	22.4	0.5	10.1	-9.7
Gambia - Gambie	1990	107.2	99.1	56.9	41.8	8.0	8.5	-0.5
	1995	44.4	46.7	25.1	23.0	-2.3	-0.4	-1.9
	2000	48.4	49.1	14.6	32.0	-0.7	0.0	-0.7
	2002	59.0	60.5	17.5	40.4	-1.5	0.0	-1.5
Ghana	1990	719.2	562.6	264.9	296.6	156.6	26.4	130.2
	1995	581.5	650.8	358.6	298.2	-69.3	10.7	-80.0
	2000	583.7	600.4	376.0	222.1	-16.8	8.6	-25.3
	2002	637.2	652.8	406.2	241.3	-15.6	4.8	-20.4
Guinea - Guinée	1990	301.6	292.8	139.0	149.7	8.8	19.6	-10.8
	1995	433.7	416.9	220.4	190.7	16.8	-2.3	19.1
	2000	141.6	153.0	92.8	57.6	-11.4	-1.4	-10.0
	2002	235.6	249.6	125.6	118.1	-14.0	-1.0	-13.0
Guinea-Bissau - Guinée-Bissau	1990	127.3	128.6	75.4	53.2	-1.3	0.0	-1.3
	1995	115.2	118.5	76.9	38.6	-3.3	0.0	-3.3
	2000	80.4	80.4	41.6	38.8	0.0	0.1	-0.1
	2002	62.2	59.4	25.8	33.6	2.8	3.2	-0.4
Kenya	1990	1145.8	1185.8	735.2	446.1	-40.0	15.4	-55.4
	1995	632.3	734.0	458.7	270.1	-101.7	-16.4	-85.3
	2000	478.3	512.1	293.0	214.3	-33.8	-4.9	-29.0
	2002	360.9	393.1	288.1	95.1	-32.2	-5.4	-26.8
Lesotho	1990	142.2	141.7	85.2	56.9	0.5	-1.5	2.0
	1995	135.2	113.7	61.6	52.1	21.5	12.6	8.9
	2000	47.1	36.7	21.8	16.1	10.4	-8.2	18.6
	2002	48.6	76.4	29.7	47.9	-27.8	-5.0	-22.9
Liberia - Libéria	1990	67.0	114.2	42.3	69.7	-47.3	-12.5	-34.8
	1995	120.1	123.5	31.1	91.1	-3.4	-3.1	-0.3
	2000	69.4	67.8	23.8	44.0	1.6	-1.9	3.5
	2002	51.8	52.5	27.0	25.5	-0.7	0.0	-0.7
Madagascar	1990	413.3	398.4	268.2	131.4	14.9	11.7	3.2
	1995	301.5	301.2	194.9	106.1	0.3	4.8	-4.5
	2000	316.7	322.2	138.7	184.6	-5.5	1.4	-6.9
	2002	368.9	372.6	125.9	247.8	-3.6	2.8	-6.4
Malawi	1990	489.3	503.4	216.2	286.6	-14.1	-5.8	-8.3
	1995	417.0	435.0	220.9	211.4	-18.0	-1.0	-17.0
	2000	443.9	446.3	269.2	170.9	-2.4	-0.1	-2.3
	2002	375.8	377.1	224.9	142.4	-1.3	2.8	-4.2
Mali	1990	482.8	481.7	312.5	153.8	1.1	1.9	-0.8
	1995	586.3	541.3	285.1	269.8	45.0	21.3	23.8
	2000	343.3	359.7	299.8	61.3	-16.4	-6.9	-9.5
	2002	464.3	472.1	256.8	161.5	-7.7	-3.8	-4.0

For sources and notes, see end of table.

Pour les sources et les notes, se reporter à la fin du tableau.

6.5 Official financial flows from bilateral and multilateral sources to developing economies (continued)
Millions of dollars

6.5 Flux financiers publics bilatéraux et multilatéraux à destination des économies en développement (suite)
En millions de dollars

Region, economic grouping, country or area / Régions, groupements économiques, pays ou zones	Year Année	Total flows Flux totaux	ODA / OA [1] APD / AP [1]			OOF [2] AASP [2]		
			Total [3]	of which DAC [4] dont CAD [4]		Total [3]	of which DAC [4] dont CAD [4]	
				Bilateral Bilatéraux	Multilateral [5] Multilatéraux [5]		Bilateral Bilatéraux	Multilateral [5] Multilatéraux [5]
Mauritania - Mauritanie	1990	225.9	237.2	106.4	106.2	-11.3	0.8	-12.1
	1995	219.0	230.4	126.0	120.2	-11.4	-9.0	-2.4
	2000	207.8	211.9	82.5	129.3	-4.2	6.8	-11.0
	2002	345.5	355.4	146.6	210.3	-9.9	-9.1	-0.8
Mauritius - Maurice	1990	107.6	88.7	75.7	12.3	18.9	16.2	2.7
	1995	3.9	23.4	11.0	13.8	-19.5	-1.2	-18.3
	2000	-17.8	20.5	12.4	7.5	-38.3	-20.7	-17.5
	2002	53.2	23.9	3.5	19.7	29.3	-2.3	31.5
Mozambique	1990	1004.2	1002.4	750.3	252.0	1.9	3.3	-1.5
	1995	1037.4	1064.2	698.3	363.7	-26.8	-23.4	-3.4
	2000	1043.5	877.0	623.5	253.5	166.5	105.2	61.2
	2002	1871.7	2057.6	1661.0	394.3	-186.0	-187.0	1.0
Namibia - Namibie	1990	121.2	121.2	39.4	81.9	..	..	0.0
	1995	193.8	191.8	147.7	43.9	2.1	2.1	0.0
	2000	154.3	152.7	96.8	54.8	1.6	-0.5	2.1
	2002	135.8	135.1	84.8	48.2	0.6	0.0	0.6
Niger	1990	401.8	396.5	254.6	138.3	5.3	6.7	-1.4
	1995	201.8	274.4	193.9	79.6	-72.6	-71.3	-1.2
	2000	186.7	211.0	105.8	105.1	-24.3	-24.3	0.0
	2002	185.1	298.5	114.5	180.8	-113.4	-113.2	-0.2
Nigeria - Nigéria	1990	1310.9	258.2	172.7	76.6	1052.6	739.4	313.2
	1995	-66.2	211.9	72.6	139.8	-278.1	-125.3	-152.8
	2000	-379.5	184.8	84.3	100.2	-564.3	-260.5	-303.8
	2002	3249.2	313.8	215.0	100.5	2935.4	3197.7	-262.3
Rwanda	1990	290.2	291.2	183.2	97.8	-1.0	-0.1	-0.9
	1995	702.4	702.1	339.2	363.1	0.3	0.1	0.2
	2000	324.1	322.0	175.4	146.5	2.1	2.2	-0.2
	2002	356.1	356.1	199.1	156.9	-0.1	0.0	-0.1
Saint Helena - Sainte-Hélène	1990	24.7	24.7	23.3	1.4	..	..	..
	1995	12.6	12.6	12.4	0.2	..	..	..
	2000	18.7	18.7	18.4	0.3	..	..	..
	2002	13.9	13.9	13.4	0.5	..	..	..
Sao Tome and Principe - Sao Tomé-et-Principe	1990	54.7	54.7	31.0	23.7	..	..	..
	1995	58.5	84.3	61.5	22.7	-25.8	-25.8	0.0
	2000	35.0	35.0	17.7	17.3	..	..	..
	2002	26.0	26.0	19.2	6.8	..	..	..
Senegal - Sénégal	1990	830.2	818.1	589.2	226.6	12.0	27.6	-15.6
	1995	639.3	665.8	399.4	253.8	-26.5	-0.4	-26.1
	2000	417.5	423.5	288.4	139.7	-6.0	9.2	-15.2
	2002	473.4	448.8	242.8	195.4	24.6	31.0	-6.4
Seychelles	1990	37.8	35.9	32.7	3.4	1.9	2.3	-0.4
	1995	16.4	13.0	11.0	2.5	3.4	-0.4	3.9
	2000	14.5	18.3	3.3	8.4	-3.8	-0.7	-3.1
	2002	5.5	7.9	3.7	4.2	-2.4	0.0	-2.4
Sierra Leone	1990	56.6	60.9	39.9	20.9	-4.3	-3.4	-0.9
	1995	201.4	206.4	59.6	146.1	-4.9	-1.4	-3.5
	2000	180.6	182.4	115.6	66.8	-1.8	-0.9	-0.9
	2002	368.6	353.4	225.3	125.5	15.2	11.2	4.0
Somalia - Somalie	1990	492.3	493.5	269.6	142.0	-1.2	-0.8	-0.4
	1995	189.1	188.9	119.2	69.7	0.2	0.2	0.0
	2000	103.8	103.8	56.4	47.3	..	..	..
	2002	193.8	193.8	102.4	47.2	..	..	..
South Africa - Afrique du Sud	1995	715.5	388.9	318.5	67.4	326.6	326.6	0.0
	2000	592.3	487.5	353.6	132.0	104.8	-94.5	199.3
	2002	435.7	656.8	375.3	280.7	-221.1	-222.2	1.2

For sources and notes, see end of table.

Pour les sources et les notes, se reporter à la fin du tableau.

6.5 Official financial flows from bilateral and multilateral sources to developing economies *(continued)* Millions of dollars

6.5 Flux financiers publics bilatéraux et multilatéraux à destination des économies en développement *(suite)* En millions de dollars

Region, economic grouping, country or area / Régions, groupements économiques, pays ou zones	Year / Année	Total flows / Flux totaux	ODA / OA [1] APD / AP [1]			OOF [2] AASP [2]		
			Total [3]	of which DAC [4] dont CAD [4]		Total [3]	of which DAC [4] dont CAD [4]	
				Bilateral Bilatéraux	Multilateral [5] Multilatéraux [5]		Bilateral Bilatéraux	Multilateral [5] Multilatéraux [5]
Swaziland	1990	34.5	54.0	36.1	17.8	-19.5	-5.3	-14.2
	1995	57.6	58.1	37.7	17.8	-0.5	0.0	-0.5
	2000	15.9	13.2	2.8	10.3	2.8	-3.5	6.2
	2002	27.7	24.7	6.6	14.3	3.0	0.2	2.9
Togo	1990	254.6	260.0	155.0	105.6	-5.4	1.3	-6.7
	1995	186.3	192.3	117.8	74.1	-6.0	-5.4	-0.6
	2000	74.3	69.8	51.9	16.4	4.5	0.4	4.1
	2002	50.9	51.0	39.2	9.0	-0.1	0.8	-0.9
Uganda - Ouganda	1990	670.2	668.1	244.4	381.0	2.1	9.4	-7.3
	1995	819.3	834.9	423.1	400.1	-15.7	-5.7	-9.9
	2000	775.9	819.4	578.2	235.6	-43.6	-46.3	2.8
	2002	607.3	637.9	466.1	166.6	-30.7	-17.3	-13.4
United Republic of Tanzania - République-Unie de Tanzanie	1990	1173.2	1173.3	844.1	326.0	-0.1	28.2	-28.2
	1995	845.5	877.4	586.7	286.2	-31.9	-9.0	-22.9
	2000	1049.1	1022.0	778.7	246.0	27.1	32.0	-4.8
	2002	1119.3	1232.8	902.8	333.5	-113.5	-108.7	-4.8
Zambia - Zambie	1990	546.1	480.1	408.9	71.2	66.0	47.2	18.8
	1995	1966.7	2033.8	439.5	1594.1	-67.1	3.7	-70.8
	2000	675.0	795.1	486.2	308.6	-120.1	-104.4	-15.8
	2002	596.3	640.6	359.5	278.9	-44.4	-6.7	-37.7
Zimbabwe	1990	448.3	339.6	295.9	34.6	108.7	14.9	93.8
	1995	453.7	491.6	347.7	147.3	-37.8	1.0	-38.8
	2000	144.8	178.1	192.6	-13.9	-33.2	-0.9	-32.3
	2002	176.9	200.6	177.8	22.5	-23.6	-13.3	-10.3
Unspecified - Non spécifiée	*1990*	*1011.1*	*994.6*	*840.4*	*145.0*	*16.5*	*5.8*	*10.6*
	1995	*1100.8*	*1066.5*	*822.6*	*243.9*	*34.3*	*30.9*	*3.4*
	2000	*1256.9*	*1255.2*	*847.7*	*394.7*	*1.7*	*6.9*	*-5.2*
	2002	*1910.2*	*1880.8*	*1202.5*	*639.6*	*29.4*	*30.8*	*-1.4*
DEVELOPING ECONOMIES: ASIA - ECONOMIES EN DEVELOPPEMENT : ASIE	1990	24390.8	17979.8	10544.6	4752.6	6411.1	2940.0	3489.6
	1995	24307.9	17506.7	11754.6	5322.2	6801.2	5251.5	1555.2
	2000	13004.5	14925.4	10146.9	4358.6	-1920.8	-4436.0	2518.1
	2002	9661.9	17998.3	10205.6	5874.6	-8336.3	-3369.5	-4942.2
West Asia - Asie occidentale	*1990*	*4540.6*	*3853.9*	*1384.5*	*279.0*	*686.7*	*423.3*	*263.4*
	1995	*3402.8*	*2734.6*	*1515.7*	*729.1*	*668.2*	*970.2*	*-302.0*
	2000	*2837.4*	*2503.9*	*1373.5*	*867.6*	*333.5*	*-593.9*	*927.4*
	2002	*5546.7*	*4287.9*	*1316.2*	*1301.4*	*1258.8*	*615.6*	*643.2*
Bahrain - Bahreïn	1990	136.2	137.0	1.9	2.4	-0.8	-0.8	0.0
	1995	47.4	49.2	1.8	0.5	-1.8	-1.8	0.0
	2000	48.9	49.1	1.6	0.0	-0.2	-0.2	0.0
	2002	70.6	70.6	1.1	2.8	..	..	0.0
Iran, Islamic Rep. of - Iran, Rép. islamique d'	1990	-95.7	105.2	34.8	36.0	-200.9	-133.9	-67.0
	1995	400.3	191.3	158.9	32.4	209.0	129.6	79.4
	2000	-582.3	130.1	112.8	17.2	-712.4	-756.8	44.4
	2002	1060.9	115.8	81.5	32.5	945.0	979.0	-34.0
Iraq	1990	700.3	63.4	-8.6	16.6	636.9	642.3	-5.4
	1995	328.8	339.3	238.9	88.3	-10.5	-10.5	0.0
	2000	100.8	100.8	84.1	16.6	..	..	..
	2002	115.8	115.8	85.1	30.3	..	..	..
Jordan - Jordanie	1990	1081.8	887.7	435.0	26.8	194.1	118.6	75.5
	1995	1032.8	540.1	392.1	145.0	492.7	410.0	82.7
	2000	552.2	552.5	385.3	168.0	-0.2	-21.4	21.2
	2002	691.7	534.3	370.9	163.2	157.5	38.2	119.3
Kuwait - Koweït	1990	5.8	5.8	2.2	3.6	0.0	0.0	0.0
	1995	19.7	3.2	2.1	1.1	16.5	16.4	0.0
	2000	-20.9	2.9	2.0	0.9	-23.8	-23.8	0.0
	2002	-21.1	4.6	3.0	1.6	-25.8	-25.8	0.0

For sources and notes, see end of table.

Pour les sources et les notes, se reporter à la fin du tableau.

6.5 Official financial flows from bilateral and multilateral sources to developing economies *(continued)* Millions of dollars

6.5 Flux financiers publics bilatéraux et multilatéraux à destination des économies en développement *(suite)* En millions de dollars

Region, economic grouping, country or area / Régions, groupements économiques, pays ou zones	Year / Année	Total flows / Flux totaux	ODA / OA [1] APD / AP [1] Total [3]	of which DAC [4] dont CAD [4] Bilateral Bilatéraux	of which DAC [4] dont CAD [4] Multilateral [5] Multilatéraux [5]	OOF [2] AASP [2] Total [3]	of which DAC [4] dont CAD [4] Bilateral Bilatéraux	of which DAC [4] dont CAD [4] Multilateral [5] Multilatéraux [5]
Lebanon - Liban	1990	229.9	252.4	64.9	39.3	-22.5	-13.6	-8.9
	1995	310.5	187.2	57.2	73.3	123.4	2.2	121.2
	2000	268.5	199.7	93.7	91.3	68.8	2.8	66.0
	2002	433.6	455.8	102.4	81.2	-22.2	-6.2	-16.0
Oman	1990	57.7	61.2	11.3	2.3	-3.5	6.0	-9.6
	1995	52.1	58.7	11.9	2.5	-6.6	-10.8	4.1
	2000	50.6	45.6	9.2	2.3	5.0	9.7	-4.7
	2002	-0.3	40.8	-0.4	1.0	-41.1	-37.9	-3.3
Palestinian territory - Territoire palestinien	1995	498.6	498.6	183.2	262.9	..	..	0.0
	2000	682.6	637.3	306.4	226.1	45.3	-0.1	45.4
	2002	1585.9	1616.5	410.2	429.4	-30.6	0.2	-30.8
Qatar	1990	1.6	1.7	1.3	0.3	0.0	0.0	0.0
	1995	618.0	2.3	2.1	0.2	615.7	615.7	0.0
	2000	-108.4	0.5	1.1	-0.6	-108.9	-108.9	0.0
	2002	-238.4	2.2	2.0	0.2	-240.6	-240.6	0.0
Saudi Arabia - Arabie saoudite	1990	39.4	40.0	12.8	27.1	-0.6	-0.6	0.0
	1995	6.7	17.3	14.5	2.2	-10.6	-10.6	0.0
	2000	57.1	31.0	18.0	11.2	26.1	26.1	0.0
	2002	-73.0	26.9	13.4	13.3	-99.9	-99.9	0.0
Syrian Arab Republic - République arabe syrienne	1990	674.1	683.2	69.4	34.8	-9.1	1.2	-10.3
	1995	326.1	359.3	158.9	73.1	-33.2	-11.3	-21.9
	2000	486.4	158.5	97.3	38.7	327.9	342.1	-14.2
	2002	68.8	80.8	25.0	51.6	-12.0	-19.1	7.1
Turkey - Turquie	1990	1297.9	1207.8	587.9	-10.7	90.0	-199.1	289.1
	1995	-328.1	313.7	180.7	-11.7	-641.8	-74.2	-567.5
	2000	1082.6	327.2	99.7	190.7	755.5	-6.2	761.6
	2002	1278.0	635.8	99.0	386.6	642.2	40.7	601.5
United Arab Emirates - Emirats arabes unis	1990	4.2	4.0	2.8	1.1	0.3	0.3	0.0
	1995	-77.6	5.5	4.8	0.4	-83.0	-83.0	0.0
	2000	-53.1	4.0	2.7	1.3	-57.1	-57.1	0.0
	2002	-8.8	4.2	3.7	0.5	-13.1	-13.1	0.0
Yemen - Yémen	1990	407.5	404.7	168.8	99.3	2.8	2.8	0.0
	1995	167.6	169.1	108.6	59.0	-1.6	-1.6	0.0
	2000	272.5	264.8	159.6	104.0	7.6	0.0	7.7
	2002	583.1	583.7	119.4	107.2	-0.6	0.0	-0.6
Other Asia - Autres économies d'Asie	*1990*	*18705.4*	*12981.0*	*8922.7*	*4051.0*	*5724.4*	*2516.7*	*3226.2*
	1995	*20137.5*	*13990.9*	*9767.6*	*4283.4*	*6146.6*	*4281.3*	*1870.9*
	2000	*9507.2*	*11762.3*	*8342.1*	*3337.8*	*-2255.1*	*-3851.0*	*1598.9*
	2002	*3525.4*	*13133.4*	*8496.7*	*4392.3*	*-9608.0*	*-3987.2*	*-5596.1*
Afghanistan	1990	130.8	130.8	100.4	31.7	..	..	..
	1995	214.3	214.3	106.1	108.2	..	..	..
	2000	140.9	140.9	87.5	52.7	..	..	..
	2002	1285.0	1285.0	985.9	275.1	..	..	..
Bangladesh	1990	2114.7	2095.1	1103.3	1002.1	19.7	21.9	-2.2
	1995	1283.5	1292.3	727.4	573.9	-8.8	-3.3	-5.4
	2000	1170.6	1171.3	616.5	519.5	-0.7	-5.3	4.6
	2002	911.3	912.8	520.8	379.8	-1.5	-18.3	16.8
Bhutan - Bhoutan	1990	46.9	46.9	20.1	27.6	..	..	0.0
	1995	71.8	71.8	55.2	16.2	..	..	0.0
	2000	53.2	53.3	33.7	20.0	-0.1	-0.1	0.0
	2002	87.2	73.5	42.9	31.8	13.8	13.8	0.0
Brunei Darussalam - Brunéi Darussalam	1990	-4.5	3.9	3.7	0.1	-8.4	-8.4	0.0
	1995	4.3	4.3	4.2	0.1	..	..	0.0
	2000	0.7	0.6	0.6	0.0	0.1	0.1	0.0
	2002	-1.5	-1.7	-1.9	0.1	0.3	0.3	0.0

For sources and notes, see end of table.

Pour les sources et les notes, se reporter à la fin du tableau.

6.5 Official financial flows from bilateral and multilateral sources to developing economies (continued)
Millions of dollars

6.5 Flux financiers publics bilatéraux et multilatéraux à destination des économies en développement (suite)
En millions de dollars

Region, economic grouping, country or area / Régions, groupements économiques, pays ou zones	Year / Année	Total flows / Flux totaux	ODA / OA [1] APD / AP [1] Total [3]	of which DAC [4] dont CAD [4] Bilateral / Bilatéraux	Multilateral [5] / Multilatéraux [5]	OOF [2] AASP [2] Total [3]	of which DAC [4] dont CAD [4] Bilateral / Bilatéraux	Multilateral [5] / Multilatéraux [5]
Cambodia - Cambodge	1990	41.6	41.6	28.5	13.1	..	..	0.0
	1995	559.0	556.0	341.2	214.8	3.0	3.0	0.0
	2000	398.0	398.4	248.0	149.7	-0.4	-0.4	0.0
	2002	490.9	486.9	272.8	191.3	4.0	4.0	0.0
China - Chine	1990	3301.8	2037.6	1465.5	577.4	1264.1	835.9	428.2
	1995	7047.1	3476.2	2476.6	958.0	3571.0	1943.0	1627.9
	2000	1180.7	1731.9	1256.2	460.4	-551.2	-2190.2	1639.1
	2002	-98.2	1475.8	1212.8	230.7	-1574.0	-1111.0	-463.1
China, Hong Kong SAR - Chine, Hong Kong RAS	1990	31.4	38.2	19.4	18.7	-6.8	..	..
	1995	2.3	17.7	11.5	6.2	-15.5	..	..
	2000	-8.4	4.3	4.2	0.1	-12.8	-12.8	0.0
	2002	1.8	4.0	4.0	0.0	-2.2	-2.2	0.0
China, Macao SAR - Chine, Macao RAS	1990	0.2	0.2	0.1	0.1	..	..	0.0
	1995	-4.0	-4.0	0.1	-4.1	..	..	0.0
	2000	0.7	0.7	0.2	0.5	..	..	..
	2002	0.9	1.0	0.4	0.7	-0.1	-0.1	0.0
China, Taiwan Province of - Chine, Taiwan Province	1990	24.6	36.3	6.3	..	-11.7	..	..
	1995	10.1	0.2	11.0	..	9.9	..	..
	2000	6.8	9.7	9.7	..	-2.9	..	..
	2002	-17.2	7.4	7.4	..	-24.7	..	..
India - Inde	1990	2907.7	1406.4	751.8	652.1	1501.2	252.9	1248.3
	1995	1780.0	1739.5	1060.8	705.6	40.6	41.4	-0.8
	2000	1344.9	1485.2	650.3	846.5	-140.3	51.6	-191.9
	2002	-1042.4	1462.7	785.3	679.9	-2505.2	-245.6	-2259.5
Indonesia - Indonésie	1990	3261.7	1722.1	1520.1	177.5	1539.6	510.3	1029.3
	1995	2707.6	1303.5	1215.8	98.5	1404.1	858.9	545.2
	2000	2321.4	1657.8	1544.0	109.5	663.6	-57.4	721.0
	2002	23.1	1308.1	1162.0	130.7	-1285.0	-1068.8	-216.2
Korea, Dem. People's Rep. of - Corée, Rép. populaire dém. de	1990	7.4	8.2	0.9	7.4	-0.9	-0.9	0.0
	1995	17.2	13.7	1.5	12.2	3.5	3.5	0.0
	2000	36.4	75.2	26.9	48.3	-38.8	0.9	-39.7
	2002	218.2	266.8	187.8	77.1	-48.6	3.3	-51.9
Korea, Republic of - Corée, République de	1990	-490.8	52.4	54.8	3.1	-543.2	-162.9	-380.3
	1995	-354.0	57.1	60.4	0.6	-411.1	-59.0	-352.2
	2000	-256.8	-198.0	-196.6	-1.5	-58.7	101.2	-159.9
	2002	-1077.3	-81.7	-79.8	-2.0	-995.6	-838.7	-156.9
Lao People's Dem. Rep. - Rép. dém. populaire lao	1990	149.9	149.9	51.2	98.4	..	..	0.0
	1995	308.7	308.6	170.0	138.5	0.1	0.1	0.0
	2000	281.4	281.8	194.9	86.1	-0.4	-0.5	0.2
	2002	278.2	278.3	177.8	98.8	0.0	0.0	0.0
Malaysia - Malaisie	1990	538.9	468.8	458.6	13.6	70.1	-6.3	76.4
	1995	400.6	108.8	106.9	8.0	291.8	412.8	-121.0
	2000	-117.6	45.4	43.3	3.3	-163.0	-89.1	-73.9
	2002	367.5	85.9	85.4	1.8	281.7	375.0	-93.3
Maldives	1990	25.3	21.2	11.6	10.2	4.1	4.1	0.0
	1995	59.3	57.9	30.4	21.5	1.3	1.3	0.0
	2000	16.3	19.3	13.3	7.2	-3.0	-1.8	-1.2
	2002	24.9	27.5	12.9	15.3	-2.5	-1.3	-1.2
Mongolia - Mongolie	1990	13.1	13.1	6.3	6.8	..	..	0.0
	1995	198.2	210.6	126.9	78.7	-12.4	-12.4	0.0
	2000	217.5	217.5	150.8	60.6	..	..	..
	2002	210.2	208.5	141.3	45.1	1.7	1.3	0.4
Myanmar	1990	186.7	163.5	83.1	80.4	23.2	23.6	-0.3
	1995	155.6	151.4	126.3	23.2	4.2	5.1	-0.9
	2000	127.0	106.8	68.1	37.8	20.2	20.2	0.0
	2002	88.6	120.5	79.1	34.0	-31.9	-31.9	0.0

For sources and notes, see end of table.

Pour les sources et les notes, se reporter à la fin du tableau.

6.5 Official financial flows from bilateral and multilateral sources to developing economies (continued)
Millions of dollars

6.5 Flux financiers publics bilatéraux et multilatéraux à destination des économies en développement (suite)
En millions de dollars

Region, economic grouping, country or area / Régions, groupements économiques, pays ou zones	Year / Année	Total flows / Flux totaux	ODA / OA [1] APD / AP [1] Total [3]	of which DAC [4] dont CAD [4] Bilateral Bilatéraux	of which DAC [4] dont CAD [4] Multilateral [5] Multilatéraux [5]	OOF [2] AASP [2] Total [3]	of which DAC [4] dont CAD [4] Bilateral Bilatéraux	of which DAC [4] dont CAD [4] Multilateral [5] Multilatéraux [5]
Nepal - Népal	1990	435.3	426.0	239.0	184.7	9.3	0.0	9.2
	1995	432.3	432.6	266.1	166.9	-0.3	0.7	-0.9
	2000	412.6	389.6	231.2	154.9	23.0	2.7	20.2
	2002	359.1	365.5	279.4	65.3	-6.3	-1.2	-5.1
Pakistan	1990	1633.8	1129.3	653.5	494.9	504.5	29.9	474.7
	1995	1244.7	823.8	360.1	528.5	421.0	299.9	121.1
	2000	766.1	702.8	475.1	226.7	63.3	74.7	-11.4
	2002	2163.7	2143.7	702.5	1397.0	20.0	210.0	-190.0
Philippines	1990	2180.6	1274.3	1102.1	171.0	906.3	411.7	494.6
	1995	679.1	905.9	764.5	132.6	-226.8	-169.5	-57.2
	2000	359.1	577.5	502.1	72.2	-218.4	-20.3	-198.1
	2002	180.9	559.7	509.1	43.7	-378.8	-223.3	-155.5
Singapore - Singapour	1990	152.1	-3.1	-3.2	0.1	155.2	193.2	-38.1
	1995	-49.0	16.7	13.9	2.8	-65.7	-65.7	0.0
	2000	-157.9	1.1	0.7	0.4	-159.0	-159.0	0.0
	2002	50.4	7.4	7.1	0.3	43.0	43.0	0.0
Sri Lanka	1990	719.8	729.8	403.8	329.5	-10.0	-1.6	-8.4
	1995	547.5	555.1	374.0	181.5	-7.6	-0.1	-7.6
	2000	253.5	276.3	240.2	25.2	-22.8	-27.2	4.4
	2002	391.7	344.0	188.5	135.6	47.7	-11.9	59.6
Thailand - Thaïlande	1990	1107.7	799.4	733.7	69.5	308.2	413.2	-104.9
	1995	1768.3	839.6	807.2	37.7	928.7	821.8	106.9
	2000	-1244.9	698.4	682.9	17.7	-1943.2	-1783.5	-159.7
	2002	-2889.9	295.5	280.4	17.9	-3185.4	-1081.5	-2103.8
Timor-Leste	1990	0.1	0.1	..	0.1	..	..	0.0
	1995	0.0	0.0	0.0	..	..	..	..
	2000	650.7	232.9	212.3	20.6	417.8	417.8	0.0
	2002	232.7	219.8	187.0	31.4	12.9	12.9	0.0
Viet Nam	1990	188.9	188.9	107.9	80.9	0.0	0.2	-0.1
	1995	1052.9	837.3	549.7	273.4	215.6	199.8	15.8
	2000	1554.3	1681.8	1246.2	419.5	-127.5	-172.5	45.1
	2002	1285.7	1276.8	746.0	511.0	8.8	-14.8	23.6
Unspecified - Non spécifiée	*1990*	*1140.5*	*1140.5*	*233.2*	*422.5*	*..*	*..*	*0.0*
	1995	*705.5*	*719.2*	*456.8*	*262.1*	*-13.7*	*0.0*	*-13.7*
	2000	*520.5*	*519.8*	*298.7*	*148.9*	*0.7*	*8.9*	*-8.2*
	2002	*0.0*	*0.0*	*0.0*	*0.0*	*0.0*	*0.0*	*0.0*
DEVELOPING ECONOMIES: OCEANIA - ECONOMIES EN DEVELOPPEMENT : OCEANIE	**1990**	**1497.3**	**1374.8**	**1214.7**	**156.8**	**122.5**	**59.9**	**62.6**
	1995	**1975.9**	**1867.7**	**1710.9**	**152.3**	**88.8**	**100.1**	**-11.3**
	2000	**1615.8**	**1569.6**	**1459.2**	**107.0**	**46.2**	**48.5**	**2.4**
	2002	**1465.3**	**1450.8**	**1399.6**	**50.4**	**14.5**	**36.2**	**-21.8**
Cook Islands - Iles Cook	1990	11.4	12.2	10.1	2.1	-0.8	-0.8	0.0
	1995	13.1	13.1	10.4	2.6	..	..	0.0
	2000	4.2	4.3	3.4	0.9	-0.2	-0.2	0.0
	2002	3.6	3.8	3.5	0.3	-0.2	-0.2	0.0
Fiji - Fidji	1990	35.8	50.5	43.5	6.5	-14.7	-0.4	-14.3
	1995	42.4	44.9	39.1	4.4	-2.5	3.6	-6.0
	2000	22.8	29.1	28.7	0.2	-6.3	-0.1	-6.2
	2002	30.9	34.1	31.3	2.5	-3.2	0.4	-3.6
French Polynesia - Polynésie française	1990	304.0	259.7	258.0	1.7	44.3	44.6	-0.3
	1995	434.3	450.9	444.4	6.5	-16.6	-16.1	-0.5
	2000	381.0	402.6	400.2	2.4	-21.6	-21.6	0.0
	2002	405.7	417.9	417.4	0.5	-12.2	-12.2	0.0
Kiribati	1990	20.2	20.2	17.7	2.5	..	..	0.0
	1995	15.4	15.4	11.4	4.0	..	..	0.0
	2000	17.9	17.9	14.8	3.1	..	..	..
	2002	21.0	20.9	18.7	2.1	0.1	0.1	0.0

For sources and notes, see end of table.

Pour les sources et les notes, se reporter à la fin du tableau.

6.5 Official financial flows from bilateral and multilateral sources to developing economies
(continued)
Millions of dollars

6.5 Flux financiers publics bilatéraux et multilatéraux à destination des économies en développement
(suite)
En millions de dollars

Region, economic grouping, country or area / Régions, groupements économiques, pays ou zones	Year / Année	Total flows / Flux totaux	ODA / OA [1] APD / AP [1] Total [3]	ODA of which DAC [4] dont CAD [4] Bilateral / Bilatéraux	ODA of which DAC [4] dont CAD [4] Multilateral [5] / Multilatéraux [5]	OOF [2] AASP [2] Total [3]	OOF of which DAC [4] dont CAD [4] Bilateral / Bilatéraux	OOF of which DAC [4] dont CAD [4] Multilateral [5] / Multilatéraux [5]
Marshall Islands - Iles Marshall	1995	38.9	38.9	32.1	6.8	..	..	0.0
	2000	57.2	57.2	47.1	10.1	..	..	..
	2002	63.9	62.4	55.4	7.0	1.5	0.0	1.5
Micronesia, Federated States of - Micronésie, Etats fédérés de	1995	78.3	77.3	71.8	5.5	1.0	1.0	0.0
	2000	101.5	101.6	96.6	5.0	-0.1	-0.1	0.0
	2002	111.8	111.7	110.1	1.6	0.2	0.2	0.0
Nauru	1990	0.2	0.2	0.2	..	..	..	..
	1995	2.8	2.8	2.2	0.0	..	..	..
	2000	4.0	4.0	3.9	0.1	..	..	..
	2002	11.7	11.7	11.6	..	..	..	..
New Caledonia - Nouvelle-Calédonie	1990	325.8	302.4	300.2	2.2	23.4	24.0	-0.6
	1995	548.8	451.2	442.3	9.0	97.6	98.7	-1.1
	2000	351.8	350.2	348.7	1.4	1.6	1.6	0.0
	2002	354.5	323.8	323.2	0.6	30.6	30.6	0.0
Niue - Nioué	1990	7.2	7.2	7.0	0.2	..	..	0.0
	1995	8.3	8.3	8.1	0.2	..	..	..
	2000	3.2	3.2	3.0	0.2	..	..	..
	2002	4.4	4.4	4.2	0.2	..	..	..
Northern Mariana Islands - Iles Mariannes du Nord	1990	63.1	63.1	61.9	1.2	..	..	..
	1995	18.8	-0.7	-0.2	-0.5	19.5	..	..
	2000	-4.5	0.2	0.0	0.2	-4.6	..	..
Palau - Palaos	1995	156.3	142.3	141.7	0.1	14.0	14.0	0.0
	2000	37.7	39.1	38.9	0.2	-1.5	-1.5	0.0
	2002	29.6	31.3	30.9	0.2	-1.7	-1.7	0.0
Papua New Guinea - Papouasie-Nouvelle-Guinée	1990	475.6	413.2	320.0	91.6	62.5	-15.3	77.8
	1995	366.1	371.0	300.5	69.6	-5.0	-1.3	-3.6
	2000	357.3	275.4	268.6	5.2	81.9	72.7	9.2
	2002	202.3	203.3	197.1	6.1	-1.0	17.8	-18.8
Samoa	1990	47.6	47.7	27.7	19.6	-0.1	-0.1	0.0
	1995	43.4	43.4	31.3	12.3	..	..	0.0
	2000	27.8	27.4	18.1	9.2	0.4	0.3	0.1
	2002	37.9	37.8	30.8	6.8	0.2	0.2	0.0
Solomon Islands - Iles Salomon	1990	46.2	45.8	31.1	14.3	0.5	0.5	0.0
	1995	47.0	47.8	36.5	10.2	-0.7	-0.7	0.0
	2000	69.6	68.4	20.8	46.3	1.2	1.2	0.0
	2002	25.4	26.3	21.3	5.0	-1.0	-1.0	0.0
Tokelau - Tokélaou	1990	4.8	4.8	4.4	0.4	..	..	..
	1995	3.7	3.7	3.5	0.3	..	..	..
	2000	3.5	3.5	3.4	0.1	..	..	..
	2002	4.8	4.8	4.6	0.2	..	..	..
Tonga	1990	29.6	29.8	24.2	5.5	-0.2	-0.2	0.0
	1995	38.9	38.9	28.8	10.0	..	..	0.0
	2000	18.9	18.8	14.8	4.0	0.0	0.0	0.0
	2002	22.4	22.3	16.7	5.5	0.1	0.1	0.0
Tuvalu	1990	5.1	5.1	4.8	0.3	..	..	..
	1995	7.9	7.9	6.3	1.6	..	..	..
	2000	4.0	4.0	3.8	0.2	..	..	..
	2002	11.7	11.7	11.2	0.6	..	..	..
Vanuatu	1990	54.4	49.8	42.1	7.7	4.6	4.6	0.0
	1995	45.2	45.6	39.6	6.1	-0.5	-0.5	0.0
	2000	45.2	45.8	28.3	17.5	-0.7	0.0	-0.7
	2002	27.0	27.5	22.4	5.2	-0.5	0.3	-0.8
Wallis and Futuna Islands - Iles Wallis et Futuna	1990	3.9	0.9	0.0	0.9	3.0	3.0	0.0
	1995	0.5	1.0	0.1	0.8	-0.4	-0.4	0.0
	2000	53.3	52.1	52.1	0.0	1.2	1.2	0.0
	2002	52.3	52.7	52.7	0.1	-0.4	-0.4	0.0

For sources and notes, see end of table.

Pour les sources et les notes, se reporter à la fin du tableau.

6.5 Official financial flows from bilateral and multilateral sources to developing economies (continued)
Millions of dollars

6.5 Flux financiers publics bilatéraux et multilatéraux à destination des économies en développement (suite)
En millions de dollars

Region, economic grouping, country or area / Régions, groupements économiques, pays ou zones	Year / Année	Total flows / Flux totaux	ODA / OA APD / AP [1] Total [3]	of which DAC [4] dont CAD [4] Bilateral / Bilatéraux	of which DAC [4] dont CAD [4] Multilateral [5] / Multilatéraux [5]	OOF [2] AASP [2] Total [3]	of which DAC [4] dont CAD [4] Bilateral / Bilatéraux	of which DAC [4] dont CAD [4] Multilateral [5] / Multilatéraux [5]
Unspecified - Non spécifiée	1990	62.4	62.4	61.9	0.1	..	..	0.0
	1995	65.9	64.0	61.1	3.0	1.9	1.9	0.0
	2000	59.5	64.7	64.0	0.7	-5.2	-5.2	0.0
	2002	0.0	0.0	0.0	0.0	0.0	0.0	0.0
DEVELOPING ECONOMIES - ECONOMIES EN DEVELOPPEMENT	1990	74209.1	56033.6	36903.9	13260.1	18178.9	8060.6	10136.7
	1995	68114.2	56300.7	38532.9	17068.0	11797.1	8875.4	2897.8
	2000	49726.5	46495.5	34086.2	11754.3	3230.9	-4946.4	8141.1
	2002	50704.1	56208.2	37150.0	16497.9	-5485.2	901.7	-6344.5
DEVELOPING ECONOMIES: UNSPECIFIED - ECONOMIES EN DEVELOPPEMENT : NON SPECIFIES	1990	6432.3	6080.4	5139.0	901.6	351.9	351.9	0.0
	1995	8377.7	8508.4	7037.0	1387.3	-130.8	-130.8	0.0
	2000	9290.4	9048.6	8061.6	1106.2	241.8	241.8	0.0
	2002	10193.3	9245.8	8172.6	1197.3	947.5	947.5	0.0

By major category - Par principales catégories

Region, economic grouping, country or area	Year	Total flows	ODA/OA Total	Bilateral	Multilateral	OOF Total	Bilateral	Multilateral
Major petroleum exporters - Principaux pays exportateurs de pétrole	1990	9518.3	4414.2	2730.1	655.2	5104.1	2432.8	2671.3
	1995	8025.1	3873.6	2877.0	787.4	4151.5	3139.3	1012.2
	2000	2613.5	3450.7	2634.5	625.3	-837.2	-1202.1	365.0
	2002	5873.4	4092.6	2355.4	1109.3	1780.8	2662.2	-881.4
Other developing economies - Autres économies en développement	1990	55365.5	42801.3	27542.5	10952.7	12567.6	5270.3	7315.7
	1995	49116.9	41397.0	26775.8	14215.8	7703.5	5706.2	1973.4
	2000	34688.9	30897.0	21044.3	9357.0	3791.9	-3998.2	7753.8
	2002	31517.7	39839.7	24598.3	13238.9	-8303.1	-2751.4	-5509.3
Major exporters of manufactures - Principaux pays exportateurs d'articles manufacturés	1990	16670.0	7693.5	5522.3	1524.7	8976.9	4478.6	4516.8
	1995	11434.5	8241.3	6168.9	1933.6	3193.3	1826.6	1372.2
	2000	6558.4	5054.2	3309.6	1702.1	1504.3	-4388.1	5895.3
	2002	-1237.5	5088.8	3326.0	1578.3	-6326.2	-2822.9	-3478.7
Remaining economies - Autres économies	1990	38695.5	35107.8	22020.1	9428.0	3590.7	791.8	2798.9
	1995	37682.4	33155.7	20607.0	12282.3	4510.2	3879.6	601.2
	2000	28130.5	25842.8	17734.7	7654.8	2287.7	389.9	1858.5
	2002	32755.1	34751.0	21272.3	11660.6	-1976.9	71.4	-2030.6
America - Amérique	1990	5966.2	4283.2	3414.0	858.2	1683.0	775.2	907.7
	1995	6770.3	5023.5	3628.9	1358.4	1746.8	986.3	731.1
	2000	5667.5	3520.8	2637.8	835.3	2146.7	-65.9	2168.7
	2002	2759.1	4034.3	3179.4	804.4	-1256.2	-425.4	-813.1
Africa - Afrique	1990	24288.3	23227.5	14143.8	5979.1	1063.8	-225.4	1289.3
	1995	21019.0	19581.3	11460.9	7960.0	1440.8	1885.4	-444.6
	2000	13324.4	13679.3	9071.5	4398.7	-355.0	112.5	-467.4
	2002	17835.6	18691.6	11321.4	6848.9	-855.9	264.6	-1120.5
West Asia - Asie occidentale	1990	1311.7	1140.1	499.9	66.1	171.6	105.0	66.6
	1995	1841.9	1225.9	632.5	481.1	616.1	412.2	203.9
	2000	1503.3	1389.5	785.4	485.4	113.9	-18.7	132.6
	2002	2711.2	2606.6	883.4	673.8	104.6	32.2	72.5
Other Asia - Autres économies d'Asie	1990	5694.5	5144.6	2809.7	2367.9	549.9	77.1	472.8
	1995	6141.1	5521.5	3234.9	2333.4	619.6	497.6	122.1
	2000	6079.0	5748.4	3844.8	1829.2	330.6	308.4	22.2
	2002	8028.4	8010.4	4525.0	3289.3	18.0	165.7	-147.7

For sources and notes, see end of table.

Pour les sources et les notes, se reporter à la fin du tableau.

6.5 **Official financial flows from bilateral and multilateral sources to developing economies** *(concluded)* Millions of dollars

6.5 **Flux financiers publics bilatéraux et multilatéraux à destination des économies en développement** *(fin)* En millions de dollars

Region, economic grouping, country or area / Régions, groupements économiques, pays ou zones	Year / Année	Total flows / Flux totaux	ODA / OA [1] APD / AP [1]			OOF [2] AASP [2]		
			Total [3]	of which DAC [4] dont CAD [4]		Total [3]	of which DAC [4] dont CAD [4]	
				Bilateral Bilatéraux	Multilateral [5] Multilatéraux [5]		Bilateral Bilatéraux	Multilateral [5] Multilatéraux [5]
By income group (per capita GDP in 2000) Par catégorie de revenus (PIB par habitant en 2000)								
High-income - Revenu élevé	1990	9452.8	2162.9	1586.1	222.1	7289.9	2943.7	4364.7
	1995	3727.8	2621.3	2196.4	285.6	1087.1	109.3	953.8
	2000	2439.7	1521.7	1199.9	198.6	918.0	-1240.5	2122.1
	2002	-1332.8	1877.6	1348.4	112.4	-3191.4	-1461.6	-1687.4
Middle-income - Revenu intermédiaire	1990	16301.4	14959.9	9432.6	1202.0	1341.8	325.7	1016.2
	1995	15619.2	10122.7	7686.5	1980.6	5496.5	4999.2	497.3
	2000	11075.9	8214.0	6117.9	1785.1	2861.9	-1809.1	4671.0
	2002	10619.9	10706.6	6442.5	2966.3	-86.8	507.5	-594.3
Low-income - Revenu faible	1990	39129.6	30092.7	19253.8	10183.9	9039.9	4433.8	4606.2
	1995	37795.1	32526.7	19770.0	12737.1	5271.4	3737.0	1534.5
	2000	23786.9	24612.0	16361.0	7998.5	-825.1	-2150.8	1325.7
	2002	28103.9	31348.1	19162.9	11269.4	-3244.2	864.8	-4109.0
MEMO ITEM: - POUR MEMOIRE :								
Least developed countries - Pays les moins avancés	1990	17470.7	16750.7	9888.0	6287.1	723.0	688.5	34.5
	1995	17105.3	17241.7	9344.1	7851.9	-133.3	-38.4	-94.9
	2000	13023.3	12682.5	7947.2	4541.4	-77.1	-79.2	-4.3
	2002	16892.6	17502.0	10364.8	6401.9	-609.4	-399.5	-209.9
Heavily indebted poor countries - Pays pauvres très endettés	1990	19407.0	17934.3	11103.6	6329.0	1475.7	1003.9	471.9
	1995	19478.1	19079.6	10658.5	8363.7	401.5	883.2	-481.7
	2000	14107.5	14658.4	9427.5	5067.7	-550.8	-226.1	-324.7
	2002	19005.1	19495.6	11439.4	7373.2	-490.4	104.5	-594.9
Landlocked countries - Pays enclavés	1990	7228.7	7049.4	4176.7	2707.9	182.3	87.9	94.4
	1995	11329.5	10747.2	5307.1	5394.4	585.3	160.5	424.8
	2000	8001.4	7655.2	4831.6	2685.1	346.2	11.5	334.7
	2002	9996.6	10148.0	6158.7	3684.2	-151.4	-32.5	-118.9
Developing economies excl. China - Economies en développement Chine non comprise	1990	70907.3	53995.9	35438.5	12682.7	16914.7	7224.7	9708.5
	1995	61067.1	52824.5	36056.3	16110.0	8226.2	6932.4	1269.8
	2000	48545.8	44763.7	32830.0	11294.0	3782.1	-2756.2	6502.0
	2002	50802.3	54732.4	35937.2	16267.3	-3911.1	2012.7	-5881.4
Sub-Saharan Africa - Afrique subsaharienne	1990	20607.1	17860.6	11453.7	5929.0	2749.4	1796.6	952.8
	1995	18611.2	18420.3	10391.8	7983.3	193.9	864.9	-670.9
	2000	11771.3	12693.1	8140.5	4376.0	-921.8	-452.0	-469.8
	2002	20955.7	18615.3	11398.7	6868.9	2340.5	3122.4	-781.9

For sources and notes, see next page.

Pour les sources et les notes, se reporter à la page suivante.

Sources: Organisation for Economic Co-operation and Development (OECD)/Development Assistance Committee (DAC): *International Development Statistics* online database.

Notes:

Official financial flows refer to net disbursements by official sources to a recipient country. *Net disbursements* refer to the actual amounts disbursed (*gross* disbursements) less repayments of principal in respect of earlier loans.

Developing economies in this table are aid recipients included in the DAC List of Aid Recipients (see the OECD/DAC *Geographical Distribution of Financial Flows to Aid Recipients, 1994-1998*).

Unspecified groups distributed by region show flows corresponding to disbursements allocated not to an individual recipient country but to a group of countries, as classified in the *Geographical Distribution of Financial Flows to Aid Recipients* of the OECD.
Such unspecified flows are not included in the categories defined by the economic groupings.

1 ODA (Official Development Assistance): Loans administered with the main objective of promoting the economic development and welfare of developing countries.

OA (Official Aid): Loans meeting the same criteria as those of ODA, but OA loans are directed to countries listed in Part II of the DAC List of Aid Recipients.

Both ODA and OA are *concessional*. According to the DAC's definitions, *concessional* loans are those that have a grant element of 25 per cent or more, whereas *non-concessional* loans carry a grant element of less than 25 per cent. The *Grant element* reflects the financial terms of a transaction: interest rate, maturity (interval to final repayment) and grace period (interval to the first repayment of capital).

Where figures under "Total ODA/OA, net" or "Total OOF, net" do not correspond to the sum of "DAC bilateral" and "DAC multilateral", the difference can be attributed to the amounts loaned by countries that are not members of DAC.

2 OOF (other official flows) are loans with a target other than rhe economic development and welfare of the aid recipient, or loans with a grant element of less than 25 per cent. They are non-concessional.

3 Includes loans from Arab countries (OPEC bilateral) and Arab agencies (OPEC multilateral). The member countries of OPEC (Organization of Petroleum Exporting Countries) are: Algeria, Indonesia, Iraq, Islamic Republic of Iran, Kuwait, the Libyan Arab Jamahiriya, Nigeria, Qatar, Saudi Arabia, United Arab Emirates and Venezuela.

4 The member countries of the DAC (Development Assistance Committee) are: Australia, Austria, Belgium, Canada, Denmark, Finland, France, Germany, Greece, Ireland, Italy, Japan, Luxembourg, the Netherlands, New Zealand, Norway, Portugal, Spain, Sweden, Switzerland, the United Kingdom and the United States. The Commission of the European Communities is also a member of the DAC.

5 DAC financial flows from multilateral sources cover the World Bank, regional development banks, other multilateral and intergovernmental agencies, concessional flows from the IMF and the Social Loans programme of the European Resettlement Fund. Not included are loans from funds administered by an international organization on behalf of a single donor government; this category is included in bilateral loans (from governments).

Sources :   Organisation de coopération et de développement économiques (OCDE)/Comité d'aide au développement (CAD) : *Statistiques sur le développement international,* base de données en ligne.

Notes :

Les flux financiers publics représentent les versements nets des organismes officiels aux pays en développement. Les *versements nets* correspondent aux montants effectivement versés (versements *bruts*) moins le remboursement du capital au titre de prêts antérieurs.

Les bénéficiares de l'aide sont des économies en développement compris dans la Liste des bénéficiaires de l'aide établie par le CAD (voir OCDE/CAD *Répartition géographique des ressources financières allouées aux pays bénéficiaires de l'aide, 1994-1998*).

Les groupes non-specifiés distribués par région montrent des flux correspondants à des versements qui ne sont pas distribués par pays bénéficiaire mais par des groupes de pays tels qu'ils sont définis dans la *Répartition géographique des ressources financières* , de l'OCDE. Ces flux non-spécifiés ne sont pas compris dans les catégories définies par des groupements économiques.

1 APD (Aide publique au développement) : Prêts dispensés dans le but de favoriser le progrès économique et social des pays en développement.

AP (Aide publique) : prêts qui obéissent aux mêmes critères que l'APD, mais l'AP est destinée à des pays inscrits dans la partie II de la Liste des bénéficiaires de l'aide, établie par le CAD.

L'APD et l'AP sont des prêts assortis de *conditions libérales* . Selon les définitions du CAD, les prêts assortis de *conditions libérales* comportent un élément de libéralité d'au moins 25 pour cent tandis que les prêts assortis de *conditions non libérales* ont un élément de libéralité inférieur à 25 pour cent. *L'élément de libéralité* résume les conditions financières d'une opération : taux d'intérêt, durée de remboursement (délai jusqu'au remboursement final) et différé d'amortissement (délai jusqu'au premier remboursement du capital).

Quand les chiffres présentés sous "Total APD / AP, montants nets" ou "Total AASP, montant net" ne correspondent pas à la somme des "CAD bilatéral" et "CAD multilatéral", la différence peut être attribuée aux montants prêtés par des pays non membres du CAD.

2 AASP (Autres apports du secteur public) : ce sont des prêts dont le but essentiel n'est pas celui du développement économique ni l'amélioration du niveau de vie du bénéficiaire de l'aide ou des prêts assortis d'un élément de libéralité inférieur à 25 pour cent. Ces transactions sont assorties des conditions du marché.

3 Y compris des prêts en provenance des pays arabes (OPEP, bilatérale) et d'organismes financés par des pays arabes (OPEP, multilatérale). Les pays membres de l'OPEP (Organisation des pays exportateurs de pétrole) sont les suivants : Algérie, Arabie saoudite, Emirats arabes unis, Indonésie, Iraq, Jamahiriya arabe libyenne, Koweït, Nigéria, Qatar, République islamique d'Iran et Vénézuela.

4 Les pays membres du CAD (Comité d'aide au développement) sont les suivants : Allemagne, Australie, Autriche, Belgique, Canada, Danemark, Espagne, Etats-Unis, Finlande, France, Grèce, Irlande, Italie, Japon, Luxembourg, Norvège, Nouvelle-Zélande, Pays-Bas, Portugal, Royaume-Uni, Suède et Suisse. La Commission de la communauté européenne est aussi membre du CAD.

5 Les apports financiers du CAD en provenance des sources multilatérales se rapportent aux organismes tels que la Banque mondiale, les banques régionales de développement, d'autres organismes multilatéraux et intergouvernementaux, et comprennent des apports concessionnels du FMI et le programme de prêts sociaux du Fonds de rétablissement européen. Ne sont pas compris les prêts provenants des fonds d'un gouvernement administrés par une organisation internationale ; cettte catégorie est incluse dans la rubrique des sources bilatérales (de gouvernements).

Developing economies / Economies en développement	Overall total [1] Total général [1]	Official sources / Sources publiques						Private sources / Sources privées			Non-guaranteed debt [9] Dette non garantie [9]
		Total [2]	Bilateral / Bilatérales				Multilateral [6] Multilatérales [6]	Total	Supplier credits [7] Crédits fournisseurs [7]	Financial markets [8] Marchés financiers [8]	
			Total [3]	DAC [4] CAD [4]	OPEC [5] OPEP [5]	Other Autres					
1980											
Debt outstanding											
(disbursed only)	324830	147445	101025	72597	14000	14428	46421	177384	24220	153164	59555
Disbursements	70883	25067	16265	11080	2493	2692	8802	45815	5887	39928	18231
Total debt service	49279	11106	7147	5298	886	964	3959	38173	6125	32047	15939
of which: amortization	26453	5952	4372	3107	534	730	1580	20501	4476	16025	9739
interest	22826	5155	2775	2190	352	233	2379	17671	1650	16022	6200
Net transfers	21604	13961	9118	5783	1608	1728	4843	7643	-238	7881	2292
1990											
Dette active											
(montants décaissés seulement)	897554	500580	306867	208026	18261	80580	193713	396974	35144	361830	56080
Déboursements	78719	44832	18996	16183	571	2242	25836	33888	3997	29891	16042
Service de la dette	94322	38622	17646	13373	1100	3174	20976	55700	5857	49843	10251
dont : amortissement	54022	21556	10495	7525	849	2121	11061	32465	4101	28365	6058
intérêts	40301	17066	7151	5848	250	1053	9915	23235	1756	21478	4194
Transferts nets	-15603	6209	1349	2810	-529	-932	4860	-21812	-1860	-19952	5791
1995											
Debt outstanding											
(disbursed only)	1117452	678151	411672	305822	13780	92070	266479	439300	31632	407669	206858
Disbursements	119656	59796	31770	25903	514	5353	28026	59860	3198	56662	53382
Total debt service	133368	66131	34555	26116	923	7517	31575	67238	6906	60331	37269
of which: amortization	80833	40863	22047	15442	718	5888	18816	39970	5078	34892	26206
interest	52536	25268	12508	10674	205	1629	12760	27268	1829	25439	11063
Net transfers	-13713	-6335	-2786	-212	-409	-2164	-3550	-7378	-3709	-3669	16113
1998											
Dette active											
(montants décaissés seulement)	1143259	652452	364490	278138	14311	72040	287962	490807	22768	468039	425578
Déboursements	124996	55391	19414	16367	545	2502	35977	69605	2753	66852	101379
Service de la dette	139760	59283	32530	25811	774	5945	26753	80477	4606	75871	88233
dont : amortissement	87495	37229	21817	17267	590	3959	15412	50266	3410	46857	62677
intérêts	52265	22055	10713	8544	184	1986	11341	30210	1196	29014	25556
Transferts nets	-14764	-3892	-13116	-9444	-229	-3443	9224	-10872	-1853	-9019	13146
1999											
Debt outstanding											
(disbursed only)	1154363	666988	365578	281665	14551	69362	301410	487375	26646	460729	450608
Disbursements	123847	53537	21287	16919	670	3699	32250	70309	3875	66434	92407
Total debt service	151557	64392	33335	25506	731	7098	31057	87165	4555	82610	121711
of which: amortization	97184	40535	22881	16940	552	5388	17654	56649	3486	53163	93103
interest	54374	23858	10455	8566	179	1710	13403	30516	1069	29447	28608
Net transfers	-27711	-10855	-12048	-8588	-62	-3399	1193	-16856	-679	-16176	-29303
2000											
Dette active											
(montants décaissés seulement)	1136804	644226	343745	249815	14013	79917	300481	492578	24248	468330	442268
Déboursements	133064	48344	17085	14676	283	2126	31259	84721	3101	81620	84271
Service de la dette	165896	66833	31575	24654	751	6170	35258	99062	5228	93834	122730
dont : amortissement	108286	43192	21946	16779	575	4592	21246	65094	3796	61297	94145
intérêts	57610	23641	9629	7875	176	1578	14012	33969	1432	32537	28585
Transferts nets	-32831	-18490	-14491	-9978	-468	-4044	-3999	-14341	-2127	-12214	-38460
2001											
Debt outstanding											
(disbursed only)	1118059	627120	321239	215765	13167	92307	305881	490939	22518	468421	408717
Disbursements	113623	47109	15843	11687	784	3373	31266	66513	3130	63383	79884
Total debt service	163253	57079	26403	19214	735	6454	30675	106175	5680	100495	118662
of which: amortization	104475	34351	17466	12423	568	4475	16885	70124	4379	65744	93341
interest	58778	22728	8938	6791	167	1979	13790	36051	1301	34750	25320
Net transfers	-49631	-9970	-10560	-7527	49	-3081	591	-39661	-2550	-37111	-38777
2002											
Dette active											
(montants décaissés seulement)	1028086	589176	283730	201198	6461	76071	305446	438910	14938	423972	324797
Déboursements	66318	45273	18262	16179	689	1393	27011	21046	1120	19925	..
Service de la dette	167389	71818	33792	26073	1038	6681	38025	95572	7255	88317	104845
dont : amortissement	112802	49195	23564	19251	839	3474	25631	63607	6208	57399	80902
intérêts	54588	22623	10228	6822	199	3207	12395	31965	1047	30918	23943
Transferts nets	-101071	-26545	-15530	-9894	-349	-5288	-11015	-74526	-6135	-68391	..

For sources and notes, see end of table 6.6E.

Pour les sources et les notes, se reporter à la fin du tableau 6.6E.

Major petroleum exporters / Principaux pays exportateurs de pétrole	Overall total [1] Total général [1]	Official sources / Sources publiques						Private sources / Sources privées			Non-guaranteed debt [9] Dette non garantie [9]
		Total [2]	Bilateral / Bilatérales				Multilateral [6] Multilatérales [6]	Total	Supplier credits [7] Crédits fournisseurs [7]	Financial markets [8] Marchés financiers [8]	
			Total [3]	DAC [4] CAD [4]	OPEC [5] OPEP [5]	Other Autres					
1980											
Debt outstanding											
(disbursed only)	59647	20478	16112	10903	1524	3685	4365	39170	8507	30663	7420
Disbursements	13180	3702	2959	1584	189	1187	743	9478	1602	7876	3151
Total debt service	11404	1762	1244	913	123	207	519	9641	2308	7333	2811
of which: amortization	6715	999	768	509	86	173	230	5716	1677	4039	2105
interest	4689	764	475	404	37	34	288	3925	631	3294	706
Net transfers	1776	1940	1716	671	65	980	224	-164	-706	543	340
1990											
Dette active											
(montants décaissés seulement)	169553	83040	58549	39540	2122	16886	24492	86513	13961	72552	14574
Déboursements	17216	8354	4139	3730	90	319	4215	8861	1286	7575	5015
Service de la dette	26330	8341	5522	3819	107	1595	2820	17988	2827	15162	2490
dont : amortissement	16361	4813	3501	2178	86	1237	1312	11548	1965	9583	1456
intérêts	9969	3528	2021	1641	21	358	1507	6441	862	5579	1034
Transferts nets	-9114	13	-1382	-90	-17	-1276	1395	-9127	-1541	-7586	2525
1995											
Debt outstanding											
(disbursed only)	209818	133950	96978	66330	2306	28342	36972	75868	10433	65435	38440
Disbursements	14421	7931	3804	3534	195	75	4127	6490	435	6055	7358
Total debt service	25354	13750	8745	4221	102	4422	5005	11604	1801	9803	6892
of which: amortization	15427	8505	5864	2158	72	3634	2641	6922	1268	5654	5403
interest	9927	5245	2882	2063	30	789	2364	4681	533	4149	1489
Net transfers	-10932	-5819	-4941	-687	93	-4347	-878	-5114	-1366	-3748	467
1998											
Dette active											
(montants décaissés seulement)	195144	127600	92805	67090	2691	23023	34795	67544	6859	60685	65658
Déboursements	14615	8907	4446	3109	74	1263	4461	5707	386	5321	9540
Service de la dette	22155	11081	6750	4396	120	2235	4331	11074	801	10272	11261
dont : amortissement	13784	6590	4183	2347	56	1780	2407	7194	643	6551	8107
intérêts	8370	4491	2567	2049	63	454	1923	3880	158	3722	3154
Transferts nets	-7540	-2174	-2305	-1288	-45	-972	131	-5366	-415	-4951	-1721
1999											
Debt outstanding											
(disbursed only)	195011	129852	93305	69137	2628	21540	36547	65159	6563	58596	57424
Disbursements	12908	8281	4185	3629	87	469	4097	4626	406	4221	3564
Total debt service	24970	12585	7756	4629	169	2958	4829	12385	994	11391	9981
of which: amortization	16121	7690	5090	2439	106	2545	2600	8431	799	7632	8560
interest	8849	4895	2666	2190	63	413	2229	3954	195	3759	1421
Net transfers	-12062	-4304	-3571	-1000	-82	-2490	-733	-7759	-588	-7170	-6417
2000											
Dette active											
(montants décaissés seulement)	194684	136299	100593	53684	2531	44378	35706	58385	5287	53098	48185
Déboursements	10710	5906	2906	2308	43	556	3000	4804	265	4540	2483
Service de la dette	23318	11815	6819	3581	181	3057	4996	11503	768	10735	11350
dont : amortissement	14403	6669	4074	1543	120	2411	2596	7734	596	7138	8662
intérêts	8915	5146	2746	2038	61	646	2400	3769	172	3598	2687
Transferts nets	-12608	-5909	-3914	-1273	-139	-2501	-1996	-6699	-503	-6196	-8867
2001											
Debt outstanding											
(disbursed only)	186612	129813	95091	47500	2483	45108	34722	56799	4898	51900	42949
Disbursements	9658	4026	1533	1307	76	150	2493	5632	451	5181	2714
Total debt service	24016	12053	7078	3598	173	3307	4975	11962	627	11335	9685
of which: amortization	15188	6887	4137	1625	117	2395	2750	8301	482	7819	8166
interest	8828	5166	2941	1974	55	912	2225	3662	145	3516	1519
Net transfers	-14358	-8027	-5545	-2292	-96	-3157	-2482	-6331	-176	-6154	-6971
2002											
Dette active											
(montants décaissés seulement)	154775	113701	79803	43769	1405	34628	33898	41074	2602	38472	32015
Déboursements	10233	6496	2993	2652	199	142	3503	3737	300	3437	..
Service de la dette	33567	16091	9805	5694	283	3829	6286	17476	1061	16414	10049
dont : amortissement	25318	10475	6369	3997	222	2150	4105	14843	951	13893	7935
intérêts	8249	5616	3436	1697	61	1679	2180	2632	111	2521	2114
Transferts nets	-23334	-9595	-6813	-3042	-84	-3687	-2782	-13739	-761	-12978	..

For sources and notes, see end of table 6.6E.

Pour les sources et les notes, se reporter à la fin du tableau 6.6E.

Other developing economies / Autres économies en développement	Overall total [1] Total général [1]	Official sources / Sources publiques						Private sources / Sources privées			Non-guaranteed debt [9] Dette non garantie [9]
		Total [2]	Bilateral / Bilatérales				Multilateral [6] Multilatérales [6]	Total	Supplier credits [7] Crédits fournisseurs [7]	Financial markets [8] Marchés financiers [8]	
			Total [3]	DAC [4] CAD [4]	OPEC [5] OPEP [5]	Other Autres					
1980											
Debt outstanding											
(disbursed only)	265183	126968	84913	61694	12476	10743	42055	138215	15713	122502	52135
Disbursements	57703	21365	13306	9497	2305	1505	8059	36338	4285	32052	15079
Total debt service	37875	9344	5903	4385	762	756	3441	28531	3818	24714	13128
of which: amortization	19738	4953	3603	2598	447	557	1350	14785	2799	11986	7633
interest	18137	4391	2300	1786	315	199	2091	13746	1019	12727	5494
Net transfers	19828	12021	7403	5112	1542	748	4619	7806	468	7338	1952
1990											
Dette active											
(montants décaissés seulement)	728001	417540	248319	168486	16139	63694	169221	310462	21184	289278	41506
Déboursements	61504	36477	14856	12453	480	1923	21621	25026	2711	22316	11027
Service de la dette	67993	30281	12125	9553	993	1578	18156	37712	3030	34682	7761
dont : amortissement	37661	16743	6994	5347	764	884	9749	20918	2136	18782	4602
intérêts	30332	13538	5130	4206	229	695	8408	16794	894	15900	3159
Transferts nets	-6489	6196	2732	2900	-513	344	3465	-12686	-320	-12366	3266
1995											
Debt outstanding											
(disbursed only)	907634	544201	314694	239491	11474	63729	229507	363432	21199	342234	168418
Disbursements	105234	51865	27966	22369	319	5278	23899	53370	2762	50607	46024
Total debt service	108015	52381	25810	21895	821	3095	26571	55634	5105	50529	30378
of which: amortization	65406	32358	16184	13284	646	2254	16175	33048	3809	29238	20804
interest	42609	20023	9626	8611	175	841	10396	22586	1296	21290	9574
Net transfers	-2780	-516	2156	475	-502	2183	-2672	-2264	-2343	79	15646
1998											
Dette active											
(montants décaissés seulement)	948115	524852	271685	211048	11620	49017	253167	423263	15909	407354	359920
Déboursements	110381	46484	14968	13258	471	1239	31516	63897	2367	61531	91839
Service de la dette	117605	48202	25780	21415	654	3710	22423	69403	3805	65598	76971
dont : amortissement	73711	30638	17634	14921	534	2179	13005	43072	2766	40306	54570
intérêts	43895	17564	8146	6494	121	1531	9418	26331	1038	25292	22402
Transferts nets	-7224	-1718	-10812	-8157	-184	-2471	9093	-5506	-1438	-4068	14867
1999											
Debt outstanding											
(disbursed only)	959352	537136	272273	212527	11923	47822	264863	422216	20082	402134	393183
Disbursements	110939	45256	17103	13289	583	3231	28153	65683	3470	62213	88843
Total debt service	126587	51807	25580	20877	563	4140	26228	74780	3561	71219	111730
of which: amortization	81062	32844	17790	14501	447	2843	15054	48218	2687	45531	84543
interest	45525	18963	7789	6376	116	1297	11174	26562	873	25689	27186
Net transfers	-15648	-6551	-8477	-7588	20	-909	1926	-9097	-91	-9006	-22886
2000											
Dette active											
(montants décaissés seulement)	942120	507928	243152	196131	11482	35539	264776	434193	18960	415232	394083
Déboursements	122354	42438	14179	12368	241	1570	28258	79916	2836	77081	81788
Service de la dette	142577	55018	24756	21073	570	3113	30262	87559	4460	83099	111381
dont : amortissement	93883	36523	17873	15236	455	2182	18650	57360	3200	54160	85483
intérêts	48695	18496	6883	5837	115	931	11612	30199	1260	28939	25898
Transferts nets	-20223	-12581	-10577	-8704	-330	-1543	-2004	-7643	-1624	-6018	-29593
2001											
Debt outstanding											
(disbursed only)	931447	497306	226147	168265	10684	47199	271159	434140	17620	416520	365768
Disbursements	103965	43083	14310	10380	708	3223	28773	60881	2679	58202	77170
Total debt service	139238	45026	19326	15616	563	3147	25700	94212	5053	89159	108977
of which: amortization	89287	27464	13329	10798	451	2080	14135	61823	3898	57925	85175
interest	49951	17562	5997	4818	112	1067	11565	32389	1155	31234	23802
Net transfers	-35273	-1942	-5015	-5236	145	76	3073	-33331	-2373	-30957	-31807
2002											
Dette active											
(montants décaissés seulement)	873311	475475	203927	157429	5056	41443	271548	397836	12336	385500	292782
Déboursements	56086	38777	15269	13528	490	1251	23507	17309	820	16489	..
Service de la dette	133823	55727	23987	20379	755	2852	31740	78096	6194	71903	94796
dont : amortissement	87484	38720	17195	15254	617	1324	21525	48763	5257	43506	72967
intérêts	46339	17006	6792	5125	139	1528	10214	29333	937	28396	21829
Transferts nets	-77737	-16950	-8718	-6852	-265	-1601	-8232	-60787	-5373	-55414	..

For sources and notes, see end of table 6.6E.

Pour les sources et les notes, se reporter à la fin du tableau 6.6E.

Major exporters of manufactures / Principaux exportateurs d'articles manufacturés	Overall total [1] Total général [1]	Official sources / Sources publiques						Private sources / Sources privées			Non-guaranteed debt [9] Dette non garantie [9]
		Total [2]	Bilateral / Bilatérales				Multilateral [6] Multilatérales [6]	Total	Supplier credits [7] Crédits fournisseurs [7]	Financial markets [8] Marchés financiers [8]	
			Total [3]	DAC [4] CAD [4]	OPEC [5] OPEP [5]	Other Autres					
1980											
Debt outstanding											
(disbursed only)	143077	50783	30875	28304	1712	859	19908	92294	8069	84225	32484
Disbursements	31602	7990	4455	3937	331	187	3535	23612	2252	21360	8754
Total debt service	23337	4379	2549	2181	254	113	1831	18958	1989	16969	8773
of which: amortization	11740	2333	1650	1352	207	91	683	9407	1481	7926	5052
interest	11598	2047	899	829	47	23	1148	9551	508	9043	3721
Net transfers	8265	3610	1906	1756	77	73	1704	4655	264	4391	-19
1990											
Dette active											
(montants décaissés seulement)	367183	160746	85744	68772	1337	15635	75002	206437	10191	196246	25390
Déboursements	38239	18061	7572	6730	48	795	10488	20178	1894	18284	8160
Service de la dette	41702	15988	6242	5217	326	699	9746	25714	1820	23894	4775
dont : amortissement	22594	8842	3592	3066	260	266	5251	13751	1227	12524	2929
intérêts	19108	7145	2650	2151	66	433	4495	11963	594	11370	1846
Transferts nets	-3463	2073	1331	1513	-278	96	742	-5536	74	-5610	3386
1995											
Debt outstanding											
(disbursed only)	479916	217328	120676	100520	469	19688	96652	262588	14913	247675	117659
Disbursements	72507	31820	21532	16670	6	4856	10288	40687	2030	38657	35207
Total debt service	71550	27881	14722	12417	157	2148	13159	43669	3650	40018	22781
of which: amortization	43662	17413	9583	7916	120	1547	7830	26249	2625	23624	16107
interest	27887	10468	5139	4501	37	601	5329	17419	1025	16394	6674
Net transfers	957	3939	6809	4253	-151	2707	-2871	-2982	-1620	-1362	12426
1998											
Dette active											
(montants décaissés seulement)	495239	207290	100545	89922	516	10106	106745	287949	10836	277114	276928
Déboursements	69637	26702	10348	9682	80	585	16354	42935	1742	41192	71769
Service de la dette	76805	27228	15666	13091	75	2499	11562	49577	2664	46913	62090
dont : amortissement	49858	18198	11512	9960	62	1491	6686	31661	1843	29818	43926
intérêts	26947	9030	4154	3131	13	1009	4877	17917	822	17095	18164
Transferts nets	-7169	-526	-5318	-3409	5	-1914	4792	-6642	-922	-5720	9680
1999											
Debt outstanding											
(disbursed only)	501977	220830	110254	95833	684	13737	110576	281148	15682	265465	302771
Disbursements	66010	25496	13190	10171	307	2712	12306	40513	3086	37427	71181
Total debt service	84043	30313	16031	13139	163	2729	14283	53730	2667	51063	89423
of which: amortization	57085	20215	11813	9530	137	2146	8402	36870	2032	34838	67327
interest	26958	10098	4217	3609	26	583	5880	16860	635	16225	22096
Net transfers	-18033	-4817	-2840	-2968	144	-17	-1977	-13217	419	-13636	-18242
2000											
Dette active											
(montants décaissés seulement)	500644	209856	98607	88109	597	9901	111249	290788	15017	275771	299709
Déboursements	81915	25041	9685	8604	75	1006	15356	56874	2359	54515	65763
Service de la dette	94738	34050	16024	13950	154	1919	18026	60688	3451	57237	93214
dont : amortissement	65192	24000	12237	10593	121	1524	11763	41192	2380	38813	72879
intérêts	29546	10050	3787	3358	34	395	6264	19496	1071	18425	20334
Transferts nets	-12823	-9009	-6339	-5347	-79	-913	-2670	-3814	-1092	-2722	-27451
2001											
Debt outstanding											
(disbursed only)	494385	205088	90920	78747	326	11846	114168	289297	13765	275532	275596
Disbursements	63264	22989	10376	7620	47	2709	12613	40275	1695	38580	65958
Total debt service	91978	25271	11158	9117	118	1923	14113	66707	4003	62703	91779
of which: amortization	61806	15796	8124	6532	95	1498	7671	46011	3000	43010	72745
interest	30171	9476	3034	2585	23	425	6442	20696	1003	19693	19034
Net transfers	-28714	-2282	-782	-1497	-70	786	-1500	-26432	-2308	-24124	-25822
2002											
Dette active											
(montants décaissés seulement)	473731	206023	91255	78500	308	12447	114768	267707	9970	257738	216409
Déboursements	35469	20878	10749	9750	46	952	10129	14591	263	14328	..
Service de la dette	82497	28267	13565	12546	79	940	14702	54231	4731	49499	77007
dont : amortissement	55115	19796	10267	9871	65	330	9529	35319	3970	31349	59188
intérêts	27382	8471	3298	2675	14	609	5173	18911	761	18150	17820
Transferts nets	-47028	-7389	-2816	-2796	-33	12	-4573	-39639	-4468	-35171	..

For sources and notes, see end of table 6.6E.

Pour les sources et les notes, se reporter à la fin du tableau 6.6E.

6.6E External long-term debt of developing economies by source of lending
Millions of dollars

6.6E Dette extérieure à long terme des économies en développement, par catégorie de prêt
Millions de dollars

Remaining countries / Autres pays	Overall total [1] / Total général [1]	Official sources / Sources publiques						Private sources / Sources privées			Non-guaranteed debt [9] / Dette non garantie [9]
		Total [2]	Bilateral / Bilatérales				Multilateral [6] / Multilatérales [6]	Total	Supplier credits [7] / Crédits fournisseurs [7]	Financial markets [8] / Marchés financiers [8]	
			Total [3]	DAC [4] / CAD [4]	OPEC [5] / OPEP [5]	Other Autres					
1980											
Debt outstanding											
(disbursed only)	122106	76185	54037	33389	10764	9884	22147	45921	7645	38276	19650
Disbursements	26101	13376	8851	5560	1973	1318	4525	12725	2033	10692	6325
Total debt service	14538	4965	3355	2203	509	643	1610	9573	1829	7745	4355
of which: amortization	7999	2620	1953	1246	240	467	667	5378	1318	4060	2581
interest	6539	2344	1401	957	268	176	943	4195	511	3684	1773
Net transfers	11563	8411	5496	3357	1465	675	2915	3152	204	2948	1971
1990											
Dette active											
(montants décaissés seulement)	360819	256794	162575	99714	14802	48059	94219	104024	10992	93032	16116
Déboursements	23265	18417	7284	5724	433	1128	11133	4848	817	4032	2867
Service de la dette	26291	14293	5883	4337	667	879	8410	11998	1210	10787	2986
dont : amortissement	15067	7901	3403	2282	504	617	4498	7167	909	6257	1673
intérêts	11224	6393	2480	2055	163	262	3912	4831	301	4530	1313
Transferts nets	-3026	4123	1401	1387	-235	248	2723	-7150	-394	-6756	-119
1995											
Debt outstanding											
(disbursed only)	427718	326873	194018	138971	11005	44041	132855	100845	6286	94559	50759
Disbursements	32728	20045	6434	5699	312	422	13611	12683	733	11951	10817
Total debt service	36465	24500	11088	9478	663	946	13412	11965	1455	10510	7597
of which: amortization	21743	14945	6600	5368	526	707	8345	6798	1184	5614	4697
interest	14722	9555	4487	4110	138	239	5068	5167	271	4896	2899
Net transfers	-3737	-4455	-4654	-3778	-351	-524	199	718	-722	1440	3220
1998											
Dette active											
(montants décaissés seulement)	452875	317562	171140	121126	11104	38910	146422	135314	5073	130241	82991
Déboursements	40744	19782	4621	3576	391	654	15161	20962	624	20338	20069
Service de la dette	40800	20974	10114	8324	579	1211	10860	19826	1140	18686	14882
dont : amortissement	23852	12441	6122	4961	472	688	6319	11412	924	10488	10644
intérêts	16948	8534	3993	3363	107	522	4541	8414	217	8197	4238
Transferts nets	-56	-1192	-5494	-4748	-189	-557	4301	1137	-516	1652	5187
1999											
Debt outstanding											
(disbursed only)	457374	316306	162019	116695	11239	34085	154287	141068	4400	136668	90412
Disbursements	44929	19759	3912	3118	276	519	15847	25170	384	24786	17662
Total debt service	42544	21494	9549	7738	400	1411	11945	21050	894	20156	22306
of which: amortization	23977	12629	5977	4971	310	696	6652	11348	656	10692	17216
interest	18567	8865	3572	2767	90	715	5293	9702	238	9463	5090
Net transfers	2385	-1735	-5637	-4620	-124	-892	3902	4120	-510	4630	-4644
2000											
Dette active											
(montants décaissés seulement)	441476	298071	144545	108021	10885	25638	153527	143405	3943	139462	94374
Déboursements	40439	17397	4494	3765	165	564	12902	23042	477	22566	16025
Service de la dette	47839	20968	8732	7122	416	1194	12236	26871	1009	25862	18167
dont : amortissement	28690	12523	5636	4643	335	658	6887	16167	820	15347	12604
intérêts	19149	8445	3097	2479	81	536	5349	10704	189	10515	5564
Transferts nets	-7400	-3572	-4238	-3358	-250	-630	666	-3829	-532	-3296	-2142
2001											
Debt outstanding											
(disbursed only)	437062	292218	135228	89518	10357	35352	156991	144843	3855	140989	90171
Disbursements	40700	20094	3934	2760	660	514	16160	20607	984	19622	11212
Total debt service	47260	19754	8168	6498	445	1224	11587	27505	1050	26456	17198
of which: amortization	27481	11669	5205	4266	356	582	6464	15812	897	14915	12430
interest	19779	8086	2963	2232	89	642	5123	11694	153	11541	4768
Net transfers	-6559	340	-4234	-3739	215	-710	4573	-6899	-66	-6833	-5985
2002											
Dette active											
(montants décaissés seulement)	399581	269452	112672	78929	4748	28995	156779	130129	2367	127763	76374
Déboursements	20617	17899	4521	3777	444	299	13378	2718	557	2161	..
Service de la dette	51325	27460	10422	7833	676	1913	17038	23865	1462	22403	17789
dont : amortissement	32368	18924	6928	5383	552	994	11996	13444	1287	12157	13779
intérêts	18957	8536	3494	2450	125	919	5042	10421	176	10246	4010
Transferts nets	-30709	-9561	-5901	-4056	-232	-1613	-3660	-21148	-905	-20242	..

For sources and notes, see next page.

Pour les sources et les notes, se reporter à la page suivante.

Sources: World Bank, *Global Development Finance 2002* (GDF2002).

Notes:

External debt data in this table are based on the Debtor Reporting System (DRS) maintained by the World Bank.

Long-term external debt is defined as debt that has an original or extended maturity of more than one year, is owed to non-residents and is repayable in foreign currency, goods or services. It is composed of public, publicly guaranteed and private non-guaranteed debt.

These series do not include data for the Republic of Korea as it was not covered in the *Global Development Finance 2002* publication. For more details, please consult the GDF2002.

1   Covers public and publicly guaranteed debt from official and private sources.

Public debt is an external obligation of a public debtor, whether it is a national government or a political subdivision (or an agency of either), or an autonomous public body.

Publicly guaranteed debt is an external obligation of a private debtor that is guaranteed for repayment by a public entity.

2   Loans from the official sector are at concessional and non-concessional terms. For definition refer to table 6.5.

3   This item covers loans from governments and their agencies (including central banks), loans from autonomous bodies and direct loans from official export credit agencies.

4   For definition refer to table 6.5.

5   For definition refer to table 6.5.

6   Includes loans and credits from the World Bank, regional development banks, and other multilateral and intergovernmental agencies. It does not include loans from funds administered by an international organization on behalf of a single donor government; this category is included in bilateral loans (from governments).

7   Includes credits from manufacturers, exporters and other suppliers of goods.

8   Loans from the financial market sector cover publicly issued or privately placed bonds, loans from private banks and other financial institutions.

9   Non-guaranteed private debt is an external obligation of a private debtor that is not guaranteed for repayment by a public entity.

Sources :   Banque mondiale, *Global Development Finance 2002* (GDF2002).

Notes :

Les données de la dette extérieure présentées dans ce tableau se basent sur le Système de notification des pays débiteurs (SNPD), géré par la Banque mondiale.

La dette extérieure à long terme a une durée de remboursement (d'origine ou différée) supérieure à une année, et son amortissement est dû en monnaies convertibles ou en nature, à des créanciers non résidents. Elle se compose de la dette publique, la dette garantie et celle non garantie du secteur privé.

Ces séries chronologiques n'incluent pas les données de la République de Corée parce que le rapport *Global Development Finance 2002* ne couvre pas ce pays. Pour plus d'informations, veuillez consulter le GDF2002.

1   Couvre la dette publique et la dette garantie par le secteur public, en provenance des sources publiques et privées.

La dette publique concerne un débiteur du secteur public, y compris un gouvernement, une entité politique (ou leurs agents d'exécution), ou d'autres organismes publics autonomes.

La dette garantie par le secteur public concerne un débiteur du secteur privé, dont l'amortissement de la dette est garanti par une entité publique.

2   Les prêts du secteur public sont assortis de conditions libérales et non libérales. Pour la définition, se reporter au tableau 6.5.

3   Cette rubrique comprend les prêts accordés par des gouvernements et des organismes publics (y compris les banques centrales), les prêts en provenance d'entités autonomes et les prêts octroyés directement par des organismes publics dans la catégorie de crédits à l'exportation.

4   Pour la définition, se reporter au tableau 6.5.

5   Pour la définition, se reporter au tableau 6.5.

6   Sont compris les prêts des sources multilatérales telles que la Banque mondiale, les banques régionales de développement, et autres organismes multilatéraux et intergouvernementaux. Ne sont pas compris les prêts provenant des fonds d'un gouvernement, administrés par une organisation internationale; cette catégorie est incluse dans la rubrique des sources bilatérales (des gouvernements).

7   Les crédits fournisseurs comprennent les crédits du secteur manufacturier, du secteur des exportations et ceux du secteur des crédits accordés par d'autres fournisseurs de biens.

8   Les prêts du secteur des marchés financiers recouvrent les émissions publiques ou privées des obligations et les prêts consentis par des banques privées et autres entités financières.

9   La dette du secteur privé non garantie concerne un débiteur du secteur privé, dont l'amortissement de la dette n'est pas garanti par une entité publique.

PART SEVEN

Indicators of development

SEPTIEME PARTIE

Indicateurs du développement

1

2

3

4

5

6

7

8

Region, economic grouping, country or area	Population [1] Total 2003 Thousands Milliers	Annual average growth rate Taux d'accroissement annuel moyen 1980-90 Percentage En pourcentage	1990-03	Area [2] Superficie [2] km²	Density Densité 2003 Inhabitants per km² Habitants par km²	Gross domestic product [3] Produit intérieur brut [3] 2003 Total Millions of dollars Millions de dollars	Per capita Par habitant Dollars	Régions, groupements économiques, pays ou zones
WORLD	**6301463**	**1.7**	**1.4**	**136026238**	**46**	**36214885**	**5747**	**MONDE**
DEVELOPED ECONOMIES	**949887**	**0.6**	**0.6**	**32473975**	**29**	**28291096**	**29784**	**ECONOMIES DEVELOPPEES**
DEVELOPING ECONOMIES	**5016745**	**2.1**	**1.7**	**80828540**	**62**	**7212862**	**1438**	**ECONOMIES EN DEVELOPPEMENT**
SOUTH-EAST EUROPE AND CIS	**334831**	**0.9**	**-0.1**	**22723723**	**15**	**710927**	**2123**	**EUROPE DU SUD-EST ET CEI**
DEVELOPED ECONOMIES: AMERICA	**325553**	**1.0**	**1.1**	**19599701**	**17**	**11711032**	**35973**	**ECONOMIES DEVELOPPEES : AMERIQUE**
Canada	31510	1.2	1.0	9970610	3	853832	27097	Canada
United States	294043	1.0	1.1	9629091	31	10857200	36924	Etats-Unis
DEVELOPED ECONOMIES: EUROPE	**466640**	**0.3**	**0.3**	**4462546**	**105**	**11548147**	**24747**	**ECONOMIES DEVELOPPEES : EUROPE**
EU 25	**454188**	**0.3**	**0.3**	**3991523**	**114**	**10999314**	**24218**	**UE 25**
EU 15	*379831*	*0.3*	*0.3*	*3242646*	*117*	*10505553*	*27659*	*UE 15*
Austria	8116	0.2	0.4	83859	97	253116	31187	Autriche
Belgium	10318	0.1	0.3	30528	338	301885	29257	Belgique
Denmark	5364	0.0	0.3	43094	124	211855	39497	Danemark
Finland	5207	0.4	0.3	338145	15	161769	31069	Finlande
France [4]	60144	0.5	0.4	551500	109	1757551	29222	France [4]
Germany	82476	0.1	0.3	357022	231	2403068	29137	Allemagne
Greece	10976	0.5	0.7	131957	83	172221	15690	Grèce
Ireland	3956	0.3	1.0	70273	56	153729	38864	Irlande
Italy	57423	0.0	0.1	301318	191	1465835	25527	Italie
Luxembourg	453	0.3	1.4	2586	175	26001	57379	Luxembourg
Netherlands	16149	0.5	0.6	41526	389	512882	31759	Pays-Bas
Portugal	10062	0.1	0.1	91982	109	147352	14645	Portugal
Spain	41060	0.4	0.4	505992	81	838620	20424	Espagne
Sweden	8876	0.3	0.2	449964	20	301129	33925	Suède
United Kingdom	59251	0.2	0.3	242900	244	1798540	30355	Royaume-Uni
New EU members 10	*74357*	*0.5*	*-0.1*	*748877*	*99*	*493761*	*6640*	*Nouveaux membres de l'UE 10*
Cyprus	802	1.1	1.3	9251	87	12861	16038	Chypre
Czech Republic	10236	0.0	-0.1	78866	130	90425	8834	République tchèque
Estonia	1323	0.8	-1.4	45100	29	8246	6232	Estonie
Hungary	9877	-0.3	-0.4	93032	106	82806	8384	Hongrie
Latvia	2307	0.9	-1.3	64600	36	10276	4453	Lettonie
Lithuania	3444	1.0	-0.6	65200	53	17918	5203	Lituanie
Malta	394	1.0	0.7	316	1248	4648	11789	Malte
Poland	38587	0.7	0.1	323250	119	206619	5355	Pologne
Slovakia	5402	0.5	0.2	49012	110	32519	6019	Slovaquie
Slovenia	1984	0.4	0.2	20250	98	27443	13831	Slovénie
Other developed Europe	**12453**	**0.7**	**0.4**	**471023**	**26**	**548833**	**44074**	**Autres économies développées d'Europe**
Andorra	71	4.6	2.0	468	152	1454	20423	Andorre
Channel Islands	145	1.0	0.1	195	743	..	..	Iles Anglo-Normandes
Faeroe Islands	47	1.1	0.0	1399	33	..	..	Iles Féroé
Gibraltar	27	0.1	0.2	6	4542	..	..	Gibraltar
Holy See	1	0.5	0.1	..	..	20	25478	Saint-Siège
Iceland	290	1.1	1.0	103000	3	10520	36329	Islande
Isle of Man	75	0.7	0.6	572	131	..	..	Ile de Man
Liechtenstein	34	1.4	1.2	160	210	1459	43485	Liechtenstein

For sources and notes, see end of table.

Pour les sources et les notes, se reporter à la fin du tableau.

Region, economic grouping, country or area	Population [1] Total 2003 Thousands Milliers	Population [1] Annual average growth rate Taux d'accroissement annuel moyen 1980-90 Percentage En pourcentage	Population [1] Annual average growth rate Taux d'accroissement annuel moyen 1990-03 Percentage En pourcentage	Area [2] Superficie [2] km²	Density Densité 2003 Inhabitants per km² Habitants par km²	Gross domestic product [3] Produit intérieur brut [3] 2003 Total Millions of dollars Millions de dollars	Gross domestic product [3] Produit intérieur brut [3] 2003 Per capita Par habitant Dollars	Régions, groupements économiques, pays ou zones
Monaco	34	1.2	1.1	1	34404	1005	29212	Monaco
Norway	4533	0.4	0.5	323877	14	221578	48880	Norvège
San Marino	28	0.7	1.4	61	452	1060	38407	Saint-Marin
Switzerland	7169	0.8	0.3	41284	174	311737	43486	Suisse
DEVELOPED ECONOMIES: ASIA	**134087**	**0.6**	**0.4**	**399974**	**335**	**4433580**	**33065**	**ECONOMIES DEVELOPPEES : ASIE**
Israel	6433	1.8	2.8	22145	291	116449	18101	Israël
Japan	127654	0.6	0.3	377829	338	4317131	33819	Japon
DEVELOPED ECONOMIES: OCEANIA	**23606**	**1.4**	**1.2**	**8011754**	**3**	**598337**	**25347**	**ECONOMIES DEVELOPPEES : OCEANIE**
Australia	19731	1.5	1.2	7741220	3	523349	26525	Australie
New Zealand	3875	0.8	1.1	270534	14	74988	19350	Nouvelle-Zélande
DEVELOPING ECONOMIES: AMERICA	**543390**	**2.0**	**1.6**	**22754693**	**24**	**1834720**	**3376**	**ECONOMIES EN DEVELOPPEMENT : AMERIQUE**
South America	*362278*	*2.0*	*1.6*	*17864926*	*20*	*953625*	*2632*	*Amérique du Sud*
Argentina	38428	1.5	1.3	2780400	14	129707	3375	Argentine
Bolivia	8808	2.2	2.2	1098581	8	7738	878	Bolivie
Brazil	178470	2.0	1.4	8547403	21	481866	2700	Brésil
Chile	15806	1.6	1.5	756626	21	71495	4523	Chili
Colombia	44222	2.1	1.8	1138914	39	77117	1744	Colombie
Ecuador	13003	2.6	1.8	283561	46	27411	2108	Equateur
Falkland Islands (Malvinas)	3	0.8	3.6	12173	0	..	..	Iles Falkland (Malvinas)
French Guiana	178	5.6	3.4	90000	2	..	..	Guyane française
Guyana	765	-0.5	0.4	214969	4	773	1010	Guyana
Paraguay	5878	3.1	2.6	406752	14	5887	1002	Paraguay
Peru	27167	2.3	1.7	1285216	21	60795	2238	Pérou
Suriname	436	1.3	0.6	163265	3	975	2239	Suriname
Uruguay	3415	0.6	0.7	175016	20	11183	3274	Uruguay
Venezuela	25699	2.6	2.1	912050	28	76951	2994	Venezuela
Other America	*181112*	*2.0*	*1.7*	*4889767*	*37*	*881095*	*4865*	*Autres économies : Amérique*
Anguilla	12	2.5	2.1	96	123	117	9877	Anguilla
Antigua and Barbuda	73	-0.1	1.2	442	165	660	9040	Antigua-et-Barbuda
Aruba	100	0.8	3.4	193	516	2000	20100	Aruba
Bahamas	314	1.9	1.6	13878	23	4539	14463	Bahamas
Barbados	270	0.3	0.4	430	629	2668	9868	Barbade
Belize	256	2.6	2.5	22696	11	861	3364	Belize
Bermuda	82	0.9	0.7	53	1539	4242	51990	Bermudes
British Virgin Islands	21	4.1	1.4	151	139	974	46567	Iles Vierges britanniques
Cayman Islands	40	4.1	3.5	264	153	1615	40018	Iles Caïmanes
Costa Rica	4173	2.7	2.4	51100	82	17482	4189	Costa Rica
Cuba	11300	0.9	0.5	110861	102	31216	2762	Cuba
Dominica	79	-0.4	0.7	751	105	258	3282	Dominique
Dominican Republic	8745	2.2	1.7	48511	180	21059	2408	République dominicaine
El Salvador	6515	1.0	1.9	21041	310	14996	2302	El Salvador
Greenland	57	1.1	0.1	2175600	0	..	..	Groenland
Grenada	80	-0.4	-0.5	344	233	342	4258	Grenade
Guadeloupe	440	1.9	0.9	1705	258	..	..	Guadeloupe
Guatemala	12347	2.5	2.7	108889	113	24239	1963	Guatemala
Haiti	8326	2.4	1.4	27750	300	2499	300	Haïti
Honduras	6941	3.2	2.8	112088	62	6799	980	Honduras
Jamaica	2651	1.1	0.9	10990	241	7427	2802	Jamaïque
Martinique	393	1.1	0.7	1102	356	..	..	Martinique
Mexico	103457	2.1	1.7	1958201	53	615051	5945	Mexique
Montserrat	4	-1.1	-10.6	102	34	37	10556	Montserrat

For sources and notes, see end of table.

Pour les sources et les notes, se reporter à la fin du tableau.

Region, economic grouping, country or area	Population¹ Total 2003 — Thousands / Milliers	Annual average growth rate / Taux d'accroissement annuel moyen 1980-90 — Percentage / En pourcentage	Annual average growth rate / Taux d'accroissement annuel moyen 1990-03 — Percentage / En pourcentage	Area² Superficie² 2003 — km²	Density / Densité 2003 — Inhabitants per km² / Habitants par km²	Gross domestic product³ / Produit intérieur brut³ 2003 Total — Millions of dollars / Millions de dollars	Per capita / Par habitant — Dollars	Régions, groupements économiques, pays ou zones
Netherlands Antilles	221	0.7	1.2	800	276	2928	13260	Antilles néerlandaises
Nicaragua	5466	2.7	2.8	130000	42	4100	750	Nicaragua
Panama	3120	2.1	2.0	75517	41	10608	3400	Panama
Puerto Rico	3879	1.0	0.7	8875	437	80731	20812	Porto Rico
Saint Kitts and Nevis	42	-0.9	0.1	261	160	373	8933	Saint-Kitts-et-Nevis
Saint Lucia	149	1.6	0.9	539	277	688	4612	Sainte-Lucie
Saint Pierre and Miquelon	6	0.5	0.1	242	26	..	..	Saint-Pierre-et-Miquelon
Saint Vincent and the Grenadines	120	0.9	0.6	388	309	376	3137	Saint-Vincent-et-les Grenadines
Trinidad and Tobago	1303	1.2	0.5	5130	254	9910	7607	Trinité-et-Tobago
Turks and Caicos Islands	21	5.1	4.1	430	48	225	10923	Iles Turques et Caïques
United States Virgin Islands	111	0.3	0.7	347	321	..	..	Iles Vierges américaines
DEVELOPING ECONOMIES: AFRICA	**850558**	**2.9**	**2.4**	**30250107**	**28**	**645195**	**759**	**ECONOMIES EN DEVELOPPEMENT : AFRIQUE**
North Africa⁵	*183598*	*2.6*	*1.9*	*8524703*	*22*	*247103*	*1346*	*Afrique du Nord⁵*
Algeria	31800	2.9	1.8	2381741	13	65172	2049	Algérie
Egypt	71931	2.4	2.0	1001449	72	76399	1062	Egypte
Libyan Arab Jamahiriya	5551	3.5	2.0	1759540	3	20207	3640	Jamahiriya arabe libyenne
Morocco	30566	2.4	1.7	446550	68	44704	1463	Maroc
Sudan	33610	2.5	2.3	2505813	13	15438	459	Soudan
Tunisia	9832	2.4	1.4	163610	60	25183	2561	Tunisie
Other Africa	*666960*	*3.0*	*2.6*	*21725404*	*31*	*398092*	*597*	*Autres économies : Afrique*
Angola	13625	2.8	2.9	1246700	11	9874	725	Angola
Benin	6736	3.0	2.8	112622	60	3510	521	Bénin
Botswana	1785	3.2	2.2	581730	3	7111	3984	Botswana
Burkina Faso	13002	2.7	2.9	274000	47	3821	294	Burkina Faso
Burundi	6825	3.2	1.2	27834	245	590	86	Burundi
Cameroon	16018	2.9	2.5	475442	34	12859	803	Cameroun
Cape Verde	463	1.9	2.2	4033	115	818	1766	Cap-Vert
Central African Republic	3865	2.5	2.2	622984	6	1257	325	République centrafricaine
Chad	8598	2.6	3.1	1284000	7	2495	290	Tchad
Comoros	768	3.1	3.0	2235	344	284	370	Comores
Congo	3724	3.3	3.2	342000	11	3908	1050	Congo
Côte d'Ivoire	16631	4.0	2.2	322463	52	14742	886	Côte d'Ivoire
Dem. Rep. of the Congo	52771	2.9	2.5	2344858	23	5669	107	Rép. dém. du Congo
Djibouti	703	5.1	2.4	23200	30	622	885	Djibouti
Equatorial Guinea	494	5.0	2.6	28051	18	2923	5915	Guinée équatoriale
Eritrea	4141	2.8	2.3	117600	35	1262	305	Erythrée
Ethiopia	70678	3.2	2.9	1104300	64	6436	91	Ethiopie
Gabon	1329	3.2	2.6	267668	5	5521	4155	Gabon
Gambia	1426	3.7	3.3	11295	126	319	224	Gambie
Ghana	20922	3.3	2.4	238533	88	7414	354	Ghana
Guinea	8480	2.6	2.5	245857	34	3598	424	Guinée
Guinea-Bissau	1493	2.4	3.0	36125	41	311	208	Guinée-Bissau
Kenya	31987	3.7	2.4	580367	55	14197	444	Kenya
Lesotho	1802	2.1	1.1	30355	59	1070	594	Lesotho
Liberia	3367	1.4	4.2	111369	30	608	181	Libéria
Madagascar	17404	2.8	2.9	587041	30	5535	318	Madagascar
Malawi	12105	4.6	2.0	118484	102	1912	158	Malawi
Mali	13007	2.5	2.8	1240192	10	3874	298	Mali
Mauritania	2893	2.3	2.2	1025520	3	1102	381	Mauritanie
Mauritius	1221	0.9	1.1	2040	599	5610	4593	Maurice
Mozambique	18863	0.9	2.7	801590	24	4196	222	Mozambique
Namibia	1987	3.4	2.8	824292	2	4585	2307	Namibie
Niger	11972	3.2	3.5	1267000	9	2723	227	Niger
Nigeria	124009	2.9	2.9	923768	134	48422	390	Nigéria
Reunion	756	1.8	1.8	2510	301	..	..	Réunion
Rwanda	8387	3.1	2.8	26338	318	1549	185	Rwanda

For sources and notes, see end of table.

Pour les sources et les notes, se reporter à la fin du tableau.

Region, economic grouping, country or area	Population[1] Total 2003 Thousands Milliers	Annual average growth rate Taux d'accroissement annuel moyen 1980-90 Percentage En pourcentage	1990-03	Area[2] Superficie[2] km²	Density Densité 2003 Inhabitants per km² Habitants par km²	Gross domestic product[3] Produit intérieur brut[3] 2003 Total Millions of dollars Millions de dollars	Per capita Par habitant Dollars	Régions, groupements économiques, pays ou zones
Saint Helena	5	0.3	-0.8	122	41	..	..	Sainte-Hélène
Sao Tome and Principe	161	2.0	2.6	964	167	58	361	Sao Tomé-et-Principe
Senegal	10095	2.9	2.5	196722	51	6475	641	Sénégal
Seychelles	81	1.0	1.0	455	178	714	8814	Seychelles
Sierra Leone	4971	2.4	1.4	71740	69	979	197	Sierra Leone
Somalia	9890	0.8	2.6	637657	16	1537	155	Somalie
South Africa	45026	2.4	1.6	1221037	37	159886	3551	Afrique du Sud
Swaziland	1077	3.7	1.9	17364	62	1781	1653	Swaziland
Togo	4909	3.3	2.9	56785	86	1850	377	Togo
Uganda	25827	3.4	3.1	241038	107	6249	242	Ouganda
United Republic of Tanzania	36977	3.3	2.7	883749	42	10024	271	République-Unie de Tanzanie
Zambia	10812	3.2	2.2	752618	14	4305	398	Zambie
Zimbabwe	12891	3.8	1.6	390757	33	2456	191	Zimbabwe
DEVELOPING ECONOMIES: ASIA	3614169	1.9	1.5	27271445	133	4717367	1305	**ECONOMIES EN DEVELOPPEMENT : ASIE**
West Asia	*249831*	*3.3*	*2.2*	*6252684*	*40*	*829304*	*3319*	*Asie occidentale*
Bahrain	724	3.5	3.1	694	1044	9085	12543	Bahreïn
Iran, Islamic Republic of	68920	3.8	1.5	1648195	42	143273	2079	Iran, Rép. islamique d'
Iraq	25175	2.9	2.9	438317	57	14952	594	Iraq
Jordan	5473	3.8	4.0	89342	61	9865	1803	Jordanie
Kuwait	2521	4.9	1.8	17818	142	34395	13641	Koweït
Lebanon	3653	0.1	2.3	10400	351	18346	5023	Liban
Oman	2851	4.5	3.4	309500	9	21064	7388	Oman
Palestinian territory	3557	3.9	3.9	6165	577	3455	971	Territoire palestinien
Qatar	610	7.5	2.1	11000	55	21161	34684	Qatar
Saudi Arabia	24217	5.7	3.0	2149690	11	207318	8561	Arabie saoudite
Syrian Arab Republic	17800	3.6	2.6	185180	96	26647	1497	République arabe syrienne
Turkey	71325	2.3	1.7	774815	92	243783	3418	Turquie
United Arab Emirates	2995	7.1	2.9	83600	36	66274	22130	Emirats arabes unis
Yemen	20010	3.9	4.0	527968	38	9686	484	Yémen
Other Asia	*3364338*	*1.9*	*1.5*	*21018761*	*160*	*3888063*	*1156*	*Autres économies : Asie*
Afghanistan	23897	-1.3	3.9	652090	37	3991	167	Afghanistan
Bangladesh	146736	2.6	2.3	143998	1019	56475	385	Bangladesh
Bhutan	2257	2.6	2.2	47000	48	684	303	Bhoutan
Brunei Darussalam	358	2.9	2.6	5765	62	4626	12920	Brunéi Darussalam
Cambodia	14144	4.1	2.9	181035	78	3927	278	Cambodge
China	1281591	1.5	0.9	9560961	134	1409848	1100	Chine
China, Hong Kong SAR	7049	1.2	1.8	1075	6558	159445	22618	Chine, Hong Kong RAS
China, Macao SAR	464	4.2	1.7	18	25775	7890	17006	Chine, Macao RAS
China, Taiwan Province of	22605	1.4	0.8	36000	628	286373	12669	Chine, Taiwan Province de
India	1065462	2.1	1.8	3287263	324	591455	555	Inde
Indonesia	219883	2.0	1.5	1904569	115	207530	944	Indonésie
Korea, Dem. People's Republic of	22664	1.5	1.0	120538	188	11207	494	Corée, Rép. populaire dém. de
Korea, Republic of	47700	1.2	0.8	99268	481	527508	11059	Corée, République de
Lao People's Dem. Rep.	5657	2.6	2.4	236800	24	2043	361	Rép. dém. populaire lao
Malaysia	24425	2.6	2.5	329758	74	103247	4227	Malaisie
Maldives	318	3.2	3.0	298	1068	719	2259	Maldives
Mongolia	2594	3.0	1.1	1566500	2	1197	461	Mongolie
Myanmar	49485	1.8	1.6	676578	73	58072	1174	Myanmar
Nepal	25164	2.3	2.3	147181	171	5860	233	Népal
Pakistan	153578	3.3	2.6	796095	193	76534	498	Pakistan
Philippines	79999	2.4	2.1	300000	267	80420	1005	Philippines
Singapore	4253	2.3	2.8	683	6227	90141	21195	Singapour
Sri Lanka	19065	1.5	0.9	65610	291	17400	913	Sri Lanka
Thailand	62833	1.6	1.1	513115	122	142832	2273	Thaïlande
Timor-Leste	778	2.6	-0.7	14874	52	338	434	Timor-Leste
Viet Nam	81377	2.2	1.6	331689	245	38301	471	Viet Nam

For sources and notes, see end of table.

Pour les sources et les notes, se reporter à la fin du tableau.

Region, economic grouping, country or area	Population[1]			Area[2]	Density	Gross domestic product[3]		Régions, groupements économiques, pays ou zones
	Total 2003	Annual average growth rate / Taux d'accroissement annuel moyen		Superficie[2]	Densité 2003	Produit intérieur brut[3] 2003		
		1980-90	1990-03			Total	Per capita / Par habitant	
	Thousands / Milliers	Percentage / En pourcentage		km²	Inhabitants per km² / Habitants par km²	Millions of dollars / Millions de dollars	Dollars	
DEVELOPING ECONOMIES: OCEANIA	**8628**	**2.3**	**2.3**	**552295**	**16**	**15580**	**1806**	**ECONOMIES EN DEVELOPPEMENT : OCEANIE**
American Samoa	62	3.8	2.1	199	311	..	..	Samoa américaines
Cook Islands	18	0.3	-0.1	236	78	135	7352	Iles Cook
Fiji	839	1.3	1.2	18274	46	2316	2761	Fidji
French Polynesia	244	2.6	1.7	4000	61	4379	17919	Polynésie française
Guam	163	2.3	1.5	549	297	..	..	Guam
Kiribati	88	2.2	1.6	726	121	69	786	Kiribati
Marshall Islands	53	3.9	1.3	181	293	112	2114	Iles Marshall
Micronesia, Federated States of	109	2.8	0.8	702	156	249	2277	Micronésie, Etats fédérés de
Nauru	13	2.4	2.5	21	622	45	3445	Nauru
New Caledonia	228	1.8	2.3	18575	12	3826	16751	Nouvelle-Calédonie
Niue	2	-3.9	-1.3	260	7	..	..	Nioué
Northern Mariana Islands	79	10.3	4.6	464	171	..	..	Iles Mariannes du Nord
Palau	21	2.4	2.3	459	45	127	6197	Palaos
Papua New Guinea	5711	2.4	2.6	462840	12	3295	577	Papouasie-Nouvelle-Guinée
Samoa	178	0.3	0.8	2831	63	322	1809	Samoa
Solomon Islands	477	3.4	3.2	28896	17	271	568	Iles Salomon
Tokelau	2	0.4	-0.3	12	127	..	..	Tokélaou
Tonga	104	0.2	0.3	650	159	168	1621	Tonga
Tuvalu	11	1.6	1.4	26	408	24	2265	Tuvalu
Vanuatu	212	2.4	2.7	12189	17	242	1142	Vanuatu
Wallis and Futuna Islands	15	2.2	0.5	200	74	..	..	Iles Wallis et Futuna
SOUTH-EAST EUROPE AND CIS	**334831**	**0.9**	**-0.1**	**22723723**	**15**	**710927**	**2123**	**EUROPE DU SUD-EST ET CEI**
South-East Europe	*54569*	*0.6*	*-0.2*	*613672*	*89*	*142031*	*2603*	*Europe du Sud-Est*
Albania	3166	2.2	-0.4	28748	110	6065	1916	Albanie
Bosnia and Herzegovina	4161	1.2	0.2	51197	81	6714	1613	Bosnie-Herzégovine
Bulgaria	7897	-0.2	-0.8	110912	71	20000	2533	Bulgarie
Croatia	4428	1.1	-0.7	56538	78	28329	6398	Croatie
Macedonia, TFYR	2056	0.6	0.6	25713	80	4575	2225	Macédoine, LERY
Romania	22334	0.5	-0.3	238391	94	56951	2550	Roumanie
Serbia and Montenegro	10527	0.6	0.2	102173	103	19397	1843	Serbie-et-Monténégro
CIS	*280263*	*0.9*	*-0.1*	*22110051*	*13*	*568896*	*2030*	*CEI*
Armenia	3061	1.4	-1.3	29800	103	2769	905	Arménie
Azerbaijan	8370	1.6	1.1	86600	97	7138	853	Azerbaïdjan
Belarus	9895	0.6	-0.3	207600	48	17496	1768	Bélarus
Georgia	5126	0.8	-0.5	69700	74	3945	770	Géorgie
Kazakhstan	15433	1.3	-0.8	2724900	6	27554	1785	Kazakhstan
Kyrgyzstan	5138	2.0	1.2	199900	26	1911	372	Kirghizistan
Moldova, Republic of	4267	0.9	-0.2	33851	126	1957	459	Moldova, République de
Russian Federation	143246	0.7	-0.3	17075400	8	433490	3026	Fédération de Russie
Tajikistan	6245	3.0	1.2	143100	44	1554	249	Tadjikistan
Turkmenistan	4867	2.5	2.2	488100	10	14978	3078	Turkménistan
Ukraine	48523	0.4	-0.6	603700	80	47289	975	Ukraine
Uzbekistan	26093	2.6	1.9	447400	58	8815	338	Ouzbékistan

For sources and notes, see end of table.

Pour les sources et les notes, se reporter à la fin du tableau.

Region, economic grouping, country or area	Population [1]			Area [2] Superficie [2]	Density Densité	Gross domestic product [3] Produit intérieur brut [3]		Régions, groupements économiques, pays ou zones
	Total 2003	Annual average growth rate Taux d'accroissement annuel moyen		2003	2003	2003		
		1980-90	1990-03			Total	Per capita Par habitant	
	Thousands Milliers	Percentage En pourcentage		km[2]	Inhabitants per km[2] Habitants par km[2]	Millions of dollars Millions de dollars	Dollars	
DEVELOPING ECONOMIES	**5016745**	**2.1**	**1.7**	**80828540**	**62**	**7212862**	**1438**	**ECONOMIES EN DEVELOPPEMENT**
By major category								*Par catégories principales*
Major petroleum exporters	593323	2.8	2.1	15121693	39	1008904	1700	Principaux pays exportateurs de pétrole
Other developing economies	4423422	2.0	1.6	65706847	67	6203958	1403	Autres économies en développement
Major exporters of manufactures	2949170	1.8	1.4	25408542	116	4731969	1605	Principaux pays exportateurs d'articles manufacturés
Remaining economies	1474252	2.5	2.2	40298305	37	1471989	998	Autres économies
America	234241	1.9	1.7	11331109	21	648014	2766	Amérique
Africa	670521	2.8	2.4	23328690	29	492091	734	Afrique
West Asia	12683	2.4	3.5	105907	120	31666	2497	Asie occidentale
Other Asia	548179	2.4	2.1	4980304	110	284638	519	Autres pays d'Asie
By income group (per capita GDP in 2000)								*Par catégories de revenus (PIB par habitant en 2000)*
High-income countries	321787	2.0	1.6	13407712	24	2524168	7844	Pays à revenu élevé
Middle-income countries	781322	2.4	1.7	24162578	32	1867438	2390	Pays à revenu intermédiaire
Low-income countries	3913636	2.0	1.7	43258250	90	2821256	721	Pays à revenu faible
MEMO ITEM:								**POUR MEMOIRE :**
LDC	718858	2.6	2.5	20740909	35	258495	360	PMA
HIPC	681308	2.8	2.4	23124908	29	287210	422	PPTE
Land-locked countries	352418	2.5	2.2	16313262	22	146280	415	Pays enclavés
Developing economies excluding China	3735154	2.3	1.9	71267579	52	5803014	1554	Economies en développement Chine non comprise
Sub-Saharan Africa	700569	2.9	2.6	24231217	29	413530	590	Afrique subsaharienne

Sources: UN/DESA/Statistics Division, World Bank, Organisation for Economic Co-operation and Development (OECD) and national sources.

Notes:

In the absence of official estimates, some regional totals have been estimated by the secretariat and applied, whenever possible, in order to ensure comparability at the total group levels.

1 Mid-year projections.

2 Total area of the country including inland water bodies. Possible variations are due to updating and revisions of the country data and not necessarily to any change of area.

3 In current prices and current exchange rates.

4 GDP data include French Guiana, Guadeloupe, Martinique, and Reunion.

5 Data for Western Sahara are included in this regional total, but are not shown separately.

Sources : ONU/DAES/Division de statistique, Banque mondiale, Organisation de coopération et de développement économique (OCDE) et sources nationales.

Notes :

Lorsqu'une estimation officielle n'est pas disponible, une estimation calculée par le secrétariat a été utilisée pour les totaux régionaux, chaque fois que possible, afin d'assurer la comparabilité des données au niveau des groupements. Il peut donc y avoir des différences entre la somme des éléments constituants et les les totaux indiqués.

1 Projections au milieu de l'année.

2 Superficie totale du pays, y compris les eaux intérieures. Les variations éventuelles résultent des mises à jour et des révisions des données par les pays et ne reflètent pas nécessairement des changements de superficie.

3 Aux prix et taux de change courants.

4 Y compris le PIB de la Guyane française, la Guadeloupe, la Martinique et la Réunion.

5 Les données pour le Sahara occidental sont comprises dans ce total régional, mais elles ne sont pas présentées séparément.

7.2 Annual average growth rates of total and per capita real gross domestic product at market prices
Percentage

Region, economic grouping, country or area	Total real product / Produit réel total [1]										
	1980-89	1980-00	1980-03	1990-00	1990-03	1995-00	1995-03	1999-00	2000-01	2001-02	2002-03
DEVELOPED ECONOMIES	3.1	2.8	2.7	2.5	2.4	3.0	2.5	3.6	1.0	1.5	2.0
DEVELOPING ECONOMIES	3.7	4.4	4.3	4.7	4.4	4.0	3.8	5.6	2.3	3.4	4.6
SOUTH-EAST EUROPE AND CIS	2.7	-2.6	-1.9	-4.6	-1.7	1.6	3.7	8.3	5.9	5.0	7.2
DEVELOPED ECONOMIES: AMERICA	3.6	3.1	3.1	3.4	3.3	4.1	3.3	3.9	0.4	2.5	2.8
Canada	3.3	2.6	2.8	3.1	3.3	4.3	3.8	5.3	1.9	3.3	2.1
United States	3.6	3.2	3.1	3.4	3.2	4.1	3.2	3.8	0.3	2.4	2.9
DEVELOPED ECONOMIES: EUROPE	2.4	2.3	2.3	2.1	2.1	2.8	2.4	3.6	1.7	1.1	0.9
EU 25	2.4	2.3	2.3	2.1	2.1	2.8	2.4	3.6	1.7	1.1	0.9
EU 15	*2.4*	*2.3*	*2.3*	*2.1*	*2.1*	*2.7*	*2.4*	*3.6*	*1.7*	*1.1*	*0.8*
Austria	2.1	2.5	2.4	2.2	2.1	2.8	2.2	3.4	0.8	1.4	0.7
Belgium	1.9	2.2	2.2	2.1	2.1	2.8	2.2	3.8	0.6	0.7	1.1
Denmark	2.1	1.9	2.0	2.5	2.4	2.7	2.3	2.9	1.4	2.1	0.0
Finland	3.4	2.0	2.1	2.6	2.8	4.8	3.7	5.1	1.2	2.2	1.9
France	2.3	2.1	2.1	1.8	1.9	2.7	2.5	3.8	2.1	1.2	0.5
Germany	2.0	2.4	2.2	1.6	1.5	1.8	1.5	2.9	0.8	0.2	-0.1
Greece	0.7	1.5	1.8	2.2	2.7	3.4	3.7	4.5	4.0	3.8	4.3
Ireland	2.8	5.1	5.7	7.5	7.7	9.9	8.6	10.1	6.2	6.9	3.4
Italy	2.4	2.0	1.9	1.6	1.6	1.9	1.7	3.1	1.8	0.4	0.3
Luxembourg	5.0	5.4	5.3	5.0	4.8	7.2	5.4	9.1	1.2	1.3	1.2
Netherlands	2.2	2.7	2.7	2.9	2.7	3.8	2.7	3.5	1.2	0.2	-0.8
Portugal	2.9	3.2	3.1	2.7	2.6	4.0	2.8	3.7	1.6	0.4	-1.3
Spain	2.9	2.9	2.9	2.6	2.8	4.0	3.5	4.2	2.8	2.0	2.4
Sweden	2.5	1.9	2.0	2.1	2.3	3.3	2.9	4.3	0.9	1.9	1.6
United Kingdom	3.2	2.5	2.6	2.7	2.7	3.1	2.8	3.8	2.1	1.7	2.3
New EU members 10	*2.0*	*3.0*	*3.1*	*2.0*	*2.5*	*4.0*	*3.7*	*4.2*	*3.1*	*2.9*	*3.4*
Cyprus	6.1	5.3	5.1	4.1	4.0	3.9	3.7	5.1	4.0	2.0	2.0
Czech Republic	1.7	0.5	0.7	1.0	1.4	0.7	1.5	3.3	3.1	2.0	2.9
Estonia	..	..	..	-0.5	1.4	4.8	5.1	7.3	6.5	6.0	4.5
Hungary	1.6	0.1	0.6	1.5	2.4	4.2	4.1	5.2	3.8	3.5	2.9
Latvia	..	..	..	-3.2	-0.1	5.3	5.9	6.8	7.9	6.1	7.0
Lithuania	..	..	..	-2.7	-0.1	4.2	4.9	4.0	6.5	6.8	8.9
Malta	3.2	4.8	4.7	4.8	4.4	4.1	3.7	4.7	3.9	1.2	2.8
Poland	2.3	1.7	2.0	4.6	4.2	5.2	3.7	4.0	1.0	1.4	2.4
Slovakia	1.5	0.5	1.0	2.6	2.9	3.6	3.5	2.0	3.8	4.4	4.2
Slovenia	..	..	..	2.8	3.1	4.5	3.9	4.1	2.9	3.0	2.6
Other developed Europe	**2.3**	**2.1**	**2.1**	**2.0**	**1.9**	**2.6**	**2.0**	**3.1**	**1.3**	**0.5**	**-0.1**
Andorra	7.3	6.2	5.9	4.5	4.5	4.1	4.3	4.9	4.4	4.3	5.2
Holy See	3.2	2.3	2.2	1.8	1.7	2.4	1.9	5.9	0.0	0.0	0.0
Iceland	3.2	2.3	2.5	2.9	3.1	5.0	4.0	5.7	2.8	-0.6	4.0
Liechtensten	2.5	2.1	2.1	1.6	1.8	3.0	2.5	4.3	1.9	1.1	0.4
Monaco	3.0	2.8	2.8	2.4	2.6	3.4	3.1	4.4	2.7	1.7	0.9
Norway	3.2	3.2	3.2	4.0	3.4	3.5	2.6	2.8	1.9	1.0	0.3
San Marino	2.4	2.4	2.5	2.8	2.9	5.0	3.7	3.2	1.8	0.4	0.2
Switzerland	1.8	1.4	1.4	0.8	1.0	1.9	1.5	3.2	0.9	0.2	-0.5
DEVELOPED ECONOMIES: ASIA	3.9	3.0	2.7	1.4	1.3	1.1	1.0	2.9	0.4	0.1	2.6
Israel	3.4	4.7	4.5	5.2	4.2	4.0	2.7	8.1	-0.9	-1.1	0.5
Japan	3.9	3.0	2.6	1.4	1.2	1.0	1.0	2.8	0.4	0.1	2.7
DEVELOPED ECONOMIES: OCEANIA	3.4	3.2	3.2	3.8	3.7	3.9	3.6	1.9	3.9	2.9	3.4
Australia	3.6	3.4	3.4	3.9	3.8	4.1	3.7	1.8	3.9	2.7	3.5
New Zealand	2.1	2.1	2.3	3.2	3.2	2.4	2.9	2.7	3.5	4.3	2.7

For sources and notes, see end of table.

7.2 Taux d'évolution annuels moyens du produit intérieur brut réel total et par habitant aux prix du marché
En pourcentage

Per capita real product / Produit réel par habitant											Régions, groupements économiques, pays ou zones
1980-89	1980-00	1980-03	1990-00	1990-03	1995-00	1995-03	1999-00	2000-01	2001-02	2002-03	
2.5	2.1	2.0	1.9	1.9	2.5	2.0	3.0	0.5	1.0	1.5	**ECONOMIES DEVELOPPEES**
1.6	2.4	2.4	3.0	2.7	2.3	2.2	3.9	0.7	1.9	3.1	**ECONOMIES EN DEVELOPPEMENT**
1.9	-2.8	-2.1	-4.6	-1.6	1.7	3.8	8.5	6.1	5.2	7.4	**EUROPE DU SUD-EST ET CEI**
2.5	2.0	2.0	2.3	2.2	3.0	2.2	2.8	-0.6	1.5	1.8	**ECONOMIES DEVELOPPEES : AMERIQUE**
2.1	1.4	1.6	2.0	2.3	3.3	2.9	4.4	1.1	2.5	1.3	Canada
2.6	2.1	2.1	2.3	2.1	3.0	2.1	2.7	-0.8	1.4	1.9	Etats-Unis
2.1	1.8	1.9	1.8	1.9	2.5	2.2	3.4	1.5	0.9	0.7	**ECONOMIES DEVELOPPEES : EUROPE**
2.1	1.9	1.9	1.8	1.9	2.5	2.2	3.4	1.6	1.0	0.8	**UE 25**
2.2	*2.0*	*2.0*	*1.7*	*1.8*	*2.4*	*2.1*	*3.3*	*1.5*	*0.9*	*0.6*	*UE 15*
1.9	2.0	2.0	1.7	1.8	2.6	2.2	3.4	0.7	1.3	0.7	Autriche
1.8	1.9	1.9	1.8	1.8	2.5	2.0	3.6	0.4	0.5	0.9	Belgique
2.1	1.7	1.7	2.1	2.0	2.3	1.9	2.6	1.1	1.8	-0.2	Danemark
2.9	1.5	1.7	2.2	2.5	4.5	3.5	4.9	1.0	2.0	1.7	Finlande
1.8	1.6	1.6	1.3	1.5	2.3	2.0	3.4	1.6	0.7	0.0	France
1.9	2.0	1.9	1.3	1.2	1.7	1.3	2.8	0.8	0.1	-0.2	Allemagne
0.2	0.9	1.2	1.4	2.0	2.6	3.1	3.8	3.6	3.6	4.2	Grèce
2.4	4.7	5.1	6.6	6.7	8.7	7.4	8.8	4.9	5.7	2.2	Irlande
2.4	1.9	1.8	1.4	1.5	1.7	1.7	3.1	1.8	0.4	0.4	Italie
4.7	4.4	4.2	3.5	3.3	5.7	4.0	7.6	-0.2	-0.1	-0.1	Luxembourg
1.6	2.1	2.1	2.3	2.1	3.3	2.1	2.9	0.7	-0.3	-1.3	Pays-Bas
2.7	3.2	3.0	2.6	2.5	3.8	2.6	3.5	1.5	0.3	-1.4	Portugal
2.4	2.5	2.5	2.2	2.5	3.5	3.1	3.8	2.5	1.8	2.2	Espagne
2.3	1.5	1.6	1.8	2.1	3.3	2.8	4.3	0.9	1.8	1.5	Suède
3.0	2.2	2.2	2.3	2.4	2.8	2.5	3.4	1.8	1.4	2.0	Royaume-Uni
1.6	*1.8*	*2.1*	*2.0*	*2.6*	*4.1*	*3.8*	*4.4*	*3.3*	*3.1*	*3.6*	*Nouveaux membres de l'UE 10*
5.0	4.0	3.8	2.7	2.7	2.8	2.8	4.2	3.1	1.2	1.2	Chypre
1.7	0.5	0.7	1.1	1.4	0.8	1.7	3.4	3.2	2.1	3.0	République tchèque
..	..	..	1.1	2.9	6.0	6.3	8.3	7.6	7.1	5.7	Estonie
2.0	0.4	1.0	1.9	2.7	4.6	4.5	5.7	4.3	3.9	3.4	Hongrie
..	..	..	-1.8	1.2	6.3	6.9	7.8	8.9	7.0	8.0	Lettonie
..	..	..	-2.0	0.5	4.6	5.3	4.3	7.0	7.4	9.6	Lituanie
2.1	3.8	3.8	4.0	3.7	3.5	3.1	4.2	3.4	0.8	2.4	Malte
1.5	1.3	1.7	4.5	4.1	5.1	3.7	4.0	1.0	1.5	2.5	Pologne
1.0	0.1	0.6	2.3	2.7	3.5	3.4	2.0	3.7	4.3	4.1	Slovaquie
..	..	..	2.4	2.9	4.5	4.0	4.2	3.0	3.0	2.7	Slovénie
1.6	**1.4**	**1.4**	**1.5**	**1.5**	**2.2**	**1.7**	**2.9**	**1.1**	**0.3**	**-0.3**	**Autres économies développées d'Europe**
2.4	2.5	2.5	2.2	2.5	3.5	3.1	3.8	2.5	1.8	2.2	Andorre
2.7	1.9	1.8	1.6	1.6	2.2	1.8	5.7	0.0	0.0	0.0	Saint-Siège
2.1	1.2	1.4	1.8	2.0	3.9	2.9	4.6	1.9	-1.5	3.2	Islande
1.0	0.7	0.8	0.3	0.6	1.7	1.4	3.2	0.9	0.2	-0.4	Liechtenstein
1.8	1.6	1.6	1.3	1.5	2.3	2.0	3.4	1.7	0.7	0.0	Monaco
2.8	2.8	2.7	3.4	2.9	3.0	2.1	2.3	1.5	0.5	-0.1	Norvège
1.7	1.2	1.3	1.3	1.5	3.6	2.5	1.9	0.7	-0.6	-0.7	Saint-Marin
1.0	0.7	0.8	0.3	0.6	1.7	1.4	3.2	0.9	0.2	-0.5	Suisse
3.3	**2.5**	**2.2**	**1.1**	**1.0**	**0.8**	**0.7**	**2.6**	**0.1**	**-0.1**	**2.4**	**ECONOMIES DEVELOPPEES : ASIE**
1.7	2.2	1.9	2.2	1.4	1.5	0.4	5.7	-3.1	-3.1	-1.5	Israël
3.3	2.6	2.3	1.1	1.0	0.8	0.8	2.6	0.2	0.0	2.6	Japon
2.0	**1.8**	**1.9**	**2.5**	**2.5**	**2.7**	**2.5**	**0.8**	**2.9**	**1.9**	**2.5**	**ECONOMIES DEVELOPPEES : OCEANIE**
2.0	1.9	2.0	2.6	2.6	2.9	2.5	0.7	2.9	1.7	2.5	Australie
1.4	1.0	1.2	1.9	2.1	1.5	2.0	1.8	2.6	3.5	1.9	Nouvelle-Zélande

Pour les sources et les notes, se reporter à la fin du tableau.

Region, economic grouping, country or area	Total real product / Produit réel total [1]										
	1980-89	1980-00	1980-03	1990-00	1990-03	1995-00	1995-03	1999-00	2000-01	2001-02	2002-03
DEVELOPING ECONOMIES: AMERICA	**1.8**	**2.5**	**2.4**	**3.3**	**2.8**	**3.0**	**2.1**	**4.0**	**0.4**	**-0.4**	**1.6**
South America	*2.0*	*2.5*	*2.4*	*3.3*	*2.6*	*2.1*	*1.3*	*3.0*	*0.4*	*-1.4*	*1.6*
Argentina	-0.2	2.2	1.9	4.2	2.2	2.7	-0.3	-0.8	-4.4	-10.9	8.7
Bolivia	-0.8	2.5	2.6	4.0	3.5	3.5	2.8	2.3	1.5	2.7	2.9
Brazil	3.1	2.4	2.4	2.9	2.6	2.0	1.9	4.5	1.5	1.5	0.6
Chile	2.5	5.9	5.6	6.6	5.4	3.8	3.2	4.2	3.1	2.1	3.3
Colombia	3.5	3.6	3.2	2.9	2.4	0.6	1.0	2.9	1.4	2.5	2.0
Ecuador	1.9	2.5	2.4	2.2	2.2	0.7	1.7	2.8	5.1	3.8	3.1
Guyana	-2.2	1.8	2.0	5.3	4.0	2.6	1.7	-1.4	1.9	1.2	-0.3
Paraguay	2.5	2.9	2.6	2.2	1.7	0.7	0.5	-0.3	2.7	-2.3	0.6
Peru	0.4	1.2	1.5	4.6	3.9	2.3	2.3	2.8	0.3	4.9	4.0
Suriname	1.0	0.1	0.4	-0.3	0.5	1.7	2.1	0.0	4.8	1.4	5.6
Uruguay	0.7	2.7	2.2	3.4	1.6	2.2	-0.8	-1.4	-3.4	-11.2	2.8
Venezuela	0.6	1.9	1.4	1.6	0.3	0.4	-1.7	3.2	2.8	-8.9	-16.7
Other America	*1.3*	*2.4*	*2.6*	*3.2*	*3.1*	*5.1*	*3.7*	*5.9*	*0.3*	*1.4*	*1.7*
Anguilla	7.6	6.2	5.6	3.7	3.3	6.0	3.6	0.0	1.4	-4.3	4.5
Antigua and Barbuda	6.9	4.8	4.5	3.3	3.1	2.6	2.6	0.9	2.2	3.0	2.5
Aruba	9.8	7.8	6.9	5.3	,4.2	4.4	2.4	3.7	-0.7	-2.6	1.5
Bahamas	4.6	1.6	1.6	1.5	1.7	4.2	2.7	4.9	-2.0	0.7	0.9
Barbados	2.2	1.4	1.4	2.1	1.7	3.7	1.8	2.3	-2.0	-2.0	1.6
Belize	3.8	5.3	5.2	3.9	4.2	4.1	4.6	7.5	5.2	3.6	4.5
Bermuda	1.6	1.5	1.6	2.8	2.5	3.1	2.1	1.9	-0.4	1.0	1.0
British Virgin Islands	5.9	7.4	7.7	7.1	8.0	10.0	10.0	9.9	10.1	10.2	10.1
Cayman Islands	8.9	5.0	4.3	0.5	0.7	1.0	1.1	1.1	1.2	1.2	1.2
Costa Rica	2.8	4.4	4.4	5.3	4.8	5.7	4.5	1.8	1.0	2.9	5.6
Cuba	4.0	-0.8	-0.4	-0.6	0.8	4.2	3.7	5.6	3.0	1.1	2.6
Dominica	4.3	3.2	2.6	2.0	1.1	2.2	0.1	1.5	-4.5	-3.6	-1.1
Dominican Republic	3.0	4.1	4.4	6.6	6.3	7.9	6.3	7.8	4.0	4.3	-0.4
El Salvador	0.3	3.1	3.2	4.8	4.0	3.3	2.7	2.2	1.7	2.1	2.0
Grenada	2.3	2.8	2.8	4.0	3.5	6.5	3.7	7.6	-5.0	0.4	0.0
Guatemala	0.4	2.9	3.0	4.1	3.8	4.0	3.4	3.6	2.3	2.3	2.1
Haiti	0.1	-0.8	-0.6	-0.8	-0.3	2.1	1.0	0.9	-1.2	-0.9	0.0
Honduras	2.7	3.1	3.1	3.2	3.0	2.6	2.6	5.0	2.6	2.5	2.0
Jamaica	1.5	2.3	2.1	0.9	0.8	-0.6	0.2	0.7	1.7	1.1	2.2
Mexico	0.8	2.4	2.5	3.1	3.0	5.3	3.7	6.6	-0.2	0.9	1.3
Montserrat	3.6	-1.6	-2.7	-9.3	-8.4	-13.4	-8.5	-3.7	-7.7	8.3	-7.7
Netherlands Antilles	-0.9	1.3	1.2	1.6	1.0	-0.2	-0.2	-2.1	0.6	0.2	0.5
Nicaragua	-1.7	0.2	0.8	3.7	3.7	5.0	4.0	4.2	3.0	1.0	2.3
Panama	1.8	3.4	3.3	4.1	3.4	3.6	2.5	2.5	0.3	0.8	1.5
Puerto Rico	4.5	4.4	4.2	4.3	4.0	4.7	3.7	5.6	-0.2	3.7	3.7
Saint Kitts and Nevis	6.0	5.2	4.8	4.5	4.0	4.0	3.1	3.4	2.1	2.0	1.2
Saint Lucia	7.5	4.7	3.9	1.9	1.2	1.8	0.4	-0.2	-5.8	2.5	0.4
Saint Vincent and the Grenadines	6.0	4.5	4.1	3.2	2.8	3.5	2.5	1.5	-0.4	1.5	2.6
Trinidad and Tobago	-3.7	0.2	1.2	4.6	5.1	8.3	6.9	11.3	2.6	2.7	3.8
Turks and Caicos Islands	6.9	5.3	5.3	4.7	5.0	6.1	5.7	6.4	6.0	2.5	2.5
DEVELOPING ECONOMIES: AFRICA	**2.6**	**2.4**	**2.6**	**2.8**	**3.1**	**3.7**	**3.6**	**3.5**	**3.6**	**3.1**	**4.0**
North Africa	*3.4*	*2.8*	*3.0*	*3.0*	*3.4*	*4.2*	*4.1*	*3.9*	*3.9*	*3.4*	*5.5*
Algeria	2.9	1.7	1.9	1.9	2.4	3.2	3.3	2.4	2.1	4.1	6.7
Egypt	6.4	4.2	4.2	4.2	4.2	5.0	4.3	3.5	3.2	3.1	4.5
Libyan Arab Jamahiriya	-1.1	-0.5	-0.2	-0.8	0.1	1.4	1.8	3.2	3.3	-0.2	4.6
Morocco	4.2	3.3	3.2	2.3	2.7	3.1	3.4	1.0	6.3	3.2	5.5
Sudan	2.8	4.0	4.4	5.0	5.4	5.9	6.2	8.3	6.4	5.5	5.8
Tunisia	3.2	4.1	4.2	4.7	4.6	5.5	4.9	4.7	4.9	1.7	5.8
Other Africa	*2.1*	*2.1*	*2.2*	*2.6*	*2.8*	*3.4*	*3.2*	*3.2*	*3.3*	*2.9*	*2.8*
Angola	3.6	1.1	1.7	1.5	3.2	5.9	6.2	3.6	5.2	13.8	4.7
Benin	3.4	3.5	3.8	4.6	4.9	5.2	5.3	5.7	5.1	6.4	5.4
Botswana	11.4	8.4	7.9	4.8	5.1	6.0	5.8	6.6	8.4	2.3	3.7
Burkina Faso	3.8	4.1	4.2	5.1	5.1	5.4	5.2	2.2	5.7	4.6	6.5
Burundi	4.4	1.1	0.8	-2.6	-1.4	-0.4	0.8	-0.9	3.2	4.5	-0.5

For sources and notes, see end of table.

			Per capita real product / Produit réel par habitant [1]								Régions, groupements économiques, pays ou zones
1980-89	1980-00	1980-03	1990-00	1990-03	1995-00	1995-03	1999-00	2000-01	2001-02	2002-03	
-0.2	**0.6**	**0.6**	**1.6**	**1.1**	**1.4**	**0.5**	**2.4**	**-1.1**	**-1.8**	**0.2**	**ECONOMIES EN DEVELOPPEMENT : AMERIQUE**
0.0	*0.7*	*0.6*	*1.7*	*1.0*	*0.5*	*-0.2*	*1.5*	*-1.0*	*-2.7*	*0.2*	*Amérique du Sud*
-1.6	0.8	0.5	2.8	0.9	1.3	-1.6	-2.0	-5.6	-12.0	7.5	Argentine
-2.9	0.2	0.4	1.7	1.3	1.3	0.7	0.2	-0.5	0.8	1.0	Bolivie
1.0	0.7	0.7	1.5	1.2	0.6	0.6	3.1	0.2	0.2	-0.6	Brésil
0.9	4.2	4.0	5.0	3.9	2.4	1.9	2.8	1.8	0.9	2.1	Chili
1.4	1.5	1.3	1.0	0.6	-1.1	-0.7	1.2	-0.3	0.9	0.4	Colombie
-0.7	0.2	0.3	0.3	0.4	-1.0	0.1	1.2	3.5	2.2	1.6	Equateur
-1.8	1.9	2.0	4.9	3.6	2.1	1.3	-1.8	1.5	0.9	-0.5	Guyana
-0.6	0.0	-0.3	-0.4	-0.9	-1.8	-1.9	-2.7	0.3	-4.6	-1.8	Paraguay
-1.9	-0.8	-0.4	2.8	2.1	0.6	0.7	1.2	-1.3	3.3	2.4	Pérou
-0.4	-0.7	-0.4	-0.8	-0.1	0.9	1.3	-0.8	4.0	0.6	4.8	Suriname
0.1	2.0	1.5	2.7	0.8	1.4	-1.6	-2.2	-4.1	-11.8	2.1	Uruguay
-2.0	-0.5	-0.9	-0.6	-1.8	-1.6	-3.6	1.2	0.8	-10.6	-18.2	Venezuela
-0.7	*0.6*	*0.7*	*1.4*	*1.4*	*3.3*	*2.0*	*4.3*	*-1.2*	*-0.1*	*0.2*	*Autres économies : Amérique*
5.2	3.3	2.9	1.5	1.2	4.1	1.7	-1.7	-0.3	-5.9	2.7	Anguilla
7.0	4.2	3.7	1.9	1.9	1.3	1.6	-0.1	1.4	2.4	2.0	Antigua-et-Barbuda
9.0	5.4	4.4	1.6	0.7	1.0	-0.5	0.9	-3.1	-4.6	-0.4	Aruba
2.6	-0.3	-0.2	-0.2	0.1	2.8	1.4	3.6	-3.2	-0.5	-0.2	Bahamas
1.9	1.1	1.0	1.7	1.4	3.3	1.5	1.9	-2.4	-2.4	1.2	Barbade
1.2	2.6	2.6	1.3	1.7	1.7	2.3	5.2	2.9	1.4	2.3	Belize
0.7	0.7	0.8	2.1	1.7	2.4	1.4	1.2	-1.1	0.3	0.3	Bermudes
1.7	4.6	5.2	5.7	6.5	8.6	8.4	8.3	8.3	8.2	8.1	Iles Vierges britanniques
4.6	1.1	0.5	-3.0	-2.7	-2.4	-2.2	-2.2	-2.0	-1.9	-1.9	Iles Caïmanes
0.0	1.7	1.8	2.7	2.3	3.1	2.1	-0.5	-1.1	0.9	3.6	Costa Rica
3.1	-1.6	-1.0	-1.1	0.3	3.8	3.3	5.3	2.7	0.8	2.3	Cuba
4.8	2.9	2.3	1.2	0.4	1.5	-0.4	1.0	-4.9	-3.9	-1.3	Dominique
0.8	2.2	2.5	4.8	4.5	6.1	4.6	6.0	2.4	2.7	-1.9	République dominicaine
-0.6	1.5	1.5	2.7	2.1	1.4	1.0	0.4	0.0	0.5	0.4	El Salvador
2.7	3.3	3.3	4.5	4.0	7.1	4.2	8.1	-4.7	0.6	0.2	Grenade
-2.1	0.3	0.4	1.4	1.1	1.2	0.7	0.9	-0.3	-0.4	-0.5	Guatemala
-2.3	-2.7	-2.5	-2.2	-1.7	0.8	-0.3	-0.5	-2.5	-2.2	-1.3	Haïti
-0.5	0.1	0.1	0.3	0.2	-0.1	-0.1	2.3	0.1	0.1	-0.4	Honduras
0.4	1.5	1.2	0.0	-0.1	-1.5	-0.6	-0.2	0.8	0.2	1.3	Jamaïque
-1.3	0.4	0.6	1.3	1.3	3.6	2.1	4.9	-1.7	-0.6	-0.2	Mexique
4.9	2.2	2.7	0.1	2.5	5.6	7.1	20.3	5.7	11.2	-12.6	Montserrat
-1.6	0.1	0.0	0.2	-0.2	-1.2	-1.1	-2.9	-0.2	-0.6	-0.4	Antilles néerlandaises
-4.3	-2.5	-1.9	0.8	0.9	2.1	1.3	1.5	0.4	-1.5	-0.2	Nicaragua
-0.4	1.3	1.2	2.0	1.3	1.6	0.5	0.5	-1.6	-1.1	-0.4	Panama
3.5	3.5	3.4	3.5	3.2	4.0	3.1	4.9	-0.8	3.1	3.2	Porto Rico
6.9	5.2	4.9	4.1	3.9	4.7	3.8	4.3	2.6	2.4	1.4	Saint-Kitts-et-Nevis
5.9	3.3	2.6	0.8	0.2	1.0	-0.3	-0.9	-6.5	1.7	-0.4	Sainte-Lucie
5.1	3.6	3.3	2.5	2.2	2.9	1.9	0.9	-1.0	0.9	2.0	Saint-Vincent-et-les Grenadines
-4.9	-0.6	0.5	3.9	4.5	7.8	6.4	10.8	2.2	2.3	3.4	Trinité-et-Tobago
1.7	0.6	0.7	0.4	0.8	2.0	1.8	2.5	2.2	-1.1	-1.1	Iles Turques et Caïques
-0.2	**-0.3**	**-0.1**	**0.3**	**0.6**	**1.3**	**1.3**	**1.2**	**1.3**	**0.8**	**1.7**	**ECONOMIES EN DEVELOPPEMENT : AFRIQUE**
0.8	*0.6*	*0.8*	*1.1*	*1.4*	*2.3*	*2.2*	*2.0*	*2.0*	*1.5*	*3.5*	*Afrique du Nord*
-0.1	-0.7	-0.4	0.0	0.5	1.6	1.7	0.8	0.4	2.4	4.9	Algérie
3.9	2.0	2.0	2.2	2.2	3.0	2.4	1.5	1.2	1.1	2.4	Egypte
-4.6	-3.0	-2.6	-2.7	-1.8	-0.5	-0.2	1.2	1.3	-2.1	2.6	Jamahiriya arabe libyenne
1.7	1.2	1.2	0.6	1.0	1.5	1.8	-0.7	4.6	1.5	3.8	Maroc
0.2	1.6	2.0	2.6	3.0	3.5	3.8	5.9	4.0	3.2	3.5	Soudan
0.7	2.1	2.3	3.1	3.2	4.3	3.7	3.5	3.7	0.6	4.7	Tunisie
-0.9	*-0.8*	*-0.5*	*-0.1*	*0.2*	*0.8*	*0.7*	*0.8*	*0.9*	*0.5*	*0.5*	*Autres économies: Afrique*
0.6	-1.6	-1.0	-1.3	0.3	3.2	3.2	0.7	2.1	10.2	1.3	Angola
0.4	0.5	0.8	1.6	2.0	2.5	2.7	3.1	2.3	3.6	2.7	Bénin
7.9	5.4	5.0	2.3	2.8	3.8	3.9	4.8	6.9	1.2	2.8	Botswana
1.1	1.2	1.3	2.1	2.1	2.4	2.2	-0.7	2.7	1.6	3.4	Burkina Faso
1.1	-1.0	-1.1	-3.5	-2.7	-1.1	-0.7	-2.5	0.8	1.5	-3.7	Burundi

Pour les sources et les notes, se reporter à la fin du tableau.

7.2 Annual average growth rates of total and per capita real gross domestic product at market prices (continued)
Percentage

Region, economic grouping, country or area	Total real product / Produit réel total [1]										
	1980-89	1980-00	1980-03	1990-00	1990-03	1995-00	1995-03	1999-00	2000-01	2001-02	2002-03
Cameroon	2.6	0.2	0.8	1.8	2.7	4.9	4.7	5.3	4.6	4.0	4.0
Cape Verde	5.6	5.1	5.2	6.1	5.9	6.6	5.9	6.7	3.0	4.7	5.0
Central African Republic	1.5	0.9	1.1	2.0	2.1	3.1	2.4	1.8	-0.4	1.5	3.3
Chad	6.7	4.4	4.4	3.2	3.9	2.9	4.6	-0.4	8.7	8.5	13.2
Comoros	3.0	0.9	0.8	-0.4	0.0	0.0	0.7	-0.8	1.6	2.8	2.4
Congo	4.0	1.5	1.5	0.7	1.4	1.8	2.5	8.1	2.9	3.5	2.0
Côte d'Ivoire	3.4	2.8	2.6	3.3	2.6	3.6	1.7	-2.7	0.1	-1.2	1.8
Dem. Rep. of the Congo	2.1	-2.9	-2.9	-4.9	-3.8	-3.8	-2.4	-6.9	-1.1	3.1	5.0
Djibouti	1.7	1.9	1.9	1.3	1.4	0.9	1.4	0.6	1.9	2.7	3.0
Equatorial Guinea	2.6	10.8	14.0	26.2	28.0	38.9	33.6	16.9	53.4	16.5	10.0
Eritrea	..	..	..	..	..	2.2	1.4	-12.0	8.7	-1.2	5.4
Ethiopia	1.7	2.5	2.8	4.5	4.4	4.7	4.2	5.4	7.8	1.2	-3.8
Gabon	0.3	1.9	1.8	2.5	1.9	0.9	0.7	2.0	2.5	-0.2	0.7
Gambia	3.5	3.6	3.7	3.6	3.9	5.7	4.9	5.6	5.9	-3.3	7.5
Ghana	2.6	4.0	4.1	4.3	4.3	4.4	4.3	3.7	4.2	4.5	4.7
Guinea	2.0	3.6	3.7	4.1	4.0	4.1	3.8	2.3	3.6	4.2	3.6
Guinea-Bissau	4.3	3.0	2.6	0.9	0.7	-3.6	-1.0	7.3	8.0	-7.0	2.3
Kenya	4.3	3.2	2.9	2.1	1.8	1.7	1.3	-0.2	1.1	1.0	1.3
Lesotho	3.8	5.0	4.7	3.9	3.4	2.2	2.3	1.5	3.3	3.8	3.9
Liberia	-2.7	-10.3	-6.9	3.7	8.0	37.7	23.3	22.2	5.1	3.2	2.7
Madagascar	0.9	1.4	1.5	2.0	2.0	3.9	2.4	4.8	6.0	-12.7	6.0
Malawi	3.1	3.7	3.5	4.2	3.3	2.7	1.7	3.3	-4.1	1.8	4.5
Mali	2.5	3.7	3.9	5.2	5.1	6.6	5.3	3.7	1.4	9.7	-1.1
Mauritania	1.5	3.1	3.4	4.6	4.5	4.1	4.3	5.0	4.6	3.3	5.4
Mauritius	6.2	5.8	5.7	5.2	5.2	5.6	5.3	9.2	5.4	1.9	4.4
Mozambique	-1.5	2.0	3.0	5.7	6.6	8.6	8.5	1.5	13.0	8.3	7.0
Namibia	2.2	3.6	3.6	4.1	3.8	3.9	3.3	3.9	0.6	3.0	4.5
Niger	-0.2	1.5	1.8	2.6	2.8	3.2	3.2	-0.3	5.9	3.0	4.1
Nigeria	1.4	3.4	3.4	2.9	3.0	3.3	3.2	5.8	2.8	0.5	5.2
Rwanda	2.1	-0.1	0.8	0.1	2.6	10.1	8.4	6.3	6.7	9.3	3.2
Sao Tome and Principe	-1.2	0.4	0.8	1.7	2.1	2.2	2.6	3.0	2.9	2.8	4.1
Senegal	3.2	2.8	3.1	3.6	4.1	5.4	5.1	5.6	5.6	2.4	6.3
Seychelles	3.7	4.8	4.5	4.6	3.8	6.9	3.7	-0.2	-1.8	0.2	3.1
Sierra Leone	1.4	-2.1	-1.9	-4.4	-2.6	-5.1	-0.9	3.8	5.4	6.3	6.6
Somalia	1.2	-1.8	-1.4	-3.3	-1.4	1.5	2.2	3.0	2.9	3.5	3.5
South Africa	1.4	1.4	1.6	2.1	2.3	2.4	2.6	3.5	2.7	3.6	1.9
Swaziland	7.5	5.7	5.2	3.3	3.1	3.4	2.9	2.1	1.8	3.6	2.2
Togo	1.8	1.9	1.9	2.2	2.1	1.5	1.5	-0.8	0.2	4.8	3.0
Uganda	3.0	5.6	5.8	7.3	6.9	6.7	6.2	4.7	6.5	5.2	5.0
United Republic of Tanzania	2.4	4.0	4.5	5.1	5.8	7.6	7.5	5.1	6.2	7.2	4.7
Zambia	1.4	0.3	0.6	0.0	1.0	2.2	2.9	3.5	4.9	3.3	4.3
Zimbabwe	3.3	3.1	2.0	2.3	-0.2	1.9	-3.4	-4.9	-8.4	-12.8	-13.2
DEVELOPING ECONOMIES: ASIA	**5.3**	**6.0**	**5.8**	**5.9**	**5.4**	**4.4**	**4.5**	**6.6**	**2.8**	**5.0**	**5.9**
West Asia	*-0.1*	*2.3*	*2.4*	*3.3*	*3.0*	*3.2*	*2.6*	*4.5*	*-0.3*	*2.3*	*4.4*
Bahrain	-0.7	3.2	3.5	4.8	4.7	4.3	4.5	5.3	4.6	5.1	4.2
Iran, Islamic Republic of	-0.1	2.3	2.7	3.5	3.8	4.0	4.4	2.8	3.2	8.0	6.7
Iraq	0.9	-6.7	-5.1	-2.4	0.5	13.0	7.8	11.0	15.0	-6.5	-21.8
Jordan	3.3	3.0	3.0	4.6	4.1	2.5	2.9	2.7	3.5	4.9	3.0
Kuwait	1.1	2.2	1.8	6.7	3.6	-2.0	-2.2	-10.1	-1.1	0.4	1.9
Lebanon	-8.7	1.3	1.9	6.3	5.0	3.3	2.8	2.0	1.4	2.0	3.0
Oman	8.2	5.8	5.5	4.5	4.2	3.2	3.6	5.5	7.5	1.7	1.1
Palestinian territory [2]	..	..	..	..	..	4.3	-2.6	-1.2	-16.0	-19.1	-1.7
Qatar	1.4	3.7	4.2	6.4	6.4	9.9	7.5	7.3	6.3	3.0	4.0
Saudi Arabia	-5.7	0.3	0.5	1.7	1.2	2.0	0.8	4.9	1.2	-9.5	4.7
Syrian Arab Republic	0.9	3.5	3.6	6.3	5.0	3.5	2.7	0.6	3.4	3.2	1.0
Turkey	5.3	4.5	4.1	3.8	3.1	3.4	2.2	7.4	-7.5	7.8	5.8
United Arab Emirates	-2.9	1.9	2.2	2.6	2.8	1.3	2.4	5.4	5.0	1.5	6.3
Yemen	..	..	..	5.5	5.2	5.5	4.8	5.1	3.9	3.3	4.2
Other Asia	*7.5*	*7.2*	*6.9*	*6.5*	*6.0*	*4.7*	*4.9*	*7.1*	*3.5*	*5.5*	*6.2*
Afghanistan	-1.0	-3.7	-3.9	-4.0	-4.3	-6.0	-5.1	-43.7	0.0	28.6	15.0
Bangladesh	3.9	4.4	4.5	4.9	5.0	5.3	5.3	5.3	4.8	5.3	5.5
Bhutan	7.7	6.5	6.5	6.2	6.4	6.6	6.7	5.6	7.3	6.6	6.5
Brunei Darussalam	-1.0	0.6	0.9	1.3	1.6	0.9	1.8	2.8	3.0	3.2	3.6
Cambodia	-1.3	3.0	3.5	5.5	5.5	4.8	5.4	7.7	6.3	5.5	4.0

For sources and notes, see end of table.

Per capita real product / Produit réel par habitant [1]											Régions, groupements économiques, pays ou zones
1980-89	1980-00	1980-03	1990-00	1990-03	1995-00	1995-03	1999-00	2000-01	2001-02	2002-03	
-0.2	-2.5	-1.9	-0.8	0.2	2.4	2.4	3.0	2.5	2.0	2.1	Cameroun
3.7	2.9	3.0	3.7	3.6	4.4	3.7	4.5	0.8	2.5	2.9	Cap-Vert
-1.0	-1.5	-1.2	-0.4	-0.1	1.0	0.6	0.1	-1.9	0.2	2.1	République centrafricaine
4.0	1.5	1.4	0.2	0.8	-0.3	1.5	-3.4	5.5	5.4	9.9	Tchad
-0.1	-2.1	-2.1	-3.3	-2.8	-2.9	-2.2	-3.6	-1.3	-0.1	-0.5	Comores
0.7	-1.8	-1.7	-2.5	-1.7	-1.4	-0.5	4.9	0.1	0.9	-0.5	Congo
-0.7	-0.4	-0.3	0.9	0.4	1.6	-0.1	-4.4	-1.6	-2.8	0.2	Côte d'Ivoire
-0.8	-5.7	-5.6	-7.3	-6.2	-5.5	-4.4	-8.8	-3.5	0.2	1.9	Rép. dém. du Congo
-3.0	-1.8	-1.6	-0.9	-0.9	-2.4	-1.3	-2.2	-0.3	0.9	1.5	Djibouti
-2.7	7.3	10.6	23.0	24.7	35.4	30.1	13.8	49.4	13.5	7.1	Guinée équatoriale
..	..	..	..	..	-0.8	-1.8	-15.0	4.8	-4.8	1.6	Erythrée
-1.5	-0.7	-0.3	1.5	1.5	2.0	1.5	2.8	5.2	-1.3	-6.1	Ethiopie
-2.8	-1.2	-1.1	-0.4	-0.7	-1.6	-1.5	-0.2	0.5	-2.0	-1.0	Gabon
-0.2	0.0	0.2	0.2	0.5	2.3	1.7	2.4	2.9	-5.9	4.7	Gambie
-0.7	1.1	1.2	1.7	1.8	2.1	2.0	1.5	1.9	2.2	2.4	Ghana
-0.6	0.6	0.9	1.2	1.4	2.0	2.0	0.7	2.0	2.7	2.1	Guinée
1.9	0.2	-0.2	-2.1	-2.2	-6.2	-3.8	4.4	4.9	-9.7	-0.7	Guinée-Bissau
0.5	0.0	-0.1	-0.5	-0.6	-0.5	-0.6	-2.0	-0.5	-0.5	-0.1	Kenya
1.6	3.3	3.1	2.5	2.3	1.0	1.4	0.7	2.8	3.5	3.8	Lesotho
-4.3	-11.5	-8.7	0.2	3.6	28.9	16.2	15.0	-0.2	-1.3	-1.2	Libéria
-1.9	-1.5	-1.4	-0.9	-0.9	0.9	-0.5	1.8	3.0	-15.2	3.0	Madagascar
-1.3	0.5	0.5	2.4	1.3	0.1	-0.7	0.8	-6.2	-0.3	2.4	Malawi
0.0	1.0	1.2	2.3	2.2	3.7	2.4	0.8	-1.5	6.5	-4.0	Mali
-0.8	0.7	0.8	1.9	1.7	1.3	1.3	2.0	1.6	0.3	2.3	Mauritanie
5.3	4.7	4.6	4.0	4.0	4.5	4.2	8.1	4.4	0.9	3.4	Maurice
-2.5	0.1	1.0	2.7	3.8	6.2	6.2	-0.4	10.8	6.3	5.1	Mozambique
-1.0	0.2	0.3	1.1	1.0	1.0	0.9	1.5	-1.3	1.4	3.1	Namibie
-3.2	-1.8	-1.5	-0.9	-0.7	-0.4	-0.4	-3.7	2.2	-0.7	0.3	Niger
-1.4	0.4	0.4	0.0	0.1	0.5	0.5	3.0	0.1	-2.0	2.6	Nigéria
-1.2	-0.9	-0.6	-1.2	-0.2	1.0	1.4	-0.8	2.2	6.6	1.8	Rwanda
-3.2	-1.9	-1.5	-0.8	-0.5	-0.4	0.0	0.4	0.3	0.3	1.6	Sao Tomé-et-Principe
0.3	0.1	0.4	1.1	1.6	2.9	2.7	3.1	3.1	0.0	3.8	Sénégal
2.6	3.7	3.4	3.5	2.7	5.8	2.7	-1.1	-2.7	-0.7	2.2	Seychelles
-1.0	-3.5	-3.4	-5.1	-3.9	-6.5	-3.3	1.0	1.8	2.0	2.2	Sierra Leone
0.5	-3.0	-2.9	-5.1	-3.9	-2.0	-1.5	-1.1	-1.2	-0.8	-0.8	Somalie
-1.0	-0.7	-0.4	0.3	0.7	0.9	1.4	2.4	1.7	2.8	1.2	Afrique du Sud
3.7	2.7	2.4	1.2	1.2	1.2	1.1	0.3	0.4	2.5	1.4	Swaziland
-1.4	-1.0	-1.0	-0.6	-0.7	-1.8	-1.5	-3.7	-2.5	2.3	0.7	Togo
-0.3	2.3	2.5	4.2	3.8	3.6	3.1	1.6	3.3	1.9	1.6	Ouganda
-0.9	0.7	1.3	2.1	3.0	5.0	5.1	2.9	4.1	5.1	2.8	République-Unie de Tanzanie
-1.7	-2.5	-2.1	-2.3	-1.1	0.0	1.1	1.8	3.4	2.1	3.2	Zambie
-0.6	0.2	-0.6	0.4	-1.8	0.4	-4.5	-5.9	-9.2	-13.3	-13.6	Zimbabwe
											ECONOMIES EN DEVELOPPEMENT : ASIE
3.3	**4.1**	**4.0**	**4.2**	**3.9**	**2.9**	**3.1**	**5.2**	**1.4**	**3.6**	**4.5**	
-3.7	*-1.0*	*-0.7*	*0.9*	*0.7*	*1.1*	*0.5*	*2.4*	*-2.3*	*0.3*	*2.3*	*Asie occidentale*
-4.0	-0.3	0.1	1.4	1.6	1.3	1.8	2.6	2.2	2.8	2.0	Bahreïn
-3.9	-0.3	0.3	1.9	2.3	2.7	3.1	1.6	2.0	6.7	5.4	Iran, Rép. islamique d'
-2.0	-9.3	-7.7	-5.2	-2.4	9.9	4.9	8.0	11.9	-9.0	-23.9	Iraq
-0.4	-1.3	-1.1	0.1	0.1	-0.9	-0.2	-0.3	0.6	2.0	0.3	Jordanie
-3.8	0.7	0.0	6.5	1.8	-7.6	-7.3	-15.3	-5.6	-3.3	-1.2	Koweït
-8.8	-0.2	0.3	3.6	2.6	1.3	0.9	0.3	-0.3	0.3	1.4	Liban
3.5	1.8	1.6	0.9	0.8	0.1	0.5	2.4	4.4	-1.3	-1.8	Oman
..	..	..	..	..	0.4	-6.2	-4.8	-19.0	-22.0	-5.1	Territoire palestinien [2]
-6.0	-0.7	0.3	4.1	4.3	7.5	5.5	5.3	4.5	1.4	2.5	Qatar
-10.9	-3.7	-3.3	-1.2	-1.7	-1.1	-2.3	1.6	-1.8	-12.2	1.7	Arabie saoudite
-2.7	0.4	0.6	3.5	2.3	0.9	0.1	-1.8	0.9	0.8	-1.3	République arabe syrienne
2.9	2.5	2.1	2.0	1.4	1.8	0.7	5.7	-8.9	6.2	4.3	Turquie
-9.5	-3.0	-2.3	-0.6	-0.1	-1.1	0.2	3.2	2.9	-0.5	4.2	Emirats arabes unis
..	..	..	1.2	1.2	1.9	1.2	1.6	0.4	-0.3	0.6	Yémen
5.6	*5.4*	*5.2*	*4.9*	*4.5*	*3.2*	*3.5*	*5.7*	*2.1*	*4.2*	*4.9*	*Autres économies : Asie*
0.8	-5.9	-6.4	-8.1	-7.9	-7.8	-7.5	-45.0	-3.1	23.9	10.3	Afghanistan
1.3	1.9	2.0	2.5	2.7	3.0	3.0	3.0	2.6	3.1	3.4	Bangladesh
4.9	4.2	4.2	4.2	4.1	3.9	3.7	2.6	4.1	3.4	3.3	Bhoutan
-3.8	-2.1	-1.8	-1.4	-1.0	-1.6	-0.6	0.4	0.6	0.9	1.3	Brunéi Darussalam
-5.3	-0.5	0.1	2.3	2.6	2.0	2.7	5.0	3.7	3.0	1.5	Cambodge

Pour les sources et les notes, se reporter à la fin du tableau.

Region, economic grouping, country or area	Total real product / Produit réel total [1]										
	1980-89	1980-00	1980-03	1990-00	1990-03	1995-00	1995-03	1999-00	2000-01	2001-02	2002-03
China	10.6	9.9	9.7	10.4	9.6	8.1	8.0	7.9	7.5	8.0	9.1
China, Hong Kong SAR	7.1	5.5	5.1	4.0	3.6	2.6	2.7	10.2	0.5	2.3	1.5
China, Macao SAR	7.5	5.5	5.0	2.1	2.4	-1.4	1.9	4.6	2.1	10.0	15.6
China, Taiwan Province of [3]	12.4	9.3	7.8	4.0	2.7	1.3	0.5	9.4	-9.6	1.3	2.5
India	5.7	5.7	5.7	6.0	5.8	5.8	5.6	3.9	5.5	4.3	7.8
Indonesia	5.7	6.0	5.4	4.2	3.5	-0.6	1.1	4.9	3.4	3.7	4.1
Korea, Dem. People's Republic of	7.9	0.8	0.6	-3.0	-1.6	-0.7	0.7	1.3	3.7	0.8	0.8
Korea, Republic of	8.9	7.6	7.2	5.8	5.5	4.0	4.7	9.3	3.1	6.3	3.1
Lao People's Dem. Rep.	4.5	5.6	5.7	6.5	6.3	6.1	6.0	5.8	5.8	5.9	5.5
Malaysia	4.9	6.9	6.6	7.0	5.9	3.6	3.6	8.3	0.4	4.1	5.2
Maldives	11.9	9.7	9.1	7.8	7.3	8.7	7.0	4.5	3.1	5.7	8.5
Mongolia	6.2	1.7	1.7	1.0	1.7	2.9	2.8	1.1	1.0	4.1	5.0
Myanmar	0.9	3.1	4.0	6.9	7.5	7.9	8.4	13.7	10.5	5.5	5.1
Nepal	4.6	4.9	4.7	4.9	4.5	4.6	4.0	6.1	4.8	-0.5	2.3
Pakistan	6.2	4.9	4.6	3.5	3.5	3.0	3.5	2.6	2.8	5.8	5.3
Philippines	0.5	2.4	2.6	3.3	3.5	3.5	3.7	6.0	3.0	4.4	4.5
Singapore	6.3	7.7	7.2	7.7	6.2	5.6	3.9	9.4	-2.4	2.2	0.5
Sri Lanka	4.1	4.6	4.5	5.3	4.7	5.1	4.0	6.0	-1.4	4.0	5.5
Thailand	7.0	7.2	6.4	4.2	3.6	-0.7	1.4	4.6	1.9	5.4	6.7
Timor-Leste	..	..	..	-1.6	-0.8	-6.4	-1.7	15.3	17.2	2.8	-2.2
Viet Nam	5.7	6.6	6.7	7.9	7.5	6.7	6.6	6.8	6.8	7.0	6.0
DEVELOPING ECONOMIES:											
OCEANIA	**3.7**	**3.7**	**3.3**	**3.0**	**2.3**	**1.1**	**0.9**	**0.4**	**-0.3**	**0.9**	**2.2**
Cook Islands	3.3	3.2	3.2	1.5	2.3	1.6	3.5	14.7	5.1	3.7	1.2
Fiji	1.3	2.5	2.6	2.7	2.8	2.3	2.8	-2.8	3.8	4.4	5.2
French Polynesia	6.3	4.3	4.0	2.9	2.6	1.8	2.0	2.7	2.1	1.9	1.9
Kiribati	1.1	2.8	3.1	5.2	4.7	6.1	4.5	2.2	2.2	0.0	2.1
Marshall Islands	8.3	3.2	2.4	-2.2	-1.5	-4.4	-1.3	-1.7	1.7	5.1	3.2
Micronesia, Federated States of	6.0	3.5	2.9	0.8	0.7	-1.5	-0.1	1.7	1.7	0.6	2.8
Nauru	5.1	-1.6	-1.9	-5.8	-4.3	-3.6	-1.9	0.0	-3.3	3.4	3.3
New Caledonia	4.6	4.0	3.4	1.6	1.2	0.2	0.2	2.1	-1.1	0.7	-0.1
Palau	0.4	3.6	3.5	4.3	3.4	1.2	1.2	1.1	4.3	1.0	1.0
Papua New Guinea	2.3	3.9	3.4	4.5	2.8	0.9	-0.1	-1.2	-3.4	-0.6	2.8
Samoa	0.9	0.5	1.0	2.2	2.9	3.4	3.8	7.0	6.1	1.9	3.0
Solomon Islands	1.8	4.1	3.0	3.2	0.7	-2.2	-3.7	-14.1	-5.0	-4.0	2.1
Tonga	4.6	2.6	2.6	2.5	2.5	2.3	2.5	6.2	1.3	1.9	1.9
Tuvalu	-0.2	4.0	3.9	4.8	3.9	7.0	3.6	0.0	6.7	-12.5	7.1
Vanuatu	4.9	3.7	3.1	2.7	1.6	1.1	-0.2	3.0	-2.0	-5.5	1.1
SOUTH-EAST EUROPE AND CIS	**2.7**	**-2.6**	**-1.9**	**-4.6**	**-1.7**	**1.6**	**3.7**	**8.3**	**5.9**	**5.0**	**7.2**
South-East Europe	*1.9*	*0.8*	*1.1*	*0.1*	*1.3*	*2.8*	*3.2*	*4.1*	*4.5*	*4.4*	*4.0*
Albania	1.9	0.0	1.0	3.8	4.9	5.0	6.0	7.7	8.0	4.8	6.0
Bosnia and Herzegovina	..	..	..	11.2	11.1	21.9	13.2	5.4	4.5	3.7	3.2
Bulgaria	3.6	-1.0	-0.7	-1.9	-0.3	-0.4	2.0	5.4	4.1	4.8	4.8
Croatia	..	..	..	0.6	1.6	3.2	3.4	2.9	3.8	5.2	4.7
Macedonia, TFYR	..	..	..	-0.8	-0.1	3.0	1.8	4.5	-4.5	0.9	3.1
Romania	1.9	-1.3	-0.9	-0.6	0.3	-2.1	0.7	2.1	5.7	4.9	4.7
Serbia and Montenegro	..	..	..	-6.0	-3.8	-2.4	-0.7	6.4	5.5	3.8	1.0
Yugoslavia, SFR (former)	1.0	..	..	..	..	..	..	..	..	..	..
CIS	*2.8*	*-2.9*	*-2.2*	*-5.1*	*-2.0*	*1.4*	*3.7*	*8.8*	*6.1*	*5.0*	*7.5*
Armenia	..	..	..	-1.9	1.4	5.1	7.2	5.9	9.6	12.9	13.9
Azerbaijan	..	..	..	-6.3	-1.5	7.3	8.8	11.1	9.9	10.6	11.2
Belarus	..	..	..	-1.7	0.5	6.7	6.0	5.8	4.7	5.0	6.8
Georgia	..	..	..	-7.1	-3.2	5.7	5.1	1.8	4.8	5.5	8.6
Kazakhstan	..	..	..	-4.1	-0.6	1.9	5.6	9.8	13.2	9.9	9.2
Kyrgyzstan	..	..	..	-4.1	-1.4	5.4	4.7	5.4	5.3	0.0	6.7
Moldova, Republic of	..	..	..	-11.2	-7.0	-2.7	0.7	2.1	6.1	7.8	6.3
Russian Federation	..	..	..	-4.7	-1.8	1.2	3.5	10.0	5.1	4.7	7.3
Tajikistan	..	..	..	-10.9	-5.6	0.9	4.9	8.3	10.3	9.3	10.6
Turkmenistan	..	..	..	-3.0	0.4	4.9	7.1	10.0	7.9	9.0	9.0
Ukraine	..	..	..	-9.5	-5.5	-1.9	1.9	5.9	9.2	3.6	8.5
USSR (former)	2.8	..	..	..	..	..	..	..	..	..	..
Uzbekistan	..	..	..	-0.2	1.3	4.1	4.2	4.0	4.5	4.2	4.4

For sources and notes, see end of table.

Per capita real product / Produit réel par habitant [1]											Régions, groupements économiques, pays ou zones
1980-89	1980-00	1980-03	1990-00	1990-03	1995-00	1995-03	1999-00	2000-01	2001-02	2002-03	
9.0	8.5	8.4	9.3	8.6	7.2	7.1	7.1	6.7	7.2	8.3	Chine
5.7	4.0	3.6	2.2	1.8	0.6	1.0	8.4	-0.9	1.1	0.5	Chine, Hong Kong RAS
3.2	2.4	2.2	0.2	0.7	-3.1	0.4	3.1	0.9	8.9	14.6	Chine, Macao RAS
10.8	8.1	6.7	3.0	1.9	0.5	-0.2	8.5	-10.2	0.7	2.2	Chine, Taiwan Province de [3]
3.5	3.6	3.7	4.0	4.0	4.0	3.8	2.2	3.8	2.7	6.2	Inde
3.6	4.2	3.7	2.6	2.0	-2.0	-0.3	3.5	2.1	2.3	2.8	Indonésie
6.3	-0.6	-0.7	-4.0	-2.5	-1.5	0.0	0.6	3.0	0.2	0.2	Corée, Rép. populaire dém. de
7.6	6.5	6.1	4.8	4.7	3.2	3.9	8.6	2.4	5.7	2.5	Corée, République de
1.8	3.0	3.1	3.9	3.8	3.6	3.5	3.4	3.3	3.5	3.1	Rép. dém. populaire lao
2.2	4.2	3.9	4.3	3.3	1.1	1.2	5.9	-1.6	2.1	3.2	Malaisie
8.4	6.3	5.8	4.6	4.2	5.5	3.9	1.4	0.1	2.6	5.3	Maldives
3.2	-0.5	-0.2	-0.1	0.5	2.0	1.8	0.1	-0.1	2.8	3.6	Mongolie
-1.0	1.3	2.3	5.2	5.9	6.3	6.9	12.1	9.0	4.1	3.7	Myanmar
2.3	2.5	2.4	2.5	2.1	2.2	1.6	3.7	2.4	-2.7	0.0	Népal
2.8	2.0	1.8	0.9	1.0	0.3	0.9	-0.1	0.3	3.3	2.8	Pakistan
-1.9	0.0	0.4	1.2	1.4	1.4	1.7	3.9	1.0	2.5	2.7	Philippines
4.0	5.0	4.5	4.6	3.4	2.6	1.3	6.7	-4.5	0.3	-1.2	Singapour
2.6	3.3	3.3	4.2	3.7	4.1	3.1	5.1	-2.3	3.1	4.6	Sri Lanka
5.3	5.7	5.1	3.0	2.5	-1.7	0.3	3.6	0.9	4.3	5.6	Thaïlande
..	..	..	-0.9	-0.2	-2.7	-0.2	17.4	15.7	-1.0	-7.2	Timor-Leste
3.4	4.5	4.7	6.1	5.8	5.2	5.2	5.3	5.4	5.6	4.6	Viet Nam
											ECONOMIES EN DEVELOPPEMENT : OCEANIE
1.4	**1.4**	**1.0**	**0.7**	**0.0**	**-1.2**	**-1.3**	**-1.8**	**-2.4**	**-1.1**	**0.2**	
3.1	2.8	3.0	1.5	2.5	2.3	4.0	15.4	5.3	3.6	0.9	Iles Cook
-0.2	1.4	1.5	1.5	1.6	1.2	1.7	-3.8	2.7	3.3	4.2	Fidji
3.5	2.1	1.8	1.1	0.9	0.1	0.3	1.0	0.5	0.4	0.4	Polynésie française
-1.0	0.9	1.2	3.5	3.1	4.5	2.9	0.7	0.7	-1.4	0.7	Kiribati
4.1	0.6	0.1	-3.5	-2.8	-5.7	-2.5	-3.0	0.5	3.8	2.0	Iles Marshall
3.0	1.4	1.1	-0.3	-0.1	-1.4	-0.2	1.7	1.3	-0.2	1.8	Micronésie, Etats fédérés de
2.8	-4.1	-4.4	-8.2	-6.7	-6.0	-4.2	-2.4	-5.6	1.1	1.0	Nauru
2.8	1.8	1.2	-0.8	-1.1	-2.0	-1.9	0.0	-3.1	-1.3	-2.0	Nouvelle-Calédonie
-2.0	1.2	1.1	1.9	1.0	-1.1	-1.1	-1.1	2.0	-1.1	-1.1	Palaos
-0.1	1.3	0.8	1.8	0.2	-1.6	-2.5	-3.6	-5.6	-2.8	0.6	Papouasie-Nouvelle-Guinée
0.6	-0.1	0.4	1.4	2.0	2.5	2.9	6.0	5.1	1.0	2.0	Samoa
-1.6	0.8	-0.2	0.0	-2.4	-5.2	-6.6	-16.7	-7.8	-6.8	-0.8	Iles Salomon
4.4	2.5	2.3	2.4	2.3	2.0	1.9	5.6	0.5	1.0	0.8	Tonga
-1.8	2.4	2.4	3.3	2.5	5.5	2.2	-1.3	5.3	-13.6	5.8	Tuvalu
2.5	1.0	0.4	-0.1	-1.1	-1.6	-2.7	0.4	-4.4	-7.8	-1.4	Vanuatu
1.9	**-2.8**	**-2.1**	**-4.6**	**-1.6**	**1.7**	**3.8**	**8.5**	**6.1**	**5.2**	**7.4**	**EUROPE DU SUD-EST ET CEI**
1.3	*1.0*	*1.3*	*0.4*	*1.5*	*2.7*	*3.2*	*4.1*	*4.5*	*4.5*	*4.1*	*Europe du Sud-Est*
-0.4	-0.8	0.4	4.5	5.3	5.5	6.1	7.7	7.7	4.1	5.2	Albanie
..	..	..	12.3	10.9	18.0	10.0	1.9	2.2	2.3	2.3	Bosnie-Herzégovine
3.7	-0.5	-0.1	-1.1	0.5	0.3	2.8	6.2	4.9	5.6	5.7	Bulgarie
..	..	..	1.6	2.3	3.2	3.3	2.7	3.8	5.4	4.9	Croatie
..	..	..	-1.4	-0.7	2.4	1.2	3.9	-5.0	0.4	2.6	Macédoine, LERY
1.4	-1.4	-0.9	-0.2	0.6	-1.9	0.8	2.3	5.9	5.1	5.0	Roumanie
..	..	..	-6.4	-4.1	-2.4	-0.7	6.5	5.6	3.9	1.1	Serbie-et-Monténégro
0.4			..	..	..	..	..	..	..	..	Yougoslavie, RSF (anc.)
1.9	*-3.2*	*-2.4*	*-5.1*	*-2.0*	*1.6*	*3.9*	*9.0*	*6.3*	*5.3*	*7.8*	*CEI*
..	..	..	-0.5	2.7	6.5	8.3	7.0	10.4	13.5	14.3	Arménie
..	..	..	-7.5	-2.7	6.3	7.8	10.2	8.9	9.6	10.2	Azerbaïdjan
..	..	..	-1.5	0.9	7.2	6.5	6.3	5.2	5.5	7.3	Bélarus
..	..	..	-6.8	-2.7	6.0	5.6	2.4	5.5	6.5	9.7	Géorgie
..	..	..	-3.4	0.2	3.1	6.6	10.9	14.0	10.3	9.4	Kazakhstan
..	..	..	-5.1	-2.6	3.8	3.1	3.8	3.8	-1.4	5.2	Kirghizistan
..	..	..	-11.0	-6.8	-2.4	0.9	2.3	6.3	7.9	6.4	Moldova, République de
..	..	..	-4.5	-1.5	1.5	4.0	10.5	5.6	5.2	8.0	Fédération de Russie
..	..	..	-12.1	-6.8	-0.3	3.8	7.2	9.3	8.4	9.8	Tadjikistan
..	..	..	-5.3	-1.7	2.9	5.2	8.1	6.1	7.3	7.4	Turkménistan
..	..	..	-9.1	-5.0	-1.2	2.7	6.8	10.1	4.5	9.3	Ukraine
1.9	..	..	..	..	..	..	..	..	..	..	URSS (anc.)
..	..	..	-2.1	-0.6	2.3	2.5	2.3	2.8	2.6	2.9	Ouzbékistan

Pour les sources et les notes, se reporter à la fin du tableau.

7.2 Annual average growth rates of total and per capita real gross domestic product at market prices *(concluded)*
Percentage

Region, economic grouping, country or area	Total real product / Produit réel total [1]										
	1980-89	1980-00	1980-03	1990-00	1990-03	1995-00	1995-03	1999-00	2000-01	2001-02	2002-03
DEVELOPING ECONOMIES	**3.7**	**4.4**	**4.3**	**4.7**	**4.4**	**4.0**	**3.8**	**5.6**	**2.3**	**3.4**	**4.6**
By major category											
Major petroleum exporters	0.1	2.2	2.3	2.8	2.6	2.1	2.2	3.7	3.2	0.8	2.9
Other developing economies	4.6	4.9	4.8	5.1	4.7	4.3	4.0	5.9	2.1	3.8	4.9
Major exporters of manufactures	5.7	5.7	5.6	5.6	5.2	4.6	4.4	6.9	2.2	4.7	5.1
Remaining economies	2.4	2.9	2.9	3.7	3.4	3.5	2.9	2.9	1.9	1.1	4.3
America	1.4	2.7	2.6	4.0	3.0	2.9	1.6	1.9	-0.6	-2.3	4.7
Africa	3.0	2.7	2.9	3.2	3.4	4.0	3.8	3.5	3.9	3.2	3.5
West Asia	-3.1	3.9	4.0	9.5	6.6	3.3	1.6	1.4	-2.3	-1.6	2.1
Other Asia	4.5	3.8	3.9	3.9	4.2	4.2	4.5	4.5	4.6	5.4	5.3
By income group (per capita GDP in 2000)											
High-income countries	2.6	4.1	3.9	4.0	3.4	3.2	2.4	6.3	-0.8	0.3	2.6
Middle-income countries	3.1	3.1	3.1	3.4	3.2	2.6	2.6	4.4	1.0	3.7	3.4
Low-income countries	5.7	6.0	6.0	6.6	6.4	5.8	5.9	5.9	5.9	5.7	7.1
MEMO ITEM:											
LDC	2.7	3.4	3.7	4.2	4.6	5.3	5.3	5.2	6.0	5.1	4.8
HIPC	2.7	3.1	3.4	3.9	4.3	5.1	5.0	5.3	5.4	4.4	4.3
Land-locked countries	2.5	10.1	9.0	-1.3	0.6	3.5	4.4	4.3	6.3	5.5	5.7
Developing economies excluding China	3.2	3.8	3.7	3.9	3.6	3.2	3.0	5.1	1.2	2.4	3.7
Sub-Saharan Africa	2.1	2.3	2.5	2.9	3.1	3.7	3.6	3.9	3.7	3.2	3.2

Sources:

United Nations, DESA, Statistics Division, Organisation for Economic Co-operation and Development (OECD), World Bank and national sources.

Notes:

In the absence of official estimates, some region totals have been estimated by the secretariat and used, whenever possible, in order to ensure comparability at the total group levels.

Prior to 1990, data refer to the former USSR and the former Yugoslavia. From 1990 onwards, data refer to the successor Republics of these two countries.

1 Growth rates are based on gross domestic product at constant market prices based on 1990 dollars.

2 GDP at 1995 constant prices.

3 GDP at 1996 constant prices.

7.2 Taux d'évolution annuels moyens du produit intérieur brut réel total et par habitant aux prix du marché *(fin)*
En pourcentage

Per capita real product / Produit réel par habitant [1]											Régions, groupements économiques, pays ou zones
1980-89	1980-00	1980-03	1990-00	1990-03	1995-00	1995-03	1999-00	2000-01	2001-02	2002-03	
1.6	**2.4**	**2.4**	**3.0**	**2.7**	**2.3**	**2.2**	**3.9**	**0.7**	**1.9**	**3.1**	**ECONOMIES EN DEVELOPPEMENT**
											Par principales catégories
-2.7	-0.4	-0.2	0.7	0.6	0.1	0.2	1.7	1.2	-1.1	1.0	Principaux pays exportateurs de pétrole
2.5	2.9	2.9	3.4	3.0	2.7	2.5	4.3	0.6	2.3	3.5	Autres économies en développement
											Principaux pays exportateurs d'articles manufacturés
3.8	4.1	4.0	4.2	3.8	3.2	3.1	5.6	1.0	3.5	4.0	
-0.1	0.5	0.5	1.4	1.1	1.3	0.8	0.8	-0.1	-0.9	2.2	Autres économies
-0.5	0.9	0.8	2.2	1.3	1.2	0.0	0.3	-2.2	-3.8	3.1	Amérique
0.2	0.0	0.2	0.7	1.0	1.6	1.5	1.2	1.6	1.0	1.3	Afrique
-4.9	-1.1	-1.0	1.4	0.3	0.2	-1.3	-1.4	-5.0	-4.2	-0.5	Asie occidentale
2.0	1.4	1.6	1.6	2.0	2.1	2.5	2.4	2.6	3.4	3.3	Autres pays d'Asie
											Par catégories de revenus (PIB par habitant en 2000)
0.6	2.3	2.1	2.4	1.8	1.6	0.9	4.7	-2.2	-1.1	1.3	Pays à revenu élevé
0.7	1.1	1.1	1.6	1.5	1.0	1.0	2.8	-0.5	2.2	1.9	Pays à revenu intermédiaire
3.6	4.0	4.1	4.8	4.6	4.1	4.2	4.2	4.3	4.1	5.5	Pays à revenu faible
											POUR MEMOIRE :
0.1	0.5	0.9	1.5	2.0	2.8	2.8	2.7	3.5	2.6	2.3	PMA
-0.2	0.3	0.6	1.4	1.8	2.6	2.6	3.0	3.0	2.1	2.0	PPTE
-0.2	5.1	4.5	-3.5	-1.6	1.2	2.1	2.1	4.1	3.3	3.4	Pays enclavés
								.			Economies en développement Chine non comprise
0.8	1.5	1.5	1.9	1.6	1.3	1.1	3.2	-0.6	0.7	1.9	
-0.8	-0.5	-0.3	0.2	0.5	1.1	1.1	1.4	1.3	0.8	0.9	Afrique subsaharienne

Sources :

Nations Unies/DAES/Division de statistique, Organisation de coopération et de développement économique (OCDE), Banque mondiale et sources nationales.

Notes :

Afin d'assurer la comparabilité des chiffres au niveau des groupements, quelques estimations de totaux régionaux ont été calculées par le secrétariat et utilisées, chaque fois que possible, lorsqu'une estimation officielle n'est pas disponible.

Avant 1990, les données comprennent l'ancienne URSS et l'ancienne Yougoslavie. À partir de 1990, les données comprennent les Républiques qui ont succédé à ces deux pays.

1 Les taux de croissance sont fondés sur le produit intérieur brut aux prix constants du marché en dollars de 1990.

2 PIB aux prix constants de 1995.

3 PIB aux prix constants de 1996.

7.3 Gross domestic product by type of expenditure and by kind of economic activity
Percentage

7.3 Produit intérieur brut par catégorie de dépense et par branche d'activité économique
En pourcentage

Region, economic grouping, country or area / Régions, groupements économiques, pays ou zones	Year / Année	Total GDP / PIB total	GDP by type of expenditure / PIB par catégorie de dépense					GDP by kind of economic activity [1] / PIB par branche d'activité économique [1]			
			Final consumption / Consommation finale		Gross capital formation / Formation brute de capital	Exports / Exportations	Less imports / Moins les importations	Agriculture	Industrial activity [2] / Activité industrielle [2]		Services
			Government / Administration Publique	Household / Ménages		Of goods and services / Des biens et services			Total	Manufacturing / Industries manufacturières	
DEVELOPED ECONOMIES - ECONOMIES DEVELOPPEES	1990	100	18	59	23	18	19	3	31	21	64
	1995	100	18	60	22	20	19	2	29	20	67
	2000	100	17	61	22	22	23	2	27	18	70
	2002	100	18	63	20	21	22	2	25	16	72
DEVELOPING ECONOMIES - ECONOMIES EN DEVELOPPEMENT	1990	100	14	60	25	24	24	15	35	19	48
	1995	100	14	60	28	28	28	13	35	19	49
	2000	100	14	59	24	33	31	11	36	18	49
	2002	100	15	58	25	35	32	12	36	18	49
DEVELOPED ECONOMIES: AMERICA - ECONOMIES DEVELOPPEES : AMERIQUE	**1990**	**100**	**18**	**66**	**18**	**11**	**12**	**2**	**27**	**18**	**70**
	1995	**100**	**16**	**67**	**18**	**13**	**14**	**2**	**26**	**18**	**72**
	2000	**100**	**15**	**68**	**21**	**14**	**17**	**1**	**24**	**16**	**75**
	2002	**100**	**16**	**69**	**18**	**12**	**15**	**1**	**23**	**14**	**78**
Canada	1990	100	23	56	22	26	26	3	30	16	62
	1995	100	22	56	19	38	35	3	29	17	62
	2000	100	19	54	21	47	41	2	29	18	62
	2002	100	19	56	21	42	38	2	29	18	62
United States - Etats-Unis	1990	100	17	67	18	10	11	2	27	18	70
	1995	100	15	68	18	11	12	2	26	18	73
	2000	100	15	69	21	11	15	1	24	16	76
	2002	100	16	70	18	10	14	1	23	14	79
DEVELOPED ECONOMIES: EUROPE - ECONOMIES DEVELOPPEES : EUROPE	**1990**	**100**	**21**	**56**	**24**	**28**	**28**	**3**	**31**	**22**	**60**
	1995	**100**	**21**	**57**	**21**	**31**	**29**	**3**	**28**	**19**	**63**
	2000	**100**	**20**	**58**	**22**	**38**	**37**	**2**	**26**	**18**	**64**
	2002	**100**	**21**	**58**	**20**	**37**	**35**	**2**	**26**	**18**	**65**
EU 25 - UE 25	**1990**	**100**	**21**	**56**	**24**	**27**	**28**	**3**	**31**	**22**	**60**
	1995	**100**	**21**	**57**	**21**	**30**	**29**	**3**	**28**	**19**	**63**
	2000	**100**	**20**	**58**	**22**	**37**	**37**	**2**	**26**	**18**	**64**
	2002	**100**	**21**	**58**	**20**	**36**	**35**	**2**	**25**	**18**	**65**
EU 15 - UE 15	*1990*	*100*	*21*	*57*	*23*	*27*	*27*	*3*	*31*	*22*	*61*
	1995	*100*	*21*	*57*	*21*	*30*	*28*	*3*	*28*	*19*	*63*
	2000	*100*	*20*	*58*	*21*	*37*	*36*	*2*	*26*	*18*	*65*
	2002	*100*	*21*	*58*	*20*	*36*	*34*	*2*	*25*	*18*	*65*
Austria - Autriche	1990	100	19	55	25	40	39	3	30	21	60
	1995	100	21	55	25	38	38	2	29	19	63
	2000	100	20	56	25	51	52	2	29	20	63
	2002	100	19	56	23	54	52	2	29	19	63
Belgium - Belgique	1990	100	21	55	23	72	70	2	29	21	63
	1995	100	22	54	20	70	66	2	27	19	66
	2000	100	21	54	22	87	84	1	25	18	66
	2002	100	23	54	20	85	81	1	24	17	67
Denmark - Danemark	1990	100	26	49	21	36	31	4	23	16	64
	1995	100	26	50	20	36	32	3	22	15	64
	2000	100	26	47	21	45	39	2	24	15	64
	2002	100	27	47	20	45	39	2	23	15	65
Finland - Finlande	1990	100	22	50	30	23	25	6	30	20	54
	1995	100	23	50	19	38	29	4	29	23	56
	2000	100	21	48	21	44	35	3	30	23	56
	2002	100	22	50	20	39	31	3	28	21	58
France	1990	100	22	55	24	21	22	3	27	19	64
	1995	100	24	55	19	23	21	3	24	17	65
	2000	100	23	54	21	29	28	3	23	17	67
	2002	100	24	55	19	27	25	3	23	17	66

For sources and notes, see end of table.

Pour les sources et les notes, se reporter à la fin du tableau.

Region, economic grouping, country or area / Régions, groupements économiques, pays ou zones	Year / Année	Total GDP / PIB total	GDP by type of expenditure / PIB par catégorie de dépense					GDP by kind of economic activity [1] / PIB par branche d'activité économique [1]			
			Final consumption / Consommation finale		Gross capital formation / Formation brute de capital	Exports / Exportations / Of goods and services / Des biens et services	Less imports / Moins les importations / Of goods and services / Des biens et services	Agriculture	Industrial activity [2] / Activité industrielle [2]		Services
			Government / Administration Publique	Household / Ménages					Total	Manufacturing / Industries manufacturières	
Germany - Allemagne	1990	100	20	56	24	25	25	2	35	27	57
	1995	100	20	56	23	25	24	1	30	21	63
	2000	100	19	58	22	35	34	1	28	21	64
	2002	100	20	58	18	37	32	1	27	21	65
Greece - Grèce	1990	100	15	72	23	18	28	10	26	15	60
	1995	100	15	73	19	18	25	9	21	12	63
	2000	100	16	69	24	26	34	7	20	11	64
	2002	100	16	67	24	21	28	6	20	11	64
Ireland - Irlande	1990	100	17	57	21	58	53	8	32	25	50
	1995	100	17	53	19	79	67	7	34	27	49
	2000	100	14	47	26	100	87	3	38	30	48
	2002	100	15	44	22	95	76	3	38	30	49
Italy - Italie	1990	100	20	57	22	20	20	3	31	23	62
	1995	100	18	59	19	27	23	3	28	21	63
	2000	100	18	60	20	28	27	3	26	19	64
	2002	100	19	60	20	27	26	2	26	18	66
Luxembourg	1990	100	19	52	26	105	101	2	29	20	70
	1995	100	19	47	22	111	98	1	23	15	84
	2000	100	16	39	24	153	132	1	17	11	82
	2002	100	18	42	22	149	131	1	18	10	88
Netherlands - Pays-Bas	1990	100	24	49	23	55	51	4	28	18	62
	1995	100	24	49	21	58	52	3	26	17	64
	2000	100	23	50	22	68	63	3	24	15	66
	2002	100	25	50	21	63	58	2	23	13	67
Portugal	1990	100	16	62	28	33	40	8	28	19	57
	1995	100	19	63	25	31	37	5	27	18	59
	2000	100	21	61	29	32	44	3	26	16	62
	2002	100	22	60	26	31	38	3	25	16	62
Spain - Espagne	1990	100	17	60	27	16	20	5	33	20	67
	1995	100	18	60	23	23	23	4	29	18	64
	2000	100	18	59	26	30	33	3	27	17	63
	2002	100	18	58	26	29	30	3	27	16	64
Sweden - Suède	1990	100	28	48	24	30	30	3	28	19	61
	1995	100	28	48	17	40	33	2	27	20	61
	2000	100	27	48	19	47	41	2	26	20	62
	2002	100	29	48	17	44	38	2	25	18	63
United Kingdom - Royaume-Uni	1990	100	20	62	21	25	27	2	32	21	60
	1995	100	20	63	17	29	30	2	29	19	62
	2000	100	19	65	18	29	31	1	25	16	66
	2002	100	21	66	17	27	30	1	24	15	67
New EU members 10 - Nouveaux membres de l'UE 10 [3]	*1990*	*100*	*20*	*51*	*27*	*41*	*39*	*11*	*42*	*27*	*42*
	1995	*100*	*21*	*56*	*23*	*39*	*40*	*5*	*32*	*21*	*51*
	2000	*100*	*20*	*59*	*27*	*48*	*54*	*4*	*30*	*19*	*55*
	2002	*100*	*20*	*60*	*23*	*48*	*52*	*3*	*28*	*18*	*58*
Cyprus - Chypre	1990	100	18	60	28	53	58	7	26	14	63
	1995	100	16	65	22	47	51	5	22	12	66
	2000	100	17	70	19	47	53	4	19	10	73
	2002	100	18	69	20	43	50	4	19	9	72
Czech Republic - République tchèque	1990	100	26	47	25	42	40	7	43	24	42
	1995	100	22	48	34	50	54	4	38	24	51
	2000	100	22	52	29	65	68	4	35	24	53
	2002	100	22	52	28	62	64	3	34	24	56

For sources and notes, see end of table.

Pour les sources et les notes, se reporter à la fin du tableau.

Region, economic grouping, country or area / Régions, groupements économiques, pays ou zones	Year Année	Total GDP PIB total	GDP by type of expenditure / PIB par catégorie de dépense					GDP by kind of economic activity [1] / PIB par branche d'activité économique [1]			
			Final consumption / Consommation finale		Gross capital formation Formation brute de capital	Exports Exportations Of goods and services	Less imports Moins les importations Des biens et services	Agriculture	Industrial activity [2] / Activité industrielle [2]		Services
			Government Administration Publique	Household Ménages					Total	Manufacturing Industries manufacturières	
Estonia - Estonie	1990	100	13	64	30	42	50	14	48	37	50
	1995	100	25	57	26	70	78	8	28	17	54
	2000	100	21	55	28	93	97	6	26	16	58
	2002	100	20	57	32	86	95	5	26	17	58
Hungary - Hongrie	1990	100	22	48	25	31	26	11	31	19	36
	1995	100	24	53	23	45	45	6	27	20	55
	2000	100	21	52	31	76	80	4	29	21	55
	2002	100	23	53	26	66	69	3	27	19	58
Latvia - Lettonie	1990	100	9	53	40	48	49	21	45	33	31
	1995	100	22	63	17	47	50	9	29	20	49
	2000	100	20	62	27	46	54	4	22	13	62
	2002	100	19	63	29	46	56	4	22	13	63
Lithuania - Lituanie	1990	100	19	57	33	52	61	27	30	21	44
	1995	100	23	66	23	52	63	11	31	19	49
	2000	100	22	64	20	46	52	7	27	18	56
	2002	100	20	63	22	54	60	6	27	17	56
Malta - Malte	1990	100	18	63	33	85	99	3	34	24	51
	1995	100	21	61	32	94	108	2	29	21	55
	2000	100	19	64	28	103	114	2	29	22	54
	2002	100	20	65	19	85	89	2	28	20	58
Poland - Pologne	1990	100	22	47	25	28	21	9	50	31	45
	1995	100	20	59	19	25	22	6	33	20	48
	2000	100	18	63	25	29	35	3	30	17	55
	2002	100	18	66	19	30	34	3	27	15	58
Slovakia - Slovaquie	1990	100	23	54	31	26	34	8	52	25	31
	1995	100	21	52	25	59	56	5	35	25	51
	2000	100	20	56	26	72	74	4	30	21	55
	2002	100	20	57	30	73	80	4	29	20	59
Slovenia - Slovénie	1990	100	18	53	17	92	79	5	38	30	48
	1995	100	20	59	23	53	55	4	31	23	48
	2000	100	20	56	27	57	61	3	32	24	54
	2002	100	21	54	24	59	57	3	31	23	55
Other developed Europe - Autres économies développées d'Europe	**1990**	**100**	**17**	**54**	**27**	**39**	**36**	**3**	**33**	**20**	**63**
	1995	**100**	**17**	**56**	**22**	**37**	**32**	**3**	**32**	**20**	**63**
	2000	**100**	**17**	**52**	**22**	**48**	**38**	**3**	**34**	**17**	**59**
	2002	**100**	**18**	**54**	**19**	**44**	**34**	**2**	**33**	**18**	**62**
Andorra - Andorre	1990	100	17	60	27	16	20	5	33	20	68
	1995	100	18	60	23	23	23	4	29	18	64
	2000	100	18	59	26	30	33	3	27	17	63
	2002	100	18	58	26	29	30	3	27	16	64
Iceland - Islande	1990	100	20	59	20	35	33	11	26	14	54
	1995	100	23	57	17	37	33	10	24	14	56
	2000	100	24	58	25	36	43	8	23	12	58
	2002	100	26	53	19	41	39	7	26	15	60
Liechtenstein	1990	100	14	56	29	37	37	3	34	24	65
	1995	100	15	59	22	36	32	3	33	23	67
	2000	100	14	60	21	48	43	3	32	23	65
	2002	100	15	60	18	45	38	3	33	23	66
Monaco	1990	100	22	55	24	21	22	3	27	19	64
	1995	100	24	55	19	23	21	3	24	17	65
	2000	100	23	54	21	29	28	2	23	17	67
	2002	100	24	54	19	27	25	3	23	17	66

For sources and notes, see end of table.

Pour les sources et les notes, se reporter à la fin du tableau.

Region, economic grouping, country or area / Régions, groupements économiques, pays ou zones	Year / Année	Total GDP / PIB total	GDP by type of expenditure / PIB par catégorie de dépense					GDP by kind of economic activity [1] / PIB par branche d'activité économique [1]			
			Final consumption / Consommation finale		Gross capital formation / Formation brute de capital	Exports / Exportations Of goods and services / Des biens et services	Less imports / Moins les importations Of goods and services / Des biens et services	Agriculture	Industrial activity [2] / Activité industrielle [2]		Services
			Government / Administration Publique	Household / Ménages					Total	Manufacturing / Industries manufacturières	
Norway - Norvège	1990	100	22	48	24	42	35	3	32	12	58
	1995	100	22	48	23	39	33	3	30	12	56
	2000	100	20	42	21	48	30	2	38	10	51
	2002	100	22	44	19	42	28	2	34	10	56
San Marino - Saint-Marin	1990	100	14	46	43	218	221	3	31	23	62
	1995	100	14	46	43	217	220	3	28	21	63
	2000	100	14	46	44	212	215	3	26	19	64
	2002	100	14	45	45	204	207	3	26	19	66
Switzerland - Suisse	1990	100	14	56	29	37	37	3	34	24	65
	1995	100	15	59	22	36	32	3	33	23	67
	2000	100	14	60	21	48	43	3	32	23	65
	2002	100	15	60	18	45	38	3	33	23	66
DEVELOPED ECONOMIES: ASIA - ECONOMIES DEVELOPPEES : ASIE	**1990**	**100**	**14**	**53**	**33**	**11**	**10**	**3**	**39**	**26**	**61**
	1995	**100**	**15**	**55**	**28**	**10**	**8**	**2**	**34**	**23**	**68**
	2000	**100**	**17**	**55**	**26**	**12**	**10**	**1**	**32**	**22**	**70**
	2002	**100**	**18**	**57**	**24**	**12**	**11**	**1**	**30**	**20**	**73**
Israel - Israël	1990	100	29	55	20	31	35	3	25	18	67
	1995	100	28	55	25	29	38	2	24	15	64
	2000	100	27	53	20	39	39	1	22	16	65
	2002	100	30	56	18	36	40	2	21	15	67
Japan - Japon	1990	100	13	53	33	11	10	3	39	27	61
	1995	100	15	55	28	9	8	2	34	23	68
	2000	100	17	55	27	11	9	1	32	22	70
	2002	100	18	57	24	11	10	1	30	20	73
DEVELOPED ECONOMIES: OCEANIA - ECONOMIES DEVELOPPEES : OCEANIE	**1990**	**100**	**19**	**59**	**22**	**18**	**18**	**4**	**27**	**13**	**62**
	1995	**100**	**18**	**60**	**22**	**21**	**21**	**4**	**25**	**13**	**63**
	2000	**100**	**18**	**60**	**21**	**25**	**24**	**4**	**24**	**12**	**65**
	2002	**100**	**18**	**60**	**24**	**21**	**23**	**4**	**22**	**11**	**63**
Australia - Australie	1990	100	19	59	22	17	17	4	27	13	62
	1995	100	19	60	22	20	20	3	26	13	63
	2000	100	18	60	22	23	23	3	24	11	64
	2002	100	18	61	24	20	22	4	22	10	62
New Zealand - Nouvelle-Zélande	1990	100	19	61	20	27	27	7	26	17	64
	1995	100	18	58	23	30	29	7	25	17	64
	2000	100	18	59	21	37	35	7	23	16	66
	2002	100	19	59	21	34	32	7	23	16	68
DEVELOPING ECONOMIES: AMERICA - ECONOMIES EN DEVELOPPEMENT : AMERIQUE	**1990**	**100**	**13**	**64**	**21**	**18**	**17**	**8**	**34**	**23**	**60**
	1995	**100**	**15**	**65**	**21**	**18**	**19**	**8**	**30**	**19**	**57**
	2000	**100**	**14**	**65**	**21**	**24**	**24**	**6**	**30**	**18**	**57**
	2002	**100**	**15**	**65**	**19**	**28**	**26**	**6**	**29**	**19**	**58**
South America - Amérique du Sud	*1990*	*100*	*14*	*62*	*20*	*13*	*10*	*8*	*37*	*25*	*60*
	1995	*100*	*16*	*64*	*22*	*12*	*14*	*8*	*31*	*19*	*55*
	2000	*100*	*16*	*64*	*19*	*15*	*15*	*7*	*31*	*17*	*54*
	2002	*100*	*17*	*62*	*18*	*21*	*17*	*8*	*32*	*18*	*53*
Argentina - Argentine	1990	100	12	68	14	10	5	8	36	27	57
	1995	100	13	69	18	10	10	5	25	16	62
	2000	100	14	70	16	11	12	5	24	15	63
	2002	100	12	61	12	27	13	10	31	20	55
Bolivia - Bolivie	1990	100	12	77	13	23	24	15	32	17	46
	1995	100	14	76	15	23	27	15	29	17	47
	2000	100	15	77	18	18	27	13	26	13	52
	2002	100	15	75	15	22	27	13	26	13	52

For sources and notes, see end of table.

Pour les sources et les notes, se reporter à la fin du tableau.

Region, economic grouping, country or area / Régions, groupements économiques, pays ou zones	Year / Année	Total GDP / PIB total	Final consumption / Consommation finale — Government / Administration Publique	Household / Ménages	Gross capital formation / Formation brute de capital	Exports / Exportations — Of goods and services / Des biens et services	Less imports / Moins les importations	Agriculture	Industrial activity [2] / Total	Manufacturing / Industries manufacturières	Services
Brazil - Brésil	1990	100	17	59	23	8	6	7	38	27	66
	1995	100	20	60	22	8	10	8	32	21	54
	2000	100	19	61	22	11	12	7	34	20	49
	2002	100	20	58	20	16	13	8	34	21	49
Chile - Chili	1990	100	11	60	26	33	30	7	39	17	49
	1995	100	11	61	26	29	27	6	38	18	50
	2000	100	13	64	22	32	30	6	35	17	54
	2002	100	13	63	22	34	32	5	35	18	54
Colombia - Colombie	1990	100	11	64	22	19	16	18	32	17	47
	1995	100	15	66	26	15	21	14	29	15	54
	2000	100	21	63	14	22	19	13	28	15	55
	2002	100	21	66	15	20	21	13	27	14	55
Ecuador - Equateur	1990	100	13	67	17	32	29	20	26	10	45
	1995	100	13	69	22	26	28	17	25	11	53
	2000	100	10	64	20	37	31	11	35	5	47
	2002	100	10	69	30	26	36	9	29	8	54
Guyana	1990	100	15	66	46	74	100	38	17	5	33
	1995	100	16	46	45	122	130	41	21	3	22
	2000	100	28	50	39	113	129	30	20	3	33
	2002	100	23	49	40	114	126	33	21	3	31
Paraguay	1990	100	6	77	23	33	40	28	26	17	47
	1995	100	7	85	24	35	51	25	26	16	49
	2000	100	10	83	22	20	34	25	26	14	49
	2002	100	8	86	19	31	44	24	25	14	51
Peru - Pérou	1990	100	9	71	18	14	13	8	26	15	57
	1995	100	10	71	25	13	18	8	28	15	54
	2000	100	11	71	20	16	18	8	28	15	56
	2002	100	10	72	18	16	17	7	28	14	57
Suriname	1990	100	25	54	21	28	27	10	27	12	61
	1995	100	20	16	52	100	88	17	36	15	40
	2000	100	6	19	69	62	56	12	26	9	56
	2002	100	7	24	79	49	58	10	19	5	61
Uruguay [4]	1990	100	14	69	11	26	20	11	32	26	63
	1995	100	12	73	15	19	19	9	29	20	66
	2000	100	13	75	14	19	21	6	27	17	71
	2002	100	13	74	12	22	20	9	27	18	70
Venezuela	1990	100	9	62	10	40	20	5	50	21	45
	1995	100	7	69	18	28	22	5	39	17	55
	2000	100	7	63	18	29	17	4	38	13	55
	2002	100	8	65	14	30	17	5	32	12	62
Other America - Autres économies d'Amérique	*1990*	*100*	*11*	*69*	*22*	*28*	*30*	*8*	*28*	*20*	*59*
	1995	*100*	*12*	*68*	*20*	*35*	*35*	*6*	*28*	*21*	*63*
	2000	*100*	*12*	*67*	*23*	*37*	*38*	*5*	*28*	*20*	*61*
	2002	*100*	*13*	*68*	*21*	*34*	*36*	*5*	*26*	*19*	*63*
Anguilla	1990	100	13	51	40	75	78	4	19	0	70
	1995	100	17	77	29	76	100	3	16	0	72
	2000	100	20	87	44	65	116	2	18	1	73
	2002	100	20	87	20	63	89	3	15	1	71
Antigua and Barbuda - Antigua-et-Barbuda	1990	100	20	44	36	87	87	4	22	3	75
	1995	100	23	46	40	78	87	4	19	2	74
	2000	100	24	31	52	64	70	4	21	2	74
	2002	100	32	22	55	54	62	4	23	2	73

For sources and notes, see end of table.

Pour les sources et les notes, se reporter à la fin du tableau.

Region, economic grouping, country or area / Régions, groupements économiques, pays ou zones	Year / Année	Total GDP / PIB total	GDP by type of expenditure / PIB par catégorie de dépense					GDP by kind of economic activity [1] / PIB par branche d'activité économique [1]			
			Final consumption / Consommation finale		Gross capital formation / Formation brute de capital	Exports / Exportations	Less imports / Moins les importations	Agriculture	Industrial activity [2] / Activité industrielle [2]		Services
			Government / Administration Publique	Household / Ménages	Formation brute de capital	Of goods and services / Des biens et services			Total	Manufacturing / Industries manufacturières	
Aruba	1990	100	13	45	31	80	69	1	15	1	78
	1995	100	20	51	31	85	87	1	15	3	81
	2000	100	20	50	25	75	70	0	15	3	82
	2002	100	25	55	22	69	71	0	16	3	80
Bahamas	1990	100	13	64	21	53	51	2	9	3	71
	1995	100	15	66	23	54	58	3	10	3	74
	2000	100	18	69	25	54	67	5	14	3	92
	2002	100	18	69	25	54	65	5	13	3	86
Barbados - Barbade	1990	100	20	64	19	49	52	5	16	7	66
	1995	100	20	62	15	58	55	5	13	6	66
	2000	100	21	67	18	50	56	4	13	5	66
	2002	100	23	66	16	48	53	3	14	5	66
Belize	1990	100	14	60	26	60	61	18	22	13	53
	1995	100	16	65	22	51	54	17	20	12	55
	2000	100	15	68	34	49	67	15	21	11	57
	2002	100	16	71	34	47	68	13	22	12	68
Bermuda - Bermudes	1990	100	12	68	16	47	43	1	13	3	82
	1995	100	12	64	14	46	37	1	11	3	87
	2000	100	11	61	20	47	39	1	11	3	88
	2002	100	11	60	21	47	40	1	11	3	88
British Virgin Islands - Iles Vierges britanniques	1990	100	14	49	26	95	84	3	13	3	76
	1995	100	14	49	26	95	84	2	14	4	86
	2000	100	11	40	25	104	80	1	14	4	86
	2002	100	11	39	24	104	78	1	15	4	86
Cayman Islands - Iles Caïmanes	1990	100	14	61	20	62	57	0	14	2	84
	1995	100	14	62	21	60	56	0	14	2	78
	2000	100	14	62	21	60	57	0	14	2	79
	2002	100	14	62	21	60	57	0	14	2	78
Costa Rica	1990	100	15	75	20	30	39	11	27	20	55
	1995	100	14	71	18	38	40	13	27	20	55
	2000	100	13	67	17	49	46	9	29	23	56
	2002	100	15	68	22	42	48	8	26	19	60
Cuba	1990	100	31	54	25	31	41	11	34	24	55
	1995	100	25	71	7	14	16	6	45	38	48
	2000	100	23	69	10	16	18	7	46	37	46
	2002	100	34	41	11	30	16	6	35	27	58
Dominica - Dominique	1990	100	20	64	41	50	75	22	15	6	52
	1995	100	21	64	31	51	67	16	18	6	58
	2000	100	23	64	28	54	69	16	20	7	57
	2002	100	21	70	22	46	60	15	18	7	58
Dominican Republic - République dominicaine	1990	100	3	79	22	44	47	12	29	20	51
	1995	100	4	79	19	35	37	9	28	18	55
	2000	100	8	78	24	45	55	9	29	17	55
	2002	100	10	77	23	38	47	9	27	16	55
El Salvador	1990	100	10	89	14	19	31	17	27	22	56
	1995	100	9	87	20	22	38	13	27	21	55
	2000	100	10	88	17	27	42	10	30	23	58
	2002	100	10	89	16	27	41	9	30	24	58
Grenada - Grenade	1990	100	21	65	42	45	72	13	15	4	53
	1995	100	18	68	36	45	67	11	17	5	61
	2000	100	15	59	49	56	80	8	19	5	59
	2002	100	19	68	41	44	73	11	18	5	59

For sources and notes, see end of table.

Pour les sources et les notes, se reporter à la fin du tableau.

Region, economic grouping, country or area / Régions, groupements économiques, pays ou zones	Year / Année	Total GDP / PIB total	GDP by type of expenditure / PIB par catégorie de dépense					GDP by kind of economic activity [1] / PIB par branche d'activité économique [1]			
			Final consumption / Consommation finale		Gross capital formation / Formation brute de capital	Exports / Exportations / Of goods and services / Des biens et services	Less imports / Moins les importations	Agriculture	Industrial activity [2] / Activité industrielle [2]		Services
			Government / Administration Publique	Household / Ménages					Total	Manufacturing / Industries manufacturières	
Guatemala	1990	100	7	84	14	20	24	26	20	15	54
	1995	100	6	86	15	19	25	24	20	14	56
	2000	100	8	85	17	20	29	23	20	13	57
	2002	100	8	87	18	16	28	22	20	13	58
Haiti - Haïti	1990	100	7	83	14	18	22	35	22	15	41
	1995	100	7	101	14	11	33	32	17	7	47
	2000	100	6	99	13	14	31	29	21	7	46
	2002	100	10	137	22	36	104	28	22	7	47
Honduras	1990	100	13	67	23	37	40	20	24	15	46
	1995	100	9	64	32	44	48	19	27	16	42
	2000	100	12	70	32	42	56	13	28	17	46
	2002	100	13	74	29	38	54	11	28	18	50
Jamaica - Jamaïque	1990	100	14	62	28	52	56	6	43	20	57
	1995	100	12	68	31	55	67	9	35	15	56
	2000	100	17	66	29	47	60	7	31	13	63
	2002	100	17	67	32	44	59	6	30	13	61
Mexico - Mexique [5]	1990	100	8	70	23	19	20	7	26	19	59
	1995	100	11	67	20	31	28	5	26	19	66
	2000	100	11	67	24	31	33	4	25	19	63
	2002	100	12	70	20	27	29	4	24	17	65
Montserrat	1990	100	18	62	74	29	83	3	34	2	55
	1995	100	23	62	35	62	82	5	12	3	77
	2000	100	51	69	46	49	114	0	17	0	69
	2002	100	45	92	50	42	129	0	21	0	71
Netherlands Antilles - Antilles néerlandaises	1990	100	39	37	29	81	86	1	14	7	85
	1995	100	25	60	24	76	85	1	15	7	81
	2000	100	24	55	28	71	78	1	12	4	82
	2002	100	23	54	30	69	76	1	12	4	83
Nicaragua	1990	100	30	63	19	16	28	18	25	17	52
	1995	100	15	78	22	19	35	21	24	17	46
	2000	100	17	76	34	24	51	19	25	14	49
	2002	100	16	78	33	23	50	18	25	15	50
Panama	1990	100	18	57	17	87	79	10	15	9	76
	1995	100	15	52	30	101	98	8	17	9	74
	2000	100	16	57	29	79	81	7	16	7	79
	2002	100	16	61	31	77	85	7	15	7	74
Puerto Rico - Porto Rico	1990	100	15	63	16	80	73	1	45	39	55
	1995	100	15	61	18	66	59	1	46	41	54
	2000	100	12	54	18	80	65	1	45	40	53
	2002	100	11	51	19	88	68	1	44	39	53
Saint Kitts and Nevis - Saint-Kitts-et-Nevis	1990	100	18	58	55	52	83	6	24	11	59
	1995	100	20	57	46	51	75	4	21	9	65
	2000	100	21	59	49	46	75	2	25	9	64
	2002	100	19	59	48	46	71	3	25	8	62
Saint Lucia - Sainte-Lucie	1990	100	15	70	25	69	78	13	15	7	63
	1995	100	17	59	25	70	70	8	16	6	68
	2000	100	19	62	26	59	67	8	16	4	70
	2002	100	22	59	23	56	60	6	15	4	69
Saint Vincent and the Grenadines - Saint-Vincent-et-les Grenadines	1990	100	19	63	28	60	70	18	20	7	52
	1995	100	20	64	30	52	66	12	21	7	56
	2000	100	20	62	27	53	62	9	20	5	60
	2002	100	21	61	30	49	60	9	21	5	59

For sources and notes, see end of table.

Pour les sources et les notes, se reporter à la fin du tableau.

Region, economic grouping, country or area / Régions, groupements économiques, pays ou zones	Year / Année	Total GDP / PIB total	Government / Administration Publique	Household / Ménages	Gross capital formation / Formation brute de capital	Exports / Exportations — Of goods and services / Des biens et services	Less imports / Moins les importations	Agriculture	Total	Manufacturing / Industries manufacturières	Services
Trinidad and Tobago - Trinité-et-Tobago	1990	100	16	55	14	49	33	3	45	13	50
	1995	100	16	49	21	54	39	2	41	16	55
	2000	100	12	54	20	59	45	1	44	17	55
	2002	100	15	56	23	50	43	1	46	19	63
Turks and Caicos Islands - Iles Turques et Caïques	1990	100	25	63	37	70	95	2	16	0	60
	1995	100	26	64	37	73	99	2	16	0	59
	2000	100	28	59	34	82	103	2	15	1	57
	2002	100	27	63	38	75	102	2	16	1	58
DEVELOPING ECONOMIES: AFRICA - ECONOMIES EN DEVELOPPEMENT : AFRIQUE	**1990**	**100**	**16**	**63**	**20**	**27**	**28**	**17**	**33**	**14**	**44**
	1995	**100**	**15**	**69**	**19**	**29**	**31**	**17**	**34**	**13**	**45**
	2000	**100**	**16**	**62**	**19**	**32**	**29**	**16**	**32**	**13**	**47**
	2002	**100**	**17**	**64**	**20**	**32**	**32**	**17**	**32**	**14**	**47**
North Africa - Afrique du Nord	*1990*	*100*	*15*	*64*	*25*	*27*	*31*	*16*	*35*	*13*	*44*
	1995	*100*	*15*	*68*	*21*	*25*	*28*	*15*	*36*	*14*	*48*
	2000	*100*	*14*	*61*	*20*	*30*	*25*	*14*	*38*	*14*	*43*
	2002	*100*	*15*	*63*	*22*	*30*	*29*	*14*	*37*	*14*	*46*
Algeria - Algérie	1990	100	16	57	29	23	25	11	46	11	38
	1995	100	17	56	32	27	31	10	46	9	40
	2000	100	14	42	23	42	21	8	55	6	33
	2002	100	15	44	31	36	26	9	49	6	36
Egypt - Egypte	1990	100	10	76	22	28	36	16	32	16	46
	1995	100	11	79	17	21	27	14	33	17	51
	2000	100	11	75	19	19	25	15	31	18	47
	2002	100	13	73	17	22	24	16	35	20	49
Libyan Arab Jamahiriya - Jamahiriya arabe libyenne	1990	100	26	33	21	50	30	7	48	8	45
	1995	100	23	59	12	30	24	9	46	7	45
	2000	100	21	46	13	36	16	8	53	6	39
	2002	100	17	58	14	48	37	10	46	6	44
Morocco - Maroc	1990	100	16	65	25	25	30	18	32	18	45
	1995	100	18	68	21	23	30	15	33	18	60
	2000	100	19	64	24	26	33	14	32	18	51
	2002	100	20	60	23	29	32	16	30	17	51
Sudan - Soudan	1990	100	13	76	26	10	25	29	16	9	51
	1995	100	6	79	20	3	7	50	13	8	35
	2000	100	6	75	18	17	16	38	15	10	39
	2002	100	6	83	18	11	17	31	21	9	43
Tunisia - Tunisie	1990	100	16	64	27	44	51	16	30	17	46
	1995	100	16	63	25	45	49	11	29	19	50
	2000	100	16	61	27	45	48	12	29	18	49
	2002	100	16	63	26	46	51	10	29	19	50
Other Africa - Autres économies d'Afrique	*1990*	*100*	*18*	*63*	*17*	*27*	*25*	*19*	*32*	*15*	*43*
	1995	*100*	*15*	*69*	*18*	*31*	*33*	*19*	*33*	*13*	*43*
	2000	*100*	*17*	*63*	*18*	*34*	*32*	*18*	*27*	*13*	*50*
	2002	*100*	*18*	*64*	*18*	*34*	*34*	*19*	*29*	*13*	*48*
Angola	1990	100	45	29	12	39	24	18	41	5	41
	1995	100	34	50	25	69	78	7	66	4	30
	2000	100	19	31	24	96	70	6	72	3	21
	2002	100	23	41	25	82	71	9	62	4	28
Benin - Bénin	1990	100	13	80	14	20	28	35	13	9	54
	1995	100	10	79	21	30	39	34	15	9	46
	2000	100	9	77	20	27	31	37	14	9	42
	2002	100	8	81	20	23	32	36	15	9	42

For sources and notes, see end of table.

Pour les sources et les notes, se reporter à la fin du tableau.

Region, economic grouping, country or area / Régions, groupements économiques, pays ou zones	Year / Année	Total GDP / PIB total	GDP by type of expenditure / PIB par catégorie de dépense					GDP by kind of economic activity [1] / PIB par branche d'activité économique [1]			
			Final consumption / Consommation finale		Gross capital formation / Formation brute de capital	Exports / Exportations	Less imports / Moins les importations	Agriculture / Agriculture	Industrial activity [2] / Activité industrielle [2]		Services
			Government / Administration Publique	Household / Ménages		Of goods and services / Des biens et services			Total	Manufacturing / Industries manufacturières	
Botswana	1990	100	24	30	39	57	50	5	59	5	33
	1995	100	29	34	26	50	40	4	47	5	44
	2000	100	30	30	19	61	40	3	46	5	46
	2002	100	33	28	25	50	36	3	47	4	47
Burkina Faso	1990	100	15	80	23	11	29	43	22	15	24
	1995	100	16	77	23	13	29	42	17	13	35
	2000	100	15	76	28	11	30	36	18	12	50
	2002	100	17	73	25	10	24	33	20	15	44
Burundi	1990	100	20	83	16	8	26	51	21	17	26
	1995	100	11	90	12	17	31	49	16	11	26
	2000	100	9	95	10	10	24	46	16	9	33
	2002	100	12	92	14	8	26	48	15	9	31
Cameroon - Cameroun	1990	100	11	77	15	18	21	18	32	19	48
	1995	100	13	68	13	24	18	23	28	20	43
	2000	100	9	63	15	28	15	22	28	20	44
	2002	100	9	66	16	25	16	23	29	20	45
Cape Verde - Cap-Vert	1990	100	19	89	44	17	69	14	20	8	59
	1995	100	23	86	41	17	66	14	17	7	61
	2000	100	25	95	33	18	70	14	16	6	64
	2002	100	21	96	19	22	58	12	18	7	71
Central African Republic - République centrafricaine	1990	100	14	88	11	17	30	43	13	7	44
	1995	100	13	84	13	14	24	43	13	7	44
	2000	100	4	90	9	13	16	55	20	10	26
	2002	100	4	90	10	13	16	52	18	9	34
Chad - Tchad	1990	100	21	96	10	18	46	39	20	17	44
	1995	100	16	88	10	23	37	35	16	13	43
	2000	100	18	92	18	18	45	38	14	11	43
	2002	100	20	90	55	14	78	38	15	13	41
Comoros - Comores	1990	100	26	80	20	12	37	42	8	4	52
	1995	100	21	80	21	17	39	43	14	5	52
	2000	100	18	83	16	21	39	41	12	5	48
	2002	100	20	82	19	20	40	42	13	5	50
Congo	1990	100	19	51	16	49	34	14	41	8	45
	1995	100	17	47	14	48	26	15	36	9	49
	2000	100	10	33	21	80	44	5	71	17	24
	2002	100	15	32	23	82	53	7	66	16	27
Côte d'Ivoire	1990	100	21	69	6	29	25	30	24	20	46
	1995	100	17	64	14	37	32	25	21	17	38
	2000	100	16	67	11	40	34	24	26	22	36
	2002	100	16	65	10	42	32	25	26	21	37
Dem. Rep. of the Congo - Rép. dém. du Congo	1990	100	18	55	22	59	55	31	31	1	38
	1995	100	5	81	10	29	24	52	17	6	30
	2000	100	8	82	11	7	7	54	18	2	29
	2002	100	6	88	9	12	15	50	19	4	31
Djibouti	1990	100	34	67	27	81	109	3	19	3	65
	1995	100	35	63	19	39	56	3	13	3	70
	2000	100	25	80	13	45	63	3	14	3	71
	2002	100	28	73	15	44	61	3	14	3	71
Equatorial Guinea - Guinée équatoriale	1990	100	40	80	17	32	69	52	8	1	36
	1995	100	17	56	76	55	104	42	10	1	41
	2000	100	7	19	38	95	58	42	10	1	41
	2002	100	5	15	13	95	28	39	10	1	44

For sources and notes, see end of table.

Pour les sources et les notes, se reporter à la fin du tableau.

7.3 **Gross domestic product by type of expenditure and by kind of economic activity** *(continued)*
Percentage

7.3 **Produit intérieur brut par catégorie de dépense et par branche d'activité économique** *(suite)*
En pourcentage

Region, economic grouping, country or area / Régions, groupements économiques, pays ou zones	Year / Année	Total GDP / PIB total	GDP by type of expenditure / PIB par catégorie de dépense					GDP by kind of economic activity [1] / PIB par branche d'activité économique [1]			
			Final consumption / Consommation finale		Gross capital formation / Formation brute de capital	Exports / Exportations	Less imports / Moins les importations	Agriculture	Industrial activity [2] / Activité industrielle [2]		Services
			Government / Administration Publique	Household / Ménages		Of goods and services / Des biens et services			Total	Manufacturing / Industries manufacturières	
Eritrea - Erythrée	1995	100	46	90	28	24	88	11	23	14	66
	2000	100	54	75	36	16	80	14	21	10	58
	2002	100	48	79	38	19	83	10	22	10	57
Ethiopia - Ethiopie	1990	100	19	73	13	8	12	28	11	8	29
	1995	100	11	83	16	14	24	61	8	5	28
	2000	100	24	79	13	16	31	52	11	7	37
	2002	100	20	76	17	15	28	45	11	7	45
Gabon	1990	100	13	50	22	46	31	8	48	6	44
	1995	100	14	42	23	59	37	9	51	5	40
	2000	100	9	36	21	66	33	6	53	4	40
	2002	100	10	40	23	61	34	8	50	4	42
Gambia - Gambie [6]	1990	100	14	82	18	43	58	23	11	6	68
	1995	100	11	88	20	45	64	26	13	5	64
	2000	100	13	84	17	48	62	39	13	5	56
	2002	100	14	83	19	54	69	40	15	6	45
Ghana	1990	100	11	85	12	15	24	48	23	10	21
	1995	100	12	76	20	25	33	39	24	9	28
	2000	100	11	77	26	37	51	35	25	9	29
	2002	100	12	82	23	44	61	35	25	9	40
Guinea - Guinée	1990	100	12	70	18	31	31	20	30	4	46
	1995	100	7	78	21	19	25	20	30	4	46
	2000	100	4	75	21	0	..	21	32	4	43
	2002	100	7	76	23	24	30	22	32	4	42
Guinea-Bissau - Guinée-Bissau	1990	100	10	87	30	10	37	45	18	7	37
	1995	100	7	94	22	12	35	43	16	7	36
	2000	100	14	95	18	32	59	59	12	9	29
	2002	100	13	95	16	28	53	58	12	10	30
Kenya	1990	100	19	62	24	26	31	25	16	10	47
	1995	100	15	69	22	33	39	26	14	8	48
	2000	100	18	77	15	27	36	17	16	11	53
	2002	100	19	72	14	27	31	14	17	11	60
Lesotho	1990	100	15	141	57	18	130	19	27	12	44
	1995	100	20	123	67	24	133	15	34	14	40
	2000	100	22	100	47	33	102	17	37	15	40
	2002	100	24	110	42	56	133	16	37	15	40
Liberia - Libéria	1990	100	13	70	11	34	28	54	17	12	31
	1995	100	13	70	11	36	29	82	5	3	14
	2000	100	13	70	11	33	27	74	9	7	17
	2002	100	13	70	11	33	27	77	7	5	16
Madagascar	1990	100	8	86	17	16	27	32	16	12	53
	1995	100	7	90	11	24	32	33	14	11	53
	2000	100	9	83	15	31	38	26	15	11	51
	2002	100	9	87	13	15	25	27	13	9	60
Malawi [7]	1990	100	14	80	15	22	32	33	22	19	45
	1995	100	19	75	17	34	45	33	22	19	45
	2000	100	12	85	14	26	37	33	22	19	45
	2002	100	26	83	10	24	43	32	20	16	47
Mali	1990	100	15	79	22	17	34	46	17	8	33
	1995	100	14	78	23	21	36	50	15	8	30
	2000	100	16	75	22	27	40	46	18	9	36
	2002	100	16	70	21	27	34	43	20	11	37

For sources and notes, see end of table.

Pour les sources et les notes, se reporter à la fin du tableau.

Region, economic grouping, country or area / Régions, groupements économiques, pays ou zones	Year / Année	Total GDP / PIB total	Final consumption / Consommation finale — Government / Administration Publique	Household / Ménages	Gross capital formation / Formation brute de capital	Exports / Exportations — Of goods and services / Des biens et services	Less imports / Moins les importations	Agriculture / Agriculture	Industrial activity / Activité industrielle — Total	Manufacturing / Industries manufacturières	Services
Mauritania - Mauritanie	1990	100	18	66	18	56	59	27	23	6	42
	1995	100	19	65	16	64	64	24	35	10	43
	2000	100	20	74	17	42	52	24	32	11	46
	2002	100	20	73	17	43	51	23	30	11	48
Mauritius - Maurice	1990	100	13	65	30	67	74	11	30	23	49
	1995	100	13	64	26	59	61	9	28	20	54
	2000	100	13	62	26	62	62	6	28	21	59
	2002	100	13	62	22	62	59	6	27	20	60
Mozambique	1990	100	12	101	19	6	38	65	25	14	11
	1995	100	10	100	31	13	52	34	14	7	52
	2000	100	14	79	34	13	39	24	24	12	51
	2002	100	20	74	21	24	39	24	25	13	50
Namibia - Namibie	1990	100	32	49	35	54	70	11	34	13	44
	1995	100	31	54	22	50	56	11	25	12	54
	2000	100	29	57	20	46	51	10	25	10	55
	2002	100	27	57	20	47	51	9	27	10	50
Niger	1990	100	17	74	13	17	21	42	21	9	40
	1995	100	16	78	14	20	28	44	17	6	39
	2000	100	12	82	13	16	23	34	18	7	40
	2002	100	12	85	11	17	25	40	17	7	43
Nigeria - Nigéria	1990	100	4	60	12	43	19	32	42	7	26
	1995	100	7	76	16	44	44	32	47	6	22
	2000	100	21	46	23	52	41	40	20	6	41
	2002	100	25	52	22	41	40	35	37	11	28
Rwanda	1990	100	10	84	14	6	14	44	24	16	33
	1995	100	9	101	14	6	29	44	16	10	40
	2000	100	9	90	18	6	23	41	20	10	40
	2002	100	9	90	18	7	24	44	19	10	39
Sao Tome and Principe - Sao Tomé-et-Principe	1990	100	37	77	35	22	70	28	16	5	55
	1995	100	28	78	41	24	72	27	20	4	53
	2000	100	28	76	44	35	83	20	17	2	63
	2002	100	25	77	43	36	80	20	19	4	61
Senegal - Sénégal	1990	100	15	76	14	25	30	20	19	13	61
	1995	100	12	79	17	32	40	20	20	13	60
	2000	100	14	73	23	30	40	19	20	12	60
	2002	100	15	74	20	29	37	17	22	14	62
Seychelles [8]	1990	100	28	52	25	62	67	5	16	10	64
	1995	100	28	51	30	-9	..	4	23	13	66
	2000	100	27	39	36	-3	..	3	26	14	67
	2002	100	29	45	37	-11	..	3	30	18	67
Sierra Leone	1990	100	8	80	10	26	24	37	16	7	46
	1995	100	9	76	6	29	19	41	10	3	48
	2000	100	10	86	6	17	20	47	30	9	23
	2002	100	10	85	6	19	20	53	31	10	17
Somalia - Somalie	1990	100	10	71	24	1	6	71	6	2	25
	1995	100	9	72	21	0	2	62	8	3	34
	2000	100	9	72	21	0	2	65	10	3	25
	2002	100	9	72	21	0	2	65	10	3	25
South Africa - Afrique du Sud	1990	100	19	59	16	23	18	4	36	22	50
	1995	100	18	63	18	23	22	4	32	19	56
	2000	100	19	63	16	29	26	3	28	17	60
	2002	100	19	62	16	33	30	4	29	18	58

For sources and notes, see end of table.

Pour les sources et les notes, se reporter à la fin du tableau.

Region, economic grouping, country or area / Régions, groupements économiques, pays ou zones	Year / Année	Total GDP / PIB total	GDP by type of expenditure / PIB par catégorie de dépense					GDP by kind of economic activity [1] / PIB par branche d'activité économique [1]			
			Final consumption / Consommation finale		Gross capital formation / Formation brute de capital	Exports / Exportations	Less imports / Moins les importations	Agri-culture	Industrial activity [2] / Activité industrielle [2]		Services
			Government / Administration Publique	Household / Ménages	Formation brute de capital	Of goods and services / Des biens et services			Total	Manu-facturing / Industries manu-facturières	
Swaziland	1990	100	18	78	19	72	88	11	35	29	37
	1995	100	19	80	20	75	93	12	36	29	32
	2000	100	20	75	20	64	79	11	31	25	27
	2002	100	19	76	20	69	83	12	32	26	28
Togo	1990	100	13	70	22	23	28	29	23	7	52
	1995	100	12	86	17	36	51	27	25	7	49
	2000	100	11	85	21	33	49	35	21	6	38
	2002	100	11	84	18	32	45	39	21	6	38
Uganda - Ouganda	1990	100	10	86	15	7	19	49	12	6	32
	1995	100	12	80	17	11	20	43	15	7	34
	2000	100	14	80	20	11	24	34	19	9	39
	2002	100	16	79	22	12	29	29	20	9	42
United Republic of Tanzania - République-Unie de Tanzanie	1990	100	10	73	42	14	39	50	15	8	29
	1995	100	15	82	19	24	40	44	13	7	39
	2000	100	7	84	18	15	23	42	15	7	38
	2002	100	6	80	19	17	23	41	15	7	38
Zambia - Zambie	1990	100	55	14	31	34	34	12	47	21	35
	1995	100	16	72	16	36	40	16	32	10	46
	2000	100	10	82	19	21	31	20	23	10	52
	2002	100	13	69	23	24	29	20	24	10	52
Zimbabwe	1990	100	20	63	18	23	23	15	30	21	47
	1995	100	18	65	20	39	41	13	26	19	51
	2000	100	24	61	13	29	27	19	25	17	57
	2002	100	22	67	8	24	22	17	24	16	59
DEVELOPING ECONOMIES: ASIA - ECONOMIES EN DEVELOPPEMENT : ASIE	**1990**	**100**	**14**	**56**	**29**	**27**	**26**	**19**	**36**	**18**	**43**
	1995	**100**	**12**	**55**	**33**	**33**	**33**	**16**	**38**	**20**	**45**
	2000	**100**	**14**	**55**	**27**	**39**	**35**	**14**	**40**	**19**	**45**
	2002	**100**	**14**	**53**	**28**	**39**	**34**	**13**	**40**	**18**	**46**
West Asia - Asie occidentale	*1990*	*100*	*20*	*56*	*25*	*29*	*30*	*13*	*39*	*13*	*48*
	1995	*100*	*18*	*55*	*25*	*32*	*30*	*13*	*40*	*14*	*48*
	2000	*100*	*19*	*52*	*22*	*38*	*32*	*10*	*42*	*12*	*49*
	2002	*100*	*19*	*49*	*23*	*42*	*33*	*9*	*45*	*12*	*48*
Bahrain - Bahreïn	1990	100	24	57	17	94	92	1	40	12	69
	1995	100	21	53	15	82	71	1	39	18	70
	2000	100	18	47	10	90	64	1	45	11	66
	2002	100	18	45	22	81	67	1	42	12	66
Iran, Islamic Rep. of - Iran, Rép. islamique d'	1990	100	13	62	39	17	31	18	28	10	53
	1995	100	16	46	30	21	13	18	34	12	47
	2000	100	14	47	34	22	17	13	36	13	49
	2002	100	14	42	40	26	23	11	39	12	48
Iraq	1990	100	26	51	23	19	18	20	32	9	54
	1995	100	22	75	3	2	2	65	6	5	49
	2000	100	16	74	11	15	15	31	6	5	67
	2002	100	17	75	10	14	15	32	5	4	65
Jordan - Jordanie [9]	1990	100	25	74	32	62	93	7	29	16	58
	1995	100	24	65	33	52	73	4	24	13	59
	2000	100	24	76	20	47	66	3	21	13	63
	2002	100	24	77	20	47	67	2	22	13	64
Kuwait - Koweït	1990	100	39	59	16	45	58	1	52	12	48
	1995	100	33	41	15	54	43	0	54	11	47
	2000	100	23	42	8	60	32	0	59	7	55
	2002	100	29	52	9	51	41	0	49	7	64

For sources and notes, see end of table.

Pour les sources et les notes, se reporter à la fin du tableau.

Region, economic grouping, country or area / Régions, groupements économiques, pays ou zones	Year / Année	Total GDP / PIB total	GDP by type of expenditure / PIB par catégorie de dépense					GDP by kind of economic activity [1] / PIB par branche d'activité économique [1]			
			Final consumption / Consommation finale		Gross capital formation / Formation brute de capital	Exports / Exportations	Less imports / Moins les importations	Agriculture / Agriculture	Industrial activity [2] / Activité industrielle [2]		Services
			Government / Administration Publique	Household / Ménages	Formation brute de capital	Of goods and services / Des biens et services			Total	Manufacturing / Industries manufacturières	
Lebanon - Liban	1990	100	46	90	39	16	91	9	21	13	70
	1995	100	10	108	36	11	65	13	33	18	62
	2000	100	31	78	29	63	101	11	22	9	71
	2002	100	31	78	29	63	101	11	22	9	74
Oman	1990	100	27	41	12	47	28	3	54	3	45
	1995	100	28	49	15	44	36	3	47	5	52
	2000	100	21	40	12	59	31	2	57	5	43
	2002	100	23	43	13	57	36	2	53	8	47
Qatar	1990	100	33	28	18	54	32	1	57	13	44
	1995	100	32	32	35	44	43	1	53	8	48
	2000	100	20	15	20	67	22	0	71	5	31
	2002	100	20	16	23	66	24	0	69	6	32
Saudi Arabia - Arabie saoudite	1990	100	32	40	21	47	39	6	53	8	40
	1995	100	26	40	21	44	31	7	53	9	40
	2000	100	26	37	19	44	25	5	53	10	42
	2002	100	26	32	15	52	25	5	61	9	33
Syrian Arab Republic - République arabe syrienne	1990	100	14	69	17	28	28	28	24	6	48
	1995	100	13	66	27	31	38	28	18	6	54
	2000	100	12	63	17	36	29	25	33	2	42
	2002	100	13	60	20	40	32	25	31	7	44
Turkey - Turquie	1990	100	11	69	24	13	18	18	32	22	50
	1995	100	11	69	25	20	24	16	32	23	52
	2000	100	14	70	24	23	31	15	29	20	57
	2002	100	14	66	21	29	30	13	30	22	59
United Arab Emirates - Emirats arabes unis	1990	100	16	39	20	65	41	2	63	7	37
	1995	100	17	49	29	68	63	3	57	9	41
	2000	100	16	51	27	68	62	3	57	10	40
	2002	100	16	48	26	64	55	3	67	10	40
Yemen - Yémen	1990	100	17	73	15	14	20	25	25	8	47
	1995	100	15	84	22	22	42	19	32	14	48
	2000	100	14	58	19	51	42	15	46	8	39
	2002	100	15	62	18	46	41	16	42	9	41
Other Asia - Autres économies d'Asie	*1990*	*100*	*12*	*57*	*31*	*26*	*25*	*21*	*35*	*20*	*42*
	1995	*100*	*11*	*55*	*35*	*33*	*34*	*16*	*38*	*22*	*44*
	2000	*100*	*13*	*55*	*29*	*39*	*36*	*15*	*39*	*21*	*44*
	2002	*100*	*13*	*54*	*29*	*38*	*35*	*14*	*39*	*21*	*45*
Afghanistan	1990	100	..	..	..	..	..	52	33	..	15
	1995	100	..	..	..	..	..	64	20	..	16
	2000	100	..	..	..	..	..	64	20	..	16
	2002	100	..	..	..	..	..	59	21	..	18
Bangladesh	1990	100	5	85	17	7	13	30	21	13	46
	1995	100	5	83	21	11	19	25	24	15	48
	2000	100	5	78	23	16	22	23	25	15	48
	2002	100	5	77	23	13	19	24	27	16	49
Bhutan - Bhoutan	1990	100	16	53	36	28	32	42	25	8	32
	1995	100	24	34	47	37	42	39	33	11	27
	2000	100	20	52	44	30	46	36	34	8	30
	2002	100	22	53	42	30	46	34	37	8	31

For sources and notes, see end of table.

Pour les sources et les notes, se reporter à la fin du tableau.

Region, economic grouping, country or area / Régions, groupements économiques, pays ou zones	Year / Année	Total GDP / PIB total	Final consumption / Consommation finale — Government / Administration Publique	Household / Ménages	Gross capital formation / Formation brute de capital	Exports / Exportations — Of goods and services / Des biens et services	Less imports / Moins les importations	Agriculture	Industrial activity[2] / Activité industrielle[2] — Total	Manufacturing / Industries manufacturières	Services
Brunei Darussalam - Brunéi Darussalam	1990	100	12	11	10	106	39	2	55	9	45
	1995	100	12	11	10	95	28	3	44	..	56
	2000	100	11	11	10	97	29	3	48	..	52
	2002	100	11	11	10	97	29	4	42	..	53
Cambodia - Cambodge	1990	100	7	90	9	2	8	51	12	8	39
	1995	100	5	92	14	34	46	49	12	7	34
	2000	100	6	83	14	50	52	38	21	15	36
	2002	100	6	76	18	54	55	35	24	17	35
China - Chine	1990	100	12	48	34	17	12	27	42	..	32
	1995	100	11	46	41	21	19	21	49	..	31
	2000	100	13	49	36	26	23	16	50	..	32
	2002	100	13	45	39	28	26	15	51	..	34
China, Hong Kong SAR - Chine, Hong Kong RAS	1990	100	8	56	29	136	129	0	24	17	77
	1995	100	9	61	36	151	156	0	15	8	87
	2000	100	10	57	29	152	148	0	14	6	89
	2002	100	11	56	25	159	150	0	12	4	91
China, Macao SAR - Chine, Macao RAS	1990	100	9	37	25	97	67	0	16	8	77
	1995	100	9	33	30	75	46	0	14	7	75
	2000	100	12	40	12	95	60	0	13	8	78
	2002	100	12	38	12	101	63	0	10	6	76
India - Inde	1990	100	12	65	25	7	8	28	25	15	37
	1995	100	11	64	27	11	12	26	25	16	39
	2000	100	13	65	23	14	15	23	24	14	44
	2002	100	13	65	23	15	16	21	24	14	46
Indonesia - Indonésie	1990	100	9	58	31	26	24	19	39	21	42
	1995	100	8	61	32	27	28	17	42	24	41
	2000	100	7	67	15	43	32	17	46	25	37
	2002	100	8	70	14	35	27	18	45	25	38
Korea, Dem. People's Rep. of - Corée, Rép. populaire dém. de	1990	100	10	73	24	10	17	22	44	24	34
	1995	100	16	73	14	8	11	22	44	24	34
	2000	100	16	73	14	8	11	22	44	24	34
	2002	100	16	73	14	8	11	22	44	24	34
Korea, Republic of - Corée, République de	1990	100	11	52	38	30	31	9	43	29	48
	1995	100	10	54	38	31	32	6	43	29	51
	2000	100	10	58	29	46	43	5	42	31	53
	2002	100	11	61	27	41	40	4	41	29	57
Lao People's Dem. Rep. - Rép. dém. populaire lao	1990	100	12	93	17	18	40	61	14	10	25
	1995	100	8	80	26	23	37	54	19	14	25
	2000	100	6	81	25	37	48	52	23	17	24
	2002	100	6	81	27	36	50	50	25	19	24
Malaysia - Malaisie	1990	100	14	52	32	75	72	15	42	24	44
	1995	100	12	48	44	94	98	13	41	26	48
	2000	100	11	42	27	125	105	9	51	33	45
	2002	100	14	44	24	115	97	10	48	31	46
Maldives	1990	100	18	36	32	92	77	17	15	8	63
	1995	100	17	37	31	93	77	11	13	8	76
	2000	100	23	33	26	90	72	8	14	8	74
	2002	100	24	30	26	86	66	9	15	8	71
Mongolia - Mongolie	1990	100	24	58	37	17	36	16	31	13	55
	1995	100	13	59	30	45	46	38	27	(suite)	36
	2000	100	16	66	33	61	77	29	22	6	51
	2002	100	15	63	32	56	66	21	23	6	60

For sources and notes, see end of table.

Pour les sources et les notes, se reporter à la fin du tableau.

Region, economic grouping, country or area / Régions, groupements économiques, pays ou zones	Year / Année	Total GDP / PIB total	GDP by type of expenditure / PIB par catégorie de dépense					GDP by kind of economic activity [1] / PIB par branche d'activité économique [1]			
			Final consumption / Consommation finale		Gross capital formation / Formation brute de capital	Exports / Exportations	Less imports / Moins les importations	Agriculture	Industrial activity [2] / Activité industrielle [2]		Services
			Government / Administration Publique	Household / Ménages	Formation brute de capital	Of goods and services / Des biens et services			Total	Manufacturing / Industries manufacturières	
Myanmar	1990	100	88	0	13	2	4	57	11	8	32
	1995	100	87	0	14	1	2	60	10	7	30
	2000	100	88	0	12	0	1	61	11	8	34
	2002	100	88	0	13	0	1	50	10	7	31
Nepal - Népal	1990	100	9	83	19	11	21	49	15	6	32
	1995	100	9	76	25	24	35	39	21	9	36
	2000	100	9	76	24	23	32	38	21	9	38
	2002	100	10	78	25	16	29	38	20	8	38
Pakistan	1990	100	14	68	19	17	19	23	23	16	43
	1995	100	13	73	19	17	21	23	22	15	46
	2000	100	10	75	16	18	19	23	21	15	48
	2002	100	11	74	16	21	20	23	24	16	53
Philippines	1990	100	10	71	24	28	33	22	35	25	44
	1995	100	11	74	22	36	44	22	32	23	46
	2000	100	12	66	20	52	51	16	32	22	52
	2002	100	12	69	19	49	50	15	33	23	53
Singapore - Singapour [10]	1990	100	10	45	36	9	..	0	33	26	68
	1995	100	9	41	34	16	..	0	33	25	65
	2000	100	11	41	32	16	..	0	34	27	64
	2002	100	13	43	21	24	..	0	34	27	67
Sri Lanka	1990	100	13	74	21	30	38	23	27	17	38
	1995	100	14	69	26	35	45	19	27	17	42
	2000	100	14	70	26	39	50	16	27	18	46
	2002	100	13	71	23	37	44	15	28	18	46
Thailand - Thaïlande	1990	100	9	57	41	34	42	13	31	22	43
	1995	100	10	54	43	43	49	11	34	24	43
	2000	100	12	57	23	68	59	10	35	28	45
	2002	100	12	58	24	64	57	9	37	29	47
Timor-Leste	1990	100	37	93	30	13	72	33	18	3	50
	1995	100	37	93	31	13	73	33	18	3	50
	2000	100	53	94	29	8	83	26	19	3	55
	2002	100	49	95	32	15	92	27	20	3	53
Viet Nam [11]	1990	100	7	88	14	-9	..	39	23	12	39
	1995	100	8	74	27	-9	..	27	29	15	44
	2000	100	6	67	29	-2	..	24	37	19	39
	2002	100	6	65	31	-2	..	25	36	19	40
DEVELOPING ECONOMIES: OCEANIA - ECONOMIES EN DEVELOPPEMENT : OCEANIE	**1990**	**100**	**34**	**69**	**37**	**29**	**69**	**18**	**21**	**7**	**58**
	1995	**100**	**32**	**64**	**30**	**35**	**62**	**18**	**22**	**6**	**57**
	2000	**100**	**33**	**73**	**27**	**32**	**64**	**18**	**23**	**6**	**57**
	2002	**100**	**33**	**73**	**29**	**30**	**64**	**17**	**22**	**6**	**59**
Cook Islands - Iles Cook [12]	1990	100	33	116	26	7	81	12	9	3	78
	1995	100	32	85	26	4	47	10	8	3	84
	2000	100	33	86	26	4	49	14	9	4	78
	2002	100	32	85	26	4	48	12	9	3	79
Fiji - Fidji	1990	100	17	70	18	60	65	20	16	11	60
	1995	100	18	71	15	61	65	19	17	11	59
	2000	100	21	72	13	69	74	19	17	11	61
	2002	100	16	71	14	58	59	18	17	11	60
French Polynesia - Polynésie française	1990	100	40	62	20	9	32	5	15	7	77
	1995	100	41	61	17	9	27	4	15	7	77
	2000	100	41	61	17	9	27	4	15	7	77
	2002	100	41	61	17	9	27	4	15	7	77

For sources and notes, see end of table.

Pour les sources et les notes, se reporter à la fin du tableau.

7.3 Gross domestic product by type of expenditure and by kind of economic activity (continued)
Percentage

7.3 Produit intérieur brut par catégorie de dépense et par branche d'activité économique (suite)
En pourcentage

Region, economic grouping, country or area / Régions, groupements économiques, pays ou zones	Year / Année	Total GDP / PIB total	GDP by type of expenditure / PIB par catégorie de dépense					GDP by kind of economic activity [1] / PIB par branche d'activité économique [1]			
			Final consumption / Consommation finale		Gross capital formation / Formation brute de capital	Exports / Exportations	Less imports / Moins les importations	Agriculture / Agriculture	Industrial activity [2] / Activité industrielle [2]		Services
			Government / Administration Publique	Household / Ménages		Of goods and services / Des biens et services	Of goods and services / Des biens et services		Total	Manufacturing / Industries manufacturières	
Kiribati	1990	100	21	45	7	59	31	18	7	0	79
	1995	100	21	45	9	57	32	22	4	2	74
	2000	100	21	45	9	57	32	17	10	0	75
	2002	100	22	45	8	59	33	15	11	0	76
Marshall Islands - Iles Marshall	1990	100	49	97	88	12	146	13	13	1	74
	1995	100	54	91	56	12	114	15	15	3	71
	2000	100	54	92	56	13	115	13	14	2	70
	2002	100	54	90	56	13	113	14	14	2	73
Micronesia, Federated States of - Micronésie, Etats fédérés de	1990	100	22	44	8	58	33	19	7	1	74
	1995	100	22	44	8	58	33	21	5	1	74
	2000	100	22	44	8	58	33	17	10	1	73
	2002	100	22	44	8	58	33	14	11	1	75
Nauru	1990	100	22	45	8	59	33	20	8	2	73
	1995	100	22	44	7	59	32	20	5	0	71
	2000	100	21	46	9	58	33	18	6	0	76
	2002	100	22	44	8	58	33	20	6	0	74
New Caledonia - Nouvelle-Calédonie [13]	1990	100	50	98	88	11	147	16	23	1	62
	1995	100	51	94	66	14	124	18	20	1	63
	2000	100	51	94	66	14	124	19	20	1	61
	2002	100	51	94	66	14	124	19	20	1	61
Palau - Palaos	1990	100	22	45	8	58	33	6	9	2	85
	1995	100	22	44	8	58	32	5	8	1	83
	2000	100	22	45	8	59	33	4	13	2	82
	2002	100	23	44	8	58	33	3	12	2	83
Papua New Guinea - Papouasie-Nouvelle-Guinée	1990	100	26	52	24	43	46	28	30	9	37
	1995	100	17	42	22	62	43	29	37	8	32
	2000	100	18	72	15	48	52	27	42	8	29
	2002	100	18	67	16	48	50	27	42	9	29
Samoa	1990	100	19	82	34	30	65	17	30	20	53
	1995	100	23	86	42	28	78	19	30	20	53
	2000	100	29	108	52	25	114	16	25	15	59
	2002	100	29	110	52	25	117	14	23	15	63
Solomon Islands - Iles Salomon	1990	100	32	58	20	47	57	37	8	3	40
	1995	100	33	49	19	58	59	40	8	3	44
	2000	100	32	49	20	59	59	43	9	3	47
	2002	100	32	49	20	59	59	40	8	3	43
Tonga	1990	100	19	94	18	34	66	30	12	5	50
	1995	100	20	107	22	20	69	25	12	4	49
	2000	100	22	97	22	16	56	24	13	5	53
	2002	100	22	101	21	16	59	24	13	4	51
Tuvalu	1990	100	46	91	82	9	127	20	10	0	50
	1995	100	50	92	58	8	108	25	17	0	58
	2000	100	53	87	53	13	107	21	14	0	57
	2002	100	53	90	58	11	111	21	21	5	58
Vanuatu	1990	100	27	60	42	45	74	20	14	6	66
	1995	100	27	49	34	46	56	25	12	5	63
	2000	100	28	51	30	47	56	21	12	5	66
	2002	100	28	51	30	48	56	23	12	4	73

For sources and notes, see end of table.

Pour les sources et les notes, se reporter à la fin du tableau.

Region, economic grouping, country or area / Régions, groupements économiques, pays ou zones	Year / Année	Total GDP / PIB total	GDP by type of expenditure / PIB par catégorie de dépense					GDP by kind of economic activity [1] / PIB par branche d'activité économique [1]				
			Final consumption / Consommation finale		Gross capital formation / Formation brute de capital	Exports / Exportations / Of goods and services / Des biens et services	Less imports / Moins les importations / Of goods and services / Des biens et services	Agriculture / Agriculture	Industrial activity [2] / Activité industrielle [2]			Services
			Government / Administration Publique	Household / Ménages					Total	Manufacturing / Industries manufacturières		
South-East Europe and CIS - Europe du Sud-Est et CEI	1990	100	20	52	30	24	26	19	44	35		32
	1995	100	19	56	25	33	33	11	34	26		48
	2000	100	17	53	20	45	35	10	32	25		47
	2002	100	18	56	22	40	36	9	31	23		51
South-East Europe - Europe du Sud-Est	*1990*	*100*	*17*	*67*	*22*	*33*	*39*	*18*	*39*	*31*		*38*
	1995	*100*	*20*	*67*	*20*	*27*	*33*	*16*	*33*	*23*		*41*
	2000	*100*	*20*	*68*	*19*	*37*	*44*	*12*	*28*	*19*		*48*
	2002	*100*	*19*	*69*	*22*	*37*	*46*	*12*	*29*	*20*		*48*
Albania - Albanie [14]	1990	100	10	73	24	-7	..	40	44	..		16
	1995	100	55	49	19	12	35	55	22	..		23
	2000	100	9	81	31	18	39	25	16	10		52
	2002	100	11	94	20	19	43	25	20	10		58
Bosnia and Herzegovina - Bosnie-Herzégovine	1990	100	20	69	19	48	56	25	25	21		41
	1995	100	25	67	20	43	55	25	25	21		41
	2000	100	28	61	24	41	54	11	24	10		48
	2002	100	24	90	21	27	62	10	22	10		50
Bulgaria - Bulgarie	1990	100	8	74	23	36	41	18	45	31		35
	1995	100	15	71	16	45	46	13	31	21		51
	2000	100	18	69	18	56	61	12	27	16		50
	2002	100	18	69	20	53	60	11	25	15		52
Croatia - Croatie	1990	100	24	66	13	78	81	10	32	..		50
	1995	100	29	65	18	39	50	9	28	20		46
	2000	100	25	60	21	48	53	7	25	18		52
	2002	100	22	60	27	46	55	7	24	..		54
Macedonia, TFYR - Macédoine, LERY	1990	100	20	70	20	27	38	8	44	34		39
	1995	100	19	70	21	33	43	11	29	22		47
	2000	100	18	74	22	49	63	10	28	17		48
	2002	100	21	72	21	43	56	10	25	16		51
Romania - Roumanie	1990	100	13	66	31	17	26	22	46	37		27
	1995	100	14	68	24	28	33	20	40	27		36
	2000	100	16	70	20	33	39	11	32	22		46
	2002	100	16	67	23	36	42	12	34	24		45
Serbia and Montenegro - Serbie-et-Monténégro	1990	100	21	65	16	11	14	18	35	26		44
	1995	100	21	67	17	7	12	16	31	22		38
	2000	100	29	70	9	9	17	20	30	21		44
	2002	100	28	69	12	16	24	18	32	20		41
CIS - CEI	*1990*	*100*	*20*	*51*	*31*	*23*	*25*	*19*	*45*	*36*		*31*
	1995	*100*	*19*	*53*	*26*	*34*	*33*	*10*	*35*	*27*		*49*
	2000	*100*	*16*	*50*	*20*	*48*	*32*	*9*	*33*	*26*		*47*
	2002	*100*	*18*	*53*	*22*	*41*	*33*	*8*	*31*	*24*		*52*
Armenia - Arménie	1990	100	17	48	47	35	46	16	50	32		27
	1995	100	12	109	19	25	64	41	31	24		28
	2000	100	12	97	19	23	51	23	32	22		37
	2002	100	10	87	20	29	46	24	33	20		35
Azerbaijan - Azerbaïdjan	1990	100	17	52	26	43	39	27	30	18		34
	1995	100	13	84	24	33	54	25	31	12		38
	2000	100	15	63	21	40	38	16	43	5		36
	2002	100	13	61	34	45	53	14	45	6		32
Belarus - Bélarus	1990	100	25	50	25	50	50	25	48	40		30
	1995	100	21	58	26	51	56	16	33	(28)		45
	2000	100	20	57	26	72	75	12	33	27		42
	2002	100	22	59	23	65	69	10	31	25		46

For sources and notes, see end of table.

Pour les sources et les notes, se reporter à la fin du tableau.

Region, economic grouping, country or area / Régions, groupements économiques, pays ou zones	Year / Année	Total GDP / PIB total	Final consumption / Consommation finale — Government / Administration Publique	Household / Ménages	Gross capital formation / Formation brute de capital	Exports / Exportations — Of goods and services / Des biens et services	Less imports / Moins les importations	Agriculture / Agriculture	Industrial activity [2] — Total	Manufacturing / Industries manufacturières	Services
Georgia - Géorgie	1990	100	16	59	30	39	45	30	33	24	33
	1995	100	9	81	26	15	31	42	12	10	41
	2000	100	8	87	21	23	39	20	21	17	54
	2002	100	10	82	21	29	41	19	23	18	52
Kazakhstan	1990	100	12	64	47	8	31	34	33	21	32
	1995	100	13	68	23	38	43	12	30	24	54
	2000	100	12	61	18	57	49	8	38	33	48
	2002	100	12	59	28	49	48	8	36	30	51
Kyrgyzstan - Kirghizistan	1990	100	26	70	25	30	51	33	37	29	28
	1995	100	20	75	19	30	43	41	19	13	35
	2000	100	21	65	21	43	49	34	28	24	31
	2002	100	19	67	18	41	45	34	21	13	36
Moldova, Republic of - Moldova, République de	1990	100	11	62	30	49	52	35	36	..	25
	1995	100	26	56	25	61	69	29	29	23	33
	2000	100	15	88	24	50	77	25	19	14	46
	2002	100	20	83	22	53	78	21	20	15	48
Russian Federation - Fédération de Russie	1990	100	21	48	31	18	18	16	46	37	32
	1995	100	19	51	26	30	26	7	35	26	52
	2000	100	15	46	19	45	24	6	34	28	50
	2002	100	18	51	21	36	25	6	31	24	55
Tajikistan - Tadjikistan	1990	100	7	62	13	57	39	30	46	35	35
	1995	100	12	66	32	126	136	37	37	34	28
	2000	100	8	70	11	83	73	27	27	24	38
	2002	100	9	73	18	66	65	26	26	22	38
Turkmenistan - Turkménistan	1990	100	23	49	40	58	70	11	81	76	12
	1995	100	8	60	34	143	146	16	62	56	18
	2000	100	9	51	42	100	102	23	42	35	35
	2002	100	9	51	42	100	102	24	44	34	32
Ukraine	1990	100	18	53	29	29	29	23	45	36	27
	1995	100	23	53	28	50	53	14	40	34	38
	2000	100	19	56	20	64	59	15	32	18	39
	2002	100	21	55	19	57	53	13	34	20	43
Uzbekistan - Ouzbékistan	1990	100	26	61	33	29	49	34	35	24	32
	1995	100	22	50	24	32	29	28	25	18	36
	2000	100	19	62	20	30	30	30	20	14	36
	2002	100	20	61	20	30	30	27	23	16	37
DEVELOPING ECONOMIES - ECONOMIES EN DEVELOPPEMENT	**1990**	**100**	**14**	**60**	**25**	**24**	**24**	**15**	**35**	**19**	**48**
	1995	**100**	**14**	**60**	**28**	**28**	**28**	**13**	**35**	**19**	**49**
	2000	**100**	**14**	**59**	**24**	**33**	**31**	**11**	**36**	**18**	**49**
	2002	**100**	**15**	**58**	**25**	**35**	**32**	**12**	**36**	**18**	**49**
By major category - Par catégories principales											
Major petroleum exporters - Principaux pays exportateurs de pétrole	1990	100	19	52	24	35	30	13	43	12	44
	1995	100	15	56	24	35	31	14	43	13	42
	2000	100	16	50	20	43	28	10	46	12	44
	2002	100	17	50	21	42	30	11	47	12	43
Other developing economies - Autres économies en développement	1990	100	13	62	26	22	22	16	33	21	50
	1995	100	13	60	28	26	28	13	33	20	50
	2000	100	14	60	25	32	31	12	34	19	50
	2002	100	14	59	26	34	32	12	35	(19)	50

For sources and notes, see end of table.

Pour les sources et les notes, se reporter à la fin du tableau.

7.3 Gross domestic product by type of expenditure and by kind of economic activity *(continued)*
Percentage

7.3 Produit intérieur brut par catégorie de dépense et par branche d'activité économique *(suite)*
En pourcentage

Region, economic grouping, country or area / Régions, groupements économiques, pays ou zones	Year / Année	Total GDP / PIB total	GDP by type of expenditure / PIB par catégorie de dépense					GDP by kind of economic activity [1] / PIB par branche d'activité économique [1]			
			Final consumption / Consommation finale		Gross capital formation / Formation brute de capital	Exports / Exportations	Less imports / Moins les importations	Agriculture / Agriculture	Industrial activity [2] / Activité industrielle [2]		Services
			Government / Administration Publique	Household / Ménages	Formation brute de capital	Of goods and services / Des biens et services			Total	Manufacturing / Industries manufacturières	
Major exporters of manufactures - Principaux pays exportateurs d'articles manufacturés	1990	100	12	59	29	21	21	15	35	23	50
	1995	100	13	57	31	28	29	13	36	22	49
	2000	100	13	58	28	34	33	11	36	21	48
	2002	100	13	57	28	35	33	11	37	20	50
Remaining economies - Autres economies	1990	100	16	67	19	24	26	17	30	18	49
	1995	100	15	69	21	22	26	14	28	17	54
	2000	100	17	67	19	25	28	13	27	16	54
	2002	100	17	65	19	30	31	15	28	17	53
America - Amérique	1990	100	13	67	18	26	25	10	33	22	55
	1995	100	13	69	21	22	24	8	29	18	58
	2000	100	14	68	18	27	28	7	29	18	59
	2002	100	14	65	19	36	34	9	30	19	57
Africa - Afrique	1990	100	16	68	20	24	28	18	29	16	46
	1995	100	16	70	19	25	29	16	28	16	51
	2000	100	16	69	19	26	29	16	27	16	50
	2002	100	16	69	18	28	31	17	28	16	51
West Asia - Asie occidentale	1990	100	33	81	35	43	92	8	26	15	63
	1995	100	15	91	35	27	68	9	30	16	61
	2000	100	29	77	26	57	89	8	22	10	69
	2002	100	28	78	26	57	89	8	22	11	70
Other Asia - Autres économies d'Asie	1990	100	20	65	19	13	17	31	24	14	41
	1995	100	19	65	21	15	20	29	22	14	44
	2000	100	24	59	20	16	18	30	24	14	44
	2002	100	25	57	20	15	17	29	24	15	44
By income group (per capita GDP in 2000) - Par catégories de revenus (PIB par habitant en 2000)											
High-income - Revenu élevé	1990	100	14	58	25	37	34	6	38	21	54
	1995	100	13	59	27	39	38	5	35	20	59
	2000	100	13	59	23	44	40	4	34	19	59
	2002	100	14	59	21	48	41	4	35	18	60
Middle-income - Revenu intermédiaire	1990	100	15	62	25	20	22	12	35	21	54
	1995	100	16	61	26	23	25	11	33	20	52
	2000	100	16	62	22	30	29	10	33	19	50
	2002	100	16	60	22	33	31	10	34	19	51
Low-income - Revenu faible	1990	100	14	60	26	16	16	27	32	15	37
	1995	100	12	59	31	21	22	24	37	16	36
	2000	100	14	57	28	25	24	20	39	15	38
	2002	100	14	55	30	25	24	19	40	16	39
MEMO ITEM: / POUR MEMOIRE :											
Least developed countries - Pays les moins avancés	1990	100	22	67	19	16	23	34	21	9	41
	1995	100	21	70	19	17	27	37	20	10	40
	2000	100	27	59	19	20	24	36	22	10	40
	2002	100	28	59	19	19	25	34	22	10	41
Heavily indebted poor countries - Pays pauvres très endettés	1990	100	23	65	18	19	25	32	22	11	42
	1995	100	21	66	19	19	25	35	21	11	40
	2000	100	26	57	19	20	23	33	25	11	39
	2002	100	27	57	19	19	23	31	24	11	40
Landlocked countries - Pays enclavés	1990	100	18	62	34	26	40	30	36	24	32
	1995	100	15	71	22	39	46	26	28	18	41
	2000	100	15	69	21	37	41	23	28	17	43
	2002	100	15	67	24	40	46	22	29	18	43

For sources and notes, see end of table.

Pour les sources et les notes, se reporter à la fin du tableau.

7.3 Gross domestic product by type of expenditure and by kind of economic activity *(concluded)*
Percentage

7.3 Produit intérieur brut par catégorie de dépense et par branche d'activité économique *(fin)*
En pourcentage

Region, economic grouping, country or area Régions, groupements économiques, pays ou zones	Year Année	Total GDP PIB total	GDP by type of expenditure PIB par catégorie de dépense					GDP by kind of economic activity [1] PIB par branche d'activité économique [1]			
			Final consumption Consommation finale		Gross capital formation Formation brute de capital	Exports Exportations Of goods and services Des biens et services	Less imports Moins les importations	Agriculture	Industrial activity [2] Activité industrielle [2]		Services
			Government Administration Publique	Household Ménages					Total	Manufacturing Industries manufacturières	
Developing economies excluding China - Economies en développement Chine non comprise	1990	100	14	61	24	25	25	14	34	19	50
	1995	100	14	62	26	29	30	12	33	19	52
	2000	100	15	61	22	35	33	10	32	18	53
	2002	100	15	61	21	37	33	11	33	18	53
Sub-Saharan Africa - Afrique subsaharienne	1990	100	17	64	18	26	25	20	30	14	44
	1995	100	15	69	18	30	32	20	32	13	43
	2000	100	17	64	18	33	32	19	26	13	49
	2002	100	18	65	18	33	34	19	28	13	47

Sources:
United Nations/DESA/Statistics Division: National Account Main Aggregates Database and national sources.

Notes:
Data in this table are shown as percentage of GDP at current prices.

1 Gross value added by economic activity is measured at basic prices. The value added data shown as percentage of GDP are calculated using total gross value added at factor cost.

2 Mining and quarrying, manufacturing, construction, electricity, gas and water.

3 Up to 1992 (inclusive), data for 10 new EU members include figures for former Czechoslovakia, which are not shown separately.

4 Household consumption expenditure 1980-2002: includes NPISHs (Non-profit institutions serving households) final consumption expenditure.

5 Household consumption expenditure 1980-1992: includes NPISHs (Non-profit institutions serving households) final consumption expenditure.

6 Exports of goods and services 1970-1993: includes net travel and tourism income.

Imports of goods and services 1970-1993: includes net freight and insurance.

7 Household consumption expenditure 1970-1996: includes changes in inventories.

8 Exports of goods and services 1994-2002: reported as exports less imports balance.

9 General government final consumption expenditure 1970-1979 and 1987-2001: includes pension payments less employees' pension contributions. Some non-capital development expenditure of the central government is included in fixed capital formation.

10 Exports 1971 - 2002: reported as exports less imports balance.

11 Exports 1970 - 2002: reported as exports less imports balance.

12 1970 - 2002 imports valued c.i.f., instead of f.o.b.

13 General government final consumption expenditure 1970-1992: includes education and health.

14 Exports 1980 - 1990: reported as exports less imports balance.

Sources :
Nations Unies/DAES/Division de statistique : Base de données des principaux agrégats des comptes nationaux et diverses sources nationales.

Notes :
Les données de ce tableau sont indiquées en pourcentage du PIB aux prix courants.

1 La valeur ajoutée brute de chaque branche d'activité est au prix de base. Les données de la valeur ajoutée indiquées sont calculées en pourcentage de la valeur ajoutée brute totale au coût des facteurs.

2 Industries extractives, industries manufacturières, construction, électricité, gaz et eau.

3 Jusqu'à l'année 1992 (comprise), les données pour les 10 nouveaux membres de l'UE comprennent les chiffres de l'ancienne Tchécoslovaquie, qui ne sont pas présentés séparément.

4 Dépense de consommation finale des ménages 1980-2002 : comprend les dépenses de consommation finale des institutions sans but lucratif au service des ménages.

5 Dépense de consommation finale des ménages 1980-1992 : comprend les dépenses de consommation finale des institutions sans but lucratif au service des ménages.

6 Exportations des biens et des services 1970-1993 : comprend les voyages nets et le revenu du tourisme.
Importations des biens et des services 1970-1993 : comprend le fret net et l'assurance.

7 Dépense de consommation finale des ménages 1970-1996 : comprend les variations des stocks.

8 Exportations 1994 - 2002 : déclarées comme la balance des exportations et des importations.

9 Dépense de consommation finale des administrations publiques 1970-1979 et 1987-2001 : comprend les paiements pour les fonds de pension, diminués des contributions pour les mêmes fonds payés par des salariés. Certaines dépenses des administrations publiques, ne contribuant pas au développement du capital, sont comprises dans la formation du capital brut.

10 Exportations 1971 - 2002 : déclarées comme la balance des exportations et des importations.

11 Exportations 1970 - 2002 : déclarées comme la balance des exportations et des importations.

12 1970 - 2002 les importations évaluées c.a.f., au lieu de f.a.b.

13 Dépense de consommation finale des administrations publiques 1970-1992 : comprend l'éducation et la santé.

14 Exportations 1980 - 1990 : déclarées comme la balance des exportations et des importations.

7.4 Selected indicators of development: population, health and environment

Country or area	Urban population (% of total population) Population urbaine (% de la population totale)	Crude birth rate per 1 000 inhabitants Taux de natalité brut pour 1 000 habitants	Crude death rate per 1 000 inhabitants Taux de mortalité brut pour 1 000 habitants	Infant mortality rate per 1 000 live births Taux de mortalité infantile pour 1 000 naissances vivantes	Life expectancy at birth Espérance de vie à la naissance	AIDS estimated deaths Décès dus au SIDA, estimations	Persons living with HIV/AIDS Personnes vivant avec VIH/SIDA
	(1)	(2)	(3)	(4)	(5)	(6)	(7)
Afghanistan	24	47	21	162	43	..	..
Albania	45	18	5	25	74	..	..
Algeria	60	23	5	44	70	..	..
American Samoa	91	..	..	..	..	..	..
Andorra	91	..	..	..	..	..	..
Angola	37	52	24	140	40	24000	350000
Anguilla	100	..	..	..	..	..	..
Antigua and Barbuda	38	..	..	..	..	..	..
Argentina	91	19	8	20	74	1800	130000
Armenia	64	10	8	17	72	100 c	2400
Aruba	45	..	..	..	..	..	..
Australia	93 a	12 a	7 a	6 a	79 a	100 c	12000
Austria	66	9	10	5	79	100 c	9900
Azerbaijan	50	18	6	29	72	100 c	1400
Bahamas	90	19	8	18	67	610	6200
Bahrain	90	20	3	14	74	..	1000 d
Bangladesh	25	29	8	64	61	650	13000
Barbados	53	12	8	11	77	..	..
Belarus	72	9	13	11	70	1000	15000
Belgium	97	11	10	4	79	100 c	8500
Belize	49	27	5	31	71	300	2500
Benin	46	42	14	93	51	8100	120000
Bermuda	100	..	..	..	..	..	..
Bhutan	9	35	9	54	63	..	100 c
Bolivia	64	29	8	56	64	290	4600
Bosnia and Herzegovina	45	10	8	14	74	..	..
Botswana	53	31	21	57	40	26000	330000
Brazil	84	20	7	38	68	8400	610000
British Virgin Islands	65	..	..	..	..	..	..
Brunei Darussalam	78	23	3	6	76	..	..
Bulgaria	70	8	15	15	71	..	..
Burkina Faso	19	48	17	93	46	44000	440000
Burundi	11	44	21	107	41	40000	390000
Cambodia	20	34	10	73	57	12000	170000
Cameroon	53	35	17	88	46	53000	920000
Canada	81	10	8	5	79	500 e	55000
Cape Verde	58	28	5	30	70	..	..
Cayman Islands	100	..	..	..	..	..	..
Central African Republic	44	38	22	100	40	22000	250000
Chad	26	48	20	115	45	14000	150000
Channel Islands	31	11	10	6	78	..	..
Chile	88	18	6	12	76	220	20000
China	41	15	7	37	71	30000	850000
China, Hong Kong SAR	100	9	6	4	80	100 c	2600
China, Macao SAR	99	10	5	9	79	..	..
China, Taiwan Province of	..	..	..	..	..	..	..
Colombia	77	22	5	26	72	5600	140000
Comoros	36	37	8	67	61	..	..
Congo	54	44	15	84	48	11000	110000
Cook Islands	73	..	..	..	..	..	..
Costa Rica	62	19	4	10	78	890	11000
Côte d'Ivoire	46	35	20	101	41	75000	770000
Croatia	60	11	12	8	74	10 g	200
Cuba	76	12	7	7	77	120	3200
Cyprus	69	13	8	8	78	..	1000 d
Czech Republic	75	9	11	6	75	10 g	500
Dem. Rep. of the Congo	33	50	21	120	42	120000	1300000
Denmark	86	12	11	5	77	100 c	3800
Djibouti	85	40	18	102	46	..	..
Dominica	73	..	..	..	..	..	..

For sources and notes, see end of table.

350

Access to improved drinking water (% of population) / Disponibilité d'eau potable (% de la population)	Access to adequate sanitation facilities (% of population) / Disponiblité de sanitaires adéquats (% de la population)	CO$_2$ emissions (1 000 metric tons of carbon) / Emissions de CO$_2$ (1 000 tonnes métriques de carbone)	CO$_2$ emissions per capita (metric tons of carbon) / Emissions de CO$_2$ par habitant (tonnes métriques de carbone)	Energy consumption: KTOE / Consommation d'énergie : KTEP	Energy consumption: kg OE per 1 dollar of GDP / Consommation d'énergie : kg EP pour 1 dollar du PIB	Pays ou zones
(8)	(9)	(10)	(11)	(12)	(13)	
13	12	906	..	..	..	Afghanistan
97	91	2860	0.9	1944	0.48	Albanie
89	92	89481	3.0	30845	0.59	Algérie
..	..	..	..	..	..	Samoa américaines
100	100	..	..	..	..	Andorre
38	44	6406	0.5	8815	1.08	Angola
..	..	..	..	..	..	Anguilla
91	95	352	4.9	..	..	Antigua-et-Barbuda
..	..	138288	3.7	56297	0.23	Argentine
..	..	3513	1.1	1938	0.83	Arménie
..	..	1925	20.6	..	..	Aruba
100	100	348983	18.2	112712	0.23	Australie
100	100	64928	8.0	30443	0.11	Autriche
78	81	29062	3.6	11728	2.25	Azerbaïdjan
97	100	1797	5.9	..	..	Bahamas
..	..	19514	28.8	6865	0.90	Bahreïn
97	48	29275	0.2	21004	. 0.39	Bangladesh
100	100	1177	4.4	..	..	Barbade
100	..	59195	5.9	24771	1.19	Bélarus
..	..	126331	12.3	56887	0.18	Belgique
92	50	781	3.3	..	..	Belize
63	23	1621	0.3	2231	0.77	Bénin
..	..	462	5.8	..	..	Bermudes
62	70	396	0.2	..	..	Bhoutan
83	70	11073	1.3	4310	0.52	Bolivie
..	..	19265	4.8	4324	0.63	Bosnie-Herzégovine
95	66	3854	2.2	..	..	Botswana
87	76	307743	1.8	190664	0.24	Brésil
..	..	59	3.0	..	..	Iles Vierges britanniques
..	..	6299	18.9	2156	..	Brunéi Darussalam
100	100	46842	5.8	19019	1.39	Bulgarie
42	29	1030	0.1	..	..	Burkina Faso
78	88	242	..	..	..	Burundi
30	17	532	..	..	..	Cambodge
58	79	6545	0.4	6569	0.60	Cameroun
100	100	576770	18.7	250035	0.34	Canada
74	71	139	0.3	..	..	Cap-Vert
..	..	286	7.8	..	..	Iles Caïmanes
70	25	271	0.1	..	..	République centrafricaine
27	29	125	..	..	..	Tchad
..	..	..	..	..	..	Iles Anglo-Normandes
93	96	59543	3.9	24708	0.29	Chili
75	40	2792482	2.2	1228574	1.02	Chine
..	..	33092	4.9	16377	0.09	Chine, Hong Kong RAS
..	..	1635	3.6	..	..	Chine, Macao RAS
..	..	..	..	93576	..	Chine, Taiwan Province de
91	86	58502	1.4	27397	0.27	Colombie
96	98	81	0.1	..	..	Comores
51	..	1811	0.5	923	0.36	Congo
..	..	29	1.6	..	..	Iles Cook
95	93	5427	1.4	3564	0.23	Costa Rica
81	52	10483	0.7	6555	0.51	Côte d'Ivoire
..	..	56591 h	12.8 h	8222	0.34	Croatie
91	98	30936	2.8	14197	..	Cuba
100	100	6428	8.2	2467	0.22	Chypre
..	..	127902	12.5	41725	0.72	République tchèque
45	21	2732	0.1	15402	3.31	Rép. dém. du Congo
100	..	52764	9.9	19749	0.09	Danemark
100	91	385	0.6	..	..	Djibouti
97	83	103	1.3	..	..	Dominique

Pour les sources et les notes, se reporter à la fin du tableau.

Country or area	Urban population (% of total population) — Population urbaine (% de la population totale)	Crude birth rate per 1 000 inhabitants — Taux de natalité brut pour 1 000 habitants	Crude death rate per 1 000 inhabitants — Taux de mortalité brut pour 1 000 habitants	Infant mortality rate per 1 000 live births — Taux de mortalité infantile pour 1 000 naissances vivantes	Life expectancy at birth — Espérance de vie à la naissance	AIDS estimated deaths — Décès dus au SIDA, estimations	Persons living with HIV/AIDS — Personnes vivant avec VIH/SIDA
	(1)	(2)	(3)	(4)	(5)	(6)	(7)
Dominican Republic	60	23	7	36	67	7800	130000
Ecuador	63	23	6	41	71	1700	20000
Egypt	42	27	6	41	69	..	8000
El Salvador	60	25	6	26	71	2100	24000
Equatorial Guinea	50	43	17	101	49	370	5900
Eritrea	21	40	12	73	53	350	55000
Estonia	70	9	14	9	72	100 c	7700
Ethiopia	16	43	18	100	45	160000	2100000
Faeroe Islands	39	..	..	..	..	..	..
Falkland Islands (Malvinas)	85	..	..	..	..	..	..
Fiji	53	24	5	18	70	..	300
Finland	61	11	10	4	78	100 c	1200
France	77	13	9	5	79	800	100000
French Guiana	76	24	4	14	75	..	..
French Polynesia	52	20	5	9	73	..	..
Gabon	85	32	11	57	57	..	..
Gambia	26	36	13	81	54	400	8400
Georgia	51	10	10	18	74	100 c	900
Germany	88	9	11	5	78	660	41000
Ghana	46	32	10	58	58	28000	360000
Gibraltar	100	..	..	..	..	..	..
Greece	61	9	10	6	78	100 c	8800
Greenland	..	..	..	..	..	..	..
Grenada	42	..	..	..	..	..	..
Guadeloupe	100	16	6	7	78	..	..
Guam	94	20	5	10	75	..	..
Guatemala	47	34	7	41	66	5200	67000
Guinea	36	43	16	102	49	..	..
Guinea-Bissau	36	50	20	120	45	1200	17000
Guyana	38	22	9	51	63	1300	18000
Haiti	39	30	15	63	50	30000	250000
Holy See	100	..	..	..	..	..	..
Honduras	46	30	6	32	69	3300	57000
Hungary	66	9	14	9	72	100 c	2800
Iceland	93	14	7	3	80	100 c	220
India	29	24	8	64	64	..	3970000
Indonesia	48	21	7	42	67	4600	120000
Iran, Islamic Rep. of	68	20	5	33	70	290	20000
Iraq	67	35	9	83	61	..	1000 d
Ireland	60	14	8	6	77	100 c	2400
Isle of Man	52	..	..	..	..	..	..
Israel	92	20	6	6	79	..	..
Italy	68	9	11	5	79	1100	100000
Jamaica	52	20	6	20	76	980	20000
Japan	66	9	8	3	82	430	12000
Jordan	79	28	4	24	71	..	1000 d
Kazakhstan	56	16	9	52	66	300	6000
Kenya	42	33	17	69	45	190000	2500000
Kiribati	50	..	..	..	..	..	..
Korea, Dem. People's Rep. of	62	16	11	45	63	..	..
Korea, Republic of	81	12	6	5	75	220	4000
Kuwait	96	20	2	11	77	..	..
Kyrgyzstan	34	22	7	37	69	100 c	500
Lao People's Dem. Rep.	22	36	13	88	54	150 f	1400
Latvia	66	8	14	14	71	100 c	5000
Lebanon	88	19	5	17	74	..	..
Lesotho	18	31	26	92	35	25000	360000
Liberia	48	50	22	147	41	..	..
Libyan Arab Jamahiriya	87	23	4	21	73	..	7000

For sources and notes, see end of table.

Access to improved drinking water (% of population) / Disponibilité d'eau potable (% de la population)	Access to adequate sanitation facilities (% of population) / Disponiblité de sanitaires adéquats (% de la population)	CO_2 emissions (1 000 metric tons of carbon) / Emissions de CO_2 (1 000 tonnes métriques de carbone)	CO_2 emissions per capita (metric tons of carbon) / Emissions de CO_2 par habitant (tonnes métriques de carbone)	Energy consumption: KTOE / Consommation d'énergie : KTEP	Energy consumption: kg OE per 1 dollar of GDP / Consommation d'énergie : kg EP pour 1 dollar du PIB	Pays ou zones
(8)	(9)	(10)	(11)	(12)	(13)	
86	67	25150	3.0	8167	0.42	République dominicaine
85	86	25469	2.1	9048	0.39	Equateur
97	98	142329	2.1	52393	0.63	Egypte
77	82	6670	1.1	4299	0.37	El Salvador
44	53	205	0.4	..	..	Guinée équatoriale
46	13	..	..	768	1.12	Erythrée
..	..	16849	12.3	4514	0.77	Estonie
24	12	5581	0.1	19934	2.39	Ethiopie
..	..	649	14.2	..	..	Iles Féroé
..	..	37	12.4	..	..	Iles Falkland (Malvinas)
47	43	726	0.9	..	..	Fidji
100	100	62283	12.0	35622	0.21	Finlande
..	..	407199	6.9	265881	0.15	France
..	..	..	..	..	..	Guyane française
..	..	..	..	..	..	Polynésie française
86	53	3502	2.8	1590	0.28	Gabon
62	37	271	0.2	..	..	Gambie
79	100	6175	1.2	2559	0.65	Géorgie
..	..	857969	10.4	346352	0.13	Allemagne
73	72	5900	0.3	8344	0.96	Ghana
..	..	216	7.9	169	..	Gibraltar
..	..	103727	9.5	29025	0.19	Grèce
..	..	..	..	..	..	Groenland
95	97	213	2.6	..	..	Grenade
..	..	..	..	7384	..	Guadeloupe
..	..	..	..	..	..	Guam
92	81	9893	0.9	7384	0.40	Guatemala
48	58	1294	0.2	..	..	Guinée
56	56	264	0.2	..	..	Guinée-Bissau
94	87	1599	2.1	..	..	Guyana
46	28	1423	0.2	2081	0.74	Haïti
..	..	..	..	..	..	Saint-Siège
88	75	4792	0.7	3426	0.71	Honduras
99	99	59009	5.9	25449	0.44	Hongrie
..	..	2316	8.2	3404	0.38	Islande
84	28	1071638	1.1	538305	1.04	Inde
78	55	269764	1.3	156086	0.70	Indonésie
92	83	310526	4.7	133960	1.13	Iran, Rép. islamique d'
85	79	76391	3.3	28996	..	Iraq
..	..	44160	11.6	15303	0.13	Irlande
..	..	..	..	..	..	Ile de Man
..	..	63144	10.5	20954	0.19	Israël
..	..	460965	8.0	172720	0.14	Italie
92	99	10787	4.2	3914	0.71	Jamaïque
..	..	1238699	9.8	516927	0.09	Japon
96	99	15561	3.1	5359	0.62	Jordanie
91	99	121363	7.8	46455	1.62	Kazakhstan
57	87	9361	0.3	15324	1.52	Kenya
48	48	26	0.3	..	..	Kiribati
100	99	188995	8.5	19537	..	Corée, Rép. populaire dém. de
92	63	427324	9.1	203498	0.30	Corée, République de
..	..	47923	21.3	22189	0.82	Koweït
77	100	4642	0.9	2536	1.11	Kirghizistan
37	30	414	0.1	..	..	Rép. dém. populaire lao
..	..	6935	2.9	4266	0.60	Lettonie
100	99	15173	4.4	5369	0.42	Liban
78	49	..	..	..	..	Lesotho
..	..	400	0.1	..	..	Libéria
72	97	57167	10.9	18704	..	Jamahiriya arabe libyenne

Pour les sources et les notes, se reporter à la fin du tableau.

Country or area	Urban population (% of total population) / Population urbaine (% de la population totale)	Crude birth rate per 1 000 inhabitants / Taux de natalité brut pour 1 000 habitants	Crude death rate per 1 000 inhabitants / Taux de mortalité brut pour 1 000 habitants	Infant mortality rate per 1 000 live births / Taux de mortalité infantile pour 1 000 naissances vivantes	Life expectancy at birth / Espérance de vie à la naissance	AIDS estimated deaths / Décès dus au SIDA, estimations	Persons living with HIV/AIDS / Personnes vivant avec VIH/SIDA
	(1)	(2)	(3)	(4)	(5)	(6)	(7)
Liechtenstein	22	..	..	..	..	..	..
Lithuania	67	9	12	9	73	100 c	1300
Luxembourg	92	13	8	5	78	100 c	..
Macedonia, TFYR	60	14	8	16	74	..	100 c
Madagascar	27	42	13	91	54	..	22000
Malawi	17	45	24	115	38	80000	850000
Malaysia	65	23	5	10	73	2500	42000
Maldives	30	36	6	38	67	..	100 c
Mali	34	50	16	119	49	11000	110000
Malta	92	12	8	7	78	100 c	..
Marshall Islands	67	..	..	..	..	..	..
Martinique	96	14	7	7	79	..	..
Mauritania	64	42	14	97	52	..	..
Mauritius	44 b	16 b	7 b	16 b	72 b	100 c	700
Mexico	76	22	5	28	73	4200	150000
Micronesia, Federated States of	30	28	6	34	69	..	..
Moldova, Republic of	46	11	11	18	69	300	5500
Monaco	100	..	..	..	..	..	..
Mongolia	57	22	7	58	64	..	100 c
Montserrat	14	..	..	..	..	..	..
Morocco	59	23	6	42	69	..	13000
Mozambique	38	41	23	122	38	60000	1100000
Myanmar	31	24	11	83	57	..	..
Namibia	33	33	18	60	44	13000	230000
Nauru	100	..	..	..	..	..	..
Nepal	16	33	10	71	60	2400	58000
Netherlands	67	12	9	5	78	110	17000
Netherlands Antilles	70	..	..	..	..	..	..
New Caledonia	62	19	5	7	75	..	..
New Zealand	86	14	8	6	78	100 c	1200
Nicaragua	58	32	5	36	70	400	5800
Niger	23	55	19	126	46	..	..
Nigeria	48	39	14	79	51	170000	3500000
Niue	37	..	..	..	..	..	..
Northern Mariana Islands	95	..	..	..	..	..	..
Norway	80	12	10	5	79	100 c	1800
Oman	79	32	3	20	72	..	1300
Pakistan	35	36	10	87	61	4500	78000
Palau	68	..	..	..	..	..	..
Palestinian territory	72	..	..	..	..	..	..
Panama	58	23	5	21	75	1900	25000
Papua New Guinea	13	32	9	62	58	880	17000
Paraguay	58	30	5	37	71	..	..
Peru	75	23	6	33	70	3900	53000
Philippines	63	25	5	29	70	720	9400
Poland	62	10	10	9	74	..	..
Portugal	56	11	11	6	76	1000	27000
Qatar	92	17	4	12	72	..	..
Reunion	92	19	5	8	75	..	..
Romania	55	10	12	20	71	350	6500
Russian Federation	73	9	15	16	67	9000	700000
Rwanda	22	44	22	112	39	49000	500000
Saint Helena	36	..	..	..	..	..	..
Saint Kitts and Nevis	32	..	..	..	..	..	..
Saint Lucia	31	20	6	15	73	..	..
Saint Pierre and Miquelon	89	..	..	..	..	..	..
Saint Vincent and the Grenadines	60	20	6	16	74	..	..
Samoa	22	29	5	26	70	..	..
San Marino	89	..	..	..	..	..	..
Sao Tome and Principe	38	33	6	32	70	..	..

For sources and notes, see end of table.

Access to improved drinking water (% of population) Disponibilité d'eau potable (% de la population)	Access to adequate sanitation facilities (% of population) Disponiblité de sanitaires adéquats (% de la population)	CO$_2$ emissions (1 000 metric tons of carbon) Emissions de CO$_2$ (1 000 tonnes métriques de carbone)	CO$_2$ emissions per capita (metric tons of carbon) Emissions de CO$_2$ par habitant (tonnes métriques de carbone)	Energy consumption: KTOE Consommation d'énergie : KTEP	Energy consumption: kg OE per 1 dollar of GDP Consommation d'énergie : kg EP pour 1 dollar du PIB	Pays ou zones
(8)	(9)	(10)	(11)	(12)	(13)	
..	..	196 h	6.1 h	..	..	Liechtenstein
..	..	..	..	8589	0.84	Lituanie
..	..	5399	12.4	4041	..	Luxembourg
..	..	11194	5.5	..	..	Macédoine, LERY
47	42	2270	0.1	..	..	Madagascar
57	76	766	0.1	..	..	Malawi
..	..	144518	6.3	51753	0.44	Malaisie
100	56	499	1.7	..	..	Maldives
65	69	557	..	..	..	Mali
100	100	2816	7.2	892	0.22	Malte
..	..	..	..	..	..	Iles Marshall
..	..	..	..	..	..	Martinique
37	33	3073	1.2	..	..	Mauritanie
100	99	2897	2.4	..	..	Maurice
88	74	424281	4.3	157308	0.42	Mexique
..	..	..	..	..	..	Micronésie, Etats fédérés de
92	99	6574	1.5	2993	1.70	Moldova, République de
100	100	90	2.7	..	..	Monaco
60	30	7502	3.0	..	..	Mongolie
..	..	48	12.3	..	..	Montserrat
80	68	36575	1.3	10753	0.25	Maroc
57	43	1181	0.1	8045	1.96	Mozambique
72	64	9156	0.2	12578	..	Myanmar
77	41	1822	1.0	1188	0.27	Namibie
..	..	136	11.2	..	..	Nauru
88	28	3403	0.1	8515	1.47	Népal
100	100	173840	10.9	77923	0.15	Pays-Bas
..	..	9937	46.2	1482	..	Antilles néerlandaises
..	..	..	..	..	..	Nouvelle-Calédonie
..	..	30662	8.1	18013	0.24	Nouvelle-Zélande
77	85	3740	0.7	2908	1.10	Nicaragua
59	20	1184	0.1	..	..	Niger
62	54	36175	0.3	95675	2.90	Nigéria
100	100	4	2.0	..	..	Nioué
..	..	..	..	..	..	Iles Mariannes du Nord
100	..	41120	9.2	26515	0.15	Norvège
39	92	19789	7.6	10825	0.69	Oman
90	62	104881	0.7	65806	0.88	Pakistan
79	100	242	12.6	..	..	Palaos
..	..	..	..	..	..	Territoire palestinien
90	92	6340	2.1	3022	..	Panama
42	82	2427	0.5	..	..	Papouasie-Nouvelle-Guinée
78	94	3663	0.7	3905	0.42	Paraguay
80	71	29564	1.1	12024	0.19	Pérou
86	83	77587	1.0	42008	0.43	Philippines
..	..	314812	8.1	89185	0.61	Pologne
..	..	63493	6.3	26392	0.20	Portugal
..	..	40715	70.1	12158	..	Qatar
..	..	..	..	..	..	Réunion
58	53	112150	5.0	36976	1.03	Roumanie
99	..	1508921 h	10.3 h	617843	1.32	Fédération de Russie
41	8	572	0.1	..	..	Rwanda
..	..	11	2.2	..	..	Sainte-Hélène
..	..	103	2.4	..	..	Saint-Kitts-et-Nevis
98	89	337	2.3	..	..	Sainte-Lucie
..	..	..	..	..	..	Saint-Pierre-et-Miquelon
93	96	169	1.4	..	..	Saint-Vincent-et-les Grenadines
99	99	139	0.8	..	..	Samoa
..	..	..	..	..	..	Saint-Marin
..	..	88	0.6	..	..	Sao Tomé-et-Principe

Pour les sources et les notes, se reporter à la fin du tableau.

Country or area	Urban population (% of total population) / Population urbaine (% de la population totale)	Crude birth rate per 1 000 inhabitants / Taux de natalité brut pour 1 000 habitants	Crude death rate per 1 000 inhabitants / Taux de mortalité brut pour 1 000 habitants	Infant mortality rate per 1 000 live births / Taux de mortalité infantile pour 1 000 naissances vivantes	Life expectancy at birth / Espérance de vie à la naissance	AIDS estimated deaths / Décès dus au SIDA, estimations	Persons living with HIV/AIDS / Personnes vivant avec VIH/SIDA
	(1)	(2)	(3)	(4)	(5)	(6)	(7)
Saudi Arabia	88	32	4	21	72	..	..
Senegal	51	37	12	61	53	2500	27000
Serbia and Montenegro	52	12	11	13	73	100 c	10000
Seychelles	50	..	..	..	..	..	..
Sierra Leone	40	50	29	177	34	11000	170000
Singapore	100	10	5	3	78	140	3400
Slovakia	58	10	10	8	74	100 c	100 c
Slovenia	51	8	10	6	76	100 c	280
Solomon Islands	17	33	5	21	69	..	..
Somalia	36	52	18	118	48	..	43000
South Africa	58	23	17	48	48	360000	5000000
Spain	77	9	9	5	79	2300	130000
Sri Lanka	21	16	7	20	73	250	4800
Sudan	41	33	12	77	56	23000	450000
Suriname	77	22	6	26	71	330	3700
Swaziland	24	34	25	78	34	12000	170000
Sweden	83	10	11	3	80	100 c	3300
Switzerland	68	9	10	5	79	100 c	19000
Syrian Arab Republic	50	28	4	22	72	..	..
Tajikistan	24	24	6	50	69	100 c	200
Thailand	32	17	7	20	69	55000	670000
Timor-Leste	8	..	..	..	..	..	..
Togo	36	38	15	81	50	12000	150000
Tokelau	..	..	..	..	..	..	..
Tonga	34	27	7	34	69	..	..
Trinidad and Tobago	76	14	7	14	71	1200	17000
Tunisia	64	17	5	23	73	..	..
Turkey	67	21	6	40	71	..	..
Turkmenistan	46	22	6	49	67	100 c	100 c
Turks and Caicos Islands	47	..	..	..	..	..	..
Tuvalu	57	..	..	..	..	..	..
Uganda	12	51	17	86	46	84000	600000
Ukraine	67	8	14	14	70	11000	250000
United Arab Emirates	85	17	2	14	75	..	..
United Kingdom	89	11	10	5	78	460	34000
United Republic of Tanzania	38	39	18	100	43	140000	1500000
United States	81	14	8	7	77	15000	900000
United States Virgin Islands	94	14	6	10	78	..	..
Uruguay	93	17	9	13	75	500 e	6300
Uzbekistan	36	22	6	37	70	100 c	740
Vanuatu	24	30	5	29	69	..	..
Venezuela	88	23	5	19	74	..	..
Viet Nam	27	20	6	34	69	..	130000
Wallis and Futuna Islands	..	..	..	..	..	..	..
Yemen	26	45	9	71	60	6600	9900
Zambia	37	42	28	105	32	120000	1200000
Zimbabwe	36	32	27	58	33	200000	2300000

For sources and notes, see next page.

Access to improved drinking water (% of population) / Disponibilité d'eau potable (% de la population)	Access to adequate sanitation facilities (% of population) / Disponiblité de sanitaires adéquats (% de la population)	CO$_2$ emissions (1 000 metric tons of carbon) / Emissions de CO$_2$ (1 000 tonnes métriques de carbone)	CO$_2$ emissions per capita (metric tons of carbon) / Emissions de CO$_2$ par habitant (tonnes métriques de carbone)	Energy consumption: KTOE / Consommation d'énergie : KTEP	Energy consumption: kg OE per 1 dollar of GDP / Consommation d'énergie : kg EP pour 1 dollar du PIB	Pays ou zones
(8)	(9)	(10)	(11)	(12)	(13)	
95	100	374616	16.9	126387	0.76	Arabie saoudite
78	70	4180	0.4	3192	0.52	Sénégal
98	100	41796	4.0	16169	1.08	Serbie-et-Monténégro
..	..	227	2.9	..	..	Seychelles
57	66	565	0.1	..	..	Sierra Leone
100	100	59088	14.7	25307	0.22	Singapour
100	100	40061	7.4	18546	0.75	Slovaquie
100	..	..	..	6951	0.28	Slovénie
71	34	165	0.4	..	..	Iles Salomon
..	..	..	..	..	..	Somalie
86	87	327518	7.4	113458	0.62	Afrique du Sud
..	..	308201	7.6	131558	0.18	Espagne
77	94	10190	0.5	8179	0.48	Sri Lanka
75	62	5225	0.2	15850	1.47	Soudan
82	93	2119	5.0	..	..	Suriname
..	..	381	0.4	..	..	Swaziland
100	100	53766	6.1	51031	0.17	Suède
100	100	43753	6.1	27139	0.08	Suisse
80	90	54226	3.3	18054	1.28	République arabe syrienne
60	90	3975	0.7	3247	2.19	Tadjikistan
84	96	198792	3.3	83339	0.45	Thaïlande
..	..	..	..	..	..	Timor-Leste
54	34	1797	0.4	1540	1.01	Togo
..	..	..	..	..	..	Tokélaou
100	..	121	1.2	..	..	Tonga
90	99	26382	20.5	9286	1.29	Trinité-et-Tobago
80	84	18407	1.9	8276	0.33	Tunisie
82	90	221716	3.2	75418	0.37	Turquie
..	..	34617	7.5	16606	3.97	Turkménistan
..	..	..	..	..	..	Iles Turques et Caïques
100	100	..	..	..	..	Tuvalu
52	79	1525	0.1	..	..	Ouganda
98	99	..	..	130743	2.62	Ukraine
..	..	58956	20.9	36072	0.64	Emirats arabes unis
100	100	544359	9.3	226508	0.17	Royaume-Uni
68	90	4308	0.1	14339	1.97	République-Unie de Tanzanie
100	100	5883119	20.6	2290410	0.25	Etats-Unis
..	..	..	..	..	..	Iles Vierges américaines
98	94	5412	1.6	2510	0.14	Uruguay
85	89	..	..	51740	2.95	Ouzbékistan
88	100	81	0.4	..	..	Vanuatu
83	68	157865	6.5	54006	0.72	Venezuela
77	47	57504	0.7	42645	1.28	Viet Nam
..	..	..	..	..	..	Iles Wallis et Futuna
69	38	8444	0.5	4107	0.67	Yémen
64	78	1826	0.2	6549	1.51	Zambie
83	62	14813	1.2	9761	1.44	Zimbabwe

Pour les sources et les notes, se reporter à la page suivante.

7.4 Selected indicators of development: population, health and environment

7.4 Quelques indicateurs de développement : population, santé et environnement

Sources:

Column (1)

United Nations, DESA, Population Division, *World Urbanization Prospects: The 2002 Revision*.

Columns (2) (3) (4) (5)

United Nations, DESA, Population Division, *World Population Prospects: The 2002 Revision*.

Column (6)

UNAIDS and United Nations, DESA, Statistics Division.

Column (7)

UNAIDS.

Columns (8) (9)

UNICEF, *The State of the World's Children 2003*.

Columns (10) (11)

United Nations, DESA, Statistics Division and

United Nations Framework Covention on Climate Change (UNFCCC)

Columns (12) (13)

International Energy Agency (IEA): Database.

Notes:

a   Including Christmas Island, Cocos (Keeling) Islands and Norfolk Island.

b   Including Agalega, Rodrigues and Saint Brandon.

c   Less than 100.

d   Less than 1000.

e   Less than 500.

f   Less than 150.

g   Less than 10.

h   Year 1999.

A year by the column number denotes the year to which a column refers.

(1)   Year 2005, estimates.

(2) (3) (5) The average value per year for the period 2000-2005.

(4)   The average value per year for the period 2000-2005. "Infant" refers to a child of age younger than 1 year.

(6)   Estimated number of adults and children who died due to AIDS during 2001.

(7)   Estimates for the end of the year 2001.

(8) (9)   Year 2000.

(10)   Year 2000. Emissions refer to total CO_2 emissions from fossil fuels, presented in thousand metric tons of carbon.

(11)   Year 2000. Emissions refer to per capita total CO_2 emissions from fossil fuels, presented in metric tons of carbon.

(12)   Year 2002. The energy consumption data correspond to the TPES series of the IEA. TPES (Total primary energy supply) measured in KTOE (kilotons of oil equivalent), (1 KTOE = 1 000 000 kg OE).

(13)   Year 2002. The energy consumption data correspond to column (12). GDP figures are taken from the World Bank series in constant 1995 US dollars.

Sources :

Colonne (1)

Nations Unies, DAES, Division de la population, *World Urbanization Prospects: The 2002 Revision*.

Colonnes (2) (3) (4) (5)

Nations Unies, DAES, Division de la population, *World Population Prospects: The 2002 Revision*.

Colonne (6)

ONUSIDA et Nations Unies, DAES, Division de statistique.

Colonne (7)

ONUSIDA.

Colonnes (8) (9)

UNICEF, *The State of the World's Children 2003*.

Colonnes (10) (11)

Nations Unies, DAES, Division de statistique et

Convention cadre des Nations Unies sur le changement climatique.

Colonnes (12) (13)

Agence internationale de l'énergie (AIE) : Base de données.

Notes :

a   Ile Christmas, Iles des Cocos (Keeling) et Ile Norfolk inclus.

b   Agalega, Rodrigues et Saint Brandon inclus.

c   Moins de 100.

d   Moins de 1000.

e   Moins de 500.

f   Moins de 150.

g   Moins de 10.

h   Année 1999.

Une année à côté du numéro de colonne indique l'année à laquelle les données se réfèrent.

(1)   Année 2005, estimations.

(2) (3) (5) La valeur moyenne par an pour la période 2000-2005.

(4)   La valeur moyenne par an pour la période 2000-2005. "Infantile" se réfère aux enfants agés de moins d'une année.

(6)   Estimations du nombre d'adultes et d'enfants morts du SIDA au cours de 2001.

(7)   Estimations pour la fin de l'année 2001.

(8) (9)   Année 2000.

(10)   Année 2000. Les émissions se réfèrent aux émissions totales de CO_2 qui sont mesurées en 1000 tonnes métriques de carbone.

(11)   Année 2000. Les émissions se réfèrent aux émissions totales par habitant de CO_2 qui sont mésurées en tonnes métriques de carbone.

(12)   Année 2002. Les données sur la consommation d'énergie correspondent à la série ATEP de l'AIE. ATEP (Approvisionnement total d'énergie primaire) est présenté en KTEP (kilotonnes d'équivalent de pétrole), (1 KTEP = 1 000 000 kg EP).

(13)   Année 2002. Les données sur la consommation d'énergie sont dérivées de la colonne (12). Les chiffres sur le PNB sont pris de la série du PNB en dollar constant de 1995 de la Banque mondiale.

Country or area	Education / Enseignement				Illiteracy rate as % of population / Taux d'analphabétisme en % de la population	Adult: female literacy rate as % of male / Adulte : taux d'alphabétisation féminin en % du masculin
	Primary: net enrolment ratio / Primaire : taux net d'inscription	Secondary / Secondaire		Tertiary: gross enrolment ratio / Troisième dégré : taux brut d'inscription		
		Net enrolment ratio / Taux net d'inscription	Female enrolment as % of male / Taux d'inscription féminine en % du masculin			
	(1)	(2)	(3)	(4)	(5)	(6)
Afghanistan	..	..	..	..	..	..
Albania	98 a	74 a	103	15 a	14	98
Algeria	95	62	108	..	30	92
Angola	..	..	78	..	..	..
Anguilla	97	99	98	..	..	..
Argentina	100	81	106	56	3	100
Armenia	85	85	106	27	1	100
Aruba	98	78	107	29	..	..
Australia	96	88	99	65	..	..
Austria	91 a	88 a	95	57 a	..	..
Azerbaijan	80	76	97	24	..	..
Bahamas	86	79	103	..	4	102
Bahrain	91	81	109	..	11	101
Bangladesh	87	44	110	6	58	72
Barbados	100	87	100	36 a	0	100
Belarus	94	78	104	62	0	100
Belgium	100 a	..	112	58 a	..	..
Belize	96 a	60 a	108	..	6	101
Benin	70 a	20 a	46	..	59	54
Bermuda	..	..	..	62 a	..	..
Bhutan	..	..	86	62 a	..	..
Bolivia	94	67 a	96	39	13	96
Bosnia and Herzegovina	..	..	..	..	..	..
Botswana	81	55 a	106	4	20	108
Brazil	97	72	110	18	12	103
British Virgin Islands	..	78	102	51	..	..
Brunei Darussalam	..	..	106	13	8	101
Bulgaria	94 a	86 a	98	40 a	1	100
Burkina Faso	35	8 a	65	1	73	55
Burundi	53	8	73	2	48	98
Cambodia	86	21	60	3	30	90
Cameroon	..	..	82	5	25	97
Canada	100 a	98 a	99	59 a	..	..
Cape Verde	99	..	105	4	24	94
Central African Republic	55 a	..	..	..	49	82
Chad	58	8 a	28 b	..	53	86
Chile	86	79	102 b	42	4	100
China	93 a	..	..	13 a	13	98
China, Hong Kong SAR	98	72	100	26	6	101
China, Macao SAR	86	72	106	66	6	99
Colombia	87	54	110	24	8	101
Comoros	56 a	..	84	..	44	80
Congo	..	..	71	4	16	99
Costa Rica	91	51	103	21	4	101
Côte d'Ivoire	63	..	..	..	48	77
Croatia	88	86	102	36	2	100
Cuba	96	83	99	27	3	100
Cyprus	95 a	88 a	102	22 a	2	100
Czech Republic	88	89	103	34	..	..
Dem. Rep. of the Congo	..	..	..	..	35	88
Denmark	99 a	89 a	105	59 a	..	..
Djibouti	34	17	62	1	32	92
Dominica	..	84 a	113 b	..	..	..
Dominican Republic	97	41	124	..	15	102
Ecuador	99 ·	50	101	..	8	99
Egypt	90	81	93	..	42	85
El Salvador	89	46	101	17	20	98
Equatorial Guinea	85	..	57	..	14	98
Eritrea	43	21	65	2	41	77
Estonia	98	92 a	102	60	0	100

For sources and notes, see end of table.

Employment Emploi		Labour force Main-d'œuvre			Migration		Pays ou zones
			of which dont				
Unemployment rate Taux de chômage	Female unemployment rate Taux de chômage féminin	Female labour force Main-d'œuvre féminine	Industry Industrie	Services	Net number of migrants (Thousands) Nombre net de migrants (Milliers)	Net migration rate per 1 000 inhabitants Taux net de migration par 1 000 habitants	
(7)	(8)	(9)	(10)	(11)	(12)	(13)	
..	..	36	..	..	1508	12.73	Afghanistan
23 a	28 a	41	..	..	-95	-6.00	Albanie
30 b	30 b	29	..	..	-100	-0.63	Algérie
..	..	46	..	..	221	3.28	Angola
..	..	..	..	..	..	..	Anguilla
18	16 b	34	23 a	76 a	60	0.31	Argentine
..	..	49	14 b	37 b	-100	-6.50	Arménie
..	..	..	..	..	..	..	Aruba
6	6	44	21 a	74 a	450	4.59	Australie
4 a	4 a	40	30 a	64 a	70	1.73	Autriche
1 a	2 a	45	11 a	49 a	-140	-3.36	Azerbaïdjan
..	..	47	..	..	..	..	Bahamas
..	..	22	..	..	18	4.89	Bahreïn
..	..	42	10 b	24 b	-300	-0.41	Bangladesh
10	12	46	20 a	56 a	-1	-0.93	Barbade
..	3 a	49	..	..	-10	-0.20	Bélarus
7	8	41	..	..	67	1.30	Belgique
..	..	24	..	..	-2	-1.19	Belize
..	..	48	..	..	-25	-0.75	Bénin
..	..	..	..	..	..	..	Bermudes
..	..	40	..	..	40	3.59	Bhoutan
5 a	6	38	28 b	67 b	-100	-2.29	Bolivie
..	..	38	..	..	200	9.77	Bosnie-Herzégovine
..	17 b	45	21 b	58 b	-6	-0.68	Botswana
9 a	12 a	36	20 a	59 a	-130	-0.15	Brésil
..	..	..	..	..	..	..	Iles Vierges britanniques
..	..	36	..	..	4	1.98	Brunéi Darussalam
19 a	18 a	48	28 a	46 a	-50	-1.26	Bulgarie
..	..	46	..	..	-64	-0.99	Burkina Faso
..	..	49	..	..	250	7.36	Burundi
2	2	51	11 a	19 a	10	0.14	Cambodge
..	..	38	..	..	-24	-0.30	Cameroun
8	7	46	23 a	74 a	775	4.94	Canada
..	..	39	..	..	-5	-2.18	Cap-Vert
..	..	..	..	..	-52	-2.69	République centrafricaine
..	..	45	..	..	31	0.73	Tchad
8	9	35	24	63	-25	-0.32	Chili
3 b	..	45	..	12 b	-1649	-0.25	Chine
7	6	37	20 a	80 a	281	8.05	Chine, Hong Kong RAS
6 a	4 a	42	31 a	69 a	10	4.34	Chine, Macao RAS
18	19 a	39	18 a	59 a	-200	-0.91	Colombie
..	..	42	..	..	..	..	Comores
..	..	44	..	..	-58	-3.14	Congo
6	8	32	23	61	84	4.07	Costa Rica
..	..	34	..	..	60	0.73	Côte d'Ivoire
15	19	44	30 a	54 a	-25	-1.13	Croatie
3	..	40	24 a	52 a	-100	-1.77	Cuba
4 a	..	39	23 a	68 a	8	1.88	Chypre
7	9	47	40 a	55 a	50	0.98	République tchèque
..	..	43	..	..	-17	-0.07	Rép. dém. du Congo
4	4	46	25 a	71 a	50	1.87	Danemark
..	..	..	..	..	-21	-6.01	Djibouti
..	..	..	..	..	..	..	Dominique
16 a	26 a	31	23 a	62 a	-61	-1.41	République dominicaine
11 a	16 a	29	24 a	68 a	-150	-2.33	Equateur
9 b	..	31	21 b	..	-150	-0.42	Egypte
6	4	37	24 a	55 a	-120	-3.72	El Salvador
..	..	36	..	..	..	..	Guinée équatoriale
..	..	47	..	..	177	8.69	Erythrée
13 a	12 a	49	33 a	60 a	-40	-6.01	Estonie

Pour les sources et les notes, se reporter à la fin du tableau.

Country or area	Education Enseignement				Illiteracy rate as % of population	Adult: female literacy rate as % of male
	Primary: net enrolment ratio Primaire : taux net d'inscription	Secondary Secondaire		Tertiary: gross enrolment ratio Troisième dégré : taux brut d'inscription	Taux d'analphabétisme en % de la population	Adulte : taux d'alphabétisation féminin en % du masculin
		Net enrolment ratio Taux net d'inscription	Female enrolment as % of male Taux d'inscription féminine en % du masculin			
	(1)	(2)	(3)	(4)	(5)	(6)
Ethiopia	46	15	62	2	57	83
Fiji	100	76	107	..	6	100
Finland	100 a	95 a	111	85 a	..	..
France	100 a	92 a	101	54 a	..	..
French Polynesia	..	..	..	..	..	..
Gabon	78 a	..	..	..	..	..
Gambia	73	28	71	..	60	78
Georgia	91	..	108	36	..	..
Germany	83	88	99	48	..	..
Ghana	60	32	82	3	25	96
Greece	95 a	85 a	102	..	3	100
Grenada	84 a	46 a	48 b	..	..	..
Guam	..	..	..	..	..	..
Guatemala	85	29	93	..	30	86
Guinea	61	..	..	..	..	..
Guinea-Bissau	54 a	..	..	..	58	65
Guyana	98 a	..	..	..	1	100
Haiti	..	..	..	..	47	101
Honduras	88 a	..	..	14	23	104
Hungary	91	92	101	44	1	100
Iceland	100 a	82 a	107	48 a	..	..
India	83 a	..	71 b	11 a	41	83
Indonesia	92	48 a	99	15	12	99
Iran, Islamic Rep. of	87	..	95	20	21	96
Iraq	93 a	33 a	..	14	60	51
Ireland	94 a	..	109	47	..	..
Israel	100	89	99	58	4	100
Italy	100 a	91 a	96	50	1	100
Jamaica	95	75	103	17	12	107
Japan	100	100	101	49	..	..
Jordan	91	80	102	31	9	100
Kazakhstan	90	84	98	39	1	100
Kenya	69 a	24	90	3	15	99
Korea, Dem. People's Rep. of	..	..	..	..	..	..
Korea, Republic of	100	89	100	82	2	100
Kuwait	85	77	106	..	17	102
Kyrgyzstan	90	..	100	45	..	..
Lao People's Dem. Rep.	83	31	73	4	33	85
Latvia	91 a	89 a	102	64	0	100
Lebanon	74 a	..	110	45	13	96
Lesotho	84	22	126	3	15	117
Liberia	83 a	25 a	..	0	43	65
Libyan Arab Jamahiriya	..	..	106	58	18	95
Lithuania	97 a	92 a	100	59 a	0	100
Luxembourg	96 a	80 a	107	10 a	..	..
Macedonia, TFYR	92 a	81 a	..	..	..	..
Madagascar	69	..	..	2	31	93
Malawi	81	29	76	..	37	77
Malaysia	95	69	110	27	11	100
Maldives	96	31 a	107	..	3	100
Mali	..	..	..	2	72	56
Malta	98 a	80 a	99	25 a	7	102
Martinique	..	..	..	..	2	100
Mauritania	67	15	76	3	58	74
Mauritius	93	62	96	11	14	101
Mexico	99	60	107	21	8	99
Micronesia, Federated States of	..	..	..	..	..	..
Moldova, Republic of	78	68	103	29	1	100
Monaco	..	..	..	10	..	..
Mongolia	87	71	120	35	1	101

For sources and notes, see end of table.

Employment Emploi		Labour force Main-d'œuvre			Migration		Pays ou zones
			of which dont				
Unemployment rate Taux de chômage	Female unemployment rate Taux de chômage féminin	Female labour force Main-d'œuvre féminine	Industry Industrie	Services	Net number of migrants (Thousands) Nombre net de migrants (Milliers)	Net migration rate per 1 000 inhabitants Taux net de migration par 1 000 habitants	
(7)	(8)	(9)	(10)	(11)	(12)	(13)	
..	..	41	..	..	-83	-0.24	Ethiopie
..	..	32	..	..	-35	-8.35	Fidji
9	9	48	27 a	67 a	20	0.77	Finlande
9	10	45	24 a	74 a	375	1.25	France
..	..	..	17 b	..	..	..	Polynésie française
..	..	45	..	..	-15	-2.28	Gabon
..	..	45	..	..	25	3.56	Gambie
11 a	11 a	47	9 a	38 a	-250	-9.72	Géorgie
9	8	42	33 a	65 a	1055	2.56	Allemagne
..	..	50	..	..	-20	-0.19	Ghana
10	15	38	23 a	61 a	150	2.74	Grèce
..	..	..	..	..	..	..	Grenade
..	..	..	9 b	64 b	..	..	Guam
3	4	30	20	38	-120	-1.97	Guatemala
..	..	47	..	..	-463	-10.97	Guinée
..	..	41	..	..	-6	-0.83	Guinée-Bissau
..	..	34	..	..	-40	-10.48	Guyana
..	..	43	..	..	-105	-2.54	Haïti
4	5	33	21 a	46 a	-30	-0.88	Honduras
6	5	45	35 a	59 a	5	0.10	Hongrie
3	3	45	23 a	69 a	1	0.69	Islande
..	..	32	..	..	-1199	-0.23	Inde
6 a	..	41	17 a	38 a	-900	-0.82	Indonésie
..	..	28	..	..	-909	-2.65	Iran, Rép. islamique d'
..	..	20	..	..	56	0.45	Iraq
4	4	35	29 a	63 a	100	5.09	Irlande
10	11	42	24 a	57	204	6.40	Israël
9	12	39	32 a	63 a	320	1.12	Italie
..	..	46	..	..	-74	-5.63	Jamaïque
5	5	42	31 a	64 a	270	0.42	Japon
13 b	21 b	26	..	..	75	2.78	Jordanie
..	..	47	..	..	-800	-10.32	Kazakhstan
..	..	46	20	62	-212	-1.34	Kenya
..	..	43	..	..	..	..	Corée, Rép. populaire dém. de
3	3	42	27 a	62 a	-80	-0.34	Corée, République de
..	1 a	32	..	..	200	16.27	Koweït
9	..	47	..	..	-20	-0.78	Kirghizistan
..	..	..	..	..	-4	-0.16	Rép. dém. populaire lao
13 a	12 a	51	26 a	59 a	-40	-3.45	Lettonie
..	..	30	..	..	35	1.93	Liban
..	..	37	..	..	-36	-4.02	Lesotho
..	..	40	..	..	194	11.88	Libéria
..	..	24	..	..	10	0.36	Jamahiriya arabe libyenne
14	14 a	48	28 a	56 a	-50	-2.90	Lituanie
3	4	37	24 a	76 a	20	8.70	Luxembourg
32	32	42	..	..	-10	-0.98	Macédoine, LERY
..	..	45	..	..	..	..	Madagascar
..	..	48	..	..	-20	-0.33	Malawi
4 a	..	38	32 b	50 b	150	1.24	Malaisie
..	..	44	19 b	50 b	..	..	Maldives
..	..	46	..	..	-242	-3.77	Mali
7 a	8 a	28	32 a	66 a	1	0.25	Malte
..	..	..	..	..	-3	-1.28	Martinique
..	..	44	..	..	30	2.10	Mauritanie
8 b	13 a	33	..	..	..	..	Maurice
2	2	34	26 a	56 a	-1500	-2.92	Mexique
..	..	..	..	..	-8	-14.02	Micronésie, Etats fédérés de
7 a	6 a	48	14 a	35 a	-40	-1.87	Moldova, République de
..	..	..	..	..	..	..	Monaco
..	..	47	14 b	15 b	-30	-2.32	Mongolie

Pour les sources et les notes, se reporter à la fin du tableau.

Country or area	Education Enseignement				Illiteracy rate as % of population	Adult: female literacy rate as % of male
	Primary: net enrolment ratio Primaire : taux net d'inscription	Secondary Secondaire		Tertiary: gross enrolment ratio Troisième dégré : taux brut d'inscription	Taux d'analphabé-tisme en % de la population	Adulte : taux d'alphabétisation féminin en % du masculin
		Net enrolment ratio Taux net d'inscription	Female enrolment as % of male Taux d'inscription féminine en % du masculin			
	(1)	(2)	(3)	(4)	(5)	(6)
Montserrat	100	95	..	..	..	..
Morocco	88	30 a	81 b	..	48	80
Mozambique	60	11	66	..	52	66
Myanmar	82	35	94	12	14	100
Namibia	78	38	114	7	16	104
Nepal	72 a	..	75	5	55	60
Netherlands	99 a	90 a	97	55 a	..	..
Netherlands Antilles	88	65	112	14	3	100
New Caledonia	..	..	..	..	..	..
New Zealand	98	92 a	109	72	..	..
Nicaragua	82	37	118	..	33	102
Niger	34	5	65	1	82	45
Nigeria	..	..	..	..	32	96
Niue	97	94	98	..	..	..
Norway	100 a	95 a	102	70 a	..	..
Oman	75	68	98	7	24	98
Pakistan	86 a	..	66 b	..	54	62
Palau	97 a	..	100 b	39 a	..	..
Palestinian territory	95	81	106	31	..	..
Panama	99	62	107	..	8	99
Papua New Guinea	77	23	79	..	34	91
Paraguay	92	50	102	19	6	100
Peru	100	66	93	32	9	97
Philippines	93	56	110	31	4	100
Poland	98	91	97	58	0	100
Portugal	..	85 a	105	50 a	7	100
Puerto Rico	..	..	..	..	6	101
Qatar	94	78	105	23	18	105
Reunion	..	..	..	..	11	104
Romania	93 a	80 a	101	27 a	2	100
Russian Federation	..	..	101	70	0	100
Rwanda	84	..	88	0	30	97
Saint Kitts and Nevis	..	91 a	143 b	..	..	..
Saint Lucia	99	70	130	..	..	..
Saint Vincent and the Grenadines	92	52	120	..	..	..
Samoa	95	61	111	7	1	100
Sao Tome and Principe	97	..	84	1	..	..
Saudi Arabia	59	53	89	22	21	97
Senegal	58	..	67	..	60	73
Serbia and Montenegro	75 a	..	101	36 a	..	..
Seychelles	100	98	105	..	..	..
Sierra Leone	..	..	70 b	2	..	..
Singapore	..	..	..	..	7	100
Slovakia	87	87	101	32	..	..
Slovenia	..	96 a	100	..	0	100
Solomon Islands	..	..	..	..	..	..
Somalia	..	..	..	..	..	..
South Africa	90	57 a	109	15	14	100
Spain	100	94	106	59	2	100
Sri Lanka	100	..	..	..	8	100
Sudan	46 a	..	89 b	..	39	89
Suriname	97	63	139	12	..	..
Swaziland	77	32	100	5	18	102
Sweden	100	99	121	76	..	..
Switzerland	99 a	88 a	94	42 a	..	..
Syrian Arab Republic	98	39	90	..	23	85
Tajikistan	98	79	82	15	1	100
Thailand	86	..	95 b	37	4	99
Timor-Leste	..	20 a	..	12	..	..
Togo	92	..	..	..	39	77

For sources and notes, see end of table.

Employment / Emploi		Labour force / Main-d'œuvre			Migration		Pays ou zones
			of which / dont		Net number of migrants (Thousands) / Nombre net de migrants (Milliers)	Net migration rate per 1 000 inhabitants / Taux net de migration par 1 000 habitants	
Unemployment rate / Taux de chômage	Female unemployment rate / Taux de chômage féminin	Female labour force / Main-d'œuvre féminine	Industry / Industrie	Services			
(7)	(8)	(9)	(10)	(11)	(12)	(13)	
..	..	..	..	..	..	..	Montserrat
..	..	35	..	..	-150	-0.99	Maroc
..	..	48	..	..	-25	-0.27	Mozambique
..	..	43	..	..	18	0.07	Myanmar
34 b	39 b	41	12 b	56	-13	-1.37	Namibie
..	..	41	..	..	-118	-0.95	Népal
3	4	41	21 a	73	150	1.86	Pays-Bas
14 b	16 b	43	18 b	81	-1	-0.46	Antilles néerlandaises
..	..	..	..	..	5	4.72	Nouvelle-Calédonie
5	5	45	23 a	68	25	1.30	Nouvelle-Zélande
11 a	9 a	37	15 a	38	-60	-2.22	Nicaragua
..	..	44	..	..	..	..	Niger
..	..	37	..	..	-94	-0.15	Nigéria
..	..	..	..	..	..	..	Nioué
4	4	47	22 a	74	50	2.21	Norvège
..	..	19	..	..	10	0.71	Oman
8 b	17 b	30	..	34	-1519	-2.00	Pakistan
..	..	..	..	..	..	..	Palaos
26 a	14	..	29 a	59 a	20	1.14	Territoire palestinien
13	18	36	16	63	11	0.71	Panama
..	..	42	..	..	..	..	Papouasie-Nouvelle-Guinée
..	..	30	17 a	51	-25	-0.86	Paraguay
9	10	32	18 a	73	-300	-2.23	Pérou
10 a	10 a	38	16 a	47	-900	-2.27	Philippines
20	21	46	31 a	50	-80	-0.41	Pologne
5	6	44	35 a	53	50	1.00	Portugal
11 a	9 a	38	22 a	76	-15	-0.80	Porto Rico
..	..	16	..	..	5	1.66	Qatar
..	..	..	..	..	5	1.33	Réunion
7 a	6 a	45	26 a	32	-25	-0.22	Roumanie
9 a	9 a	49	..	..	250	0.35	Fédération de Russie
..	..	49	..	..	-20	-0.49	Rwanda
..	..	..	..	..	..	..	Saint-Kitts-et-Nevis
..	..	..	..	..	-5	-6.73	Sainte-Lucie
..	..	..	..	..	-5	-8.37	Saint-Vincent-et-les Grenadines
..	..	..	..	..	-12	-13.54	Samoa
..	..	..	..	..	-2	-2.52	Sao Tomé-et-Principe
..	..	18	..	..	150	1.26	Arabie saoudite
..	..	43	..	..	-50	-1.00	Sénégal
22 a	22 a	43	..	..	-100	-1.90	Serbie-et-Monténégro
..	..	..	..	..	..	..	Seychelles
..	..	37	..	..	429	17.58	Sierra Leone
3	3 a	39	25 a	74 a	250	11.92	Singapour
19	19	48	38 a	56 a	8	0.30	Slovaquie
6 a	6 a	47	38 a	51 a	5	0.50	Slovénie
..	..	46	..	..	..	..	Iles Salomon
..	..	43	..	..	350	7.19	Somalie
30 a	33 a	38	..	..	..	..	Afrique du Sud
11	16	37	32 a	62 a	400	1.95	Espagne
8 a	11 a	37	..	..	-160	-1.68	Sri Lanka
..	..	30	..	..	55	0.33	Soudan
..	..	34	..	..	-17	-7.84	Suriname
..	..	38	..	..	-6	-1.13	Swaziland
5	5	48	24 a	74 a	50	1.13	Suède
3	3	41	26 a	70 a	20	0.56	Suisse
..	24 a	28	..	..	-9	-0.10	République arabe syrienne
..	..	45	..	..	-306	-9.84	Tadjikistan
2	2	46	21	33	-45	-0.14	Thaïlande
..	..	45	..	..	114	29.24	Timor-Leste
..	..	40	..	..	-9	-0.37	Togo

Pour les sources et les notes, se reporter à la fin du tableau.

Country or area	Education Enseignement				Illiteracy rate as % of population	Adult: female literacy rate as % of male
	Primary: net enrolment ratio	Secondary Secondaire		Tertiary: gross enrolment ratio		
		Net enrolment ratio	Female enrolment as % of male			
	Primaire : taux net d'inscription	Taux net d'inscription	Taux d'inscription féminine en % du masculin	Troisième dégré : taux brut d'inscription	Taux d'analphabétisme en % de la population	Adulte : taux d'alphabétisation féminin en % du masculin
	(1)	(2)	(3)	(4)	(5)	(6)
Tonga	100	72 a	113	4	..	..
Trinidad and Tobago	94	68	110	7	1	100
Tunisia	97	68	104	23	26	93
Turkey	88	..	76	25	14	96
Turkmenistan	88	..	..	..	..	..
Turks and Caicos Islands	..	76	103	..	..	..
Uganda	..	14 a	77	3	30	86
Ukraine	82	91	100	58	0	100
United Arab Emirates	81	72	106	..	22	108
United Kingdom	100 a	95 a	125	59 a	..	..
United Republic of Tanzania	54	..	..	1 a	22	96
United States	93	85	99	81	..	..
Uruguay	90	72	114	37	2	101
Uzbekistan	..	..	97	9	1	100
Vanuatu	93	28	103	4	..	..
Venezuela	92	57	116	27	7	101
Viet Nam	94	65	92	10	7	101
Yemen	67 a	..	42 b	..	50	63
Zambia	66	20	80	2 a	19	95
Zimbabwe	83	40	89	4	9	97

For sources and notes, see next page.

Employment Emploi		Labour force Main-d'œuvre			Migration		Pays ou zones
			of which dont		Net number of migrants (Thousands) Nombre net de migrants (Milliers)	Net migration rate per 1 000 inhabitants Taux net de migration par 1 000 habitants	
Unemployment rate Taux de chômage	Female unemployment rate Taux de chômage féminin	Female labour force Main-d'œuvre féminine	Industry Industrie	Services			
(7)	(8)	(9)	(10)	(11)	(12)	(13)	
..	..	..	..	..	-5	-9.68	Tonga
..	..	35	..	..	-19	-2.92	Trinité-et-Tobago
..	..	32	..	..	-40	-0.82	Tunisie
11	10	38	24 a	43 a	-250	-0.71	Turquie
..	..	46	..	..	-10	-0.41	Turkménistan
..	..	..	..	..	..	..	Iles Turques et Caïques
..	..	48	..	..	-207	-1.62	Ouganda
11 a	11 a	49	31 a	44 a	-500	-2.05	Ukraine
..	..	16	33 b	59	75	5.06	Emirats arabes unis
5	4	44	25 a	73 a	715	2.42	Royaume-Uni
..	..	49	..	..	-345	-1.89	République-Unie de Tanzanie
6	6	46	22 a	75 a	6000	4.10	Etats-Unis
17	20 a	42	24 a	72	-10	-0.59	Uruguay
..	..	47	20 b	..	-100	-0.77	Ouzbékistan
..	..	..	..	..	-1	-0.83	Vanuatu
13 a	15 a	35	22 a	68	40	0.31	Venezuela
..	..	49	..	..	-100	-0.25	Viet Nam
..	..	28	..	..	-75	-0.76	Yémen
..	..	45	..	..	-141	-2.62	Zambie
..	..	45	..	..	-10	-0.16	Zimbabwe

Pour les sources et les notes, se reporter à la page suivante.

7.5 Selected indicators of development: education, employment, gender equality and migration

7.5 Quelques indicateurs de développement : enseignement, emploi, égalité entre hommes et femmes et migration

Sources:

Columns (1) (2) (3) (4) (5) (6)

UNESCO, Database.

Columns (7) (8) (9) (10) (11)

World Bank, *World Development Indicators Online*.

Columns (12) (13)

UN/DESA/Population Division, *World Population Prospects: The 2002 Revision*.

Sources :

Colonnes (1) (2) (3) (4) (5) (6)

UNESCO, Base de données.

Colonnes (7) (8) (9) (10) (11)

Banque mondiale, *World Development Indicators Online*.

Colonnes (12) (13)

ONU/DAES/Division de la population, *World Population Prospects: The 2002 Revision*.

Notes:

a Refers to 2001

b Refers to 2000

A year by the column number denotes the year to which data refer.

Notes :

a Se réfère à 2001

b Se réfère à 2000

Une année à côté du numéro de colonne indique l'année à laquelle les données se réfèrent.

(1) (2) (4) Year 2002. Net enrolment ratio is defined as number of pupils in the official age group for a given level of education enrolled in that level expressed as a percentage of the total population in that age group.
Gross enrolment ratio is defined as total enrolment in a specific level of education, regardless of age, expressed as a percentage of the official school-age population corresponding to the same level of education in a given school year.

(1) (2) (4) Année 2002. Le taux net d'inscription est défini comme le nombre d'étudiants en âge d'être scolarisés pour un niveau particulier d'enseignement qui sont inscrits à ce niveau d'éducation, exprimé en pourcentage de la population totale de cet âge.
Le taux brut d'inscription est défini comme taux d'inscription totale (l'age n'est pas pris en compte) à un niveau particulier d'enseignement et est exprimé en pourcentage de la population en age de scolarité pour un niveau donné durant une année scolaire.

(3) Year 2001. The indicator presents the ratio of female enrolment in secondary education as a percentage of male enrolment in the same level of education.

(3) Année 2001. Cet indicateur présente le taux d'inscription féminine dans l'enseignement secondaire en pourcentage d'inscription masculine dans le même niveau d'enseignement.

(5) Year 2002. The indicator presents the illiteracy rate as a percentage of total population of a country or an area.

(5) Année 2002. Cet indicateur présente le taux d'analphabétisme en pourcentage de la population totale d'un pays ou d'une zone.

(6) Year 2003. The indicator presents the literacy rate of adult (age 15 and above) females as a percentage of literate adult males.

(6) Année 2003. Cet indicateur présente le taux d'alphabétisation féminine en pourcentage d'alphabétisation masculine pour des adultes de 15 ans ou plus.

(7) (8) Year 2002.

(7) (8) Année 2002.

(9) Year 2002. The indicator represents the percentage of female labour force.

(9) Année 2002. Cet indicateur présente le pourcentage de la main-d'œuvre féminine.

(10) Year 2002. The indicator presents the percentage of the labour force employed in industry.

(10) Année 2002. Cet indicateur présente le pourcentage de la main-d'œuvre employé dans l'industrie.

(11) Year 2002. The indicator presents the percentage of the labour force employed in the services sector.

(11) Année 2002. Cet indicateur présente le pourcentage de la main-d'œuvre employé dans le secteur des services.

(12) Data are estimated and represent the value in thousands for the period 2000-2005 (from 1 July 2000 to 1 July 2005).

(12) Les données sont estimées et représentent le nombre, en milliers, pour la période 2000-2005 (1 juillet 2000 au 1 juillet 2005).

(13) Data are estimated and represent the average value per year for the period 2000-2005.

(13) Les données sont estimées et représentent la valeur moyenne par année pour la période 2000-2005.

Country or area	Main telephone lines per 100 inhabitants Lignes téléphoniques principales par 100 habitants	Outgoing international calls per inhabitant (minutes) Appels internationaux sortants par habitant (minutes)	Incoming international calls per inhabitant (minutes) Appels internationaux entrants par habitant (minutes)	Mobile phone subscribers per 100 inhabitants Abonnements au téléphone mobile par 100 habitants	Cost of a 3-minute mobile phone call (dollars) Coût d'un appel de 3 minutes : téléphone mobile (dollars)	Cost of a 3-minute fixed-line phone call (dollars) Coût d'un appel de 3 minutes : réseau fixe (dollars)
	(1)	(2)	(3)	(4)	(5)	(6)
Afghanistan	0.1	..	..	0	..	..
Albania	7.1	20	130	28	0.627 a	0.021
Algeria	6.1	7 a	..	1	0.082	0.038
American Samoa	25.2 a	..	..	..	0.300	..
Andorra	53.1	..	..	40	0.397 a	0.084 a
Angola	0.6	2	5	1	0.207	0.090
Antigua and Barbuda	48.8	199	455	49	..	..
Argentina	21.9	12	..	18	..	0.029
Armenia	14.3	10	15	2	0.508	0.021
Aruba	35.0 a	202 a	..	50 a	1.006	0.089
Australia	55.5	114 a	97 a	64	1.582	0.120
Austria	48.2	155	102	84	2.009	0.189
Azerbaijan	11.3	4	10	11	0.302	0.102
Bahamas	40.6	216 a	358 a	39	..	..
Bahrain	26.1	297	270	58	0.395	0.055
Bangladesh	0.5	..	3	1	0.311	0.029
Barbados	49.4	299 a	293	36	1.110	..
Belarus	29.9	24	25	5	0.128	0.008
Belgium	49.4	174	..	79	1.132	0.142
Belize	11.4	42	110	19	1.275	0.150
Benin	0.9	3 a	5 a	3	1.033	0.095
Bermuda	86.2	..	..	46	0.750 a	0.200
Bhutan	2.8	9 a	..	..	..	0.021
Bolivia	6.4	5	15 a	11	..	..
Bosnia and Herzegovina	23.7	24 a	..	20	0.617 a	0.028
Botswana	8.3	37	27	25	0.616	0.017
Brazil	22.3	5	7 a	20	0.572 a	0.028 a
Brunei Darussalam	25.6	72 a	..	40 a	0.168 a	..
Bulgaria	36.8	18	27	33	..	0.020
Burkina Faso	0.5	2	2	1	0.861	0.102
Burundi	0.3	..	1 a	1	0.928	0.077
Cambodia	0.3	1	2	3	0.676 a	0.030
Cameroon	0.7	1 a	..	4	1.076	0.057
Canada	64.3	260	..	38	0.484 a	..
Cape Verde	15.6	19	103	10	0.895	0.038
Cayman Islands	84.9 a	738	787	38 a	..	..
Central African Republic	0.2	1	..	0	0.430	0.430
Chad	0.2	0 a	..	0	..	0.108
Chile	23.0	18	30	43	..	0.104
China	16.7	1 a	3 a	16	0.145 a	0.027
China, Hong Kong SAR	56.5	587	257	94	0.185	..
China, Macao SAR	39.9	344	256	63	0.523	..
China, Taiwan Province of	58.2	96	73	106	0.519	0.046
Colombia	17.9	7 a	..	11	0.419 a	0.029 a
Comoros	1.3	5	19	..	..	0.143
Congo	0.7	..	..	7	..	..
Costa Rica	25.1	31	38	11	0.319 a	0.027
Côte d'Ivoire	2.0	4	7	6	1.937	0.224
Croatia	41.7	82	96	54	..	0.088
Cuba	5.1 a	3 a	25	0	1.200 a	0.090 a
Cyprus	68.8	358	229	58	0.443	0.033
Czech Republic	36.2	39	67	85	0.450 a	0.128
Dem. Rep. of the Congo	..	..	..	1	..	..
Denmark	68.9	147	..	83	0.508 a	0.084 a
Djibouti	1.5	9	..	2	0.844	0.197

For sources and notes, see end of table.

Personal computers per 1 000 inhabitants Ordinateurs personnels par 1 000 habitants	Internet users per 1 000 inhabitants Utilisateurs d'Internet par 1 000 habitants	Internet hosts per 100 000 inhabitants Hébergeurs d'Internet par 100 000 habitants	Total telecommunications revenue (millions of dollars) Revenu total en télé-communications (millions de dollars)	Annual investment in telecommunications (millions of dollars) Investissement annuel dans les télécommunications (millions de dollars)	Television sets per 1 000 inhabitants Postes téléviseurs par 1 000 habitants	Pays ou zones
(7)	(8)	(9)	(10)	(11)	(12)	
..	..	..	..	..	14 a	Afghanistan
12	4	6	251	32	318	Albanie
8	16	3	362 a	96 a	171	Algérie
..	..	1247	..	..	268 a	Samoa américaines
..	..	3388	..	..	..	Andorre
2	3	0	..	..	20	Angola
..	128	797	..	..	449 a	Antigua-et-Barbuda
82	112	1355	7547	869 a	322 a	Argentine
16	16	75	82	23	232	Arménie
..	226 a	1038	98 a	..	218 a	Aruba
565	482	13042	13382 a	4663 a	727	Australie
374	415	4569	5245	1562 a	646	Autriche
..	37	14	86	29	332	Azerbaïdjan
..	192	10	..	..	244 a	Bahamas
159	246	199	489	84	425	Bahreïn
3	2	..	524	80	62	Bangladesh
104	112	60	181	44	346	Barbade
..	82	41	215	62	363 a	Bélarus
241	328	3250	6878	754	541	Belgique
127	109	544	56	30	175	Belize
2	7	8	62 a	26 a	34	Bénin
523	464 a	10051	90 a	15 a	1077 a	Bermudes
14	14	180	11 a	3	29	Bhoutan
23	32	17	389 a	162 a	..	Bolivie
..	26	150	209 a	64 a	..	Bosnie-Herzégovine
41	35	94	183	12	44	Botswana
75	82	1287	20428 a	5205	345 a	Brésil
77	102 a	2463	..	..	611 a	Brunéi Darussalam
52	81	423	911	407	..	Bulgarie
2	2	3	63	24	12	Burkina Faso
1	1	..	15 a	30 a	31	Burundi
2	2	10	..	..	7 a	Cambodge
6	4	3	..	80	35	Cameroun
487	513	9531	21015	3629	684 a	Canada
78	36	11	48	15	102	Cap-Vert
..	..	4244	..	..	213 a	Iles Caïmanes
2	1	0	11	..	5	République centrafricaine
2	2	0	..	..	5	Tchad
119	238	898	2421	589	523	Chili
28	46	12	50994	25040	350	Chine
422	430	5867	6255	1065	522	Chine, Hong Kong RAS
208	260	34	231	40	290	Chine, Macao RAS
395	381	9637	9591	2626	442	Chine, Taiwan Province de
49	46	129	3876	1530 a	303	Colombie
6	4	2	10	4	24	Comores
4	2	1	..	..	13	Congo
197	193	187	364	249	..	Costa Rica
9	5	27	399	138	47	Côte d'Ivoire
174	180	678	1240	182	..	Croatie
32	11 a	10	787 a	144 a	250 a	Cuba
270	294	377	347	99	379	Chypre
177	256	2232	3270	811	542 a	République tchèque
..	1	0	..	..	2	Rép. dém. du Congo
577	513	15567	4217 a	1280 a	856 a	Danemark
15	7	76	23 a	..	78	Djibouti

Pour les sources et les notes, se reporter à la fin du tableau.

Country or area	Main telephone lines per 100 inhabitants Lignes téléphoniques principales par 100 habitants	Outgoing international calls per inhabitant (minutes) Appels internationaux sortants par habitant (minutes)	Incoming international calls per inhabitant (minutes) Appels internationaux entrants par habitant (minutes)	Mobile phone subscribers per 100 inhabitants Abonnements au téléphone mobile par 100 habitants	Cost of a 3-minute mobile phone call (dollars) Coût d'un appel de 3 minutes : téléphone mobile (dollars)	Cost of a 3-minute fixed-line phone call (dollars) Coût d'un appel de 3 minutes : réseau fixe (dollars)
	(1)	(2)	(3)	(4)	(5)	(6)
Dominica	30.4	126 a	..	12	0.104 a	0.104
Dominican Republic	11.0	27	208 a	21	0.398 a	0.064
Ecuador	11.0	5 a	44 a	12	..	0.030
Egypt	11.5	4	15	7	0.167	0.016
El Salvador	10.3	24 a	124 a	14	..	0.070 a
Equatorial Guinea	1.7	9 a	..	6	..	..
Eritrea	0.9	1	6	..	..	0.029
Estonia	35.1	76	76 a	65	0.427 a	0.090
Ethiopia	0.5	..	1	0	0.252	0.023
Faeroe Islands	48.2	..	..	64	..	..
Fiji	11.9	28	83	11	0.301	0.055
Finland	52.3	90	..	87	0.464 a	0.132
France	57.2	79	126	65	0.764	0.125
French Guiana	30.2 a	..	..	50	..	..
French Polynesia	21.9	76 a	..	38	3.251	0.302
Gabon	2.5	21	..	22	0.646	0.215
Gambia	2.9	10	..	8	0.669 a	0.028
Georgia	13.1	12 a	19 a	10	0.393	0.027
Germany	65.2	123	..	73	1.104	0.094
Ghana	1.3	3	7	2	0.945	0.025
Gibraltar	87.7	607 a	..	44	..	..
Greece	49.1	78	89	85	..	0.074
Greenland	44.7	258 a	..	35	..	..
Grenada	31.6	272	351	7	0.544 a	0.089
Guadeloupe	48.7 a	..	..	74	..	..
Guam	50.9 a	..	..	21 a	2.400	..
Guatemala	7.1	12	68	13	0.382 a	0.084 a
Guinea	0.3	1	6	1	0.607	0.076
Guinea-Bissau	0.9	..	..	..	..	..
Guyana	9.2	21	79 a	10	0.582	0.003
Haiti	1.6	..	..	2	..	..
Honduras	4.8	..	..	5	0.759 a	0.064
Hungary	36.1	24	36	68	0.681 a	0.132
Iceland	65.3	129 a	153 a	91	0.349 a	0.093
India	4.0	1	2	1	0.120 a	0.016
Indonesia	3.7	1	2	6	0.105	0.026
Iran, Islamic Rep. of	18.7	4	3	3	0.662 a	0.006
Iraq	2.8	..	..	0	..	..
Ireland	50.2	355	..	76	1.232 a	0.142
Israel	45.3	180	123	96	0.208	0.016
Italy	48.1	82 a	96 a	94	..	0.105 a
Jamaica	16.9	52	177	53	0.620	0.065
Japan	55.8	22	15	64	0.558	0.068
Jordan	12.7	37	44	23	0.761	0.042
Kazakhstan	13.0	8	16	6	0.669	..
Kenya	1.0	1	1	4	0.571	0.094
Kiribati	5.1	7 a	18 a	1	0.978	0.098
Korea, Dem. People's Rep. of	2.1	..	..	..	..	..
Korea, Republic of	48.9	22	19	68	0.302	0.031
Kuwait	20.4	80	..	52	0.387 a	..
Kyrgyzstan	7.7	4	9	1	..	0.090
Lao People's Dem. Rep.	1.1	1 a	4 a	1	0.050 a	0.015 a
Latvia	30.1	20	50	39	0.048	0.113
Lebanon	19.9	27 a	..	23	0.429	0.098
Lesotho	1.3	..	..	5	..	0.106

For sources and notes, see end of table.

Personal computers per 1 000 inhabitants Ordinateurs personnels par 1 000 habitants	Internet users per 1 000 inhabitants Utilisateurs d'Internet par 1 000 habitants	Internet hosts per 100 000 inhabitants Hébergeurs d'Internet par 100 000 habitants	Total telecommunications revenue (millions of dollars) Revenu total en télé-communications (millions de dollars)	Annual investment in telecommunications (millions of dollars) Investissement annuel dans les télécommunications (millions de dollars)	Television sets per 1 000 inhabitants Postes téléviseurs par 1 000 habitants	Pays ou zones
(7)	(8)	(9)	(10)	(11)	(12)	
90	160	595	..	..	225 a	Dominique
..	61	553	..	288 a	..	République dominicaine
31	42	21	448 a	..	237	Equateur
17	28	5	2395	666	229	Egypte
25	46	4	587 a	163 a	231 a	El Salvador
7	4	1	19 a	..	..	Guinée équatoriale
3	2	22	17	1	50	Erythrée
210	328	4676	419	73 a	502	Estonie
1	1	0	104	29	7	Ethiopie
..	524	4308	33 a	..	..	Iles Féroé
49	61	96	71	38	117	Fidji
442	509	23431	4728	730	670	Finlande
347	314	2329	32024	5472	632	France
166	143	1	..	..	..	Guyane française
292	146	1525	136 a	..	229	Polynésie française
19	19	6	129	11	138	Gabon
14	19	43	30	4	15	Gambie
32	15	62	135	..	357	Géorgie
431	436	3143	58208	6632	661	Allemagne
4	8	1	128	59	51	Ghana
..	225 a	1836	..	..	..	Gibraltar
82	135	1460	4847 a	1232	499 a	Grèce
..	441	5142	80 a	..	..	Groenland
132	142	13	..	..	349 a	Grenade
255	115	93	..	..	289 a	Guadeloupe
..	312	81	..	..	269	Guam
14	33	82	448 a	..	142 a	Guatemala
5	5	3	29 a	1 a	17	Guinée
..	11	2	..	..	40	Guinée-Bissau
27	142	7	80	..	97 a	Guyana
..	10	..	..	..	54	Haïti
14	25	2	390	53	119	Honduras
108	158	1916	3720	686	466 a	Hongrie
451	648	23702	174 a	37 a	..	Islande
7	16	8	7645 a	3512 a	84	Inde
12	21	29	2167 a	1703 a	151 a	Indonésie
75	48	5	1270	1825	173	Iran, Rép. islamique d'
8	1	..	..	..	..	Iraq
421	280	3472	3245	..	694	Irlande
243	301	2212	3690	1441	342	Israël
231	352	1191	35241 a	7289 a	..	Italie
54	228	49	548	136	369	Jamaïque
382	449	7267	117971 a	15775	785	Japon
38	58	77	761	193	177	Jordanie
..	16	104	602	87	341 a	Kazakhstan
6	13	9	622	45	45	Kenya
11	23	40	4 a	..	36	Kiribati
..	..	..	..	..	162	Corée, Rép. populaire dém. de
494	552	856	21737	6507	357 a	Corée, République de
121	106	138	857	..	402 a	Koweït
13	30	116	43	6	48 a	Kirghizistan
3	3	5	27	11	54	Rép. dém. populaire lao
172	133	1524	237	92	850	Lettonie
81	117	211	..	..	354	Liban
..	10	2	14	7	35	Lesotho

Pour les sources et les notes, se reporter à la fin du tableau.

Country or area	Main telephone lines per 100 inhabitants — Lignes téléphoniques principales par 100 habitants	Outgoing international calls per inhabitant (minutes) — Appels internationaux sortants par habitant (minutes)	Incoming international calls per inhabitant (minutes) — Appels internationaux entrants par habitant (minutes)	Mobile phone subscribers per 100 inhabitants — Abonnements au téléphone mobile par 100 habitants	Cost of a 3-minute mobile phone call (dollars) — Coût d'un appel de 3 minutes : téléphone mobile (dollars)	Cost of a 3-minute fixed-line phone call (dollars) — Coût d'un appel de 3 minutes : réseau fixe (dollars)
	(1)	(2)	(3)	(4)	(5)	(6)
Liberia	0.2	2 a	..	0 a	..	..
Libyan Arab Jamahiriya	13.0	8 a	..	1	..	..
Liechtenstein	58.3	1257	1308 a	33	1.757 a	0.112 a
Lithuania	27.0	10	33 a	48	..	0.136
Luxembourg	79.7	1037 a	655 a	106	0.351	0.875
Macedonia, TFYR	27.1	31	93	18	..	0.015 a
Madagascar	0.4	..	1	1	0.527	0.073
Malawi	0.7	3	2	1	0.861	0.059
Malaysia	19.0	40	43	38	0.426	0.032
Maldives	10.2	25	37	15	0.527	0.059
Mali	0.5	1 a	6 a	1	1.228 a	0.070 a
Malta	52.3	110	175	70	0.978 a	0.116
Marshall Islands	8.2	13	43	1	0.300	..
Martinique	44.5 a	..	..	82	..	..
Mauritania	1.2	4 a	..	9	..	0.126
Mauritius	27.0	31	52	29	0.100	0.043
Mexico	14.7	20	57	26	0.825 a	0.158 a
Micronesia, Federated States of	8.7 a	22 a	49 a	2	1.800	..
Moldova, Republic of	16.1	12	30	8	..	0.015
Mongolia	5.3	2	..	9	0.946	0.016
Morocco	3.8	9 a	..	21	0.653	0.147
Mozambique	0.5	1	..	1	1.003	0.079
Myanmar	0.7	..	1	0	0.013	0.048
Namibia	6.5	32	28	8	0.638	0.031
Nauru	16.0 a	..	..	13 a	..	..
Nepal	1.4	1	3	0	0.231	0.013
Netherlands	61.8	161 a	..	75	..	0.107 a
Netherlands Antilles	37.2 a	..	..	..	..	..
New Caledonia	23.2	85 a	..	36	0.538 a	0.269 a
New Zealand	44.8	245	176 a	62	1.792	..
Nicaragua	3.2	3	15	4	..	0.084
Niger	0.2	1 a	..	0	0.225 a	0.102 a
Nigeria	0.6	1	2 a	1	1.079 a	0.107
Northern Mariana Islands	..	..	..	..	..	..
Norway	73.4	121	153	84	0.396 a	0.153
Oman	9.2	65	..	18	1.974	0.074
Pakistan	2.5	1	10	1	0.289	0.020
Palestinian territory	8.7	11	17	9	..	0.048
Panama	12.9	15 a	40 a	18	..	0.120 a
Papua New Guinea	1.1	5 a	..	0	0.577	0.077
Paraguay	4.7	5	12	29	0.252 a	0.088 a
Peru	6.2	5	41	9	..	0.080
Philippines	4.2	2	33	19	0.464	..
Poland	30.1	22 a	31 a	36	..	..
Portugal	42.1	52	97 a	83	0.964 a	0.113
Puerto Rico	33.1	..	..	47	..	..
Qatar	28.6	378	218	43	0.593	..
Reunion	41.0 a	..	..	66	..	..
Romania	19.4	10	40	24	..	0.112
Russian Federation	24.2	8	7	12	..	..
Rwanda	0.3	1 a	..	1	1.241	0.088
Saint Kitts and Nevis	50.0	240	466	11	..	..
Saint Lucia	32.0	98	256	9	..	0.089
Saint Vincent and the Grenadines	23.4	90	374	9	..	..
Samoa	6.5	40	105	2	0.266	0.033

For sources and notes, see end of table.

Personal computers per 1 000 inhabitants — Ordinateurs personnels par 1 000 habitants	Internet users per 1 000 inhabitants — Utilisateurs d'Internet par 1 000 habitants	Internet hosts per 100 000 inhabitants — Hébergeurs d'Internet par 100 000 habitants	Total telecommunications revenue (millions of dollars) — Revenu total en télé-communications (millions de dollars)	Annual investment in telecommunications (millions of dollars) — Investissement annuel dans les télécommunications (millions de dollars)	Television sets per 1 000 inhabitants — Postes téléviseurs par 1 000 habitants	Pays ou zones
(7)	(8)	(9)	(10)	(11)	(12)	
..	0 a	0	..	..	..	Libéria
23	22	2	..	..	..	Jamahiriya arabe libyenne
..	585	11421	27 a	..	512	Liechtenstein
110	144	1577	442	92 a	487	Lituanie
594	370	3870	317	69	605	Luxembourg
..	48	153	218 a	..	..	Macédoine, LERY
4	3	3	96	..	18	Madagascar
1	3	0	32	..	6	Malawi
147	320	352	4792	1009	210	Malaisie
71	53	..	65	8	131	Maldives
1	2	2	92	18 a	27	Mali
255	303	1857	113 a	31 a	566	Malte
56	24	9	7	..	..	Iles Marshall
200	154	82	..	..	169 a	Martinique
11	4	3	66	..	41	Mauritanie
149	103	286	163	59	333	Maurice
82	98	1087	16938	3179	278 a	Mexique
..	51	539	11 a	..	22	Micronésie, Etats fédérés de
18	34	50	96	72	295 a	Moldova, République de
28	21	5	57	5	79	Mongolie
17	24	9	1549	644	165	Maroc
5	3	11	128	59	17	Mozambique
5	1	..	11	2	8	Myanmar
71	27	198	120	9	79	Namibie
..	26 a	414	..	..	..	Nauru
4	3	5	84	21 a	8 a	Népal
467	506	19371	13138 a	2633 a	648	Pays-Bas
..	..	51	..	..	..	Antilles néerlandaises
..	223	2641	77 a	..	504	Nouvelle-Calédonie
413	484	10983	1988	263	550	Nouvelle-Zélande
28	17	63	101	41	119 a	Nicaragua
1	1	1	18 a	..	10	Niger
7	4	1	1217	..	68	Nigéria
..	..	21	..	..	..	Iles Mariannes du Nord
528	503	5618	5135 a	2589	879 a	Norvège
37	71	27	509	127	591	Oman
4 a	10	9	1442	169	79	Pakistan
36	30	..	103 a	34 a	148	Territoire palestinien
38	41 a	246	..	..	191	Panama
59	14	10	..	..	20 a	Papouasie-Nouvelle-Guinée
35	17	75	309 a	82 a	..	Paraguay
43	90	73	1395 a	175 a	172	Pérou
28	44	48	2729	697	182	Philippines
106	230	1703	..	..	422 a	Pologne
135	194	1594	6468	1975	413 a	Portugal
..	175	23	2598 a	..	339	Porto Rico
178	113	28	450	71	469	Qatar
71	202	0	..	..	188	Réunion
83	101	189	1727	302	697	Roumanie
89	41	279	6956 a	1015	..	Fédération de Russie
..	3	15	20 a	..	8	Rwanda
191	213	4	..	..	234 a	Saint-Kitts-et-Nevis
150	82 a	18	..	..	292 a	Sainte-Lucie
120	60	3 a	..	..	..	Saint-Vincent-et-les Grenadines
7	22	3162	12	..	144	Samoa

Pour les sources et les notes, se reporter à la fin du tableau.

Country or area	Main telephone lines per 100 inhabitants Lignes téléphoniques principales par 100 habitants	Outgoing international calls per inhabitant (minutes) Appels internationaux sortants par habitant (minutes)	Incoming international calls per inhabitant (minutes) Appels internationaux entrants par habitant (minutes)	Mobile phone subscribers per 100 inhabitants Abonnements au téléphone mobile par 100 habitants	Cost of a 3-minute mobile phone call (dollars) Coût d'un appel de 3 minutes : téléphone mobile (dollars)	Cost of a 3-minute fixed-line phone call (dollars) Coût d'un appel de 3 minutes : réseau fixe (dollars)
	(1)	(2)	(3)	(4)	(5)	(6)
San Marino	76.3	3719	3015	62	..	..
Sao Tome and Principe	4.1	8	26	1	..	0.165
Saudi Arabia	15.1	87	37	23	0.400	0.040
Senegal	2.2	7 a	16 a	5	0.572	0.169
Serbia and Montenegro	23.3	29	61	26	0.312 a	0.009
Seychelles	26.9	101 a	..	55	0.486 a	0.150
Sierra Leone	0.5	2 a	..	1	0.540	0.029
Singapore	46.3	472	273 a	80	0.335	0.022
Slovakia	26.8	36	27 a	54	0.645 a	0.122 a
Slovenia	40.5	53	..	84	..	0.066
Solomon Islands	1.5	13 a	..	0	0.907	0.068
Somalia	1.0	..	..	0	..	..
South Africa	10.7	12	18	30	0.484	0.094
Spain	43.4	90 a	85 a	82	..	0.068 a
Sri Lanka	4.7	3	17	5	0.220	0.034
Sudan	2.0	1	7	1	0.139 a	0.034
Suriname	16.4	55	86	23	0.562	0.049
Swaziland	3.4	22	18	7	0.490	0.038
Sweden	73.6	..	..	89	..	0.110 a
Switzerland	74.4	356 a	..	79	0.769	0.154
Syrian Arab Republic	12.3	10 a	19 a	2	0.233	0.012
Tajikistan	3.7	2	6	0	..	0.011
Thailand	10.5	5	5	26	0.209	0.070
Togo	1.0	4	12	4	0.710	0.102
Tonga	11.3	31 a	..	3	0.095	0.055
Trinidad and Tobago	25.0	52 a	113 a	28	1.438	0.037
Tunisia	11.7	20	41	6	0.528	0.021
Turkey	28.1	10	17	35	0.494	0.125
Turkmenistan	7.7	5	..	0	..	..
Tuvalu	6.8 a	86 a	..	..	..	..
Uganda	0.2	0 a	..	2	0.606	0.209
Ukraine	21.6	8	7	8	..	..
United Arab Emirates	29.1	505	..	65	0.245	..
United Kingdom	59.1	152	130 a	84	0.672	0.179
United Republic of Tanzania	0.5	..	1	2	0.544	0.121
United States	64.6	140	49	49	..	..
United States Virgin Islands	63.5 a	..	..	38 a	..	..
Uruguay	28.0	25 a	..	19	..	..
Uzbekistan	6.6	2	..	1	0.358	0.005 a
Vanuatu	3.3	14 a	..	2	0.862	0.216
Venezuela	11.3	11 a	..	26	0.659 a	0.040
Viet Nam	4.8	1	7	2	0.353	0.024
Yemen	2.8	2	10	2	0.171	0.017
Zambia	0.8	1	3 a	1	0.904	0.091
Zimbabwe	2.5	7 a	..	3	0.403 a	0.013

For sources and notes, see next page.

Personal computers per 1 000 inhabitants Ordinateurs personnels par 1 000 habitants		Internet users per 1 000 inhabitants Utilisateurs d'Internet par 1 000 habitants		Internet hosts per 100 000 inhabitants Hébergeurs d'Internet par 100 000 habitants	Total telecommunications revenue (millions of dollars) Revenu total en télé-communications (millions de dollars)		Annual investment in telecommunications (millions of dollars) Investissement annuel dans les télécommunications (millions de dollars)		Television sets per 1 000 inhabitants Postes téléviseurs par 1 000 habitants		Pays ou zones
(7)		(8)		(9)	(10)		(11)		(12)		
760		531		5967	..		..		863		Saint-Marin
..		73		708	7		4		93		Sao Tomé-et-Principe
137		65		67	6279		1541		279		Arabie saoudite
20		10		8	234		109		40		Sénégal
27		60		158	358	a	212		..		Serbie-et-Monténégro
161		145		329	..		..		253		Seychelles
..		2		6	..		..		13		Sierra Leone
622		504		8126	3349		433		303		Singapour
180		160		1599	940	a	126	a	409	a	Slovaquie
301		376		1793	678		150		366		Slovénie
41		5		106	12	a	..		11		Iles Salomon
..		9		..	..		..		15		Somalie
73		68		438	5339		712		177		Afrique du Sud
196		193		1450	29797		5242		560	a	Espagne
13		11		12	335		82		121		Sri Lanka
6		3		..	179		108	a	383		Soudan
42	a	42		5	56		33		242		Suriname
24		19		129	35		10	a	34		Swaziland
621		573		9495	7824		1482	a	962	a	Suède
709		351		7703	9596		1633		563		Suisse
19		13		0	433	a	175	a	182		République arabe syrienne
..		1		5	8		..		348	a	Tadjikistan
40		78		162	4141		1513		283		Thaïlande
31		41		2	42		30		123		Togo
20		29		19642	..		..		71		Tonga
80		106		554	299	a	110	a	350		Trinité-et-Tobago
34		52		4	579		306		210		Tunisie
45		73		230	5196	a	198		423		Turquie
..		2	a	42	56	a	7		181	a	Turkménistan
..		131		89949	1	a	..		..		Tuvalu
3		4		9	112		..		16		Ouganda
19		18		143	1559	a	466		..		Ukraine
120		271		1394	2181		312		213		Emirats arabes unis
406		423		4850	72836		13433		966	a	Royaume-Uni
4		2		5	221		9	a	44		République-Unie de Tanzanie
659		551		39988	294000		29620	a	926	a	Etats-Unis
..		273		3567	..		..		..		Iles Vierges américaines
109	a	119	a	2324	714	a	..		..		Uruguay
..		11		1	196	a	41	a	277	a	Ouzbékistan
15		35		273	12	a	..		13		Vanuatu
61		51		96	2934		674		183	a	Venezuela
10		18		1	1400		..		197		Viet Nam
7		5		1	144		74		308		Yémen
7		5		15	69	a	5	a	61		Zambie
52		43		21	207	a	..		66		Zimbabwe

Pour les sources et les notes, se reporter à la page suivante.

7.6 Information and communication technology indicators by country

7.6 Indicateurs des technologies de l'information et de la communication par pays

Sources:

International Telecommunication Union (ITU), *World Telecommunication Indicators*, database.

Notes:

The data presented refer to the year 2002 unless otherwise indicated by "a".

a   Data refer to the year 2001.

Column number:

(5)   "Three-minute mobile phone call" refers to a local call from a cellular phone during peak hours. Its cost is expressed in dollars.

(6)   "Three-minute fixed-line phone call" refers to a local call from a residential phone during peak hours. Its cost is expressed in dollars.

(8)   Estimates.

(9)   Internet hosts refer to the number of computers in an economy that are directly linked to the worldwide Internet network. This statistic is based on the country code in the host address and thus may not correspond to the actual physical location.

(10)   Refers to the earnings of enterprises that are directly making available facilities for providing telecommunications services to the public (not including revenues of resellers). This includes revenues from fixed telephone, mobile, text (telex, telegraph and facsimile), communications leased circuits; and data communications services. Some countries include telecommunications-related revenue such as directory advertising and equipment rental or sales. Others include value-added telecommunications services such as the provision of electronic mail or online services. This indicator is expressed in millions of dollars.

(11)   Refers to expenditures associated with acquiring ownership of telecommunication equipment infrastructure (including supporting land and buildings and intellectual and non-tangible property such as computer software). These include expenditures on initial installations and on additions to existing installations. This indicator is expressed in millions of dollars.

Sources :

Union internationale de télécommunication (UIT) , *World Telecommunication Indicators*, base de données.

Notes :

Les données présentées se réfèrent à l'année 2002. Les exceptions sont marquées par "a".

a   Les données se réfèrent à l'année 2001.

Numéro de colonnes :

(5)   L'appel de trois minutes par téléphone mobile se réfère à un appel local d'un téléphone portable aux heures de pointe. Le coût est exprimé en dollars.

(6)   L'appel de trois minutes par téléphone du réseau fixe se réfère à un appel local d'un téléphone résidentiel aux heures de pointe. Le coût est exprimé en dollars.

(8)   Estimations.

(9)   Les hébergeurs d'Internet sont définis comme les ordinateurs dans une économie qui sont directement liés au réseau mondial d'Internet. Ces statistiques se basent sur les codes des pays dans les adresses d'hébergeurs et ne correspondent pas toujours à l'emplacement physique de l'ordinateur.

(10)   Se réfère aux revenus des entreprises qui sont fournisseurs directs de services de télécommunication au public (revenus des reventes exclus). Cela comprend des revenus de téléphone fixe, de communications de mobiles, de transmission de textes (télex, télégraphe, télécopie), des circuit en location (en bail) et de services de transmission de données. Quelques pays y incluent d'autres revenus liés aux télécommunications comme les publicités dans les annuaires et la location ou la vente d'équipements. D'autres y incluent les services tenant lieu de valeur ajoutée, comme courrier électronique ou autres services en ligne. Cet indicateur est présenté en millions de dollars.

(11)   Comprend les dépenses associées à l'acquisition d'équipements et d'infrastructures des télécommunications (y compris des terrains, des bâtiments, la propriété intellectuelle et autre propriété comme des logiciels etc.). Cela inclut les dépenses pour des installations initiales et toutes les additions aux installations existantes. L'indicateur est présenté en millions de dollars.

PART EIGHT

Special studies

HUITIEME PARTIE

Etudes spéciales

1

2

3

4

5

6

7

8

	1980	1990	1994	1995	1996	1997	1998	1999	2001	2002
Algeria - Algérie										
Exports										
Value	63	59	40	46	57	63	45	57	88	87
Unit value	133	88	62	66	77	75	55	63	97	90
Quantum	47	67	65	70	74	84	82	90	90	96
Imports										
Value	115	107	102	112	97	95	103	100	106	118
Unit value	79	119	108	114	114	106	108	106	96	100
Quantum	146	90	95	98	84	89	95	95	110	118
Terms of trade	168	74	58	58	67	71	51	60	101	90
Purchasing power of exports	80	49	37	41	50	59	41	54	91	87
Angola										
Exportations										
Valeur	..	49	38	47	64	63	45	65	83	96
Valeur unitaire	..	82	48	63	90	69	43	63	86	89
Volume	..	60	80	74	72	92	103	104	96	108
Importations										
Valeur	..	52	48	48	67	85	68	102	105	125
Valeur unitaire	..	87	70	78	104	101	97	105	98	71
Volume	..	60	68	62	65	85	71	97	107	176
Termes de l'échange	..	94	68	81	86	68	45	59	87	125
Pouvoir d'achat des exportations	..	56	54	60	62	63	46	62	84	135
Argentina - Argentine										
Exports										
Value	30	47	59	80	90	100	100	89	101	98
Unit value	85	75	106	109	116	109	99	91	97	94
Quantum	36	63	56	73	78	92	101	98	104	104
Imports										
Value	42	16	86	80	94	121	125	101	81	36
Unit value	80	118	109	119	116	109	104	100	97	95
Quantum	52	14	79	67	81	111	120	101	83	38
Terms of trade	106	64	97	92	100	100	95	91	99	99
Purchasing power of exports	38	40	55	67	78	92	96	89	104	103
Bangladesh										
Exportations										
Valeur	12	26	42	58	63	76	80	85	..	..
Valeur unitaire	255	190	80	85	91	96	99	100	..	..
Volume	5	14	52	68	69	79	81	86	..	..
Importations										
Valeur	31	43	55	78	79	83	83	92	..	..
Valeur unitaire	170	171	70	76	82	84	87	92	..	..
Volume	18	25	79	102	97	98	96	100	..	..
Termes de l'échange	150	111	114	112	111	113	114	108	..	..
Pouvoir d'achat des exportations	7	15	59	76	76	90	92	93	..	..
Benin - Bénin										
Exports										
Value	16	73	101	107	135	106	104	108	95	114
Unit value	57	107	91	129	113	110	114	112	100	107
Quantum	28	69	111	83	119	97	91	96	95	106
Imports										
Value	54	43	70	122	107	111	120	122	98	111
Unit value	66	100	113	121	120	111	115	112	100	105
Quantum	82	43	62	100	89	100	105	109	98	105
Terms of trade	86	107	81	106	94	99	99	100	100	102
Purchasing power of exports	24	73	89	88	112	96	91	96	95	109

For sources and notes, see end of table.

Pour les sources et les notes, se reporter à la fin du tableau.

	1980	1990	1994	1995	1996	1997	1998	1999	2001	2002
Bolivia - Bolivie										
Exportations										
Valeur	77	75	84	90	92	95	90	86	105	106
Valeur unitaire	150	101	94	101	111	110	100	96	95	93
Volume	51	75	89	89	83	86	90	89	110	113
Importations										
Valeur	36	38	66	78	89	101	108	96	93	97
Valeur unitaire	80	99	103	113	111	106	102	98	97	95
Volume	45	38	64	69	80	95	107	98	96	102
Termes de l'échange	188	102	92	89	100	103	98	98	98	98
Pouvoir d'achat des exportations	96	76	81	79	83	89	88	87	108	111
Botswana										
Exports										
Value	19	66	68	79	94	105	72	97	90	93
Unit value	81	105	103	109	105	108	101	102	93	91
Quantum	23	63	66	73	89	97	71	95	97	101
Imports										
Value	28	79	66	77	70	91	97	90	73	79
Unit value	97	107	115	122	112	110	101	102	92	90
Quantum	29	74	58	63	62	83	95	88	80	88
Terms of trade	84	98	89	89	94	98	100	101	101	101
Purchasing power of exports	19	62	59	65	83	95	71	96	98	103
Brazil - Brésil										
Exportations										
Valeur	37	57	79	84	87	96	93	87	106	110
Valeur unitaire	116	99	106	117	117	119	112	98	97	92
Volume	32	58	74	72	74	81	83	89	109	119
Importations										
Valeur	43	38	61	92	97	111	103	88	100	85
Valeur unitaire	157	149	105	106	108	104	98	95	97	95
Volume	27	26	58	86	90	107	106	93	103	89
Termes de l'échange	74	66	101	110	108	114	114	103	100	97
Pouvoir d'achat des exportations	23	38	75	80	80	93	95	92	109	115
Burkina Faso										
Exports										
Value	43	73	51	132	111	111	153	122	112	113
Unit value	76	139	123	148	141	129	122	109	107	100
Quantum	57	52	41	89	79	86	125	112	105	114
Imports										
Value	59	88	57	74	106	96	120	111	107	121
Unit value	117	117	101	113	115	106	98	97	91	91
Quantum	50	75	56	66	92	91	123	115	118	133
Terms of trade	65	119	122	131	122	121	125	113	117	110
Purchasing power of exports	37	62	50	117	97	105	156	126	123	125
Burundi										
Exportations										
Valeur	131	150	242	211	80	173	129	109	77	60
Valeur unitaire	702	440	413	440	270	264	206	131	60	60
Volume	19	34	58	48	30	65	63	83	129	101
Importations										
Valeur	114	156	152	158	86	82	107	80	94	87
Valeur unitaire	304	343	241	269	227	241	170	113	82	73
Volume	37	45	63	59	38	34	63	71	115	120
Termes de l'échange	231	128	171	164	119	110	121	116	73	82
Pouvoir d'achat des exportations	43	44	100	79	35	72	76	96	94	83

For sources and notes, see end of table.

Pour les sources et les notes, se reporter à la fin du tableau.

	1980	1990	1994	1995	1996	1997	1998	1999	2001	2002
Cameroon - Cameroun										
Exports										
Value	90	131	97	106	105	110	120	99	137	148
Unit value	154	104	100	113	102	101	91	78	98	94
Quantum	59	125	97	94	102	109	132	127	140	158
Imports										
Value	108	94	73	81	82	91	100	89	124	121
Unit value	192	128	118	125	124	116	109	111	93	94
Quantum	56	73	62	64	67	79	93	80	134	128
Terms of trade	80	81	84	90	83	87	84	71	105	100
Purchasing power of exports	47	102	82	85	85	95	110	90	147	158
Cape Verde - Cap-Vert										
Exportations										
Valeur	40	53	41	78	119	132	98	108	93	104
Valeur unitaire	78	102	113	126	124	119	118	117	102	110
Volume	51	52	36	62	96	112	84	92	91	94
Importations										
Valeur	29	59	91	110	102	102	99	107	101	121
Valeur unitaire	78	102	113	126	124	119	118	117	102	110
Volume	38	58	80	87	82	86	84	91	99	110
Termes de l'échange	100	100	100	100	100	100	100	100	100	100
Pouvoir d'achat des exportations	51	52	36	62	96	112	84	92	91	94
Central African Republic - République centrafricaine										
Exports										
Value	72	75	94	106	91	101	94	91	89	91
Unit value	344	437	212	247	217	165	141	120	103	113
Quantum	21	17	44	43	42	61	67	76	86	81
Imports										
Value	69	132	119	149	121	120	125	112	92	103
Unit value	132	184	106	128	130	110	114	112	100	107
Quantum	53	72	112	116	93	109	110	100	92	96
Terms of trade	261	238	199	193	166	150	124	107	103	106
Purchasing power of exports	55	41	88	83	70	92	83	81	89	85
Chad - Tchad										
Exportations										
Valeur	39	103	81	133	130	129	143	133	103	101
Valeur unitaire	104	104	83	113	124	112	120	109	121	119
Volume	37	99	98	118	105	116	119	122	85	85
Importations										
Valeur	23	91	56	116	105	106	113	100	215	316
Valeur unitaire	96	93	107	122	135	121	119	114	76	72
Volume	24	97	52	95	78	87	95	88	283	439
Termes de l'échange	108	112	77	92	92	92	101	95	159	165
Pouvoir d'achat des exportations	40	111	75	109	97	107	120	116	136	140
Chile - Chili										
Exports										
Value	24	44	60	83	82	93	85	89	95	95
Unit value	146	116	110	141	115	113	94	91	89	88
Quantum	17	38	55	59	71	83	91	98	106	108
Imports										
Value	31	42	64	86	103	113	107	86	96	93
Unit value	60	102	96	104	105	100	94	91	96	94
Quantum	52	41	67	83	99	112	114	95	100	99
Terms of trade	243	114	114	136	110	113	100	100	93	93
Purchasing power of exports	41	43	63	81	78	93	90	98	99	101

For sources and notes, see end of table.

Pour les sources et les notes, se reporter à la fin du tableau.

382

	1980	1990	1994	1995	1996	1997	1998	1999	2001	2002
China - Chine										
Exportations										
Valeur	7	25	49	60	61	73	74	78	107	131
Valeur unitaire	101	97	100	105	107	108	104	101	98	95
Volume	7	26	48	57	56	68	71	78	109	137
Importations										
Valeur	9	24	51	59	62	63	62	74	108	131
Valeur unitaire	86	95	98	103	101	98	94	97	95	93
Volume	10	25	52	57	61	65	66	76	114	141
Termes de l'échange	117	102	102	102	107	110	110	104	103	102
Pouvoir d'achat des exportations	8	26	49	58	60	75	78	81	112	140
China, Hong Kong SAR - Chine, Hong Kong RAS										
Exports										
Value	10	41	75	86	90	93	86	86	94	99
Unit value	92	101	106	110	110	108	104	101	98	95
Quantum	11	40	70	78	82	87	83	86	96	104
Imports										
Value	11	39	76	91	93	98	87	84	94	98
Unit value	92	101	106	111	110	107	102	100	97	93
Quantum	11	38	72	81	85	91	85	85	97	105
Terms of trade	100	100	100	99	100	100	102	101	101	102
Purchasing power of exports	11	40	71	77	82	87	85	86	97	107
China, Taiwan Province of - Chine, Taiwan Province de										
Exportations										
Valeur	..	45	63	75	78	82	75	82	83	88
Valeur unitaire	..	70	74	80	87	88	92	93	105	107
Volume	..	65	85	94	90	93	81	88	79	83
Importations										
Valeur	..	39	61	74	72	81	75	79	77	81
Valeur unitaire	..	72	79	89	90	89	91	90	94	91
Volume	..	54	77	84	81	91	82	88	82	89
Termes de l'échange	..	97	94	91	97	99	101	104	111	117
Pouvoir d'achat des exportations	..	63	79	85	87	92	82	91	88	97
Colombia - Colombie										
Exports										
Value	30	52	65	77	81	88	83	89	94	91
Unit value	84	78	89	92	97	98	85	88	91	89
Quantum	36	67	72	84	84	90	98	101	103	103
Imports										
Value	41	48	103	120	119	133	127	92	111	110
Unit value	75	96	98	106	108	109	103	99	97	96
Quantum	55	50	105	113	110	123	123	93	115	115
Terms of trade	112	81	91	86	90	90	83	89	94	93
Purchasing power of exports	40	54	66	73	75	81	81	90	97	95
Comoros - Comores										
Exportations										
Valeur	163	261	164	165	90	82	57	68	199	276
Valeur unitaire	139	153	90	137	133	117	111	115	127	131
Volume	117	171	183	120	68	70	52	59	157	212
Importations										
Valeur	40	72	73	87	79	77	65	111	137	118
Valeur unitaire	125	178	176	159	156	133	123	119	96	93
Volume	32	40	42	55	51	57	53	93	142	127
Termes de l'échange	111	86	51	86	85	88	90	97	132	140
Pouvoir d'achat des exportations	130	147	93	104	57	62	47	57	207	297

For sources and notes, see end of table.

Pour les sources et les notes, se reporter à la fin du tableau.

	1980	1990	1994	1995	1996	1997	1998	1999	2001	2002
					Congo					
Exports										
Value	37	39	39	47	54	67	55	63	80	90
Unit value	92	74	60	64	77	70	49	67	85	83
Quantum	40	53	64	74	70	96	112	94	94	108
Imports										
Value	121	134	136	144	334	199	146	177	125	127
Unit value	95	117	112	123	120	110	125	104	100	88
Quantum	127	114	121	117	278	181	117	171	125	144
Terms of trade	97	63	53	52	64	64	39	64	85	95
Purchasing power of exports	39	34	34	38	45	61	44	61	80	102
					Costa Rica					
Exportations										
Valeur	17	25	49	59	64	74	94	114	86	90
Valeur unitaire	83	81	99	114	108	112	110	105	95	93
Volume	21	31	49	52	60	66	86	108	90	97
Importations										
Valeur	24	31	59	64	68	78	98	99	103	113
Valeur unitaire	102	108	101	109	109	106	101	98	96	95
Volume	24	29	58	59	62	73	97	101	107	118
Termes de l'échange	81	75	98	104	99	105	108	107	99	97
Pouvoir d'achat des exportations	17	23	49	55	59	70	93	116	89	95
					Côte d'Ivoire					
Exports										
Value	81	79	71	98	114	114	118	120	102	136
Unit value	144	103	102	122	128	115	119	117	99	129
Quantum	56	77	69	81	89	99	100	102	102	105
Imports										
Value	125	87	80	122	121	116	139	115	101	102
Unit value	71	72	83	100	108	98	102	99	100	109
Quantum	175	121	96	122	112	118	137	117	101	94
Terms of trade	203	143	123	121	118	117	117	119	99	118
Purchasing power of exports	114	110	85	98	106	116	117	121	102	124
				Dem. Rep. of the Congo - Rép. dém. du Congo						
Exportations										
Valeur	299	306	165	217	217	156	155	123	124	159
Valeur unitaire	355	225	264	268	250	212	276	111	94	99
Volume	84	136	63	81	87	74	56	111	132	161
Importations										
Valeur	147	168	64	101	136	109	119	107	68	95
Valeur unitaire	422	261	397	336	465	315	421	107	87	90
Volume	35	64	16	30	29	35	28	100	78	105
Termes de l'échange	84	86	67	80	54	67	66	104	108	110
Pouvoir d'achat des exportations	71	117	42	65	47	50	37	115	142	177
				Dominican Republic - République dominicaine						
Exports										
Value	100	76	67	90	98	105	91	83	83	86
Unit value	121	97	100	106	105	106	100	99	98	98
Quantum	82	78	67	85	93	99	91	84	85	88
Imports										
Value	22	28	47	49	56	65	76	81	80	82
Unit value	69	101	106	108	109	106	99	97	97	97
Quantum	32	28	44	46	51	61	77	83	83	85
Terms of trade	175	96	94	98	96	100	101	102	101	101
Purchasing power of exports	144	75	63	84	89	99	92	86	86	89

For sources and notes, see end of table.

Pour les sources et les notes, se reporter à la fin du tableau.

	1980	1990	1994	1995	1996	1997	1998	1999	2001	2002
Ecuador - Equateur										
Exportations										
Valeur	50	55	78	87	99	107	85	90	95	102
Valeur unitaire	164	96	86	87	94	95	81	83	89	91
Volume	31	57	90	101	106	112	106	108	106	112
Importations										
Valeur	61	50	97	112	106	133	150	81	144	173
Valeur unitaire	77	84	98	108	106	105	100	97	97	96
Volume	79	60	100	104	100	126	150	84	149	180
Termes de l'échange	213	114	88	81	89	90	80	86	92	95
Pouvoir d'achat des exportations	65	66	79	81	94	101	85	93	98	107
Egypt - Egypte										
Exports										
Value	65	106	74	74	75	84	67	76	88	100
Unit value	107	83	96	100	100	105	99	93	101	91
Quantum	61	127	78	73	76	79	67	81	88	110
Imports										
Value	35	120	73	84	93	94	115	114	91	90
Unit value	50	82	80	86	90	98	101	96	102	93
Quantum	69	146	91	98	104	96	114	119	89	96
Terms of trade	214	101	120	117	111	108	98	97	99	98
Purchasing power of exports	130	129	93	86	84	85	66	79	86	108
El Salvador										
Exportations										
Valeur	73	44	63	75	77	103	94	88	91	93
Valeur unitaire	78	64	83	109	106	108	109	101	94	93
Volume	93	68	76	69	73	95	87	87	97	100
Importations										
Valeur	25	33	59	75	70	79	82	83	102	103
Valeur unitaire	83	76	85	90	93	95	98	96	97	97
Volume	31	44	70	84	75	82	84	86	105	106
Termes de l'échange	94	84	98	121	113	114	111	105	97	96
Pouvoir d'achat des exportations	87	57	75	83	82	108	96	92	94	96
Equatorial Guinea - Guinée équatoriale										
Exports										
Value	..	6	6	8	16	45	40	65	149	171
Unit value	..	87	44	50	62	69	52	79	68	71
Quantum	..	7	13	15	26	65	77	82	220	241
Imports										
Value	..	14	8	11	65	73	70	94	162	95
Unit value	..	231	119	136	166	187	140	100	183	191
Quantum	..	6	7	8	39	39	50	94	89	50
Terms of trade	..	38	37	37	37	37	37	79	37	37
Purchasing power of exports	..	2	5	6	10	24	29	64	81	90
Eritrea - Erythrée										
Exportations										
Valeur	..	..	343	428	506	282	149	92	101	275
Valeur unitaire	..	..	112	119	115	111	101	99	98	99
Volume	..	..	305	361	438	253	147	93	103	278
Importations										
Valeur	..	..	121	123	157	149	153	100	129	164
Valeur unitaire	..	..	108	117	117	110	106	103	98	100
Volume	..	..	111	105	134	136	144	98	132	164
Termes de l'échange	..	..	104	102	99	101	95	96	100	99
Pouvoir d'achat des exportations	..	..	316	367	432	256	140	89	103	275

For sources and notes, see end of table.

Pour les sources et les notes, se reporter à la fin du tableau.

	1980	1990	1994	1995	1996	1997	1998	1999	2001	2002
					Ethiopia - Ethiopie					
Exports										
Value	..	61	77	87	86	121	115	96	94	99
Unit value	..	116	110	157	124	132	147	120	92	82
Quantum	..	53	70	56	69	91	79	80	101	121
Imports										
Value	..	86	82	91	111	88	120	122	144	132
Unit value	..	96	97	104	108	104	98	96	99	97
Quantum	..	89	84	88	103	85	123	127	145	136
Terms of trade	..	121	113	151	115	127	150	126	93	84
Purchasing power of exports	..	64	79	84	79	116	118	101	95	102
					Gabon					
Exportations										
Valeur	88	90	95	110	129	123	78	97	108	85
Valeur unitaire	248	166	126	143	168	149	105	104	141	154
Volume	36	54	75	77	77	82	74	94	76	55
Importations										
Valeur	68	92	76	89	96	111	111	85	86	102
Valeur unitaire	81	106	106	114	114	102	102	99	100	109
Volume	84	87	72	78	85	109	109	85	86	93
Termes de l'échange	306	157	119	125	148	147	103	104	141	142
Pouvoir d'achat des exportations	109	84	90	96	114	121	77	98	108	78
					Gambia - Gambie					
Exports										
Value	193	199	237	113	76	34	129	76	56	61
Unit value	93	106	110	115	115	115	111	108	88	83
Quantum	208	188	215	99	66	30	116	70	64	74
Imports										
Value	88	100	113	97	138	148	122	102	72	79
Unit value	51	106	110	115	115	115	111	108	88	83
Quantum	173	95	103	85	120	129	110	95	81	95
Terms of trade	182	100	100	100	100	100	100	100	100	100
Purchasing power of exports	378	188	215	99	66	30	116	70	64	74
					Ghana					
Exportations										
Valeur	76	54	86	104	101	99	108	104	95	111
Valeur unitaire	44	98	98	112	114	114	118	103	98	109
Volume	172	55	87	93	88	87	92	101	96	102
Importations										
Valeur	38	40	71	64	71	78	86	117	83	94
Valeur unitaire	21	98	104	105	105	100	95	94	95	97
Volume	181	41	68	61	67	78	91	125	88	97
Termes de l'échange	210	100	95	106	108	113	124	110	103	112
Pouvoir d'achat des exportations	361	55	83	99	96	98	114	111	100	114
					Guatemala					
Exports										
Value	56	43	56	80	75	87	96	89	91	83
Unit value	109	98	104	125	111	111	108	99	94	94
Quantum	52	44	55	64	68	79	89	90	97	89
Imports										
Value	33	34	58	69	66	80	97	91	117	127
Unit value	82	85	98	106	107	99	97	96	96	96
Quantum	41	40	60	65	61	81	100	95	122	132
Terms of trade	133	115	106	118	104	112	111	103	98	97
Purchasing power of exports	69	51	58	75	70	88	99	92	95	86

For sources and notes, see end of table.

Pour les sources et les notes, se reporter à la fin du tableau.

	1980	1990	1994	1995	1996	1997	1998	1999	2001	2002
					Guinea - Guinée					
Exportations										
Valeur	..	101	99	105	106	103	104	95	110	133
Valeur unitaire	..	180	157	138	129	130	116	110	94	95
Volume	..	56	63	76	83	79	90	87	117	140
Importations										
Valeur	..	114	109	134	106	101	88	91	98	109
Valeur unitaire	..	148	157	154	165	149	145	143	94	95
Volume	..	77	70	87	64	68	60	63	104	115
Termes de l'échange	..	122	100	90	78	87	80	77	100	100
Pouvoir d'achat des exportations	..	68	63	68	65	69	72	67	117	140
					Guinea-Bissau - Guinée-Bissau					
Exports										
Value	18	31	139	71	45	78	43	82	101	87
Unit value	65	140	116	113	115	106	89	102	115	136
Quantum	27	22	120	63	39	73	48	80	88	64
Imports										
Value	112	174	333	270	177	181	128	104	126	119
Unit value	52	96	93	110	113	109	102	104	104	130
Quantum	215	182	358	245	156	166	126	100	121	91
Terms of trade	125	146	124	102	102	98	88	98	110	105
Purchasing power of exports	34	32	149	65	40	72	42	79	97	67
					Haiti - Haïti					
Exportations										
Valeur	71	50	26	35	28	67	101	105	86	88
Valeur unitaire	146	127	94	103	99	99	107	102	97	97
Volume	49	40	28	34	29	67	94	103	89	91
Importations										
Valeur	36	32	24	63	64	63	77	99	98	109
Valeur unitaire	65	96	85	91	97	92	97	94	96	97
Volume	56	33	28	69	66	68	79	105	102	112
Termes de l'échange	225	132	110	114	103	108	110	108	101	100
Pouvoir d'achat des exportations	110	53	30	38	29	72	104	111	90	91
					Honduras					
Exports										
Value	60	60	61	88	95	105	111	84	96	96
Unit value	103	71	82	105	95	113	110	101	94	91
Quantum	58	85	75	84	101	93	101	84	102	105
Imports										
Value	35	33	37	58	64	75	89	94	103	104
Unit value	91	91	92	109	106	102	97	95	96	96
Quantum	39	36	40	53	61	74	92	98	107	109
Terms of trade	113	78	89	96	89	111	114	106	98	95
Purchasing power of exports	66	66	66	81	90	103	115	89	100	100
					India - Inde					
Exportations										
Valeur	20	42	59	72	78	83	79	84	102	116
Valeur unitaire	96	121	114	108	103	117	107	101	94	92
Volume	21	35	52	67	76	71	74	83	108	127
Importations										
Valeur	29	46	52	67	74	80	83	91	98	110
Valeur unitaire	134	141	96	100	104	103	91	96	96	104
Volume	22	32	55	67	71	78	91	95	102	105
Termes de l'échange	72	86	119	108	99	114	117	105	98	88
Pouvoir d'achat des exportations	15	30	62	72	75	80	86	87	107	112

For sources and notes, see end of table.

Pour les sources et les notes, se reporter à la fin du tableau.

	1980	1990	1994	1995	1996	1997	1998	1999	2001	2002
					Indonesia - Indonésie					
Exports										
Value	35	41	64	73	80	86	79	78	91	94
Unit value	157	93	90	103	109	104	81	65	90	96
Quantum	22	44	71	71	74	83	97	121	101	98
Imports										
Value	..	65	95	121	128	124	82	72	93	76
Unit value	..	98	106	114	112	105	99	98	96	96
Quantum	..	66	90	106	115	119	82	73	96	79
Terms of trade	..	95	85	90	98	99	82	66	94	100
Purchasing power of exports	..	42	61	64	72	82	79	80	95	97
					Jordan - Jordanie					
Exportations										
Valeur	30	56	75	93	96	97	95	96	121	146
Valeur unitaire	95	89	96	111	117	114	107	105	101	102
Volume	32	63	78	84	82	85	89	92	119	144
Importations										
Valeur	52	57	74	80	93	89	83	81	105	109
Valeur unitaire	108	95	85	96	103	101	100	98	102	105
Volume	48	60	87	84	91	89	83	83	103	104
Termes de l'échange	88	94	113	116	114	113	107	107	99	97
Pouvoir d'achat des exportations	28	59	89	97	93	96	95	99	118	139
					Kenya					
Exports										
Value	72	60	92	108	119	118	116	101	112	122
Unit value	139	94	89	107	105	122	122	102	103	109
Quantum	52	63	103	101	113	97	95	99	109	112
Imports										
Value	68	72	67	96	95	106	103	91	103	104
Unit value	138	134	83	103	97	107	111	104	101	111
Quantum	50	53	81	93	98	98	93	88	102	94
Terms of trade	101	70	106	104	109	114	110	98	102	98
Purchasing power of exports	52	44	110	105	123	110	104	97	111	110
					Korea, Republic of - Corée, République de					
Exportations										
Valeur	10	38	56	73	75	79	77	83	87	94
Valeur unitaire	128	156	151	162	141	128	102	100	87	83
Volume	8	24	37	45	54	62	75	84	100	113
Importations										
Valeur	14	44	64	84	94	90	58	75	88	95
Valeur unitaire	112	117	110	117	112	105	87	87	91	88
Volume	12	37	58	72	84	86	67	85	97	108
Termes de l'échange	114	134	137	139	125	122	117	114	95	95
Pouvoir d'achat des exportations	9	32	51	62	67	75	88	96	96	108
					Lesotho					
Exports										
Value	26	28	65	73	85	89	88	78	128	166
Unit value	131	102	117	124	115	115	105	105	87	77
Quantum	20	27	56	59	74	78	84	74	148	216
Imports										
Value	59	92	117	135	137	141	119	107	94	108
Unit value	100	102	117	124	115	115	105	106	87	77
Quantum	59	91	100	109	120	122	113	102	108	140
Terms of trade	131	100	100	100	100	100	100	100	100	100
Purchasing power of exports	26	27	56	59	74	77	84	74	147	215

For sources and notes, see end of table.

Pour les sources et les notes, se reporter à la fin du tableau.

	1980	1990	1994	1995	1996	1997	1998	1999	2001	2002
Madagascar										
Exportations										
Valeur	49	39	55	62	62	63	65	71	113	59
Valeur unitaire	55	68	73	82	84	83	90	88	105	99
Volume	89	57	75	75	73	76	73	80	108	59
Importations										
Valeur	77	57	55	63	63	70	69	74	96	60
Valeur unitaire	66	84	94	103	103	98	96	99	89	87
Volume	116	68	58	61	61	71	72	75	108	69
Termes de l'échange	83	81	78	79	82	85	94	89	117	114
Pouvoir d'achat des exportations	74	46	58	59	60	64	68	72	127	68
Malawi										
Exports										
Value	78	110	90	107	127	142	114	119	118	107
Unit value	98	126	92	112	118	123	100	104	97	100
Quantum	79	87	98	95	108	115	114	115	122	107
Imports										
Value	83	108	92	89	117	147	97	127	106	131
Unit value	60	85	103	106	105	105	97	98	97	101
Quantum	138	127	90	84	112	140	100	130	109	129
Terms of trade	163	148	90	106	112	118	103	106	100	99
Purchasing power of exports	130	129	88	100	121	135	117	122	122	106
Malaysia - Malaisie										
Exportations										
Valeur	13	30	60	75	80	80	75	86	90	95
Valeur unitaire	75	113	119	127	130	119	107	103	96	95
Volume	18	27	50	59	61	67	70	84	93	100
Importations										
Valeur	13	36	73	95	96	96	71	80	90	97
Valeur unitaire	105	110	108	117	116	107	100	98	98	97
Volume	13	32	67	81	82	90	71	81	92	100
Termes de l'échange	71	103	110	109	112	112	107	104	98	98
Pouvoir d'achat des exportations	13	27	55	64	68	75	74	87	91	98
Mali										
Exports										
Value	37	65	61	80	79	102	102	104	132	161
Unit value	149	155	114	137	134	114	114	102	109	105
Quantum	25	42	54	58	59	89	90	101	121	153
Imports										
Value	74	102	100	130	130	125	129	102	124	126
Unit value	128	115	113	125	121	107	102	101	111	105
Quantum	58	88	88	105	108	117	126	101	112	120
Terms of trade	116	135	101	110	111	107	112	101	98	100
Purchasing power of exports	29	57	54	64	65	96	100	103	119	153
Mauritania - Mauritanie										
Exportations										
Valeur	54	125	136	139	137	113	98	104	97	90
Valeur unitaire	99	145	131	139	135	140	124	110	94	78
Volume	55	86	103	100	102	81	79	95	103	115
Importations										
Valeur	88	68	124	152	143	135	111	94	115	110
Valeur unitaire	137	149	135	136	144	136	120	106	96	88
Volume	64	46	92	112	99	99	92	89	120	125
Termes de l'échange	72	97	97	102	94	103	103	103	98	88
Pouvoir d'achat des exportations	40	84	100	102	95	83	81	98	101	102

For sources and notes, see end of table.

Pour les sources et les notes, se reporter à la fin du tableau.

	1980	1990	1994	1995	1996	1997	1998	1999	2001	2002
Mauritius - Maurice										
Exports										
Value	28	77	86	99	116	102	106	102	105	116
Unit value	74	88	91	100	107	106	97	95	96	81
Quantum	38	87	96	99	108	96	109	107	109	143
Imports										
Value	29	77	92	94	109	105	99	107	95	104
Unit value	80	95	102	113	118	116	103	98	97	83
Quantum	37	81	90	84	93	90	96	109	98	125
Terms of trade	93	93	89	89	91	92	95	96	99	98
Purchasing power of exports	35	81	85	88	98	88	103	104	108	139
Mexico - Mexique										
Exportations										
Valeur	11	24	37	48	58	66	71	82	95	97
Valeur unitaire	171	95	94	98	99	99	94	95	96	98
Volume	6	26	39	49	58	67	75	86	99	98
Importations										
Valeur	12	24	45	42	51	63	72	81	96	97
Valeur unitaire	56	93	98	106	103	102	100	100	97	98
Volume	22	26	47	39	50	62	71	81	99	99
Termes de l'échange	305	102	96	93	96	97	94	95	99	100
Pouvoir d'achat des exportations	19	26	37	45	56	65	70	82	98	99
Morocco - Maroc										
Exports										
Value	35	61	80	99	99	101	103	106	103	113
Unit value	110	107	98	114	119	109	108	107	99	105
Quantum	32	57	82	86	83	93	95	99	104	107
Imports										
Value	37	60	72	87	84	83	89	86	96	103
Unit value	122	126	123	128	130	115	102	103	96	98
Quantum	30	48	59	68	65	72	87	83	100	105
Terms of trade	90	85	80	89	91	95	106	103	103	107
Purchasing power of exports	29	49	65	77	76	88	101	102	107	115
Mozambique										
Exportations										
Valeur	77	35	43	46	60	61	63	72	193	..
Valeur unitaire	173	168	133	142	114	117	112	113	99	..
Volume	45	21	32	32	52	52	56	64	194	..
Importations										
Valeur	69	76	88	61	66	64	68	98	92	117
Valeur unitaire	72	96	82	94	99	101	96	96	98	97
Volume	96	79	108	65	66	63	71	103	94	120
Termes de l'échange	240	175	163	151	115	115	116	118	101	..
Pouvoir d'achat des exportations	107	36	53	49	60	60	65	76	197	..
Myanmar										
Exports										
Value	..	20	49	52	46	53	65	69	145	..
Unit value	..	136	127	150	142	128	118	109	143	..
Quantum	..	15	38	35	32	42	56	63	101	..
Imports										
Value	..	11	37	56	57	86	112	97	120	..
Unit value	..	54	68	70	86	102	102	99	102	..
Quantum	..	21	55	80	66	84	110	97	117	..
Terms of trade	..	252	188	216	164	126	115	110	140	..
Purchasing power of exports	..	37	72	75	53	52	64	69	142	..

For sources and notes, see end of table.　　　　Pour les sources et les notes, se reporter à la fin du tableau.

	1980	1990	1994	1995	1996	1997	1998	1999	2001	2002
					Namibia - Namibie					
Exportations										
Valeur	..	82	99	107	107	101	93	93	89	83
Valeur unitaire	156	128	114	114	113	114	104	99	94	88
Volume	..	64	87	93	95	89	90	94	95	94
Importations										
Valeur	..	75	91	104	108	113	106	104	100	..
Valeur unitaire	139	138	129	138	125	124	109	105	95	..
Volume	..	54	71	75	86	91	98	99	105	..
Termes de l'échange	112	93	88	83	90	92	96	95	99	..
Pouvoir d'achat des exportations	..	60	77	77	86	82	86	89	94	..
					Nicaragua					
Exports										
Value	70	51	52	71	72	89	89	85	92	92
Unit value	120	124	102	116	106	109	108	98	89	87
Quantum	58	41	51	61	68	82	82	86	103	106
Imports										
Value	49	35	48	55	64	80	83	103	99	99
Unit value	74	80	83	90	93	100	95	93	97	97
Quantum	66	44	58	61	69	80	87	110	102	103
Terms of trade	162	155	123	129	114	108	113	105	92	90
Purchasing power of exports	94	64	63	79	78	·89	93	90	95	95
					Niger					
Exportations										
Valeur	200	100	80	102	115	96	118	101	..	..
Valeur unitaire	189	137	106	119	105	96	100	97	..	..
Volume	106	73	75	86	109	100	118	104	..	..
Importations										
Valeur	151	99	83	95	114	95	120	100	..	..
Valeur unitaire	82	83	89	98	99	96	101	104	..	..
Volume	184	119	94	97	115	99	118	97	..	..
Termes de l'échange	230	165	119	121	106	100	99	94	..	..
Pouvoir d'achat des exportations	244	120	90	104	116	100	117	98	..	..
					Nigeria - Nigéria					
Exports										
Value	124	65	45	59	77	73	47	66	82	72
Unit value	87	77	55	60	73	69	43	59	86	90
Quantum	142	84	81	99	106	105	108	112	96	80
Imports										
Value	191	65	76	94	74	109	106	98	133	87
Unit value	48	87	98	108	84	106	98	99	97	99
Quantum	398	74	77	87	87	103	108	99	137	87
Terms of trade	181	89	56	55	86	65	44	59	89	91
Purchasing power of exports	258	75	46	54	91	69	48	66	85	73
					Oman					
Exportations										
Valeur	22	..	51	56	68	70	51	67	102	103
Valeur unitaire	121	..	57	61	73	70	45	65	86	91
Volume	18	..	90	91	93	101	114	103	118	113
Importations										
Valeur	..	..	..	..	..	..	..	..	..	..
Valeur unitaire	..	..	..	..	..	..	..	..	..	..
Volume	..	..	..	..	..	..	..	..	..	..
Termes de l'échange	..	..	..	..	..	..	..	..	..	..
Pouvoir d'achat des exportations	..	..	..	..	..	..	..	..	..	..

For sources and notes, see end of table.

Pour les sources et les notes, se reporter à la fin du tableau.

	1980	1990	1994	1995	1996	1997	1998	1999	2001	2002
					Pakistan					
Exports										
Value	29	62	82	89	103	97	94	93	102	110
Unit value	101	100	97	118	114	115	117	109	94	90
Quantum	29	62	84	75	90	84	80	85	109	122
Imports										
Value	49	68	82	105	112	107	86	94	94	103
Unit value	78	92	90	99	95	97	86	93	94	95
Quantum	63	74	91	107	117	110	100	101	100	109
Terms of trade	129	109	107	119	120	119	136	118	100	95
Purchasing power of exports	37	67	90	90	108	100	110	101	109	116
					Panama					
Exportations										
Valeur	42	40	68	73	84	84	91	96	106	98
Valeur unitaire	75	66	96	96	98	99	100	101	97	97
Volume	56	60	71	76	86	85	91	95	109	102
Importations										
Valeur	43	46	71	74	82	89	101	104	88	88
Valeur unitaire	65	96	87	96	96	96	97	95	97	98
Volume	66	47	82	77	85	93	104	109	90	90
Termes de l'échange	115	69	110	100	101	104	103	106	100	99
Pouvoir d'achat des exportations	65	41	78	76	87	88	94	100	109	100
				Papua New Guinea - Papouasie-Nouvelle-Guinée						
Exports										
Value	49	56	126	127	121	103	85	92	87	74
Unit value	31	37	49	69	68	75	86	97	103	128
Quantum	159	152	256	184	178	137	98	95	84	58
Imports										
Value	..	..	..	..	..	..	..	..	..	..
Unit value	..	..	..	..	..	..	..	..	..	..
Quantum	..	..	..	..	..	..	..	..	..	..
Terms of trade	..	..	..	..	..	..	..	..	..	..
Purchasing power of exports	..	..	..	..	..	..	..	..	..	..
					Paraguay					
Exportations										
Valeur	36	110	94	106	120	125	117	85	114	134
Valeur unitaire	90	92	107	110	110	110	109	101	97	97
Volume	40	120	88	96	109	114	107	84	118	139
Importations										
Valeur	30	66	104	136	139	151	121	84	97	102
Valeur unitaire	132	89	85	93	93	93	100	97	97	97
Volume	23	74	122	146	150	163	121	87	100	105
Termes de l'échange	68	103	125	119	119	119	110	104	100	100
Pouvoir d'achat des exportations	27	124	110	114	129	135	117	88	117	138
					Peru - Pérou					
Exports										
Value	56	46	64	79	85	98	83	88	101	110
Unit value	167	113	115	132	129	131	109	98	92	96
Quantum	34	41	55	60	65	75	76	89	109	115
Imports										
Value	28	39	75	105	106	116	112	92	102	102
Unit value	68	99	97	107	108	103	98	95	96	97
Quantum	41	39	78	98	98	112	114	96	106	106
Terms of trade	246	114	118	124	119	128	111	103	96	99
Purchasing power of exports	82	47	65	74	78	95	84	92	105	113

For sources and notes, see end of table.

Pour les sources et les notes, se reporter à la fin du tableau.

392

	1980	1990	1994	1995	1996	1997	1998	1999	2001	2002
Philippines										
Exportations										
Valeur	14	20	33	44	51	63	74	92	82	92
Valeur unitaire	337	83	81	81	86	89	97	107	95	100
Volume	4	25	41	54	60	70	76	86	86	92
Importations										
Valeur	22	35	61	77	92	104	85	88	94	100
Valeur unitaire	340	95	104	101	106	108	111	104	99	96
Volume	7	37	59	76	87	97	77	85	95	105
Termes de l'échange	99	87	78	80	81	83	87	102	96	104
Pouvoir d'achat des exportations	4	21	32	44	48	58	67	88	83	96
Rwanda										
Exports										
Value	230	208	55	99	115	166	114	114	162	106
Unit value	99	70	85	109	96	128	96	83	75	66
Quantum	232	297	65	91	120	130	118	138	216	161
Imports										
Value	124	136	57	113	122	141	135	118	118	96
Unit value	174	174	94	99	104	98	87	89	93	95
Quantum	71	78	61	114	118	144	155	133	127	101
Terms of trade	57	40	90	110	93	131	111	93	81	69
Purchasing power of exports	132	119	58	100	111	'170	131	128	174	112
Samoa										
Exportations										
Valeur	..	62	25	62	71	106	102	143	109	..
Valeur unitaire	..	61	80	82	75	89	105	123	129	..
Volume	..	102	32	76	94	119	98	117	85	..
Importations										
Valeur	..	..	..	..	..	..	..	..	..	..
Valeur unitaire	..	..	..	..	..	..	..	..	..	..
Volume	..	..	..	..	..	..	..	..	..	..
Termes de l'échange	..	..	..	..	..	..	..	..	..	..
Pouvoir d'achat des exportations	..	..	..	..	..	..	..	..	..	..
Sao Tome and Principe - Sao Tomé-et-Principe										
Exports										
Value	..	160	215	186	178	193	173	80	95	182
Unit value	..	99	124	113	143	147	117	116	107	129
Quantum	..	162	173	165	124	131	148	69	89	141
Imports										
Value	..	72	103	99	76	55	57	129	96	105
Unit value	..	98	107	113	115	108	96	102	92	93
Quantum	..	74	96	88	66	50	60	126	105	113
Terms of trade	..	101	116	100	124	136	122	114	116	138
Purchasing power of exports	..	164	201	164	155	179	180	78	104	195
Saudi Arabia - Arabie saoudite										
Exportations										
Valeur	141	57	55	65	78	78	50	65	88	94
Valeur unitaire	100	86	56	62	74	70	45	65	87	92
Volume	141	67	98	104	106	112	111	100	101	102
Importations										
Valeur	..	..	..	..	..	..	..	..	..	..
Valeur unitaire	..	..	..	..	..	..	..	..	..	..
Volume	..	..	..	..	..	..	..	..	..	..
Termes de l'échange	..	..	..	..	..	..	..	..	..	..
Pouvoir d'achat des exportations	..	..	..	..	..	..	..	..	..	..

For sources and notes, see end of table.

Pour les sources et les notes, se reporter à la fin du tableau.

	1980	1990	1994	1995	1996	1997	1998	1999	2001	2002
Senegal - Sénégal										
Exports										
Value	52	83	86	108	107	98	105	112	109	116
Unit value	160	186	149	175	164	120	120	116	100	111
Quantum	32	45	58	62	65	82	88	96	109	105
Imports										
Value	69	80	67	93	95	88	96	103	114	128
Unit value	101	108	112	112	99	95	92	101	104	115
Quantum	69	74	60	83	95	92	104	102	110	111
Terms of trade	158	172	133	156	166	126	131	115	97	96
Purchasing power of exports	51	77	77	97	108	103	114	110	105	101
Seychelles										
Exportations										
Valeur	..	29	27	28	72	59	63	75	112	118
Valeur unitaire	..	92	100	110	110	104	103	111	95	101
Volume	..	32	27	25	66	56	61	67	117	116
Importations										
Valeur	..	55	60	68	111	99	112	127	139	123
Valeur unitaire	..	118	106	107	107	107	94	109	95	101
Volume	..	46	57	64	104	93	119	117	147	122
Termes de l'échange	..	78	95	103	103	97	109	103	100	100
Pouvoir d'achat des exportations	..	25	25	26	68	55	67	69	118	117
Sierra Leone										
Exports										
Value	1716	1056	888	324	359	132	51	48	223	373
Unit value	8	6	12	11	14	12	72	90	98	113
Quantum	21451	17601	7518	2915	2589	1074	71	54	227	331
Imports										
Value	286	100	101	89	141	62	63	54	122	177
Unit value	31	25	34	33	29	33	80	115	75	69
Quantum	921	398	295	267	493	191	79	47	162	256
Terms of trade	26	24	35	33	49	38	90	78	131	164
Purchasing power of exports	5536	4224	2598	970	1256	404	64	42	297	541
Singapore - Singapour										
Exportations										
Valeur	14	38	70	86	91	91	80	83	88	91
Valeur unitaire	123	115	113	120	119	112	97	96	93	91
Volume	11	33	62	72	76	81	82	87	95	100
Importations										
Valeur	18	45	76	93	98	98	78	83	86	87
Valeur unitaire	97	99	107	115	114	107	93	93	96	96
Volume	18	46	72	81	86	92	84	88	90	90
Termes de l'échange	127	116	106	104	105	105	105	103	96	94
Pouvoir d'achat des exportations	14	39	66	75	79	85	86	89	92	95
South Africa - Afrique du Sud										
Exports										
Value	85	79	84	93	97	103	88	89	98	99
Unit value	144	120	118	123	115	113	103	100	93	96
Quantum	59	66	72	75	85	92	85	89	105	104
Imports										
Value	66	62	79	103	102	111	98	90	95	99
Unit value	114	115	110	116	107	106	99	98	93	93
Quantum	58	54	72	88	95	105	100	92	102	106
Terms of trade	126	104	107	106	107	106	105	102	100	103
Purchasing power of exports	75	68	77	80	91	97	89	91	105	107

For sources and notes, see end of table.

Pour les sources et les notes, se reporter à la fin du tableau.

	1980	1990	1994	1995	1996	1997	1998	1999	2001	2002
Sri Lanka										
Exportations										
Valeur	20	35	59	70	75	85	89	85	89	87
Valeur unitaire	68	75	89	99	102	105	110	101	96	93
Volume	29	47	66	71	74	82	81	84	92	93
Importations										
Valeur	29	37	66	74	76	82	..	..	..	..
Valeur unitaire	78	91	90	100	102	100	..	..	..	..
Volume	37	41	74	74	74	82	..	..	..	..
Termes de l'échange	87	82	99	99	100	105	..	..	..	..
Pouvoir d'achat des exportations	25	39	66	70	74	86	..	..	..	..
Sudan - Soudan										
Exports										
Value	30	21	28	31	34	33	33	43	94	102
Unit value	144	131	78	108	88	107	108	91	102	116
Quantum	21	16	36	29	39	31	30	47	92	88
Imports										
Value	102	40	79	79	100	102	123	91	151	161
Unit value	158	131	78	108	88	107	108	91	102	97
Quantum	64	30	102	73	113	95	114	100	148	166
Terms of trade	91	100	100	100	100	100	100	100	100	119
Purchasing power of exports	19	16	36	29	39	31	30	47	92	106
Swaziland										
Exportations										
Valeur	41	61	87	95	94	106	107	103	116	103
Valeur unitaire	98	86	100	115	108	112	103	101	90	81
Volume	42	71	86	83	87	94	104	102	129	128
Importations										
Valeur	60	63	80	96	101	102	104	102	108	94
Valeur unitaire	98	86	100	115	108	112	103	101	90	81
Volume	61	74	80	84	94	91	101	101	120	116
Termes de l'échange	100	100	100	100	100	100	100	100	100	100
Pouvoir d'achat des exportations	42	71	86	83	87	94	104	102	129	127
Syrian Arab Republic - République arabe syrienne										
Exports										
Value	45	91	66	77	86	85	62	75	113	120
Unit value	329	110	79	99	104	82	60	75	89	95
Quantum	14	83	83	78	83	103	104	100	127	126
Imports										
Value	..	..	..	..	..	..	..	..	..	..
Unit value	..	..	..	..	..	..	..	..	..	..
Quantum	..	..	..	..	..	..	..	..	..	..
Terms of trade	..	..	..	..	..	..	..	..	..	..
Purchasing power of exports	..	..	..	..	..	..	..	..	..	..
Thailand - Thaïlande										
Exportations										
Valeur	9	33	66	82	81	83	79	85	94	100
Valeur unitaire	97	96	107	116	127	122	106	102	99	91
Volume	10	35	62	70	64	68	74	83	96	109
Importations										
Valeur	15	53	88	114	117	102	69	81	100	104
Valeur unitaire	64	81	88	100	111	106	98	95	108	102
Volume	23	66	99	115	105	96	71	86	93	102
Termes de l'échange	152	119	120	117	114	115	109	107	91	90
Pouvoir d'achat des exportations	15	41	74	82	73	78	81	89	87	98

For sources and notes, see end of table.   Pour les sources et les notes, se reporter à la fin du tableau.

	1980	1990	1994	1995	1996	1997	1998	1999	2001	2002
Togo										
Exports										
Value	93	74	90	104	121	117	116	108	98	118
Unit value	123	140	96	113	109	106	116	113	105	109
Quantum	76	53	94	92	111	111	100	95	94	108
Imports										
Value	114	120	46	122	137	133	121	101	106	119
Unit value	104	105	101	114	118	106	101	99	99	105
Quantum	109	114	45	108	116	125	119	102	108	114
Terms of trade	118	133	95	99	93	99	114	114	106	104
Purchasing power of exports	89	70	89	92	103	110	114	109	99	112
Tunisia - Tunisie										
Exportations										
Valeur	38	60	80	94	94	95	98	100	113	118
Valeur unitaire	110	107	98	114	119	109	108	107	99	105
Volume	35	56	81	82	79	87	91	94	115	112
Importations										
Valeur	41	64	77	92	90	93	97	99	111	111
Valeur unitaire	89	98	105	119	120	113	112	110	97	101
Volume	46	66	73	77	75	82	87	90	115	110
Termes de l'échange	124	109	93	96	99	97	96	97	102	104
Pouvoir d'achat des exportations	43	62	76	78	79	84	87	91	117	116
Turkey - Turquie										
Exports										
Value	10	47	65	78	84	95	97	96	113	124
Unit value	120	120	114	129	123	117	112	105	98	96
Quantum	9	39	57	60	68	81	87	91	115	130
Imports										
Value	15	41	43	66	80	89	84	75	76	91
Unit value	110	110	104	122	115	105	101	96	100	98
Quantum	13	37	41	54	69	84	83	78	76	93
Terms of trade	109	109	110	106	107	111	111	110	98	98
Purchasing power of exports	10	42	62	64	72	90	96	100	113	127
Uganda - Ouganda										
Exportations										
Valeur	..	33	89	100	128	121	109	113	99	96
Valeur unitaire	..	169	138	209	175	156	139	117	89	83
Volume	..	20	64	48	73	77	78	97	111	116
Importations										
Valeur	..	19	57	69	78	86	92	87	104	72
Valeur unitaire	..	116	105	106	111	100	100	97	99	95
Volume	..	16	54	65	70	86	92	90	105	76
Termes de l'échange	..	146	132	197	158	156	139	120	90	87
Pouvoir d'achat des exportations	..	29	85	94	115	121	109	116	100	101
United Republic of Tanzania - République-Unie de Tanzanie										
Exports										
Value	..	50	78	103	118	113	89	82	117	132
Unit value	..	101	110	97	101	150	123	108	106	110
Quantum	..	49	71	106	117	76	72	76	111	120
Imports										
Value	..	90	99	110	91	88	95	102	112	111
Unit value	..	94	102	99	106	152	125	109	86	84
Quantum	..	95	96	111	86	58	76	94	131	132
Terms of trade	..	107	107	97	96	99	98	99	123	131
Purchasing power of exports	..	53	76	103	112	75	71	75	136	157

For sources and notes, see end of table.

Pour les sources et les notes, se reporter à la fin du tableau.

	1980	1990	1994	1995	1996	1997	1998	1999	2001	2002
Uruguay										
Exportations										
Valeur	46	74	83	92	104	119	121	97	90	81
Valeur unitaire	121	117	110	122	119	117	117	103	97	96
Volume	38	63	76	75	88	102	103	95	93	84
Importations										
Valeur	48	39	80	83	96	108	110	97	88	57
Valeur unitaire	86	101	101	105	106	105	98	93	96	96
Volume	56	38	80	79	90	103	112	104	92	59
Termes de l'échange	141	116	110	116	112	112	120	110	101	100
Pouvoir d'achat des exportations	54	73	83	87	98	114	123	104	94	84
Venezuela										
Exports										
Value	60	55	51	58	73	68	54	63	86	77
Unit value	131	86	64	71	80	73	52	68	81	86
Quantum	46	64	79	82	91	94	105	93	106	89
Imports										
Value	73	45	57	78	61	90	98	87	111	73
Unit value	85	96	101	112	109	103	102	100	97	97
Quantum	86	47	56	70	56	87	96	87	115	75
Terms of trade	154	90	64	64	73	70	51	68	84	89
Purchasing power of exports	71	57	50	52	67	66	53	63	89	79
Yemen - Yémen										
Exportations										
Valeur	..	..	..	..	..	..	..	..	..	..
Valeur unitaire	..	..	..	..	..	..	..	..	..	..
Volume	..	..	..	..	..	..	..	..	..	..
Importations										
Valeur	..	68	90	68	88	87	93	86	99	..
Valeur unitaire	..	135	149	161	161	176	88	90	102	..
Volume	..	50	60	42	55	49	106	96	97	..
Termes de l'échange	..	..	..	..	..	..	..	..	..	..
Pouvoir d'achat des exportations	..	..	..	..	..	..	..	..	..	..
Zambia - Zambie										
Exports										
Value	196	197	139	156	156	138	153	160	148	140
Unit value	198	211	177	220	169	163	114	88	112	108
Quantum	99	93	79	71	92	84	135	181	132	129
Imports										
Value	110	123	60	70	84	82	109	83	132	126
Unit value	89	102	117	116	111	115	101	101	105	116
Quantum	123	120	51	61	76	72	108	82	125	109
Terms of trade	222	207	151	190	152	141	113	87	107	93
Purchasing power of exports	220	193	119	135	140	119	152	158	141	120
Zimbabwe										
Exportations										
Valeur	73	90	98	110	125	112	90	98	63	121
Valeur unitaire	241	196	145	149	163	158	109	100	97	99
Volume	30	46	68	74	77	71	82	98	65	123
Importations										
Valeur	80	102	124	147	155	181	145	117	96	156
Valeur unitaire	284	201	148	154	167	163	112	103	96	98
Volume	28	51	84	96	93	111	129	114	100	159
Termes de l'échange	85	98	98	97	97	96	97	97	101	101
Pouvoir d'achat des exportations	26	45	66	72	75	68	80	95	65	123

For sources and notes, see end of table.

Pour les sources et les notes, se reporter à la fin du tableau.

Sources:

Asian Development Bank (ADB): *Key Indicators of Developing Asian and Pacific Countries, 2003*; UN, Economic Commission for Latin America and the Caribbean (ECLAC); IMF: *International Financial Statistics (IFS), on-line*; UN/DESA/SD: *Monthly Bulletin of Statistics (MBS), 2004*; World Bank: *World Bank Africa Database on CD-ROM, 2004;* World Trade Organization (WTO) and national sources.

Notes:

Regional and overall indices are presented in Part II of this *Handbook*, while the detailed annual data for individual countries and territories are shown in table 8.1.

In some instances these indices may differ from the estimates published in official sources, since the main aim has been to provide tentative estimates for most developing countries on a comparable basis.

Definitions:

Values indices:

Current value of exports (f.o.b.) or of imports (c.i.f.) converted to dollars and expressed as a percentage of the average for the base period (2000).

Unit value indices:

Official data and UNCTAD secretariat estimates (see appendix of TD/138/Supp.1).

Quantum indices:

The ratio of the export (or import) value index to the corresponding unit value index.

Terms of trade:

The "net barter" terms of trade, defined as percentage ratio of the export unit value index to the import unit value index.

Purchasing power of exports:

The value index of exports deflated by the import unit value index.

Sources :

Banque de développement de l'Asie : *Key Indicators of Developing Asian and Pacific Countries, 2003*; ONU, Economic Commission for Latin America and the Caribbean (ECLAC); FMI: International Financial Statistics (IFS), on-line; ONU/DAES/DS: *Monthly Bulletin of Statistics (MBS)*, *2004*; Banque mondiale: *World Bank Africa Database on CD-ROM, 2004;* Organisation mondiale du commerce (OMC) et sources nationales.

Notes :

Les indices totaux et régionaux sont présentés dans la partie II de ce *Manuel*, tandis que les données annuelles détaillées pour les pays et territoires en développement individuels sont présentées dans le tableau 8.1.

Dans certains cas ces indices peuvent différer des estimations publiées dans les sources officielles, le but principal étant de fournir des estimations approximatives et comparables pour la plupart des pays en développement.

Définitions :

Indices des valeurs :

Valeurs courantes des exportations (f.a.b.) ou des importations (c.a.f.) converties en dollars et exprimées en pourcentage de la moyenne de la période de base (2000).

Indices de la valeur unitaire :

Données officielles et estimations du secrétariat de la CNUCED (voir appendice du document TD/138/Supp.1).

Indices du quantum :

Représentent le rapport de l'indice de la valeur des exportations (ou des importations) à l'indice de la valeur unitaire correspondant.

Terme de l'échange :

Il s'agit de ce qu'on appelle le "troc net", défini comme étant le rapport de l'indice de la valeur unitaire des exportations et de l'indice de la valeur unitaire des importations exprimé en pourcentage.

Pouvoir d'achat des exportations :

Indice de la valeur des exportations corrigé par l'indice de la valeur unitaire des importations.

Country or area [1] / Pays ou zones [1]	1992			2002		
	Number of commodities exported [2] / Nombre de produits exportés [2]	Diversification index [3] / Indice de diversification [3]	Concentration index [4] / Indice de concentration [4]	Number of commodities exported [2] / Nombre de produits exportés [2]	Diversification index [3] / Indice de diversification [3]	Concentration index [4] / Indice de concentration [4]
WORLD - MONDE	**223**	**0.422**	**0.139**	**224**	**0.419**	**0.157**
DEVELOPED ECONOMIES - ECONOMIES DEVELOPPEES	**231**	**0.353**	**0.098**	**231**	**0.348**	**0.115**
Faeroe Islands - Iles Féroé	12	0.732	0.631	13	0.734	0.682
Norway - Norvège	218	0.631	0.367	215	0.662	0.426
Iceland - Islande	69	0.893	0.499	96	0.844	0.373
Israel - Israël	195	0.559	0.256	199	0.583	0.327
Andorra - Andorre	..	..	..	64	0.624	0.275
Ireland - Irlande	223	0.562	0.129	226	0.634	0.229
Finland - Finlande	214	0.516	0.222	221	0.553	0.219
Cyprus - Chypre	147	0.631	0.189	153	0.599	0.188
Latvia - Lettonie	..	..	..	199	0.649	0.169
Switzerland - Suisse	221	0.514	0.102	223	0.528	0.166
New Zealand - Nouvelle-Zélande	211	0.647	0.165	214	0.647	0.151
Japan - Japon	224	0.432	0.140	224	0.398	0.149
Slovakia - Slovaquie	–	–	–	218	0.457	0.136
Luxembourg	..	..	..	199	0.565	0.135
Australia - Australie	233	0.595	0.154	233	0.562	0.133
Canada	235	0.406	0.125	234	0.384	0.132
Hungary - Hongrie	213	0.438	0.069	217	0.356	0.130
Estonia - Estonie	..	..	..	209	0.541	0.122
Belgium - Belgique	..	..	..	234	0.362	0.121
Spain - Espagne	232	0.344	0.142	234	0.331	0.119
Sweden - Suède	229	0.406	0.107	231	0.375	0.115
Slovenia - Slovénie	212	0.434	0.083	209	0.453	0.108
Czech Republic - République tchèque	–	–	–	226	0.385	0.108
Portugal	219	0.528	0.106	225	0.458	0.107
Germany - Allemagne	236	0.274	0.084	236	0.268	0.105
United Kingdom - Royaume-Uni	235	0.241	0.066	235	0.238	0.096
Greece - Grèce	212	0.636	0.118	215	0.533	0.095
Netherlands - Pays-Bas	234	0.345	0.061	235	0.389	0.087
France	237	0.263	0.064	236	0.268	0.087
Poland - Pologne	222	0.498	0.076	229	0.448	0.084
United States - Etats-Unis	236	0.290	0.081	235	0.256	0.084
Denmark - Danemark	226	0.451	0.078	226	0.400	0.084
Austria - Autriche	227	0.388	0.061	230	0.357	0.070
Italy - Italie	234	0.342	0.056	234	0.362	0.056
DEVELOPING ECONOMIES - ECONOMIES EN DEVELOPPEMENT	**199**	**0.601**	**0.250**	**210**	**0.545**	**0.234**
DEVELOPING ECONOMIES: AMERICA - ECONOMIES EN DEVELOPPEMENT : AMERIQUE	**195**	**0.591**	**0.230**	**213**	**0.520**	**0.199**
Venezuela	193	0.786	0.555	194	0.783	0.749
Jamaica - Jamaïque	93	0.825	0.521	98	0.859	0.625
Belize	45	0.798	0.356	14	0.910	0.609
Greenland - Groenland	15	0.929	0.556	27	0.913	0.502
Saint Vincent and the Grenadines - Saint-Vincent-et-les Grenadines	..	..	..	24	0.808	0.444
Dominica - Dominique	..	..	..	18	0.871	0.397
Ecuador - Equateur	117	0.839	0.467	151	0.769	0.392
Paraguay	61	0.861	0.362	94	0.839	0.376
Grenada - Grenade	..	..	..	28	0.757	0.361
Saint Lucia - Sainte-Lucie	47	0.814	0.567	50	0.684	0.359
Guyana	..	..	..	66	0.859	0.310
Panama	75	0.775	0.452	120	0.730	0.305
Anguilla	..	..	..	25	0.578	0.297
Chile - Chili	195	0.786	0.308	201	0.776	0.274

For sources and notes, see end of table 8.2B.

Pour les sources et les notes, se reporter à la fin du tableau 8.2B.

Country or area [1] Pays ou zones [1]	1992			2002		
	Number of commodities exported [2] Nombre de produits exportés [2]	Diversification index [3] Indice de diversification [3]	Concentration index [4] Indice de concentration [4]	Number of commodities exported [2] Nombre de produits exportés [2]	Diversification index [3] Indice de diversification [3]	Concentration index [4] Indice de concentration [4]
Bolivia - Bolivie	81	0.856	0.318	130	0.790	0.253
Peru - Pérou	162	0.816	0.266	190	0.780	0.247
Colombia - Colombie	189	0.669	0.238	201	0.605	0.217
Costa Rica	142	0.715	0.303	175	0.651	0.211
Honduras	90	0.848	0.457	131	0.821	0.198
Guatemala	137	0.710	0.219	168	0.672	0.193
Uruguay	149	0.697	0.176	150	0.720	0.186
Nicaragua	63	0.853	0.289	137	0.769	0.179
Barbados - Barbade	83	0.701	0.223	89	0.691	0.168
Argentina - Argentine	211	0.647	0.153	220	0.568	0.143
Mexico - Mexique	221	0.406	0.153	229	0.390	0.127
El Salvador	113	0.713	0.238	164	0.656	0.125
Brazil - Brésil	220	0.505	0.088	225	0.480	0.089
AFRICA - AFRIQUE	**116**	**0.818**	**0.569**	**123**	**0.788**	**0.492**
Sao Tome and Principe - Sao Tomé-et-Principe	..	..	..	8	0.702	0.918
Sierra Leone	..	..	..	12	0.703	0.857
Burundi	..	..	..	12	0.802	0.650
Malawi	..	..	..	50	0.912	0.605
Burkina Faso	..	..	..	53	0.822	0.602
Sudan - Soudan	..	..	..	54	0.815	0.589
Eritrea - Erythrée	..	..	..	32	0.728	0.589
Guinea - Guinée	..	..	..	32	0.930	0.547
Rwanda	..	..	..	7	0.870	0.504
Zambia - Zambie	..	..	..	103	0.852	0.504
Seychelles	13	0.890	0.617	12	0.877	0.488
Niger	..	..	..	38	0.913	0.471
Cameroon - Cameroun	..	..	..	89	0.849	0.463
Benin - Bénin	23	0.858	0.563	42	0.887	0.456
Swaziland	..	..	..	135	0.818	0.452
Côte d'Ivoire	..	..	..	138	0.827	0.430
Ethiopia - Ethiopie	..	..	..	36	0.836	0.405
Lesotho	..	..	..	32	0.882	0.352
Togo	..	..	..	59	0.856	0.318
United Republic of Tanzania - République-Unie de Tanzanie	..	..	..	92	0.893	0.307
Kenya	143	0.796	0.300	166	0.749	0.303
Senegal - Sénégal	108	0.814	0.238	122	0.751	0.290
Uganda - Ouganda	..	..	..	89	0.851	0.288
Mauritius - Maurice	128	0.829	0.332	154	0.806	0.275
Egypt - Egypte	170	0.688	0.361	175	0.704	0.251
Tunisia - Tunisie	174	0.671	0.211	190	0.637	0.186
Morocco - Maroc	153	0.748	0.160	172	0.733	0.161
Zimbabwe	171	0.741	0.330	188	0.739	0.142
South Africa - Afrique du Sud	..	..	..	227	0.525	0.112
DEVELOPING ECONOMIES: ASIA - ECONOMIES EN DEVELOPPEMENT : ASIE	**212**	**0.573**	**0.212**	**217**	**0.530**	**0.220**
Saudi Arabia - Arabie saoudite	207	0.840	0.730	206	0.859	0.851
Iran, Islamic Rep. of - Iran, Rép. islamique d'	..	..	..	187	0.839	0.834
Bahrain - Bahreïn	..	..	..	124	0.883	0.678
Oman	115	0.810	0.824	164	0.754	0.658
Syrian Arab Republic - République arabe syrienne	100	0.819	0.586	99	0.811	0.634
Qatar	95	0.847	0.641	117	0.847	0.550
Maldives	..	..	..	10	0.503	0.423
Philippines	187	0.657	0.293	204	0.634	0.417
China, Macao SAR - Chine, Macao RAS	139	0.798	0.308	116	0.838	0.350
Mongolia - Mongolie	..	..	..	42	0.896	0.345
Singapore - Singapour	226	0.483	0.184	224	0.495	0.249

For sources and notes, see end of table 8.2B.

Pour les sources et les notes, se reporter à la fin du tableau 8.2B.

Country or area [1] Pays ou zones [1]	1992			2002		
	Number of commodities exported [2] Nombre de produits exportés [2]	Diversification index [3] Indice de diversification [3]	Concentration index [4] Indice de concentration [4]	Number of commodities exported [2] Nombre de produits exportés [2]	Diversification index [3] Indice de diversification [3]	Concentration index [4] Indice de concentration [4]
Viet Nam	..	..	..	196	0.631	0.239
Sri Lanka	129	0.788	0.232	163	0.772	0.223
Pakistan	145	0.827	0.227	178	0.807	0.220
Malaysia - Malaisie	222	0.545	0.156	224	0.502	0.216
Jordan - Jordanie	154	0.633	0.247	176	0.645	0.159
China, Taiwan Province of - Chine, Taiwan Province	219	0.486	0.089	219	0.486	0.153
Korea, Republic of - Corée, République de	214	0.475	0.109	217	0.420	0.148
India - Inde	215	0.617	0.140	227	0.562	0.130
Lebanon - Liban	..	..	..	171	0.644	0.126
Indonesia - Indonésie	207	0.634	0.195	227	0.505	0.120
China, Hong Kong SAR - Chine, Hong Kong RAS	231	0.504	0.090	227	0.500	0.119
Turkey - Turquie	202	0.660	0.119	222	0.562	0.094
China - Chine	..	..	..	233	0.455	0.085
DEVELOPING ECONOMIES: OCEANIA - ECONOMIES EN DEVELOPPEMENT : OCEANIE	**60**	**0.878**	**0.497**	**56**	**0.862**	**0.479**
French Polynesia - Polynésie française	..	..	..	33	0.856	0.691
New Caledonia - Nouvelle-Calédonie	..	..	..	55	0.914	0.671
Samoa	..	..	..	27	0.869	0.602
Fiji - Fidji	95	0.788	0.355	112	0.787	0.268
SOUTH-EAST EUROPE AND CIS - EUROPE DU SUD-EST ET CEI	**210**	**0.660**	**0.233**	**210**	**0.671**	**0.269**
Azerbaijan - Azerbaïdjan	..	..	..	93	0.832	0.689
Armenia - Arménie	..	..	..	68	0.830	0.434
Kyrgyzstan - Kirghizistan	..	..	..	115	0.782	0.345
Russian Federation - Fédération de Russie	..	..	..	225	0.692	0.307
Albania - Albanie	..	..	..	80	0.814	0.292
Moldova, Republic of - Moldova, République de	..	..	..	125	0.791	0.284
Belarus - Bélarus	..	..	..	203	0.549	0.168
Macedonia, TFYR - Macédoine, LERY	..	..	..	158	0.674	0.152
Ukraine	..	..	..	211	0.597	0.133
Romania - Roumanie	202	0.561	0.125	207	0.576	0.122
Croatia - Croatie	212	0.537	0.108	210	0.507	0.119
Bulgaria - Bulgarie	..	..	..	208	0.535	0.104
Serbia and Montenegro - Serbie-et-Monténégro	187	0.524	0.090	203	0.558	0.091
MEMO ITEM: - POUR MEMOIRE						
Least developed countries - Pays les moins avancés	42	0.898	0.584	69	0.876	0.526
Landlocked countries - Pays enclavés	82	0.846	0.479	129	0.825	0.452
Heavily indebted poor countries - Pays pauvres très endettés	76	0.868	0.532	124	0.797	0.416
High-income - Revenu élevé	208	0.566	0.246	214	0.531	0.254
Middle-income - Revenu intermédiaire	190	0.651	0.273	203	0.573	0.239
Low-income - Revenu faible	186	0.636	0.237	207	0.550	0.195

For sources and notes, see end of table 8.2B.

Pour les sources et les notes, se reporter à la fin du tableau 8.2B.

Country or area [1] Pays ou zones [1]	1992			2002		
	Number of commodities imported [2] Nombre de produits importés [2]	Diversification index [3] Indice de diversification [3]	Concentration index [4] Indice de concentration [4]	Number of commodities imported [2] Nombre de produits importés [2]	Diversification index [3] Indice de diversification [3]	Concentration index [4] Indice de concentration [4]
WORLD - MONDE	**231**	**0.258**	**0.083**	**232**	**0.263**	**0.103**
DEVELOPED ECONOMIES - ECONOMIES DEVELOPPEES	**235**	**0.205**	**0.074**	**235**	**0.205**	**0.088**
Israel - Israël	227	0.272	0.148	226	0.300	0.191
Ireland - Irlande	229	0.272	0.068	231	0.334	0.146
Belgium - Belgique	..	..	..	235	0.266	0.110
Faeroe Islands - Iles Féroé	160	0.488	0.125	162	0.443	0.108
Greece - Grèce	230	0.273	0.088	232	0.282	0.105
United States - Etats-Unis	236	0.214	0.096	237	0.194	0.102
Japan - Japon	234	0.344	0.106	235	0.273	0.099
Andorra - Andorre	..	..	..	167	0.509	0.096
Luxembourg	..	..	..	222	0.372	0.095
Canada	235	0.228	0.094	236	0.219	0.090
Switzerland - Suisse	231	0.249	0.062	230	0.280	0.090
Cyprus - Chypre	213	0.324	0.078	211	0.338	0.090
New Zealand - Nouvelle-Zélande	221	0.251	0.072	225	0.248	0.090
Hungary - Hongrie	222	0.277	0.063	227	0.279	0.087
Iceland - Islande	201	0.374	0.085	202	0.362	0.086
Netherlands - Pays-Bas	234	0.183	0.051	234	0.215	0.086
Australia - Australie	229	0.237	0.064	229	0.214	0.085
Spain - Espagne	236	0.161	0.071	236	0.179	0.083
Italy - Italie	235	0.183	0.077	234	0.198	0.080
United Kingdom - Royaume-Uni	237	0.165	0.058	235	0.199	0.079
Slovakia - Slovaquie	–	–	–	228	0.271	0.076
Czech Republic - République tchèque	–	–	–	232	0.247	0.074
Finland - Finlande	225	0.226	0.057	232	0.177	0.074
Germany - Allemagne	236	0.146	0.055	236	0.132	0.067
Estonia - Estonie	..	..	..	221	0.322	0.067
Portugal	231	0.213	0.071	232	0.196	0.067
Sweden - Suède	232	0.192	0.053	230	0.178	0.065
Poland - Pologne	225	0.314	0.088	232	0.253	0.065
France	238	0.131	0.053	236	0.141	0.062
Austria - Autriche	235	0.225	0.063	234	0.217	0.060
Norway - Norvège	229	0.277	0.053	233	0.267	0.058
Latvia - Lettonie	..	..	..	214	0.347	0.057
Slovenia - Slovénie	229	0.257	0.057	228	0.284	0.057
Denmark - Danemark	233	0.238	0.049	232	0.237	0.055
DEVELOPING ECONOMIES - ECONOMIES EN DEVELOPPEMENT	**221**	**0.386**	**0.096**	**225**	**0.390**	**0.139**
DEVELOPING ECONOMIES: AMERICA - ECONOMIES EN DEVELOPPEMENT : AMERIQUE	**217**	**0.354**	**0.101**	**223**	**0.324**	**0.093**
Belize	158	0.507	0.096	153	0.559	0.269
Guyana	147	0.521	0.112	169	0.508	0.178
Honduras	190	0.435	0.107	197	0.671	0.168
Costa Rica	202	0.375	0.114	212	0.328	0.135
Paraguay	174	0.409	0.101	187	0.426	0.124
Greenland - Groenland	152	0.506	0.136	150	0.509	0.111
Jamaica - Jamaïque	205	0.391	0.099	197	0.376	0.109
Panama	201	0.322	0.101	201	0.324	0.101
Anguilla	..	..	..	106	0.493	0.101
Saint Lucia - Sainte-Lucie	157	0.455	0.065	153	0.492	0.090
Nicaragua	182	0.434	0.120	192	0.383	0.088
Grenada - Grenade	..	..	..	145	0.483	0.086
Mexico - Mexique	230	0.323	0.094	231	0.285	0.086
Uruguay	206	0.340	0.090	206	0.368	0.086
Chile - Chili	214	0.282	0.084	227	0.286	0.085
Guatemala	204	0.385	0.104	213	0.357	0.084
Bolivia - Bolivie	190	0.426	0.084	198	0.457	0.084

For sources and notes, see end of table.   Pour les sources et les notes, se reporter à la fin du tableau.

Country or area [1] Pays ou zones [1]	1992			2002		
	Number of commodities imported [2] Nombre de produits importés [2]	Diversification index [3] Indice de diversification [3]	Concentration index [4] Indice de concentration [4]	Number of commodities imported [2] Nombre de produits importés [2]	Diversification index [3] Indice de diversification [3]	Concentration index [4] Indice de concentration [4]
Brazil - Brésil	227	0.380	0.132	229	0.313	0.081
Peru - Pérou	214	0.379	0.079	218	0.340	0.081
Dominica - Dominique	..	..	..	130	0.482	0.080
Saint Vincent and the Grenadines - Saint-Vincent-et-les Grenadines	..	..	..	144	0.471	0.078
Colombia - Colombie	216	0.386	0.060	222	0.363	0.074
Ecuador - Equateur	197	0.427	0.093	208	0.356	0.073
Venezuela	222	0.341	0.081	217	0.317	0.070
El Salvador	198	0.386	0.109	210	0.370	0.069
Argentina - Argentine	224	0.272	0.063	219	0.401	0.068
Barbados - Barbade	182	0.415	0.084	188	0.375	0.062
AFRICA - AFRIQUE	**203**	**0.437**	**0.099**	**207**	**0.433**	**0.108**
Sierra Leone	..	..	..	135	0.684	0.371
Senegal - Sénégal	190	0.416	0.085	196	0.493	0.220
Guinea - Guinée	..	..	..	153	0.591	0.198
Seychelles	149	0.464	0.137	126	0.609	0.175
Côte d'Ivoire	..	..	..	195	0.504	0.159
Sao Tome and Principe - Sao Tomé-et-Principe	..	..	..	54	0.595	0.158
Togo	..	..	..	134	0.622	0.155
Burkina Faso	..	..	..	153	0.562	0.155
Niger	..	..	..	146	0.611	0.144
Rwanda	..	..	..	138	0.485	0.143
Benin - Bénin	135	0.613	0.193	158	0.600	0.143
Malawi	..	..	..	176	0.550	0.142
Uganda - Ouganda	..	..	..	176	0.496	0.141
Burundi	..	..	..	111	0.543	0.134
Kenya	193	0.542	0.169	205	0.431	0.123
Ethiopia - Ethiopie	..	..	..	179	0.450	0.120
South Africa - Afrique du Sud	..	..	..	230	0.297	0.116
Zambia - Zambie	..	..	..	199	0.480	0.105
Egypt - Egypte	214	0.472	0.079	215	0.480	0.105
United Republic of Tanzania - République-Unie de Tanzanie	..	..	..	192	0.462	0.105
Cameroon - Cameroun	..	..	..	187	0.459	0.104
Eritrea - Erythrée	..	..	..	151	0.468	0.104
Mauritius - Maurice	201	0.419	0.086	200	0.438	0.094
Morocco - Maroc	224	0.403	0.105	220	0.386	0.089
Swaziland	..	..	..	204	0.449	0.087
Sudan - Soudan	..	..	..	191	0.479	0.086
Tunisia - Tunisie	217	0.401	0.071	220	0.380	0.079
Lesotho	..	..	..	181	0.553	0.079
Zimbabwe	199	0.477	0.126	212	0.411	0.072
DEVELOPING ECONOMIES: ASIA - ECONOMIES EN DEVELOPPEMENT : ASIE	**225**	**0.387**	**0.095**	**228**	**0.402**	**0.152**
Bahrain - Bahreïn	..	..	..	204	0.528	0.308
Philippines	222	0.385	0.161	228	0.472	0.305
Malaysia - Malaisie	232	0.388	0.120	234	0.401	0.262
India - Inde	203	0.532	0.195	224	0.513	0.248
Singapore - Singapour	229	0.335	0.107	228	0.376	0.203
China, Taiwan Province of - Chine, Taiwan Province	231	0.291	0.085	232	0.369	0.165
Pakistan	201	0.491	0.120	219	0.496	0.159
China, Macao SAR - Chine, Macao RAS	187	0.563	0.136	183	0.586	0.147
Korea, Republic of - Corée, République de	229	0.364	0.107	235	0.344	0.139
Iran, Islamic Rep. of - Iran, Rép. islamique d'	..	..	..	201	0.493	0.128
Indonesia - Indonésie	229	0.441	0.063	230	0.468	0.119
China, Hong Kong SAR - Chine, Hong Kong RAS	232	0.377	0.065	228	0.400	0.118
Lebanon - Liban	..	..	..	216	0.388	0.117

For sources and notes, see end of table.

Pour les sources et les notes, se reporter à la fin du tableau.

Country or area [1] / Pays ou zones [1]	1992			2002		
	Number of commodities imported [2] / Nombre de produits importés [2]	Diversification index [3] / Indice de diversification [3]	Concentration index [4] / Indice de concentration [4]	Number of commodities imported [2] / Nombre de produits importés [2]	Diversification index [3] / Indice de diversification [3]	Concentration index [4] / Indice de concentration [4]
China - Chine	..	..	..	234	0.3855	0.113
Oman	197	0.467	0.144	216	0.421	0.109
Jordan - Jordanie	205	0.414	0.096	209	0.337	0.100
Viet Nam	..	..	..	217	0.424	0.100
Maldives	..	..	..	146	0.480	0.100
Sri Lanka	215	0.463	0.089	215	0.480	0.100
Syrian Arab Republic - République arabe syrienne	189	0.490	0.075	178	0.520	0.098
Saudi Arabia - Arabie saoudite	230	0.381	0.109	227	0.359	0.088
Qatar	187	0.414	0.102	208	0.397	0.084
Turkey - Turquie	232	0.353	0.096	228	0.331	0.078
DEVELOPING ECONOMIES: OCEANIA - ECONOMIES EN DEVELOPPEMENT : OCEANIE	**160**	**0.489**	**0.115**	**148**	**0.553**	**0.249**
French Polynesia - Polynésie française	..	..	..	174	0.425	0.149
Samoa	..	..	..	128	0.534	0.118
New Caledonia - Nouvelle-Calédonie	..	..	..	182	0.387	0.109
Fiji - Fidji	190	0.424	0.115	190	0.441	0.101
SOUTH-EAST EUROPE AND CIS - EUROPE DU SUD-EST ET CEI	**225**	**0.492**	**0.201**	**225**	**0.396**	**0.100**
Ukraine	..	..	..	220	0.429	0.213
Armenia - Arménie	..	..	..	189	0.569	0.192
Macedonia, TFYR - Macédoine, LERY	..	..	..	209	0.400	0.176
Bulgaria - Bulgarie	218	0.414	0.142	219	0.402	0.154
Belarus - Bélarus	..	..	..	220	0.424	0.147
Kyrgyzstan - Kirghizistan	..	..	..	176	0.538	0.136
Azerbaijan - Azerbaïdjan	..	..	..	191	0.533	0.133
Moldova, Republic of - Moldova, République de	..	..	..	198	0.501	0.110
Croatia - Croatie	226	0.330	0.061	229	0.264	0.072
Serbia and Montenegro - Serbie-et-Monténégro	221	0.376	0.096	223	0.322	0.071
Romania - Roumanie	220	0.429	0.119	225	0.335	0.066
Albania - Albanie	..	..	..	196	0.464	0.063
Russian Federation - Fédération de Russie	..	..	..	230	0.381	0.057
MEMO ITEM: - POUR MEMOIRE						
Least developed countries - Pays les moins avancés	161	0.537	0.133	178	0.545	0.135
Landlocked countries - Pays enclavés	157	0.538	0.151	186	0.499	0.122
Heavily indebted poor countries - Pays pauvres très endettés	174	0.503	0.136	195	0.492	0.123
High-income - Revenu élevé	225	0.362	0.093	228	0.368	0.132
Middle-income - Revenu intermédiaire	221	0.387	0.095	222	0.375	0.135
Low-income - Revenu faible	213	0.449	0.107	224	0.441	0.152

For sources and notes, see next page.

Pour les sources et les notes, se reporter à la page suivante.

Sources: UNCTAD secretariat calculations based on United Nations Statistics Division (Comtrade database).

Notes:

1 Within each group shown, countries are ranked according to the concentration index in 2002.

2 Number of products (at the three-digit level of SITC, Revision 2) exported (or imported) by country; this figure includes only those products that are greater than 100,000 dollars or more than 0.3 per cent of the country's total exports (or imports).

Data for the country groupings are calculated as weighted averages of individual countries data, including those that are estimated and not shown separately.

3 Diversification index that ranges from 0 to 1, reveals the extend of the differences between the structure of trade of the country and the world average. The index value closer to 1 indicates a bigger difference from the world average.

Diversification index is computed by measuring absolute deviation of the country share from world structure, as follows:

$$S_j = \frac{\sum_i \left| h_{ij} - h_i \right|}{2}$$

where h_{ij} = share of commodity _i_ in total exports (or imports) of country _j_

h_i = share of commodity _i_ in total world exports (or imports).

This index is a modified Finger-Kreinin measure of similarity in trade. For more information, please consult the article of Finger, J. M. and M. E. Kreinin (1979), "A measure of 'export similarity' and its possible uses" in the _Economic Journal_, 89: 905-12.

4 The Herfindahl-Hirschmann index is a measure of the degree of market concentration. It has been normalized to obtain values ranking from 0 to 1 (maximum concentration), according to the following formula:

$$H_j = \frac{\sqrt{\sum_{i=1}^{239} \left(\frac{x_i}{X} \right)^2} - \sqrt{1/239}}{1 - \sqrt{1/239}}$$

where H_j = country index

x_i = value of exports of product _i_

$$X = \sum_{i=1}^{239} x_i$$

and 239 = number of products (at the three-digit level of SITC, Revision 2) .

Sources : Calculs du secrétariat de la CNUCED fondés sur des données de la Division de statistique des Nations Unies (base de données COMTRADE).

Notes :

1 A l'intérieur de chaque groupe, les pays sont classés d'après l'indice de concentration en 2002.

2 Nombre de produits (position à trois chiffres de la CTCI, révision 2) exportés (ou importés) par chaque pays ; cependant, seuls les produits ayant une valeur supérieure à 100.000 dollars ou comptant pour plus de 0,3 pour cent des exportations (ou des importations) totales du pays sont inclus.

Les indices de concentration et de diversification calculés au niveau des groupes de pays et du monde sont les moyennes arithmétiques des indices respectifs des pays, pondérées par la valeur de leurs exportations.

3 L'indice de diversification, dont la valeur est comprise entre 0 et 1, indique si la structure par produits des exportations d'un pays diverge peu ou beaucoup de la structure par produits des exportations totales dans le monde. Plus l'indice est proche de 1, plus la divergence est forte (les produits exportés par le pays sont très différents des produits exportés dans l'ensemble du monde.

L'indice de diversification mesure la déviation absolue de la structure du pays par rapport à la structure mondiale comme ci-dessous :

$$S_j = \frac{\sum_i \left| h_{ij} - h_i \right|}{2}$$

où h_{ij} = part du produit _i_ dans le total des exportations (ou importations) du pays _j_

h_i = part du produit _i_ dans le total des exportations (ou importations) mondiales.

Cet indice est une variante de l'indicateur de Finger-Kreinin sur la similarité de la structure du commerce. Pour plus d'information, veuillez consulter l'article de Finger, J. M. et M. E. Kreinin (1979), "A measure of 'export similarity' and its possible uses", dans l'_Economic Journal_, 89: 905-12.

4 L'indice Herfindahl-Hirschmann mesure le degré de concentration des marchés. Il a été normalisé afin d'obtenir des valeurs comprises entre 0 et 1 (concentration maximale), d'après la formule suivante:

$$H_j = \frac{\sqrt{\sum_{i=1}^{239} \left(\frac{x_i}{X} \right)^2} - \sqrt{1/239}}{1 - \sqrt{1/239}}$$

où H_j = indice du pays

x_i = valeur des exportations du produit _i_

$$X = \sum_{i=1}^{239} x_i$$

et 239 = nombre de groupes de produits (position à trois chiffres de la CTCI, révision 2).

SITC group [1] Groupes de la CTCI [1]	Market concentration index of exports [2] Indice de concentration des exportations [2]			Structural change index of exports [3] (1992 = 0) Indice de changement structurel des exportations [3] (1992 = 0)		
	1995	2000	2002	1995	2000	2002
261 Silk	0.615	0.763	0.813	0.082	0.258	0.318
264 Jute, other textile bast fibres	0.823	0.793	0.764	0.113	0.113	0.136
633 Cork manufactures	0.643	0.614	0.633	0.050	0.094	0.076
244 Cork, natural, raw, waste	0.587	0.520	0.599	0.078	0.138	0.092
044 Maize (corn), unmilled	0.689	0.550	0.523	0.224	0.124	0.121
268 Wool (exc tops), animal hair	0.428	0.467	0.511	0.126	0.174	0.138
424 Other fixed vegetable oils	0.456	0.418	0.482	0.083	0.217	0.212
896 Works of art, etc	0.401	0.444	0.465	0.089	0.161	0.147
045 Cereals nes, unmilled	0.442	0.487	0.443	0.257	0.172	0.218
232 Natural rubber, gums	0.430	0.450	0.440	0.098	0.181	0.196
222 Seeds for soft fixed oils	0.483	0.432	0.439	0.120	0.203	0.212
885 Watches and clocks	0.376	0.401	0.420	0.072	0.147	0.147
792 Aircraft, etc	0.405	0.404	0.410	0.133	0.135	0.132
281 Iron ore and concentrates	0.377	0.410	0.400	0.046	0.131	0.128
323 Briquettes, coke and semi-coke	0.318	0.387	0.399	0.362	0.542	0.495
265 Vegetb fibre, exc cotton, jute	0.377	0.439	0.396	0.181	0.530	0.389
883 Developed cinema film	0.320	0.310	0.391	0.245	0.344	0.397
267 Other man-made fibres	0.403	0.391	0.377	0.315	0.334	0.354
714 Engines and motors nes	0.368	0.381	0.368	0.075	0.105	0.115
072 Cocoa	0.311	0.324	0.367	0.158	0.224	0.258
524 Radioactive etc materials	0.358	0.358	0.364	0.123	0.176	0.188
212 Furskins, raw	0.345	0.367	0.363	0.269	0.306	0.264
831 Travel goods, handbags, etc	0.343	0.356	0.362	0.129	0.232	0.232
322 Coal, lignite and peat	0.334	0.339	0.354	0.106	0.268	0.283
774 Electro-medical, xray equip	0.353	0.351	0.352	0.072	0.176	0.151
726 Print and bookbind machy, parts	0.338	0.331	0.351	0.062	0.113	0.103
271 Fertilizers, crude	0.308	0.328	0.348	0.149	0.318	0.277
289 Prec metal ores, waste nes	0.421	0.333	0.346	0.476	0.493	0.469
662 Clay, refractory building prdts	0.341	0.354	0.346	0.082	0.208	0.222
763 Sound recorders, phonographs	0.294	0.366	0.341	0.232	0.258	0.328
012 Meat dried, salted, smoked	0.343	0.331	0.328	0.122	0.244	0.230
667 Pearl, prec, semi-prec stones	0.322	0.319	0.326	0.122	0.453	0.324
712 Steam engines, turbines	0.341	0.338	0.324	0.225	0.274	0.196
042 Rice	0.325	0.302	0.319	0.164	0.163	0.184
848 Headgear, non-textile clothing	0.234	0.279	0.318	0.184	0.251	0.280
894 Toys, sporting goods, etc	0.277	0.327	0.317	0.112	0.231	0.196
584 Cellulose, derivatives, etc	0.337	0.319	0.309	0.107	0.198	0.219
785 Cycles, etc, motorized or not	0.319	0.337	0.308	0.081	0.195	0.206
871 Optical instruments	0.304	0.318	0.308	0.197	0.344	0.269
263 Cotton	0.343	0.298	0.306	0.339	0.330	0.365
786 Trailers, non-motor vehicl nes	0.225	0.293	0.305	0.154	0.380	0.324
043 Barley, unmilled	0.289	0.333	0.304	0.173	0.266	0.360
292 Crude vegetb materials nes	0.325	0.300	0.303	0.086	0.174	0.150
251 Pulp and waste paper	0.352	0.343	0.302	0.090	0.208	0.160
041 Wheat etc, unmilled	0.376	0.339	0.299	0.153	0.212	0.315
683 Nickel	0.285	0.282	0.295	0.216	0.319	0.305
572 Explosives, pyrotechnic prdts	0.270	0.318	0.295	0.231	0.390	0.329
411 Animal oils and fats	0.357	0.266	0.294	0.114	0.208	0.153
793 Ships, boats, etc	0.311	0.310	0.294	0.154	0.226	0.266
874 Measuring, controlg instruments	0.307	0.330	0.293	0.062	0.156	0.115
025 Eggs, yolks, fresh, prsrvd	0.339	0.316	0.293	0.151	0.280	0.259
666 Pottery	0.225	0.285	0.291	0.134	0.280	0.283
515 Organo-inorgan compounds, etc	0.242	0.327	0.291	0.101	0.326	0.263
882 Photogr and cinema supplies	0.299	0.292	0.290	0.051	0.201	0.161
722 Tractors non-road	0.301	0.296	0.290	0.101	0.146	0.121
351 Electric current	0.475	0.375	0.289	0.226	0.424	0.372
074 Tea and mate	0.283	0.303	0.289	0.148	0.237	0.264
274 Sulphur, unroastd iron pyrites	0.390	0.356	0.289	0.235	0.318	0.427

For sources and notes, see end of table 8.3B.

Pour les sources et les notes, se reporter à la fin du tableau 8.3B.

SITC group [1] Groupes de la CTCI [1]	Market concentration index of exports [2] Indice de concentration des exportations [2]			Structural change index of exports [3] (1992 = 0) Indice de changement structurel des exportations [3] (1992 = 0)		
	1995	2000	2002	1995	2000	2002
781 Passengr motor vehicl, exc bus	0.292	0.287	0.288	0.115	0.219	0.158
851 Footwear	0.262	0.282	0.286	0.164	0.266	0.258
745 Non-electr machy, tools nes	0.298	0.285	0.285	0.071	0.179	0.141
881 Photogr apparatus, equip nes	0.340	0.330	0.285	0.107	0.232	0.262
551 Essential oils, perfume, etc	0.241	0.272	0.284	0.055	0.217	0.255
211 Hides skins, exc furs, raw	0.269	0.289	0.283	0.107	0.201	0.192
248 Wood, shaped, rail sleepers	0.318	0.331	0.283	0.106	0.230	0.193
736 Metal working machy, tools	0.300	0.302	0.280	0.137	0.220	0.132
696 Cutlery	0.227	0.251	0.280	0.126	0.308	0.348
223 Seeds for other fixed oils	0.321	0.205	0.278	0.289	0.371	0.326
884 Optical goods nes	0.260	0.288	0.278	0.092	0.199	0.137
681 Silver, platinum, etc	0.255	0.317	0.277	0.250	0.360	0.323
047 Other cereal meals, flour	0.241	0.283	0.275	0.272	0.349	0.328
246 Pulpwood, chips, woodwaste	0.337	0.315	0.275	0.160	0.258	0.337
724 Textile, leather machinery	0.305	0.277	0.274	0.066	0.182	0.155
725 Paper etc mill machinery	0.259	0.259	0.273	0.094	0.138	0.130
723 Civil engineering equip, etc	0.294	0.284	0.273	0.150	0.201	0.189
112 Alcoholic beverages	0.294	0.287	0.272	0.097	0.162	0.182
654 Other woven textile fabric	0.297	0.272	0.272	0.091	0.187	0.190
553 Perfumery, cosmetics, etc	0.321	0.280	0.272	0.061	0.196	0.181
341 Gas, natural and manufactured	0.326	0.282	0.271	0.186	0.215	0.285
687 Tin	0.266	0.304	0.271	0.178	0.352	0.289
742 Pumps for liquids, etc	0.302	0.291	0.270	0.055	0.138	0.158
655 Knitted, etc, fabric	0.255	0.269	0.268	0.087	0.258	0.207
728 Oth machy for spec industries	0.279	0.306	0.266	0.115	0.242	0.127
721 Agricult machinry exc tractor	0.270	0.276	0.265	0.072	0.154	0.132
872 Medical instruments nes	0.276	0.280	0.265	0.074	0.159	0.174
431 Procesd animl and veg oil, etc	0.276	0.267	0.264	0.166	0.240	0.294
023 Butter	0.258	0.260	0.264	0.139	0.351	0.270
247 Other wood rough, squared	0.277	0.247	0.263	0.203	0.315	0.375
713 Intern combust piston engines	0.295	0.277	0.262	0.098	0.166	0.155
024 Cheese and curd	0.307	0.270	0.260	0.070	0.191	0.180
762 Radio-broadcast receivers	0.275	0.258	0.260	0.174	0.276	0.337
121 Tobacco, unmanufactd, refuse	0.298	0.264	0.260	0.122	0.186	0.233
277 Natural abrasives nes	0.238	0.251	0.259	0.322	0.565	0.528
783 Road motor vehicles nes	0.304	0.267	0.258	0.244	0.306	0.266
233 Rubber, synthetic, reclaimed	0.251	0.270	0.258	0.210	0.299	0.236
585 Plastic materials nes	0.265	0.288	0.258	0.267	0.314	0.332
266 Synthetic fibres for spinning	0.238	0.266	0.257	0.229	0.373	0.322
873 Meters and counters nes	0.257	0.273	0.256	0.156	0.286	0.310
613 Fur skins tanned, dressed	0.224	0.253	0.256	0.173	0.302	0.303
423 Fixed vegetable oils, soft	0.230	0.245	0.255	0.139	0.224	0.231
727 Food machinery, non-demestic	0.257	0.251	0.255	0.062	0.137	0.087
122 Tobacco, manufactured	0.312	0.294	0.254	0.121	0.202	0.320
659 Floor coverings, etc	0.282	0.249	0.254	0.091	0.340	0.224
621 Materials of rubber	0.293	0.265	0.253	0.134	0.226	0.198
784 Motor vehicl parts, acces nes	0.282	0.271	0.251	0.128	0.181	0.168
598 Miscel chemical prdts nes	0.260	0.259	0.248	0.071	0.219	0.181
776 Transistors, valves, etc	0.284	0.263	0.247	0.068	0.188	0.219
845 Outer garments knit nonelastic	0.205	0.235	0.246	0.104	0.253	0.259
037 Fish etc prepd, prsrvd nes	0.183	0.244	0.245	0.198	0.314	0.294
782 Lorries, spec motor vehicl nes	0.277	0.253	0.244	0.163	0.286	0.276
751 Office machines	0.276	0.284	0.244	0.131	0.196	0.330
743 Pumps nes, centrifuges, etc	0.256	0.254	0.243	0.053	0.176	0.155
531 Synth dye, natrl indigo, lakes	0.293	0.248	0.242	0.095	0.251	0.255
035 Fish salted, dried, smoked	0.272	0.235	0.241	0.132	0.215	0.237
761 Television receivers	0.200	0.231	0.241	0.123	0.345	0.324
514 Nitrogen-function compounds	0.242	0.227	0.241	0.126	0.219	0.346

For sources and notes, see end of table 8.3B.

Pour les sources et les notes, se reporter à la fin du tableau 8.3B.

SITC group [1] Groupes de la CTCI [1]	Market concentration index of exports [2] Indice de concentration des exportations [2]			Structural change index of exports [3] (1992=0) Indice de changement structurel des exportations [3] (1992=0)		
	1995	2000	2002	1995	2000	2002
897 Gold, silver ware, jewellery	0.253	0.261	0.240	0.110	0.187	0.198
001 Live animals for food	0.228	0.225	0.240	0.123	0.254	0.218
291 Crude animal materials nes	0.213	0.242	0.240	0.113	0.218	0.200
737 Metal working machinery nes	0.264	0.253	0.240	0.121	0.193	0.137
591 Pesticides, disinfectants	0.258	0.245	0.237	0.124	0.188	0.201
658 Textile articles nes	0.193	0.213	0.236	0.100	0.232	0.235
694 Stell, copper nails, nuts, etc	0.226	0.240	0.235	0.074	0.180	0.114
685 Lead	0.221	0.223	0.233	0.162	0.349	0.306
611 Leather	0.210	0.236	0.233	0.152	0.186	0.176
749 Non-electr machy parts, acces	0.262	0.241	0.233	0.074	0.174	0.164
081 Feeding stuff for animals	0.233	0.242	0.232	0.090	0.180	0.160
676 Railway rails etc, iron, steel	0.218	0.226	0.231	0.212	0.324	0.248
892 Printed matter	0.238	0.232	0.231	0.084	0.183	0.168
541 Medicinal, pharmaceutical prdts	0.222	0.222	0.230	0.057	0.140	0.195
775 Household type equip nes	0.221	0.217	0.230	0.107	0.208	0.241
511 Hydrocarbons nes, derivtives	0.248	0.232	0.228	0.248	0.308	0.280
744 Mechanical handling equipment	0.239	0.232	0.227	0.102	0.166	0.144
022 Milk and cream	0.280	0.241	0.226	0.091	0.278	0.280
652 Cotton fabrics, woven	0.201	0.209	0.226	0.111	0.218	0.212
287 Base metals ores, conc nes	0.222	0.232	0.225	0.140	0.263	0.239
847 Textile clothing accessoris nes	0.212	0.223	0.225	0.143	0.272	0.254
073 Chocolate and products	0.245	0.221	0.223	0.126	0.288	0.245
899 Other manufactured goods	0.220	0.223	0.223	0.083	0.233	0.241
056 Vegtb etc prsrvd, preprd	0.209	0.210	0.222	0.159	0.266	0.252
844 Under garments non-knit	0.200	0.223	0.222	0.151	0.279	0.283
718 Oth power generating machinery	0.281	0.222	0.221	0.161	0.326	0.301
523 Other inorganic chemicals	0.221	0.221	0.220	0.132	0.242	0.172
054 Vegtb etc fresh, simply prsrvd	0.231	0.223	0.219	0.124	0.279	0.234
843 Women's outwear non-knit	0.207	0.206	0.219	0.131	0.267	0.271
791 Railway vehicles	0.245	0.237	0.219	0.292	0.356	0.280
533 Pigments, paints, varnishes etc	0.222	0.221	0.219	0.092	0.228	0.180
516 Other organic chemicals	0.225	0.219	0.218	0.118	0.243	0.223
812 Plumbg, heatg, lightg equip	0.205	0.211	0.217	0.120	0.279	0.253
697 Base metal household equip	0.182	0.195	0.216	0.082	0.228	0.228
778 Electrical machinery nes	0.234	0.243	0.216	0.109	0.189	0.202
895 Office supplies nes	0.227	0.226	0.215	0.068	0.192	0.178
582 Prdts of condensation, etc	0.223	0.222	0.214	0.136	0.266	0.220
592 Starch, inulin, gluten, etc	0.209	0.211	0.214	0.102	0.231	0.205
634 Veneers, plywood, etc	0.270	0.233	0.214	0.140	0.300	0.296
562 Fertilizers, manufactured	0.208	0.219	0.214	0.150	0.246	0.205
689 Non-fer base metals nes	0.223	0.203	0.213	0.250	0.309	0.309
628 Rubber articles nes	0.229	0.226	0.213	0.063	0.203	0.181
663 Mineral manufactures nes	0.223	0.223	0.213	0.117	0.235	0.190
513 Carboxylic acids, etc	0.235	0.219	0.211	0.150	0.260	0.252
011 Meat, fresh, chilled, frozen	0.210	0.227	0.210	0.115	0.267	0.235
583 Polymerization, etc, prdts	0.216	0.213	0.210	0.086	0.252	0.187
641 Paper and paperboard	0.224	0.218	0.210	0.060	0.145	0.140
711 Steam boilers and auxil parts	0.245	0.222	0.209	0.143	0.321	0.354
898 Musical instruments and parts	0.254	0.230	0.209	0.082	0.226	0.196
282 Iron and steel scrap	0.273	0.203	0.209	0.117	0.291	0.268
772 Switchgear etc, parts nes	0.240	0.224	0.209	0.086	0.232	0.207
699 Base metal manufactures nes	0.201	0.216	0.208	0.075	0.229	0.182
752 Automatic data processing equip	0.247	0.219	0.207	0.135	0.308	0.362
335 Residual petroleum prdts nes	0.274	0.227	0.207	0.117	0.222	0.235
269 Waste of textile fabrics	0.259	0.230	0.207	0.119	0.273	0.286
741 Heating, cooling equipment	0.230	0.225	0.207	0.071	0.207	0.200
333 Crude petroleum	0.213	0.203	0.206	0.143	0.210	0.213
759 Office, adp machy parts, acces	0.242	0.215	0.205	0.111	0.271	0.283

For sources and notes, see end of table 8.3B.

Pour les sources et les notes, se reporter à la fin du tableau 8.3B.

SITC group [1] Groupes de la CTCI [1]	Market concentration index of exports [2] Indice de concentration des exportations [2]			Structural change index of exports [3] (1992=0) Indice de changement structurel des exportations [3] (1992=0)		
	1995	2000	2002	1995	2000	2002
695 Tools	0.216	0.204	0.205	0.071	0.205	0.171
111 Non alcoholic beverages nes	0.216	0.209	0.205	0.153	0.316	0.283
091 Margarine and shortening	0.230	0.175	0.201	0.203	0.437	0.345
842 Men's outwear non-knit	0.196	0.199	0.201	0.132	0.293	0.299
771 Electric power machinery nes	0.188	0.204	0.201	0.109	0.241	0.218
061 Sugar and honey	0.200	0.191	0.200	0.218	0.299	0.308
664 Glass	0.216	0.212	0.200	0.116	0.291	0.205
656 Lace, ribbon, tulle, etc	0.191	0.207	0.199	0.157	0.309	0.287
657 Spec textile fabrics, products	0.207	0.206	0.199	0.112	0.239	0.163
679 Iron, steel castings unworked	0.183	0.207	0.198	0.146	0.287	0.251
288 Non-ferrous metal scrap nes	0.209	0.189	0.198	0.164	0.228	0.220
612 Leather, etc, manufactures	0.189	0.189	0.198	0.323	0.490	0.375
773 Electricity distributing equip	0.194	0.216	0.198	0.079	0.214	0.205
532 Dyes nes, tanning products	0.227	0.205	0.198	0.112	0.224	0.242
014 Meat prepd, prsrvd nes, etc	0.193	0.189	0.197	0.151	0.351	0.302
653 Woven man-made fib fabric	0.218	0.201	0.197	0.104	0.252	0.247
278 Other crude minerals	0.197	0.213	0.197	0.106	0.228	0.189
048 Cereal etc preparations	0.205	0.200	0.197	0.102	0.237	0.205
671 Pig iron, etc	0.203	0.209	0.195	0.309	0.373	0.335
893 Articles of plastic nes	0.179	0.197	0.193	0.122	0.298	0.226
071 Coffee and substitutes	0.188	0.189	0.193	0.171	0.221	0.232
672 Iron, steel primary forms	0.179	0.189	0.192	0.206	0.401	0.325
554 Soap, cleansing, etc preps	0.214	0.196	0.190	0.109	0.281	0.246
057 Fruit, nuts, fresh, dried	0.192	0.181	0.190	0.090	0.163	0.140
764 Telecom equip, parts, acces	0.214	0.186	0.190	0.125	0.278	0.289
716 Rotating electric plant	0.211	0.191	0.189	0.113	0.215	0.221
678 Iron, steel tubes, pipes, etc	0.205	0.188	0.189	0.134	0.234	0.193
686 Zinc	0.195	0.198	0.188	0.209	0.303	0.262
674 Iron, steel univ, plate, sheet	0.214	0.190	0.188	0.117	0.289	0.225
821 Furniture and parts thereof	0.199	0.188	0.188	0.122	0.297	0.270
665 Glassware	0.208	0.190	0.187	0.111	0.227	0.185
661 Lime, cement and building prdts	0.205	0.197	0.187	0.148	0.290	0.300
642 Paper and paperboard, cut	0.202	0.185	0.187	0.092	0.231	0.227
512 Alcohols, phenols, etc	0.213	0.200	0.187	0.176	0.250	0.246
098 Edible products, preps nes	0.217	0.194	0.186	0.089	0.239	0.208
625 Rubber tyres,tubes, etc	0.198	0.194	0.186	0.096	0.208	0.194
682 Copper	0.172	0.185	0.185	0.092	0.221	0.184
691 Structures and parts nes	0.187	0.179	0.183	0.177	0.314	0.286
245 Fuel wood nes, charcoal	0.170	0.176	0.181	0.265	0.425	0.456
522 Inorg chem elmnt, oxides, etc	0.172	0.181	0.179	0.142	0.259	0.222
046 Wheat etc, meal or flour	0.206	0.179	0.176	0.262	0.393	0.359
692 Metal tanks, boxes, etc	0.199	0.173	0.173	0.106	0.233	0.208
677 Iron, steel wire, exc w rod	0.167	0.173	0.170	0.177	0.297	0.202
846 Under garments knitted	0.170	0.172	0.167	0.121	0.245	0.242
693 Wire products, non-electric	0.172	0.173	0.166	0.113	0.286	0.233
635 Wood manufactures nes	0.144	0.163	0.166	0.140	0.295	0.253
651 Textile yarn	0.156	0.161	0.164	0.125	0.280	0.238
058 Fruit prsrvd, preprd	0.164	0.163	0.162	0.101	0.216	0.203
273 Stone, sand and gravel	0.160	0.159	0.161	0.102	0.270	0.223
036 Shell fish fresh, frozen	0.168	0.155	0.161	0.132	0.226	0.240
673 Iron, steel shapes, etc	0.168	0.160	0.157	0.141	0.253	0.211
034 Fish, fresh, chilled, frozen	0.154	0.156	0.157	0.177	0.260	0.244
684 Aluminium	0.166	0.163	0.157	0.107	0.199	0.183
062 Sugar preps non-chocolate	0.160	0.156	0.153	0.174	0.338	0.289
075 Spices	0.195	0.183	0.152	0.218	0.271	0.276
334 Petroleum products, refined	0.146	0.133	0.131	0.144	0.235	0.276

For sources and notes, see end of table 8.3B.

Pour les sources et les notes, se reporter à la fin du tableau 8.3B.

SITC group [1] Groupes de la CTCI [1]	Market concentration index of imports [2] Indice de concentration des importations [2]			Structural change index of imports [3] (1992 = 0) Indice de changement structurel des importations [3] (1992 = 0)		
	1995	2000	2002	1995	2000	2002
246 Pulpwood, chips, woodwaste	0.736	0.721	0.677	0.050	0.088	0.110
896 Works of art, etc	0.445	0.534	0.525	0.182	0.267	0.212
244 Cork, natural, raw, waste	0.360	0.465	0.506	0.200	0.273	0.289
012 Meat dried, salted, smoked	0.512	0.408	0.482	0.095	0.254	0.155
883 Developed cinema film	0.318	0.371	0.429	0.266	0.254	0.282
261 Silk	0.313	0.333	0.376	0.080	0.252	0.384
894 Toys, sporting goods, etc	0.314	0.359	0.370	0.091	0.142	0.125
045 Cereals nes, unmilled	0.272	0.342	0.360	0.297	0.205	0.285
289 Prec metal ores, waste nes	0.391	0.404	0.356	0.171	0.285	0.217
212 Furskins, raw	0.294	0.361	0.351	0.282	0.345	0.338
264 Jute, other textile bast fibres	0.260	0.322	0.350	0.376	0.378	0.478
848 Headgear, non-textile clothing	0.304	0.360	0.344	0.089	0.180	0.173
871 Optical instruments	0.244	0.271	0.343	0.283	0.389	0.463
763 Sound recorders, phonographs	0.308	0.391	0.342	0.116	0.172	0.136
845 Outer garments knit nonelastic	0.296	0.338	0.341	0.125	0.240	0.237
036 Shell fish fresh, frozen	0.423	0.372	0.340	0.052	0.137	0.169
667 Pearl, prec, semi-prec stones	0.317	0.327	0.334	0.135	0.425	0.307
781 Passengr motor vehicl, exc bus	0.289	0.352	0.333	0.124	0.227	0.205
524 Radioactive etc materials	0.345	0.363	0.333	0.111	0.275	0.311
844 Under garments non-knit	0.316	0.364	0.331	0.123	0.216	0.188
821 Furniture and parts thereof	0.249	0.318	0.328	0.121	0.273	0.253
897 Gold, silver ware, jewellery	0.288	0.326	0.323	0.098	0.189	0.189
762 Radio-broadcast receivers	0.292	0.337	0.320	0.104	0.186	0.189
851 Footwear	0.312	0.333	0.319	0.103	0.163	0.154
761 Television receivers	0.227	0.277	0.317	0.170	0.303	0.298
666 Pottery	0.300	0.320	0.317	0.086	0.165	0.175
843 Women's outwear non-knit	0.299	0.339	0.313	0.083	0.196	0.170
658 Textile articles nes	0.230	0.287	0.312	0.128	0.250	0.257
281 Iron ore and concentrates	0.276	0.279	0.307	0.120	0.218	0.241
515 Organo-inorgan compounds, etc	0.198	0.318	0.303	0.097	0.267	0.259
842 Men's outwear non-knit	0.270	0.320	0.303	0.102	0.221	0.196
681 Silver, platinum, etc	0.300	0.346	0.301	0.127	0.217	0.262
831 Travel goods, handbags, etc	0.319	0.315	0.301	0.079	0.120	0.134
268 Wool (exc tops), animal hair	0.231	0.305	0.294	0.118	0.282	0.267
846 Under garments knitted	0.265	0.301	0.293	0.115	0.225	0.218
697 Base metal household equip	0.213	0.277	0.291	0.138	0.236	0.234
248 Wood, shaped, rail sleepers	0.266	0.291	0.290	0.116	0.214	0.223
613 Fur skins tanned, dressed	0.297	0.310	0.289	0.255	0.325	0.336
037 Fish etc prepd, prsrvd nes	0.274	0.297	0.284	0.123	0.205	0.166
112 Alcoholic beverages	0.212	0.278	0.282	0.087	0.194	0.180
635 Wood manufactures nes	0.247	0.274	0.276	0.112	0.261	0.250
714 Engines and motors nes	0.258	0.293	0.272	0.161	0.202	0.193
711 Steam boilers and auxil parts	0.153	0.182	0.269	0.419	0.449	0.531
774 Electro-medical, xray equip	0.203	0.236	0.267	0.138	0.158	0.145
247 Other wood rough, squared	0.359	0.269	0.266	0.110	0.318	0.377
633 Cork manufactures	0.261	0.265	0.265	0.096	0.193	0.200
782 Lorries, spec motor vehicl nes	0.212	0.257	0.262	0.199	0.236	0.232
752 Automatic data processing equip	0.267	0.268	0.261	0.111	0.192	0.193
001 Live animals for food	0.217	0.242	0.258	0.188	0.259	0.244
885 Watches and clocks	0.276	0.266	0.258	0.070	0.131	0.124
265 Vegetb fibre, exc cotton, jute	0.212	0.244	0.257	0.238	0.485	0.478
211 Hides skins, exc furs, raw	0.269	0.275	0.257	0.174	0.242	0.279
341 Gas, natural and manufactured	0.273	0.271	0.254	0.186	0.288	0.282
812 Plumbg, heatg, lightg equip	0.204	0.254	0.253	0.120	0.263	0.238
034 Fish, fresh, chilled, frozen	0.312	0.285	0.252	0.092	0.149	0.172
689 Non-fer base metals nes	0.282	0.270	0.252	0.110	0.161	0.194
333 Crude petroleum	0.250	0.252	0.250	0.076	0.172	0.177
881 Photogr apparatus, equip nes	0.239	0.265	0.249	0.132	0.214	0.195

For sources and notes, see end of table.

Pour les sources et les notes, se reporter à la fin du tableau.

SITC group [1] / Groupes de la CTCI [1]	Market concentration index of imports [2] / Indice de concentration des importations [2]			Structural change index of imports [3] (1992 = 0) / Indice de changement structurel des importations [3] (1992 = 0)		
	1995	2000	2002	1995	2000	2002
322 Coal, lignite and peat	0.276	0.257	0.247	0.122	0.197	0.186
873 Meters and counters nes	0.253	0.251	0.246	0.272	0.337	0.315
232 Natural rubber, gums	0.249	0.243	0.242	0.074	0.196	0.206
634 Veneers, plywood, etc	0.217	0.241	0.241	0.127	0.243	0.252
792 Aircraft, etc	0.165	0.239	0.239	0.190	0.256	0.255
659 Floor coverings, etc	0.241	0.233	0.237	0.101	0.275	0.286
713 Intern combust piston engines	0.238	0.252	0.233	0.108	0.194	0.147
784 Motor vehicl parts, acces nes	0.230	0.241	0.233	0.123	0.207	0.169
722 Tractors non-road	0.235	0.247	0.232	0.190	0.257	0.235
274 Sulphur, unroastd iron pyrites	0.213	0.208	0.232	0.203	0.400	0.412
014 Meat prepd, prsrvd nes, etc	0.215	0.226	0.232	0.132	0.279	0.258
899 Other manufactured goods	0.200	0.214	0.229	0.067	0.161	0.195
514 Nitrogen-function compounds	0.171	0.174	0.229	0.144	0.222	0.259
785 Cycles, etc, motorized or not	0.194	0.220	0.228	0.144	0.251	0.259
847 Textile clothing accessoris nes	0.215	0.232	0.227	0.147	0.231	0.222
245 Fuel wood nes, charcoal	0.199	0.226	0.224	0.193	0.339	0.277
773 Electricity distributing equip	0.202	0.227	0.222	0.093	0.196	0.184
323 Briquettes, coke and semi-coke	0.183	0.206	0.221	0.222	0.378	0.297
611 Leather	0.214	0.224	0.220	0.130	0.240	0.261
686 Zinc	0.214	0.214	0.220	0.141	0.239	0.222
661 Lime, cement and building prdts	0.163	0.227	0.219	0.197	0.326	0.315
071 Coffee and substitutes	0.244	0.251	0.219	0.085	0.146	0.154
696 Cutlery	0.201	0.227	0.218	0.080	0.181	0.179
288 Non-ferrous metal scrap nes	0.210	0.219	0.216	0.109	0.283	0.243
775 Household type equip nes	0.181	0.208	0.216	0.108	0.196	0.194
023 Butter	0.260	0.226	0.215	0.170	0.294	0.254
035 Fish salted, dried, smoked	0.228	0.226	0.215	0.125	0.204	0.169
759 Office, adp machy parts, acces	0.261	0.240	0.215	0.133	0.198	0.227
072 Cocoa	0.245	0.232	0.214	0.121	0.220	0.231
222 Seeds for soft fixed oils	0.220	0.233	0.213	0.079	0.334	0.276
025 Eggs, yolks, fresh, prsrvd	0.268	0.201	0.213	0.145	0.258	0.253
043 Barley, unmilled	0.199	0.235	0.213	0.289	0.400	0.333
024 Cheese and curd	0.268	0.214	0.211	0.085	0.260	0.229
872 Medical instruments nes	0.181	0.205	0.211	0.103	0.195	0.179
712 Steam engines, turbines	0.168	0.198	0.211	0.428	0.552	0.487
771 Electric power machinery nes	0.188	0.229	0.210	0.117	0.197	0.193
764 Telecom equip, parts, acces	0.183	0.208	0.210	0.142	0.168	0.154
776 Transistors, valves, etc	0.249	0.211	0.209	0.106	0.172	0.271
572 Explosives, pyrotechnic prdts	0.172	0.207	0.209	0.205	0.251	0.267
694 Stell, copper nails, nuts, etc	0.215	0.222	0.209	0.061	0.191	0.175
062 Sugar preps non-chocolate	0.159	0.198	0.208	0.217	0.230	0.225
058 Fruit prsrvd, preprd	0.221	0.214	0.207	0.112	0.158	0.146
251 Pulp and waste paper	0.208	0.202	0.206	0.061	0.166	0.194
351 Electric current	0.240	0.318	0.206	0.319	0.511	0.509
011 Meat, fresh, chilled, frozen	0.259	0.225	0.206	0.134	0.226	0.232
292 Crude vegetb materials nes	0.220	0.206	0.205	0.095	0.194	0.188
671 Pig iron, etc	0.225	0.226	0.205	0.116	0.253	0.208
884 Optical goods nes	0.223	0.236	0.205	0.109	0.185	0.240
075 Spices	0.186	0.198	0.204	0.111	0.148	0.158
751 Office machines	0.265	0.226	0.204	0.146	0.175	0.161
266 Synthetic fibres for spinning	0.196	0.199	0.203	0.145	0.206	0.200
683 Nickel	0.243	0.227	0.203	0.178	0.218	0.239
056 Vegtb etc prsrvd, preprd	0.214	0.201	0.203	0.133	0.218	0.190
287 Base metals ores, conc nes	0.231	0.207	0.202	0.128	0.239	0.253
291 Crude animal materials nes	0.230	0.225	0.201	0.096	0.217	0.258
724 Textile, leather machinery	0.162	0.154	0.200	0.146	0.204	0.239
541 Medicinal, pharmaceutical prdts	0.146	0.166	0.200	0.074	0.210	0.236
054 Vegtb etc fresh, simply prsrvd	0.209	0.200	0.199	0.109	0.231	0.210

For sources and notes, see end of table.

Pour les sources et les notes, se reporter à la fin du tableau.

SITC group [1] Groupes de la CTCI [1]	Market concentration index of imports [2] Indice de concentration des importations [2]			Structural change index of imports [3] (1992 = 0) Indice de changement structurel des importations [3] (1992 = 0)		
	1995	2000	2002	1995	2000	2002
513 Carboxylic acids, etc	0.145	0.173	0.199	0.107	0.208	0.227
682 Copper	0.165	0.186	0.198	0.112	0.231	0.248
625 Rubber tyres,tubes, etc	0.179	0.205	0.197	0.093	0.222	0.198
687 Tin	0.226	0.216	0.197	0.128	0.200	0.257
895 Office supplies nes	0.191	0.204	0.196	0.092	0.162	0.132
716 Rotating electric plant	0.157	0.192	0.196	0.141	0.219	0.235
277 Natural abrasives nes	0.210	0.204	0.195	0.150	0.325	0.272
663 Mineral manufactures nes	0.176	0.205	0.195	0.113	0.261	0.234
044 Maize (corn), unmilled	0.212	0.194	0.193	0.262	0.328	0.314
057 Fruit, nuts, fresh, dried	0.213	0.195	0.193	0.082	0.195	0.184
655 Knitted, etc, fabric	0.215	0.189	0.192	0.125	0.289	0.325
699 Base metal manufactures nes	0.168	0.199	0.190	0.096	0.235	0.197
516 Other organic chemicals	0.182	0.209	0.190	0.111	0.217	0.196
874 Measuring, controlg instruments	0.169	8.193	0.190	0.126	0.219	0.185
628 Rubber articles nes	0.173	0.188	0.190	0.109	0.221	0.201
612 Leather, etc, manufactures	0.185	0.179	0.189	0.146	0.242	0.283
111 Non alcoholic beverages nes	0.173	0.189	0.189	0.190	0.327	0.240
736 Metal working machy, tools	0.194	0.214	0.188	0.216	0.243	0.220
695 Tools	0.170	0.187	0.188	0.110	0.194	0.188
898 Musical instruments and parts	0.183	0.183	0.186	0.113	0.188	0.176
282 Iron and steel scrap	0.208	0.183	0.186	0.149	0.307	0.294
778 Electrical machinery nes	0.180	0.188	0.184	0.086	0.203	0.204
585 Plastic materials nes	0.163	0.157	0.184	0.222	0.296	0.267
512 Alcohols, phenols, etc	0.162	0.171	0.183	0.112	0.239	0.254
122 Tobacco, manufactured	0.188	0.196	0.183	0.207	0.303	0.295
641 Paper and paperboard	0.186	0.186	0.183	0.085	0.191	0.176
665 Glassware	0.174	0.196	0.183	0.109	0.232	0.206
737 Metal working machinery nes	0.165	0.166	0.182	0.229	0.282	0.255
672 Iron, steel primary forms	0.176	0.188	0.182	0.123	0.269	0.266
267 Other man-made fibres	0.146	0.167	0.181	0.189	0.315	0.299
893 Articles of plastic nes	0.170	0.184	0.181	0.120	0.249	0.224
684 Aluminium	0.192	0.186	0.180	0.115	0.210	0.192
744 Mechanical handling equipment	0.142	0.196	0.180	0.202	0.277	0.242
511 Hydrocarbons nes, derivtives	0.171	0.172	0.178	0.157	0.274	0.232
223 Seeds for other fixed oils	0.197	0.195	0.178	0.201	0.323	0.369
749 Non-electr machy parts, acces	0.170	0.184	0.176	0.113	0.208	0.189
679 Iron, steel castings unworked	0.168	0.171	0.176	0.152	0.274	0.257
073 Chocolate and products	0.182	0.177	0.176	0.128	0.191	0.185
772 Switchgear etc, parts nes	0.169	0.184	0.176	0.105	0.201	0.218
718 Oth power generating machinery	0.171	0.183	0.175	0.246	0.398	0.341
233 Rubber, synthetic, reclaimed	0.149	0.168	0.174	0.123	0.251	0.224
677 Iron, steel wire, exc w rod	0.185	0.175	0.173	0.101	0.230	0.216
424 Other fixed vegetable oils	0.159	0.160	0.172	0.220	0.277	0.311
743 Pumps nes, centrifuges, etc	0.146	0.171	0.168	0.120	0.191	0.176
745 Non-electr machy, tools nes	0.141	0.169	0.168	0.139	0.198	0.171
674 Iron, steel univ, plate, sheet	0.143	0.152	0.168	0.101	0.211	0.239
725 Paper etc mill machinery	0.154	0.180	0.168	0.234	0.261	0.223
728 Oth machy for spec industries	0.166	0.177	0.167	0.195	0.249	0.209
892 Printed matter	0.158	0.164	0.166	0.108	0.217	0.188
721 Agricult machinry exc tractor	0.166	0.174	0.164	0.157	0.212	0.186
583 Polymerization, etc, prdts	0.155	0.160	0.164	0.078	0.232	0.238
664 Glass	0.161	0.169	0.163	0.131	0.250	0.225
662 Clay, refractory building prdts	0.174	0.174	0.163	0.131	0.310	0.298
121 Tobacco, unmanufactd, refuse	0.176	0.160	0.163	0.140	0.260	0.252
651 Textile yarn	0.164	0.158	0.163	0.100	0.227	0.231
273 Stone, sand and gravel	0.188	0.167	0.163	0.121	0.303	0.281
621 Materials of rubber	0.161	0.167	0.161	0.109	0.250	0.240
522 Inorg chem elmnt, oxides, etc	0.163	0.165	0.161	0.105	0.192	0.178

For sources and notes, see end of table.

Pour les sources et les notes, se reporter à la fin du tableau.

**8.3B   Import concentration and structural change
indices by product**
(concluded)

**8.3B   Indices de concentration et de changement
structurel des importations par produits**
(fin)

SITC group [1] Groupes de la CTCI [1]	Market concentration index of imports [2] Indice de concentration des importations [2]			Structural change index of imports [3] (1992 = 0) Indice de changement structurel des importations [3] (1992 = 0)		
	1995	2000	2002	1995	2000	2002
685 Lead	0.178	0.171	0.161	0.148	0.300	0.250
263 Cotton	0.167	0.157	0.161	0.191	0.334	0.328
693 Wire products, non-electric	0.167	0.173	0.160	0.100	0.234	0.215
642 Paper and paperboard, cut	0.147	0.161	0.160	0.100	0.240	0.214
786 Trailers, non-motor vehicl nes	0.168	0.206	0.159	0.177	0.292	0.252
882 Photogr and cinema supplies	0.178	0.175	0.158	0.101	0.178	0.203
654 Other woven textile fabric	0.181	0.167	0.158	0.124	0.241	0.275
726 Print and bookbind machy, parts	0.167	0.174	0.158	0.182	0.208	0.184
742 Pumps for liquids, etc	0.151	0.162	0.157	0.110	0.194	0.187
691 Structures and parts nes	0.158	0.154	0.156	0.232	0.334	0.315
562 Fertilizers, manufactured	0.190	0.148	0.156	0.094	0.254	0.230
793 Ships, boats, etc	0.158	0.180	0.156	0.296	0.359	0.363
783 Road motor vehicles nes	0.213	0.189	0.156	0.269	0.371	0.337
278 Other crude minerals	0.168	0.168	0.155	0.094	0.185	0.173
791 Railway vehicles	0.177	0.226	0.154	0.338	0.483	0.392
334 Petroleum products, refined	0.139	0.175	0.154	0.161	0.230	0.231
335 Residual petroleum prdts nes	0.153	0.159	0.152	0.154	0.311	0.338
551 Essential oils, perfume, etc	0.143	0.157	0.152	0.108	0.202	0.212
048 Cereal etc preparations	0.154	0.150	0.152	0.137	0.235	0.210
271 Fertilizers, crude	0.139	0.157	0.151	0.165	0.293	0.250
656 Lace, ribbon, tulle, etc	0.155	0.160	0.148	0.129	0.284	0.305
652 Cotton fabrics, woven	0.157	0.157	0.148	0.139	0.259	0.295
592 Starch, inulin, gluten, etc	0.161	0.156	0.147	0.090	0.200	0.184
676 Railway rails etc, iron, steel	0.154	0.175	0.146	0.345	0.374	0.346
582 Prdts of condensation, etc	0.152	0.145	0.146	0.089	0.222	0.216
723 Civil engineering equip, etc	0.149	0.167	0.146	0.204	0.296	0.259
074 Tea and mate	0.157	0.150	0.145	0.168	0.203	0.230
423 Fixed vegetable oils, soft	0.151	0.131	0.145	0.213	0.248	0.235
553 Perfumery, cosmetics, etc	0.144	0.144	0.144	0.104	0.195	0.182
673 Iron, steel shapes, etc	0.156	0.169	0.143	0.137	0.266	0.233
598 Miscel chemical prdts nes	0.137	0.142	0.143	0.097	0.233	0.209
532 Dyes nes, tanning products	0.131	0.139	0.142	0.147	0.202	0.227
657 Spec textile fabrics, products	0.143	0.140	0.140	0.100	0.230	0.232
584 Cellulose, derivatives, etc	0.145	0.139	0.139	0.092	0.241	0.257
046 Wheat etc, meal or flour	0.144	0.093	0.138	0.308	0.494	0.503
653 Woven man-made fib fabric	0.172	0.150	0.137	0.139	0.282	0.308
741 Heating, cooling equipment	0.118	0.134	0.137	0.155	0.240	0.221
531 Synth dye, natrl indigo, lakes	0.146	0.142	0.135	0.097	0.155	0.159
692 Metal tanks, boxes, etc	0.129	0.133	0.134	0.171	0.263	0.239
022 Milk and cream	0.180	0.139	0.133	0.146	0.271	0.258
411 Animal oils and fats	0.144	0.135	0.132	0.199	0.339	0.329
678 Iron, steel tubes, pipes, etc	0.125	0.150	0.130	0.172	0.270	0.257
081 Feeding stuff for animals	0.153	0.131	0.129	0.106	0.228	0.188
098 Edible products, preps nes	0.149	0.124	0.128	0.113	0.211	0.179
523 Other inorganic chemicals	0.128	0.142	0.127	0.092	0.209	0.192
554 Soap, cleansing, etc preps	0.127	0.120	0.126	0.106	0.232	0.183
591 Pesticides, disinfectants	0.142	0.129	0.125	0.126	0.224	0.220
061 Sugar and honey	0.124	0.115	0.122	0.170	0.196	0.173
041 Wheat etc, unmilled	0.140	0.116	0.121	0.284	0.372	0.389
533 Pigments, paints, varnishes etc	0.119	0.120	0.118	0.102	0.231	0.202
091 Margarine and shortening	0.134	0.113	0.118	0.258	0.425	0.370
431 Procesd animl and veg oil, etc	0.159	0.118	0.117	0.191	0.341	0.304
047 Other cereal meals, flour	0.104	0.097	0.115	0.354	0.469	0.473
727 Food machinery, non-demestic	0.123	0.110	0.112	0.201	0.234	0.217
269 Waste of textile fabrics	0.122	0.090	0.099	0.206	0.378	0.397
042 Rice	0.103	0.096	0.090	0.312	0.323	0.312

For sources and notes, see next page.   Pour les sources et les notes, se reporter à la page suivante.

8.3 Concentration and structural change indices of exports and imports by product

8.3 Indices de concentration et de changement structurel des exportations et des importations par produits

Sources:

UN/DESA/Statistics Division (COMTRADE database and estimates).

Indices are calculated from the data set that includes not only official country trade data reported to the COMTRADE but also estimates provided by the United Nations Statistics Division for all the other countries.

Notes:

1   Products are ranked according to the concentration index in 2002.

2   Market concentration index:

The Herfindahl-Hirschmann index is a measure of the degree of market concentration. It has been normalized to obtain values ranking from 0 to 1 (maximum concentration), according to the following formula:

$$H_i = \frac{\sqrt{\sum_{j=1}^{n} (\frac{x_{ij}}{X_j})^2} - \sqrt{\frac{1}{n}}}{1 - \sqrt{\frac{1}{n}}}$$

where

H_i = value of concentration index for product i

x_{ij} = value of exports or imports for country j and product i

$$X_j = \sum_{i=1}^{n} x_{ij} \quad \text{and}$$

n = 242 maximum number of individual markets (countries) over the period from 1990 to 2002.

An index value that is close to 1 indicates a very concentrated market. On the contrary, values closer to 0 reflect a more equal distribution of market shares among exporters or importers.

3   Structural change index:

This index, ranging from 0 to 1 reveals the structural change in trade for a particular product as compared to the reference year (1992 = 0).

An index value close to 1 indicates a significant change in the composition of exporters (importers). On the contrary, values closer to 0 would demonstrate a higher degree of "traditionality" in the markets over the period concerned. The value is calculated as follows:

$$I_i = \frac{\sum_{j=1}^{n} \left| S^1_{ij} - S^0_{ij} \right|}{2}$$

where

I_i = Value of structure index for product i

S^0_{ij} = Share of trade of product i for country j in 1992

S^1_{ij} = Share of trade of product i for the country j in the concerned year

Sources :

ONU/DAES/Division de statistique (Base de donnés COMTRADE et estimations).

Les indices sont calculés à partir de données n'incluant pas seulement les données officielles que les pays fournissent à la COMTRADE, mais aussi à partir d'estimations produites par la division de statistique des Nations Unies pour tous les autres pays.

Notes :

1   Les produits sont classés d'après l'indice de concentration en 2002.

2   Indice de concentration :

L'indice Herfindahl-Hirschmann mesure le degré de concentration des marchés. Il a été normalisé afin d'obtenir des valeurs comprises entre 0 et 1 (concentration maximale), d'après la formule suivante :

$$H_i = \frac{\sqrt{\sum_{j=1}^{n} (\frac{x_{ij}}{X_j})^2} - \sqrt{\frac{1}{n}}}{1 - \sqrt{\frac{1}{n}}}$$

où

H_i = Valeur de l'indice de concentration pour le produit i

x_{ij} = Valeur des exportations ou des importations du pays j pour le produit i

$$X_j = \sum_{i=1}^{n} x_{ij} \quad \text{et}$$

n = 242 Nombre maximum de marchés (pays) sur la période allant de 1990 à 2002.

Un indice proche de 1 indique une concentration très forte du marché pour ce produit en particulier. En revanche, une valeur proche de 0 démontre une répartition plus homogène du commerce entre les exportateurs ou les importateurs.

3   Indice de changement structurel :

Cet indice, dont la valeur est comprise entre 0 et 1, représente les changements de structure du commerce par rapport à une année de référence(1992 = 0).
Une valeur proche de 1 indique un important changement structurel du commerce de ce produit, c'est à dire, une grande variation des parts de marché au sein des exportateurs ou importateurs, par rapport à l'année de référence.
Plus la valeur de l'indice est proche de 0, plus la structure du commerce de ce produit est stable. Il est calculé comme suit :

$$I_i = \frac{\sum_{j=1}^{n} \left| S^1_{ij} - S^0_{ij} \right|}{2}$$

où

I_i = Valeur de l'indice de changement structurel, pour le produit i

S^0_{ij} = Part du commerce du produit i pour le pays j par rapport au commerce total de ce produit pour l'année 1992

S^1_{ij} = Part du commerce du produit i pour le pays j, par rapport au commerce total de ce produit pour l'année concernée

Markets / Marchés	Year / Année	MFN rate - Simple average / Droit NPF - Moyenne simple						MFN rate - Weighted average / Droit NPF - Moyenne pondérée					
		Total of non-agricultural and non-fuel products / Total des produits non-agricoles et non-pétroliers	Ores and metals / Minérais et métaux	Manufactured products / Produits manufacturés	Chemical products / Produits chimiques	Machinery and transport equipment / Machines et matériel de transport	Other manufactured products / Produits manufacturés divers	Total of non-agricultural and non-fuel products / Total des produits non-agricoles et non-pétroliers	Ores and metals / Minérais et métaux	Manufactured products / Produits manufacturés	Chemical products / Produits chimiques	Machinery and transport equipment / Machines et matériel de transport	Other manufactured products / Produits manufacturés divers
SITC Rev.2 / CTCI Rév.2		5+6+7+8 +27+28	27+28+68	(5+6+7+8) - 68	5	7	(6+8) - 68	5+6+7+8 +27+28	27+28+68	(5+6+7+8) - 68	5	7	(6+8) - 68
Albania - Albanie	1997	16.1	12.2	16.2	12.4	8.9	20.6	15.2	15.1	15.2	12.3	9.8	18.7
	2001	10.5	8.3	10.6	7.6	6.0	13.6	11.6	9.5	11.6	8.1	7.2	14.9
Algeria - Algérie	1993	24.4	12.1	24.8	13.2	16.8	32.0	18.7	11.5	18.8	13.7	16.5	23.8
	1997	23.5	11.5	23.9	15.5	17.3	29.6	19.4	12.1	19.4	10.0	18.3	25.2
	1998	23.3	11.4	23.7	15.1	17.1	29.4	18.6	12.1	18.6	9.0	17.2	25.3
	2001	21.7	11.4	22.0	13.8	16.8	27.1	16.7	13.1	16.7	9.2	16.9	20.3
	2002	18.6	12.3	18.9	15.7	12.2	22.7	13.2	13.5	13.3	12.1	10.8	18.8
	2003	18.1	11.9	18.4	14.3	11.9	22.5	..	..	..	..	..	..
Angola	2002	8.0	9.5	7.9	4.8	3.8	10.6	5.7	5.7	5.6	6.8	4.0	8.6
Antigua and Barbuda - Antigua-et-Barbuda	1996	20.6	16.0	20.6	14.5	20.6	21.6	25.0	13.6	25.1	19.1	31.0	20.7
	1999	17.2	12.8	17.2	11.3	17.9	18.0	22.1	11.4	22.2	14.7	29.8	16.4
	2000	10.1	4.3	10.3	6.3	8.9	12.3	16.9	9.8	16.9	16.1	17.2	16.8
	2001	8.6	3.9	8.8	5.7	8.0	10.2	14.4	8.0	14.4	12.6	16.0	12.8
	2002	8.6	3.9	8.8	5.7	8.0	10.2	14.4	8.0	14.4	12.6	16.0	12.8
	2003	8.6	3.9	8.8	5.7	8.0	10.2	·..	..	..	..	..	..
Argentina - Argentine	1992	13.8	8.1	14.1	9.4	13.6	16.0	13.5	6.5	13.6	8.5	14.5	14.8
	1993	12.5	6.0	12.8	7.6	14.6	13.9	13.4	5.2	13.5	7.7	14.7	14.2
	1995	12.7	6.5	13.0	8.3	9.9	15.9	12.0	5.9	12.1	8.9	11.3	15.8
	1996	13.4	6.3	13.8	8.3	13.4	15.9	14.2	5.8	14.4	8.8	15.5	16.2
	1997	13.6	6.3	13.9	8.3	14.5	15.7	14.7	6.0	14.9	9.3	16.1	15.9
	1998	15.9	9.1	16.3	11.3	15.2	18.4	16.3	8.5	16.4	12.4	16.8	18.2
	1999	15.8	9.1	16.1	11.4	14.9	18.2	15.3	8.6	15.4	12.5	15.2	17.7
	2000	15.7	9.0	16.0	11.4	14.7	18.1	15.1	8.4	15.2	12.4	15.0	17.6
	2001	13.0	8.5	13.2	11.0	14.5	13.5	14.1	7.3	14.2	12.1	15.4	14.1
	2002	14.5	7.3	14.8	9.7	15.0	16.5	12.7	5.1	13.1	10.9	13.9	15.0
	2003	15.2	5.9	15.6	8.3	14.0	18.8	..	..	..	..	..	..
Armenia - Arménie	2001	2.2	0.0	2.3	0.1	1.4	3.5	1.3	0.0	1.3	0.0	2.4	1.2
Australia - Australie	1991	13.6	2.6	14.1	5.0	11.5	18.2	11.7	5.1	11.8	5.5	9.9	16.6
	1993	10.1	2.4	10.4	4.4	9.3	13.0	10.0	4.9	10.1	5.0	9.4	12.9
	1996	6.5	1.1	6.7	1.9	4.0	9.5	5.4	2.2	5.4	1.8	4.5	8.4
	1997	6.1	1.1	6.3	1.9	4.0	8.8	5.4	2.2	5.4	1.9	4.6	8.0
	1998	5.8	1.1	6.0	1.9	3.9	8.2	5.2	2.1	5.2	1.8	4.5	7.5
	1999	5.5	1.1	5.6	1.9	3.9	7.7	4.8	2.4	4.9	1.8	4.2	7.3
	2000	5.2	1.1	5.3	1.9	3.9	7.1	4.7	2.4	4.7	1.7	4.2	7.0
	2001	4.8	1.1	5.0	1.5	3.2	6.9	4.5	2.3	4.5	1.7	3.9	6.8
	2002	4.8	1.0	5.0	1.5	3.2	7.0	4.6	2.2	4.6	1.7	4.0	6.8
	2003	4.8	1.0	5.0	1.5	3.2	7.0	..	..	..	..	..	..
Azerbaijan - Azerbaïdjan	2002	8.3	4.4	8.3	3.9	5.2	11.3	6.9	3.4	7.0	6.0	4.0	10.5
Bahamas	1999	32.1	34.3	32.1	34.0	35.6	30.0	32.1	28.7	32.1	26.9	38.5	27.6
	2002	31.6	33.3	31.6	33.5	34.6	29.6	30.3	26.9	30.4	24.6	36.8	26.1
Bahrain - Bahreïn	1999	7.7	5.4	7.8	5.3	9.5	8.1	8.9	5.4	9.6	6.2	12.4	7.9
	2001	7.7	5.4	7.8	5.3	9.5	8.1	9.3	5.3	10.0	6.2	13.0	8.0
Bangladesh	1989	118.1	45.0	121.3	62.7	69.2	160.5	108.8	57.5	110.1	52.5	74.7	143.6
	1994	82.7	61.2	83.8	68.6	77.3	91.6	86.3	67.5	86.5	70.1	78.0	92.7
	1999	21.6	14.4	22.0	16.6	13.4	27.4	22.4	13.1	22.4	13.7	12.2	28.5
	2000	21.6	14.4	22.0	16.6	13.3	27.4	21.6	12.8	21.6	14.1	11.5	28.1
	2002	20.4	12.8	20.7	14.9	12.4	26.2	20.4	9.1	20.5	11.2	11.4	27.5
	2003	19.2	13.0	19.5	14.6	12.9	23.9	..	..	..	..	..	..

For sources and notes, see end of table.

Pour les sources et les notes, se reporter à la fin du tableau.

Markets / Marchés	Year / Année	MFN rate - Simple average / Droit NPF - Moyenne simple						MFN rate - Weighted average / Droit NPF - Moyenne pondérée					
		Total of non-agricultural and non-fuel products / Total des produits non-agricoles et non-pétroliers	Ores and metals / Minérais et métaux	Manu-factured products / Produits manu-facturés	Chemical products / Produits chimiques	Machinery and transport equipment / Machines et matériel de transport	Other manu-factured products / Produits manu-facturés divers	Total of non-agricultural and non-fuel products / Total des produits non-agricoles et non-pétroliers	Ores and metals / Minérais et métaux	Manu-factured products / Produits manu-facturés	Chemical products / Produits chimiques	Machinery and transport equipment / Machines et matériel de transport	Other manu-factured products / Produits manu-facturés divers
SITC Rev.2 / CTCI Rév.2		5+6+7+8 +27+28	27+28+68	(5+6+7+8) - 68	5	7	(6+8) - 68	5+6+7+8 +27+28	27+28+68	(5+6+7+8) - 68	5	7	(6+8) - 68
Barbados - Barbade	1996	21.2	19.4	21.2	14.5	18.9	22.7	22.8	21.4	22.8	17.4	24.3	23.6
	1999	17.9	16.2	17.9	11.4	16.4	19.2	22.4	19.1	22.4	14.2	27.8	21.5
	2000	17.9	16.2	17.9	11.4	16.4	19.2	21.6	18.2	21.6	14.3	26.1	21.1
	2001	9.5	5.8	9.6	6.5	8.0	11.3	14.8	8.9	14.8	13.8	11.3	17.9
	2002	9.5	5.8	9.6	6.5	8.0	11.3	14.3	9.6	14.3	14.0	11.2	17.1
	2003	9.5	5.8	9.6	6.5	8.0	11.3	..	..	..	..	..	..
Belarus - Bélarus	1996	12.4	9.9	12.6	6.0	11.9	15.2	10.3	5.0	10.5	7.0	11.1	11.5
	1997	12.9	8.9	13.2	7.0	12.7	15.5	11.0	7.0	11.2	8.6	11.6	12.0
	2002	11.1	8.2	11.2	6.7	10.6	13.1	10.2	8.1	10.4	8.0	10.6	11.2
Belize	1996	21.2	19.6	21.2	14.5	18.8	22.8	18.9	22.8	18.8	12.6	21.0	20.2
	1999	17.8	16.4	17.8	11.1	16.1	19.2	17.1	21.6	16.6	14.2	27.4	14.5
	2001	8.9	4.3	9.0	5.5	7.5	10.9	11.2	15.8	11.2	9.7	10.4	12.3
	2002	8.9	4.3	9.0	5.5	7.5	10.9	11.0	15.0	10.9	9.3	10.2	12.3
	2003	8.9	4.3	9.0	5.5	7.5	10.9	..	..	..	..	..	..
Benin - Bénin	2001	11.8	7.5	12.0	6.3	8.5	15.4	12.3	6.6	12.4	4.8	10.3	16.4
	2002	11.7	7.5	11.9	6.3	8.5	15.3	12.4	7.1	12.5	5.2	11.7	16.5
	2003	11.7	7.3	11.9	6.3	8.6	15.3	..	..	..	..	..	..
Bermuda - Bermudes	2001	19.3	19.9	19.3	20.1	23.9	17.1	26.4	20.2	26.4	1.8	32.4	19.3
Bhutan - Bhoutan	1996	15.5	17.8	15.5	9.2	12.0	19.5	16.7	12.3	16.8	28.8	14.3	19.0
	2002	16.5	17.4	16.5	12.7	11.3	20.0	15.0	16.3	15.0	26.3	11.2	19.2
Bolivia - Bolivie	1993	9.8	10.0	9.8	10.0	9.0	10.0	9.3	10.0	9.3	10.0	8.8	9.9
	1994	10.0	10.0	10.0	10.0	10.0	10.0	9.9	10.0	9.9	10.0	10.0	9.8
	1995	9.7	10.0	9.7	10.0	8.6	10.0	9.4	10.0	9.4	10.0	8.9	9.9
	1996	9.7	10.0	9.7	10.0	8.6	10.0	9.1	10.0	9.1	10.0	8.7	9.7
	1997	9.7	10.0	9.7	10.0	8.6	10.0	9.1	10.0	9.1	10.0	8.7	9.7
	1998	9.7	10.0	9.7	10.0	8.6	10.0	8.9	10.0	8.9	10.0	8.3	9.6
	1999	9.7	10.0	9.7	10.0	8.6	10.0	9.0	10.0	9.0	10.0	8.2	9.8
	2000	9.2	9.9	9.2	9.9	6.7	9.9	8.2	10.0	8.2	9.7	6.4	9.7
	2001	9.2	9.9	9.2	9.9	6.7	9.9	8.6	10.0	8.6	9.7	6.8	9.8
	2002	9.6	10.0	9.6	10.7	7.1	10.2	9.0	10.0	9.0	10.3	6.3	10.6
Bosnia and Herzegovina - Bosnie-Herzégovine	2001	6.4	1.8	6.6	2.8	6.2	8.2	7.8	5.0	7.8	6.5	7.6	8.4
Brazil - Brésil	1989	46.7	22.6	47.6	38.7	44.5	52.0	35.3	12.8	37.1	33.9	40.9	33.7
	1990	34.0	10.7	34.8	24.9	38.5	36.9	26.9	6.9	28.1	21.4	32.9	25.8
	1991	27.6	6.9	28.4	18.4	31.1	30.8	22.2	5.0	23.1	16.3	28.4	20.7
	1992	22.7	5.4	23.4	15.1	26.8	25.0	19.8	3.4	20.7	13.4	25.9	17.4
	1993	15.0	2.9	15.5	11.3	19.6	15.4	15.8	1.6	16.3	10.7	20.4	13.0
	1994	13.7	3.3	14.1	7.9	19.5	14.2	15.5	2.8	15.9	6.9	21.1	12.7
	1995	13.8	6.0	14.2	8.4	16.8	15.2	13.7	5.4	13.9	8.1	16.2	13.9
	1996	14.2	6.3	14.6	8.3	17.7	15.5	17.0	5.8	17.2	8.0	21.6	14.5
	1997	13.9	6.2	14.2	8.5	16.9	15.2	16.1	5.8	16.3	8.4	20.1	13.9
	1998	16.8	9.2	17.1	11.5	19.3	18.2	17.8	9.2	17.9	11.3	20.9	16.5
	1999	16.5	9.1	16.8	11.5	18.4	18.1	15.4	8.6	15.6	11.4	17.2	16.1
	2000	16.3	9.0	16.6	11.4	17.6	18.1	14.7	8.2	14.8	11.0	16.1	15.7
	2001	14.7	8.6	15.0	10.9	12.8	17.4	12.2	7.8	12.3	10.1	12.5	14.4
	2002	14.4	7.5	14.7	9.8	14.8	16.4	11.9	6.8	12.0	8.7	12.8	14.3
	2003	14.0	7.4	14.3	9.7	14.6	15.9	..	..	..	..	..	..

For sources and notes, see end of table.

Pour les sources et les notes, se reporter à la fin du tableau.

Markets / Marchés	Year / Année	MFN rate - Simple average / Droit NPF - Moyenne simple						MFN rate - Weighted average / Droit NPF - Moyenne pondérée					
		Total of non-agricultural and non-fuel products / Total des produits non-agricoles et non-pétroliers	Ores and metals / Minérais et métaux	Manufactured products / Produits manufacturés	Chemical products / Produits chimiques	Machinery and transport equipment / Machines et matériel de transport	Other manufactured products / Produits manufacturés divers	Total of non-agricultural and non-fuel products / Total des produits non-agricoles et non-pétroliers	Ores and metals / Minérais et métaux	Manufactured products / Produits manufacturés	Chemical products / Produits chimiques	Machinery and transport equipment / Machines et matériel de transport	Other manufactured products / Produits manufacturés divers
SITC Rev.2 / CTCI Rév.2		5+6+7+8 +27+28	27+28+68	(5+6+7+8) - 68	5	7	(6+8) - 68	5+6+7+8 +27+28	27+28+68	(5+6+7+8) - 68	5	7	(6+8) - 68
Brunei Darussalam - Brunéi Darussalam	1992	2.5	0.0	2.6	0.6	2.5	3.3	4.4	0.0	4.4	2.3	6.2	2.6
	2001	3.1	0.0	3.2	0.3	9.6	1.6	10.6	0.0	10.7	1.1	19.0	0.9
	2002	3.1	0.0	3.2	0.3	9.6	1.6	10.6	0.0	10.7	1.1	19.0	0.9
Bulgaria - Bulgarie	2001	11.4	3.9	11.7	8.2	7.8	14.5	10.3	1.6	10.9	8.5	7.4	14.9
	2003	9.0	2.7	9.2	7.4	5.8	11.2	..	..	..	..	..	..
Burkina Faso	1993	24.6	20.1	25.0	28.3	17.0	27.0	20.2	10.3	20.3	16.4	21.1	21.8
	2001	11.8	7.5	12.0	6.3	8.5	15.4	11.4	8.0	11.5	5.3	11.2	15.3
	2002	11.7	7.5	11.9	6.3	8.5	15.3	11.5	8.7	11.5	5.0	12.1	15.5
	2003	11.7	7.3	11.9	6.3	8.6	15.3	..	..	..	..	..	..
Burundi	2002	21.8	11.9	22.1	12.3	17.0	27.6	19.9	13.5	20.1	14.8	20.2	23.3
Cambodia - Cambodge	2001	16.2	11.6	16.3	10.7	17.9	17.7	14.6	11.7	14.6	9.6	21.0	13.3
	2002	16.2	11.6	16.3	10.7	17.9	17.7	14.2	8.7	14.2	6.4	19.3	13.4
Cameroon - Cameroun	1994	17.9	15.4	18.1	11.3	14.1	22.1	13.6	11.3	13.8	7.3	15.2	16.3
	1995	17.5	12.1	17.7	10.6	14.0	21.7	13.3	10.8	13.5	8.1	14.9	15.3
	2001	17.3	11.7	17.5	10.6	14.0	21.4	13.2	11.6	13.2	9.6	11.8	16.6
	2002	17.3	11.7	17.5	10.6	14.0	21.4	14.2	11.4	14.2	9.5	13.5	17.6
Canada	1989	10.2	3.8	10.5	8.5	7.3	12.5	7.6	2.3	7.7	8.7	6.4	10.3
	1993	10.0	3.8	10.3	8.4	7.1	12.1	7.5	2.0	7.7	8.8	6.3	10.1
	1995	9.1	3.4	9.3	7.4	6.4	11.2	7.1	2.0	7.2	7.7	6.1	9.2
	1996	7.4	1.4	7.6	4.4	4.9	9.8	5.3	0.8	5.5	5.7	4.4	7.7
	1997	6.9	1.3	7.1	4.2	4.4	9.2	4.9	0.9	5.0	5.4	4.0	7.1
	1998	5.1	0.7	5.2	3.1	2.3	7.2	3.5	0.6	3.5	3.7	2.8	5.1
	1999	4.8	0.7	5.0	2.9	2.2	6.8	3.2	0.6	3.3	3.3	2.6	4.7
	2000	4.7	0.7	4.8	2.8	2.2	6.6	3.1	0.6	3.1	3.2	2.5	4.5
	2001	4.6	0.7	4.7	2.7	2.2	6.4	3.2	0.6	3.2	3.0	2.6	4.5
	2002	4.4	0.7	4.5	2.7	2.2	6.1	3.2	0.7	3.3	2.9	2.8	4.4
	2003	4.3	0.7	4.4	2.6	2.2	5.9	..	..	..	..	..	..
Central African Republic - République centrafricaine	1995	17.5	12.1	17.7	10.6	14.0	21.7	14.6	19.0	14.6	7.8	14.4	18.7
	1997	17.5	12.1	17.7	10.6	14.0	21.7	14.6	16.7	14.6	7.0	14.9	19.3
	2001	17.3	11.7	17.5	10.6	14.0	21.4	15.9	21.0	15.9	9.3	17.1	18.7
	2002	17.3	11.7	17.5	10.6	14.0	21.4	15.7	18.7	15.8	9.3	17.1	18.2
Chad - Tchad	1995	17.5	12.1	17.7	10.6	14.0	21.7	15.1	12.4	15.1	7.5	14.8	17.6
	1997	17.5	12.1	17.7	10.6	14.0	21.7	15.1	12.4	15.1	7.5	14.8	17.6
	2001	17.3	11.7	17.5	10.6	14.0	21.4	11.8	10.3	11.8	7.8	11.5	14.3
	2002	17.3	11.7	17.5	10.6	14.0	21.4	13.0	8.6	13.0	8.3	11.9	15.6
Chile - Chili	1992	11.0	11.0	11.0	11.0	10.9	11.0	10.9	11.0	10.9	11.0	10.9	11.0
	1993	11.0	11.0	11.0	11.0	10.9	11.0	10.9	11.0	10.9	11.0	10.9	11.0
	1994	11.0	11.0	11.0	11.0	10.9	11.0	10.9	11.0	10.9	11.0	10.9	11.0
	1995	11.0	11.0	11.0	11.0	10.9	11.0	10.9	11.0	10.9	11.0	10.9	11.0
	1997	11.0	11.0	11.0	11.0	10.9	11.0	11.0	11.0	11.0	11.0	10.9	11.0
	1998	11.0	11.0	11.0	11.0	10.9	11.0	10.9	11.0	10.9	11.0	10.9	11.0
	1999	10.0	10.0	10.0	10.0	9.9	10.0	9.9	10.0	9.9	10.0	9.9	10.0
	2000	9.0	9.0	9.0	9.0	9.0	9.0	9.0	9.0	9.0	9.0	9.0	9.0
	2001	8.0	8.0	8.0	8.0	8.0	8.0	8.0	8.0	8.0	8.0	8.0	8.0
	2002	7.0	7.0	7.0	7.0	6.9	7.0	6.9	7.0	6.9	7.0	6.9	7.0

For sources and notes, see end of table.   Pour les sources et les notes, se reporter à la fin du tableau.

Markets / Marchés	Year / Année	MFN rate - Simple average / Droit NPF - Moyenne simple						MFN rate - Weighted average / Droit NPF - Moyenne pondérée					
		Total of non-agricultural and non-fuel products / Total des produits non-agricoles et non-pétroliers	Ores and metals / Minérais et métaux	Manu-factured products / Produits manu-facturés	Chemical products / Produits chimiques	Machinery and transport equipment / Machines et matériel de transport	Other manu-factured products / Produits manu-facturés divers	Total of non-agricultural and non-fuel products / Total des produits non-agricoles et non-pétroliers	Ores and metals / Minérais et métaux	Manu-factured products / Produits manu-facturés	Chemical products / Produits chimiques	Machinery and transport equipment / Machines et matériel de transport	Other manu-factured products / Produits manu-facturés divers
SITC Rev.2 / CTCI Rév.2		5+6+7+8 +27+28	27+28+68	(5+6+7+8) - 68	5	7	(6+8) - 68	5+6+7+8 +27+28	27+28+68	(5+6+7+8) - 68	5	7	(6+8) - 68
China - Chine	1992	42.2	17.7	43.0	27.2	32.6	52.5	34.8	7.7	35.6	22.2	34.0	43.5
	1993	39.3	16.8	39.9	26.1	31.3	48.1	32.1	7.4	32.8	24.1	34.1	33.7
	1994	35.2	15.4	35.8	23.3	27.9	43.4	29.8	7.8	30.4	21.5	29.8	34.3
	1996	22.0	7.5	22.5	14.1	19.7	26.7	17.8	5.8	18.2	14.6	16.1	22.6
	1997	16.5	5.3	16.9	11.1	16.2	19.4	14.3	4.8	14.7	12.8	13.2	17.4
	1998	16.5	5.3	16.9	11.1	16.3	19.3	14.2	5.2	14.6	12.9	13.5	17.0
	1999	16.1	5.3	16.5	11.1	16.2	18.6	13.5	5.3	13.8	12.8	12.8	16.0
	2000	15.8	5.3	16.2	11.1	16.2	18.0	13.1	5.2	13.5	13.0	12.8	14.9
	2001	14.7	4.5	15.1	10.2	15.4	16.7	12.4	4.2	12.8	12.5	12.5	13.7
	2003	10.6	3.8	10.8	7.3	10.0	12.4	..	..	..	..	..	..
China, Taiwan Province of - Chine, Taiwan Province de	1989	10.2	4.0	10.4	9.0	11.6	10.5	10.2	4.5	10.5	6.5	12.8	9.1
	1992	6.5	1.7	6.7	4.1	6.8	7.5	6.3	1.8	6.4	3.7	7.8	5.4
	1996	6.3	1.5	6.5	4.0	6.5	7.3	5.3	1.4	5.4	3.3	6.8	4.7
	1999	6.3	1.5	6.5	4.0	6.6	7.4	4.5	1.4	4.6	3.8	4.7	4.7
	2000	6.1	1.5	6.2	3.9	6.0	7.2	2.9	1.4	3.0	3.3	2.5	3.8
	2001	6.0	1.5	6.2	3.9	6.0	7.2	2.9	1.3	3.0	3.5	2.4	3.9
	2002	5.9	1.4	6.1	3.8	5.7	7.0	3.0	1.2	3.1	3.4	2.8	3.6
	2003	5.2	1.1	5.4	3.4	5.1	6.2	..	..	..	..	..	..
Colombia - Colombie	1991	6.3	2.2	6.4	3.4	5.1	8.1	6.0	1.1	6.0	3.9	8.7	4.6
	1992	12.0	6.7	12.2	8.2	10.2	14.5	10.3	7.7	10.4	7.7	11.2	11.8
	1994	12.0	6.7	12.2	8.1	10.3	14.4	11.4	7.9	11.5	7.7	12.5	12.3
	1995	13.5	7.2	13.8	10.6	12.7	15.4	12.0	5.5	12.1	9.4	12.8	12.9
	1996	11.7	6.4	11.9	7.7	9.8	14.2	10.7	6.0	10.8	7.3	11.5	12.2
	1997	11.7	6.4	11.9	7.7	9.8	14.2	10.9	6.0	10.9	7.6	11.7	12.2
	1999	11.8	6.4	12.0	7.8	9.9	14.3	9.9	6.4	10.0	7.9	9.4	12.6
	2000	11.8	6.4	12.0	7.8	9.9	14.3	10.4	6.6	10.5	7.9	10.7	12.5
	2001	11.8	6.4	12.0	7.8	9.9	14.3	10.2	7.0	10.3	8.1	9.8	12.8
	2002	11.8	6.3	12.0	7.8	9.9	14.3	10.8	6.9	10.8	8.3	10.9	12.9
Congo	1994	17.4	13.6	17.6	10.9	14.1	21.4	14.6	16.1	14.6	9.6	14.4	17.3
	1997	15.3	10.9	15.5	6.6	13.0	19.7	17.0	10.8	17.0	15.9	13.5	20.1
	2001	17.3	11.7	17.5	10.6	14.0	21.4	15.9	11.8	15.9	11.2	13.4	22.3
	2002	17.3	11.7	17.5	10.6	14.0	21.4	16.2	10.7	16.3	11.2	14.4	21.0
Costa Rica	1995	9.5	5.8	9.6	5.8	4.6	12.9	8.3	6.1	8.3	6.4	7.7	9.9
	1999	5.4	1.3	5.5	1.3	2.5	8.3	4.5	2.5	4.5	3.6	2.6	7.1
	2000	4.5	1.4	4.7	1.2	2.1	6.9	3.8	1.6	3.8	2.9	1.9	6.6
	2001	4.5	1.3	4.6	1.2	2.0	6.8	3.7	2.0	3.7	3.0	1.6	6.8
	2002	4.8	1.0	4.9	1.3	2.2	7.3	4.1	1.4	4.1	3.5	2.0	7.8
Côte d'Ivoire	1993	21.7	16.4	21.8	13.0	19.3	25.8	22.4	16.9	22.5	8.6	28.9	23.7
	1996	18.6	12.8	18.8	12.4	12.0	23.8	14.1	14.0	14.1	9.7	12.0	19.7
	2001	11.8	7.5	12.0	6.3	8.5	15.4	10.7	7.7	10.7	5.3	10.2	14.4
	2002	11.7	7.5	11.9	6.3	8.5	15.3	10.5	7.6	10.6	5.5	10.2	14.2
	2003	11.7	7.3	11.9	6.3	8.6	15.3	..	..	..	..	..	..
Croatia - Croatie	2001	10.1	5.6	10.2	7.0	8.8	11.9	11.0	5.9	11.1	10.1	9.8	12.7
Cuba	1993	12.8	5.6	13.1	11.1	11.0	14.6	12.9	5.1	12.9	10.0	12.3	14.7
	1997	11.1	5.4	11.3	9.3	9.8	12.7	10.3	3.7	10.3	7.2	9.9	11.8
	2002	11.2	5.3	11.4	9.1	9.9	12.8	10.9	3.9	10.9	7.1	11.2	12.1
	2003	11.3	5.1	11.5	9.0	9.9	13.0	..	..	..	..	..	..
Cyprus - Chypre	2002	4.2	1.6	4.3	4.7	2.3	5.0	5.0	4.8	5.0	2.8	5.6	5.0
Czech Republic - République tchèque	1996	5.9	1.6	6.1	5.3	5.6	6.6	6.1	1.9	6.2	5.0	6.2	6.7
	1999	5.2	2.2	5.3	4.5	5.8	5.5	5.8	2.8	5.8	4.0	6.2	6.0
	2002	4.5	1.2	4.6	4.1	3.8	5.1	4.5	1.6	4.5	3.7	4.1	5.4
	2003	4.5	1.2	4.6	4.1	3.8	5.1	..	..	..	..	..	..

For sources and notes, see end of table.

Pour les sources et les notes, se reporter à la fin du tableau.

Markets / Marchés	Year / Année	MFN rate - Simple average / Droit NPF - Moyenne simple						MFN rate - Weighted average / Droit NPF - Moyenne pondérée					
		Total of non-agricultural and non-fuel products / Total des produits non-agricoles et non-pétroliers	of which: / dont :					Total of non-agricultural and non-fuel products / Total des produits non-agricoles et non-pétroliers	of which: / dont :				
			Ores and metals / Minérais et métaux	Manu-factured products / Produits manu-facturés	Of which: / dont :				Ores and metals / Minérais et métaux	Manu-factured products / Produits manu-facturés	Of which: / dont :		
					Chemical products / Produits chimiques	Machinery and transport equipment / Machines et matériel de transport	Other manu-factured products / Produits manu-facturés divers				Chemical products / Produits chimiques	Machinery and transport equipment / Machines et matériel de transport	Other manu-factured products / Produits manu-facturés divers
SITC Rev.2 / CTCI Rév.2		5+6+7+8 +27+28	27+28+68	(5+6+7+8) - 68	5	7	(6+8) - 68	5+6+7+8 +27+28	27+28+68	(5+6+7+8) - 68	5	7	(6+8) - 68
Czechoslovakia (former) - Tchécoslovaquie (anc.)	1992	8.9	1.6	9.2	5.2	11.4	9.7	8.7	2.2	8.8	5.0	9.3	9.0
Dem. Rep. of the Congo - Rép. dém. du Congo	2003	11.8	8.8	11.9	7.7	8.3	14.9	..	..	..	..	..	..
Dominica - Dominique	1996	20.3	17.1	20.3	14.5	18.5	21.6	18.7	22.3	18.7	14.1	23.5	18.4
	1999	16.9	13.8	16.9	11.3	16.0	18.0	16.4	16.9	16.4	11.6	22.0	15.0
	2000	13.2	13.7	13.2	8.7	12.4	14.7	15.0	14.4	15.0	9.0	21.8	12.6
	2001	8.0	3.7	8.1	6.1	5.8	9.7	11.2	5.2	11.2	10.1	10.1	12.3
	2002	8.0	3.7	8.1	6.2	5.8	9.7	12.4	5.0	12.5	11.0	10.7	14.4
	2003	8.0	3.7	8.1	6.2	5.8	9.7	..	..	..	..	..	..
Dominican Republic - République dominicaine	1997	14.1	7.6	14.4	8.3	10.2	18.2	14.3	9.5	14.3	8.7	14.9	16.1
	2000	17.5	9.2	17.9	9.9	13.1	22.6	18.2	11.2	18.3	9.9	18.2	21.1
	2001	7.7	4.5	7.8	4.3	5.5	10.1	8.6	5.1	8.7	4.0	8.6	11.0
	2002	7.8	4.5	7.9	4.3	5.4	10.1	8.6	5.2	8.6	3.9	8.6	11.0
	2003	7.8	4.5	7.9	4.3	5.4	10.1	..	..	..	..	..	..
Ecuador - Equateur	1993	9.4	3.7	9.6	6.0	6.7	12.1	8.3	4.3	8.3	4.7	9.8	7.7
	1994	12.0	6.5	12.2	7.5	9.5	15.0	11.6	7.3	11.7	6.9	13.7	10.9
	1995	12.6	6.5	12.9	9.4	10.9	14.9	11.3	5.7	11.3	6.5	12.9	11.9
	1996	11.5	5.9	11.7	7.1	8.9	14.4	11.3	5.7	11.3	5.8	14.2	11.4
	1997	11.5	5.9	11.7	7.1	8.9	14.4	11.1	5.6	11.1	6.0	13.0	11.9
	1998	11.5	5.9	11.7	7.1	9.0	14.4	10.8	5.8	10.8	6.2	12.2	11.9
	1999	13.4	7.9	13.6	8.5	10.8	16.5	11.3	7.5	11.3	7.5	12.0	13.8
	2002	11.4	5.9	11.6	7.2	8.7	14.4	10.8	6.2	10.8	7.0	10.9	12.8
Egypt - Egypte	1995	28.4	13.8	28.9	14.1	19.1	37.9	21.9	11.2	22.2	11.4	27.2	22.9
	1998	21.7	12.8	22.1	13.0	12.6	28.4	17.2	9.6	17.5	10.9	19.4	18.9
	2002	19.9	12.6	20.3	12.7	14.0	26.2	16.5	10.9	16.7	10.9	15.8	21.1
El Salvador	1995	9.5	5.9	9.6	6.0	4.0	13.0	8.7	6.0	8.7	7.6	7.1	11.1
	1997	7.4	1.7	7.6	1.9	2.8	11.5	6.7	2.8	6.7	5.2	5.4	9.3
	1998	3.8	1.7	3.9	1.8	2.7	5.1	5.5	3.0	5.6	5.5	4.7	6.5
	2000	6.6	1.1	6.7	1.4	2.2	10.5	5.4	1.6	5.4	4.5	3.5	8.1
	2001	6.6	1.1	6.8	1.4	2.2	10.5	5.9	1.7	6.0	4.6	3.9	8.5
	2002	6.3	1.0	6.5	1.5	2.2	10.0	10.3	1.1	10.4	4.7	2.8	15.3
Equatorial Guinea - Guinée équatoriale	1998	17.4	12.0	17.6	10.3	13.8	21.6	13.5	7.1	13.6	15.0	11.7	17.6
	2001	17.3	11.7	17.5	10.6	14.0	21.4	12.5	9.9	12.6	14.9	10.4	17.0
	2002	17.3	11.7	17.5	10.6	14.0	21.4	13.9	8.2	14.0	15.7	12.5	16.9
Estonia - Estonie	1995	0.1	0.0	0.1	0.0	0.1	0.1	0.5	0.0	0.5	0.0	1.3	0.0
	2000	0.1	0.0	0.1	0.4	0.0	0.0	0.0	0.0	0.0	0.1	0.0	0.0
	2001	0.1	0.0	0.1	0.4	0.0	0.0	0.0	0.0	0.0	0.1	0.0	0.0
	2002	0.1	0.0	0.1	0.4	0.0	0.0	0.0	0.0	0.0	0.1	0.0	0.0
	2003	0.1	0.0	0.1	0.4	0.0	0.0	..	..	..	..	..	..
Ethiopia - Ethiopie	1995	27.4	13.6	27.9	16.4	14.6	37.1	18.0	11.0	18.0	9.5	19.3	21.2
	2001	18.6	10.0	18.9	10.8	12.4	24.5	15.1	9.1	15.2	8.8	13.9	19.2
	2002	18.6	10.0	18.9	10.8	12.4	24.5	15.6	8.6	15.7	7.9	14.8	20.0

For sources and notes, see end of table.　　　　Pour les sources et les notes, se reporter à la fin du tableau.

Markets / Marchés	Year / Année	MFN rate - Simple average / Droit NPF - Moyenne simple						MFN rate - Weighted average / Droit NPF - Moyenne pondérée					
		Total of non-agricultural and non-fuel products / Total des produits non-agricoles et non-pétroliers	Ores and metals / Minérais et métaux	Manufactured products / Produits manufacturés	Chemical products / Produits chimiques	Machinery and transport equipment / Machines et matériel de transport	Other manufactured products / Produits manufacturés divers	Total of non-agricultural and non-fuel products / Total des produits non-agricoles et non-pétroliers	Ores and metals / Minérais et métaux	Manufactured products / Produits manufacturés	Chemical products / Produits chimiques	Machinery and transport equipment / Machines et matériel de transport	Other manufactured products / Produits manufacturés divers
SITC Rev.2 / CTCI Rév.2		5+6+7+8 +27+28	27+28+68	(5+6+7+8) - 68	5	7	(6+8) - 68	5+6+7+8 +27+28	27+28+68	(5+6+7+8) - 68	5	7	(6+8) - 68
European Union (15) - Union européenne (15)	1988	5.8	2.5	6.0	7.6	4.9	5.9	5.4	1.7	5.7	7.8	5.7	5.0
	1989	5.8	2.5	6.0	7.6	4.9	5.9	5.3	1.7	5.6	7.7	5.6	5.0
	1990	8.1	2.5	8.4	7.5	5.0	10.0	7.1	1.7	7.4	7.4	5.9	8.9
	1991	6.7	2.5	6.9	7.5	5.0	7.4	6.4	1.7	6.6	7.6	5.9	7.3
	1992	6.8	2.5	7.0	7.7	5.1	7.5	6.8	1.7	7.0	7.7	6.3	7.5
	1993	6.7	2.5	7.0	7.5	5.1	7.5	6.7	1.7	6.9	7.5	6.0	7.6
	1994	6.7	2.5	6.9	7.5	5.0	7.4	6.5	1.9	6.7	7.6	5.9	7.3
	1995	6.1	2.3	6.3	6.6	4.5	6.9	6.1	2.0	6.2	5.9	5.8	6.8
	1996	5.2	2.0	5.4	5.0	3.5	6.2	4.8	1.8	5.0	4.0	4.2	6.0
	1997	5.3	1.9	5.5	5.7	3.5	6.2	4.8	1.8	5.0	4.7	4.2	6.0
	1998	4.8	1.8	4.9	4.8	2.8	5.8	4.0	1.9	4.1	3.7	2.9	5.6
	1999	4.4	1.6	4.5	4.4	2.3	5.4	3.6	1.9	3.6	3.1	2.6	5.2
	2000	4.2	1.6	4.3	4.1	2.3	5.2	3.3	1.8	3.3	2.8	2.3	4.8
	2001	4.3	1.6	4.4	4.9	2.3	5.0	3.4	1.9	3.5	3.5	2.4	4.8
	2002	4.4	1.6	4.6	4.7	2.3	5.4	3.6	1.9	3.7	3.2	2.6	5.2
Gabon	1995	17.5	12.1	17.7	10.6	14.0	21.7	15.1	16.5	15.2	9.9	14.8	17.8
	1998	17.4	12.0	17.6	10.3	13.8	21.6	13.4	15.8	13.5	8.5	11.8	18.8
	2001	17.3	11.7	17.5	10.6	14.0	21.4	13.6	20.0	13.6	10.2	12.2	18.2
	2002	17.3	11.7	17.5	10.6	14.0	21.4	13.5	17.7	13.5	10.3	12.2	18.0
Georgia - Géorgie	1999	10.3	11.8	10.2	11.7	5.8	11.4	8.3	10.6	8.3	6.9	6.7	10.9
Ghana	1993	14.0	10.9	14.1	11.1	10.1	16.7	9.2	9.8	9.2	9.7	8.4	10.4
	2000	13.8	11.7	13.9	11.7	5.3	17.9	8.9	10.2	8.9	11.2	5.2	13.3
Grenada - Grenade	1996	20.4	16.5	20.4	14.5	19.2	21.6	21.5	14.3	21.6	18.4	28.0	19.4
	1999	17.0	13.3	17.0	11.4	16.8	18.0	16.7	10.5	16.8	14.2	21.2	15.4
	2001	17.0	13.3	17.1	11.5	16.8	17.9	16.2	12.4	16.3	14.3	20.3	15.1
	2002	9.0	5.6	9.1	6.3	7.8	10.4	11.3	7.7	11.3	13.2	9.8	12.0
	2003	9.0	5.6	9.1	6.3	7.8	10.4	..	..	..	..	..	..
Guatemala	1995	9.5	5.9	9.6	6.0	4.2	12.9	8.0	6.4	8.0	6.3	7.4	10.0
	1997	7.9	2.5	8.0	2.6	3.6	11.7	6.5	3.2	6.5	4.4	5.7	9.0
	1998	7.8	1.4	8.0	1.6	2.8	12.4	6.0	2.9	6.0	3.8	5.5	7.9
	2000	6.6	1.1	6.8	1.4	2.5	10.4	5.1	2.0	5.1	3.4	4.7	6.8
	2001	6.3	1.1	6.4	1.4	2.5	9.8	5.8	2.1	5.8	3.7	5.6	7.5
	2002	5.6	1.0	5.7	1.5	2.5	8.6	5.7	2.0	5.7	3.6	5.4	7.5
Guinea-Bissau - Guinée-Bissau	2001	11.8	7.5	12.0	6.3	8.5	15.4	12.4	8.7	12.4	5.7	10.0	15.9
	2002	11.7	7.5	11.9	6.3	8.5	15.3	12.6	9.4	12.6	8.7	10.9	16.1
	2003	11.7	7.3	11.9	6.3	8.6	15.3	..	..	..	..	..	..
Guyana	1996	21.4	19.0	21.4	15.6	18.9	22.9	18.4	21.2	18.4	13.9	20.4	18.9
	1999	18.0	15.8	18.0	12.5	16.4	19.3	15.6	16.5	15.6	10.7	19.7	14.7
	2000	18.0	15.8	18.0	12.5	16.4	19.2	16.1	16.2	16.1	12.1	20.3	14.9
	2001	9.2	5.7	9.3	6.3	7.7	11.0	9.7	6.6	9.8	8.7	9.6	10.5
	2002	9.2	5.7	9.3	6.3	7.7	11.0	10.0	9.2	10.0	9.1	9.7	10.8
	2003	9.2	5.7	9.3	6.3	7.7	11.0	..	..	..	..	..	..
Honduras	1995	9.4	5.8	9.5	5.7	4.0	12.9	7.5	6.6	7.5	5.0	4.7	12.0
	1999	6.9	2.0	7.0	2.3	3.4	10.2	5.9	3.3	5.9	3.9	4.1	9.2
	2000	6.7	2.0	6.8	2.2	3.5	9.9	6.0	3.8	6.0	2.4	8.0	8.5
	2001	6.4	2.0	6.5	2.1	3.3	9.4	5.4	3.9	5.4	2.2	8.0	7.6
	2002	5.2	1.0	5.4	1.3	2.4	8.0	..	..	..	..	..	..
Hungary - Hongrie	1991	11.5	3.9	11.7	9.6	16.4	10.7	11.7	4.1	11.9	6.8	15.2	10.5
	1993	9.7	4.0	9.9	8.5	10.7	10.1	10.4	2.8	10.4	6.3	12.9	9.7
	1996	8.7	3.2	8.8	7.1	9.9	9.1	9.1	2.4	9.2	6.1	11.1	8.7
	1997	8.3	3.0	8.4	6.6	9.6	8.6	8.7	2.6	8.7	5.6	9.8	8.3
	2002	7.0	2.5	7.1	5.2	8.8	7.1	8.0	2.8	8.0	4.2	9.0	7.3

For sources and notes, see end of table.

Pour les sources et les notes, se reporter à la fin du tableau.

Markets / Marchés	Year / Année	MFN rate - Simple average / Droit NPF - Moyenne simple						MFN rate - Weighted average / Droit NPF - Moyenne pondérée					
		Total of non-agricultural and non-fuel products / Total des produits non-agricoles et non-pétroliers	of which: / dont :					Total of non-agricultural and non-fuel products / Total des produits non-agricoles et non-pétroliers	of which: / dont :				
			Ores and metals / Minérais et métaux	Manu-factured products / Produits manu-facturés	Of which: / dont :				Ores and metals / Minérais et métaux	Manu-factured products / Produits manu-facturés	Of which: / dont :		
					Chemical products / Produits chimiques	Machinery and transport equipment / Machines et matériel de transport	Other manu-factured products / Produits manu-facturés divers				Chemical products / Produits chimiques	Machinery and transport equipment / Machines et matériel de transport	Other manu-factured products / Produits manu-facturés divers
SITC Rev.2 / CTCI Rév.2		5+6+7+8 +27+28	27+28+68	(5+6+7+8) - 68	5	7	(6+8) - 68	5+6+7+8 +27+28	27+28+68	(5+6+7+8) - 68	5	7	(6+8) - 68
Iceland - Islande	1993	3.4	0.0	3.5	0.8	3.9	4.3	4.9	0.0	5.1	3.4	4.6	5.8
	1996	2.5	0.0	2.6	0.7	1.3	3.7	2.8	0.0	2.8	3.2	0.7	5.1
	2001	2.5	0.0	2.6	1.0	1.3	3.8	2.9	0.0	3.1	3.3	0.8	5.4
	2003	2.5	0.0	2.5	0.7	1.3	3.7	..	..	..	..	..	..
India - Inde	1990	83.0	67.8	83.7	77.5	75.8	89.0	70.5	74.1	70.8	78.7	74.0	64.0
	1992	59.1	55.4	59.4	62.0	51.3	61.6	41.5	25.8	44.2	60.0	51.6	29.8
	1997	30.8	24.0	31.1	29.7	26.1	33.6	21.0	25.2	21.1	25.2	21.4	18.6
	1999	33.7	27.1	34.0	34.5	29.2	35.8	31.1	28.1	31.6	28.7	26.9	36.1
	2001	31.3	26.4	31.6	34.1	28.2	32.1	28.0	25.1	28.4	30.3	22.8	31.7
Indonesia - Indonésie	1989	22.5	7.1	23.1	9.4	18.1	30.0	14.7	4.2	15.3	6.3	19.3	15.6
	1990	18.6	6.9	19.0	9.4	16.9	23.3	15.1	3.9	15.6	7.1	19.5	13.7
	1993	17.9	6.9	18.3	8.9	16.1	22.5	14.0	4.2	14.3	8.5	16.3	14.2
	1995	15.6	6.4	16.0	7.5	13.1	20.1	12.6	3.6	12.9	6.7	15.8	11.6
	1996	11.9	5.3	12.2	7.1	8.4	15.5	9.0	2.9	9.2	8.1	9.3	9.8
	1999	10.8	5.0	11.0	6.8	8.1	13.7	7.8	3.0	8.0	6.9	7.6	9.6
	2000	8.7	4.9	8.9	5.9	5.4	11.4	6.5	2.9	6.6	5.5	6.1	8.5
	2001	6.8	4.3	6.9	4.9	4.6	8.6	5.3	2.5	5.4	4.2	5.3	6.8
	2002	6.8	4.3	7.0	4.9	4.7	8.6	6.0	2.9	6.1	5.4	5.2	8.1
Iran, Islamic Rep. of - Iran, Rép. islamique d'	2000	7.3	2.8	7.5	1.6	6.2	10.1	3.8	1.6	3.8	0.9	5.0	3.8
Israel - Israël	1993	8.4	1.0	8.7	3.4	5.1	11.9	5.4	2.0	5.4	5.2	4.7	6.0
Jamaica - Jamaïque	1996	20.1	16.4	20.1	14.6	17.9	21.5	20.8	17.2	20.9	16.9	22.3	20.9
	1999	16.7	13.2	16.7	11.5	15.4	17.9	18.4	14.7	18.4	14.1	21.2	18.1
	2000	5.4	1.4	5.5	1.9	3.8	7.5	9.9	1.1	9.9	6.6	10.5	10.7
	2001	5.4	1.4	5.5	1.9	3.8	7.5	9.3	0.7	9.3	6.0	9.1	10.8
	2002	5.4	1.4	5.5	1.9	3.8	7.5	9.3	0.7	9.3	6.0	9.1	10.8
	2003	5.4	1.4	5.5	1.9	3.8	7.5	..	..	..	..	..	..
Japan - Japon	1988	4.8	4.1	4.8	4.8	1.9	6.0	4.1	1.6	4.2	4.8	1.2	5.6
	1989	4.5	2.1	4.7	4.5	1.8	5.8	3.5	0.7	3.9	4.2	1.0	5.3
	1990	3.8	1.9	3.9	4.4	0.2	5.1	2.8	0.6	3.0	3.9	0.1	4.7
	1991	3.7	1.9	3.8	4.3	0.1	5.1	2.9	0.7	3.2	3.7	0.1	5.0
	1992	3.7	1.9	3.8	4.3	0.1	5.1	3.1	0.6	3.4	3.6	0.1	5.6
	1993	3.7	1.9	3.8	4.3	0.1	5.1	3.3	0.6	3.5	3.7	0.1	5.8
	1994	3.7	1.9	3.8	4.3	0.1	5.1	3.2	0.7	3.4	3.7	0.1	5.8
	1995	3.5	1.9	3.6	3.7	0.0	5.0	2.8	0.5	3.0	2.9	0.0	5.6
	1996	3.3	1.7	3.4	3.3	0.1	4.8	2.6	0.3	2.8	2.5	0.1	5.4
	1997	3.1	1.6	3.3	3.2	0.1	4.5	2.4	0.4	2.6	2.3	0.1	5.0
	1998	3.0	1.4	3.1	3.1	0.1	4.4	2.2	0.3	2.4	2.2	0.1	4.8
	1999	2.9	1.3	3.0	2.9	0.1	4.2	2.1	0.4	2.3	1.9	0.1	4.7
	2000	2.8	1.3	2.9	2.9	0.1	4.0	2.0	0.5	2.1	1.8	0.1	4.5
	2001	2.7	1.3	2.8	2.9	0.1	3.9	2.1	0.3	2.2	1.9	0.1	4.5
	2002	2.6	1.3	2.7	2.8	0.1	3.8	1.9	0.4	2.0	1.8	0.1	4.3
	2003	3.7	1.9	3.8	3.8	0.1	5.4	..	..	..	..	..	..
Jordan - Jordanie	2000	21.8	16.0	22.1	18.0	14.4	26.6	19.8	14.3	19.8	13.9	18.7	24.2
	2001	14.0	11.0	14.2	7.5	11.5	17.6	12.8	9.3	12.8	7.3	12.9	15.1
	2002	14.1	11.0	14.2	7.5	11.5	17.7	13.0	8.7	13.1	7.7	12.9	15.6
	2003	12.0	6.6	12.2	2.7	10.4	16.4	..	..	..	..	..	..
Kazakhstan	1996	9.2	8.5	9.3	3.7	1.1	14.5	..	..	..	..	..	..

For sources and notes, see end of table.

Pour les sources et les notes, se reporter à la fin du tableau.

Markets / Marchés	Year / Année	MFN rate - Simple average / Droit NPF - Moyenne simple						MFN rate - Weighted average / Droit NPF - Moyenne pondérée					
		Total of non-agricultural and non-fuel products / Total des produits non-agricoles et non-pétroliers	Ores and metals / Minérais et métaux	Manu-factured products / Produits manu-facturés	Chemical products / Produits chimiques	Machinery and transport equipment / Machines et matériel de transport	Other manu-factured products / Produits manu-facturés divers	Total of non-agricultural and non-fuel products / Total des produits non-agricoles et non-pétroliers	Ores and metals / Minérais et métaux	Manu-factured products / Produits manu-facturés	Chemical products / Produits chimiques	Machinery and transport equipment / Machines et matériel de transport	Other manu-factured products / Produits manu-facturés divers
SITC Rev.2 / CTCI Rév.2		5+6+7+8 +27+28	27+28+68	(5+6+7+8) - 68	5	7	(6+8) - 68	5+6+7+8 +27+28	27+28+68	(5+6+7+8) - 68	5	7	(6+8) - 68
Kenya	1994	34.4	28.3	34.6	30.0	25.5	39.8	23.7	26.3	23.7	18.1	24.4	28.1
	2000	17.7	12.7	17.9	11.7	13.4	23.1	12.9	7.7	12.9	7.1	12.3	19.0
	2001	18.9	12.0	19.2	10.9	11.8	25.2	12.5	4.5	12.5	6.3	11.2	19.4
Korea, Republic of - Corée, République de	1988	18.2	13.4	18.6	18.6	18.2	18.7	16.1	8.5	17.0	17.3	16.4	17.7
	1989	14.3	7.4	14.6	14.3	14.8	14.7	12.5	4.5	13.5	12.4	14.4	13.0
	1990	12.3	7.0	12.6	12.4	12.6	12.7	10.9	4.7	11.4	11.4	11.5	11.3
	1992	10.5	6.0	10.8	10.6	10.7	10.8	9.4	4.4	9.8	10.1	9.7	9.8
	1995	7.5	4.5	7.7	7.8	7.7	7.7	7.1	3.7	7.3	7.5	7.4	7.2
	1996	8.3	4.4	8.5	11.8	7.6	7.7	7.3	3.6	7.5	9.6	7.3	7.2
	1999	7.8	4.3	8.0	7.5	7.2	8.4	5.9	2.9	6.2	7.1	5.5	7.0
	2002	7.9	4.2	8.0	10.9	5.9	7.8	4.8	2.8	5.0	8.5	3.3	6.3
Kyrgyzstan - Kirghizistan	2002	8.4	7.0	8.5	7.6	7.0	9.4	7.1	5.4	7.1	4.8	6.9	8.8
Lao People's Dem. Rep. - Rép. dém. populaire lao	2000	7.9	5.8	8.0	6.3	7.2	8.9	12.6	5.0	12.6	9.2	16.6	8.4
	2001	8.0	5.9	8.1	6.3	7.5	8.9	11.9	5.0	12.0	10.6	14.8	8.4
Latvia - Lettonie	1996	2.6	0.5	2.7	1.1	1.6	3.7	2.6	0.5	2.6	1.8	0.9	4.2
	1997	3.5	0.5	3.6	1.1	1.4	5.5	2.8	0.5	2.8	1.9	0.9	4.9
	2001	2.1	0.5	2.2	0.8	0.4	3.4	1.5	0.5	1.5	0.6	0.1	3.2
Lebanon - Liban	1999	9.8	4.1	10.0	4.7	7.7	12.8	12.6	4.6	12.7	6.7	13.5	14.4
	2000	13.6	6.5	13.9	7.4	11.5	17.2	16.0	6.4	16.2	10.6	15.7	18.7
	2001	4.8	2.0	4.9	2.3	3.8	6.2	6.7	2.1	6.8	5.6	5.3	8.2
	2002	4.1	1.9	4.2	2.3	3.6	5.1	6.0	4.0	6.1	5.8	5.1	7.0
Libyan Arab Jamahiriya - Jamahiriya arabe libyenne	1996	18.6	8.3	18.8	6.9	21.3	22.1	25.1	3.4	25.6	10.2	35.0	17.9
	2002	16.8	7.7	17.0	6.5	19.3	19.9	28.6	7.3	28.7	8.2	39.1	16.1
Lithuania - Lituanie	1995	2.8	0.0	2.9	0.7	0.5	4.5	2.0	0.0	2.1	0.4	0.7	4.0
	1997	2.7	0.0	2.8	0.6	0.4	4.5	2.0	0.0	2.0	0.7	0.6	4.3
	2002	2.5	0.0	2.6	0.5	0.4	4.3	1.9	0.0	1.9	0.5	0.6	4.2
	2003	2.4	0.0	2.5	0.5	0.4	4.1	..	..	..	..	..	..
Macedonia, TFYR - Macédoine, LERY	2001	13.6	7.6	13.8	7.3	11.5	17.1	12.9	8.4	13.0	10.8	11.6	15.5
Madagascar	1995	7.3	2.1	7.5	0.9	7.7	9.7	6.3	0.7	6.3	0.8	8.9	6.3
	2001	4.6	1.5	4.7	0.6	4.5	6.3	4.4	0.7	4.4	0.9	5.4	5.1
Malawi	1994	31.8	15.4	32.7	25.0	26.8	36.8	26.3	10.9	26.6	13.4	26.7	34.0
	1996	27.4	14.8	28.0	20.1	23.2	32.7	19.4	13.3	19.5	6.8	19.9	31.1
	1997	25.7	13.9	26.2	19.8	22.1	30.1	21.0	4.1	21.2	11.9	20.1	27.3
	1998	20.3	10.4	20.6	11.1	17.2	25.3	16.4	2.4	16.6	8.2	14.8	23.3
	2001	12.9	8.0	13.1	6.1	9.4	17.0	11.6	5.7	11.7	5.5	11.8	14.5
Malaysia - Malaisie	1988	14.1	5.9	14.5	5.5	11.1	18.9	10.8	4.8	11.0	4.7	10.9	13.6
	1991	14.3	6.0	14.6	6.9	10.4	19.0	10.9	5.7	11.0	9.9	10.3	13.2
	1993	11.8	5.4	12.1	6.0	9.2	15.4	9.3	5.5	9.4	9.3	8.9	10.9
	1996	9.0	2.4	9.3	2.7	5.9	13.0	5.5	4.4	5.5	4.5	4.9	8.1
	1997	9.4	2.4	9.7	3.7	6.5	13.2	5.7	4.4	5.8	4.8	5.2	8.1
	2001	9.3	2.4	9.6	3.0	7.0	12.9	5.2	4.3	5.2	4.4	4.3	9.2
	2002	9.3	2.4	9.6	3.0	7.0	12.9	5.2	4.6	5.3	4.5	4.4	9.0
Maldives	2000	20.6	24.3	20.4	14.7	23.9	21.1	21.4	19.2	21.5	19.8	23.8	19.9
	2001	20.6	24.3	20.4	14.7	23.9	21.1	21.4	18.3	21.5	20.5	23.8	19.9
	2002	20.6	24.2	20.4	14.7	23.9	21.1	21.6	18.1	21.7	20.1	23.4	20.7
	2003	20.6	24.3	20.4	14.7	23.9	21.2	..	..	..	..	..	..
Mali	1995	14.8	16.9	14.7	3.3	8.4	21.2	8.6	12.0	8.5	2.0	9.0	11.7
	2001	11.8	7.5	12.0	6.3	8.5	15.4	10.6	9.0	10.7	5.2	9.3	15.2
	2002	11.7	7.5	11.9	6.3	8.5	15.3	10.6	9.0	10.7	5.2	9.3	15.2
	2003	11.7	7.3	11.9	6.3	8.6	15.3	..	..	..	..	..	..

For sources and notes, see end of table.

Pour les sources et les notes, se reporter à la fin du tableau.

Markets / Marchés	Year / Année	MFN rate - Simple average / Droit NPF - Moyenne simple						MFN rate - Weighted average / Droit NPF - Moyenne pondérée					
		Total of non-agricultural and non-fuel products / Total des produits non-agricoles et non-pétroliers	Ores and metals / Minérais et métaux	Manufactured products / Produits manufacturés	Chemical products / Produits chimiques	Machinery and transport equipment / Machines et matériel de transport	Other manufactured products / Produits manufacturés divers	Total of non-agricultural and non-fuel products / Total des produits non-agricoles et non-pétroliers	Ores and metals / Minérais et métaux	Manufactured products / Produits manufacturés	Chemical products / Produits chimiques	Machinery and transport equipment / Machines et matériel de transport	Other manufactured products / Produits manufacturés divers
SITC Rev.2 / CTCI Rév.2		5+6+7+8 +27+28	27+28+68	(5+6+7+8) - 68	5	7	(6+8) - 68	5+6+7+8 +27+28	27+28+68	(5+6+7+8) - 68	5	7	(6+8) - 68
Malta - Malte	1997	7.9	7.9	7.9	7.3	7.2	8.3	9.3	4.6	9.3	4.4	10.9	7.8
	2000	7.8	7.9	7.8	7.3	7.1	8.4	10.3	4.5	10.3	4.2	11.7	8.0
	2002	6.2	2.5	6.3	6.5	4.7	6.9	4.4	5.5	4.4	4.7	3.6	7.2
	2003	6.2	2.5	6.3	6.5	4.7	6.9	..	..	..	..	..	..
Mauritania - Mauritanie	2001	10.5	5.6	10.7	4.9	8.3	13.7	9.8	5.1	9.9	9.4	8.9	12.1
Mauritius - Maurice	1995	31.7	15.9	32.2	22.0	31.5	36.1	23.0	16.4	23.1	20.6	38.6	17.0
	1997	30.6	16.1	31.1	22.0	30.7	34.5	19.0	12.3	19.1	19.8	25.5	15.1
	1998	30.6	22.6	31.1	24.9	30.0	33.7	27.0	23.8	27.1	36.6	27.9	25.1
	2002	18.6	0.9	19.2	6.1	14.2	26.0	14.2	2.1	14.4	14.1	13.5	14.9
Mexico - Mexique	1991	13.7	10.0	13.9	11.2	13.7	14.9	12.9	8.1	13.0	9.8	13.7	13.3
	1995	13.1	9.8	13.2	10.8	11.3	14.8	11.7	8.8	11.8	9.5	11.1	13.6
	1997	13.9	9.6	14.1	9.9	11.1	16.8	12.4	8.3	12.4	8.8	11.3	15.4
	1998	13.8	9.4	14.0	9.6	10.9	16.8	12.1	8.8	12.2	8.7	10.8	15.4
	1999	17.0	12.4	17.2	12.3	14.3	20.2	15.1	12.0	15.2	11.5	14.0	18.3
	2000	17.0	12.4	17.2	12.3	14.1	20.1	14.6	11.9	14.6	11.4	13.2	18.1
	2001	17.0	12.4	17.2	12.3	14.0	20.1	14.5	12.2	14.5	11.6	12.9	18.3
	2002	17.1	12.4	17.3	12.6	14.0	20.3	14.5	12.3	14.6	11.9	12.8	18.6
	2003	17.1	12.3	17.3	12.4	14.0	20.4	..	..	..	..	..	..
Moldova, Republic of - Moldova, République de	1996	4.9	2.9	4.9	3.4	1.0	7.0	2.3	1.9	2.3	1.4	1.1	3.6
	2000	4.3	2.0	4.3	3.5	1.5	5.7	2.8	1.8	2.8	1.5	1.3	4.0
	2001	4.1	1.3	4.2	3.4	1.5	5.5	2.9	1.6	2.9	1.7	1.1	4.2
Montserrat	1996	19.8	15.8	19.8	14.5	16.7	21.3	15.4	7.0	15.5	19.8	10.7	18.5
	1999	16.4	12.9	16.4	11.2	14.3	17.7	16.5	11.2	16.5	14.6	11.9	19.2
Morocco - Maroc	1993	64.5	27.9	65.9	49.5	55.3	75.7	53.6	17.8	55.1	45.9	51.9	64.1
	1997	18.4	9.3	18.7	12.5	10.7	24.2	17.7	3.9	18.1	12.2	10.9	25.8
	2000	27.9	23.8	28.1	26.1	13.1	34.9	25.9	12.8	26.3	25.6	15.5	35.6
	2001	27.7	23.7	27.9	25.8	13.0	34.6	25.8	12.8	26.1	25.2	15.5	35.4
	2002	27.5	24.1	27.7	24.6	13.0	34.7	25.4	12.7	25.8	24.1	15.2	35.1
	2003	27.1	23.9	27.3	23.2	12.7	34.5	..	..	..	..	..	..
Mozambique	1994	5.0	5.0	5.0	5.0	5.0	5.0	5.0	5.0	5.0	5.0	5.0	5.0
	1997	14.5	4.4	14.9	4.9	9.4	20.6	15.4	4.3	15.5	12.0	10.6	21.3
	2001	12.9	4.4	13.2	4.7	8.8	17.9	12.2	6.4	12.3	10.2	9.6	16.4
	2002	11.2	4.3	11.5	4.4	8.1	15.4	8.8	6.4	8.9	7.7	7.4	10.7
	2003	11.2	4.3	11.5	4.4	8.1	15.4	..	..	..	..	..	..
Nepal - Népal	1993	18.0	7.4	18.4	8.9	18.0	21.9	20.8	5.2	21.0	8.5	25.6	22.7
	1998	17.5	7.5	17.9	8.8	17.4	21.4	29.2	5.1	29.9	9.2	44.9	22.8
	1999	12.9	7.2	13.2	9.7	12.1	14.9	15.1	7.2	15.2	10.9	21.9	12.1
	2000	13.4	9.5	13.5	12.1	11.8	14.6	19.5	5.4	19.9	12.0	33.2	11.8
	2002	13.6	10.2	13.7	12.2	11.9	15.0	17.2	5.5	17.3	13.6	19.3	15.9
	2003	13.7	10.2	13.8	12.3	12.0	15.2	..	..	..	..	..	..
New Zealand - Nouvelle-Zélande	1992	8.9	2.4	9.1	2.4	10.9	10.8	9.3	3.5	9.6	5.5	9.5	11.3
	1993	8.4	2.4	8.6	2.1	9.7	10.5	9.0	3.4	9.3	4.4	9.7	10.9
	1996	6.1	1.7	6.3	1.4	6.6	7.8	7.3	2.2	7.5	2.9	8.1	8.6
	1997	5.3	1.3	5.5	1.2	5.8	6.9	6.2	2.4	6.4	2.3	6.4	8.0
	1998	4.5	0.9	4.6	0.9	4.9	5.8	5.3	1.8	5.5	1.8	5.4	7.1
	1999	3.7	0.8	3.9	0.8	4.1	4.9	4.6	1.6	4.7	1.7	4.8	5.8
	2000	2.9	0.6	3.0	0.6	3.1	3.8	3.6	1.3	3.7	1.3	3.8	4.5
	2002	3.6	0.8	3.7	0.8	3.9	4.8	4.6	1.8	4.7	1.8	4.8	5.8
	2003	3.6	0.8	3.7	0.8	3.9	4.7	..	..	..	..	..	..

For sources and notes, see end of table.

Pour les sources et les notes, se reporter à la fin du tableau.

Markets / Marchés	Year / Année	MFN rate - Simple average / Droit NPF - Moyenne simple						MFN rate - Weighted average / Droit NPF - Moyenne pondérée					
		Total of non-agricultural and non-fuel products / Total des produits non-agricoles et non-pétroliers	Ores and metals / Minérais et métaux	Manufactured products / Produits manufacturés	Chemical products / Produits chimiques	Machinery and transport equipment / Machines et matériel de transport	Other manufactured products / Produits manufacturés divers	Total of non-agricultural and non-fuel products / Total des produits non-agricoles et non-pétroliers	Ores and metals / Minérais et métaux	Manufactured products / Produits manufacturés	Chemical products / Produits chimiques	Machinery and transport equipment / Machines et matériel de transport	Other manufactured products / Produits manufacturés divers
SITC Rev.2 / CTCI Rév.2		5+6+7+8 +27+28	27+28+68	(5+6+7+8) - 68	5	7	(6+8) - 68	5+6+7+8 +27+28	27+28+68	(5+6+7+8) - 68	5	7	(6+8) - 68
Nicaragua	1995	9.4	5.8	9.5	5.8	4.1	12.9	7.6	6.3	7.6	6.5	5.1	10.9
	1998	4.8	1.2	4.9	1.3	1.9	7.3	5.0	3.8	5.1	3.9	4.0	7.2
	1999	9.7	6.2	9.8	6.2	6.8	12.3	9.6	10.0	9.6	8.0	8.2	12.1
	2000	3.1	0.9	3.2	0.9	1.5	4.7	3.9	2.3	3.9	3.0	3.5	4.8
	2001	3.9	0.9	4.0	1.1	1.8	6.0	4.5	2.2	4.5	3.8	3.6	5.6
	2002	3.9	0.8	4.0	1.1	1.8	5.9	4.5	2.2	4.5	3.9	3.7	5.5
Niger	2001	11.8	7.5	12.0	6.3	8.5	15.4	12.4	5.5	12.7	6.2	12.9	16.2
	2002	11.7	7.5	11.9	6.3	8.5	15.3	12.4	5.4	12.6	6.0	11.5	16.8
	2003	11.7	7.3	11.9	6.3	8.6	15.3	..	..	..	..	..	..
Nigeria - Nigéria	1988	33.6	22.5	34.2	18.5	18.2	45.9	21.3	18.7	21.4	18.5	18.9	27.1
	1989	35.6	29.9	36.1	19.1	19.5	48.5	22.3	15.8	22.4	19.0	19.8	28.5
	1990	35.8	30.0	36.2	19.0	20.1	48.5	22.5	16.6	22.6	18.9	20.6	28.1
	1992	34.5	23.1	35.0	22.6	20.1	45.2	23.1	16.6	23.3	22.3	20.6	27.8
	1995	27.0	11.4	27.7	11.5	12.3	34.9	19.5	10.3	19.6	12.4	17.8	23.9
	1996	23.4	16.6	23.7	13.2	12.7	31.9	14.9	9.8	15.1	14.4	12.9	17.9
	1997	23.4	16.6	23.7	13.2	12.7	31.9	15.1	10.0	15.3	15.1	12.9	18.0
	1998	23.4	16.6	23.7	13.2	12.7	31.9	15.1	10.0	15.3	15.1	12.9	18.0
	1999	25.3	18.8	25.6	17.6	16.3	32.2	18.5	14.6	18.6	18.9	16.7	20.6
	2000	25.3	18.8	25.6	17.6	16.3	32.2	18.1	15.4	18.2	17.0	17.5	20.3
	2001	25.3	18.8	25.6	17.6	16.3	32.2	18.2	15.4	18.2	17.1	17.5	20.3
	2002	26.7	17.4	27.1	16.1	15.4	35.7	15.5	9.8	15.5	11.8	16.5	17.3
Norway - Norvège	1988	6.5	0.5	6.8	5.0	5.1	8.2	5.5	0.4	5.8	6.2	3.6	8.5
	1993	6.5	0.4	6.8	5.0	5.2	8.2	5.7	0.3	6.1	6.0	4.2	8.5
	1995	6.2	0.4	6.4	4.7	4.8	7.7	5.4	0.4	5.7	5.8	4.3	7.3
	1996	5.7	0.4	5.9	4.8	4.0	7.2	4.6	0.3	4.9	6.7	3.1	6.9
	1998	3.6	0.3	3.7	3.5	0.7	5.0	2.3	0.3	2.4	5.2	0.7	4.1
	2000	2.4	0.3	2.5	1.4	0.3	3.8	1.6	0.3	1.7	3.1	0.1	3.7
	2001	2.3	0.3	2.3	1.0	0.3	3.6	1.5	0.3	1.6	2.1	0.2	3.5
	2002	1.8	0.2	1.9	0.7	0.1	3.0	1.3	0.2	1.3	1.4	0.1	2.9
	2003	0.8	0.0	0.8	0.3	0.0	1.3	..	..	..	..	..	..
Oman	1992	5.1	5.0	5.1	5.0	5.0	5.2	5.4	5.7	5.4	4.5	5.0	6.5
	1997	4.9	4.9	4.9	4.8	4.8	5.0	4.9	4.9	4.9	4.7	5.0	4.8
	2002	7.1	5.4	7.1	5.6	7.0	7.8	6.5	5.2	6.5	7.4	6.1	7.1
Pakistan	1995	51.9	37.2	52.4	43.3	45.5	58.3	49.5	28.6	50.0	42.1	52.6	56.0
	1998	47.7	36.8	48.1	42.0	38.7	53.8	43.8	28.0	44.1	39.3	44.0	50.6
	2001	20.4	12.1	20.6	14.9	19.6	23.1	21.9	9.2	22.2	13.8	28.6	21.6
	2002	17.4	10.6	17.5	13.9	16.4	19.3	18.6	8.6	18.8	13.3	23.1	18.4
	2003	17.1	9.9	17.3	13.6	16.1	19.1	..	..	..	..	..	..
Panama	1997	10.9	12.9	11.0	6.4	9.5	13.1	11.0	11.4	11.0	6.7	9.6	14.4
	1998	7.6	8.9	7.6	4.9	7.0	8.9	8.5	5.6	8.5	5.4	9.1	8.7
	2000	7.1	8.7	7.1	4.1	6.8	8.3	7.7	6.9	7.7	4.9	7.8	8.6
	2001	6.8	8.4	6.8	3.4	6.8	8.0	7.4	6.5	7.4	4.7	7.8	8.2
Papua New Guinea - Papouasie-Nouvelle-Guinée	1997	16.7	13.3	16.9	9.5	9.9	22.3	13.8	20.3	13.7	14.1	10.5	20.2
	2002	4.9	0.0	5.0	1.1	0.3	8.3	3.1	0.0	3.1	2.4	0.1	7.7
	2003	4.1	0.0	4.2	0.9	0.3	7.0	..	..	..	..	..	..

For sources and notes, see end of table.

Pour les sources et les notes, se reporter à la fin du tableau.

Markets / Marchés	Year / Année	MFN rate - Simple average / Droit NPF - Moyenne simple						MFN rate - Weighted average / Droit NPF - Moyenne pondérée					
		Total of non-agricultural and non-fuel products / Total des produits non-agricoles et non-pétroliers	Ores and metals / Minérais et métaux	Manu-factured products / Produits manu-facturés	Chemical products / Produits chimiques	Machinery and transport equipment / Machines et matériel de transport	Other manu-factured products / Produits manu-facturés divers	Total of non-agricultural and non-fuel products / Total des produits non-agricoles et non-pétroliers	Ores and metals / Minérais et métaux	Manu-factured products / Produits manu-facturés	Chemical products / Produits chimiques	Machinery and transport equipment / Machines et matériel de transport	Other manu-factured products / Produits manu-facturés divers
SITC Rev.2 / CTCI Rév.2		5+6+7+8 +27+28	27+28+68	(5+6+7+8) - 68	5	7	(6+8) - 68	5+6+7+8 +27+28	27+28+68	(5+6+7+8) - 68	5	7	(6+8) - 68
Paraguay	1991	15.0	5.6	15.3	5.3	11.8	20.2	14.4	3.1	14.4	8.8	14.0	17.4
	1994	7.7	2.1	7.8	1.1	7.1	10.5	8.1	0.8	8.1	3.1	9.0	8.9
	1995	11.1	6.0	11.3	8.0	6.6	14.4	10.4	6.8	10.4	9.3	9.5	12.4
	1996	11.2	6.0	11.4	7.8	6.1	14.8	9.4	8.1	9.4	8.2	8.7	11.4
	1997	11.4	6.0	11.6	7.9	7.1	14.8	9.9	8.2	9.9	8.5	9.2	11.8
	1998	11.4	6.0	11.7	7.9	7.6	14.7	10.2	8.2	10.2	8.8	9.6	12.1
	1999	13.4	8.8	13.6	10.6	8.1	16.9	10.5	10.7	10.5	10.3	9.1	12.8
	2000	13.4	8.8	13.7	10.7	8.7	16.7	11.7	8.8	11.7	11.1	10.0	14.0
	2001	13.1	7.9	13.4	9.8	9.8	16.1	11.9	8.5	11.9	10.3	10.8	14.1
	2002	12.8	7.3	13.1	9.2	9.8	15.8	11.3	7.2	11.4	9.7	9.9	14.3
	2003	12.9	7.3	13.1	9.3	9.8	15.8	..	..	..	..	..	..
Peru - Pérou	1993	17.9	15.4	18.0	15.5	16.0	19.7	16.6	15.0	16.6	15.7	16.0	18.3
	1995	16.5	15.0	16.6	15.0	15.3	17.6	15.4	15.0	15.4	15.0	15.2	15.8
	1997	13.2	12.0	13.3	12.0	12.3	14.1	12.3	12.0	12.3	12.0	12.2	12.7
	1998	13.2	12.0	13.2	12.0	12.3	14.1	12.3	12.0	12.3	12.0	12.2	12.7
	1999	13.2	12.0	13.2	12.0	12.3	14.1	12.3	12.0	12.3	12.0	12.2	12.8
	2000	13.2	12.0	13.2	12.0	12.3	14.1	12.3	12.0	12.3	12.0	12.2	12.8
Philippines	1988	27.5	17.1	28.0	16.9	23.7	33.6	23.1	12.8	23.4	19.6	22.5	27.7
	1989	27.6	17.2	28.0	16.9	23.7	33.6	23.1	12.8	23.4	19.6	22.5	27.7
	1990	19.2	13.8	19.5	12.5	15.1	23.6	14.8	10.8	14.9	12.7	13.4	20.1
	1992	19.2	13.8	19.5	12.5	15.1	23.6	14.8	10.8	14.9	12.7	13.4	20.1
	1993	21.8	11.4	22.3	12.7	15.2	28.3	15.1	9.5	15.2	12.2	13.3	21.9
	1994	21.3	11.3	21.6	12.7	14.8	27.5	14.8	9.5	15.0	12.2	13.2	21.2
	1995	19.4	12.9	19.7	12.5	14.1	24.4	14.1	9.5	14.2	12.1	12.4	20.3
	1998	10.0	3.9	10.2	4.6	7.0	13.5	5.6	3.9	5.7	5.9	4.3	10.6
	1999	9.1	3.8	9.2	4.5	6.9	11.9	5.7	3.9	5.7	5.8	4.5	9.7
	2000	7.2	3.3	7.3	3.9	5.0	9.5	3.5	3.4	3.5	5.1	2.1	7.3
	2001	6.8	3.3	7.0	3.8	4.5	9.0	3.2	3.7	3.2	4.9	1.8	6.9
	2002	5.2	2.7	5.3	3.1	3.5	6.8	2.1	2.9	2.1	4.3	1.1	5.3
	2003	4.3	2.7	4.3	3.1	3.1	5.2	..	..	..	..	..	..
Poland - Pologne	1991	11.8	6.7	12.0	11.4	9.3	13.3	10.6	3.9	10.9	12.2	9.4	11.6
	1992	11.8	6.7	12.0	11.3	9.3	13.3	10.6	3.9	10.9	12.2	9.4	11.6
	1995	9.6	6.5	9.7	12.7	13.1	7.4	10.2	5.5	10.4	11.4	12.2	8.2
	1996	13.7	6.8	14.0	11.8	12.5	15.4	12.9	5.1	13.1	10.5	13.9	13.4
	1997	11.6	5.8	11.9	9.3	9.9	13.5	10.2	4.5	10.4	8.9	9.7	11.7
	1998	11.1	5.7	11.3	9.2	9.2	12.9	9.6	5.1	9.7	8.7	8.5	11.3
	1999	10.6	5.5	10.9	9.1	8.8	12.3	9.1	5.8	9.2	8.5	7.9	10.9
	2000	10.3	5.4	10.5	8.8	8.9	11.8	8.6	5.5	8.7	7.7	7.6	10.5
	2001	9.7	5.1	10.0	8.8	8.1	11.1	8.1	5.5	8.2	7.5	6.5	10.1
	2002	9.7	5.1	9.9	8.8	8.1	11.0	8.2	5.9	8.3	7.4	6.7	10.3
	2003	9.7	5.1	9.9	8.8	8.1	11.0	..	..	..	..	..	..
Romania - Roumanie	1991	17.3	6.8	17.7	16.5	16.3	18.7	15.8	2.8	17.9	15.4	20.1	16.6
	1999	16.0	6.7	16.4	15.9	14.6	17.3	14.1	5.6	14.3	13.9	12.1	15.9
	2001	16.1	6.6	16.4	14.5	14.0	18.1	14.7	3.9	15.0	10.9	12.6	17.7
Russian Federation - Fédération de Russie	1993	8.7	7.1	8.8	5.3	6.3	10.9	7.2	3.7	7.5	7.6	6.3	8.7
	1994	12.1	6.9	12.4	5.7	12.1	14.9	9.2	3.5	9.5	5.8	8.8	11.8
	1996	11.4	10.0	11.5	5.7	11.4	13.9	9.1	5.4	9.3	7.7	8.1	11.9
	1997	13.0	9.0	13.2	7.0	12.8	15.6	11.5	5.7	11.8	9.3	11.2	13.9
	2001	10.0	8.2	10.2	6.5	10.2	11.8	9.0	6.4	9.3	8.5	8.6	10.8
	2002	9.7	8.6	9.8	6.6	8.9	11.6	8.8	6.8	9.0	8.7	7.9	11.0

For sources and notes, see end of table.

Pour les sources et les notes, se reporter à la fin du tableau.

Markets / Marchés	Year / Année	MFN rate - Simple average / Droit NPF - Moyenne simple						MFN rate - Weighted average / Droit NPF - Moyenne pondérée					
		Total of non-agricultural and non-fuel products / Total des produits non-agricoles et non-pétroliers	Ores and metals / Minérais et métaux	Manu-factured products / Produits manu-facturés	Chemical products / Produits chimiques	Machinery and transport equipment / Machines et matériel de transport	Other manu-factured products / Produits manu-facturés divers	Total of non-agricultural and non-fuel products / Total des produits non-agricoles et non-pétroliers	Ores and metals / Minérais et métaux	Manu-factured products / Produits manu-facturés	Chemical products / Produits chimiques	Machinery and transport equipment / Machines et matériel de transport	Other manu-factured products / Produits manu-facturés divers
SITC Rev.2 / CTCI Rév.2		5+6+7+8 +27+28	27+28+68	(5+6+7+8) - 68	5	7	(6+8) - 68	5+6+7+8 +27+28	27+28+68	(5+6+7+8) - 68	5	7	(6+8) - 68
Rwanda	1993	33.1	24.9	33.6	17.8	24.8	42.6	25.2	17.2	25.5	15.2	25.2	29.4
	2001	9.5	6.7	9.7	5.7	7.2	12.1	7.0	5.4	7.0	4.8	8.2	6.8
	2003	9.5	6.7	9.7	5.7	7.2	12.1	..	..	..	..	..	..
Saint Kitts and Nevis - Saint-Kitts-et-Nevis	1996	20.8	16.0	20.8	14.5	21.3	21.6	23.7	15.7	23.8	17.6	34.2	19.9
	1999	17.3	12.8	17.4	11.0	18.5	18.1	19.1	10.9	19.1	14.4	32.6	15.7
	2000	8.8	2.4	9.1	5.1	7.8	11.0	13.3	4.4	13.4	13.1	12.5	14.0
	2001	8.8	2.4	9.1	5.1	7.8	11.0	12.1	5.6	12.1	12.0	11.2	12.9
	2002	8.8	2.4	9.1	5.1	7.8	11.0	12.1	5.6	12.1	12.0	11.2	12.9
	2003	8.8	2.4	9.1	5.1	7.8	11.0	..	..	..	..	..	..
Saint Lucia - Sainte-Lucie	1996	20.5	16.5	20.6	14.5	20.5	21.5	20.8	14.1	20.9	15.8	25.7	20.1
	1999	17.1	13.3	17.1	11.3	17.3	18.0	17.6	13.1	17.6	13.5	24.3	15.5
	2000	17.1	13.3	17.1	11.5	17.3	17.9	17.7	13.1	17.7	14.2	24.3	15.6
	2001	7.5	2.1	7.6	5.6	5.2	9.4	11.6	1.5	11.7	13.2	11.6	11.4
	2002	7.5	2.1	7.6	5.6	5.2	9.4	12.3	1.4	12.4	13.3	10.8	13.3
	2003	7.5	2.1	7.6	5.6	5.2	9.4	..	..	..	..	..	..
Saint Vincent and the Grenadines Saint-Vincent-et-les Grenadines	1996	20.1	15.5	20.1	14.5	18.4	21.4	20.2	18.8	20.2	16.0	23.3	19.9
	1999	16.7	12.2	16.7	11.3	15.9	17.7	16.5	13.0	16.5	12.0	20.1	16.4
	2000	16.7	12.2	16.7	11.5	15.9	17.7	16.5	14.5	16.6	12.6	22.3	15.5
	2001	8.5	4.3	8.6	5.7	7.4	10.2	12.2	6.8	12.3	10.1	11.4	13.3
	2002	8.5	4.3	8.6	5.7	7.4	10.2	11.3	7.0	11.3	11.2	10.5	11.9
	2003	8.5	4.3	8.6	5.7	7.4	10.2	..	..	..	..	..	..
Saudi Arabia - Arabie saoudite	1994	12.2	12.2	12.2	11.8	11.8	12.5	11.5	13.4	11.5	8.9	11.0	12.9
	1999	12.1	12.2	12.1	11.8	11.8	12.4	11.5	13.3	11.5	8.3	11.3	13.0
	2000	12.1	12.2	12.1	11.8	11.8	12.3	11.4	13.1	11.4	8.4	11.4	12.6
	2003	6.1	5.5	6.1	6.0	5.3	6.4	..	..	..	..	..	..
Senegal - Sénégal	2001	11.8	7.5	12.0	6.3	8.5	15.4	10.3	6.8	10.4	5.7	10.5	13.1
	2002	11.7	7.5	11.9	6.3	8.5	15.3	10.2	6.9	10.3	5.7	10.5	13.2
	2003	11.7	7.3	11.9	6.3	8.6	15.3	..	..	..	..	..	..
Serbia and Montenegro - Serbie-et-Monténégro	2001	13.5	8.3	13.7	7.6	10.9	17.0	..	..	..	..	..	..
Seychelles	2000	25.1	22.5	25.1	28.7	20.8	25.6	18.5	21.3	18.5	22.7	17.3	21.0
	2001	24.8	22.5	24.8	28.7	20.8	25.1	18.5	21.3	18.5	22.7	17.3	21.0
Singapore - Singapour	1989	0.4	0.0	0.5	0.0	0.6	0.6	0.6	0.0	0.6	0.0	0.9	0.3
Slovakia - Slovaquie	2002	20.7	6.6	21.3	19.2	18.6	23.0	23.1	5.6	23.6	18.7	21.5	28.0
Slovenia - Slovénie	1999	10.0	3.2	10.3	7.5	10.7	11.1	11.9	4.4	12.1	9.0	13.6	11.6
	2001	9.7	3.0	9.9	7.5	9.5	10.9	10.4	4.8	10.6	9.0	10.4	11.3
	2002	9.6	3.0	9.9	7.5	9.4	10.9	10.3	4.8	10.5	9.0	10.1	11.3
	2003	9.6	3.0	9.9	7.5	9.4	10.9	..	..	..	..	..	..
Solomon Islands - Iles Salomon	1995	39.1	7.9	40.3	16.3	20.4	56.5	34.0	10.9	34.1	24.7	27.2	42.7
South Africa (Customs Union) - Afrique du Sud (Union douanière)	1988	11.9	3.9	12.2	8.8	7.5	15.4	12.2	4.4	12.3	7.0	14.6	9.9
	1990	10.8	3.8	11.1	8.6	7.7	13.6	10.9	5.9	10.9	7.1	12.3	10.5
	1991	10.5	3.5	10.8	8.4	7.9	13.1	11.8	5.7	11.9	6.9	14.2	9.9
	1993	17.2	3.9	17.7	8.9	8.2	24.4	14.0	5.7	14.1	7.8	15.2	15.4
	1996	14.9	1.8	15.6	3.2	4.6	24.4	8.8	1.1	9.0	3.5	7.4	14.7
	1997	7.0	2.0	7.2	3.0	5.7	9.8	6.0	1.8	6.2	2.9	5.6	9.0
	1999	5.7	1.7	5.8	2.9	3.4	8.4	4.9	1.4	5.0	3.0	4.7	6.9
	2001	7.9	1.4	8.2	2.5	3.2	12.4	5.9	0.9	6.0	2.5	5.4	9.1

For sources and notes, see end of table.

Pour les sources et les notes, se reporter à la fin du tableau.

Markets / Marchés	Year / Année	MFN rate - Simple average / Droit NPF - Moyenne simple						MFN rate - Weighted average / Droit NPF - Moyenne pondérée					
		Total of non-agricultural and non-fuel products / Total des produits non-agricoles et non-pétroliers	Ores and metals / Minérais et métaux	Manufactured products / Produits manufacturés	Chemical products / Produits chimiques	Machinery and transport equipment / Machines et matériel de transport	Other manufactured products / Produits manufacturés divers	Total of non-agricultural and non-fuel products / Total des produits non-agricoles et non-pétroliers	Ores and metals / Minérais et métaux	Manufactured products / Produits manufacturés	Chemical products / Produits chimiques	Machinery and transport equipment / Machines et matériel de transport	Other manufactured products / Produits manufacturés divers
SITC Rev.2 / CTCI Rév.2		5+6+7+8 +27+28	27+28+68	(5+6+7+8) - 68	5	7	(6+8) - 68	5+6+7+8 +27+28	27+28+68	(5+6+7+8) - 68	5	7	(6+8) - 68
Sri Lanka	1990	26.0	11.4	26.4	12.3	14.1	36.4	24.1	7.4	24.3	7.8	14.4	35.9
	1993	22.5	12.0	22.8	12.2	15.7	29.3	26.4	11.8	26.5	9.5	18.4	34.2
	1994	22.5	12.0	22.8	12.2	15.7	29.3	26.9	11.6	27.0	9.8	20.2	34.1
	1997	18.2	11.7	18.4	11.6	14.4	22.3	21.5	10.7	21.5	9.9	20.2	24.3
	2000	7.9	5.5	7.9	6.1	6.1	9.3	5.2	6.3	5.2	5.3	6.5	4.6
	2001	7.9	5.5	7.9	6.1	6.1	9.3	5.2	6.3	5.1	5.4	6.5	4.6
Sudan - Soudan	1996	4.3	1.8	4.4	2.3	1.6	6.3	4.0	3.9	4.0	3.2	1.8	7.6
	2002	22.6	16.9	22.9	14.4	14.5	29.3	18.9	11.3	18.9	15.2	15.5	29.6
Suriname	1996	20.0	17.1	20.1	14.9	16.9	21.6	18.5	17.1	18.5	18.8	17.4	20.0
	1999	16.6	13.8	16.6	11.9	14.2	18.0	15.3	12.0	15.3	14.1	14.7	16.0
	2000	12.5	13.7	12.5	9.3	8.7	14.6	12.1	14.8	12.1	8.8	10.0	14.5
Syrian Arab Republic - République arabe syrienne	2002	19.8	6.9	20.3	5.5	15.1	27.6	16.6	5.6	16.6	3.6	30.6	10.8
Tajikistan - Tadjikistan	2002	8.1	8.7	8.1	5.2	5.3	10.3	7.5	6.2	8.4	5.1	5.0	11.9
Thailand - Thaïlande	1989	39.9	17.8	40.9	32.0	35.2	48.3	34.1	10.7	34.9	31.0	39.7	25.9
	1991	39.9	17.8	40.9	32.1	35.2	48.3	33.8	12.2	34.2	31.4	37.9	26.6
	1993	45.4	18.8	46.5	36.7	34.0	55.1	36.0	14.1	36.5	38.4	34.9	38.9
	1995	20.2	10.3	20.6	14.0	13.3	26.0	15.6	8.7	15.6	15.2	15.6	15.9
	2000	15.5	6.5	15.8	11.1	12.1	19.1	10.0	5.4	10.1	10.5	8.8	12.3
	2001	14.6	6.1	14.9	6.2	12.4	18.9	10.5	4.2	10.6	9.8	8.8	14.7
Togo	2001	11.8	7.5	12.0	6.3	8.5	15.4	11.1	5.9	11.2	6.1	11.2	12.8
	2002	11.7	7.5	11.9	6.3	8.5	15.3	10.1	5.8	10.2	5.4	9.7	12.2
	2003	11.7	7.3	11.9	6.3	8.6	15.3	..	..	..	..	..	..
Trinidad and Tobago - Trinité-et-Tobago	1991	16.4	8.0	16.5	11.3	12.7	19.9	13.7	6.8	14.1	13.0	13.9	14.7
	1992	16.4	8.0	16.5	11.3	12.7	19.9	13.9	7.7	14.2	13.2	14.3	14.5
	1996	8.3	3.6	8.4	4.5	6.3	10.7	7.0	3.4	7.2	8.0	6.7	7.6
	1999	17.3	15.5	17.4	11.4	17.0	18.3	16.6	15.6	16.7	13.4	19.0	15.7
	2001	6.2	1.4	6.3	2.1	4.9	8.4	4.5	3.2	4.5	6.3	3.3	6.5
	2002	6.3	1.4	6.4	2.1	5.1	8.5	5.4	1.4	5.5	7.2	4.5	6.8
	2003	6.3	1.4	6.4	2.1	5.1	8.5	..	..	..	..	..	..
Tunisia - Tunisie	1990	28.5	21.4	28.8	24.2	25.0	31.9	28.1	19.7	28.5	22.6	24.8	33.0
	1992	28.6	21.5	28.9	23.6	25.3	32.1	28.3	20.0	28.6	22.6	24.7	32.7
	1995	28.9	21.5	29.2	21.2	26.4	33.1	30.2	20.2	30.4	20.6	26.4	35.4
	1998	28.4	24.2	28.6	23.5	19.8	34.0	27.8	21.9	27.9	22.3	21.0	35.5
	2002	27.4	24.3	27.5	23.3	18.7	32.6	25.6	22.9	25.7	21.1	18.2	32.5
	2003	22.1	15.8	22.4	14.5	14.5	28.3	..	..	..	..	..	..
Turkey - Turquie	1993	9.3	6.1	9.5	8.0	7.9	10.6	7.4	1.9	7.8	8.1	7.4	8.2
	1995	8.4	4.0	8.6	7.8	6.3	9.8	6.9	2.3	7.3	8.3	6.0	8.2
	1997	5.6	1.9	5.8	5.7	3.6	6.7	5.5	1.6	5.8	5.8	5.3	6.5
	1999	6.3	1.6	6.5	5.4	2.5	8.5	5.1	1.9	5.3	5.0	4.0	7.7
	2003	4.3	1.6	4.5	4.7	2.2	5.2	..	..	..	..	..	..
Turkmenistan - Turkménistan	2002	4.0	1.4	4.0	0.7	1.2	6.3	1.1	2.9	1.1	0.5	0.9	1.6
Uganda - Ouganda	1994	16.1	11.8	16.2	11.0	13.7	18.9	14.9	15.3	14.9	6.2	15.2	17.2
	2000	8.5	8.0	8.5	7.1	3.8	10.9	7.0	7.2	7.0	4.7	6.3	8.6
	2001	8.4	8.0	8.4	7.1	3.6	10.7	6.8	7.1	6.8	4.2	5.9	8.9
	2002	8.3	8.0	8.3	7.0	3.5	10.6	6.7	6.9	6.7	4.2	6.2	8.4
	2003	7.9	7.7	7.9	5.9	3.2	10.5	..	..	..	..	..	..
Ukraine	1995	6.6	1.9	6.7	5.3	4.7	8.0	4.3	3.0	4.3	2.5	3.9	5.6
	1997	7.4	1.9	7.5	6.0	5.4	8.9	5.0	1.6	5.2	4.2	4.8	6.3
	2002	7.0	3.5	7.1	5.3	5.8	8.2	6.2	2.2	6.4	5.5	5.6	7.7

For sources and notes, see end of table.

Pour les sources et les notes, se reporter à la fin du tableau.

Markets / Marchés	Year / Année	MFN rate - Simple average / Droit NPF - Moyenne simple						MFN rate - Weighted average / Droit NPF - Moyenne pondérée					
		Total of non-agricultural and non-fuel products / Total des produits non-agricoles et non-pétroliers	of which: / dont :					Total of non-agricultural and non-fuel products / Total des produits non-agricoles et non-pétroliers	of which: / dont :				
			Ores and metals / Minérais et métaux	Manu-factured products / Produits manu-facturés	Of which: / dont :				Ores and metals / Minérais et métaux	Manu-factured products / Produits manu-facturés	Of which: / dont :		
					Chemical products / Produits chimiques	Machinery and transport equipment / Machines et matériel de transport	Other manu-factured products / Produits manu-facturés divers				Chemical products / Produits chimiques	Machinery and transport equipment / Machines et matériel de transport	Other manu-factured products / Produits manu-facturés divers
SITC Rev.2 / CTCI Rév.2		5+6+7+8 +27+28	27+28+68	(5+6+7+8) - 68	5	7	(6+8) - 68	5+6+7+8 +27+28	27+28+68	(5+6+7+8) - 68	5	7	(6+8) - 68
United Republic of Tanzania - République-Unie de Tanzanie	1993	19.0	19.2	19.0	17.2	11.1	22.8	15.0	18.1	15.0	22.2	10.1	16.5
	1997	22.6	28.9	22.4	27.0	17.6	22.7	18.3	24.3	18.3	16.2	16.2	22.5
	1998	22.9	29.3	22.7	27.1	17.9	23.0	19.7	26.6	19.6	19.6	17.9	22.5
	2000	15.9	12.0	16.2	7.9	13.1	20.5	13.0	10.4	13.0	8.4	11.0	18.3
	2003	12.9	7.0	13.3	3.7	8.9	18.5	..	..	..	..	..	..
United States - Etats-Unis	1989	5.9	2.3	6.1	5.0	3.7	7.4	4.5	1.4	4.6	5.2	3.1	6.7
	1990	5.9	2.3	6.1	5.0	3.7	7.4	4.6	1.3	4.7	5.2	3.1	6.9
	1991	5.9	2.3	6.0	5.0	3.7	7.3	4.7	1.2	4.7	5.3	3.1	7.0
	1992	5.9	2.3	6.0	5.0	3.7	7.3	4.8	1.4	4.8	5.3	3.1	7.2
	1993	5.9	2.3	6.0	5.0	3.7	7.3	4.7	1.4	4.7	5.2	3.1	7.1
	1995	5.3	2.1	5.5	4.0	3.4	6.8	4.1	1.4	4.2	3.8	3.0	6.2
	1996	5.0	1.9	5.2	4.0	3.0	6.5	4.0	1.4	4.0	3.7	2.8	6.0
	1997	4.9	1.6	5.1	4.3	2.7	6.3	3.9	1.4	3.9	4.0	2.6	5.9
	1998	4.3	1.5	4.5	3.6	2.2	5.7	3.4	1.3	3.4	3.2	2.2	5.4
	1999	4.0	1.3	4.1	3.5	1.8	5.3	3.1	1.2	3.2	3.1	2.0	5.0
	2000	3.9	1.3	4.0	3.4	1.7	5.2	2.9	1.1	3.0	3.0	1.8	4.8
	2001	3.8	1.3	3.9	3.3	1.7	5.0	3.1	1.1	3.1	2.8	2.0	4.7
	2002	3.7	1.3	3.8	3.1	1.7	4.9	3.0	1.4	3.0	2.6	2.1	4.6
	2003	3.6	1.3	3.7	3.0	1.7	4.7	..	..	..	..	..	..
Uruguay	1992	5.6	4.9	5.6	4.2	5.4	6.2	5.8	5.4	5.8	4.7	5.1	7.4
	1995	11.3	6.1	11.5	8.1	6.3	14.8	11.9	7.7	11.9	8.7	11.3	14.5
	1996	11.6	6.1	11.9	8.1	6.5	15.4	11.2	6.7	11.3	8.6	9.5	15.4
	1997	11.8	6.1	12.1	8.1	7.6	15.3	11.5	6.7	11.6	8.7	10.2	15.3
	1998	14.0	8.8	14.3	10.7	9.1	17.7	13.6	8.9	13.6	11.0	12.1	17.2
	1999	14.2	8.8	14.4	10.8	9.7	17.6	13.7	8.8	13.7	11.8	11.6	17.5
	2000	14.4	9.0	14.6	10.9	10.4	17.8	14.4	9.6	14.4	12.5	12.8	17.4
	2001	14.2	8.4	14.5	10.7	11.1	17.3	14.1	9.3	14.2	12.4	12.7	16.9
	2002	13.3	7.3	13.6	9.4	10.7	16.3	12.7	6.4	12.8	10.7	11.7	15.5
Uzbekistan - Ouzbékistan	2001	11.7	9.3	11.8	8.9	4.9	15.6	6.2	6.9	6.2	8.0	2.9	10.8
Venezuela	1992	16.4	8.2	16.7	10.2	12.7	20.7	16.4	6.9	16.5	9.5	18.1	16.7
	1995	13.5	7.3	13.8	10.6	12.6	15.4	13.2	7.5	13.3	10.7	13.6	14.4
	1997	12.0	6.7	12.2	8.1	10.2	14.4	13.4	7.3	13.5	8.8	14.9	13.2
	1998	12.0	6.6	12.2	8.1	10.3	14.4	13.2	7.0	13.3	8.9	14.3	13.2
	1999	12.0	6.7	12.3	8.1	10.4	14.5	12.7	7.2	12.7	9.1	12.6	14.5
	2000	12.0	6.7	12.2	8.1	10.3	14.4	13.2	8.5	13.3	9.3	14.0	14.2
	2002	12.4	6.7	12.6	8.2	10.4	15.1	13.5	8.5	13.6	10.0	13.9	15.2
Viet Nam	1994	13.5	1.2	13.9	3.8	6.4	20.4	13.1	0.5	13.1	2.8	11.6	19.9
	1999	15.4	1.7	15.8	3.8	9.4	22.7	14.6	1.6	14.6	4.7	12.9	20.9
	2001	15.4	1.8	15.8	3.7	9.9	22.6	16.1	1.5	16.2	4.0	19.9	17.9
	2002	15.4	1.8	15.8	3.7	9.7	22.6	15.0	1.1	15.1	4.1	15.5	19.0
Yemen - Yémen	2000	12.2	12.7	12.3	9.5	11.2	13.7	12.9	12.4	12.9	8.4	13.8	13.2
Zambia - Zambie	1993	25.6	20.6	25.8	20.5	22.9	28.8	20.0	20.1	20.0	11.3	21.2	23.2
	1997	13.4	9.6	13.6	7.0	10.8	17.1	11.6	6.5	11.9	6.5	11.9	15.4
	2002	11.4	6.8	11.5	6.2	6.5	15.3	8.3	4.8	8.3	5.5	7.8	10.2
	2003	13.0	9.3	13.2	6.3	10.4	16.8	..	..	..	..	..	..
Zimbabwe	1996	41.9	30.5	42.3	33.0	37.9	47.3	39.2	31.9	39.3	32.1	39.6	43.0
	1997	24.0	9.4	24.5	8.3	15.7	33.9	15.7	8.5	16.0	9.2	16.4	22.3
	1998	21.2	9.6	21.7	8.4	15.2	29.0	15.2	8.4	15.5	9.1	16.1	20.9
	2001	19.1	8.6	19.5	7.9	13.3	26.1	13.9	7.8	14.2	7.4	16.2	18.1

For sources and notes, see end of table.

Pour les sources et les notes, se reporter à la fin du tableau.

**8.4   Average applied import MFN tariff
rates on non-agricultural and non-fuel
products**

**8.4   Droits de douane moyens NPF appliqués
à l'importation des produits non-agricoles
et non-pétroliers**

Sources: UNCTAD TRAINS database.

Notes: Product categories are defined in terms of SITC Revision 2, and all
corresponding Harmonized System (HS) 6-digit codes have been
aggregated for each category.

MFN: Most Favoured Nation import tariff rate.

Simple average: simple average for each product category calculated from
simple average at HS 6-digit level.

Weighted average: weighted average for each product category
calculated from simple average at HS 6-digit level. Country's own
imports at HS 6-digit level for corresponding years are used as
weights. Where imports are not reported, mirror imports have been
compiled using exports of partner countries.

Sources : Base de données TRAINS de la CNUCED.

Notes : Les catégories de produits sont définies sur la base de la CTCI, révision 2, et pour
chaque catégorie, les codes à 6 chiffres du Système harmonisé (SH) correspondants
ont été agrégés.

NPF : droit de douane appliqué à la Nation la plus favorisée.

Moyenne simple : moyenne arithmétique, pour chaque catégorie de produits,
calculée à partir des moyennes arithmétiques au niveau du code à 6 chiffres du SH.

Moyenne pondérée : Moyenne arithmétique pondérée, pour chaque catégorie de
produits, calculée à partir des moyennes simples au niveau
du code à 6 chiffres du SH. Pour chaque année, on a utilisé les importations
de chaque marché au niveau du code à 6 chiffres du SH comme
coefficient de pondération. Lorsque les importations n'étaient pas disponibles,
elles ont été evaluées par les données miroir basées sur les exportations des
pays partenaires.

8.5 Instability indices and trends in free-market prices for selected commodities

8.5 Indices d'instabilité et tendances des prix sur le marché libre d'une sélection de produits de base

Product Produit	Price instability indices [1] Indices d'instabilité des prix [1]			Price trends [2] Tendances des prix [2]							
				In current dollars En dollars courants				In constant dollars [3] En dollars constants [3]			
	1970-79	1980-89	1990-99	1970-79	1980-89	1990-99	2000-03	1970-79	1980-89	1990-99	2000-03
				Annual average rate of change, per cent Taux de variation annuel en pourcentage							
ALL COMMODITIES	**17.3**	**14.2**	**9.3**	**10.5**	**-1.8**	**-0.4**	**0.5**	**-0.5**	**-5.0**	**0.1**	**-2.0**
All food	**22.2**	**14.5**	**10.7**	**10.9**	**-3.7**	**0.7**	**0.6**	**0.0**	**-7.0**	**1.3**	**-1.8**
Food and tropical beverages	*23.0*	*15.6*	*11.0*	*11.0*	*-3.6*	*0.3*	*-0.6*	*0.0*	*-6.9*	*0.9*	*-3.0*
Food	*30.4*	*21.9*	*9.8*	*8.6*	*-3.7*	*-0.7*	*-0.1*	*-2.3*	*-7.0*	*-0.2*	*-2.5*
Wheat	27.8	11.0	15.5	10.4	-2.7	0.1	9.0	-0.5	-6.0	0.6	6.5
Maize	19.8	13.7	11.2	8.2	-4.7	0.0	6.2	-2.7	-7.9	0.6	3.7
Rice	34.5	21.9	10.9	10.6	-4.9	-0.5	-0.1	-0.7	-8.2	0.0	-2.5
Sugar	58.1	50.6	19.5	7.9	-7.5	-2.7	-5.0	-3.1	-10.8	-2.2	-7.4
Beef	15.5	7.1	6.8	5.8	-0.6	-5.3	2.8	-5.2	-3.9	-4.7	0.3
Bananas	12.2	13.3	16.6	9.5	1.5	-1.7	-5.9	-1.9	-1.8	-1.1	-8.3
Pepper	16.3	31.7	17.6	16.2	12.0	19.7	-13.6	5.2	8.7	20.2	-16.0
Soybean meal	22.3	15.2	13.2	8.7	-0.8	-0.6	3.7	-2.2	-4.0	-0.1	1.2
Fishmeal	26.7	18.4	16.8	8.9	-1.1	2.8	13.9	-2.0	-4.3	3.4	11.4
Tropical beverages	*20.0*	*12.7*	*19.5*	*18.3*	*-3.7*	*5.2*	*-2.7*	*7.3*	*-7.0*	*5.8*	*-5.2*
Coffee	23.7	14.5	26.6	18.0	-2.1	6.7	-9.0	7.0	-5.4	7.3	-11.4
Cocoa	22.5	14.8	12.3	22.9	-4.9	2.6	23.8	11.9	-8.2	3.1	21.3
Tea	13.0	17.2	11.2	10.1	-2.2	2.7	-8.0	-0.8	-5.5	3.2	-10.5
Vegetable oilseeds and oils	**19.4**	**18.8**	**10.0**	**10.3**	**-4.2**	**4.2**	**11.4**	**-0.6**	**-7.5**	**4.8**	**8.9**
Soybeans	19.3	13.7	9.8	9.4	-1.2	-0.1	7.6	-1.5	-4.5	0.5	5.2
Soybean oil	23.2	19.2	11.7	10.0	-3.9	2.2	17.7	-0.9	-7.2	2.7	15.2
Sunflower oil	22.1	18.3	12.1	9.3	-4.7	2.9	14.6	-1.7	-8.0	3.5	12.1
Groundnut oil	17.9	24.8	14.0	11.5	-3.6	0.9	15.9	0.6	-6.9	1.4	13.4
Copra	34.4	27.7	15.5	12.0	-3.3	6.8	2.4	1.0	-6.6	7.3	-0.1
Coconut oil	31.8	29.5	15.2	9.5	-3.7	7.6	4.0	-1.7	-6.9	8.1	1.5
Palm kernel oil	33.2	28.0	15.2	11.6	-4.9	7.6	4.1	0.6	-8.2	8.1	1.7
Palm oil	19.7	22.2	14.7	11.2	-6.2	6.7	13.9	0.2	-9.5	7.3	11.5
Cotton oil	16.9	14.0	9.7	9.7	-2.1	-0.3	19.2	-2.3	-5.5	0.3	16.7
Agricultural raw materials	**11.9**	**10.2**	**9.2**	**12.5**	**0.6**	**-1.9**	**1.5**	**1.5**	**-2.7**	**-1.4**	**-1.0**
Linseed oil	45.2	22.9	17.3	12.0	-2.3	1.9	18.8	1.0	-5.6	2.4	16.3
Tobacco	9.1	5.5	9.0	11.0	2.2	-0.5	-4.4	0.1	-1.1	0.1	-6.8
Cotton	..	14.0	16.5	..	-3.5	-1.6	2.1	..	-6.8	-1.0	-0.4
Wool	..	19.0	19.4	..	15.4	-3.6	-25.6	..	6.8	-3.1	-21.9
Jute	10.0	25.5	19.1	3.9	0.1	-2.1	-6.7	-7.0	-3.1	-1.5	-9.4
Sisal	41.4	6.3	11.2	15.0	-1.0	4.7	0.1	4.0	-4.3	5.2	-2.4
Hides and skins	23.1	11.8	8.7	15.3	9.7	-0.9	-4.7	4.3	6.4	-0.3	-7.2
Non-coniferous woods	12.0	9.7	5.0	12.1	1.4	2.0	3.7	1.1	-1.9	2.6	1.2
Tropical logs	16.1	15.8	6.6	14.1	3.2	-3.9	3.5	3.1	-0.1	-3.4	1.0
Tropical sawnwood	13.7	11.2	17.9	11.6	0.1	0.7	0.6	0.6	-3.2	1.2	-1.8
Plywood	19.7	14.3	20.0	9.8	4.8	1.5	-0.7	-1.1	1.5	2.1	-3.2
Rubber	17.2	17.0	26.9	13.8	-2.1	-0.9	16.9	2.8	-5.4	-0.3	14.4
Minerals, ores and metals	**12.0**	**16.4**	**9.2**	**8.1**	**1.7**	**-2.1**	**-0.5**	**-2.9**	**-1.6**	**-1.5**	**-3.0**
Phosphate rock	45.0	11.5	9.1	17.1	-2.5	0.6	-4.5	6.1	-5.8	1.1	-7.0
Manganese ore	15.1	18.8	12.1	12.4	2.1	-9.1	1.9	1.5	-1.2	-8.5	-0.6
Iron ore	15.1	5.1	5.2	12.1	-2.1	-1.4	3.1	1.1	-5.4	-0.9	0.7
Aluminium	13.6	23.2	13.1	9.1	4.3	0.6	-3.2	-1.9	1.0	1.1	-5.6
Copper	21.3	22.7	14.8	2.7	3.3	-3.9	-0.7	-8.2	0.0	-3.3	-3.1
Nickel	4.3	35.8	16.8	9.4	6.7	-3.8	4.1	-1.5	3.4	-3.3	1.6
Lead	20.2	26.0	16.8	13.5	-1.9	-1.1	3.3	2.5	-5.2	-0.6	0.9
Zinc	35.9	19.3	11.8	8.7	5.9	-1.9	-10.3	-2.3	2.6	-1.4	-12.7
Tin	11.5	14.8	6.9	17.2	-10.1	-0.7	-3.8	6.2	-13.5	-0.1	-6.2
Tungsten	26.8	14.0	15.7	13.6	-12.5	-1.4	-5.0	2.6	-15.7	-0.8	-7.4
Gold	22.9	14.3	8.0	21.6	-2.6	-2.6	9.1	10.5	-5.8	-2.1	6.7
Silver	20.9	21.7	9.1	19.1	-10.7	2.7	-0.1	8.0	-13.9	3.3	-2.5
Crude petroleum	25.8	12.8	15.2	28.2	-10.7	-1.6	1.0	17.0	-14.0	-1.1	-1.4

For sources and notes, see next page.

Pour les sources et les notes, se reporter à la page suivante.

Sources:

UNCTAD calculations based on UNCTAD Monthly Commodity Price database.

Notes:

1. The measure of price instability is

$$1/n \sum_{t=1}^{n} \left[\left(\left| Y(t) - y(t) \right| \right) / y(t) \right] * 100$$

Where

$Y(t)$ is the observed magnitude of the variable.

$y(t)$ is the magnitude estimated by fitting an exponential trend to the observed value and

n is the number of observations.

Accordingly, instability is measured as the percentage deviation of the variables concerned from their exponential trend levels for a given period.

2. The growth rate of each period has been calculated using the formula:

$$\log(p) = a + b(t)$$

Where

p is the price index and t is time.

3. Constant 1985 dollars (current dollars divided by the United Nations unit value index of manufactured goods exported by developed economies).

Sources :

Calculs du secrétariat de la CNUCED fondés sur la Base de données des prix mensuels des produits de base, de la CNUCED.

Notes :

1. L'indice d'instabilité des prix est calculé selon

$$1/n \sum_{t=1}^{n} \left[\left(\left| Y(t) - y(t) \right| \right) / y(t) \right] * 100$$

où

$Y(t)$ est la valeur observée de la variable.

$y(t)$ est la valeur estimée par ajustement à la tendance exponentielle des valeurs observées et

n est le nombre d'observations.

L'instabilité est le pourcentage de déviation des variables en question par rapport à la ligne de tendance exponentielle pour une période donnée.

2. Le taux de croissance de chaque période a été calculé selon la formule :

$$\log(p) = a + b(t)$$

où

p est l'indice de prix et t le temps.

3. Dollars constants 1985 (dollar courant divisé par l'index des Nations Unies de la valeur unitaire des exportations des produits manufacturés par les économies développées).

Region, country or area / Régions pays ou zones	Year / Année	Total Fleet (thousands of DWT) [1] / Flotte totale (milliers de TPL) [1]	As percentage of world total fleet / En pourcentage de la flotte mondiale					As percentage of the country total fleet / En pourcentage de la flotte totale du pays				
			Oil tankers / Petroliers	Bulk carriers / Vraquiers	General cargo / Navires de charge classiques	Container ships / Porte-conteneurs	Other types / Autres navires	Oil tankers / Petroliers	Bulk carriers / Vraquiers	General cargo / Navires de charge classique	Container ships / Porte-conteneurs	Other types / Autres navires
WORLD - MONDE	1990	651282.0	100.0	100.0	100.0	100.0	100.0	37.6	35.3	15.7	3.6	7.8
	1995	722670.6	100.0	100.0	100.0	100.0	100.0	36.7	35.5	14.2	5.7	7.9
	2000	794963.6	100.0	100.0	100.0	100.0	100.0	35.6	34.8	12.5	8.4	8.6
	2003	856974.4	100.0	100.0	100.0	100.0	100.0	37.0	35.9	11.1	10.6	5.5
DEVELOPED ECONOMIES - ECONOMIES DEVELOPPEES	1990	261515.0	42.4	38.8	30.7	52.3	48.8	39.7	34.1	12.0	4.7	9.5
	1995	268745.3	39.2	34.9	30.1	45.1	45.4	38.7	33.3	11.5	6.9	9.7
	2000	278777.0	39.7	29.5	29.3	40.4	41.2	40.4	29.3	10.5	9.7	10.1
	2003	300130.0	39.2	31.1	28.9	38.0	39.4	41.4	31.8	9.1	11.5	6.2
DEVELOPING ECONOMIES - ECONOMIES EN DEVELOPPEMENT	1990	346262.0	54.2	55.0	54.4	44.3	41.3	38.3	36.5	16.0	3.0	6.0
	1995	426047.5	58.8	62.6	58.5	53.4	47.9	36.6	37.7	14.1	5.1	6.4
	2000	501208.6	59.3	69.3	64.4	58.9	55.3	33.5	38.2	12.8	7.9	7.6
	2003	540928.4	59.8	67.8	64.8	61.5	55.1	35.0	38.5	11.4	10.3	4.8
DEVELOPED ECONOMIES: AMERICA - ECONOMIES DEVELOPPEES : AMERIQUE	1990	25735.0	6.6	0.8	2.1	11.7	5.6	62.6	7.5	8.2	10.7	11.0
	1995	21909.5	4.3	0.9	1.8	8.9	4.5	52.6	10.6	8.4	16.7	11.6
	2000	29833.0	6.0	1.7	1.7	5.8	3.9	56.9	15.5	5.5	13.1	9.0
	2003	44607.5	7.6	3.5	2.7	6.0	3.5	54.3	23.9	5.8	12.2	3.8
Canada	1990	700.0	0.1	0.0	0.1	0.0	0.5	40.7	8.1	13.4	1.0	36.7
	1995	666.7	0.1	0.0	0.1	0.0	0.5	25.3	19.1	13.6	0.3	41.8
	2000	1168.0	0.2	0.1	0.1	0.0	0.5	46.1	14.0	10.4	0.2	29.4
	2003	3123.6	0.2	0.6	0.1	0.0	0.8	23.5	59.4	4.2	0.1	12.8
United States - Etats-Unis	1990	25035.0	6.5	0.8	2.0	11.7	5.1	63.2	7.5	8.1	11.0	10.2
	1995	21242.8	4.3	0.9	1.7	8.9	4.0	53.5	10.3	8.3	17.3	10.7
	2000	28665.0	5.8	1.6	1.5	5.8	3.4	57.3	15.6	5.3	13.6	8.2
	2003	41483.8	7.4	2.9	2.6	6.0	2.7	56.6	21.2	6.0	13.1	3.1
DEVELOPED ECONOMIES: EUROPE - ECONOMIES DEVELOPPEES : EUROPE	1990	190311.0	29.7	29.9	22.4	33.1	35.7	38.2	36.1	12.0	4.1	9.5
	1995	213048.1	30.3	29.3	24.9	31.6	32.9	37.7	35.3	12.0	6.1	8.8
	2000	226258.0	31.2	25.3	25.0	32.4	30.9	39.0	30.9	11.0	9.6	9.4
	2003	235612.6	29.6	25.3	23.6	30.5	29.4	39.8	33.1	9.5	11.7	5.9
European Union 25 - Union européenne 25	1990	144637.0	20.2	23.6	20.1	32.4	24.9	34.3	37.5	14.2	5.3	8.7
	1995	178834.2	23.7	26.3	21.5	31.4	23.3	35.2	37.8	12.4	7.2	7.5
	2000	192493.0	25.7	22.5	21.1	32.2	22.0	37.8	32.3	10.9	11.2	7.8
	2003	205591.5	25.3	22.6	19.1	30.0	22.7	39.0	33.8	8.8	13.2	5.2
European Union 15 - Union européenne 15	*1990*	*98801.0*	*14.7*	*13.7*	*12.3*	*30.8*	*23.0*	*36.3*	*31.8*	*12.7*	*7.4*	*11.8*
	1995	*103319.2*	*15.7*	*11.6*	*9.8*	*25.9*	*19.6*	*40.4*	*28.8*	*9.7*	*10.3*	*10.8*
	2000	*107636.0*	*15.8*	*8.1*	*10.2*	*26.6*	*18.2*	*41.5*	*20.9*	*9.4*	*16.6*	*11.6*
	2003	*128225.3*	*18.0*	*9.1*	*11.2*	*25.1*	*20.9*	*44.4*	*21.9*	*8.2*	*17.7*	*7.7*
Austria - Autriche	1990	234.0	0.0	0.1	0.1	0.0	0.0	0.0	52.1	47.9	0.0	0.0
	1995	130.0	0.0	0.0	0.1	0.0	0.0	0.0	5.2	94.8	0.0	0.0
	2000	121.0	0.0	0.0	0.1	0.0	0.0	0.0	0.0	100.0	0.0	0.0
	2003	41.2	0.0	0.0	0.0	0.0	0.0	0.0	0.0	92.2	7.8	0.0
Belgium - Belgique	1990	3116.0	0.1	0.8	0.1	0.9	1.5	6.5	59.2	2.9	7.0	24.3
	1995	249.2	0.0	0.0	0.0	0.0	0.4	1.5	0.0	4.1	0.0	94.4
	2000	171.0	0.0	0.0	0.0	0.0	0.2	4.1	0.0	0.6	0.0	95.3
	2003	1937.6	0.2	0.1	0.0	0.4	1.4	31.8	17.8	0.1	16.4	33.9
Denmark - Danemark	1990	8787.0	1.2	0.3	0.8	6.0	6.0	32.8	7.5	9.2	16.0	34.5
	1995	7617.2	0.8	0.4	0.8	5.2	3.0	26.2	12.1	11.0	28.3	22.5
	2000	8455.0	0.7	0.2	0.8	5.4	1.9	24.6	7.9	9.6	42.8	15.2
	2003	9173.2	1.0	0.0	0.4	5.4	1.3	34.9	0.8	4.5	53.1	6.7
Finland - Finlande	1990	983.0	0.1	0.1	0.3	0.0	0.5	24.8	18.9	29.0	0.0	27.3
	1995	1158.0	0.2	0.0	0.3	0.0	0.3	44.0	10.4	29.9	0.0	15.7
	2000	1215.0	0.2	0.0	0.4	0.0	0.3	42.0	11.0	30.2	0.0	16.8
	2003	1146.5	0.2	0.0	0.4	0.0	0.3	44.8	8.2	34.2	1.2	11.6
France	1990	5574.0	1.4	0.3	0.5	2.3	1.0	60.3	11.0	9.7	9.6	9.5
	1995	6201.6	1.5	0.2	0.4	1.5	1.0	65.3	8.7	6.4	10.0	9.7
	2000	6883.0	1.5	0.4	0.3	0.7	1.3	60.3	14.8	4.9	6.7	13.4
	2003	6389.2	1.3	0.2	0.3	0.7	1.6	63.8	10.8	3.9	9.8	11.7

For sources and notes, see end of table.

Pour les sources et les notes, se reporter à la fin du tableau.

Region, country or area / Régions pays ou zones	Year / Année	Total Fleet (thousands of DWT)[1] / Flotte totale (milliers de TPL)[1]	As percentage of world total fleet / En pourcentage de la flotte mondiale					As percentage of the country total fleet / En pourcentage de la flotte totale du pays				
			Oil tankers / Petroliers	Bulk carriers / Vraquiers	General cargo / Navires de charge classiques	Container ships / Porte-conteneurs	Other types / Autres navires	Oil tankers / Petroliers	Bulk carriers / Vraquiers	General cargo / Navires de charge classique	Container ships / Porte-conteneurs	Other types / Autres navires
Germany - Allemagne	1995	6599.7	0.0	0.2	1.4	10.0	1.1	0.3	6.0	21.6	62.5	9.5
	2000	7773.0	0.0	0.0	0.9	9.6	0.5	0.6	0.1	11.6	82.9	4.8
	2003	6902.2	0.1	0.0	0.4	6.7	0.5	4.0	0.0	4.9	87.8	3.3
Germany (former Dem. Rep.) - Allemagne (anc. Rép. Dém.)	1990	1731.0	0.0	0.2	0.9	0.5	0.3	0.6	30.0	54.7	7.2	7.6
Germany (former Federal Rep.) - Allemagne (anc. Rép. fédérale)	1990	5369.0	0.1	0.3	1.6	9.4	1.5	3.4	11.7	29.8	41.3	13.8
Greece - Grèce	1990	37205.0	6.2	7.9	2.5	1.3	1.8	41.0	48.9	6.8	0.8	2.5
	1995	52064.7	9.4	8.9	2.0	2.0	2.4	48.1	43.8	3.9	1.6	2.6
	2000	44618.0	9.1	5.3	0.8	3.1	1.8	57.9	32.8	1.9	4.6	2.8
	2003	54481.5	9.9	6.5	0.5	2.4	0.9	57.4	37.0	0.8	4.0	0.8
Ireland - Irlande	1990	188.0	0.0	0.0	0.1	0.1	0.1	5.9	7.4	49.5	13.3	23.9
	1995	199.9	0.0	0.0	0.1	0.0	0.1	7.1	0.0	60.0	5.1	27.8
	2000	176.0	0.0	0.0	0.1	0.0	0.1	0.0	20.5	49.4	4.0	26.1
	2003	446.0	0.0	0.0	0.2	0.0	0.1	3.6	31.7	50.2	2.9	11.6
Italy - Italie	1990	11840.0	1.8	1.8	1.3	1.7	2.9	37.8	35.6	10.9	3.4	12.3
	1995	8843.8	1.3	1.1	0.7	1.0	2.8	37.5	32.0	7.7	4.5	18.3
	2000	10366.0	1.0	1.4	1.0	1.2	2.8	27.2	37.1	9.6	7.7	18.3
	2003	10575.4	1.4	0.8	1.4	0.9	2.7	42.9	24.6	12.4	7.8	12.2
Luxembourg	1990	6.0	0.0	0.0	0.0	0.0	0.0	50.0	0.0	0.0	0.0	50.0
	1995	1297.6	0.0	0.2	0.1	0.2	1.3	0.4	29.7	5.2	6.0	58.7
	2000	1427.0	0.2	0.0	0.1	0.0	1.1	38.9	0.6	4.0	2.0	54.4
	2003	1365.6	0.2	0.0	0.1	0.2	0.8	55.5	0.0	4.6	10.7	29.2
Netherlands - Pays-Bas	1990	4725.0	0.2	0.2	1.8	2.5	2.4	12.0	11.6	38.0	12.5	26.0
	1995	5315.4	0.3	0.1	2.0	2.4	2.1	15.5	4.9	38.3	18.6	22.7
	2000	6911.0	0.1	0.0	3.2	2.8	2.3	4.0	0.2	45.9	27.2	22.7
	2003	7920.0	0.2	0.1	3.8	2.2	2.8	8.7	3.9	45.6	25.1	16.7
Portugal	1990	1322.0	0.3	0.2	0.1	0.1	0.2	54.2	28.0	8.4	1.7	7.8
	1995	1417.9	0.3	0.1	0.2	0.0	0.2	62.3	16.5	11.9	1.0	8.3
	2000	1718.0	0.2	0.2	0.4	0.1	0.3	37.6	27.5	21.2	2.1	11.6
	2003	1608.0	0.3	0.1	0.3	0.0	0.3	53.8	19.2	14.9	2.6	9.5
Spain - Espagne	1990	6185.0	1.2	0.7	0.7	0.4	1.5	49.2	25.3	11.7	1.6	12.0
	1995	1282.4	0.1	0.0	0.2	0.2	0.9	27.6	7.2	19.1	7.8	38.3
	2000	2142.0	0.4	0.0	0.3	0.2	0.7	51.8	3.3	15.1	6.3	23.5
	2003	2586.5	0.4	0.0	0.4	0.3	1.4	49.6	1.7	13.7	9.0	26.1
Sweden - Suède	1990	2942.0	0.3	0.3	1.0	0.3	1.1	24.5	21.8	33.1	2.4	18.2
	1995	2384.3	0.3	0.0	1.0	0.0	1.1	28.4	3.1	43.4	0.0	25.2
	2000	1822.0	0.1	0.0	1.0	0.0	0.9	8.9	2.2	53.8	0.0	35.0
	2003	2116.5	0.2	0.0	1.2	0.0	0.6	29.0	2.9	55.3	0.0	12.8
United Kingdom - Royaume-Uni	1990	8594.0	1.7	0.6	0.7	5.3	2.3	49.0	15.0	7.8	14.5	13.7
	1995	8557.5	1.5	0.4	0.5	3.3	2.8	47.0	12.3	6.3	15.9	18.6
	2000	13838.0	2.3	0.6	0.8	3.5	3.9	46.7	11.2	5.8	17.1	19.2
	2003	21535.8	2.6	1.1	1.8	6.0	6.1	38.4	15.1	8.0	25.1	13.5
New Eu members 10 - Nouveaux membres de l'UE 10	**1990**	**45836.0**	**5.6**	**9.9**	**7.8**	**1.6**	**1.9**	**29.8**	**49.9**	**17.3**	**0.8**	**2.1**
	1995	**75515.0**	**8.0**	**14.7**	**11.7**	**5.5**	**3.8**	**28.1**	**50.1**	**15.9**	**3.0**	**2.8**
	2000	**84857.0**	**9.9**	**14.3**	**10.9**	**5.6**	**3.8**	**33.0**	**46.7**	**12.8**	**4.4**	**3.1**
	2003	**77366.2**	**7.3**	**13.5**	**7.9**	**4.8**	**1.8**	**29.9**	**53.6**	**9.7**	**5.6**	**1.1**
Cyprus - Chypre	1990	32985.0	4.3	7.3	4.7	1.4	1.2	31.8	50.7	14.7	1.0	1.9
	1995	40378.0	3.1	8.9	6.5	4.2	1.6	20.1	56.9	16.4	4.3	2.3
	2000	36165.0	2.5	7.2	5.2	4.2	1.8	19.7	54.7	14.4	7.8	3.4
	2003	35331.7	2.2	7.0	3.8	3.5	0.6	19.4	60.8	10.1	8.9	0.8
Czech Republic - République tchèque	1995	226.5	0.0	0.1	0.1	0.0	0.0	0.0	73.1	26.9	0.0	0.0
Czechoslovakia (former) - Tchécoslovaquie (anc.)	1990	510.0	0.0	0.2	0.1	0.0	0.0	0.0	77.5	22.5	0.0	0.0
Estonia - Estonie	1995	595.2	0.0	0.1	0.2	0.0	0.2	2.6	43.5	37.9	0.0	16.0
	2000	281.0	0.0	0.0	0.2	0.0	0.1	3.9	17.1	58.0	0.0	21.0
	2003	226.6	0.0	0.0	0.1	0.0	0.1	6.8	21.3	48.4	0.0	23.5

For sources and notes, see end of table.

Pour les sources et les notes, se reporter à la fin du tableau.

Region, country or area / Régions pays ou zones	Year / Année	Total Fleet (thousands of DWT)[1] / Flotte totale (milliers de TPL)[1]	As percentage of world total fleet / En pourcentage de la flotte mondiale					As percentage of the country total fleet / En pourcentage de la flotte totale du pays				
			Oil tankers / Petroliers	Bulk carriers / Vraquiers	General cargo / Navires de charge classiques	Container ships / Porte-conteneurs	Other types / Autres navires	Oil tankers / Petroliers	Bulk carriers / Vraquiers	General cargo / Navires de charge classique	Container ships / Porte-conteneurs	Other types / Autres navires
Hungary - Hongrie	1990	143.0	0.0	0.0	0.1	0.0	0.0	0.0	20.3	79.7	0.0	0.0
	1995	65.0	0.0	0.0	0.1	0.0	0.0	0.0	0.0	100.0	0.0	0.0
	2003	10.0	0.0	0.0	0.0	0.0	0.0	0.0	0.0	100.0	0.0	0.0
Latvia - Lettonie	1995	881.0	0.2	0.0	0.3	0.0	0.2	56.1	0.0	33.5	0.0	10.4
	2000	81.0	0.0	0.0	0.0	0.0	0.1	14.8	0.0	40.7	0.0	44.4
	2003	53.1	0.0	0.0	0.0	0.0	0.1	7.5	0.0	21.2	0.0	71.3
Lithuania - Lituanie	1995	562.4	0.0	0.1	0.2	0.0	0.3	2.4	28.5	42.1	0.0	27.1
	2000	420.0	0.0	0.1	0.2	0.0	0.1	1.7	34.8	51.7	0.0	11.9
	2003	402.5	0.0	0.0	0.2	0.0	0.2	1.8	28.9	49.9	0.0	19.4
Malta - Malte	1990	7756.0	1.2	1.4	1.5	0.0	0.3	38.4	40.2	19.5	0.1	1.8
	1995	29629.1	4.7	4.6	3.8	1.3	1.2	42.4	40.2	13.2	1.8	2.4
	2000	46330.0	7.4	6.6	5.2	1.4	1.6	45.0	39.4	11.2	2.0	2.4
	2003	40998.4	5.1	6.4	3.8	1.3	0.7	39.6	47.9	8.7	2.9	0.9
Poland - Pologne	1990	4442.0	0.1	1.1	1.3	0.2	0.4	4.9	58.1	30.9	1.1	5.0
	1995	3176.7	0.0	0.9	0.6	0.0	0.3	0.3	75.4	19.3	0.0	5.0
	2000	1561.0	0.0	0.5	0.0	0.0	0.2	0.6	90.6	1.9	0.0	6.9
	2003	300.3	0.0	0.1	0.0	0.0	0.1	5.3	66.8	6.1	0.0	21.8
Slovakia - Slovaquie	2000	19.0	0.0	0.0	0.0	0.0	0.0	0.0	0.0	100.0	0.0	0.0
	2003	42.8	0.0	0.0	0.0	0.0	0.0	0.0	76.2	23.8	0.0	0.0
Slovenia - Slovénie	1995	1.1	0.0	0.0	0.0	0.0	0.0	0.0	0.0	20.8	0.0	79.2
	2003	0.7	0.0	0.0	0.0	0.0	0.0	0.0	0.0	0.0	0.0	100.0
Other developed Europe - Autres économies développées d'Europe	*1990*	*45674.0*	*9.5*	*6.3*	*2.4*	*0.6*	*10.7*	*50.8*	*31.7*	*5.3*	*0.3*	*11.9*
	1995	*34213.8*	*6.6*	*3.0*	*3.4*	*0.2*	*9.6*	*50.9*	*22.7*	*10.2*	*0.2*	*16.0*
	2000	*33765.0*	*5.5*	*2.9*	*4.0*	*0.3*	*8.9*	*46.3*	*23.4*	*11.7*	*0.5*	*18.1*
	2003	*30021.0*	*4.3*	*2.7*	*4.6*	*0.5*	*6.7*	*45.3*	*28.1*	*14.5*	*1.6*	*10.5*
Gibraltar	1990	3849.0	1.3	0.3	0.1	0.0	0.1	79.6	15.9	3.7	0.0	0.8
	1995	579.4	0.2	0.0	0.0	0.0	0.0	92.5	0.0	5.9	0.0	1.6
	2000	922.0	0.2	0.0	0.1	0.1	0.1	70.5	2.9	10.3	7.6	8.7
	2003	1255.9	0.2	0.0	0.5	0.3	0.0	38.0	2.4	36.1	22.6	0.9
Iceland - Islande	1990	135.0	0.0	0.0	0.1	0.0	0.1	0.7	4.4	52.6	0.0	43.0
	1995	107.0	0.0	0.0	0.0	0.0	0.1	2.1	0.6	34.4	0.0	62.9
	2000	15.0	0.0	0.0	0.0	0.0	0.0	20.0	6.7	20.0	0.0	53.3
	2003	72.8	0.0	0.0	0.0	0.0	0.1	0.6	0.9	2.3	0.0	96.1
Norway - Norvège	1990	41207.0	8.2	5.8	2.1	0.6	10.5	48.9	32.6	5.3	0.3	12.9
	1995	32867.2	6.4	2.8	3.3	0.2	9.4	51.4	21.7	10.3	0.3	16.3
	2000	31994.0	5.3	2.6	3.8	0.2	8.8	46.9	22.2	11.9	0.3	18.8
	2003	27652.2	4.1	2.4	4.1	0.1	6.5	47.5	27.2	13.9	0.3	11.1
Switzerland - Suisse	1990	483.0	0.0	0.2	0.0	0.0	0.0	0.0	88.4	7.0	0.0	4.6
	1995	660.2	0.0	0.2	0.0	0.0	0.0	0.0	93.9	1.9	0.0	4.2
	2000	834.0	0.0	0.3	0.0	0.0	0.0	0.0	91.7	5.5	0.0	2.8
	2003	1040.1	0.0	0.3	0.0	0.1	0.0	0.0	84.3	3.8	11.4	0.5
DEVELOPED ECONOMIES: ASIA - ECONOMIES DEVELOPPEES : ASIE	**1990**	**41437.0**	**5.6**	**7.2**	**5.9**	**6.9**	**6.7**	**33.3**	**39.9**	**14.6**	**3.9**	**8.2**
	1995	**29504.2**	**4.1**	**3.9**	**3.2**	**4.3**	**6.1**	**36.8**	**34.2**	**11.2**	**5.9**	**11.8**
	2000	**20163.0**	**2.4**	**2.1**	**2.6**	**2.1**	**5.0**	**33.8**	**29.4**	**12.8**	**6.9**	**17.1**
	2003	**17468.3**	**1.8**	**1.9**	**2.3**	**1.5**	**4.8**	**32.6**	**34.0**	**12.7**	**7.8**	**12.9**
Israel - Israël	1990	609.0	0.0	0.0	0.1	1.9	0.0	0.2	8.5	18.6	72.2	0.5
	1995	720.7	0.0	0.0	0.1	1.5	0.0	0.3	2.5	9.8	86.9	0.5
	2000	712.0	0.0	0.0	0.0	1.0	0.0	0.4	0.0	1.0	98.2	0.4
	2003	891.6	0.0	0.0	0.0	1.0	0.0	0.3	0.0	0.3	98.9	0.5
Japan - Japon	1990	40828.0	5.6	7.2	5.8	5.1	6.7	33.8	40.4	14.6	2.9	8.3
	1995	28783.5	4.1	3.9	3.1	2.7	6.1	37.8	35.0	11.2	3.9	12.1
	2000	19451.0	2.4	2.1	2.6	1.0	5.0	35.0	30.5	13.2	3.6	17.7
	2003	16576.7	1.8	1.9	2.3	0.5	4.8	34.3	35.8	13.4	2.9	13.6

For sources and notes, see end of table.

Pour les sources et les notes, se reporter à la fin du tableau.

Region, country or area / Régions pays ou zones	Year / Année	Total Fleet (thousands of DWT)[1] / Flotte totale (milliers de TPL)[1]	As percentage of world total fleet / En pourcentage de la flotte mondiale					As percentage of the country total fleet / En pourcentage de la flotte totale du pays				
			Oil tankers / Petroliers	Bulk carriers / Vraquiers	General cargo / Navires de charge classiques	Container ships / Porte-conteneurs	Other types / Autres navires	Oil tankers / Petroliers	Bulk carriers / Vraquiers	General cargo / Navires de charge classique	Container ships / Porte-conteneurs	Other types / Autres navires
DEVELOPED ECONOMIES: OCEANIA - ECONOMIES DEVELOPPEES : OCEANIE	**1990**	**4032.0**	**0.5**	**0.8**	**0.3**	**0.6**	**0.9**	**30.4**	**48.5**	**6.6**	**3.5**	**11.0**
	1995	**4283.4**	**0.4**	**0.7**	**0.2**	**0.3**	**1.9**	**26.6**	**40.2**	**4.2**	**3.1**	**25.9**
	2000	**2523.0**	**0.2**	**0.4**	**0.1**	**0.1**	**1.3**	**19.8**	**40.2**	**3.0**	**1.9**	**35.2**
	2003	**2441.7**	**0.2**	**0.3**	**0.1**	**0.0**	**1.7**	**22.4**	**38.7**	**5.0**	**0.4**	**33.4**
Australia - Australie	1990	3730.0	0.5	0.8	0.2	0.5	0.8	29.5	51.3	4.8	3.4	11.0
	1995	3975.9	0.4	0.7	0.1	0.3	1.8	25.5	42.4	3.0	3.3	25.8
	2000	2356.0	0.1	0.4	0.1	0.1	1.2	17.3	42.4	2.5	2.0	35.8
	2003	2277.3	0.1	0.3	0.1	0.0	1.6	20.3	40.8	4.9	0.4	33.6
New Zealand - Nouvelle-Zélande	1990	302.0	0.1	0.0	0.1	0.1	0.1	41.4	13.9	29.1	4.6	10.9
	1995	307.6	0.0	0.0	0.1	0.0	0.1	41.2	12.1	19.5	0.0	27.2
	2000	167.0	0.0	0.0	0.0	0.0	0.1	54.5	10.2	9.0	0.0	26.3
	2003	164.4	0.0	0.0	0.0	0.0	0.1	52.4	10.4	6.7	0.0	30.6
DEVELOPING ECONOMIES: AMERICA - ECONOMIES EN DEVELOPPEMENT : AMERIQUE	**1990**	**117878.0**	**18.0**	**17.2**	**22.5**	**14.9**	**15.5**	**37.3**	**33.5**	**19.5**	**3.0**	**6.7**
	1995	**180826.3**	**25.6**	**24.9**	**27.3**	**24.6**	**19.4**	**37.5**	**35.3**	**15.5**	**5.6**	**6.1**
	2000	**262257.3**	**31.1**	**37.6**	**32.1**	**30.2**	**26.3**	**33.6**	**39.6**	**12.2**	**7.7**	**6.9**
	2003	**277099.4**	**28.3**	**37.7**	**31.0**	**31.0**	**30.0**	**32.3**	**41.8**	**10.6**	**10.1**	**5.1**
South America - Amérique du Sud	*1990*	*17260.0*	*2.3*	*3.2*	*2.9*	*0.9*	*2.3*	*32.9*	*42.2*	*17.1*	*1.3*	*6.6*
	1995	*12446.2*	*1.9*	*1.8*	*1.1*	*0.9*	*2.3*	*40.8*	*36.6*	*9.0*	*2.8*	*10.8*
	2000	*9540.0*	*1.4*	*1.2*	*1.0*	*0.4*	*1.5*	*42.2*	*33.6*	*10.6*	*2.9*	*10.7*
	2003	*9532.9*	*1.4*	*0.9*	*1.0*	*0.3*	*2.6*	*46.3*	*28.6*	*9.5*	*2.5*	*13.1*
Argentina - Argentine	1990	2872.0	0.4	0.4	0.7	0.3	0.5	33.1	30.6	25.0	2.3	8.9
	1995	757.5	0.1	0.0	0.2	0.1	0.4	24.5	13.9	24.2	6.5	30.9
	2000	384.0	0.1	0.0	0.1	0.0	0.1	39.1	13.5	34.4	0.0	13.0
	2003	488.8	0.0	0.0	0.1	0.0	0.5	18.9	10.6	22.1	0.0	48.4
Bolivia - Bolivie	1990	16.0	0.0	0.0	0.0	0.0	0.0	0.0	0.0	100.0	0.0	0.0
	2000	259.0	0.0	0.0	0.1	0.0	0.0	15.8	19.3	54.4	1.5	8.9
	2003	654.6	0.2	0.0	0.1	0.0	0.1	72.9	2.1	19.7	0.3	5.0
Brazil - Brésil	1990	10005.0	1.4	2.3	0.9	0.5	1.0	33.1	51.7	8.8	1.1	5.2
	1995	8543.3	1.4	1.4	0.4	0.6	0.7	44.2	43.1	5.0	2.9	4.8
	2000	6152.0	1.0	0.9	0.4	0.3	0.3	46.0	41.0	6.0	3.1	3.9
	2003	5139.3	0.7	0.7	0.4	0.2	0.4	44.4	41.6	6.6	3.6	3.9
Chile - Chili	1990	883.0	0.0	0.2	0.2	0.0	0.2	0.7	62.7	22.9	0.0	13.7
	1995	1038.8	0.1	0.2	0.1	0.1	0.4	13.2	51.1	10.5	2.1	23.1
	2000	881.0	0.1	0.1	0.1	0.1	0.3	18.8	42.0	10.1	8.7	20.3
	2003	1128.5	0.1	0.1	0.1	0.1	0.4	38.9	29.1	10.3	4.5	17.1
Colombia - Colombie	1990	541.0	0.0	0.1	0.3	0.0	0.0	3.0	29.0	64.3	0.0	3.7
	1995	171.4	0.0	0.0	0.1	0.0	0.0	5.6	0.0	83.0	0.0	11.3
	2000	103.0	0.0	0.0	0.1	0.0	0.0	9.7	0.0	60.2	0.0	30.1
	2003	88.1	0.0	0.0	0.1	0.0	0.1	11.0	0.0	60.1	0.0	28.9
Ecuador - Equateur	1990	523.0	0.1	0.0	0.2	0.0	0.1	40.0	8.8	46.1	0.0	5.2
	1995	209.3	0.0	0.0	0.0	0.0	0.1	62.5	0.0	21.9	0.0	15.6
	2000	440.0	0.1	0.0	0.0	0.0	0.1	86.4	0.0	0.9	0.0	12.7
	2003	452.5	0.1	0.0	0.0	0.0	0.1	84.6	0.0	0.6	0.0	14.8
Falkland Islands (Malvinas) - Iles Falkland (Malvinas)	1990	4.0	0.0	0.0	0.0	0.0	0.0	0.0	0.0	0.0	0.0	100.0
	1995	11.8	0.0	0.0	0.0	0.0	0.0	0.0	0.0	5.4	0.0	94.6
	2000	36.0	0.0	0.0	0.0	0.0	0.1	0.0	0.0	2.8	0.0	97.2
	2003	37.3	0.0	0.0	0.0	0.0	0.1	0.0	0.0	1.3	0.0	98.7
Guyana	1990	11.0	0.0	0.0	0.0	0.0	0.0	0.0	0.0	45.5	0.0	54.5
	1995	12.9	0.0	0.0	0.0	0.0	0.0	0.0	0.0	54.7	0.0	45.3
	2000	15.0	0.0	0.0	0.0	0.0	0.0	0.0	0.0	60.0	0.0	40.0
	2003	30.1	0.0	0.0	0.0	0.0	0.0	7.0	0.0	69.3	0.0	23.8
Paraguay	1990	42.0	0.0	0.0	0.0	0.0	0.0	2.4	0.0	57.1	0.0	40.5
	1995	40.0	0.0	0.0	0.0	0.0	0.0	7.1	0.0	83.9	0.0	8.9
	2000	52.0	0.0	0.0	0.0	0.0	0.0	17.3	0.0	76.9	3.8	1.9
	2003	47.2	0.0	0.0	0.0	0.0	0.0	8.2	0.0	84.7	4.6	2.5

For sources and notes, see end of table.

Pour les sources et les notes, se reporter à la fin du tableau.

Region, country or area / Régions pays ou zones	Year / Année	Total Fleet (thousands of DWT)[1] / Flotte totale (milliers de TPL)[1]	As percentage of world total fleet / En pourcentage de la flotte mondiale					As percentage of the country total fleet / En pourcentage de la flotte totale du pays				
			Oil tankers / Petroliers	Bulk carriers / Vraquiers	General cargo / Navires de charge classiques	Container ships / Porte-conteneurs	Other types / Autres navires	Oil tankers / Petroliers	Bulk carriers / Vraquiers	General cargo / Navires de charge classique	Container ships / Porte-conteneurs	Other types / Autres navires
Peru - Pérou	1990	807.0	0.1	0.1	0.2	0.0	0.1	40.5	26.8	26.6	0.0	6.1
	1995	343.7	0.1	0.0	0.1	0.0	0.1	43.8	14.7	21.7	0.0	19.8
	2000	222.0	0.0	0.0	0.1	0.0	0.1	26.6	0.0	36.5	0.0	36.9
	2003	147.6	0.0	0.0	0.0	0.0	0.2	18.4	0.0	25.1	0.0	56.6
Suriname	1990	16.0	0.0	0.0	0.0	0.0	0.0	18.8	0.0	62.5	12.5	6.3
	1995	9.0	0.0	0.0	0.0	0.0	0.0	33.6	0.0	38.3	19.6	8.5
	2000	6.0	0.0	0.0	0.0	0.0	0.0	50.0	0.0	50.0	0.0	0.0
	2003	6.8	0.0	0.0	0.0	0.0	0.0	49.9	0.0	46.4	0.0	3.7
Uruguay	1990	157.0	0.0	0.0	0.0	0.1	0.0	59.9	0.0	2.5	21.7	15.9
	1995	149.5	0.0	0.0	0.0	0.1	0.0	62.4	0.0	1.8	18.8	16.9
	2000	40.0	0.0	0.0	0.0	0.0	0.0	20.0	0.0	10.0	0.0	70.0
	2003	50.6	0.0	0.0	0.0	0.0	0.1	21.6	0.0	13.7	0.0	64.7
Venezuela	1990	1383.0	0.3	0.1	0.3	0.0	0.2	54.9	17.9	20.0	0.1	7.2
	1995	1159.1	0.2	0.1	0.1	0.0	0.5	51.1	16.2	7.9	0.1	24.7
	2000	950.0	0.1	0.1	0.1	0.0	0.4	38.8	22.0	8.1	0.1	30.9
	2003	1261.3	0.2	0.1	0.1	0.0	0.7	53.7	15.9	3.9	0.1	26.4
Other America - Autres économies d'Amérique	*1990*	*100618.0*	*15.6*	*14.0*	*19.6*	*14.0*	*13.3*	*38.1*	*32.0*	*19.9*	*3.3*	*6.7*
	1995	*168380.1*	*23.6*	*23.1*	*26.2*	*23.7*	*17.1*	*37.2*	*35.2*	*16.0*	*5.8*	*5.8*
	2000	*252717.3*	*29.7*	*36.4*	*31.1*	*29.8*	*24.8*	*33.2*	*39.8*	*12.3*	*7.9*	*6.7*
	2003	*267566.6*	*26.9*	*36.8*	*30.1*	*30.8*	*27.4*	*31.8*	*42.3*	*10.7*	*10.4*	*4.8*
Anguilla	1990	4.0	0.0	0.0	0.0	0.0	0.0	0.0	0.0	75.0	0.0	25.0
	1995	3.6	0.0	0.0	0.0	0.0	0.0	0.0	0.0	97.4	0.0	2.6
	2000	1.3	0.0	0.0	0.0	0.0	0.0	0.0	0.0	100.0	0.0	0.0
	2003	0.9	0.0	0.0	0.0	0.0	0.0	0.0	0.0	100.0	0.0	0.0
Antigua and Barbuda - Antigua-et-Barbuda	1990	608.0	0.0	0.0	0.5	0.1	0.1	1.0	0.8	83.2	5.1	9.9
	1995	2441.2	0.0	0.1	1.4	2.0	0.1	0.2	6.7	58.5	33.1	1.4
	2000	5462.0	0.0	0.1	2.2	4.3	0.1	0.1	5.6	39.8	53.3	1.1
	2003	7851.1	0.0	0.2	2.8	4.9	0.2	0.6	7.8	34.2	56.3	1.2
Bahamas	1990	22365.0	5.2	2.8	2.0	1.1	1.9	56.5	28.6	9.3	1.2	4.3
	1995	36717.0	7.5	3.1	6.1	2.0	3.4	54.1	21.4	17.0	2.3	5.3
	2000	46453.0	9.0	3.1	7.4	2.4	5.0	55.1	18.4	15.8	3.5	7.3
	2003	47750.3	8.2	3.1	7.0	2.2	7.7	54.1	20.2	13.9	4.2	7.6
Barbados - Barbade	1990	8.0	0.0	0.0	0.0	0.0	0.0	0.0	0.0	100.0	0.0	0.0
	1995	414.1	0.0	0.0	0.2	0.0	0.1	18.4	20.4	54.0	0.0	7.2
	2000	1172.0	0.2	0.1	0.1	0.1	0.1	54.6	22.5	12.0	3.0	7.8
	2003	694.6	0.1	0.1	0.1	0.0	0.2	28.1	45.3	14.4	0.0	12.2
Belize	1995	710.7	0.0	0.0	0.5	0.0	0.1	4.6	4.4	78.2	1.7	11.2
	2000	2589.0	0.2	0.1	1.5	0.1	0.2	24.0	11.4	56.2	3.2	5.2
	2003	1782.5	0.1	0.1	1.0	0.0	0.6	13.3	15.5	54.2	1.1	15.9
Bermuda - Bermudes	1990	7800.0	2.7	0.1	0.2	0.1	1.3	85.0	3.7	2.4	0.4	8.5
	1995	4797.0	1.2	0.2	0.2	0.4	1.4	67.5	9.1	3.5	3.2	16.6
	2000	9398.0	1.5	1.3	0.3	0.7	0.8	46.3	39.4	3.4	4.9	6.1
	2003	6488.4	0.4	1.2	0.3	0.6	2.1	17.8	55.2	3.7	8.1	15.3
British Virgin Islands - Iles Vierges britanniques	1990	5.0	0.0	0.0	0.0	0.0	0.0	0.0	0.0	80.0	0.0	20.0
	1995	4.1	0.0	0.0	0.0	0.0	0.0	0.0	0.0	79.0	0.0	21.0
	2000	8.0	0.0	0.0	0.0	0.0	0.0	0.0	0.0	12.5	0.0	87.5
	2003	158.4	0.0	0.0	0.0	0.0	0.0	79.4	0.0	19.1	0.0	1.5
Cayman Islands - Iles Caïmanes	1990	570.0	0.0	0.1	0.2	0.0	0.2	20.4	27.2	34.7	0.0	17.7
	1995	487.7	0.0	0.1	0.2	0.0	0.1	1.8	39.0	42.1	0.4	16.7
	2000	2805.0	0.2	0.4	0.3	0.1	1.1	19.3	39.9	11.9	1.4	27.5
	2003	4437.0	0.8	0.4	0.6	0.0	0.3	57.0	26.1	13.7	0.0	3.2
Costa Rica	1990	6.0	0.0	0.0	0.0	0.0	0.0	0.0	0.0	33.3	0.0	66.7
	1995	2.2	0.0	0.0	0.0	0.0	0.0	0.0	0.0	0.0	0.0	100.0
	2000	4.0	0.0	0.0	0.0	0.0	0.0	0.0	75.0	0.0	0.0	25.0
	2003	0.8	0.0	0.0	0.0	0.0	0.0	0.0	0.0	0.0	0.0	100.0

For sources and notes, see end of table.

Pour les sources et les notes, se reporter à la fin du tableau.

Region, country or area / Régions pays ou zones	Year / Année	Total Fleet (thousands of DWT)[1] / Flotte totale (milliers de TPL)[1]	As percentage of world total fleet / En pourcentage de la flotte mondiale					As percentage of the country total fleet / En pourcentage de la flotte totale du pays				
			Oil tankers / Petroliers	Bulk carriers / Vraquiers	General cargo / Navires de charge classiques	Container ships / Porte-conteneurs	Other types / Autres navires	Oil tankers / Petroliers	Bulk carriers / Vraquiers	General cargo / Navires de charge classique	Container ships / Porte-conteneurs	Other types / Autres navires
Cuba	1990	1115.0	0.0	0.0	0.7	0.0	0.3	10.5	9.0	65.2	0.0	15.3
	1995	490.2	0.0	0.0	0.3	0.0	0.2	18.7	0.1	53.1	0.0	28.1
	2000	80.0	0.0	0.0	0.1	0.0	0.0	6.3	0.0	86.3	0.0	7.5
	2003	110.0	0.0	0.0	0.0	0.0	0.1	29.0	5.7	20.0	0.0	45.3
Dominica - Dominique	1990	4.0	0.0	0.0	0.0	0.0	0.0	0.0	0.0	100.0	0.0	0.0
	1995	1.9	0.0	0.0	0.0	0.0	0.0	0.0	0.0	100.0	0.0	0.0
	2000	2.0	0.0	0.0	0.0	0.0	0.0	0.0	0.0	100.0	0.0	0.0
	2003	44.3	0.0	0.0	0.0	0.0	0.0	41.5	1.1	46.3	0.0	11.1
Dominican Republic - République dominicaine	1990	52.0	0.0	0.0	0.0	0.0	0.0	3.8	36.5	59.6	0.0	0.0
	1995	11.2	0.0	0.0	0.0	0.0	0.0	14.5	0.0	76.9	0.0	8.6
	2000	8.0	0.0	0.0	0.0	0.0	0.0	0.0	0.0	87.5	0.0	12.5
	2003	11.9	0.0	0.0	0.0	0.0	0.0	0.0	0.0	90.9	0.0	9.1
El Salvador	2003	1.7	0.0	0.0	0.0	0.0	0.0	0.0	0.0	0.0	0.0	100.0
Grenada - Grenade	1990	1.0	0.0	0.0	0.0	0.0	0.0	0.0	0.0	0.0	0.0	100.0
	1995	8.4	0.0	0.0	0.0	0.0	0.0	0.0	0.0	100.0	0.0	0.0
	2000	1.0	0.0	0.0	0.0	0.0	0.0	0.0	0.0	100.0	0.0	0.0
	2003	1.0	0.0	0.0	0.0	0.0	0.0	0.0	0.0	95.5	0.0	4.5
Guatemala	1990	7.0	0.0	0.0	0.0	0.0	0.0	0.0	0.0	85.7	0.0	14.3
	2000	4.0	0.0	0.0	0.0	0.0	0.0	0.0	0.0	0.0	0.0	100.0
	2003	3.5	0.0	0.0	0.0	0.0	0.0	0.0	0.0	0.0	0.0	100.0
Haiti - Haïti	1990	1.0	0.0	0.0	0.0	0.0	0.0	0.0	0.0	0.0	0.0	100.0
	1995	0.2	0.0	0.0	0.0	0.0	0.0	0.0	0.0	0.0	0.0	100.0
	2000	1.0	0.0	0.0	0.0	0.0	0.0	0.0	0.0	100.0	0.0	0.0
	2003	1.0	0.0	0.0	0.0	0.0	0.0	0.0	0.0	82.3	0.0	17.7
Honduras	1990	1046.0	0.1	0.0	0.7	0.1	0.1	17.1	9.0	67.7	1.2	5.0
	1995	1695.8	0.1	0.1	1.1	0.0	0.2	10.4	13.3	69.6	0.4	6.4
	2000	1317.0	0.1	0.1	0.8	0.0	0.2	19.7	12.7	57.3	0.4	10.0
	2003	999.8	0.1	0.0	0.5	0.0	0.2	31.4	11.4	45.2	0.6	11.4
Jamaica - Jamaïque	1990	21.0	0.0	0.0	0.0	0.0	0.0	14.3	19.0	38.1	23.8	4.8
	1995	6.1	0.0	0.0	0.0	0.0	0.0	53.9	0.0	46.1	0.0	0.0
	2000	3.0	0.0	0.0	0.0	0.0	0.0	100.0	0.0	0.0	0.0	0.0
	2003	78.9	0.0	0.0	0.0	0.0	0.0	3.9	89.0	0.0	0.0	7.1
Mexico - Mexique	1990	1803.0	0.3	0.1	0.1	0.1	1.2	46.6	14.8	4.4	0.7	33.5
	1995	1494.1	0.3	0.0	0.1	0.4	1.0	47.2	0.0	5.0	9.8	38.0
	2000	1180.0	0.3	0.0	0.0	0.0	0.6	64.0	0.0	1.9	0.0	34.1
	2003	1251.9	0.3	0.0	0.1	0.0	0.6	69.2	1.1	5.3	0.0	24.5
Montserrat	1990	1.0	0.0	0.0	0.0	0.0	0.0	0.0	0.0	100.0	0.0	0.0
Nicaragua	1990	3.0	0.0	0.0	0.0	0.0	0.0	0.0	0.0	100.0	0.0	0.0
	1995	1.5	0.0	0.0	0.0	0.0	0.0	0.0	0.0	79.2	0.0	20.8
	2000	1.0	0.0	0.0	0.0	0.0	0.0	0.0	0.0	100.0	0.0	0.0
	2003	1.8	0.0	0.0	0.0	0.0	0.0	0.0	0.0	65.6	0.0	34.4
Panama	1990	62184.0	7.0	10.4	14.1	12.1	7.8	27.7	38.3	23.1	4.6	6.4
	1995	109514.4	13.7	18.1	13.2	18.5	9.8	33.2	42.3	12.3	7.0	5.1
	2000	172355.0	17.8	29.6	14.6	21.9	16.0	29.3	47.4	8.4	8.5	6.4
	2003	186860.2	16.8	30.1	14.2	22.8	14.5	28.5	49.6	7.2	11.0	3.7
Saint Kitts and Nevis - Saint-Kitts-et-Nevis	1990	1.0	0.0	0.0	0.0	0.0	0.0	0.0	0.0	0.0	0.0	100.0
	1995	0.6	0.0	0.0	0.0	0.0	0.0	0.0	0.0	100.0	0.0	0.0
	2000	1.0	0.0	0.0	0.0	0.0	0.0	0.0	0.0	100.0	0.0	0.0
	2003	0.6	0.0	0.0	0.0	0.0	0.0	0.0	0.0	100.0	0.0	0.0
Saint Lucia - Sainte-Lucie	1990	2.0	0.0	0.0	0.0	0.0	0.0	0.0	0.0	100.0	0.0	0.0
	1995	1.7	0.0	0.0	0.0	0.0	0.0	0.0	0.0	100.0	0.0	0.0
Saint Vincent and the Grenadines - Saint-Vincent-et-les Grenadines	1990	2995.0	0.2	0.5	1.1	0.4	0.3	18.6	36.9	36.9	2.9	4.6
	1995	9556.3	0.8	1.6	2.9	0.4	0.6	21.5	41.7	31.6	1.7	3.5
	2000	9866.0	0.3	1.7	3.9	0.3	0.7	8.0	46.4	39.1	2.0	4.6
	2003	9027.7	0.2	1.5	3.4	0.2	0.8	6.8	51.0	35.7	2.3	4.2

For sources and notes, see end of table.

Pour les sources et les notes, se reporter à la fin du tableau.

8.6   World merchant fleet by flag of registration
      and type of ship
      (continued)

8.6   Flotte marchande mondiale par pavillons
      d'immatriculation et par types de navires
      (suite)

Region, country or area / Régions pays ou zones	Year / Année	Total Fleet (thousands of DWT) [1] / Flotte totale (milliers de TPL) [1]	As percentage of world total fleet / En pourcentage de la flotte mondiale					As percentage of the country total fleet / En pourcentage de la flotte totale du pays				
			Oil tankers / Petroliers	Bulk carriers / Vraquiers	General cargo / Navires de charge classiques	Container ships / Porte-conteneurs	Other types / Autres navires	Oil tankers / Petroliers	Bulk carriers / Vraquiers	General cargo / Navires de charge classique	Container ships / Porte-conteneurs	Other types / Autres navires
Trinidad and Tobago - Trinité-et-Tobago	1990	13.0	0.0	0.0	0.0	0.0	0.0	0.0	0.0	46.2	0.0	53.8
	1995	19.9	0.0	0.0	0.0	0.0	0.0	0.0	0.0	37.9	0.0	62.1
	2000	6.0	0.0	0.0	0.0	0.0	0.0	16.7	0.0	0.0	0.0	83.3
	2003	8.2	0.0	0.0	0.0	0.0	0.0	0.0	0.0	4.9	0.0	95.1
Turks and Caicos Islands - Iles Turques et Caïques	1990	3.0	0.0	0.0	0.0	0.0	0.0	0.0	0.0	33.3	0.0	66.7
	1995	0.4	0.0	0.0	0.0	0.0	0.0	0.0	0.0	39.8	0.0	60.2
	2003	0.2	0.0	0.0	0.0	0.0	0.0	0.0	0.0	100.0	0.0	0.0
DEVELOPING ECONOMIES: AFRICA - ECONOMIES EN DEVELOPPEMENT : AFRIQUE	**1990**	**106851.0**	**23.6**	**13.8**	**7.6**	**9.6**	**14.2**	**54.2**	**29.7**	**7.2**	**2.1**	**6.8**
	1995	**104832.7**	**21.3**	**11.6**	**6.1**	**10.2**	**14.6**	**53.8**	**28.3**	**6.0**	**4.0**	**8.0**
	2000	**86383.3**	**13.5**	**8.5**	**6.4**	**11.9**	**15.2**	**44.2**	**27.1**	**7.4**	**9.3**	**12.0**
	2003	**87864.9**	**13.6**	**6.8**	**6.0**	**14.8**	**9.9**	**49.2**	**23.7**	**6.5**	**15.2**	**5.3**
North Africa - Afrique du Nord	*1990*	*5494.0*	*0.8*	*0.5*	*1.3*	*0.0*	*2.2*	*35.5*	*18.9*	*24.6*	*0.2*	*20.7*
	1995	*4871.9*	*0.6*	*0.5*	*1.1*	*0.0*	*1.6*	*32.2*	*24.8*	*23.6*	*0.2*	*19.2*
	2000	*4361.0*	*0.3*	*0.4*	*1.1*	*0.1*	*1.4*	*22.5*	*28.3*	*25.5*	*2.1*	*21.5*
	2003	*3294.8*	*0.2*	*0.3*	*0.8*	*0.1*	*1.6*	*19.3*	*32.0*	*22.6*	*3.8*	*22.3*
Algeria - Algérie	1990	1062.0	0.0	0.1	0.3	0.0	0.9	4.3	23.9	27.9	0.0	43.9
	1995	1111.1	0.0	0.1	0.3	0.0	0.8	4.7	25.9	26.7	0.0	42.7
	2000	1063.0	0.0	0.1	0.3	0.0	0.7	2.8	27.1	26.2	0.0	43.9
	2003	938.5	0.0	0.1	0.2	0.0	0.9	5.4	30.7	16.3	0.0	47.5
Egypt - Egypte	1990	1825.0	0.2	0.2	0.7	0.0	0.2	27.2	31.0	36.6	0.0	5.3
	1995	1919.3	0.1	0.3	0.5	0.0	0.2	20.0	44.9	28.3	0.0	6.8
	2000	2010.0	0.1	0.3	0.5	0.1	0.2	18.0	45.9	26.9	2.9	6.3
	2003	1688.1	0.1	0.2	0.4	0.1	0.2	22.5	43.8	23.7	3.4	6.5
Libyan Arab Jamahiriya - Jamahiriya arabe libyenne	1990	1468.0	0.5	0.0	0.1	0.0	0.0	91.6	0.0	6.8	0.0	1.6
	1995	1222.5	0.4	0.0	0.1	0.0	0.1	89.4	0.0	7.2	0.0	3.4
	2000	661.0	0.2	0.0	0.1	0.0	0.1	81.2	0.0	12.9	0.0	5.9
	2003	115.8	0.0	0.0	0.1	0.0	0.1	8.5	0.0	64.3	0.0	27.2
Morocco - Maroc	1990	618.0	0.0	0.1	0.1	0.0	0.5	3.1	26.4	24.4	1.6	44.5
	1995	380.1	0.0	0.0	0.1	0.0	0.4	6.6	0.0	26.7	2.6	64.1
	2000	398.0	0.0	0.0	0.1	0.1	0.3	5.0	0.0	30.2	8.5	56.3
	2003	391.6	0.0	0.0	0.1	0.1	0.3	30.3	0.0	21.3	17.4	31.0
Sudan - Soudan	1990	79.0	0.0	0.0	0.1	0.0	0.0	1.3	0.0	97.5	0.0	1.3
	1995	61.8	0.0	0.0	0.1	0.0	0.0	2.0	0.0	96.7	0.0	1.3
	2000	52.0	0.0	0.0	0.1	0.0	0.0	1.9	0.0	98.1	0.0	0.0
	2003	29.0	0.0	0.0	0.0	0.0	0.0	4.2	0.0	92.9	0.0	2.8
Tunisia - Tunisie	1990	442.0	0.0	0.0	0.1	0.0	0.5	10.6	13.1	13.8	0.0	62.4
	1995	177.1	0.0	0.0	0.1	0.0	0.1	7.4	33.1	34.0	0.0	25.6
	2000	177.0	0.0	0.0	0.0	0.0	0.1	18.1	14.7	21.5	0.0	45.8
	2003	131.8	0.0	0.0	0.0	0.0	0.1	57.1	20.0	3.7	0.0	19.1
Other Africa - Autres économies d'Afrique	*1990*	*101357.0*	*22.8*	*13.4*	*6.3*	*9.5*	*12.0*	*55.2*	*30.3*	*6.3*	*2.2*	*6.0*
	1995	*99960.7*	*20.7*	*11.1*	*5.0*	*10.2*	*13.0*	*54.8*	*28.5*	*5.1*	*4.2*	*7.4*
	2000	*82022.3*	*13.1*	*8.0*	*5.3*	*11.8*	*13.8*	*45.4*	*27.1*	*6.4*	*9.7*	*11.5*
	2003	*84570.1*	*13.4*	*6.4*	*5.3*	*14.7*	*8.3*	*50.4*	*23.4*	*5.9*	*15.7*	*4.7*
Angola	1990	122.0	0.0	0.0	0.1	0.0	0.0	1.6	0.0	87.7	0.0	10.7
	1995	116.1	0.0	0.0	0.1	0.0	0.0	2.3	0.0	85.9	0.0	11.8
	2000	70.0	0.0	0.0	0.0	0.0	0.0	7.1	0.0	68.6	0.0	24.3
	2003	32.1	0.0	0.0	0.0	0.0	0.0	7.0	0.0	38.4	0.0	54.6
Benin - Bénin	1990	5.0	0.0	0.0	0.0	0.0	0.0	0.0	0.0	80.0	0.0	20.0
	1995	0.2	0.0	0.0	0.0	0.0	0.0	0.0	0.0	0.0	0.0	100.0
	2003	0.2	0.0	0.0	0.0	0.0	0.0	0.0	0.0	0.0	0.0	100.0
Cameroon - Cameroun	1990	39.0	0.0	0.0	0.0	0.0	0.0	0.0	0.0	87.2	0.0	12.8
	1995	40.2	0.0	0.0	0.0	0.0	0.0	0.0	0.0	83.4	0.0	16.6
	2000	5.3	0.0	0.0	0.0	0.0	0.0	0.0	0.0	5.7	0.0	94.3
	2003	365.8	0.1	0.0	0.0	0.0	0.0	97.6	0.0	0.5	0.0	1.9

For sources and notes, see end of table.

Pour les sources et les notes, se reporter à la fin du tableau.

Region, country or area / Régions pays ou zones	Year / Année	Total Fleet (thousands of DWT)[1] / Flotte totale (milliers de TPL)[1]	As percentage of world total fleet / En pourcentage de la flotte mondiale					As percentage of the country total fleet / En pourcentage de la flotte totale du pays				
			Oil tankers / Petroliers	Bulk carriers / Vraquiers	General cargo / Navires de charge classiques	Container ships / Porte-conteneurs	Other types / Autres navires	Oil tankers / Petroliers	Bulk carriers / Vraquiers	General cargo / Navires de charge classique	Container ships / Porte-conteneurs	Other types / Autres navires
Cape Verde - Cap-Vert	1990	30.0	0.0	0.0	0.0	0.0	0.0	3.3	0.0	90.0	0.0	6.7
	1995	21.5	0.0	0.0	0.0	0.0	0.0	2.6	0.0	79.9	0.0	17.5
	2000	24.0	0.0	0.0	0.0	0.0	0.0	4.2	0.0	79.2	0.0	16.7
	2003	20.6	0.0	0.0	0.0	0.0	0.0	17.0	0.0	70.8	0.0	12.2
Comoros - Comores	1990	3.0	0.0	0.0	0.0	0.0	0.0	0.0	0.0	100.0	0.0	0.0
	1995	3.0	0.0	0.0	0.0	0.0	0.0	0.0	0.0	77.6	0.0	22.4
	2000	31.0	0.0	0.0	0.0	0.0	0.0	0.0	0.0	100.0	0.0	0.0
	2003	598.8	0.0	0.1	0.2	0.0	0.1	23.1	40.9	32.0	0.0	4.0
Congo	1990	11.0	0.0	0.0	0.0	0.0	0.0	0.0	0.0	0.0	0.0	100.0
	1995	15.1	0.0	0.0	0.0	0.0	0.0	0.0	0.0	27.1	0.0	72.9
	2003	0.7	0.0	0.0	0.0	0.0	0.0	0.0	0.0	0.0	0.0	100.0
Côte d'Ivoire	1990	100.0	0.0	0.0	0.1	0.0	0.0	0.0	0.0	85.0	0.0	15.0
	1995	41.9	0.0	0.0	0.0	0.0	0.0	2.8	0.0	82.2	0.0	15.0
	2000	5.0	0.0	0.0	0.0	0.0	0.0	20.0	0.0	0.0	0.0	80.0
	2003	5.1	0.0	0.0	0.0	0.0	0.0	23.0	0.0	0.0	0.0	77.0
Dem. Rep. of the Congo - Rép. dém. du Congo	1990	76.0	0.0	0.0	0.1	0.0	0.0	0.0	0.0	80.3	0.0	19.7
	1995	15.8	0.0	0.0	0.0	0.0	0.0	0.0	0.0	3.8	0.0	96.2
Djibouti	1995	4.8	0.0	0.0	0.0	0.0	0.0	0.0	0.0	92.7	0.0	7.3
	2000	4.0	0.0	0.0	0.0	0.0	0.0	0.0	0.0	100.0	0.0	0.0
	2003	4.2	0.0	0.0	0.0	0.0	0.0	0.0	0.0	89.3	0.0	10.7
Equatorial Guinea - Guinée équatoriale	1990	7.0	0.0	0.0	0.0	0.0	0.0	0.0	0.0	100.0	0.0	0.0
	1995	3.3	0.0	0.0	0.0	0.0	0.0	0.0	0.0	100.0	0.0	0.0
	2000	25.0	0.0	0.0	0.0	0.0	0.0	0.0	0.0	68.0	0.0	32.0
	2003	18.1	0.0	0.0	0.0	0.0	0.0	0.0	0.0	39.2	0.0	60.8
Ethiopia - Ethiopie	1990	91.0	0.0	0.0	0.1	0.0	0.0	6.6	0.0	92.3	0.0	1.1
	1995	98.7	0.0	0.0	0.1	0.0	0.0	5.9	0.0	94.1	0.0	0.0
	2000	110.0	0.0	0.0	0.1	0.0	0.0	3.6	0.0	96.4	0.0	0.0
	2003	101.3	0.0	0.0	0.1	0.0	0.0	3.6	0.0	96.4	0.0	0.0
Gabon	1990	29.0	0.0	0.0	0.0	0.0	0.0	0.0	0.0	89.7	0.0	10.3
	1995	43.8	0.0	0.0	0.0	0.0	0.0	1.7	87.9	5.7	0.0	4.8
	2000	8.0	0.0	0.0	0.0	0.0	0.0	12.5	0.0	50.0	0.0	37.5
	2003	7.8	0.0	0.0	0.0	0.0	0.0	9.5	0.0	49.6	0.0	40.9
Gambia - Gambie	1990	2.0	0.0	0.0	0.0	0.0	0.0	0.0	0.0	0.0	0.0	100.0
	1995	2.7	0.0	0.0	0.0	0.0	0.0	0.0	0.0	0.0	0.0	100.0
	2000	2.0	0.0	0.0	0.0	0.0	0.0	0.0	0.0	0.0	0.0	100.0
	2003	1.7	0.0	0.0	0.0	0.0	0.0	0.0	0.0	0.0	0.0	100.0
Ghana	1990	110.0	0.0	0.0	0.1	0.0	0.1	0.9	0.0	66.4	0.0	32.7
	1995	96.0	0.0	0.0	0.0	0.0	0.1	1.2	0.3	42.6	0.0	55.9
	2000	94.0	0.0	0.0	0.0	0.0	0.1	9.6	0.0	19.1	0.0	71.3
	2003	96.5	0.0	0.0	0.0	0.0	0.1	11.9	0.3	23.7	0.0	64.1
Guinea - Guinée	1990	3.0	0.0	0.0	0.0	0.0	0.0	0.0	0.0	0.0	0.0	100.0
	1995	2.4	0.0	0.0	0.0	0.0	0.0	0.0	0.0	11.8	0.0	88.2
	2000	5.0	0.0	0.0	0.0	0.0	0.0	0.0	0.0	0.0	0.0	100.0
	2003	7.4	0.0	0.0	0.0	0.0	0.0	31.5	0.0	3.9	0.0	64.6
Guinea-Bissau - Guinée-Bissau	1990	2.0	0.0	0.0	0.0	0.0	0.0	0.0	0.0	0.0	0.0	100.0
	1995	2.7	0.0	0.0	0.0	0.0	0.0	0.0	0.0	20.0	0.0	80.0
	2000	3.0	0.0	0.0	0.0	0.0	0.0	0.0	0.0	33.3	0.0	66.7
	2003	2.2	0.0	0.0	0.0	0.0	0.0	0.0	0.0	10.2	0.0	89.8
Kenya	1990	4.0	0.0	0.0	0.0	0.0	0.0	0.0	0.0	0.0	0.0	100.0
	1995	17.0	0.0	0.0	0.0	0.0	0.0	37.8	0.0	9.0	0.0	53.2
	2000	19.0	0.0	0.0	0.0	0.0	0.0	42.1	0.0	10.5	0.0	47.4
	2003	15.5	0.0	0.0	0.0	0.0	0.0	49.1	0.0	12.7	0.0	38.2
Liberia - Libéria	1990	99226.0	22.7	13.3	5.3	8.5	11.2	55.9	30.9	5.5	2.0	5.7
	1995	97888.6	20.4	11.1	4.2	9.6	12.4	55.3	29.0	4.4	4.0	7.2
	2000	80062.0	12.9	8.0	4.6	11.3	13.2	45.7	27.7	5.8	9.5	11.3
	2003	82085.1	13.1	6.3	4.7	14.6	7.5	50.4	23.7	5.4	16.1	4.3

For sources and notes, see end of table.

Pour les sources et les notes, se reporter à la fin du tableau.

Region, country or area / Régions pays ou zones	Year / Année	Total Fleet (thousands of DWT) [1] / Flotte totale (milliers de TPL) [1]	As percentage of world total fleet — En pourcentage de la flotte mondiale					As percentage of the country total fleet — En pourcentage de la flotte totale du pays				
			Oil tankers / Petroliers	Bulk carriers / Vraquiers	General cargo / Navires de charge classiques	Container ships / Porte-conteneurs	Other types / Autres navires	Oil tankers / Petroliers	Bulk carriers / Vraquiers	General cargo / Navires de charge classique	Container ships / Porte-conteneurs	Other types / Autres navires
Madagascar	1990	92.0	0.0	0.0	0.1	0.0	0.0	7.6	0.0	82.6	0.0	9.8
	1995	40.8	0.0	0.0	0.0	0.0	0.0	41.5	0.0	43.2	0.0	15.3
	2000	48.0	0.0	0.0	0.0	0.0	0.0	35.4	0.0	50.0	0.0	14.6
	2003	33.1	0.0	0.0	0.0	0.0	0.0	21.2	0.0	57.5	0.0	21.3
Mauritania - Mauritanie	1990	22.0	0.0	0.0	0.0	0.0	0.0	0.0	0.0	9.1	0.0	90.9
	1995	19.4	0.0	0.0	0.0	0.0	0.0	0.0	0.0	9.6	0.0	90.4
	2000	23.0	0.0	0.0	0.0	0.0	0.0	0.0	0.0	4.3	0.0	95.7
	2003	23.3	0.0	0.0	0.0	0.0	0.0	0.0	0.0	3.1	0.0	96.9
Mauritius - Maurice	1990	141.0	0.0	0.0	0.0	0.1	0.0	0.0	56.0	19.9	20.6	3.5
	1995	324.7	0.0	0.0	0.2	0.2	0.0	26.0	0.8	50.1	21.2	1.9
	2000	106.0	0.0	0.0	0.0	0.1	0.0	0.0	4.7	13.2	65.1	17.0
	2003	60.1	0.0	0.0	0.0	0.0	0.1	0.0	22.1	25.3	0.0	52.6
Mozambique	1990	29.0	0.0	0.0	0.0	0.0	0.0	6.9	0.0	69.0	0.0	24.1
	1995	27.2	0.0	0.0	0.0	0.0	0.0	1.5	0.0	60.9	0.0	37.6
	2000	24.0	0.0	0.0	0.0	0.0	0.0	0.0	0.0	45.8	0.0	54.2
	2003	27.7	0.0	0.0	0.0	0.0	0.0	0.0	0.0	38.2	0.0	61.8
Nigeria - Nigéria	1990	727.0	0.2	0.0	0.2	0.0	0.1	60.0	0.0	33.8	0.0	6.2
	1995	724.6	0.2	0.0	0.2	0.0	0.1	68.6	0.0	25.2	0.0	6.2
	2000	685.0	0.2	0.0	0.1	0.0	0.1	75.6	0.0	16.9	0.0	7.4
	2003	675.9	0.2	0.0	0.0	0.0	0.1	85.4	2.0	6.6	0.0	6.1
Saint Helena - Sainte-Hélène	1990	2.0	0.0	0.0	0.0	0.0	0.0	0.0	0.0	0.0	0.0	100.0
	2003	1.0	0.0	0.0	0.0	0.0	0.0	0.0	0.0	0.0	0.0	100.0
Sao Tome and Principe - Sao Tomé-et-Principe	1990	1.0	0.0	0.0	0.0	0.0	0.0	0.0	0.0	0.0	0.0	100.0
	1995	2.5	0.0	0.0	0.0	0.0	0.0	0.0	0.0	51.6	0.0	48.4
	2000	197.0	0.0	0.0	0.2	0.0	0.0	5.6	8.1	77.7	2.5	6.1
	2003	104.8	0.0	0.0	0.1	0.0	0.0	8.1	27.5	62.5	0.0	1.9
Senegal - Sénégal	1990	38.0	0.0	0.0	0.0	0.0	0.0	0.0	0.0	44.7	0.0	55.3
	1995	26.5	0.0	0.0	0.0	0.0	0.0	0.0	0.0	25.2	0.0	74.8
	2000	25.0	0.0	0.0	0.0	0.0	0.0	0.0	0.0	8.0	0.0	92.0
	2003	23.3	0.0	0.0	0.0	0.0	0.0	1.2	0.0	6.7	0.0	92.1
Seychelles	1990	2.0	0.0	0.0	0.0	0.0	0.0	0.0	0.0	100.0	0.0	0.0
	1995	4.2	0.0	0.0	0.0	0.0	0.0	0.0	0.0	78.5	0.0	21.5
	2000	21.0	0.0	0.0	0.0	0.0	0.0	0.0	0.0	57.1	0.0	42.9
	2003	70.1	0.0	0.0	0.0	0.0	0.0	50.6	0.0	25.5	0.0	23.9
Sierra Leone	1990	15.0	0.0	0.0	0.0	0.0	0.0	6.7	0.0	20.0	0.0	73.3
	1995	15.1	0.0	0.0	0.0	0.0	0.0	12.1	0.0	6.2	0.0	81.6
	2000	8.0	0.0	0.0	0.0	0.0	0.0	0.0	0.0	50.0	0.0	50.0
	2003	22.5	0.0	0.0	0.0	0.0	0.0	74.8	0.0	4.2	0.0	21.0
Somalia - Somalie	1990	19.0	0.0	0.0	0.0	0.0	0.0	0.0	0.0	68.4	0.0	31.6
	1995	16.5	0.0	0.0	0.0	0.0	0.0	0.0	0.0	68.0	0.0	32.0
	2000	8.0	0.0	0.0	0.0	0.0	0.0	25.0	0.0	62.5	0.0	12.5
	2003	5.7	0.0	0.0	0.0	0.0	0.0	26.6	0.0	42.7	0.0	30.7
South Africa - Afrique du Sud	1990	299.0	0.0	0.0	0.0	0.9	0.2	0.3	0.0	0.0	72.2	27.4
	1995	293.7	0.0	0.0	0.0	0.5	0.2	0.8	0.0	0.0	67.6	31.6
	2000	368.0	0.0	0.0	0.0	0.4	0.1	1.4	0.0	0.0	71.2	27.4
	2003	107.4	0.0	0.0	0.0	0.0	0.2	4.0	0.0	0.1	27.6	68.3
Togo	1990	78.0	0.0	0.0	0.0	0.0	0.1	1.3	0.0	26.9	0.0	73.1
	1995	0.1	0.0	0.0	0.0	0.0	0.0	0.0	0.0	0.0	0.0	100.0
	2000	3.0	0.0	0.0	0.0	0.0	0.0	0.0	0.0	100.0	0.0	0.0
	2003	10.6	0.0	0.0	0.0	0.0	0.0	0.0	0.0	36.3	0.0	63.7
Uganda - Ouganda	2000	3.0	0.0	0.0	0.0	0.0	0.0	0.0	0.0	100.0	0.0	0.0
United Republic of Tanzania - République-Unie de Tanzanie	1990	32.0	0.0	0.0	0.0	0.0	0.0	12.5	0.0	71.9	0.0	15.6
	1995	51.5	0.0	0.0	0.0	0.0	0.0	18.0	0.0	76.5	0.0	5.5
	2000	36.0	0.0	0.0	0.0	0.0	0.0	22.2	0.0	66.7	0.0	11.1
	2003	41.6	0.0	0.0	0.0	0.0	0.0	33.3	0.0	59.7	0.0	7.0

For sources and notes, see end of table.

Pour les sources et les notes, se reporter à la fin du tableau.

Region, country or area / Régions pays ou zones	Year / Année	Total Fleet (thousands of DWT) [1] / Flotte totale (milliers de TPL) [1]	As percentage of world total fleet — En pourcentage de la flotte mondiale					As percentage of the country total fleet — En pourcentage de la flotte totale du pays				
			Oil tankers / Petroliers	Bulk carriers / Vraquiers	General cargo / Navires de charge classiques	Container ships / Porte-conteneurs	Other types / Autres navires	Oil tankers / Petroliers	Bulk carriers / Vraquiers	General cargo / Navires de charge classique	Container ships / Porte-conteneurs	Other types / Autres navires
DEVELOPING ECONOMIES: ASIA - ECONOMIES EN DEVELOPPEMENT : ASIE	**1990**	**117993.0**	**12.5**	**23.1**	**23.5**	**19.5**	**11.2**	**25.9**	**45.1**	**20.3**	**3.9**	**4.8**
	1995	**137823.1**	**12.0**	**25.6**	**24.6**	**18.5**	**13.0**	**23.0**	**47.7**	**18.3**	**5.5**	**5.4**
	2000	**150954.0**	**14.7**	**23.0**	**25.5**	**16.7**	**13.4**	**27.6**	**42.0**	**16.8**	**7.4**	**6.1**
	2003	**173526.6**	**17.8**	**22.9**	**27.2**	**15.6**	**14.3**	**32.6**	**40.6**	**14.8**	**8.1**	**3.9**
West Asia - Asie occidentale	*1990*	*24951.0*	*5.6*	*2.4*	*4.0*	*2.3*	*2.0*	*55.4*	*22.0*	*16.3*	*2.1*	*4.1*
	1995	*25089.3*	*3.5*	*3.6*	*4.6*	*1.1*	*2.2*	*37.3*	*37.0*	*18.9*	*1.8*	*5.0*
	2000	*26514.0*	*3.6*	*3.0*	*5.1*	*2.2*	*2.2*	*38.1*	*31.6*	*19.0*	*5.6*	*5.8*
	2003	*25248.4*	*4.0*	*2.1*	*4.1*	*1.7*	*1.8*	*49.8*	*25.5*	*15.3*	*5.9*	*3.4*
Bahrain - Bahreïn	1990	49.0	0.0	0.0	0.0	0.0	0.0	4.1	0.0	55.1	0.0	40.8
	1995	242.1	0.0	0.0	0.1	0.0	0.1	40.1	5.4	40.8	0.0	13.7
	2000	450.0	0.1	0.0	0.1	0.1	0.1	34.0	13.3	21.8	22.2	8.7
	2003	352.9	0.0	0.0	0.0	0.1	0.1	43.5	16.9	1.2	28.3	10.1
Iran, Islamic Rep. of - Iran, Rép. islamique d'	1990	8692.0	2.5	0.8	0.6	0.0	0.3	71.3	20.4	6.6	0.0	1.7
	1995	4975.0	0.9	0.7	0.6	0.0	0.3	49.3	34.2	13.3	0.0	3.1
	2000	7207.0	1.4	0.7	0.9	0.3	0.2	55.6	27.1	12.6	2.5	2.2
	2003	8335.9	1.7	0.6	0.7	0.3	0.2	66.1	21.2	8.4	3.0	1.4
Iraq	1990	1797.0	0.6	0.0	0.1	0.0	0.2	86.4	0.0	6.7	0.0	7.0
	1995	1503.8	0.5	0.0	0.1	0.0	0.1	87.4	0.0	7.2	0.0	5.3
	2000	835.0	0.2	0.0	0.1	0.0	0.1	79.0	0.0	12.6	0.0	8.4
	2003	206.8	0.0	0.0	0.1	0.0	0.1	41.5	0.0	26.6	0.0	32.0
Jordan - Jordanie	1990	64.0	0.0	0.0	0.0	0.0	0.0	0.0	68.8	25.0	0.0	6.3
	1995	33.6	0.0	0.0	0.0	0.0	0.0	0.0	99.3	0.0	0.0	0.7
	2000	59.0	0.0	0.0	0.0	0.0	0.0	0.0	30.5	57.6	11.9	0.0
	2003	385.2	0.1	0.0	0.1	0.0	0.0	75.3	0.0	21.4	1.7	1.6
Kuwait - Koweït	1990	2944.0	0.8	0.0	0.5	0.6	0.5	68.5	0.0	17.5	5.0	9.1
	1995	3250.1	0.9	0.0	0.4	0.2	0.6	74.5	0.0	11.5	2.8	11.2
	2000	3813.0	1.0	0.0	0.3	0.3	0.5	76.9	0.7	6.8	6.0	9.6
	2003	3716.4	1.0	0.0	0.2	0.3	0.6	81.9	0.7	4.3	6.1	7.0
Lebanon - Liban	1990	473.0	0.0	0.0	0.4	0.0	0.0	4.9	15.6	78.0	0.0	1.5
	1995	424.0	0.0	0.1	0.3	0.0	0.0	0.5	32.5	65.6	0.3	1.1
	2000	546.0	0.0	0.1	0.2	0.0	0.0	0.2	57.1	40.8	0.0	1.8
	2003	246.6	0.0	0.0	0.2	0.0	0.0	0.6	32.6	63.4	0.0	3.5
Oman	1990	12.0	0.0	0.0	0.0	0.0	0.0	0.0	0.0	58.3	0.0	41.7
	1995	11.1	0.0	0.0	0.0	0.0	0.0	4.1	0.0	26.9	0.0	68.9
	2000	13.0	0.0	0.0	0.0	0.0	0.0	0.0	0.0	46.2	0.0	53.8
	2003	8.8	0.0	0.0	0.0	0.0	0.0	13.9	0.0	11.5	0.0	74.5
Qatar	1990	556.0	0.1	0.0	0.1	0.4	0.0	53.6	0.0	27.0	16.4	3.1
	1995	773.6	0.1	0.1	0.2	0.2	0.0	25.1	34.9	26.5	11.8	1.6
	2000	1079.0	0.1	0.1	0.2	0.3	0.0	34.8	25.0	19.1	18.9	2.2
	2003	795.9	0.2	0.0	0.1	0.2	0.1	63.7	0.0	7.3	25.4	3.6
Saudi Arabia - Arabie saoudite	1990	2716.0	0.7	0.0	0.6	0.3	0.4	63.1	1.7	24.2	2.8	8.3
	1995	1414.7	0.2	0.0	0.6	0.3	0.4	29.4	0.0	44.9	8.3	17.4
	2000	1523.0	0.1	0.0	0.6	0.3	0.5	27.6	0.0	37.2	13.2	21.9
	2003	1961.8	0.4	0.0	0.4	0.2	0.1	71.1	0.0	17.6	7.9	3.3
Syrian Arab Republic - République arabe syrienne	1990	116.0	0.0	0.0	0.1	0.0	0.0	0.0	0.0	96.6	0.0	3.4
	1995	558.7	0.0	0.0	0.5	0.0	0.0	0.0	15.1	84.9	0.0	0.0
	2000	697.0	0.0	0.0	0.7	0.0	0.0	0.3	5.7	93.8	0.0	0.1
	2003	688.9	0.0	0.0	0.6	0.0	0.0	0.4	11.2	87.0	1.2	0.2
Turkey - Turquie	1990	6360.0	0.6	1.5	1.3	0.0	0.2	22.8	55.0	20.4	0.0	1.8
	1995	10345.1	0.6	2.7	1.6	0.0	0.3	14.4	67.5	16.1	0.1	1.9
	2000	9159.0	0.4	2.1	1.8	0.3	0.5	12.4	62.1	19.2	2.3	3.9
	2003	7541.7	0.3	1.4	1.7	0.4	0.3	14.7	57.9	21.4	4.3	1.7
United Arab Emirates - Emirats arabes unis	1990	1158.0	0.2	0.0	0.2	0.9	0.2	50.2	4.7	18.7	18.8	7.6
	1995	1530.9	0.4	0.0	0.2	0.3	0.2	62.7	4.0	15.3	9.3	8.7
	2000	1102.0	0.1	0.0	0.2	0.5	0.2	36.1	0.1	19.6	31.7	12.5
	2003	1007.4	0.2	0.0	0.1	0.3	0.3	48.6	6.4	8.8	22.5	13.8

For sources and notes, see end of table.

Pour les sources et les notes, se reporter à la fin du tableau.

8.6 World merchant fleet by flag of registration and type of ship (continued)

8.6 Flotte marchande mondiale par pavillons d'immatriculation et par types de navires (suite)

Region, country or area / Régions pays ou zones	Year / Année	Total Fleet (thousands of DWT)[1] / Flotte totale (milliers de TPL)[1]	As percentage of world total fleet / En pourcentage de la flotte mondiale					As percentage of the country total fleet / En pourcentage de la flotte totale du pays				
			Oil tankers / Petroliers	Bulk carriers / Vraquiers	General cargo / Navires de charge classiques	Container ships / Porte-conteneurs	Other types / Autres navires	Oil tankers / Petroliers	Bulk carriers / Vraquiers	General cargo / Navires de charge classique	Container ships / Porte-conteneurs	Other types / Autres navires
Yemen - Yémen	1990	14.0	0.0	0.0	0.0	0.0	0.0	21.4	0.0	35.7	0.0	42.9
	1995	26.6	0.0	0.0	0.0	0.0	0.0	12.0	0.0	11.5	0.0	76.5
	2000	31.0	0.0	0.0	0.0	0.0	0.0	25.8	0.0	9.7	0.0	64.5
Other Asia - Autres économies d'Asie	*1990*	*93042.0*	*6.8*	*20.7*	*19.5*	*17.3*	*9.1*	*17.9*	*51.3*	*21.4*	*4.4*	*5.0*
	1995	*112733.7*	*8.4*	*22.0*	*20.0*	*17.4*	*10.8*	*19.8*	*50.1*	*18.2*	*6.3*	*5.5*
	2000	*124440.0*	*11.2*	*19.9*	*20.4*	*14.5*	*11.2*	*25.4*	*44.2*	*16.4*	*7.8*	*6.2*
	2003	*148278.2*	*13.9*	*20.8*	*23.1*	*14.0*	*12.5*	*29.6*	*43.1*	*14.8*	*8.5*	*4.0*
Bangladesh	1990	620.0	0.0	0.0	0.5	0.0	0.0	13.5	0.0	84.4	0.0	2.1
	1995	520.5	0.0	0.0	0.4	0.0	0.0	16.3	1.7	78.6	0.0	3.4
	2000	505.0	0.0	0.0	0.4	0.0	0.0	21.0	1.8	71.7	1.6	4.0
	2003	605.6	0.0	0.0	0.4	0.1	0.0	19.2	1.5	66.4	10.2	2.9
Brunei Darussalam - Brunéi Darussalam	1990	349.0	0.0	0.0	0.0	0.0	0.7	0.0	0.0	0.9	0.0	99.1
	1995	352.5	0.0	0.0	0.0	0.0	0.6	0.1	0.0	1.2	0.0	98.7
	2000	349.0	0.0	0.0	0.0	0.0	0.5	0.0	0.0	0.9	0.0	99.1
	2003	422.5	0.0	0.0	0.0	0.0	0.9	0.4	0.0	0.6	0.0	99.0
Cambodia - Cambodge	1990	4.0	0.0	0.0	0.0	0.0	0.0	0.0	0.0	25.0	0.0	75.0
China - Chine	1990	20755.0	1.1	3.6	7.6	4.6	1.7	13.0	40.3	37.3	5.3	4.2
	1995	24933.6	1.4	4.4	7.2	4.1	1.7	14.9	44.8	29.7	6.7	3.9
	2000	23808.0	1.3	4.0	6.4	2.6	1.4	15.4	46.5	26.6	7.4	4.1
	2003	26824.5	1.5	3.9	6.7	2.9	1.8	18.2	45.1	23.7	9.8	3.2
China, Hong Kong SAR - Chine, Hong Kong RAS	1990	11176.0	0.8	3.5	0.5	2.5	0.5	16.7	71.0	4.4	5.3	2.5
	1995	15257.2	0.5	4.7	0.8	2.3	0.2	7.9	79.4	5.5	6.3	0.9
	2000	17778.0	0.6	4.7	1.3	2.5	0.2	9.3	73.7	7.0	9.3	0.6
	2003	34466.6	2.2	7.3	2.1	3.0	0.5	20.5	65.2	5.8	7.8	0.7
India - Inde	1990	10497.0	1.2	2.4	1.6	0.0	1.0	27.5	52.1	15.3	0.0	5.1
	1995	11613.6	1.7	2.1	0.8	0.3	1.3	39.5	46.1	7.3	1.0	6.2
	2000	10570.0	1.6	1.6	0.6	0.2	1.3	42.6	42.4	5.3	1.4	8.2
	2003	11363.3	2.2	1.1	0.4	0.1	1.2	61.0	29.7	3.2	1.2	4.9
Indonesia - Indonésie	1990	2910.0	0.4	0.1	1.3	0.4	0.5	33.2	6.9	47.2	3.4	9.3
	1995	3626.2	0.5	0.1	1.7	0.2	0.6	33.0	8.7	47.2	2.2	8.8
	2000	4262.0	0.5	0.2	2.0	0.2	0.5	30.2	12.5	46.2	2.8	8.3
	2003	4809.3	0.5	0.2	2.2	0.3	0.7	31.7	12.9	43.3	4.8	7.3
Korea, Dem. People's Rep. of - Corée, Rép. populaire dém. de	1990	656.0	0.0	0.1	0.5	0.0	0.1	3.0	19.1	70.6	0.0	7.3
	1995	1011.9	0.1	0.1	0.5	0.0	0.1	23.3	17.2	54.4	0.0	5.1
	2000	843.0	0.0	0.0	0.7	0.0	0.1	1.4	12.3	79.4	0.0	6.9
	2003	1311.0	0.0	0.1	1.1	0.0	0.1	2.8	15.5	76.2	1.7	3.7
Korea, Republic of - Corée, République de	1990	12462.0	0.5	3.7	1.3	3.2	1.4	8.9	68.5	10.9	6.1	5.5
	1995	10637.0	0.3	2.6	0.9	3.2	1.4	7.3	63.4	9.2	12.6	7.6
	2000	9058.0	0.4	1.9	1.2	1.2	0.9	12.7	58.2	13.6	9.0	6.5
	2003	10433.7	0.6	1.9	1.2	0.9	1.4	18.1	56.4	11.0	7.8	6.6
Malaysia - Malaisie	1990	2460.0	0.1	0.3	0.7	1.0	1.2	12.5	25.8	27.5	9.5	24.8
	1995	4748.4	0.3	0.7	0.8	1.0	1.9	14.7	37.0	16.4	9.0	22.9
	2000	7692.0	0.5	1.0	0.8	1.3	2.5	20.0	36.1	10.8	11.1	22.0
	2003	8063.8	0.9	0.8	0.8	0.9	2.5	34.0	31.7	9.0	10.6	14.8
Maldives	1990	123.0	0.0	0.0	0.1	0.0	0.0	8.1	43.9	45.5	0.0	2.4
	1995	130.7	0.0	0.0	0.1	0.0	0.0	9.7	15.0	69.5	0.0	5.9
	2000	112.0	0.0	0.0	0.1	0.0	0.0	6.3	0.0	90.2	0.0	3.6
	2003	84.0	0.0	0.0	0.1	0.0	0.0	14.7	0.0	81.6	0.0	3.7
Myanmar	1990	1246.0	0.0	0.4	0.2	0.1	0.0	0.8	75.1	20.1	2.0	1.9
	1995	696.2	0.0	0.1	0.2	0.1	0.2	0.7	53.7	28.9	3.6	13.0
	2000	656.0	0.0	0.1	0.2	0.0	0.0	0.8	60.1	37.2	0.0	2.0
	2003	650.9	0.0	0.1	0.2	0.0	0.0	0.7	66.5	30.6	0.0	2.1
Pakistan	1990	508.0	0.0	0.0	0.4	0.0	0.0	17.7	0.0	80.1	0.0	2.2
	1995	624.2	0.0	0.1	0.3	0.0	0.0	14.6	34.0	49.6	0.0	1.8
	2000	381.0	0.0	0.0	0.2	0.1	0.0	23.9	0.0	61.7	11.0	3.4
	2003	498.6	0.1	0.0	0.2	0.0	0.0	54.9	0.0	36.9	5.5	2.7

For sources and notes, see end of table.

Pour les sources et les notes, se reporter à la fin du tableau.

Region, country or area / Régions pays ou zones	Year / Année	Total Fleet (thousands of DWT) [1] / Flotte totale (milliers de TPL) [1]	As percentage of world total fleet / En pourcentage de la flotte mondiale					As percentage of the country total fleet / En pourcentage de la flotte totale du pays				
			Oil tankers / Petroliers	Bulk carriers / Vraquiers	General cargo / Navires de charge classiques	Container ships / Porte-conteneurs	Other types / Autres navires	Oil tankers / Petroliers	Bulk carriers / Vraquiers	General cargo / Navires de charge classique	Container ships / Porte-conteneurs	Other types / Autres navires
Philippines	1990	14159.0	0.3	4.9	1.9	0.4	0.4	5.0	79.4	13.6	0.7	1.3
	1995	13504.2	0.1	4.2	2.0	0.5	0.4	1.8	79.9	15.0	1.6	1.8
	2000	9956.0	0.1	2.7	1.9	0.1	0.6	2.2	74.3	18.9	0.8	3.8
	2003	6944.3	0.1	1.5	1.5	0.1	0.5	6.2	68.3	21.0	0.8	3.7
Singapore - Singapour	1990	12965.0	2.3	1.7	1.7	4.7	1.0	43.4	30.6	13.5	8.5	4.1
	1995	21020.7	3.4	2.6	2.1	5.4	1.6	43.4	31.5	10.2	10.6	4.3
	2000	33742.0	5.8	3.2	2.5	6.0	2.7	48.8	26.2	7.5	11.9	5.5
	2003	36393.0	5.3	3.4	3.4	5.4	2.2	46.5	28.4	8.8	13.3	2.9
Sri Lanka	1990	528.0	0.1	0.1	0.2	0.0	0.0	26.3	35.6	37.1	0.0	0.6
	1995	325.7	0.0	0.1	0.1	0.0	0.0	1.3	55.3	42.2	0.0	1.2
	2000	238.0	0.0	0.1	0.1	0.0	0.0	1.3	63.0	32.4	0.0	3.4
	2003	187.3	0.0	0.0	0.1	0.0	0.0	39.6	0.0	43.8	11.1	5.5
Thailand - Thaïlande	1990	912.0	0.1	0.0	0.6	0.3	0.1	16.7	1.9	69.4	7.0	5.0
	1995	2670.0	0.1	0.3	1.4	0.2	0.2	13.6	24.3	55.3	3.0	3.8
	2000	3034.0	0.2	0.3	1.3	0.3	0.2	22.8	24.1	42.7	6.1	4.3
	2003	3411.2	0.2	0.3	1.7	0.3	0.3	15.9	27.8	45.9	6.8	3.6
Viet Nam	1990	712.0	0.0	0.0	0.5	0.0	0.3	4.8	3.4	68.1	0.0	23.7
	1995	1061.1	0.0	0.0	0.6	0.0	0.6	3.1	3.4	58.8	0.0	34.7
	2000	1456.0	0.1	0.1	0.8	0.0	0.3	15.0	13.4	53.3	2.2	16.1
	2003	1808.7	0.1	0.1	1.1	0.0	0.1	23.9	15.4	56.5	0.9	3.3
DEVELOPING ECONOMIES: OCEANIA - ECONOMIES EN DEVELOPPEMENT : OCEANIE	**1990**	**3540.0**	**0.2**	**0.9**	**0.8**	**0.3**	**0.4**	**11.0**	**58.0**	**23.8**	**2.1**	**5.1**
	1995	**2565.4**	**0.0**	**0.5**	**0.6**	**0.1**	**0.8**	**2.9**	**54.2**	**23.9**	**1.2**	**17.8**
	2000	**1614.0**	**0.0**	**0.3**	**0.4**	**0.1**	**0.4**	**1.5**	**52.0**	**25.7**	**2.2**	**18.6**
	2003	**2437.4**	**0.0**	**0.4**	**0.6**	**0.0**	**0.9**	**3.8**	**54.8**	**22.9**	**1.2**	**17.3**
Fiji - Fidji	1990	53.0	0.0	0.0	0.0	0.0	0.0	11.3	0.0	69.8	0.0	18.9
	1995	26.9	0.0	0.0	0.0	0.0	0.0	13.4	0.0	40.3	0.0	46.3
	2000	25.0	0.0	0.0	0.0	0.0	0.0	16.0	0.0	24.0	0.0	60.0
	2003	16.6	0.0	0.0	0.0	0.0	0.0	44.0	0.0	22.0	0.0	34.0
Kiribati	1990	3.0	0.0	0.0	0.0	0.0	0.0	0.0	0.0	100.0	0.0	0.0
	1995	7.1	0.0	0.0	0.0	0.0	0.0	43.0	0.0	47.3	0.0	9.8
	2000	3.0	0.0	0.0	0.0	0.0	0.0	0.0	0.0	100.0	0.0	0.0
	2003	4.1	0.0	0.0	0.0	0.0	0.0	0.0	0.0	84.0	0.0	16.0
Nauru	1990	41.0	0.0	0.0	0.0	0.0	0.0	0.0	65.9	34.1	0.0	0.0
Papua New Guinea - Papouasie-Nouvelle-Guinée	1990	35.0	0.0	0.0	0.0	0.0	0.0	8.6	14.3	48.6	0.0	28.6
	1995	52.3	0.0	0.0	0.0	0.0	0.0	9.7	0.0	84.3	0.0	6.1
	2000	80.0	0.0	0.0	0.1	0.0	0.0	3.8	0.0	80.0	0.0	16.3
	2003	84.3	0.0	0.0	0.1	0.0	0.0	13.8	6.5	75.4	0.0	4.3
Samoa	1990	35.0	0.0	0.0	0.0	0.0	0.0	0.0	0.0	97.1	0.0	2.9
	1995	6.5	0.0	0.0	0.0	0.0	0.0	0.0	0.0	93.3	0.0	6.7
Solomon Islands - Iles Salomon	1990	6.0	0.0	0.0	0.0	0.0	0.0	0.0	0.0	66.7	0.0	33.3
	1995	5.7	0.0	0.0	0.0	0.0	0.0	0.0	0.0	54.9	0.0	45.1
	2000	6.0	0.0	0.0	0.0	0.0	0.0	0.0	0.0	33.3	0.0	66.7
	2003	4.6	0.0	0.0	0.0	0.0	0.0	0.0	0.0	40.6	0.0	59.4
Tonga	1990	50.0	0.0	0.0	0.0	0.1	0.0	0.0	0.0	34.0	60.0	6.0
	1995	15.3	0.0	0.0	0.0	0.0	0.0	0.0	0.0	72.4	0.0	27.6
	2000	30.0	0.0	0.0	0.0	0.0	0.0	0.0	0.0	63.3	0.0	36.7
	2003	228.2	0.0	0.0	0.1	0.0	0.0	10.0	31.2	53.9	0.0	4.9
Tuvalu	1990	1.0	0.0	0.0	0.0	0.0	0.0	0.0	0.0	100.0	0.0	0.0
	1995	93.1	0.0	0.0	0.0	0.0	0.1	0.0	0.0	37.8	0.0	62.2
	2000	78.0	0.0	0.0	0.0	0.0	0.1	0.0	0.0	44.9	0.0	55.1
	2003	93.4	0.0	0.0	0.0	0.0	0.0	53.5	0.0	41.7	0.0	4.8
Vanuatu	1990	3316.0	0.2	0.9	0.7	0.2	0.3	11.5	60.9	21.5	1.4	4.6
	1995	2358.6	0.0	0.5	0.5	0.1	0.7	2.7	59.0	21.2	1.3	15.9
	2000	1392.0	0.0	0.3	0.3	0.1	0.3	1.2	60.3	20.5	2.5	15.4
	2003	2006.2	0.0	0.4	0.3	0.0	0.8	0.0	62.8	16.1	1.4	19.6

For sources and notes, see end of table.

Pour les sources et les notes, se reporter à la fin du tableau.

Region, country or area / Régions pays ou zones	Year / Année	Total Fleet (thousands of DWT) [1] / Flotte totale (milliers de TPL) [1]	As percentage of world total fleet / En pourcentage de la flotte mondiale					As percentage of the country total fleet / En pourcentage de la flotte totale du pays				
			Oil tankers / Petroliers	Bulk carriers / Vraquiers	General cargo / Navires de charge classiques	Container ships / Porte-conteneurs	Other types / Autres navires	Oil tankers / Petroliers	Bulk carriers / Vraquiers	General cargo / Navires de charge classique	Container ships / Porte-conteneurs	Other types / Autres navires
South-East Europe and CIS - Europe du Sud-Est et CEI	1990	43505.0	3.3	6.2	14.9	3.4	10.0	18.7	33.0	34.9	1.9	11.6
	1995	27877.9	2.0	2.5	11.4	1.5	6.7	18.8	23.2	42.0	2.2	13.7
	2000	14978.0	1.0	1.2	6.2	0.7	3.5	18.3	21.3	41.6	3.0	15.8
	2003	15916.1	1.0	1.2	6.3	0.5	5.5	20.3	22.9	37.6	2.7	16.4
South-East Europe - Europe du Sud-Est	*1990*	*14145.0*	*0.9*	*3.3*	*3.9*	*0.7*	*0.5*	*15.0*	*53.9*	*28.0*	*1.3*	*1.8*
	1995	*5814.8*	*0.4*	*0.9*	*2.0*	*0.4*	*0.4*	*19.2*	*38.2*	*35.9*	*2.5*	*4.2*
	2000	*3461.0*	*0.1*	*0.6*	*1.0*	*0.2*	*0.3*	*11.0*	*51.9*	*27.8*	*3.0*	*6.4*
	2003	*3082.6*	*0.1*	*0.6*	*0.6*	*0.1*	*0.4*	*9.1*	*64.3*	*18.5*	*2.2*	*5.9*
Albania - Albanie	1990	75.0	0.0	0.0	0.1	0.0	0.0	0.0	0.0	100.0	0.0	0.0
	1995	81.0	0.0	0.0	0.1	0.0	0.0	0.0	0.0	100.0	0.0	0.0
	2000	24.0	0.0	0.0	0.0	0.0	0.0	0.0	0.0	95.8	0.0	4.2
	2003	97.6	0.0	0.0	0.1	0.0	0.0	0.0	0.0	98.6	0.0	1.4
Bulgaria - Bulgarie	1990	1954.0	0.2	0.4	0.4	0.1	0.1	23.5	49.6	22.5	0.9	3.4
	1995	1642.3	0.1	0.3	0.4	0.2	0.1	21.2	47.5	24.1	4.1	3.1
	2000	1445.0	0.1	0.3	0.3	0.1	0.1	18.5	56.2	18.0	4.6	2.7
	2003	1077.2	0.0	0.3	0.1	0.1	0.0	3.0	78.7	10.5	6.2	1.7
Croatia - Croatie	1995	372.8	0.0	0.0	0.2	0.2	0.0	2.4	8.4	66.3	16.8	6.0
	2000	1036.0	0.0	0.3	0.2	0.0	0.0	1.2	73.5	19.7	2.7	3.0
	2003	1221.6	0.0	0.3	0.2	0.0	0.1	12.3	73.8	11.7	0.0	2.2
Romania - Roumanie	1990	6089.0	0.5	1.4	1.6	0.1	0.3	18.8	51.9	26.8	0.3	2.3
	1995	3718.8	0.3	0.5	1.3	0.0	0.3	20.4	37.9	36.6	0.4	4.6
	2000	956.0	0.0	0.1	0.5	0.0	0.2	10.7	23.2	49.6	0.8	15.7
	2003	686.3	0.0	0.1	0.2	0.0	0.3	14.2	34.1	32.0	0.0	19.8
Yugoslavia, SFR (former) - Yougoslavie, RSF (anc.)	1990	6027.0	0.2	1.5	1.8	0.6	0.1	8.6	58.0	30.2	2.4	0.8
CIS - CEI	*1990*	*29360.0*	*2.4*	*2.9*	*11.0*	*2.7*	*9.5*	*20.4*	*22.9*	*38.2*	*2.2*	*16.3*
	1995	*22063.1*	*1.6*	*1.7*	*9.4*	*1.1*	*6.3*	*18.7*	*19.3*	*43.7*	*2.1*	*16.2*
	2000	*11517.0*	*0.8*	*0.5*	*5.3*	*0.5*	*3.1*	*20.5*	*12.1*	*45.8*	*3.0*	*18.7*
	2003	*12833.5*	*0.9*	*0.5*	*5.7*	*0.4*	*5.1*	*23.0*	*13.0*	*42.2*	*2.8*	*19.0*
Azerbaijan - Azerbaïdjan	1995	504.1	0.1	0.0	0.1	0.0	0.3	48.2	0.0	20.6	0.0	31.2
	2000	503.0	0.1	0.0	0.1	0.0	0.2	46.3	0.0	20.5	0.0	33.2
	2003	508.1	0.1	0.0	0.1	0.0	0.3	46.0	0.0	22.2	0.0	31.9
Georgia - Géorgie	1995	407.7	0.1	0.1	0.0	0.0	0.0	54.4	39.2	0.9	0.0	5.4
	2000	142.0	0.0	0.0	0.1	0.0	0.0	8.5	0.0	77.5	0.0	14.1
	2003	1106.0	0.0	0.1	0.7	0.0	0.1	6.0	33.0	56.5	0.4	4.1
Kazakhstan	1995	5.8	0.0	0.0	0.0	0.0	0.0	0.0	0.0	22.2	0.0	77.8
	2000	6.0	0.0	0.0	0.0	0.0	0.0	0.0	0.0	16.7	0.0	83.3
	2003	10.6	0.0	0.0	0.0	0.0	0.0	0.0	0.0	23.6	0.0	76.4
Russian Federation - Fédération de Russie	1995	15794.1	1.3	1.1	6.1	0.8	4.9	22.3	18.1	39.5	2.1	17.9
	2000	9393.0	0.7	0.4	4.2	0.5	2.3	21.5	13.1	45.1	3.3	16.9
	2003	9901.9	0.8	0.4	4.2	0.4	4.0	26.1	11.5	40.0	3.2	19.2
Turkmenistan - Turkménistan	1995	22.3	0.0	0.0	0.0	0.0	0.0	22.4	0.0	36.1	0.0	41.5
	2000	33.0	0.0	0.0	0.0	0.0	0.0	9.1	9.1	45.5	0.0	36.4
	2003	39.5	0.0	0.0	0.0	0.0	0.0	21.2	8.5	39.2	0.0	31.1
Ukraine	1995	5275.8	0.0	0.5	3.2	0.3	1.0	2.3	23.2	61.6	2.5	10.5
	2000	1440.0	0.0	0.1	0.8	0.0	0.5	6.3	11.1	55.9	2.1	24.7
	2003	1267.3	0.0	0.1	0.7	0.0	0.6	4.4	12.6	55.5	3.2	24.2
USSR (former) - URSS (anc.)	1990	29360.0	2.4	2.9	11.0	2.7	9.5	20.4	22.9	38.2	2.2	16.3
Major open-registry countries - Principaux pays de libre immatriculation	*1990*	*224560.0*	*41.8*	*33.9*	*26.3*	*23.2*	*23.4*	*45.6*	*34.7*	*12.0*	*2.4*	*5.3*
	1995	*321282.7*	*50.7*	*46.5*	*34.3*	*36.1*	*30.5*	*41.8*	*37.1*	*11.0*	*4.6*	*5.4*
	2000	*392155.0*	*51.2*	*56.1*	*37.6*	*41.9*	*38.8*	*37.0*	*39.5*	*9.6*	*7.2*	*6.8*
	2003	*399514.1*	*45.7*	*54.1*	*33.6*	*45.1*	*33.1*	*36.2*	*41.7*	*8.0*	*10.2*	*3.9*

For sources and notes, see end of table.

Pour les sources et les notes, se reporter à la fin du tableau.

8.6 World merchant fleet by flag of registration and type of ship

8.6 Flotte marchande mondiale par pavillons d'immatriculation et par types de navires

Sources: UNCTAD Review of Maritime Transport.

The Review of Maritime Transport is one of UNCTAD's flagship publications, published annually since 1968. It reports on the worldwide evolution of shipping, ports and multimodal transport related to the major traffics of liquid bulk, dry bulk and containers.

From 1979 to 1993:
Lloyd's Register of Shipping - Statistical Tables (London) and supplementary data regarding the Great Lakes fleets of the United States and Canada and the United States Reserve Fleet.

From 1994 to 2002:
Lloyd's Maritime Information Services (London).

Year 2003:
Lloyd's Register-Fairplay.

Flag of registration:
The designations employed and the presentation of material in this table refer to flags of registration and do not imply the expression of any opinion by the Secretariat of the United Nations concerning the legal status of any country or territory, or of its authorities, or concerning the delimitation of its frontiers.

Former USSR:
All republics of the former USSR that have not established new shipping registers.

A ship owner who registers his or her vessel in an open-registry country does not need to have any conection with a country of registry. The number of open-registry countries has varied over the years, but five consistently appear (Bermuda, Bahamas, Cyprus, Liberia, and Panama). For the current list, please consult the UNCTAD Review of Maritime Transport.

A "0.0" indicates that data are not available or that the amount is negligible.

1 DWT (deadweight ton) is a weight measure of a vessel's carrying capacity. It includes cargo, fuel and stores.

Sources : Etude sur les transports maritimes de la CNUCED.

L´Etude sur les transports maritimes est une des publications phares de la CNUCED qui paraît chaque année depuis 1968. Elle rend compte de l´évolution mondiale du transport multimodal, portuaire et maritime concernant les principaux trafics de vracs liquides, de vracs secs et de conteneurs.

De 1979 à 1993 :
Le registre maritime de la Lloyd - Tableaux statistiques (Londres) et les données supplémentaires concernant les flottes des Grands Lacs des Etats-Unis et du Canada et la flotte de réserve des Etats-Unis.

De 1994 à 2002 :
Services d'Information Maritimes De Lloyd (Londres).

Année 2003 :
Lloyd's Register-Fairplay.

Pavillon d'immatriculation :
Les désignations employées dans ce tableau et la présentation des données qui y figurent concernent les pavillons d'immatriculation et n'impliquent, de la part du Secrétariat de l'Organisation des Nations Unies, aucune prise de position quant au statut juridique de tel ou tel pays ou territoire, ou de ses autorités, ni quant au tracé de ses frontières.

Ex-URSS :
Ensemble des républiques de l'ex-URSS qui n'ont pas créé de nouveaux registres maritimes.

Un propriétaire qui enregistre son navire dans un pays "libre d'immatriculation" ne doit avoir aucune relation avec ce pays. Le nombre de pays "libre d'immatriculation" a changé au cours des années, mais néanmoins cinq d'entre eux apparaissent constamment (Bahamas, Bermudes, Chypre, Libéria, Panama). Pour obtenir la liste courante des pays de libre immatriculation, veuillez consulter l'Etude sur les transports maritimes de la CNUCED.

Un "0.0" indique que les données ne sont pas disponibles ou que le total est négligeable.

1 TPL (tonne de port en lourd) est une mesure de poids de la capacité de charge d'un navire. Il inclut la cargaison, le carburant et les magasins.

كيفية الحصول على منشورات الامم المتحدة

يمكن الحصول على منشورات الامم المتحدة من المكتبات ودور التوزيع في جميع انحاء العالم . استعلم عنها من المكتبة التي تتعامل معها
أو اكتب الى : الامم المتحدة ،قسم البيع في نيويورك او في جنيف .

如何购取联合国出版物

联合国出版物在全世界各地的书店和经售处均有发售。请向书店询问或写信到纽约或日内瓦的联合国销售组。

HOW TO OBTAIN UNITED NATIONS PUBLICATIONS

United Nations publications may be obtained from bookstores and distributors throughout the world. Consult your bookstore or write to: United Nations, Sales Section, New York or Geneva.

COMMENT SE PROCURER LES PUBLICATIONS DES NATIONS UNIES

Les publications des Nations Unies sont en vente dans les librairies et les agences dépositaires du monde entier. Informez-vous auprès de votre libraire ou adressez-vous à : Nations Unies, Section des ventes, New York ou Genève.

КАК ПОЛУЧИТЬ ИЗДАНИЯ ОРГАНИЗАЦИИ ОБЪЕДИНЕННЫХ НАЦИИ

Издания Организации Объединенных Наций можно купить в книжных магазинах и агентствах во всех районах мира. Наводите справки об изданиях в вашем книжном магазине или пишите по адресу: Организация Объединенных Наций, Секция по продаже изданий, Нью-Йорк или Женева.

CÓMO CONSEGUIR PUBLICACIONES DE LAS NACIONES UNIDAS

Las publicaciones de las Naciones Unidas están en venta en librerías y casas distribuidoras en todas partes del mundo. Consulte a su librero o diríjase a: Naciones Unidas, Sección de Ventas, Nueva York o Ginebra.

Printed at United Nations, Geneva
GE.04-53462–January 2005–4,270

TD/STAT.29

United Nations publication
Sales No. E/F.05.II.D.4

ISBN 92-1-012058-2
ISSN 0251-9461